UNIFORM CRIME REPORTS

for the United States

1995

SUMMARY

CRIME INDEX

CRIMES CLEARED

PERSONS ARRESTED

TOPICAL STUDIES

LAW ENFORCEMENT PERSONNEL

PRINTED ANNUALLY

Federal Bureau of Investigation
U.S. Department of Justice
Washington, D.C. 20535

APPENDICES

ADVISORY:

Committee on Uniform Crime Records
International Association of Chiefs of Police;
Committee on Uniform Crime Reporting
National Sheriffs' Association;
Criminal Justice Information Services Advisory Policy Board

For sale by the U.S. Government Printing Office
Superintendent of Documents, Mail Stop: SSOP, Washington, DC 20402-9328
ISBN 0-16-048756-0

PREFACE

Crime in the United States has undergone many changes over the years. It has grown from the small booklet that was first published in 1930 to the large publication it is today. Through the years more tables have been added, and data collection has been expanded. Many law enforcement agencies have been involved in the Uniform Crime Reporting (UCR) Program's changes. As the National Incident-Based Reporting System (NIBRS) has been developed in recent years, agencies across the country are changing the way they collect and report crime data, and state-level UCR programs are adopting NIBRS.

This year the FBI UCR has experienced a different kind of change. The Program is in the process of moving from its traditional residence in Washington, D.C., to its new home in Clarksburg, West Virginia. The undertaking is enormous. It involves moving a Program that has been in place for over 60 years and all that it comprises—computers, equipment, files, furniture, publications, libraries, and most of all people.

Most important is how this change affects longtime contributors to and users of the UCR Program. Hopefully, it does not and it will not affect them at all. It has been the desire of the UCR staff that while the program is experiencing an internal change, externally the change should be transparent. Contributors are still collecting and reporting data. They are still getting the assistance they need from the Program's components. Information is still being disseminated to the Program's users. In other words, in spite of the change, the Program is conducting business as usual, which speaks to the importance placed on the entire data collecting and reporting process. It speaks to the worth of the Program and the value of all contributing agencies. And it speaks to the dedication of all of the men and women who make this publication possible.

Thus while change is constantly with us, what remains unchanged is a commitment to those people and their programs that assist in reducing crime.

CRIME FACTORS

Each year when *Crime in the United States* is published, many entities—news media, tourism agencies, and other groups with an interest in crime in our Nation—compile rankings of cities and counties based on their Crime Index figures. These simplistic and/or incomplete analyses often create misleading perceptions which adversely affect cities and counties, along with their residents. Assessing criminality and law enforcement's response from jurisdiction to jurisdiction must encompass many elements, some of which, while having significant impact, are not readily measurable nor applicable pervasively among all locales. Geographic and demographic factors specific to each jurisdiction must be considered and applied if crime assessment is to approach completeness and accuracy. There are several sources of information which may assist the responsible researcher. The U.S. Bureau of the Census data, for example, can be utilized to better understand the makeup of a locale's population. The transience of the population, its racial and ethnic makeup, its composition by age and gender, education levels, and prevalent family structures are all key factors in assessing and better understanding the crime issue.

Local chambers of commerce, planning offices, or similar entities provide information regarding the economic and cultural makeup of cities and counties. Understanding a jurisdiction's industrial/economic base, its dependence upon neighboring jurisdictions, its transportation system, its economic dependence on nonresidents (such as tourists and convention attendees), its proximity to military installations, etc., all help in better gauging and interpreting the crime known to and reported by law enforcement.

The strength (personnel and other resources) and the aggressiveness of a jurisdiction's law enforcement agency are also key factors. While information pertaining to the number of sworn and civilian law enforcement employees can be found in this publication, assessment of the law enforcement emphases is, of course, much more difficult. For example, one city may report more crime than a comparable one, not because there is more crime, but rather because its law enforcement agency through proactive efforts identifies more offenses. Attitudes of the citizens toward crime and their crime reporting practices, especially concerning more minor offenses, have an impact on the volume of crimes known to police.

It is incumbent upon all data users to become as well educated as possible about how to categorize and quantify the nature and extent of crime in the United States and in any of the over 16,000 jurisdictions represented by law enforcement contributors to this Program. Valid assessments are only possible with careful study and analysis of the various unique conditions affecting each local law enforcement jurisdiction.

Historically, the causes and origins of crime have been the subjects of investigation by varied disciplines. Some factors which are known to affect the volume and type of crime occurring from place to place are:

Population density and degree of urbanization.

Variations in composition of the population, particularly youth concentration.

Stability of population with respect to residents' mobility, commuting patterns, and transient factors.

Modes of transportation and highway system.

Economic conditions, including median income, poverty level, and job availability.

Cultural factors and educational, recreational, and religious characteristics.

Family conditions with respect to divorce and family cohesiveness.

Climate.

Effective strength of law enforcement agencies.

Administrative and investigative emphases of law enforcement.

Policies of other components of the criminal justice system (i.e., prosecutorial, judicial, correctional, and probational).

Citizens' attitudes toward crime.

Crime reporting practices of the citizenry.

The Uniform Crime Reports give a nationwide view of crime based on statistics contributed by state and local law enforcement agencies. Population size is the only correlate of crime utilized in this publication. While the other factors listed above are of equal concern, no attempt is made to relate them to the data presented. *The reader is, therefore, cautioned against comparing statistical data of individual reporting units from cities, counties, metropolitan areas, states, or colleges and universities solely on the basis of their population coverage or student enrollment.*

Data users are cautioned against comparisons of crime trends presented in this report and those estimated by the National Crime Victimization Survey (NCVS), administered by the Bureau of Justice Statistics. Because of differences in methodology and crime coverage, the two programs examine the Nation's crime problem from somewhat different perspectives, and their results are not strictly comparable. The definitional and procedural differences can account for many of the apparent discrepancies in results from the two programs.

CONTENTS

SECTION I

Summary of the Uniform Crime Reporting Program

The Uniform Crime Reporting Program is a nationwide, cooperative statistical effort of over 16,000 city, county, and state law enforcement agencies voluntarily reporting data on crimes brought to their attention. During 1995, law enforcement agencies active in the Program represented nearly 251 million United States inhabitants or 95 percent of the total population as established by the Bureau of the Census. The coverage amounted to 97 percent of the United States population in Metropolitan Statistical Areas (MSAs), 90 percent of the population in cities outside metropolitan areas, and 88 percent of the rural population.

Since 1930, the FBI has administered the Program and issued periodic assessments of the nature and type of crime in the Nation. While the Program's primary objective is to generate a reliable set of criminal statistics for use in law enforcement administration, operation, and management, its data have over the years become one of the country's leading social indicators. The American public looks to Uniform Crime Reports for information on fluctuations in the level of crime, while criminologists, sociologists, legislators, municipal planners, the press, and other students of criminal justice use the statistics for varied research and planning purposes.

Historical Background

Recognizing a need for national crime statistics, the International Association of Chiefs of Police (IACP) formed the Committee on Uniform Crime Records in the 1920s to develop a system of uniform police statistics. Establishing offenses known to law enforcement as the appropriate measure, the Committee evaluated various crimes on the basis of their seriousness, frequency of occurrence, pervasiveness in all geographic areas of the country, and likelihood of being reported to law enforcement. After studying state criminal codes and making an evaluation of the recordkeeping practices in use, the Committee in 1929 completed a plan for crime reporting which became the foundation of the Uniform Crime Reporting (UCR) Program.

Seven offenses were chosen to serve as an Index for gauging fluctuations in the overall volume and rate of crime. Known collectively as the Crime Index, these offenses included the violent crimes of murder and nonnegligent manslaughter, forcible rape, robbery, and aggravated assault and the property crimes of burglary, larceny-theft, and motor vehicle theft. By congressional mandate, arson was added as the eighth Index offense in 1979.

During the early planning of the Program, it was recognized that the differences among criminal codes precluded a mere aggregation of state statistics to arrive at a national total.

Further, because of the variances in punishment for the same offenses in different state codes, no distinction between felony and misdemeanor crimes was possible. To avoid these problems and provide nationwide uniformity in crime reporting, standardized offense definitions by which law enforcement agencies were to submit data, without regard for local statutes, were formulated. The definitions used by the Program are set forth in Appendix II of this publication.

In January 1930, 400 cities collectively representing 20 million inhabitants in 43 states began participating in the UCR Program. Congress enacted Title 28, Section 534, of the United States Code authorizing the Attorney General to gather crime information that same year. The Attorney General, in turn, designated the FBI to serve as the national clearinghouse for the data collected. Since that time, data based on uniform classifications and procedures for reporting have been obtained from the Nation's law enforcement agencies.

Advisory Groups

Providing vital links between local law enforcement and the FBI in the conduct of the UCR Program are the Criminal Justice Information Systems Committees of the IACP and the National Sheriffs' Association. The IACP, as it has since the Program began, represents the thousands of police departments nationwide. The NSA encourages sheriffs throughout the country to participate fully in the Program. Both committees serve in advisory capacities concerning the UCR Program's operation.

To function in an advisory capacity concerning UCR policy and provide suggestions on UCR data usage, a Data Providers' Advisory Policy Board (APB) was established in August 1988. The Board operated until 1993 when a new Board to address all FBI criminal justice information services was approved. The Board functions in an advisory capacity concerning UCR policy and on data collection and use. The UCR Subcommittee of the Board ensures continuing emphasis on UCR-related issues.

The Association of State Uniform Crime Reporting Programs and committees on UCR within individual state law enforcement associations are also active in promoting interest in the UCR Program. These organizations foster widespread and more intelligent use of uniform crime statistics and lend assistance to contributors when the needs arise.

Redesign of UCR

While throughout the years the UCR Program remained virtually unchanged in terms of the data collected and disseminated, a broad utility had evolved for UCR by the 1980s. Recognizing the need for improved statistics, law enforcement called for a thorough evaluative study that would modernize the UCR Program. The FBI fully concurred with the need for an updated Program and lent its complete support, formulating a comprehensive three-phase redesign effort. The Bureau of Justice Statistics (BJS), the Department of Justice agency responsible for funding criminal justice information projects, agreed to underwrite the first two phases. Conducted by an independent contractor, these phases were structured to determine what, if any, changes should be made to the current Program. The third phase would involve implementation of the changes identified. Abt Associates Inc. of Cambridge, Massachusetts, overseen by the FBI, BJS, and a Steering Committee comprised of prestigious individuals representing a myriad of disciplines, commenced the first phase in 1982.

During the first phase, the historical evolution of the UCR Program was examined. All aspects of the Program, including the objectives and intended user audience, data items, reporting mechanisms, quality control, publications and user services, and relationships with other criminal justice data systems, were studied.

Early in 1984, a conference on the future of UCR, held in Elkridge, Maryland, launched the second phase of the study, which would examine potential futures for UCR and conclude with a set of recommended changes. Attendees at this conference reviewed work conducted during the first phase and discussed the potential changes that should be considered during phase two.

Findings from the evaluation's first phase and input on alternatives for the future were also major topics of discussion at the seventh National UCR Conference in July 1984. Overlapping phases one and two was a survey of law enforcement agencies.

Phase two ended in early 1985 with the production of a draft "Blueprint for the Future of the Uniform Crime Reporting Program." The study's Steering Committee reviewed the draft report at a March 1985, meeting and made various recommendations for revision. The Committee members, however, endorsed the report's concepts.

In April 1985, the phase two recommendations were presented at the eighth National UCR Conference. While various considerations for the final report were set forth, the overall concept for the revised Program was unanimously approved. The joint IACP/NSA Committee on UCR also issued a resolution endorsing the Blueprint.

The final report, the "Blueprint for the Future of the Uniform Crime Reporting Program," was released in the summer of 1985. It specifically outlined recommendations for an expanded, improved UCR Program to meet informational needs into the next century. There were three recommended areas of enhancement to the UCR Program. First, reporting of offenses and arrests would be made by means of an incident-based system. Second, collection of data would be accomplished on two levels. Agencies in level one would report important details about those offenses comprising the current Crime Index, their victims, and arrestees. Law enforcement agencies covering populations of over 100,000 and a sampling of smaller agencies would be included in level two, which would collect expanded detail on all significant offenses. The third proposal involved introducing a quality assurance program.

To begin implementation, the FBI awarded a contract to develop new offense definitions and data elements for the redesigned system. The work involved: (a) revision of the definitions of certain Index offenses; (b) identification of additional significant offenses to be reported; (c) refining definitions for both; and (d) development of data elements (incident details) for all UCR offenses in order to fulfill the requirements of incident-based reporting versus the current summary reporting.

Concurrent with the preparation of the data elements, the FBI studied the various state systems to select an experimental site for implementation of the redesigned Program. In view of its long-standing incident-based Program and well-established staff dedicated solely to UCR, the South Carolina Law Enforcement Division (SLED) was chosen. The SLED agreed to adapt its existing system to meet the requirements of the redesigned Program and collect data on both offenses and arrests relating to the newly defined offenses.

To assist SLED with the pilot project, offense definitions and data elements developed under the private contract were put at the staff's disposal. Also, FBI automated data processing personnel developed "Automated Data Capture Specifications" for use in adapting the state's data processing procedures to incorporate the revised system. The BJS supplied funding to facilitate software revisions needed at the state level. Testing of the new Program was completed in late 1987.

Following the completion of the pilot project conducted by SLED, the FBI produced a draft set of guidelines for an enhanced UCR Program. Law enforcement executives from around the country were then invited to a conference in Orange Beach, Alabama, where the guidelines were presented for final review.

During the conference, three overall endorsements were passed without dissent. First, that there be established a new, incident-based national crime reporting system; second, that the FBI manage this Program; and third, that an Advisory Policy Board composed of law enforcement executives be formed to assist in the direction and implementation of the new Program.

Information about the redesigned UCR Program, called the National Incident-Based Reporting System, or NIBRS, is contained in four documents produced subsequent to the Orange Beach Conference. Volume 1, *Data Collection Guidelines,* contains a system overview and descriptions of the offenses, offense codes, reports, data elements, and data values used in the system. Volume 2, *Data Submission Specifications,* is for the use of state and local systems personnel who are responsible for preparing magnetic tapes/floppy disks/etc., for submission to the FBI. Volume 3, *Approaches to Implementing an Incident-Based Reporting (IBR) System,* is for use by computer programmers, analysts, etc., responsible for developing a state or local IBR system which will meet NIBRS' reporting requirements. Volume 4, *Error Message Manual,* contains designations of mandatory and optional data elements, data element edits, and error messages.

A NIBRS edition of the *UCR Handbook* has been produced to assist law enforcement agency data contributors implementing NIBRS within their departments. This document is geared toward familiarizing local and state law enforcement personnel with the definitions, policies, and procedures of NIBRS. It does not contain the technical coding and data transmission requirements presented in Volumes 1 through 4.

NIBRS will collect data on each single incident and arrest within 22 crime categories. For each offense known to police within these categories, incident, victim, property, offender, and arrestee information will be gathered when available. The goal of the redesign is to modernize crime information by collecting data presently maintained in law enforcement records; the enhanced UCR Program is, therefore, a by-product of current records systems. The integrity of UCR's long-running statistical series will, of course, be maintained.

It became apparent during the development of the prototype system that the level one and level two reporting proposed in the "Blueprint" may not be the most practical approach. Many state and local law enforcement administrators indicated that the collection of data on all pertinent offenses could be handled with more ease than could the extraction of selected ones. While "Limited" participation, equivalent to the "Blueprint's" level one, will remain an option, it appears that most reporting jurisdictions, upon implementation, will go immediately to "Full" participation, meeting all NIBRS data submission requirements.

Implementing NIBRS will be at a pace commensurate with the resources, abilities, and limitations of the contributing law enforcement agencies. The FBI was able to accept NIBRS data as of January 1989, and 10 state-level UCR Programs (Colorado, Idaho, Iowa, Massachusetts, Michigan, North Dakota, South Carolina, Utah, Vermont, and Virginia) are now supplying data in the NIBRS format. An additional 22 state agencies, 3 local law enforcement agencies in states not having state-level programs, and 3 federal agencies (the Departments of Commerce and Defense-Air Force and the FBI) have submitted test tapes or disks containing the expanded data. Eleven other state agencies, agencies in the District of Columbia and Guam, and other federal agencies are in various stages of planning and development.

Recent Developments

HATE CRIME STATISTICS — To comply with The Violent Crime Control and Law Enforcement Act of 1994 (Crime Act), Public Law 103-322, enacted September 13, 1994, the UCR Program, beginning January 1, 1997, will add to its hate crime data collection crimes motivated by bias against persons with disabilities. In the Hate Crime Statistics Act of l990, the types of bias to be reported were limited to those based on "race, religion, sexual orientation, or ethnicity." The Crime Act amended the earlier legislation to include disabilities as a factor to be considered in bias-motivated crimes. In UCR, disability bias is defined as: A preformed negative opinion of or attitude toward a group of persons based on their physical or mental impairments/challenges, whether such disability is temporary or permanent, congenital, or acquired by heredity, accident, injury, advanced age, or illness.

UCR RELOCATION—The UCR Program has undergone many changes over the past 60 plus years, but perhaps the most dramatic change is the one it is experiencing this year. The Program is in the final stages of moving from its traditional residence in Washington, D.C., to its new home in Clarksburg, West Virginia. This enormous undertaking involves moving computers, equipment, files, furniture, publications, and libraries—many years' accumulation of resources. As of August 5, 1996, the general mailing address for the Criminal Justice Information Services Division became:

Federal Bureau of Investigation
Criminal Justice Information Services Division
Attention: Uniform Crime Reports
1000 Custer Hollow Road
Clarksburg, West Virginia 26306

CHART 2.1

CRIME CLOCK
1995

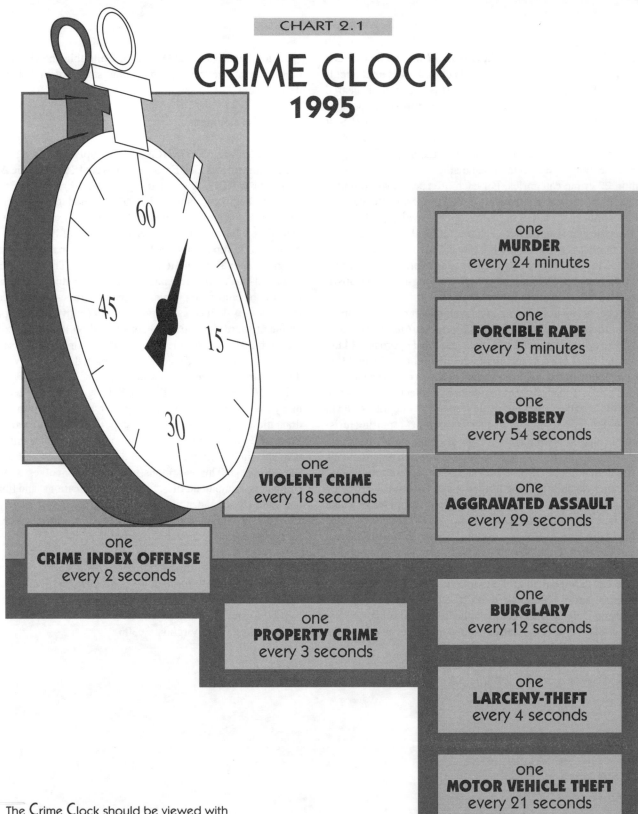

one
MURDER
every 24 minutes

one
FORCIBLE RAPE
every 5 minutes

one
ROBBERY
every 54 seconds

one
VIOLENT CRIME
every 18 seconds

one
AGGRAVATED ASSAULT
every 29 seconds

one
CRIME INDEX OFFENSE
every 2 seconds

one
PROPERTY CRIME
every 3 seconds

one
BURGLARY
every 12 seconds

one
LARCENY-THEFT
every 4 seconds

one
MOTOR VEHICLE THEFT
every 21 seconds

The Crime Clock should be viewed with care. Being the most aggregate representation of UCR data, it is designed to convey the annual reported crime experience by showing the relative frequency of occurrence of the Index Offenses. This mode of display should not be taken to imply a regularity in the commission of the Part I Offenses; rather, it represents the annual ratio of crime to fixed time intervals.

SECTION II
Crime Index Offenses Reported

CRIME INDEX TOTAL

DEFINITION

The Crime Index is composed of selected offenses used to gauge fluctuations in the overall volume and rate of crime reported to law enforcement. The offenses included are the violent crimes of murder and nonnegligent manslaughter, forcible rape, robbery, and aggravated assault and the property crimes of burglary, larceny-theft, motor vehicle theft, and arson.

	TREND	
Year	Number of offenses[1]	Rate per 100,000 inhabitants[1]
1994	13,989,543	5,373.5
1995	13,867,143	5,277.6
Percent change	−.9	−1.8

[1]Does not include arson. See page 57.

The Crime Index total, 13.9 million offenses in 1995, was the lowest serious crime count since 1987. The 1-percent decline in the total, 1995 versus 1994, was the fourth consecutive annual decline. Among the Nation's cities collectively, the Index decreased 2 percent, with the greatest decrease, 6 percent, reported in cities having a million or more inhabitants. Similar to the national experience, the suburban counties recorded a 1-percent decrease, but rural county law enforcement agencies registered a 4-percent rise.

Five- and 10-year percent changes showed the 1995 national total was 7 percent lower than the 1991 level but 5 percent higher than the 1986 total.

Geographically, the largest volume of Crime Index offenses was reported in the most populous Southern States, which accounted for 38 percent of the total. Following were the Western States with 25 percent, the Midwestern States with 21 percent, and the Northeastern States with 16 percent. All regions except the west showed Crime Index decreases during 1995 as compared to 1994 figures. (See Tables 3 and 4.)

As in previous years, Crime Index offenses occurred most frequently in August and least often in February.

Table 2.1—Crime Index Total by Month, 1991–1995

[Percent distribution]

Months	1991	1992	1993	1994	1995
January	7.9	8.3	8.0	7.6	8.1
February	7.4	7.8	6.9	7.1	7.2
March	8.1	8.2	8.1	8.2	8.2
April	8.0	8.0	7.9	8.1	7.8
May	8.4	8.3	8.2	8.5	8.4
June	8.5	8.4	8.6	8.5	8.5
July	9.1	9.0	9.1	9.1	9.0
August	9.2	9.0	9.2	9.4	9.2
September	8.4	8.4	8.4	8.5	8.5
October	8.7	8.5	8.6	8.8	8.8
November	8.0	8.0	8.1	8.3	8.2
December	8.3	8.1	9.1	7.9	8.0

Rate

Crime rates relate the incidence of crime to population. In 1995, there were an estimated 5,278 Crime Index offenses for each 100,000 in United States population, the lowest rate since 1985. The Crime Index rate was highest in the Nation's metropolitan areas and lowest in the rural counties. (See Tables 1 and 2.) The national 1995 Crime Index rate fell 2 percent from the 1994 rate, 11 percent from the 1991 level, and 4 percent from the 1986 rate.

Regionally, the Crime Index rates ranged from 6,083 in the West to 4,180 in the Northeast. Two-year percent changes (1995 versus 1994) showed rate declines in all regions. (See Table 4.)

Nature

The Crime Index is composed of violent and property crime categories, and in 1995, 13 percent of the Index offenses reported to law enforcement were violent crimes and 87 percent, property crimes. Larceny-theft was the offense with the highest volume, while murder accounted for the fewest offenses. (See Chart 2.3.)

Property estimated in value at $15.6 billion was stolen in connection with all Crime Index offenses, with the greatest losses due to thefts of motor vehicles; jewelry and precious metals; and televisions, radios, stereos, etc. Law enforcement agencies nationwide recorded a 35-percent recovery rate for dollar losses in connection with stolen property. The highest recovery percentages were for stolen motor vehicles, consumable goods, clothing and furs, livestock, and firearms. (See Table 24.)

Law Enforcement Response

Law enforcement agencies nationwide recorded a 21-percent clearance rate for the collective Crime Index offenses in 1995 and made an estimated 2.9 million arrests for Index crimes. Crimes can be cleared by arrest or by exceptional means when some element beyond law enforcement control precludes the placing of formal charges against the offender. The arrest of one person may clear several crimes, or several persons may be arrested in connection with the clearance of one offense.

The Index clearance rate has remained relatively stable throughout the past 10-year period. As in 1995, the clearance rates in both 1991 and 1986 were 21 percent.

The number of persons arrested for Index crimes decreased 1 percent in 1995 when compared to 1994. Juvenile arrests for Index crimes decreased 2 percent, while those of adults showed virtually no change. By gender, arrests of males decreased 2 percent, but arrests of females increased 2 percent for the 2-year period. (See Tables 36 and 37.)

Between 1994 and 1995, the number of persons arrested for the individual offenses composing the Index decreased for murder and motor vehicle theft, 6 percent; forcible rape, 5 percent; burglary, 4 percent; arson, 3 percent; and robbery, 2 percent. The number of larceny-theft arrests showed virtually no change, while those for aggravated assault increased 1 percent during the same 2-year period.

As in previous years, larceny-theft arrests accounted for the highest volume of Crime Index arrests at 1.5 million. (See Table 29.)

6

CRIME INDEX TOTAL

CHART 2.2

PERCENT CHANGE FROM 1991

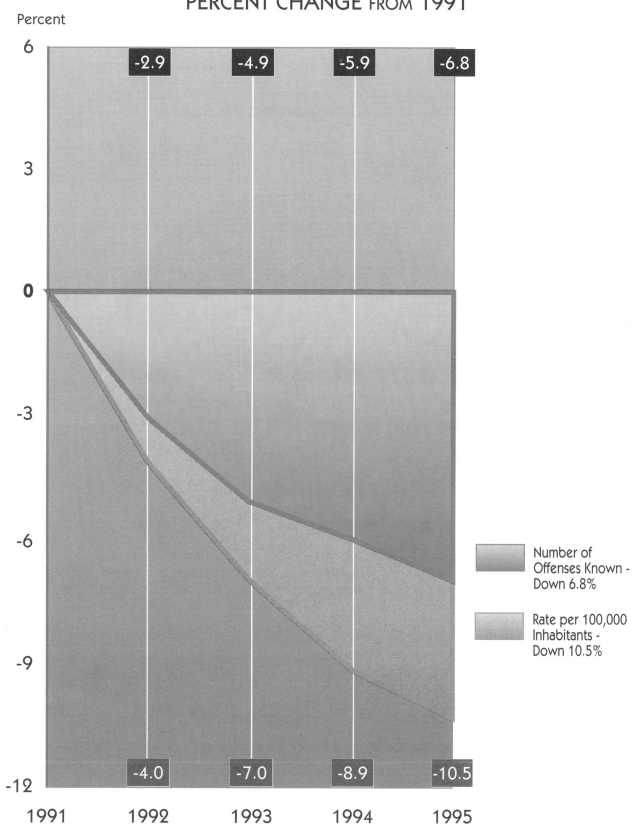

Percent

6

3

0

-3

-6

-9

-12

-2.9   -4.9   -5.9   -6.8

-4.0   -7.0   -8.9   -10.5

1991   1992   1993   1994   1995

Number of
Offenses Known -
Down 6.8%

Rate per 100,000
Inhabitants -
Down 10.5%

CHART 2.3

CRIME INDEX OFFENSES
1995
Percent Distribution

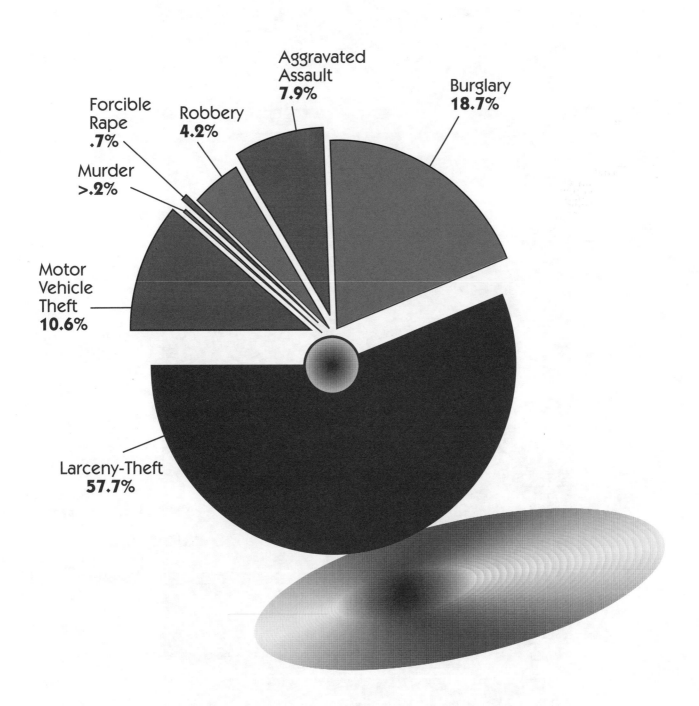

Aggravated
Assault
7.9%

Forcible
Rape
.7%

Robbery
4.2%

Burglary
18.7%

Murder
>.2%

Motor
Vehicle
Theft
10.6%

Larceny-Theft
57.7%

REGIONAL VIOLENT
AND PROPERTY CRIME RATES
1995

CHART 2.4

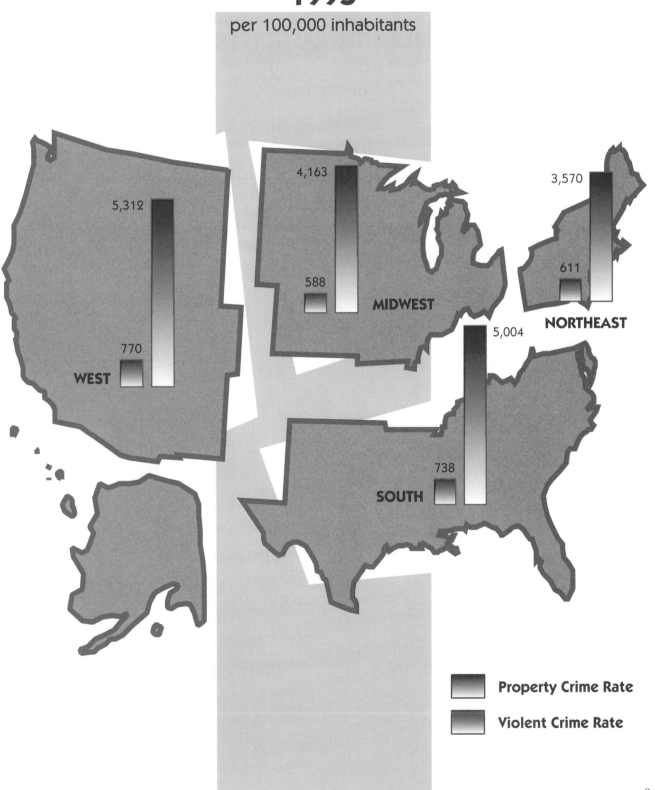

per 100,000 inhabitants

WEST 5,312 770

MIDWEST 4,163 588

NORTHEAST 3,570 611

SOUTH 5,004 738

Property Crime Rate

Violent Crime Rate

VIOLENT CRIME TOTAL

DEFINITION

Violent crime is composed of four offenses: murder and nonnegligent manslaughter, forcible rape, robbery, and aggravated assault. All violent crimes involve force or threat of force.

	— TREND —	
Year	*Number of offenses*	*Rate per 100,000 inhabitants*
1994	1,857,670	713.6
1995	1,798,785	684.6
Percent change	−3.2	−4.1

The number of violent crimes reported to law enforcement during 1995 was estimated at 1.8 million offenses, showing a decrease of 3 percent from 1994. The 1995 estimated total was 6 percent below the 1991 level, but 21 percent above that of 1986. From 1994 to 1995, the Nation's cities collectively recorded a 5-percent decrease in violent crime, and the suburban counties experienced a 2-percent drop. An increase of 4 percent was reported in the rural counties.

Regionally, the South, the most populous region, accounted for 38 percent of all violent crimes reported to law enforcement in 1995. Lesser volumes of 25 percent for the West, 20 percent for the Midwest, and 17 percent for the Northeast were recorded. All four regions experienced decreases in the number of violent crimes reported from 1994 to 1995. The Northeast registered an 8-percent decline; the West, 3 percent; the South, 2 percent; and the Midwest, 1 percent. (See Table 4.)

Violent crimes occurred most frequently in August. The lowest total was experienced in the month of February.

Table 2.2—Violent Crime Total by Month, 1991–1995
[Percent distribution]

Months	1991	1992	1993	1994	1995
January	7.6	8.0	8.0	7.7	7.9
February	7.0	7.6	6.7	7.3	7.1
March	7.8	8.1	8.2	8.4	8.1
April	7.8	8.3	8.0	8.3	8.0
May	8.6	8.7	8.4	8.5	8.5
June	8.7	8.5	8.7	8.6	8.5
July	9.2	9.0	9.3	9.1	9.1
August	9.5	8.9	9.1	9.2	9.2
September	8.8	8.5	8.4	8.6	8.8
October	8.8	8.6	8.6	8.7	8.9
November	8.0	7.8	7.8	7.8	8.0
December	8.2	8.0	8.9	7.6	7.9

Rate

A violent crime rate of 685 per 100,000 inhabitants was registered nationally in 1995, the lowest rate since 1989. Two- and 5-year trends showed the 1995 rate was 4 percent lower than in 1994 and 10 percent below the 1991 rate. It was, however, 11 percent above the 1986 figure. The Nation's metropolitan areas collectively registered 774 offenses per 100,000 population, the highest violent crime rate. The rate in cities outside metropolitan areas was 483, and for rural counties, it was 234.

Geographically, the violent crime rates ranged from 770 per 100,000 inhabitants of the Western States to 588 per 100,000 inhabitants of the Midwestern States. All regions registered rate declines: the Northeast, 8 percent; the West, 4 percent; the South, 3 percent; and the Midwest, 2 percent. (See Table 4.)

Nature

Aggravated assaults accounted for 61 percent of the violent crimes reported to law enforcement during 1995. Robberies comprised 32 percent; forcible rapes, 5 percent; and murders, 1 percent.

While data concerning weapons used in connection with forcible rape are not collected, firearms were the weapons used in 30 percent of all murders, robberies, and aggravated assaults, collectively, in 1995. Knives or cutting instruments were used in 15 percent; other dangerous weapons in 24 percent; and personal weapons (hands, fists, feet, etc.) in 31 percent. The proportion of violent crimes committed with firearms has remained relatively constant in recent years. During the past 5 years, the proportions ranged from 31 percent in 1991 to 30 percent in 1995. Historically, the 1990s have become the decade most prone to firearm use for violent crime. (Refer to Section V, Weapons Used in Violent Crime.)

Law Enforcement Response

The overall violent crime clearance rate was 45 percent in 1995. Among the violent offenses, the 1995 clearance rates ranged from 65 percent for murder to 25 percent for robbery. Over half of all forcible rapes and aggravated assaults were cleared.

There were an estimated 796,250 persons arrested for violent crimes in 1995. Violent crime arrests accounted for 5 percent of the arrests for all offenses and 27 percent of those for Index crimes. Males made up 85 percent of all violent crime arrestees; whites, 54 percent; and adults, 81 percent. (See Tables 38, 42, and 43.)

The total number of arrests for violent crimes showed virtually no change from 1994 to 1995. Juvenile arrests (under age 18) decreased 3 percent, while adult arrests increased 1 percent. Overall violent crime arrests declined 1 percent in the Nation's cities, while a 3-percent rise was recorded in suburban counties. Like the Nation, the rural counties showed virtually no change from 1994 to 1995. (See Section IV, Persons Arrested.)

VIOLENT CRIME

CHART 2.5
PERCENT CHANGE FROM 1991

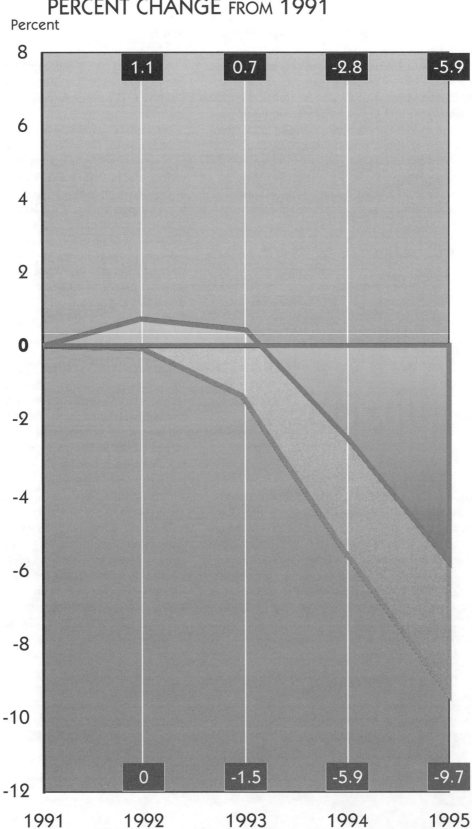

Percent

| | 1.1 | 0.7 | -2.8 | -5.9 |

Number of
Offenses Known -
Down 5.9%

Rate per 100,000
Inhabitants -
Down 9.7%

| | 0 | -1.5 | -5.9 | -9.7 |

1991   1992   1993   1994   1995

12

MURDER AND NONNEGLIGENT MANSLAUGHTER

DEFINITION

Murder and nonnegligent manslaughter, as defined in the Uniform Crime Reporting Program, is the willful (nonnegligent) killing of one human being by another.

The classification of this offense, as for all other Crime Index offenses, is based solely on police investigation as opposed to the determination of a court, medical examiner, coroner, jury, or other judicial body. Not included in the count for this offense classification are deaths caused by negligence, suicide, or accident; justifiable homicides; and attempts to murder or assaults to murder, which are scored as aggravated assaults.

TREND		
Year	Number of offenses	Rate per 100,000 inhabitants
1994	23,326	9.0
1995	21,597	8.2
Percent change	−7.4	−8.9

The number of persons murdered in 1995 was estimated at 21,597, down 7 percent from the 1994 count and 13 percent below the 1991 total. The 1995 total was, however, 5 percent above the 1986 level. (See Table 1.)

The murder volumes decreased 9 percent in suburban counties and 8 percent in the Nation's cities in 1995 from the 1994 level. The greatest decrease—14 percent—was registered in cities with populations of 50,000 to 99,999. In the rural counties, murder increased 2 percent for the 2-year period.

When viewing the four regions of the Nation, the Southern States, the most populous region, accounted for 42 percent of the murders. The Western States reported 24 percent; the Midwestern States, 20 percent; and the Northeastern States, 15 percent. All the regions showed declines in the number of murders reported from 1994 to 1995. The greatest drop was in the Northeast, 13 percent. Decreases in the remaining regions were 8 percent in the Midwest, 7 percent in the South, and 3 percent in the West. (See Tables 3 and 4.)

Monthly figures showed that the greatest number of murders occurred in the month of August in 1995, while the fewest occurred in February. (See Table 2.3.)

decrease of 13 percent, and the West, the smallest, a 4-percent drop. (See Table 4.)

The Nation's metropolitan areas reported a 1995 murder rate of 9 victims per 100,000 inhabitants. In the rural counties and in cities outside metropolitan areas, the rate was 5 per 100,000.

Nature

Supplemental data were provided by contributing agencies for 20,043 of the estimated 21,597 murders in 1995. Submitted monthly, the data consist of the age, sex, and race of both victims and offenders; the types of weapons used; the relationships of victims to the offenders; and the circumstances surrounding the murders.

Based on this information, 77 percent of the murder victims in 1995 were males; and 88 percent were persons 18 years of age or older. Forty-five percent were aged 20 through 34. Considering victims for whom race was known, 49 percent were black, 48 percent were white, and the remainder were persons of other races.

Table 2.3—Murder by Month, 1991–1995

[Percent distribution]

Months	1991	1992	1993	1994	1995
January	8.0	8.1	8.1	8.2	8.3
February	7.0	7.5	6.7	7.6	6.8
March	7.7	8.2	7.9	8.8	7.7
April	7.8	8.0	7.6	8.1	8.4
May	8.1	8.5	7.8	8.2	7.9
June	8.6	7.9	8.6	8.3	8.2
July	9.1	9.1	9.3	9.0	8.9
August	9.4	9.1	9.2	9.2	9.8
September	8.8	8.7	8.3	8.3	8.7
October	8.6	8.0	8.4	8.5	8.8
November	7.8	8.1	8.2	7.9	8.1
December	9.0	8.8	9.8	8.0	8.5

Table 2.4—Murder Victims by Race and Sex, 1995

Race of Victims	Sex of Victims			
	Total	Male	Female	Unknown
Total White Victims	9,613	6,939	2,674	—
Total Black Victims	9,694	7,913	1,781	—
Total Other Race Victims	542	387	155	—
Total Unknown Race	194	117	44	33
Total Victims[1]	20,043	15,356	4,654	33

[1]Total murder victims for whom supplemental data were received.

Rate

Down 9 percent from 1994, the national murder rate in 1995 was 8 per 100,000 inhabitants, the lowest rate since 1985. Five- and 10-year trends showed the 1995 rate was 16 percent lower than in 1991 and 5 percent below the 1986 rate.

On a regional basis, the South averaged 10 murders for every 100,000 people; the West, 9 per 100,000; the Midwest, 7 per 100,000; and the Northeast, 6 per 100,000. Compared to 1994, murder rates in 1995 declined in all of the four geographic regions, with the Northeast experiencing the greatest change, a

Supplemental data were also reported for 22,434 murder offenders in 1995. Of those for whom sex and age were reported, 91 percent of the offenders were males, and 85 percent were persons 18 years of age or older. Sixty-eight percent were aged 17 through 34. Of offenders for whom race was known, 53 percent were black, 45 percent were white, and the remainder were persons of other races.

Murder is most frequently intraracial among victims and offenders. In 1995, data based on incidents involving one victim and one offender showed that 94 percent of the black murder victims were slain by black offenders, and 84 percent of the white murder victims were killed by white offenders. Likewise, males were most often slain by males (89 percent in single victim/single offender situations). These same data showed, however, that 9 of every 10 female victims were murdered by males.

MURDER

CHART 2.6

PERCENT CHANGE FROM 1991

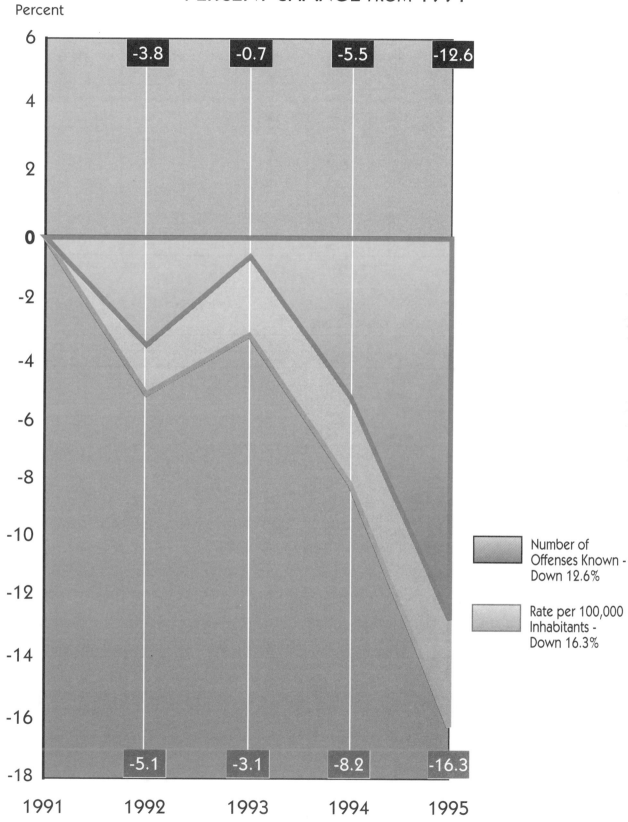

Percent

-3.8   -0.7   -5.5   -12.6

-5.1   -3.1   -8.2   -16.3

6
4
2
0
-2
-4
-6
-8
-10
-12
-14
-16
-18

1991   1992   1993   1994   1995

Number of
Offenses Known -
Down 12.6%

Rate per 100,000
Inhabitants -
Down 16.3%

15

Table 2.5—Age, Sex, and Race of Murder Victims, 1995

Age	Total	Sex			Race			
		Male	Female	Unknown	White	Black	Other	Unknown
Total	20,043	15,356	4,654	33	9,613	9,694	542	194
Percent distribution[1]	100.0	76.6	23.2	.2	48.0	48.4	2.7	1.0
Under 18[2]	2,428	1,735	693	—	1,142	1,185	85	16
Under 22[2]	5,445	4,337	1,107	1	2,377	2,876	157	35
18 and over[2]	17,278	13,401	3,875	2	8,339	8,382	446	111
Infant (under 1)	249	139	110	—	149	90	7	3
1 to 4	411	224	187	—	225	176	9	1
5 to 8	103	52	51	—	55	43	5	—
9 to 12	103	59	44	—	59	34	9	1
13 to 16	953	742	211	—	422	489	35	7
17 to 19	2,116	1,816	299	1	840	1,201	61	14
20 to 24	3,559	3,051	508	—	1,446	2,016	80	17
25 to 29	2,814	2,248	566	—	1,223	1,508	67	16
30 to 34	2,526	1,919	606	1	1,174	1,269	65	18
35 to 39	1,966	1,408	558	—	970	929	54	13
40 to 44	1,517	1,118	399	—	846	620	34	17
45 to 49	993	763	230	—	556	405	25	7
50 to 54	645	476	169	—	395	216	28	6
55 to 59	471	356	115	—	286	162	22	1
60 to 64	352	264	88	—	218	121	11	2
65 to 69	292	200	92	—	187	97	6	2
70 to 74	222	121	101	—	152	65	4	1
75 and over	414	180	234	—	278	126	9	1
Unknown	337	220	86	31	132	127	11	67

[1] Because of rounding, may not add to total.
[2] Does not include unknown ages.

Table 2.6—Age, Sex, and Race of Murder Offenders, 1995

Age	Total	Sex			Race			
		Male	Female	Unknown	White	Black	Other	Unknown
Total	22,434	14,609	1,400	6,425	7,071	8,285	418	6,660
Percent distribution[1]	100.0	65.1	6.2	28.6	31.5	36.9	1.9	29.7
Under 18[2]	2,169	2,044	125	—	861	1,225	66	17
Under 22[2]	5,875	5,580	295	—	2,274	3,413	151	37
18 and over[2]	12,468	11,246	1,219	3	5,846	6,219	322	81
Infant (under 1)	—	—	—	—	—	—	—	—
1 to 4	—	—	—	—	—	—	—	—
5 to 8	—	—	—	—	—	—	—	—
9 to 12	29	25	4	—	12	17	—	—
13 to 16	1,268	1,182	86	—	492	723	40	13
17 to 19	2,875	2,749	126		1,117	1,675	69	14
20 to 24	3,555	3,329	226	—	1,398	2,067	73	17
25 to 29	2,017	1,812	204	1	939	995	69	14
30 to 34	1,573	1,345	228	—	794	716	50	13
35 to 39	1,136	966	170	—	612	480	36	8
40 to 44	813	690	121	2	496	291	20	6
45 to 49	501	425	76	—	295	189	13	4
50 to 54	305	263	42	—	184	113	5	3
55 to 59	199	175	24	—	122	68	7	2
60 to 64	134	120	14	—	80	47	4	3
65 to 69	91	86	5	—	60	29	1	1
70 to 74	64	54	10	—	44	19	1	—
75 and over	77	69	8	—	62	15	—	—
Unknown	7,797	1,319	56	6,422	364	841	30	6,562

[1] Because of rounding, may not add to total.
[2] Does not include unknown ages.

As in previous years, firearms were the weapons used in approximately 7 of every 10 murders committed in the Nation. Of those murders for which weapons were reported, 59 percent were by handguns, 5 percent by shotguns, and 3 percent by rifles. Other or unknown types of firearms accounted for another 5 percent of the total murders. Among the remaining weapons, knives or cutting instruments were employed in 13 percent of the murders; personal weapons (hands, fists, feet, etc.) in 6 percent; blunt objects (clubs, hammers, etc.) in 5 percent; and other dangerous weapons, such as poison, explosives, etc., in the remainder. (See Table 2.13.) A state-by-state breakdown of weapons used in connection with murder is shown in Table 20.

Table 2.7—Victim/Offender Relationship by Age, 1995

[Single Victim/Single Offender]

Age of Victim	Age of Offender			
	Total	Under 18	18 and over	Unknown
Total	10,032	967	8,390	675
Under 18	1,265	304	893	68
18 and over	8,655	655	7,418	582
Unknown	112	8	79	25

Table 2.8—Victim/Offender Relationship by Race and Sex,[1] 1995

[Single Victim/Single Offender]

Race of Victim	Total	Race of Offender				Sex of Offender		
		White	Black	Other	Unknown	Male	Female	Unknown
White Victims	4,954	4,124	699	60	71	4,443	440	71
Black Victims	4,764	281	4,422	15	46	4,165	553	46
Other Race Victims	253	50	44	153	6	224	23	6
Unknown Race.................................	61	21	10	—	30	30	1	30

Sex of Victim	Total	Race of Offender				Sex of Offender		
		White	Black	Other	Unknown	Male	Female	Unknown
Male Victims	7,382	3,077	4,055	155	95	6,503	784	95
Female Victims	2,589	1,378	1,110	73	28	2,329	232	28
Unknown Sex.................................	61	21	10	—	30	30	1	30

[1] Data based on 10,032 incidents.

Historical statistics on relationships of victims to offenders showed that the majority of murder victims knew their killers. During the 1990s, however, the relationship percentages have changed; in 1995, 15 percent of victims were killed by strangers, and 39 percent of victims were killed by persons whose relationships were unknown, for a collective total of 55 percent. Less than half of murder victims in 1995 were related to or acquainted with their assailants, 11 and 34 percent, respectively. Among all female murder victims in 1995, 26 percent were slain by husbands or boyfriends. Three percent of the male victims were killed by wives or girlfriends.

Considering circumstances, arguments resulted in 28 percent of the murders during the year. Eighteen percent occurred as a result of felonious activities such as robbery, arson, etc., while another 1 percent were suspected to have been the result of some felonious activity. Six percent were juvenile gang killings, which were up 38 percent in volume over the past 5 years. Table 2.14 shows murder circumstances for the same timeframe.

Table 2.9—Murder, Types of Weapons Used, 1995

[Percent distribution by region]

Region	Total all weapons[1]	Firearms	Knives or cutting instruments	Unknown or other dangerous weapons	Personal weapons (hands, fists, feet, etc.)
Total	100.0	68.0	13.0	12.8	6.3
Northeastern States . .	100.0	65.2	15.5	11.7	7.6
Midwestern States . . .	100.0	67.9	12.3	14.7	5.2
Southern States	100.0	68.3	12.0	13.1	6.6
Western States	100.0	70.6	12.1	11.7	5.6

[1] Because of rounding, percentages may not add to totals.

Table 2.10—Murder Victims, Types of Weapons Used, 1991–1995

Weapons	1991	1992	1993	1994	1995
Total	21,676	22,716	23,180	22,084	20,043
Total Firearms	14,373	15,489	16,136	15,463	13,673
Handguns	11,497	12,580	13,212	12,775	11,198
Rifles	745	706	757	724	637
Shotguns	1,124	1,111	1,057	953	917
Other guns	30	42	37	19	29
Firearms–not stated	977	1,050	1,073	992	892
Knives or cutting instruments	3,430	3,296	2,967	2,802	2,538
Blunt objects (clubs, hammers, etc.)	1,099	1,040	1,022	912	904
Personal weapons (hands, fists, feet, etc.)[1]	1,202	1,131	1,151	1,165	1,182
Poison	12	13	9	10	12
Explosives	16	19	23	10	190
Fire	195	203	217	196	166
Narcotics	22	24	22	22	22
Drowning	40	29	23	25	29
Strangulation	327	314	331	287	232
Asphyxiation	113	115	111	113	135
Other weapons or weapons not stated	847	1,043	1,168	1,079	960

[1] Pushed is included in personal weapons.

Table 2.11—Murder Victims, Types of Weapons Used, 1995

Age	Total	Firearms	Knives or cutting instruments	Blunt objects (clubs, hammers, etc.)	Personal[1] weapons (hands, fists, feet, etc.)	Poison	Explosives	Fire	Narcotics	Strangulation	Asphyxiation	Other[2] weapon or weapon not stated
Total	20,043	13,673	2,538	904	1,182	12	190	166	22	232	135	989
Percent distribution	100.0	68.2	12.7	4.5	5.9	.1	.9	.8	.1	1.2	.7	4.9
Under 18[3]	2,428	1,482	148	73	391	4	28	53	5	32	66	146
Under 22[3]	5,445	3,998	408	139	439	5	30	63	8	51	68	236
18 and over[3]	17,278	12,013	2,353	816	763	8	162	108	17	195	68	775
Infant (under 1)	249	8	3	14	143	1	5	3	2	1	33	36
1 to 4	411	61	14	22	194	2	19	21	1	4	21	52
5 to 8	103	41	5	4	15	—	3	16	1	2	2	14
9 to 12	103	67	7	6	9	1	1	5	—	3	1	3
13 to 16	953	789	72	16	17	—	—	8	1	14	8	28
17 to 19	2,116	1,788	175	43	36	—	1	3	—	16	1	53
20 to 24	3,559	2,922	323	82	66	1	7	12	4	34	7	101
25 to 29	2,814	2,147	349	80	75	1	17	9	1	20	9	106
30 to 34	2,526	1,744	375	104	108	—	14	14	2	38	8	119
35 to 39	1,966	1,246	337	106	108	1	17	16	4	27	7	97
40 to 44	1,517	956	226	91	107	—	24	9	2	15	7	80
45 to 49	993	592	165	80	58	2	30	7	1	13	2	43
50 to 54	645	368	101	52	33	2	22	8	—	10	8	41
55 to 59	471	247	89	49	37	—	13	4	—	7	4	21
60 to 64	352	178	70	30	25	—	8	4	—	3	4	30
65 to 69	292	140	59	29	23	1	4	3	—	3	2	28
70 to 74	222	80	44	27	27	—	5	10	1	5	3	20
75 and over	414	121	87	54	73	—	—	9	2	12	7	49
Unknown	337	178	37	15	28	—	—	5	—	5	1	68

[1] Pushed is included in personal weapons.
[2] Includes drowning.
[3] Does not include unknown ages.

Table 2.12—Murder Circumstances by Relationship,[1] 1995

Circumstances	Total	Husband	Wife	Mother	Father	Son	Daughter	Brother	Sister	Other Family	Acquaintance	Friend	Boyfriend	Girlfriend	Neighbor	Employee	Employer	Stranger	Unknown
Total[2]	20,043	267	732	114	148	281	226	124	24	382	5,347	584	191	482	175	7	18	3,036	7,905
Felony type total	3,535	6	11	11	11	25	23	4	2	44	935	69	5	22	38	1	4	1,052	1,272
Rape	79	—	1	—	—	1	1	—	1	2	29	2	—	1	2	—	—	17	22
Robbery	1,855	—	1	3	3	—	—	2	—	20	318	22	—	5	16	1	2	763	699
Burglary	123	—	1	1	1	—	1	—	—	1	20	2	1	2	6	—	—	48	39
Larceny-theft	23	—	—	—	—	—	—	—	—	1	5	1	—	—	—	—	—	13	3
Motor vehicle theft	49	—	—	—	—	—	—	—	—	—	12	2	—	2	—	—	2	24	7
Arson	109	1	2	3	1	3	2	1	1	6	21	—	—	2	7	—	—	9	50
Prostitution and commercialized vice	9	—	—	—	—	—	—	—	—	—	2	—	—	—	—	—	—	4	3
Other sex offenses	30	—	1	—	—	—	—	—	—	—	16	2	—	—	2	—	—	5	4
Narcotic drug laws	1,010	2	2	2	—	2	2	—	—	2	445	34	2	5	2	—	—	125	385
Gambling	22	—	—	—	—	—	—	—	—	—	17	—	—	—	—	—	—	2	3
Other – not specified	226	3	3	2	6	19	17	1	—	12	50	4	2	5	3	—	—	42	57
Suspected felony type	114	—	1	1	—	—	2	—	—	1	27	1	—	1	—	—	—	14	66
Other than felony type total	10,592	243	649	86	124	245	187	114	21	294	3,899	460	171	425	119	6	10	1,576	1,963
Romantic triangle	280	15	40	—	—	—	2	—	—	2	147	15	11	23	1	—	—	13	11
Child killed by babysitter	23	—	—	—	—	1	—	—	—	3	17	1	—	—	—	—	—	—	1
Brawl due to influence of alcohol	254	4	7	2	2	2	1	5	—	7	112	20	3	8	4	—	—	49	28
Brawl due to influence of narcotics	185	2	1	—	—	—	—	1	—	1	80	6	—	2	1	—	—	20	71
Argument over money or property	338	4	3	4	4	1	—	7	1	20	200	35	4	2	4	1	1	24	23
Other arguments	5,188	181	407	43	83	52	26	88	11	183	1,859	284	138	321	80	2	5	684	741
Gangland killings	85	—	—	—	—	—	—	—	1	1	23	1	1	—	1	—	—	30	28
Juvenile gang killings	1,157	—	—	1	—	—	—	—	—	2	600	7	1	1	—	—	—	257	289
Institutional killings	30	—	—	—	—	—	—	—	—	—	19	—	—	—	—	—	—	1	9
Sniper attack	13	—	—	—	—	—	—	—	—	—	3	—	1	—	—	—	—	2	7
Other – not specified	3,039	37	191	36	35	189	158	13	8	75	839	91	13	68	28	3	4	496	755
Unknown	5,802	18	71	16	13	11	14	6	1	43	486	54	15	34	18	—	4	394	4,604

[1] Relationship is that of victim to offender.
[2] Total murder victims for whom supplemental homicide data were received.

Table 2.13—Murder Circumstances by Weapon, 1995

Circumstances	Total murder victims[1]	Total firearms	Handguns	Rifles	Shotguns	Other guns or type not stated	Knives or cutting instruments	Blunt objects (clubs, hammers, etc.)	Personal weapons (hands, fists, feet, etc.)	Poison	Pushed or thrown out window	Explosives	Fire	Narcotics	Drowning	Strangulation	Asphyxiation	Other
Total[1]	20,043	13,673	11,198	637	917	921	2,538	904	1,178	12	4	190	166	22	29	232	135	960
Felony type total	3,535	2,472	2,170	59	146	97	362	187	194	—	—	10	99	10	7	52	25	117
Rape	79	10	9	1	—	—	16	7	26	—	—	—	—	—	2	13	1	4
Robbery	1,855	1,382	1,218	23	80	61	206	111	83	—	—	—	1	—	2	18	13	39
Burglary	123	59	49	2	6	2	28	12	15	—	—	—	—	—	—	5	—	4
Larceny-theft	23	15	13	—	1	1	5	—	2	—	—	—	—	—	—	1	—	—
Motor vehicle theft	49	32	20	3	5	4	4	5	—	—	—	—	—	—	—	1	—	7
Arson	109	2	—	—	2	—	2	3	—	—	—	6	90	—	—	2	—	4
Prostitution and commercialized vice	9	2	2	—	—	—	3	—	—	—	—	—	2	—	—	—	—	2
Other sex offenses	30	4	1	3	—	—	9	4	6	—	—	—	—	—	—	5	1	1
Narcotic drug laws	1,010	855	776	20	33	26	65	26	22	—	—	3	1	9	—	5	4	20
Gambling	22	19	19	—	—	—	2	—	—	—	—	—	—	—	—	—	—	1
Other – not specified	226	92	63	7	19	3	22	19	40	—	—	1	5	1	3	2	6	35
Suspected felony type	114	71	56	2	4	9	11	9	7	—	—	—	2	—	1	2	3	8
Other than felony type total	10,592	7,108	5,681	456	582	389	1,598	450	741	8	3	176	35	11	18	77	80	287
Romantic triangle	280	216	161	21	21	13	42	5	7	—	—	—	2	—	—	1	—	7
Child killed by babysitter	23	—	—	—	—	—	—	3	16	—	—	—	—	—	—	—	2	2
Brawl due to influence of alcohol	254	132	105	10	12	5	69	22	27	—	—	—	—	—	1	1	1	1
Brawl due to influence of narcotics	185	149	120	7	9	13	15	4	3	—	—	—	—	1	—	2	—	11
Argument over money or property	338	244	206	12	14	12	45	25	13	—	—	—	2	1	—	1	—	7
Other arguments	5,188	3,389	2,770	205	308	106	1,094	248	295	2	—	2	12	—	2	53	13	78
Gangland killings	85	83	72	4	2	5	2	—	—	—	—	—	—	—	—	—	—	—
Juvenile gang killings	1,157	1,114	973	68	38	35	31	4	5	—	—	—	—	—	—	—	—	2
Institutional killings	30	—	—	—	—	—	14	2	10	—	—	—	—	—	—	1	—	2
Sniper attack	13	11	6	1	2	2	—	—	—	—	—	—	—	—	—	—	—	2
Other – not specified	3,039	1,769	1,267	128	176	198	286	137	365	6	3	174	19	9	15	18	64	174
Unknown	5,802	4,022	3,291	120	185	426	567	258	236	4	1	4	30	1	3	101	27	548

[1] Total murder victims for whom supplemental homicide data were received.

Table 2.14—Murder Circumstances, 1991–1995

Circumstances	1991	1992	1993	1994	1995
Total[1]	21,676	22,716	23,180	22,084	20,043
Felony type total:	4,636	4,917	4,461	4,070	3,535
Rape	132	138	115	78	79
Robbery	2,226	2,266	2,305	2,076	1,855
Burglary	197	212	179	157	123
Larceny-theft	32	41	31	30	23
Motor vehicle theft	53	66	61	53	49
Arson	138	148	154	132	109
Prostitution and commercialized vice	20	32	18	14	9
Other sex offenses	47	34	28	41	30
Narcotic drug laws	1,353	1,302	1,295	1,239	1,010
Gambling	33	20	10	12	22
Other – not specified	405	658	265	238	226
Suspected felony type	210	280	145	136	114
Other than felony type total: . . .	11,220	11,244	12,210	11,691	10,592
Romantic triangle	314	334	440	371	280
Child killed by babysitter . . .	32	36	34	22	23
Brawl due to influence of alcohol	500	429	383	316	254
Brawl due to influence of narcotics	254	253	261	211	185
Argument over money or property	520	483	445	387	338
Other arguments	6,108	6,066	6,289	5,820	5,188
Gangland killings	206	137	142	111	85
Juvenile gang killings	840	813	1,145	1,157	1,157
Institutional killings	19	18	15	14	30
Sniper attack	12	33	7	2	13
Other – not specified	2,415	2,642	3,049	3,280	3,039
Unknown	5,610	6,275	6,364	6,187	5,802

[1] Total number of murder victims for whom supplemental homicide information was received.

Table 2.15—Murder Circumstances by Victim Sex, 1995

Circumstances	Total murder victims[1]	Male	Female	Unknown
Total[1]	20,043	15,356	4,654	33
Felony type total:	3,535	2,815	719	1
Rape	79	7	72	—
Robbery	1,855	1,570	284	1
Burglary	123	63	60	—
Larceny-theft	23	20	3	—
Motor vehicle theft	49	37	12	—
Arson	109	56	53	—
Prostitution and commercialized vice	9	2	7	—
Other sex offenses	30	14	16	—
Narcotic drug laws	1,010	883	127	—
Gambling	22	22	—	—
Other – not specified	226	141	85	—
Suspected felony type	114	73	41	—
Other than felony type total:	10,592	8,020	2,570	2
Romantic triangle	280	187	93	—
Child killed by babysitter	23	16	7	—
Brawl due to influence of alcohol	254	228	26	—
Brawl due to influence of narcotics	185	163	22	—
Argument over money or property	338	299	38	1
Other arguments	5,188	3,908	1,280	—
Gangland killings	85	75	10	—
Juvenile gang killings	1,157	1,090	67	—
Institutional killings	30	28	2	—
Sniper attack	13	13	—	—
Other – not specified	3,039	2,013	1,025	1
Unknown	5,802	4,448	1,324	30

[1] Total number of murder victims for whom supplemental homicide information was received.

Law Enforcement Response

The 1995 clearance rate for murder, 65 percent for law enforcement agencies nationwide, is higher than for any other Crime Index offense. Eighty percent of murders in rural counties, 66 percent of those in suburban counties, and 63 percent in the Nation's cities were cleared. Among the city population groups, those with populations under 25,000 reported the most successful clearance rate, 81 percent. (See Table 25.)

Regionally, the highest murder clearance rates were registered in the South and the Midwest, each with 70 percent. Following were the Northeastern States with 59 percent and the Western States with 58 percent.

The proportion of juvenile involvement, as measured by clearances, was lower for murder than for any other Index crime. Persons under 18 years of age accounted for 9 percent of the willful killings cleared by law enforcement nationally in 1995. Only persons in this young age group also accounted for 9 percent of clearances in the Nation's cities and suburban counties. They accounted for 7 percent of the rural county clearances.

Law enforcement agencies made an estimated 21,230 arrests for murder in 1995. Fifty-six percent of the arrestees in 1995 were under 25 years of age, with the 18- to 24-year age group accounting for 41 percent of the total. (See Table 38.)

Ninety-one percent of those arrested for murder in 1995 were males and 9 percent, females. Blacks comprised 54 percent of the total; whites, 43 percent; and the remainder, other races.

The 1995 murder arrest total was 6 percent lower than the 1994 count. During the 2-year period, arrests of adults decreased 4 percent and those of juveniles dropped 14 percent. Arrests of females for murder were down 11 percent, and those of males, down 6 percent.

Long-term trends indicate the 1995 murder arrest total was 15 percent below the 1991 level but 8 percent higher than the 1986 figure.

Justifiable Homicide

Certain willful killings are classified as justifiable or excusable, based on law enforcement investigation. In Uniform Crime Reporting, justifiable homicide is defined as and limited to the killing of a felon by a law enforcement officer in the line of duty, or the killing by a private citizen of a felon during the commission of a felony. These offenses are tabulated independently and are not included in the murder counts.

In 1995, the total number of justifiable homicides decreased 20 percent. The justifiable homicide total was 651 in 1995 and 815 in 1994. Compared to the 1991 count of 698, the 1995 total was down 7 percent. Of justifiable homicides in 1995, 383 involved law enforcement officers and 268 were by private citizens. Data on weapons showed that handguns were the weapons used most often in justifiable homicides. (See Tables 2.16 and 2.17.)

Table 2.16—Justifiable Homicide by Weapon, Law Enforcement,[1] 1991–1995

Year	Total	Total fire-arms	Hand-guns	Rifles	Shot-guns	Fire-arms type not stated	Knives or other cutting instru-ments	Other danger-ous weapons	Personal weapons
1991 ...	367	361	319	10	25	7	1	3	2
1992 ...	418	411	357	22	21	11	4	1	2
1993 ...	455	451	391	22	26	12	—	2	2
1994 ...	462	460	404	21	29	6	—	1	1
1995 ...	383	380	345	12	19	4	—	3	—

[1] The killing of a felon by a law enforcement officer in the line of duty.

Table 2.17—Justifiable Homicide by Weapon, Private Citizen,[1] 1991–1995

Year	Total	Total fire-arms	Hand-guns	Rifles	Shot-guns	Fire-arms type not stated	Knives or other cutting instru-ments	Other danger-ous weapons	Personal weapons
1991 ...	331	296	243	15	25	13	29	4	2
1992 ...	351	311	264	20	24	3	31	5	4
1993 ...	357	313	254	15	33	11	28	9	7
1994 ...	353	316	260	17	29	10	19	13	5
1995 ...	268	230	179	18	25	8	24	10	4

[1] The killing of a felon, during the commission of a felony, by a private citizen.

FORCIBLE RAPE

DEFINITION

Forcible rape, as defined in the Program, is the carnal knowledge of a female forcibly and against her will. Assaults or attempts to commit rape by force or threat of force are also included; however, statutory rape (without force) and other sex offenses are excluded.

TREND		
Year	Number of offenses	Rate per 100,000 inhabitants
1994	102,216	39.3
1995	97,464	37.1
Percent change	−4.6	−5.6

The 97,464 forcible rapes reported to law enforcement agencies across the Nation during 1995 represented the lowest total since 1989. The 1995 count was 5 percent lower than in 1994, 9 percent below the 1991 level, but 7 percent higher than the 1986 volume.

Geographically, 39 percent of the forcible rape total in 1995 was accounted for by the most populous Southern States, 25 percent by the Midwestern States, 23 percent by the Western States, and 13 percent by the Northeastern States. Two-year trends showed that forcible rapes declined in all regions. The Northeast and Midwest each registered decreases of 6 percent; the South, 5 percent; and the West, 2 percent. (See Tables 3 and 4.)

Monthly totals show the lowest rape volume occurred in December, while the most forcible rapes were reported during August. (See Table 2.18.)

Table 2.18—Forcible Rape by Month, 1991–1995
[Percent distribution]

Months	1991	1992	1993	1994	1995
January	7.1	7.0	7.7	7.5	7.7
February	7.0	7.6	6.9	7.3	7.1
March	7.9	8.6	8.5	8.3	8.5
April	8.3	8.5	8.2	8.4	7.9
May	9.2	8.9	8.9	8.9	8.8
June	9.2	8.7	9.2	9.2	8.5
July	9.5	9.4	9.7	9.7	9.4
August	9.7	9.6	9.3	9.6	9.9
September	8.8	8.7	8.3	8.7	8.8
October	8.6	8.4	8.1	8.5	8.8
November	7.8	7.6	7.5	7.3	7.8
December	6.8	7.0	7.7	6.5	6.8

Rate

By Uniform Crime Reporting definition, the victims of forcible rape are always female, and in 1995, an estimated 72 of every 100,000 females in the country were reported rape victims. The 1995 female forcible rape rate was 6 percent lower than the 1994 rate and 13 percent lower than the 1991 rate.

The highest rate in 1995 was recorded in the Nation's metropolitan areas where it was 76 victims per 100,000 females. In cities outside metropolitan areas, the rate was 73 per 100,000 females, and in rural counties, it was 49 per 100,000 females. Although metropolitan areas record the highest rape rates, they have shown the only rate decline over the past 10 years (1986–1995), 10 percent. During this same time, the rate increased in cities outside metropolitan areas by 70 percent and in rural counties by 40 percent.

Geographically, in 1995, the highest female rape rate was in the Southern States, which recorded 80 victims per 100,000 females. The Midwestern States followed closely with a rate of 78; the Western States registered 75; and the Northeastern States, 49. For the 2-year period, 1994 and 1995, the changes in the forcible rape rates ranged from a decline of 7 percent in the Midwest to a 4-percent decrease in the West.

Over the last 10 years, regional increases in the female forcible rape rate were 13 percent in the Midwest and 1 percent in the South. Forcible rape rate decreases were reported in the Northeast and West, 11 and 13 percent, respectively, for the same timeframe.

Nature

Rapes by force constitute the greatest percentage of total forcible rapes, 87 percent of the 1995 incidents. The remainder were attempts or assaults to commit forcible rape. The number of rapes by force decreased 5 percent in 1995 from the 1994 volume, and attempts to rape decreased 6 percent.

As for all other Crime Index offenses, complaints of forcible rape made to law enforcement agencies are sometimes found to be false or baseless. In such cases, law enforcement agencies "unfound" the offenses and exclude them from crime counts. The "unfounded" rate, or percentage of complaints determined through investigation to be false, is higher for forcible rape than for any other Index crime. In 1995, 8 percent of forcible rape complaints were "unfounded," while the average for all Index crimes was 2 percent.

Law Enforcement Response

In 1995, over half of the forcible rapes reported to law enforcement nationwide and in cities were cleared by arrest or exceptional means. Rural and suburban county law enforcement clearance rates, each at 52 percent, were slightly higher than the cities' rate, 51 percent. (See Table 25.)

Geographically, forcible rape clearance rates in 1995 were 46 percent in the West, 49 percent in the Midwest, 50 percent in the Northeast, and 56 percent in the South. (See Table 26.)

Of the total clearances for forcible rape in the country as a whole, 15 percent involved only persons under 18 years of age. The percentage of juvenile involvement varied by community type, ranging from 13 percent in the Nation's cities to 22 percent in suburban counties. (See Table 28.)

Law enforcement agencies nationwide made an estimated 34,650 arrests for forcible rape in 1995. Of the forcible rape arrestees, about 4 of every 10 were under age 25. Over half of those arrested were white. (See Tables 29, 41, and 43.)

The number of arrests for forcible rape declined 5 percent nationwide from 1994 to 1995. Arrests fell 4 percent in the Nation's cities, 6 percent in the suburban counties, and 14 percent in the rural counties. (See Tables 36, 44, 50, and 56.)

FORCIBLE RAPE

CHART 2.7
PERCENT CHANGE FROM 1991

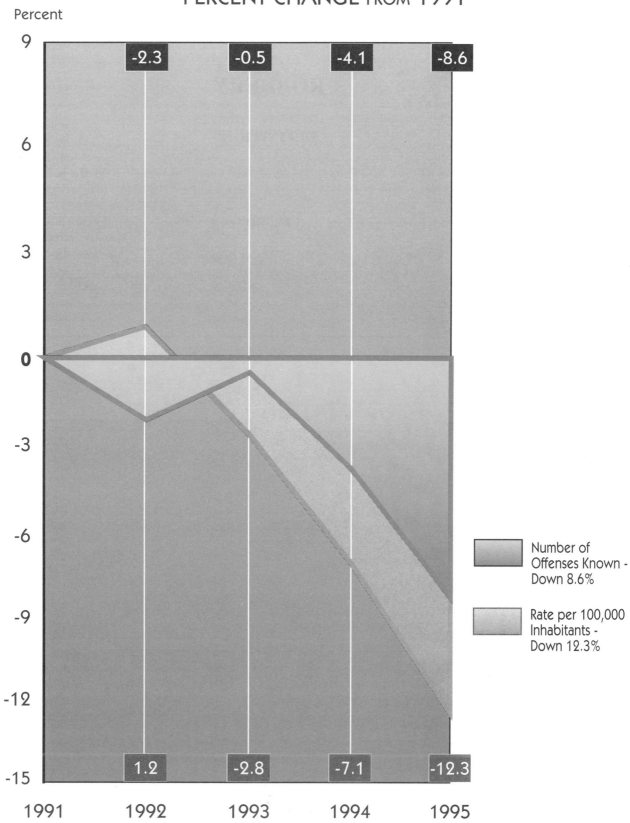

Percent

-2.3   -0.5   -4.1   -8.6

1.2   -2.8   -7.1   -12.3

Number of
Offenses Known -
Down 8.6%

Rate per 100,000
Inhabitants -
Down 12.3%

1991   1992   1993   1994   1995

ROBBERY

DEFINITION

Robbery is the taking or attempting to take anything of value from the care, custody, or control of a person or persons by force or threat of force or violence and/or by putting the victim in fear.

TREND		
Year	Number of offenses	Rate per 100,000 inhabitants
1994	618,949	237.7
1995	580,545	220.9
Percent change	−6.2	−7.1

The 1995 estimated robbery total, 580,545, was the lowest since 1989. Nationally, the 1995 robbery volume was down 6 percent from the 1994 total. In the Nation's cities, robberies decreased 7 percent. The largest decline—12 percent—was experienced in cities with a million or more inhabitants. During the same period, the robbery volume dropped 3 percent in the suburban counties but increased 1 percent in the rural counties. (See Table 12.)

Regionally, the Southern States, the most populous region, accounted for 34 percent of all reported robberies. The Western States followed with 24 percent, the Northeastern States with 23 percent, and the Midwestern States with 19 percent. (See Table 3.) Two-year trends show the number of robberies in 1995 was down in all regions as compared to 1994. The declines ranged from 11 percent in the Northeast to 3 percent in the South.

Chart 2.8 depicts the national trend in the robbery volume, as well as the robbery rate, for the years 1991–1995. In 1995, the number of robbery offenses was 16 percent lower than in 1991 but 7 percent higher than in 1986.

Monthly volume figures for 1995 show robberies occurred most frequently in October and least often in February.

Table 2.19—Robbery by Month, 1991–1995
[Percent distribution]

Months	1991	1992	1993	1994	1995
January	8.7	9.0	8.8	8.7	8.6
February	7.5	8.0	7.1	7.7	7.3
March	8.0	8.1	8.3	8.6	8.1
April	7.4	7.8	7.4	8.0	7.5
May	7.8	7.9	7.5	8.0	7.8
June	7.8	7.9	8.1	8.0	8.0
July	8.4	8.4	8.7	8.5	8.5
August	8.8	8.6	8.8	8.8	8.9
September	8.5	8.3	8.4	8.3	8.5
October	9.2	8.7	9.0	8.8	9.2
November	8.7	8.3	8.5	8.2	8.7
December	9.2	9.0	9.4	8.4	8.9

Rate

The national robbery rate in 1995 was 221 per 100,000 people, 7 percent lower than in 1994. In metropolitan areas, the 1995 rate was 268; in cities outside metropolitan areas, it was 72; and in the rural areas, it was 17. With 768 robberies per 100,000 inhabitants, the highest rate was recorded in cities with populations 1 million and over. (See Table 16.)

Robbery rates per 100,000 inhabitants declined in all regions from 1994 to 1995. The rates of 260 in the Northeast and 242 in the West were down 11 and 6 percent, respectively. The South's rate of 212 was 4 percent lower; and the Midwest's rate of 182 was down 9 percent. (See Table 4.)

Nature

Losses estimated at $507 million were attributed to robberies during 1995. The value of property stolen averaged $873 per robbery, up from $801 in 1994. Average dollar losses in 1995 ranged from $400 taken during robberies of convenience stores to $4,015 per bank robbery. (See Table 23.) The impact of this violent crime on its victims cannot be measured in terms of monetary loss alone. While the object of a robbery is to obtain money or property, the crime always involves force or threat of force, and many victims suffer serious personal injury.

Robberies on streets or highways accounted for more than half (54 percent) of the offenses in this category during 1995. Robberies of commercial and financial establishments accounted for 21 percent, and those occurring at residences, 11 percent. The remainder were miscellaneous types. All robbery types declined in 1995 as compared to 1994 totals. The decreases ranged from 10 percent for convenience store robberies to 4 percent for those of gas or service stations. (See Table 23.)

Table 2.20—Robbery, Percent Distribution, 1995
[By region]

	United States Total	North-eastern States	Mid-western States	Southern States	Western States
Total[1]	100.0	100.0	100.0	100.0	100.0
Street/highway	54.3	64.1	61.6	50.7	48.8
Commercial house	12.3	9.0	10.4	12.4	15.5
Gas or service station .	2.3	1.9	2.8	2.3	2.4
Convenience store	5.2	2.9	3.8	6.6	5.6
Residence	10.8	10.1	9.6	13.5	8.4
Bank	1.6	.9	1.3	1.3	2.6
Miscellaneous	13.4	11.0	10.6	13.3	16.6

[1] Because of rounding, percentages may not add to totals.

ROBBERY

CHART 2.8

PERCENT CHANGE FROM 1991

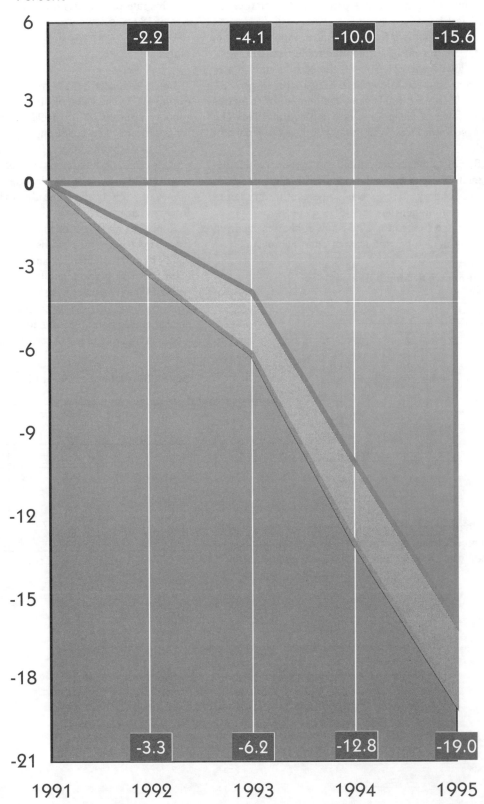

Percent

-2.2   -4.1   -10.0   -15.6

6

3

0

-3

-6

-9

-12

-15

-18

-21

Number of
Offenses Known -
Down 15.6%

Rate per 100,000
Inhabitants -
Down 19.0%

-3.3   -6.2   -12.8   -19.0

1991   1992   1993   1994   1995

Table 2.21—Robbery, Percent Distribution, 1995

[By population group]

	Group I (55 cities, 250,000 and over; population 39,629,000)	Group II (136 cities, 100,000 to 249,999; population 20,081,000)	Group III (341 cities, 50,000 to 99,999; population 23,166,000)	Group IV (616 cities, 25,000 to 49,999; population 21,191,000)	Group V (1,481 cities, 10,000 to 24,999; population 23,280,000)	Group VI (5,839 cities under 10,000; population 20,038,000)	County agencies (3,637 agencies; population 74,008,000)
Total[1]	100.0	100.0	100.0	100.0	100.0	100.0	100.0
Street/highway	62.9	54.8	50.9	42.6	38.8	31.0	36.5
Commercial house	10.7	12.9	13.1	13.8	13.6	14.0	16.1
Gas or service station	1.5	2.2	2.8	3.3	3.9	3.4	3.9
Convenience store	2.9	5.8	6.2	7.9	9.0	10.5	9.2
Residence	9.9	10.6	9.7	10.5	11.8	12.4	15.9
Bank	1.1	1.7	2.0	2.5	2.3	2.4	2.1
Miscellaneous	10.8	12.0	15.4	19.3	20.7	26.3	16.3

[1] Because of rounding, percentages may not add to totals.

Firearms were the weapons used in 41 percent of robberies in 1995. Strong-armed tactics were used in another 41 percent, knives or cutting instruments in 9 percent, and other dangerous weapons in the remainder. A comparison of 1994 and 1995 robbery totals by weapon showed those by strong-arm tactics decreased 3 percent; those by firearms were down 8 percent; those by knives or cutting instruments declined 10 percent; and those by other dangerous weapons dropped 12 percent. A state-by-state breakdown of weapons used in robberies in 1995 is shown in Table 21.

Table 2.22—Robbery, Types of Weapons Used, 1995

[Percent distribution by region]

Region	Total all weapons[1]	Armed			
		Firearms	Knives or cutting instruments	Other weapons	Strong-armed
Total	100.0	41.0	9.1	9.2	40.7
Northeastern States	100.0	33.3	11.7	10.4	44.6
Midwestern States	100.0	45.6	7.8	9.0	37.7
Southern States	100.0	45.1	6.5	8.9	39.6
Western States	100.0	38.9	10.4	8.4	42.2

[1] Because of rounding, percentages may not add to totals.

Law Enforcement Response

The 1995 robbery clearance rate was 25 percent nationally. The highest robbery clearance rate—40 percent—was registered by rural county law enforcement agencies. In suburban counties, the rate was 28 percent, and in the Nation's cities, it was 24 percent. (See Table 25.) Regional robbery clearance percentages ranged from 21 percent in the Northeast to 27 percent in the South. (See Table 26.)

Persons under the age of 18, exclusively, were the offenders in 20 percent of all 1995 robbery clearances. This age group accounted for 22 percent of the suburban county clearances, 20 percent of those in the Nation's cities, and 14 percent of those by rural county agencies. (See Table 28.)

Two percent fewer persons were arrested for robbery in 1995 than in 1994. For the 2-year period, arrests of adults for robbery also declined 2 percent, and those of juveniles decreased 1 percent. The number of robbery arrests dropped 3 percent in the Nation's cities but increased 11 percent in the rural counties and 1 percent in suburban counties.

Considering the 5-year period, 1991–1995, total arrests and arrests of males for robbery were each down 7 percent, while arrests of females were up 3 percent. For the same timespan, arrests of persons 18 years of age and older decreased 15 percent, but juvenile arrests rose 18 percent.

Sixty-four percent of all robbery arrestees in 1995 were under 25 years of age, and 91 percent were males. Fifty-nine percent of those arrested were black, 39 percent were white, and the remainder were of other races.

Street Robbery

Down 17%

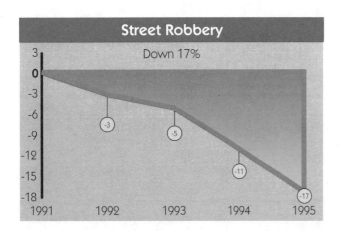

Commercial House Robbery

Down 16%

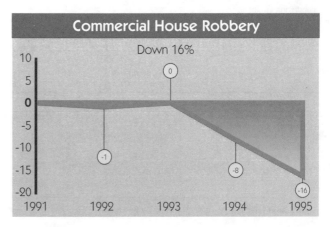

Gas Station Robbery

Down 25%

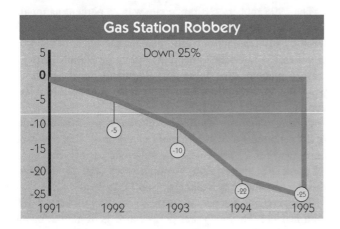

Convenience Store Robbery

Down 33%

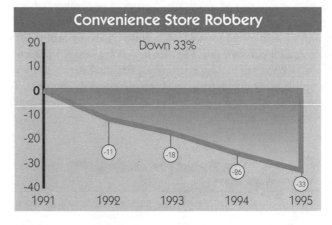

Residence Robbery

Down 5%

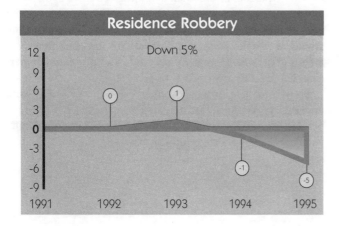

Bank Robbery

Down 22%

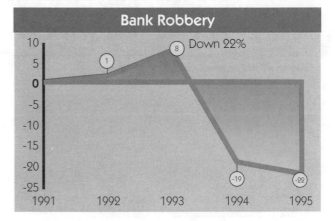

AGGRAVATED ASSAULT

DEFINITION

Aggravated assault is an unlawful attack by one person upon another for the purpose of inflicting severe or aggravated bodily injury. This type of assault is usually accompanied by the use of a weapon or by means likely to produce death or great bodily harm. Attempts are included since it is not necessary that an injury result when a gun, knife, or other weapon is used which could and probably would result in serious personal injury if the crime were successfully completed.

	TREND	
Year	Number of offenses	Rate per 100,000 inhabitants
1994	1,113,179	427.6
1995	1,099,179	418.3
Percent change	−1.3	−2.2

For the second consecutive year, aggravated assaults declined 1 percent to a total of 1,099,179 offenses in 1995. Aggravated assaults in 1995 accounted for 61 percent of the violent crimes.

Geographic distribution figures show that 40 percent of the aggravated assault volume was accounted for by the most populous Southern Region. Following were the Western Region with 25 percent, the Midwestern Region with 20 percent, and the Northeastern Region with 15 percent. Among the regions, only the Midwest registered an increase in the number of reported aggravated assaults. (See Table 4.)

The 1995 monthly figures show that the greatest number of aggravated assaults was recorded during July, while the lowest volume occurred during February.

Table 2.23—Aggravated Assault by Month, 1991–1995

[Percent distribution]

Months	1991	1992	1993	1994	1995
January	6.9	7.3	7.5	7.2	7.6
February	6.6	7.3	6.5	7.0	7.1
March	7.7	8.0	8.1	8.3	8.1
April	8.1	8.7	8.3	8.5	8.3
May	9.1	9.2	8.9	8.8	8.8
June	9.3	8.9	9.1	8.9	8.8
July	9.7	9.4	9.6	9.5	9.4
August	9.9	9.1	9.2	9.4	9.3
September	9.0	8.6	8.3	8.9	8.9
October	8.6	8.5	8.5	8.7	8.8
November	7.6	7.6	7.4	7.7	7.6
December	7.6	7.4	8.6	7.3	7.4

The Nation's cities collectively experienced a decrease of 3 percent in the aggravated assault volume from 1994 to 1995. Among city population groupings, both cities with populations over a million and cities with populations from 250,000 to 499,999 recorded 5-percent declines. The number of aggravated assaults decreased 1 percent in suburban counties but increased 6 percent in the rural counties during the same 2-year period. (See Table 12.)

Five- and 10-year trends for the country as a whole showed aggravated assaults 1 percent higher than in 1991 and 32 percent above the 1986 experience. (See Table 1.)

Rate

There were 418 reported victims of aggravated assault for every 100,000 people nationwide in 1995, the lowest rate since 1989. The rate was 2 percent lower than in 1994 and 3 percent below the 1991 rate. The 1995 rate was, however, 21 percent above the 1986 rate.

Higher than the national average, the rate in metropolitan areas was 459 per 100,000 in 1995. Cities outside metropolitan areas experienced a rate of 369, and rural counties, a rate of 187.

Regionally, the aggravated assault rate was 319 per 100,000 people in the Northeast, 359 in the Midwest, 474 in the South, and 481 in the West. Compared to 1994 rates, 1995 aggravated assault rates were down in all regions except the Midwest, which registered a 3-percent increase. (See Table 4.)

Nature

Thirty-three percent of the aggravated assaults in 1995 were committed with blunt objects or other dangerous weapons. Of the remaining weapon categories, personal weapons such as hands, fists, and feet were used in 26 percent of the assaults; firearms in 23 percent; and knives or cutting instruments in the remainder.

Three of the four categories of weapons decreased in use during 1995, with personal weapons (hands, fists, feet, etc.) showing the only increase, less than 1 percent. Those aggravated assaults involving firearms decreased 9 percent; assaults with knives or cutting instruments, 2 percent; and those with blunt objects or other dangerous weapons, 1 percent.

Table 2.24—Aggravated Assault, Types of Weapons Used, 1995

[Percent distribution by region]

Region	Total all weapons[1]	Firearms	Knives or cutting instruments	Other weapons (clubs, blunt objects, etc.)	Personal weapons
Total	100.0	22.9	18.3	32.9	25.9
Northeastern States	100.0	14.3	21.1	35.3	29.3
Midwestern States	100.0	25.4	19.7	34.0	20.9
Southern States	100.0	25.4	18.8	34.3	21.5
Western States	100.0	22.1	14.4	29.2	34.3

AGGRAVATED ASSAULT

CHART 2.10

PERCENT CHANGE FROM 1991

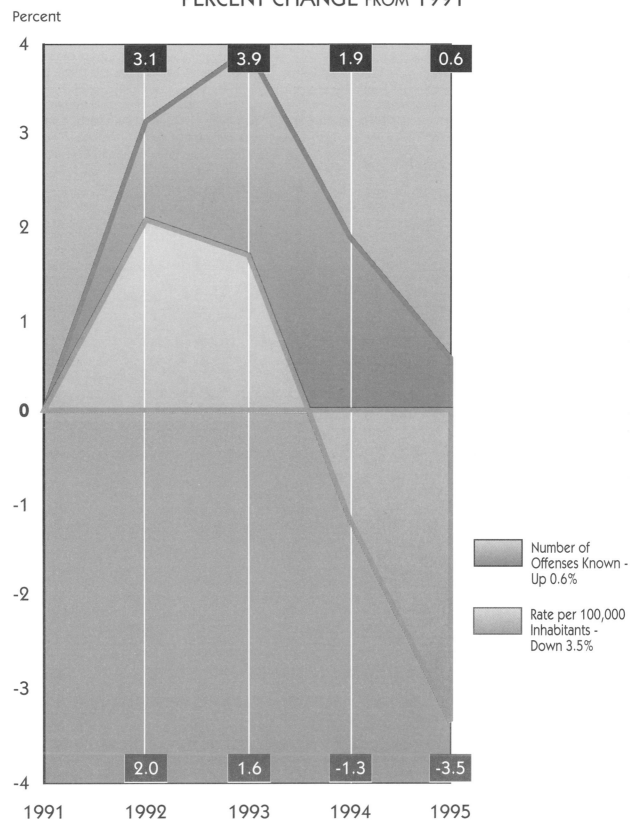

Percent

4 ·
3.1 · 3.9 · 1.9 · 0.6

3 ·

2 ·

1 ·

0

-1 ·

-2 ·

-3 ·

2.0 · 1.6 · -1.3 · -3.5
-4 ·

1991 · 1992 · 1993 · 1994 · 1995

Number of Offenses Known - Up 0.6%

Rate per 100,000 Inhabitants - Down 3.5%

Law Enforcement Response

Law enforcement agencies nationwide recorded a 56-percent aggravated assault clearance rate during 1995. The cities collectively reported 54 percent cleared, while the suburban and rural county law enforcement agencies cleared 60 and 64 percent, respectively. Among the city groupings, those with populations under 10,000 recorded the highest assault clearance rate, 66 percent. (See Table 25.)

Regional clearance percentages for aggravated assault were 58 percent in the West, 57 percent in the South, 53 percent in the Midwest, and 51 percent in the Northeast.

Thirteen percent of the clearances reported nationally and in cities involved only persons under age 18. Persons in this age group were identified as the assailants in 14 percent of the clearances in the suburban counties and 10 percent of those in the rural counties.

Seven of every 10 violent crime arrests were for aggravated assault in 1995. Of the over 437,000 arrestees, whites comprised 60 percent; blacks, 38 percent; and all other races, the remainder. Eighty-two percent of the arrestees were males, and 85 percent, adults.

Total aggravated assault arrests were up 1 percent in 1995 from the 1994 total. During this 2-year period, the number of adult arrests increased 2 percent, while arrests of persons under age 18 decreased 3 percent. A comparison of 1991 and 1995 figures showed increases of 8 percent for both total arrests and those of adults. Juvenile aggravated assault arrests increased 11 percent.

PROPERTY CRIME TOTAL

DEFINITION

Property crime includes the offenses of burglary, larceny-theft, motor vehicle theft, and arson. The object of the theft-type offenses is the taking of money or property, but there is no force or threat of force against the victims. Arson is included since it involves the destruction of property; its victims may be subjected to force.

Year	Number of offenses[1]	Rate per 100,000 inhabitants[1]
TREND		
1994	12,131,873	4,660.0
1995	12,068,358	4,593.0
Percent change	−.5	−1.4

[1]Does not include arson. See page 57.

Estimated at 12.1 million offenses, property crime declined 1 percent in 1995 to its lowest total since 1987. Five- and 10-year trends show the 1995 volume was 7 percent lower than the 1991 level but was 3 percent higher than in 1986.

During 1995, 38 percent of all property crimes were recorded in the Southern States. Following were the Western States with 25 percent, the Midwestern States with 21 percent, and the Northeastern States with 15 percent.

A comparison of 1994 and 1995 regional property crime volumes showed declines of 3 percent in the Northeast and 1 percent in the Midwest. The volume of property crime increased 1 percent in the West and showed virtually no change in the South. (See Table 4.)

The Nation's cities collectively recorded a 1-percent property crime decrease, with the greatest drop (6 percent) in cities with populations of a million or more. The suburban counties also experienced a 1-percent decline, while rural county law enforcement agencies recorded an increase of 4 percent. (See Table 12.)

As in previous years, 1995 monthly figures show more property crime occurred in August, while the lowest total was recorded in February.

Table 2.25—Property Crime Total by Month, 1991–1995

[Percent distribution]

Months	1991	1992	1993	1994	1995
January	7.9	8.4	8.0	7.6	8.1
February	7.4	7.8	6.9	7.1	7.2
March	8.2	8.2	8.1	8.2	8.2
April	8.0	8.0	7.9	8.0	7.8
May	8.3	8.2	8.1	8.5	8.4
June	8.4	8.4	8.6	8.5	8.5
July	9.1	9.0	9.1	9.2	9.0
August	9.2	9.1	9.2	9.4	9.2
September	8.4	8.4	8.4	8.5	8.5
October	8.7	8.5	8.6	8.8	8.8
November	8.0	8.0	8.1	8.3	8.2
December	8.4	8.1	9.1	7.9	8.0

Rate

In 1995, there were an estimated 4,593 property crimes for every 100,000 United States inhabitants. The 1995 property crime rate was 1 percent lower than the 1994 rate and 11 percent under the 1991 rate.

Geographically, 1995 property crime rates decreased in all regions from the previous year. The rate of 3,570 per 100,000 in the Northeast showed the largest decline, 3 percent. The rate

of 5,004 in the South represented a 2-percent decrease; and the rates of 5,312 in the West and 4,163 in the Midwest were each down 1 percent.

Property crime rates for 1995 were 4,986 in metropolitan areas, 4,833 in cities outside metropolitan areas, and 1,850 in rural counties. By population group, the highest rate—8,241— was recorded in cities with populations from 250,000 to 499,999. (See Tables 2 and 16.)

Nature

The total dollar value of property stolen in connection with property crimes in 1995 was estimated at $15.1 billion. The average loss per offense in 1995 was $1,251 up slightly compared to $1,248 in 1994.

Larceny-theft accounted for 66 percent of all property crime in 1995. Burglary accounted for 22 percent and motor vehicle theft for 12 percent. Based on information from 11,887 law enforcement agencies who provided detailed arson data, more than 80,000 arson offenses were reported in 1995. The average dollar loss of property damaged due to reported arsons was $11,151.

Law Enforcement Response

Property crimes generally have lower clearance rates than violent crimes, and in 1995, the overall property crime clearance rate was 18 percent, as compared to 45 percent for violent crime. Geographically, the Midwest's and South's 1995 property crime clearance rates equaled the Nation's, 18 percent. Rates of 17 percent were recorded in both the Northeast and West. (See Table 26.)

Twenty-five percent of the property crimes cleared by law enforcement nationwide and in cities in 1995 involved only young people under age 18. The juvenile percentage was 26 percent in suburban counties and 22 percent in rural counties. (See Table 28.)

The estimated 2,128,600 persons arrested for property crimes in 1995 accounted for 14 percent of all arrestees. Property crime arrests in 1995 were 1 percent below the 1994 level, 8 percent lower than the 1991 total, but 2 percent above the 1986 experience. Compared to 1994 totals, arrests of juveniles and adults for property crimes declined 2 and 1 percent, respectively, nationwide. (See Tables 32, 34, and 36.)

In 1995, 73 percent of all property crime arrestees were males, 65 percent of the total were white, and 65 percent were over the age of 18.

PROPERTY CRIME

CHART 2.11
PERCENT CHANGE FROM 1991

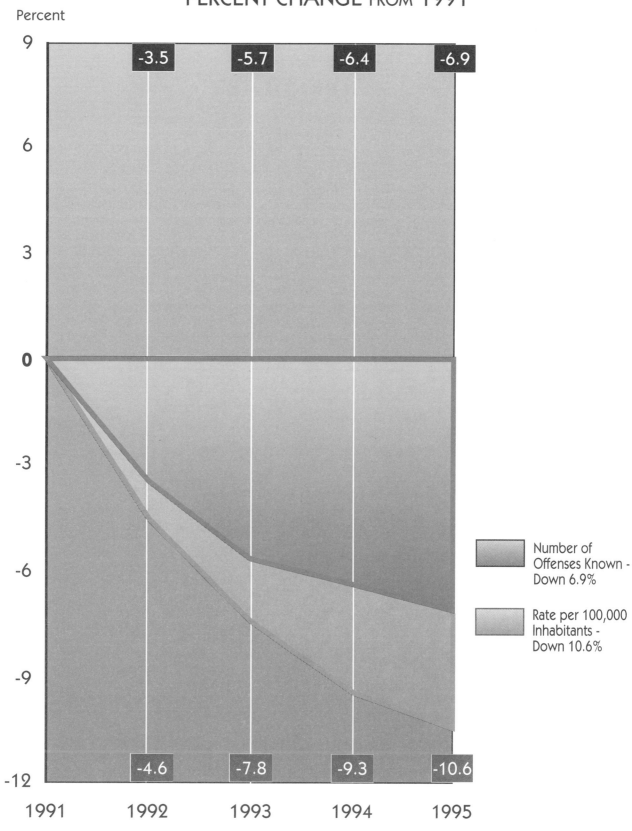

Percent

	1991	1992	1993	1994	1995
		-3.5	-5.7	-6.4	-6.9
		-4.6	-7.8	-9.3	-10.6

Number of Offenses Known - Down 6.9%

Rate per 100,000 Inhabitants - Down 10.6%

BURGLARY

DEFINITION

The Uniform Crime Reporting Program defines burglary as the unlawful entry of a structure to commit a felony or theft. The use of force to gain entry is not required to classify an offense as burglary. Burglary in this Program is categorized into three subclassifications: forcible entry, unlawful entry where no force is used, and attempted forcible entry.

	TREND	
Year	Number of offenses	Rate per 100,000 inhabitants
1994	2,712,774	1,042.0
1995	2,594,995	987.6
Percent change	−4.3	−5.2

The estimated 2.6 million burglaries in the United States during 1995 represented the lowest total in the past two decades. Distribution figures for the regions showed that the highest burglary volume in 1995 (40 percent) occurred in the most populous Southern States. The Western States followed with 25 percent, the Midwestern States with 20 percent, and the Northeastern States with 15 percent. (See Table 3.)

The greatest number of burglaries was recorded during August of 1995, while the lowest count was in February.

Table 2.26—Burglary by Month, 1991–1995
[Percent distribution]

Months	1991	1992	1993	1994	1995
January	8.1	8.6	8.3	7.9	8.4
February	7.3	7.7	6.9	7.1	7.2
March	8.1	8.2	8.2	8.2	8.2
April	7.9	7.8	7.7	8.0	7.7
May	8.3	8.2	8.0	8.5	8.4
June	8.2	8.1	8.4	8.3	8.3
July	9.2	9.0	9.0	9.2	9.0
August	9.2	9.0	9.1	9.4	9.2
September	8.6	8.4	8.5	8.6	8.5
October	8.6	8.3	8.4	8.6	8.8
November	8.0	8.2	8.1	8.4	8.3
December	8.6	8.3	9.3	7.9	8.0

Overall, the burglary volume dropped 4 percent in 1995 from the 1994 total. Among the Nation's cities, decreases were registered in all groupings; the largest decrease was in cities with populations of 1 million and over which showed a 9-percent decline. The suburban counties also showed a decrease, 5 percent; however, an increase of 2 percent was reported for the rural counties. (See Table 12.)

All four regions of the United States reported decreases in burglary volumes during 1995 as compared to the 1994 figures. The Northeastern States experienced a 6-percent decline; the Southern States, a 5-percent decrease; the Midwestern States, a 4-percent decline; and the Western States, a 3-percent drop. (See Table 4.)

Longer term national trends show burglary down 18 percent from the 1991 level and down 20 percent from the 1986 volume.

Rate

Lower than in any other year of the past two decades, the burglary rate was 988 per 100,000 inhabitants nationwide in 1995. The rate was 5 percent lower than in 1994, down 21 percent from the 1991 level, and 27 percent below the 1986 rate. In 1995, for every 100,000 in population, the rate was 1,048 in the metropolitan areas, 924 in the cities outside metropolitan areas, and 634 in the rural counties.

Regionally, the burglary rate was 1,137 in the Southern States, 1,111 in the Western States, 841 in the Midwestern States, and 758 in the Northeastern States. A comparison of 1994 and 1995 rates showed decreases of 6 percent in both the Northeast and the South, 5 percent in the Midwest, and 4 percent in the West. (See Table 4.)

Nature

Two of every 3 burglaries in 1995 were residential in nature. Sixty-seven percent of all burglaries involved forcible entry, 25 percent were unlawful entries (without force), and the remainder were forcible entry attempts. Offenses for which time of occurrence was reported showed that 52 percent of burglaries happened during daytime hours and 48 percent at night. More residential burglaries (59 percent) occurred during the daytime, while 61 percent of nonresidential burglaries occurred during nighttime hours.

The value of property stolen in burglaries was estimated at $3.3 billion in 1995, and the average dollar loss per burglary was $1,259. The average loss for residential offenses was $1,211 and for nonresidential offenses, $1,257. Compared to 1994 losses, the 1995 average loss for both residential and nonresidential property decreased.

Both residential and nonresidential burglary volumes also showed declines from 1994 to 1995, 4 and 5 percent, respectively. (See Table 23.)

BURGLARY

CHART 2.12

PERCENT CHANGE FROM 1991

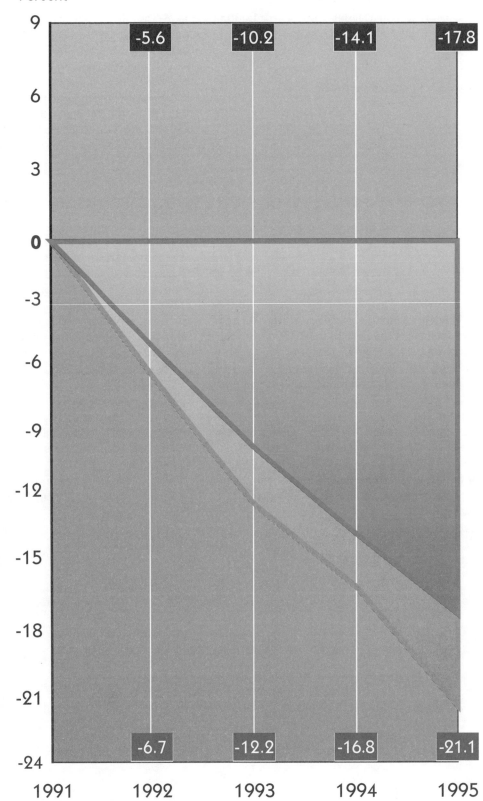

Percent

-5.6	-10.2	-14.1	-17.8

Number of
Offenses Known -
Down 17.8%

Rate per 100,000
Inhabitants -
Down 21.1%

-6.7	-12.2	-16.8	-21.1

1991   1992   1993   1994   1995

BURGLARY Percent Change from 1991

CHART 2.13

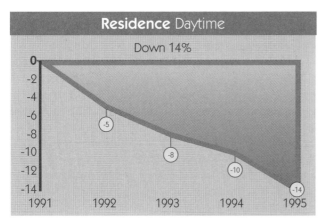

Residence Daytime
Down 14%

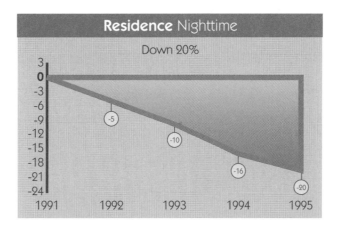

Residence Nighttime
Down 20%

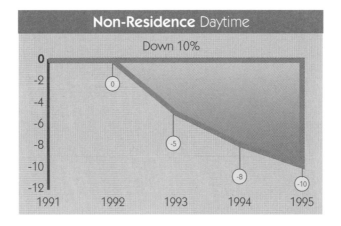

Non-Residence Daytime
Down 10%

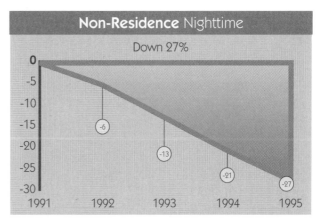

Non-Residence Nighttime
Down 27%

Law Enforcement Response

Nationwide in 1995, a 13-percent clearance rate was recorded for burglaries brought to the attention of law enforcement agencies across the country. Geographically, in the South, the clearance rate was 15 percent; in both the Northeast and Midwest, it was 13 percent; and in the West, it was 12 percent. (See Table 26.)

Rural county law enforcement agencies cleared 16 percent of the burglaries in their jurisdictions. Agencies in suburban counties cleared 15 percent, and those in cities, 13 percent. (See Table 25.)

Adults were involved in 79 percent of all burglary offenses cleared; the remaining 21 percent involved only young people under 18 years of age. Persons under age 18 accounted for 21 percent of the burglary clearances in cities, 22 percent of those in rural counties, and 24 percent of those in suburban counties. The highest degree of juvenile involvement was recorded in the Nation's smallest cities (under 10,000 in population) where young persons under 18 years of age accounted for 26 percent of the clearances. (See Table 28.)

In the UCR Program, several persons may be arrested in connection with the clearance of one crime, or the arrest of one individual may clear numerous offenses. The latter is often true in cases of burglary, for which an estimated 386,500 arrests were made in 1995.

Arrest trends between 1994 and 1995 show total burglary arrests were down 4 percent. Arrests of adults were down 3 percent, and those of persons under 18 years of age decreased 6 percent. For the same 2-year time period, total burglary arrest trends showed decreases of 5 percent in cities; 3 percent in rural counties; and 2 percent in suburban counties.

Eighty-nine percent of the burglary arrestees during 1995 were males, and 62 percent of the total were under 25 years of age. Among all burglary arrestees, whites accounted for 67 percent, blacks for 31 percent, and other races for the remainder.

LARCENY–THEFT

DEFINITION

Larceny-theft is the unlawful taking, carrying, leading, or riding away of property from the possession or constructive possession of another. It includes crimes such as shoplifting, pocket-picking, purse-snatching, thefts from motor vehicles, thefts of motor vehicle parts and accessories, bicycle thefts, etc., in which no use of force, violence, or fraud occurs. In the Uniform Crime Reporting Program, this crime category does not include embezzlement, "con" games, forgery, and worthless checks. Motor vehicle theft is also excluded from this category inasmuch as it is a separate Crime Index offense.

TREND		
Year	Number of offenses	Rate per 100,000 inhabitants
1994	7,879,812	3,026.7
1995	8,000,631	3,044.9
Percent change	+1.5	+.6

Larceny-theft, estimated at 8 million offenses during 1995, comprised 58 percent of the Crime Index total and 66 percent of the property crimes. Similar to the experience in previous years, larceny-thefts were recorded most often during August and least frequently in February.

Table 2.27—Larceny–Theft by Month, 1991–1995

[Percent distribution]

Months	1991	1992	1993	1994	1995
January	7.8	8.2	7.7	7.4	7.9
February	7.5	7.8	6.8	7.1	7.1
March	8.2	8.3	8.0	8.1	8.2
April	8.1	8.1	8.0	8.1	7.8
May	8.4	8.2	8.2	8.5	8.5
June	8.5	8.5	8.7	8.6	8.7
July	9.2	9.1	9.2	9.2	9.1
August	9.3	9.1	9.3	9.5	9.3
September	8.3	8.4	8.3	8.5	8.5
October...............	8.7	8.6	8.6	8.9	8.8
November	7.9	7.9	8.0	8.3	8.1
December	8.2	8.0	9.1	7.9	8.0

Viewed geographically, the Southern States, the most populous region, recorded 38 percent of the larceny-theft total. The Western States recorded 25 percent; the Midwestern States, 22 percent; and the Northeastern States, 15 percent. (See Table 3.)

The 1995 volume of larceny-thefts nationwide was 2 percent higher than the 1994 total. By community type, increases of 1 percent were recorded both in cities collectively and suburban counties, and a 6-percent rise was experienced in the rural counties.

Larceny volumes increased in all four geographic regions. The increases were 3 percent in the West and 1 percent in the Midwest, Northeast, and South.

Long-term national trends indicate larceny was up 10 percent when compared to the 1986 total but was 2 percent below the 1991 level. (See Table 1.)

Rate

The 1995 larceny-theft rate was 3,045 per 100,000 U.S. inhabitants. Two-, 5-, and 10-year trends showed the rate was 1 percent higher than the rates in 1994 and 1986 but 6 percent below the 1991 rate. The 1995 rate was 3,278 per 100,000 inhabitants of metropolitan areas; 3,669 per 100,000 population in cities outside metropolitan areas; and 1,091 per 100,000 people in the rural counties. (See Tables 1 and 2.)

By region, the 1995 larceny-theft rate per 100,000 people in the West was up 2 percent, and the Northeast's rate rose 1 percent. Showing virtually no change from 1994 were the rates in the Midwest and the South. (See Table 4.) The regional rates ranged from 2,296 per 100,000 people in the Northeast to 3,435 per 100,000 population in the West.

Nature

During 1995, the average value of property stolen due to larceny-theft was $535, up from $505 in 1994. When the average value was applied to the estimated number of larceny-thefts, the loss to victims nationally was nearly $4.3 billion for the year. This estimated dollar loss is considered conservative since many offenses in the larceny category, particularly if the value of the stolen goods is small, never come to law enforcement attention. Losses under $50 and those over $200 jointly accounted for 77 percent of the thefts reported to law enforcement. The remainder involved losses ranging from $50 to $200.

Losses of goods and property reported stolen as a result of pocket-picking averaged $350; purse-snatching, $279; and shoplifting, $108. Thefts from buildings resulted in an average loss of $891; from motor vehicles, $531; and from coin-operated machines, $283. The average value loss due to thefts of motor vehicle accessories was $329 and for thefts of bicycles, $286. (See Table 23.)

Thefts of motor vehicle parts, accessories, and contents made up the largest portion of reported larcenies—36 percent. Also contributing to the high volume of thefts were shoplifting, accounting for 15 percent; thefts from buildings, 13 percent; and bicycle thefts, 6 percent. The remainder was distributed among pocket-picking, purse-snatching, thefts from coin-operated machines, and all other types of larceny-thefts. Table 2.28 presents the distribution of larceny-theft by type and geographic region.

Table 2.28—Larceny Analysis by Region, 1995

[Percent distribution]

	United States Total	North- eastern States	Mid- western States	Southern States	Western States
Total[1]	100.0	100.0	100.0	100.0	100.0
Pocket-picking	.6	2.0	.3	.5	.4
Purse-snatching	.6	1.2	.6	.6	.5
Shoplifting	15.1	14.6	13.6	14.6	16.8
From motor vehicles (except accessories)	24.3	22.7	22.3	22.0	29.7
Motor vehicle accessories ..	12.1	11.1	13.1	12.9	10.7
Bicycles	6.3	7.9	6.7	5.3	6.6
From buildings	12.5	17.6	15.8	9.8	12.2
From coin-operated machines	.6	.7	.5	.7	.6
All others	27.9	22.2	27.1	33.7	22.5

[1] Because of rounding, percentages may not add to totals.

LARCENY-THEFT

CHART 2.14

PERCENT CHANGE FROM 1991

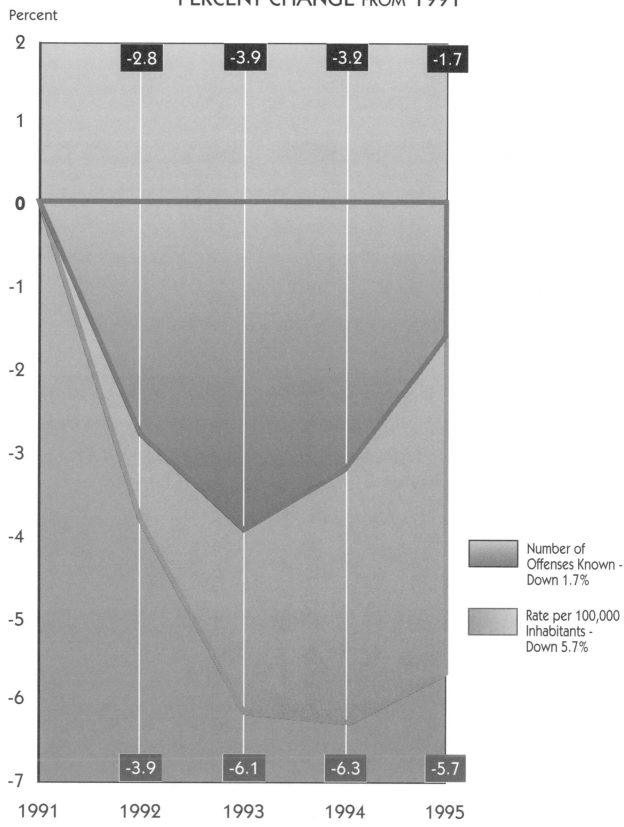

Percent

-2.8   -3.9   -3.2   -1.7

-3.9   -6.1   -6.3   -5.7

2
1
0
-1
-2
-3
-4
-5
-6
-7

1991   1992   1993   1994   1995

Number of
Offenses Known -
Down 1.7%

Rate per 100,000
Inhabitants -
Down 5.7%

45

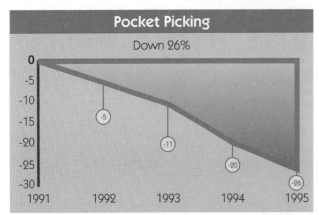

Pocket Picking
Down 26%

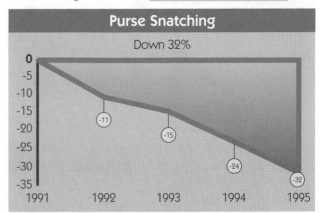

Purse Snatching
Down 32%

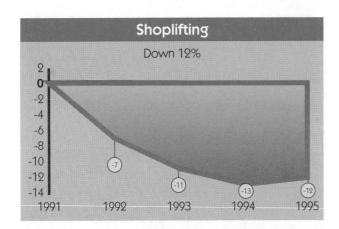

Shoplifting
Down 12%

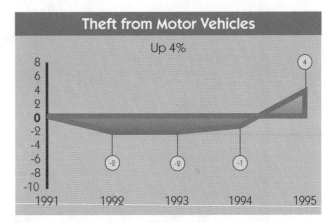

Theft from Motor Vehicles
Up 4%

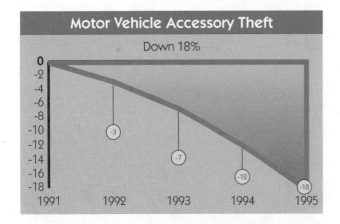

Motor Vehicle Accessory Theft
Down 18%

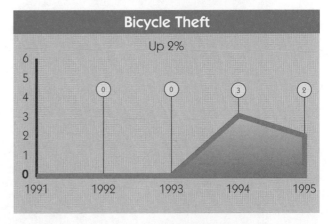

Bicycle Theft
Up 2%

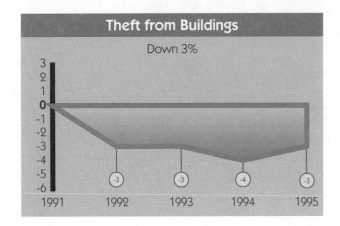

Theft from Buildings
Down 3%

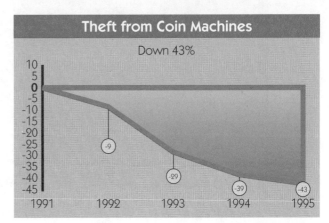

Theft from Coin Machines
Down 43%

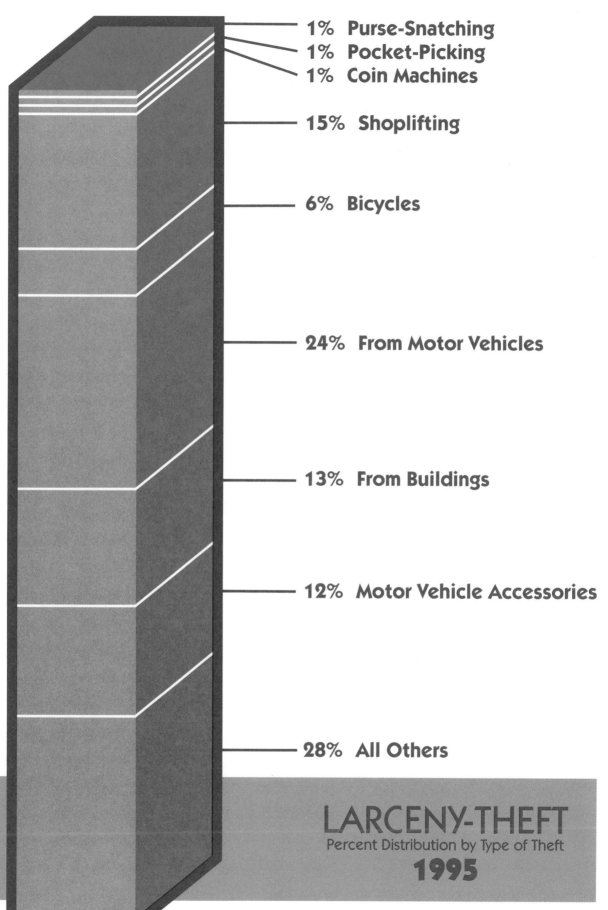

CHART 2.16

1% Purse-Snatching
1% Pocket-Picking
1% Coin Machines

15% Shoplifting

6% Bicycles

24% From Motor Vehicles

13% From Buildings

12% Motor Vehicle Accessories

28% All Others

LARCENY-THEFT
Percent Distribution by Type of Theft
1995

Law Enforcement Response

A 20-percent larceny-theft clearance rate was recorded nationally and in cities during 1995. The highest rate, 25 percent, was reported by law enforcement agencies in cities from 10,000 to 24,999 in population. Suburban and rural counties each recorded an 18-percent clearance rate.

Three of the four geographic regions recorded 20-percent larceny-theft clearance rates in 1995. A 19-percent clearance rate was reported in the West. (See Table 26.)

Twenty-six percent of the larceny-theft clearances nationally and in cities involved only offenders under 18 years of age. Twenty-seven percent of those in suburban counties and 21 percent of those in rural counties were accounted for by persons in this age group.

Between 1994 and 1995, the total number of persons arrested for larceny-theft, as well as arrests of males and those of adults, showed virtually no change. During this same period, arrests of females and of juveniles (persons under 18 years of age) each increased 1 percent.

For the 5-year period, 1991–1995, total larceny-theft arrests declined 5 percent. Male and female arrests also decreased, 7 and 1 percent, respectively. During the same timespan, arrests of adults dropped 10 percent, while arrests of persons under the age of 18 were up 6 percent.

Larceny-theft not only comprised the largest portion of Crime Index offenses reported to law enforcement, but this offense also accounted for 52 percent of the arrests for Index crimes and 72 percent of those for property crimes in 1995. Forty-six percent of the larceny arrests were of persons under 21 years of age, and 33 percent of the arrestees were under 18. Females, who were arrested for this offense more often than for any other in 1995, comprised 33 percent of all larceny-theft arrestees.

Whites accounted for 65 percent of the total larceny-theft arrestees, blacks for 32 percent, and all other races for the remainder.

MOTOR VEHICLE THEFT

DEFINITION

Defined as the theft or attempted theft of a motor vehicle, this offense category includes the stealing of automobiles, trucks, buses, motorcycles, motorscooters, snowmobiles, etc. The definition excludes the taking of a motor vehicle for temporary use by those persons having lawful access.

TREND		
Year	Number of offenses	Rate per 100,000 inhabitants
1994	1,539,287	591.3
1995	1,472,732	560.5
Percent change	−4.3	−5.2

The nearly 1.5 million thefts of motor vehicles occurring in the United States during 1995 represented the lowest total since 1989. The regional distribution of thefts in 1995 showed 33 percent of the volume was in the Southern States, 30 percent in the Western States, 19 percent in the Midwestern States, and 18 percent in the Northeastern States. (See Table 3.)

The 1995 monthly figures show that the greatest numbers of motor vehicle thefts were recorded during the months of August and October, while the lowest count was in February.

Table 2.29—Motor Vehicle Theft by Month, 1991–1995
[Percent distribution]

Months	1991	1992	1993	1994	1995
January	8.3	8.8	8.5	8.2	8.6
February	7.5	7.9	7.3	7.4	7.5
March	8.2	8.2	8.2	8.5	8.2
April	7.8	7.8	7.8	8.0	7.8
May	8.1	8.1	7.9	8.2	8.2
June	8.2	8.2	8.4	8.3	8.2
July	8.7	8.8	8.9	8.9	8.6
August	8.9	8.9	8.9	9.1	8.9
September	8.3	8.2	8.4	8.4	8.4
October................	8.7	8.6	8.6	8.8	8.9
November	8.5	8.3	8.3	8.4	8.5
December	8.8	8.2	8.8	7.8	8.2

Motor vehicle thefts declined 4 percent nationally from 1994 to 1995. The Nation's cities collectively experienced a 6-percent decline, but among city population groupings, the changes ranged from a 12-percent decline in cities with populations of 1 million or more to a 4-percent increase in those with populations under 10,000. During the same 2-year period, a 2-percent decrease in the volume of motor vehicle thefts occurred in the suburban counties, while rural counties registered an increase of 8 percent.

Geographically, decreases in motor vehicle thefts were recorded in the Northeast, 14 percent, and in the West, 3 percent. Both the South and Midwest regions showed decreases of 1 percent. (See Table 4.)

The accompanying chart shows that the volume of motor vehicle thefts in 1995 declined 11 percent from the 1991 volume.

Rate

The 1995 national motor vehicle theft rate—560 per 100,000 people—was 5 percent lower than in 1994 and 15 percent below the 1991 rate. The 1995 rate was 10 percent above the 1986 rate.

For every 100,000 inhabitants living in metropolitan areas, there were 660 motor vehicle thefts reported in 1995. The rate in cities outside metropolitan areas was 240 and in rural counties, 125. As in previous years, the highest rates were in the Nation's most heavily populated municipalities, indicating that this offense is primarily a large-city problem. For every 100,000 inhabitants in cities with populations over 250,000, the 1995 motor vehicle theft rate was 1,310. The Nation's smallest cities, those with fewer than 10,000 inhabitants, recorded a rate of 261 per 100,000.

Declining among all regions in comparison to 1994, motor vehicle theft rates ranged from 766 per 100,000 people in the Western States to 451 in the Midwestern States. The Southern States' rate was 530, and the Northeastern States' rate was 516. The Northeast reported the greatest rate decrease, 14 percent. The West reported a decrease of 4 percent; the South, a decrease of 3 percent; and the Midwest, a decrease of 2 percent.

An estimated average of 1 of every 139 registered motor vehicles was stolen nationwide during 1995. Regionally, this rate was greatest in the West where 1 of every 100 motor vehicles registered was stolen. The other three regions reported lesser rates—1 per 190 in the Midwest, 1 per 148 in the South, and 1 per 132 in the Northeast.

Nature

The estimated value of motor vehicles stolen nationwide in 1995 was nearly $7.6 billion. At the time of theft, the average value per vehicle was $5,129. The recovery percentage for the value of vehicles stolen was higher than for any other property type. Relating the value of vehicles stolen to the value of those recovered resulted in a 62-percent recovery rate for 1995. (See Tables 23 and 24.)

Seventy-eight percent of all motor vehicles reported stolen during the year were automobiles, 16 percent were trucks or buses, and the remainder were other types.

Table 2.30—Motor Vehicle Theft, 1995
[Percent distribution by region]

Region	Total[1]	Autos	Trucks and buses	Other vehicles
Total	100.0	78.4	16.3	5.4
Northeastern States	100.0	92.8	4.4	2.9
Midwestern States	100.0	75.1	18.2	6.7
Southern States	100.0	82.9	12.1	5.0
Western States	100.0	71.5	22.9	5.5

[1]Because of rounding, percentages may not add to totals.

MOTOR VEHICLE THEFT

CHART 2.17
PERCENT CHANGE FROM 1991

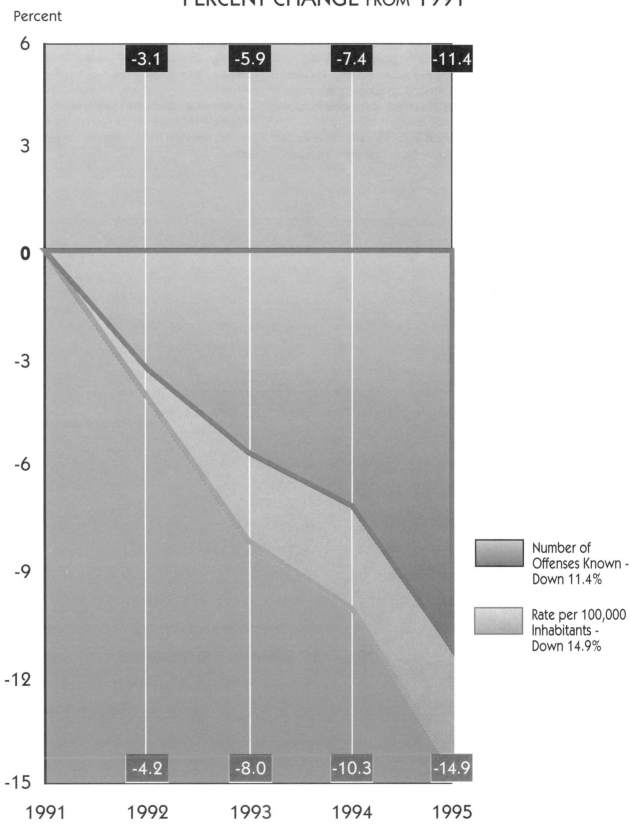

Percent

-3.1   -5.9   -7.4   -11.4

-4.2   -8.0   -10.3   -14.9

1991   1992   1993   1994   1995

Number of
Offenses Known -
Down 11.4%

Rate per 100,000
Inhabitants -
Down 14.9%

Law Enforcement Response

Law enforcement agencies nationwide recorded a 14-percent motor vehicle theft clearance rate for 1995. Those in cities cleared 13 percent; those in suburban counties cleared 16 percent; and rural county agencies cleared 32 percent.

Regional clearance percentages for motor vehicle theft were 17 percent in both the Southern and Midwestern States, 12 percent in the Western States, and 10 percent in the Northeastern States.

Persons in the under-18 age group accounted for 24 percent of the motor vehicle thefts cleared both nationally and in cities. They were responsible for 22 percent of the clearances in both suburban and rural counties.

During 1995, law enforcement agencies nationwide made an estimated 191,900 arrests for motor vehicle theft. Males accounted for 87 percent of those arrested. Fifty-nine percent of the arrestees were white, 38 percent were black, and the remainder were of other races.

A large proportion of motor vehicle theft arrestees was accounted for by the younger segment of the population. In 1995, 58 percent of all persons arrested for this offense were under 21 years of age, and those under 18 comprised 42 percent of the total. Between 1994 and 1995, arrests of persons under age 18 were down 9 percent. Arrests of juvenile males decreased 10 percent, and those of young females decreased 5 percent.

Total motor vehicle theft arrests in 1995 were down 6 percent from the 1994 level and 13 percent lower than in 1991. Compared to the 1986 level, however, the arrest total increased 18 percent.

ARSON

DEFINITION

Arson is defined by the Uniform Crime Reporting Program as any willful or malicious burning or attempt to burn, with or without intent to defraud, a dwelling house, public building, motor vehicle or aircraft, personal property of another, etc.

Only fires determined through investigation to have been willfully or maliciously set are classified as arsons. Fires of suspicious or unknown origins are excluded.

A total of 94,926 arson offenses was reported by 12,261 law enforcement agencies across the country; these agencies furnished from 1 to 12 months of reports during 1995. Among these reporting agencies, 11,887 provided the detailed information—type of structure, estimated monetary value of the property damaged, etc.—from which the tables on the accompanying pages were tabulated. Further information regarding arson offenses and trends is presented in Tables 12 through 15 and arson clearances in Tables 25 through 28. Since only 8,940 agencies, covering 72 percent of the United States population, submitted reports for all 12 months of the year, the data user should be aware that, while conservative indicators, the figures do not represent the Nation's total arson experience.

The number of arson offenses reported nationally decreased 4 percent in 1995 from the 1994 total. While arson dropped 5 percent in the Nation's cities collectively, changes among the population groupings ranged from a 16-percent decrease in cities with populations over one million to a 3-percent increase in those with populations under 10,000. The suburban counties registered a decline of 3 percent, while an increase of 7 percent was experienced in the rural counties. (See Table 12.)

Geographically, arson decreased 10 percent in the Midwest and 5 percent in the Northeast and West. The South showed a 1-percent increase.

By property type nationally, decreases were shown in the number of arsons of mobile property, 5 percent; structures, 3 percent; and all other property, 2 percent. (See Table 15.)

Table 2.31—Arson Rate, Population Group, 1995
[8,940 agencies; 1995 estimated population 188,804,000; rate per 100,000 inhabitants]

Group	Rate
Total	44.8
Total cities	53.0
Group I (cities 250,000 and over)	83.3
(cities 1,000,000 and over)	81.4
(cities 500,000 to 999,999)	75.0
(cities 250,000 to 499,999)	94.6
Group II (cities 100,000 to 249,999)	59.6
Group III (cities 50,000 to 99,999)	42.4
Group IV (cities 25,000 to 49,999)	35.6
Group V (cities 10,000 to 24,999)	28.5
Group VI (cities under 10,000)	34.5
Suburban counties	31.4
Rural counties	20.6
Suburban area	31.1

Caution is recommended when viewing arson trend information. The percent change figures may have been influenced by improved arson reporting procedures. It is expected that year-to-year statistical comparability will improve as collection continues.

Rate

Since population coverage for arson data is lower than for the other Crime Index offenses, arson rates per 100,000 inhabitants are tabulated independently. Based only on figures from law enforcement agencies supplying 12 months of statistics for all Index crimes, including arson, the 1995 rates are shown in Table 2.31.

The rates ranged from 95 per 100,000 inhabitants in cities with populations 250,000 to 499,999 to 21 per 100,000 rural county inhabitants. The suburban counties and all cities collectively recorded rates of 31 and 53 per 100,000 inhabitants, respectively. Overall, the 1995 national arson rate was 45 per 100,000 population.

Regionally, the highest arson rate was registered in the Northeastern States with 52 offenses per 100,000 population. Following were the Western States with a rate of 50 per 100,000, the Midwestern States with 43 per 100,000, and the Southern States with 40 per 100,000.

Nature

As in previous years, structures were the most frequent targets of arsonists in 1995 and comprised 53 percent of the reported incidents. Twenty-six percent of the arsons were directed at mobile property (motor vehicles, trailers, etc.), while other types of property (crops, timber, etc.) accounted for 22 percent.

Residential property was involved in 60 percent of the structural arsons during the year, with 43 percent of such offenses directed at single-family dwellings. Twenty percent of all targeted structural property was either uninhabited or abandoned at the time the arson occurred.

Motor vehicles comprised 94 percent of all mobile property at which arsons were directed.

Table 2.32—Arson, Type of Property, 1995
[11,887 agencies; 1995 estimated population 199,302,000]

Property classification	Number of offenses	Percent distribution[1]
Total	80,182	100.0
Total structure	42,226	52.7
Single occupancy residential	17,955	22.4
Other residential	7,461	9.3
Storage	3,788	4.7
Industrial/manufacturing	605	.8
Other commercial	4,322	5.4
Community/public	4,696	5.9
Other structure	3,399	4.2
Total mobile	20,459	25.5
Motor vehicles	19,223	24.0
Other mobile	1,236	1.5
Other	17,497	21.8

[1] Because of rounding, percentages may not add to total.

Table 2.33—Arson, Structures Not in Use, 1995
[11,887 agencies; 1995 estimated population 199,302,000]

Type of structure	Number of offenses	Percent not in use
Total	42,226	19.8
Single occupancy residential	17,955	21.7
Other residential	7,461	16.4
Storage	3,788	21.9
Industrial/manufacturing	605	26.4
Other commercial	4,322	21.8
Community/public	4,696	10.2
Other structure	3,399	23.6

The monetary value of property damaged due to reported arsons averaged $11,151 per incident in 1995. The overall average for all types of structures was $17,704. Mobile properties averaged $4,561 per incident, and other targets averaged $3,042.

Table 2.34—Arson, Monetary Value of Property Damaged, 1995
[11,887 agencies; 1995 estimated population 199,302,000]

Property classification	Number of offenses	Average damage
Total	80,182	$11,151
Total structure	42,226	17,704
Single occupancy residential	17,955	15,856
Other residential	7,461	12,560
Storage	3,788	18,332
Industrial/manufacturing	605	80,732
Other commercial	4,322	37,069
Community/public	4,696	14,903
Other structure	3,399	6,080
Total mobile	20,459	4,561
Motor vehicles	19,223	4,181
Other mobile	1,236	10,459
Other	17,497	3,042

Law Enforcement Response

The 1995 arson clearance rate was 16 percent nationwide and 15 percent in cities. Rural county law enforcement agencies cleared 22 percent; and those in suburban counties, 18 percent. Agencies in cities with fewer than 10,000 inhabitants showed the highest rate, clearing 25 percent of the arson offenses brought to their attention. (See Table 25.)

Regionally, the Southern States recorded a clearance rate of 20 percent; the Midwestern States, 16 percent; the Western States, 15 percent; and the Northeastern States, 11 percent.

Forty-seven percent of all 1995 arson clearances involved only young people under age 18, a higher percentage of juvenile involvement than for any other Index crime. Persons in this age group accounted for 45 percent of structural arson clearances, 28 percent of the clearances for arsons of mobile property, and 62 percent of those of all other property. Juveniles

were the offenders in 50 percent of the city, 44 percent of the suburban county, and 28 percent of the rural county arson clearances.

The accompanying tables show clearance data for only those 11,887 law enforcement agencies which were able to furnish breakdowns by type for the structural and mobile classifications. As can be seen, the highest clearance rate (33 percent) was recorded for arsons of community/public structures, while the lowest rate (8 percent) was registered for motor vehicles.

Table 2.35—Arson Offenses Cleared by Arrest,[1] 1995
[11,887 agencies;[2] 1995 estimated population 199,302,000]

Property classification	Number of offenses	Percent cleared by arrest
Total	80,182	18.5
Total structure	42,226	22.9
Single occupancy residential	17,955	23.3
Other residential	7,461	24.0
Storage	3,788	18.6
Industrial/manufacturing	605	17.4
Other commercial	4,322	16.6
Community/public	4,696	33.1
Other structure	3,399	18.0
Total mobile	20,459	8.4
Motor vehicles	19,223	7.8
Other mobile	1,236	16.7
Other	17,497	19.6

[1] Includes offenses cleared by exceptional means.
[2] To be included in this table, it was necessary that arson clearances be reported by property classification.

An estimated 20,000 arrests for arson were made during 1995. Fifty-two percent of the arrestees were under 18 years of age and 68 percent were under 25. Males comprised 84 percent of all arson arrestees. Seventy-four percent of those arrested were white, 24 percent were black, and the remainder were of other races.

Table 2.36—Arson Offenses Cleared by Arrest[1] of Persons under 18 Years of Age, 1995
[11,887 agencies;[2] 1995 estimated population 199,302,000]

Property classification	Total clearances	Percent under 18
Total	14,808	47.2
Total structure	9,666	45.3
Single occupancy residential	4,178	36.6
Other residential	1,793	34.5
Storage	705	64.1
Industrial/manufacturing	105	45.7
Other commercial	718	37.7
Community/public	1,554	73.6
Other structure	613	51.5
Total mobile	1,709	28.1
Motor vehicles	1,502	26.5
Other mobile	207	39.6
Other	3,433	62.0

[1] Includes offenses cleared by exceptional means.
[2] To be included in this table, it was necessary that arson clearances be reported by property classification.

Trends for 1995 versus 1994 show arson arrests down 3 percent nationally and 2 percent in cities. Suburban counties recorded the largest decrease, 8 percent. Virtually no change occurred in the rural counties.

Nationwide, arrests of juveniles for arson were down 8 percent, while adult arrests showed a 3-percent increase from 1994 to 1995. During the same period, male arrests decreased 4 percent but female arrests rose 5 percent. The 1995 arson arrest total for all ages was 6 percent higher than in 1991 and 7 percent above the 1986 level.

Crime Index Tabulations

This Section's tabular portions present data on crime in the United States as a whole; geographic divisions; individual states; Metropolitan Statistical Areas; cities, towns, and counties; and college and university campuses. Also furnished in the following tables are national averages for the value of property stolen in connection with Crime Index offenses; further breakdowns by type for the robbery, burglary, larceny-theft, and arson classifications; information on the types of weapons used; and data on the type and value of property stolen and recovered.

Although the total number of crimes occurring throughout the Nation is unknown, information on those reported to law enforcement gives a reliable indication of criminal activity. In reviewing the tables in this report, it must be remembered, however, that many factors can cause the volume and type of crime to vary from place to place. Even though population, one of these factors, is used in computing crime rates, all communities are affected to some degree by seasonal or transient populations. Since counts of current, permanent population are used in their construction, crime rates do not account for short-term population variables, such as an influx of day workers, tourists, shoppers, etc. A further discussion of various factors contributing to the amount of crime in a given area is shown on page iv of this publication.

National data can serve as a guide for the law enforcement administrator in analyzing the local crime count, as well as the performance of the jurisdiction's law enforcement agency. The analysis, however, should not end with a comparison based on data presented in this publication. It is only through an appraisal of local conditions that a true assessment of the community crime problem or the effectiveness of the law enforcement operation is possible.

National estimates of the volume and rate per 100,000 inhabitants for all Crime Index offenses covering the past two decades are set forth in Table 1, "Index of Crime, United States, 1976–1995."

Table 2, "Index of Crime, United States, 1995," shows current year estimates for MSAs, rural counties, and cities and towns outside metropolitan areas. See Appendix III for the definitions of these community types.

Provided in Table 3, "Index of Crime, Regional Offense and Population Distribution, 1995," are data showing the geographical distribution of estimated Index crimes and population. When utilizing figures presented on a regional basis in this publication, the reader is cautioned to consider each region's proportion of the total United States population. For example, although the Southern States accounted for the largest volume of Crime Index offenses in 1995, they also represented the greatest regional population.

Note

The collection of statistics on arson as a Crime Index offense began in 1979. However, 1995 annual figures are not available for inclusion in tables presenting statistics for the total United States. Arson totals reported by individual law enforcement agencies are displayed in Tables 8 through 11. Two-year arson trends are shown in Tables 12 through 15.

Table 1.—Index of Crime, United States, 1976–1995

Population[1]	Crime Index total[2]	Modified Crime Index total[3]	Violent crime[4]	Property crime[4]	Murder and non-negligent man-slaughter	Forcible rape	Robbery	Aggravated assault	Burglary	Larceny-theft	Motor vehicle theft	Arson[3]
					Number of Offenses							
Population by year:												
1976–214,659,000	11,349,700		1,004,210	10,345,500	18,780	57,080	427,810	500,530	3,108,700	6,270,800	966,000	
1977–216,332,000	10,984,500		1,029,580	9,955,000	19,120	63,500	412,610	534,350	3,071,500	5,905,700	977,700	
1978–218,059,000	11,209,000		1,085,550	10,123,400	19,560	67,610	426,930	571,460	3,128,300	5,991,000	1,004,100	
1979–220,099,000	12,249,500		1,208,030	11,041,500	21,460	76,390	480,700	629,480	3,327,700	6,601,000	1,112,800	
1980–225,349,264	13,408,300		1,344,520	12,063,700	23,040	82,990	565,840	672,650	3,795,200	7,136,900	1,131,700	
1981–229,146,000	13,423,800		1,361,820	12,061,900	22,520	82,500	592,910	663,900	3,779,700	7,194,400	1,087,800	
1982–231,534,000	12,974,400		1,322,390	11,652,000	21,010	78,770	553,130	669,480	3,447,100	7,142,500	1,062,400	
1983–233,981,000	12,108,600		1,258,090	10,850,500	19,310	78,920	506,570	653,290	3,129,900	6,712,800	1,007,900	
1984–236,158,000	11,881,800		1,273,280	10,608,500	18,690	84,230	485,010	685,350	2,984,400	6,591,900	1,032,200	
1985–238,740,000	12,431,400		1,328,800	11,102,600	18,980	88,670	497,870	723,250	3,073,300	6,926,400	1,102,900	
1986–241,077,000	13,211,900		1,489,170	11,722,700	20,610	91,460	542,780	834,320	3,241,400	7,257,200	1,224,100	
1987–243,400,000	13,508,700		1,484,000	12,024,700	20,100	91,110	517,700	855,090	3,236,200	7,499,900	1,288,700	
1988–245,807,000	13,923,100		1,566,220	12,356,900	20,680	92,490	542,970	910,090	3,218,100	7,705,900	1,432,900	
1989–248,239,000	14,251,400		1,646,040	12,605,400	21,500	94,500	578,330	951,710	3,168,200	7,872,400	1,564,800	
1990–248,709,873	14,475,600		1,820,130	12,655,500	23,440	102,560	639,270	1,054,860	3,073,900	7,945,700	1,635,900	
1991–252,177,000	14,872,900		1,911,770	12,961,100	24,700	106,590	687,730	1,092,740	3,157,200	8,142,200	1,661,700	
1992–255,082,000	14,438,200		1,932,270	12,505,900	23,760	109,060	672,480	1,126,970	2,979,900	7,915,200	1,610,800	
1993–257,908,000	14,144,800		1,926,020	12,218,800	24,530	106,010	659,870	1,135,610	2,834,800	7,820,900	1,563,100	
1994–260,341,000[5]	13,989,500		1,857,670	12,131,900	23,330	102,220	618,950	1,113,180	2,712,800	7,879,800	1,539,300	
1995–262,755,000	13,867,100		1,798,790	12,068,400	21,600	97,460	580,550	1,099,180	2,595,000	8,000,600	1,472,700	
Percent change: number of offenses:												
1995/1994	–.9		–3.2	–.5	–7.4	–4.6	–6.2	–1.3	–4.3	+1.5	–4.3	
1995/1991	–6.8		–5.9	–6.9	–12.6	–8.6	–15.6	+.6	–17.8	–1.7	–11.4	
1995/1986	+5.0		+20.8	+2.9	+4.8	+6.6	+7.0	+31.7	–19.9	+10.2	+20.3	
					Rate per 100,000 Inhabitants							
Year:												
1976	5,287.3		467.8	4,819.5	8.8	26.6	199.3	233.2	1,448.2	2,921.3	450.0	
1977	5,077.6		475.9	4,601.7	8.8	29.4	190.7	247.0	1,419.8	2,729.9	451.9	
1978	5,140.3		497.8	4,642.5	9.0	31.0	195.8	262.1	1,434.6	2,747.4	460.5	
1979	5,565.5		548.9	5,016.6	9.7	34.7	218.4	286.0	1,511.9	2,999.1	505.6	
1980	5,950.0		596.6	5,353.3	10.2	36.8	251.1	298.5	1,684.1	3,167.0	502.2	
1981	5,858.2		594.3	5,263.9	9.8	36.0	258.7	289.7	1,649.5	3,139.7	474.7	
1982	5,603.6		571.1	5,032.5	9.1	34.0	238.9	289.2	1,488.8	3,084.8	458.8	
1983	5,175.0		537.7	4,637.4	8.3	33.7	216.5	279.2	1,337.7	2,868.9	430.8	
1984	5,031.3		539.2	4,492.1	7.9	35.7	205.4	290.2	1,263.7	2,791.3	437.1	
1985	5,207.1		556.6	4,650.5	7.9	37.1	208.5	302.9	1,287.3	2,901.2	462.0	
1986	5,480.4		617.7	4,862.6	8.6	37.9	225.1	346.1	1,344.6	3,010.3	507.8	
1987	5,550.0		609.7	4,940.3	8.3	37.4	212.7	351.3	1,329.6	3,081.3	529.4	
1988	5,664.2		637.2	5,027.1	8.4	37.6	220.9	370.2	1,309.2	3,134.9	582.9	
1989	5,741.0		663.1	5,077.9	8.7	38.1	233.0	383.4	1,276.3	3,171.3	630.4	
1990	5,820.3		731.8	5,088.5	9.4	41.2	257.0	424.1	1,235.9	3,194.8	657.8	
1991	5,897.8		758.1	5,139.7	9.8	42.3	272.7	433.3	1,252.0	3,228.8	659.0	
1992	5,660.2		757.5	4,902.7	9.3	42.8	263.6	441.8	1,168.2	3,103.0	631.5	
1993	5,484.4		746.8	4,737.6	9.5	41.1	255.9	440.3	1,099.2	3,032.4	606.1	
1994[5]	5,373.5		713.6	4,660.0	9.0	39.3	237.7	427.6	1,042.0	3,026.7	591.3	
1995	5,277.6		684.6	4,593.0	8.2	37.1	220.9	418.3	987.6	3,044.9	560.5	
Percent change: rate per 100,000 inhabitants:												
1995/1994	–1.8		–4.1	–1.4	–8.9	–5.6	–7.1	–2.2	–5.2	+.6	–5.2	
1995/1991	–10.5		–9.7	–10.6	–16.3	–12.3	–19.0	–3.5	–21.1	–5.7	–14.9	
1995/1986	–3.7		+10.8	–5.5	–4.7	–2.1	–1.9	+20.9	–26.6	+1.1	+10.4	

[1]Populations are Bureau of the Census provisional estimates as of July 1, except 1980 and 1990 which are the decennial census counts.

[2]Because of rounding, the offenses may not add to totals.

[3]Although arson data are included in the trend and clearance tables, sufficient data are not available to estimate totals for this offense.

[4]Violent crimes are offenses of murder, forcible rape, robbery, and aggravated assault. Property crimes are offenses of burglary, larceny-theft, and motor vehicle theft. Data are not included for the property crime of arson.

[5]The 1994 figures have been adjusted. See "Crime Trends," page 368 for details.

Complete data for 1995 were not available for the states of Illinois, Kansas, and Montana; therefore, it was necessary that their crime counts be estimated. See "Offense Estimation," pages 367–368 for details.

All rates were calculated on the offenses before rounding.

Table 2.—Index of Crime, United States, 1995

Area	Population[1]	Crime Index total	Modified Crime Index total[2]	Violent crime[3]	Property crime[3]	Murder and non-negligent manslaughter	Forcible rape	Robbery	Aggravated assault	Burglary	Larceny–theft	Motor vehicle theft	Arson[2]
United States Total	262,755,000	13,867,143		1,798,785	12,068,358	21,597	97,464	580,545	1,099,179	2,594,995	8,000,631	1,472,732	
Rate per 100,000 inhabitants ..		5,277.6		684.6	4,593.0	8.2	37.1	220.9	418.3	987.6	3,044.9	560.5	
Metropolitan Statistical													
Area	209,080,950												
Area actually reporting[4]	97.1%	11,828,339		1,600,330	10,228,009	18,816	79,817	555,716	945,981	2,153,487	6,711,866	1,362,656	
Estimated totals	100.0%	12,044,788		1,619,116	10,425,672	18,983	81,321	559,658	959,154	2,191,552	6,853,440	1,380,680	
Rate per 100,000 inhabitants ..		5,760.8		774.4	4,986.4	9.1	38.9	267.7	458.7	1,048.2	3,277.9	660.4	
Cities outside metropolitan													
areas	21,787,777												
Area actually reporting[4]	90.4%	1,046,366		94,285	952,081	920	7,364	14,027	71,974	182,012	723,171	46,898	
Estimated totals	100.0%	1,158,110		105,163	1,052,947	1,014	8,186	15,592	80,371	201,326	799,439	52,182	
Rate per 100,000 inhabitants ..		5,315.4		482.7	4,832.7	4.7	37.6	71.6	368.9	924.0	3,669.2	239.5	
Rural Counties	31,885,273												
Area actually reporting[4]	88.0%	599,692		66,024	533,668	1,384	7,287	4,797	52,556	181,260	316,377	36,031	
Estimated totals	100.0%	664,245		74,506	589,739	1,600	7,957	5,295	59,654	202,117	347,752	39,870	
Rate per 100,000 inhabitants ..		2,083.2		233.7	1,849.6	5.0	25.0	16.6	187.1	633.9	1,090.6	125.0	

[1]Populations are Bureau of the Census provisional estimates as of July 1, 1995, and are subject to change.

[2]Although arson data are included in the trend and clearance tables, sufficient data are not available to estimate totals for this offense.

[3]Violent crimes are offenses of murder, forcible rape, robbery, and aggravated assault. Property crimes are offenses of burglary, larceny-theft, and motor vehicle theft. Data are not included for the property crime of arson.

[4]The percentage representing area actually reporting will not coincide with the ratio between reported and estimated crime totals, since these data represent the sum of the calculations for individual states which have varying populations, portions reporting, and crime rates.

Complete data were not available for 1995 for the states of Illinois, Kansas, and Montana; therefore it was necessary that their crime counts be estimated. See "Offense Estimation," pages 367–368 for details.

Table 3.—Index of Crime, Regional Offense and Population Distribution, 1995

Region	Population	Crime Index total	Modified Crime Index total[1]	Violent crime[2]	Property crime[2]	Murder and non-negligent manslaughter	Forcible rape	Robbery	Aggravated assault	Burglary	Larceny–theft	Motor vehicle theft	Arson[1]
United States Total3	**100.0**	**100.0**		**100.0**	**100.0**	**100.0**	**100.0**	**100.0**	**100.0**	**100.0**	**100.0**	**100.0**	
Northeastern States	19.6	15.5		17.5	15.2	14.7	13.2	23.1	14.9	15.0	14.8	18.0	
Midwestern States	23.5	21.2		20.2	21.3	19.6	25.5	19.4	20.2	20.0	22.2	18.9	
Southern States	35.0	38.0		37.7	38.1	41.7	38.6	33.6	39.7	40.3	38.3	33.1	
Western States	21.9	25.3		24.7	25.4	23.9	22.8	24.0	25.2	24.7	24.7	30.0	

[1]Although arson data are included in the trend and clearance tables, sufficient data are not available to estimate totals for this offense.

[2]Violent crimes are offenses of murder, forcible rape, robbery, and aggravated assault. Property crimes are offenses of burglary, larceny-theft, and motor vehicle theft. Data are not included for the property crime of arson.

[3]Because of rounding, the percentages may not add to totals.

Complete data were not available for 1995 for the states of Illinois, Kansas, and Montana; therefore it was necessary that their crime counts be estimated. See "Offense Estimation," pages 367–368 for details.

Table 4. — Index of Crime: Region, Geographic Division, and State, 1994–1995

Area	Year	Population[1]	Crime Index total		Modified Crime Index total[2]		Violent crime[3]		Property crime[3]		Murder and non-negligent manslaughter	
			Number	Rate per 100,000	Number	Rate per 100,000	Number	Rate per 100,000	Number	Rate per 100,000	Number	Rate per 100,000
United States4, 5, 8	1994	260,341,000	13,989,543	5,373.5			1,857,670	713.6	12,131,873	4,660.0	23,326	9.0
	1995	262,755,000	13,867,143	5,277.6			1,798,785	684.6	12,068,358	4,593.0	21,597	8.2
Percent change			–.9	–1.8			–3.2	–4.1	–.5	–1.4	–7.4	–8.9
Northeast...............	1994	51,396,000	2,232,897	4,344.5			340,312	662.1	1,892,585	3,682.4	3,644	7.1
	1995	51,466,000	2,151,488	4,180.4			314,233	610.6	1,837,255	3,569.8	3,173	6.2
Percent change			–3.6	–3.8			–7.7	–7.8	–2.9	–3.1	–12.9	–12.7
New England	1994	13,270,000	548,893	4,136.3			64,910	489.1	483,983	3,647.2	520	3.9
	1995	13,312,000	544,546	4,090.6			62,312	468.1	482,234	3,622.6	459	3.4
Percent change			–.8	–1.1			–4.0	–4.3	–.4	–.7	–11.7	–12.8
Connecticut	1994	3,275,000	148,946	4,548.0			14,916	455.5	134,030	4,092.5	215	6.6
	1995	3,275,000	147,481	4,503.2			13,293	405.9	134,188	4,097.3	150	4.6
Percent change			–1.0	–1.0			–10.9	–10.9	+.1	+.1	–30.2	–30.3
Maine	1994	1,240,000	40,582	3,272.7			1,611	129.9	38,971	3,142.8	28	2.3
	1995	1,241,000	40,763	3,284.7			1,631	131.4	39,132	3,153.3	25	2.0
Percent change			+.4	+.4			+1.2	+1.2	+.4	+.3	–10.7	–13.0
Massachusetts	1994	6,041,000	268,281	4,441.0			42,749	707.6	225,532	3,733.4	214	3.5
	1995	6,074,000	263,710	4,341.6			41,739	687.2	221,971	3,654.4	217	3.6
Percent change			–1.7	–2.2			–2.4	–2.9	–1.6	–2.1	+1.4	+2.9
New Hampshire	1994	1,137,000	31,165	2,741.0			1,328	116.8	29,837	2,624.2	16	1.4
	1995	1,148,000	30,484	2,655.4			1,314	114.5	29,170	2,540.9	21	1.8
Percent change			–2.2	–3.1			–1.1	–2.0	–2.2	–3.2	+31.3	+28.6
Rhode Island	1994	997,000	41,067	4,119.1			3,744	375.5	37,323	3,743.5	41	4.1
	1995	990,000	42,021	4,244.5			3,643	368.0	38,378	3,876.6	33	3.3
Percent change			+2.3	+3.0			–2.7	–2.0	+2.8	+3.6	–19.5	–19.5
Vermont	1994	580,000	18,852	3,250.3			562	96.9	18,290	3,153.4	6	1.0
	1995	585,000	20,087	3,433.7			692	118.3	19,395	3,315.4	13	2.2
Percent change			+6.6	+5.6			+23.1	+22.1	+6.0	+5.1	+116.7	+120.0
Middle Atlantic	1994	38,125,000	1,684,004	4,417.1			275,402	722.4	1,408,602	3,694.7	3,124	8.2
	1995	38,153,000	1,606,942	4,211.8			251,921	660.3	1,355,021	3,551.5	2,714	7.1
Percent change			–4.6	–4.6			–8.5	–8.6	–3.8	–3.9	–13.1	–13.4
New Jersey	1994	7,904,000	368,400	4,660.9			48,544	614.2	319,856	4,046.8	396	5.0
	1995	7,945,000	373,708	4,703.7			47,652	599.8	326,056	4,103.9	409	5.1
Percent change			+1.4	+.9			–1.8	–2.3	+1.9	+1.4	+3.3	+2.0
New York	1994	18,169,000	921,278	5,070.6			175,433	965.6	745,845	4,105.0	2,016	11.1
	1995	18,136,000	827,025	4,560.1			152,683	841.9	674,342	3,718.3	1,550	8.5
Percent change			–10.2	–10.1			–13.0	–12.8	–9.6	–9.4	–23.1	–23.4
Pennsylvania	1994	12,052,000	394,326	3,271.9			51,425	426.7	342,901	2,845.2	712	5.9
	1995	12,072,000	406,209	3,364.9			51,586	427.3	354,623	2,937.6	755	6.3
Percent change			+3.0	+2.8			+.3	+.1	+3.4	+3.2	+6.0	+6.8

See footnotes at end of table.

Table 4. — Index of Crime: Region, Geographic Division, and State, 1994–1995 — Continued

	Forcible rape		Robbery		Aggravated assault		Burglary		Larceny-theft		Motor vehicle theft		Arson[2]	
	Number	Rate per 100,000	Number	Rate per 100,000	Number	Rate per 100,000	Number	Rate per 100,000	Number	Rate per 100,000	Number	Rate per 100,000	Number	Rate per 100,000
	102,216	**39.3**	**618,949**	**237.7**	**1,113,179**	**427.6**	**2,712,774**	**1,042.0**	**7,879,812**	**3,026.7**	**1,539,287**	**591.3**		
	97,464	37.1	580,545	220.9	1,099,179	418.3	2,594,995	987.6	8,000,631	3,044.9	1,472,732	560.5		
	–4.6	–5.6	–6.2	–7.1	–1.3	–2.2	–4.3	–5.2	+1.5	+.6	–4.3	–5.2		
	13,606	**26.5**	**149,713**	**291.3**	**173,349**	**337.3**	**413,144**	**803.8**	**1,171,613**	**2,279.6**	**307,828**	**598.9**		
	12,828	24.9	133,944	260.3	164,288	319.2	390,180	758.1	1,181,573	2,295.8	265,502	515.9		
	–5.7	–6.0	–10.5	–10.6	–5.2	–5.4	–5.6	–5.7	+.9	+.7	–13.7	–13.9		
	3,789	28.6	17,837	134.4	42,764	322.3	109,952	828.6	301,393	2,271.2	72,638	547.4		
	3,565	26.8	16,108	121.0	42,180	316.9	106,270	798.3	313,059	2,351.7	62,905	472.5		
	–5.9	–6.3	–9.7	–10.0	–1.4	–1.7	–3.3	–3.7	+3.9	+3.5	–13.4	–13.7		
	806	24.6	6,150	187.8	7,745	236.5	29,142	889.8	84,721	2,586.9	20,167	615.8		
	776	23.7	5,345	163.2	7,022	214.4	29,095	888.4	87,401	2,668.7	17,692	540.2		
	–3.7	–3.7	–13.1	–13.1	–9.3	–9.3	–.2	–.2	+3.2	+3.2	–12.3	–12.3		
	318	25.6	278	22.4	987	79.6	8,938	720.8	28,257	2,278.8	1,776	143.2		
	265	21.4	334	26.9	1,007	81.1	9,015	726.4	28,444	2,292.0	1,673	134.8		
	–16.7	–16.4	+20.1	+20.1	+2.0	+1.9	+.9	+.8	+.7	+.6	–5.8	–5.9		
	1,825	30.2	10,160	168.2	30,550	505.7	53,222	881.0	129,962	2,151.3	42,348	701.0		
	1,759	29.0	9,137	150.4	30,626	504.2	49,669	817.7	135,586	2,232.2	36,716	604.5		
	–3.6	–4.0	–10.1	–10.6	+.2	–.3	–6.7	–7.2	+4.3	+3.8	–13.3	–13.8		
	407	35.8	308	27.1	597	52.5	5,275	463.9	22,260	1,957.8	2,302	202.5		
	333	29.0	314	27.4	646	56.3	4,806	418.6	22,698	1,977.2	1,666	145.1		
	–18.2	–19.0	+1.9	+1.1	+8.2	+7.2	–8.9	–9.8	+2.0	+1.0	–27.6	–28.3		
	273	27.4	870	87.3	2,560	256.8	9,101	912.8	23,039	2,310.8	5,183	519.9		
	267	27.0	914	92.3	2,429	245.4	9,234	932.7	24,780	2,503.0	4,364	440.8		
	–2.2	–1.5	+5.1	+5.7	–5.1	–4.4	+1.5	+2.2	+7.6	+8.3	–15.8	–15.2		
	160	27.6	71	12.2	325	56.0	4,274	736.9	13,154	2,267.9	862	148.6		
	165	28.2	64	10.9	450	76.9	4,451	760.9	14,150	2,418.8	794	135.7		
	+3.1	+2.2	–9.9	–10.7	+38.5	+37.3	+4.1	+3.3	+7.6	+6.7	–7.9	–8.7		
	9,817	25.7	131,876	345.9	130,585	342.5	303,192	795.3	870,220	2,282.5	235,190	616.9		
	9,263	24.3	117,836	308.9	122,108	320.0	283,910	744.1	868,514	2,276.4	202,597	531.0		
	–5.6	–5.4	–10.6	–10.7	–6.5	–6.6	–6.4	–6.4	–.2	–.3	–13.9	–13.9		
	1,972	24.9	22,762	288.0	23,414	296.2	72,074	911.9	195,618	2,474.9	52,164	660.0		
	1,927	24.3	22,486	283.0	22,830	287.4	69,533	875.2	206,339	2,597.1	50,184	631.6		
	–2.3	–2.4	–1.2	–1.7	–2.5	–3.0	–3.5	–4.0	+5.5	+4.9	–3.8	–4.3		
	4,700	25.9	86,617	476.7	82,100	451.9	164,650	906.2	452,322	2,489.5	128,873	709.3		
	4,290	23.7	72,492	399.7	74,351	410.0	146,562	808.1	425,184	2,344.4	102,596	565.7		
	–8.7	–8.5	–16.3	–16.2	–9.4	–9.3	–11.0	–10.8	–6.0	–5.8	–20.4	–20.2		
	3,145	26.1	22,497	186.7	25,071	208.0	66,468	551.5	222,280	1,844.3	54,153	449.3		
	3,046	25.2	22,858	189.3	24,927	206.5	67,815	561.8	236,991	1,963.1	49,817	412.7		
	–3.1	–3.4	+1.6	+1.4	–.6	–.7	+2.0	+1.9	+6.6	+6.4	–8.0	–8.1		

Table 4. — Index of Crime: Region, Geographic Division, and State, 1994–1995 — Continued

Area	Year	Population[1]	Crime Index total		Modified Crime Index total[2]		Violent crime[3]		Property crime[3]		Murder and non-negligent manslaughter	
			Number	Rate per 100,000	Number	Rate per 100,000	Number	Rate per 100,000	Number	Rate per 100,000	Number	Rate per 100,000
Midwest4, 5	**1994**	**61,394,000**	**2,955,629**	**4,814.2**			**367,912**	**599.3**	**2,587,717**	**4,214.9**	**4,627**	**7.5**
	1995	**61,804,000**	**2,936,313**	**4,751.0**			**363,105**	**587.5**	**2,573,208**	**4,163.5**	**4,242**	**6.9**
Percent change			**-.7**	**-1.3**			**-1.3**	**-2.0**	**-.6**	**-1.2**	**-8.3**	**-8.0**
East North Central[4]	1994	43,184,000	2,138,168	4,951.3			283,562	656.6	1,854,606	4,294.7	3,647	8.4
	1995	43,456,000	2,099,366	4,831.0			282,165	649.3	1,817,201	4,181.7	3,314	7.6
Percent change			-1.8	-2.4			-.5	-1.1	-2.0	-2.6	-9.1	-9.5
Illinois[4]	1994	11,752,000	661,150	5,625.9			112,928	960.9	548,222	4,664.9	1,378	11.7
	1995	11,830,000	645,408	5,455.7			117,836	996.1	527,572	4,459.6	1,221	10.3
Percent change			-2.4	-3.0			+4.3	+3.7	-3.8	-4.4	-11.4	-12.0
Indiana	1994	5,752,000	264,180	4,592.8			30,205	525.1	233,975	4,067.7	453	7.9
	1995	5,803,000	268,768	4,631.5			30,451	524.7	238,317	4,106.8	466	8.0
Percent change			+1.7	+.8			+.8	-.1	+1.9	+1.0	+2.9	+1.3
Michigan	1994	9,496,000	517,076	5,445.2			72,751	766.1	444,325	4,679.1	927	9.8
	1995	9,549,000	494,903	5,182.8			65,680	687.8	429,223	4,495.0	808	8.5
Percent change			-4.3	-4.8			-9.7	-10.2	-3.4	-3.9	-12.8	-13.3
Ohio	1994	11,102,000	495,310	4,461.4			53,930	485.8	441,380	3,975.7	662	6.0
	1995	11,151,000	491,223	4,405.2			53,799	482.5	437,424	3,922.7	600	5.4
Percent change			-.8	-1.3			-.2	-.7	-.9	-1.3	-9.4	-10.0
Wisconsin	1994	5,082,000	200,452	3,944.4			13,748	270.5	186,704	3,673.8	227	4.5
	1995	5,123,000	199,064	3,885.7			14,399	281.1	184,665	3,604.6	219	4.3
Percent change			-.7	-1.5			+4.7	+3.9	-1.1	-1.9	-3.5	-4.4
West North Central[4, 5]	1994	18,210,000	817,461	4,489.1			84,350	463.2	733,111	4,025.9	980	5.4
	1995	18,348,000	836,947	4,561.5			80,940	441.1	756,007	4,120.4	928	5.1
Percent change			+2.4	+1.6			-4.0	-4.8	+3.1	+2.3	-5.3	-5.6
Iowa	1994	2,829,000	103,389	3,654.6			8,914	315.1	94,475	3,339.5	47	1.7
	1995	2,842,000	116,575	4,101.9			10,071	354.4	106,504	3,747.5	51	1.8
Percent change			+12.8	+12.2			+13.0	+12.5	+12.7	+12.2	+8.5	+5.9
Kansas[4, 5]	1994	2,554,000	123,791	4,846.9			11,314	443.0	112,477	4,404.0	170	6.7
	1995	2,565,000	125,350	4,886.9			10,792	420.7	114,558	4,466.2	159	6.2
Percent change			+1.3	+.8			-4.6	-5.0	+1.9	+1.4	-6.5	-7.5
Minnesota	1994	4,567,000	198,253	4,341.0			16,397	359.0	181,856	3,982.0	147	3.2
	1995	4,610,000	207,327	4,497.3			16,416	356.1	190,911	4,141.2	182	3.9
Percent change			+4.6	+3.6			+.1	-.8	+5.0	+4.0	+23.8	+21.9
Missouri	1994	5,278,000	280,138	5,307.7			39,240	743.5	240,898	4,564.2	554	10.5
	1995	5,324,000	272,617	5,120.5			35,339	663.8	237,278	4,456.8	469	8.8
Percent change			-2.7	-3.5			-9.9	-10.7	-1.5	-2.4	-15.3	-16.2
Nebraska	1994	1,623,000	72,068	4,440.4			6,322	389.5	65,746	4,050.9	51	3.1
	1995	1,637,000	74,393	4,544.5			6,253	382.0	68,140	4,162.5	48	2.9
Percent change			+3.2	+2.3			-1.1	-1.9	+3.6	+2.8	-5.9	-6.5
North Dakota	1994	638,000	17,455	2,735.9			522	81.8	16,933	2,654.1	1	.2
	1995	641,000	18,373	2,866.3			556	86.7	17,817	2,779.6	6	.9
Percent change			+5.3	+4.8			+6.5	+6.0	+5.2	+4.7	+500.0	+350.0
South Dakota	1994	721,000	22,367	3,102.2			1,641	227.6	20,726	2,874.6	10	1.4
	1995	729,000	22,312	3,060.6			1,513	207.5	20,799	2,853.1	13	1.8
Percent change			-.2	-1.3			-7.8	-8.8	+.4	-.7	+30.0	+28.6

See footnotes at end of table.

Table 4. — Index of Crime: Region, Geographic Division, and State, 1994–1995 — Continued

Forcible rape		Robbery		Aggravated assault		Burglary		Larceny-theft		Motor vehicle theft		Arson[2]	
Number	Rate per 100,000	Number	Rate per 100,000	Number	Rate per 100,000	Number	Rate per 100,000	Number	Rate per 100,000	Number	Rate per 100,000	Number	Rate per 100,000
26,455	**43.1**	**122,815**	**200.0**	**214,015**	**348.6**	**544,097**	**886.2**	**1,761,409**	**2,869.0**	**282,211**	**459.7**		
24,812	**40.1**	**112,350**	**181.8**	**221,701**	**358.7**	**519,928**	**841.3**	**1,774,505**	**2,871.2**	**278,775**	**451.1**		
-6.2	**-7.0**	**-8.5**	**-9.1**	**+3.6**	**+2.9**	**-4.4**	**-5.1**	**+.7**	**+.1**	**-1.2**	**-1.9**		
19,102	44.2	99,571	230.6	161,242	373.4	387,885	898.2	1,247,454	2,888.7	219,267	507.8		
18,189	41.9	90,183	207.5	170,479	392.3	368,058	847.0	1,233,720	2,839.0	215,423	495.7		
-4.8	-5.2	-9.4	-10.0	+5.7	+5.1	-5.1	-5.7	-1.1	-1.7	-1.8	-2.4		
3,913	33.3	43,788	372.6	63,849	543.3	118,116	1,005.1	363,888	3,096.4	66,218	563.5		
4,313	36.5	39,139	330.8	73,163	618.5	108,555	917.6	357,143	3,019.0	61,874	523.0		
+10.2	+9.6	-10.6	-11.2	+14.6	+13.8	-8.1	-8.7	-1.9	-2.5	-6.6	-7.2		
2,046	35.6	7,490	130.2	20,216	351.5	48,921	850.5	160,043	2,782.4	25,011	434.8		
1,930	33.3	7,844	135.2	20,211	348.3	47,676	821.6	163,618	2,819.5	27,023	465.7		
-5.7	-6.5	+4.7	+3.8	—	-.9	-2.5	-3.4	+2.2	+1.3	+8.0	+7.1		
6,720	70.8	21,733	228.9	43,371	456.7	91,849	967.2	290,172	3,055.7	62,304	656.1		
5,917	62.0	17,885	187.3	41,070	430.1	86,872	909.7	280,712	2,939.7	61,639	645.5		
-11.9	-12.4	-17.7	-18.2	-5.3	-5.8	-5.4	-5.9	-3.3	-3.8	-1.1	-1.6		
5,231	47.1	20,821	187.5	27,216	245.1	96,175	866.3	297,792	2,682.3	47,413	427.1		
4,835	43.4	19,931	178.7	28,433	255.0	93,539	838.8	297,624	2,669.0	46,261	414.9		
-7.6	-7.9	-4.3	-4.7	+4.5	+4.0	-2.7	-3.2	-.1	-.5	-2.4	-2.9		
1,192	23.5	5,739	112.9	6,590	129.7	32,824	645.9	135,559	2,667.4	18,321	360.5		
1,194	23.3	5,384	105.1	7,602	148.4	31,416	613.2	134,623	2,627.8	18,626	363.6		
+.2	-.9	-6.2	-6.9	+15.4	+14.4	-4.3	-5.1	-.7	-1.5	+1.7	+.9		
7,353	40.4	23,244	127.6	52,773	289.8	156,212	857.8	513,955	2,822.4	62,944	345.7		
6,623	36.1	22,167	120.8	51,222	279.2	151,870	827.7	540,785	2,947.4	63,352	345.3		
-9.9	-10.6	-4.6	-5.3	-2.9	-3.7	-2.8	-3.5	+5.2	+4.4	+.6	-.1		
666	23.5	1,327	46.9	6,874	243.0	18,872	667.1	70,507	2,492.3	5,096	180.1		
619	21.8	1,507	53.0	7,894	277.8	21,527	757.5	78,645	2,767.2	6,332	222.8		
-7.1	-7.2	+13.6	+13.0	+14.8	+14.3	+14.1	+13.6	+11.5	+11.0	+24.3	+23.7		
1,055	41.3	2,940	115.1	7,149	279.9	28,635	1,121.2	75,459	2,954.5	8,383	328.2		
938	36.6	2,775	108.2	6,920	269.8	27,404	1,068.4	78,855	3,074.3	8,299	323.5		
-11.1	-11.4	-5.6	-6.0	-3.2	-3.6	-4.3	-4.7	+4.5	+4.1	-1.0	-1.4		
2,725	59.7	5,370	117.6	8,155	178.6	36,157	791.7	131,344	2,875.9	14,355	314.3		
2,593	56.2	5,702	123.7	7,939	172.2	36,756	797.3	138,414	3,002.5	15,741	341.5		
-4.8	-5.9	+6.2	+5.2	-2.6	-3.6	+1.7	+.7	+5.4	+4.4	+9.7	+8.7		
1,955	37.0	12,178	230.7	24,553	465.2	55,577	1,053.0	158,283	2,998.9	27,038	512.3		
1,711	32.1	10,863	204.0	22,296	418.8	49,649	932.6	162,430	3,050.9	25,199	473.3		
-12.5	-13.2	-10.8	-11.6	-9.2	-10.0	-10.7	-11.4	+2.6	+1.7	-6.8	-7.6		
500	30.8	1,223	75.4	4,548	280.2	10,963	675.5	48,547	2,991.2	6,236	384.2		
317	19.4	1,067	65.2	4,821	294.5	10,344	631.9	52,044	3,179.2	5,752	351.4		
-36.6	-37.0	-12.8	-13.5	+6.0	+5.1	-5.6	-6.5	+7.2	+6.3	-7.8	-8.5		
149	23.4	71	11.1	301	47.2	2,070	324.5	13,899	2,178.5	964	151.1		
146	22.8	64	10.0	340	53.0	2,248	350.7	14,421	2,249.8	1,148	179.1		
-2.0	-2.6	-9.9	-9.9	+13.0	+12.3	+8.6	+8.1	+3.8	+3.3	+19.1	+18.5		
303	42.0	135	18.7	1,193	165.5	3,938	546.2	15,916	2,207.5	872	120.9		
299	41.0	189	25.9	1,012	138.8	3,942	540.7	15,976	2,191.5	881	120.9		
-1.3	-2.4	+40.0	+38.5	-15.2	-16.1	+.1	-1.0	+.4	-.7	+1.0	—		

Table 4. — Index of Crime: Region, Geographic Division, and State, 1994–1995 — Continued

Area	Year	Population[1]	Crime Index total Number	Rate per 100,000	Modified Crime Index total[2] Number	Rate per 100,000	Violent crime[3] Number	Rate per 100,000	Property crime[3] Number	Rate per 100,000	Murder and non-negligent manslaughter Number	Rate per 100,000
South5	**1994**	**90,692,000**	**5,303,092**	**5,847.4**			**691,481**	**762.4**	**4,611,611**	**5,084.9**	**9,708**	**10.7**
	1995	**91,890,000**	**5,275,936**	**5,741.6**			**677,702**	**737.5**	**4,598,234**	**5,004.1**	**9,010**	**9.8**
Percent change			**−.5**	**−1.8**			**−2.0**	**−3.3**	**−.3**	**−1.6**	**−7.2**	**−8.4**
South Atlantic	1994	46,398,000	2,908,194	6,267.9			385,734	831.4	2,522,460	5,436.6	4,674	10.1
	1995	46,995,000	2,882,559	6,133.8			379,065	806.6	2,503,494	5,327.1	4,262	9.1
Percent change			−.9	−2.1			−1.7	−3.0	−.8	−2.0	−8.8	−9.9
Delaware	1994	706,000	34,592	4,899.7			4,621	654.5	29,971	4,245.2	33	4.7
	1995	717,000	36,988	5,158.7			5,198	725.0	31,790	4,433.8	25	3.5
Percent change			+6.9	+5.3			+12.5	+10.8	+6.1	+4.4	−24.2	−25.5
District of Columbia[6]	1994	570,000	63,186	11,085.3			15,177	2,662.6	48,009	8,422.6	399	70.0
	1995	554,000	67,441	12,173.5			14,744	2,661.4	52,697	9,512.1	360	65.0
Percent change			+6.7	+9.8			−2.9	—	+9.8	+12.9	−9.8	−7.1
Florida	1994	13,953,000	1,151,121	8,250.0			160,016	1,146.8	991,105	7,103.2	1,165	8.3
	1995	14,166,000	1,090,999	7,701.5			151,711	1,071.0	939,288	6,630.6	1,037	7.3
Percent change			−5.2	−6.6			−5.2	−6.6	−5.2	−6.7	−11.0	−12.0
Georgia	1994	7,055,000	424,029	6,010.3			47,103	667.7	376,926	5,342.7	703	10.0
	1995	7,201,000	432,322	6,003.6			47,317	657.1	385,005	5,346.5	683	9.5
Percent change			+2.0	−.1			+.5	−1.6	+2.1	+.1	−2.8	−5.0
Maryland	1994	5,006,000	306,496	6,122.6			47,457	948.0	259,039	5,174.6	579	11.6
	1995	5,042,000	317,382	6,294.8			49,757	986.9	267,625	5,307.9	596	11.8
Percent change			+3.6	+2.8			+4.8	+4.1	+3.3	+2.6	+2.9	+1.7
North Carolina	1994	7,070,000	397,705	5,625.2			46,308	655.0	351,397	4,970.3	772	10.9
	1995	7,195,000	405,764	5,639.5			46,508	646.4	359,256	4,993.1	677	9.4
Percent change			+2.0	+.3			+.4	−1.3	+2.2	+.5	−12.3	−13.8
South Carolina	1994	3,664,000	219,870	6,000.8			37,756	1,030.5	182,114	4,970.4	353	9.6
	1995	3,673,000	222,723	6,063.8			36,067	981.9	186,656	5,081.8	292	7.9
Percent change			+1.3	+1.0			−4.5	−4.7	+2.5	+2.2	−17.3	−17.7
Virginia	1994	6,552,000	265,200	4,047.6			23,437	357.7	241,763	3,689.9	571	8.7
	1995	6,618,000	264,005	3,989.2			23,921	361.5	240,084	3,627.7	503	7.6
Percent change			−.5	−1.4			+2.1	+1.1	−.7	−1.7	−11.9	−12.6
West Virginia	1994	1,822,000	46,067	2,528.4			3,931	215.8	42,136	2,312.6	99	5.4
	1995	1,828,000	44,935	2,458.2			3,842	210.2	41,093	2,248.0	89	4.9
Percent change			−2.5	−2.8			−2.3	−2.6	−2.5	−2.8	−10.1	−9.3
East South Central[5]	1994	15,890,000	728,628	4,585.4			97,717	615.0	630,911	3,970.5	1,636	10.3
	1995	16,066,000	739,184	4,600.9			95,082	591.8	644,102	4,009.1	1,656	10.3
Percent change			+1.4	+.3			−2.7	−3.8	+2.1	+1.0	+1.2	—
Alabama	1994	4,219,000	206,859	4,903.0			28,844	683.7	178,015	4,219.4	501	11.9
	1995	4,253,000	206,188	4,848.1			26,894	632.4	179,294	4,215.7	475	11.2
Percent change			−.3	−1.1			−6.8	−7.5	+.7	−.1	−5.2	−5.9
Kentucky[5]	1994	3,827,000	127,716	3,337.2			16,991	444.0	110,725	2,893.3	244	6.4
	1995	3,860,000	129,377	3,351.7			14,079	364.7	115,298	2,987.0	276	7.2
Percent change			+1.3	+.4			−17.1	−17.9	+4.1	+3.2	+13.1	+12.5
Mississippi	1994	2,669,000	129,101	4,837.1			13,177	493.7	115,924	4,343.3	409	15.3
	1995	2,697,000	121,755	4,514.5			13,560	502.8	108,195	4,011.7	348	12.9
Percent change			−5.7	−6.7			+2.9	+1.8	−6.7	−7.6	−14.9	−15.7
Tennessee	1994	5,175,000	264,952	5,119.8			38,705	747.9	226,247	4,371.9	482	9.3
	1995	5,256,000	281,864	5,362.7			40,549	771.5	241,315	4,591.2	557	10.6
Percent change			+6.4	+4.7			+4.8	+3.2	+6.7	+5.0	+15.6	+14.0
West South Central	1994	28,404,000	1,666,270	5,866.3			208,030	732.4	1,458,240	5,133.9	3,398	12.0
	1995	28,828,000	1,654,193	5,738.1			203,555	706.1	1,450,638	5,032.0	3,092	10.7
Percent change			−.7	−2.2			−2.2	−3.6	−.5	−2.0	−9.0	−10.8
Arkansas	1994	2,453,000	117,713	4,798.7			14,598	595.1	103,115	4,203.6	294	12.0
	1995	2,484,000	116,521	4,690.9			13,741	553.2	102,780	4,137.7	259	10.4
Percent change			−1.0	−2.2			−5.9	−7.0	−.3	−1.6	−11.9	−13.3
Louisiana	1994	4,315,000	287,857	6,671.1			42,369	981.9	245,488	5,689.2	856	19.8
	1995	4,342,000	289,873	6,676.0			43,741	1,007.4	246,132	5,668.6	740	17.0
Percent change			+.7	+.1			+3.2	+2.6	+.3	−.4	−13.6	−14.1
Oklahoma[7]	1994	3,258,000	181,475	5,570.1			21,225	651.5	160,250	4,918.7	226	6.9
	1995	3,278,000	183,463	5,596.8			21,770	664.1	161,693	4,932.7	400	12.2
Percent change			+1.1	+.5			+2.6	+1.9	+.9	+.3	+77.0	+76.8
Texas	1994	18,378,000	1,079,225	5,872.4			129,838	706.5	949,387	5,165.9	2,022	11.0
	1995	18,724,000	1,064,336	5,684.3			124,303	663.9	940,033	5,020.5	1,693	9.0
Percent change			−1.4	−3.2			−4.3	−6.0	−1.0	−2.8	−16.3	−18.2

See footnotes at end of table.

Table 4. — Index of Crime: Region, Geographic Division, and State, 1994–1995 — Continued

Forcible rape		Robbery		Aggravated assault		Burglary		Larceny-theft		Motor vehicle theft		Arson[2]	
Number	Rate per 100,000	Number	Rate per 100,000	Number	Rate per 100,000	Number	Rate per 100,000	Number	Rate per 100,000	Number	Rate per 100,000	Number	Rate per 100,000
39,405	**43.4**	**200,671**	**221.3**	**441,697**	**487.0**	**1,094,445**	**1,206.8**	**3,022,655**	**3,332.9**	**494,511**	**545.3**		
37,583	**40.9**	**195,143**	**212.4**	**435,966**	**474.4**	**1,044,918**	**1,137.1**	**3,066,121**	**3,336.7**	**487,195**	**530.2**		
−4.6	**−5.8**	**−2.8**	**−4.0**	**−1.3**	**−2.6**	**−4.5**	**−5.8**	**+1.4**	**+.1**	**−1.5**	**−2.8**		
19,142	41.3	118,277	254.9	243,641	525.1	590,540	1,272.8	1,659,930	3,577.6	271,990	586.2		
18,667	39.7	115,741	246.3	240,395	511.5	559,772	1,191.1	1,680,341	3,575.6	263,381	560.4		
−2.5	−3.9	−2.1	−3.4	−1.3	−2.6	−5.2	−6.4	+1.2	−.1	−3.2	−4.4		
546	77.3	1,213	171.8	2,829	400.7	6,198	877.9	20,828	2,950.1	2,945	417.1		
575	80.2	1,425	198.7	3,173	442.5	6,491	905.3	22,329	3,114.2	2,970	414.2		
+5.3	+3.8	+17.5	+15.7	+12.2	+10.4	+4.7	+3.1	+7.2	+5.6	+.8	−.7		
249	43.7	6,311	1,107.2	8,218	1,441.8	10,037	1,760.9	29,711	5,212.5	8,261	1,449.3		
292	52.7	6,864	1,239.0	7,228	1,304.7	10,185	1,838.4	32,319	5,833.8	10,193	1,839.9		
+17.3	+20.6	+8.8	+11.9	−12.0	−9.5	+1.5	+4.4	+8.8	+11.9	+23.4	+27.0		
7,301	52.3	45,871	328.8	105,679	757.4	237,341	1,701.0	626,578	4,490.6	127,186	911.5		
6,887	48.6	42,485	299.9	101,302	715.1	215,657	1,522.4	612,311	4,322.4	111,320	785.8		
−5.7	−7.1	−7.4	−8.8	−4.1	−5.6	−9.1	−10.5	−2.3	−3.7	−12.5	−13.8		
2,448	34.7	15,703	222.6	28,249	400.4	81,406	1,153.9	256,208	3,631.6	39,312	557.2		
2,539	35.3	14,777	205.2	29,318	407.1	76,324	1,059.9	264,872	3,678.3	43,809	608.4		
+3.7	+1.7	−5.9	−7.8	+3.8	+1.7	−6.2	−8.1	+3.4	+1.3	+11.4	+9.2		
2,035	40.7	20,147	402.5	24,696	493.3	52,234	1,043.4	168,608	3,368.1	38,197	763.0		
2,130	42.2	21,334	423.1	25,697	509.7	53,320	1,057.5	178,126	3,532.8	36,179	717.6		
+4.7	+3.7	+5.9	+5.1	+4.1	+3.3	+2.1	+1.4	+5.6	+4.9	−5.3	−6.0		
2,334	33.0	12,811	181.2	30,391	429.9	104,118	1,472.7	225,937	3,195.7	21,342	301.9		
2,320	32.2	12,896	179.2	30,615	425.5	101,995	1,417.6	234,911	3,264.9	22,350	310.6		
−.6	−2.4	+.7	−1.1	+.7	−1.0	−2.0	−3.7	+4.0	+2.2	+4.7	+2.9		
1,991	54.3	6,817	186.1	28,595	780.4	46,678	1,274.0	122,252	3,336.6	13,184	359.8		
1,737	47.3	6,461	175.9	27,577	750.8	46,083	1,254.6	126,416	3,441.8	14,157	385.4		
−12.8	−12.9	−5.2	−5.5	−3.6	−3.8	−1.3	−1.5	+3.4	+3.2	+7.4	+7.1		
1,868	28.5	8,704	132.8	12,294	187.6	41,855	638.8	181,619	2,772.0	18,289	279.1		
1,799	27.2	8,718	131.7	12,901	194.9	39,388	595.2	181,333	2,740.0	19,363	292.6		
−3.7	−4.6	+.2	−.8	+4.9	+3.9	−5.9	−6.8	−.2	−1.2	+5.9	+4.8		
370	20.3	772	42.4	2,690	147.6	10,673	585.8	28,189	1,547.1	3,274	179.7		
388	21.2	781	42.7	2,584	141.4	10,329	565.0	27,724	1,516.6	3,040	166.3		
+4.9	+4.4	+1.2	+.7	−3.9	−4.2	−3.2	−3.6	−1.6	−2.0	−7.1	−7.5		
6,594	41.5	25,889	162.9	63,598	400.2	166,355	1,046.9	402,194	2,531.1	62,362	392.5		
6,112	38.0	27,163	169.1	60,151	374.4	162,566	1,011.9	412,983	2,570.5	68,553	426.7		
−7.3	−8.4	+4.9	+3.8	−5.4	−6.4	−2.3	−3.3	+2.7	+1.6	+9.9	+8.7		
1,487	35.2	7,223	171.2	19,633	465.3	44,064	1,044.4	119,951	2,843.1	14,000	331.8		
1,350	31.7	7,900	185.8	17,169	403.7	43,586	1,024.8	120,967	2,844.3	14,741	346.6		
−9.2	−9.9	+9.4	+8.5	−12.6	−13.2	−1.1	−1.9	+.8	—	+5.3	+4.5		
1,350	35.3	3,595	93.9	11,802	308.4	28,718	750.4	73,449	1,919.2	8,558	223.6		
1,231	31.9	4,001	103.7	8,571	222.0	28,389	735.5	76,906	1,992.4	10,003	259.1		
−8.8	−9.6	+11.3	+10.4	−27.4	−28.0	−1.1	−2.0	+4.7	+3.8	+16.9	+15.9		
1,212	45.4	4,336	162.5	7,220	270.5	34,493	1,292.4	70,621	2,646.0	10,810	405.0		
1,054	39.1	3,530	130.9	8,628	319.9	30,505	1,131.1	67,967	2,520.1	9,723	360.5		
−13.0	−13.9	−18.6	−19.4	+19.5	+18.3	−11.6	−12.5	−3.8	−4.8	−10.1	−11.0		
2,545	49.2	10,735	207.4	24,943	482.0	59,080	1,141.6	138,173	2,670.0	28,994	560.3		
2,477	47.1	11,732	223.2	25,783	490.5	60,086	1,143.2	147,143	2,799.5	34,086	648.5		
−2.7	−4.3	+9.3	+7.6	+3.4	+1.8	+1.7	+.1	+6.5	+4.9	+17.6	+15.7		
13,669	48.1	56,505	198.9	134,458	473.4	337,550	1,188.4	960,531	3,381.7	160,159	563.9		
12,804	44.4	52,239	181.2	135,420	469.8	322,580	1,119.0	972,797	3,374.5	155,261	538.6		
−6.3	−7.7	−7.5	−8.9	+.7	−.8	−4.4	−5.8	+1.3	−.2	−3.1	−4.5		
1,028	41.9	3,158	128.7	10,118	412.5	26,911	1,097.1	68,478	2,791.6	7,726	315.0		
925	37.2	3,122	125.7	9,435	379.8	24,763	996.9	69,935	2,815.4	8,082	325.4		
−10.0	−11.2	−1.1	−2.3	−6.8	−7.9	−8.0	−9.1	+2.1	+.9	+4.6	+3.3		
1,923	44.6	11,530	267.2	28,060	650.3	55,188	1,279.0	164,081	3,802.6	26,219	607.6		
1,855	42.7	11,662	268.6	29,484	679.0	53,481	1,231.7	166,667	3,838.5	25,984	598.4		
−3.5	−4.3	+1.1	+.5	+5.1	+4.4	−3.1	−3.7	+1.6	+.9	−.9	−1.5		
1,616	49.6	4,174	128.1	15,209	466.8	40,764	1,251.2	104,025	3,192.9	15,461	474.6		
1,461	44.6	3,788	115.6	16,121	491.8	41,694	1,271.9	103,727	3,164.5	16,272	496.4		
−9.6	−10.1	−9.2	−9.8	+6.0	+5.4	+2.3	+1.7	−.3	−.9	+5.2	+4.6		
9,102	49.5	37,643	204.8	81,071	441.1	214,687	1,168.2	623,947	3,395.1	110,753	602.6		
8,563	45.7	33,667	179.8	80,380	429.3	202,642	1,082.3	632,468	3,377.8	104,923	560.4		
−5.9	−7.7	−10.6	−12.2	−.9	−2.7	−5.6	−7.4	+1.4	−.5	−5.3	−7.0		

Table 4. — Index of Crime: Region, Geographic Division, and State, 1994–1995 — Continued

Area	Year	Population[1]	Crime Index total		Modified Crime Index total[2]		Violent crime[3]		Property crime[3]		Murder and non-negligent manslaughter	
			Number	Rate per 100,000	Number	Rate per 100,000	Number	Rate per 100,000	Number	Rate per 100,000	Number	Rate per 100,000
West[4, 8]	1994	56,859,000	3,497,925	6,151.9			457,965	805.4	3,039,960	5,346.5	5,347	9.4
	1995	57,596,000	3,503,406	6,082.7			443,745	770.4	3,059,661	5,312.3	5,172	9.0
Percent change			+.2	−1.1			−3.1	−4.3	+.6	−.6	−3.3	−4.3
Mountain[4]	1994	15,214,000	927,716	6,097.8			88,451	581.4	839,265	5,516.4	1,112	7.3
	1995	15,645,000	994,536	6,356.9			87,718	560.7	906,818	5,796.2	1,126	7.2
Percent change			+7.2	+4.2			−.8	−3.6	+8.0	+5.1	+1.3	−1.4
Arizona	1994	4,075,000	322,926	7,924.6			28,653	703.1	294,273	7,221.4	426	10.5
	1995	4,218,000	346,450	8,213.6			30,095	713.5	316,355	7,500.1	439	10.4
Percent change			+7.3	+3.6			+5.0	+1.5	+7.5	+3.9	+3.1	−1.0
Colorado	1994	3,656,000	194,440	5,318.4			18,632	509.6	175,808	4,808.8	199	5.4
	1995	3,747,000	202,199	5,396.3			16,494	440.2	185,705	4,956.1	216	5.8
Percent change			+4.0	+1.5			−11.5	−13.6	+5.6	+3.1	+8.5	+7.4
Idaho	1994	1,133,000	46,192	4,077.0			3,238	285.8	42,954	3,791.2	40	3.5
	1995	1,163,000	51,189	4,401.5			3,745	322.0	47,444	4,079.4	48	4.1
Percent change			+10.8	+8.0			+15.7	+12.7	+10.5	+7.6	+20.0	+17.1
Montana[4]	1994	856,000	42,961	5,018.8			1,516	177.1	41,445	4,841.7	28	3.3
	1995	870,000	46,153	5,304.9			1,484	170.6	44,669	5,134.4	26	3.0
Percent change			+7.4	+5.7			−2.1	−3.7	+7.8	+6.0	−7.1	−9.1
Nevada	1994	1,457,000	97,290	6,677.4			14,597	1,001.9	82,693	5,675.6	170	11.7
	1995	1,530,000	100,664	6,579.3			14,461	945.2	86,203	5,634.2	163	10.7
Percent change			+3.5	−1.5			−.9	−5.7	+4.2	−.7	−4.1	−8.5
New Mexico	1994	1,654,000	102,346	6,187.8			14,708	889.2	87,638	5,298.5	177	10.7
	1995	1,685,000	108,312	6,428.0			13,804	819.2	94,508	5,608.8	148	8.8
Percent change			+5.8	+3.9			−6.1	−7.9	+7.8	+5.9	−16.4	−17.8
Utah	1994	1,908,000	101,142	5,300.9			5,810	304.5	95,332	4,996.4	56	2.9
	1995	1,951,000	118,832	6,090.8			6,415	328.8	112,417	5,762.0	76	3.9
Percent change			+17.5	+14.9			+10.4	+8.0	+17.9	+15.3	+35.7	+34.5
Wyoming	1994	476,000	20,419	4,289.7			1,297	272.5	19,122	4,017.2	16	3.4
	1995	480,000	20,737	4,320.2			1,220	254.2	19,517	4,066.0	10	2.1
Percent change			+1.6	+.7			−5.9	−6.7	+2.1	+1.2	−37.5	−38.2
Pacific[8]	1994	41,645,000	2,570,209	6,171.7			369,514	887.3	2,200,695	5,284.4	4,235	10.2
	1995	41,951,000	2,508,870	5,980.5			356,027	848.7	2,152,843	5,131.8	4,046	9.6
Percent change			−2.4	−3.1			−3.6	−4.4	−2.2	−2.9	−4.5	−5.9
Alaska	1994	606,000	34,591	5,708.1			4,644	766.3	29,947	4,941.7	38	6.3
	1995	604,000	34,753	5,753.8			4,656	770.9	30,097	4,982.9	55	9.1
Percent change			+.5	+.8			+.3	+.6	+.5	+.8	+44.7	+44.4
California	1994	31,431,000	1,940,497	6,173.8			318,395	1,013.0	1,622,102	5,160.8	3,703	11.8
	1995	31,589,000	1,841,984	5,831.1			305,154	966.0	1,536,830	4,865.1	3,531	11.2
Percent change			−5.1	−5.6			−4.2	−4.6	−5.3	−5.7	−4.6	−5.1
Hawaii	1994	1,179,000	78,763	6,680.5			3,091	262.2	75,672	6,418.3	50	4.2
	1995	1,187,000	85,447	7,198.6			3,509	295.6	81,938	6,902.9	56	4.7
Percent change			+8.5	+7.8			+13.5	+12.7	+8.3	+7.6	+12.0	+11.9
Oregon	1994	3,086,000	194,307	6,296.4			16,067	520.6	178,240	5,775.8	150	4.9
	1995	3,141,000	206,173	6,563.9			16,408	522.4	189,765	6,041.5	129	4.1
Percent change			+6.1	+4.2			+2.1	+.3	+6.5	+4.6	−14.0	−16.3
Washington	1994	5,343,000	322,051	6,027.5			27,317	511.3	294,734	5,516.3	294	5.5
	1995	5,431,000	340,513	6,269.8			26,300	484.3	314,213	5,785.5	275	5.1
Percent change			+5.7	+4.0			−3.7	−5.3	+6.6	+4.9	−6.5	−7.3
Puerto Rico[8]	·1994		116,248				25,385		90,863		980	
	1995		106,088				22,450		83,638		864	
Percent change			−8.7				−11.6		−8.0		−11.8	

[1]Populations are Bureau of the Census provisional estimates as of July 1 and are subject to change and may not add to totals due to rounding.

[2]Although arson data are included in the trend and clearance tables, sufficient data are not available to estimate totals for this offense.

[3]Violent crimes are offenses of murder, forcible rape, robbery, and aggravated assault. Property crimes are offenses of burglary, larceny–theft, and motor vehicle theft. Data are not included for the property crime of arson.

[4]Complete data for 1995 were not available for the states of Illinois, Kansas, and Montana; therefore, it was necessary that their crime counts be estimated. See "Offense Estimation," pages 367–368 for details.

[5]The 1994 figures have been adjusted. See "Crime Trends," page 368 for details.

[6]Includes offenses reported by the Zoological Police.

[7]The increase in murders was the result of the bombing of the Alfred P. Murrah Federal Building in Oklahoma City.

[8]The 1995 Bureau of the Census population estimate for Puerto Rico was not available prior to publication; therefore, no population or rates per 100,000 inhabitants are provided. Data for Puerto Rico are not included in totals.

Offense totals are based on all reporting agencies and estimates for unreported areas.

Table 4. — Index of Crime: Region, Geographic Division, and State, 1994–1995 — Continued

Forcible rape		Robbery		Aggravated assault		Burglary		Larceny-theft		Motor vehicle theft		Arson[2]	
Number	Rate per 100,000	Number	Rate per 100,000	Number	Rate per 100,000	Number	Rate per 100,000	Number	Rate per 100,000	Number	Rate per 100,00	Number	Rate per 100,000
22,750	**40.0**	**145,750**	**256.3**	**284,118**	**499.7**	**661,088**	**1,162.7**	**1,924,135**	**3,384.0**	**454,737**	**799.8**		
22,241	**38.6**	**139,108**	**241.5**	**277,244**	**481.3**	**639,969**	**1,111.1**	**1,978,432**	**3,435.0**	**441,260**	**766.1**		
−2.2	**−3.5**	**−4.6**	**−5.8**	**−2.4**	**−3.7**	**−3.2**	**−4.4**	**+2.8**	**+1.5**	**−3.0**	**−4.2**		
6,426	42.2	19,755	129.8	61,158	402.0	168,191	1,105.5	582,707	3,830.1	88,367	580.8		
6,343	40.5	20,466	130.8	59,783	382.1	173,282	1,107.6	636,242	4,066.7	97,294	621.9		
−1.3	−4.0	+3.6	+.8	−2.2	−5.0	+3.0	+.2	+9.2	+6.2	+10.1	+7.1		
1,465	36.0	6,601	162.0	20,161	494.7	60,157	1,476.2	190,649	4,678.5	43,467	1,066.7		
1,418	33.6	7,329	173.8	20,909	495.7	59,762	1,416.8	207,763	4,925.6	48,830	1,157.7		
−3.2	−6.7	+11.0	+7.3	+3.7	+.2	−.7	−4.0	+9.0	+5.3	+12.3	+8.5		
1,579	43.2	3,910	106.9	12,944	354.0	33,843	925.7	127,600	3,490.2	14,365	392.9		
1,480	39.5	3,604	96.2	11,194	298.7	35,001	934.1	136,184	3,634.5	14,520	387.5		
−6.3	−8.6	−7.8	−10.0	−13.5	−15.6	+3.4	+.9	+6.7	+4.1	+1.1	−1.4		
316	27.9	209	18.4	2,673	235.9	8,147	719.1	32,597	2,877.1	2,210	195.1		
330	28.4	279	24.0	3,088	265.5	9,069	779.8	35,560	3,057.6	2,815	242.0		
+4.4	+1.8	+33.5	+30.4	+15.5	+12.5	+11.3	+8.4	+9.1	+6.3	+27.4	+24.0		
233	27.2	280	32.7	975	113.9	6,178	721.7	32,817	3,833.8	2,450	286.2		
225	25.9	289	33.2	944	108.5	6,271	720.8	35,718	4,105.5	2,680	308.0		
−3.4	−4.8	+3.2	+1.5	−3.2	−4.7	+1.5	−.1	+8.8	+7.1	+9.4	+7.6		
1,001	68.7	5,134	352.4	8,292	569.1	19,735	1,354.5	51,893	3,561.6	11,065	759.4		
937	61.2	4,966	324.6	8,395	548.7	20,235	1,322.5	54,563	3,566.2	11,405	745.4		
−6.4	−10.9	−3.3	−7.9	+1.2	−3.6	+2.5	−2.4	+5.1	+.1	+3.1	−1.8		
866	52.4	2,329	140.8	11,336	685.4	21,945	1,326.8	57,343	3,466.9	8,350	504.8		
954	56.6	2,604	154.5	10,098	599.3	24,383	1,447.1	61,478	3,648.5	8,647	513.2		
+10.2	+8.0	+11.8	+9.7	−10.9	−12.6	+11.1	+9.1	+7.2	+5.2	+3.6	+1.7		
806	42.2	1,213	63.6	3,735	195.8	15,089	790.8	74,554	3,907.4	5,689	298.2		
834	42.7	1,309	67.1	4,196	215.1	15,623	800.8	89,202	4,572.1	7,592	389.1		
+3.5	+1.2	+7.9	+5.5	+12.3	+9.9	+3.5	+1.3	+19.6	+17.0	+33.5	+30.5		
160	33.6	79	16.6	1,042	218.9	3,097	650.6	15,254	3,204.6	771	162.0		
165	34.4	86	17.9	959	199.8	2,938	612.1	15,774	3,286.3	805	167.7		
+3.1	+2.4	+8.9	+7.8	−8.0	−8.7	−5.1	−5.9	+3.4	+2.5	+4.4	+3.5		
16,324	39.2	125,995	302.5	222,960	535.4	492,897	1,183.6	1,341,428	3,221.1	366,370	879.7		
15,898	37.9	118,642	282.8	217,441	518.3	466,687	1,112.5	1,342,190	3,199.4	343,966	819.9		
−2.6	−3.3	−5.8	−6.5	−2.5	−3.2	−5.3	−6.0	+.1	−.7	−6.1	−6.8		
418	69.0	886	146.2	3,302	544.9	4,848	800.0	21,824	3,601.3	3,275	540.4		
485	80.3	937	155.1	3,179	526.3	5,055	836.9	21,891	3,624.3	3,151	521.7		
+16.0	+16.4	+5.8	+6.1	−3.7	−3.4	+4.3	+4.6	+.3	+.6	−3.8	−3.5		
10,984	34.9	112,160	356.8	191,548	609.4	384,257	1,222.5	929,640	2,957.7	308,205	980.6		
10,554	33.4	104,611	331.2	186,458	590.3	353,895	1,120.3	902,456	2,856.9	280,479	887.9		
−3.9	−4.3	−6.7	−7.2	−2.7	−3.1	−7.9	−8.4	−2.9	−3.4	−9.0	−9.5		
359	30.4	1,221	103.6	1,461	123.9	14,029	1,189.9	55,260	4,687.0	6,383	541.4		
336	28.3	1,553	130.8	1,564	131.8	13,832	1,165.3	59,907	5,046.9	8,199	690.7		
−6.4	−6.9	+27.2	+26.3	+7.0	+6.4	−1.4	−2.1	+8.4	+7.7	+28.5	+27.6		
1,333	43.2	4,264	138.2	10,320	334.4	33,970	1,100.8	122,506	3,969.7	21,764	705.2		
1,309	41.7	4,332	137.9	10,638	338.7	34,640	1,102.8	133,075	4,236.7	22,050	702.0		
−1.8	−3.5	+1.6	−.2	+3.1	+1.3	+2.0	+.2	+8.6	+6.7	+1.3	−.5		
3,230	60.5	7,464	139.7	16,329	305.6	55,793	1,044.2	212,198	3,971.5	26,743	500.5		
3,214	59.2	7,209	132.7	15,602	287.3	59,265	1,091.2	224,861	4,140.3	30,087	554.0		
−.5	−2.1	−3.4	−5.0	−4.5	−6.0	+6.2	+4.5	+6.0	+4.3	+12.5	+10.7		
396		17,625		6,384		31,160		42,062		17,641			
324		15,753		5,509		27,689		39,960		15,989			
−18.2		−10.6		−13.7		−11.1		−5.0		−9.4			

Table 5. — Index of Crime, State, 1995

Area	Population	Crime Index total	Modified Crime Index total[1]	Violent crime[2]	Property crime[3]	Murder and non-negligent man-slaughter	Forcible rape	Robbery	Aggra-vated assault	Burglary	Larceny–theft	Motor vehicle theft	Arson[1]
ALABAMA													
Metropolitan Statistical													
Area	2,873,679												
Area actually reporting	99.5%	165,126		21,477	143,649	381	1,031	7,043	13,022	34,281	96,344	13,024	
Estimated totals	100.0%	165,927		21,571	144,356	381	1,034	7,071	13,085	34,425	96,854	13,077	
Cities outside metropolitan areas	600,368												
Area actually reporting	94.2%	29,001		3,917	25,084	47	194	686	2,990	5,274	18,731	1,079	
Estimated totals	100.0%	30,783		4,158	26,625	50	206	728	3,174	5,598	19,882	1,145	
Rural	778,953												
Area actually reporting	93.5%	8,863		1,089	7,774	41	103	94	851	3,332	3,957	485	
Estimated totals	100.0%	9,478		1,165	8,313	44	110	101	910	3,563	4,231	519	
State Total	**4,253,000**	**206,188**		**26,894**	**179, 294**	**475**	**1,350**	**7,900**	**17,169**	**43,586**	**120,967**	**14,741**	
Rate per 100,000 inhabitants		4,848.1		632.4	4,215.7	11.2	31.7	185.8	403.7	1,024.8	2,844.3	346.6	
ALASKA													
Metropolitan Statistical													
Area	253,500												
Area actually reporting	100.0%	18,305		2,510	15,795	29	242	777	1,462	2,521	11,152	2,122	
Cities outside metropolitan areas	160,347												
Area actually reporting	71.5%	7,391		743	6,648	4	49	87	603	783	5,452	413	
Estimated totals	100.0%	10,338		1,040	9,298	6	69	122	843	1,095	7,625	578	
Rural	190,153												
Area actually reporting	100.0%	6,110		1,106	5,004	20	174	38	874	1,439	3,114	451	
State Total	**604,000**	**34,753**		**4,656**	**30,097**	**55**	**485**	**937**	**3,179**	**5,055**	**21,891**	**3,151**	
Rate per 100,000 inhabitants		5,753.8		770.9	4,982.9	9.1	80.3	155.1	526.3	836.9	3,624.3	521.7	
ARIZONA													
Metropolitan Statistical													
Area	3,569,716												
Area actually reporting	99.5%	313,825		27,367	286,458	411	1,290	7,088	18,578	53,588	186,030	46,840	
Estimated totals	100.0%	315,306		27,464	287,842	411	1,295	7,111	18,647	53,875	186,939	47,028	
Cities outside metropolitan areas	322,660												
Area actually reporting	94.0%	22,065		1,473	20,592	13	65	174	1,221	3,481	15,871	1,240	
Estimated totals	100.0%	23,470		1,567	21,903	14	69	185	1,299	3,703	16,881	1,319	
Rural	325,624												
Area actually reporting	100.0%	7,674		1,064	6,610	14	54	33	963	2,184	3,943	483	
State Total	**4,218,000**	**346,450**		**30,095**	**316,355**	**439**	**1,418**	**7,329**	**20,909**	**59,762**	**207,763**	**48,830**	
Rate per 100,000 inhabitants		8,213.6		713.5	7,500.1	10.4	33.6	173.8	495.7	1,416.8	4,925.6	1,157.7	
ARKANSAS													
Metropolitan Statistical													
Area	1,117,263												
Area actually reporting	99.7%	71,776		9,296	62,480	133	565	2,386	6,212	13,537	43,541	5,402	
Estimated totals	100.0%	71,989		9,314	62,675	133	566	2,391	6,224	13,575	43,684	5,416	
Cities outside metropolitan areas	543,421												
Area actually reporting	99.7%	30,512		3,117	27,395	71	215	628	2,203	6,480	19,323	1,592	
Estimated totals	100.0%	30,610		3,127	27,483	71	216	630	2,210	6,501	19,385	1,597	
Rural	823,316												
Area actually reporting	100.0%	13,922		1,300	12,622	55	143	101	1,001	4,687	6,866	1,069	
State Total	**2,484,000**	**116,521**		**13,741**	**102,780**	**259**	**925**	**3,122**	**9,435**	**24,763**	**69,935**	**8,082**	
Rate per 100,000 inhabitants		4,690.9		553.2	4,137.7	10.4	37.2	125.7	379.8	996.9	2,815.4	325.4	
CALIFORNIA													
Metropolitan Statistical													
Area	30,526,853												
Area actually reporting	99.9%	1,787,962		298,148	1,489,814	3,474	10,195	103,921	180,558	340,058	873,924	275,832	
Estimated totals	100.0%	1,788,424		298,210	1,490,214	3,475	10,197	103,942	180,596	340,147	874,167	275,900	
Cities outside metropolitan areas	439,439												
Area actually reporting	98.9%	31,352		3,669	27,683	21	169	511	2,968	6,698	18,658	2,327	
Estimated totals	100.0%	31,688		3,708	27,980	21	171	516	3,000	6,770	18,858	2,352	
Rural	622,708												
Area actually reporting	100.0%	21,872		3,236	18,636	35	186	153	2,862	6,978	9,431	2,227	
State Total	**31,589,000**	**1,841,984**		**305,154**	**1,536,830**	**3,531**	**10,554**	**104,611**	**186,458**	**353,895**	**902,456**	**280,479**	
Rate per 100,000 inhabitants		5,831.1		966.0	4,865.1	11.2	33.4	331.2	590.3	1,120.3	2,856.9	887.9	

See footnotes at end of table.

Table 5. — Index of Crime, State, 1995 — Continued

Area	Population	Crime Index total	Modified Crime Index total[1]	Violent crime[2]	Property crime[3]	Murder and non-negligent man-slaughter	Forcible rape	Robbery	Aggra-vated assault	Burglary	Larceny–theft	Motor vehicle theft	Arson[1]
COLORADO													
Metropolitan Statistical Area	3,048,311												
Area actually reporting	99.4%	166,247		14,364	151,883	179	1,311	3,440	9,434	29,050	109,665	13,168	
Estimated totals	100.0%	167,288		14,447	152,841	179	1,318	3,459	9,491	29,201	110,408	13,232	
Cities outside metropolitan areas	320,980												
Area actually reporting	94.0%	22,587		1,220	21,367	17	102	113	988	2,863	17,737	767	
Estimated totals	100.0%	24,016		1,297	22,719	18	108	120	1,051	3,044	18,859	816	
Rural	377,709												
Area actually reporting	93.7%	10,206		703	9,503	18	51	23	611	2,582	6,479	442	
Estimated totals	100.0%	10,895		750	10,145	19	54	25	652	2,756	6,917	472	
State Total	**3,747,000**	**202,199**		**16,494**	**185,705**	**216**	**1,480**	**3,604**	**11,194**	**35,001**	**136,184**	**14,520**	
Rate per 100,000 inhabitants		5,396.3		440.2	4,956.1	5.8	39.5	96.2	298.7	934.1	3,634.5	387.5	
CONNECTICUT													
Metropolitan Statistical Area	3,014,589												
Area actually reporting	100.0%	141,215		12,651	128,564	146	727	5,275	6,503	27,522	83,798	17,244	
Cities outside metropolitan areas	66,991												
Area actually reporting	100.0%	2,472		166	2,306	—	6	40	120	455	1,699	152	
Rural	193,420												
Area actually reporting	100.0%	3,794		476	3,318	4	43	30	399	1,118	1,904	296	
State Total	**3,275,000**	**147,481**		**13,293**	**134,188**	**150**	**776**	**5,345**	**7,022**	**29,095**	**87,401**	**17,692**	
Rate per 100,000 inhabitants		4,503.2		405.9	4,097.3	4.6	23.7	163.2	214.4	888.4	2,668.7	540.2	
DELAWARE													
Metropolitan Statistical Area	594,552												
Area actually reporting	99.9%	31,627		4,274	27,353	13	461	1,338	2,462	5,198	19,302	2,853	
Estimated totals	100.0%	31,638		4,275	27,363	13	461	1,338	2,463	5,199	19,310	2,854	
Cities outside metropolitan areas	30,443												
Area actually reporting	100.0%	1,981		194	1,787	—	16	46	132	279	1,464	44	
Rural	92,005												
Area actually reporting	100.0%	3,369		729	2,640	12	98	41	578	1,013	1,555	72	
State Total	**717,000**	**36,988**		**5,198**	**31,790**	**25**	**575**	**1,425**	**3,173**	**6,491**	**22,329**	**2,970**	
Rate per 100,000 inhabitants		5,158.7		725.0	4,433.8	3.5	80.2	198.7	442.5	905.3	3,114.2	414.2	
DISTRICT OF COLUMBIA[4]													
Metropolitan Statistical Area	554,000												
Area actually reporting	100.0%	67,441		14,744	52,697	360	292	6,864	7,228	10,185	32,319	10,193	
Cities outside metropolitan areas	NONE												
Rural	NONE												
State Total	**554,000**	**67,441**		**14,744**	**52,697**	**360**	**292**	**6,864**	**7,228**	**10,185**	**32,319**	**10,193**	
Rate per 100,000 inhabitants		12,173.5		2,661.4	9,512.1	65.0	52.7	1,239.0	1,304.7	1,838.4	5,833.8	1,839.9	
FLORIDA													
Metropolitan Statistical Area	13,170,589												
Area actually reporting	99.9%	1,041,488		144,884	896,604	969	6,482	41,502	95,931	203,509	584,555	108,540	
Estimated totals	100.0%	1,042,096		144,950	897,146	969	6,484	41,523	95,974	203,622	584,918	108,606	
Cities outside metropolitan areas	220,980												
Area actually reporting	94.5%	17,563		2,251	15,312	19	63	469	1,700	3,602	10,780	930	
Estimated totals	100.0%	18,586		2,382	16.204	20	67	496	1,799	3,812	11,408	984	
Rural	774,431												
Area actually reporting	98.1%	29,742		4,296	25,446	47	330	457	3,462	8,067	15,682	1,697	
Estimated totals	100.0%	30,317		4,379	25,938	48	336	466	3,529	8,223	15,985	1,730	
State Total	**14,166,000**	**1,090,999**		**151,711**	**939,288**	**1,037**	**6,887**	**42,485**	**101,302**	**215,657**	**612,311**	**111,320**	
Rate per 100,000 inhabitants		7,701.5		1,071.0	6,630.6	7.3	48.6	299.9	715.1	1,522.4	4,322.4	785.8	

See footnotes at end of table.

Table 5. — Index of Crime, State, 1995 — Continued

Area	Population	Crime Index total	Modified Crime Index total[1]	Violent crime[2]	Property crime[3]	Murder and non-negligent man-slaughter	Forcible rape	Robbery	Aggra-vated assault	Burglary	Larceny–theft	Motor vehicle theft	Arson[1]
GEORGIA													
Metropolitan Statistical													
Area	4,906,892												
Area actually reporting	97.2%	326,375		35,240	291,135	492	1,958	12,787	20,003	54,958	198,536	37,641	
Estimated totals	100.0%	334,319		35,839	298,480	499	2,002	12,987	20,351	56,212	203,693	38,575	
Cities outside metropolitan areas ...	876,169												
Area actually reporting	92.5%	55,552		6,506	49,046	73	236	1,264	4,933	9,304	37,384	2,358	
Estimated totals	100.0%	60,048		7,032	53,016	79	255	1,366	5,332	10,057	40,410	2,549	
Rural......................	1,417,939												
Area actually reporting	92.6%	35,165		4,119	31,046	97	261	393	3,368	9,316	19,242	2,488	
Estimated totals	100.0%	37,955		4,446	33,509	105	282	424	3,635	10,055	20,769	2,685	
State Total	**7,201,000**	**432,322**		**47,317**	**385,005**	**683**	**2,539**	**14,777**	**29,318**	**76,324**	**264,872**	**43,809**	
Rate per 100,000													
inhabitants		6,003.6		657.1	5,346.5	9.5	35.3	205.2	407.1	1,059.9	3,678.3	608.4	
HAWAII													
Metropolitan Statistical													
Area	880,266												
Area actually reporting	100.0%	67,145		2,882	64,263	38	217	1,371	1,256	10,127	46,696	7,440	
Cities outside metropolitan areas	40,578												
Area actually reporting	100.0%	2,618		138	2,480	4	29	34	71	452	1,936	92	
Rural......................	266,156												
Area actually reporting	100.0%	15,684		489	15,195	14	90	148	237	3,253	11,275	667	
State Total	**1,187,000**	**85,447**		**3,509**	**81,938**	**56**	**336**	**1,553**	**1,564**	**13,832**	**59,907**	**8,199**	
Rate per 100,000													
inhabitants		7,198.6		295.6	6,902.9	4.7	28.3	130.8	131.8	1,165.3	5,046.9	690.7	
IDAHO													
Metropolitan Statistical													
Area	356,980												
Area actually reporting	100.0%	18,440		1,308	17,132	11	111	117	1,069	2,981	13,089	1,062	
Cities outside metropolitan areas ...	406,066												
Area actually reporting	99.2%	23,305		1,464	21,841	22	133	114	1,195	3,595	17,110	1,136	
Estimated totals	100.0%	23,499		1,476	22,023	22	134	115	1,205	3,625	17,253	1,145	
Rural......................	399,954												
Area actually reporting	98.7%	9,132		949	8,183	15	84	46	804	2,432	5,151	600	
Estimated totals	100.0%	9,250		961	8,289	15	85	47	814	2,463	5,218	608	
State Total	**1,163,000**	**51,189**		**3,745**	**47,444**	**48**	**330**	**279**	**3,088**	**9,069**	**35,560**	**2,815**	
Rate per 100,000													
inhabitants		4,401.5		322.0	4,079.4	4.1	28.4	24.0	265.5	779.8	3,057.6	242.0	
ILLINOIS[5]													
State Total	**11,830,000**	**645,408**		**117,836**	**527,572**	**1,221**	**4,313**	**39,139**	**73,163**	**108,555**	**357,143**	**61,874**	
Rate per 100,000													
inhabitants		5,455.7		996.1	4,459.6	10.3	36.5	330.8	618.5	917.6	3,019.0	523.0	
INDIANA													
Metropolitan Statistical													
Area	4,160,993												
Area actually reporting	80.5%	188,152		22,355	165,797	387	1,415	6,902	13,651	33,341	111,094	21,362	
Estimated totals	100.0%	216,879		24,566	192,313	404	1,569	7,341	15,252	37,899	130,506	23,908	
Cities outside metropolitan areas ...	591,323												
Area actually reporting	68.7%	22,139		2,320	19,819	17	113	278	1,912	3,252	15,290	1,277	
Estimated totals	100.0%	32,208		3,375	28,833	25	164	404	2,782	4,731	22,244	1,858	
Rural......................	1,050,684												
Area actually reporting	46.7%	9,192		1,172	8,020	17	92	46	1,017	2,357	5,076	587	
Estimated totals	100.0%	19,681		2,510	17,171	37	197	99	2,177	5,046	10,868	1,257	
State Total	**5,803,000**	**268,768**		**30,451**	**238,317**	**466**	**1,930**	**7,844**	**20,211**	**47,676**	**163,618**	**27,023**	
Rate per 100,000													
inhabitants		4,631.5		524.7	4,106.8	8.0	33.3	135.2	348.3	821.6	2,819.5	465.7	

See footnotes at end of table.

Table 5. — Index of Crime, State, 1995 — Continued

Area	Population	Crime Index total	Modified Crime Index total[1]	Violent crime[2]	Property crime[3]	Murder and non-negligent man-slaughter	Forcible rape	Robbery	Aggra-vated assault	Burglary	Larceny–theft	Motor vehicle theft	Arson[1]
IOWA													
Metropolitan Statistical Area	1,251,310												
Area actually reporting	96.5%	71,672		6,926	64,746	42	453	1,307	5,124	12,234	48,322	4,190	
Estimated totals	100.0%	73,042		7,021	66.021	42	460	1,317	5,202	12,522	49,232	4,267	
Cities outside metropolitan areas	705,792												
Area actually reporting	89.9%	28,558		2,216	26,342	6	97	159	1,954	4,807	20,303	1,232	
Estimated totals	100.0%	31,750		2,464	29,286	7	108	177	2,172	5,344	22,572	1,370	
Rural	884,898												
Area actually reporting	92.0%	10,837		539	10,298	2	47	12	478	3,367	6,292	639	
Estimated totals	100.0%	11,783		586	11,197	2	51	13	520	3,661	6,841	695	
State Total	**2,842,000**	**116,575**		**10,071**	**106,504**	**51**	**619**	**1,507**	**7,894**	**21,527**	**78,645**	**6,332**	
Rate per 100,000 inhabitants		4,101.9		354.4	3,747.5	1.8	21.8	53.0	277.8	757.5	2,767.2	222.8	
KANSAS[5]													
State Total	**2,565,000**	**125,350**		**10,792**	**114,558**	**159**	**938**	**2,775**	**6,920**	**27,404**	**78,855**	**8,299**	
Rate per 100,000 inhabitants		4,886.9		420.7	4,466.2	6.2	36.6	108.2	269.8	1,068.4	3,074.3	323.5	
KENTUCKY[6]													
Metropolitan Statistical Area	1,864,313												
Area actually reporting	99.1%	86,122		10,302	75,820	113	602	3,378	6,209	17,665	51,137	7,018	
Estimated totals	100.0%	86,847		10,342	76,505	113	604	3,395	6,230	17,791	51,655	7,059	
Cities outside metropolitan areas	643,407												
Area actually reporting	94.3%	24,180		2,096	22,084	34	172	432	1,458	4,399	16,349	1,336	
Estimated totals	100.0%	25,643		2,222	23,421	36	182	458	1,546	4,665	17,339	1,417	
Rural	1,352,280												
Area actually reporting	99.5%	16,809		1,507	15,302	126	443	147	791	5,906	7,876	1,520	
Estimated totals	100.0%	16,887		1,515	15,372	127	445	148	795	5,933	7,912	1,527	
State Total	**3,860,000**	**129,377**		**14,079**	**115,298**	**276**	**1,231**	**4,001**	**8,571**	**28,389**	**76,906**	**10,003**	
Rate per 100,000 inhabitants		3,351.7		364.7	2,987.0	7.2	31.9	103.7	222.0	735.5	1,992.4	259.1	
LOUISIANA													
Metropolitan Statistical Area	3,260,660												
Area actually reporting	96.5%	239,026		35,328	203,698	648	1,561	10,761	22,358	43,618	136,013	24,067	
Estimated totals	100.0%	245,485		36,088	209,397	655	1,596	10,918	22,919	44,805	140,040	24,552	
Cities outside metropolitan areas	396,731												
Area actually reporting	82.8%	22,996		3,146	19,850	29	103	457	2,557	4,143	14,963	744	
Estimated totals	100.0%	27,779		3,800	23,979	35	124	552	3,089	5,005	18,075	899	
Rural	684,609												
Area actually reporting	98.5%	16,368		3,797	12,571	49	133	189	3,426	3,618	8,428	525	
Estimated totals	100.0%	16,609		3,853	12,756	50	135	192	3,476	3,671	8,552	533	
State Total	**4,342,000**	**289,873**		**43,741**	**246,132**	**740**	**1,855**	**11,662**	**29,484**	**53,481**	**166,667**	**25,984**	
Rate per 100,000 inhabitants		6,676.0		1,007.4	5,668.6	17.0	42.7	268.6	679.0	1,231.7	3,838.5	598.4	
MAINE													
Metropolitan Statistical Area	459,495												
Area actually reporting	100.0%	19,390		926	18,464	14	125	249	538	3,840	13,863	761	
Cities outside metropolitan areas	434,317												
Area actually reporting	98.5%	15,138		511	14,627	2	87	75	347	2,756	11,285	586	
Estimated totals	100.0%	15,362		518	14,844	2	88	76	352	2,797	11,452	595	
Rural	347,188												
Area actually reporting	100.0%	6,011		187	5,824	9	52	9	117	2,378	3,129	317	
State Total	**1,241,000**	**40,763**		**1,631**	**39,132**	**25**	**265**	**334**	**1,007**	**9,015**	**28,444**	**1,673**	
Rate per 100,000 inhabitants		3,284.7		131.4	3,153.3	2.0	21.4	26.9	81.1	726.4	2,292.0	134.8	

See footnotes at end of table.

Table 5. — Index of Crime, State, 1995 — Continued

Area	Population	Crime Index total	Modified Crime Index total[1]	Violent crime[2]	Property crime[3]	Murder and non-negligent man-slaughter	Forcible rape	Robbery	Aggra-vated assault	Burglary	Larceny–theft	Motor vehicle theft	Arson[1]
MARYLAND													
Metropolitan Statistical													
Area	4,678,669												
Area actually reporting	99.9%	301,257		47,558	253,699	576	1,969	20,960	24,053	50,002	168,169	35,528	
Estimated totals	100.0%	301,317		47,564	253,753	576	1,969	20,963	24,056	50,011	168,209	35,533	
Cities outside metropolitan areas	98,063												
Area actually reporting	100.0%	9,203		1,133	8,070	6	65	259	803	1,545	6,138	387	
Rural	265,268												
Area actually reporting	100.0%	6,862		1,060	5,802	14	96	112	838	1,764	3,779	259	
State Total	**5,042,000**	**317,382**		**49,757**	**267,625**	**596**	**2,130**	**21,334**	**25,697**	**53,320**	**178,126**	**36,179**	
Rate per 100,000 inhabitants		6,294.8		986.9	5,307.9	11.8	42.2	423.1	509.7	1,057.5	3,532.8	717.6	
MASSACHUSETTS													
Metropolitan Statistical													
Area	5,777,763												
Area actually reporting	92.1%	235,757		37,285	198,472	209	1,551	8,776	26,749	44,290	119,814	34,368	
Estimated totals	100.0%	249,733		39,060	210,673	214	1,624	9,040	28,182	47,004	127,670	35,999	
Cities outside metropolitan areas	283,829												
Area actually reporting	59.1%	8,200		1,558	6,642	2	79	56	1,421	1,565	4,660	417	
Estimated totals	100.0%	13,875		2,636	11,239	3	134	95	2,404	2,648	7,885	706	
Rural	12,408												
Area actually reporting	100.0%	102		43	59	—	1	2	40	17	31	11	
State Total	**6,074,000**	**263,710**		**41,739**	**221,971**	**217**	**1,759**	**9,137**	**30,626**	**49,669**	**135,586**	**36,716**	
Rate per 100,000 inhabitants		4,341.6		687.2	3,654.4	3.6	29.0	150.4	504.2	817.7	2,232.2	604.5	
MICHIGAN													
Metropolitan Statistical													
Area	7,879,086												
Area actually reporting	91.6%	418,188		58,920	359,268	761	4,339	17,231	36,589	72,057	230,744	56,467	
Estimated totals	100.0%	447,203		61,567	385,636	780	4,608	17,731	38,448	76,245	249,950	59,441	
Cities outside metropolitan areas	618,889												
Area actually reporting	82.8%	17,877		1,064	16,813	2	259	58	745	2,127	13,838	848	
Estimated totals	100.0%	21,586		1,285	20,301	2	313	70	900	2,568	16,709	1,024	
Rural	1,051,025												
Area actually reporting	97.1%	25,345		2,745	22,600	25	967	82	1,671	7,822	13,639	1,139	
Estimated totals	100.0%	26,114		2,828	23,286	26	996	84	1,722	8,059	14,053	1,174	
State Total	**9,549,000**	**494.903**		**65,680**	**429,223**	**808**	**5,917**	**17,885**	**41,070**	**86,872**	**280,712**	**61,639**	
Rate per 100,000 inhabitants		5,182.8		687.8	4,495.0	8.5	62.0	187.3	430.1	909.7	2,939.7	645.5	
MINNESOTA													
Metropolitan Statistical													
Area	3,203,336												
Area actually reporting	99.9%	161,367		14,432	146,935	167	1,906	5,564	6,795	26,991	106,955	12,989	
Estimated totals	100.0%	161,528		14,439	147,089	167	1,907	5,566	6,799	27,012	107,078	12,999	
Cities outside metropolitan areas	539,366												
Area actually reporting	96.2%	25,779		965	24,814	3	310	95	557	3,527	19,931	1,356	
Estimated totals	100.0%	26,794		1,003	25,791	3	322	99	579	3,666	20,716	1,409	
Rural	867,298												
Area actually reporting	100.0%	19,005		974	18,031	12	364	37	561	6,078	10,620	1,333	
State Total	**4,610,000**	**207,327**		**16,416**	**190,911**	**182**	**2,593**	**5,702**	**7,939**	**36,756**	**138,414**	**15,741**	
Rate per 100,000 inhabitants		4,497.3		356.1	4,141.2	3.9	56.2	123.7	172.2	797.3	3,002.5	341.5	
MISSISSIPPI													
Metropolitan Statistical													
Area	944,140												
Area actually reporting	75.3%	48,496		4,409	44,087	126	372	2,033	1,878	11,237	27,191	5,659	
Estimated totals	100.0%	56,001		4,904	51,097	144	440	2,160	2,160	13,482	31,495	6,120	
Cities outside metropolitan areas	649,923												
Area actually reporting	68.4%	33,954		3,812	30,142	62	290	802	2,658	7,380	20,804	1,958	
Estimated totals	100.0%	49,675		5,577	44,098	91	424	1,173	3,889	10,797	30,436	2,865	
Rural	1,102,937												
Area actually reporting	24.8%	3,985		763	3,222	28	47	49	639	1,543	1,496	183	
Estimated totals	100.0%	16,079		3,079	13,000	113	190	197	2,579	6,226	6,036	738	
State Total	**2,697,000**	**121,755**		**13,560**	**108,195**	**348**	**1,054**	**3,530**	**8,628**	**30,505**	**67,967**	**9,723**	
Rate per 100,000 inhabitants		4,514.5		502.8	4,011.7	12.9	39.1	130.9	319.9	1,131.1	2,520.1	360.5	

See footnotes at end of table.

Table 5. — Index of Crime, State, 1995 — Continued

Area	Population	Crime Index total	Modified Crime Index total[1]	Violent crime[2]	Property crime[3]	Murder and non-negligent man-slaughter	Forcible rape	Robbery	Aggra-vated assault	Burglary	Larceny-theft	Motor vehicle theft	Arson[1]
MISSOURI													
Metropolitan Statistical Area	3,623,162												
Area actually reporting	95.9%	225,687		30,688	194,999	390	1,362	10,397	18,539	39,003	133,316	22,680	
Estimated totals	100.0%	230,183		31,031	199,152	395	1,391	10,465	18,780	39,837	136,282	23,033	
Cities outside metropolitan areas	495,870												
Area actually reporting	89.5%	24,354		1,734	22,620	18	126	254	1,336	3,746	17,709	1,165	
Estimated totals	100.0%	27,222		1,938	25,284	20	141	284	1,493	4,187	19,795	1,302	
Rural	1,204,968												
Area actually reporting	55.4%	8,421		1,312	7,109	30	99	63	1,120	3,114	3,517	478	
Estimated totals	100.0%	15,212		2,370	12,842	54	179	114	2,023	5,625	6,353	864	
State Total	**5,324,000**	**272,617**		**35,339**	**237,278**	**469**	**1,711**	**10,863**	**22,296**	**49,649**	**162,430**	**25,199**	
Rate per 100,000 inhabitants		5,120.5		663.8	4,456.8	8.8	32.1	204.0	418.8	932.6	3,050.9	473.3	
MONTANA[5]													
State Total	**870,000**	**46,153**		**1,484**	**44,669**	**26**	**225**	**289**	**944**	**6,271**	**35,718**	**2,680**	
Rate per 100,000 inhabitants		5,304.9		170.6	5,134.4	3.0	25.9	33.2	108.5	720.8	4,105.5	308.0	
NEBRASKA													
Metropolitan Statistical Area	830,170												
Area actually reporting	100.0%	50,010		5,220	44,790	32	177	981	4,030	6,814	33,303	4,673	
Cities outside metropolitan areas	390,944												
Area actually reporting	98.4%	18,096		701	17,395	8	93	67	533	2,208	14,493	694	
Estimated totals	100.0%	18,389		713	17,676	8	95	68	542	2,244	14,727	705	
Rural	415,886												
Area actually reporting	99.4%	5,957		318	5,639	8	45	18	247	1,278	3,989	372	
Estimated totals	100.0%	5,994		320	5,674	8	45	18	249	1,286	4,014	374	
State Total	**1,637,000**	**74,393**		**6,253**	**68,140**	**48**	**317**	**1,067**	**4,821**	**10,344**	**52,044**	**5,752**	
Rate per 100,000 inhabitants		4,544.5		382.0	4,162.5	2.9	19.4	65.2	294.5	631.9	3,179.2	351.4	
NEVADA													
Metropolitan Statistical Area	1,305,265												
Area actually reporting	100.0%	92,266		13,378	78,888	154	859	4,877	7,488	18,439	49,423	11,026	
Cities outside metropolitan areas	47,865												
Area actually reporting	59.2%	1,404		151	1,253	1	15	13	122	237	966	50	
Estimated totals	100.0%	2,370		255	2,115	2	25	22	206	400	1,631	84	
Rural	176,870												
Area actually reporting	99.2%	5,979		821	5,158	7	53	66	695	1,385	3,480	293	
Estimated totals	100.0%	6,028		828	5,200	7	53	67	701	1,396	3,509	295	
State Total	**1,530,000**	**100,664**		**14,461**	**86,203**	**163**	**937**	**4,966**	**8,395**	**20,235**	**54,563**	**11,405**	
Rate per 100,000 inhabitants		6,579.3		945.2	5,634.2	10.7	61.2	324.6	548.7	1,322.5	3,566.2	745.4	
NEW HAMPSHIRE													
Metropolitan Statistical Area	674,927												
Area actually reporting	87.8%	16,837		726	16,111	11	154	245	316	2,824	12,167	1,120	
Estimated totals	100.0%	18,849		799	18,050	12	172	259	356	3,162	13,637	1,251	
Cities outside metropolitan areas	324,539												
Area actually reporting	68.7%	7,344		289	7,055	2	98	36	153	960	5,846	249	
Estimated totals	100.0%	10,686		421	10,265	3	143	52	223	1,397	8,506	362	
Rural	148,534												
Area actually reporting	92.7%	880		88	792	6	17	3	62	229	514	49	
Estimated totals	100.0%	949		94	855	6	18	3	67	247	555	53	
State Total	**1,148,000**	**30,484**		**1,314**	**29,170**	**21**	**333**	**314**	**646**	**4,806**	**22,698**	**1,666**	
Rate per 100,000 inhabitants		2,655.4		114.5	2,540.9	1.8	29.0	27.4	56.3	418.6	1,977.2	145.1	

See footnotes at end of table.

Table 5. — Index of Crime, State, 1995 — Continued

Area	Population	Crime Index total	Modified Crime Index total[1]	Violent crime[2]	Property crime[3]	Murder and non-negligent man-slaughter	Forcible rape	Robbery	Aggra-vated assault	Burglary	Larceny-theft	Motor vehicle theft	Arson[1]
NEW JERSEY													
Metropolitan Statistical													
Area	7,945,000												
Area actually reporting	100.0%	373,708		47,652	326,056	409	1,927	22,486	22,830	69,533	206,339	50,184	
Cities outside metropolitan areas	NONE												
Rural	NONE												
State Total	**7,945,000**	**373,708**		**47,652**	**326,056**	**409**	**1,927**	**22,486**	**22,830**	**69,533**	**206,339**	**50,184**	
Rate per 100,000 inhabitants		4,703.7		599.8	4,103.9	5.1	24.3	283.0	287.4	875.2	2,597.1	631.6	
NEW MEXICO													
Metropolitan Statistical													
Area	949,733												
Area actually reporting	77.3%	59,072		6,690	52,382	72	449	1,977	4,192	12,184	33,995	6,203	
Estimated totals	100.0%	64,766		7,441	57,325	85	507	2,072	4,777	13,938	36,847	6,540	
Cities outside metropolitan areas	435,709												
Area actually reporting	83.7%	28,648		3,874	24,774	22	238	376	3,238	6,175	17,415	1,184	
Estimated totals	100.0%	34,214		4,626	29,588	26	284	449	3,867	7,375	20,799	1,414	
Rural	299,558												
Area actually reporting	61.4%	5,733		1,067	4,666	23	100	51	893	1,886	2,354	426	
Estimated totals	100.0%	9,332		1,737	7,595	37	163	83	1,454	3,070	3,832	693	
State Total	**1,685,000**	**108,312**		**13,804**	**94,508**	**148**	**954**	**2,604**	**10,098**	**24,383**	**61,478**	**8,647**	
Rate per 100,000 inhabitants		6,428.0		819.2	5,608.8	8.8	56.6	154.5	599.3	1,447.1	3,648.5	513.2	
NEW YORK													
Metropolitan Statistical													
Area	16,634,301												
Area actually reporting	99.6%	779,907		148,148	631,759	1,510	3,949	71,994	70,695	135,628	394,878	101,253	
Estimated totals	100.0%	782,293		148,359	633,934	1,510	3,957	72,061	70,831	136,000	396,514	101,420	
Cities outside metropolitan areas	648,525												
Area actually reporting	92.5%	23,693		2,065	21,628	15	182	306	1,562	3,962	17,108	558	
Estimated totals	100.0%	25,608		2,232	23,376	16	197	331	1,688	4,282	18,491	603	
Rural	853,174												
Area actually reporting	100.0%	19,124		2,092	17,032	24	136	100	1,832	6,280	10,179	573	
State Total	**18,136,000**	**827,025**		**152,683**	**674,342**	**1,550**	**4,290**	**72,492**	**74,351**	**146,562**	**425,184**	**102,596**	
Rate per 100,000 inhabitants		4,560.1		841.9	3,718.3	8.5	23.7	399.7	410.0	808.1	2,344.4	565.7	
NORTH CAROLINA													
Metropolitan Statistical													
Area	4,790,671												
Area actually reporting	99.5%	298,647		34,802	263,845	462	1,692	10,580	22,068	70,353	176,236	17,256	
Estimated totals	100.0%	299,795		34,901	264,894	463	1,697	10,602	22,139	70,641	176,947	17,306	
Cities outside metropolitan areas	739,827												
Area actually reporting	94.5%	57,114		6,623	50,491	75	274	1,649	4,625	12,921	35,201	2,369	
Estimated totals	100.0%	60,431		7,008	53,423	79	290	1,745	4,894	13,671	37,245	2,507	
Rural	1,664,502												
Area actually reporting	98.8%	45,013		4,546	40,467	133	329	543	3,541	17,479	20,480	2,508	
Estimated totals	100.0%	45,538		4,599	40,939	135	333	549	3,582	17,683	20,719	2,537	
State Total	**7,195,000**	**405,764**		**46,508**	**359,256**	**677**	**2,320**	**12,896**	**30,615**	**101,995**	**234,911**	**22,350**	
Rate per 100,000 inhabitants		5,639.5		646.4	4,993.1	9.4	32.2	179.2	425.5	1,417.6	3,264.9	310.6	
NORTH DAKOTA													
Metropolitan Statistical													
Area	269,821												
Area actually reporting	99.8%	11,096		347	10,749	1	69	55	222	1,293	8,726	730	
Estimated totals	100.0%	11,115		348	10,767	1	69	55	223	1,295	8,741	731	
Cities outside metropolitan areas	148,710												
Area actually reporting	86.0%	4,404		118	4,286	3	47	5	63	346	3,716	224	
Estimated totals	100.0%	5,120		137	4,983	3	55	6	73	402	4,321	260	
Rural	222,469												
Area actually reporting	92.5%	1,978		66	1,912	2	20	3	41	510	1,257	145	
Estimated totals	100.0%	2,138		71	2,067	2	22	3	44	551	1,359	157	
State Total	**641,000**	**18,373**		**556**	**17,817**	**6**	**146**	**64**	**340**	**2,248**	**14,421**	**1,148**	
Rate per 100,000 inhabitants		2,866.3		86.7	2,779.6	.9	22.8	10.0	53.0	350.7	2,249.8	179.1	

See footnotes at end of table.

Table 5. — Index of Crime, State, 1995 — Continued

Area	Population	Crime Index total	Modified Crime Index total[1]	Violent crime[2]	Property crime[3]	Murder and non-negligent man-slaughter	Forcible rape	Robbery	Aggra-vated assault	Burglary	Larceny-theft	Motor vehicle theft	Arson[1]
OHIO													
Metropolitan Statistical													
Area	9,055,329												
Area actually reporting	82.1%	380,707		45,912	334,795	536	3,979	18,364	23,033	73,275	221,400	40,120	
Estimated totals	100.0%	433,347		49,667	383,680	562	4,358	19,363	25,384	81,917	258,079	43,684	
Cities outside metropolitan areas	768,703												
Area actually reporting	61.1%	23,037		1,412	21,625	9	172	290	941	3,728	16,955	942	
Estimated totals	100.0%	37,726		2,313	35,413	15	282	475	1,541	6,105	27,765	1,543	
Rural	1,326,968												
Area actually reporting	56.4%	11,358		1,025	10,333	13	110	52	850	3,110	6,640	583	
Estimated totals	100.0%	20,150		1,819	18,331	23	195	93	1,508	5,517	11,780	1,034	
State Total	**11,151,000**	**491,223**		**53,799**	**437,424**	**600**	**4,835**	**19,931**	**28,433**	**93,539**	**297,624**	**46,261**	
Rate per 100,000 inhabitants		4,405.2		482.5	3,922.7	5.4	43.4	178.7	255.0	838.8	2,669.0	414.9	
OKLAHOMA[7]													
Metropolitan Statistical													
Area	1,972,582												
Area actually reporting	100.0%	134,363		15,837	118,526	308	1,114	3,299	11,116	28,597	76,524	13,405	
Cities outside metropolitan areas	670,899												
Area actually reporting	99.5%	37,666		4,383	33,283	41	244	425	3,673	8,758	22,483	2,042	
Estimated totals	100.0%	37,858		4,405	33,453	41	245	427	3,692	8,803	22,598	2,052	
Rural	634,519												
Area actually reporting	100.0%	11,242		1,528	9,714	51	102	62	1,313	4,294	4,605	815	
State Total	**3,278,000**	**183,463**		**21,770**	**161,693**	**400**	**1,461**	**3,788**	**16,121**	**41,694**	**103,727**	**16,272**	
Rate per 100,000 inhabitants		5,596.8		664.1	4,932.7	12.2	44.6	115.6	491.8	1,271.9	3,164.3	496.4	
OREGON													
Metropolitan Statistical													
Area	2,199,850												
Area actually reporting	97.6%	153,490		13,962	139,528	96	1,010	3,840	9,016	24,482	96,665	18,381	
Estimated totals	100.0%	156,564		14,129	142,435	97	1,026	3,887	9,119	24,949	98,811	18,675	
Cities outside metropolitan areas	435,008												
Area actually reporting	99.2%	33,682		1,204	32,478	11	127	338	728	5,232	25,141	2,105	
Estimated totals	100.0%	33,942		1,214	32,728	11	128	341	734	5,272	25,335	2,121	
Rural	506,142												
Area actually reporting	87.6%	13,725		933	12,792	18	136	91	688	3,871	7,822	1,099	
Estimated totals	100.0%	15,667		1,065	14,602	21	155	104	785	4,419	8,929	1,254	
State Total	**3,141,000**	**206,173**		**16,408**	**189,765**	**129**	**1,309**	**4,332**	**10,638**	**34,640**	**133,075**	**22,050**	
Rate per 100,000 inhabitants		6,563.9		522.4	6,041.5	4.1	41.7	137.9	338.7	1,102.8	4,236.7	702.0	
PENNSYLVANIA													
Metropolitan Statistical													
Area	10,231,136												
Area actually reporting	95.2%	353,510		47,406	306,104	708	2,543	22,206	21,949	56,699	203,086	46,319	
Estimated totals	100.0%	366,619		48,625	317,994	716	2,606	22,495	22,808	58,435	212,071	47,488	
Cities outside metropolitan areas	780,447												
Area actually reporting	83.4%	18,727		1,462	17,265	11	155	214	1,082	2,891	13,420	954	
Estimated totals	100.0%	22,464		1,754	20,710	13	186	257	1,298	3,468	16,098	1,144	
Rural	1,060,417												
Area actually reporting	100.0%	17,126		1,207	15,919	26	254	106	821	5,912	8,822	1,185	
State Total	**12,072,000**	**406,209**		**51,586**	**354,623**	**755**	**3,046**	**22,858**	**24,927**	**67,815**	**236,991**	**49,817**	
Rate per 100,000 inhabitants		3,364.9		427.3	2,937.6	6.3	25.2	189.3	206.5	561.8	1963.1	412.7	
PUERTO RICO[6]													
Metropolitan Statistical													
Area													
Area actually reporting	100.0%	93,577		20,250	73,327	797	271	14,803	4,379	23,235	35,020	15,072	
Cities outside metropolitan areas													
Area actually reporting	100.0%	12,511		2,200	10,311	67	53	950	1,130	4,454	4,940	917	
Total		**106,088**		**22,450**	**83,638**	**864**	**324**	**15,753**	**5,509**	**27,689**	**39,960**	**15,989**	

See footnotes at end of table.

Table 5. — Index of Crime, State, 1995 — Continued

Area	Population	Crime Index total	Modified Crime Index total[1]	Violent crime[2]	Property crime[3]	Murder and non-negligent man-slaughter	Forcible rape	Robbery	Aggra-vated assault	Burglary	Larceny-theft	Motor vehicle theft	Arson[1]
RHODE ISLAND													
Metropolitan Statistical													
Area	910,980												
Area actually reporting	100.0%	38,606		3,328	35,278	32	243	869	2,184	8,548	22,511	4,219	
Cities outside metropolitan areas	79,020												
Area actually reporting	100.0%	3,383		310	3,073	1	22	45	242	679	2,249	145	
Rural													
Area actually reporting	100.0%	32		5	27	—	2	—	3	7	20	—	
State Total	**990,000**	**42,021**		**3,643**	**38,378**	**33**	**267**	**914**	**2,429**	**9,234**	**24,780**	**4,364**	
Rate per 100,000													
inhabitants		4,244.5		368.0	3,876.6	3.3	27.0	92.3	245.4	932.7	2,503.0	440.8	
SOUTH CAROLINA													
Metropolitan Statistical													
Area	2,563,353												
Area actually reporting	99.0%	164,547		25,283	139,264	193	1,257	5,007	18,826	33,163	94,780	11,321	
Estimated totals	100.0%	166,115		25,453	140,662	194	1,266	5,040	18,953	33,421	95,844	11,397	
Cities outside metropolitan areas	322,947												
Area actually reporting	98.9%	24,255		4,634	19,621	30	131	748	3,725	4,334	14,270	1,017	
Estimated totals	100.0%	24,529		4,685	19,844	30	132	756	3,767	4,383	14,432	1,029	
Rural	786,700												
Area actually reporting	100.0%	32,079		5,929	26,150	68	339	665	4,857	8,279	16,140	1,731	
State Total	**3,673,000**	**222,723**		**36,067**	**186,656**	**292**	**1,737**	**6,461**	**27,577**	**46,083**	**126,416**	**14,157**	
Rate per 100,000													
inhabitants		6,063.8		981.9	5,081.8	7.9	47.3	175.9	750.8	1,254.6	3,441.8	385.4	
SOUTH DAKOTA													
Metropolitan Statistical													
Area	242,267												
Area actually reporting	90.8%	11,079		875	10,204	5	158	144	568	1,889	7,915	400	
Estimated totals	100.0%	11,622		918	10,704	5	169	146	598	2,026	8,253	425	
Cities outside metropolitan areas	192,936												
Area actually reporting	74.0%	6,076		324	5,752	2	67	26	229	904	4,607	241	
Estimated totals	100.0%	8,209		438	7,771	3	91	35	309	1,221	6,224	326	
Rural	293,797												
Area actually reporting	64.0%	1,587		100	1,487	3	25	5	67	445	959	83	
Estimated totals	100.0%	2,481		157	2,324	5	39	8	105	695	1,499	130	
State Total	**729,000**	**22,312**		**1,513**	**20,799**	**13**	**299**	**189**	**1,012**	**3,942**	**15,976**	**881**	
Rate per 100,000													
inhabitants		3,060.6		207.5	2,853.1	1.8	41.0	25.9	138.8	540.7	2,191.5	120.9	
TENNESSEE													
Metropolitan Statistical													
Area	3,537,662												
Area actually reporting	81.7%	206,478		31,862	174,616	414	1,978	10,673	18,797	41,329	104,218	29,069	
Estimated totals	100.0%	230,433		34,476	195,957	450	2,172	11,070	20,784	46,431	118,639	30,887	
Cities outside metropolitan areas	624,195												
Area actually reporting	78.5%	24,718		2,981	21,737	29	143	388	2,421	5,030	15,324	1,383	
Estimated totals	100.0%	31,493		3,798	27,695	37	182	494	3,085	6,409	19,524	1,762	
Rural	1,094,143												
Area actually reporting	47.1%	9,396		1,072	8,324	33	58	79	902	3,415	4,232	677	
Estimated totals	100.0%	19,938		2,275	17,663	70	123	168	1,914	7,246	8,980	1,437	
State Total	**5,256,000**	**281,864**		**40,549**	**241,315**	**557**	**2,477**	**11,732**	**25,783**	**60,086**	**147,143**	**34,086**	
Rate per 100,000													
inhabitants		5,362.7		771.5	4,591.2	10.6	47.1	223.2	490.5	1,143.2	2,799.5	648.5	
TEXAS													
Metropolitan Statistical													
Area	15,737,893												
Area actually reporting	100.0%	966,382		113,291	853,091	1,530	7,729	32,659	71,373	178,201	574,021	100,869	
Cities outside metropolitan areas	1,376,791												
Area actually reporting	99.8%	66,356		7,206	59,150	79	528	793	5,806	13,448	43,266	2,436	
Estimated totals	100.0%	66,470		7,217	59,253	79	528	794	5,816	13,473	43,340	2,440	
Rural	1,609,316												
Area actually reporting	100.0%	31,484		3,795	27,689	84	306	214	3,191	10,968	15,107	1,614	
State Total	**18,724,000**	**1,064,336**		**124,303**	**940,033**	**1,693**	**8,563**	**33,667**	**80,380**	**202,642**	**632,468**	**104,923**	
Rate per 100,000													
inhabitants		5,684.3		663.9	5,020.5	9.0	45.7	179.8	429.3	1,082.3	3,377.8	560.4	

See footnotes at end of table.

Table 5. — Index of Crime, State, 1995 — Continued

Area	Population	Crime Index total	Modified Crime Index total[1]	Violent crime[2]	Property crime[3]	Murder and non-negligent man-slaughter	Forcible rape	Robbery	Aggra-vated assault	Burglary	Larceny–theft	Motor vehicle theft	Arson[1]
UTAH													
Metropolitan Statistical													
Area	1,502,498												
Area actually reporting	98.0%	98,509		5,290	93,219	51	683	1,241	3,315	12,561	74,017	6,641	
Estimated totals	100.0%	100,301		5,394	94,907	51	697	1,257	3,389	12,790	75,372	6,745	
Cities outside metropolitan areas	239,733												
Area actually reporting	95.6%	12,475		655	11,820	13	86	36	520	1,615	9,694	511	
Estimated totals	100.0%	13,044		686	12,358	14	90	38	544	1,689	10,135	534	
Rural	208,769												
Area actually reporting	87.5%	4,801		293	4,508	10	41	12	230	1,001	3,233	274	
Estimated totals	100.0%	5,487		335	5,152	11	47	14	263	1,144	3,695	313	
State Total	**1,951,000**	**118,832**		**6,415**	**112,417**	**76**	**834**	**1,309**	**4,196**	**15,623**	**89,202**	**7,592**	
Rate per 100,000 inhabitants		6,090.8		328.8	5,762.0	3.9	42.7	67.1	215.1	800.8	4,572.1	389.1	
VERMONT													
Metropolitan Statistical													
Area	144,343												
Area actually reporting	95.8%	7,855		218	7,637	2	64	35	117	1,719	5,623	295	
Estimated totals	100.0%	8,164		225	7,939	2	66	36	121	1,771	5,862	306	
Cities outside metropolitan areas	201,816												
Area actually reporting	89.4%	7,147		248	6,899	2	64	19	163	1,028	5,586	285	
Estimated totals	100.0%	7,991		277	7,714	2	72	21	182	1,149	6,246	319	
Rural	238,841												
Area actually reporting	85.0%	3,343		162	3,181	8	23	6	125	1,301	1,736	144	
Estimated totals	100.0%	3,932		190	3,742	9	27	7	147	1,531	2,042	169	
State Total	**585,000**	**20,087**		**692**	**19,395**	**13**	**165**	**64**	**450**	**4,451**	**14,150**	**794**	
Rate per 100,000 inhabitants		3,433.7		118.3	3,315.4	2.2	28.2	10.9	76.9	760.9	2,418.8	135.7	
VIRGINIA													
Metropolitan Statistical													
Area	5,143,246												
Area actually reporting	100.0%	232,264		20,901	211,363	424	1,529	8,303	10,645	33,031	160,615	17,717	
Cities outside metropolitan areas	419,001												
Area actually reporting	100.0%	15,745		1,318	14,427	19	108	232	959	2,139	11,671	617	
Rural	1,055,753												
Area actually reporting	100.0%	15,996		1,702	14,294	60	162	183	1,297	4,218	9,047	1,029	
State Total	**6,618,000**	**264,005**		**23,921**	**240,084**	**503**	**1,799**	**8,718**	**12,901**	**39,388**	**181,333**	**19,363**	
Rate per 100,000 inhabitants		3,989.2		361.5	3,627.7	7.6	27.2	131.7	194.9	595.2	2,740.0	292.6	
WASHINGTON													
Metropolitan Statistical													
Area	4,503,997												
Area actually reporting	99.1%	283,711		22,985	260,726	231	2,681	6,794	13,279	48,584	184,910	27,232	
Estimated totals	100.0%	286,856		23,158	263,698	232	2,706	6,850	13,370	49,025	187,135	27,538	
Cities outside metropolitan areas	423,529												
Area actually reporting	91.2%	33,782		1,911	31,871	17	271	268	1,355	4,873	25,549	1,449	
Estimated totals	100.0%	37,062		2,097	34,965	19	297	294	1,487	5,346	28,029	1,590	
Rural	503,474												
Area actually reporting	100.0%	16,595		1,045	15,550	24	211	65	745	4,894	9,697	959	
State Total	**5,431,000**	**340,513**		**26,300**	**314,213**	**275**	**3,214**	**7,209**	**15,602**	**59,265**	**224,861**	**30,087**	
Rate per 100,000 inhabitants		6,269.8		484.3	5,785.5	5.1	59.2	132.7	287.3	1,091.2	4,140.3	554.0	
WEST VIRGINIA													
Metropolitan Statistical													
Area	763,721												
Area actually reporting	100.0%	26,093		2,131	23,962	35	226	614	1,256	5,513	16,743	1,706	
Cities outside metropolitan areas	280,238												
Area actually reporting	99.4%	8,641		589	8,052	11	51	111	416	1,584	6,068	400	
Estimated totals	100.0%	8,697		593	8,104	11	51	112	419	1,594	6,107	403	
Rural	784,041												
Area actually reporting	100.0%	10,145		1,118	9,027	43	111	55	909	3,222	4,874	931	
State Total	**1,828,000**	**44,935**		**3,842**	**41,093**	**89**	**388**	**781**	**2,584**	**10,329**	**27,724**	**3,040**	
Rate per 100,000 inhabitants		2,458.2		210.2	2,248.0	4.9	21.2	42.7	141.4	565.0	1,516.6	166.3	

See footnotes at end of table.

Table 5. — Index of Crime, State, 1995 — Continued

Area	Population	Crime Index total	Modified Crime Index total[1]	Violent crime[2]	Property crime[3]	Murder and non-negligent man-slaughter	Forcible rape	Robbery	Aggra-vated assault	Burglary	Larceny–theft	Motor vehicle theft	Arson[1]
WISCONSIN													
Metropolitan Statistical													
Area	3,485,853												
Area actually reporting	100.0%	154,474		12,244	142,230	181	911	5,220	5,932	22,704	102,850	16,676	
Cities outside metropolitan areas . . .	652,239												
Area actually reporting	99.4%	27,423		1,012	26,411	8	137	128	739	3,041	22,383	987	
Estimated totals	100.0%	27,593		1,019	26,574	8	138	129	744	3,060	22,521	993	
Rural	984,908												
Area actually reporting	97.2%	16,523		1,104	15,419	29	141	34	900	5,495	8,994	930	
Estimated totals	100.0%	16,997		1,136	15,861	30	145	35	926	5,652	9,252	957	
State Total	**5,123,000**	**199,064**		**14,399**	**184,665**	**219**	**1,194**	**5,384**	**7,602**	**31,416**	**134,623**	**18,626**	
Rate per 100,000 inhabitants		3,885.7		281.1	3,604.6	4.3	23.3	105.1	148.4	613.2	2,627.8	363.6	
WYOMING													
Metropolitan Statistical													
Area	143,158												
Area actually reporting	100.0%	7,308		348	6,960	5	45	49	249	1,067	5,542	351	
Cities outside metropolitan areas . . .	211,184												
Area actually reporting	99.4%	10,573		607	9,966	2	77	32	496	1,273	8,351	342	
Estimated totals	100.0%	10,631		610	10,021	2	77	32	499	1,280	8,397	344	
Rural	125,658												
Area actually reporting	100.0%	2,798		262	2,536	3	43	5	211	591	1,835	110	
State Total	**480,000**	**20,737**		**1,220**	**19,517**	**10**	**165**	**86**	**959**	**2,938**	**15,774**	**805**	
Rate per 100,000 inhabitants		4,320.2		254.2	4,066.0	2.1	34.4	17.9	199.8	612.1	3,286.3	167.7	

[1]Although arson data were included in the trend and clearance tables, sufficient data are not available to estimate totals for this offense.

[2]Violent crimes are offenses of murder, forcible rape, robbery, and aggravated assault.

[3]Property crimes are offenses of burglary, larceny-theft, and motor vehicle theft. Data are not included for the property crime of arson.

[4]Includes offenses reported by the Zoological Police.

[5]Complete data were not available for the states of Illinois, Kansas, and Montana; therefore, it was necessary that their crime counts be estimated. See "Offense Estimation," pages 367–368 for details.

[6]Aggravated assault figures for 1995 are not comparable to 1994. See "Crime Trends," page 368 for details.

[7]The increase in murders was the result of the bombing of the Alfred P. Murrah Federal Building in Oklahoma City.

[8]The 1995 Bureau of the Census population estimate for Puerto Rico was not available prior to publication; therefore, no population or rates per 100,000 inhabitants are provided.

Table 6. — Index of Crime, Metropolitan Statistical Areas, 1995

Metropolitan Statistical Area	Population	Crime Index total	Modified Crime Index total[1]	Violent crime[2]	Property crime[3]	Murder and non-negligent man-slaughter	Forcible rape	Robbery	Aggra-vated assault	Burglary	Larceny–theft	Motor vehicle theft	Arson[1]
Abilene, Tx. M.S.A.	**124,197**												
(Includes Taylor County.)													
City of Abilene	112,105	6,049		696	5,353	5	80	131	480	1,044	4,095	214	
Total area actually reporting . .	100.0%	6,377		735	5,642	5	89	134	507	1,154	4,266	222	
Rate per 100,000 inhabitants . . .		5,134.6		591.8	4,542.8	4.0	71.7	107.9	408.2	929.2	3,434.9	178.7	
Akron, Oh. M.S.A.	**673,983**												
(Includes Portage and Summit Counties.)													
City of Akron	222,864	15,901		2,268	13,633	18	209	875	1,166	2,792	8,824	2,017	
Total area actually reporting . .	79.9%	26,564		3,024	23,540	22	269	1,008	1,725	4,421	16,505	2,614	
Estimated total	100.0%	30,240		3,271	26,969	24	299	1,073	1,875	5,100	19,013	2,856	
Rate per 100,000 inhabitants . . .		4,486.8		485.3	4,001.4	3.6	44.4	159.2	278.2	756.7	2,821.0	423.7	
Albany, Ga. M.S.A.	**119,388**												
(Includes Dougherty and Lee Counties.)													
City of Albany	82,739	8,151		770	7,381	14	70	335	351	1,905	5,105	371	
Total area actually reporting . .	99.3%	9,118		821	8,297	16	74	343	388	2,160	5,729	408	
Estimated total	100.0%	9,187		826	8,361	16	74	345	391	2,169	5,778	414	
Rate per 100,000 inhabitants . . .		7,695.1		691.9	7,003.2	13.4	62.0	289.0	327.5	1,816.8	4,839.7	346.8	
Albany-Schenectady-Troy, N.Y. M.S.A.	**873,624**												
(Includes Albany, Montgomery, Rensselaer, Saratoga, Schenectady, and Schoharie Counties.)													
City of :													
Albany	104,637	8,329		1,227	7,102	7	61	548	611	2,038	4,460	604	
Schenectady	64,157	3,976		504	3,472	8	33	240	223	1,066	2,222	184	
Troy	52,510	3,054		275	2,779	1	27	147	100	794	1,824	161	
Total area actually reporting . .	98.0%	34,367		3,359	31,008	26	178	1,099	2,056	7,172	22,227	1,609	
Estimated total	100.0%	34,971		3,412	31,559	26	180	1,116	2,090	7,266	22,642	1,651	
Rate per 100,000 inhabitants . . .		4,003.0		390.6	3,612.4	3.0	20.6	127.7	239.2	831.7	2,591.7	189.0	
Albuquerque, N.M. M.S.A.	**658,142**												
(Includes Bernalillo, Sandoval, and Valencia Counties.)													
City of Albuquerque[4]	419,714				36,818	53	296	1,623		8,362	23,461	4,995	
Total area actually reporting . .	78.2%	46,274		5,339	40,935	55	334	1,691	3,259	9,322	26,346	5,267	
Estimated total	100.0%	49,505		5,788	43,717	64	370	1,748	3,606	10,431	27,828	5,458	
Rate per 100,000 inhabitants . . .		7,521.9		879.4	6,642.5	9.7	56.2	265.6	547.9	1,584.9	4,228.3	829.3	
Alexandria, La. M.S.A.	**127,269**												
(Includes Rapides Parish.)													
City of Alexandria	46,269	4,926		668	4,258	7	27	107	527	863	3,186	209	
Total area actually reporting . .	96.8%	8,082		1,027	7,055	12	41	132	842	1,764	4,860	431	
Estimated total	100.0%	8,356		1,063	7,293	12	42	139	870	1,810	5,033	450	
Rate per 100,000 inhabitants . . .		6,565.6		835.2	5,730.4	9.4	33.0	109.2	683.6	1,422.2	3,954.6	353.6	
Amarillo, Tx. M.S.A.	**200,745**												
(Includes Potter and Randall Counties.)													
City of Amarillo	168,142	13,293		1,380	11,913	16	84	242	1,038	2,419	8,883	611	
Total area actually reporting . .	100.0%	14,243		1,479	12,764	19	95	250	1,115	2,653	9,445	666	
Rate per 100,000 inhabitants . . .		7,095.1		736.8	6,358.3	9.5	47.3	124.5	555.4	1,321.6	4,705.0	331.8	
Anchorage, Ak. M.S.A.	**253,500**												
(Includes Anchorage Borough.)													
Total area actually reporting . .	100.0%	18,305		2,510	15,795	29	242	777	1,462	2,521	11,152	2,122	
Rate per 100,000 inhabitants . . .		7,220.9		990.1	6,230.8	11.4	95.5	306.5	576.7	994.5	4,399.2	837.1	
Ann Arbor, Mi. M.S.A.	**514,930**												
(Includes Lenawee, Livingston and Washtenaw Counties.)													
City of Ann Arbor	109,424	5,414		472	4,942	3	43	132	294	1,083	3,644	215	
Total area actually reporting . .	97.7%	20,281		1,846	18,435	14	219	392	1,221	3,884	13,186	1,365	
Estimated total	100.0%	20,845		1,896	18,949	14	223	402	1,257	3,961	13,562	1,426	
Rate per 100,000 inhabitants . . .		4,048.1		368.2	3,679.9	2.7	43.3	78.1	244.1	769.2	2,633.8	276.9	
Anniston, Al. M.S.A.	**117,811**												
(Includes Calhoun County.)													
City of Anniston	27,425	4,215		640	3,575	6	25	169	440	1,025	2,343	207	
Total area actually reporting . .	100.0%	6,698		1,002	5,696	9	43	216	734	1,576	3,820	300	
Rate per 100,000 inhabitants . . .		5,685.4		850.5	4,834.9	7.6	36.5	183.3	623.0	1,337.7	3,242.5	254.6	

See footnotes at end of table.

79

Metropolitan Statistical Area	Population	Crime Index total	Modified Crime Index total[1]	Violent crime[2]	Property crime[3]	Murder and non-negligent manslaughter	Forcible rape	Robbery	Aggravated assault	Burglary	Larceny-theft	Motor vehicle theft	Arson[1]
Appleton-Oshkosh-Neenah, Wi. M.S.A.	338,240												
(Includes Calumet, Outagamie, and Winnebago Counties.)													
City of:													
Appleton	7,155	2,305		35	2,270	1	2	9	23	261	1,921	88	
Neenah	24,574	858		65	793	—	1	2	62	94	670	29	
Oshkosh	56,682	2,900		99	2,801	—	18	15	66	455	2,268	78	
Total area actually reporting	100.0%	9,920		320	9,600	3	38	37	242	1,277	8,013	310	
Rate per 100,000 inhabitants		2,932.8		94.6	2,838.2	.9	11.2	10.9	71.5	377.5	2,369.0	91.7	
Asheville, N.C. M.S.A.	207,140												
(Includes Buncombe County.)													
City of Asheville	65,397	5,093		554	4,539	12	48	157	337	1,018	3,166	355	
Total area actually reporting	91.1%	7,662		862	6,800	15	65	185	597	1,812	4,462	526	
Estimated total	100.0%	8,354		922	7,432	16	69	197	640	2,009	4,863	560	
Rate per 100,000 inhabitants		4,033.0		445.1	3,587.9	7.7	33.3	95.1	309.0	969.9	2,347.7	270.3	
Athens, Ga. M.S.A.	136,072												
(Includes Clarke, Madison, and Oconee Counties.)													
City of Athens-Clarke County	91,242	7,133		785	6,348	10	49	224	502	1,039	4,889	420	
Total area actually reporting	84.3%	8,170		852	7,318	11	52	237	552	1,193	5,688	437	
Estimated total	100.0%	9,170		928	8,242	12	58	263	595	1,373	6,292	577	
Rate per 100,000 inhabitants		6,739.1		682.0	6,057.1	8.8	42.6	193.3	437.3	1,009.0	4,624.0	424.0	
Atlanta, Ga. M.S.A.	3,399,930												
(Includes Barrow, Bartow, Carroll, Cherokee, Cobb, Coweta, DeKalb, Douglas, Fayette, Forsyth, Fulton, Gwinnett, Henry, Newton, Paulding, Pickens, Rockdale, Spalding, and Walton Counties.)													
City of Atlanta	404,337	69,011		14,744	54,267	184	441	5,260	8,859	11,694	34,221	8,352	
Total area actually reporting	97.5%	240,058		27,048	213,010	351	1,398	9,762	15,537	39,380	142,716	30,914	
Estimated total	100.0%	245,636		27,469	218,167	356	1,428	9,901	15,784	40,216	146,427	31,524	
Rate per 100,000 inhabitants		7,224.7		807.9	6,416.8	10.5	42.0	291.2	464.2	1,182.8	4,306.8	927.2	
Atlantic City, N.J. M.S.A.	331,700												
(Includes Atlantic and Cape May Counties.)													
City of Atlantic City	36,752	10,102		949	9,153	15	42	554	338	1,245	7,554	354	
Total area actually reporting	100.0%	26,659		2,283	24,376	23	179	915	1,166	4,689	18,651	1,036	
Rate per 100,000 inhabitants		8,037.1		688.3	7,348.8	6.9	54.0	275.9	351.5	1,413.6	5,622.9	312.3	
Augusta-Aiken, Ga.-S.C. M.S.A.	454,945												
(Includes Columbia, McDuffie, and Richmond Counties, Ga., and Aiken and Edgefield Counties, S.C.)													
City of:													
Augusta, Ga.	44,358	4,233		375	3,858	7	17	175	176	1,043	2,250	565	
Aiken, S.C.	24,990	1,679		171	1,508	4	9	59	99	355	1,081	72	
Total area actually reporting	99.8%	21,687		2,605	19,082	34	192	674	1,705	4,653	12,031	2,398	
Estimated total	100.0%	21,734		2,610	19,124	34	192	675	1,709	4,661	12,063	2,400	
Rate per 100,000 inhabitants		4,777.3		573.7	4,203.6	7.5	42.2	148.4	375.6	1,024.5	2,651.5	527.5	
Austin-San Marcos, Tx. M.S.A.	982,121												
(Includes Bastrop, Caldwell, Hays, Travis, and Williamson Counties.)													
City of:													
Austin	523,691	42,586		4,050	38,536	46	308	1,336	2,360	7,521	27,434	3,581	
San Marcos	31,603	1,472		129	1,343	1	19	21	88	221	1,068	54	
Total area actually reporting	100.0%	59,430		5,692	53,738	55	494	1,514	3,629	11,368	38,040	4,330	
Rate per 100,000 inhabitants		6,051.2		579.6	5,471.6	5.6	50.3	154.2	369.5	1,157.5	3,873.2	440.9	
Bakersfield, Ca. M.S.A.	612,393												
(Includes Kern County.)													
City of Bakersfield	192,021	13,806		1,298	12,508	29	39	604	626	2,862	7,883	1,763	
Total area actually reporting	98.6%	34,641		4,460	30,181	71	172	1,121	3,096	8,127	18,037	4,017	
Estimated total	100.0%	35,103		4,522	30,581	72	174	1,142	3,134	8,216	18,280	4,085	
Rate per 100,000 inhabitants		5,732.1		738.4	4,993.7	11.8	28.4	186.5	511.8	1,341.6	2,985.0	667.1	
Baltimore, Md. M.S.A.	2,480,270												
(Includes Baltimore City and Anne Arundel, Baltimore, Carroll, Harford, Howard, and Queen Anne's Counties.)													
City of Baltimore	712,209	94,855		21,495	73,360	325	683	11,353	9,134	16,569	45,619	11,172	
Total area actually reporting	100.0%	184,765		33,133	151,632	392	1,188	15,054	16,499	31,279	100,315	20,038	
Rate per 100,000 inhabitants		7,449.4		1,335.9	6,113.5	15.8	47.9	607.0	665.2	1,261.1	4,044.5	807.9	

See footnotes at end of table.

Table 6. — Index of Crime, Metropolitan Statistical Areas, 1995 — Continued

Metropolitan Statistical Area	Population	Crime Index total	Modified Crime Index total[1]	Violent crime[2]	Property crime[3]	Murder and non-negligent man-slaughter	Forcible rape	Robbery	Aggra-vated assault	Burglary	Larceny-theft	Motor vehicle theft	Arson[1]
Bangor, Me. M.S.A.	**67,149**												
(Includes part of Penobscot and Waldo Counties.)													
City of Bangor	32,029	1,583		41	1,542	1	6	20	14	151	1,343	48	
Total area actually reporting ..	100.0%	2,273		66	2,207	2	7	24	33	246	1,895	66	
Rate per 100,000 inhabitants ...		3,385.0		98.3	3,286.7	3.0	10.4	35.7	49.1	366.3	2,822.1	98.3	
Barnstable-Yarmouth, Ma. M.S.A.	**142,476**												
(Includes part of Barnstable County.)													
City of:													
Barnstable	42,811	2,119		874	1,245	3	25	21	825	497	636	112	
Yarmouth	22,451	1,000		95	905	—	5	13	77	284	568	53	
Total area actually reporting ..	100.0%	5,916		1,127	4,789	4	34	44	1,045	1,675	2,871	243	
Rate per 100,000 inhabitants ...		4,152.3		791.0	3,361.3	2.8	23.9	30.9	733.5	1,175.6	2,015.1	170.6	
Baton Rouge, La. M.S.A.	**561,752**												
(Includes Ascension, East Baton Rouge, Livingston, and West Baton Rouge Parishes.)													
City of Baton Rouge	229,027	30,794		6,551	24,243	65	173	1,394	4,919	5,164	15,796	3,283	
Total area actually reporting ..	97.6%	47,764		7,671	40,093	91	241	1,639	5,700	8,241	27,580	4,272	
Estimated total	100.0%	48,645		7,786	40,859	92	245	1,660	5,789	8,390	28,137	4,332	
Rate per 100,000 inhabitants ...		8,659.5		1,386.0	7,273.5	16.4	43.6	295.5	1,030.5	1,493.5	5,008.8	771.2	
Beaumont-Port Arthur, Tx. M.S.A.	**379,744**												
(Includes Hardin, Jefferson, and Orange Counties.)													
City of:													
Beaumont	117,187	11,181		1,230	9,951	14	189	420	607	1,749	7,414	788	
Port Arthur	59,902	4,238		715	3,523	13	11	147	544	1,286	1,920	317	
Total area actually reporting ..	100.0%	23,592		2,626	20,966	37	299	714	1,576	4,858	14,545	1,563	
Rate per 100,000 inhabitants ...		6,212.6		691.5	5,521.1	9.7	78.7	188.0	415.0	1,279.3	3,830.2	411.6	
Bellingham, Wa. M.S.A.	**147,802**												
(Includes Whatcom County.)													
City of Bellingham	58,059	4,705		217	4,488	2	51	43	121	549	3,764	175	
Total area actually reporting ..	100.0%	8,447		491	7,956	5	114	74	298	1,454	6,166	336	
Rate per 100,000 inhabitants ...		5,715.1		332.2	5,382.9	3.4	77.1	50.1	201.6	983.7	4,171.8	227.3	
Benton Harbor, Mi. M.S.A.	**162,625**												
(Includes Berrien County.)													
City of Benton Harbor	13,259	2,525		852	1,673	13	31	156	652	614	869	190	
Total area actually reporting ..	87.9%	9,282		1,516	7,766	22	142	250	1,102	1,839	5,298	629	
Estimated total	100.0%	10,211		1,600	8,611	23	149	267	1,161	1,965	5,917	729	
Rate per 100,000 inhabitants ...		6,278.9		983.9	5,295.0	14.1	91.6	164.2	713.9	1,208.3	3,638.4	448.3	
Bergen-Passaic, N.J. M.S.A.	**1,310,934**												
(Includes Bergen and Passaic Counties.)													
City of Passaic	56,332	4,378		837	3,541	2	22	450	363	709	1,971	861	
Total area actually reporting ..	100.0%	46,589		4,291	42,298	28	161	1,868	2,234	7,659	28,275	6,364	
Rate per 100,000 inhabitants ...		3,553.9		327.3	3,226.6	2.1	12.3	142.5	170.4	584.2	2,156.9	485.5	
Binghamton, N.Y. M.S.A.	**262,319**												
(Includes Broome and Tioga Counties.)													
City of Binghamton	51,050	2,847		170	2,677	3	15	79	73	352	2,316	9	
Total area actually reporting ..	100.0%	7,412		496	6,916	6	51	115	324	1,218	5,588	110	
Rate per 100,000 inhabitants ...		2,825.6		189.1	2,636.5	2.3	19.4	43.8	123.5	464.3	2,130.2	41.9	
Birmingham, Al. M.S.A.	**880,597**												
(Includes Blount, Jefferson, St. Clair, and Shelby Counties.)													
City of Birmingham	270,728	33,037		6,649	26,388	121	248	2,158	4,122	6,399	16,309	3,680	
Total area actually reporting ..	99.5%	56,938		9,405	47,533	158	378	3,014	5,855	11,283	30,780	5,470	
Estimated total	100.0%	57,186		9,434	47,752	158	379	3,023	5,874	11,328	30,938	5,486	
Rate per 100,000 inhabitants ...		6,494.0		1,071.3	5,422.7	17.9	43.0	343.3	667.0	1,286.4	3,513.3	623.0	
Bismarck, N.D. M.S.A.	**88,568**												
(Includes Burleigh and Morton Counties.)													
City of Bismarck	52,839	2,199		67	2,132	—	4	11	52	264	1,738	130	
Total area actually reporting ..	100.0%	3,040		147	2,893	—	16	15	116	339	2,371	183	
Rate per 100,000 inhabitants ...		3,432.4		166.0	3,266.4	—	18.1	16.9	131.0	382.8	2,677.0	206.6	
Boise, Id. M.S.A.	**356,980**												
(Includes Ada and Canyon Counties.)													
City of Boise	149,856	8,873		645	8,228	3	53	76	513	1,424	6,311	493	
Total area actually reporting ..	100.0%	18,440		1,308	17,132	11	111	117	1,069	2,981	13,089	1,062	
Rate per 100,000 inhabitants ...		5,165.6		366.4	4,799.1	3.1	31.1	32.8	299.5	835.1	3,666.6	297.5	

See footnotes at end of table.

Table 6. — Index of Crime, Metropolitan Statistical Areas, 1995 — Continued

Metropolitan Statistical Area	Population	Crime Index total	Modified Crime Index total[1]	Violent crime[2]	Property crime[3]	Murder and non-negligent man-slaughter	Forcible rape	Robbery	Aggra-vated assault	Burglary	Larceny-theft	Motor vehicle theft	Arson[1]
Boston, Ma.-N.H. M.S.A.	**3,432,914**												
(Includes Part of Bristol, Essex, Middlesex, Plymouth, Suffolk, and Worcester Counties, Ma., and part of Rockingham County, N.H.)													
City of Boston, Ma.	550,715	52,278		9,569	42,709	96	379	3,597	5,497	6,671	26,002	10,036	
Total area actually reporting	92.8%	140,903		21,169	119,734	133	819	5,802	14,415	23,540	75,473	20,721	
Estimated total	100.0%	148,460		22,129	126,331	136	858	5,945	15,190	25,008	79,721	21,602	
Rate per 100,000 inhabitants		4,324.6		644.6	3,680.0	4.0	25.0	173.2	442.5	728.5	2,322.3	629.3	
Boulder-Longmont, Co. M.S.A.	**255,815**												
(Includes Boulder County.)													
City of:													
Boulder	87,743	6,423		188	6,235	3	29	53	103	1,209	4,757	269	
Longmont	57,664	2,922		110	2,812	2	25	28	55	448	2,198	166	
Total area actually reporting	99.5%	13,545		625	12,920	9	112	102	402	2,530	9,792	598	
Estimated total	100.0%	13,631		633	12,998	9	113	104	407	2,542	9,853	603	
Rate per 100,000 inhabitants		5,328.5		247.4	5,081.0	3.5	44.2	40.7	159.1	993.7	3,851.6	235.7	
Brazoria, Tx. M.S.A.	**215,501**												
(Includes Brazoria County.)													
Total area actually reporting	100.0%	6,632		700	5,932	10	85	70	535	1,372	4,133	427	
Rate per 100,000 inhabitants		3,077.5		324.8	2,752.7	4.6	39.4	32.5	248.3	636.7	1,917.9	198.1	
Bremerton, Wa. M.S.A.	**224,024**												
(Includes Kitsap County.)													
City of Bremerton	43,015	2,230		193	2,037	3	55	46	89	414	1,451	172	
Total area actually reporting	100.0%	10,038		927	9,111	7	182	102	636	1,928	6,566	617	
Rate per 100,000 inhabitants		4,480.8		413.8	4,067.0	3.1	81.2	45.5	283.9	860.6	2,930.9	275.4	
Bridgeport, Ct. M.S.A.	**452,933**												
(Includes part of Fairfield and New Haven Counties.)													
City of Bridgeport	133,057	10,386		1,585	8,801	33	46	840	666	2,338	3,947	2,516	
Total area actually reporting	100.0%	20,311		2,057	18,254	40	93	1,009	915	4,173	10,590	3,491	
Rate per 100,000 inhabitants		4,484.3		454.2	4,030.2	8.8	20.5	222.8	202.0	921.3	2,338.1	770.8	
Brownsville-Harlingen-San Benito, Tx. M.S.A.	**302,530**												
(Includes Cameron County.)													
City of:													
Brownsville	115,029	8,408		817	7,591	7	26	204	580	1,264	5,793	534	
Harlingen	56,567	4,774		367	4,407	1	2	52	312	951	3,152	304	
San Benito	23,756	1,669		121	1,548	—	16	10	95	341	1,134	73	
Total area actually reporting	100.0%	17,997		1,583	16,414	17	61	299	1,206	3,781	11,562	1,071	
Rate per 100,000 inhabitants		5,948.8		523.3	5,425.6	5.6	20.2	98.8	398.6	1,249.8	3,821.8	354.0	
Bryan-College Station, Tx. M.S.A.	**132,844**												
(Includes Brazos County.)													
City of:													
Bryan	61,900	4,273		477	3,796	4	50	69	354	763	2,799	234	
College Station	58,351	2,655		150	2,505	1	29	45	75	313	2,107	85	
Total area actually reporting	100.0%	8,008		668	7,340	6	87	118	457	1,296	5,703	341	
Rate per 100,000 inhabitants		6,028.1		502.8	5,525.3	4.5	65.5	88.8	344.0	975.6	4,293.0	256.7	
Buffalo-Niagara Falls, N.Y. M.S.A.	**1,189,157**												
(Includes Erie and Niagara Counties.)													
City of:													
Buffalo	312,395	28,757		6,333	22,424	62	261	2,836	3,174	7,092	11,124	4,208	
Niagara Falls	60,406	4,590		479	4,111	2	39	286	152	1,194	2,526	391	
Total area actually reporting	99.6%	59,212		9,042	50,170	72	381	3,539	5,050	12,388	31,220	6,562	
Estimated total	100.0%	59,385		9,058	50,327	72	382	3,544	5,060	12,415	31,338	6,574	
Rate per 100,000 inhabitants		4,993.9		761.7	4,232.2	6.1	32.1	298.0	425.5	1,044.0	2,635.3	552.8	
Burlington, Vt. M.S.A.	**144,343**												
(Includes part of Chittenden, Franklin, and Grand Isle Counties.)													
City of Burlington	38,431	3,421		74	3,347	—	14	17	43	834	2,393	120	
Total area actually reporting	95.8%	7,855		218	7,637	2	64	35	117	1,719	5,623	295	
Estimated total	100.0%	8,164		225	7,939	2	66	36	121	1,771	5,862	306	
Rate per 100,000 inhabitants		5,656.0		155.9	5,500.1	1.4	45.7	24.9	83.8	1,226.9	4,061.2	212.0	
Casper, Wy. M.S.A.	**64,421**												
(Includes Natrona County.)													
City of Casper	49,605	3,281		166	3,115	3	14	21	128	566	2,360	189	
Total area actually reporting	100.0%	4,082		217	3,865	5	15	23	174	749	2,871	245	
Rate per 100,000 inhabitants		6,336.4		336.8	5,999.6	7.8	23.3	35.7	270.1	1,162.7	4,456.6	380.3	

See footnotes at end of table.

Table 6. — Index of Crime, Metropolitan Statistical Areas, 1995 — Continued

Metropolitan Statistical Area	Population	Crime Index total	Modified Crime Index total[1]	Violent crime[2]	Property crime[3]	Murder and non-negligent man-slaughter	Forcible rape	Robbery	Aggra-vated assault	Burglary	Larceny-theft	Motor vehicle theft	Arson[1]
Charleston-North Charleston, S.C. M.S.A.	523,555												
(Includes Berkeley, Charleston, and Dorchester Counties.)													
City of:													
Charleston	77,043	7,955		1,184	6,771	12	46	345	781	1,069	4,812	890	
North Charleston	67,886	10,330		1,746	8,584	10	69	453	1,214	1,513	5,852	1,219	
Total area actually reporting ..	99.7%	36,269		4,968	31,301	32	272	1,117	3,547	6,256	21,769	3,276	
Estimated total	100.0%	36,383		4,980	31,403	32	273	1,119	3,556	6,275	21,846	3,282	
Rate per 100,000 inhabitants ...		6,949.2		951.2	5,998.0	6.1	52.1	213.7	679.2	1,198.5	4,172.6	626.9	
Charleston, W.V. M.S.A.	254,383												
(Includes Kanawha and Putnam Counties.)													
City of Charleston	56,204	5,486		659	4,827	9	47	287	316	908	3,529	390	
Total area actually reporting ..	100.0%	10,340		985	9,355	16	86	362	521	2,114	6,411	830	
Rate per 100,000 inhabitants ...		4,064.7		387.2	3,677.5	6.3	33.8	142.3	204.8	831.0	2,520.2	326.3	
Charlotte-Gastonia-Rock Hill, N.C.-S.C. M.S.A.	1,280,512												
(Includes Cabarrus, Gaston, Lincoln, Mecklenburg, Rowan, and Union Counties, N.C., and York County, S.C.)													
City of:													
Charlotte-Mecklenburg, N.C.	544,146	52,110		9,228	42,882	89	366	2,949	5,824	9,959	29,273	3,650	
Gastonia, N.C.	60,137	5,835		703	5,132	12	28	236	427	1,122	3,760	250	
Rock Hill, S.C.	47,121	3,191		688	2,503	2	14	88	584	470	1,907	126	
Total area actually reporting ..	100.0%	85,835		13,300	72,535	147	546	3,729	8,878	17,604	49,876	5,055	
Rate per 100,000 inhabitants ...		6,703.2		1,038.6	5,664.5	11.5	42.6	291.2	693.3	1,374.8	3,895.0	394.8	
Charlottesville, Va. M.S.A.	142,090												
(Includes Albemarle, Fluvanna, and Greene Counties and Charlottesville City.)													
City of Charlottesville	41,447	2,844		272	2,572	2	19	82	169	341	2,104	127	
Total area actually reporting ..	100.0%	5,995		436	5,559	11	35	104	286	784	4,530	245	
Rate per 100,000 inhabitants ...		4,219.2		306.8	3,912.3	7.7	24.6	73.2	201.3	551.8	3,188.1	172.4	
Cheyenne, Wy. M.S.A.	78,737												
(Includes Laramie County.)													
City of Cheyenne	54,051	2,547		99	2,448	—	19	23	57	237	2,136	75	
Total area actually reporting ..	100.0%	3,226		131	3,095	—	30	26	75	318	2,671	106	
Rate per 100,000 inhabitants ...		4,097.2		166.4	3,930.8	—	38.1	33.0	95.3	403.9	3,392.3	134.6	
Chico-Paradise, Ca. M.S.A.	193,216												
(Includes Butte County.)													
City of:													
Chico	43,861	3,415		196	3,219	1	34	59	102	625	2,349	245	
Paradise	26,521	777		66	711	1	7	5	53	145	520	46	
Total area actually reporting ..	100.0%	9,746		734	9,012	5	80	141	508	2,353	5,816	843	
Rate per 100,000 inhabitants ...		5,044.1		379.9	4,664.2	2.6	41.4	73.0	262.9	1,217.8	3,010.1	436.3	
Cincinnati, Oh.-Ky.-In. M.S.A. ...	1,590,080												
(Includes Brown, Clermont, Hamilton, and Warren Counties, Oh.; Boone, Campbell, Gallatin, Grant, Kenton, and Pendleton Counties, Ky., and Dearborn and Ohio Counties, In.)													
City of Cincinnati, Oh.	359,749	26,931		4,640	22,291	50	408	2,155	2,027	5,366	15,012	1,913	
Total area actually reporting ..	87.6%	64,453		7,019	57,434	66	685	2,889	3,379	11,325	42,518	3,591	
Estimated total	100.0%	70,426		7,424	63,002	69	728	2,993	3,634	12,352	46,654	3,996	
Rate per 100,000 inhabitants ...		4,429.1		466.9	3,962.2	4.3	45.8	188.2	228.5	776.8	2,934.1	251.3	
Clarksville-Hopkinsville, Tn.-Ky. M.S.A.	188,455												
(Includes Christian County, Ky., and Montgomery County, Tn.)													
City of:													
Clarksville, Tn.	93,557	5,462		770	4,692	11	132	140	487	1,166	3,281	245	
Hopkinsville, Ky.	32,561	2,040		179	1,861	6	19	75	79	434	1,337	90	
Total area actually reporting ..	99.3%	9,132		1,205	7,927	18	156	233	798	2,052	5,450	425	
Estimated total	100.0%	9,188		1,208	7,980	18	156	234	800	2,062	5,490	428	
Rate per 100,000 inhabitants ...		4,875.4		641.0	4,234.4	9.6	82.8	124.2	424.5	1,094.2	2,913.2	227.1	
Colorado Springs, Co. M.S.A.	463,765												
(Includes El Paso County.)													
City of Colorado Springs	324,441	21,949		1,566	20,383	18	207	416	925	3,446	15,549	1,388	
Total area actually reporting ..	99.9%	25,761		1,928	23,833	24	229	446	1,229	4,238	17,967	1,628	
Estimated total	100.0%	25,800		1,931	23,869	24	229	447	1,231	4,244	17,995	1,630	
Rate per 100,000 inhabitants ...		5,563.2		416.4	5,146.8	5.2	49.4	96.4	265.4	915.1	3,880.2	351.5	

See footnotes at end of table.

Table 6. — Index of Crime, Metropolitan Statistical Areas, 1995 — Continued

Metropolitan Statistical Area	Population	Crime Index total	Modified Crime Index total[1]	Violent crime[2]	Property crime[3]	Murder and non-negligent man-slaughter	Forcible rape	Robbery	Aggra-vated assault	Burglary	Larceny–theft	Motor vehicle theft	Arson[1]
Columbia, Mo. M.S.A.	**122,536**												
(Includes Boone County.)													
City of Columbia	74,717	4,749		487	4,262	2	40	120	325	522	3,566	174	
Total area actually reporting ..	100.0%	6,262		559	5,703	2	46	127	384	772	4,702	229	
Rate per 100,000 inhabitants...		5,110.3		456.2	4,654.1	1.6	37.5	103.6	313.4	630.0	3,837.2	186.9	
Columbia, S.C. M.S.A.	**488,077**												
(Includes Lexington and Richland Counties.)													
City of Columbia	104,457	12,832		2,176	10,656	9	89	677	1,401	2,256	7,559	841	
Total area actually reporting ..	100.0%	32,566		4,858	27,708	42	293	1,301	3,222	6,803	18,421	2,484	
Rate per 100,000 inhabitants...		6,672.3		995.3	5,677.0	8.6	60.0	266.6	660.1	1,393.8	3,774.2	508.9	
Columbus, Ga.-Al. M.S.A.	**282,299**												
(Includes Chattahoochee, Harris, and Muscogee Counties, Ga., and Russell County, Al.)													
City of Columbus, Ga.......	190,328	12,417		983	11,434	20	34	432	497	2,201	8,350	883	
Total area actually reporting ..	99.8%	14,702		1,281	13,421	26	74	485	696	2,722	9,606	1,093	
Estimated total	100.0%	14,753		1,284	13,469	26	74	486	698	2,729	9,642	1,098	
Rate per 100,000 inhabitants...		5,226.0		454.8	4,771.2	9.2	26.2	172.2	247.3	966.7	3,415.5	388.9	
Columbus, Oh. M.S.A.	**1,427,757**												
(Includes Delaware, Fairfield, Franklin, Licking, Madison, and Pickaway Counties.)													
City of Columbus	638,729	58,715		6,624	52,091	77	636	3,329	2,582	13,146	31,905	7,040	
Total area actually reporting ..	86.6%	82,256		9,185	73,071	90	840	3,858	4,397	17,181	47,490	8,400	
Estimated total	100.0%	88,018		9,587	78,431	93	884	3,965	4,645	18,176	51,470	8,785	
Rate per 100,000 inhabitants...		6,164.8		671.5	5,493.3	6.5	61.9	277.7	325.3	1,273.0	3,605.0	615.3	
Corpus Christi, Tx. M.S.A.	**383,668**												
(Includes Nueces and San Patricio Counties.)													
City of Corpus Christi	280,605	29,274		2,764	26,510	31	216	504	2,013	3,785	21,271	1,454	
Total area actually reporting ..	100.0%	32,651		3,037	29,614	37	242	527	2,231	4,751	23,245	1,618	
Rate per 100,000 inhabitants...		8,510.2		791.6	7,718.7	9.6	63.1	137.4	581.5	1,238.3	6,058.6	421.7	
Cumberland, Md.-W.V. M.S.A. ...	**101,724**												
(Includes Allegany County, Md. and Mineral County, W.V.)													
City of Cumberland, Md.	24,072	1,360		276	1,084	—	7	12	257	201	850	33	
Total area actually reporting ..	100.0%	2,795		435	2,360	2	18	19	396	493	1,777	90	
Rate per 100,000 inhabitants...		2,747.6		427.6	2,320.0	2.0	17.7	18.7	389.3	484.6	1,746.9	88.5	
Dallas, Tx. M.S.A.	**2,849,397**												
(Includes Collin, Dallas, Denton, Ellis, Henderson, Kaufman, and Rockwall Counties.)													
City of Dallas	1,042,088	98,624		15,969	82,655	276	852	5,899	8,942	16,705	49,068	16,882	
Total area actually reporting ..	100.0%	187,248		23,343	163,905	340	1,422	7,376	14,205	33,008	107,292	23,605	
Rate per 100,000 inhabitants...		6,571.5		819.2	5,752.3	11.9	49.9	258.9	498.5	1,158.4	3,765.4	828.4	
Danbury, Ct. M.S.A.	**163,856**												
(Includes part of Fairfield and Litchfield Counties.)													
City of Danbury	64,675	3,742		152	3,590	2	10	90	50	521	2,679	390	
Total area actually reporting ..	100.0%	5,508		207	5,301	3	17	101	86	905	3,915	481	
Rate per 100,000 inhabitants...		3,361.5		126.3	3,235.2	1.8	10.4	61.6	52.5	552.3	2,389.3	293.6	
Danville, Va. M.S.A.	**111,066**												
(Includes Pittsylvania County and Danville City.)													
City of Danville	54,773	2,462		259	2,203	3	22	123	111	409	1,697	97	
Total area actually reporting ..	100.0%	3,263		311	2,952	4	34	125	148	629	2,174	149	
Rate per 100,000 inhabitants...		2,937.9		280.0	2,657.9	3.6	30.6	112.5	133.3	566.3	1,957.4	134.2	
Dayton-Springfield, Oh. M.S.A. .	**961,196**												
(Includes Clark, Greene, Miami, and Montgomery Counties.)													
City of:													
Dayton	179,327	18,949		2,425	16,524	39	237	1,360	789	4,022	9,357	3,145	
Springfield	70,698	6,666		1,432	5,234	3	73	288	1,068	964	3,822	448	
Total area actually reporting ..	85.6%	47,377		4,895	42,482	51	467	1,965	2,412	8,295	29,229	4,958	
Estimated total	100.0%	50,658		5,103	45,555	53	497	2,019	2,534	8,963	31,423	5,169	
Rate per 100,000 inhabitants...		5,270.3		530.9	4,739.4	5.5	51.7	210.1	263.6	932.5	3,269.2	537.8	
Daytona Beach, Fl. M.S.A.	**447,211**												
(Includes Flagler and Volusia Counties.)													
City of Daytona Beach	65,631	7,027		1,225	5,802	6	73	310	836	1,678	3,487	637	
Total area actually reporting ..	100.0%	23,398		3,132	20,266	11	206	579	2,336	5,789	12,849	1,628	
Rate per 100,000 inhabitants...		5,232.0		700.3	4,531.6	2.5	46.1	129.5	522.3	1,294.5	2,873.1	364.0	

See footnotes at end of table.

Table 6. — Index of Crime, Metropolitan Statistical Areas, 1995 — Continued

Metropolitan Statistical Area	Population	Crime Index total	Modified Crime Index total[1]	Violent crime[2]	Property crime[3]	Murder and non-negligent manslaughter	Forcible rape	Robbery	Aggravated assault	Burglary	Larceny-theft	Motor vehicle theft	Arson[1]
Decatur, Al. M.S.A.	**138,990**												
(Includes Lawrence and Morgan Counties.)													
City of Decatur	52,887	3,458		172	3,286	7	17	60	88	674	2,467	145	
Total area actually reporting ..	98.5%	4,542		229	4,313	13	22	63	131	1,037	3,068	208	
Estimated total	100.0%	4,649		242	4,407	13	23	67	139	1,056	3,136	215	
Rate per 100,000 inhabitants...		3,344.8		174.1	3,170.7	9.4	16.5	48.2	100.0	759.8	2,256.3	154.7	
Denver, Co. M.S.A.	**1,832,547**												
(Includes Adams, Arapahoe, Denver, Douglas, and Jefferson Counties.)													
City of Denver	505,843	34,769		4,357	30,412	81	320	1,413	2,543	7,410	17,761	5,241	
Total area actually reporting ..	99.7%	102,139		9,383	92,756	126	725	2,589	5,943	18,039	65,045	9,672	
Estimated total	100.0%	102,463		9,409	93,054	126	727	2,595	5,961	18,086	65,276	9,692	
Rate per 100,000 inhabitants...		5,591.3		513.4	5,077.9	6.9	39.7	141.6	325.3	986.9	3,562.0	528.9	
Des Moines, Ia. M.S.A.	**418,189**												
(Includes Dallas, Polk, and Warren Counties.)													
City of Des Moines	194,654	16,108		1,005	15,103	19	127	312	547	1,933	11,911	1,259	
Total area actually reporting ..	98.5%	24,519		1,446	23,073	22	162	370	892	3,444	17,879	1,750	
Estimated total	100.0%	24,787		1,462	23,325	22	163	372	905	3,483	18,080	1,762	
Rate per 100,000 inhabitants...		5,927.2		349.6	5,577.6	5.3	39.0	89.0	216.4	832.9	4,323.4	421.3	
Detroit, Mi. M.S.A.	**4,333,106**												
(Includes Lapeer, Macomb, Monroe, Oakland, St. Claire, and Wayne Counties.)													
City of Detroit	997,297	119,065		24,011	95,054	475	1,104	10,076	12,356	22,366	43,415	29,273	
Total area actually reporting ..	91.4%	248,776		36,603	212,173	554	2,194	12,512	21,343	40,193	126,718	45,262	
Estimated total	100.0%	266,200		38,168	228,032	564	2,329	12,831	22,444	42,558	138,340	47,134	
Rate per 100,000 inhabitants...		6,143.4		880.8	5,262.6	13.0	53.7	296.1	518.0	982.2	3,192.6	1,087.8	
Dothan, Al. M.S.A.	**135,573**												
(Includes Dale and Houston Counties.)													
City of Dothan	56,241	2,807		236	2,571	2	5	103	126	687	1,744	140	
Total area actually reporting ..	96.7%	4,359		546	3,813	13	22	132	379	973	2,628	212	
Estimated total	100.0%	4,597		574	4,023	13	23	140	398	1,016	2,779	228	
Rate per 100,000 inhabitants...		3,390.8		423.4	2,967.4	9.6	17.0	103.3	293.6	749.4	2,049.8	168.2	
Dubuque, Ia. M.S.A.	**88,678**												
(Includes Dubuque County.)													
City of Dubuque	59,355	1,784		25	1,759	—	8	6	11	382	1,296	81	
Total area actually reporting ..	100.0%	2,093		29	2,064	—	9	6	14	459	1,505	100	
Rate per 100,000 inhabitants...		2,360.2		32.7	2,327.5	—	10.1	6.8	15.8	517.6	1,697.2	112.8	
Duluth-Superior, Mn.-Wi. M.S.A.	**243,123**												
(Includes St. Louis County, Mn., and Douglas County, Wi.)													
City of:													
Duluth, Mn.	84,781	4,872		394	4,478	4	105	68	217	765	3,430	283	
Superior, Wi.	27,768	1,958		85	1,873	—	19	13	53	261	1,530	82	
Total area actually reporting ..	100.0%	10,136		612	9,524	5	186	89	332	1,928	7,076	520	
Rate per 100,000 inhabitants...		4,169.1		251.7	3,917.4	2.1	76.5	36.6	136.6	793.0	2,910.5	213.9	
Dutchess County, N.Y. M.S.A. ...	**260,997**												
(Includes Dutchess County.)													
Total area actually reporting ..	98.9%	7,700		1,108	6,592	14	52	284	758	1,360	4,913	319	
Estimated total	100.0%	7,800		1,117	6,683	14	52	287	764	1,376	4,981	326	
Rate per 100,000 inhabitants...		2,988.5		428.0	2,560.6	5.4	19.9	110.0	292.7	527.2	1,908.5	124.9	
Eau Claire, Wi. M.S.A.	**143,087**												
(Includes Chippewa and Eau Claire Counties.)													
City of Eau Claire	58,947	3,091		151	2,940	—	1	19	131	452	2,367	121	
Total area actually reporting ..	100.0%	5,057		222	4,835	2	8	24	188	832	3,804	199	
Rate per 100,000 inhabitants...		3,534.2		155.2	3,379.1	1.4	5.6	16.8	131.4	581.5	2,658.5	139.1	
El Paso, Tx. M.S.A.	**677,329**												
(Includes El Paso County.)													
City of El Paso	590,215	41,692		4,948	36,744	37	242	1,076	3,593	3,828	29,034	3,882	
Total area actually reporting ..	100.0%	44,862		5,432	39,430	42	287	1,144	3,959	4,466	30,856	4,108	
Rate per 100,000 inhabitants...		6,623.4		802.0	5,821.4	6.2	42.4	168.9	584.5	659.4	4,555.5	606.5	
Enid, Ok. M.S.A.	**57,279**												
(Includes Garfield County.)													
City of Enid	46,132	4,371		436	3,935	2	24	72	338	903	2,789	243	
Total area actually reporting ..	100.0%	4,571		451	4,120	2	26	72	351	1,010	2,862	248	
Rate per 100,000 inhabitants...		7,980.2		787.4	7,192.9	3.5	45.4	125.7	612.8	1,763.3	4,996.6	433.0	

See footnotes at end of table.

Table 6. — Index of Crime, Metropolitan Statistical Areas, 1995 — Continued

Metropolitan Statistical Area	Population	Crime Index total	Modified Crime Index total[1]	Violent crime[2]	Property crime[3]	Murder and non-negligent man-slaughter	Forcible rape	Robbery	Aggra-vated assault	Burglary	Larceny-theft	Motor vehicle theft	Arson[1]
Eugene-Springfield, Or. M.S.A...	304,323												
(Includes Lane County.)													
City of:													
Eugene	120,226	11,876		726	11,150	3	41	273	409	2,036	8,444	670	
Springfield	48,648	5,601		216	5,385	2	26	90	98	917	4,056	412	
Total area actually reporting ..	100.0%	22,013		1,229	20,784	12	125	413	679	4,234	15,093	1,457	
Rate per 100,000 inhabitants...		7,233.4		403.8	6,829.6	3.9	41.1	135.7	223.1	1,391.3	4,959.5	478.8	
Evansville-Henderson, In.-Ky. M.S.A.	289,156												
(Includes Posey, Vanderburgh, and Warrick Counties, In., and Henderson County, Ky.)													
City of:													
Evansville, In.	130,600	7,478		724	6,754	5	33	154	532	1,537	4,772	445	
Henderson, Ky.	27,093	1,723		132	1,591	1	18	38	75	327	1,170	94	
Total area actually reporting ..	93.3%	11,656		1,088	10,568	9	69	202	808	2,253	7,688	627	
Estimated total	100.0%	12,271		1,135	11,136	9	73	213	840	2,368	8,085	683	
Rate per 100,000 inhabitants...		4,243.7		392.5	3,851.2	3.1	25.2	73.7	290.5	818.9	2,796.1	236.2	
Fargo-Moorhead, N.D.-Mn. M.S.A.	162,341												
(Includes Cass County, N.D. and Clay County, Mn.)													
City of:													
Fargo, N.D.	79,788	3,559		102	3,457	—	36	21	45	376	2,833	248	
Moorhead, Mn.	33,383	1,651		69	1,582	1	9	8	51	166	1,352	64	
Total area actually reporting ..	100.0%	6,195		206	5,989	3	55	30	118	764	4,840	385	
Rate per 100,000 inhabitants...		3,816.0		126.9	3,689.1	1.8	33.9	18.5	72.7	470.6	2,981.4	237.2	
Fayetteville, N.C. M.S.A.	291,434												
(Includes Cumberland County.)													
City of Fayetteville	85,484	10,481		1,662	8,819	19	64	484	1,095	2,098	5,972	749	
Total area actually reporting ..	100.0%	23,397		2,783	20,614	34	168	841	1,740	5,655	13,357	1,602	
Rate per 100,000 inhabitants...		8,028.2		954.9	7,073.3	11.7	57.6	288.6	597.0	1,940.4	4,583.2	549.7	
Fayetteville-Springdale-Rogers, Ar. M.S.A.	245,526												
(Includes Benton and Washington Counties.)													
City of:													
Fayetteville	49,841	2,632		157	2,475	3	24	21	109	341	2,013	121	
Springdale	37,014	1,616		77	1,539	—	20	15	42	236	1,168	135	
Rogers	30,847	1,440		63	1,377	1	14	10	38	184	1,139	54	
Total area actually reporting ..	99.1%	8,628		485	8,143	10	73	59	343	1,321	6,393	429	
Estimated total	100.0%	8,763		497	8,266	10	74	62	351	1,345	6,483	438	
Rate per 100,000 inhabitants...		3,569.1		202.4	3,366.6	4.1	30.1	25.3	143.0	547.8	2,640.5	178.4	
Fitchburg-Leominster, Ma. M.S.A.	136,112												
(Includes part of Middlesex and Worcester Counties.)													
City of:													
Fitchburg	36,926	2,357		599	1,758	3	44	71	481	634	937	187	
Leominster	38,448	1,724		145	1,579	—	11	27	107	420	1,024	135	
Total area actually reporting ..	78.2%	4,904		907	3,997	5	61	106	735	1,301	2,331	365	
Estimated total	100.0%	5,811		1,022	4,789	5	66	123	828	1,477	2,841	471	
Rate per 100,000 inhabitants...		4,269.3		750.9	3,518.4	3.7	48.5	90.4	608.3	1,085.1	2,087.3	346.0	
Flint, Mi. M.S.A.	435,639												
(Includes Genesee County.)													
City of Flint	138,934	17,338		3,892	13,446	41	206	1,030	2,615	4,137	7,346	1,963	
Total area actually reporting ..	87.1%	28,968		4,938	24,030	50	325	1,268	3,295	6,154	14,840	3,036	
Estimated total	100.0%	30,777		5,118	25,659	52	358	1,288	3,420	6,505	15,985	3,169	
Rate per 100,000 inhabitants...		7,064.8		1,174.8	5,890.0	11.9	82.2	295.7	785.1	1,493.2	3,669.3	727.4	
Florence, Al. M.S.A.	136,776												
(Includes Colbert and Lauderdale Counties.)													
City of Florence	37,066	2,085		168	1,917	4	8	40	116	366	1,495	56	
Total area actually reporting ..	98.7%	4,372		351	4,021	7	21	67	256	742	3,168	111	
Estimated total	100.0%	4,462		361	4,101	7	21	70	263	758	3,226	117	
Rate per 100,000 inhabitants...		3,262.3		263.9	2,998.3	5.1	15.4	51.2	192.3	554.2	2,358.6	85.5	
Florence, S.C. M.S.A.	121,462												
(Includes Florence County.)													
City of Florence	32,466	3,677		584	3,093	4	22	167	391	671	2,287	135	
Total area actually reporting ..	100.0%	7,954		1,226	6,728	14	65	246	901	1,690	4,680	358	
Rate per 100,000 inhabitants...		6,548.6		1,009.4	5,539.2	11.5	53.5	202.5	741.8	1,391.4	3,853.1	294.7	
Fort Collins-Loveland, Co. M.S.A.	217,633												
(Includes Larimer County.)													
City of:													
Fort Collins	101,416	5,573		458	5,115	2	66	30	360	790	4,132	193	
Loveland	45,061	1,665		107	1,558	2	25	13	67	263	1,225	70	
Total area actually reporting ..	100.0%	9,588		655	8,933	4	144	53	454	1,438	7,136	359	
Rate per 100,000 inhabitants...		4,405.6		301.0	4,104.6	1.8	66.2	24.4	208.6	660.7	3,278.9	165.0	

See footnotes at end of table.

Table 6. — Index of Crime, Metropolitan Statistical Areas, 1995 — Continued

Metropolitan Statistical Area	Population	Crime Index total	Modified Crime Index total[1]	Violent crime[2]	Property crime[3]	Murder and non-negligent man-slaughter	Forcible rape	Robbery	Aggra-vated assault	Burglary	Larceny–theft	Motor vehicle theft	Arson[1]
Fort Lauderdale, Fl. M.S.A.	1,404,094												
(Includes Broward County.)													
City of Fort Lauderdale	165,328	25,036		2,293	22,743	27	102	1,113	1,051	4,876	14,836	3,031	
Total area actually reporting	100.0%	114,222		11,905	102,317	82	535	4,243	7,045	20,789	67,809	13,719	
Rate per 100,000 inhabitants		8,134.9		847.9	7,287.0	5.8	38.1	302.2	501.7	1,480.6	4,829.4	977.1	
Fort Myers-Cape Coral, Fl. M.S.A.	373,045												
(Includes Lee County.)													
City of:													
Fort Myers	51,259	6,327		1,190	5,137	7	54	334	795	1,047	3,212	878	
Cape Coral	86,265	3,487		197	3,290	1	20	36	140	802	2,295	193	
Total area actually reporting	100.0%	20,393		2,429	17,964	16	227	632	1,554	4,228	11,561	2,175	
Rate per 100,000 inhabitants		5,466.6		651.1	4,815.5	4.3	60.9	169.4	416.6	1,133.4	3,099.1	583.0	
Fort Pierce-Port St. Lucie, Fl. M.S.A.	282,528												
(Includes Martin and St. Lucie Counties.)													
City of:													
Fort Pierce	37,336	5,075		990	4,085	11	54	231	694	1,383	2,291	411	
Port St. Lucie	71,473	2,701		210	2,491	—	22	30	158	740	1,651	100	
Total area actually reporting	100.0%	16,205		2,292	13,913	19	158	390	1,725	3,981	9,054	878	
Rate per 100,000 inhabitants		5,735.7		811.2	4,924.5	6.7	55.9	138.0	610.6	1,409.1	3,204.6	310.8	
Fort Smith, Ar.-Ok. M.S.A.	187,227												
(Includes Crawford and Sebastian Counties, Ar., and Sequoyah County, Ok.)													
City of Fort Smith, Ar.	75,421	6,532		514	6,018	4	54	94	362	709	4,841	468	
Total area actually reporting	100.0%	9,407		778	8,629	12	68	104	594	1,551	6,407	671	
Rate per 100,000 inhabitants		5,024.4		415.5	4,608.8	6.4	36.3	55.5	317.3	828.4	3,422.0	358.4	
Fort Walton Beach, Fl. M.S.A.	163,264												
(Includes Okaloosa County.)													
City of Fort Walton Beach	24,576	1,219		123	1,096	1	11	31	80	191	852	53	
Total area actually reporting	100.0%	5,570		547	5,023	3	40	96	408	1,015	3,782	226	
Rate per 100,000 inhabitants		3,411.7		335.0	3,076.6	1.8	24.5	58.8	249.9	621.7	2,316.5	138.4	
Fort Wayne, In. M.S.A.	473,219												
(Includes Adams, Allen, De Kalb, Huntington, and Whitley Counties.)													
City of Fort Wayne	184,985	12,765		931	11,834	23	84	594	230	1,800	8,081	1,953	
Total area actually reporting	83.1%	17,061		1,335	15,726	30	105	642	558	2,541	10,848	2,337	
Estimated total	100.0%	19,876		1,552	18,324	32	120	686	714	2,994	12,743	2,587	
Rate per 100,000 inhabitants		4,200.2		328.0	3,872.2	6.8	25.4	145.0	150.9	632.7	2,692.8	546.7	
Fort Worth-Arlington, Tx. M.S.A.	1,587,352												
(Includes Johnson, Parker, and Tarrant Counties.)													
City of:													
Fort Worth	460,321	39,667		5,344	34,323	108	332	1,965	2,939	7,334	22,128	4,861	
Arlington	292,324	20,404		2,576	17,828	9	154	521	1,892	3,224	12,306	2,298	
Total area actually reporting	100.0%	93,527		10,870	82,657	148	767	3,005	6,950	16,569	56,117	9,971	
Rate per 100,000 inhabitants		5,892.0		684.8	5,207.2	9.3	48.3	189.3	437.8	1,043.8	3,535.3	628.2	
Fresno, Ca. M.S.A.	838,851												
(Includes Fresno and Madera Counties.)													
City of Fresno	388,495	46,267		5,659	40,608	71	212	2,166	3,210	7,638	20,552	12,418	
Total area actually reporting	100.0%	71,858		9,974	61,884	117	412	2,816	6,629	14,080	31,546	16,258	
Rate per 100,000 inhabitants		8,566.2		1,189.0	7,377.2	13.9	49.1	335.7	790.2	1,678.5	3,760.6	1,938.1	
Gadsden, Al. M.S.A.	100,719												
(Includes Etowah County.)													
City of Gadsden	46,925	5,276		772	4,504	8	31	175	558	1,170	2,936	398	
Total area actually reporting	100.0%	6,653		851	5,802	9	38	195	609	1,475	3,880	447	
Rate per 100,000 inhabitants		6,605.5		844.9	5,760.6	8.9	37.7	193.6	604.7	1,464.5	3,852.3	443.8	
Gainesville, Fl. M.S.A.	195,999												
(Includes Alachua County.)													
City of Gainesville	89,146	10,003		1,334	8,669	8	61	329	936	1,829	6,281	559	
Total area actually reporting	100.0%	19,134		2,777	16,357	13	152	564	2,048	3,766	11,464	1,127	
Rate per 100,000 inhabitants		9,762.3		1,416.8	8,345.5	6.6	77.6	287.8	1,044.9	1,921.4	5,849.0	575.0	
Galveston-Texas City, Tx. M.S.A.	239,102												
(Includes Galveston County.)													
City of:													
Galveston	60,339	6,660		1,367	5,293	15	55	356	941	1,234	3,337	722	
Texas City	42,446	4,587		565	4,022	7	33	129	396	1,358	2,295	369	
Total area actually reporting	100.0%	17,116		2,415	14,701	32	142	574	1,667	3,992	9,226	1,483	
Rate per 100,000 inhabitants		7,158.5		1,010.0	6,148.4	13.4	59.4	240.1	697.2	1,669.6	3,858.6	620.2	
Glens Falls, N.Y. M.S.A.	121,897												
(Includes Warren and Washington Counties.)													
City of Glens Falls	13,537	1,039		217	822	—	5	12	200	174	636	12	
Total area actually reporting	100.0%	3,758		443	3,315	5	19	20	399	697	2,538	80	
Rate per 100,000 inhabitants		3,082.9		363.4	2,719.5	4.1	15.6	16.4	327.3	571.8	2,082.1	65.6	

See footnotes at end of table.

Table 6. — Index of Crime, Metropolitan Statistical Areas, 1995 — Continued

Metropolitan Statistical Area	Population	Crime Index total	Modified Crime Index total[1]	Violent crime[2]	Property crime[3]	Murder and non-negligent man-slaughter	Forcible rape	Robbery	Aggra-vated assault	Burglary	Larceny–theft	Motor vehicle theft	Arson[1]
Goldsboro, N.C. M.S.A.	**111,183**												
(Includes Wayne County.)													
City of Goldsboro	45,807	4,073		632	3,441	8	20	148	456	731	2,526	184	
Total area actually reporting	100.0%	6,296		882	5,414	12	35	185	650	1,484	3,589	341	
Rate per 100,000 inhabitants...		5,662.7		793.3	4,869.4	10.8	31.5	166.4	584.6	1,334.7	3,228.0	306.7	
Grand Forks, N.D.-Mn. M.S.A. ...	**104,256**												
(Includes Grand Forks County, N.D. and Polk County, Mn.)													
City of Grand Forks, N.D. ...	50,403	3,202		53	3,149	—	6	17	30	328	2,594	227	
Total area actually reporting ..	99.6%	4,759		154	4,605	—	22	23	109	649	3,645	311	
Estimated total	100.0%	4,778		155	4,623	—	22	23	110	651	3,660	312	
Rate per 100,000 inhabitants...		4,582.9		148.7	4,434.3	—	21.1	22.1	105.5	624.4	3,510.6	299.3	
Green Bay, Wi. M.S.A.	**208,939**												
(Includes Brown County.)													
City of Green Bay	103,536	4,868		509	4,359	4	75	70	360	555	3,616	188	
Total area actually reporting ..	100.0%	8,228		608	7,620	4	96	88	420	1,051	6,267	302	
Rate per 100,000 inhabitants...		3,938.0		291.0	3,647.0	1.9	45.9	42.1	201.0	503.0	2,999.4	144.5	
Greensboro-Winston-Salem-High Point, N.C. M.S.A.	**1,127,217**												
(Includes Alamance, Davidson, Davie, Forsythe, Guilford, Randolph, Stokes, and Yadkin Counties.)													
City of:													
Greensboro................	199,635	18,044		2,098	15,946	36	88	785	1,189	3,671	11,067	1,208	
Winston-Salem	157,870	19,636		2,398	17,238	23	142	926	1,307	4,644	11,304	1,290	
High Point	73,484	7,073		894	6,179	11	26	280	577	1,861	3,893	425	
Total area actually reporting ..	99.6%	72,220		7,890	64,330	99	360	2,461	4,970	17,864	42,442	4,024	
Estimated total	100.0%	72,538		7,917	64,621	99	361	2,468	4,989	17,927	42,658	4,036	
Rate per 100,000 inhabitants...		6,435.1		702.3	5,732.8	8.8	32.0	218.9	442.6	1,590.4	3,784.4	358.0	
Greenville, N.C. M.S.A.	**116,162**												
(Includes Pitt County.)													
City of Greenville	50,198	5,423		517	4,906	4	27	227	259	1,389	3,302	215	
Total area actually reporting ..	99.6%	8,839		933	7,906	8	53	295	577	2,570	4,977	359	
Estimated total	100.0%	8,873		936	7,937	8	53	296	579	2,577	5,000	360	
Rate per 100,000 inhabitants...		7,638.5		805.8	6,832.7	6.9	45.6	254.8	498.4	2,218.5	4,304.3	309.9	
Greenville-Spartanburg-Anderson, S.C. M.S.A.	**876,762**												
(Includes Anderson, Cherokee, Greenville, Pickens, and Spartanburg Counties.)													
City of:													
Greenville..............	59,955	6,321		931	5,390	4	42	202	683	949	4,133	308	
Spartanburg	45,833	6,697		1,370	5,327	6	24	271	1,069	1,146	3,748	433	
Anderson	29,795	3,045		567	2,478	5	22	123	417	773	1,553	152	
Total area actually reporting ..	97.5%	51,132		8,887	42,245	64	365	1,384	7,074	10,591	28,621	3,033	
Estimated total	100.0%	52,510		9,037	43,473	65	373	1,413	7,186	10,817	29,556	3,100	
Rate per 100,000 inhabitants...		5,989.1		1,030.7	4,958.4	7.4	42.5	161.2	819.6	1,233.7	3,371.0	353.6	
Hagerstown, Md. M.S.A.	**127,509**												
(Includes Washington County.)													
City of Hagerstown	38,786	2,132		295	1,837	2	14	57	222	340	1,374	123	
Total area actually reporting ..	100.0%	3,504		497	3,007	5	28	66	398	635	2,172	200	
Rate per 100,000 inhabitants...		2,748.0		389.8	2,358.3	3.9	22.0	51.8	312.1	498.0	1,703.4	156.9	
Hamilton-Middletown, Oh. M.S.A.	**314,164**												
(Includes Butler County.)													
City of:													
Hamilton	65,198	5,078		868	4,210	11	72	236	549	1,097	2,715	398	
Middletown	48,741	3,006		188	2,818	2	28	79	79	556	2,162	100	
Total area actually reporting ..	77.8%	13,776		1,406	12,370	13	125	379	889	2,675	8,978	717	
Estimated total	100.0%	15,234		1,493	13,741	14	140	401	938	2,999	9,934	808	
Rate per 100,000 inhabitants...		4,849.1		475.2	4,373.8	4.5	44.6	127.6	298.6	954.6	3,162.0	257.2	
Hartford, Ct. M.S.A.	**1,048,246**												
(Includes all of Hartford County, Ct. and part of Litchfield, Middlesex, New London, Tolland, and Windham Counties.)													
City of Hartford	124,196	16,573		2,599	13,974	33	112	1,278	1,176	3,137	8,278	2,559	
Total area actually reporting ..	100.0%	49,784		5,059	44,725	48	292	2,056	2,663	9,756	29,275	5,694	
Rate per 100,000 inhabitants...		4,749.3		482.6	4,266.7	4.6	27.9	196.1	254.0	930.7	2,792.8	543.2	

See footnotes at end of table.

Table 6. — Index of Crime, Metropolitan Statistical Areas, 1995 — Continued

Metropolitan Statistical Area	Population	Crime Index total	Modified Crime Index total[1]	Violent crime[2]	Property crime[3]	Murder and non-negligent man-slaughter	Forcible rape	Robbery	Aggra-vated assault	Burglary	Larceny–theft	Motor vehicle theft	Arson[1]
Hickory-Morganton, N.C. M.S.A.	311,177												
(Includes Alexander, Burke, Caldwell, and Catawba Counties.)													
City of:													
Hickory	30,099	3,425		386	3,039	2	19	142	223	606	2,276	157	
Morganton	17,677	1,175		86	1,089	4	4	26	52	232	808	49	
Total area actually reporting ..	100.%	13,297		1,133	12,164	21	74	270	768	3,314	8,252	598	
Rate per 100,000 inhabitants...		4,273.1		364.1	3,909.0	6.7	23.8	86.8	246.8	1,065.0	2,651.9	192.2	
Honolulu, Hi. M.S.A............	880,266												
(Includes Honolulu County.)													
Total area actually reporting ..	100.0%	67,145		2,882	64,263	38	217	1,371	1,256	10,127	46,696	7,440	
Rate per 100,000 inhabitants...		7,627.8		327.4	7,300.4	4.3	24.7	155.7	142.7	1,150.4	5.304.8	845.2	
Houma, La. M.S.A.	188,441												
(Includes Lafourche and Terrebonne Parishes.)													
City of Houma	31,507	1,600		238	1,362	—	16	68	154	282	1,000	80	
Total area actually reporting ..	100.0%	8,476		1,036	7,440	7	66	173	790	1,910	5,055	475	
Rate per 100,000 inhabitants...		4,498.0		549.8	3,948.2	3.7	35.0	91.8	419.2	1,013.6	2,682.5	252.1	
Houston, Tx. M.S.A.	3,721,515												
(Includes Chambers, Fort Bend, Harris, Liberty, Montgomery, and Waller Counties.)													
City of Houston	1,734,335	131,602		22,260	109,342	316	837	9,222	11,885	24,830	61,976	22,536	
Total area actually reporting ..	100.0%	209,664		31,861	177,803	446	1,562	11,463	18,390	41,961	103,759	32,083	
Rate per 100,000 inhabitants...		5,633.8		856.1	4,777.7	12.0	42.0	308.0	494.2	1,127.5	2,788.1	862.1	
Huntington-Ashland, W.V.-Ky.-Oh. M.S.A.	318,169												
(Includes Cabell and Wayne Counties, W.V.; Boyd, Carter and Greenup Counties, Ky., and Lawrence County, Oh.)													
City of:													
Huntington, W.V.	53,965	3,385		281	3,104	3	67	103	108	696	2,232	176	
Ashland, Ky.	24,168	1,267		83	1,184	—	6	9	68	221	914	49	
Total area actually reporting ..	79.1%	8,517		565	7,952	7	97	144	317	1,866	5,594	492	
Estimated total	100.0%	10,202		672	9,530	8	111	172	381	2,197	6,733	600	
Rate per 100,000 inhabitants...		3,206.5		211.2	2,995.3	2.5	34.9	54.1	119.7	690.5	2,116.2	188.6	
Huntsville, Al. M.S.A.	318,682												
(Includes Limestone and Madison Counties.)													
City of Huntsville	161,617	13,102		1,275	11,827	10	56	384	825	2,413	8,393	1,021	
Total area actually reporting ..	99.7%	16,546		1,649	14,897	16	73	429	1,131	3,230	10,453	1,214	
Estimated total	100.0%	16,593		1,655	14,938	16	73	431	1,135	3,238	10,483	1,217	
Rate per 100,000 inhabitants...		5,206.8		519.3	4,687.4	5.0	22.9	135.2	356.2	1,016.1	3,289.5	381.9	
Iowa City, Ia. M.S.A............	100,462												
(Includes Johnson County.)													
City of Iowa City	60,934	2,654		247	2,407	—	15	33	199	480	1,852	75	
Total area actually reporting ..	100.0%	3,794		343	3,451	1	21	40	281	715	2,630	106	
Rate per 100,000 inhabitants...		3,776.6		341.4	3,435.1	1.0	20.9	39.8	279.7	711.7	2,617.9	105.5	
Jackson, Mi. M.S.A.	154,136												
(Includes Jackson County.)													
City of Jackson	39,451	2,739		263	2,476	1	59	66	137	324	2,055	97	
Total area actually reporting ..	98.6%	6,381		673	5,708	3	140	97	433	936	4,495	277	
Estimated total	100.0%	6,482		682	5,800	3	141	99	439	950	4,562	288	
Rate per 100,000 inhabitants...		4,205.4		442.5	3,762.9	1.9	91.5	64.2	284.8	616.3	2,959.7	186.8	
Jackson, Ms. M.S.A.	416,187												
(Includes Hinds, Madison, and Rankin Counties.)													
City of Jackson	195,123	23,046		2,667	20,379	92	186	1,469	920	5,455	10,868	4,056	
Total area actually reporting ..	82.3%	27,124		2,927	24,197	101	217	1,542	1,067	6,494	13,414	4,289	
Estimated total	100.0%	31,251		3,165	28,086	104	243	1,620	1,198	7,335	16,235	4,516	
Rate per 100,000 inhabitants...		7,508.9		760.5	6,748.4	25.0	58.4	389.2	287.9	1,762.4	3,900.9	1,085.1	
Jackson, Tn. M.S.A.	83,849												
(Includes Madison County.)													
City of Jackson	54,931	5,439		895	4,544	9	44	208	634	1,011	3,210	323	
Total area actually reporting ..	100.0%	6,403		1,045	5,358	14	58	220	753	1,271	3,690	397	
Rate per 100,000 inhabitants...		7,636.3		1,246.3	6,390.1	16.7	69.2	262.4	898.0	1,515.8	4,400.8	473.5	
Jacksonville, Fl. M.S.A.	989,038												
(Includes Clay, Duval, Nassau, and St. Johns Counties.)													
City of Jacksonville	679,148	61,129		9,596	51,533	86	625	2,920	5,965	12,491	33,306	5,736	
Total area actually reporting ..	100.0%	74,750		11,558	63,192	93	773	3,172	7,520	15,094	41,703	6,395	
Rate per 100,000 inhabitants...		7,557.8		1,168.6	6,389.2	9.4	78.2	320.7	760.3	1,526.1	4,216.5	646.6	

See footnotes at end of table.

Table 6. — Index of Crime, Metropolitan Statistical Areas, 1995 — Continued

Metropolitan Statistical Area	Population	Crime Index total	Modified Crime Index total[1]	Violent crime[2]	Property crime[3]	Murder and non-negligent man-slaughter	Forcible rape	Robbery	Aggra-vated assault	Burglary	Larceny–theft	Motor vehicle theft	Arson[1]
Jacksonville, N.C. M.S.A.	**150,257**												
(Includes Onslow County.)													
City of Jacksonville	58,111	2,683		277	2,406	2	28	73	174	499	1,817	90	
Total area actually reporting	100.0%	6,327		413	5,914	6	51	117	239	1,567	4,062	285	
Rate per 100,000 inhabitants		4,210.8		274.9	3935.9	4.0	33.9	77.9	159.1	1,042.9	2,703.4	189.7	
Jamestown, N.Y. M.S.A.	**141,908**												
(Includes Chautauqua County.)													
City of Jamestown	34,325	2,037		152	1,885	3	13	57	79	462	1,347	76	
Total area actually reporting	100.0%	5,305		397	4,908	3	23	80	291	1,152	3,587	169	
Rate per 100,000 inhabitants		3,738.3		279.8	3,458.6	2.1	16.2	56.4	205.1	811.8	2,527.7	119.1	
Janesville-Beloit, Wi. M.S.A.	**147,130**												
(Includes Rock County.)													
City of:													
Janesville	57,320	3,146		183	2,963	1	20	33	129	559	2,266	138	
Beloit	36,939	1,970		133	1,837	1	21	60	51	263	1,457	117	
Total area actually reporting	100.0%	6,274		404	5,870	3	52	100	249	1,067	4,497	306	
Rate per 100,000 inhabitants		4,264.3		274.6	3,989.7	2.0	35.3	68.0	169.2	725.2	3,056.5	208.0	
Jersey City, N.J. M.S.A.	**555,254**												
(Includes Hudson County.)													
City of Jersey City	227,195	18,053		4,331	13,722	25	92	2,306	1,908	3,810	6,397	3,515	
Total area actually reporting	100.0%	35,162		5,952	29,210	40	121	3,091	2,700	6,765	15,663	6,782	
Rate per 100,000 inhabitants		6,332.6		1,071.9	5,260.7	7.2	21.8	556.7	486.3	1,218.4	2,820.9	1,221.4	
Johnson City-Kingsport-Bristol, Tn.-Va. M.S.A.	**456,911**												
(Includes Carter, Hawkins, Sullivan, Unicoi, and Washington Counties, Tn., and Bristol City and Scott and Washington Counties, Va.)													
City of:													
Johnson City, Tn.	52,380	3,292		265	3,027	2	24	48	191	514	2,349	164	
Kingsport, Tn.	39,078	1,819		247	1,572	3	10	20	214	281	1,189	102	
Bristol, Tn.	25,346	1,112		105	1,007	—	4	12	89	153	814	40	
Total area actually reporting	94.1%	11,719		1,246	10,473	19	91	116	1,020	2,408	7,425	640	
Estimated total	100.0%	12,897		1,375	11,522	21	100	137	1,117	2,633	8,167	722	
Rate per 100,000 inhabitants		2,822.7		300.9	2,521.7	4.6	21.9	30.0	244.5	576.3	1,787.4	158.0	
Joplin, Mo. M.S.A.	**142,975**												
(Includes Jasper and Newton Counties.)													
City of Joplin	43,265	3,202		224	2,978	2	24	58	140	739	2,051	188	
Total area actually reporting	76.1%	5,501		429	5,072	2	34	76	317	1,219	3,580	273	
Estimated total	100.0%	6,386		496	5,890	3	40	87	366	1,398	4,147	345	
Rate per 100,000 inhabitants		4,466.5		346.9	4,119.6	2.1	28.0	60.8	256.0	977.8	2,900.5	241.3	
Kalamazoo-Battle Creek, Mi. M.S.A.	**445,090**												
(Includes Calhoun, Kalamazoo, and Van Buren Counties.)													
City of:													
Kalamazoo	82,099	7,296		1,352	5,944	7	53	310	982	1,160	4,280	504	
Battle Creek	77,053	5,394		798	4,596	7	50	192	549	1,076	3,118	402	
Total area actually reporting	99.2%	25,492		3,236	22,256	32	288	642	2,274	4,665	15,984	1,607	
Estimated total	100.0%	25,649		3,250	22,399	32	289	645	2,284	4,686	16,089	1,624	
Rate per 100,000 inhabitants		5,762.7		730.2	5,032.5	7.2	64.9	144.9	513.2	1,052.8	3,614.8	364.9	
Kenosha, Wi. M.S.A.	**138,919**												
(Includes Kenosha County.)													
City of Kenosha	85,808	3,194		312	2,882	5	35	93	179	647	2,003	232	
Total area actually reporting	100.0%	4,981		387	4,594	5	44	108	230	947	3,324	323	
Rate per 100,000 inhabitants		3,585.5		278.6	3,307.0	3.6	31.7	77.7	165.6	681.7	2,392.8	232.5	
Killeen-Temple, Tx. M.S.A.	**292,573**												
(Includes Bell and Coryell Counties.)													
City of:													
Killeen	84,416	4,880		447	4,433	3	75	176	193	949	3,204	280	
Temple	53,067	3,170		271	2,899	5	72	61	133	523	2,153	223	
Total area actually reporting	100.0%	12,665		1,150	11,515	13	202	294	641	2,416	8,393	706	
Rate per 100,000 inhabitants		4,328.8		393.1	3,935.8	4.4	69.0	100.5	219.1	825.8	2,868.7	241.3	
Kokomo, In. M.S.A.	**100,223**												
(Includes Howard and Tipton Counties.)													
City of Kokomo	46,435	2,600		155	2,445	3	25	40	87	317	2,044	84	
Total area actually reporting	83.5%	3,175		248	2,927	3	32	42	171	441	2,374	112	
Estimated total	100.0%	3,774		293	3,481	3	35	51	204	534	2,783	164	
Rate per 100,000 inhabitants		3,765.6		292.3	3,473.3	3.0	34.9	50.9	203.5	532.8	2776.8	163.6	
La Crosse, Wi.-Mn. M.S.A.	**121,109**												
(Includes La Crosse County, Wi. and Houston County, Mn.)													
City of La Crosse, Wi.	51,287	3,038		54	2,984	—	14	14	26	170	2,707	107	
Total area actually reporting	100.0%	4,579		187	4,392	2	24	18	143	333	3,887	172	
Rate per 100,000 inhabitants		3,780.9		154.4	3,626.5	1.7	19.8	14.9	118.1	275.0	3,209.5	142.0	

See footnotes at end of table.

Table 6. — Index of Crime, Metropolitan Statistical Areas, 1995 — Continued

Metropolitan Statistical Area	Population	Crime Index total	Modified Crime Index total[1]	Violent crime[2]	Property crime[3]	Murder and non-negligent man-slaughter	Forcible rape	Robbery	Aggra-vated assault	Burglary	Larceny–theft	Motor vehicle theft	Arson[1]
Lafayette, In. M.S.A.	**168,211**												
(Includes Clinton and Tippecanoe Counties.)													
City of Lafayette	46,283	3,221		162	3,059	1	26	36	99	500	2,411	148	
Total area actually reporting	80.6%	6,396		441	5,955	3	53	52	333	830	4,871	254	
Estimated total	100.0%	7,697		540	7,157	3	59	70	408	1,006	5,786	365	
Rate per 100,000 inhabitants		4,575.8		321.0	4,254.8	1.8	35.1	41.6	242.6	598.1	3,439.7	217.0	
Lafayette, La. M.S.A.	**363,592**												
(Includes Acadia, Lafayette, St. Landry, and St. Martin Parishes.)													
City of Lafayette	102,921	10,006		1,022	8,984	8	63	279	672	1,624	6,680	680	
Total area actually reporting	99.4%	18,114		2,156	15,958	16	123	375	1,642	3,419	11,548	991	
Estimated total	100.0%	18,251		2,174	16,077	16	124	378	1,656	3,442	11,635	1,000	
Rate per 100,000 inhabitants		5,019.6		597.9	4,421.7	4.4	34.1	104.0	455.5	946.7	3,200.0	275.0	
Lake Charles, La. M.S.A.	**174,419**												
(Includes Calcasieu Parish.)													
City of Lake Charles	72,877	5,510		667	4,843	9	44	171	443	972	3,377	494	
Total area actually reporting	85.4%	11,968		1,498	10,470	12	88	282	1,116	2,220	7,474	776	
Estimated total	100.0%	13,658		1,718	11,940	13	95	322	1,288	2,506	8,543	891	
Rate per 100,000 inhabitants		7,830.6		985.0	6,845.6	7.5	54.5	184.6	738.5	1,436.8	4,898.0	510.8	
Lansing-East Lansing, Mi. M.S.A.	**438,551**												
(Includes Clinton, Eaton, and Ingham Counties.)													
City of:													
Lansing	120,256	9,784		1,643	8,141	13	148	344	1,138	1,502	5,940	699	
East Lansing	50,802	1,941		104	1,837	—	24	21	59	273	1,444	120	
Total area actually reporting	83.1%	20,043		2,248	17,795	16	304	413	1,515	3,105	13,474	1,216	
Estimated total	100.0%	22,393		2,483	19,910	19	348	438	1,678	3,568	14,957	1,385	
Rate per 100,000 inhabitants		5106.1		566.2	4,540.0	4.3	79.4	99.9	382.6	813.6	3,410.5	315.8	
Laredo, Tx. M.S.A.	**166,135**												
(Includes Webb County.)													
City of Laredo	152,736	10,150		1,107	9,043	14	22	174	897	1,628	6,529	886	
Total area actually reporting	100.0%	10,618		1,149	9,469	16	25	177	931	1,827	6,728	914	
Rate per 100,000 inhabitants		6,391.2		691.6	5,699.6	9.6	15.0	106.5	560.4	1,099.7	4,049.7	550.2	
Las Cruces, N.M. M.S.A.	**158,381**												
(Includes Dona Ana County.)													
City of Las Cruces	72,374	6,647		667	5,980	5	67	101	494	1,394	4,206	380	
Total area actually reporting	98.6%	8,858		888	7,970	12	88	137	651	2,127	5,325	518	
Estimated total	100.0%	9,004		904	8,100	12	89	139	664	2,154	5,419	527	
Rate per 100,000 inhabitants		5,685.0		570.8	5,114.2	7.6	56.2	87.8	419.2	1,360.0	3,421.5	332.7	
Las Vegas, Nv.-Az. M.S.A.	**1,128,410**												
(Includes Clark and Nye Counties, Nv. and Mohave County, Az.)													
City of Las Vegas, Nv.	793,432	60,178		9,523	50,655	118	571	3,712	5,122	12,219	30,445	7,991	
Total area actually reporting	100.0%	83,599		12,253	71,346	138	750	4,450	6,915	17,500	43,466	10,380	
Rate per 100,000 inhabitants		7,408.6		1,085.9	6,322.7	12.2	66.5	394.4	612.8	1,550.9	3,852.0	919.9	
Lawrence, Ma.-N.H. M.S.A.	**298,872**												
(Includes part of Essex County, Ma. and Rockingham County, N.H.)													
City of Lawrence, Ma.	63,461	5,688		1,172	4,516	6	13	283	870	1,234	1,349	1,933	
Total area actually reporting	85.0%	11,081		1,426	9,655	6	49	346	1,025	2,077	4,659	2,919	
Estimated total	100.0%	12,198		1,477	10,721	7	59	355	1,056	2,267	5,457	2,997	
Rate per 100,000 inhabitants		4,081.3		494.2	3,587.2	2.3	19.7	118.8	353.3	758.5	1,825.9	1,002.8	
Lawton, Ok. M.S.A.	**118,347**												
(Includes Comanche County.)													
City of Lawton	86,606	7,798		1,431	6,367	10	56	176	1,189	1,689	4,254	424	
Total area actually reporting	100.0%	8,493		1,575	6,918	11	61	176	1,327	1,831	4,600	487	
Rate per 100,000 inhabitants		7,176.4		1,330.8	5,845.5	9.3	51.5	148.7	1,121.3	1,547.1	3,886.9	411.5	
Lewiston-Auburn, Me. M.S.A.	**103,962**												
(Includes part of Androscoggin County.)													
City of:													
Lewiston	37,415	2,485		150	2,335	4	18	63	65	535	1,752	48	
Auburn	23,382	838		7	831	1	2	3	1	149	647	35	
Total area actually reporting	100.0%	4,267		180	4,087	7	25	68	80	903	3,054	130	
Rate per 100,000 inhabitants		4,104.4		173.1	3,931.2	6.7	24.0	65.4	77.0	868.6	2,937.6	125.0	
Lexington, Ky. M.S.A.[5]	**434,551**												
(Includes Bourbon, Clark, Fayette, Jessamine, Scott, and Woodford Counties.)													
City of Lexington	239,660	15,933		2,099	13,834	14	131	636	1,318	2,978	9,912	944	
Total area actually reporting	99.9%	23,748		2,498	21,250	23	188	729	1,558	4,383	15,499	1,368	
Estimated total	100.0%	23,777		2,500	21,277	23	188	730	1,559	4,388	15,519	1,370	
Rate per 100,000 inhabitants		5,471.6		575.3	4,896.3	5.3	43.3	168.0	358.8	1,009.8	3,571.3	315.3	

See footnotes at end of table.

Table 6. — Index of Crime, Metropolitan Statistical Areas, 1995 — Continued

Metropolitan Statistical Area	Population	Crime Index total	Modified Crime Index total[1]	Violent crime[2]	Property crime[3]	Murder and non-negligent man-slaughter	Forcible rape	Robbery	Aggra-vated assault	Burglary	Larceny-theft	Motor vehicle theft	Arson[1]
Lima, Oh. M.S.A.[6]	**156,540**												
(Includes Allen and Auglaize Counties.)													
City of Lima[6]	44,569				2,733	6	36	194		834	1,763	136	
Total area actually reporting ..	83.0%	6,777		1,762	5,015	6	68	217	1,471	1,298	3,490	227	
Estimated total	100.0%	7,836		1,841	5,995	6	75	238	1,522	1,451	4,243	301	
Rate per 100,000 inhabitants ...		5,005.7		1,176.1	3,829.7	3.8	47.9	152.0	972.3	926.9	2,710.5	192.3	
Lincoln, Nb. M.S.A.	**227,695**												
(Includes Lancaster County.)													
City of Lincoln	204,828	14,433		1,331	13,102	2	80	122	1,127	1,880	10,765	457	
Total area actually reporting ..	100.0%	15,760		1,363	14,397	2	81	126	1,154	2,064	11,842	491	
Rate per 100,000 inhabitants ...		6,921.5		598.6	6,322.9	.9	35.6	55.3	506.8	906.5	5,200.8	215.6	
Little Rock-North Little Rock, Ar. M.S.A.	**544,763**												
(Includes Faulkner, Lonoke, Pulaski, and Saline Counties.)													
City of:													
Little Rock	180,821	22,212		3,699	18,513	53	172	1,056	2,418	3,701	13,069	1,743	
North Little Rock	62,983	7,221		834	6,387	10	47	315	462	1,267	4,601	519	
Total area actually reporting ..	99.8%	41,604		5,713	35,891	87	316	1,559	3,751	7,603	25,289	2,999	
Estimated total	100.0%	41,682		5,719	35,963	87	316	1,561	3,755	7,617	25,342	3,004	
Rate per 100,000 inhabitants ...		7,651.4		1,049.8	6,601.6	16.0	58.0	286.5	689.3	1,398.2	4,651.9	551.4	
Longview-Marshall, Tx. M.S.A. ..	**207,648**												
(Includes Gregg, Harrison, and Upshur Counties.)													
City of:													
Longview	74,644	5,527		511	5,016	2	78	163	268	1,041	3,482	493	
Marshall	23,763	2,079		203	1,876	4	15	32	152	420	1,343	113	
Total area actually reporting ..	100.0%	11,473		1,136	10,337	13	143	232	748	2,466	7,044	827	
Rate per 100,000 inhabitants ...		5,525.2		547.1	4,978.1	6.3	68.9	111.7	360.2	1,187.6	3,392.3	398.3	
Los Angeles-Long Beach, Ca. M.S.A.	**9,196,040**												
(Includes Los Angeles County.)													
City of:													
Los Angeles	3,466,211	266,204		70,518	195,686	849	1,590	29,134	38,945	41,325	108,149	46,212	
Long Beach	436,034	30,657		5,649	25,008	80	171	2,774	2,624	5,577	14,011	5,420	
Total area actually reporting ..	100.0%	564,803		130,824	433,979	1,682	3,179	52,389	73,574	96,768	234,891	102,320	
Rate per 100,000 inhabitants ...		6,141.8		1,422.6	4,719.2	18.3	34.6	569.7	800.1	1,052.3	2,554.3	1,112.7	
Louisville, Ky-In. M.S.A.[5]	**989,707**												
(Includes Bullitt, Jefferson, and Oldham Counties, Ky., and Clark, Floyd, Harrison, and Scott Counties, In.)													
City of Louisville, Ky.	272,638	19,491		3,260	16,231	50	135	1,592	1,483	4,471	8,800	2,960	
Total area actually reporting ..	93.9%	46,779		7,024	39,755	64	277	2,204	4,479	9,461	25,333	4,961	
Estimated total	100.0%	49,220		7,209	42,011	66	288	2,238	4,617	9,792	27,053	5,166	
Rate per 100,000 inhabitants ...		4,973.2		728.4	4,244.8	6.7	29.1	226.1	466.5	989.4	2,733.4	522.0	
Lowell, Ma.-N.H. M.S.A.	**280,167**												
(Includes part of Middlesex County, Ma. and Hillsborough County, N.H.)													
City of Lowell, Ma.	96,578	6,266		1,528	4,738	8	68	226	1,226	1,159	2,449	1,130	
Total area actually reporting ..	79.0%	9,402		1,752	7,650	8	90	259	1,395	1,682	4,315	1,653	
Estimated total	100.0%	11,138		1,952	9,186	9	100	289	1,554	2,013	5,330	1,843	
Rate per 100,000 inhabitants ...		3,975.5		696.7	3,278.8	3.2	35.7	103.2	554.7	718.5	1,902.4	657.8	
Lubbock, Tx. M.S.A.	**234,071**												
(Includes Lubbock County.)													
City of Lubbock	198,128	13,406		1,905	11,501	19	122	297	1,467	2,441	8,086	974	
Total area actually reporting ..	100.0%	15,526		2,129	13,397	20	137	305	1,667	2,764	9,573	1,060	
Rate per 100,000 inhabitants ...		6,633.0		909.6	5,723.5	8.5	58.5	130.3	712.2	1,180.8	4,089.8	452.9	
Lynchburg, Va. M.S.A.	**204,934**												
(Includes Lynchburg and Bedford Cities and Amherst, Bedford, and Campbell Counties.)													
City of Lynchburg	67,160	3,414		497	2,917	5	17	124	351	471	2,263	183	
Total area actually reporting ..	100.0%	6,252		824	5,428	11	37	141	635	1,001	4,125	302	
Rate per 100,000 inhabitants ...		3,050.7		402.1	2,648.7	5.4	18.1	68.8	309.9	488.4	2,012.8	147.4	
Macon, Ga. M.S.A.	**313,771**												
(Includes Bibb, Houston, Jones, Peach, and Twiggs Counties.)													
City of Macon	111,450	11,070		868	10,202	25	82	390	371	1,901	7,386	915	
Total area actually reporting ..	99.9%	20,008		1,763	18,245	31	145	550	1,037	3,462	13,433	1,350	
Estimated total	100.0%	20,023		1,764	18,259	31	145	550	1,038	3,464	13,444	1,351	
Rate per 100,000 inhabitants ...		6,381.4		562.2	5,819.2	9.9	46.2	175.3	330.8	1,104 .0	4,284.7	430.6	

See footnotes at end of table.

Metropolitan Statistical Area	Population	Crime Index total	Modified Crime Index total[1]	Violent crime[2]	Property crime[3]	Murder and non-negligent man-slaughter	Forcible rape	Robbery	Aggra-vated assault	Burglary	Larceny-theft	Motor vehicle theft	Arson[1]
Madison, Wi. M.S.A.	**386,241**												
(Includes Dane County.)													
City of Madison	196,156	9,287		617	8,670	5	67	282	263	1,459	6,478	733	
Total area actually reporting ..	100.0%	15,366		1,001	14,365	5	100	338	558	2,161	11,252	952	
Rate per 100,000 inhabitants...		3,978.3		259.2	3,719.2	1.3	25.9	87.5	144.5	559.5	2,913.2	246.5	
Manchester, N.H. M.S.A.	**167,916**												
(Includes part of Hillsborough, Merrimack, and Rockingham Counties.)													
City of Manchester	97,785	4,349		227	4,122	3	29	160	35	886	2,930	306	
Total area actually reporting ..	97.1%	5,605		253	5,352	4	31	170	48	1,140	3,837	375	
Estimated total	100.0%	5,722		257	5,465	4	32	171	50	1,160	3,922	383	
Rate per 100,000 inhabitants...		3,407.7		153.1	3,254.6	2.4	19.1	101.8	29.8	690.8	2,335.7	228.1	
Mansfield, Oh. M.S.A.	**176,339**												
(Includes Crawford and Richland Counties.)													
City of Mansfield	53,426	4,868		1,142	3,726	5	48	144	945	1,147	2,397	182	
Total area actually reporting ..	92.4%	8,423		1,253	7,170	7	51	169	1,026	1,950	4,900	320	
Estimated total	100.0%	8,956		1,293	7,663	7	54	180	1,052	2,027	5,279	357	
Rate per 100,000 inhabitants...		5,078.9		733.2	4,345.6	4.0	30.6	102.1	596.6	1,149.5	2,993.7	202.5	
McAllen-Edinburg-Mission, Tx. M.S.A.	**469,699**												
(Includes Hidalgo County.)													
City of:													
McAllen	97,093	12,591		683	11,908	5	29	145	504	1,762	9,193	953	
Edinburg	37,165	2,135		211	1,924	4	9	28	170	386	1,393	145	
Mission................	39,160	2,656		71	2,585	1	1	27	42	689	1,717	179	
Total area actually reporting ..	100.0%	31,689		2,582	29,107	36	156	502	1,888	7,449	19,224	2,434	
Rate per 100,000 inhabitants...		6,746.7		549.7	6,196.9	7.7	33.2	106.9	402.0	1,585.9	4,092.8	518.2	
Medford-Ashland, Or. M.S.A. ...	**165,257**												
(Includes Jackson County.)													
City of:													
Medford	53,548	5,233		330	4,903	5	30	43	252	677	3,920	306	
Ashland	17,253	1,060		24	1,036	1	6	9	8	132	861	43	
Total area actually reporting ..	99.3%	10,300		775	9,525	8	65	92	610	1,580	7,358	587	
Estimated total	100.0%	10,368		778	9,590	8	65	93	612	1,590	7,406	594	
Rate per 100,000 inhabitants...		6,273.9		470.8	5,803.1	4.8	39.3	56.3	370.3	962.1	4,481.5	359.4	
Melbourne-Titusville-Palm Bay, Fl. M.S.A.	**450,264**												
(Includes Brevard County.)													
City of:													
Melbourne	69,062	5,817		789	5,028	3	43	133	610	1,198	3,476	354	
Titusville	41,688	2,872		435	2,437	—	13	64	358	652	1,618	167	
Palm Bay	76,286	4,010		496	3,514	2	14	50	430	784	2,520	210	
Total area actually reporting ..	100.0%	25,711		3,505	22,206	17	179	530	2,779	5,351	15,381	1,474	
Rate per 100,000 inhabitants...		5,710.2		778.4	4,931.8	3.8	39.8	117.7	617.2	1,188.4	3,416.0	327.4	
Memphis, Tn.-Ar.-Ms. M.S.A. ...	**1,072,051**												
(Includes Fayette, Shelby, and Tipton Counties, Tn.; Crittenden County, Ar., and DeSoto County, Ms.)													
City of Memphis, Tn	623,902	65,597		11,039	54,558	181	785	5,779	4,294	16,026	24,695	13,837	
Total area actually reporting ..	86.2%	82,319		12,902	69,417	204	893	6,250	5,555	19,524	33,999	15,894	
Estimated total	100.0%	87,474		13,432	74,042	214	937	6,335	5,946	20,764	37,015	16,263	
Rate per 100,000 inhabitants...		8,159.5		1,252.9	6,906.6	20.0	87.4	590.9	554.6	1,936.8	3,452.7	1,517.0	
Merced, Ca. M.S.A.	**197,836**												
(Includes Merced County.)													
City of Merced	60,651	4,545		540	4,005	2	27	140	371	1,097	2,394	514	
Total area actually reporting ..	100.0%	11,129		1,433	9,696	11	73	238	1,111	3,031	5,567	1,098	
Rate per 100,000 inhabitants...		5,625.4		724.3	4,901.0	5.6	36.9	120.3	561.6	1,532.1	2,813.9	555.0	
Miami, Fl. M.S.A.	**2,055,953**												
(Includes Dade County.)													
City of Miami	378,720	59,170		12,927	46,243	110	198	5,676	6,943	9,874	27,537	8,832	
Total area actually reporting ..	99.7%	252,749		38,725	214,024	311	1,067	15,263	22,084	41,595	132,316	40,113	
Estimated total	100.0%	253,276		38,782	214,494	311	1,069	15,281	22,121	41,693	132,631	40,170	
Rate per 100,000 inhabitants...		12,319.2		1,886.3	10,432.8	15.1	52.0	743.3	1,075.9	2,027.9	6,451.1	1,953.8	
Middlesex-Somerset-Hunterdon, N.J. M.S.A.	**1,074,285**												
(Includes Hunterdon, Middlesex, and Somerset Counties.)													
Total area actually reporting ..	100.0%	34,658		2,613	32,045	14	121	1,016	1,462	6,435	22,592	3,018	
Rate per 100,000 inhabitants...		3,226.1		243.2	2,982.9	1.3	11.3	94.6	136.1	599.0	2,103.0	280.9	

See footnotes at end of table.

Table 6. — Index of Crime, Metropolitan Statistical Areas, 1995 — Continued

Metropolitan Statistical Area	Population	Crime Index total	Modified Crime Index total[1]	Violent crime[2]	Property crime[3]	Murder and non-negligent man-slaughter	Forcible rape	Robbery	Aggra-vated assault	Burglary	Larceny-theft	Motor vehicle theft	Arson[1]
Milwaukee-Waukesha, Wi. M.S.A.	1,457,771												
(Includes Milwaukee, Ozaukee, Washington, and Waukesha Counties.)													
City of:													
Milwaukee	622,467	52,679		6,737	45,942	138	370	3,650	2,579	8,366	26,231	11,345	
Waukesha	60,623	1,823		86	1,737	1	13	15	57	216	1,433	88	
Total area actually reporting . .	100.0%	79,010		7,775	71,235	146	443	4,047	3,139	11,665	46,634	12,936	
Rate per 100,000 inhabitants . . .		5,419.9		533.3	4,886.6	10.0	30.4	277.6	215.3	800.2	3,199.0	887.4	
Minneapolis-St. Paul, Mn.-Wi. M.S.A.	2,715,317												
(Includes Anoka, Carver, Chisago, Dakota, Hennepin, Isanti, Ramsey, Scott, Sherburne, and Wright Counties, Mn.; and Pierce and St. Croix Counties, Wi.)													
City of:													
Minneapolis, Mn	357,709	41,299		7,076	34,223	96	578	3,550	2,852	8,024	21,710	4,489	
St. Paul, Mn	264,539	20,256		2,536	17,720	25	233	930	1,348	4,272	11,219	2,229	
Total area actually reporting . .	99.9%	143,402		13,294	130,108	156	1,551	5,388	6,199	23,826	94,215	12,067	
Estimated total	100.0%	143,563		13,301	130,262	156	1,552	5,390	6,203	23,847	94,338	12,077	
Rate per 100,000 inhabitants . . .		5,287.2		489.9	4,797.3	5.7	57.2	198.5	228.4	878.2	3,474.3	444.8	
Mobile, Al. M.S.A.	516,267												
(Includes Baldwin and Mobile Counties.)													
City of Mobile[4]	206,138	18,915		2,332	16,583	56	106	1,384	786	4,236	10,416	1,931	
Total area actually reporting . .	100.0%	31,934		4,129	27,805	91	200	1,896	1,942	7,467	17,490	2,848	
Rate per 100,000 inhabitants . . .		6,185.6		799.8	5,385.8	17.6	38.7	367.3	376.2	1,446.3	3,387.8	551.7	
Modesto, Ca. M.S.A.	408,806												
(Includes Stanislaus County.)													
City of Modesto	177,244	15,425		1,368	14,057	13	76	387	892	2,814	9,262	1,981	
Total area actually reporting . .	100.0%	31,011		3,794	27,217	32	176	698	2,888	6,621	16,856	3,740	
Rate per 100,000 inhabitants . . .		7,585.7		928.1	6,657.7	7.8	43.1	170.7	706.4	1,619.6	4,123.2	914.9	
Monmouth-Ocean, N.J. M.S.A. . . .	1,040,351												
(Includes Monmouth and Ocean Counties.)													
Total area actually reporting . .	100.0%	35,552		2,494	33,058	23	181	779	1,511	6,192	25,093	1,773	
Rate per 100,000 inhabitants . . .		3,417.3		239.7	3,177.6	2.2	17.4	74.9	145.2	595.2	2,412.0	170.4	
Monroe, La. M.S.A.	147,361												
(Includes Ouachita Parish.)													
City of Monroe	57,406	6,940		1,017	5,923	7	36	107	867	1,145	4,576	202	
Total area actually reporting . .	100.0%	10,563		1,304	9,259	9	58	142	1,095	2,036	6,832	391	
Rate per 100,000 inhabitants . . .		7,168.1		884.9	6,283.2	6.1	39.4	96.4	743.1	1,381.6	4,636.2	265.3	
Montgomery, Al. M.S.A.	317,942												
(Includes Autauga, Elmore, and Montgomery Counties.)													
City of Montgomery	197,046	13,184		1,409	11,775	35	85	564	725	3,085	7,390	1,300	
Total area actually reporting . .	99.6%	17,473		1,943	15,530	50	117	662	1,114	4,140	9,843	1,547	
Estimated total	100.0%	17,544		1,951	15,593	50	117	664	1,120	4,153	9,888	1,552	
Rate per 100,000 inhabitants . . .		5,518.0		613.6	4,904.4	15.7	36.8	208.8	352.3	1,306.2	3,110.0	488.1	
Myrtle Beach S.C. M.S.A.	153,250												
(Includes Horry County.)													
City of Myrtle Beach	28,115	5,389		576	4,813	1	31	195	349	982	3,591	240	
Total area actually reporting . .	99.7%	15,214		1,775	13,439	11	104	390	1,270	2,804	9,734	901	
Estimated total	100.0%	15,243		1,778	13,465	11	104	391	1,272	2,809	9,754	902	
Rate per 100,000 inhabitants . . .		9,946.5		1,160.2	8,786.3	7.2	67.9	255.1	830.0	1,833.0	6,364.8	588.6	
Naples, Fl. M.S.A.	179,114												
(Includes Collier County.)													
City of Naples	21,597	1,390		128	1,262	—	2	20	106	214	994	54	
Total area actually reporting . .	100.0%	10,157		1,308	8,849	18	88	239	963	2,471	5,693	685	
Rate per 100,000 inhabitants . . .		5,670.7		730.3	4,940.4	10.0	49.1	133.4	537.6	1,379.6	3,178.4	382.4	
Nashua, N.H. M.S.A.	161,975												
(Includes part of Hillsborough County.)													
City of Nashua	80,401	2,563		66	2,497	—	23	13	30	339	1,951	207	
Total area actually reporting . .	98.6%	4,183		170	4,013	3	44	25	98	572	3,172	269	
Estimated total	100.0%	4,239		172	4,067	3	45	25	99	581	3,213	273	
Rate per 100,000 inhabitants . . .		2,617.1		106.2	2,510.9	1.9	27.8	15.4	61.1	358.7	1,983.6	168.5	

See footnotes at end of table.

Metropolitan Statistical Area	Population	Crime Index total	Modified Crime Index total[1]	Violent crime[2]	Property crime[3]	Murder and non-negligent man-slaughter	Forcible rape	Robbery	Aggra-vated assault	Burglary	Larceny–theft	Motor vehicle theft	Arson[1]
Nashville, Tn. M.S.A.	**1,086,715**												
(Includes Cheatham, Davidson, Dickson, Robertson, Rutherford, Sumner, Williamson, and Wilson Counties.)													
City of Nashville	523,681	56,090		9,376	46,714	105	487	2,675	6,109	8,236	30,363	8,115	
Total area actually reporting ..	81.2%	70,398		10,898	59,500	119	596	2,827	7,356	11,011	39,615	8,874	
Estimated total	100.0%	78,921		11,826	67,095	130	661	2,972	8,063	12,694	44,920	9,481	
Rate per 100,000 inhabitants...		7,262.3		1,088.2	6,174.1	12.0	60.8	273.5	742.0	1,168.1	4,133.6	872.4	
Nassau-Suffolk, N.Y. M.S.A.	**2,619,026**												
(Includes Nassau and Suffolk Counties.)													
Total area actually reporting ..	99.9%	75,612		5,556	70,056	53	166	2,364	2,973	11,878	48,762	9,416	
Estimated total	100.0%	75,732		5,566	70,166	53	166	2,367	2,980	11,897	48,845	9,424	
Rate per 100,000 inhabitants...		2,891.6		212.5	2,679.1	2.0	6.3	90.4	113.8	454.3	1,865.0	359.8	
Newark, N.J. M.S.A.	**1,943,842**												
(Includes Essex, Morris, Sussex, Union, and Warren Counties.)													
City of Newark	260,232	40,367		10,371	29,996	102	216	5,480	4,573	7,369	12,762	9,865	
Total area actually reporting ..	100.0%	113,417		20,051	93,366	175	579	10,841	8,456	21,242	50,853	21,271	
Rate per 100,000 inhabitants...		5,834.7		1,031.5	4,803.2	9.0	29.8	557.7	435.0	1,092.8	2,616.1	1,094.3	
New Bedford, Ma. M.S.A.	**175,051**												
(Includes part of Bristol and Plymouth Counties.)													
City of New Bedford	95,139	5,155		1,156	3,999	6	64	237	849	1,498	1,858	643	
Total area actually reporting ..	97.6%	8,637		1,785	6,852	6	77	259	1,443	2,414	3,577	861	
Estimated total	100.0%	8,765		1,801	6,964	6	78	261	1,456	2,439	3,649	876	
Rate per 100,000 inhabitants...		5,007.1		1,028.8	3,978.3	3.4	44.6	149.1	831.8	1,393.3	2,084.5	500.4	
New Haven-Meriden, Ct. M.S.A. .	**561,285**												
(Includes part of Middlesex and New Haven Counties.)													
City of:													
New Haven..............	119,604	15,174		2,229	12,945	21	98	953	1,157	2,965	7,465	2,515	
Meriden	56,928	3,427		192	3,235	1	5	92	94	927	2,032	276	
Total area actually reporting ..	100.0%	33,063		2,985	30,078	29	152	1,248	1,556	6,436	19,307	4,335	
Rate per 100,000 inhabitants...		5,890.6		531.8	5,358.8	5.2	27.1	222.3	277.2	1,146.7	3,439.8	772.3	
New London-Norwich, Ct.-R.I. M.S.A.	**302,334**												
(Includes part of Middlesex and New London Counties, Ct., and Washington County, R.I.)													
City of:													
New London, Ct	22,792	1,344		205	1,139	2	12	73	118	205	831	103	
Norwich, Ct.	35,504	1,766		204	1,562	—	28	55	121	335	1,125	102	
Total area actually reporting ..	100.0%	9,086		854	8,232	9	92	195	558	1,776	5,899	557	
Rate per 100,000 inhabitants...		3,005.3		282.5	2,722.8	3.0	30.4	64.5	184.6	587.4	1,951.2	184.2	
New Orleans, La. M.S.A.	**1,317,092**												
(Includes Jefferson, Orleans, Plaquemines, St. Charles, St. James, St. John the Baptist, and St. Tammany Parishes.)													
City of New Orleans	487,179	53,399		10,876	42,523	363	487	5,349	4,677	10,236	22,454	9,833	
Total area actually reporting ..	94.8%	104,663		17,206	87,457	426	792	7,149	8,839	18,674	53,700	15,083	
Estimated total	100.0%	108,140		17,577	90,563	431	814	7,235	9,097	19,357	55,841	15,365	
Rate per 100,000 inhabitants...		8,210.5		1,334.5	6,876.0	32.7	61.8	549.3	690.7	1,469.7	4,239.7	1,166.6	
New York, N.Y. M.S.A.	**8,595,280**												
(Includes Bronx, Kings, New York, Putnam, Queens, Richmond, Rockland, and Westchester Counties.)													
City of New York	7,319,546	444,758		115,153	329,605	1,177	2,374	59,280	52,322	73,889	183,037	72,679	
Total area actually reporting ..	99.8%	486,589		119,650	366,939	1,220	2,502	61,392	54,536	80,342	209,293	77,304	
Estimated total	100.0%	487,312		119,714	367,598	1,220	2,505	61,412	54,577	80,455	209,788	77,355	
Rate per 100,000 inhabitants...		5,669.5		1,392.8	4,276.7	14.2	29.1	714.5	635.0	936.0	2,440.7	900.0	

See footnotes at end of table.

Table 6. — Index of Crime, Metropolitan Statistical Areas, 1995 — Continued

Metropolitan Statistical Area	Population	Crime Index total	Modified Crime Index total[1]	Violent crime[2]	Property crime[3]	Murder and non-negligent man-slaughter	Forcible rape	Robbery	Aggra-vated assault	Burglary	Larceny-theft	Motor vehicle theft	Arson[1]
Norfolk-Virginia Beach-Newport News, Va.-N.C. M.S.A. ...	**1,546,051**												
(Includes Gloucester, Isle of Wight, James City, Mathews, and York Counties; Chesapeake, Hampton, Newport News, Portsmouth, Poquoson, Suffolk, Virginia Beach, and Williamsburg Cities, Va; and Currituck County, N.C.)													
City of:													
Norfolk, Va.	243,857	20,602		2,393	18,209	53	177	1,293	870	3,134	12,747	2,328	
Virginia Beach, Va.	435,959	20,280		968	19,312	16	99	479	374	2,915	15,244	1,153	
Newport News, Va.	180,930	11,239		1,750	9,489	28	139	538	1,045	1,669	7,181	639	
Total area actually reporting ...	100.0%	85,857		8,865	76,992	163	661	3,993	4,048	12,982	57,542	6,468	
Rate per 100,000 inhabitants ...		5,553.3		573.4	4,979.9	10.5	42.8	258.3	261.8	839.7	3,721.9	418.4	
Ocala, Fl. M.S.A.	**223,162**												
(Includes Marion County.)													
City of Ocala	54,037	6,847		826	6,021	3	43	224	556	1,169	4,549	303	
Total area actually reporting ..	100.0%	14,154		2,419	11,735	12	164	338	1,905	3,300	7,842	593	
Rate per 100,000 inhabitants ...		6,342.5		1,084.0	5,258.5	5.4	73.5	151.5	853.6	1,478.7	3,514.0	265.7	
Odessa-Midland, Tx. M.S.A.	**241,762**												
(Includes Ector and Midland Counties.)													
City of:													
Odessa	96,547	6,759		1,125	5,634	4	37	113	971	1,269	4,034	331	
Midland	97,973	4,838		473	4,365	8	68	88	309	1,004	3,074	287	
Total area actually reporting ..	100.0%	13,557		1,692	11,865	14	120	220	1,338	2,772	8,362	731	
Rate per 100,000 inhabitants ...		5,607.6		699.9	4,907.7	5.8	49.6	91.0	553.4	1,146.6	3,458.8	302.4	
Oklahoma City, Ok. M.S.A. [7]	**1,013,827**												
(Includes Canadian, Cleveland, Logan, McClain, Oklahoma, and Pottawatomie Counties.)													
City of Oklahoma City[7]	466,232	53,625		6,027	47,598	227	473	1,603	3,724	10,420	32,063	5,115	
Total area actually reporting ..	100.0%	80,151		8,197	71,954	245	659	1,974	5,319	16,210	48,627	7,117	
Rate per 100,000 inhabitants ...		7,905.8		808.5	7,097.3	24.2	65.0	194.7	524.6	1,598.9	4,796.4	702.0	
Olympia, Wa. M.S.A.	**190,320**												
(Includes Thurston County.)													
City of Olympia	40,378	2,511		157	2,354	1	25	23	108	327	1,886	141	
Total area actually reporting ..	100.0%	8,623		565	8,058	4	104	93	364	1,863	5,635	560	
Rate per 100,000 inhabitants ...		4,530.8		296.9	4,233.9	2.1	54.6	48.9	191.3	978.9	2,960.8	294.2	
Omaha, Nb.-Ia. M.S.A.	**668,267**												
(Includes Cass, Douglas, Sarpy, and Washington Counties, Nb., and Pottawattamie County, Ia.)													
City of Omaha, Nb.	348,089	27,324		3,585	23,739	27	80	808	2,670	3,883	16,071	3,785	
Total area actually reporting ..	96.2%	36,836		4,117	32,719	30	124	906	3,057	5,162	23,223	4,334	
Estimated total	100.0%	37,440		4,168	33,272	30	129	910	3,099	5,338	23,558	4,376	
Rate per 100,000 inhabitants ...		5,602.6		623.7	4,978.8	4.5	19.3	136.2	463.7	798.8	3,525.2	654.8	
Orange County, Ca. M.S.A.	**2,555,945**												
(Includes Orange County.)													
Total area actually reporting ..	100.0%	119,418		13,117	106,301	166	543	4,759	7,649	22,312	66,191	17,798	
Rate per 100,000 inhabitants ...		4,672.2		513.2	4,159.0	6.5	21.2	186.2	299.3	872.9	2.589.7	696.3	
Orlando, Fl. M.S.A.	**1,382,263**												
(Includes Lake, Orange, Osceola, and Seminole Counties.)													
City of Orlando	179,649	20,750		3,772	16,978	19	141	1,048	2,564	3,862	11,255	1,861	
Total area actually reporting ..	100.0%	98,466		13,920	84,546	79	662	3,381	9,798	20,914	55,666	7,966	
Rate per 100,000 inhabitants ...		7,123.5		1,007.0	6,116.5	5.7	47.9	244.6	708.8	1,513.0	4,027.2	576.3	
Owensboro, Ky. M.S.A.	**90,916**												
(Includes Daviess County.)													
City of Owensboro	54,107	3,136		104	3,032	3	14	44	43	522	2,400	110	
Total area actually reporting ..	100.0%	3,869		124	3,745	5	17	48	54	741	2,857	147	
Rate per 100,000 inhabitants ...		4,255.6		136.4	4,119.2	5.5	18.7	52.8	59.4	815.0	3,142.5	161.7	
Panama City, Fl. M.S.A.	**142,051**												
(Includes Bay County.)													
City of Panama City	38,571	3,304		419	2,885	3	24	81	311	589	2,150	146	
Total area actually reporting ..	100.0%	8,897		904	7,993	8	70	126	700	1,692	5,942	359	
Rate per 100,000 inhabitants ...		6,263.2		636.4	5,626.9	5.6	49.3	88.7	492.8	1,191.1	4,183.0	252.7	
Pensacola, Fl. M.S.A.	**376,420**												
(Includes Escambia and Santa Rosa Counties.)													
City of Pensacola	60,941	4,584		705	3,879	6	34	141	524	931	2,747	201	
Total area actually reporting ..	100.0%	21,920		3,945	17,975	17	206	626	3,096	5,058	11,894	1,023	
Rate per 100,000 inhabitants ...		5,823.3		1,048.0	4,775.3	4.5	54.7	166.3	822.5	1,343.7	3,159.8	271.8	

See footnotes at end of table.

Table 6. — Index of Crime, Metropolitan Statistical Areas, 1995 — Continued

Metropolitan Statistical Area	Population	Crime Index total	Modified Crime Index total[1]	Violent crime[2]	Property crime[3]	Murder and non-negligent man-slaughter	Forcible rape	Robbery	Aggra-vated assault	Burglary	Larceny-theft	Motor vehicle theft	Arson[1]
Phoenix-Mesa, Az. M.S.A.	**2,560,109**												
(Includes Maricopa and Pinal Counties.)													
City of:													
Phoenix	1,085,706	118,126		11,590	106,536	214	411	3,693	7,272	20,953	62,422	23,161	
Mesa...................	324,654	28,877		2,638	26,239	17	128	507	1,986	4,764	16,991	4,484	
Total area actually reporting ..	99.7%	224,885		19,544	205,341	305	826	5,353	13,060	41,305	125,892	38,144	
Estimated total	100.0%	225,508		19,585	205,923	305	828	5,363	13,089	41,426	126,274	38,223	
Rate per 100,000 inhabitants...		8,808.5		765.0	8,043.5	11.9	32.3	209.5	511.3	1,618.1	4,932.4	1,493.0	
Pine Bluff, Ar. M.S.A.	**85,093**												
(Includes Jefferson County.)													
City of Pine Bluff	58,703	5,586		1,325	4,261	14	60	381	870	1,658	1,899	704	
Total area actually reporting ..	100.0%	6,319		1,412	4,907	17	64	387	944	1,882	2,259	766	
Rate per 100,000 inhabitants...		7,426.0		1,659.4	5,766.6	20.0	75.2	454.8	1,109.4	2,211.7	2,654.7	900.2	
Pittsfield, Ma. M.S.A.	**98,529**												
(Includes part of Berkshire County.)													
City of Pittsfield	46,690	1,352		167	1,185	—	12	30	125	334	749	102	
Total area actually reporting ..	85.0%	1,867		254	1,613	—	15	31	208	453	1,029	131	
Estimated total	100.0%	2,319		311	2,008	—	17	40	254	541	1,283	184	
Rate per 100,000 inhabitants...		2,353.6		315.6	2,038.0	—	17.3	40.6	257.8	549.1	1,302.2	186.7	
Portland, Me. M.S.A.	**237,052**												
(Includes part of Cumberland and York Counties.)													
City of Portland	61,803	4,814		460	4,354	3	70	107	280	984	3,133	237	
Total area actually reporting ..	100.0%	11,464		645	10,819	5	88	150	402	2,352	7,941	526	
Rate per 100,000 inhabitants...		4,836.1		272.1	4,564.0	2.1	37.1	63.3	169.6	992.2	3,349.9	221.9	
Portland-Vancouver, Or.-Wa. M.S.A.	**1,708,678**												
(Includes Clackamas, Columbia, Multnomah, and Yamhill Counties, Or., and Clark County, Wa.)													
City of:													
Portland, Or.............	458,623	55,348		8,833	46,515	43	426	2,298	6,066	7,813	29,589	9,113	
Vancouver, Wa.	52,700	5,804		625	5,179	1	85	145	394	1,039	3,410	730	
Total area actually reporting ..	97.2%	112,315		12,266	100,049	63	886	3,311	8,006	17,801	66,459	15,789	
Estimated total	100.0%	115,133		12,420	102,713	64	901	3,354	8,101	18,229	68,426	16,058	
Rate per 100,000 inhabitants...		6,738.1		726.9	6,011.3	3.7	52.7	196.3	474.1	1,066.8	4,004.6	939.8	
Providence-Fall River-Warwick, R.I.-Ma. M.S.A.	**951,143**												
(Includes part of Bristol, Kent, Newport, Providence, and Washington Counties, R.I., and part of Bristol County, Ma.)													
City of:													
Providence, R.I.	149,805	13,998		1,222	12,776	25	97	570	530	3,534	7,150	2,092	
Fall River, Ma.	89,913	4,024		568	3,456	2	29	149	388	1,019	2,061	376	
Warwick, R.I............	85,711	3,830		255	3,575	1	12	23	219	527	2,654	394	
Total area actually reporting ..	100.0%	41,568		3,702	37,866	33	265	930	2,474	9,068	24,302	4,496	
Rate per 100,000 inhabitants...		4,370.3		389.2	3,981.1	3.5	27.9	97.8	260.1	953.4	2,555.0	472.7	
Provo-Orem, Ut. M.S.A.	**297,574**												
(Includes Utah County.)													
City of:													
Provo	90,514	3,952		130	3,822	1	23	17	89	470	3,157	195	
Orem	76,079	3,844		70	3,774	—	11	9	50	350	3,276	148	
Total area actually reporting ..	100.0%	13,543		437	13,106	2	77	45	313	1,693	10,819	594	
Rate per 100,000 inhabitants...		4,551.1		146.9	4,404.3	.7	25.9	15.1	105.2	568.9	3,635.7	199.6	
Pueblo, Co. M.S.A.	**130,841**												
(Includes Pueblo County.)													
City of Pueblo	102,971	7,822		1,367	6,455	8	46	182	1,131	1,468	4,475	512	
Total area actually reporting ..	100.0%	8,798		1,403	7,395	10	49	184	1,160	1,720	5,124	551	
Rate per 100,000 inhabitants...		6,724.2		1,072.3	5,651.9	7.6	37.5	140.6	886.6	1,314.6	3,916.2	421.1	
Punta Gorda, Fl. M.S.A.	**128,422**												
(Includes Charlotte County.)													
City of Punta Gorda........	12,286	413		35	378	—	1	8	26	77	274	27	
Total area actually reporting ..	100.0%	4,112		353	3,759	7	23	89	234	922	2,625	212	
Rate per 100,000 inhabitants...		3,201.9		274.9	2,927.1	5.5	17.9	69.3	182.2	717.9	2,044.0	165.1	
Racine, Wi. M.S.A.	**183,167**												
(Includes Racine County.)													
City of Racine	86,708	6,165		817	5,348	11	23	373	410	1,105	3,720	523	
Total area actually reporting ..	100.0%	8,942		902	8,040	11	31	404	456	1,549	5,817	674	
Rate per 100,000 inhabitants...		4,881.9		492.4	4,389.4	6.0	16.9	220.6	249.0	845.7	3,175.8	368.0	

See footnotes at end of table.

Table 6. — Index of Crime, Metropolitan Statistical Areas, 1995 — Continued

Metropolitan Statistical Area	Population	Crime Index total	Modified Crime Index total[1]	Violent crime[2]	Property crime[3]	Murder and non-negligent man-slaughter	Forcible rape	Robbery	Aggra-vated assault	Burglary	Larceny-theft	Motor vehicle theft	Arson[1]
Raleigh-Durham-Chapel Hill, N.C.. M.S.A.	**981,561**												
(Includes Chatham, Durham, Franklin, Johnston, Orange, and Wake Counties.)													
City of:													
Raleigh	240,891	17,523		2,039	15,484	18	104	648	1,269	3,682	10,565	1,237	
Durham	145,975	15,866		1,835	14,031	24	82	904	825	4,522	8,376	1,133	
Chapel Hill.............	47,438	2,657		275	2,382	—	14	86	175	526	1,751	105	
Total area actually reporting ..	99.9%	59,156		5,888	53,268	88	297	2,045	3,458	14,078	35,558	3,632	
Estimated total	100.0%	59,165		5,889	53,276	88	297	2,045	3,459	14,080	35,564	3,632	
Rate per 100,000 inhabitants...		6,027.6		600.0	5,427.7	9.0	30.3	208.3	352.4	1,434.4	3,623.2	370.0	
Rapid City, S.D. M.S.A.	**87,544**												
(Includes Pennington County.)													
City of Rapid City	58,248	4,145		267	3,878	—	48	55	164	680	3,088	110	
Total area actually reporting ..	96.5%	4,856		336	4,520	—	84	59	193	833	3,549	138	
Estimated total	100.0%	4,939		341	4,598	—	84	59	198	853	3,604	141	
Rate per 100,000 inhabitants...		5,641.7		389.5	5,252.2	—	96.0	67.4	226.2	974.4	4,116.8	161.1	
Redding, Ca. M.S.A.	**160,824**												
(Includes Shasta County.)													
City of Redding	73,272	5,333		508	4,825	2	71	100	335	1,247	3,143	435	
Total area actually reporting ..	100.0%	8,814		1,020	7,794	8	96	136	780	2,168	4,819	807	
Rate per 100,000 inhabitants...		5,480.5		634.2	4,846.3	5.0	59.7	84.6	485.0	1,348.1	2,996.4	501.8	
Reno, Nv. M.S.A.	**297,109**												
(Includes Washoe County.)													
City of Reno.............	152,294	10,947		1,097	9,850	14	94	421	568	1,846	7,193	811	
Total area actually reporting ..	100.0%	17,609		1,706	15,903	21	138	542	1,005	3,230	11,399	1,274	
Rate per 100,000 inhabitants...		5,926.8		574.2	5,352.6	7.1	46.4	182.4	338.3	1,087.1	3,836.6	428.8	
Richland-Kennewick-Pasco, Wa. M.S.A.	**174,837**												
(Includes Benton and Franklin Counties.)													
City of:													
Richland	36,328	1,684		89	1,595	—	21	8	60	240	1,281	74	
Kennewick	48,892	3,628		217	3,411	2	20	53	142	406	2,772	233	
Pasco	23,608	2,124		182	1,942	3	27	34	118	272	1,495	175	
Total area actually reporting ..	96.6%	9,300		633	8,667	11	88	104	430	1,384	6,698	585	
Estimated total	100.0%	9,744		657	9,087	11	91	112	443	1,446	7,013	628	
Rate per 100,000 inhabitants...		5,573.2		375.8	5,197.4	6.3	52.0	64.1	253.4	827.1	4,011.2	359.2	
Richmond-Petersburg, Va. M.S.A.	**925,899**												
(Includes Colonial Heights, Hopewell, Petersburg, and Richmond cities, and Charles City, Chesterfield, Dinwiddie, Goochland, Hanover, Henrico, New Kent, Powhatan, and Prince George Counties.)													
City of:													
Richmond..............	203,133	20,984		3,500	17,484	120	171	1,491	1,718	4,260	10,848	2,376	
Petersburg	41,346	3,204		523	2,681	9	25	242	247	614	1,859	208	
Total area actually reporting ..	100.0%	49,502		5,586	43,916	156	355	2,158	2,917	8,697	31,437	3,782	
Rate per 100,000 inhabitants...		5,346.4		603.3	4,743.1	16.8	38.3	233.1	315.0	939.3	3,395.3	408.5	
Riverside-San Bernardino, Ca. M.S.A.	**2,906,920**												
(Includes Riverside and San Bernardino Counties.)													
City of:													
Riverside	242,859	19,683		3,809	15,874	34	117	1,010	2,648	4,232	8,545	3,097	
San Bernardino	182,632	19,319		3,928	15,391	67	101	1,442	2,318	3,991	7,897	3,503	
Total area actually reporting ..	100.0%	186,309		27,484	158,825	358	1,042	7,760	18,324	46,680	81,662	30,483	
Rate per 100,000 inhabitants...		6,409.2		945.5	5,463.7	12.3	35.8	266.9	630.4	1,605.8	2,809.2	1,048.6	
Roanoke, Va. M.S.A.	**230,902**												
(Includes Roanoke and Salem Cities, and Botetourt and Roanoke Counties.)													
City of Roanoke...........	97,616	5,846		526	5,320	13	35	251	227	889	4,091	340	
Total area actually reporting ..	100.0%	8,639		711	7,928	15	60	287	349	1,265	6,205	458	
Rate per 100,000 inhabitants...		3,741.4		307.9	3,433.5	6.5	26.0	124.3	151.1	547.9	2,687.3	198.4	
Rochester, Mn. M.S.A.	**113,972**												
(Includes Olmsted County.)													
City of Rochester	76,482	3,524		244	3,280	1	70	56	117	594	2,548	138	
Total area actually reporting ..	100.0%	4,201		289	3,912	1	92	59	137	802	2,939	171	
Rate per 100,000 inhabitants...		3,686.0		253.6	3,432.4	.9	80.7	51.8	120.2	703.7	2,578.7	150.0	

See footnotes at end of table.

Table 6. — Index of Crime, Metropolitan Statistical Areas, 1995 — Continued

Metropolitan Statistical Area	Population	Crime Index total	Modified Crime Index total[1]	Violent crime[2]	Property crime[3]	Murder and non-negligent man-slaughter	Forcible rape	Robbery	Aggra-vated assault	Burglary	Larceny–theft	Motor vehicle theft	Arson[1]
Rochester, N.Y. M.S.A.	1,088,591												
(Includes Genesee, Livingston, Monroe, Ontario, Orleans, and Wayne Counties.)													
City of Rochester	230,749	22,722		2,553	20,169	53	150	1,576	774	5,089	12,871	2,209	
Total area actually reporting . .	99.5%	49,300		3,705	45,595	68	287	1,879	1,471	8,732	33,539	3,324	
Estimated total	100.0%	49,488		3,722	45,766	68	288	1,884	1,482	8,761	33,668	3,337	
Rate per 100,000 inhabitants . . .		4,546.1		341.9	4,204.2	6.2	26.5	173.1	136.1	804.8	3,092.8	306.5	
Rocky Mount, N.C. M.S.A.	142,784												
(Includes Edgecombe and Nash Counties.)													
City of Rocky Mount	52,858	5,346		699	4,647	16	28	216	439	1,236	3,189	222	
Total area actually reporting . .	99.6%	8,754		1,004	7,750	26	42	316	620	2,265	5,088	397	
Estimated total	100.0%	8,790		1,007	7,783	26	42	317	622	2,272	5,113	398	
Rate per 100,000 inhabitants . . .		6,156.2		705.3	5,450.9	18.2	29.4	222.0	435.6	1,591.2	3,580.9	278.7	
Sacramento, Ca. M.S.A.	1,448,719												
(Includes El Dorado, Placer, and Sacramento Counties.)													
City of Sacramento	375,845	38,803		4,280	34,523	57	158	2,129	1,936	8,003	18,538	7,982	
Total area actually reporting . .	100.0%	103,093		11,829	91,264	114	549	4,211	6,955	22,817	49,965	18,482	
Rate per 100,000 inhabitants . . .		7,116.1		816.5	6,299.6	7.9	37.9	290.7	480.1	1,575.0	3,448.9	1,275.7	
Saginaw-Bay City-Midland, Mi. M.S.A.	404,537												
(Includes Bay, Midland, and Saginaw Counties.)													
City of:													
Saginaw	71,000	6,054		1,568	4,486	16	101	374	1,077	1,638	2,509	339	
Bay City	38,603	2,336		382	1,954	—	46	59	277	308	1,482	164	
Midland	39,788	1,148		87	1,061	—	24	2	61	101	927	33	
Total area actually reporting . .	92.7%	17,698		2,910	14,788	30	300	550	2,030	3,305	10,577	906	
Estimated total	100.0%	19,082		3,034	16,048	31	311	575	2,117	3,493	11,500	1,055	
Rate per 100,000 inhabitants . . .		4,717.0		750.0	3,967.0	7.7	76.9	142.1	523.3	863.5	2,842.8	260.8	
St. Cloud, Mn. M.S.A.	158,386												
(Includes Benton and Stearns Counties.)													
City of St. Cloud	51,262	3,228		191	3,037	1	69	33	88	466	2,398	173	
Total area actually reporting . .	100.0%	5,316		253	5,063	2	80	36	135	848	3,915	300	
Rate per 100,000 inhabitants . . .		3,356.4		159.7	3,196.6	1.3	50.5	22.7	85.2	535.4	2,471.8	189.4	
St. Joseph, Mo. M.S.A.	98,841												
(Includes Andrew and Buchanan Counties.)													
City of St. Joseph	72,336	4,965		252	4,713	1	9	51	191	738	3,805	170	
Total area actually reporting . .	95.5%	5,384		363	5,021	3	11	53	296	843	3,997	181	
Estimated total	100.0%	5,603		379	5,224	3	12	57	307	876	4,151	197	
Rate per 100,000 inhabitants . . .		5,668.7		383.4	5,285.3	3.0	12.1	57.7	310.6	886.3	4,199.7	199.3	
Salem, Or. M.S.A.	310,903												
(Includes Marion and Polk Counties.)													
City of Salem	117,466	12,346		432	11,914	9	65	247	111	1,852	8,967	1,095	
Total area actually reporting . .	99.0%	23,737		918	22,819	18	125	360	415	3,748	16,914	2,157	
Estimated total	100.0%	23,925		928	22,997	18	126	363	421	3,777	17,045	2,175	
Rate per 100,000 inhabitants . . .		7,695.3		298.5	7,396.8	5.8	40.5	116.8	135.4	1,214.8	5,482.4	699.6	
Salinas, Ca. M.S.A.	353,693												
(Includes Monterey County.)													
City of Salinas	120,416	8,329		1,508	6,821	15	49	494	950	1,181	4,797	843	
Total area actually reporting . .	100.0%	18,052		2,878	15,174	26	105	770	1,977	3,348	10,375	1,451	
Rate per 100,000 inhabitants . . .		5,103.9		813.7	4,290.2	7.4	29.7	217.7	559.0	946.6	2,933.3	410.2	
Salt Lake City-Ogden, Ut. M.S.A.	1,204,924												
(Includes Davis, Salt Lake, and Weber Counties.)													
City of:													
Salt Lake City	175,765	22,115		1,375	20,740	27	148	564	636	2,950	15,467	2,323	
Ogden	69,290	6,194		422	5,772	5	31	114	272	858	4,498	416	
Total area actually reporting . .	97.6%	84,966		4,853	80,113	49	606	1,196	3,002	10,868	63,198	6,047	
Estimated total	100.0%	86,758		4,957	81,801	49	620	1,212	3,076	11,097	64,553	6,151	
Rate per 100,000 inhabitants . . .		7,200.3		411.4	6,788.9	4.1	51.5	100.6	255.3	921.0	5,357.4	510.5	
San Angelo, Tx. M.S.A.	103,149												
(Includes Tom Green County.)													
City of San Angelo	90,396	4,902		401	4,501	3	26	31	341	739	3,624	138	
Total area actually reporting . .	100.0%	5,231		481	4,750	4	32	32	413	806	3,800	144	
Rate per 100,000 inhabitants . . .		5,071.3		466.3	4,605.0	3.9	31.0	31.0	400.4	781.4	3,684.0	139.6	

See footnotes at end of table.

Metropolitan Statistical Area	Population	Crime Index total	Modified Crime Index total[1]	Violent crime[2]	Property crime[3]	Murder and non-negligent man-slaughter	Forcible rape	Robbery	Aggra-vated assault	Burglary	Larceny–theft	Motor vehicle theft	Arson[1]
San Antonio, Tx. M.S.A.	1,464,356												
(Includes Bexar, Comal,													
Guadalupe, and Wilson Counties.)													
City of San Antonio	999,900	79,931		5;178	74,753	142	658	2,345	2,033	13,961	52,370	8,422	
Total area actually reporting . .	100.0%	98,074		7,092	90,982	159	795	2,542	3,596	17,266	64,231	9,485	
Rate per 100,000 inhabitants . . .		6,697.4		484.3	6,213.1	10.9	54.3	173.6	245.6	1,179.1	4,386.3	647.7	
San Diego, Ca. M.S.A.	2,645,313												
(Includes San Diego County.)													
City of San Diego	1,157,771	64,235		11,077	53,158	91	346	3,244	7,396	10,311	30,505	12,342	
Total area actually reporting . .	100.0%	133,073		21,018	112,055	198	724	5,892	14,204	25,829	62,829	23,397	
Rate per 100,000 inhabitants . . .		5,030.5		794.5	4,236.0	7.5	27.4	222.7	536.9	976.4	2,375.1	884.5	
San Francisco, Ca. M.S.A.	1,654,212												
(Includes Marin, San Francisco,													
and San Mateo Counties.)													
City of San Francisco	738,371	60,474		10,903	49,571	99	304	6,469	4,031	7,127	34,153	8,291	
Total area actually reporting . .	100.0%	96,503		14,628	81,875	141	500	7,599	6,388	12,901	57,353	11,621	
Rate per 100,000 inhabitants . . .		5,833.8		884.3	4,949.5	8.5	30.2	459.4	386.2	779.9	3,467.1	702.5	
San Jose, Ca. M.S.A.	1,565,059												
(Includes Santa Clara County.)													
City of San Jose	822,845	36,096		6,649	29,447	38	387	1,209	5,015	5,477	19,745	4,225	
Total area actually reporting . .	100.0%	66,430		9,618	56,812	56	568	1,960	7,034	10,222	40,062	6,528	
Rate per 100,000 inhabitants . . .		4,244.6		614.5	3,630.0	3.6	36.3	125.2	449.4	653.1	2,559.8	417.1	
San Luis Obispo-Atascadero-													
Paso Robles, Ca. M.S.A.	224,831												
(Includes San Luis Obispo County.)													
City of:													
San Luis Obispo	40,510	2,031		316	1,715	—	20	20	276	378	1,244	93	
Atascadero	24,353	981		99	882	—	5	9	85	268	556	58	
Paso Robles	17,534	947		153	794	1	8	9	135	249	493	52	
Total area actually reporting . .	100.0%	9,030		1,546	7,484	8	66	87	1,385	1,965	5,153	366	
Rate per 100,000 inhabitants . . .		4,016.4		687.6	3,328.7	3.6	29.4	38.7	616.0	874.0	2,291.9	162.8	
Santa Barbara-Santa Maria-													
Lompoc, Ca. M.S.A.	382,403												
(Includes Santa Barbara County.)													
City of:													
Santa Barbara	86,056	4,075		577	3,498	5	33	107	432	665	2,588	245	
Santa Maria	66,263	3,795		399	3,396	5	28	98	268	614	2,534	248	
Lompoc	41,724	2,216		228	1,988	—	16	70	142	440	1,418	130	
Total area actually reporting . .	100.0%	15,091		1,781	13,310	11	130	312	1,328	3,358	9,099	853	
Rate per 100,000 inhabitants . . .		3,946.4		465.7	3,480.6	2.9	34.0	81.6	347.3	878.1	2,379.4	223.1	
Santa Cruz-Watsonville, Ca. M.S.A.	236,151												
(Includes Santa Cruz County.)													
City of:													
Santa Cruz	48,740	4,068		485	3,583	4	14	104	363	603	2,753	227	
Watsonville	32,252	2,824		529	2,295	1	18	98	412	359	1,747	189	
Total area actually reporting . .	100.0%	13,663		1,757	11,906	8	77	286	1,386	2,306	8,874	726	
Rate per 100,000 inhabitants . . .		5,785.7		744.0	5,041.7	3.4	32.6	121.1	586.9	976.5	3,757.8	307.4	
Santa Rosa, Ca. M.S.A.	412,251												
(Includes Sonoma County.)													
City of Santa Rosa	117,550	7,325		683	6,642	4	64	193	422	1,183	4,925	534	
Total area actually reporting . .	100.0%	19,497		1,953	17,544	15	140	349	1,449	4,183	12,158	1,203	
Rate per 100,000 inhabitants . . .		4,729.4		473.7	4,255.7	3.6	34.0	84.7	351.5	1,014.7	2,949.2	291.8	
Sarasota-Bradenton, Fl. M.S.A. . . .	525,837												
(Includes Manatee and Sarasota													
Counties.)													
City of:													
Sarasota	55,241	6,236		878	5,358	7	45	346	480	1,297	3,783	278	
Bradenton	47,463	4,281		761	3,520	4	36	233	488	996	2,238	286	
Total area actually reporting . .	100.0%	34,346		4,632	29,714	21	193	1,043	3,375	7,678	20,357	1,679	
Rate per 100,000 inhabitants . . .		6,531.7		880.9	5,650.8	4.0	36.7	198.4	641.8	1,460.1	3,871.4	319.3	
Savannah, Ga. M.S.A.	281,353												
(Includes Bryan, Chatham, and													
Effingham Counties.)													
City of Savannah	143,505	12,016		1,390	10,626	27	76	840	447	1,946	7,669	1,011	
Total area actually reporting . .	90.9%	18,179		1,909	16,270	38	109	945	817	2,991	11,852	1,427	
Estimated total	100.0%	19,380		2,000	17,380	39	117	976	868	3,207	12,577	1,596	
Rate per 100,000 inhabitants . . .		6,888.1		710.9	6,177.3	13.9	41.6	346.9	308.5	1,139.8	4,470.2	567.3	
Sheboygan, Wi. M.S.A.	107,892												
(Includes Sheboygan County.)													
City of Sheboygan	50,774	2,704		90	2,614	—	11	27	52	344	2,188	82	
Total area actually reporting . .	100.0%	3,910		139	3,771	1	16	29	93	527	3,127	117	
Rate per 100,000 inhabitants . . .		3,624.0		128.8	3,495.2	.9	14.8	26.9	86.2	488.5	2,898.3	108.4	

See footnotes at end of table.

Table 6. — Index of Crime, Metropolitan Statistical Areas, 1995 — Continued

Metropolitan Statistical Area	Population	Crime Index total	Modified Crime Index total[1]	Violent crime[2]	Property crime[3]	Murder and non-negligent man-slaughter	Forcible rape	Robbery	Aggra-vated assault	Burglary	Larceny-theft	Motor vehicle theft	Arson[1]
Sherman-Denison, Tx. M.S.A.	**99,096**												
(Includes Grayson County.)													
City of:													
Sherman	32,132	2,587		284	2,303	2	51	53	178	398	1,775	130	
Denison	21,902	1,538		150	1,388	2	11	30	107	242	1,084	62	
Total area actually reporting . .	100.0%	5,195		483	4,712	6	70	88	319	965	3,486	261	
Rate per 100,000 inhabitants . . .		5,242.4		487.4	4,755.0	6.1	70.6	88.8	321.9	973.8	3,517.8	263.4	
Shreveport-Bossier City, La. M.S.A.	**380,734**												
(Includes Bossier, Caddo, and													
Webster Parishes.)													
City of:													
Shreveport	199,007	22,338		2,592	19,746	61	112	776	1,643	3,787	14,637	1,322	
Bossier City	54,759	3,495		477	3,018	6	16	51	404	518	2,344	156	
Total area actually reporting . .	100.0%	29,396		3,430	25,966	75	152	869	2,334	5,354	18,964	1,648	
Rate per 100,000 inhabitants . . .		7,720.9		900.9	6,820.0	19.7	39.9	228.2	613.0	1,406.2	4,980.9	432.8	
Sioux City, Ia.-Nb. M.S.A.	**119,632**												
(Includes Woodbury County, Ia.													
and Dakota County, Nb.)													
City of Sioux City, Ia.	83,115	8,178		1,429	6,749	2	52	129	1,246	1,351	4,956	442	
Total area actually reporting . .	97.4%	9,198		1,514	7,684	3	59	135	1,317	1,561	5,618	505	
Estimated total	100.0%	9,328		1,521	7,807	3	59	136	1,323	1,580	5,716	511	
Rate per 100,000 inhabitants . . .		7,797.2		1,271.4	6,525.8	2.5	49.3	113.7	1,105.9	1,320.7	4,778.0	427.1	
Sioux Falls, S.D. M.S.A.	**154,723**												
(Includes Lincoln and													
Minnehaha Counties.)													
City of Sioux Falls	110,385	5,766		501	5,265	5	70	82	344	904	4,136	225	
Total area actually reporting . .	87.5%	6,223		539	5,684	5	74	85	375	1,056	4,366	262	
Estimated total	100.0%	6,683		577	6,106	5	85	87	400	1,173	4,649	284	
Rate per 100,000 inhabitants . . .		4,319.3		372.9	3,946.4	3.2	54.9	56.2	258.5	758.1	3,004.7	183.6	
South Bend, In. M.S.A.	**257,699**												
(Includes St. Joseph County.)													
City of South Bend	106,024	10,013		980	9,033	26	86	389	479	2,406	5,920	707	
Total area actually reporting . .	82.8%	12,625		1,076	11,549	27	98	417	534	2,951	7,761	837	
Estimated total	100.0%	14,785		1,236	13,549	28	105	441	662	3,171	9,368	1,010	
Rate per 100,000 inhabitants . . .		5,737.3		479.6	5,257.7	10.9	40.7	171.1	256.9	1,230.5	3,635.2	391.9	
Spokane, Wa. M.S.A.	**402,394**												
(Includes Spokane County.)													
City of Spokane	195,956	16,484		1,586	14,898	23	132	471	960	2,966	11,000	932	
Total area actually reporting . .	98.8%	26,586		2,034	24,552	26	199	568	1,241	4,939	18,102	1,511	
Estimated total	100.0%	26,935		2,053	24,882	26	202	574	1,251	4,988	18,349	1,545	
Rate per 100,000 inhabitants . . .		6,693.7		510.2	6,183.5	6.5	50.2	142.6	310.9	1,239.6	4,560.0	384.0	
Springfield, Mo. M.S.A.	**291,507**												
(Includes Christian, Greene, and													
Webster Counties.)													
City of Springfield	151,032	12,092		829	11,263	5	82	145	597	2,123	8,440	700	
Total area actually reporting . .	100.0%	14,552		935	13,617	8	110	162	655	2,802	9,955	860	
Rate per 100,000 inhabitants . . .		4,992.0		320.7	4,671.2	2.7	37.7	55.6	224.7	961.2	3,415.0	295.0	
Springfield, Ma. M.S.A.	**536,015**												
(Includes part of Franklin,													
Hampden, and Hampshire													
Counties.)													
City of Springfield	149,978	11,165		2,307	8,858	19	134	748	1,406	2,490	3,798	2,570	
Total area actually reporting . .	94.4%	24,383		3,914	20,469	27	229	1,043	2,615	4,783	11,586	4,100	
Estimated total	100.0%	25,306		4,031	21,275	27	234	1,060	2,710	4,962	12,105	4,208	
Rate per 100,000 inhabitants . . .		4,721.1		752.0	3,969.1	5.0	43.7	197.8	505.6	925.7	2,258.3	785.1	
Stamford-Norwalk, Ct. M.S.A. . . .	**331,629**												
(Includes part of Fairfield County.)													
City of:													
Stamford	107,199	6,051		511	5,540	4	14	231	262	935	3,999	606	
Norwalk	78,710	3,987		263	3,724	5	7	130	121	755	2,546	423	
Total area actually reporting . .	100.0%	12,992		896	12,096	9	35	389	463	2,155	8,737	1,204	
Rate per 100,000 inhabitants . . .		3,917.6		270.2	3,647.4	2.7	10.6	117.3	139.6	649.8	2,634.6	363.1	
Stockton-Lodi, Ca. M.S.A.	**520,771**												
(Includes San Joaquin County.)													
City of:													
Stockton	223,752	20,782		3,187	17,595	42	133	1,228	1,784	3,836	10,278	3,481	
Lodi	52,686	3,492		388	3,104	2	19	68	299	462	2,234	408	
Total area actually reporting . .	100.0%	37,801		4,818	32,983	62	227	1,560	2,969	7,489	19,952	5,542	
Rate per 100,000 inhabitants . . .		7,258.7		925.2	6,333.5	11.9	43.6	299.6	570.1	1,438.1	3,831.2	1,064.2	
Sumter, S.C. M.S.A.	**106,961**												
(Includes Sumter County.)													
City of Sumter	42,878	3,076		505	2,571	5	12	155	333	714	1,658	199	
Total area actually reporting . .	100.0%	6,695		1,167	5,528	11	36	235	885	1,792	3,288	448	
Rate per 100,000 inhabitants . . .		6,259.3		1,091.1	5,168.2	10.3	33.7	219.7	827.4	1,675.4	3,074.0	418.8	

See footnotes at end of table.

Metropolitan Statistical Area	Population	Crime Index total	Modified Crime Index total[1]	Violent crime[2]	Property crime[3]	Murder and non-negligent man-slaughter	Forcible rape	Robbery	Aggra-vated assault	Burglary	Larceny-theft	Motor vehicle theft	Arson[1]
Syracuse, N.Y. M.S.A.	**753,840**												
(Includes Cayuga, Madison, Onondaga, and Oswego Counties.)													
City of Syracuse	159,603	11,340		1,467	9,873	18	84	633	732	3,048	6,032	793	
Total area actually reporting	99.6%	27,586		2,267	25,319	21	165	767	1,314	6,297	17,767	1,255	
Estimated total	100.0%	27,693		2,276	25,417	21	165	770	1,320	6,314	17,840	1,263	
Rate per 100,000 inhabitants		3,673.6		301.9	3,371.7	2.8	21.9	102.1	175.1	837.6	2,366.5	167.5	
Tacoma, Wa. M.S.A.	**649,584**												
(Includes Pierce County.)													
City of Tacoma	186,074	21,766		3,223	18,543	28	171	925	2,099	3,655	12,250	2,638	
Total area actually reporting	99.5%	46,777		5,659	41,118	53	385	1,401	3,820	8,367	27,864	4,887	
Estimated total	100.0%	47,013		5,672	41,341	53	387	1,405	3,827	8,400	28,031	4,910	
Rate per 100,000 inhabitants		7,237.4		873.2	6,364.2	8.2	59.6	216.3	589.1	1,293.1	4,315.2	755.9	
Tallahassee, Fl. M.S.A.	**257,233**												
(Includes Gadsden and Leon Counties.)													
City of Tallahassee	135,759	16,611		1,929	14,682	12	119	607	1,191	2,800	10,751	1,131	
Total area actually reporting	100.0%	22,939		2,964	19,975	19	176	826	1,943	4,419	13,957	1,599	
Rate per 100,000 inhabitants		8,917.6		1,152.3	7,765.3	7.4	68.4	321.1	755.3	1,717.9	5,425.8	621.6	
Tampa-St. Petersburg-Clearwater, Fl. M.S.A.	**2,189,459**												
(Includes Hernando, Hillsborough, Pasco, and Pinellas Counties.)													
City of:													
Tampa	289,882	41,112		8,735	32,377	47	277	2,626	5,785	6,622	19,773	5,982	
St. Petersburg	242,228	22,899		5,174	17,725	30	172	1,417	3,555	4,217	12,076	1,432	
Clearwater	101,362	7,249		1,083	6,166	4	48	257	774	1,420	4,452	294	
Total area actually reporting	99.9%	155,979		24,522	131,457	145	1,013	6,032	17,332	28,851	88,242	14,364	
Estimated total	100.0%	156,060		24,531	131,529	145	1,013	6,035	17,338	28,866	88,290	14,373	
Rate per 100,000 inhabitants		7,127.8		1,120.4	6,007.4	6.6	46.3	275.6	791.9	1,318.4	4,032.5	656.5	
TerreHaute, In. M.S.A.	**150,980**												
(Includes Clay, Vermillion, and Vigo Counties.)													
City of Terre Haute	60,733	5,448		336	5,112	7	32	116	181	1,078	3,751	283	
Total area actually reporting	80.5%	8,146		673	7,473	11	46	126	490	1,617	5,426	430	
Estimated total	100.0%	9,066		746	8,320	12	52	142	540	1,790	6,014	516	
Rate per 100,000 inhabitants		6,004.8		494.1	5,510.7	7.9	34.4	94.1	357.7	1,185.6	3,983.3	341.8	
Texarkana, Tx.-Texarkana, Ar. M.S.A.	**124,710**												
(Includes Bowie County, Tx., and Miller County, Ar.)													
City of:													
Texarkana, Tx.	33,071	2,587		325	2,262	2	27	82	214	493	1,641	128	
Texarkana, Ar.	23,211	2,302		242	2,060	2	23	62	155	343	1,622	95	
Total area actually reporting	100.0%	6,399		730	5,669	7	68	165	490	1,248	4,113	308	
Rate per 100,000 inhabitants		5,131.1		585.4	4,545.7	5.6	54.5	132.3	392.9	1,000.7	3,298.1	247.0	
Toledo, Oh. M.S.A.	**616,641**												
(Includes Fulton, Lucas, and Wood Counties.)													
City of Toledo	323,972	27,196		2,873	24,323	35	278	1,414	1,146	6,298	14,821	3,204	
Total area actually reporting	92.3%	35,537		3,283	32,254	36	346	1,505	1,396	7,593	21,038	3,623	
Estimated total	100.0%	37,424		3,425	33,999	37	358	1,543	1,487	7,866	22,379	3,754	
Rate per 100,000 inhabitants		6,069.0		555.4	5,513.6	6.0	58.1	250.2	241.1	1,275.6	3,629.2	608.8	
Trenton, N.J. M.S.A.	**331,135**												
(Includes Mercer County.)													
City of Trenton	84,879	6,371		1,330	5,041	16	80	486	748	1,275	2,370	1,396	
Total area actually reporting	100.0%	14,908		1,772	13,136	20	124	668	960	2,717	7,772	2,647	
Rate per 100,000 inhabitants		4,502.1		535.1	3,967.0	6.0	37.4	201.7	289.9	820.5	2,347.1	799.4	
Tucson, Az. M.S.A.	**757,195**												
(Includes Pima County.)													
City of Tucson	449,981	54,706		5,427	49,279	65	292	1,192	3,878	5,995	37,235	6,049	
Total area actually reporting	99.0%	73,376		6,603	66,773	92	394	1,445	4,672	8,645	50,675	7,453	
Estimated total	100.0%	73,974		6,642	67,332	92	396	1,454	4,700	8,761	51,042	7,529	
Rate per 100,000 inhabitants		9,769.5		877.2	8,892.3	12.2	52.3	192.0	620.7	1,157.0	6,740.9	994.3	
Tulsa, Ok. M.S.A.	**747,659**												
(Includes Creek, Osage, Rogers, Tulsa, and Wagoner Counties.)													
City of Tulsa	377,152	27,824		4,359	23,465	30	255	947	3,127	6,072	12,991	4,402	
Total area actually reporting	100.0%	40,274		5,516	34,758	44	361	1,076	4,035	9,203	20,072	5,483	
Rate per 100,000 inhabitants		5,386.7		737.8	4,648.9	5.9	48.3	143.9	539.7	1,230.9	2,684.6	733.4	

See footnotes at end of table.

Metropolitan Statistical Area	Population	Crime Index total	Modified Crime Index total[1]	Violent crime[2]	Property crime[3]	Murder and non-negligent manslaughter	Forcible rape	Robbery	Aggravated assault	Burglary	Larceny-theft	Motor vehicle theft	Arson[1]
Tuscaloosa, Al. M.S.A.	**158,311**												
(Includes Tuscaloosa County.)													
City of Tuscaloosa	80,440	10,597		809	9,788	10	61	284	454	1,319	8,176	293	
Total area actually reporting	100.0%	13,790		1,128	12,662	12	83	323	710	1,959	10,216	487	
Rate per 100,000 inhabitants		8,710.7		712.5	7,998.2	7.6	52.4	204.0	448.5	1,237.4	6,453.1	307.6	
Tyler, Tx. M.S.A.	**161,923**												
(Includes Smith County.)													
City of Tyler	81,704	7,229		705	6,524	7	47	166	485	1,169	4,928	427	
Total area actually reporting	100.0%	10,336		1,046	9,290	11	83	198	754	2,112	6,538	640	
Rate per 100,000 inhabitants		6,383.3		646.0	5,737.3	6.8	51.3	122.3	465.7	1,304.3	4,037.7	395.2	
Utica-Rome, N.Y. M.S.A.	**313,399**												
(Includes Herkimer and Oneida Counties.)													
City of:													
Utica	63,978	3,212		188	3,024	10	13	124	41	600	2,184	240	
Rome	44,152	1,009		55	954	2	6	31	16	185	724	45	
Total area actually reporting	98.8%	9,664		776	8,888	14	59	195	508	1,997	6,471	420	
Estimated total	100.0%	9,794		787	9,007	14	59	199	515	2,017	6,561	429	
Rate per 100,000 inhabitants		3,125.1		251.1	2,874.0	4.5	18.8	63.5	164.3	643.6	2,093.5	136.9	
Vallejo-Fairfield-Napa, Ca. M.S.A.	**484,975**												
(Includes Napa and Solano Counties.)													
City of:													
Vallejo	112,044	9,040		1,631	7,409	13	52	508	1,058	1,670	4,701	1,038	
Fairfield	84,197	5,709		823	4,886	4	39	264	516	902	3,428	556	
Napa	63,763	2,981		300	2,681	2	12	39	247	413	2,030	238	
Total area actually reporting	100.0%	26,282		3,757	22,525	30	159	1,024	2,544	4,931	14,979	2,615	
Rate per 100,000 inhabitants		5,419.2		774.7	4,644.6	6.2	32.8	211.1	524.6	1,,016.8	3,088.6	539.2	
Ventura Ca. M.S.A.	**706,270**												
(Includes Ventura County.)													
City of Ventura	96,772	4,592		327	4,265	1	25	119	182	1,139	2,719	407	
Total area actually reporting	100.0%	25,190		3,049	22,141	26	171	833	2,019	5,143	14,465	2,533	
Rate per 100,000 inhabitants		3,566.6		431.7	3,134.9	3.7	24.2	117.9	285.9	728.2	2,048.1	358.6	
Victoria, Tx. M.S.A.	**80,933**												
(Includes Victoria County.)													
City of Victoria	61,724	4,537		616	3,921	4	30	55	527	956	2,724	241	
Total area actually reporting	100.0%	5,130		660	4,470	6	39	60	555	1,139	3,062	269	
Rate per 100,000 inhabitants		6,338.6		815.5	5,523.1	7.4	48.2	74.1	685.8	1,407.3	3,783.4	332.4	
Vineland-Millville-Bridgeton, N.J. M.S.A.	**139,521**												
(Includes Cumberland County.)													
City of:													
Vineland	54,956	4,055		454	3,601	3	35	208	208	787	2,531	283	
Millville	26,665	1,996		303	1,693	1	24	92	186	443	1,128	122	
Bridgeton	19,136	1,944		416	1,528	1	16	120	279	383	989	156	
Total area actually reporting	100.0%	9,078		1,338	7,740	6	93	431	808	1,923	5,158	659	
Rate per 100,000 inhabitants		6,506.5		959.0	5,547.6	4.3	66.7	308.9	579.1	1,378.3	3,696.9	472.3	
Visalia-Tulare-Porterville, Ca. M.S.A.	**344,978**												
(Includes Tulare County.)													
City of:													
Visalia	85,500	6,562		727	5,835	5	27	160	535	999	4,156	680	
Tulare	38,757	2,358		411	1,947	7	13	58	333	423	1,202	322	
Porterville	32,590	2,357		184	2,173	3	12	44	125	527	1,299	347	
Total area actually reporting	100.0%	19,429		2,395	17,034	39	90	386	1,880	4,163	10,658	2,213	
Rate per 100,000 inhabitants		5,632.0		694.2	4,937.7	11.3	26.1	111.9	545.0	1,206.7	3,089.5	641.5	
Waco, Tx. M.S.A.	**200,878**												
(Includes McLennan County.)													
City of Waco	107,885	10,064		1,508	8,556	16	131	457	904	1,900	5,553	1,103	
Total area actually reporting	100.0%	13,727		1,873	11,854	25	155	506	1,187	2,690	7,855	1,309	
Rate per 100,000 inhabitants		6,833.5		932.4	5,901.1	12.4	77.2	251.9	590.9	1,339.1	3,910.3	651.6	

See footnotes at end of table.

Metropolitan Statistical Area	Population	Crime Index total	Modified Crime Index total[1]	Violent crime[2]	Property crime[3]	Murder and non-negligent man-slaughter	Forcible rape	Robbery	Aggra-vated assault	Burglary	Larceny–theft	Motor vehicle theft	Arson[1]
Washington, D.C.-Md.-Va.-W.V. M.S.A.	4,486,417												
(Includes District of Columbia; Calvert, Charles, Frederick, Montgomery, and Prince Georges Counties, Md.; Alexandria, Fairfax, Falls Church, Fredericksburg, Manassas, and Manassas Park Cities, and Arlington, Clarke, Culpeper, Fairfax, Fauquier, King George, Loudoun, Prince William, Spotsylvania, Stafford, and Warren Counties, Va.; and Berkeley and Jefferson Counties, W.V.)													
City of Washington, D.C.	554,000	67,401		14,744	52,657	360	292	6,864	7,228	10,184	32,281	10,192	
Total area actually reporting ..	99.9%	250,749		32,136	218,613	600	1,365	14,191	15,980	35,708	151,251	31,654	
Estimated total	100.0%	250,809		32,142	218,667	600	1,365	14,194	15,983	35,717	151,291	31,659	
Rate per 100,000 inhabitants...		5,590.4		716.4	4,874.0	13.4	30.4	316.4	356.3	796.1	3,372.2	705.7	
Waterbury, Ct. M.S.A.	182,683												
(Includes part of Litchfield and New Haven Counties.)													
City of Waterbury	103,523	8,799		526	8,273	9	32	260	225	2,049	4,923	1,301	
Total area actually reporting ..	100.0%	10,949		600	10,349	9	46	278	267	2,434	6,407	1,508	
Rate per 100,000 inhabitants...		5,993.4		328.4	5,665.0	4.9	25.2	152.2	146.2	1,332.4	3,507.2	825.5	
Waterloo-Cedar Falls, Ia. M.S.A.	124,270												
(Includes Black Hawk County.)													
City of:													
Waterloo................	66,843	5,445		459	4,986	2	38	126	293	1,258	3,465	263	
Cedar Falls	34,063	1,424		100	1,324	—	—	15	85	180	1,093	51	
Total area actually reporting ..	100.0%	7,498		579	6,919	3	45	142	389	1,645	4,952	322	
Rate per 100,000 inhabitants...		6,033.6		465.9	5,567.7	2.4	36.2	114.3	313.0	1,323.7	3,984.9	259.1	
Wausau, Wi. M.S.A.	140,552												
(Includes Marathon County.)													
City of Wausau	39,113	1,484		41	1,443	—	9	3	29	141	1,230	72	
Total area actually reporting ..	100.0%	3,621		123	3,498	—	32	6	85	423	2,908	167	
Rate per 100,000 inhabitants...		2,576.3		87.5	2,488.8	—	22.8	4.3	60.5	301.0	2,069.0	118.8	
West Palm Beach-Boca Raton, Fl. M.S.A.	969,103												
(Includes Palm Beach County.)													
City of:													
West Palm Beach	76,608	12,086		1,290	10,796	29	55	624	582	2,071	7,138	1,587	
Boca Raton	67,436	3,154		193	2,961	1	7	71	114	799	1,805	357	
Total area actually reporting ..	100.0%	83,074		9,445	73,629	63	382	2,486	6,514	17,805	47,330	8,494	
Rate per 100,000 inhabitants...		8,572.3		974.6	7,597.6	6.5	39.4	256.5	672.2	1,837.3	4,883.9	876.5	
Wheeling, W.V.-Oh. M.S.A.	158,467												
(Includes Marshall and Ohio Counties, W.V. and Belmont County, Oh.)													
City of Wheeling, W.V.	34,080	1,285		201	1,084	2	11	40	148	275	739	70	
Total area actually reporting ..	95.0%	3,164		288	2,876	9	25	54	200	713	1,986	177	
Estimated total	100.0%	3,480		311	3,169	9	27	60	215	759	2,211	199	
Rate per 100,000 inhabitants...		2,196.0		196.3	1,999.8	5.7	17.0	37.9	135.7	479.0	1,395.2	125.6	
Wichita Falls, Tx. M.S.A.	134,476												
(Includes Archer and Wichita Counties.)													
City of Wichita Falls	99,606	7,011		861	6,150	8	90	211	552	1,183	4,601	366	
Total area actually reporting ..	100.0%	7,771		898	6,873	9	95	212	582	1,429	5,053	391	
Rate per 100,000 inhabitants...		5,778.7		667.8	5,110.9	6.7	70.6	157.6	432.8	1,062.6	3,757.5	290.8	
Wilmington, N.C. M.S.A.	196,830												
(Includes Brunswick and New Hanover Counties.)													
City of Wilmington	63,758	7,087		575	6,512	7	32	225	311	1,490	4,603	419	
Total area actually reporting ..	99.6%	13,796		1,108	12,688	10	56	290	752	3,378	8,571	739	
Estimated total	100.0%	13,855		1,113	12,742	10	56	291	756	3,390	8,611	741	
Rate per 100,000 inhabitants...		7,039.1		565.5	6,473.6	5.1	28.5	147.8	384.1	1,722.3	4,374.8	376.5	
Worcester, Ma.-Ct. M.S.A.	479,929												
(Includes part of Windham County, Ct. and Hampden and Worcester Counties, Ma.)													
City of Worcester, Ma.	166,290	11,386		1,782	9,604	5	82	431	1,264	2,523	5,790	1,291	
Total area actually reporting ..	97.2%	18,293		3,097	15,196	10	119	500	2,468	4,078	9,378	1,740	
Estimated total	100.0%	18,696		3,148	15,548	10	121	508	2,509	4,156	9,605	1,787	
Rate per 100,000 inhabitants...		3,895.6		655.9	3,239.6	2.1	25.2	105.8	522.8	866.0	2,001.3	372.3	

See footnotes at end of table.

Metropolitan Statistical Area	Population	Crime Index total	Modified Crime Index total[1]	Violent crime[2]	Property crime[3]	Murder and non-negligent man-slaughter	Forcible rape	Robbery	Aggra-vated assault	Burglary	Larceny–theft	Motor vehicle theft	Arson[1]
Yakima, Wa. M.S.A.	**211,099**												
(Includes Yakima County.)													
City of Yakima	62,996	8,461		714	7,747	6	50	163	495	1,680	5,507	560	
Total area actually reporting . .	97.9%	16,771		1,206	15,565	13	128	213	852	4,013	10,390	1,162	
Estimated total	100.0%	17,112		1,225	15,887	13	131	219	862	4,061	10,631	1,195	
Rate per 100,000 inhabitants . . .		8,106.1		580.3	7,525.9	6.2	62.1	103.7	408.3	1,923.7	5,036.0	566.1	
Yolo Ca. M.S.A.	**147,156**												
(Includes Yolo County.)													
Total area actually reporting . .	100.0%	9,774		1,167	8,607	9	47	184	927	1,613	6,025	969	
Rate per 100,000 inhabitants . . .		6,641.9		793.0	5,848.9	6.1	31.9	125.0	629.9	1,096.1	4,094.3	658.5	
Yuba City, Ca. M.S.A.	**135,864**												
(Includes Sutter and Yuba Counties.)													
City of Yuba City	32,604	2,776		351	2,425	—	18	28	305	589	1,627	209	
Total area actually reporting . .	100.0%	8,605		1,690	6,915	6	55	98	1,531	1,885	4,270	760	
Rate per 100,000 inhabitants . . .		6,333.5		1,243.9	5,089.6	4.4	40.5	72.1	1,126.9	1,387.4	3,142.8	559.4	
San Juan, Puerto Rico M.S.A.[8] . .		**65,577**		**15,443**	**50,134**	**635**	**176**	**11,983**	**2,649**	**15,058**	**22,670**	**12,406**	
Total area actually reporting . .	100.0%												
Aguadilla, Puerto Rico M.S.A.[8] . .		**3,669**		**509**	**3,160**	**17**	**17**	**219**	**256**	**1,152**	**1,759**	**249**	
Total area actually reporting . .	100.0%												
Arecibo, Puerto Rico M.S.A.[8]		**3,798**		**586**	**3,212**	**19**	**12**	**327**	**228**	**1,325**	**1,434**	**453**	
Total area actually reporting . .	100.0%												
Caguas, Puerto Rico M.S.A.[8]		**8,597**		**1,778**	**6,819**	**46**	**29**	**1,274**	**429**	**2,609**	**3,120**	**1,090**	
Total area actually reporting . .	100.0%												
Mayaguez, Puerto Rico M.S.A.[8] . .		**4,919**		**628**	**4,291**	**13**	**19**	**254**	**342**	**1,315**	**2,758**	**218**	
Total area actually reporting . .	100.0%												
Ponce, Puerto Rico M.S.A.[8]		**7,017**		**1,306**	**5,711**	**67**	**18**	**746**	**475**	**1,776**	**3,279**	**656**	
Total area actually reporting . .	100.0%												

[1]Although arson data are included in the trend and clearance tables, sufficient data are not available to estimate totals for this offense.

[2]Violent crimes are offenses of murder, forcible rape, robbery, and aggravated assault.

[3]Property crimes are offenses of burglary, larceny-theft, and motor vehicle theft. Data are not included for the property crime of arson.

[4]Due to reporting changes or annexations, figures are not comparable to previous years.

[5]Aggravated assault figures for 1995 are not comparable to 1994. See "Crime Trends," page 368 for details.

[6]Aggravated assault data furnished by the police department were not in accordance with national Uniform Crime Reporting guidelines; therefore, the figures were excluded from the aggravated assault, violent crime, and Crime Index total categories.

[7]The increase in murders was the result of the bombing of the Alfred P. Murrah Federal Building in Oklahoma City.

[8]The 1995 Bureau of the Census population estimate for Puerto Rico was not available prior to publication; therefore, no population or rates per 100,000 inhabitants are provided.

Complete data were not available for the states of Delaware, Illinois, Kansas, Montana, and Pennsylvania. See "Offense Estimation," pages 367–368 for details.

Table 7.—Offense Analysis, United States, 1991–1995

Classification	1991	1992	1993	1994	1995
Murder	24,700	23,760	24,530	23,330	21,600
Forcible rape	106,590	109,060	106,010	102,220	97,460
Robbery:					
Total	687,730	672,480	659,870	618,950	580,550
Street/highway	386,948	374,157	360,799	337,758	315,413
Commercial house	81,485	79,717	82,385	76,130	71,463
Gas or service station	16,992	16,752	15,391	13,436	13,428
Convenience store	37,871	35,312	34,817	31,831	30,023
Residence	67,640	67,619	67,914	67,389	62,973
Bank	10,930	11,121	11,856	8,961	9,175
Miscellaneous	85,863	87,802	86,708	83,446	78,077
Burglary:					
Total	3,157,200	2,979,900	2,834,800	2,712,800	2,595,000
Residence (dwelling):	2,089,148	1,972,919	1,883,907	1,814,172	1,735,881
Night	660,458	629,462	591,404	556,647	530,365
Day	903,885	863,812	827,731	805,992	763,977
Unknown	524,805	479,645	464,772	451,533	441,539
Nonresidence (store, office, etc.):	1,068,052	1,006,981	950,893	898,628	859,119
Night	503,850	469,929	440,653	400,856	374,504
Day	257,627	258,914	242,340	242,758	235,745
Unknown	306,575	278,138	267,900	255,014	248,871
Larceny–theft (except motor vehicle theft):					
Total	8,142,200	7,915,200	7,820,900	7,879,800	8,000,600
By type:					
Pocket-picking	86,239	78,194	72,775	63,716	51,100
Purse-snatching	84,135	74,858	68,447	60,476	51,150
Shoplifting	1,337,681	1,253,766	1,200,910	1,178,223	1,204,567
From motor vehicles (except accessories)	1,836,654	1,792,386	1,827,643	1,865,813	1,940,333
Motor vehicle accessories	1,152,401	1,107,131	1,090,850	1,014,214	964,368
Bicycles	465,182	468,584	478,485	496,637	500,627
From buildings	1,168,237	1,106,809	1,028,997	1,026,961	1,004,010
From coin-operated machines	81,186	72,087	61,686	53,147	49,689
All others	1,930,484	1,961,384	1,991,106	2,120,612	2,234,756
By value:					
Over $200	2,910,299	2,844,553	2,865,453	2,946,988	3,061,607
$50 to $200	1,930,796	1,874,226	1,829,138	1,845,866	1,864,188
Under $50	3,301,105	3,196,421	3,126,309	3,086,946	3,074,805
Motor Vehicle Theft	1,661,700	1,610,800	1,563,100	1,539,300	1,472,700

Note: Because of rounding, offenses may not add to totals.

Table 8. — Number of Offenses Known to the Police, Cities and Towns 10,000 and over in Population, 1995

*Arson is shown only if 12 months of arson data were received. Dashes (—) indicate zero data. The Modified Crime Index total is the sum of the Crime Index offenses, including arson.

City by state	Population	Crime Index total	Modified* Crime Index total	Murder and non-negligent man-slaughter	Forcible rape	Robbery	Aggravated assault	Burglary	Larceny-theft	Motor vehicle theft	Arson*
ALABAMA											
Alabaster	17,399	139		1	2	7	20	12	88	9	
Albertville	17,284	116		2	2	3	10	14	63	22	
Alexander City	15,216	987		5	6	33	60	155	701	27	
Anniston	27,425	4,215		6	25	169	440	1,025	2,343	207	
Athens	18,855	683		—	2	11	52	101	483	34	
Auburn	36,151	1,980		—	17	22	66	292	1,531	52	
Bessemer	32,078	4,268	4,303	15	20	219	596	1,103	1,932	383	35
Birmingham	270,728	33,037	33,320	121	248	2,158	4,122	6,399	16,309	3,680	283
Cullman	18,226	821		1	8	5	32	129	598	48	
Daphne	14,595	599		2	3	6	30	79	464	15	
Decatur	52,887	3,458		7	17	60	88	674	2,467	145	
Dothan	56,241	2,807		2	5	103	126	687	1,744	140	
Enterprise	21,443	1,198		2	14	28	33	239	858	24	
Eufaula	13,834	638		3	1	7	5	79	530	13	
Fairfield	12,486	1,716		2	5	79	113	260	1,140	117	
Fairhope	10,608	568		—	—	9	59	145	335	20	
Florence	37,066	2,085		4	8	40	116	366	1,495	56	
Fort Payne	12,858	440		1	—	3	3	78	342	13	
Gadsden	46,925	5,276		8	31	175	558	1,170	2,936	398	
Hartselle	11,758	338		—	2	2	1	59	257	17	
Homewood	24,061	1,649		—	4	77	30	200	1,218	120	
Hoover	42,302	2,063		—	1	69	23	205	1,588	177	
Hueytown	15,549	523		1	2	8	41	77	344	50	
Huntsville	161,617	13,102	13,152	10	56	384	825	2,413	8,393	1,021	50
Jacksonville	11,075	424		—	4	9	9	115	275	12	
Jasper	13,961	1,214		5	3	19	114	202	779	92	
Leeds	10,107	503		—	4	8	25	63	382	21	
Madison	20,404	576		—	1	9	28	120	379	39	
Mobile[1]	206,138	18,915	19,002	56	106	1,384	786	4,236	10,416	1,931	87
Montgomery	197,046	13,184	13,256	35	85	564	725	3,085	7,390	1,300	72
Mountain Brook	20,305	519		1	1	12	17	79	384	25	
Muscle Shoals	10,319	578		—	1	2	3	16	549	7	
Northport	20,392	797		—	4	16	69	127	554	27	
Opelika	24,009	2,076		1	7	51	427	474	1,066	50	
Oxford	10,506	1,113		—	4	22	204	177	668	38	
Ozark	13,311	906		5	4	14	168	107	570	38	
Pelham	12,145	362		—	—	10	12	39	275	26	
Phenix City[1]	29,146	1,286		3	23	41	113	237	735	134	
Prattville	24,312	1,247		5	9	30	83	244	814	62	
Prichard	33,531	4,159		16	47	337	519	1,098	1,653	489	
Saraland	12,332	680		2	2	15	8	65	570	18	
Scottsboro	14,724	395		—	1	3	15	59	298	19	
Selma	24,845	3,887		6	28	213	642	744	2,090	164	
Sheffield	10,360	714		—	8	12	39	97	544	14	
Sylacauga	13,949	949		1	4	22	110	186	603	23	
Talladega	19,338	829		1	4	24	14	142	614	30	
Troy	14,104	1,060		1	6	20	47	169	800	17	
Tuscaloosa	80,440	10,597	10,604	10	61	284	454	1,319	8,176	293	7
Vestavia Hills	20,014	292		—	1	18	1	58	192	22	
Tuskegee	12,240	749		1	4	17	143	214	366	4	
ALASKA											
Anchorage	253,500	18,305	18,401	29	242	777	1,462	2,521	11,152	2,122	96
Fairbanks	34,207	2,146	2,149	2	24	55	159	279	1,470	157	3
ARIZONA											
Apache Junction	22,103	1,510	1,521	—	10	8	128	306	920	138	11
Avondale	21,374	1,941	1,952	3	6	34	119	568	998	213	11
Bullhead City	28,129	2,672	2,684	—	5	53	156	678	1,514	266	12
Casa Grande	21,827	3,526	3,539	2	11	45	231	399	2,626	212	13
Chandler	123,410	8,080	8,164	9	32	119	243	1,677	4,882	1,118	84

See footnotes at end of table.

City by State	Population	Crime Index total	Modified* Crime Index total	Murder and non-negligent man-slaughter	Forcible rape	Robbery	Aggravated assault	Burglary	Larceny–theft	Motor vehicle theft	Arson*
ARIZONA — Continued											
Flagstaff	52,487	5,569	5,595	1	9	40	261	631	4,410	217	26
Gilbert	52,866	2,798	2,815	—	8	14	175	729	1,656	216	17
Glendale	174,349	15,468	15,587	9	53	320	1,018	2,850	8,489	2,729	119
Kingman	16,502	2,069		—	6	27	105	351	1,506	74	
Lake Havasu City	33,014	1,890	1,902	—	7	12	86	403	1,277	105	12
Mesa	324,654	28,877	29,021	17	128	507	1,986	4,764	16,991	4,484	144
Nogales	21,041	1,308	1,316	3	—	49	75	412	573	196	8
Paradise Valley	14,267	675	677	1	2	3	9	378	246	36	2
Payson	10,148	575	575	2	8	2	30	81	429	23	—
Peoria	72,600	3,284	3,296	3	10	33	129	856	1,935	318	12
Phoenix	1,085,706	118,126	118,397	214	411	3,693	7,272	20,953	62,422	23,161	271
Prescott	31,452	2,295	2,310	2	13	25	115	311	1,733	96	15
Prescott Valley	13,614	1,077	1,086	—	8	2	64	213	726	64	9
Scottsdale	157,788	10,816	10,861	6	18	138	296	2,076	6,627	1,655	45
Sierra Vista	39,613	1,447	1,454	1	1	17	22	182	1,114	110	7
Tempe	149,352	14,723	14,780	7	49	299	478	2,103	9,374	2,413	57
Tucson	449,981	54,706	54,983	65	292	1,192	3,878	5,995	37,235	6,049	277
ARKANSAS											
Arkadelphia	10,613	213	213	—	—	1	—	16	182	14	—
Benton	22,167	1,092	1,095	2	12	13	80	103	802	80	3
Bentonville	13,679	710	710	—	—	—	10	93	598	9	—
Blytheville	17,554	2,680	2,719	10	22	95	279	745	1,399	130	39
Cabot	11,905	368	369	—	—	2	8	59	279	20	1
Camden	14,404	870	875	5	9	15	87	151	557	46	5
Conway	34,375	2,099	2,104	—	14	25	69	217	1,715	59	5
El Dorado	24,180	1,666	1,680	3	5	39	66	404	1,001	148	14
Fayetteville	49,841	2,632	2,640	3	24	21	109	341	2,013	121	8
Forrest City	13,509	1,675	1,684	3	6	36	315	303	942	70	9
Fort Smith	75,421	6,532	6,541	4	54	94	362	709	4,841	468	9
Harrison	11,017	457	457	1	3	1	13	63	343	33	—
Hope	10,207	703	706	5	6	25	35	205	415	12	3
Hot Springs	36,094	3,867	3,892	9	37	127	125	927	2,439	203	25
Jacksonville	29,957	2,167	2,179	2	14	46	145	421	1,427	112	12
Jonesboro	50,843	3,026	3,040	3	26	81	137	684	1,922	173	14
Little Rock	180,821	22,212	22,382	53	172	1,056	2,418	3,701	13,069	1,743	170
Magnolia	11,916	455	455	2	2	11	20	135	270	15	—
Mountain Home	10,136	159	165	—	2	—	4	14	127	12	6
North Little Rock	62,983	7,221	7,253	10	47	315	462	1,267	4,601	519	32
Paragould	21,527	612	613	—	5	3	11	105	441	47	1
Pine Bluff	58,703	5,586	5,663	14	60	381	870	1,658	1,899	704	77
Rogers	30,847	1,440	1,442	1	14	10	38	184	1,139	54	2
Russellville	23,536	1,648	1,655	—	15	20	92	234	1,187	100	7
Searcy	18,302	948	948	1	3	6	4	54	840	40	—
Sherwood	20,711	882	882	—	2	10	39	131	627	73	—
Springdale	37,014	1,616	1,625	—	20	15	42	236	1,168	135	9
Stuttgart	10,376	806	807	—	12	20	198	146	399	31	1
Texarkana	23,211	2,302	2,310	2	23	62	155	343	1,622	95	8
Van Buren	17,105	936	936	—	1	4	6	165	712	48	—
West Helena	10,021	383	386	3	4	21	6	178	143	28	3
West Memphis	27,864	2,952	2,965	9	24	186	200	812	1,284	437	13
CALIFORNIA											
Agoura Hills	25,491	697	702	1	2	17	64	161	377	75	5
Alameda	79,067	4,224	4,255	4	18	248	207	574	2,754	419	31
Albany	16,961	781	785	1	3	63	82	136	413	83	4
Alhambra	84,835	3,622	3,649	3	26	388	119	733	1,634	719	27
Anaheim	283,552	17,399	17,456	25	76	1,011	1,363	3,141	8,764	3,019	57
Antioch	73,386	3,499	3,521	2	9	130	436	914	1,634	374	22
Apple Valley	52,255	2,852	2,868	6	14	76	159	843	1,382	372	16

Table 8. — Number of Offenses Known to the Police, Cities and Towns 10,000 and over in Population, 1995 — Continued

City by State	Population	Crime Index total	Modified* Crime Index total	Murder and non-negligent man-slaughter	Forcible rape	Robbery	Aggravated assault	Burglary	Larceny–theft	Motor vehicle theft	Arson*
CALIFORNIA — Continued											
Arcadia	50,908	2,257	2,269	1	15	93	83	408	1,395	262	12
Arcata	15,528	1,385	1,388	—	12	3	67	209	1,017	77	3
Arroyo Grande	15,223	612	620	2	—	10	67	119	399	15	8
Artesia	15,665	929	935	3	3	88	107	163	396	169	6
Arvin	10,212	364	379	1	—	6	15	90	219	33	15
Atascadero	24,353	981	997	—	5	9	85	268	556	58	16
Atwater	23,484	1,437	1,443	—	11	29	162	419	685	131	6
Auburn	11,925	561	561	—	4	7	42	123	347	38	—
Avenal	12,161	338	349	1	1	7	46	149	113	21	11
Azusa	43,310	2,045	2,056	3	12	89	139	416	972	414	11
Bakersfield	192,021	13,806	13,945	29	39	604	626	2,862	7,883	1,763	139
Baldwin Park	73,128	2,095	2,108	7	23	162	229	746	271	657	13
Banning	23,569	1,278	1,326	—	8	50	315	308	370	227	48
Barstow	19,953	1,783	1,794	5	16	73	68	404	1,031	186	11
Beaumont	10,697	672	679	—	5	16	92	140	316	103	7
Bell	35,866	1,209	1,218	3	5	158	139	225	297	382	9
Bell Gardens	42,645	2,038	2,049	10	11	198	173	509	601	536	11
Bellflower	67,002	4,245	4,269	10	30	284	604	865	1,385	1,067	24
Belmont	25,278	677	678	3	8	16	49	95	461	45	1
Benicia	27,161	881	896	2	6	16	45	205	525	82	15
Berkeley	100,332	11,407	11,458	10	33	619	591	1,538	7,541	1,075	51
Beverly Hills	33,295	2,733	2,739	—	5	196	70	575	1,700	187	6
Brawley	21,937	1,457	1,467	1	1	35	145	491	706	78	10
Brea	34,846	1,933	1,946	—	2	37	77	290	1,299	228	13
Buena Park	73,036	3,944	3,990	3	21	170	188	767	1,954	841	46
Burbank	100,166	4,234	4,251	6	20	188	289	597	2,246	888	17
Burlingame	27,787	1,360	1,367	—	4	34	56	222	908	136	7
Calabasas	75,565	557	558	—	6	12	71	107	300	61	1
Calexico	24,390	1,791	1,808	1	1	72	99	422	904	292	17
Camarillo	57,019	1,642	1,650	1	8	34	73	272	1,091	163	8
Campbell	37,501	1,906	1,938	—	18	50	89	294	1,278	177	32
Capitola	10,017	1,212	1,217	—	1	12	45	84	1,028	425	5
Carlsbad	65,790	3,506	3,523	3	14	92	217	785	1,940	455	17
Carpinteria	13,725	372	375	—	2	1	44	146	153	26	3
Carson	90,477	4,415	4,448	15	21	310	812	788	1,584	885	33
Cathedral City	34,908	2,202	2,221	3	16	49	354	483	978	319	19
Ceres	30,083	2,565	2,574	1	9	57	189	444	1,550	315	9
Cerritos	55,061	3,964	3,988	3	5	183	239	655	1,890	989	24
Chico	43,861	3,415	3,479	1	34	59	102	625	2,349	245	64
Chino	65,106	4,099	4,165	3	21	123	654	666	1,925	707	66
Chino Hills	45,184	1,656	1,666	1	10	44	59	457	910	175	10
Chula Vista	150,005	9,069	9,123	12	34	405	636	1,662	4,524	1,796	54
Claremont	34,296	1,478	1,490	1	5	42	97	356	813	164	12
Clearlake	13,100	1,338	1,344	2	10	18	127	459	636	86	6
Clovis	60,584	3,728	3,751	1	23	76	178	639	2,279	532	23
Coachella	18,701	798	800	4	6	37	128	203	311	109	2
Colton	41,446	3,217	3,236	7	14	199	160	914	1,234	689	19
Commerce	12,418	1,920	1,927	2	4	119	158	200	911	526	7
Compton	96,962	6,357	6,378	79	45	840	826	1,616	1,554	1,397	21
Concord	112,451	7,696	7,713	4	50	156	452	1,378	4,830	826	17
Corcoran	13,862	487	489	1	4	6	96	132	215	33	2
Corona	93,365	5,423	5,441	4	24	214	503	1,252	2,327	1,099	18
Coronado	21,940	863	865	—	3	28	32	134	532	134	2
Costa Mesa	98,922	6,336	6,359	2	25	171	241	1,111	3,984	802	23
Covina	44,867	2,304	2,320	2	15	122	67	417	1,180	501	16
Cudahy	23,156	789	794	2	7	86	193	125	186	190	5
Culver City	39,483	2,097	2,097	3	9	203	46	305	1,200	331	—
Cupertino	42,905	1,547	1,559	—	11	43	104	215	1,088	86	12
Cypress	46,652	2,091	2,109	2	9	76	81	368	1,283	272	18
Daly City	94,509	3,003	3,019	3	14	188	141	333	1,796	528	16
Dana Point	33,623	1,217	1,223	2	8	21	133	240	734	79	6

City by State	Population	Crime Index total	Modified* Crime Index total	Murder and non-negligent man-slaughter	Forcible rape	Robbery	Aggravated assault	Burglary	Larceny–theft	Motor vehicle theft	Arson*
CALIFORNIA — Continued											
Danville	38,904	829	832	—	—	9	14	191	592	23	3
Davis	48,517	2,908	2,912	1	4	22	26	245	2,452	158	4
Delano	27,823	2,059	2,064	6	12	77	143	478	1,038	305	5
Desert Hot Springs	14,478	1,830	1,843	1	6	68	167	624	826	138	13
Diamond Bar	59,123	1,573	1,580	2	7	60	153	391	723	237	7
Dinuba	13,621	806	814	1	—	10	81	213	422	79	· 8
Dixon	11,628	671	683	—	1	13	36	154	426	41	12
Downey	100,391	4,791	4,843	7	19	353	198	848	2,097	1,269	52
Duarte	22,566	816	818	—	3	38	146	137	365	127	2
Dublin	26,271	777	779	—	1	14	33	124	509	96	2
East Palo Alto	25,975	1,255	1,282	6	13	156	150	251	546	133	27
El Cajon	93,124	6,148	6,207	3	32	235	706	1,189	3,195	788	59
El Centro	37,782	2,801	2,823	4	13	77	241	1,069	1,183	214	22
El Cerrito	22,653	1,834	1,862	—	1	141	61	281	1,135	215	28
El Monte	105,187	5,167	5,222	30	33	531	801	996	1,782	994	55
El Segundo	15,663	1,140	1,144	—	4	32	24	216	656	208	4
Escondido	116,934	7,993	8,038	11	36	252	581	1,450	4,346	1,317	45
Eureka	27,354	4,297	4,322	2	35	61	169	592	3,017	421	25
Fairfield	84,197	5,709	5,759	4	39	264	516	902	3,428	556	50
Fillmore	12,461	335	340	1	2	3	50	92	162	25	5
Folsom	39,802	1,080	1,083	—	3	11	72	280	611	103	3
Fontana	104,258	6,276	6,302	13	66	470	978	1,372	1,788	1,589	26
Foster City	29,620	634	638	1	5	10	30	83	472	33	4
Fountain Valley	55,745	2,763	2,780	1	7	84	71	384	1,856	360	17
Fremont	184,498	8,606	8,652	2	32	199	981	1,424	4,855	1,113	46
Fresno	388,495	46,267	47,594	· 71	212	2,166	3,210	7,638	20,552	12,418	1,327
Fullerton	117,450	6,490	6,519	6	39	198	247	1,113	4,024	863	29
Galt	12,936	596	599	—	1	8	59	116	313	99	3
Gardena	53,747	3,376	3,393	8	27	529	371	569	1,174	698	17
Garden Grove	148,702	7,740	7,766	6	39	347	532	1,293	3,994	1,529	26
Gilroy	33,789	2,369	2,419	2	10	56	386	405	1,332	178	50
Glendale	179,378	7,958	8,002	8	22	351	384	1,315	4,552	1,326	44
Glendora	52,218	1,587	1,598	—	11	56	74	343	929	174	11
Grand Terrace	11,681	487	489	—	2	20	12	103	216	134	2
Grover City	12,194	457	457	—	3	5	38	116	273	22	—
Hanford	34,149	2,200	2,214	2	5	29	347	360	1,213	244	14
Hawaiian Gardens	13,289	1,085	1,088	3	4	115	102	, 381	287	193	3
Hawthorne	75,707	6,401	6,471	16	39	766	1,052	966	2,418	1,144	70
Hayward	116,171	7,981	8,065	12	45	349	449	1,235	4,372	1,519	84
Hemet	41,823	3,769	3,799	4	22	143	204	1,306	1,536	554	30
Hercules	19,713	537	542	1	4	15	91	78	265	83	5
Hermosa Beach	18,953	848	853	1	2	18	42	174	496	115	5
Hesperia	59,428	3,269	3,289	4	16	80	212	875	1,533	549	20
Highland	39,412	2,250	2,274	8	22	136	153	634	946	351	24
Hillsborough	11,284	106	106	—	—	1	5	16	81	3	—
Hollister	22,108	1,188	1,206	2	12	22	270	200	596	86	18
Huntington Beach	190,171	8,093	8,117	8	44	176	338	2,084	4,474	969	24
Huntington Park	55,992	3,945	3,957	11	9	464	232	469	1,221	1,539	12
Indio	39,653	1,926		6	19	141	221	507	485	547	
Inglewood	110,638	6,817	6,870	40	60	1,067	814	1,096	2,095	1,645	53
Irvine	126,255	4,707	4,740	2	14	75	122	894	3,191	409	33
La Canada-Flintridge	19,933	456	461	—	1	14	30	134	226	51	5
Lafayette	24,117	703	705	—	3	14	6	161	492	27	2
Laguna Beach	24,043	1,188	1,192	2	5	19	120	303	654	85	4
Laguna Hills	48,545	997	1,006	—	6	18	48	209	634	82	9
Laguna Niguel	56,966	1,139	1,150	—	3	19	67	229	747	74	11
La Habra	53,933	2,557	2,578	3	11	90	377	510	1,238	328	21
Lake Elsinore	22,840	2,277	2,283	1	12	53	214	606	1,055	336	6
Lake Forest	60,195	1,714	1,726	2	7	51	125	372	979	178	12
Lakewood	79,815	4,367	4,382	6	10	284	425	623	2,005	1,014	15
La Mesa	54,589	2,963	2,998	1	4	113	156	622	1,543	524	35

Table 8. — Number of Offenses Known to the Police, Cities and Towns 10,000 and over in Population, 1995 — Continued

City by State	Population	Crime Index total	Modified* Crime Index total	Murder and non-negligent man-slaughter	Forcible rape	Robbery	Aggravated assault	Burglary	Larceny–theft	Motor vehicle theft	Arson*
CALIFORNIA — Continued											
La Mirada	46,575	1,526	1,536	2	9	50	137	342	645	341	10
Lancaster	119,785	6,269	6,312	9	49	301	961	1,414	2,579	956	43
La Palma	16,088	755	765	—	—	22	53	129	396	155	10
La Puente	39,223	1,460	1,471	9	15	146	312	233	452	293	11
La Quinta	17,327	1,130	1,139	1	3	12	79	392	564	79	9
La Verne	33,273	1,046	1,051	1	2	19	47	263	579	135	5
Lawndale	29,056	1,545	1,576	2	7	172	281	275	452	356	31
Lemoore	15,201	750	751	1	3	9	44	155	443	95	1
Livermore	63,680	2,755	2,788	2	14	47	147	616	1,675	254	33
Lodi	52,686	3,492	3,499	2	19	68	299	462	2,234	408	7
Loma Linda	18,570	1,024	1,028	—	6	22	25	239	407	325	4
Lomita	20,810	782	788	—	3	38	159	166	285	131	6
Lompoc	41,724	2,216	2,270	—	16	70	142	440	1,418	130	54
Long Beach	436,034	30,657	30,848	80	171	2,774	2,624	5,577	14,011	5,420	191
Los Alamitos	12,073	650	652	—	5	16	28	162	354	85	2
Los Altos	28,346	476	476	—	3	18	30	114	302	9	—
Los Angeles	3,466,211	266,204	269,583	849	1,590	29,134	38,945	41,325	108,149	46,212	3,379
Los Banos	18,027	1,242	1,246	1	12	11	80	391	674	73	4
Los Gatos	29,375	860	874	1	5	17	44	170	585	38	14
Lynwood	65,134	3,587	3,639	25	24	454	742	661	857	824	52
Madera	33,883	3,288	3,296	8	46	180	391	907	1,265	491	8
Malibu	11,534	524	524	1	3	9	47	104	307	53	—
Manhattan Beach	33,455	1,770	1,771	1	5	71	59	281	1,137	216	1
Manteca	44,402	3,000	3,014	2	20	44	143	520	1,898	373	14
Marina	15,510	769	784	—	6	34	63	143	472	51	15
Martinez	32,852	1,546	1,556	2	1	25	39	382	942	155	10
Marysville	13,243	1,562	1,567	1	8	25	315	218	826	169	5
Maywood	27,486	985	990	4	5	90	125	147	403	211	5
Menlo Park	39,655	1,390	1,392	1	11	48	77	281	898	74	2
Merced	60,651	4,545	4,567	2	27	140	371	1,097	2,394	514	22
Mission Viejo	84,234	2,222	2,236	—	7	51	140	484	1,356	184	14
Millbrae	20,973	636	643	—	2	23	72	87	370	82	7
Mill Valley	13,256	504	507	—	—	2	27	104	358	13	3
Milpitas	56,208	2,466	2,467	2	22	63	92	377	1,657	253	1
Modesto	177,244	15,425	15,658	13	76	387	892	2,814	9,262	1,981	233
Monrovia	38,958	1,668	1,671	4	6	100	114	347	848	249	3
Montclair	28,687	2,885	2,890	5	15	123	150	435	1,625	532	5
Montebello	61,828	3,171	3,210	6	21	252	314	396	1,441	741	39
Monterey	29,962	2,081	2,091	2	8	52	185	414	1,305	115	10
Monterey Park	58,212	2,366	2,366	3	4	262	139	548	903	507	—
Moorpark	29,163	532	538	2	3	6	51	125	288	57	6
Moraga	16,274	270	274	—	—	2	10	61	189	8	4
Morena Valley	140,011	9,187	9,224	16	44	390	852	2,200	4,566	1,119	37
Morgan Hill	26,902	1,361	1,367	—	5	32	49	335	871	69	6
Mountain View	66,143	2,945	2,957	1	7	125	233	324	2,052	203	12
Murrieta	33,233	789	793	—	5	18	36	175	452	103	4
Napa	63,763	2,981	3,012	2	12	39	247	413	2,030	238	31
National City	57,827	4,270	4,283	10	32	286	449	670	1,877	946	13
Newark	39,767	2,867	2,879	2	6	69	172	343	2,043	232	12
Newport Beach	71,023	3,552	3,566	2	17	33	177	890	2,134	299	14
Norco	24,762	1,252	1,263	—	4	35	101	234	668	210	11
Norwalk	101,250	4,819	4,844	16	23	370	680	794	1,664	1,272	25
Novato	49,041	2,017	2,027	3	8	32	169	368	1,315	122	10
Oceanside	146,964	7,587	7,622	23	72	409	1,041	1,861	2,997	1,184	35
Ontario	135,503	10,383	10,466	21	70	550	905	1,856	4,830	2,151	83
Orange	117,372	4,936	4,976	6	15	194	368	968	2,477	908	40
Orinda	17,502	298	299	3	1	4	8	62	209	11	1
Oroville	13,185	823	823	1	6	18	37	175	412	174	—
Oxnard	146,596	7,771	7,790	11	65	419	948	1,335	4,102	891	19
Pacifica	39,705	1,120	1,128	1	8	26	191	135	683	76	8
Pacific Grove	16,604	602	604	1	3	7	63	181	326	21	2

Table 8. — Number of Offenses Known to the Police, Cities and Towns 10,000 and over in Population, 1995 — Continued

City by State	Population	Crime Index total	Modified* Crime Index total	Murder and non-negligent man-slaughter	Forcible rape	Robbery	Aggravated assault	Burglary	Larceny–theft	Motor vehicle theft	Arson*
CALIFORNIA — Continued											
Palmdale	103,943	5,134	5,184	7	38	289	823	1,067	2,123	787	50
Palm Desert	26,688	3,047	3,060	1	6	28	143	869	1,791	209	13
Palm Springs	39,834	3,627	3,652	5	29	111	359	970	1,626	527	25
Palo Alto	57,211	3,156	3,183	—	13	57	41	504	2,390	151	27
Palos Verdes Estates	14,014	236	237	—	1	3	14	68	133	17	1
Paradise	26,521	777	779	1	7	5	53	145	520	46	2
Paramount	52,471	3,737	3,769	14	10	277	570	655	1,236	975	32
Pasadena	134,844	9,399	9,456	12	53	721	635	1,713	5,232	1,033	57
Paso Robles	17,534	947	951	1	8	9	135	249	493	52	4
Perris	30,508	2,099	2,099	6	14	105	307	558	720	389	—
Petaluma	46,187	1,721	1,747	1	13	21	209	263	1,111	103	26
Pico Rivera	62,880	2,782	2,798	9	18	256	476	465	968	590	16
Piedmont	11,639	340	347	—	—	7	1	65	231	36	7
Pinole	18,547	1,034	1,034	—	5	64	102	162	558	143	—
Pittsburg	52,297	2,193	2,201	9	19	141	164	594	981	285	8
Placentia	43,218	1,385	1,402	1	5	37	101	314	728	199	17
Pleasant Hill	31,794	2,009	2,017	1	4	53	105	386	1,318	142	8
Pleasanton	57,972	2,029	2,035	2	4	22	43	343	1,449	166	6
Pomona	144,593	8,468	8,510	32	59	614	1,016	1,786	3,454	1,507	42
Porterville	32,590	2,357	2,359	3	12	44	125	527	1,299	347	2
Port Hueneme	23,084	751	752	—	3	38	67	160	433	50	1
Rancho Cucamonga	115,376	4,843	4,864	7	22	179	158	998	2,498	981	21
Rancho Mirage	10,407	662	665	2	—	7	28	239	353	33	3
Rancho Palos Verdes	44,053	678	688	—	2	18	49	169	353	87	10
Red Bluff	13,351	1,445	1,465	—	4	19	136	203	1,029	54	20
Redding	73,272	5,333	5,354	2	71	100	335	1,247	3,143	435	21
Redlands	64,850	3,658	3,677	1	18	129	312	700	1,682	816	19
Redondo Beach	64,559	3,506	3,509	4	13	119	256	672	1,989	453	3
Redwood City	68,126	3,024	3,032	6	14	109	282	394	1,883	336	8
Reedley	16,967	916	925	1	4	28	123	126	500	134	9
Rialto	83,939	4,558	4,583	10	25	290	750	1,475	963	1,045	25
Richmond	88,386	8,127	8,216	26	70	702	1,177	1,392	3,772	988	89
Ridgecrest	29,545	1,154	1,211	—	6	17	185	238	644	64	57
Riverbank	12,078	592	595	1	5	9	57	131	316	73	3
Riverside	242,859	19,683	19,927	34	117	1,010	2,648	4,232	8,545	3,097	244
Rocklin	26,349	865	866	—	—	11	29	176	549	100	1
Rohnert Park	38,741	1,827	1,848	—	15	24	106	604	964	114	21
Rosemead	52,285	2,284	2,297	6	8	228	267	537	817	421	13
Roseville	53,285	3,197	3,204	1	14	68	208	658	1,801	447	7
Sacramento	375,845	38,803	39,005	57	158	2,129	1,936	8,003	18,538	7,982	202
Salinas	120,416	8,329	8,385	15	49	494	950	1,181	4,797	843	56
San Anselmo	12,154	362	365	—	3	3	4	106	234	12	3
San Bernardino	182,632	19,319	19,507	67	101	1,442	2,318	3,991	7,897	3,503	188
San Bruno	40,757	1,754	1,754	2	7	54	71	202	1,247	171	—
San Carlos	28,216	691	694	—	3	8	21	117	508	34	3
San Clemente	45,376	1,542	1,558	1	8	44	162	306	884	137	16
San Diego	1,157,771	64,235	64,465	91	346	3,244	7,396	10,311	30,505	12,342	230
San Dimas	35,824	1,255	1,260	2	11	39	194	288	581	140	5
San Fernando	23,113	1,213	1,215	2	5	89	127	203	542	245	2
San Francisco	738,371	60,474	60,907	99	304	6,469	4,031	7,127	34,153	8,291	433
San Gabriel	38,173	1,484	1,491	4	8	145	150	292	700	185	7
Sanger	18,031	978	982	3	3	23	167	211	428	143	4
San Jacinto	20,823	1,019	1,021	—	11	32	94	398	351	133	2
San Jose	822,845	36,096	36,635	38	387	1,209	5,015	5,477	19,745	4,225	539
San Juan Capistrano	29,238	1,249	1,260	—	5	29	126	214	767	108	11
San Leandro	69,839	5,737	5,766	4	20	250	295	825	3,490	853	29
San Luis Obispo	40,510	2,031	2,139	—	20	20	276	378	1,244	93	108
San Marino	13,576	254	257	5	—	14	8	63	145	19	3
San Mateo	88,277	3,562	3,585	6	17	109	247	585	2,315	283	23
San Pablo	27,015	2,658	2,678	8	17	210	440	484	1,167	332	20
San Rafael	48,889	2,546	2,566	1	20	64	164	367	1,684	246	20

Table 8. — Number of Offenses Known to the Police, Cities and Towns 10,000 and over in Population, 1995 — Continued

City by State	Population	Crime Index total	Modified* Crime Index total	Murder and non-negligent man-slaughter	Forcible rape	Robbery	Aggravated assault	Burglary	Larceny–theft	Motor vehicle theft	Arson*
CALIFORNIA — Continued											
San Ramon	40,104	1,074	1,081	—	4	20	24	170	787	69	7
Santa Ana	292,289	15,190	15,514	72	66	1,234	1,141	2,182	7,396	3,099	324
Santa Barbara	86,056	4,075	4,090	5	33	107	432	665	2,588	245	15
Santa Clara	95,037	4,674	4,701	3	19	104	397	637	3,044	470	27
Santa Clarita	124,298	3,929	3,947	4	28	92	554	910	1,821	520	18
Santa Cruz	48,740	4,068	4,086	4	14	104	363	603	2,753	227	18
Santa Fe Springs	16,369	2,370	2,372	4	3	106	182	448	1,096	531	2
Santa Maria	66,263	3,795	3,815	5	28	98	268	614	2,534	248	20
Santa Monica	87,484	8,071	8,142	8	48	522	507	1,112	4,795	1,079	71
Santa Paula	25,823	1,303	1,314	—	10	54	114	317	720	88	11
Santa Rosa	117,550	7,325	7,392	4	64	193	422	1,183	4,925	534	67
Saratoga	30,005	537	538	—	2	9	43	114	350	19	1
Seal Beach	25,057	819	823	3	2	27	86	155	454	92	4
Seaside	32,347	1,401	1,409	3	7	84	318	143	759	87	8
Selma	16,499	1,139	1,140	—	4	40	196	223	504	172	1
Sierra Madre	11,549	210	210	—	—	2	15	48	128	17	—
Simi Valley	107,486	2,908	2,941	4	12	57	123	626	1,759	327	33
South El Monte	22,204	1,153	1,160	5	8	114	194	230	389	213	7
South Gate	92,369	4,240	4,263	15	23	455	356	802	1,251	1,338	23
South Lake Tahoe	22,227	1,413	1,423	—	6	25	107	396	807	72	10
South Pasadena	24,964	779	786	—	1	59	8	160	366	185	7
South San Francisco	56,860	2,099	2,114	1	8	68	144	265	1,336	277	15
Stanton	30,290	1,925	1,958	3	20	124	214	467	831	266	33
Stockton	223,752	20,782	20,896	42	133	1,228	1,784	3,836	10,278	3,481	114
Suisun City	27,497	1,071	1,080	—	5	38	135	248	539	106	9
Sunnyvale	120,185	3,777	3,788	3	29	110	112	459	2,714	350	11
Temecula	39,844	1,729	1,738	—	9	39	144	361	978	198	9
Temple City	33,904	892	898	—	2	53	132	232	357	116	6
Thousand Oaks	111,539	2,747	2,772	—	23	59	154	447	1,755	309	25
Torrance	138,914	7,637	7,675	5	10	393	283	1,294	4,216	1,436	38
Tracy	44,961	2,625	2,637	—	12	37	279	504	1,511	282	12
Tulare	38,757	2,358	2,433	7	13	58	333	423	1,202	322	75
Turlock	46,593	4,086	4,146	3	21	93	226	863	2,391	489	60
Tustin	58,774	3,134	3,158	3	12	76	114	656	1,914	359	24
Twenty-Nine Palms	13,572	784	794	2	14	18	60	298	315	77	10
Twin Cities	20,218	643	647	—	3	5	11	125	459	40	4
Ukiah	14,634	1,129	1,142	—	6	14	48	211	798	52	13
Union City	55,661	2,920	2,948	3	17	135	141	563	1,758	303	28
Upland	62,137	4,847	4,884	12	11	185	309	1,175	2,472	683	37
Vacaville	83,425	3,328	3,345	3	22	99	212	602	2,089	301	17
Vallejo	112,044	9,040	9,110	13	52	508	1,058	1,670	4,701	1,038	70
Ventura	96,772	4,592	4,616	1	25	119	182	1,139	2,719	407	24
Victorville	50,375	4,000	4,022	8	19	169	193	816	1,899	896	22
Visalia	85,500	6,562	6,574	5	27	160	535	999	4,156	680	12
Walnut	32,507	826	831	1	6	46	100	233	348	92	5
Walnut Creek	62,342	3,143	3,154	1	8	32	90	702	2,135	175	11
Watsonville	32,252	2,824	2,833	1	18	98	412	359	1,747	189	9
West Covina	103,817	5,502	5,576	10	24	361	253	780	2,980	1,094	74
West Hollywood	34,616	3,956	3,976	1	13	344	330	574	2,087	607	20
Westminster	80,152	4,803	4,822	6	23	208	172	870	2,466	1,058	19
West Sacramento	30,254	2,524	2,545	2	24	117	464	547	919	451	21
Whittier	80,215	3,810	3,825	4	13	228	227	677	2,075	586	15
Windsor	13,670	597	600	—	4	14	37	135	374	33	3
Woodland	43,013	1,988	2,006	2	11	30	299	420	978	248	18
Yorba Linda	61,806	1,225	1,243	—	6	19	50	219	808	123	18
Yuba City	32,604	2,776	2,787	—	18	28	305	589	1,627	209	11
Yucaipa	36,741	1,464	1,476	—	6	21	77	425	722	213	12
Yucca Valley	14,232	795	806	—	6	13	52	287	360	77	11

Table 8. — Number of Offenses Known to the Police, Cities and Towns 10,000 and over in Population, 1995 — Continued

City by State	Population	Crime Index total	Modified* Crime Index total	Murder and non-negligent man-slaughter	Forcible rape	Robbery	Aggravated assault	Burglary	Larceny-theft	Motor vehicle theft	Arson*
COLORADO											
Arvada	97,821	3,773	3,802	1	21	56	189	704	2,635	167	29
Aurora	256,957	16,902		18	138	549	1,253	2,436	11,173	1,335	
Boulder	87,743	6,423	6,455	3	29	53	103	1,209	4,757	269	32
Brighton	16,415	919	919	—	1	5	24	116	710	63	—
Broomfield	28,110	1,241	1,260	3	6	8	95	174	914	41	19
Canon City	14,346	842	845	1	13	7	7	75	704	35	3
Castle Rock	12,347	356	361	—	1	—	3	63	277	12	5
Colorado Springs	324,441	21,949	22,092	18	207	416	925	3,446	15,549	1,388	143
Commerce City	18,154	2,108	2,119	1	8	37	213	281	1,417	151	11
Denver	505,843	34,769	35,158	81	320	1,413	2,543	7,410	17,761	5,241	389
Englewood	33,538	2,506	2,543	3	14	46	127	364	1,719	233	37
Federal Heights	10,485	797	799	1	4	13	13	89	626	51	2
Fort Collins	101,416	5,573	5,618	2	66	30	360	790	4,132	193	45
Fountain	12,594	546	562	—	7	5	11	80	418	25	16
Golden	14,331	701	713	—	2	3	19	103	539	35	12
Grand Junction	32,548	3,868	3,901	3	17	38	172	527	2,964	147	33
Lafayette	17,705	900	923	—	15	4	59	148	633	41	23
Lakewood	129,167	7,348	7,405	6	49	130	361	1,153	5,207	442	57
Littleton	38,759	1,764	1,783	1	9	14	86	360	1,178	116	19
Longmont	57,664	2,922	2,944	2	25	28	55	448	2,198	166	22
Louisville[1]	17,836			—	—	4		114	364	20	8
Loveland	45,061	1,665	1,676	2	25	13	67	263	1,225	70	11
Montrose	10,224	931	939	—	5	4	17	105	780	20	8
Northglenn	28,173	1,838	1,849	—	10	14	63	178	1,448	125	11
Pueblo	102,971	7,822	7,884	8	46	182	1,131	1,468	4,475	512	62
Sterling	10,558	595	603	—	4	—	27	88	460	16	8
Thornton	64,649	4,564		1	32	46	253	591	3,381	260	
Wheat Ridge	31,657	2,222	2,237	1	5	39	60	311	1,656	150	15
CONNECTICUT											
Ansonia	18,156	449	451	—	7	16	41	50	307	28	2
Avon	13,951	269	272	—	1	—	—	56	205	7	3
Berlin	16,804	422	422	1	—	2	1	81	293	44	—
Bethel	17,806	189	189	1	1	5	16	53	102	11	—
Bloomfield	19,505	918	921	—	7	31	46	175	553	106	3
Branford	27,948	555	556	1	3	2	9	66	431	43	1
Bridgeport	133,057	10,386	10,959	33	46	840	666	2,338	3,947	2,516	573
Bristol	60,647	2,226	2,234	1	19	50	285	447	1,192	232	8
Brookfield	14,326	252	252	—	—	2	5	54	173	18	—
Cheshire	26,005	537	545	2	—	2	—	116	383	34	8
Clinton	13,159	210	212	—	—	2	2	71	135	—	2
Coventry	10,232	182	183	—	—	3	2	42	120	15	1
Cromwell	12,662	376	377	—	2	9	7	49	283	26	1
Danbury	64,675	3,742	3,754	2	10	90	50	521	2,679	390	12
Darien	18,470	329	329	—	1	6	1	57	246	18	—
Derby	12,055	682	684	—	23	9	28	136	435	51	2
East Hampton	10,746	202	202	—	—	3	5	41	146	7	—
East Hartford	50,511	2,548	2,561	—	12	93	161	417	1,475	390	13
East Haven Town	26,471	1,281	1,283	—	1	24	3	212	872	169	2
East Windsor	10,090	333	345	—	2	3	11	77	188	52	12
Enfield	45,585	1,510	1,521	1	—	10	20	268	1,042	169	11
Fairfield	54,228	1,832	1,842	2	—	19	9	377	1,238	187	10
Farmington	20,632	734	735	—	4	8	14	121	540	47	1
Glastonbury	27,934	638	638	—	6	5	3	106	492	26	—
Greenwich	59,329	1,393	1,397	—	10	17	47	175	1,046	98	4
Groton Town	35,150	957	962	2	20	17	36	157	675	50	5
Guilford	20,095	463	465	—	7	3	13	80	332	28	2
Hamden	53,089	2,713	2,713	—	18	50	25	321	1,857	442	—
Hartford	124,196	16,573	16,738	33	112	1,278	1,176	3,137	8,278	2,559	165
Madison Town	15,677	295	296	—	—	1	6	80	191	17	1
Manchester	51,265	3,108	3,139	—	28	74	86	737	2,031	152	31

See footnotes at end of table.

Table 8. — Number of Offenses Known to the Police, Cities and Towns 10,000 and over in Population, 1995 — Continued

City by State	Population	Crime Index total	Modified* Crime Index total	Murder and non-negligent man-slaughter	Forcible rape	Robbery	Aggravated assault	Burglary	Larceny–theft	Motor vehicle theft	Arson*
CONNECTICUT — Continued											
Meriden	56,928	3,427	3,428	1	5	92	94	927	2,032	276	1
Middletown	42,615	1,846	1,850	—	3	31	29	246	1,329	208	4
Milford	49,092	2,192	2,198	1	5	42	10	272	1,637	225	6
Monroe	17,150	307	312	—	—	1	20	66	203	17	5
Naugatuck	30,968	896	902	—	9	6	18	157	620	86	6
New Britain	69,887	5,186	5,192	7	16	236	329	1,338	2,660	600	6
New Canaan	18,134	216	216	—	—	2	4	42	156	12	—
New Haven	119,604	15,174	15,282	21	98	953	1,157	2,965	7,465	2,515	108
Newington	29,242	1,040	1,043	—	4	12	32	115	775	102	3
New London	22,792	1,344	1,346	2	12	73	118	205	831	103	2
New Milford	24,721	717	726	—	3	2	7	97	567	41	9
Newtown	21,093	308	309	—	—	2	6	101	188	11	1
North Branford	13,159	231	231	—	1	1	4	46	155	24	—
North Haven	22,525	848	853	1	—	10	14	133	609	81	5
Norwalk	78,710	3,987	3,994	5	7	130	121	755	2,546	423	7
Norwich	35,504	1,766	1,782	—	28	55	121	335	1,125	102	16
Orange	12,990	776	776	—	1	6	9	111	606	43	—
Plainfield	14,526	218	222	2	—	4	12	48	130	22	4
Plainville	17,412	558	558	—	4	7	7	100	383	57	—
Plymouth	12,122	342	347	—	2	3	24	84	209	20	5
Ridgefield Town	21,235	164	166	—	—	—	2	36	117	9	2
Rocky Hill	16,571	539	540	—	—	10	5	61	373	90	1
Seymour	14,465	252	255	—	2	—	24	64	144	18	3
Shelton	36,905	528	530	—	—	5	11	128	309	75	2
Simsbury	22,046	301	303	—	—	—	—	65	215	21	2
Southington	38,562	1,212	1,213	1	10	18	16	206	869	92	1
South Windsor	22,115	302	303	—	—	9	11	62	197	23	1
Stamford	107,199	6,051	6,086	4	14	231	262	935	3,999	606	35
Stonington	16,841	478	480	—	1	5	6	67	392	7	2
Stratford	50,137	1,901	1,911	2	3	56	38	409	1,169	224	10
Suffield	11,440	171	174	—	1	—	1	19	139	11	3
Torrington	33,789	827	830	—	1	10	50	130	541	95	3
Trumbull	32,501	1,140	1,151	1	—	17	7	125	891	99	11
Vernon	30,351	687	688	—	3	22	30	111	468	53	1
Wallingford	41,334	1,261	1,264	—	—	5	40	207	911	98	3
Waterbury	103,523	8,799	8,813	9	32	260	225	2,049	4,923	1,301	14
Waterford	17,850	850	853	—	6	17	22	68	701	36	3
Watertown	20,978	548	548	—	1	5	16	95	380	51	—
West Hartford	60,180	2,202	2,208	—	6	69	46	425	1,477	179	6
West Haven	52,848	2,987	2,996	2	3	62	27	508	1,946	439	9
Westport	24,779	672	680	—	2	2	19	99	516	34	8
Wethersfield	25,680	635	640	—	6	20	27	92	423	67	5
Willimantic	15,418	1,129	1,139	—	3	27	47	257	759	36	10
Wilton	16,231	203	203	—	1	1	2	50	139	10	—
Windsor	27,849	871	873	—	12	25	10	125	631	68	2
Windsor Locks	12,371	277	277	1	—	4	10	44	185	33	—
Wolcott	13,870	474	474	—	4	5	4	81	334	46	—
DELAWARE[2]											
Dover	29,190	2,533	2,569	3	25	92	134	322	1,822	135	36
DISTRICT OF COLUMBIA											
Washington	554,000	67,402	67,524	361	292	6,864	7,228	10,184	32,281	10,192	122
FLORIDA											
Altamonte Springs	36,835	2,882	2,889	2	7	84	89	435	1,988	277	7
Apopka	15,855	1,921	1,927	—	9	56	133	99	1,514	110	6
Belle Glade	16,663	2,587	2,592	1	13	109	360	638	1,287	179	5
Boca Raton	67,436	3,154	3,169	1	7	71	114	799	1,805	357	15
Boynton Beach	52,012	5,774	5,788	1	17	181	487	832	3,517	739	14

See footnotes at end of table.

Table 8. — Number of Offenses Known to the Police, Cities and Towns 10,000 and over in Population, 1995 — Continued

City by State	Population	Crime Index total	Modified* Crime Index total	Murder and non-negligent man-slaughter	Forcible rape	Robbery	Aggravated assault	Burglary	Larceny–theft	Motor vehicle theft	Arson*
FLORIDA — Continued											
Bradenton	47,463	4,281	4,287	4	36	233	488	996	2,238	286	6
Cape Coral	86,265	3,487	3,496	1	20	36	140	802	2,295	193	9
Casselberry	20,860	1,310	1,313	1	4	36	97	217	833	122	3
Clearwater	101,362	7,249	7,274	4	48	257	774	1,420	4,452	294	25
Cocoa Beach	12,252	1,127	1,129	1	3	19	39	173	844	48	2
Coconut Creek	30,116	1,290	1,298	1	7	16	53	330	725	158	8
Cooper City	28,504	724	733	—	7	18	28	141	487	43	9
Coral Springs	94,026	4,859	4,864	—	25	80	207	789	3,376	382	5
Crestview	14,658	623	626	—	5	12	50	68	459	29	3
Dania	14,152	2,350	2,357	3	8	87	184	355	1,433	280	7
Davie	58,189	3,413	3,420	1	10	68	195	690	2,128	321	7
Daytona Beach	65,631	7,027	7,050	6	73	310	836	1,678	3,487	637	23
Deerfield Beach	47,563	3,223	3,230	4	26	74	211	540	1,939	429	7
De Land	18,329	2,646	2,648	—	10	74	181	614	1,629	138	2
Delray Beach	51,805	6,767	6,779	—	28	231	570	1,197	3,924	817	12
Edgewater	18,345	667	671	—	3	1	59	74	502	28	4
Eustis	15,337	441	442	—	2	2	44	53	308	32	1
Fernandina Beach	10,495	635	637	2	5	17	63	102	420	26	2
Fort Lauderdale	165,328	25,036	25,102	27	102	1,113	1,051	4,876	14,836	3,031	66
Fort Myers	51,259	6,327	6,335	7	54	334	795	1,047	3,212	878	8
Fort Pierce	37,336	5,075	5,095	11	54	231	694	1,383	2,291	411	20
Fort Walton Beach	24,576	1,219	1,224	1	11	31	80	191	852	53	5
Gainesville	89,146	10,003	10,029	8	61	329	936	1,829	6,281	559	26
Gulfport	11,795	1,117	1,123	1	4	60	117	229	660	46	6
Hallandale	30,437	2,719	2,728	1	15	156	326	602	1,265	354	9
Hialeah	197,084	15,654	15,718	17	41	809	993	2,433	7,637	3,724	64
Holly Hill	11,500	918	918	2	3	22	34	224	578	55	—
Hollywood	126,900	12,146	12,164	5	63	518	537	2,024	7,515	1,484	18
Jacksonville	679,148	61,129	61,524	86	625	2,920	5,965	12,491	33,306	5,736	395
Jacksonville Beach	18,439	1,605	1,607	1	14	48	143	281	1,041	77	2
Jupiter	27,993	1,461	1,462	—	3	22	68	218	1,048	102	1
Key West	25,067	3,051	3,051	1	10	87	72	582	1,898	401	—
Kissimmee	36,962	4,094	4,114	5	30	156	365	864	2,455	219	20
Lady Lake	14,709	176	178	—	1	3	21	62	83	6	2
Lake City	10,189	1,475	1,477	—	5	43	168	222	989	48	2
Lakeland	72,343	9,941	9,960	2	50	315	647	2,097	5,601	1,229	19
Lake Wales	10,411	897	898	1	—	23	73	208	531	61	1
Lake Worth	32,018	4,093	4,094	2	8	159	261	1,011	2,172	480	1
Largo	68,755	3,160	3,168	3	24	73	291	644	2,009	116	8
Lauderdale Lakes	28,067	2,958	2,966	2	17	145	216	478	1,529	571	8
Leesburg	19,713	1,471	1,473	1	9	37	171	358	835	60	2
Lighthouse Point	10,640	345	345	—	1	5	5	49	258	27	—
Margate	48,174	2,519	2,528	1	16	53	133	581	1,485	250	9
Melbourne	69,062	5,817	5,849	3	43	133	610	1,198	3,476	354	32
Miami	378,720	59,170	59,407	110	198	5,676	6,943	9,874	27,537	8,832	237
Miami Beach	91,529	16,897	16,911	1	52	707	803	2,501	10,177	2,656	14
Miami Shores	11,015	993	994	—	2	59	40	229	498	165	1
Miami Springs	13,996	1,293	1,294	1	3	81	61	225	775	147	1
Miramar	48,717	2,981	2,993	3	19	146	202	660	1,600	351	12
Naples	21,597	1,390	1,391	—	2	20	106	214	994	54	1
New Port Richey	15,322	894	895	—	1	4	76	156	623	34	1
New Smyrna Beach	18,049	863	866	—	4	17	56	181	559	46	3
Niceville	12,045	281	283	—	1	2	20	45	207	6	2
North Lauderdale	27,831	1,570	1,573	1	7	81	83	322	923	153	3
North Miami	54,321	6,812	6,824	8	24	517	412	1,638	3,045	1,168	12
North Miama Beach	38,909	3,391	3,399	3	13	222	211	1,008	1,417	517	8
North Palm Beach	11,160	543	545	—	—	11	16	144	338	34	2
North Port	14,437	403	404	—	4	4	37	87	263	8	1
Oakland Park	29,604	4,025	4,026	1	13	150	270	730	2,312	549	1
Ocala	54,037	6,847	6,863	3	43	224	556	1,169	4,549	303	16
Ocoee	15,209	1,012	1,014	—	9	17	97	229	586	74	2

Table 8. — Number of Offenses Known to the Police, Cities and Towns 10,000 and over in Population, 1995 — Continued

City by State	Population	Crime Index total	Modified* Crime Index total	Murder and non-negligent man-slaughter	Forcible rape	Robbery	Aggravated assault	Burglary	Larceny-theft	Motor vehicle theft	Arson*
FLORIDA — Continued											
Opa Locka	16,592	3,001	3,010	5	27	265	376	632	1,315	381	9
Orange Park	10,492	440	440	—	4	9	22	99	273	33	—
Orlando	179,649	20,750	20,806	19	141	1,048	2,564	3,862	11,255	1,861	56
Ormond Beach	32,235	1,298	1,300	—	6	22	8	292	875	95	2
Oviedo	14,015	728	733	—	3	4	56	163	479	23	5
Palatka	11,131	1,789	1,793	1	8	72	215	367	1,044	82	4
Palm Bay	76,286	4,010	4,011	2	14	50	430	784	2,520	210	1
Palmetto	10,259	843	845	—	5	29	51	172	543	43	2
Panama City	38,571	3,304	3,314	3	24	81	311	589	2,150	146	10
Pembroke Pines	82,742	4,502	4,507	—	7	122	87	495	3,341	450	5
Pensacola	60,941	4,584	4,599	6	34	141	524	931	2,747	201	15
Pinellas Park	45,756	3,255	3,276	—	15	68	226	545	2,260	141	21
Plantation	75,889	6,047	6,065	5	23	140	212	725	4,126	816	18
Plant City	23,341	2,256	2,263	1	22	69	312	424	1,151	277	7
Pompano Beach	76,875	8,772	8,784	3	30	402	1,060	2,019	4,487	771	12
Port Orange	40,133	864	866	—	6	4	45	3	798	8	2
Port St. Lucie	71,473	2,701	2,714	—	22	30	158	740	1,651	100	13
Punta Gorda	12,286	413	413	—	1	8	26	77	274	27	—
Riviera Beach	27,065	4,072	4,100	—	24	244	554	1,660	1,279	311	28
Rockledge	18,013	1,156	1,158	1	5	21	72	234	760	63	2
Royal Palm Beach	19,668	828	829	—	2	7	23	143	577	76	1
Safety Harbor	16,169	656	661	—	1	10	41	161	414	29	5
St. Cloud	14,995	978	986	—	10	1	61	233	642	31	8
St. Petersburg	242,228	22,899	23,031	30	172	1,417	3,555	4,217	12,076	1,432	132
Sanford	34,987	3,114	3,117	3	19	170	351	806	1,496	269	3
Sarasota	55,241	6,236	6,260	7	45	346	480	1,297	3,783	278	24
Satellite Beach	10,805	429	430	—	2	1	13	81	323	9	1
Sebastian	11,766	733	735	—	—	4	41	166	508	14	2
South Daytona	12,504	320	320	—	1	3	29	125	124	38	—
South Miami	11,029	1,214	1,216	1	1	75	97	238	661	141	2
Stuart	12,780	1,292	1,298	2	6	19	106	207	905	47	6
Sunrise	76,183	5,085	5,092	1	16	159	167	681	3,498	563	7
Sweetwater	14,715	161	161	—	—	—	21	22	66	52	—
Tallahassee	135,759	16,611	16,641	12	119	607	1,191	2,800	10,751	1,131	30
Tamarac	48,546	2,330	2,333	1	5	53	82	341	1,496	352	3
Tampa	289,882	41,112	41,324	47	277	2,626	5,785	6,622	19,773	5,982	212
Tarpon Springs	19,679	973	978	—	11	26	153	174	579	30	5
Temple Terrace	16,604	539	539	1	1	27	10	75	377	48	—
Titusville	41,688	2,872	2,877	—	13	64	358	652	1,618	167	5
Venice	16,977	541	543	2	5	1	44	67	405	17	2
Vero Beach	18,414	1,425	1,427	3	10	27	77	270	980	58	2
West Palm Beach	76,608	12,086	12,107	29	55	624	582	2,071	7,138	1,587	21
Wilton Manors	12,044	1,167	1,171	1	4	36	49	229	722	126	4
Winter Garden	11,286	902	906	—	9	23	115	182	513	60	4
Winter Park	23,786	1,880	1,885	1	9	66	125	369	1,208	102	5
Winter Springs	28,773	821	825	1	10	16	87	207	463	37	4
GEORGIA											
Albany	82,739	8,151	8,192	14	70	335	351	1,905	5,105	371	41
Alpharetta	21,347	939	940	—	1	5	6	101	762	64	1
Americus	17,769	1,138	1,141	3	—	28	3	134	941	29	3
Athens-Clarke County	91,242	7,133	7,155	10	49	224	502	1,039	4,889	420	22
Atlanta	404,337	69,011	69,237	184	441	5,260	8,859	11,694	34,221	8,352	226
Augusta	44,358	4,233	4,243	7	17	175	176	1,043	2,250	565	10
Bainbridge	11,463	1,246	1,248	—	4	32	62	229	882	37	2
Brunswick	18,091	2,100	2,107	4	14	70	216	423	1,287	86	7
Carrollton	17,497	1,644	1,646	1	15	29	90	174	1,265	70	2
Cartersville	13,682	768	772	—	5	23	101	167	427	45	4
College Park	22,934	3,460	3,460	12	15	151	189	571	1,743	779	—
Columbus	190,328	12,417	12,441	20	34	432	497	2,201	8,350	883	24
Cordele[1]	12,143			2	7	25		155	743	39	4

See footnotes at end of table.

Table 8. — Number of Offenses Known to the Police, Cities and Towns 10,000 and over in Population, 1995 — Continued

City by State	Population	Crime Index total	Modified* Crime Index total	Murder and non-negligent man-slaughter	Forcible rape	Robbery	Aggravated assault	Burglary	Larceny–theft	Motor vehicle theft	Arson*
GEORGIA — Continued											
Covington	11,614	1,266	1,267	—	7	25	84	139	954	57	1
Dalton	22,841	1,451	1,457	2	4	15	146	139	1,042	103	6
Douglas	11,716	1,900	1,905	1	4	33	240	238	1,319	65	5
Douglasville	13,959	1,426	1,434	—	10	17	109	70	1,104	116	8
Dublin	18,295	1,308	1,308	2	5	30	74	209	936	52	—
Duluth	12,862	471	471	—	2	12	15	96	317	29	—
East Point	33,281	4,257	4,283	9	25	212	139	942	2,302	628	26
Forest Park	16,710	2,200	2,209	3	20	101	136	284	1,394	262	9
Gainesville	19,878	2,164	2,177	—	11	35	87	261	1,668	102	13
Griffin	22,868	2,432	2,442	2	22	73	280	337	1,551	167	10
Hinesville	27,567	2,105	2,105	3	13	41	61	277	1,630	80	—
Jesup	10,290	623		—	4	11	58	150	382	18	—
Kennesaw	10,625	317	317	—	2	3	14	37	259	2	—
La Grange	27,591	3,098	3,110	3	12	63	165	480	2,048	327	12
Lawrenceville	21,691	1,056	1,068	1	2	7	52	152	760	82	12
Lilburn	10,218	550	552	3	—	5	7	70	429	36	2
Macon	111,450	11,070	11,120	25	82	390	371	1,901	7,386	915	50
Marietta	51,330	6,042	6,059	8	31	167	438	692	4,023	683	17
Milledgeville	18,756	1,195	1,199	—	8	36	94	171	855	31	4
Monroe	13,563	662	662	—	5	4	30	105	500	18	—
Moultrie	15,720	1,292	1,305	—	7	64	76	259	821	65	13
Newnan	15,609	1,272	1,273	2	2	34	41	201	906	86	1
Peachtree City	25,600	333	334	—	—	4	2	28	280	19	1
Perry	10,417	692	695	—	1	8	2	84	595	2	3
Powder Springs	10,763	262	262	—	1	5	15	40	186	15	—
Riverdale	10,380	1,216	1,216	2	3	40	25	121	902	123	—
Rome	31,843	3,873	3,909	4	13	93	444	650	2,557	112	36
Roswell	56,044	2,603	2,608	—	5	37	45	403	1,940	173	5
St. Marys	11,715	780	790	1	3	5	22	101	630	18	10
Savannah	143,505	12,016	12,079	27	76	840	447	1,946	7,669	1,011	63
Smyrna	33,076	2,928	2,929	4	23	95	64	369	2,042	331	1
Snellville	14,752	534	534	—	1	1	1	71	449	11	—
Statesboro	18,669	1,177	1,177	1	4	30	29	186	876	51	—
Thomasville	18,774	1,787	1,799	2	3	42	49	384	1,221	86	12
Tifton	14,980	1,656	1,656	2	5	47	130	227	1,194	51	—
Valdosta	45,713	3,478	3,481	4	31	124	234	660	2,267	158	3
Vidalia	11,797	1,126	1,131	5	11	29	145	155	733	48	5
Warner Robins	48,680	3,554	3,554	3	40	90	137	585	2,481	218	—
Waycross	17,931	1,664	1,674	1	3	29	42	179	1,360	50	10
HAWAII											
Hilo	40,578	2,618	2,625	4	29	34	71	452	1,936	92	7
Honolulu	880,266	67,145	67,444	38	217	1,371	1,256	10,127	46,696	7,440	299
IDAHO											
Blackfoot	11,049	599	605	1	3	1	13	108	441	32	6
Boise	149,856	8,873	8,926	3	53	76	513	1,424	6,311	493	53
Caldwell	24,604	1,822	1,839	—	6	8	133	180	1,400	95	17
Coeur d'Alene	29,210	2,817	2,846	2	24	14	242	395	2,013	127	29
Idaho Falls	51,250	3,260	3,275	2	13	18	201	466	2,402	158	15
Lewiston	30,893	1,835	1,847	1	7	9	38	267	1,428	85	12
Meridian	14,951	930	933	—	3	2	29	147	700	49	3
Moscow	19,409	762	765	4	8	3	12	54	667	14	3
Nampa	36,268	3,086	3,113	2	22	17	157	439	2,317	132	27
Pocatello	50,948	2,522	2,548	3	22	24	157	405	1,759	152	26
Post Falls	10,651	1,004	1,011	—	3	4	28	159	769	41	7
Rexburg	14,890	481	481	—	2	—	9	19	442	9	—
Twin Falls	32,403	2,963	2,973	2	9	15	119	555	2,120	143	10

Table 8. — Number of Offenses Known to the Police, Cities and Towns 10,000 and over in Population, 1995 — Continued

City by State	Population	Crime Index total	Modified* Crime Index total	Murder and non-negligent man-slaughter	Forcible rape	Robbery	Aggravated assault	Burglary	Larceny–theft	Motor vehicle theft	Arson*
ILLINOIS[2, 3]											
Aurora	113,058			24		231	576	1,151	3,756	492	65
Chicago	2,749,881			824		30,086	39,205	40,239	121,487	36,197	1,241
Rockford	144,214			19		751	962	3,616	8,681	1,301	60
Springfield	106,641			11		564	1,024	2,487	6,183	515	57
INDIANA											
Bedford	14,289	772	776	1	5	4	86	84	545	47	4
Beech Grove	13,147	569	576	—	2	9	5	86	419	48	7
Bloomington	63,114	3,134	3,144	1	21	39	499	478	1,943	153	10
Carmel	31,689	862	874	1	5	2	40	70	710	34	12
Clarksville	21,777	2,311	2,313	1	10	21	18	137	1,941	183	2
Connersville	16,744	1,027		—	1	9	41	177	728	71	
Crawfordsville	14,392	989	994	—	5	8	25	151	771	29	5
Crown Point	18,186	519	522	—	1	—	100	63	312	43	3
Dyer	12,035	343	343	—	1	5	21	26	263	27	—
Evansville	130,600	7,478	7,550	5	33	154	532	1,537	4,772	445	72
Fort Wayne	184,985	12,765	12,864	23	84	594	230	1,800	8,081	1,953	99
Goshen	25,570	1,536	1,553	2	10	15	111	185	1,121	92	17
Greenfield	13,140	239	243	—	—	4	1	31	187	16	4
Greenwood	30,601	1,130	1,132	—	3	7	1	90	965	64	2
Griffith	18,708	911	914	1	3	15	90	75	591	136	3
Hammond	83,571	7,176	7,246	15	43	349	705	1,193	3,572	1,299	70
Highland	22,813	1,094	1,096	1	1	9	46	77	774	186	2
Hobart	24,428	1,699	1,708	—	2	18	2	150	1,296	231	9
Huntington	17,093	666	668	2	—	2	192	61	386	23	2
Indianapolis[4]		36,469	36,807	99	457	2,523	3,636	7,797	15,941	6,016	338
Jasper	10,951	339	340	1	1	2	48	35	244	8	1
Kokomo	46,435	2,600	2,610	3	25	40	87	317	2,044	84	10
Lafayette	46,283	3,221	3,236	1	26	36	99	500	2,411	148	15
Lake Station	14,306	678	681	1	—	12	10	80	483	92	3
La Porte	23,116	1,390	1,390	—	3	6	298	101	922	60	—
Lawrence	27,417	1,318	1,323	2	4	70	219	248	629	146	5
Marion	32,598	2,992	2,996	1	28	60	564	414	1,787	138	4
Martinsville	12,450	571	571	—	1	2	34	70	430	34	—
Merrillville	27,897	1,338	1,339	—	2	33	60	67	940	236	1
Michigan City	34,199	2,741	2,769	2	14	109	70	497	1,690	359	28
Muncie	72,040	3,565	3,584	2	17	136	163	729	2,371	147	19
Munster	20,582	772	774	—	—	10	33	36	590	103	2
New Albany	38,256	2,929	2,964	—	3	26	237	435	2,081	147	35
New Castle	18,882	1,403	1,405	1	7	2	8	215	1,119	51	2
New Haven	11,071	287	288	1	4	13	13	39	189	28	1
Noblesville	20,231	619	619	—	2	2	80	52	463	20	—
Plainfield	15,772	520	521	—	2	2	11	52	424	29	1
Portage	31,321	1,331	1,342	3	9	17	38	168	919	177	11
Richmond	39,154	2,252	2,374	2	12	46	57	372	1,645	118	122
Schererville	24,703	706	707	—	—	5	8	66	541	86	1
South Bend	106,024	10,013	10,135	26	86	389	479	2,406	5,920	707	122
Speedway	12,363	1,082	1,083	—	16	35	5	52	893	81	1
Terre Haute	60,733	5,448	5,457	7	32	116	181	1,078	3,751	283	9
Valparaiso	26,170	1,007	1,015	—	3	4	81	99	779	41	8
Vincennes	19,964	922	927	2	8	3	13	213	657	26	5
Wabash	12,359	309	312	1	—	—	57	44	191	16	3
Warsaw	13,048	812	813	—	5	7	20	85	664	31	1
IOWA											
Ames	46,776	1,673	1,678	—	5	4	39	150	1,418	57	5
Ankeny	21,305	746	748	—	—	—	9	82	640	15	2
Bettendorf	30,780	1,230	1,237	1	6	13	131	187	830	62	7
Boone	12,736	529	535	—	—	—	7	34	467	21	6
Burlington	27,699	2,098	2,107	—	4	28	125	462	1,373	106	9
Cedar Falls	34,063	1,424	1,436	—	—	15	85	180	1,093	51	12

See footnotes at end of table.

Table 8. — Number of Offenses Known to the Police, Cities and Towns 10,000 and over in Population, 1995 — Continued

City by State	Population	Crime Index total	Modified* Crime Index total	Murder and non-negligent man-slaughter	Forcible rape	Robbery	Aggravated assault	Burglary	Larceny–theft	Motor vehicle theft	Arson*
IOWA — Continued											
Coralville	11,707	608	614	—	3	3	6	97	482	17	6
Davenport	97,410	9,355	9,416	6	56	376	1,329	1,570	5,464	554	61
Des Moines	194,654	16,108	16,272	19	127	312	547	1,933	11,911	1,259	164
Dubuque	59,355	1,784	1,807	—	8	6	11	382	1,296	81	23
Fairfield	10,303	454	456	—	2	1	21	123	293	14	2
Fort Dodge	25,415	1,916	1,927	—	9	35	145	335	1,291	101	11
Fort Madison	12,457	648	651	—	1	6	5	99	513	24	3
Indianola	12,611	478	484	—	—	—	11	81	368	18	6
Iowa City	60,934	2,654	2,667	—	15	33	199	480	1,852	75	13
Marion	22,654	713	722	1	—	2	10	76	604	20	9
Marshalltown	25,052	1,113	1,121	—	2	6	99	196	760	50	8
Mason City	28,949	2,635	2,640	—	10	20	292	405	1,838	70	5
Muscatine	24,046	1,399	1,405	1	17	8	120	451	746	56	6
Newton	14,983	738	740	—	—	3	7	89	591	48	2
Oskaloosa	11,118	307	310	—	1	2	30	60	196	18	3
Ottumwa	24,742	1,471	1,476	1	1	5	52	259	1,111	42	5
Sioux City	83,115	8,178	8,223	2	52	129	1,246	1,351	4,956	442	45
Spencer	11,192	294	294	—	—	—	3	14	268	9	—
Urbandale	28,379	1,032	1,038	—	—	10	9	115	849	49	6
Waterloo	66,843	5,445	5,497	2	38	126	293	1,258	3,465	263	52
West Des Moines	37,414	1,794	1,805	—	—	16	97	294	1,291	96	11
KANSAS[2]											
Topeka	121,165	15,931		9	89	504	905	5,894	7,535	995	
Wichita	311,675	25,625		41	203	895	1,046	5,364	15,429	2,647	
KENTUCKY[5]											
Ashland	24,168	1,267	1,267	—	6	9	68	221	914	49	—
Bowling Green	45,842	3,574	3,579	2	34	87	210	657	2,412	172	5
Campbellsville	22,606	473	473	1	3	13	13	110	303	30	—
Covington	42,190	3,533	3,634	3	27	179	156	805	2,171	192	101
Danville	15,789	755	757	1	4	16	33	145	525	31	2
Elizabethtown	20,536	1,259	1,266	2	1	21	104	156	917	58	7
Erlanger	16,133	503	503	—	3	9	9	53	400	29	—
Florence	21,979	1,378	1,378	—	2	29	40	159	1,090	58	—
Fort Thomas	16,258	196	197	—	1	—	3	50	135	7	1
Frankfort	28,955	1,324	1,327	3	8	35	41	209	953	75	3
Georgetown	13,037	945	948	—	9	5	53	142	697	39	3
Glasgow	13,413	51	51	—	1	—	1	11	21	17	—
Henderson	27,093	1,723	1,736	1	18	38	75	327	1,170	94	13
Hopkinsville	32,561	2,040	2,058	6	19	75	79	434	1,337	90	18
Independence	12,086	190	191	—	1	2	3	52	120	12	1
Lexington	239,660	15,933	16,041	14	131	636	1,318	2,978	9,912	944	108
Louisville	272,638	19,491	19,873	50	135	1,592	1,483	4,471	8,800	2,960	382
Madisonville	19,008	1,494	1,502	2	6	8	300	155	950	73	8
Mayfield	10,343	290	293	1	8	12	25	66	164	14	3
Middlesboro	10,822	740	742	2	3	4	13	108	572	38	2
Murray	14,993	528	529	—	1	1	19	87	394	26	1
Newport	18,546	1,603	1,612	2	7	38	97	331	1,039	89	9
Nicholasville	16,259	812	813	—	1	8	17	123	605	58	1
Owensboro	54,107	3,136		3	14	44	43	522	2,400	110	
Paducah	26,979	2,591	2,598	3	17	65	183	442	1,723	158	7
Radcliff	20,050	844	846	3	10	24	116	190	483	18	2
Richmond	24,047	1,277	1,281	1	10	23	53	230	868	92	4
St. Matthews	15,644	869	870	—	4	24	4	95	687	55	1
Shively	15,298	839	839	—	6	59	8	172	460	134	—
Somerset	12,183	827	830	1	5	5	40	94	651	31	3
LOUISIANA											
Abbeville	11,867	674		3	4	14	72	182	398	1	
Alexandria	46,269	4,926	4,931	7	27	107	527	863	3,186	209	5

See footnotes at end of table.

Table 8. — Number of Offenses Known to the Police, Cities and Towns 10,000 and over in Population, 1995 — Continued

City by State	Population	Crime Index total	Modified* Crime Index total	Murder and non-negligent man-slaughter	Forcible rape	Robbery	Aggravated assault	Burglary	Larceny-theft	Motor vehicle theft	Arson*
LOUISIANA — Continued											
Bastrop	14,794	1,053	1,055	1	3	37	79	196	711	26	2
Baton Rouge	229,027	30,794	31,002	65	173	1,394	4,919	5,164	15,796	3,283	208
Bogalusa	15,008	1,419	1,436	3	7	26	101	317	922	43	17
Bossier City	54,759	3,495	3,520	6	16	51	404	518	2,344	156	25
Crowley	14,577	799	799	1	1	5	94	119	548	31	—
De Ridder	10,256	346		—	1	3	30	40	271	1	
Eunice	11,497	756	757	1	3	5	226	188	311	22	1
Gretna	17,479	1,636	1,641	3	16	118	140	378	767	214	5
Hammond	17,764	3,875	3,887	—	26	114	153	616	2,704	262	12
Houma	31,507	1,600	1,601	—	16	68	154	282	1,000	80	1
Jennings	11,951	1,153	1,153	2	3	24	187	147	773	17	—
Kenner	73,347	5,503	5,503	6	28	198	496	763	3,317	695	
Lafayette	102,921	10,006	10,032	8	63	279	672	1,624	6,680	680	26
Lake Charles	72,877	5,510	5,530	9	44	171	443	972	3,377	494	20
Minden	13,900	489	491	—	4	8	49	119	292	17	2
Monroe	57,406	6,940	6,940	7	36	107	867	1,145	4,576	202	—
Morgan City	14,019	740	747	—	6	30	7	188	474	35	7
Natchitoches	16,867	1,451	1,452	1	17	45	158	281	908	41	1
New Iberia	33,868	1,383	1,383	2	2	28	47	430	813	61	—
New Orleans	487,179	53,399		363	487	5,349	4,677	10,236	22,454	9,833	
Opelousas	19,425	1,457	1,457	1	10	31	91	332	922	70	—
Pineville	12,087	938	940	1	1	5	24	193	680	34	2
Ruston	20,248	1,629	1,630	1	5	25	150	305	1,117	26	1
Shreveport	199,007	22,338	22,538	61	112	776	1,643	3,787	14,637	1,322	200
Slidell	29,854	2,701	2,701	—	9	44	253	336	1,884	175	—
Thibodaux	14,300	916	919	—	4	20	201	167	491	33	3
West Monroe	14,439	1,277	1,279	—	6	15	72	108	1,019	57	2
Westwego	10,996	1,044	1,051	2	7	46	107	215	585	82	7
MAINE											
Auburn	23,382	838	838	1	2	3	1	149	647	35	—
Augusta	19,786	1,159	1,168	—	3	11	16	216	858	55	9
Bangor	32,029	1,583	1,595	1	6	20	14	151	1,343	48	12
Biddeford	20,432	1,361	1,366	—	12	11	11	267	1,001	59	5
Brunswick	21,093	618	626	—	2	2	5	92	500	17	8
Gorham	11,960	312	313	—	—	—	17	85	194	16	1
Lewiston	37,415	2,485	2,501	4	18	63	65	535	1,752	48	16
Orono	10,598	133	133	—	—	2	1	18	110	2	—
Portland	61,803	4,814	4,904	3	70	107	280	984	3,133	237	90
Presque Isle	10,042	343	344	—	—	—	2	38	296	7	1
Saco	15,398	740	744	—	3	8	12	204	492	21	4
Sanford	20,796	903	903	1	2	6	10	221	618	45	—
Scarborough	12,629	564	564	1	3	3	20	107	413	17	—
South Portland	22,614	1,477	1,477	—	1	15	26	150	1,254	31	—
Waterville	16,246	782	782	—	7	5	13	102	625	30	—
Westbrook	15,749	776	785	—	1	6	9	137	548	75	9
Windham	13,134	499	502	—	1	3	8	97	369	21	3
York	11,589	333	333	—	1	1	1	74	245	11	—
MARYLAND											
Aberdeen	13,554	930	938	1	12	25	90	107	653	42	8
Annapolis	35,421	2,911	2,942	2	18	177	241	511	1,826	136	31
Baltimore	712,209	94,855	95,760	325	683	11,353	9,134	16,569	45,619	11,172	905
Baltimore City Sheriff		1	1	—	—	—	1	—	—	—	—
Cambridge	11,756	882	891	2	7	37	135	157	513	31	9
Cumberland	24,072	1,360	1,373	—	7	12	257	201	850	33	13
Easton	11,054	841	847	1	4	12	99	133	560	32	6
Frederick	46,965	2,593	2,610	3	18	116	376	350	1,596	134	17
Greenbelt	20,859	1,472		1	8	59	49	142	994	219	
Hagerstown	38,786	2,132	2,180	2	14	57	222	340	1,374	123	48
Hyattsville	14,636	1,070		—	3	63	24	166	694	120	

Table 8. — Number of Offenses Known to the Police, Cities and Towns 10,000 and over in Population, 1995 — Continued

City by State	Population	Crime Index total	Modified* Crime Index total	Murder and non-negligent man-slaughter	Forcible rape	Robbery	Aggravated assault	Burglary	Larceny-theft	Motor vehicle theft	Arson*
MARYLAND — Continued											
Laurel	21,722	1,366		2	3	79	38	171	933	140	
Salisbury	22,363	3,081	3,099	2	28	155	279	604	1,867	146	18
Takoma Park (Montgomery County)	12,839	610		1	3	56	23	121	327	79	
Takoma Park (Prince George's County)	5,141	522		—	4	48	18	94	279	79	
Westminster	14,616	1,145	1,164	—	2	18	42	163	870	50	19
MASSACHUSETTS											
Acushnet	10,070	318	321	—	2	2	119	74	106	15	3
Agawam	27,722	693	711	—	7	5	82	67	425	107	18
Andover	30,874	914	927	—	1	6	23	144	618	122	13
Arlington	46,272	603	610	—	4	15	64	100	356	64	7
Barnstable	42,811	2,119	2,126	3	25	21	825	497	636	112	7
Belchertown	10,916	192	203	—	3	—	27	42	111	9	11
Bellingham	15,323	388	391	—	1	1	49	98	213	26	3
Belmont	25,630	338	342	—	—	5	79	70	163	21	4
Beverly	38,966	1,353	1,353	—	7	23	8	603	597	115	—
Boston	550,715	52,278	52,905	96	379	3,597	5,497	6,671	26,002	10,036	627
Bourne	17,033	857	873	—	6	9	184	161	436	61	16
Braintree	34,855	1,318	1,330	1	4	30	97	188	748	250	12
Bridgewater	22,596	269	271	—	1	2	32	51	150	33	2
Brockton	87,888	6,359	6,444	6	39	312	870	1,522	2,341	1,269	85
Brookline	56,367	1,875	1,886	—	4	41	217	176	1,182	255	11
Burlington	24,158	990		—	2	8	45	104	686	145	
Cambridge	100,428	5,606	5,630	3	35	295	463	953	3,313	544	24
Carver	11,261	339	341	—	2	3	17	99	177	41	2
Chelmsford	33,574	816	820	—	6	3	13	114	594	86	4
Chelsea	25,866	3,050	3,071	2	22	170	1,073	469	789	525	21
Clinton	13,774	414	420	1	3	5	85	51	244	25	6
Concord	17,703	250	251	—	1	1	12	32	204	—	1
Danvers	25,602	1,267	1,271	—	3	16	26	161	924	137	4
Dartmouth	28,691	1,849	1,858	—	7	10	272	491	953	116	9
Dedham	24,498	677	701	—	3	9	31	73	416	145	24
Dennis	14,700	802	804	—	1	5	53	336	378	29	2
Dracut	26,536	706	717	—	5	12	40	115	360	174	11
Duxbury	14,775	93	96	—	1	—	6	16	66	4	3
East Bridgewater	11,808	344	345	—	2	6	31	83	184	38	1
East Longmeadow	13,728	515	515	—	—	8	23	71	355	58	—
Easton	20,877	449	454	—	1	5	8	91	291	53	5
Everett	34,325	1,638	1,668	1	9	60	148	430	575	415	30
Fairhaven	17,005	891	913	—	—	9	177	229	432	44	22
Fall River	89,913	4,024	4,541	2	29	149	388	1,019	2,061	376	517
Fitchburg	36,926	2,357	2,400	3	44	71	481	634	937	187	43
Foxborough	15,075	334	355	—	1	1	2	73	234	23	21
Framingham	67,381	1,972	1,985	4	13	44	132	539	1,131	109	13
Franklin	25,958	417	417	1	8	1	34	55	295	23	—
Gloucester	29,256	904	976	1	3	1	122	214	489	74	72
Grafton	13,580	230	256	—	2	3	83	59	71	12	26
Greenfield	18,940	976	977	2	11	16	240	135	525	47	1
Harvard	12,844	63	64	—	1	—	2	17	41	2	1
Harwich	10,894	403	407	—	—	2	29	148	210	14	4
Haverhill	53,251	3,189	3,214	1	18	46	253	964	1,346	561	25
Hingham	21,078	431	445	—	4	7	19	85	287	29	14
Holden	15,239	196	196	1	2	1	51	30	105	6	—
Holliston	13,400	119	119	—	—	—	1	21	95	2	—
Hull	11,128	264	265	—	1	—	63	51	136	13	1
Ipswich	12,572	295	295	—	2	5	10	72	201	5	—
Lawrence	63,461	5,688	5,764	6	13	283	870	1,234	1,349	1,933	76
Leicester	10,616	206	217	—	—	1	15	46	109	35	11
Leominster	38,448	1,724	1,739	—	11	27	107	420	1,024	135	15
Lexington	30,039	416	419	—	—	3	—	80	321	12	3
Longmeadow	15,886	266	266	—	1	1	3	23	221	17	—

Table 8. — Number of Offenses Known to the Police, Cities and Towns 10,000 and over in Population, 1995 — Continued

City by State	Population	Crime Index total	Modified* Crime Index total	Murder and non-negligent man-slaughter	Forcible rape	Robbery	Aggravated assault	Burglary	Larceny–theft	Motor vehicle theft	Arson*
MASSACHUSETTS — Continued											
Lowell	96,578	6,266	6,334	8	68	226	1,226	1,159	2,449	1,130	68
Ludlow	19,329	468	473	—	2	12	26	104	245	79	5
Lynn	78,739	6,225	6,269	9	17	333	1,053	1,086	2,384	1,343	44
Malden	52,085	1,979	1,986	—	10	74	373	423	727	372	7
Mansfield	17,462	495	495	—	4	4	96	85	262	44	—
Marblehead	21,149	352	355	—	4	1	11	56	268	12	3
Marlborough	33,459	692	706	—	12	4	31	123	479	43	14
Marshfield	22,897	465	465	—	1	1	48	73	306	36	—
Medfield	10,846	105	105	—	5	—	5	30	55	10	—
Medford	55,974	1,940	1,949	1	10	27	434	297	946	225	9
Medway	10,228	175	175	—	—	—	25	57	83	10	—
Melrose	27,372	525	533	—	2	13	2	127	336	45	8
Methuen	41,187	1,705	1,783	—	19	33	67	171	889	526	78
Milford	26,419	245	253	—	—	3	—	59	118	65	8
Millbury	12,740	214	214	—	1	4	65	63	63	18	—
Milton	26,497	347	349	1	—	10	8	67	232	29	2
Natick	31,632	710	711	—	5	1	15	94	509	86	1
Needham	28,386	293	298	—	3	2	26	38	205	19	5
New Bedford	95,139	5,155	5,225	6	64	237	849	1,498	1,858	643	70
Newton	85,824	2,102	2,120	—	3	14	160	278	1,469	178	18
North Adams	15,569	1,021	1,053	—	16	6	429	217	320	33	32
Northampton	29,036	775	793	—	8	13	44	100	531	79	18
North Andover	24,138	488	494	—	1	5	30	58	338	56	6
North Attleboro	26,394	947	951	—	6	10	27	64	755	85	4
Northborough	12,427	199	201	—	—	1	7	59	123	9	2
Northbridge	13,931	465	468	—	2	1	120	121	194	27	3
North Reading	12,441	140	140	—	—	1	3	40	75	21	—
Norton	15,036	330	361	—	5	—	23	79	200	23	31
Norwood	29,563	528	537	—	—	8	37	74	349	60	9
Palmer	12,379	501	507	—	2	6	147	126	186	34	6
Peabody	48,255	1,998	2,001	1	11	40	59	327	1,348	212	3
Pembroke	15,465	431	437	—	2	2	59	75	267	26	6
Pepperell	10,467	178	179	—	—	—	10	41	116	11	1
Pittsfield	46,690	1,352	1,353	—	12	30	125	334	749	102	1
Plymouth	48,504	1,707	1,785	—	11	20	104	376	1,057	139	78
Quincy	84,498	3,221	3,275	—	19	54	210	799	1,636	503	54
Randolph	30,997	711	713	—	3	14	19	210	354	111	2
Raynham	10,399	673	675	1	3	12	34	106	443	74	2
Reading	23,368	291	296	—	1	2	7	59	191	31	5
Salem	37,701	2,172	2,185	—	10	35	36	281	1,625	185	13
Sandwich	16,424	385	397	—	—	1	13	87	276	8	12
Saugus	27,058	1,617	1,631	—	5	28	203	172	904	305	14
Scituate	17,851	187	197	—	1	1	6	51	124	4	10
Seekonk	13,751	1,009	1,011	—	6	2	113	144	645	99	2
Sharon	15,982	146	146	—	1	—	2	43	92	8	—
Somerset	18,609	482	494	—	9	1	54	68	337	13	12
Somerville	69,316	3,049	3,077	3	4	97	390	582	1,352	621	28
Southbridge	18,561	669	676	—	7	4	327	136	180	15	7
South Hadley	17,217	277	281	—	—	—	22	43	181	31	4
Spencer	12,131	227	245	3	—	8	10	91	100	15	18
Springfield	149,978	11,165	11,742	19	134	748	1,406	2,490	3,798	2,570	577
Stoneham	23,020	552	554	—	5	7	22	127	322	69	2
Stoughton	27,581	719	722	1	5	20	37	169	375	112	3
Swampscott	14,455	380	381	—	—	4	3	122	243	8	1
Swansea	16,244	628	660	—	2	4	97	125	322	78	32
Taunton	51,905	2,070		—	7	68	239	479	1,037	240	
Tewksbury	28,268	840	842	—	3	8	19	133	527	150	2
Uxbridge	10,850	283	289	—	3	2	80	86	100	12	6
Wakefield	25,737	415	419	—	5	5	5	120	240	40	4
Walpole	20,819	388	390	—	1	1	42	43	280	21	2
Waltham	55,090	1,609	1,621	—	16	16	163	301	983	130	12

Table 8. — Number of Offenses Known to the Police, Cities and Towns 10,000 and over in Population, 1995 — Continued

City by State	Population	Crime Index total	Modified* Crime Index total	Murder and non-negligent manslaughter	Forcible rape	Robbery	Aggravated assault	Burglary	Larceny–theft	Motor vehicle theft	Arson*
MASSACHUSETTS — Continued											
Ware	10,119	173	174	—	3	—	29	51	67	23	1
Wareham	20,453	1,206	1,263	1	7	5	61	407	675	50	57
Watertown	31,608	1,222		1	1	8	116	128	896	72	
Wellesley	27,414	457	463	—	4	—	16	196	220	21	6
Westborough	14,725	413	423	—	2	6	43	72	249	41	10
Westfield	38,394	1,062	1,081	—	15	21	161	200	581	84	19
Westford	16,994	199	200	—	1	1	9	41	136	11	1
Weston	10,573	120	120	—	1	2	7	41	64	5	—
Westport	14,601	248	270	—	—	—	34	55	134	25	22
West Springfield	28,284	1,980	2,002	2	14	30	153	264	1,133	384	22
Westwood	12,934	168	168	—	—	3	3	29	108	25	—
Weymouth	55,692	1,442	1,457	—	8	16	95	257	786	280	15
Wilbraham	12,977	264	277	—	—	6	29	48	142	39	13
Wilmington	18,299	521	524	—	3	1	61	75	323	58	3
Winchester	21,011	312	314	—	2	1	9	44	235	21	2
Woburn	36,572	1,274	1,284	1	6	20	25	201	843	178	10
Worcester	166,290	11,386		5	82	431	1,264	2,523	5,790	1,291	
Yarmouth	22,451	1,000	1,005	—	5	13	77	284	568	53	5
MICHIGAN											
Adrian	22,681	941	943	3	18	8	23	98	758	33	2
Albion	10,253	757	765	—	11	25	117	151	434	19	8
Allen Park	30,326	1,253	1,259	1	8	19	60	201	746	218	6
Alpena	11,348	444	451	—	9	2	18	57	337	21	7
Ann Arbor	109,424	5,414	5,435	3	43	132	294	1,083	3,644	215	21
Auburn Hills	18,989	1,283	1,292	1	6	10	108	181	845	132	9
Battle Creek	77,053	5,394	5,434	7	50	192	549	1076	3,118	402	40
Bay City	38,603	2,336	2,359	—	46	59	277	308	1,482	164	23
Benton Harbor	13,259	2,525	2,602	13	31	156	652	614	869	190	77
Benton Township	17,635	2,409	2,420	7	35	46	164	407	1,593	157	11
Berkley	16,653	435	438	—	1	8	17	58	329	22	3
Berrien Springs-Oronoko	12,067	369	375	—	3	1	32	72	240	21	6
Beverly Hills	10,937	264	265	—	—	2	11	15	229	7	1
Big Rapids	12,645	579	581	—	8	5	17	83	449	17	2
Birmingham	20,619	763	765	—	3	3	22	75	620	40	2
Blackman Township	21,055	671	675	—	5	1	25	82	532	26	4
Bloomfield Township	43,644	1,395	1,402	2	3	13	46	145	1,089	97	7
Brownstown Township	19,328	946	956	1	10	13	103	183	522	114	10
Buena Vista Township	11,199	1,121	1,130	1	12	39	120	225	662	62	9
Burton	27,581	2,122	2,133	2	24	72	108	325	1,389	202	11
Cadillac	10,501	655	665	—	3	—	25	41	540	46	10
Canton Township	58,613	2,021		—	19	25	80	288	1,434	175	
Chesterfield Township	26,618	1,071	1,072	—	—	7	16	133	841	74	1
Clawson	14,337	364	366	—	2	3	10	44	281	24	2
Clinton Township	88,235	2,627	2,647	2	79	58	203	361	1,649	275	20
Davison Township	15,073	494	496	—	4	5	19	83	352	31	2
Dearborn	86,667	7,164	7,183	2	18	166	379	625	4,685	1,289	19
Dearborn Heights	58,613	3,124	3,139	—	25	114	124	447	1,863	551	15
Detroit	997,297	119,065	120,216	475	1,104	10,076	12,356	22,366	43,415	29,273	1,151
De Witt Township	10,734	328	329	—	10	2	15	63	219	19	1
East Lansing	50,602	1,941	1,950	—	24	21	59	273	1,444	120	9
Emmett Township	11,058	464	467	—	2	6	25	94	325	12	3
Escanaba	13,675	696	696	1	4	—	15	56	605	15	—
Farmington	10,343	387	388	—	2	4	20	42	296	23	1
Farmington Hills	79,585	3,038	3,057	1	18	37	186	419	2,124	253	19
Ferndale	23,351	1,511	1,521	1	13	61	179	260	817	180	10
Flint	138,934	17,338	17,684	41	206	1,030	2,615	4,137	7,346	1,963	346
Fraser	14,163	661	661	—	8	10	32	66	484	61	—
Garden City	31,203	913	913	1	4	17	43	113	675	60	—
Genesee Township	24,755	989	993	1	14	21	134	211	515	93	4
Grand Blanc Township	26,091	1,014	1,015	2	16	5	53	167	702	69	1

Table 8. — Number of Offenses Known to the Police, Cities and Towns 10,000 and over in Population, 1995 — Continued

City by State	Population	Crime Index total	Modified* Crime Index total	Murder and non-negligent man-slaughter	Forcible rape	Robbery	Aggravated assault	Burglary	Larceny-theft	Motor vehicle theft	Arson*
MICHIGAN — Continued											
Grand Haven	12,928	716	727	—	1	4	21	44	631	15	11
Grand Rapids	191,457	14,556	14,666	24	109	662	1,669	3,113	8,089	890	110
Grandville	17,044	585	592	—	12	1	20	101	426	25	7
Green Oak Township	11,922	226	226	—	1	1	10	51	147	16	—
Grosse Ile Township	10,048	145	147	—	—	—	1	21	115	8	2
Grosse Pointe Park	12,672	391	392	—	—	23	8	30	276	54	1
Hamburg Township	13,442	106	106	—	1	—	2	23	75	5	—
Hamtramck	16,575	2,265	2,267	5	14	110	262	538	734	602	2
Harper Woods	14,342	1,752	1,755	—	3	25	35	131	1,286	272	3
Hazel Park	19,036	1,466	1,473	2	19	58	119	211	835	222	7
Highland Park	20,164	3,077	3,098	11	55	247	497	661	925	681	21
Huron Township	10,733	285	288	—	2	1	15	76	151	40	3
Jackson	39,451	2,739	2,764	1	59	66	137	324	2,055	97	25
Kalamazoo	82,099	7,296	7,393	7	53	310	982	1,160	4,280	504	97
Kalamazoo Township	21,553	939	944	—	16	22	47	157	601	96	5
Kentwood	40,118	2,149	2,158	—	22	40	127	345	1,498	117	9
Lansing	120,256	9,784	9,839	13	148	344	1,138	1,502	5,940	699	55
Lincoln Park	40,675	2,672	2,694	1	1	85	137	338	1,734	376	22
Livonia	100,975	3,682		1	29	80	156	551	2,433	432	
Madison Heights	32,092	1,994	2,025	—	8	17	103	206	1,312	348	31
Marquette	22,319	690	699	—	7	—	13	59	585	26	9
Melvindale	10,887	526	527	—	—	12	26	125	275	88	1
Meridian Township	36,626	2,009	2,022	1	15	14	46	254	1,633	46	13
Midland	39,788	1,148	1,162	—	24	2	61	101	927	33	14
Monroe	23,547	992	1,004	—	7	16	71	156	689	53	12
Mount Clemens	18,998	1,198	1,209	1	27	47	112	191	757	63	11
Mount Morris Township	25,892	1,616	1,625	3	20	74	149	418	708	244	9
Mount Pleasant	23,993	861	865	—	2	4	36	119	656	44	4
Mundy Township	11,827	493	494	—	3	8	11	70	387	14	1
Muskegon	40,865	4,611	4,636	3	30	197	478	951	2,715	237	25
Muskegon Heights	14,095	991	996	1	15	68	152	226	482	47	5
Niles	12,463	890	897	1	9	20	52	158	602	48	7
Niles Township	13,180	149	153	—	—	1	1	24	118	5	4
Northville Township	17,788	553	556	—	4	2	17	69	417	44	3
Norton Shores	22,184	906	909	—	1	10	28	141	694	32	3
Novi	38,897	1,974	1,980	—	17	12	126	200	1,518	101	6
Oak Park	32,034	1,992	1,995	2	23	74	240	204	1,111	338	3
Oscoda Township	14,661	276	278	—	3	3	15	56	188	11	2
Owosso	16,711	583	587	—	15	3	76	82	377	30	4
Pittsfield Township	18,154	1,687	1,695	—	9	28	58	231	1,206	155	8
Plymouth Township	24,297	489	493	1	5	1	9	97	348	28	4
Portage	42,763	2,312	2,318	—	18	17	74	258	1,871	74	6
Port Huron	33,560	1,721	1,751	2	51	28	202	400	940	98	30
River Rouge	10,647	1,007	1,025	2	3	40	142	232	472	116	18
Roseville	51,879	3,259	3,272	—	13	53	120	193	2,543	337	13
Royal Oak	68,812	2,489	2,503	—	10	37	102	266	1,856	218	14
Saginaw	71,000	6,054	6,191	16	101	374	1,077	1,638	2,509	339	137
Saginaw Township	38,722	1,423	1,438	—	3	17	70	142	1,151	40	15
Sault Ste. Marie	14,911	435	438	—	2	—	4	90	318	21	3
Shelby Township	49,997	1,678	1,682	—	3	4	79	260	1,213	119	4
Southfield	80,234	6,052	6,074	5	29	170	363	739	3,492	1,254	22
Sturgis	10,480	368	369	—	4	2	16	39	298	9	1
Summit Township	21,710	466	467	—	2	5	48	80	315	16	1
Sumpter Township	11,190	320	321	—	2	—	17	90	170	41	1
Taylor	68,923	5,135	5,173	4	48	133	324	877	2,781	968	38
Thomas Township	11,271	337	338	—	1	2	13	30	284	7	1
Traverse City	15,783	808	816	—	14	6	31	84	652	21	8
Trenton	19,909	532	533	—	4	7	30	71	375	45	1
Troy	79,469	3,587	3,605	3	8	25	139	428	2,743	241	18
Van Buren Township	21,588	716	717	—	3	9	24	62	533	85	1
Warren	143,420	7,257	7,314	—	34	217	1,054	910	3,661	1,381	57

125

City by State	Population	Crime Index total	Modified* Crime Index total	Murder and non-negligent man-slaughter	Forcible rape	Robbery	Aggravated assault	Burglary	Larceny–theft	Motor vehicle theft	Arson*
MICHIGAN — Continued											
Wayne	19,398	1,238	1,256	—	19	30	150	170	698	171	18
Westland	85,696	4,087	4,102	5	57	64	304	684	2,332	641	15
White Lake Township	23,228	778	783	1	3	6	56	94	569	49	5
Woodhaven	11,992	637	639	—	—	2	23	73	478	61	2
Wyandotte	29,688	716		—	3	3	13	88	544	65	
MINNESOTA											
Albert Lea	18,050	690	698	—	—	3	19	91	552	25	8
Andover	20,186	643	647	—	5	1	16	128	447	46	4
Anoka	16,843	959	968	—	7	5	21	146	730	50	9
Apple Valley	40,162	1,320	1,331	1	14	6	21	161	1,057	60	11
Austin	21,958	1,000	1,003	—	13	3	32	143	770	39	3
Bemidji	12,484	1,364	1,370	—	10	9	26	83	1,116	120	6
Blaine	42,347	2,435	2,437	7	7	14	39	238	2,003	127	2
Bloomington	85,987	4,841	4,852	2	32	87	96	454	3,793	377	11
Brainerd	13,660	1,396	1,400	—	8	6	31	233	1,018	100	4
Brooklyn Center	27,817	2,493	2,509	1	27	50	39	259	1,889	228	16
Brooklyn Park	59,339	3,418	3,435	1	33	96	214	554	2,261	259	17
Burnsville	55,599	2,897	2,910	—	27	34	30	300	2,340	166	13
Champlin	20,745	458	463	—	9	7	23	56	341	22	5
Chanhassen	15,273	365	365	—	1	—	4	46	297	17	—
Chaska	13,621	454	457	—	9	6	15	46	370	8	3
Cloquet	11,145	538	543	—	8	—	14	71	408	37	5
Columbia Heights	18,346	1,210	1,219	—	16	39	34	218	794	109	9
Coon Rapids	62,951	2,477	2,496	1	33	19	44	307	1,885	188	19
Cottage Grove	27,081	696	703	1	14	7	32	103	516	23	7
Crystal	23,107	1,028	1,034	2	9	22	27	155	743	70	6
Duluth	84,781	4,872	4,902	4	105	68	217	765	3,430	283	30
Eagan	57,528	1,754	1,771	1	16	10	34	229	1,300	164	17
Eden Prairie	48,392	1,570	1,582	1	7	5	26	164	1,287	80	12
Edina	46,954	1,493	1,502	—	3	8	24	254	1,145	59	9
Elk River	13,241	666	668	—	5	1	7	96	535	22	2
Fairmont	11,198	558	561	—	5	1	14	112	417	9	3
Faribault	18,058	1,180	1,195	—	21	6	26	217	841	69	15
Fergus Falls	12,603	540	544	—	14	2	13	77	408	26	4
Fridley	26,483	2,045	2,057	3	21	34	56	292	1,467	172	12
Golden Valley	20,829	799	800	1	2	22	11	156	558	49	1
Ham Lake	10,492	452	461	—	5	1	9	113	293	31	9
Hastings	16,525	726	728	—	7	2	24	70	582	41	2
Hibbing	17,829	337	338	—	8	—	2	60	249	18	1
Hopkins	15,891	771	779	—	8	17	29	108	535	74	8
Hutchinson	12,672	587	587	—	6	1	20	34	514	12	—
Inver Grove Heights	24,731	983	999	—	5	6	42	154	714	62	16
Lakeville	33,737	1,028	1,052	—	3	9	7	151	818	40	24
Lino Lakes	11,776	271	272	—	5	—	3	41	199	23	1
Mankato	31,699	2,534	2,543	—	26	23	30	459	1,870	126	9
Maple Grove	47,090	1,197	1,198	—	10	4	32	163	934	54	1
Maplewood	33,877	2,296	2,301	—	13	23	39	242	1,860	119	5
Marshall	12,304	445	450	—	8	—	21	64	335	17	5
Mendota Heights	10,878	224	228	—	1	—	5	43	167	8	4
Minneapolis	357,709	41,299		96	578	3,550	2,852	8,024	21,710	4,489	
Moorhead	33,383	1,651	1,654	1	9	8	51	166	1,352	64	3
Mound	10,100	245	251	—	7	4	10	39	176	9	6
Mounds View	13,112	610	614	—	4	7	41	76	440	42	4
New Brighton	21,809	779	784	1	9	8	12	122	581	46	5
New Hope	21,336	696	698	—	5	15	20	81	532	43	2
New Ulm	13,674	549	557	—	2	—	8	95	432	12	8
Northfield	16,099	752	756	1	2	2	12	105	586	44	4
North Mankato	11,502	325	327	—	1	1	2	25	282	14	2
North St. Paul	12,773	531	538	—	10	6	16	53	409	37	7
Oakdale	23,661	879	883	—	15	6	34	109	667	48	4

Table 8. — Number of Offenses Known to the Police, Cities and Towns 10,000 and over in Population, 1995 — Continued

City by State	Population	Crime Index total	Modified* Crime Index total	Murder and non-negligent man-slaughter	Forcible rape	Robbery	Aggravated assault	Burglary	Larceny–theft	Motor vehicle theft	Arson*
MINNESOTA — Continued											
Owatonna	20,321	697	697	—	9	3	12	72	577	24	—
Plymouth	60,709	1,849	1,919	—	17	15	51	287	1,388	91	70
Prior Lake	13,405	440	441	—	1	4	14	19	365	37	1
Ramsey	15,848	429	430	—	4	6	15	71	303	30	1
Red Wing	15,890	797	803	1	18	5	10	114	595	54	6
Richfield	34,754	1,802	1,824	1	32	62	69	288	1,188	162	22
Robbinsdale	14,182	692	695	—	4	30	11	131	477	39	3
Rochester	76,482	3,524	3,532	1	70	56	117	594	2,548	138	8
Roseville	33,386	2,297	2,302	—	12	27	21	202	1,918	117	5
St. Cloud	51,262	3,228	3,260	1	69	33	88	466	2,398	173	32
St. Louis Park	42,890	1,845	1,857	—	16	33	42	256	1,392	106	12
St. Paul	264,539	20,256	20,580	25	233	930	1,348	4,272	11,219	2,229	324
Savage	14,009	381	385	—	3	3	8	64	285	18	4
Shakopee	13,170	766	767	—	9	8	23	78	594	54	1
Shoreview	27,206	455	468	—	5	2	12	80	324	32	13
South Lake Minnetonka	10,985	282	287	—	5	3	5	44	207	18	5
South St. Paul	19,754	1,007	1,009	1	24	10	43	113	747	69	2
Stillwater	16,106	587	590	—	6	—	24	108	427	22	3
Vadnais Heights	13,379	351	354	—	3	3	14	65	235	31	3
West St. Paul	19,036	1,182	1,182	2	7	12	27	86	968	80	—
White Bear Lake	24,718	1,128	1,135	—	3	3	10	158	861	93	7
Willmar	18,671	1,125	1,133	—	28	5	33	171	806	82	8
Winona	25,871	1,489	1,496	—	5	5	8	182	1,226	63	7
Woodbury	29,428	996	1,003	—	5	5	10	192	753	31	7
MISSISSIPPI											
Greenville	44,859	5,354	5,414	16	85	134	301	1,201	3,435	182	60
Greenwood	18,982	1,780		8	8	71	30	498	1,059	106	
Gulfport	66,372	5,155	5,219	7	41	150	152	800	3,677	328	64
Hattiesburg	48,192	3,453		4	27	70	147	887	2,180	138	
Indianola	12,199	945		5	6	14	44	289	568	19	
Jackson	195,123	23,046	23,154	92	186	1,469	920	5,455	10,868	4,056	108
Long Beach	16,982	643	644	—	3	3	11	110	492	24	1
Madison	12,384	262	262	—	—	4	—	16	239	3	—
McComb	12,258	1,023	1,023	2	4	19	189	247	519	43	—
Meridian	43,055	2,625	2,647	5	26	114	154	678	1,452	196	22
Moss Point	18,163	1,361	1,388	2	15	25	68	472	709	70	27
Natchez	19,482	1,759	1,759	2	24	20	91	311	1,276	35	—
Oxford	10,197	498	498	—	2	9	28	59	375	25	—
Pascagoula	29,348	2,711	2,715	2	13	74	105	688	1,657	172	4
Picayune	12,120	721	726	1	1	14	62	102	511	30	5
Ridgeland	14,235	1,032	1,032	—	1	23	16	91	854	47	—
Southaven	19,532	1,301	1,306	—	2	25	18	150	921	185	5
Starkville	19,738	1,270	1,271	2	9	17	67	193	935	47	1
Tupelo	33,333	2,792	2,792	1	14	80	96	498	1,894	209	—
Vicksburg[1]	28,417			7	32	59		724	1,711	279	8
MISSOURI											
Arnold	20,257	717	719	2	7	6	87	119	463	33	2
Ballwin	22,087	392	392	—	3	1	15	62	300	11	—
Bellefontaine Neighbors	10,864	521	522	—	1	12	10	37	416	45	1
Belton	20,871	773	775	1	3	9	35	102	579	44	2
Berkeley	12,805	760	761	—	7	28	60	159	399	107	1
Blue Springs	41,287	2,165	2,170	1	12	31	82	247	1,696	96	5
Bridgeton	17,931	1,303	1,303	—	2	27	38	139	948	149	—
Cape Girardeau	36,249	2,693	2,695	2	16	52	151	282	2,098	92	2
Carthage	11,158	567	570	—	2	7	8	115	420	15	3
Chesterfield	42,666	982	990	—	—	11	27	123	795	26	8
Clayton	13,824	713	719	—	—	12	5	175	500	21	6
Columbia	74,717	4,749	4,775	2	40	120	325	522	3,566	174	26
Crestwood	11,261	692	692	1	—	4	1	28	633	25	—

See footnotes at end of table.

City by State	Population	Crime Index total	Modified* Crime Index total	Murder and non-negligent man-slaughter	Forcible rape	Robbery	Aggravated assault	Burglary	Larceny–theft	Motor vehicle theft	Arson*
MISSOURI — Continued											
Creve Coeur	12,176	472	472	—	3	7	13	46	352	51	—
Excelsior Springs	11,080	547	550	—	4	5	9	97	401	31	3
Farmington	12,266	668	668	—	5	3	12	60	569	19	—
Ferguson	22,783	1,240	1,242	1	6	45	55	215	769	149	2
Florissant	51,846	1,378	1,381	2	9	33	31	163	1,047	93	3
Fulton	10,572	473	473	—	5	8	20	71	359	10	—
Gladstone	27,916	973	980	—	3	29	56	135	677	73	7
Grandview	25,594	928	943	1	4	53	67	220	460	123	15
Hannibal	18,261	967	983	1	10	14	81	192	617	52	16
Hazelwood	15,929	802	809	—	5	15	33	106	536	107	7
Independence	112,642	8,981	9,041	2	40	146	442	1,382	6,309	660	60
Jefferson City	37,252	1,805	1,810	1	9	37	42	221	1,424	71	5
Jennings	16,129	1,057	1,065	1	6	53	61	231	531	174	8
Joplin	43,265	3,202	3,216	2	24	58	140	739	2,051	188	14
Kansas City	445,549	52,575	53,054	107	470	3,346	5,811	9,748	26,301	6,792	479
Kennett	11,343	987	987	2	6	18	37	137	590	197	—
Kirksville	17,436	612	612	—	6	—	2	94	490	20	—
Kirkwood	28,530	679	683	1	4	19	33	100	489	33	4
Lebanon	10,468	750	751	—	2	1	40	152	496	59	1
Lees Summit	47,438	1,659	1,671	1	10	22	28	314	1,187	97	12
Liberty	21,952	811	815	—	4	6	35	91	634	41	4
Maplewood	10,326	740	744	—	1	15	39	92	533	60	4
Marshall	12,524	337	338	—	1	1	2	50	278	5	1
Maryland Heights	26,257	1,097	1,097	2	4	9	82	142	784	74	—
Maryville	10,601	242	244	1	3	—	1	35	197	5	2
Mexico	11,320	264	264	1	—	3	24	68	163	5	—
Moberly	12,690	721	722	1	1	19	64	104	518	14	1
O'Fallon	20,235	840	840	1	4	7	21	135	647	25	—
Overland	18,474	1,049	1,051	1	1	15	17	132	834	49	2
Park Hills	13,203	293	294	—	3	—	40	72	159	19	1
Poplar Bluff	17,478	1,421	1,432	—	6	20	56	249	1,035	55	11
Raytown	30,200	1,127	1,132	—	6	39	50	188	736	108	5
Richmond Heights	10,543	1,192	1,197	3	—	20	22	49	1,056	42	5
Rolla	14,905	739	742	—	4	11	19	113	564	28	3
St. Charles	56,830	2,382	2,412	—	18	42	153	484	1,545	140	30
St. Joseph	72,336	4,965	4,994	1	9	51	191	738	3,805	170	29
St. Louis	371,425	59,736	60,505	204	273	5,136	6,839	10,692	28,587	8,005	769
St. Peters	46,812	1,851	1,863	—	3	35	50	179	1,517	67	12
Sedalia	20,431	1,454	1,454	1	—	10	66	267	1,041	69	—
Sikeston	18,084	1,190	1,200	2	6	22	63	210	822	65	10
Springfield	151,032	12,092	12,189	5	82	145	597	2,123	8,440	700	97
University City	41,133	2,749	2,769	1	16	129	101	464	1,697	341	20
Warrensburg	16,784	740	743	1	3	7	18	116	560	35	3
Washington	11,431	580	586	—	3	2	30	86	443	16	6
Webster Groves	23,258	389	395	—	2	10	10	79	270	18	6
MONTANA[3]											
Havre	10,223	770	772	—	5	1	16	57	636	55	2
Missoula	46,106	4,118	4,128	3	14	29	76	355	3,471	170	10
NEBRASKA											
Beatrice	12,435	757	762	—	4	1	9	71	644	28	5
Bellevue	41,630	1,557	1,582	2	2	20	24	190	1,218	101	25
Columbus	20,691	807	813	3	6	6	10	86	652	44	6
Fremont	23,960	1,141	1,141	—	1	6	58	169	865	42	—
Grand Island	41,502	3,498	3,500	—	28	17	119	473	2,723	138	2
Hastings	23,154	1,008	1,009	1	6	3	17	108	834	39	1
Kearney	26,442	1,419	1,430	—	7	—	58	160	1,151	43	11
La Vista	10,725	456	456	—	—	1	4	26	411	14	—
Lincoln	204,828	14,433	14,538	2	80	122	1,127	1,880	10,765	457	105
Norfolk	22,628	1,285	1,291	2	14	4	22	96	1,082	65	6

See footnotes at end of table.

Table 8. — Number of Offenses Known to the Police, Cities and Towns 10,000 and over in Population, 1995 — Continued

City by State	Population	Crime Index total	Modified* Crime Index total	Murder and non-negligent man-slaughter	Forcible rape	Robbery	Aggravated assault	Burglary	Larceny–theft	Motor vehicle theft	Arson*
NEBRASKA — Continued											
North Platte	23,370	1,807	1,822	—	5	11	52	252	1,422	65	15
Omaha	348,089	27,324	27,565	27	80	808	2,670	3,883	16,071	3,785	241
Papillion	10,910	330	333	—	1	5	5	27	280	12	3
Scottsbluff	14,191	933	934	—	—	5	35	114	739	40	1
South Sioux City	10,373	497	497	—	—	3	8	57	398	31	—
NEVADA											
Boulder Ciy	13,747	483	493	—	3	5	21	117	316	21	10
Henderson	107,107	4,982	5,020	3	79	124	110	917	3,061	688	38
Las Vegas Metropolitan Police Department Jurisdiction	793,432	60,178	60,574	118	571	3,712	5,122	12,219	30,445	7,991	396
North Las Vegas	67,769	6,565	6,658	11	66	464	1,077	1,300	2,727	920	93
Reno	152,294	10,947	11,016	14	94	421	568	1,846	7,193	811	69
Sparks	63,255	4,162		4	34	95	177	744	2,830	278	
NEW HAMPSHIRE											
Bedford	12,952	184	184	1	1	1	3	34	132	12	—
Berlin	10,993	199	208	1	—	—	4	31	160	3	9
Claremont	13,438	738	740	—	18	5	9	96	574	36	2
Concord	36,548	1,392	1,407	—	15	19	16	173	1,116	53	15
Derry	30,525	927	963	—	9	10	11	204	555	138	36
Dover	25,131	683	687	—	11	3	14	51	585	19	4
Durham	12,184	199	205	—	6	1	3	29	156	4	6
Exeter	12,869	248	250	—	2	—	3	35	200	8	2
Goffstown	15,076	274	274	—	—	—	4	44	217	9	—
Hudson	20,137	428	436	2	1	3	10	83	302	27	8
Keene	22,127	981	1,006	—	22	8	57	99	767	28	25
Lebanon	12,586	659	663	—	—	1	14	53	576	15	4
Manchester	97,785	4,349	4,395	3	29	160	35	886	2,930	306	46
Milford	12,160	451	456	—	19	3	46	42	330	11	5
Nashua	80,401	2,563	2,601	—	23	13	30	339	1,951	207	38
Somersworth	11,882	458	459	—	6	2	1	64	373	12	1
NEW JERSEY											
Aberdeen Township	17,826	575	586	—	8	8	36	124	348	51	11
Asbury Park	15,686	1,460	1,465	2	11	147	130	245	799	126	5
Atlantic City	36,752	10,102	10,240	15	42	554	338	1,245	7,554	354	138
Barnegat Township	12,599	317	322	—	2	5	23	44	228	15	5
Bayonne	62,593	1,844	1,855	2	7	119	127	283	1,036	270	11
Beachwood	10,034	362	364	—	—	7	9	86	250	10	2
Belleville	34,728	1,607	1,614	—	2	68	114	288	807	328	7
Bellmawr	12,342	428	428	—	3	8	20	56	307	34	—
Bergenfield	25,014	399	400	—	2	21	14	48	287	27	1
Berkeley Heights	12,291	111	111	—	—	—	4	11	90	6	—
Berkeley Township	38,433	816	825	2	2	10	37	169	567	29	9
Bernards Township	18,489	271	272	—	—	—	14	45	194	18	1
Bloomfield	45,737	2,023	2,027	1	6	123	66	360	1,007	460	4
Branchburg Township	11,703	237	238	—	3	2	6	34	184	8	1
Brick Township	68,459	1,887	1,919	—	5	23	74	430	1,256	99	32
Bridgeton	19,136	1,944	1,959	1	16	120	279	383	989	156	15
Bridgewater Township	34,949	1,027	1,031	—	—	11	8	137	769	102	4
Brigantine	12,058	626	628	—	6	11	51	126	414	18	2
Burlington Township	12,747	828	829	2	1	28	41	147	558	51	1
Camden	83,296	12,223	12,590	58	88	1,593	1,486	3,199	3,785	2,014	367
Carteret	19,229	646	647	2	14	33	38	137	364	58	1
Cedar Grove Township	12,233	325	329	—	—	1	29	87	189	19	4
Cherry Hill Township	72,273	3,422	3,429	1	14	75	55	552	2,294	431	7
Cinnaminson Township	14,926	458	460	—	4	16	15	86	262	75	2
Clark Township	15,009	319	320	—	1	3	5	28	245	37	1
Cliffside Park	20,944	475	475	1	2	6	27	120	272	47	—
Clifton	74,386	2,627	2,630	3	5	76	70	456	1,514	503	3
Clinton Township	11,070	128	129	—	—	—	3	36	75	14	1

Table 8. — Number of Offenses Known to the Police, Cities and Towns 10,000 and over in Population, 1995 — Continued

City by State	Population	Crime Index total	Modified* Crime Index total	Murder and non-negligent man-slaughter	Forcible rape	Robbery	Aggravated assault	Burglary	Larceny–theft	Motor vehicle theft	Arson*
NEW JERSEY — Continued											
Collingswood	14,426	786	787	—	4	37	38	151	430	126	1
Cranford Township	23,223	526	528	—	1	2	23	71	403	26	2
Delran Township	13,488	466	466	—	1	11	25	42	336	51	—
Denville Township	14,307	172	172	—	1	—	8	13	142	8	—
Deptford Township	25,311	1,735	1,741	1	—	31	59	219	1,241	184	6
Dover	14,573	464	465	—	6	12	21	84	292	49	1
Dover Township	78,653	3,093	3,117	—	15	60	111	575	2,201	131	24
Dumont	17,448	307	307	—	—	1	9	40	248	9	—
East Brunswick Township	45,373	1,389	1,392	—	8	12	39	147	1,070	113	3
East Hanover Township	10,282	399	399	—	—	5	7	18	318	51	—
East Orange	73,225	7,396	7,468	12	65	1,222	674	1,663	2,539	1,221	72
East Windsor Township	22,974	503	506	1	6	9	12	62	369	44	3
Eatontown	13,084	761	764	2	1	5	17	65	632	39	3
Edison Township	92,398	3,257	3,275	1	6	92	133	549	2,050	426	18
Egg Harbor Township	25,123	1,710	1,726	—	13	26	69	339	1,162	101	16
Elizabeth	106,849	9,638	9,669	18	46	936	345	2,076	4,229	1,988	31
Elmwood Park	17,903	695	697	—	4	23	14	103	486	65	2
Englewood	25,018	1,365	1,372	—	2	40	68	243	869	143	7
Evesham Township	36,144	1,007	1,016	—	5	11	31	263	622	75	9
Ewing Township	35,135	1,563	1,575	—	7	53	47	233	890	333	12
Fair Lawn	31,345	604	604	1	4	16	15	74	454	40	—
Fairview	10,623	342	342	—	1	15	23	77	172	54	—
Florence Township	10,507	260	265	2	—	4	12	41	185	16	5
Fort Lee	32,233	1,288	1,292	—	3	32	64	221	858	110	4
Franklin Lakes	10,371	100	100	—	—	1	—	32	67	—	—
Franklin Township (Gloucester County)	15,185	568	572	1	4	10	34	167	306	46	4
Franklin Township (Somerset County)	45,992	1,624	1,635	—	6	52	42	451	928	145	11
Freehold	11,657	618	622	—	4	27	41	56	471	19	4
Freehold Township	25,852	855	856	—	—	5	16	33	755	46	1
Galloway Township	23,882	932	936	—	8	13	33	166	652	60	4
Garfield	26,580	1,013	1,015	1	3	31	42	176	570	190	2
Glassboro	17,474	1,244	1,250	—	16	43	75	241	791	78	6
Glen Rock	11,410	134	134	—	—	1	3	14	113	3	—
Gloucester City	12,428	470	471	—	—	9	20	73	312	56	1
Gloucester Township	56,065	2,490	2,513	—	18	41	111	504	1,517	299	23
Hackensack	37,635	2,269	2,276	1	13	76	91	288	1,504	296	7
Haddonfield	11,643	346	350	—	1	2	4	34	291	14	4
Haddon Township	15,460	727	735	—	1	21	21	116	512	56	8
Hamilton Township (Atlantic County)	16,389	1,345	1,357	2	13	22	75	243	922	68	12
Hamilton Township (Mercer County)	88,964	2,566	2,591	3	15	73	70	518	1,507	380	25
Hammonton	12,375	349	357	—	1	5	19	66	226	32	8
Hanover Township	11,951	225	226	—	—	2	16	27	156	24	1
Harrison	13,240	979	980	—	—	47	20	147	428	337	1
Hasbrouck Heights	11,781	328	328	—	1	7	5	41	223	51	—
Hawthorne	18,170	322	322	—	1	4	1	33	263	20	—
Hazlet Township	22,992	289	290	—	—	2	12	44	203	28	1
Highland Park	12,960	379	379	—	1	5	12	46	292	23	—
Hillsborough Township	30,970	589	593	—	1	3	—	142	427	16	4
Hillside Township	21,593	1,776	1,785	—	11	146	65	286	879	389	9
Hoboken	33,536	2,581	2,582	3	1	75	158	365	1,480	499	1
Holmdel Township	12,064	294	295	1	1	4	12	41	230	5	1
Hopatcong	16,127	278	280	—	—	—	24	54	191	9	2
Hopewell Township	11,911	180	180	—	—	—	2	47	124	7	—
Howell Township	40,792	885	901	—	2	4	31	176	612	60	16
Irvington	61,936	7,215	7,240	11	56	1,061	674	1,702	2,074	1,637	25
Jackson Township	34,225	1,790	1,798	—	—	8	28	120	1,603	31	8
Jefferson Township	18,465	269	272	—	—	3	15	43	189	19	3
Jersey City	227,195	18,053	18,157	25	92	2,306	1,908	3,810	6,397	3,515	104
Keansburg	11,803	471	473	—	17	6	36	71	319	22	2
Kearny	36,010	2,400	2,405	1	5	102	83	398	1,456	355	5
Lacey Township	22,801	494	498	—	—	7	20	81	373	13	4

City by State	Population	Crime Index total	Modified* Crime Index total	Murder and non-negligent man-slaughter	Forcible rape	Robbery	Aggravated assault	Burglary	Larceny–theft	Motor vehicle theft	Arson*
NEW JERSEY — Continued											
Lakewood	46,393	2,760	2,790	2	28	160	106	531	1,719	214	30
Lawrence Township	26,503	1,749	1,750	—	5	23	36	220	1,112	353	1
Lincoln Park	11,142	170	171	1	—	2	6	25	122	14	1
Linden	36,753	1,966	1,975	1	2	82	71	312	1,099	399	9
Lindenwold	18,577	1,118	1,126	—	12	75	72	259	548	152	8
Little Egg Harbor Township	13,729	629	636	—	5	—	23	146	436	19	7
Little Falls Township	11,860	579	579	—	—	6	22	87	349	115	—
Livingston Township	27,010	1,069	1,069	—	1	13	21	137	763	134	—
Lodi	22,719	767	773	—	2	19	41	107	503	95	6
Long Branch	28,022	2,183	2,195	5	16	124	139	486	1,275	138	12
Lower Township	21,313	669	679	—	10	9	29	99	496	26	10
Lyndhurst Township	19,066	624	626	1	1	6	14	56	430	116	2
Madison	15,844	318	318	—	—	10	4	58	231	15	—
Mahwah Township	18,694	377	378	—	1	3	4	51	301	17	1
Manalapan Township	27,952	344	345	—	3	4	16	52	251	18	1
Manchester Township	37,049	402	424	1	3	3	25	78	278	14	22
Mantua Township	10,562	413	418	—	3	3	7	58	314	28	5
Manville	10,537	239	239	—	—	3	8	44	179	5	—
Maple Shade Township	19,664	876	879	—	3	27	18	151	505	172	3
Maplewood Township	21,978	1,053	1,056	1	3	56	33	157	577	226	3
Marlboro Township	29,269	453	454	—	1	2	26	114	295	15	1
Medford Township	21,011	424	436	—	—	2	12	89	304	17	12
Metuchen	13,075	378	384	—	—	5	13	73	273	14	6
Middlesex	13,433	284	287	—	2	6	9	24	230	13	3
Middle Township	15,120	793	798	—	9	16	24	298	414	32	5
Middletown Township	71,341	1,158	1,162	—	2	5	31	201	865	54	4
Millburn Township	18,909	1,113	1,114	—	—	22	8	142	790	151	1
Millville	26,665	1,996	1,999	1	24	92	186	443	1,128	122	3
Monroe Township (Gloucester County)	28,003	1,000	1,008	1	4	20	25	277	579	94	8
Monroe Township (Middlesex County)	23,186	329	334	—	1	3	20	83	206	16	5
Montclair	38,297	2,115	2,119	4	8	95	118	298	1,238	354	4
Montgomery Township	10,333	224	225	—	3	3	6	57	151	4	1
Montville Township	16,159	320	322	—	1	2	—	50	239	28	2
Moorestown Township	16,496	689	700	—	3	23	22	108	474	59	11
Morristown	16,491	1,022	1,025	—	4	56	51	146	719	46	3
Morris Township	20,668	334	336	1	3	1	13	56	227	33	2
Mount Holly	10,889	756	760	—	13	65	66	150	427	35	4
Mount Laurel Township	30,984	882	885	—	2	19	16	177	570	98	3
Mount Olive Township	22,046	372	372	—	5	2	25	60	264	16	—
Neptune Township	29,450	1,765	1,773	—	8	59	74	370	1,107	147	8
Newark	260,232	40,367	40,618	102	216	5,480	4,573	7,369	12,762	9,865	251
New Brunswick	41,480	3,857	3,870	4	3	264	178	858	2,292	258	13
New Milford	16,114	319	323	1	1	—	15	84	206	12	4
New Providence	12,106	193	194	—	1	2	—	15	152	23	1
North Arlington	14,185	400	400	—	1	2	6	56	282	53	—
North Bergen Township	50,289	2,362	2,366	4	6	76	74	454	1,190	558	4
North Brunswick Township	32,597	1,109	1,120	—	4	34	32	188	739	112	11
North Hanover Township	10,228	79	79	—	—	1	6	30	36	6	—
North Plainfield	19,381	884	885	—	5	22	14	157	598	88	1
Nutley	27,506	737	751	1	4	17	39	184	376	116	14
Oakland	12,202	132	133	—	2	2	3	25	93	7	1
Ocean City	15,099	1,429	1,432	1	4	26	20	328	1,037	13	3
Ocean Township (Monmouth County)	26,217	1,065	1,072	—	3	15	28	194	785	40	7
Old Bridge	58,841	1,404	1,416	—	15	24	57	227	931	150	12
Orange	30,376	3,292	3,303	6	22	438	203	663	1,298	662	11
Palisades Park	15,201	329	329	1	2	9	11	155	96	55	—
Paramus	25,272	3,423	3,444	1	2	36	69	162	2,566	587	21
Parsippany-Troy Hills Township	50,223	1,641	1,647	—	12	8	38	391	1,070	122	6
Passaic	56,332	4,378	4,384	2	22	450	363	709	1,971	861	6
Paterson	139,007	9,339	9,435	12	45	829	771	2,231	4,047	1,404	96
Pemberton Township	32,082	986	997	—	21	21	63	344	454	83	11

131

Table 8. — Number of Offenses Known to the Police, Cities and Towns 10,000 and over in Population, 1995 — Continued

City by State	Population	Crime Index total	Modified* Crime Index total	Murder and non-negligent man-slaughter	Forcible rape	Robbery	Aggravated assault	Burglary	Larceny–theft	Motor vehicle theft	Arson*
NEW JERSEY — Continued											
Pennsauken	36,201	2,266	2,276	—	2	108	86	565	1,026	479	10
Pennsville Township	14,118	408	413	—	5	6	5	53	328	11	5
Pequannock Township	13,304	261	263	—	—	1	17	41	189	13	2
Perth Amboy	40,677	2,826	2,847	2	1	163	199	711	1,494	256	21
Phillipsburg	15,927	414	414	—	—	8	14	100	268	24	—
Pine Hill	10,625	339	344	—	5	8	20	75	198	33	5
Piscataway Township	49,062	1,111	1,117	—	7	46	84	186	719	69	6
Plainfield	45,025	3,303	3,306	3	36	359	359	829	1,474	243	3
Plainsboro Township	14,806	346	352	—	1	3	11	52	250	29	6
Pleasantville	17,161	1,388	1,390	2	13	90	199	337	656	91	2
Point Pleasant	18,658	534	535	1	—	3	16	100	400	14	1
Pompton Lakes	11,060	183	183	—	1	—	4	43	126	9	—
Princeton	11,921	680	680	—	1	12	12	153	492	10	—
Princeton Township	13,563	212	212	—	1	2	3	56	142	8	—
Rahway	25,893	995	998	—	1	52	21	175	632	114	3
Ramsey	14,588	323	323	—	—	4	11	29	259	20	—
Randolph Township	20,691	239	239	—	1	1	10	10	207	10	—
Raritan Township	15,984	406	406	—	2	3	26	60	291	24	—
Readington Township	13,715	232	233	—	—	6	4	62	156	4	1
Red Bank	10,244	632	632	—	2	11	19	49	527	24	—
Ridgefield	10,170	169	169	—	—	3	6	24	105	31	—
Ridgefield Park	12,580	219	220	—	—	7	9	46	134	23	1
Ridgewood	24,741	310	311	—	—	3	17	29	247	14	1
Ringwood	13,307	155	155	1	—	3	12	18	118	3	—
River Edge	10,955	164	164	—	—	2	5	33	113	11	—
Rockaway Township	20,275	993	997	1	1	10	18	54	844	65	4
Roselle	20,678	791	795	1	5	29	33	174	433	116	4
Roselle Park	12,973	387	387	—	—	9	12	108	208	50	—
Roxbury Township	21,163	438	439	—	5	2	15	49	334	33	1
Rutherford	17,812	332	332	—	2	4	8	54	190	74	—
Saddle Brook Township	13,881	390	391	—	1	3	7	46	272	61	1
Sayreville	36,593	891	902	1	8	18	48	167	578	71	11
Scotch Plains Township	21,712	390	391	—	4	8	10	75	257	36	1
Secaucus	15,449	1,157	1,157	—	1	9	26	60	828	233	—
Somers Point	11,550	411	412	—	5	7	22	107	249	21	1
Somerville	12,256	539	541	—	1	19	13	87	396	23	2
South Brunswick Township	26,871	631	633	—	4	2	24	152	403	46	2
South Orange	16,633	936	936	1	2	55	33	155	457	233	—
South Plainfield	21,089	840	843	—	—	16	10	70	678	66	3
South River	13,928	249	254	1	2	6	17	54	157	12	5
Sparta Township	15,514	214	216	—	—	—	15	48	144	7	2
Springfield	13,770	504	504	—	—	4	13	52	269	166	—
Stafford Township	13,721	653	669	—	4	1	19	110	469	50	16
Summit	20,296	781	783	1	1	4	10	111	604	50	2
Teaneck Township	39,494	1,144	1,164	1	8	30	90	237	710	68	20
Tenafly	13,357	219	229	—	—	3	3	78	122	13	10
Tinton Falls	13,317	375	377	—	1	5	17	88	242	22	2
Totowa	10,431	523	525	—	1	6	11	36	413	56	2
Trenton	84,879	6,371	6,407	16	80	486	748	1,275	2,370	1,396	36
Union City	56,600	3,107	3,111	4	6	248	170	689	1,513	477	4
Union Township	51,331	2,950	2,964	—	6	139	91	434	1,740	540	14
Ventnor City	10,846	552	552	1	2	7	17	140	371	14	—
Vernon Township	21,712	475	476	—	—	4	15	85	353	18	1
Verona	13,800	263	264	—	—	2	5	38	177	41	1
Vineland	54,956	4,055	4,078	3	35	208	208	787	2,531	283	23
Voorhees Township	25,593	1,292	1,300	1	7	37	19	169	937	122	8
Wallington	10,541	284	285	—	—	11	5	49	184	35	1
Wall Township	21,181	412	412	—	1	4	9	76	311	11	—
Wanaque	10,180	177	178	—	—	2	8	34	126	7	1
Warren Township	11,641	237	237	—	1	—	7	32	174	23	—
Washington Township (Gloucester County)	44,002	1,474	1,483	—	12	30	42	297	978	115	9

Table 8. — Number of Offenses Known to the Police, Cities and Towns 10,000 and over in Population, 1995 — Continued

City by State	Population	Crime Index total	Modified* Crime Index total	Murder and non-negligent man-slaughter	Forcible rape	Robbery	Aggravated assault	Burglary	Larceny-theft	Motor vehicle theft	Arson*
NEW JERSEY — Continued											
Washington Township (Morris County) ..	16,151	211	212	—	—	—	7	32	163	9	1
Waterford Township	11,399	299	302	—	2	1	16	64	198	18	3
Wayne Township	49,388	2,805	2,808	—	3	25	44	163	2,122	448	3
Weehawken Township	12,863	719	720	—	1	20	29	100	388	181	1
West Caldwell	10,579	274	275	—	1	2	5	32	221	13	1
West Deptford Township	20,321	803	809	—	4	5	65	116	564	49	6
Westfield	29,492	616	616	—	—	11	6	106	467	26	—
West Milford Township	26,706	468	471	—	5	2	13	118	313	17	3
West New York....................	36,747	1,520	1,530	1	1	75	81	371	726	265	10
West Orange	39,688	1,619	1,621	1	2	76	75	327	774	364	2
West Paterson	11,430	343	344	—	4	7	9	70	203	50	1
West Windsor Township	16,466	468	470	—	2	4	11	51	343	57	2
Westwood	10,357	210	212	—	1	2	6	42	153	6	2
Willingboro Township	37,149	1,366	1,378	1	13	42	57	264	817	172	12
Winslow Township	31,353	1,053	1,067	1	10	49	105	285	519	84	14
Woodbridge Township	96,988	4,568	4,596	2	13	105	259	718	2,899	572	28
Woodbury	10,626	777	779	—	8	16	26	168	487	72	2
Wyckoff	16,049	142	143	—	2	—	2	23	113	2	1
NEW MEXICO											
Alamogordo	30,183	1,341	1,342	2	19	14	71	239	952	44	1
Albuquerque[1]	419,714			53	296	1,623		8,362	23,461	4,995	229
Artesia	11,963	418	420	—	—	5	23	187	196	7	2
Clovis	36,767	2,102	2,111	2	13	20	134	470	1,392	71	9
Deming..........................	13,657	1,041	1,042	1	4	18	86	276	599	57	1
Gallup...........................	20,338	2,858	2,866	2	15	63	264	257	2,128	129	8
Hobbs...........................	30,268	2,459	2,469	2	18	36	369	554	1,443	37	10
Las Cruces	72,374	6,647	6,687	5	67	101	494	1,394	4,206	380	40
Portales	12,510	593	594	—	2	2	21	237	308	23	1
Rio Rancho	42,269	1,120	1,125	—	16	11	107	239	679	68	5
Roswell	48,283	3,939	3,967	5	23	43	321	862	2,579	106	28
Silver City	11,723	868	878	2	1	6	58	168	605	28	10
NEW YORK											
Albany	104,637	8,329	8,370	7	61	548	611	2,038	4,460	604	41
Amherst Town	107,042	2,843	2,847	1	8	54	22	215	2,331	212	4
Auburn	30,736	1,343	1,345	—	8	26	37	174	1,082	16	2
Batavia	16,049	783	785	—	4	13	9	105	641	11	2
Beacon	13,505	494	497	1	4	28	140	105	200	16	3
Bethlehem Town	27,788	999	1,000	—	1	10	18	113	842	15	1
Binghamton	51,050	2,847	2,859	3	15	79	73	352	2,316	9	12
Blooming Grove Town	11,866	167		—	—	—	—	49	111	7	—
Brighton Town	34,750	1,236	1,238	—	5	18	13	186	946	68	2
Buffalo	312,395	28,757	29,319	62	261	2,836	3,174	7,092	11,124	4,208	562
Camillus Town and Village	23,827	333		—	—	2	4	69	252	6	—
Canandaigua......................	11,184	379	379	—	4	5	7	43	316	4	—
Carmel Town	29,064	419	423	—	1	1	7	89	302	19	4
Cheektowaga Town	94,322	3,882	3,900	2	10	105	270	565	2,432	498	18
Cicero Town......................	23,826	343	343	—	—	4	22	45	265	7	—
Clarkstown Town	79,291	2,602	2,605	2	4	40	118	261	1,979	198	3
Clay Town	54,789	632	640	—	—	1	—	115	514	2	8
Colonie Town	72,782	3,664	3,673	1	9	36	23	393	3,049	153	9
Cortland	19,952	1,065	1,067	—	3	7	34	146	855	20	2
Cortlandt Town	28,611	295	298	1	—	3	40	49	191	11	3
Depew Village	17,942	578	584	—	2	10	48	101	366	51	6
Dewitt Town	21,990	979	986	—	—	12	14	172	735	46	7
Dobbs Ferry Village................	10,211	238	239	—	—	6	30	21	160	21	1
Dunkirk	13,876	661	675	—	2	13	24	140	471	11	14
East Aurora-Aurora Town	27,094	260	260	—	—	1	13	51	187	8	—
Eastchester Town	18,694	405	405	—	1	6	11	20	304	63	—

See footnotes at end of table.

Table 8. — Number of Offenses Known to the Police, Cities and Towns 10,000 and over in Population, 1995 — Continued

City by State	Population	Crime Index total	Modified* Crime Index total	Murder and non-negligent man-slaughter	Forcible rape	Robbery	Aggravated assault	Burglary	Larceny–theft	Motor vehicle theft	Arson*
NEW YORK — Continued											
East Fishkill Town	22,289	324	326	—	—	—	8	75	233	8	2
East Greenbush Town	14,195	365	367	1	—	3	15	39	294	13	2
East Hampton Town	14,109	554	554	—	2	4	17	199	315	17	—
Ellicott Town	10,773	388	392	—	1	3	27	65	289	3	4
Endicott Village	13,432	676	678	—	—	12	43	91	520	10	2
Evans Town	15,376	410	413	—	1	1	46	79	260	23	3
Fallsburg Town	10,752	341	352	1	—	7	13	132	176	12	11
Fishkill Town	15,831	269	272	—	—	—	12	32	213	12	3
Floral Park Village	16,370	181	181	—	1	11	—	63	84	22	—
Fredonia Village	10,396	244		—	—	1	8	18	211	6	
Freeport Village	39,827	1,624	1,631	3	12	133	95	292	873	216	7
Fulton	12,984	633	638	—	3	5	19	115	479	12	5
Garden City Village	21,959	682	682	—	1	14	5	58	501	103	—
Gates Town	28,827	1,107	1,108	—	—	21	9	189	822	66	1
Geddes Town	11,052	290	290	—	2	2	1	63	220	2	—
Geneva	14,242	567	572	—	3	14	41	70	431	8	5
Glen Cove	23,829	401	402	—	2	18	17	79	244	41	1
Glens Falls	13,537	1,039	1,048	—	5	12	200	174	636	12	9
Glenville Town	21,594	460		1	3	—	24	105	305	22	
Gloversville	17,284	877	884	—	6	16	26	132	646	51	7
Goshen	11,598	65	65	—	—	2	4	17	37	5	—
Greece Town	90,882	3,110		1	12	36	88	327	2,464	182	
Greenburgh Town	40,927	1,646	1,648	1	2	48	39	211	1,101	244	2
Hamburg Town	40,740	1,911	1,923	—	9	19	196	293	1,216	178	12
Hamburg Village	10,337	308		—	—	3	41	37	219	8	
Harrison Town	23,321	595	599	—	1	7	3	90	426	68	4
Haverstraw Town	23,472	609	610	—	1	20	62	134	372	20	1
Hempstead Village	44,648	2,236	2,259	9	33	249	426	346	972	201	23
Irondequoit Town	52,827	3,115	3,119	2	4	67	12	362	2,500	168	4
Ithaca	29,188	1,806	1,814	—	5	48	17	330	1,366	40	8
Jamestown	34,325	2,037	2,057	3	13	57	79	462	1,347	76	20
Johnson City Village	15,931	1,132	1,140	1	13	11	65	165	862	15	8
Kenmore Vllage	16,591	496	498	—	1	19	43	58	347	28	2
Kent Town	13,294	243	245	—	—	—	7	62	168	6	2
Kingston	23,377	1,173	1,175	3	15	25	33	168	886	43	2
Lackawanna	20,114	894	906	—	3	39	233	99	414	106	12
Lancaster Town	14,068	356		—	1	1	1	56	270	27	
Lancaster Village	13,496	218	219	—	1	3	19	52	122	21	1
Lockport	25,659	1,428		2	3	24	202	264	861	72	
Long Beach	34,153	981	984	—	—	33	137	150	526	135	3
Lynbrook Village	19,559	357	358	—	—	2	7	63	249	36	1
Mamaroneck Town	11,503	279	280	—	2	4	4	26	187	56	1
Mamaroneck Village	17,627	566	566	—	—	20	16	88	370	72	—
Manlius Town	35,156	533	535	—	1	2	6	112	402	10	2
Massena Village	11,845	138	138	1	1	4	14	23	90	5	—
Middletown	24,751	1,362	1,366	—	12	42	92	254	912	50	4
Mount Pleasant Town	25,266	482	486	—	4	2	30	78	336	32	4
Mount Vernon	65,742	3,981	4,001	6	21	493	385	766	1,557	753	20
Newburgh Town	24,263	1,142	1,152	—	3	5	11	161	919	43	10
New Castle Town	16,790	176	176	—	—	2	3	25	130	16	—
New Hartford Town and Village	21,937	1,066	1,066	—	1	11	3	132	908	11	—
New Paltz Town and Village	16,710	389		—	6	3	20	55	294	11	
New Rochelle	66,642	2,431	2,439	2	8	110	83	340	1,629	259	8
New Windsor Town	23,133	543	549	—	2	3	79	86	343	30	6
New York	7,319,546	444,758		1,177	2,374	59,280	52,322	73,889	183,037	72,679	
Niagara Falls	60,406	4,590	4,644	2	39	286	152	1,194	2,526	391	54
Niskayuna Town	19,210	543	543	—	—	2	38	80	306	17	—
North Greenbush Town	10,982	169	169	—	—	1	17	42	103	6	—
North Tonawanda	32,874	894	896	—	4	4	8	140	697	41	2
Ogden Town	17,055	390	390	—	—	1	4	71	309	5	—
Ogdensburg	13,150	586	586	—	—	—	3	84	476	23	—

Table 8. — Number of Offenses Known to the Police, Cities and Towns 10,000 and over in Population, 1995 — Continued

City by State	Population	Crime Index total	Modified* Crime Index total	Murder and non-negligent man-slaughter	Forcible rape	Robbery	Aggravated assault	Burglary	Larceny–theft	Motor vehicle theft	Arson*
NEW YORK — Continued											
Olean	17,007	817	819	—	6	17	1	138	645	10	2
Oneida	11,187	490	495	—	3	2	5	107	356	17	5
Oneonta	13,033	469	472	1	6	7	33	82	338	2	3
Orangetown Town	35,133	1,109	1,118	—	2	28	89	219	730	41	9
Orchard Park Town	24,842	724	728	—	3	6	31	116	528	40	4
Ossining Village	22,671	672	676	2	6	51	53	145	386	29	4
Oswego	18,680	775	777	—	—	3	2	146	588	36	2
Peekskill	20,352	997		—	6	54	84	238	576	39	
Plattsburgh	20,902	485		2	4	4	94	16	357	8	
Port Chester Village	24,628	725	725	—	2	31	46	55	522	69	
Port Washington Village	14,901	383	384	—	1	3	9	32	316	22	1
Poughkeepsie	29,385	1,609	1,625	8	26	184	108	348	821	114	16
Poughkeepsie Town	39,619	1,977	1,985	—	2	30	146	213	1,524	62	8
Ramapo Town	66,640	1,397	1,401	—	3	30	23	294	1,008	39	4
Rochester	230,749	22,722	23,074	53	150	1,576	774	5,089	12,871	2,209	352
Rockville Centre Village	25,014	625	631	1	—	20	13	90	460	41	6
Rome	44,152	1,009	1,018	2	6	31	16	185	724	45	9
Rotterdam Town	28,637	1,258	1,262	1	3	12	1	155	1,046	40	4
Saratoga Springs	26,069	1,585	1,592	1	9	17	260	264	1,011	23	7
Scarsdale Village	16,935	300	300	—	—	6	2	28	236	28	—
Schenectady	64,157	3,976	4,019	8	33	240	223	1,066	2,222	184	43
Schodack Town	10,434	223	223	—	1	1	5	66	142	8	—
Shawangunk Town	10,166	154	154	—	—	—	22	17	109	6	—
Southampton Town	37,442	1,609	1,613	1	11	26	48	493	967	63	4
Southold Town	17,917	742	748	—	—	23	2	222	487	8	6
Spring Valley Village	23,060	1,769	1,772	3	11	152	81	243	1,164	115	3
Stony Point Town	12,923	102	102	—	—	—	3	28	68	3	—
Suffern Village	11,342	312	314	—	—	3	6	62	231	10	2
Syracuse	159,603	11,340	11,438	18	84	633	732	3,048	6,032	793	98
Tarrytown Village	10,351	334	337	1	2	6	33	39	209	44	3
Tonawanda	17,373	561		—	3	11	58	65	390	34	
Tonawanda Town	65,845	1,773	1,775	—	6	28	120	192	1,296	131	2
Troy	52,510	3,054	3,063	1	27	147	100	794	1,824	161	9
Ulster Town	12,433	703	703	1	2	9	46	57	575	13	—
Utica	63,978	3,212	3,238	10	13	124	41	600	2,184	240	26
Warwick Town	15,635	178	178	—	—	—	3	44	129	2	—
Watertown	27,818	1,192	1,209	—	20	18	31	281	830	12	17
Webster Town and Village	37,408	793	797	—	3	7	3	110	621	49	4
West Seneca Town	48,242	1,433	1,457	—	6	32	79	221	997	98	24
White Plains	49,680	2,507	2,508	2	2	69	64	153	2,058	159	1
Yonkers	183,156	8,364	8,433	9	25	730	373	1,400	4,140	1,687	69
Yorktown Town	33,753	667	667	—	2	1	5	91	550	18	—
NORTH CAROLINA											
Albemarle	17,544	1,423	1,436	—	12	25	119	388	840	39	13
Archdale	11,580	291	293	1	—	5	7	119	150	9	2
Asheboro	18,787	1,700	1,701	3	3	32	97	317	1,160	88	1
Asheville	65,397	5,093	5,104	12	48	157	337	1,018	3,166	355	11
Boone	13,971	610	610	—	—	3	25	93	458	31	—
Burlington	44,578	2,440	2,447	4	3	89	191	510	1,540	103	7
Carrboro	14,006	1,057	1,061	—	1	17	44	158	786	51	4
Cary	61,849	2,210	2,226	2	6	29	48	381	1,671	73	16
Chapel Hill	47,438	2,657	2,671	—	14	86	175	526	1,751	105	14
Charlotte-Mecklenburg	544,146	52,110	52,455	89	366	2,949	5,824	9,959	29,273	3,650	345
Concord	31,440	1,820	1,830	2	5	40	92	368	1,248	65	10
Durham	145,975	15,866	15,930	24	82	904	825	4,522	8,376	1,133	64
Eden	16,087	1,127	1,134	—	6	33	61	254	709	64	7
Elizabeth City	17,376	1,281	1,283	1	9	28	109	288	786	60	2
Fayetteville	85,484	10,481	10,542	19	64	484	1,095	2,098	5,972	749	61
Garner	17,418	1,099	1,103	—	3	4	45	138	854	55	4

City by State	Population	Crime Index total	Modified* Crime Index total	Murder and non-negligent man-slaughter	Forcible rape	Robbery	Aggravated assault	Burglary	Larceny–theft	Motor vehicle theft	Arson*
NORTH CAROLINA — Continued											
Gastonia	60,137	5,835	5,867	12	28	236	427	1,122	3,760	250	32
Goldsboro	45,807	4,073	4,086	8	20	148	456	731	2,526	184	13
Graham	11,175	878	878	1	1	19	143	172	503	39	—
Greensboro	199,635	18,044	18,177	36	88	785	1,189	3,671	11,067	1,208	133
Greenville	50,198	5,423	5,434	4	27	227	259	1,389	3,302	215	11
Havelock	21,494	600	602	2	1	11	76	112	380	18	2
Henderson	16,319	1,996	2,013	3	6	73	315	447	1,053	99	17
Hickory	30,099	3,425	3,447	2	19	142	223	606	2,276	157	22
High Point	73,484	7,073	7,115	11	26	280	577	1,861	3,893	425	42
Jacksonville	58,111	2,683	2,691	2	28	73	174	499	1,817	90	8
Kannapolis	31,203	1,043	1,056	1	13	42	77	211	639	60	13
Kernersville	13,413	894	899	2	4	11	71	168	594	44	5
Kings Mountain	10,398	810	815	1	3	25	74	148	525	34	5
Kinston	25,673	2,783	2,804	5	9	132	267	621	1,632	117	21
Laurinburg	13,343	1,305	1,316	2	8	45	85	353	760	52	11
Lenoir	14,904	1,289	1,293	1	4	26	86	272	856	44	4
Lexington	18,873	1,618	1,634	1	7	43	155	416	930	66	16
Lumberton	19,526	2,623	2,637	1	7	91	177	730	1,462	155	14
Matthews	15,164	604	606	—	4	9	27	126	416	22	2
Monroe	19,771	1,703	1,707	4	5	43	130	339	1,110	72	4
Mooresville	12,158	721	723	2	6	15	69	106	514	9	2
Morganton	17,677	1,175	1,176	4	4	26	52	232	808	49	1
New Bern	18,409	2,305	2,318	2	9	56	247	458	1,440	93	13
Newton	11,172	778	783	1	6	24	36	211	474	26	5
Raleigh	240,891	17,523	17,626	18	104	648	1,269	3,682	10,565	1,237	103
Reidsville	12,607	1,011	1,016	2	9	22	128	184	630	36	5
Roanoke Rapids	16,856	1,235	1,241	—	3	26	39	172	927	68	6
Rocky Mount	52,858	5,346	5,363	16	28	216	439	1,236	3,189	222	17
Salisbury	28,291	2,015	2,031	2	10	65	162	396	1,274	106	16
Sanford	16,527	2,577	2,586	10	7	59	117	405	1,885	94	9
Shelby	16,067	2,022	2,032	2	11	137	192	453	1,161	66	10
Tarboro	10,990	779	787	1	5	21	63	176	496	17	8
Thomasville	17,983	1,371	1,375	—	4	50	66	342	874	35	4
Wilmington	63,758	7,087	7,129	7	32	225	311	1,490	4,603	419	42
Wilson	39,534	4,196	4,221	8	32	141	250	1,277	2,190	298	25
Winston-Salem	157,870	19,636	19,780	23	142	926	1,307	4,644	11,304	1,290	144
NORTH DAKOTA											
Bismarck	52,839	2,199	2,199	—	4	11	52	264	1,738	130	—
Dickinson	16,266	494	495	—	4	1	13	26	427	23	1
Fargo	79,788	3,559	3,571	—	36	21	45	376	2,833	248	12
Grand Forks	50,403	3,202	3,214	—	6	17	30	328	2,594	227	12
Jamestown	15,437	450	456	—	17	1	3	42	365	22	6
Mandan	15,901	629	630	—	9	4	53	30	494	39	1
Minot	35,518	1,606	1,615	1	17	1	15	147	1,361	64	9
West Fargo	13,835	498	502	1	4	1	5	111	351	25	4
Williston	12,808	468	468	—	6	—	2	26	405	29	—
OHIO											
Akron	222,864	15,901	16,049	18	209	875	1,166	2,792	8,824	2,017	148
Amherst	11,149	476	476	—	4	9	—	28	414	21	—
Ashland	21,205	626	628	—	2	4	3	62	535	20	2
Athens	21,112	584	585	—	5	1	29	82	443	24	1
Aurora	10,735	263	264	—	—	1	6	35	214	7	1
Barberton	27,906	1,603	1,613	—	13	28	216	269	997	80	10
Beavercreek	37,905	1,493	1,536	—	13	35	3	226	1,165	51	43
Bedford Heights	11,880	539	543	1	5	20	75	74	252	112	4
Bellefontaine	12,698	502	502	—	11	10	9	93	365	14	—
Berea	18,877	618	624	—	4	19	18	103	430	44	6
Bexley	13,443	532	532	1	—	19	4	95	381	32	—
Bowling Green	27,975	960	964	—	14	7	12	134	760	33	4

Table 8. — Number of Offenses Known to the Police, Cities and Towns 10,000 and over in Population, 1995 — Continued

City by State	Population	Crime Index total	Modified* Crime Index total	Murder and non-negligent man-slaughter	Forcible rape	Robbery	Aggravated assault	Burglary	Larceny–theft	Motor vehicle theft	Arson*
OHIO — Continued											
Brecksville	12,590	128	128	—	—	—	1	10	114	3	—
Brooklyn	11,147	555	556	—	1	9	—	17	417	111	1
Bucyrus	13,256	970	976	—	1	3	7	236	684	39	6
Cambridge	11,761	971	975	—	2	6	6	102	813	42	4
Centerville	21,836	674	694	—	—	3	5	126	500	40	20
Chillicothe	22,395	1,951	1,962	2	18	21	45	314	1,493	58	11
Cincinnati	359,749	26,931	27,330	50	408	2,155	2,027	5,366	15,012	1,913	399
Cleveland	495,074	38,665	39,344	129	689	4,224	3,108	7,693	13,764	9,058	679
Cleveland Heights	51,704	1,453		1	—	30	1	151	1,065	205	—
Columbus	638,729	58,715	59,630	77	636	3,329	2,582	13,146	31,905	7,040	915
Conneaut	13,270	305	305	1	—	—	6	45	244	9	—
Cuyahoga Falls	55,952	1,962	1,993	—	6	23	81	221	1,514	117	31
Dayton	179,327	18,949	19,209	39	237	1,360	789	4,022	9,357	3,145	260
Dover	12,061	388	388	—	1	1	3	45	324	14	—
Dublin	21,852	767	767	—	2	5	4	174	552	30	—
Englewood	11,325	543	543	—	—	4	2	55	453	29	—
Fairborn	30,058	1,153	1,155	1	5	22	37	173	849	66	2
Fairfield	41,072	2,265		—	7	42	137	384	1,575	120	
Fremont	18,212	1,574	1,587	1	7	39	71	214	1,136	106	13
Gahanna	31,107	861	867	—	7	12	19	165	616	42	6
Garfield Heights	31,006	1,104	1,116	—	13	66	40	207	630	148	12
Girard	11,505	312	321	1	1	3	5	37	230	35	9
Goshen Township	13,044	188	192	—	2	4	8	48	111	15	4
Grove City	22,782	827	827	—	3	17	18	89	669	31	—
Hamilton	65,198	5,078	5,125	11	72	236	549	1,097	2,715	398	47
Hilliard	16,795	596	607	—	6	7	8	102	455	18	11
Huber Heights	40,852	1,691	1,702	1	20	35	18	278	1,263	76	11
Jackson Township	32,951	1,419	1,431	—	1	21	30	180	1,100	87	12
Kent	28,802	1,149	1,166	—	6	24	81	196	767	75	17
Kettering	59,618	2,198	2,215	1	19	28	32	364	1,645	109	17
Lakewood	57,314	1,547	1,557	1	8	46	23	195	1,108	166	10
Lancaster[6]	35,965			1	3	22		208	1,285	67	—
Lebanon	11,697	565	570	1	4	6	23	88	421	22	5
Liberty Township	13,509	579	586	—	1	31	6	82	356	103	7
Lima[6]	44,569			6	36	194		834	1,763	136	30
Lorain	71,231	1,861	1,867	2	37	99	58	559	947	159	6
Madison Township (Lake County)	18,446	455	462	—	3	1	17	107	309	18	7
Madison Township (Montgomery County)	21,169	1,206	1,222	1	13	34	122	167	749	120	16
Mansfield	53,426	4,868	4,909	5	48	144	945	1,147	2,397	182	41
Marietta	15,223	657	660	1	8	6	8	81	538	15	3
Marion	34,763	2,523	2,537	2	25	37	41	560	1,749	109	14
Mason	13,342	381	381	—	4	4	4	47	311	11	—
Massillon	31,431	1,418	1,424	2	11	51	54	259	971	70	6
Mentor	50,278	1,590	1,603	—	10	18	25	174	1,241	122	13
Miamisburg	18,200	1,226	1,228	—	6	12	12	225	864	107	2
Miami Township	23,157	686	688	—	11	1	9	120	526	19	2
Middletown	48,741	3,006	3,028	2	28	79	79	556	2,162	100	22
Montgomery	10,144	262	264	—	—	2	—	37	217	6	2
New Philadelphia	16,708	444	446	—	3	7	19	30	381	4	2
Niles	21,459	1,212	1,212	1	1	21	120	131	801	137	—
North Ridgeville	22,518	335	335	—	2	5	13	81	205	29	—
Norton	11,835	388	392	—	3	2	9	85	269	20	4
Norwalk	15,271	381	382	—	1	5	—	73	299	3	1
Norwood	22,474	1,590	1,593	—	4	58	20	204	1,243	61	3
Oregon	18,356	1,153	1,162	—	6	27	73	149	839	59	9
Oxford	19,540	688	691	—	3	3	12	158	493	19	3
Perkins Township	11,087	569	570	—	1	13	6	62	475	12	1
Perrysburg	13,909	411	411	—	3	1	14	68	316	9	—
Perry Township	31,139	916	919	1	3	16	73	192	579	52	3
Piqua	20,872	1,223	1,227	—	7	12	8	198	954	44	4

See footnotes at end of table.

Table 8. — Number of Offenses Known to the Police, Cities and Towns 10,000 and over in Population, 1995 — Continued

City by State	Population	Crime Index total	Modified* Crime Index total	Murder and non-negligent man-slaughter	Forcible rape	Robbery	Aggravated assault	Burglary	Larceny-theft	Motor vehicle theft	Arson*
OHIO — Continued											
Poland Township	11,302	140	142	—	—	—	6	38	84	12	2
Portsmouth	24,011	1,724		3	19	48	98	454	1,012	90	
Randolph Township	13,896	323		—	4	3	18	26	252	20	
Reading	11,804	368	369	—	3	3	4	56	270	32	1
Salem	12,897	80	80	—	—	—	6	7	63	4	—
Sandusky	30,304	2,609	2,616	1	21	53	38	569	1,789	138	7
Seven Hills	12,094	114	114	—	—	2	6	29	69	8	—
Shaker Heights	30,682	1,005	1,010	—	5	71	15	244	544	126	5
Sharonville	14,030	950	953	—	1	14	8	159	741	27	3
Sheffield Lake	10,258	687		—	5	9	453	48	161	11	
Shelby	10,228	466	467	—	—	1	4	92	355	14	1
Springdale	10,679	1,228	1,230	—	7	32	6	78	1,077	28	2
Springfield	70,698	6,666	6,716	3	73	288	1,068	964	3,822	448	50
Springfield Township (Hamilton Couny)	39,567	1,170	1,174	—	12	45	84	202	788	39	4
Stow	30,317	644	653	—	4	6	6	60	546	22	9
Streetsboro	10,660	360	363	—	2	2	2	56	271	27	3
Strongsville	40,311	865	869	—	4	4	8	152	625	72	4
Sylvania Township	23,305	1,189	1,194	—	2	10	17	161	910	89	5
Tallmadge	15,383	687	710	—	3	7	26	138	473	40	23
Tiffin	18,611	714	716	—	3	5	48	106	539	13	2
Toledo	323,972	27,196	27,688	35	278	1,414	1,146	6,298	14,821	3,204	492
Troy	20,494	898	908	—	12	22	14	130	680	40	10
Twinsburg	12,496	312	312	1	1	1	13	44	234	18	—
Union Township (Butler County)	40,795	1,365	1,394	—	3	15	34	315	963	35	29
Union Township (Clermont County)	34,285	2,140	2,156	—	14	21	7	185	1,803	110	16
University Heights	14,319	324	330	—	5	24	27	45	201	22	6
Upper Arlington	36,242	905	913	—	9	14	11	120	730	21	8
Urbana	11,809	570	574	—	12	10	22	85	421	20	4
Vandalia	14,058	593	597	1	4	7	10	94	444	33	4
Van Wert	11,536	707	717	—	10	1	31	111	532	22	10
Vermilion	11,416	305	307	2	2	1	5	35	251	9	2
Wadsworth	16,910	435	442	—	3	6	8	59	339	20	7
Warrensville Heights	15,808	804	808	1	5	55	68	166	382	127	4
Washington Court House	13,338	483	483	—	6	6	2	166	284	19	—
West Carrollton	14,449	688	691	2	4	7	26	114	478	57	3
Westerville	34,986	918	933	1	6	18	15	132	730	16	15
Westlake	30,503	545	545	—	4	5	7	102	359	68	—
Whitehall	21,188	2,006	2,013	—	12	83	396	247	1,138	130	7
Wickliffe	13,845	362	362	—	1	5	17	25	270	44	—
Wilmington	11,618	626		—	4	7	20	56	517	22	
Worthington	15,111	515	518	1	—	14	3	99	376	22	3
Xenia	24,164	1,435	1,441	—	13	30	45	155	1,152	40	6
Youngstown	92,179	7,050	7,325	66	62	650	791	2,043	2,465	973	275
OKLAHOMA											
Ada	15,952	951	955	—	7	10	70	210	596	58	4
Altus	22,439	1,530	1,536	2	5	21	243	350	885	24	6
Ardmore	23,740	2,448	2,456	3	6	46	118	696	1,463	116	8
Bartlesville	33,846	1,644	1,655	—	5	20	124	256	1,172	67	11
Bethany	20,089	1,070	1,077	1	14	19	190	165	619	62	7
Bixby	10,817	206	206	—	—	1	13	39	126	27	—
Broken Arrow	66,082	2,291	2,291	—	16	26	112	503	1,442	192	—
Chickasha	15,249	1,205	1,214	—	11	26	163	351	548	106	9
Claremore	15,664	743	756	1	11	3	32	138	519	39	13
Del City	23,898	1,417	1,425	2	5	32	23	397	845	113	8
Duncan	22,304	1,362	1,368	1	5	17	49	275	943	72	6
Durant	13,315	905	907	—	11	2	33	158	649	52	2
Edmond	61,599	2,018	2,073	—	11	31	70	455	1,328	123	55
Elk City	10,653	518	519	1	8	2	13	133	331	30	1
El Reno	15,896	902	905	—	6	19	51	196	496	134	3
Enid	46,132	4,371	4,403	2	24	72	338	903	2,789	243	32

Table 8. — Number of Offenses Known to the Police, Cities and Towns 10,000 and over in Population, 1995 — Continued

City by State	Population	Crime Index total	Modified* Crime Index total	Murder and non-negligent man-slaughter	Forcible rape	Robbery	Aggravated assault	Burglary	Larceny–theft	Motor vehicle theft	Arson*
OKLAHOMA — Continued											
Guthrie	10,662	712	730	—	11	10	58	183	400	50	18
Lawton	86,606	7,798	7,833	10	56	176	1,189	1,689	4,254	424	35
McAlester	17,728	871	874	3	4	17	56	209	524	58	3
Miami	13,486	935	943	—	7	6	25	200	620	77	8
Midwest City	53,801	3,616	3,624	1	18	72	207	709	2,183	426	8
Moore	42,854	1,784	1,794	—	9	29	129	409	1,026	182	10
Muskogee	39,201	3,700	3,719	9	44	102	312	1,018	1,942	273	19
Mustang	11,648	402	405	—	1	4	18	130	227	22	3
Norman	87,825	4,482	4,488	2	39	47	142	870	3,065	317	6
Oklahoma City[7]	466,232	53,625	53,979	227	473	1,603	3,724	10,420	32,063	5,115	354
Okmulgee	13,658	1,072	1,084	—	12	25	125	232	624	54	12
Owasso	13,061	449	454	2	4	9	27	88	288	31	5
Ponca City	26,229	1,342	1,355	4	16	17	69	265	881	90	13
Sand Springs	16,597	723	727	—	3	4	24	133	490	69	4
Sapulpa	18,599	1,247	1,253	1	7	16	98	272	757	96	6
Shawnee	28,050	1,902	1,907	1	15	22	91	401	1,238	134	5
Stillwater	37,744	1,829	1,842	—	9	14	91	351	1,314	50	13
Tahlequah	11,473	714	715	—	7	4	9	134	501	59	1
The Village	10,930	949	962	—	3	14	29	102	765	36	13
Tulsa	377,152	27,824	28,095	30	255	947	3,127	6,072	12,991	4,402	271
Weatherford	10,221	371	373	—	1	3	11	81	267	8	2
Woodward	12,303	462	462	—	1	—	50	141	258	12	—
Yukon	21,822	846	859	—	6	5	23	126	663	23	13
OREGON											
Albany	32,351	3,056	3,066	1	12	34	33	375	2,369	232	10
Ashland	17,253	1,060	1,072	1	6	9	8	132	861	43	12
Astoria	10,369	642	647	1	4	5	22	144	433	33	5
Beaverton	60,424	3,317	3,348	1	18	68	135	421	2,307	367	31
Bend	24,377	3,385	3,399	1	10	31	95	381	2,699	168	14
Coos Bay	17,625	1,561	1,566	—	6	15	15	235	1,193	97	5
Corvallis	47,068	2,904	2,937	1	25	24	39	446	2,244	125	33
Dallas	10,866	409	411	1	2	3	2	37	340	24	2
Eugene	120,226	11,876	11,969	3	41	273	409	2,036	8,444	670	93
Forest Grove	15,796	896	899	—	7	13	15	153	624	84	3
Gladstone	10,990	623	633	—	3	13	11	112	388	96	10
Grants Pass	19,672	2,437	2,448	—	5	33	36	384	1,731	248	11
Gresham	79,994	4,713	4,742	4	45	104	185	835	2,743	797	29
Hermiston	11,253	711	713	—	3	8	11	106	526	57	2
Klamath Falls	19,162	1,394	1,410	—	4	35	84	326	823	122	16
La Grande	12,930	518	526	1	3	6	12	77	392	27	8
Lake Oswego	33,724	965	975	—	—	12	30	210	657	56	10
Lebanon	11,991	1,444	1,453	—	3	12	11	144	1,208	66	9
McMinnville	20,654	1,479	1,494	—	15	13	42	219	1,097	93	15
Medford	53,548	5,233	5,291	5	30	43	252	677	3,920	306	58
Milwaukie	20,773	1,199	1,207	—	6	26	37	190	714	226	8
North Bend	10,138	623	625	—	—	2	—	94	498	29	2
Ontario	10,528	1,164	1,174	—	—	7	72	149	872	64	10
Oregon City	16,385	1,402	1,415	—	1	32	67	227	933	142	13
Pendleton	15,973	826	834	—	3	12	10	134	595	72	8
Portland	458,623	55,348	55,834	43	426	2,298	6,066	7,813	29,589	9,113	486
Roseburg	17,967	1,837	1,863	—	4	20	32	302	1,379	100	26
Salem	117,466	12,346	12,402	9	65	247	111	1,852	8,967	1,095	56
Springfield	48,648	5,601	5,629	2	26	90	98	917	4,056	412	28
The Dalles	10,428	1,070	1,075	—	5	7	22	168	801	67	5
Tigard	36,141	2,710	2,724	—	5	59	22	290	2,130	204	14
Tualatin	18,807	1,210	1,215	—	2	14	12	173	919	90	5
West Linn	18,899	510	515	—	4	1	66	82	330	27	5
Woodburn	14,201	1,192	1,205	1	5	13	37	125	864	147	13

See footnotes at end of table.

Table 8. — Number of Offenses Known to the Police, Cities and Towns 10,000 and over in Population, 1995 — Continued

City by State	Population	Crime Index total	Modified* Crime Index total	Murder and non-negligent man-slaughter	Forcible rape	Robbery	Aggravated assault	Burglary	Larceny–theft	Motor vehicle theft	Arson*
PENNSYLVANIA[2]											
Allentown	105,513	7,031	7,075	7	48	414	307	1,435	4,174	646	44
Erie	108,577	5,706	5,740	6	56	341	269	1,015	3,623	396	34
Philadelphia	1,529,848	108,278	110,628	432	773	13,612	7,155	16,165	46,332	23,809	2,350
Pittsburgh	354,780	21,748	21,961	58	243	2,077	1,096	3,598	11,289	3,387	213
RHODE ISLAND											
Barrington	15,780	373	378	—	—	1	2	29	336	5	5
Bristol	21,533	371	371	—	—	3	11	73	265	19	—
Burrillville	16,739	219	219	—	2	1	12	44	145	15	—
Central Falls	15,103	561	561	—	8	19	82	166	187	99	—
Coventry	31,185	697	720	—	1	1	16	189	469	21	23
Cranston	76,780	2,890	2,907	—	18	44	68	774	1,696	290	17
Cumberland	29,953	752	753	—	1	2	124	126	469	30	1
East Greenwich	11,902	252	258	—	2	3	3	42	191	11	6
East Providence	49,707	1,432	1,444	—	13	34	340	923	122	12	
Johnston	27,379	781	785	1	4	4	25	158	504	85	4
Lincoln	18,613	718	720	—	—	3	9	93	519	94	2
Middletown	19,825	429	433	1	3	3	19	56	334	13	4
Narragansett	14,931	461	461	—	7	3	46	93	293	19	—
Newport	24,044	2,289	2,348	—	15	36	211	474	1,456	97	59
North Kingstown	23,704	584	586	—	2	1	40	153	353	35	2
North Providence	33,102	820	823	—	10	15	47	215	440	93	3
North Smithfield	10,826	218	218	—	—	1	44	37	122	14	—
Pawtucket	68,517	3,367	3,391	2	30	116	164	885	1,734	436	24
Portsmouth	17,172	265	267	—	2	2	10	46	188	17	2
Providence	149,805	13,998	14,545	25	97	570	530	3,534	7,150	2,092	547
Scituate	10,102	131	134	—	1	—	7	27	95	1	3
Smithfield	19,767	282	283	1	2	1	12	38	202	26	1
South Kingstown	24,547	629	631	—	10	1	13	90	484	31	2
Tiverton	14,580	352	353	—	1	4	2	96	232	17	1
Warren	11,334	297	297	—	1	—	1	47	229	19	—
Warwick	85,711	3,830	3,874	1	12	23	219	527	2,654	394	44
Westerly	21,530	357	358	1	—	1	3	86	249	17	1
West Warwick	29,364	1,320	1,320	—	2	7	394	208	653	56	—
Woonsocket	40,465	1,095	1,108	1	5	28	78	251	636	96	13
SOUTH CAROLINA											
Aiken	24,990	1,679	1,681	4	9	59	99	355	1,081	72	2
Anderson	29,795	3,045	3,051	5	22	123	417	773	1,553	152	6
Beaufort	10,769	1,495	1,499	—	6	41	87	242	1,080	39	4
Bennettsville	10,515	968	973	1	7	49	194	164	524	29	5
Cayce	10,520	1,213	1,213	1	10	34	75	194	821	78	—
Charleston	77,043	7,955	7,975	12	46	345	781	1,069	4,812	890	20
Clemson	11,143	441	442	—	1	5	29	79	307	20	1
Columbia	104,457	12,832	12,873	9	89	677	1,401	2,256	7,559	841	41
Conway	11,080	1,224	1,225	1	13	34	135	164	815	62	1
Easley	19,701	966	969	1	4	16	75	179	670	21	3
Florence	32,466	3,677	3,688	4	22	167	391	671	2,287	135	11
Gaffney	16,001	909	922	1	5	37	180	177	455	54	13
Goose Creek	27,521	713	720	—	1	6	52	115	512	27	7
Greenville	59,955	6,321	6,348	4	42	202	683	949	4,133	308	27
Greenwood	23,219	2,811	2,815	2	11	64	586	485	1,524	139	4
Greer	12,034	1,060	1,065	1	11	33	129	211	599	76	5
Hanahan	12,917	710	713	—	3	12	40	153	436	66	3
Hartsville	10,236	1,063	1,067	2	7	30	152	159	668	45	4
Irmo	12,826	326	329	—	1	2	15	76	221	11	3
Laurens	10,310	752	755	1	5	22	132	159	401	32	3
Mauldin	13,159	414	415	—	4	6	47	56	288	13	1
Mount Pleasant	34,509	1,496	1,496	—	10	18	43	204	1,163	58	—
Myrtle Beach	28,115	5,389	5,392	1	31	195	349	982	3,591	240	3
Newberry	10,607	686	688	3	2	13	130	47	482	9	2

See footnotes at end of table.

Table 8. — Number of Offenses Known to the Police, Cities and Towns 10,000 and over in Population, 1995 — Continued

City by State	Population	Crime Index total	Modified* Crime Index total	Murder and non-negligent man-slaughter	Forcible rape	Robbery	Aggravated assault	Burglary	Larceny–theft	Motor vehicle theft	Arson*
SOUTH CAROLINA — Continued											
North Augusta	17,661	974	974	—	2	18	40	148	695	71	—
North Charleston	67,886	10,330	10,354	10	69	453	1,214	1,513	5,852	1,219	24
Orangeburg	13,795	1,341	1,342	—	8	58	137	229	860	49	1
Rock Hill	47,121	3,191	3,205	2	14	88	584	470	1,907	126	14
Simpsonville	12,993	317	318	—	1	4	16	42	237	17	1
Spartanburg	45,833	6,697	6,713	6	24	271	1,069	1,146	3,748	433	16
Summerville	22,572	1,677	1,686	—	14	27	113	333	1,081	109	9
Sumter	42,878	3,076	3,093	5	12	155	333	714	1,658	199	17
Union	10,153	190	190	—	2	11	45	34	95	3	—
West Columbia	12,120	1,197	1,204	2	4	25	107	239	738	82	7
SOUTH DAKOTA											
Aberdeen	25,369	1,060	1,069	—	24	2	26	185	784	39	9
Brookings	17,432	623	623	1	4	2	3	94	501	18	—
Mitchell	14,085	622	634	—	7	2	18	94	477	24	12
Pierre	13,738	767	771	—	5	7	28	99	604	24	4
Rapid City	58,248	4,145	4,158	—	48	55	164	680	3,088	110	13
Sioux Falls	110,385	5,766	5,792	5	70	82	344	904	4,136	225	26
Vermillion	10,493	503	503	—	15	1	7	54	416	10	—
Yankton	13,756	432	433	—	1	1	24	51	331	24	1
TENNESSEE											
Athens[1]	14,031			1	—	20	53			64	9
Bartlett	33,281	1,117	1,118	—	4	13	62	159	810	69	1
Brentwood	21,578	541	541	—	—	4	22	82	424	9	—
Bristol	25,346	1,112	1,117	—	4	12	89	153	814	40	5
Brownsville	10,611	931	931	3	17	35	123	272	393	88	—
Chattanooga	154,641	14,269	14,357	28	62	532	1,330	2,595	8,341	1,381	88
Clarksville	93,557	5,462	5,466	11	132	140	487	1,166	3,281	245	4
Collierville	19,849	737		—	1	4	19	78	576	59	
Columbia	35,453	2,923	2,930	3	20	67	222	648	1,834	129	7
Franklin	25,719	1,594	1,595	1	18	24	105	129	1,213	104	1
Gallatin	21,284	1,490		2	9	19	187	258	951	64	
Germantown	34,527	901		—	1	5	18	65	771	41	
Goodlettsville	12,105	1,602	1,602	—	6	29	70	136	1,184	177	—
Greeneville	14,279	847	852	—	1	12	18	155	588	73	5
Hendersonville	37,198	1,412	1,414	—	9	13	70	380	940	—	2
Humboldt	10,896	948	953	1	10	17	150	144	587	39	5
Jackson	54,931	5,439	5,470	9	44	208	634	1,011	3,210	323	31
Johnson City	52,380	3,292		2	24	48	191	514	2,349	164	
Kingsport	39,078	1,819	1,829	3	10	20	214	281	1,189	102	10
Knoxville	171,960	13,667	13,793	19	110	716	2,335	2,810	5,898	1,779	126
LaVergne	11,199	533		—	5	5	127	72	264	60	
Lawrenceburg	11,776	894		1	1	5	58	231	554	44	
Maryville	22,820	598	606	—	19	17	17	94	411	40	8
McMinnville	12,288	937	938	1	10	17	107	164	570	68	1
Memphis	623,902	65,597	66,308	181	785	5,779	4,294	16,026	24,695	13,837	711
Millington	17,347	980	984	—	1	23	57	278	538	83	4
Morristown	22,363	1,577	1,600	1	6	16	193	167	1,059	135	23
Nashville	523,681	56,090		105	487	2,675	6,109	8,236	30,363	8,115	
Oak Ridge	28,650	1,429	1,435	—	10	17	74	159	1,089	80	6
Red Bank	12,001	762		—	8	16	74	150	455	59	
Sevierville	10,363	543	545	1	2	6	25	65	379	65	2
Shelbyville	15,925	738	739	—	2	21	69	186	434	26	1
Smyrna	17,123	997	1,003	2	3	22	48	151	718	53	6
Springfield	14,242	1,226	1,226	1	4	10	170	132	851	58	—
Tullahoma	18,022	1,005		3	8	9	12	184	734	55	—
Union City	10,990	952	956	—	5	8	62	233	616	28	4
TEXAS											
Abilene	112,105	6,049	6,072	5	80	131	480	1,044	4,095	214	23

See footnotes at end of table.

Table 8. — Number of Offenses Known to the Police, Cities and Towns 10,000 and over in Population, 1995 — Continued

City by State	Population	Crime Index total	Modified* Crime Index total	Murder and non-negligent man-slaughter	Forcible rape	Robbery	Aggravated assault	Burglary	Larceny–theft	Motor vehicle theft	Arson*
TEXAS — Continued											
Alama	10,680	397	398	1	—	10	24	102	228	32	1
Alice	20,751	1,257	1,273	1	8	16	102	300	783	47	16
Allen	27,699	997	1,002	—	8	8	19	179	747	36	5
Alvin	21,942	873	879	—	5	18	34	133	637	46	6
Amarillo	168,142	13,293	13,378	16	84	242	1,038	2,419	8,883	611	85
Andrews	10,934	386	387	1	—	2	14	71	291	7	1
Angleton	19,038	673	676	1	9	6	76	146	396	39	3
Arlington	292,324	20,404	20,471	9	154	521	1,892	3,224	12,306	2,298	67
Athens	11,300	678	678	2	—	10	64	202	359	41	—
Austin	523,691	42,586	43,077	46	308	1,336	2,360	7,521	27,434	3,581	491
Balch Springs	19,320	1,368	1,371	2	20	19	72	276	858	121	3
Bay City	19,245	1,467	1,475	—	7	32	130	294	980	24	8
Baytown	68,724	3,995	4,020	6	33	112	238	668	2,513	425	25
Beaumont	117,187	11,181	11,234	14	189	420	607	1,749	7,414	788	53
Bedford	45,690	1,601	1,606	1	15	25	96	385	966	113	5
Beeville	12,732	773	777	—	—	3	72	215	465	18	4
Bellaire	14,944	440	440	—	2	14	12	115	254	43	—
Belton	14,204	448	449	—	2	7	20	98	286	35	1
Benbrook	21,390	374	378	—	7	7	9	60	267	24	4
Big Spring	23,458	1,071	1,080	2	17	17	68	233	701	33	9
Borger	15,197	563	569	1	4	5	33	83	416	21	6
Brenham	12,787	928	934	1	13	16	104	125	646	23	6
Brownsville	115,029	8,408	8,428	7	26	204	580	1,264	5,793	534	20
Brownwood	19,129	1,324	1,332	—	10	5	111	252	919	27	8
Bryan	61,900	4,273	4,292	4	50	69	354	763	2,799	234	19
Burkburnett	10,485	230	246	1	—	—	4	57	158	10	16
Burleson	18,475	647	649	—	4	7	23	95	472	46	2
Canyon	11,977	217	219	1	1	—	8	23	177	7	2
Carrollton	96,035	3,824	3,845	2	28	68	209	709	2,424	384	21
Cedar Hill	25,372	813	821	—	3	10	10	221	496	73	8
Cleburne	23,650	1,588	1,592	1	7	16	69	163	1,238	94	4
College Station	58,351	2,655	2,657	1	29	45	75	313	2,107	85	2
Colleyville	18,898	271	271	—	1	2	6	53	200	9	—
Conroe	31,471	2,348	2,357	—	14	61	201	329	1,581	162	9
Converse	11,597	284	289	—	7	3	28	91	138	17	5
Coppell	24,875	746	751	2	3	5	18	221	472	25	5
Copperas Cove	28,952	1,389	1,400	1	17	24	40	235	1,035	37	11
Corpus Christi	280,605	29,274	29,469	31	216	504	2,013	3,785	21,271	1,454	195
Corsicana	23,337	1,641	1,651	1	29	35	48	305	1,142	81	10
Dallas	1,042,088	98,624	100,051	276	852	5,899	8,942	16,705	49,068	16,882	1,427
Deer Park	30,366	803	805	2	5	8	56	192	480	60	2
Del Rio	36,037	2,253	2,257	1	1	37	233	425	1,460	96	4
Denison	21,902	1,538	1,559	2	11	30	107	242	1,084	62	21
Denton	70,513	4,021	4,049	1	45	53	279	640	2,823	180	28
DeSoto	35,561	1,679	1,691	—	11	35	54	390	1,041	148	12
Dickinson	10,620	667	678	2	7	14	24	127	448	45	11
Donna	14,750	1,219	1,227	3	5	27	39	358	705	82	8
Dumas	13,872	459	460	—	6	3	48	75	316	11	1
Duncanville	37,128	2,154	2,174	2	14	34	127	340	1,327	310	20
Eagle Pass	25,395	1,594	1,597	1	7	18	91	555	846	76	3
Edinburg	37,165	2,135	2,144	4	9	28	170	386	1,393	145	9
El Campo	10,606	558	558	2	5	16	25	136	350	24	—
El Paso	590,215	41,692	41,988	37	242	1,076	3,593	3,828	29,034	3,882	296
Ennis	14,571	666	667	1	1	17	74	99	438	36	1
Euless	40,715	1,463	1,486	1	20	28	72	262	953	127	23
Farmers Branch	25,070	1,641	1,648	1	6	37	61	301	1,003	232	7
Flower Mound	28,432	586	593	—	5	6	53	145	354	23	7
Forest Hill	12,316	706	711	1	11	39	63	122	374	96	5
Fort Worth	460,321	39,667	40,026	108	332	1,965	2,939	7,334	22,128	4,861	359
Freeport	12,324	581	583	3	2	4	51	110	358	53	2
Friendswood	28,946	587	598	1	3	8	27	127	394	27	11

Table 8. — Number of Offenses Known to the Police, Cities and Towns 10,000 and over in Population, 1995 — Continued

City by State	Population	Crime Index total	Modified* Crime Index total	Murder and non-negligent man-slaughter	Forcible rape	Robbery	Aggravated assault	Burglary	Larceny–theft	Motor vehicle theft	Arson*
TEXAS — Continued											
Frisco	10,990	304	306	—	1	3	22	77	194	7	2
Gainesville	14,429	702	707	2	6	9	29	118	502	36	5
Galena Park	10,414	326	326	1	4	2	11	84	186	38	—
Galveston	60,339	6,660	6,721	15	55	356	941	1,234	3,337	722	61
Garland	197,875	11,418	11,486	7	102	271	580	2,146	7,244	1,068	68
Gatesville	12,201	190	194	—	2	6	22	53	99	8	4
Georgetown	17,929	739	740	—	13	6	27	128	532	33	1
Grand Prairie	110,958	6,448	6,451	12	28	140	515	1,065	3,714	974	3
Grapevine	37,369	1,130	1,132	1	15	9	42	246	725	92	2
Greenville	23,056	2,673	2,703	1	8	68	261	638	1,581	116	30
Groves	17,152	996	996	1	4	7	14	189	740	41	—
Haltom City	35,124	1,954	1,965	2	35	36	131	389	1,110	251	11
Harker Heights	18,183	829	829	—	5	12	28	159	589	36	—
Harlingen	56,567	4,774	4,786	1	2	52	312	951	3,152	304	12
Henderson	11,977	1,108	1,108	—	1	26	103	182	739	57	—
Hereford	15,132	838	838	—	2	4	88	114	606	24	—
Hewitt	10,634	274	274	—	2	4	5	82	177	4	—
Houston	1,734,335	131,602	133,094	316	837	9,222	11,885	24,830	61,976	22,536	1,492
Humble	13,344	1,637	1,638	1	2	51	54	154	1,126	249	1
Huntsville	29,540	1,239	1,243	1	9	38	103	162	859	67	4
Hurst	35,919	2,206	2,214	—	26	42	193	274	1,498	173	8
Irving	168,022	9,787	9,828	5	56	213	557	1,344	6,723	889	41
Jacinto City	10,273	457	458	—	1	21	14	80	272	69	1
Jacksonville	12,787	911	912	1	11	19	49	189	608	34	1
Keller	19,174	328	335	—	3	1	9	64	242	9	7
Kerrville	19,350	834	838	—	16	11	38	123	596	50	4
Kilgore	11,574	1,064	1,067	1	11	14	61	168	752	57	3
Killeen	84,416	4,880	5,013	3	75	176	193	949	3,204	280	133
Kingsville	26,192	1,389	1,403	1	6	9	109	273	949	42	14
Lake Jackson	25,555	860	862	—	3	4	15	74	691	73	2
La Marque	15,061	849	852	2	3	26	16	254	472	76	3
Lamesa	10,762	578	579	—	1	3	102	122	339	11	1
Lancaster	23,933	1,476	1,499	3	12	21	100	392	811	137	23
La Porte	31,504	884	890	1	8	14	72	230	500	59	6
Laredo	152,736	10,150	10,234	14	22	174	897	1,628	6,529	886	84
League City	37,798	1,255	1,255	2	16	16	21	233	892	75	—
Leon Valley	10,556	610	610	—	3	12	25	57	458	55	—
Levelland	14,786	553	553	2	2	5	21	38	465	20	—
Lewisville	52,106	3,403	3,416	5	16	53	91	516	2,426	296	13
Live Oak	11,163	366	368	—	3	11	29	29	263	31	2
Lockhart	10,129	622	624	—	6	2	80	154	363	17	2
Longview	74,644	5,527	5,555	2	78	163	268	1,041	3,482	493	28
Lubbock	198,128	13,406	13,476	19	122	297	1,467	2,441	8,086	974	70
Lufkin	32,256	2,127	2,132	5	12	32	161	321	1,520	76	5
Mansfield	19,552	646	648	—	1	9	71	144	392	29	2
Marshall	23,763	2,079	2,081	4	15	32	152	420	1,343	113	2
McAllen	97,093	12,591	12,629	5	29	145	504	1,762	9,193	953	38
McKinney	27,023	1,598	1,598	2	22	36	117	269	1,045	107	—
Mercedes	14,612	433	435	—	7	5	141	93	143	44	2
Mesquite	115,770	7,293	7,403	1	20	89	491	825	5,195	672	110
Midland	97,973	4,838	4,863	8	68	88	309	1,004	3,074	287	25
Mineral Wells	14,924	1,063	1,076	2	6	5	86	252	644	68	13
Mission	39,160	2,656	2,661	1	1	27	42	689	1,717	179	5
Missouri City	46,176	1,427	1,434	—	11	38	60	472	749	97	7
Mount Pleasant	13,128	852	857	1	4	14	78	131	555	69	5
Nacogdoches	32,353	1,417	1,433	1	8	25	237	237	867	42	16
Nederland	17,244	795	796	—	7	7	10	116	623	32	1
New Braunfels	31,739	1,929	1,935	—	18	21	180	292	1,352	66	6
North Richland Hills	56,515	2,340	2,340	1	17	49	91	364	1,646	172	—
Odessa	96,547	6,759	6,813	4	37	113	971	1,269	4,034	331	54
Orange	20,275	1,655	1,673	3	29	81	123	367	966	86	18

Table 8. — Number of Offenses Known to the Police, Cities and Towns 10,000 and over in Population, 1995 — Continued

City by State	Population	Crime Index total	Modified* Crime Index total	Murder and non-negligent man-slaughter	Forcible rape	Robbery	Aggravated assault	Burglary	Larceny–theft	Motor vehicle theft	Arson*
TEXAS — Continued											
Palestine	18,644	1,482	1,491	3	14	27	155	314	933	36	9
Pampa	19,922	1,052	1,052	2	1	11	52	247	675	64	—
Paris	25,012	2,958	2,971	5	13	52	458	403	1,932	95	13
Pasadena	131,726	6,821	6,890	15	63	176	801	1,225	3,661	880	69
Pearland	25,405	712	714	1	1	12	45	116	489	48	2
Pecos	11,885	328	330	1	1	4	13	87	216	6	2
Pharr	37,264	2,740	2,756	4	20	50	165	446	1,771	284	16
Plainview	22,745	1,428	1,436	1	19	15	100	325	937	31	8
Plano	160,357	7,654	7,665	4	38	92	513	1,345	5,282	380	11
Port Arthur	59,902	4,238	4,322	13	11	147	544	1,286	1,920	317	84
Portland	13,898	441	443	—	2	—	10	78	337	14	2
Port Lavaca	11,768	585	589	—	14	3	46	136	361	25	4
Port Neches	13,747	580	583	—	4	2	19	144	376	35	3
Richardson	80,475	3,835	3,858	1	14	87	130	574	2,777	252	23
Richmond	12,848	641	644	5	9	33	79	162	299	54	3
Robstown	13,542	729	736	2	1	11	53	260	358	44	7
Rockwall	13,952	454	456	—	—	2	25	60	346	21	2
Rosenberg	21,931	1,581	1,649	1	27	39	129	279	992	114	68
Round Rock	42,215	1,236	1,241	—	19	19	44	209	893	52	5
Rowlett	31,726	1,154	1,160	—	9	15	57	252	776	45	6
San Angelo	90,396	4,902		3	26	31	341	739	3,624	138	
San Antonio	999,900	79,931	80,765	142	658	2,345	2,033	13,961	52,370	8,422	834
San Benito	23,756	1,669	1,678	—	16	10	95	341	1,134	73	9
San Juan	13,337	832	834	1	1	14	39	277	433	67	2
San Marcos	31,603	1,472	1,477	1	19	21	88	221	1,068	54	5
Schertz	12,932	351	357	—	10	7	21	65	239	9	6
Seagoville	10,246	603	604	1	11	9	81	116	326	59	1
Seguin	20,239	1,500	1,500	2	11	13	81	236	1,102	55	—
Sherman	32,132	2,587	2,598	2	51	53	178	398	1,775	130	11
Snyder	12,388	370	373	1	2	2	29	72	255	9	3
Socorro	27,056	439	440	—	1	4	63	133	196	42	1
South Houston	15,006	902	905	1	—	32	52	183	468	166	3
Southlake	12,577	359	360	—	1	4	23	72	251	8	1
Stafford	10,729	710	710	2	3	12	34	104	454	101	—
Stephenville	14,477	678	680	—	6	5	22	65	563	17	2
Sugar Land	31,452	1,261	1,268	1	4	27	76	240	846	67	7
Sulphur Srings	14,809	879	881	2	18	8	117	116	575	43	2
Sweetwater	12,204	623	630	—	7	12	67	128	393	16	7
Taylor	12,348	451	454	—	4	5	90	63	269	20	3
Temple	53,067	3,170	3,191	5	72	61	133	523	2,153	223	21
Terrell	13,275	1,002	1,004	2	5	37	56	241	580	81	2
Texarkana	33,071	2,587	2,613	2	27	82	214	493	1,641	128	26
Texas City	42,446	4,587	4,607	7	33	129	396	1,358	2,295	369	20
The Colony	26,973	805	835	2	8	25	50	140	559	21	30
Tyler	81,704	7,229	7,273	7	47	166	485	1,169	4,928	427	44
Universal City	13,893	733	737	—	6	14	78	87	516	32	4
University Park	22,835	586	590	—	—	9	5	45	490	37	4
Uvalde	15,906	609	612	—	—	4	56	185	344	20	3
Vernon	11,954	433	441	1	2	8	35	123	251	13	8
Victoria	61,724	4,537	4,555	4	30	55	527	956	2,724	241	18
Vidor	11,569	477	481	—	—	4	33	74	337	29	4
Village	12,628	199	199	—	—	7	3	76	110	3	—
Waco	107,885	10,064	10,129	16	131	457	904	1,900	5,553	1,103	65
Watauga	23,615	613	613	—	5	9	14	159	396	30	—
Waxahachie	19,968	1,343	1,353	—	2	19	67	214	976	65	10
Weatherford	18,252	675	679	—	14	6	33	93	485	44	4
Weslaco	25,658	2,582	2,589	1	3	38	135	692	1,450	263	7
West University Place	14,111	193	194	—	—	7	1	52	122	11	1
White Settlement	16,812	1,013	1,014	—	4	26	34	123	751	75	1
Wichita Falls	99,606	7,011	7,117	8	90	211	552	1,183	4,601	366	106
Wylie	10,124	349	351	—	3	2	17	73	240	14	2

Table 8. — Number of Offenses Known to the Police, Cities and Towns 10,000 and over in Population, 1995 — Continued

City by State	Population	Crime Index total	Modified* Crime Index total	Murder and non-negligent man-slaughter	Forcible rape	Robbery	Aggravated assault	Burglary	Larceny–theft	Motor vehicle theft	Arson*
UTAH											
American Fork	18,604	745	745	—	2	3	46	91	567	36	—
Bountiful	37,911	1,199	1,211	—	11	13	32	165	925	53	12
Brigham City	16,992	739	740	—	4	1	17	66	630	21	1
Cedar City	16,102	896	898	—	—	1	20	75	770	30	2
Centerville	14,089	378	379	—	2	—	9	67	287	13	1
Clearfield	23,871	765	772	—	9	2	30	98	577	49	7
Farmington	10,389	235	236	—	4	3	14	27	176	11	1
Kaysville	17,249	530	534	1	2	5	5	79	413	25	4
Layton	54,633	2,086	2,099	—	10	14	54	275	1,627	106	13
Lehi	10,803	314	314	—	1	3	17	47	220	26	—
Logan	36,891	1,684	1,688	—	12	4	28	193	1,409	38	4
Midvale	12,355	1,376	1,385	4	3	18	67	147	1,019	118	9
Murray	34,116	3,872	3,878	1	21	35	70	394	3,123	228	6
North Ogden	13,375	273	274	—	1	—	9	37	221	5	1
Ogden	69,290	6,194	6,207	5	31	114	272	858	4,498	416	13
Orem	76,079	3,844	3,852	—	11	9	50	350	3,276	148	8
Payson	11,081	498	498	—	13	1	10	50	390	34	—
Pleasant Grove	21,270	602	607	1	5	—	7	91	458	40	5
Provo	90,514	3,952	3,963	1	23	17	89	470	3,157	195	11
Roy	27,985	1,223	1,234	—	4	9	82	196	896	36	11
St. George	39,827	2,270	2,279	1	20	7	112	316	1,644	170	9
Salt Lake City	175,765	22,115	22,205	27	148	564	636	2,950	15,467	2,323	90
Sandy	87,331	4,280	4,293	1	15	30	117	665	3,288	164	13
South Jordan	17,292	673	677	—	5	3	11	137	453	64	4
South Ogden	13,264	637	642	1	2	4	32	82	478	38	5
South Salt Lake	11,448	2,326	2,342	—	17	29	99	312	1,609	260	16
Spanish Fork	13,826	802	805	—	2	1	8	224	552	15	3
Springville	16,117	714	718	—	3	3	21	74	591	22	4
Tooele	15,130	835	835	—	2	6	62	128	589	48	—
West Jordan	51,105	2,834	2,848	2	15	18	81	427	2,141	150	14
VERMONT											
Bennington	17,341	514	515	—	5	—	25	85	383	16	1
Brattleboro	12,700	742	744	—	13	8	11	119	542	49	2
Burlington	38,431	3,421	3,428	—	14	17	43	834	2,393	120	7
Colchester	15,284	612	617	—	4	3	14	133	436	22	5
Essex	17,117	616	623	—	3	—	1	87	510	15	7
Rutland	17,639	679	682	1	4	4	19	89	530	32	3
South Burlington	13,283	933	934	—	7	1	12	109	762	42	1
VIRGINIA											
Alexandria	114,015	7,418	7,439	2	30	291	331	934	4,647	1,183	21
Alexandria State Police	—	3	3	—	1	—	—	—	2	—	—
Blacksburg	35,585	785	787	1	6	8	51	90	604	25	2
Bristol	18,250	696	710	1	—	8	61	131	462	33	14
Bristol State Police	—	4	4	—	—	—	2	1	—	1	—
Charlottesville	41,447	2,844	2,871	2	19	82	169	341	2,104	127	27
Charlottesville State Police	—	2	2	—	—	—	—	1	1	—	—
Chesapeake	182,395	8,538	8,674	10	71	357	383	1,478	5,645	594	136
Chesapeake State Police	—	7	7	—	—	—	2	—	2	3	—
Christiansburg	17,708	645	652	—	3	4	15	93	507	23	7
Colonial Heights	16,612	795	800	—	—	13	19	69	656	38	5
Colonial Heights State Police	—	1	1	—	—	—	—	—	1	—	—
Danville	54,773	2,462	2,471	3	22	123	111	409	1,697	97	9
Danville State Police	—	1	1	—	—	—	—	—	1	—	—
Fairfax City	20,862	1,112	1,112	—	9	26	55	117	833	72	—
Fredericksburg	22,383	590	596	2	8	15	63	65	418	19	6
Front Royal	13,556	701	703	—	7	5	14	90	531	54	2
Hampton	141,034	7,045	7,107	14	40	264	236	829	5,199	463	62
Hampton State Police	—	11	11	—	—	1	—	—	6	4	—
Harrisonburg	33,601	1,286	1,290	—	7	20	29	163	1,004	63	4

Table 8. — Number of Offenses Known to the Police, Cities and Towns 10,000 and over in Population, 1995 — Continued

City by State	Population	Crime Index total	Modified* Crime Index total	Murder and non-negligent man-slaughter	Forcible rape	Robbery	Aggravated assault	Burglary	Larceny–theft	Motor vehicle theft	Arson*
VIRGINIA — Continued											
Harrisonburg State Police	—	3	3	—	—	—	—	—	2	1	—
Herndon	18,018	789	789	—	4	11	5	69	677	23	—
Hopewell	24,699	1,805	1,805	1	13	54	381	213	1,077	66	—
Hopewell State Police	—	2	2	—	—	—	—	—	2	—	—
Leesburg	19,976	741	741	2	10	10	16	69	590	44	—
Lynchburg	67,160	3,414	3,465	5	17	124	351	471	2,263	183	51
Lynchburg State Police	—	1	1	—	—	1	—	—	—	—	—
Manassas	32,193	1,246	1,248	1	10	40	46	157	901	91	2
Martinsville	15,977	1,260	1,263	4	1	52	77	163	891	72	3
Newport News	180,930	11,239	11,318	28	139	538	1,045	1,669	7,181	639	79
Newport News State Police	—	2	2	—	—	—	1	—	—	1	—
Norfolk	243,857	20,602	20,743	53	177	1,293	870	3,134	12,747	2,328	141
Norfolk State Police	—	10	10	1	—	—	1	—	3	5	—
Petersburg	41,346	3,204	3,206	9	25	242	247	614	1,859	208	2
Petersburg State Police	—	2	2	—	1	—	—	—	—	1	—
Poquoson	11,801	174	176	—	1	—	35	13	121	4	2
Portsmouth	104,505	8,969	9,115	34	77	842	549	1,639	4,953	875	146
Portsmouth State Police	—	1	1	—	—	—	—	—	1	—	—
Radford	15,947	396	398	—	2	1	30	120	223	20	2
Radford State Police	—	2	2	—	—	—	—	—	2	—	—
Richmond	203,133	20,984	21,172	120	171	1,491	1,718	4,260	10,848	2,376	188
Richmond State Police	—	13	13	—	—	—	1	—	12	—	—
Roanoke	97,616	5,846	5,911	13	35	251	227	889	4,091	340	65
Roanoke State Police	—	2	2	—	—	—	—	—	1	1	—
Salem	24,461	715	720	1	6	8	14	78	578	30	5
Staunton	25,090	834	836	—	5	13	39	106	653	18	2
Staunton State Police	—	3	3	—	2	—	—	1	—	—	—
Suffolk	55,475	3,548	3,583	4	30	155	286	547	2,307	219	35
Suffolk State Police	—	5	5	—	—	—	—	—	5	—	—
Vienna	15,946	482	482	—	—	12	7	52	383	28	—
Virginia Beach	435,959	20,280	20,491	16	99	479	374	2,915	15,244	1,153	211
Virginia Beach State Police	—	13	13	—	—	—	—	1	10	2	—
Waynesboro	18,937	934	949	2	10	8	41	143	691	39	15
Williamsburg	12,686	529	529	—	—	8	59	45	385	32	—
Winchester	24,035	1,612	1,618	—	13	23	98	174	1,248	56	6
Winchester State Police	—	2	2	—	—	—	—	—	1	1	—
WASHINGTON											
Aberdeen	17,129	2,211	2,230	2	19	9	51	234	1,826	70	19
Anacortes	13,082	554	558	—	1	1	10	75	445	22	4
Auburn	37,084	3,431	3,462	2	26	63	99	365	2,447	429	31
Bellevue	85,626	5,289	5,326	—	22	52	95	681	4,095	344	37
Bellingham	58,059	4,705	4,743	2	51	43	121	549	3,764	175	38
Bonney Lake	10,395	475	478	—	3	5	10	61	376	20	3
Bothell	13,259	945	966	1	5	10	20	153	682	74	21
Bremerton	43,015	2,230	2,238	3	55	46	89	414	1,451	172	8
Burien	29,148	2,773	2,782	1	17	57	97	413	1,753	435	9
Centralia	12,843	1,543	1,555	1	4	12	59	265	1,074	128	12
Des Moines	19,120	1,221	1,223	1	17	37	35	199	767	165	2
Edmonds	30,840	1,315	1,322	—	7	28	28	222	941	89	7
Ellensburg	13,720	840	844	—	7	4	26	84	692	27	4
Federal Way	74,001	6,431	6,469	3	71	173	167	878	4,296	843	38
Kelso	12,445	1,127	1,140	2	20	24	37	211	764	69	13
Kennewick	48,892	3,628	3,653	2	20	53	142	406	2,772	233	25
Kent	41,802	4,772	4,805	1	39	146	84	730	3,075	697	33
Kirkland	42,951	2,197	2,213	2	24	36	41	245	1,666	183	16
Lacey	23,163	1,254	1,256	—	15	22	36	239	887	55	2
Longview	33,243	2,818	2,856	1	15	45	100	520	1,931	206	38
Lynnwood	31,061	3,125	3,146	4	10	70	45	305	2,447	244	21
Moses Lake	13,725	1,670	1,680	1	27	16	143	217	1,208	58	10
Mountlake Terrace	19,969	1,056	1,080	2	9	8	21	154	747	115	24

Table 8. — Number of Offenses Known to the Police, Cities and Towns 10,000 and over in Population, 1995 — Continued

City by State	Population	Crime Index total	Modified* Crime Index total	Murder and non-negligent man-slaughter	Forcible rape	Robbery	Aggravated assault	Burglary	Larceny–theft	Motor vehicle theft	Arson*
WASHINGTON — Continued											
Mount Vernon	21,020	2,343	2,367	1	12	21	27	243	1,954	85	24
Oak Harbor	19,014	629	637	—	15	10	16	42	529	17	8
Olympia	40,378	2,511	2,516	1	25	23	108	327	1,886	141	5
Pasco	23,608	2,124	2,127	3	27	34	118	272	1,495	175	3
Port Angeles	19,221	1,210	1,219	1	7	15	28	240	862	57	9
Puyallup	27,338	2,303	2,338	3	10	34	49	196	1,800	211	35
Redmond	40,415	1,587	1,613	—	13	27	34	243	1,179	91	26
Renton	44,247	3,946	3,970	9	27	108	107	611	2,525	559	24
Richland	36,328	1,684	1,706	—	21	8	60	240	1,281	74	22
Sea Tac	24,505	2,287	2,295	2	26	69	92	393	1,334	371	8
Seattle	529,526	55,507	55,753	41	260	2,213	2,390	7,689	35,970	6,944	246
Spokane	195,956	16,484	16,558	23	132	471	960	2,966	11,000	932	74
Tacoma	186,074	21,766	21,903	28	171	925	2,099	3,655	12,250	2,638	137
Tukwila	12,788	3,950	3,952	4	27	108	103	391	2,898	419	2
Tumwater	11,702	857	860	—	9	6	27	168	586	61	3
Vancouver	52,700	5,804	5,839	1	85	145	394	1,039	3,410	730	35
Walla Walla	29,669	2,931	2,955	—	32	33	222	431	2,121	92	24
Wenatchee	23,693	2,282	2,300	—	20	18	67	328	1,747	102	18
Yakima	62,996	8,461	8,508	6	50	163	495	1,680	5,507	560	47
WEST VIRGINIA											
Beckley	18,513	1,386	1,404	2	9	28	112	164	1,003	68	18
Bluefield	12,634	331	333	3	—	11	23	102	184	8	2
Charleston	56,204	5,486	5,568	9	47	287	316	908	3,529	390	82
Clarksburg	17,736	449	449	1	4	6	8	69	349	12	—
Fairmont	20,694	644	651	1	5	10	16	109	469	34	7
Huntington	53,965	3,385	3,450	3	67	103	108	696	2,232	176	65
Martinsburg	14,970	1,146	1,146	1	—	25	16	164	890	50	—
Morgantown	26,604	1,403	1,413	—	19	17	64	310	944	49	10
Moundsville	10,836	506	506	—	—	4	4	122	345	31	—
Parkersburg	33,210	1,606	1,630	1	17	17	68	329	1,076	98	24
St. Albans	10,858	296	298	—	1	1	—	75	201	18	2
South Charleston	13,453	460	460	—	1	9	10	58	343	39	—
Vienna	11,066	419	420	—	3	—	1	21	388	6	1
Weirton	21,552	386	398	—	4	3	27	84	251	17	12
Wheeling	34,080	1,285	1,295	2	11	40	148	275	739	70	10
WISCONSIN											
Appleton	70,155	2,305	2,308	1	2	9	23	261	1,921	88	3
Ashwaubenon	17,410	970	971	—	6	4	4	65	869	22	1
Baraboo	10,343	494	495	—	1	5	5	41	423	19	1
Beaver Dam	14,944	680	689	—	2	—	41	34	584	19	9
Beloit	36,939	1,970	1,982	1	21	60	51	263	1,457	117	12
Brookfield	37,111	1,414	1,432	—	1	14	3	124	1,203	69	18
Brown Deer	11,993	558	560	—	—	9	8	37	469	35	2
Caledonia	22,762	451	461	—	—	7	3	69	340	32	10
Cedarburg	10,747	203	204	—	—	1	1	33	164	4	1
Chippewa Falls	13,484	444	451	—	2	—	14	62	349	17	7
Cudahy	18,411	612	642	1	2	7	21	85	448	48	30
De Pere	19,028	624	627	—	1	2	11	95	484	31	3
Eau Claire	58,947	3,091	3,139	—	1	19	131	452	2,367	121	48
Everest	14,226	518	525	—	5	1	25	60	400	27	7
Fitchburg	17,180	593	593	—	3	15	14	117	415	29	—
Fond du Lac	39,657	2,167	2,176	1	4	12	25	156	1,922	47	9
Fort Atkinson	11,291	427	429	—	2	2	5	45	359	14	2
Fox Valley	15,512	422	425	—	—	1	4	52	356	9	3
Franklin	21,901	600	602	—	6	10	12	95	437	40	2
Germantown	16,361	447	451	—	2	5	2	39	391	8	4
Glendale	13,310	1,044	1,045	—	—	36	6	72	846	84	1
Grand Chute	14,866	868	868	2	4	2	20	47	773	20	—
Green Bay	103,536	4,868	4,902	4	75	70	360	555	3,616	188	34

147

Table 8. — Number of Offenses Known to the Police, Cities and Towns 10,000 and over in Population, 1995 — Continued

City by State	Population	Crime Index total	Modified* Crime Index total	Murder and non-negligent man-slaughter	Forcible rape	Robbery	Aggravated assault	Burglary	Larceny–theft	Motor vehicle theft	Arson*
WISCONSIN — Continued											
Greendale	14,742	786	786	—	1	2	14	13	735	21	—
Greenfield	32,309	1,263	1,268	2	3	19	8	190	926	115	5
Janesville	57,320	3,146	3,168	1	20	33	129	559	2,266	138	22
Kaukauna	12,006	287	287	—	1	5	18	36	218	9	—
Kenosha	85,808	3,194	3,221	5	35	93	179	647	2,003	232	27
La Crosse	51,287	3,038	3,044	—	14	14	26	170	2,707	107	6
Madison	196,156	9,287	9,335	5	67	282	263	1,459	6,478	733	48
Manitowoc	33,342	1,355	1,360	—	13	4	28	139	1,134	37	5
Marinette	12,364	443	444	—	5	—	7	42	383	6	1
Marshfield	19,791	636	639	—	9	1	1	87	513	25	3
Menasha	15,682	572	574	—	4	1	7	54	499	7	2
Menasha Town	14,517	280	282	—	—	—	1	42	228	9	2
Menomonee Falls	28,677	757	759	—	1	8	9	124	550	65	2
Monomonie	15,049	867	873	1	4	1	2	109	726	24	6
Mequon	21,651	171	172	—	—	1	—	20	136	14	1
Merrill	10,213	477	478	—	—	—	—	44	424	9	1
Middleton	14,565	386	389	—	4	7	2	46	317	10	3
Milwaukee	622,467	52,679	53,234	138	370	3,650	2,579	8,366	26,231	11,345	555
Monroe	10,633	390	391	—	3	4	10	56	289	28	1
Mount Pleasant	21,804	812	813	—	3	16	16	140	592	45	1
Muskego	20,131	156	156	—	—	4	—	24	120	8	—
Neenah	24,574	858	860	—	1	2	62	94	670	29	2
New Berlin	36,222	563	592	—	—	2	19	119	400	23	29
Oak Creek	19,453	837	846	—	5	16	38	64	652	62	9
Oconomowoc	11,871	412	413	—	—	1	10	54	333	14	1
Onalaska	12,786	425	425	—	1	4	7	26	363	24	—
Oshkosh	56,682	2,900	2,904	—	18	15	66	455	2,268	78	4
Platteville	10,293	247	247	—	3	1	4	21	211	7	—
Pleasant Prairie	13,452	459	460	—	2	2	11	37	396	11	1
Plover	11,870	226	227	—	1	—	4	40	176	5	1
Port Washington	10,030	285	291	—	—	1	5	36	238	5	6
Racine	86,708	6,165	6,214	11	23	373	410	1,105	3,720	523	49
River Falls	11,613	619	623	—	3	1	14	30	559	12	4
Sheboygan	50,774	2,704	2,747	—	11	27	52	344	2,188	82	43
Shorewood	13,631	581	581	—	1	29	8	68	454	21	—
South Milwaukee	20,369	775	795	—	—	4	11	119	606	35	20
Stevens Point	21,440	1,337	1,342	2	14	2	45	170	1,069	35	5
Stoughton	10,402	384	385	—	2	2	18	51	303	8	1
Sun Prairie	17,548	589	604	—	3	7	17	40	499	23	15
Superior	27,768	1,958	1,980	—	19	13	53	261	1,530	82	22
Two Rivers	13,294	283	286	—	3	—	20	35	217	8	3
Watertown	20,853	925	943	—	7	7	16	148	713	34	18
Waukesha	60,623	1,823	1,831	1	13	15	57	216	1,433	88	8
Wausau	39,113	1,484	1,491	—	9	3	29	141	1,230	72	7
Wauwatosa	48,078	2,254	2,264	—	6	93	12	258	1,657	228	10
West Allis	61,753	2,883	2,927	1	8	74	75	496	2,010	219	44
West Bend	27,435	1,310	1,314	—	2	4	22	95	1,145	42	4
Whitefish Bay	14,180	277	277	—	—	3	3	24	238	9	—
Whitewater	13,779	368	378	—	4	1	13	45	296	9	10
Wisconsin Rapids	18,493	921	923	—	1	—	15	160	721	24	2
WYOMING											
Casper	49,605	3,281	3,321	3	14	21	128	566	2,360	189	40
Cheyenne	54,051	2,547	2,558	—	19	23	57	237	2,136	75	11
Evanston	12,092	763	763	—	3	4	23	116	594	23	—
Gillette	18,918	1,156	1,168	—	11	2	51	148	917	27	12
Green River	13,545	612	616	—	1	1	19	75	501	15	4

Table 8. — Number of Offenses Known to the Police, Cities and Towns 10,000 and over in Population, 1995 — Continued

City by State	Population	Crime Index total	Modified* Crime Index total	Murder and non-negligent man-slaughter	Forcible rape	Robbery	Aggravated assault	Burglary	Larceny–theft	Motor vehicle theft	Arson*
WYOMING — Continued											
Laramie	27,451	985	986	—	9	1	43	92	806	34	1
Riverton	10,144	707	708	1	2	2	19	88	580	15	1
Rock Springs	20,313	1,477	1,477	1	8	8	115	137	1,137	71	—
Sheridan	14,922	619	625	—	9	4	15	71	497	23	6

[1]Due to reporting changes or annexations, figures are not comparable to previous years.

[2]Complete data for 1995 were not available for the states of Delaware, Illinois, Kansas, Montana, and Pennsylvania. See "Offense Estimation," pages 367–368 for details.

[3]Forcible rape figures furnished by the state-level Uniform Crime Reporting (UCR) Program administered by the Illinois Department of State Police were not in accordance with national UCR guidelines. Therefore, the figures were excluded from the forcible rape, Crime Index total, and Modified Crime Index total categories.

[4]Indianapolis/Marion County, Indiana is a unified city–county government with a total population of 772,792.

[5]Aggravated assault figures for 1994 furnished by the state-level Uniform Crime Reporting (UCR) Program administered by the Kentucky State Police were not in accordance with national UCR guidelines; therefore, the 1995 figures, which are in accordance with the national UCR guidelines, cannot be compared to the 1994 figures,

[6]Aggravated assault data furnished by the police department were not in accordance with national Uniform Crime Reporting guidelines; therefore, the figures were excluded from the aggravated assault, Crime Index total, and Modified Crime Index total categories.

[7]The increase in murders was the result of the bombing of the Alfred P. Murrah Federal Building in Oklahoma City.

Table 9. — Number of Offenses Known to the Police, Universities and Colleges, 1995

*Arson is shown only if 12 months of arson data were received. Dashes (—) indicate zero data.

University/College	Student enrollment[1]	Violent[2] crime total	Violent crime				Property[3] crime total	Property crime			
			Murder and non-negligent manslaughter	Forcible rape	Robbery	Aggravated assault		Burglary	Larceny–theft	Motor vehicle theft	Arson*
ALABAMA											
Alabama State University	5,037	16	—	—	9	7	169	4	161	4	
Auburn University, Main Campus	21,226	1	—	—	—	1	348	16	330	2	
Jacksonville State University	7,553	—	—	—	—	—	102	2	99	1	
Talladega College	976	3	—	—	—	3	52	10	42	—	
Troy State University..............	6,458	—	—	—	—	—	94	5	87	2	
University of Alabama:											
Huntsville	7,492	1	—	—	1	—	87	6	81	—	—
Tuscaloosa	[4]	10	—	2	5	3	453	16	426	11	
University of Montevallo	3,282	—	—	—	—	—	29	—	28	1	
University of North Alabama	5,221	7	—	—	4	3	61	5	56	—	
University of South Alabama	12,386	4	—	—	3	1	75	16	58	1	
University of West Alabama	2,320	2	—	—	—	2	11	—	11	—	
ALASKA											
University of Alaska, Fairbanks	7,703	21	1	8	1	11	106	3	99	4	—
ARIZONA											
Arizona State University:											
Tempe.....................	42,189	53	1	8	4	40	1,484	386	1,061	37	4
West	4,681	—	—	—	—	—	38	11	27	—	3
Arizona Western College...........	5,647	1	—	—	—	1	56	6	50	—	—
Central Arizona College	4,369	1	—	1	—	—	65	14	50	1	—
Northern Arizona University	19,242	17	—	1	—	16	602	64	523	15	2
Pima Community College	27,960	4	—	—	—	4	146	48	80	18	—
University of Arizona	35,306	21	—	4	6	11	1,069	160	830	79	9
Yavapai College	4,953	—	—	—	—	—	74	12	62	—	
ARKANSAS											
Arkansas State University	9,631	4	—	1	2	1	195	26	167	2	1
Henderson State University	4,033	2	—	—	—	2	56	11	45	—	1
Southern Arkansas University	2,957	3	—	—	1	2	56	5	50	1	—
University of Arkansas:											
Fayetteville..................	14,495	9	—	1	4	4	290	56	224	10	—
Little Rock	11,451	9	—	1	2	6	152	20	127	5	—
Medical Science...............	1,864	4	—	—	1	3	156	4	146	6	1
Monticello	2,394	—	—	—	—	—	40	5	34	1	—
Pine Bluff...................	3,823	15	—	—	—	15	162	49	109	4	—
University of Central Arkansas	9,192	6	—	1	—	5	89	11	77	1	3
CALIFORNIA											
Allen Hancock College	7,384	1	—	—	—	1	45	8	37	—	1
Cabrillo Community College	12,212	7	—	—	1	6	67	23	44	—	—
California State Polytechnic University:											
Pomona	16,304	3	1	—	1	1	301	28	223	50	—
San Luis Obispo	15,440	5	—	2	2	1	508	41	464	3	6
California State University:											
Bakersfield...................	5,086	5	—	—	—	5	52	12	35	5	—
Chico	14,232	7	—	2	1	4	345	28	307	10	4
Dominguez Hills	9,744	5	—	—	3	2	118	63	40	15	2
Fresno......................	17,293	6	—	—	1	5	480	40	358	82	6
Fullerton....................	22,097	6	—	1	—	5	489	10	446	33	—
Hayward	12,567	6	—	1	3	2	188	34	138	16	—
Long Beach	26,277	22	—	1	3	18	462	69	345	48	1
Los Angeles	18,224	9	—	1	4	4	457	23	351	83	1
Monterey Bay	[4]	13	—	1	1	11	50	10	36	4	—
Northridge	24,310	19	—	5	5	9	482	57	350	75	—
Sacramento..................	22,726	7	—	2	4	1	340	37	269	34	—
San Bernardino	11,864	12	—	2	2	8	334	108	198	28	1
San Jose	[4]	18	—	3	7	8	389	33	336	20	—
San Marcos	2,736	1	—	—	1	—	30	3	27	—	—
Stanislaus	5,877	—	—	—	—	—	136	3	130	3	—
College of the Sequoias............	8,483	4	—	—	—	4	81	39	37	5	1
Contra Costa Community College	6,710	40	—	—	16	24	451	36	386	29	—
El Camino College	21,763	9	—	—	3	6	262	32	213	17	2

See footnotes at end of table.

Table 9. — Number of Offenses Known to the Police, Universities and Colleges, 1995 — Continued

University/College	Student enrollment[1]	Violent[2] crime total	Violent crime				Property[3] crime total	Property crime			
			Murder and non-negligent manslaughter	Forcible rape	Robbery	Aggravated assault		Burglary	Larceny–theft	Motor vehicle theft	Arson*
CALIFORNIA — Continued											
Foothill-De Anza College	35,807	—	—	—	—	—	199	22	171	6	1
Fresno Community College	16,962	19	—	—	2	17	290	14	224	52	—
Humboldt State University	7,049	3	—	—	—	3	330	23	303	4	—
Kings River Community College	6,065	4	—	2	—	2	46	1	42	3	2
Los Angeles City College	15,433	17	—	—	8	9	91	31	54	6	—
Marin Community College	11,708	1	—	—	—	1	62	3	59	—	—
Pasadena Community College	21,787	8	—	—	5	3	238	4	223	11	3
San Bernardino Community College ..	9,878	3	—	—	2	1	140	19	112	9	—
San Diego State University	28,372	20	—	3	3	14	598	43	446	109	3
San Francisco State University	26,260	12	—	—	5	7	461	19	402	40	20
San Jose/Evergreen Community College	9,524	2	—	—	1	1	87	13	68	6	—
Santa Rosa Junior College	20,869	3	—	—	—	3	95	13	79	3	—
Sonoma State University	6,611	2	—	—	1	1	187	25	159	3	—
University of California:											
Berkeley	29,634	35	—	2	24	9	1,477	80	1,363	34	4
Davis	22,442	8	—	1	2	5	1,303	116	1,174	13	5
Hastings College of the Law	1,234	—	—	—	—	—	42	2	40	—	—
Irvine	17,073	11	—	1	1	9	837	46	752	39	3
Lawrence Livermore Laboratory ...	[4]	—	—	—	—	—	23	—	23	—	—
Los Angeles	35,110	35	—	7	13	15	1,621	334	1,154	133	3
Riverside	8,590	46	—	—	3	43	400	107	251	42	—
Sacramento...................	3,744	4	—	1	2	1	281	19	240	22	1
San Diego	17,774	—	—	—	—	—	698	65	540	93	2
San Francisco Medical School	3,729	6	—	1	—	5	624	27	578	19	1
Santa Barbara.................	17,834	8	—	2	—	6	569	46	513	10	2
Santa Cruz...................	10,117	5	—	1	—	4	269	65	201	3	3
West Valley College	10,550	4	—	—	2	2	144	56	86	2	—
COLORADO											
Auraria Higher Education Center	[4]	11	—	—	4	7	393	23	364	6	1
Colorado School of Mines	3,677	—	—	—	—	—	57	4	53	—	3
Colorado State University	27,130	14	—	3	2	9	472	38	430	4	5
Fort Lewis College	4,015	2	—	2	—	—	89	4	83	2	—
University of Colorado:											
Boulder.......................	27,862	10	—	8	2	—	814	141	665	8	18
Colorado Springs...............	6,606	—	—	—	—	—	84	1	83	—	—
Health Sciences	2,500	1	—	—	—	1	238	14	221	3	2
University of Northern Colorado	12,226	6	—	4	—	2	265	31	230	4	2
University of Southern Colorado	5,182	—	—	—	—	—	66	13	53	—	—
CONNECTICUT											
Central Connecticut State University ..	11,959	3	—	1	—	2	102	6	88	8	—
Eastern Connecticut State University ..	4,523	—	—	—	—	—	144	1	142	1	—
Southern Connecticut State University.....................	11,652	3	—	1	—	2	176	56	109	11	—
University of Connecticut:											
Avery Point	[4]	2	—	—	—	2	16	4	12	—	—
Health Center.................	[4]	—	—	—	—	—	137	10	120	7	—
Storrs	[4]	14	—	4	3	7	445	87	347	11	2
Western Connecticut State University.....................	5,583	3	—	3	—	—	133	43	89	1	3
Yale University	10,916	15	—	—	8	7	755	256	494	5	—
DELAWARE[5]											
FLORIDA											
Florida A&M University	10,084	22	1	—	7	14	421	10	391	20	1
Florida Atlantic University	17,487	5	—	—	1	4	234	10	219	5	1
Florida International University	26,547	3	—	—	—	3	434	79	317	38	2
Santa Fe Community College	12,640	—	—	—	—	—	74	—	71	3	—
University of Central Florida	25,592	2	—	—	—	2	275	41	230	4	—
University of Florida	38,277	30	—	2	4	24	1,301	56	1,168	77	8
University of North Florida..........	9,884	5	—	1	—	4	99	14	85	—	—
University of South Florida:											
St. Petersburg.................	[4]	2	—	—	—	2	39	3	36	—	—
Sarasota.....................	[4]	3	—	—	—	3	52	2	50	—	—
Tampa.......................	36,043	17	—	—	3	14	672	39	606	27	3

See footnotes at end of table.

Table 9. — Number of Offenses Known to the Police, Universities and Colleges, 1995 — Continued

University/College	Student enrollment[1]	Violent[2] crime total	Violent crime				Property[3] crime total	Property crime			
			Murder and non-negligent man-slaughter	Forcible rape	Robbery	Aggravated assault		Burglary	Larceny–theft	Motor vehicle theft	Arson*
FLORIDA — Continued											
University of West Florida	7,801	2	—	1	—	1	66	6	60	—	—
GEORGIA											
Abraham Baldwin College	2,751	—	—	—	—	—	51	1	49	1	—
Agnes Scott College	595	2	—	—	—	2	37	2	35	—	—
Albany State College	3,062	3	—	—	—	3	54	20	33	1	—
Armstrong State College	2,830	—	—	—	—	—	73	1	72	—	—
Augusta College	5,651	1	—	—	1	—	57	—	55	2	—
Berry College	1,701	—	—	—	—	—	56	2	53	1	1
Brunswick College	1,912	—	—	—	—	—	10	—	10	—	—
Clark Atlanta University	5,193	12	—	1	2	9	203	33	164	6	—
Clayton State College	4,903	—	—	—	—	—	41	—	38	3	—
Columbus College	5,526	2	—	—	—	2	61	3	58	—	—
Dalton College	3,003	—	—	—	—	—	4	—	4	—	—
Emory University	10,899	4	—	—	3	1	747	45	693	9	—
Fort Valley State College	2,823	4	—	—	3	1	38	1	37	—	—
Georgia College	5,655	5	—	1	—	4	66	1	65	—	—
Georgia Institute of Technology	12,901	15	—	—	11	4	1,176	231	845	100	—
Georgia Southern University	14,138	—	—	—	—	—	278	3	273	2	—
Georgia Southwestern College	2,532	2	—	—	—	2	18	1	17	—	—
Georgia State University	23,730	7	—	—	5	2	673	19	652	2	—
Gordon College	2,157	—	—	—	—	—	1	—	1	—	—
Kennesaw College	11,901	—	—	—	—	—	42	1	39	2	—
Medical College of Georgia	2,546	1	—	—	—	1	235	6	192	37	1
Mercer University	5,160	2	—	—	—	2	104	3	99	2	—
Middle Georgia College	2,168	1	—	—	—	1	59	7	52	—	—
North Georgia College	2,877	—	—	—	—	—	9	—	9	—	—
Reinhardt College	942	—	—	—	—	—	25	4	21	—	—
Savannah State College	2,759	19	—	—	1	18	20	4	13	3	—
Southern College of Technology	3,952	—	—	—	—	—	51	7	43	1	—
South Georgia College	1,267	—	—	—	—	—	23	6	17	—	—
Valdosta State University	9,126	6	—	—	4	2	200	34	162	4	—
Wesleyan College	424	1	—	—	—	1	10	—	10	—	—
West Georgia College	8,306	4	—	1	—	3	218	57	160	1	2
ILLINOIS[5]											
INDIANA											
Ball State University	20,390	20	—	7	2	11	709	83	618	8	—
Indiana State University	11,641	19	—	1	—	18	332	12	311	9	1
Indiana University:											
Bloomington	35,594	18	—	9	4	5	861	132	712	17	1
Gary	5,639	—	—	—	—	—	34	1	31	2	—
Indianapolis	26,766	5	—	2	3	—	616	7	600	9	—
New Albany	5,464	1	—	—	—	1	41	—	40	1	—
Purdue University	36,172	53	2	3	1	47	960	27	921	12	1
IOWA											
Iowa State University	24,990	6	—	3	1	2	344	37	302	5	10
University of Northern Iowa	12,956	3	—	2	1	—	163	6	156	1	3
KANSAS[5]											
KENTUCKY[6]											
Eastern Kentucky University	16,038	6	—	—	5	1	204	7	194	3	—
Jefferson Community College........	10,301	1	—	—	1	—	2	—	2	—	—
Kentucky State University...........	2,563	2	—	—	2	—	32	4	27	1	1
Morehead State University	8,693	1	—	1	—	—	154	7	147	—	—
Murray State University	7,936	2	—	—	2	—	95	11	84	—	2
Northern Kentucky University	11,958	—	—	—	—	—	115	5	110	—	—
University of Kentucky	23,622	10	—	3	6	1	936	87	833	16	4
University of Louisville	20,721	11	—	2	5	4	365	19	332	14	4
Western Kentucky University	14,728	5	—	—	1	4	208	1	204	3	2
LOUISIANA											
Grambling State University	7,610	57	—	—	4	53	207	81	124	2	6

See footnotes at end of table.

Table 9. — Number of Offenses Known to the Police, Universities and Colleges, 1995 — Continued

University/College	Student enrollment[1]	Violent[2] crime total	Violent crime				Property[3] crime total	Property crime			
			Murder and non-negligent man-slaughter	Forcible rape	Robbery	Aggravated assault		Burglary	Larceny–theft	Motor vehicle theft	Arson*
LOUISIANA — Continued											
Louisiana State University:											
Baton Rouge	26,010	11	—	—	4	7	738	146	580	12	—
Medical Center	3,217	—	—	—	—	—	104	1	102	1	—
Shreveport	4,237	—	—	—	—	—	20	2	18	—	—
Louisiana Tech. University	9,947	1	—	—	1	—	188	30	153	5	—
McNeese State University	8,701	—	—	—	—	—	131	43	82	6	—
Nichols State University	7,196	—	—	—	—	—	71	46	25	—	1
Northeast Louisiana University	11,379	7	—	—	—	7	301	3	293	5	—
Northwestern State University	8,761	4	—	—	—	4	200	35	164	1	—
Southeastern Louisiana University	13,818	3	—	—	—	3	203	16	186	1	—
Southern University and A & M College, Baton Rouge	9,904	23	—	—	6	17	293	44	216	33	2
University of Southwestern Louisiana	16,789	13	—	—	2	11	279	74	200	5	2
MAINE											
University of Maine:											
Farmington	2,338	—	—	—	—	—	44	12	32	—	—
Orono	11,001	5	—	2	2	1	197	10	185	2	6
University of Southern Maine	9,628	—	—	—	—	—	123	2	115	6	—
MARYLAND											
Bowie State University	4,896	4	—	—	—	4	51	29	22	—	—
Coppin State University	3,380	1	—	—	—	1	81	1	76	4	—
Frostburg State University	5,443	3	—	1	—	2	69	2	67	—	—
Morgan State University	5,766	32	—	1	19	12	215	75	133	7	1
St. Mary's College	1,565	2	—	—	—	2	45	4	41	—	—
Salisbury State University	6,048	2	—	—	1	1	184	8	173	3	1
Towson State University	14,551	8	—	2	2	4	442	72	366	4	—
University of Baltimore	5,204	6	—	—	2	4	204	17	182	5	—
University of Maryland:											
Baltimore City	4	29	—	—	18	11	523	31	477	15	—
Baltimore County	10,315	6	—	—	2	4	233	51	176	6	—
College Park	32,493	46	—	5	12	29	1,408	223	1,111	74	10
Eastern Shore	2,925	12	—	1	—	11	116	14	102	—	—
MASSACHUSETTS											
Boston College	14,713	9	—	4	—	5	271	12	251	8	—
Boston University	29,072	22	—	1	9	12	745	64	654	27	—
Brandeis University	4,008	6	—	—	1	5	143	4	137	2	—
Emerson College	3,409	3	—	1	—	2	94	6	88	—	—
Framingham State College	5,149	2	—	—	—	2	37	16	21	—	—
Massachusetts College of Art	2,145	2	—	—	—	2	39	4	34	1	—
Massachusetts Institute of Technology	9,774	19	—	—	3	16	847	42	786	19	—
North Adams State College	1,775	5	—	—	—	5	34	3	31	—	—
Northeastern University	25,086	16	—	—	10	6	470	30	427	13	—
Tufts University—Medford	8,324	3	—	—	—	3	156	5	147	4	—
University of Massachusetts:											
Amherst	24,825	17	—	9	4	4	794	270	497	27	—
Harbor Campus, Boston	13,340	1	—	—	1	—	102	5	97	—	—
Worcester	637	9	—	1	—	8	150	3	146	1	—
Wentworth Institute of Technology	2,799	2	—	—	—	2	63	2	60	1	—
MICHIGAN											
Central Michigan University	23,390	7	—	5	—	2	348	7	336	5	2
Eastern Michigan University	23,321	17	—	1	7	9	515	15	489	11	11
Ferris State University	10,258	6	—	4	—	2	284	20	256	8	3
Grand Valley State University	13,553	1	—	1	—	—	156	8	148	—	3
Hope College	2,825	—	—	—	—	—	182	12	169	1	1
Lansing Community College	16,816	—	—	—	—	—	150	8	142	—	—
Macomb Community College	25,809	—	—	—	—	—	102	6	90	6	—
Michigan State University	40,254	31	—	9	3	19	1,301	259	999	43	—
Northern Michigan University	7,898	4	—	3	—	1	104	1	103	—	—
Oakland Community College	26,324	4	—	1	—	3	75	1	72	2	—
Oakland University	13,165	1	—	—	1	—	126	4	118	4	—
Saginaw Valley State University	7,037	1	—	1	—	—	90	2	87	1	—
University of Michigan:											
Ann Arbor	36,543	43	—	5	14	24	1,842	131	1,665	46	17

See footnotes at end of table.

Table 9. — Number of Offenses Known to the Police, Universities and Colleges, 1995 — Continued

University/College	Student enrollment[1]	Violent[2] crime total	Murder and non-negligent man-slaughter	Forcible rape	Robbery	Aggravated assault	Property[3] crime total	Burglary	Larceny–theft	Motor vehicle theft	Arson*
			Violent crime					Property crime			
MICHIGAN — Continued											
Flint	6,236	—	—	—	—	5	134	1	130	3	—
Western Michigan University	25,673	8	—	—	3	5	559	5	549	5	17
MINNESOTA											
University of Minnesota:											
Duluth	9,417	4	—	3	—	1	194	6	188	—	—
Twin Cities...................	51,478	18	—	7	5	6	1,336	66	1,263	7	11
MISSISSIPPI											
Itawamba Community College	3,088	—	—	—	—	—	30	14	15	1	—
Mississippi State University	14,152	25	—	—	5	20	295	35	259	1	—
University of Mississippi:											
Medical Center	1,817	—	—	—	—	—	143	—	135	8	—
Oxford	11,038	6	—	1	1	4	233	58	175	—	—
MISSOURI											
Lincoln University	3,512	6	—	—	1	5	84	12	71	1	1
University of Missouri, St. Louis	15,588	—	—	—	—	—	148	3	134	11	—
Washington University	11,655	1	—	—	1	—	283	5	276	2	1
MONTANA[5]											
NEBRASKA											
University of Nebraska:											
Kearney	7,584	1	—	—	—	1	86	8	77	1	—
Lincoln	23,854	1	—	—	—	1	723	65	654	4	—
NEVADA											
University of Nevada:											
Las Vegas	18,954	10	—	1	1	8	475	110	337	28	2
Reno	12,379	4	—	—	1	3	241	93	139	9	2
NEW HAMPSHIRE											
University of New Hampshire........	15,394	7	—	2	1	4	263	39	222	2	4
NEW JERSEY											
Brookdale Community College	12,257	—	—	—	—	—	89	6	79	4	—
Essex County College	8,735	11	—	—	8	3	58	2	40	16	—
Kean College	11,387	13	—	2	3	8	237	30	187	20	2
Middlesex County College	11,767	—	—	—	—	—	64	1	61	2	—
Monmouth College	4,422	4	—	3	—	1	125	9	116	—	—
Montclair State College	12,748	8	—	—	2	6	269	23	212	34	—
New Jersey Institute of Technology ...	7,504	2	—	—	2	—	98	11	75	12	—
Rowan College...................	8,936	10	—	1	2	7	200	51	131	18	—
Rutgers University:											
Camden	4,833	4	—	—	3	1	115	10	93	12	—
Newark	9,477	5	—	—	3	2	296	4	281	11	3
New Brunswick	33,464	26	—	7	10	9	744	26	699	19	5
Stockton State College	5,683	5	—	1	—	4	106	18	86	2	—
Trenton State College	6,946	3	—	1	2	—	137	5	128	4	1
University of Medicine and Dentistry:											
Camden	[4]	1	—	—	—	1	13	1	12	—	—
Newark	4,020	17	—	—	1	16	542	23	496	23	—
Piscataway	[4]	—	—	—	—	—	48	1	46	1	—
William Paterson College	9,669	2	—	1	—	1	132	5	117	10	1
NEW MEXICO											
Eastern New Mexico University	3,854	3	—	2	—	1	47	8	38	1	—
New Mexico State University	15,643	5	—	2	—	3	442	32	380	30	4
University of New Mexico	24,572	32	—	6	8	18	823	96	685	42	4

See footnotes at end of table.

Table 9. — Number of Offenses Known to the Police, Universities and Colleges, 1995 — Continued

University/College	Student enrollment[1]	Violent[2] crime total	Murder and non-negligent man-slaughter	Forcible rape	Robbery	Aggravated assault	Property[3] crime total	Burglary	Larceny–theft	Motor vehicle theft	Arson*
NEW YORK											
Cornell University	[4]	10	—	—	1	9	664	105	552	7	2
Ithaca College	5,688	—	—	—	—	—	165	1	164	—	—
Rensselaer Polytechnic Institute	6,520	7	—	—	1	6	261	28	231	2	1
State University of New York:											
Albany	16,622	8	—	—	4	4	456	118	335	3	
Buffalo	24,943	28	—	1	8	19	817	231	562	24	
College of Technology	[4]	3	—	—	2	1	89	31	56	2	
Downstate Medical Center	[4]	6	—	—	3	3	197	3	187	7	—
Maritime College	822	—	—	—	—	—	56	41	15	—	1
Stony Brook	17,621	15	—	—	2	8	5	773	62	691	20
State University of New York Agricultural and Technical College:											
Alfred	3,493	11	—	5	—	6	189	51	137	1	2
Canton	2,081	—	—	—	—	—	95	1	94	—	—
Farmingdale	6,717	8	—	—	4	4	119	38	75	6	—
Morrisville	[4]	9	—	1	—	8	134	19	115	—	
State University of New York College:											
Brockport	9,148	14	—	8	—	6	146	32	113	1	
Buffalo	11,528	13	—	3	4	6	245	40	188	17	4
Cortland	6,827	4	—	2	2	—	154	17	137	—	
Environmental Science and Forestry	1,736	—	—	—	—	—	30	2	28	—	—
Geneseo	5,754	3	—	1	1	1	157	15	140	2	—
New Paltz	7,852	5	—	3	—	2	116	1	114	1	—
Oneonta	5,829	8	—	2	—	6	86	13	73	—	—
Optometry	264	—	—	—	—	—	7	—	7	—	—
Oswego	8,817	7	—	2	—	5	220	20	200	—	—
Plattsburgh	6,174	1	—	1	—	—	133	—	133	—	—
Potsdam	4,294	—	—	—	—	—	144	12	132	—	4
Purchase	3,751	2	—	—	1	1	175	14	153	8	—
Utica-Rome	2,544	—	—	—	—	—	24	1	23	—	—
Syracuse University	18,971	2	—	—	—	2	445	—	445	—	—
NORTH CAROLINA											
Appalachian State University	12,236	8	—	2	1	5	183	13	168	2	1
Beaufort County Community College . .	1,212	—	—	—	—	—	5	—	5	—	—
Davidson College	1,614	—	—	—	—	—	67	20	45	2	—
Duke University	11,352	13	—	1	3	9	948	86	851	11	1
East Carolina University	18,076	16	—	2	5	9	379	36	341	2	—
Elizabeth City State University	2,099	3	—	—	1	2	69	39	29	1	—
Fayetteville State University	4,109	6	1	—	1	4	75	7	68	—	—
Mars Hill College	1,325	1	—	—	—	1	23	9	14	—	—
North Carolina A & T State University, Greensboro	8,136	23	—	1	2	20	349	73	270	6	6
North Carolina Central University, Durham	5,692	14	—	—	6	8	287	24	251	12	9
North Carolina School of the Arts	644	—	—	—	—	—	35	8	27	—	—
North Carolina State University, Raleigh	28,223	26	—	—	10	16	768	46	710	12	12
Pembroke State University	3,017	2	—	—	—	2	59	17	41	1	—
Pfeiffer College	1,057	1	—	—	—	1	6	2	4	—	—
Queens College	1,543	1	—	—	1	—	21	2	19	—	—
University of North Carolina:											
Asheville	3,165	—	—	—	—	—	51	3	48	—	—
Chapel Hill	24,565	18	—	1	7	10	744	42	693	9	13
Charlotte	15,648	8	—	—	3	5	329	60	262	7	1
Greensboro	12,658	13	—	2	2	9	289	54	230	5	3
Wilmington	8,472	9	—	—	1	8	358	11	345	2	4
Wake Forest University	5,728	1	—	—	1	—	278	53	224	1	1
Western Carolina University	6,790	11	—	1	—	10	136	8	127	1	3
Winston-Salem State University	2,915	3	—	—	2	1	43	18	23	2	—
NORTH DAKOTA											
University of North Dakota	11,499	4	—	2	1	1	270	4	261	5	—
OHIO											
Bowling Green State University	17,669	11	—	5	2	4	468	25	440	3	1

See footnotes at end of table.

Table 9. — Number of Offenses Known to the Police, Universities and Colleges, 1995 — Continued

University/College	Student enrollment[1]	Violent[2] crime total	Violent crime				Property[3] crime total	Property crime			
			Murder and non-negligent man-slaughter	Forcible rape	Robbery	Aggravated assault		Burglary	Larceny–theft	Motor vehicle theft	Arson*
OHIO — Continued											
Kent State University, Main Campus	21,413	2	—	1	1	—	377	26	348	3	—
Lakeland Community College	8,698	3	—	—	—	3	47	—	47	—	—
Marietta College	1,318	—	—	—	—	—	50	19	30	1	1
Miami University	15,624	4	—	1	—	3	408	2	406	—	1
Ohio State University	49,542	29	—	3	13	13	1,616	228	1,359	29	9
Ohio University	19,461	7	—	—	—	7	310	13	295	2	—
University of Cincinnati	28,758	30	—	1	6	23	776	85	685	6	7
University of Toledo	23,107	10	—	—	2	8	395	34	357	4	—
Wright State University	16,029	2	—	1	—	1	320	10	304	6	2
Youngstown State University	13,979	2	—	—	2	—	119	1	114	4	—
OKLAHOMA											
Cameron University	6,081	—	—	—	—	—	38	2	36	—	—
East Central University	4,501	4	—	—	—	4	35	5	30	—	—
Murray State College	1,601	—	—	—	—	—	17	4	13	—	—
Northeastern Oklahoma State University	8,994	9	—	—	—	9	148	38	108	2	1
Oklahoma State University: Main Campus	18,807	2	1	—	1	—	271	67	197	7	2
Okmulgee	2,175	—	—	—	—	—	54	5	48	1	1
Southeastern Oklahoma State University	4,004	4	—	—	—	4	31	—	31	—	1
Tulsa Junior College	18,604	—	—	—	—	—	69	—	68	1	—
University Center, Tulsa	[4]	1	—	1	—	—	32	1	30	1	—
University of Central Oklahoma	16,076	4	—	1	—	3	109	7	98	4	—
University of Oklahoma: Health Science Center	2,971	1	—	—	—	1	50	—	50	—	—
Norman	22,043	17	—	—	4	13	660	137	507	16	2
PENNSYLVANIA[5]											
RHODE ISLAND											
Brown University	7,801	8	—	2	5	1	465	60	402	3	—
University of Rhode Island	14,151	2	—	—	—	2	278	19	251	8	6
SOUTH CAROLINA											
Clemson University	16,290	9	—	1	3	5	448	21	424	3	2
Francis Marion University	3,898	4	—	1	1	2	92	3	88	1	—
Medical University of South Carolina	2,256	2	—	—	—	2	526	22	500	4	3
South Carolina State University	4,693	28	—	—	11	17	135	43	89	3	2
The Citadel	4,441	1	—	—	—	1	110	11	96	3	—
Trident Technical College	9,623	1	—	—	—	1	69	—	66	3	—
Winthrop University	5,164	1	—	—	1	—	75	7	68	—	—
SOUTH DAKOTA											
South Dakota State University	9,707	4	—	2	1	1	109	51	58	—	—
TENNESSEE											
East Tennessee State University	11,439	7	—	2	2	3	153	7	145	1	—
Middle Tennessee State University	17,120	3	—	—	—	3	292	13	275	4	2
University of Tennessee: Knoxville	25,914	16	2	2	5	7	546	30	516	—	2
Martin	5,608	6	—	2	1	3	93	2	90	1	—
TEXAS											
Alamo Community College	[4]	3	—	—	1	2	401	5	381	15	—
Alvin Community College	3,645	1	—	—	1	—	10	1	9	—	—
Amarillo College	6,724	2	—	—	2	—	64	11	53	—	—
Amarillo Technical Center	498	—	—	—	—	—	3	1	1	1	—
Angelo State University	6,276	—	—	—	—	—	58	4	53	—	—
Austin College	1,123	1	—	—	—	1	42	2	38	2	2
Baylor University	12,241	1	—	—	—	1	188	22	164	2	4
Baylor University Medical Center	[4]	3	—	—	2	1	235	9	222	4	1

See footnotes at end of table.

Table 9. — Number of Offenses Known to the Police, Universities and Colleges, 1995 — Continued

University/College	Student enrollment[1]	Violent[2] crime total	Murder and non-negligent man-slaughter	Forcible rape	Robbery	Aggravated assault	Property[3] crime total	Burglary	Larceny–theft	Motor vehicle theft	Arson*
TEXAS — Continued											
Central Texas College	14,547	3	—	2	—	1	63	4	58	1	1
College of the Mainland	4,034	1	—	—	1	—	42	1	41	—	—
Eastfield College	8,722	1	—	—	—	1	107	3	98	6	1
East Texas State University, Commerce	7,752	7	—	4	1	2	111	19	92	—	—
Grayson County Junior College	4	—	—	—	—	—	25	3	21	1	—
Hardin-Simmons University	2,133	—	—	—	—	—	50	17	32	1	—
Houston Baptist University	2,130	1	—	—	1	—	24	2	22	—	—
Houston Community College	45,893	6	—	—	1	5	186	9	166	11	—
Lamar University, Beaumont	9,787	12	—	—	2	10	138	14	120	4	—
Laredo Community College	7,019	1	—	—	—	—	54	4	43	7	—
McLennan Community College	5,435	—	—	—	—	—	20	—	20	—	—
Midwestern State University	5,828	2	—	1	—	1	83	20	62	1	—
North Lake College	6,196	—	—	—	—	—	39	—	38	1	1
Paris Junior College	2,617	1	—	1	—	—	38	4	34	—	1
Prairie View A & M University	5,849	12	—	1	1	10	261	53	198	10	1
Rice University	4,139	7	—	2	—	5	231	14	206	11	—
Richland College	12,069	1	—	—	—	1	112	2	96	14	—
Southern Methodist University	9,014	3	—	—	—	3	153	1	142	10	3
South Plains College	5,671	1	—	—	—	1	27	19	8	—	—
Southwestern University	1,238	—	—	—	—	—	28	2	26	—	8
Southwest Texas State University	20,889	7	—	3	1	3	341	57	280	4	3
Stephen F. Austin State University	12,206	5	—	—	—	5	230	24	204	2	1
Sul Ross State University	3,145	3	—	2	—	1	63	27	36	—	1
Tarleton State University	6,460	—	—	—	—	—	62	11	51	—	—
Texas A & M University:											
College Station	42,018	7	—	3	3	1	714	66	642	6	1
Corpus Christi	5,152	1	—	1	—	—	47	5	42	—	—
Galveston	1,237	—	—	—	—	—	6	—	6	—	—
Kingsville	6,545	1	—	—	1	—	154	38	116	—	—
Texas Christian University	6,706	4	—	2	1	1	133	36	91	6	—
Texas College Osteo. Med.	416	—	—	—	—	—	32	—	32	—	—
Texas Southern University	10,078	19	—	1	12	6	242	34	200	8	1
Texas State Technical College:											
Harlingen	4	—	—	—	—	—	52	13	39	—	—
Waco	3,430	6	—	—	2	4	246	53	191	2	—
Texas Tech. University:											
Health Science Center	1,430	1	—	—	—	1	185	1	183	1	—
Lubbock	24,083	3	—	3	—	—	535	14	518	3	—
Texas Woman's University	10,090	2	—	1	1	—	72	3	69	—	—
Trinity University	2,478	2	—	—	1	1	194	76	117	1	5
Tyler Junior College	7,993	1	—	—	—	1	107	37	68	2	—
University of Houston:											
Central Campus	33,022	9	—	—	6	3	447	7	420	20	—
Clearlake	7,228	2	—	1	—	1	29	1	28	—	—
Downtown Campus	7,715	4	—	—	—	4	140	2	135	3	—
University of North Texas	25,605	2	—	—	1	1	321	19	299	3	1
University of Texas:											
Arlington	23,373	3	—	—	3	—	305	28	269	8	1
Austin	47,957	3	—	2	1	—	650	16	619	15	3
Brownsville and Texas Southmost College	7,770	1	—	—	—	1	61	3	41	17	—
Dallas	8,487	—	—	—	—	—	77	2	75	—	1
El Paso	17,196	4	—	—	—	4	242	7	218	17	1
Health Science Center, San Antonio	2,790	—	—	—	—	—	113	—	113	—	—
Health Science Center, Tyler	3,183	—	—	—	—	—	21	—	20	1	—
Houston	4	2	—	1	—	1	296	2	293	1	—
Medical Branch	2,327	6	—	1	4	1	311	6	304	1	—
Pan American	15,104	2	—	1	—	1	136	—	127	9	—
Permian Basin	2,315	—	—	—	—	—	14	1	13	—	—
San Antonio	17,579	4	—	2	—	2	277	36	237	4	1
Southwestern Medical School	1,700	2	—	—	1	1	136	1	134	1	—
Tyler	3,917	1	—	1	—	—	42	8	33	1	—
West Texas State University	6,633	3	—	2	1	—	99	14	85	—	—
UTAH											
Brigham Young University	31,511	8	—	—	1	7	636	9	624	3	—
College of Eastern Utah	3,135	5	—	1	—	4	32	3	29	—	—
Salt Lake Community College	18,534	1	—	—	—	1	150	6	143	1	—

See footnotes at end of table.

Table 9. — Number of Offenses Known to the Police, Universities and Colleges, 1995 — Continued

University/College	Student enrollment[1]	Violent[2] crime total	Violent crime				Property[3] crime total	Property crime			
			Murder and non-negligent man-slaughter	Forcible rape	Robbery	Aggravated assault		Burglary	Larceny–theft	Motor vehicle theft	Arson*
UTAH — Continued											
Southern Utah University	4,754	6	—	—	—	6	60	27	32	1	—
University of Utah	26,906	26	—	1	4	21	875	33	823	19	2
Utah State University	20,371	2	—	2	—	—	284	17	267	—	—
Utah Valley State College	13,293	4	—	—	—	4	119	8	110	1	—
Weber State University	14,230	3	—	1	—	2	148	7	140	1	—
VERMONT											
University of Vermont	10,230	5	—	—	2	3	264	16	247	1	1
VIRGINIA											
Christopher Newport College	4,705	—	—	—	—	—	31	1	30	—	—
Clinch Valley College	1,839	5	—	—	—	5	8	3	5	—	—
College of William and Mary	7,547	23	—	2	—	21	274	2	271	1	7
George Mason University	21,774	15	—	5	3	7	542	76	460	6	4
Hampton University	5,769	10	—	—	2	8	70	4	64	2	—
James Madison University	11,680	5	—	—	—	5	190	78	112	—	—
Longwood College	3,351	1	—	—	—	1	88	—	87	1	—
Mary Washington College	3,727	11	—	7	—	4	142	36	105	1	1
Norfolk State University	8,667	11	—	—	4	7	187	26	159	2	6
Northern Virginia Community College . .	37,655	15	—	—	—	15	176	4	168	4	—
Old Dominion University	16,490	11	—	—	6	5	386	3	357	26	—
Radford University	9,105	5	—	3	1	1	190	9	181	—	—
Thomas Nelson Community College . .	7,483	—	—	—	—	—	17	—	17	—	—
University of Richmond	4,258	5	—	—	—	5	93	6	87	—	—
University of Virginia	21,421	9	—	—	4	5	744	17	722	5	3
Virginia Commonwealth University . . .	21,523	8	—	—	6	2	764	10	743	11	2
Virginia Military Institute	1,179	—	—	—	—	—	11	4	7	—	—
Virginia Polytechnic Institute and State University	25,842	18	—	2	1	15	400	8	389	3	2
Virginia State University	4,007	4	—	1	1	2	37	2	35	—	1
Virginia Western Community College	6,136	—	—	—	—	—	13	—	13	—	—
WASHINGTON											
Central Washington University	8,468	4	—	1	1	2	276	22	251	3	1
Eastern Washington University	8,360	4	—	3	—	1	119	9	109	1	—
University of Washington	33,719	13	—	2	5	6	1,055	90	933	32	—
Washington State University	19,314	7	—	2	1	4	513	60	444	9	11
Western Washington University	10,598	6	—	2	2	2	242	22	220	—	—
WEST VIRGINIA											
Concord College	2,623	—	—	—	—	—	31	16	14	1	—
Glenville State College	2,269	—	—	—	—	—	11	1	10	—	—
Marshall University	12,659	4	—	2	1	1	165	2	162	1	3
West Liberty State College	2,381	3	—	—	—	3	31	5	26	—	6
West Virginia State College	4,519	3	—	2	—	1	36	4	32	—	—
West Virginia Tech	2,697	—	—	—	—	—	30	3	27	—	—
West Virginia University	22,500	12	—	1	4	7	392	56	327	9	2
WISCONSIN											
University of Wisconsin:											
Eau Claire	10,395	2	—	—	—	2	161	8	152	1	3
Green Bay	5,712	—	—	—	—	—	103	—	103	—	—
La Crosse	8,663	3	—	2	—	1	175	39	136	—	—
Madison	39,361	7	—	—	5	2	795	39	728	28	9
Milwaukee	22,604	5	—	1	1	3	391	29	359	3	—
Oshkosh	10,611	3	—	—	—	3	126	—	125	1	9
Parkside	5,050	—	—	—	—	—	93	2	88	3	—
Platteville	5,305	2	—	1	1	—	104	1	102	1	3
Stout	7,512	—	—	—	—	—	246	38	203	5	—
Superior	2,624	—	—	—	—	—	45	1	44	—	—
Whitewater	10,850	2	—	1	1	—	153	7	146	—	2

See footnotes at end of table.

158

Table 9. — Number of Offenses Known to the Police, Universities and Colleges, 1995 — Continued

University/College	Student enrollment[1]	Violent[2] crime total	Violent crime				Property[3] crime total	Property crime			
			Murder and non-negligent man-slaughter	Forcible rape	Robbery	Aggravated assault		Burglary	Larceny–theft	Motor vehicle theft	Arson*
WYOMING											
Sheridan College	2,155	—	—	—	—	—	2	2	—	—	—
University of Wyoming	12,022	3	—	2	—	1	240	9	228	3	—

[1]The student enrollment figures provided by the United States Department of Education are for the 1994–1995 school year. The enrollment figure includes full-time and part-time students. See Appendix I for details.

[2]Violent crimes are offenses of murder, forcible rape, robbery, and aggravated assault.

[3]Property crimes are offenses of burglary, larceny–theft, and motor vehicle theft. Data are not included for the property crime of arson.

[4]Student enrollment figures were not available.

[5]Complete data for 1995 were not available for the states of Delaware, Illinois, Kansas, Montana, and Pennsylvania. See "Offense Estimation," pages 367–368 for details.

[6]Aggravated assault figures for 1994 furnished by the state-level Uniform Crime Reporting (UCR) Program administered by the Kentucky State Police were not in accordance with national UCR guidelines; therefore, the 1995 figures, which are in accordance with the national UCR guidelines, cannot be compared to the 1994 figures.

NOTE: Caution should be exercised in making any inter-campus comparisons or ranking schools, as university/college crime statistics are affected by a variety of factors. These include: demographic characteristics of the surrounding community, ratio of male to female students, number of on-campus residents, accessibility of outside visitors, size of enrollment, etc.

Table 10. — Number of Offenses Known to the Police, Suburban Counties, 1995

[The data shown in this table do not reflect county totals but are the number of offenses reported by the sheriff's office, county police department, or state police.]

*Arson is shown only if 12 months of arson data were received. Dashes (—) indicate zero data. The Modified Crime Index total is the sum of the Crime Index offenses, including arson.

County by State	Crime Index total	Modified* Crime Index total	Murder and non-negligent manslaughter	Forcible rape	Robbery	Aggravated assault	Burglary	Larceny–theft	Motor vehicle theft	Arson*
ALABAMA										
Autauga	177		—	1	5	4	75	73	19	
Baldwin	886		7	6	20	68	359	379	47	
Blount	302		—	2	6	1	144	136	13	
Calhoun	645		1	6	10	48	207	340	33	
Colbert	157		1	—	2	22	60	62	10	
Dale	179		4	6	7	34	45	71	12	
Elmore	815		1	2	11	70	330	353	48	
Etowah	405		1	6	5	7	157	216	13	
Houston	250	251	1	6	4	23	77	128	11	1
Jefferson	6,111		11	57	190	544	1,508	3,365	436	
Lauderdale	338		1	4	1	52	123	141	16	
Lawrence	35		1	—	—	2	8	21	3	
Limestone	307		1	—	5	36	78	155	32	
Madison	1,800		5	14	20	186	485	1,003	87	
Mobile	3,220		3	22	70	289	952	1,686	198	
Montgomery	921		3	10	17	127	227	475	62	
Morgan	526		4	2	1	38	254	193	34	
Russell	521		—	10	3	48	161	257	42	
St. Clair	402		2	2	2	19	172	184	21	
Shelby	239		3	8	9	7	97	88	27	
Tuscaloosa	1,884		2	14	18	179	481	1,035	155	
ARIZONA										
Maricopa	7,039	7,054	28	33	91	426	1,526	4,017	918	15
Mohave	2,311	2,358	5	11	23	85	859	1,145	183	47
Pima	15,418	15,569	24	81	177	653	2,166	11,148	1,169	151
ARKANSAS										
Benton	811	816	1	9	4	58	206	499	34	5
Crawford	490	491	2	3	4	80	206	139	56	1
Crittenden	770	775	1	3	24	214	228	242	58	5
Faulkner	520	520	2	1	—	36	202	252	27	—
Jefferson	556	559	3	4	6	59	175	251	58	3
Lonoke	145	145	2	1	1	—	57	40	44	—
Miller	103	103	1	1	1	12	42	41	5	—
Pulaski	3,006	3,028	14	39	69	417	915	1,328	224	22
Saline	570	572	—	9	10	23	231	241	56	2
Sebastian	289	291	—	3	1	16	77	176	16	2
Washington	401	404	5	3	—	30	124	201	38	3
CALIFORNIA										
Alameda	5,169	5,203	13	35	214	1,069	872	2,159	807	34
Alameda Highway Patrol	129		—	—	12	4		26	87	
Butte	3,455	3,604	1	29	56	293	1,304	1,742	30	149
Butte Highway Patrol	388		—	—	1	1	1	78	307	
Contra Costa	6,207	6,264	21	49	194	397	1,798	3,745	3	57
Contra Costa Highway Patrol	135		—	—	—			22	113	
El Dorado	2,986	2,999	3	25	26	267	1,086	1,559	20	13
El Dorado Highway Patrol	300		—	—	—	2	—	48	250	
Fresno	8,980	9,000	24	77	205	1,421	2,456	3,212	1,585	20
Fresno Highway Patrol	150		—	—	—		7	17	126	
Kern	15,578	16,580	34	108	398	1,912	4,019	7,451	1,656	1,002
Kern Highway Patrol	162		—	—	—			63	99	
Los Angeles	39,946	40,393	227	286	3,657	9,970	7,694	11,099	7,013	447
Los Angeles Highway Patrol	922		—	—	—	317	17	126	462	
Madera	2,629	2,705	3	28	43	542	1,116	876	21	76
Madera Highway Patrol	183		—	—	—			7	176	
Marin	1,688	1,700	2	8	28	192	404	1,048	6	12
Marin Highway Patrol	77		—	—	—	3	—	7	67	
Merced	2,622	2,625	8	20	42	281	922	1,345	4	3
Merced Highway Patrol	316		—	—	—			22	294	
Monterey	2,766	2,803	3	22	56	174	861	1,628	22	37
Napa	694	697	—	8	8	61	244	367	6	3
Napa Highway Patrol	66		—	—	—			14	52	

Table 10. — Number of Offenses Known to the Police, Suburban Counties, 1995 — Continued

County by State	Crime Index total	Modified* Crime Index total	Murder and non-negligent man-slaughter	Forcible rape	Robbery	Aggravated assault	Burglary	Larceny–theft	Motor vehicle theft	Arson*
CALIFORNIA — Continued										
Orange	4,019	4,055	5	34	77	506	886	2,011	500	36
Orange Highway Patrol	77	—	—	—	—	49	—	9	19	
Placer	3,641	3,661	6	22	22	294	1,151	2,119	27	20
Placer Highway Patrol	313	—	—	—	—	5	—	85	223	
Riverside	19,996	20,118	44	78	430	2,004	5,578	9,229	2,633	122
Riverside Highway Patrol	50	—	—	—	—	8	1	3	38	
Sacramento	37,077	37,186	46	305	1,871	3,736	10,395	20,355	369	109
Sacramento Highway Patrol	9,576	—	—	—	4	15	23	1,011	8,523	
San Bernardino	12,981	13,073	44	88	354	1,027	4,725	4,829	1,914	92
San Bernardino Highway Patrol	66	—	—	—	—	9	1	11	45	
San Diego	24,427	24,550	44	148	822	2,957	6,963	9,877	3,616	123
San Diego Highway Patrol	124	—	—	—	1	9	5	37	72	
San Joaquin	5,739	5,799	16	37	155	339	1,791	3,301	100	60
San Joaquin Highway Patrol	949	—	—	—	—	—	—	146	803	
San Luis Obispo	2,243	2,259	5	25	22	632	606	950	3	16
San Luis Obispo Highway Patrol	133	—	—	—	—	2	—	42	89	
San Mateo	3,055	3,064	4	33	62	83	813	1,765	295	9
San Mateo Highway Patrol	103	—	—	—	—	—	—	24	79	
Santa Barbara	3,405	3,423	1	45	22	380	1,323	1,613	21	18
Santa Barbara Highway Patrol	210	—	—	—	—	—	—	51	159	
Santa Clara	3,150	3,151	6	34	56	375	627	1,880	172	1
Santa Clara Highway Patrol	97	—	—	—	—	—	—	5	92	
Santa Cruz	4,281	4,330	3	40	69	513	1,088	2,567	1	49
Santa Cruz Highway Patrol	322	—	—	—	—	1	—	73	248	
Shasta	2,142	2,207	6	23	26	212	782	1,030	63	65
Shasta Highway Patrol	259	—	—	—	—	3	—	30	226	
Sonoma	4,803	4,860	8	40	74	487	1,465	2,704	25	57
Sonoma Highway Patrol	469	—	—	—	—	19	1	153	296	
Stanislaus	5,572	5,782	11	60	131	1,360	1,957	1,981	72	210
Stanislaus Highway Patrol	737	—	—	—	—	—	—	71	666	
Sutter[1]			2	9	12		313	531	40	2
Sutter Highway Patrol	61	—	—	—	—	—	—	4	57	
Tulare	4,817	5,235	20	34	84	656	1,556	2,467	—	418
Tulare Highway Patrol	710	—	—	—	—	2	—	54	654	
Ventura	2,096	2,128	6	17	38	231	551	1,072	181	32
Ventura Highway Patrol	37	—	—	—	—	—	—	16	21	
Yolo	645	651	4	7	13	119	232	255	15	6
Yolo Highway Patrol	88	—	—	—	—	—	2	23	63	
Yuba	2,403	2,431	3	20	33	388	726	1,214	19	28
Yuba Highway Patrol	275	—	—	—	—	—	—	18	257	
COLORADO										
Adams	4,022	4,058	4	35	53	225	849	2,429	427	36
Arapahoe	3,185	3,226	1	18	42	25	733	2,241	125	41
Boulder	1,056	1,078	2	29	4	76	342	538	65	22
Douglas	1,339	1,354	—	2	4	56	280	957	40	15
El Paso	2,466	2,472	6	14	22	257	605	1,377	185	6
Jefferson	4,746	4,800	6	27	37	82	977	3,390	227	54
Larimer	1,570	1,588	—	50	7	17	299	1,120	77	18
Pueblo	909	917	2	3	2	29	239	595	39	8
Weld	1,077	1,095	2	17	4	50	290	603	111	18
DELAWARE[2]										
FLORIDA										
Alachua	6,498	6,527	4	79	196	859	1,579	3,347	434	29
Bay	3,620	3,625	2	35	22	312	699	2,426	124	5
Brevard	7,264	7,318	8	71	124	933	1,638	4,079	411	54
Broward	10,304	10,355	16	93	366	1,254	2,081	5,167	1,327	51
Charlotte	3,699	3,700	7	22	81	208	845	2,351	185	1
Clay	3,986	3,986	1	63	45	458	512	2,667	240	—
Collier	8,766	8,805	18	86	219	857	2,257	4,698	631	39
Dade	130,812	130,924	160	668	6,406	11,326	20,510	71,286	20,456	112
Escambia	13,121	13,171	10	134	453	2,059	3,051	6,795	619	50
Flagler	796	798	—	2	6	56	210	498	24	2
Gadsden	999	1,004	1	9	45	112	293	442	97	5
Hernando	4,154	4,170	3	31	37	468	961	2,497	157	16
Hillsborough	36,724	36,819	26	198	894	2,901	7,035	21,528	4,142	95
Lake	3,326	3,337	5	65	30	481	1,009	1,502	234	11
Lee	10,158	10,171	8	153	259	609	2,318	5,727	1,084	13

See footnotes at end of table.

Table 10. — Number of Offenses Known to the Police, Suburban Counties, 1995 — Continued

County by State	Crime Index total	Modified* Crime Index total	Murder and non-negligent man-slaughter	Forcible rape	Robbery	Aggravated assault	Burglary	Larceny–theft	Motor vehicle theft	Arson*
FLORIDA — Continued										
Leon	3,429	3,451	2	40	111	465	1,028	1,515	268	22
Manatee	11,601	11,652	5	57	318	1,543	2,619	6,457	602	51
Marion	7,058	7,079	9	120	107	1,328	2,106	3,114	274	21
Martin	4,553	4,579	2	52	76	528	979	2,749	167	26
Nassau	1,355	1,360	1	47	16	204	407	588	92	5
Okaloosa	3,411	3,411	2	23	50	254	700	2,245	137	—
Osceola	4,612	4,623	6	53	76	416	1,688	2,108	265	11
Palm Beach	31,608	31,788	28	201	593	2,804	7,190	17,820	2,972	180
Pasco	9,790	9,850	14	74	118	922	2,135	5,954	573	60
Pinellas	12,954	13,044	8	103	205	1,144	2,537	8,283	674	90
St. Johns	2,905	2,910	2	11	50	426	777	1,526	113	5
Santa Rosa	3,404	3,412	1	29	26	465	892	1,811	180	8
Sarasota	9,778	9,826	3	39	110	702	2,322	6,173	429	48
Seminole	5,450	5,458	3	40	121	413	1,485	2,983	405	8
GEORGIA										
Barrow	573	574	1	5	5	25	182	311	44	1
Bibb	1,580	1,580	1	—	23	22	288	1,137	109	—
Bryan	241	241	1	—	2	5	44	172	17	—
Carroll	1,640	1,653	4	17	17	116	365	1,007	114	13
Catoosa	829	830	—	1	4	15	126	581	102	1
Chatham Police Department	3,164	3,179	4	20	45	199	618	2,053	225	15
Chattahoochee	18	18	1	1	1	4	6	4	1	—
Cherokee	1,752	1,764	2	8	13	82	431	1,099	117	12
Clayton Police Department	10,149	10,205	4	60	211	437	1,728	6,573	1,136	56
Cobb Police Department	16,767	16,814	10	90	332	537	2,733	11,465	1,600	47
Columbia	1,961	1,961	1	14	17	60	309	1,418	142	—
Coweta	1,228	1,236	4	12	10	115	263	713	111	8
Dade	152	152	—	—	—	11	42	84	15	—
DeKalb Police Department	47,356	47,557	54	171	1,836	891	7,893	29,284	7,227	201
Dougherty Police Department	393	393	2	4	—	5	110	261	11	—
Douglas	2,049	2,065	1	7	27	79	276	1,472	187	16
Fayette	629	631	—	1	1	7	159	415	46	2
Forsyth	2,613	2,638	—	8	11	180	513	1,739	162	25
Fulton Police Department	5,735	5,767	7	87	167	416	970	2,525	1,563	32
Gwinnett Police Department	14,175	14,301	13	179	326	552	2,685	6,457	3,963	126
Harris	149	150	2	3	—	2	65	69	8	1
Henry Police Department	2,740	2,744	6	20	30	178	575	1,743	188	4
Houston	1,477	1,477	1	11	15	344	252	798	56	—
Jones	274	274	1	2	—	32	82	147	10	—
Lee	389	389	—	—	7	14	105	244	19	—
McDuffie	373	374	2	—	6	18	78	232	37	1
Newton	1,096	1,097	—	8	13	72	321	596	86	1
Oconee	375	376	—	—	2	18	85	256	14	1
Paulding	1,387	1,399	—	6	6	36	259	964	116	12
Peach	267	267	—	4	8	69	49	125	12	—
Pickens	293	293	—	3	2	113	63	97	15	—
Richmond	6,964	6,966	10	92	288	686	1,281	3,550	1,057	2
Rockdale	1,802	1,803	1	9	19	111	329	1,160	173	1
Spalding	835	835	2	7	12	79	214	474	47	—
Twiggs	86	86	—	—	—	—	33	51	2	—
Walker	1,235	1,326	1	13	8	58	338	715	102	91
Walton	1,036		—	8	3	106	264	570	85	
IDAHO										
Ada	2,120	2,143	3	16	9	122	427	1,389	154	23
Canyon	945	955	3	7	3	60	206	569	97	10
ILLINOIS[2]										
INDIANA										
Allen	1,982	1,984	3	10	21	18	424	1,255	251	2
Allen State Police	149	149	—	6	3	25	18	81	16	—
Clark	482		—	—	3	—	115	337	27	—
Clark State Police	197	197	—	2	1	30	35	92	37	—

See footnotes at end of table.

162

Table 10. — Number of Offenses Known to the Police, Suburban Counties, 1995 — Continued

County by State	Crime Index total	Modified* Crime Index total	Murder and non-negligent man-slaughter	Forcible rape	Robbery	Aggravated assault	Burglary	Larceny–theft	Motor vehicle theft	Arson*
INDIANA — Continued										
Dearborn	442	442	—	—	—	157	89	179	17	—
Dearborn State Police	74	74	—	5	2	14	22	29	2	—
Elkhart	2,303	2,327	—	6	25	429	547	1,151	145	24
Elkhart State Police	186	187	—	1	2	51	35	78	19	1
Hancock	468	470	—	1	6	—	116	329	16	2
Hancock State Police	20	20	—	1	2	4	1	6	6	—
Howard	532	534	—	7	2	74	115	312	22	2
Howard State Police	26	26	—	—	—	6	6	11	3	—
Huntington	143	144	—	—	3	26	48	66	—	1
Huntington State Police	16	16	—	1	—	2	1	10	2	—
Lake	709	709	—	2	4	61	115	307	220	—
Lake State Police	300	300	1	2	3	42	17	101	134	—
Marion[3]	19,893	19,960	15	122	514	97	3,558	13,689	1,898	67
Marion State Police	390	390	1	7	2	75	6	173	126	—
Porter	895	896	—	3	6	19	137	631	99	1
Porter State Police	62	62	—	—	5	13	—	25	19	—
St. Joseph	2,414	2,418	1	10	27	29	503	1,750	94	4
St. Joseph State Police	156	157	—	2	1	25	40	58	30	1
Scott	193	193	—	5	2	19	44	112	11	—
Scott State Police	59	59	—	1	1	14	9	25	9	—
Tippecanoe	1,062	1,066	—	12	6	119	194	681	50	4
Tippecanoe State Police	126	126	—	1	—	21	13	77	14	—
Vanderburgh	937	942	—	8	2	110	85	707	25	5
Vanderburgh State Police	68	68	—	1	—	8	4	52	3	—
Vigo	1,354	1,367	2	8	7	142	323	794	78	13
Vigo State Police	253	256	—	3	2	34	40	145	29	3
Warrick	599	607	—	2	1	21	115	451	9	8
Warrick State Police	39	39	—	2	—	8	4	23	2	—
IOWA										
Black Hawk	337	339	1	5	—	7	187	132	5	2
Dubuque	248	251	—	1	—	1	72	157	17	3
Johnson	532	534	1	3	4	76	138	296	14	2
Linn	556	560	—	—	2	58	161	286	49	4
Polk	1,753	1,763	1	18	17	103	410	1,010	194	10
Scott	494	494	—	5	3	8	142	322	14	—
Warren	401	406	1	3	3	17	135	215	27	5
Woodbury	348	349	—	6	2	60	104	159	17	1
KANSAS[2]										
KENTUCKY[4]										
Bell	11	11	—	—	—	—	3	6	2	—
Bell State Police	144	147	3	6	—	14	40	64	17	3
Boone	254	255	—	1	1	34	40	162	16	1
Boone Police Department	675	687	—	9	8	47	170	399	42	12
Boone State Police	4	4	—	—	—	—	—	2	2	—
Bourbon	10	10	—	—	—	—	3	7	—	—
Bourbon State Police	97	98	—	2	—	4	30	51	10	1
Boyd	295	296	—	2	5	4	94	173	17	1
Boyd Police Department	30	31	—	—	—	1	4	23	2	1
Boyd State Police	228	230	2	2	2	3	72	130	17	2
Bullitt	461	462	—	—	1	6	194	227	33	1
Bullitt State Police	69	75	1	2	1	1	19	40	5	6
Campbell	3	3	—	—	—	—	1	2	—	—
Campbell Police Department	255	261	1	2	2	7	92	144	7	6
Carter State Police	262	270	—	5	6	27	94	105	25	8
Christian	365	371	1	2	5	27	120	176	34	6
Christian County Police Department	2	2	—	1	—	—	—	—	1	—
Christian State Police	33	37	—	1	4	2	10	11	5	4
Clark	253	254	—	—	2	3	81	147	20	1
Clark State Police	40	40	1	1	1	—	15	16	6	—
Daviess	549	550	2	—	4	9	139	372	23	1
Daviess State Police	184	194	—	3	—	2	80	85	14	10
Gallatin	6	6	—	—	—	—	3	2	1	—
Gallatin State Police	24	26	—	—	2	4	6	9	3	2
Grant	9	10	—	—	—	—	5	4	—	1
Grant State Police	302	304	1	6	2	13	74	176	30	2
Greenup	159	160	—	—	—	3	59	90	7	1

See footnotes at end of table.

163

Table 10. — Number of Offenses Known to the Police, Suburban Counties, 1995 — Continued

County by State	Crime Index total	Modified* Crime Index total	Murder and non-negligent manslaughter	Forcible rape	Robbery	Aggravated assault	Burglary	Larceny–theft	Motor vehicle theft	Arson*
KENTUCKY[4] — Continued										
Greenup State Police	103	115	—	—	1	5	36	52	9	12
Henderson	294	296	—	—	4	5	74	202	9	2
Henderson State Police	129	140	2	—	1	9	45	66	6	11
Jessamine	246	246	—	—	1	5	84	136	20	—
Jessamine State Police	41	42	2	3	—	3	18	10	5	1
Kenton Police Department	235	237	—	2	—	7	70	143	13	2
Kenton State Police	3	3	—	1	—	—	2	—	—	—
Madison	196	196	—	—	1	2	80	102	11	—
Madison State Police	295	296	1	12	5	11	109	119	38	1
Oldham	102	102	—	—	2	2	19	74	5	—
Oldham Police Department	535	537	—	3	7	17	143	342	23	2
Oldham State Police	42	42	1	2	2	7	2	26	2	—
Pendleton	14	14	—	—	—	—	8	3	3	—
Pendleton State Police	100	102	1	17	—	7	28	43	4	2
Scott	145	145	—	—	—	6	48	78	13	—
Scott State Police	28	29	—	1	4	1	8	13	1	1
Woodford Police Department	193	196	2	2	1	8	64	106	10	3
Woodford State Police	11	11	—	5	1	—	2	3	—	—
LOUISIANA										
Acadia	540	540	—	2	1	63	121	320	33	—
Ascension	1,637	1,637	1	8	13	61	403	1,104	47	—
Bossier	942	943	3	4	11	97	206	585	36	1
Caddo	1,579	1,579	2	13	16	69	513	871	95	—
Calcasieu	5,862	5,885	3	44	107	643	1,114	3,692	259	23
East Baton Rouge	10,789	10,811	15	45	168	348	1,761	7,727	725	22
Jefferson	29,354	29,547	29	152	1,160	2,050	4,497	17,975	3,491	193
Lafayette	1,587	1,591	—	16	25	182	420	902	42	4
Lafourche	1,968	1,971	3	8	39	112	314	1,374	118	3
Livingston	779	786	4	9	9	115	354	259	29	7
Ouachita	2,281	2,282	2	16	20	149	774	1,188	132	1
Plaquemines	663	663	4	1	10	57	180	367	44	—
Rapides	1,969	1,971	4	12	13	204	644	912	180	2
St. Charles	1,939	1,946	—	20	46	314	392	1,048	119	7
St. James	521	521	1	2	8	74	107	324	5	—
St. John the Baptist	1,822	1,828	10	17	85	112	320	1,192	86	6
St. Landry	813	819	2	10	4	76	226	448	47	6
St. Martin	758	758	1	7	4	12	132	584	18	—
St. Tammany	3,847	3,869	7	44	52	349	911	2,224	260	22
Terrebonne	3,865	3,886	4	40	48	320	1,078	2,132	243	21
Webster	234	234	3	3	3	15	87	105	18	—
West Baton Rouge	752	752	3	2	13	51	148	500	35	—
MAINE										
Androscoggin	400	402	1	—	1	4	127	241	26	2
Androscoggin State Police	44	44	1	1	—	3	11	24	4	—
Cumberland	739	745	—	7	1	8	280	397	46	6
Cumberland State Police	187	187	1	1	—	6	60	107	12	—
MARYLAND										
Allegany	86	86	—	—	—	14	20	51	1	—
Allegany State Police	558	566	1	5	5	89	112	318	28	8
Anne Arundel Police Department	18,237	18,360	15	89	583	829	2,979	12,033	1,709	123
Anne Arundel State Police	147	147	—	4	3	10	7	106	17	—
Baltimore County	7	7	—	—	—	1	—	6	—	—
Baltimore County Police Department	45,916	46,336	38	248	2,468	4,909	7,505	25,371	5,377	420
Baltimore County State Police	111	111	—	1	1	17	6	67	19	—
Calvert	1,041	1,041	3	17	3	113	234	642	29	—
Calvert State Police	518	528	1	5	5	90	104	290	23	10
Carroll	29	29	—	—	—	2	1	25	1	—
Carroll State Police	1,950	1,961	1	26	24	123	430	1,236	110	11
Cecil	659	659	1	3	6	50	170	388	41	—
Cecil State Police	1,060	1,081	1	6	10	129	267	572	75	21
Charles	5,060	5,060	10	34	142	496	898	3,042	438	—
Charles State Police	64	107	—	3	5	13	4	31	8	43
Frederick	1,021	1,021	1	8	5	78	249	617	63	—
Frederick State Police	1,144	1,183	—	13	18	85	154	812	62	39
Harford	3,218	3,218	4	34	71	229	687	2,029	164	—
Harford State Police	912	953	—	10	35	59	212	519	77	41

See footnotes at end of table.

Table 10. — Number of Offenses Known to the Police, Suburban Counties, 1995 — Continued

County by State	Crime Index total	Modified* Crime Index total	Murder and non-negligent man-slaughter	Forcible rape	Robbery	Aggravated assault	Burglary	Larceny–theft	Motor vehicle theft	Arson*
MARYLAND — Continued										
Howard Police Department	8,979	8,979	3	32	209	363	1,426	6,105	841	—
Howard State Police	75	122	—	1	4	19	5	43	3	47
Montgomery	29	29	—	—	—	29	—	—	—	—
Montgomery Police Department	34,005	34,401	20	215	1,015	1,109	4,671	23,682	3,293	396
Montgomery State Police	40	40	—	—	—	12	—	23	5	—
Prince George's Police Department	50,821	51,174	127	361	3,812	3,626	8,685	24,611	9,599	353
Prince George's State Police	164	164	—	—	8	23	9	87	37	—
Queen Anne's	361	361	—	3	4	15	78	231	30	—
Queen Anne's State Police	392	409	—	12	3	42	67	243	25	17
Washington	875	875	2	7	4	88	200	521	53	—
Washington State Police	432	478	1	6	5	76	87	238	19	46
MASSACHUSETTS										
Barnstable State Police	46		—	1	1	28	—	7	9	
Berkshire State Police	87		—	2	—	16	26	35	8	
Bristol State Police	111		—	2	—	37	2	6	64	
Essex State Police	79		—	1	8	22	4	18	26	
Hampden State Police	55		—	—	—	22	12	15	6	
Hampshire State Police	35		—	—	—	9	10	13	3	
Middlesex State Police	55		—	1	—	18	3	10	23	
Norfolk State Police	23		—	—	—	10	—	3	10	
Plymouth State Police	138		—	—	1	60	—	14	63	
Suffolk State Police	401		—	—	4	34	22	294	47	
MICHIGAN										
Allegan	1,176	1,188	2	16	4	94	290	694	76	12
Allegan State Police	584	592	—	23	5	64	206	263	23	8
Bay	763	763	1	7	6	27	161	512	49	—
Bay State Police	653	662	1	27	9	73	121	387	35	9
Berrien	824	838	—	25	17	86	246	401	49	14
Berrien State Police	725	741	1	29	5	60	150	438	42	16
Calhoun	119	120	—	3	1	21	38	51	5	1
Calhoun State Police	335	342	5	21	4	27	76	186	16	7
Clinton	315	317	—	11	—	17	69	202	16	2
Clinton State Police	65	67	—	3	—	4	15	41	2	2
Ingham	1,520	1,531	—	34	5	113	288	977	103	11
Ingham State Police	227	230	1	11	1	7	17	179	11	3
Jackson	1,269	1,292	2	44	11	133	252	749	78	23
Jackson State Police	435	438	—	22	9	72	73	237	22	3
Kalamazoo	2,456	2,463	3	42	22	89	484	1,659	157	7
Kalamazoo State Police	24	25	—	3	—	1	6	12	2	1
Kent	4,400	4,415	7	57	28	223	857	3,027	201	15
Kent State Police	699	708	—	10	1	31	125	502	30	9
Lenawee	793	799	1	9	1	30	219	487	46	6
Lenawee State Police	303	309	—	6	1	28	81	174	13	6
Livingston	580	580	—	4	4	22	129	360	61	—
Livingston State Police	765	771	—	19	5	61	160	477	43	6
Macomb	2,364	2,364	2	37	13	87	379	1,661	185	—
Macomb State Police	162	166	—	22	1	20	31	78	10	4
Midland	416	420	2	18	2	38	109	233	14	4
Midland State Police	16	16	—	2	—	1	2	10	1	—
Monroe	3,453	3,486	8	45	17	201	660	2,279	243	33
Monroe State Police	496	509	—	8	7	24	128	289	40	13
Muskegon	1,612	1,617	2	21	5	67	338	1,087	92	5
Muskegon State Police	433	440	—	10	1	38	108	253	23	7
Oakland	7,014	7,110	4	79	42	581	1,142	4,788	378	96
Oakland State Police	426	435	—	20	4	39	117	196	50	9
Ottawa	2,408	2,427	—	49	11	59	400	1,790	99	19
Ottawa State Police	391	394	—	18	3	23	74	258	15	3
Saginaw	1,577		3	10	21	169	215	1,072	87	
Saginaw State Police	617	626	5	42	15	60	109	344	42	9
Van Buren	871	875	2	7	4	44	280	415	119	4
Van Buren State Police	857	875	4	22	12	87	312	363	57	18
Washtenaw	3,332	3,375	4	54	96	347	914	1,500	417	43
Washtenaw State Police	420	423	—	17	11	65	135	164	28	3
Wayne	53	53	2	—	1	4	3	43	—	—
Wayne State Police	151	168	—	16	7	46	23	47	12	17

Table 10. — Number of Offenses Known to the Police, Suburban Counties, 1995 — Continued

County by State	Crime Index total	Modified* Crime Index total	Murder and non-negligent man-slaughter	Forcible rape	Robbery	Aggravated assault	Burglary	Larceny-theft	Motor vehicle theft	Arson*
MINNESOTA										
Anoka	546	552	—	7	2	17	169	288	63	6
Benton	406	413	1	5	2	15	125	232	26	7
Carver	426	426	4	7	3	10	89	280	33	—
Chisago	1,120	1,122	1	27	7	28	207	767	83	2
Clay	142	143	1	4	—	8	44	67	18	1
Dakota	217	220	—	7	—	12	51	118	29	3
Hennepin	266	268	—	11	1	23	43	165	23	2
Houston	135	135	2	—	—	8	27	91	7	—
Isanti	346	349	—	11	1	11	119	154	50	3
Olmsted	543	545	—	21	2	16	184	289	31	2
Polk	244	244	—	—	1	6	134	90	13	—
Ramsey	337	344	—	1	2	13	51	246	24	7
St. Louis	956	961	1	33	2	30	365	468	57	5
Scott	308	309	—	7	—	8	63	204	26	1
Sherburne	543	543	—	7	2	14	123	339	58	—
Stearns	823	826	—	3	1	7	188	556	68	3
Washington	1,281	1,288	—	8	1	26	334	812	100	7
Wright	1,306	1,313	—	9	4	16	242	947	88	7
MISSISSIPPI										
Forrest	404	410	4	—	4	41	116	221	18	6
Hinds	601	601	2	9	10	12	244	263	61	—
Madison	720	740	3	13	14	47	202	383	58	20
Rankin	842	850	4	5	11	40	340	406	36	8
MISSOURI										
Andrew	187	188	1	—	1	50	52	82	1	1
Boone	872	880	—	6	5	45	191	583	42	8
Buchanan	232	234	1	2	1	55	53	110	10	2
Cass	622	629	1	7	5	84	185	295	45	7
Christian	519	524	—	12	1	1	142	335	28	5
Clay	184	194	—	3	—	2	89	83	7	10
Franklin	1,560	1,560	1	21	12	128	592	677	129	—
Greene	1,463	1,464	3	10	10	37	385	919	99	1
Jackson	788	800	—	2	11	41	218	476	40	12
Jasper	682	682	—	6	6	110	203	321	36	—
Jefferson	3,474	3,535	2	48	12	144	933	1,991	344	61
St. Charles	1,784	1,794	3	17	14	143	373	1,128	106	10
St. Louis County Police Department	14,696	14,787	21	62	274	632	1,887	10,523	1,297	91
Webster	222	224	—	3	2	13	108	70	26	2
MONTANA[2]										
NEBRASKA										
Cass	270	282	—	—	—	2	63	190	15	12
Cass State Patrol	9	9	—	—	—	2	2	5	—	—
Dakota	175	176	1	1	1	3	49	105	15	1
Douglas	1,832	1,836	—	9	10	102	221	1,383	107	4
Douglas State Patrol	7	7	—	—	—	1	—	4	2	—
Lancaster	576	586	—	1	4	22	114	408	27	10
Lancaster State Patrol	27	27	—	—	—	4	5	15	3	—
Sarpy	879	896	—	2	3	21	111	695	47	17
Sarpy State Patrol	5	5	—	—	—	—	—	5	—	—
Washington	172	174	—	—	—	5	37	122	8	2
NEVADA										
Nye	639	648	1	—	6	76	227	296	33	9
Washoe	2,255	2,277	3	10	25	257	547	1,237	176	22
NEW HAMPSHIRE										
Rockingham State Police	37	38	2	3	—	8	8	12	4	1
Strafford State Police	25	25	—	—	—	3	12	10	—	—

See footnotes at end of table.

Table 10. — Number of Offenses Known to the Police, Suburban Counties, 1995 — Continued

County by State	Crime Index total	Modified* Crime Index total	Murder and non-negligent man-slaughter	Forcible rape	Robbery	Aggravated assault	Burglary	Larceny–theft	Motor vehicle theft	Arson*
NEW JERSEY										
Atlantic State Police	939	954	1	4	12	39	133	699	51	15
Bergen State Police	282	282	—	1	3	25	18	176	59	—
Burlington State Police	746	752	1	11	13	63	159	432	67	6
Camden State Police	60	61	—	2	1	14	1	37	5	1
Cape May State Police	557	561	1	5	9	37	161	315	29	4
Cumberland State Police	1,081	1,099	1	18	11	135	308	510	98	18
Essex Police Department	594	597	3	8	124	87	42	225	105	3
Essex State Police	83	86	—	—	7	16	6	43	11	3
Gloucester State Police	24	24	—	—	—	9	1	10	4	—
Hudson State Police	45	45	—	—	—	8	5	26	6	—
Hunterdon State Police	224	230	—	—	1	13	76	125	9	6
Mercer State Police	287	287	—	—	3	6	28	220	30	—
Middlesex State Police	168	170	—	1	5	22	8	105	27	2
Monmouth State Police	313	315	1	3	—	20	53	204	32	2
Morris State Police	43	43	—	1	1	16	7	15	3	—
Ocean State Police	130	133	—	1	1	10	25	88	5	3
Passaic State Police	67	67	—	—	—	4	2	35	26	—
Salem State Police	505	516	1	7	6	44	153	250	44	11
Somerset State Police	22	22	—	—	2	1	5	11	3	—
Sussex State Police	660	666	—	5	3	31	220	356	45	6
Union State Police	61	61	—	—	2	12	10	32	5	—
Warren State Police	263	268	—	4	6	27	77	127	22	5
NEW MEXICO										
Sandoval	283	283	—	6	2	76	76	110	13	—
NEW YORK										
Albany	223	223	—	—	2	59	45	104	13	—
Albany State Police	345	345	—	1	4	18	85	227	10	—
Broome	727	732	—	6	5	22	194	466	34	5
Broome State Police	612	619	1	9	2	24	177	387	12	7
Cayuga	468	484	—	2	1	32	162	262	9	16
Cayuga State Police	556	561	1	5	3	111	104	315	17	5
Chautauqua	1,127	1,129	—	5	1	92	327	647	55	2
Chautauqua State Police	374	375	—	1	4	21	77	266	5	1
Chemung	397	397	—	—	1	33	74	281	8	—
Chemung State Police	361	367	—	—	3	49	78	220	11	6
Dutchess	1,012	1,020	—	5	16	43	266	643	39	8
Dutchess State Police	1,179	1,183	5	12	12	167	181	761	41	4
Erie	1,915	1,936	1	3	14	74	233	1,550	40	21
Erie State Police	912	916	—	4	12	60	248	545	43	4
Genesee	544	551	—	11	1	14	148	350	20	7
Genesee State Police	203	204	—	2	2	15	46	136	2	1
Herkimer	22	22	—	—	—	3	—	19	—	—
Herkimer State Police	416	427	—	2	4	14	196	187	13	11
Livingston	630	635	2	1	1	44	107	469	6	5
Livingston State Police	104	104	1	1	2	19	23	56	2	—
Madison	119	119	—	—	—	13	27	78	1	—
Madison State Police	496	500	—	7	3	24	166	285	11	4
Nassau	24,886	25,113	17	70	877	903	3,483	15,075	4,461	227
Nassau State Police	30		—	—	5	4	—	20	1	
Niagara	1,558	1,561	3	7	12	55	365	915	201	3
Niagara State Police	373	377	—	1	2	22	87	230	31	4
Oneida	976	980	—	24	4	153	282	487	26	4
Oneida State Police	1,082	1,094	1	3	6	78	327	641	26	12
Onondaga	2,968		—	19	47	115	638	2,003	146	
Onondaga State Police	1,085	1,090	1	3	9	18	223	807	24	5
Ontario	1,152	1,161	4	9	12	14	233	839	41	9
Ontario State Police	445	446	1	1	2	10	52	376	3	1
Orange State Police	1,375	1,398	2	13	19	73	219	931	118	23
Orleans	185	185	1	3	—	2	37	139	3	—
Orleans State Police	88	89	—	—	2	15	20	45	6	1
Oswego	754	796	—	11	1	15	195	500	32	42
Oswego State Police	801	801	1	8	1	77	254	446	14	—
Putnam	292	294	1	2	4	12	108	153	12	2
Putnam State Police	185	188	—	1	9	6	46	109	14	3
Rensselaer	423	452	—	2	1	61	141	191	27	29
Rensselaer State Police	626	628	—	5	1	30	213	363	14	2
Rockland	141		—	—	6	7	3	116	9	

Table 10. — Number of Offenses Known to the Police, Suburban Counties, 1995 — Continued

County by State	Crime Index total	Modified* Crime Index total	Murder and non-negligent man-slaughter	Forcible rape	Robbery	Aggravated assault	Burglary	Larceny-theft	Motor vehicle theft	Arson*
NEW YORK — Continued										
Rockland State Police	63	67	2	3	3	9	9	21	16	4
Saratoga	1,154	1,164	—	2	14	79	283	740	36	10
Saratoga State Police	721	728	1	5	3	52	137	478	45	7
Schenectady	1	1	—	—	—	1	—	—	—	—
Schenectady State Police............	118	118	—	—	—	14	36	62	6	—
Schoharie	65	67	—	—	—	—	20	41	4	2
Schoharie State Police	268	275	—	—	—	23	99	139	7	7
Tioga......................	204		1	2	1	7	70	116	7	
Tioga State Police	138	138	—	2	—	2	37	95	2	—
Warren	1,079	1,082	1	9	5	36	181	821	26	3
Warren State Police	221	221	2	—	2	9	39	163	6	—
Washington	373	376	—	—	—	34	81	247	11	3
Washington State Police	263	263	2	—	—	27	77	154	3	—
Wayne	804		—	20	9	24	182	546	23	
Wayne State Police	655	665	—	4	3	43	142	430	33	10
Westchester	495	499	—	2	12	26	32	393	30	4
Westchester State Police	626	634	4	4	9	76	107	381	45	8
NORTH CAROLINA										
Alamance	1,214	1,219	1	3	18	53	521	570	48	5
Alexander	604	608	1	1	—	19	216	340	27	4
Brunswick	1,311	1,325	1	1	19	88	586	513	103	14
Buncombe	2,207	2,229	3	14	24	243	705	1,076	142	22
Burke	1,457	1,465	1	9	15	112	481	755	84	8
Cabarrus	933	939	3	3	12	35	317	538	25	6
Caldwell	1,354	1,363	7	6	11	146	431	698	55	9
Catawba	1,792	1,796	2	19	8	27	622	1,034	80	4
Chatham	933	934	2	1	18	75	336	448	53	1
Cumberland	10,707	10,843	13	93	277	458	3,073	6,005	788	136
Currituck	525	526	2	1	1	20	157	337	7	1
Davidson	2,510	2,536	2	14	23	105	1,051	1,211	104	26
Davie	649	654	2	5	10	44	226	322	40	5
Durham	1,246	1,251	3	—	9	187	283	674	90	5
Edgecombe	829	839	6	4	25	30	311	416	37	10
Forsyth	3,764	3,839	—	19	44	299	1,018	2,258	126	75
Franklin	926	936	9	7	10	71	350	423	56	10
Gaston	2,656	2,701	13	21	29	306	906	1,250	131	45
Guilford	3,771	3,802	6	15	56	326	1,107	2,100	161	31
Johnston	1,660	1,670	8	13	29	23	587	868	132	10
Lincoln	1,233	1,246	—	4	13	36	412	709	59	13
Nash	1,325	1,344	1	3	45	55	419	707	95	19
New Hanover	3,071	3,080	1	13	27	231	758	1,879	162	9
Onslow	3,428	3,441	4	23	43	53	1,015	2,104	186	13
Orange	1,246	1,248	4	7	23	29	437	669	77	2
Pitt	2,048	2,064	3	18	39	149	955	797	87	16
Randolph	2,135	2,146	—	8	13	98	698	1,228	90	11
Rowan	1,803	1,823	3	14	12	207	617	870	80	20
Stokes	795	799	3	8	11	83	257	389	44	4
Union	1,776	1,783	6	7	18	83	591	1,011	60	7
Wake	3,048	3,089	6	31	60	185	975	1,562	229	41
Wayne	1,876	1,894	4	12	29	159	665	867	140	18
Yadkin	604	605	—	3	3	20	184	372	22	1
NORTH DAKOTA										
Burleigh	89	89	—	1	—	2	26	56	4	—
Cass	204	206	—	1	—	4	54	121	24	2
Grand Forks	260	263	—	3	—	19	69	152	17	3
Morton	123	123	—	2	—	9	19	83	10	—
OHIO										
Allen......................	1,822	1,829	—	20	22	263	274	1,181	62	7
Ashtabula	1,478	1,495	—	18	8	29	356	968	99	17
Auglaize	379	379	—	10	1	13	115	224	16	—
Clermont	1,329	1,355	—	39	4	62	345	815	64	26
Columbiana	512	514	1	6	2	8	153	297	45	2
Crawford	243	243	1	1	1	1	91	132	16	—
Delaware	535	539	2	3	2	4	183	308	33	4
Franklin	4,436	4,452	5	58	172	80	912	2,742	467	16
Fulton	321	324	—	3	2	—	84	209	23	3

Table 10. — Number of Offenses Known to the Police, Suburban Counties, 1995 — Continued

County by State	Crime Index total	Modified* Crime Index total	Murder and non-negligent man-slaughter	Forcible rape	Robbery	Aggravated assault	Burglary	Larceny-theft	Motor vehicle theft	Arson*
OHIO — Continued										
Geauga	474	475	—	6	1	8	93	350	16	1
Greene	361	361	—	6	2	5	81	250	17	—
Hamilton	7,955	8,020	2	50	138	164	1,060	6,170	371	65
Jefferson	365	365	1	1	—	—	100	255	8	—
Lake	903	911	1	5	2	16	143	692	44	8
Licking	1,055	1,055	—	10	11	95	232	631	76	—
Lorain	1,148	1,164	—	21	24	101	529	442	31	16
Lucas	1,515	1,524	—	23	24	30	386	969	83	9
Mahoning	140		—	—	—	—	33	107	—	
Medina	541	545	1	5	8	18	132	332	45	4
Miami	697	697	1	10	3	14	225	363	81	—
Pickaway	735	738	—	9	4	14	222	455	31	3
Portage	1,269	1,272	2	16	13	30	269	852	87	3
Richland	1,098	1,104	1	1	9	57	319	668	43	6
Stark	3,530	3,540	4	28	75	122	1,113	1,966	222	10
Trumbull	244	244	1	1	3	13	65	110	51	—
Wood	530	530	—	4	1	14	127	350	34	—
OKLAHOMA										
Canadian	165	166	1	6	2	4	76	66	10	1
Cleveland	324	325	3	2	7	11	164	127	10	1
Comanche	657	658	1	5	—	138	140	310	63	1
Creek	715	717	2	3	—	104	318	240	48	2
Garfield	166	178	—	2	—	13	97	51	3	12
Logan	592	595	—	8	10	94	211	228	41	3
McClain	127	127	1	1	1	25	48	50	1	—
Oklahoma	329	332	—	1	4	49	104	145	26	3
Osage	384	384	—	8	5	63	142	137	29	—
Pottawatomie	543	559	3	2	5	64	190	233	46	16
Rogers	502	504	1	—	2	20	168	286	25	2
Sequoyah	371	375	5	2	—	34	194	112	24	4
Tulsa	1,738	1,755	3	34	33	207	430	797	234	17
Wagoner	582	586	3	5	1	23	236	258	56	4
OREGON										
Clackamas	10,033	10,065	3	59	150	160	1,823	6,210	1,628	32
Clackamas State Police	94	129	1	7	1	19	13	33	20	35
Columbia	381	382	1	—	2	13	108	206	51	1
Columbia State Police	22		—	3	—	9	1	7	2	
Jackson	2,274	2,287	2	11	24	211	502	1,387	137	13
Jackson State Police	247	276	1	12	—	38	51	115	30	29
Lane	2,189	2,194	4	26	27	80	756	1,104	192	5
Lane State Police	360	400	2	17	5	50	86	152	48	40
Marion	4,822	4,848	5	24	49	84	969	3,122	569	26
Marion State Police	251	298	—	7	3	44	7	162	28	47
Multnomah	1,097	1,102	—	14	23	119	221	595	125	5
Multnomah State Police	58	60	—	5	1	11	—	30	11	2
Polk	581	585	—	4	3	16	150	363	45	4
Polk State Police	5	10	—	1	—	2	—	2	—	5
Washington	5,484	5,501	3	35	86	75	1,060	3,627	598	17
Washington State Police	42	52	—	1	—	12	3	17	9	10
Yamhill	961	974	—	13	6	14	268	579	81	13
Yamhill State Police	27	29	—	—	—	3	5	13	6	2
PENNSYLVANIA[2]										
RHODE ISLAND										
Kent	222	222	—	6	—	77	31	103	5	—
Providence (Chepachet State Police)	58	59	—	5	—	6	10	22	15	1
Providence (Lincoln Woods State Police)	119	119	—	9	—	13	10	68	19	—
Washington	181	182	—	1	—	29	31	104	16	1
SOUTH CAROLINA										
Aiken	3,829	3,841	8	45	79	498	1,122	1,750	327	12
Anderson	5,595	5,636	6	35	91	704	1,448	2,903	408	41
Berkeley	3,950	3,978	3	51	72	420	969	2,157	278	28
Charleston	5,124	5,133	2	43	131	549	1,145	2,838	416	9

See footnotes at end of table.

Table 10. — Number of Offenses Known to the Police, Suburban Counties, 1995 — Continued

County by State	Crime Index total	Modified* Crime Index total	Murder and non-negligent man-slaughter	Forcible rape	Robbery	Aggravated assault	Burglary	Larceny–theft	Motor vehicle theft	Arson*
SOUTH CAROLINA — Continued										
Cherokee	1,268	1,276	2	3	28	281	317	556	81	8
Dorchester	2,300	2,311	2	26	29	266	518	1,328	131	11
Edgefield	363	366	1	5	7	32	108	188	22	3
Florence	3,188	3,215	3	31	39	373	836	1,717	189	27
Greenville	10,955	11,042	16	112	279	1,650	2,496	5,701	701	87
Horry Police Department	6,146	6,152	7	52	111	658	1,168	3,667	483	6
Lexington	5,736	5,754	8	64	131	544	1,743	2,864	382	18
Pickens	1,103	1,107	1	15	7	100	263	662	55	4
Richland	8,843	8,870	21	120	380	957	1,987	4,361	1,017	27
Spartanburg	10,112	10,160	18	76	237	1,415	2,168	5,614	584	48
Sumter	3,575	3,592	6	24	79	540	1,067	1,611	248	17
York	3,115	3,140	3	35	40	469	780	1,633	155	25
SOUTH DAKOTA										
Minnehaha	358	360	—	4	3	25	128	164	34	2
Pennington	711	711	—	36	4	29	153	461	28	—
TENNESSEE										
Carter	504	513	2	·10	1	21	176	261	33	9
Knox	4,095	4,160	7	29	69	158	1,228	2,261	343	65
Madison	964	969	5	14	12	119	260	480	74	5
Marion	531		3	13	9	84	34	363	25	
Montgomery	813		—	—	—	195	235	351	32	
Robertson	448	448	2	7	4	33	128	267	7	—
Rutherford	1,549	1,563	5	28	8	140	504	756	108	14
Shelby	7,437	7,502	12	67	180	538	1,584	3,986	1,070	65
Sullivan	1,556		3	18	15	148	440	840	92	
Sumner	1,149	1,156	1	5	3	118	435	534	53	7
Washington	738	742	1	3	4	48	280	366	36	4
TEXAS										
Archer	59	62	—	—	—	1	28	27	3	3
Bastrop	754	760	1	13	5	119	288	273	55	6
Bell	1,101	1,124	4	26	6	150	257	596	62	23
Bexar	5,618	5,715	8	38	73	516	1,233	3,271	479	97
Bowie	822	828	1	14	11	71	266	394	65	6
Brazoria	1,623	1,632	3	60	9	238	526	678	109	9
Brazos	359	366	1	5	1	27	154	155	16	7
Caldwell	195	195	—	6	—	31	48	108	2	—
Cameron	1,552	1,555	8	2	23	136	824	506	53	3
Chambers	448	449	2	5	6	19	112	261	43	1
Collin	719	722	1	9	7	100	207	347	48	3
Comal	979	994	—	14	1	121	257	555	31	15
Coryell	134	134	—	—	—	10	60	59	5	—
Dallas	635	661	—	1	16	103	144	321	50	26
Denton	713	713	1	11	4	39	210	394	54	—
Ector	1,119	1,122	—	6	17	16	305	695	80	3
Ellis	1,118	1,119	2	9	10	67	522	429	79	1
El Paso	2,053	2,073	5	44	58	265	448	1,091	142	20
Fort Bend	2,287	2,350	2	31	53	208	762	1,066	165	63
Galveston	1,305	1,327	3	15	16	149	400	605	117	22
Grayson	856	862	2	8	5	17	298	470	56	6
Gregg	593	594	3	17	7	105	139	273	49	1
Guadalupe	1,165	1,165	—	6	3	281	334	476	65	—
Hardin	368	373	1	5	3	10	119	212	18	5
Harris	34,955	35,396	69	375	1,305	3,479	8,504	15,614	5,609	441
Harrison	903	922	2	5	5	43	318	467	63	19
Hays	1,012	1,020	2	14	6	100	292	541	57	8
Henderson	1,144	1,145	7	18	4	77	439	540	59	1
Hidalgo	5,182	5,267	16	79	143	580	2,361	1,690	313	85
Hood	750	756	1	2	2	48	235	437	25	6
Hunt	921	942	1	8	7	86	368	383	68	21
Jefferson	727	736	2	28	4	29	192	422	50	9
Johnson	865	866	—	11	1	52	336	384	81	1
Kaufman	950	962	1	9	4	73	315	460	88	12
Liberty	752	753	4	18	9	37	361	279	44	1
Lubbock	997	1,003	1	10	2	159	194	573	58	6
McLennan	793	794	4	1	9	43	274	411	51	1
Midland	642	644	2	9	2	39	177	380	33	2

170

Table 10. — Number of Offenses Known to the Police, Suburban Counties, 1995 — Continued

County by State	Crime Index total	Modified* Crime Index total	Murder and non-negligent man-slaughter	Forcible rape	Robbery	Aggravated assault	Burglary	Larceny–theft	Motor vehicle theft	Arson*
TEXAS — Continued										
Montgomery	5,600	5,679	15	69	77	485	1,516	2,952	486	79
Nueces	234	236	2	6	4	18	52	120	32	2
Orange	956	961	3	12	7	115	274	454	91	5
Parker	988	988	3	24	5	78	272	541	65	—
Potter	284	288	2	7	—	47	77	135	16	4
Randall	358	363	—	3	6	22	117	182	28	5
Rockwall	198	200	1	4	2	26	60	96	9	2
San Patricio	418	419	1	—	2	14	157	227	17	1
Smith	2,462	2,544	4	33	30	238	784	1,180	193	82
Tarrant	1,324	1,340	2	8	15	216	363	637	83	16
Taylor	214	218	—	9	1	21	58	119	6	4
Tom Green	271	277	1	6	1	72	63	123	5	6
Travis	4,131	4,153	3	50	61	251	1,171	2,386	209	22
Upshur	409	410	—	12	2	23	172	167	33	1
Victoria	593	595	2	9	5	28	183	338	28	2
Waller	116	116	—	—	3	16	56	37	4	—
Webb	413	414	2	3	2	34	195	156	21	1
Wichita	204	223	—	2	1	18	79	94	10	19
Williamson	2,192	2,227	1	19	13	192	648	1,195	124	35
Wilson	203	231	5	—	—	21	108	66	3	28
UTAH										
Salt Lake	21,152	21,251	5	156	198	981	2,587	15,947	1,278	99
Utah	913	929	—	15	6	46	203	600	43	16
Weber	1,029	1,033	—	14	1	36	175	767	36	4
VERMONT										
Rockingham State Police	151	162	1	3	1	4	57	81	4	11
St. Albans State Police	745	773	—	27	2	26	230	417	43	28
VIRGINIA										
Albemarle Police Department	1,970	1,985	6	14	17	69	332	1,439	93	15
Albemarle State Police	5	5	—	—	—	—	—	3	2	—
Amherst	480	483	3	6	4	43	107	301	16	3
Amherst State Police	9	9	—	—	—	2	—	3	4	—
Arlington Police Department	10,928	10,969	11	32	316	433	929	7,843	1,364	41
Arlington State Police	11	11	—	—	—	1	—	8	2	—
Bedford	770	770	3	2	1	17	198	530	19	—
Bedford State Police	13	13	—	—	—	—	—	9	4	—
Botetourt	278	280	—	2	3	12	47	195	19	2
Botetourt State Police	5	5	—	—	—	—	—	2	3	—
Campbell	1,049	1,051	—	6	6	174	172	646	45	2
Campbell State Police	19	19	—	—	—	1	1	9	8	—
Charles City	23	23	—	—	—	3	2	17	1	—
Charles City State Police	12	12	—	—	—	—	10	1	1	—
Chesterfield Police Department	8,408	8,478	7	63	113	112	1,322	6,431	360	70
Chesterfield State Police	18	18	—	—	1	4	—	9	4	—
Clarke	188	190	—	4	—	2	33	134	15	2
Clarke State Police	9	9	—	—	—	7	—	1	1	—
Culpeper	329	333	3	1	2	15	57	227	24	4
Culpeper State Police	16	16	—	—	—	2	—	11	3	—
Dinwiddie	335	339	2	4	9	21	95	195	9	4
Fairfax Police Department	27,043	27,261	15	77	447	348	2,189	21,984	1,983	218
Fairfax State Police	28	28	—	—	1	6	2	16	3	—
Fauquier	654	663	1	5	11	41	176	372	48	9
Fauquier State Police	33	33	—	—	—	—	4	25	4	—
Fluvanna	169	172	3	1	—	9	54	92	10	3
Fluvanna State Police	3	3	—	—	1	—	—	2	—	—
Gloucester	500	500	—	6	2	13	112	353	14	—
Gloucester State Police	7	7	—	—	—	—	—	7	—	—
Goochland	167	167	1	1	—	12	61	79	13	—
Goochland State Police	8	8	—	—	—	—	3	5	—	—
Greene	250	254	—	1	—	34	40	167	8	4
Greene State Police	1	1	—	—	—	—	—	1	—	—
Hanover	1,291	1,294	—	7	6	41	164	1,037	36	3
Hanover State Police	24	24	—	1	—	4	—	15	4	—
Henrico Police Department	9,492	9,589	15	55	198	264	1,618	6,793	549	97
Henrico State Police	33	33	—	1	—	2	1	28	1	—
Isle of Wight	441	449	—	5	3	26	110	276	21	8

Table 10. — Number of Offenses Known to the Police, Suburban Counties, 1995 — Continued

County by State	Crime Index total	Modified* Crime Index total	Murder and non-negligent man-slaughter	Forcible rape	Robbery	Aggravated assault	Burglary	Larceny–theft	Motor vehicle theft	Arson*
VIRGINIA — Continued										
Isle of Wight State Police	4	4	—	—	—	—	2	2	—	—
James City Police Department	1,072	1,074	—	8	22	59	117	832	34	2
James City State Police	3	3	—	—	—	—	—	—	3	—
King George	261	261	—	—	1	23	57	159	21	—
King George State Police	5	5	—	—	—	—	1	4	—	—
Loudoun	2,146	2,149	5	19	14	92	268	1,611	137	3
Loudoun State Police	23	23	—	—	—	1	1	20	1	—
Mathews	58	58	—	2	—	7	14	32	3	—
New Kent	291	292	—	6	3	15	60	173	34	1
New Kent State Police	15	15	—	—	3	2	2	8	—	—
Pittsylvania	683	686	1	12	1	32	196	411	30	3
Powhatan	168	168	—	3	—	5	47	103	10	—
Powhatan State Police	13	13	—	—	—	9	—	3	1	—
Prince George	463		—	4	5	16	99	319	20	—
Prince George State Police	5	5	—	—	—	2	—	2	1	—
Prince William Police Department	9,667	9,756	12	73	198	354	1,417	7,001	612	89
Prince William State Police	39	39	—	—	3	2	5	25	4	—
Roanoke Police Department	1,534	1,544	1	17	21	88	232	1,118	57	10
Roanoke State Police	8	8	—	—	—	1	2	5	—	—
Scott	292	295	2	6	1	26	78	160	19	3
Scott State Police	7	8	1	—	—	2	—	3	1	1
Spotsylvania	1,907	1,907	3	8	18	38	247	1,478	115	—
Spotsylvania State Police	50	50	—	—	—	4	—	41	5	—
Stafford	1,510	1,556	—	21	23	61	180	1,132	93	46
Stafford State Police	23	23	—	1	—	4	—	18	—	—
Washington	591	600	3	6	3	76	102	353	48	9
Washington State Police	23	27	1	—	—	6	—	10	6	4
York	1,367	1,383	1	3	20	35	143	1,121	44	16
York State Police	7	7	—	—	—	2	—	3	2	—
WASHINGTON										
Benton	1,151	1,160	3	18	6	77	304	697	46	9
Clark	7,888	7,926	3	102	187	250	1,639	4,909	798	38
Franklin	356	358	2	2	—	25	99	197	31	2
Island	809	815	3	9	9	31	230	506	21	6
King	19,261	19,497	14	272	340	649	3,687	12,094	2,205	236
Kitsap	6,355	6,439	4	118	46	511	1,234	4,067	375	84
Pierce	19,860	19,996	22	187	414	1,587	4,087	11,789	1,774	136
Snohomish	7,222	7,251	10	219	105	256	1,928	3,944	760	29
Spokane	9,478	9,521	3	61	96	267	1,886	6,603	562	43
Thurston	3,599	3,615	3	51	40	169	1,076	1,984	276	16
Whatcom	2,169	2,187	1	53	16	99	726	1,167	107	18
Yakima	3,943	3,999	3	49	27	121	1,598	1,795	350	56
WEST VIRGINIA										
Brooke	85	85	—	—	1	—	31	48	5	—
Brooke State Police	7	7	—	1	—	2	1	1	2	—
Cabell	867	872	1	5	11	15	219	575	41	5
Cabell State Police	221	221	—	2	1	6	54	119	39	—
Hancock	105	107	—	1	1	8	27	61	7	2
Hancock State Police	7	7	—	—	—	—	—	5	2	—
Kanawha	1,746	1,755	4	15	39	64	559	889	176	9
Kanawha State Police	714	714	—	6	10	72	161	383	82	—
Marshall	153	153	1	4	2	7	68	61	10	—
Marshall State Police	13	13	1	—	—	1	9	1	1	—
Mineral	31	32	—	1	—	2	16	11	1	1
Mineral State Police	135	141	—	1	—	19	54	51	10	6
Ohio	139	139	1	—	4	17	35	76	6	—
Ohio State Police	40	40	—	—	—	—	11	26	3	—
Putnam	537	543	2	2	4	9	133	353	34	6
Putnam State Police	130	131	1	9	—	20	22	66	12	1
Wayne	128	129	1	—	1	18	46	50	12	1
Wayne State Police	305	308	—	4	—	40	110	111	40	3
Wood	321	321	—	—	2	31	72	208	8	—
Wood State Police	82	82	—	—	—	1	36	36	9	—
WISCONSIN										
Brown	1,634	1,643	—	14	11	45	335	1,169	60	9
Calumet	191	193	—	1	—	18	32	130	10	2

172

Table 10. — Number of Offenses Known to the Police, Suburban Counties, 1995 — Continued

County by State	Crime Index total	Modified* Crime Index total	Murder and non-negligent man-slaughter	Forcible rape	Robbery	Aggravated assault	Burglary	Larceny–theft	Motor vehicle theft	Arson*
WISCONSIN — Continued										
Chippewa	433	433	1	—	—	26	104	285	17	—
Dane	1,255	1,275	—	16	9	192	201	776	61	20
Douglas	407	407	—	3	—	5	243	139	17	—
Eau Claire	441	449	1	1	4	12	146	253	24	8
Kenosha	1,025	1,039	—	5	13	36	219	677	75	14
La Crosse	339	342	—	3	—	89	32	194	21	3
Marathon	598	599	—	6	—	13	109	433	37	1
Milwaukee	210	210	—	—	1	12	1	177	19	—
Outagamie	353	353	—	2	1	5	72	250	23	—
Ozaukee	214	215	2	2	1	3	34	158	14	1
Pierce	392	392	—	—	—	11	128	228	25	—
Racine	826	827	—	5	7	18	119	626	51	1
Rock	593	602	1	9	5	44	151	349	34	9
St. Croix	599	602	1	3	1	38	173	336	47	3
Sheboygan	652	659	1	5	—	32	142	444	28	7
Washington	754	762	—	2	1	27	190	491	43	8
Waukesha	986	996	—	2	—	64	171	690	59	10
Winnebago	376	379	—	3	1	9	99	245	19	3
WYOMING										
Laramie	635	639	—	11	2	18	71	507	26	4
Natrona	549	553	—	1	2	31	150	323	42	4

[1]Due to reporting changes figures are not comparable to previous years.

[2]Complete data for 1995 were not available for the states of Delaware, Illinois, Kansas, Montana, and Pennsylvania. See "Offense Estimation," pages 367–368 for details.

[3]Indianapolis/Marion County, Indiana, is a unified city–county government with a total population of 772,792.

[4]Aggravated assault figures for 1994 furnished by the state-level Uniform Crime Reporting (UCR) Program administered by the Kentucky State Police were not in accordance with national UCR guidelines; therefore, the 1995 figures, which are in accordance with the national UCR guidelines, cannot be compared to the 1994 figures.

Table 11. — Number of Offenses Known to the Police, Rural Counties 25,000 and over in Population, 1995

[The data shown in this table do not reflect county totals but are the number of offenses reported by the sheriff's office, county police department, or state police.]

*Arson is shown only if 12 months of arson data were received. Dashes (—) indicate zero data. The Modified Crime Index total is the sum of the Crime Index offenses, including arson.

County by State	Crime Index total	Modified* Crime Index total	Murder and non-negligent man-slaughter	Forcible rape	Robbery	Aggravated assault	Burglary	Larceny–theft	Motor vehicle theft	Arson*
ALABAMA										
Cullman	1,039		2	15	3	94	297	530	98	
De Kalb	412		1	—	2	3	159	241	6	
Jackson	454		1	6	3	23	201	174	46	
Lee	805		5	8	4	80	292	381	35	
Marshall	306		3	1	—	9	126	167	—	
Talladega	105		—	7	3	1	41	50	3	
Walker	100		—	—	—	—	41	38	21	
ARIZONA										
Apache	254	257	2	—	4	26	82	133	7	3
Navajo	650	654	—	12	2	75	226	302	33	4
Yavapai	2,611	2,622	5	10	8	334	777	1,306	171	11
ARKANSAS										
Garland	298	299	1	6	4	6	76	161	44	1
Independence	1,250	1,251	—	8	2	53	180	932	75	1
Pope	599	604	1	6	1	4	188	360	39	5
White	778	786	6	11	10	18	294	337	102	8
CALIFORNIA										
Calaveras	1,303	1,307	3	7	3	126	592	571	1	4
Calaveras Highway Patrol	99		—	—	—	—	—	35	64	
Humboldt	1,949	1,971	6	17	31	24	964	879	28	22
Humboldt Highway Patrol	225		—	—	—	2	—	1	222	
Imperial	1,361	1,412	3	9	14	426	371	530	8	51
Imperial Highway Patrol	117		—	—	—	—	—	16	101	
Kings	904	911	2	11	18	155	305	404	9	7
Kings Highway Patrol	105		—	—	—	1	—	11	93	
Lake	880	880	1	6	13	129	445	281	5	—
Lake Highway Patrol	112		—	—	—	7	—	15	90	
Mendocino	1,621	1,637	3	34	16	412	633	516	7	16
Mendocino Highway Patrol	142		—	—	—	—	—	25	117	
Nevada	2,146	2,148	1	16	10	247	545	1,253	74	2
Nevada Highway Patrol	138		—	—	—	4	—	43	91	
Tehama	863	923	3	4	5	138	313	397	3	60
Tehama Highway Patrol	78		—	—	—	1	—	3	74	
Tuolumne	1,854	1,863	—	13	8	319	729	782	3	9
Tuolumne Highway Patrol	150		—	—	—	—	—	15	135	
DELAWARE¹										
FLORIDA										
Citrus	2,034	2,067	1	5	9	183	637	1,116	83	33
Columbia	1,838	1,840	1	24	20	284	368	1,020	121	2
Highlands	2,309	2,319	1	18	34	232	733	1,098	193	10
Indian River	3,372	3,375	3	46	69	278	825	1,961	190	3
Jackson	939	942	1	9	14	143	231	512	29	3
Monroe	4,005	4,016	—	17	35	329	742	2,726	156	11
Okeechobee	1,191	1,196	6	21	16	163	396	517	72	5
Putnam	3,935	3,953	9	82	51	433	1,193	1,986	181	18
Sumter	964	967	1	—	13	204	356	332	58	3
Walton	458	459	2	7	2	39	186	194	28	1
GEORGIA										
Floyd Police Department	1,303	1,322	9	14	6	63	420	733	58	19
Glynn Police Department	3,028	3,039	3	7	54	234	448	2,160	122	11
Gordon	975		—	2	4	20	238	597	114	
Hall	3,036	3,047	9	26	19	201	778	1,705	298	11
Liberty	531	536	—	6	14	18	146	304	43	5
Lowndes	1,099	1,108	—	10	15	25	192	791	66	9
Whitfield	1,238	1,253	—	9	6	57	272	751	143	15

See footnotes at end of table.

Table 11. — Number of Offenses Known to the Police, Rural Counties 25,000 and over in Population, 1995 — Continued

County by State	Crime Index total	Modified* Crime Index total	Murder and non-negligent man-slaughter	Forcible rape	Robbery	Aggravated assault	Burglary	Larceny–theft	Motor vehicle theft	Arson*
HAWAII										
Hawaii Police Department	4,456	4,482	6	20	38	103	1,116	2,945	228	26
Kauai Police Department	2,637	2,657	3	22	17	30	541	1,931	93	20
Maui Police Department	8,591	8,621	5	48	93	104	1,596	6,399	346	30
IDAHO										
Bonneville	858	862	—	9	4	64	169	560	52	4
Kootenai	1,391	1,400	1	17	5	122	459	718	69	9
ILLINOIS[1]										
INDIANA										
Bartholomew	271	281	—	1	5	—	54	198	13	10
Bartholomew State Police	25	25	—	—	—	4	5	8	8	—
Grant...........................	455	458	2	1	1	40	124	266	21	3
Grant State Police	26	26	—	—	—	3	5	14	4	—
Henry	517	525	1	8	4	5	135	348	16	8
Henry State Police	33	33	1	—	1	3	12	13	3	—
La Grange	177	177	—	—	2	25	36	103	11	—
La Grange State Police	79	79	—	2	1	11	14	46	5	—
La Porte	1,024	1,025	1	2	9	50	251	651	60	1
La Porte State Police	86	86	—	1	1	27	—	40	17	—
Lawrence	333	334	1	3	2	46	95	171	15	1
Lawrence State Police	25	25	—	—	—	5	11	7	2	—
Wayne..........................	555	557	1	2	2	1	176	346	27	2
Wayne State Police	37	38	1	1	—	3	3	26	3	1
KANSAS[1]										
KENTUCKY[2]										
Knox...........................	6	6	—	—	—	—	—	5	1	—
Knox State Police	365	369	3	5	2	17	141	118	79	4
McCracken......................	733	742	—	5	11	30	193	431	63	9
McCracken State Police	3	8	—	—	—	—	1	1	1	5
LOUISIANA										
Avoyelles	695	698	—	20	6	239	110	311	9	3
Iberia	890	890	2	10	11	52	162	623	30	—
Tangipahoa......................	1,906	1,906	14	16	53	609	229	953	32	—
Vermilion	468	469	1	3	3	18	126	310	7	1
Vernon	823	827	1	11	7	122	111	542	29	4
MAINE										
Aroostook.......................	132	132	—	—	2	—	62	59	9	—
Aroostook State Police	370	372	—	9	1	7	173	163	17	2
Hancock	399	399	—	—	—	5	123	259	12	—
Hancock State Police...............	40	40	4	2	—	4	16	11	3	—
Kennebec	458	459	—	6	2	10	197	224	19	1
Kennebec State Police	239	239	—	3	1	13	104	98	20	—
Penobscot	668	668	—	4	—	10	199	427	28	—
Penobscot State Police	255	257	—	6	—	13	65	156	15	2
Somerset........................	384	384	—	3	—	12	152	190	27	—
Somerset State Police	93	93	1	1	—	4	34	44	9	—
Waldo	212	213	—	—	—	6	87	107	12	1
Waldo State Police.................	31	31	—	—	—	1	11	16	3	—
York	524	525	—	3	1	9	257	217	37	1
York State Police	231	231	—	1	—	3	122	90	15	—

See footnotes at end of table.

Table 11. — Number of Offenses Known to the Police, Rural Counties 25,000 and over in Population, 1995 — Continued

County by State	Crime Index total	Modified* Crime Index total	Murder and non-negligent man-slaughter	Forcible rape	Robbery	Aggravated assault	Burglary	Larceny–theft	Motor vehicle theft	Arson*
MARYLAND										
Garrett	277	277	—	1	—	27	70	168	11	—
Garrett State Police	273	279	1	4	—	24	63	160	21	6
St. Mary's	1,944	1,949	1	13	36	195	451	1,202	46	5
St. Mary's State Police	409	434	2	10	15	63	86	209	24	25
Wicomico	1,111	1,111	1	8	18	115	306	653	10	—
Wicomico State Police	525	553	1	6	14	51	166	250	37	28
MICHIGAN										
Barry	324	324	—	2	2	17	123	160	20	—
Barry State Police	637	641	1	31	5	55	211	301	33	4
Cass	283	285	—	8	3	19	102	138	13	2
Cass State Police	123	126	—	11	2	11	38	52	9	3
Grand Traverse	1,088	1,098	—	24	1	55	167	808	33	10
Grand Traverse State Police	413	413	—	15	1	19	83	281	14	—
Hillsdale	396	400	3	19	3	28	99	220	24	4
Hillsdale State Police	215	219	—	30	1	14	55	100	15	4
Isabella	304	310	—	3	2	15	70	200	14	6
Isabella State Police	354	354	—	15	1	24	107	186	21	—
Mecosta	581	589	—	26	—	55	162	325	13	8
Mecosta State Police	100	101	—	16	—	4	25	52	3	1
Montcalm	704	706	1	26	2	63	202	366	44	2
Montcalm State Police	386	390	—	36	1	42	141	151	15	4
St. Joseph	539	543	1	5	4	25	150	326	28	4
St. Joseph State Police	314	320	—	16	—	11	92	186	9	6
Sanilac	380	386	—	41	1	52	100	176	10	6
Sanilac State Police	276	287	—	20	—	23	94	128	11	11
Shiawassee	532	533	—	11	1	76	113	306	25	1
Shiawassee State Police	290	295	1	4	3	35	74	163	10	5
Tuscola	228	229	1	3	1	13	66	112	32	1
Tuscola State Police	295	298	1	22	—	15	110	123	24	3
MINNESOTA										
Beltrami	584	588	2	10	2	13	170	349	38	4
Crow Wing	996	998	1	19	2	28	373	500	73	2
Otter Tail	725	728	1	11	—	22	259	395	37	3
MISSOURI										
Cole	424	427	—	3	1	27	105	273	15	3
Pulaski	201	207	2	2	14	89	53	22	19	6
MONTANA[1]										
Flathead	1,261	1,275	7	30	1	61	348	722	92	14
Gallatin	622	625	—	3	—	20	99	443	57	3
NEVADA										
Carson City	2,245	2,252	1	21	31	224	446	1,427	95	7
Douglas	1,085	1,094	1	2	12	114	226	667	63	9
NEW HAMPSHIRE										
Hillsboro State Police	24	25	1	3	1	3	9	6	1	1
NEW MEXICO										
McKinley	334	335	—	10	6	36	66	175	41	1
San Juan	1,175	1,180	2	9	9	175	388	529	63	5
NEW YORK										
Allegany State Police	502	518	1	4	—	67	202	221	7	16
Cattaraugus	651	674	—	3	3	109	252	239	45	23
Cattaraugus State Police	519	520	2	3	3	36	149	313	13	1
Chenango	515		1	—	1	70	164	270	9	
Chenango State Police	228		—	3	1	29	70	122	3	
Clinton	23	23	—	—	—	5	—	18	—	—
Clinton State Police	1,181	1,189	4	5	4	163	297	688	20	8
Columbia	409	413	—	2	2	18	137	236	14	4

See footnotes at end of table.

Table 11. — Number of Offenses Known to the Police, Rural Counties 25,000 and over in Population, 1995 — Continued

County by State	Crime Index total	Modified* Crime Index total	Murder and non-negligent man-slaughter	Forcible rape	Robbery	Aggravated assault	Burglary	Larceny-theft	Motor vehicle theft	Arson*
NEW YORK — Continued										
Columbia State Police	446	448	1	3	5	42	133	249	13	2
Delaware State Police	484	488	1	1	—	21	221	226	14	4
Franklin State Police	500		—	9	6	72	188	210	15	
Fulton	878		—	3	9	43	413	382	28	
Fulton State Police	139	140	—	—	—	8	55	76	—	1
Greene	78	81	—	—	—	1	32	45	—	3
Greene State Police	676	678	1	1	4	196	210	254	10	2
Jefferson	525		—	17	4	13	135	342	14	
Jefferson State Police	558	563	1	3	3	29	127	380	15	5
Otsego	117	125	—	1	—	11	43	57	5	8
Otsego State Police	575	575	—	4	3	32	172	360	4	—
St. Lawrence	575	576	—	2	2	40	172	336	23	1
St. Lawrence State Police	651	656	—	12	8	57	192	360	22	5
Steuben State Police	768	771	2	7	2	40	207	489	21	3
Sullivan	779	785	—	3	4	113	330	301	28	6
Sullivan State Police	891	906	3	10	7	75	394	384	18	15
Tompkins	674	674	—	6	4	15	208	401	40	—
Tompkins State Police	356	356	—	2	2	34	92	200	26	—
Ulster	174	177	—	2	2	13	59	94	4	3
Ulster State Police	967	984	2	9	8	166	309	427	46	17
Wyoming	559	560	—	2	3	62	256	224	12	1
Wyoming State Police	120	120	2	—	1	44	33	34	6	—
NORTH CAROLINA										
Beaufort	944	952	1	8	8	82	361	441	43	8
Carteret	906	913	2	3	7	14	294	530	56	7
Cleveland	2,237	2,244	7	29	52	143	726	1,148	132	7
Columbus	1,341	1,373	4	16	23	106	621	469	102	32
Craven	1,546	1,547	5	19	19	156	361	890	96	1
Duplin	979	984	3	8	4	150	390	366	58	5
Halifax	1,090	1,099	4	11	22	74	465	446	68	9
Harnett	2,325	2,358	8	13	25	161	882	1,083	153	33
Haywood	827	857	1	8	3	64	333	384	34	30
Henderson	1,289	1,298	1	10	8	42	475	659	94	9
Iredell	1,629	1,648	2	15	25	90	582	819	96	19
Jackson	588	593	—	2	2	29	297	241	17	5
Lee	888	895	2	3	12	50	280	475	66	7
Lenoir	922	930	1	6	13	82	361	400	59	8
Moore	896	944	3	6	14	82	356	375	60	48
Pender	699	700	4	11	6	67	265	321	25	1
Richmond	911	923	7	5	18	76	343	413	49	12
Robeson	1,568	1,582	16	8	15	181	761	515	72	14
Rockingham	1,530	1,542	1	4	17	130	507	780	91	12
Rutherford	1,074	1,079	3	7	11	63	362	565	63	5
Sampson	1,330	1,346	4	8	23	166	514	528	87	16
Stanly	727	727	5	—	5	11	276	401	29	—
Surry	994	998	—	6	6	86	370	440	86	4
Wilkes	913	935	5	15	8	105	296	436	48	22
OHIO										
Ashland	264	265	1	1	—	3	120	127	12	1
Coshocton	478	484	—	1	—	29	66	358	24	6
Darke	369	378	1	17	4	14	181	147	5	9
Huron	357	359	—	3	1	16	142	174	21	2
Logan	454	457	2	4	2	7	109	310	20	3
Muskingum	1,108	1,116	—	8	5	49	248	756	42	8
Preble	592	597	—	15	3	88	128	323	35	5
Ross	1,248	1,248	1	2	10	7	411	741	76	—
Shelby	293	293	—	3	2	25	70	186	7	—
Tuscarawas	294	295	4	2	1	10	111	127	39	1
OREGON										
Coos	1,121	1,133	1	25	5	26	318	667	79	12
Coos State Police	55	56	—	2	1	9	12	27	4	1
Deschutes	1,293	1,298	—	8	4	4	358	830	89	5
Deschutes State Police	180	190	—	7	—	22	44	75	32	10
Josephine State Police	73	82	—	2	1	21	15	14	20	9
Klamath	1,501	1,509	3	3	22	66	379	928	100	8
Klamath State Police	192	214	—	7	8	32	49	63	33	22

Table 11. — Number of Offenses Known to the Police, Rural Counties 25,000 and over in Population, 1995 — Continued

County by State	Crime Index total	Modified* Crime Index total	Murder and non-negligent man-slaughter	Forcible rape	Robbery	Aggravated assault	Burglary	Larceny–theft	Motor vehicle theft	Arson*
OREGON — Continued										
Linn	2,175	2,186	2	12	9	107	648	1,260	137	11
Linn State Police	48	53	—	4	—	19	3	15	7	5
PENNSYLVANIA¹										
RHODE ISLAND										
Newport	32	32	—	2	—	3	7	20	—	—
SOUTH CAROLINA										
Beaufort	5,898	5,911	6	39	94	401	1,283	3,869	206	13
Chesterfield	814	818	2	8	29	118	281	308	68	4
Colleton	1,108	1,114	1	12	29	130	356	501	79	6
Darlington	1,947	1,955	4	14	42	247	625	853	162	8
Georgetown	1,683	1,692	4	21	36	235	452	836	99	9
Greenwood	1,518	1,524	1	13	28	234	429	762	51	6
Kershaw	1,403	1,416	2	10	32	162	339	790	68	13
Lancaster	1,637	1,646	2	20	35	143	444	909	84	9
Laurens	1,467	1,478	3	7	17	307	404	649	80	11
Oconee	1,117	1,117	—	8	10	153	298	596	52	—
Orangeburg	3,539	3,563	8	45	124	680	871	1,618	193	24
Williamsburg	801	810	3	17	31	167	227	275	81	9
TENNESSEE										
Bradley	764	764	—	5	8	74	249	367	61	—
Greene	1,265	1,265	4	6	8	127	585	414	121	—
Hamblen	353	355	—	1	4	1	116	209	22	2
McMinn	691	691	7	—	2	56	252	347	27	—
Monroe	327		1	1	1	37	98	145	44	
TEXAS										
Anderson	547	563	1	7	2	61	217	236	23	16
Angelina	718	719	—	8	4	15	228	434	29	1
Polk	620	622	1	—	10	18	266	294	31	2
Rusk	579	590	1	11	4	61	235	238	29	11
Starr	913	916	10	3	16	212	357	263	52	3
Van Zandt	521	523	2	9	1	24	200	201	84	2
Wise	567	572	—	4	4	47	194	289	29	5
UTAH										
Cache	752	753	—	1	2	12	61	649	27	1
VERMONT										
Bethel State Police	389	394	—	1	—	16	173	182	17	5
Bradford State Police	202	202	—	2	1	5	79	101	14	—
Brattleboro State Police	180	180	2	2	1	4	79	79	13	—
Derby State Police	389	395	2	3	1	16	164	189	14	6
Middlebury State Police	211	212	1	3	—	6	83	111	7	1
Middlesex State Police	333	346	—	—	1	18	152	148	14	13
Rutland State Police	686	702	1	4	2	17	202	431	29	16
St. Johnsbury State Police	369	376	—	1	—	21	128	202	17	7
Shaftsbury State Police	261	279	2	3	—	12	99	131	14	18
Williston State Police	323	355	—	4	—	10	142	162	5	32
VIRGINIA										
Accomack	276	276	—	1	21	20	65	145	24	—
Accomack State Police	24	25	—	—	—	2	3	11	8	1
Augusta	911	919	2	4	4	25	205	630	41	8
Augusta State Police	37	37	—	1	—	4	—	20	12	—
Buchanan	318	320	—	1	—	50	106	125	36	2
Buchanan State Police	71	76	—	2	—	4	27	31	7	5
Carroll	301	304	—	3	1	29	105	135	28	3
Carroll State Police	14	14	—	—	—	—	—	10	4	—
Franklin	362	363	—	3	2	18	100	203	36	1
Franklin State Police	5	5	—	—	—	—	—	4	1	—
Frederick	1,137	1,137	—	11	6	30	227	790	73	—

See footnotes at end of table.

Table 11. — Number of Offenses Known to the Police, Rural Counties 25,000 and over in Population, 1995 — Continued

County by State	Crime Index total	Modified* Crime Index total	Murder and non-negligent man-slaughter	Forcible rape	Robbery	Aggravated assault	Burglary	Larceny–theft	Motor vehicle theft	Arson*
VIRGINIA — Continued										
Frederick State Police	28	28	1	—	2	3	3	17	2	—
Halifax	558	560	5	6	8	145	138	230	26	2
Halifax State Police	40	40	—	—	—	7	4	15	14	—
Henry	1,709	1,716	8	11	54	73	520	890	153	7
Henry State Police	15	16	—	—	—	2	—	7	6	1
Rockingham	423	426	3	7	1	4	127	274	7	3
Rockingham State Police	38	39	—	—	—	2	1	9	26	1
Tazewell	466	468	—	5	1	113	103	229	15	2
Tazewell State Police	30	30	—	—	—	2	6	16	6	—
Wise	240	245	1	1	—	3	83	133	19	5
Wise State Police	22	28	1	1	—	3	5	5	7	6
WASHINGTON										
Chelan	1,217	1,221	1	12	2	51	283	809	59	4
Clallam	820	831	—	13	4	49	231	477	46	11
Cowlitz	1,132	1,155	1	12	6	72	321	645	75	23
Douglas	738	739	2	14	5	28	204	456	29	1
Grant	1,083	1,083	3	9	6	42	389	551	83	—
Grays Harbor	571	579	3	5	1	26	188	299	49	8
Lewis	1,046	1,051	—	16	4	53	356	538	79	5
Mason	1,877	1,878	3	24	10	66	618	1,040	116	1
Skagit	1,577	1,581	2	12	—	—	404	1,100	59	4
Stevens	690	692	2	5	3	24	218	405	33	2
WEST VIRGINIA										
Berkeley	921	922	1	5	5	19	238	599	54	1
Berkeley State Police	731	741	1	5	12	108	213	328	64	10
Fayette	230	235	1	1	5	19	80	106	18	5
Fayette State Police	241	242	3	1	2	16	80	125	14	1
Harrison	270	274	1	3	1	25	80	146	14	4
Harrison State Police	126	126	—	1	—	1	56	54	14	—
Jefferson	250	250	1	—	2	1	94	138	14	—
Jefferson State Police	505	507	2	1	3	4	132	341	22	2
Logan	125	128	1	2	3	12	55	36	16	3
Logan State Police	531	535	—	4	4	3	152	262	106	4
McDowell	50	51	2	1	2	11	8	24	2	1
McDowell State Police	53	53	6	3	3	5	19	9	8	—
Marion	230	232	—	2	3	8	58	140	19	2
Marion State Police	68	68	—	—	—	1	25	33	9	—
Mercer	480	480	1	—	—	56	167	200	56	—
Mercer State Police	125	127	1	10	2	5	47	42	18	2
Mingo	103	108	4	—	1	21	22	43	12	5
Mingo State Police	243	253	1	1	2	37	71	73	58	10
Monongalia	358	360	2	4	2	1	86	246	17	2
Monongalia State Police.	384	384	—	2	—	2	175	139	66	—
Raleigh	1,583	1,585	2	—	11	351	263	873	83	2
Raleigh State Police	259	259	—	—	1	47	41	150	20	—
WISCONSIN										
Barron	404	413	—	8	—	29	114	228	25	9
Clark	371	378	2	8	—	5	119	215	22	7
Columbia	465	469	2	4	2	13	87	317	40	4
Dodge	240	241	1	5	1	4	68	149	12	1
Fond du Lac	380	384	—	—	—	6	128	219	27	4
Grant	345	347	1	7	—	38	75	198	26	2
Jefferson	459	462	—	7	2	12	84	306	48	3
Manitowoc	430	436	—	7	1	23	120	255	24	6
Marinette	678	683	2	5	1	3	381	260	26	5
Polk	472	477	1	5	2	10	283	143	28	5
Portage	537	537	—	4	3	26	132	339	33	—
Shawano	555	558	—	2	—	12	147	357	37	3
Waupaca	568	570	1	5	1	7	209	320	25	2
Wood	476	476	1	1	1	13	128	313	19	—

Table 11. — Number of Offenses Known to the Police, Rural Counties 25,000 and over in Population, 1995 — Continued

County by State	Crime Index total	Modified* Crime Index total	Murder and non-negligent man-slaughter	Forcible rape	Robbery	Aggravated assault	Burglary	Larceny–theft	Motor vehicle theft	Arson*
STATE AGENCIES										
Alaska State Police	6,110	6,183	20	174	38	874	1,439	3,114	451	73
Arizona Department of Public Safety ...	36	36	—	—	—	20	1	15	—	—
Connecticut State Police	9,823	9,898	11	110	75	1,032	2,896	4,934	765	75
Minnesota Highway Patrol	144	144	—	—	4	2	1	113	24	—
OTHER AREAS										
American Samoa	508	520	1	4	4	117	253	124	5	12
Guam	8,381	8,411	7	112	127	242	2,149	5,077	667	30
Virgin Islands	8,432	8,494	21	60	482	1,472	2,893	2,903	601	62

[1]Complete data for 1995 were not available for the states of Delaware, Illinois, Kansas, Montana, and Pennsylvania. See "Offense Estimation," pages 367–368 for details.

[2]Aggravated assault figures for 1994 furnished by the state-level Uniform Crime Reporting (UCR) Program administered by the Kentucky State Police were not in accordance with national UCR guidelines; therefore, the 1995 figures, which are in accordance with the national UCR guidelines, cannot be compared to the 1994 figures.

Table 12.—Crime Trends, Offenses Known to the Police, Population Group, 1994–1995

[1995 estimated population]

Population group	Crime Index total	Modified Crime Index total[1]	Violent crime[2]	Property crime[3]	Murder and non-negligent man-slaughter	Forcible rape	Robbery	Aggravated assault	Burglary	Larceny-theft	Motor vehicle theft	Arson[1]
TOTAL ALL AGENCIES:												
11,813 agencies;												
population 230,021,000:												
1994	**12,614,588**	**12,708,530**	**1,709,373**	**10,905,215**	**21,550**	**90,216**	**586,133**	**1,011,474**	**2,445,982**	**7,026,079**	**1,433,154**	**93,942**
1995	**12,462,083**	**12,552,401**	**1,637,991**	**10,824,092**	**19,959**	**85,277**	**548,146**	**984,609**	**2,332,331**	**7,126,878**	**1,364,883**	**90,318**
Percent change	**–1.2**	**–1.2**	**–4.2**	**–.7**	**–7.4**	**–5.5**	**–6.5**	**–2.7**	**–4.6**	**+1.4**	**–4.8**	**–3.9**
TOTAL CITIES: 8,195 cities;												
population 154,419,000:												
1994	**10,143,177**	**10,218,480**	**1,426,072**	**8,717,105**	**17,384**	**66,565**	**530,139**	**811,984**	**1,841,672**	**5,672,888**	**1,202,545**	**75,303**
1995	**9,986,388**	**10,058,137**	**1,356,882**	**8,629,506**	**16,028**	**63,262**	**493,746**	**783,846**	**1,746,554**	**5,747,708**	**1,135,244**	**71,749**
Percent change	**–1.5**	**–1.6**	**–4.9**	**–1.0**	**–7.8**	**–5.0**	**–6.9**	**–3.5**	**–5.2**	**+1.3**	**–5.6**	**–4.7**
GROUP I												
64 cities, 250,000 and over;												
population 46,175,000:												
1994	4,079,057	4,114,898	767,287	3,311,770	10,361	27,280	337,938	391,708	718,971	1,939,326	653,473	35,841
1995	3,950,152	3,983,088	719,535	3,230,617	9,614	26,179	308,799	374,943	674,623	1,950,618	605,376	32,936
Percent change	–3.2	–3.2	–6.2	–2.5	–7.2	–4.0	–8.6	–4.3	–6.2	+.6	–7.4	–8.1
8 cities, 1,000,000 and over;												
population 20,085,000:												
1994	1,602,764	1,617,828	369,593	1,233,171	4,752	7,670	174,342	182,829	267,446	677,065	288,660	15,064
1995	1,499,829	1,512,526	338,618	1,161,211	4,181	7,145	154,170	173,122	244,417	662,976	253,818	12,697
Percent change	–6.4	–6.5	–8.4	–5.8	–12.0	–6.8	–11.6	–5.3	–8.6	–2.1	–12.1	–15.7
19 cities, 500,000 to 999,999;												
population 12,830,000:												
1994	1,148,847	1,158,689	181,372	967,475	2,699	9,002	78,254	91,417	204,406	597,812	165,257	9,842
1995	1,158,303	1,167,534	175,813	982,490	2,572	8,994	74,336	89,911	199,373	616,704	166,413	9,231
Percent change	+.8	+.8	–3.1	+1.6	–4.7	–.1	–5.0	–1.6	–2.5	+3.2	+.7	–6.2
37 cities, 250,000 to 499,999;												
population 13,259,000:												
1994	1,327,446	1,338,381	216,322	1,111,124	2,910	10,608	85,342	117,462	247,119	664,449	199,556	10,935
1995	1,292,020	1,303,028	205,104	1,086,916	2,861	10,040	80,293	111,910	230,833	670,938	185,145	11,008
Percent change	–2.7	–2.6	–5.2	–2.2	–1.7	–5.4	–5.9	–4.7	–6.6	+1.0	–7.2	+.7
GROUP II												
143 cities, 100,000 to 249,999;												
population 20,924,000:												
1994	1,615,912	1,628,887	213,442	1,402,470	2,797	10,828	76,621	123,196	317,650	896,513	188,307	12,975
1995	1,582,893	1,595,341	203,038	1,379,855	2,543	10,360	72,428	117,707	295,288	905,902	178,665	12,448
Percent change	–2.0	–2.1	–4.9	–1.6	–9.1	–4.3	–5.5	–4.5	–7.0	+1.0	–5.1	–4.1
GROUP III												
341 cities, 50,000 to 99,999;												
population 23,165,000:												
1994	1,418,430	1,427,409	165,599	1,252,831	1,723	9,576	52,031	102,269	265,407	837,747	149,677	8,979
1995	1,394,615	1,403,399	161,071	1,233,544	1,484	9,000	50,533	100,054	250,964	839,319	143,261	8,784
Percent change	–1.7	–1.7	–2.7	–1.5	–13.9	–6.0	–2.9	–2.2	–5.4	+.2	–4.3	–2.2
GROUP IV												
616 cities, 25,000 to 49,999;												
population 21,241,000:												
1994	1,101,931	1,108,796	109,753	992,178	936	7,049	30,593	71,175	203,070	694,833	94,275	6,865
1995	1,105,095	1,111,963	107,761	997,334	890	6,896	29,918	70,057	197,973	709,279	90,082	6,868
Percent change	+.3	+.3	–1.8	+.5	–4.9	–2.2	–2.2	–1.6	–2.5	+2.1	–4.4	—

See footnotes at end of table.

Table 12.—Crime Trends, Offenses Known to the Police, Population Group, 1994–1995 — Continued

Population group	Crime Index total	Modified Crime Index total[1]	Violent crime[2]	Property crime[3]	Murder and non-negligent man-slaughter	Forcible rape	Robbery	Aggravated assault	Burglary	Larceny-theft	Motor vehicle theft	Arson[1]
GROUP V												
1,484 cities, 10,000 to 24,999; population 23,327,000:												
1994	1,056,785	1,062,471	97,482	959,303	927	6,985	21,801	67,769	187,476	699,502	72,325	5,686
1995	1,065,772	1,071,361	94,053	971,719	871	6,315	20,875	65,992	182,184	718,033	71,502	5,589
Percent change	+.9	+.8	−3.5	+1.3	−6.0	−9.6	−4.2	−2.6	−2.8	+2.6	−1.1	−1.7
Group VI												
5,547 cities under 10,000; population 19,588,000:												
1994	871,062	876,019	72,509	798,553	640	4,847	11,155	55,867	149,098	604,967	44,488	4,957
1995	887,861	892,985	71,424	816,437	626	4,512	11,193	55,093	145,522	624,557	46,358	5,124
Percent change	+1.9	+1.9	−1.5	+2.2	−2.2	−6.9	+.3	−1.4	−2.4	+3.2	+4.2	+3.4
SUBURBAN COUNTIES												
1,245 agencies; population 50,770,000;												
1994	1,952,131	1,966,775	226,566	1,725,565	2,937	16,877	51,579	155,173	441,810	1,083,858	199,897	14,644
1995	1,933,561	1,947,838	221,994	1,711,567	2,681	15,669	49,938	153,706	420,420	1,094,689	196,458	14,277
Percent change	−1.0	−1.0	−2.0	−.8	−8.7	−7.2	−3.2	−.9	−4.8	+1.0	−1.7	−2.5
RURAL COUNTIES[4]												
2,373 agencies; population 24,832,000:												
1994	519,280	523,275	56,735	462,545	1,229	6,774	4,415	44,317	162,500	269,333	30,712	3,995
1995	542,134	546,426	59,115	483,019	1,250	6,346	4,462	47,057	165,357	284,481	33,181	4,292
Percent change	+4.4	+4.4	+4.2	+4.4	+1.7	−6.3	+1.1	+6.2	+1.8	+5.6	+8.0	+7.4
SUBURBAN AREA[5]												
5,795 agencies; population 93,763,000:												
1994	3,817,181	3,843,072	391,439	3,425,742	4,308	27,473	93,592	266,066	767,153	2,303,205	355,384	25,891
1995	3,795,747	3,821,074	379,312	3,416,435	3,910	25,428	90,460	259,514	733,573	2,336,606	346,256	25,327
Percent change	−.6	−.6	−3.1	−.3	−9.2	−7.4	−3.3	−2.5	−4.4	+1.5	−2.6	−2.2

[1] The number of agency reports used in arson trends is less than used in compiling trends for other Crime Index offenses. It is not necessary to report arson by property classification to be included in this table. The Modified Crime Index total is the sum of the Crime Index offenses, including arson.

[2] Violent crimes are offenses of murder, forcible rape, robbery, and aggravated assault.

[3] Property crimes are offenses of burglary, larceny-theft, and motor vehicle theft. Data are not included for the property crime of arson.

[4] Includes state police agencies with no county breakdowns.

[5] Includes suburban city and county law enforcement agencies within metropolitan areas. Excludes central cities. Suburban cities and counties are also included in other groups.

Forcible rape figures furnished by the state-level Uniform Crime Reporting (UCR) Program administered by the Illinois State Police were not in accordance with national UCR guidelines and were excluded from the forcible rape, violent crime, Crime Index total, and Modified Crime Index total categories.

Aggravated assault figures for 1994 furnished by the state level Uniform Crime Reporting (UCR) Program administered by the Kentucky State Police were not in accordance with national UCR guidelines and were excluded for both years from the aggravated assault, violent crime, Crime Index total, and Modified Crime Index total categories.

Complete data for 1995 were not available for the states of Delaware, Illinois, Kansas, and Montana. See "Offense Estimation," pages 367–368 for details.

Table 13.—Crime Trends, Offenses Known to the Police, Suburban and Nonsuburban Cities,[1] Population Group, 1994–1995

[1995 estimated population]

Population group	Crime Index total	Modified Crime Index total[2]	Violent crime[3]	Property crime[4]	Murder and non-negligent man-slaughter	Forcible rape	Robbery	Aggravated assault	Burglary	Larceny-theft	Motor vehicle theft	Arson[2]
Suburban Cities												
TOTAL SUBURBAN CITIES:												
4,550 cities;												
population 42,993,000:												
1994	1,865,050	1,876,297	164,873	1,700,177	1,371	10,596	42,013	110,893	325,343	1,219,347	155,487	11,247
1995	1,862,186	1,873,236	157,318	1,704,868	1,229	9,759	40,522	105,808	313,153	1,241,917	149,798	11,050
Percent change	−.2	−.2	−4.6	+.3	−10.4	−7.9	−3.5	−4.6	−3.7	+1.9	−3.7	−1.8
GROUP IV												
433 cities, 25,000 to 49,999;												
population 14,742,000:												
1994	667,183	671,379	64,794	602,389	517	3,786	19,516	40,975	121,512	411,163	69,714	4,196
1995	660,273	664,463	62,228	598,045	474	3,685	18,969	39,100	116,439	416,498	65,108	4,190
Percent change	−1.0	−1.0	−4.0	−.7	−8.3	−2.7	−2.8	−4.6	−4.2	+1.3	−6.6	−.1
GROUP V												
1,073 cities, 10,000 to 24,999;												
population 16,850,000:												
1994	677,501	681,299	61,090	616,411	554	4,207	15,082	41,247	119,328	441,757	55,326	3,798
1995	676,460	680,051	57,474	618,986	467	3,753	14,145	39,109	114,600	450,868	53,518	3,591
Percent change	−.2	−.2	−5.9	+.4	−15.7	−10.8	−6.2	−5.2	−4.0	+2.1	−3.3	−5.5
GROUP VI												
3,044 cities under 10,000;												
population 11,401,000:												
1994	520,366	523,619	38,989	481,377	300	2,603	7,415	28,671	84,503	366,427	30,447	3,253
1995	525,453	528,722	37,616	487,837	288	2,321	7,408	27,599	82,114	374,551	31,172	3,269
Percent change	+1.0	+1.0	−3.5	+1.3	−4.0	−10.8	−.1	−3.7	−2.8	+2.2	+2.4	+.5
Nonsuburban Cities												
TOTAL NONSUBURBAN CITIES:												
3,097 cities;												
population 21,163,000:												
1994	1,164,728	1,170,989	114,871	1,049,857	1,132	8,285	21,536	83,918	214,301	779,955	55,601	6,261
1995	1,196,542	1,203,073	115,920	1,080,622	1,158	7,964	21,464	85,334	212,526	809,952	58,144	6,531
Percent change	+2.7	+2.7	+.9	+2.9	+2.3	−3.9	−.3	+1.7	−.8	+3.8	+4.6	+4.3
GROUP IV												
183 cities, 25,000 to 49,999;												
population 6,499,000:												
1994	434,748	437,417	44,959	389,789	419	3,263	11,077	30,200	81,558	283,670	24,561	2,669
1995	444,822	447,500	45,533	399,289	416	3,211	10,949	30,957	81,534	292,781	24,974	2,678
Percent change	+2.3	+2.3	+1.3	+2.4	−.7	−1.6	−1.2	+2.5	—	+3.2	+1.7	+.3
GROUP V												
411 cities, 10,000 to 24,999;												
population 6,477,000:												
1994	379,284	381,172	36,392	342,892	373	2,778	6,719	26,522	68,148	257,745	16,999	1,888
1995	389,312	391,310	36,579	352,733	404	2,562	6,730	26,883	67,584	267,165	17,984	1,998
Percent change	+2.6	+2.7	+.5	+2.9	+8.3	−7.8	+.2	+1.4	−.8	+3.7	+5.8	+5.8
GROUP VI												
2,503 cities under 10,000;												
population 8,187,000:												
1994	350,696	352,400	33,520	317,176	340	2,244	3,740	27,196	64,595	238,540	14,041	1,704
1995	362,408	364,263	33,808	328,600	338	2,191	3,785	27,494	63,408	250,006	15,186	1,855
Percent change	+3.3	+3.4	+.9	+3.6	−.6	−2.4	+1.2	+1.1	−1.8	+4.8	+8.2	+8.9

[1] Suburban places are within Metropolitan Statistical Areas (MSAs) and include suburban city and county law enforcement agencies within the metropolitan area. Central cities are excluded. Nonsuburban places are outside MSAs.

[2] The number of agencies used in arson trends is less than used in compiling trends for other Crime Index offenses. It is not necessary to report arson by property classification to be included in this table. The Modified Crime Index total is the sum of the Crime Index offenses, including arson.

[3] Violent crimes are offenses of murder, forcible rape, robbery, and aggravated assault.

[4] Property crimes are offenses of burglary, larceny-theft, and motor vehicle theft. Data are not included for the property crime of arson.

Forcible rape figures furnished by the state-level Uniform Crime Reporting (UCR) Program administered by the Illinois State Police were not in accordance with national UCR guidelines and were excluded from the forcible rape, violent crime, Crime Index total, and Modified Crime Index total categories.

Aggravated assault figures for 1994 furnished by the state level Uniform Crime Reporting (UCR) Program administered by the Kentucky State Police were not in accordance with national UCR guidelines and were excluded for both years from the aggravated assault, violent crime, Crime Index total, and Modified Crime Index total categories.

Complete data for 1995 were not available for the states of Delaware, Illinois, Kansas, and Montana. See "Offense Estimation," pages 367–368 for details.

Table 14.—Crime Trends, Offenses Known to the Police, Suburban and Nonsuburban Counties, Population Group, 1994–1995

[1995 estimated population]

Population group	Crime Index total	Modified Crime Index total[1]	Violent crime[2]	Property crime[3]	Murder and non-negligent man-slaughter	Forcible rape	Robbery	Aggravated assault	Burglary	Larceny-theft	Motor vehicle theft	Arson[1]
Suburban Counties[4]												
100,000 and over												
121 counties; population 30,456,000:												
1994	1,408,087	1,418,494	169,479	1,238,608	1,977	10,679	45,103	111,720	299,089	788,627	150,892	10,407
1995	1,384,386	1,394,195	164,862	1,219,524	1,854	10,048	43,633	109,327	280,466	791,158	147,900	9,809
Percent change	−1.7	−1.7	−2.7	−1.5	−6.2	−5.9	−3.3	−2.1	−6.2	+.3	−2.0	−5.7
25,000 to 99,999												
345 counties; population 17,595,000:												
1994	423,555	426,508	43,632	379,923	747	4,628	4,922	33,335	116,706	237,159	26,058	2,953
1995	427,068	430,109	43,760	383,308	601	4,157	4,849	34,153	113,856	242,808	26,644	3,041
Percent change	+.8	+.8	+.3	+.9	−19.5	−10.2	−1.5	+2.5	−2.4	+2.4	+2.2	+3.0
Under 25,000												
773 counties; population 2,590,000:												
1994	118,163	119,440	13,142	105,021	211	1,550	1,518	9,863	25,323	56,903	22,795	1,277
1995	119,902	121,328	13,034	106,868	217	1,431	1,418	9,968	25,453	59,657	21,758	1,426
Percent change	+1.5	+1.6	−.8	+1.8	+2.8	−7.7	−6.6	+1.1	+.5	+4.8	−4.5	+11.7
Nonsuburban counties[4]												
25,000 and over												
249 counties; population 9,949,000:												
1994	206,682	208,036	21,937	184,745	383	2,228	2,124	17,202	63,728	109,465	11,552	1,354
1995	218,194	219,756	22,695	195,499	415	2,086	2,163	18,031	65,824	117,666	12,009	1,562
Percent change	+5.6	+5.6	+3.5	+5.8	+8.4	−6.4	+1.8	+4.8	+3.3	+7.5	+4.0	+15.4
10,000 to 24,999												
632 counties; population 10,131,000:												
1994	176,918	178,086	20,634	156,284	474	2,074	1,394	16,692	58,014	88,704	9,566	1,168
1995	184,714	185,943	21,449	163,265	420	1,865	1,377	17,787	58,622	94,089	10,554	1,229
Percent change	+4.4	+4.4	+3.9	+4.5	−11.4	−10.1	−1.2	+6.6	+1.0	+6.1	+10.3	+5.2
Under 10,000												
1,382 counties; population 4,244,000:												
1994	106,143	107,391	10,937	95,206	321	2,077	648	7,891	32,606	54,853	7,747	1,248
1995	108,829	110,127	11,590	97,239	355	1,980	674	8,581	32,912	55,687	8,640	1,298
Percent change	+2.5	+2.5	+6.0	+2.1	+10.6	−4.7	+4.0	+8.7	+.9	+1.5	+11.5	+4.0

[1] The number of agencies used in arson trends is less than used in compiling trends for other Crime Index offenses. It is not necessary to report arson by property classification to be included in this table. The Modified Crime Index total is the sum of the Crime Index offenses, including arson.

[2] Violent crimes are offenses of murder, forcible rape, robbery, and aggravated assault.

[3] Property crimes are offenses of burglary, larceny-theft, and motor vehicle theft. Data are not included for the property crime of arson.

[4] Offenses include sheriffs' and county law enforcement agencies. State police offenses are not included.

Forcible rape figures furnished by the state-level Uniform Crime Reporting (UCR) Program administered by the Illinois State Police were not in accordance with national UCR guidelines and were excluded from the forcible rape, violent crime, Crime Index total, and Modified Crime Index total categories.

Aggravated assault figures for 1994 furnished by the state level Uniform Crime Reporting (UCR) Program administered by the Kentucky State Police were not in accordance with national UCR guidelines and were excluded for both years from the aggravated assault, violent crime, Crime Index total, and Modified Crime Index total categories.

Complete data for 1995 were not available for the states of Delaware, Illinois, Kansas, and Montana. See "Offense Estimation," pages 367–368 for details.

Table 15.—Crime Trends, Offenses Known Breakdown, Population Group, 1994–1995

[1995 estimated population]

Population group	Forcible rape: Rape by force	Forcible rape: Assault to rape–attempts	Robbery: Firearm	Robbery: Knife or cutting instrument	Robbery: Other weapon	Robbery: Strong-armed	Aggravated assault: Firearm	Aggravated assault: Knife or cutting instrument	Aggravated assault: Other weapon	Aggravated assault: Hands, fists, feet, etc.	Burglary: Forcible entry	Burglary: Unlawful entry	Burglary: Attempted forcible entry	Motor vehicle theft: Autos	Motor vehicle theft: Trucks and buses	Motor vehicle theft: Other vehicles	Arson[1]: Structure	Arson[1]: Mobile	Arson[1]: Other
TOTAL ALL AGENCIES: 11,538 agencies; population 226,378,000:																			
1994	77,728	11,247	242,692	55,421	56,482	228,504	243,286	180,597	322,136	254,286	1,625,535	602,836	187,561	1,124,216	224,465	76,857	46,821	23,031	20,200
1995	73,596	10,516	223,022	49,639	49,871	222,218	221,355	177,571	319,911	255,508	1,537,534	586,152	178,335	1,061,967	220,703	74,071	45,471	21,953	19,737
Percent change	-5.3	-6.5	-8.1	-10.4	-11.7	-2.8	-9.0	-1.7	-.7	+.5	-5.4	-2.8	-4.9	-5.5	-1.7	-3.6	-2.9	-4.7	-2.3
TOTAL CITIES: 7,978 cities; population 152,621,000:																			
1994	57,023	8,825	218,676	51,420	49,405	208,099	201,574	151,495	257,443	193,300	1,224,279	448,037	149,962	964,758	179,553	52,883	37,667	18,368	15,748
1995	54,295	8,305	199,075	45,404	44,600	201,822	181,007	148,287	254,068	192,893	1,152,962	431,226	142,825	902,661	176,116	50,839	36,328	17,341	15,183
Percent change	-4.8	-5.9	-9.0	-11.7	-9.7	-3.0	-10.2	-2.1	-1.3	-.2	-5.8	-3.8	-4.8	-6.4	-1.9	-3.9	-3.6	-5.6	-3.6
GROUP I																			
64 cities, 250,000 and over; population 46,175,000:																			
1994	23,433	3,847	148,962	33,663	28,706	126,607	117,408	79,883	130,530	63,887	507,367	156,178	55,426	535,222	99,712	18,539	17,423	10,116	5,400
1995	22,425	3,754	132,520	28,797	27,309	120,173	103,967	78,089	126,994	65,893	478,223	142,731	53,669	487,280	99,346	18,750	16,281	9,186	5,100
Percent change	-4.3	-2.4	-11.0	-14.5	-4.9	-5.1	-11.4	-2.2	-2.7	+3.1	-5.7	-8.6	-3.2	-9.0	-.4	+1.1	-6.6	-9.2	-5.6
8 cities, 1,000,000 and over; population 20,085,000:																			
1994	6,500	1,170	74,264	20,469	15,367	64,242	50,656	40,704	59,165	32,304	180,011	64,059	23,376	244,254	38,214	6,192	6,665	4,392	2,381
1995	6,025	1,120	64,821	16,424	14,209	58,716	44,842	38,655	56,077	33,548	160,053	60,467	23,897	209,530	38,392	5,896	5,857	3,671	1,928
Percent change	-7.3	-4.3	-12.7	-19.8	-7.5	-8.6	-11.5	-5.0	-5.2	+3.9	-11.1	-5.6	+2.2	-14.2	+.5	-4.8	-12.1	-16.4	-19.0
19 cities, 500,000 to 999,999; population 12,830,000:																			
1994	7,741	1,261	37,624	6,202	6,264	28,164	28,373	17,518	31,687	13,839	150,145	40,015	14,246	132,208	26,641	6,408	4,650	2,769	1,285
1995	7,754	1,240	34,222	5,846	6,362	27,906	25,557	17,227	32,388	14,739	152,770	33,819	12,784	132,141	27,795	6,477	4,542	2,767	1,040
Percent change	+.2	-1.7	-9.0	-5.7	+1.6	-.9	-9.9	-1.7	+2.2	+6.5	+1.7	-15.5	-10.3	-.1	+4.3	+1.1	-2.3	-.1	-19.1
37 cities, 250,000 to 499,999; population 13,259,000:																			
1994	9,192	1,416	37,074	6,992	7,075	34,201	38,379	21,661	39,678	17,744	177,211	52,104	17,804	158,760	34,857	5,939	6,108	2,955	1,734
1995	8,646	1,394	33,477	6,527	6,738	33,551	33,568	22,207	38,529	17,606	165,400	48,445	16,988	145,609	33,159	6,377	5,882	2,748	2,132
Percent change	-5.9	-1.6	-9.7	-6.7	-4.8	-1.9	-12.5	+2.5	-2.9	-.8	-6.7	-7.0	-4.6	-8.3	-4.9	+7.4	-3.7	-7.0	+23.0
GROUP II																			
143 cities, 100,000 to 249,999; population 20,924,000:																			
1994	9,352	1,466	30,936	7,788	7,629	30,142	32,786	22,306	40,857	27,130	217,314	73,569	26,266	149,704	29,319	9,049	6,950	3,079	2,655
1995	8,947	1,401	29,366	6,996	6,766	29,178	30,680	21,204	41,272	24,419	201,118	69,321	24,351	142,329	28,230	7,931	6,762	3,113	2,349
Percent change	-4.3	-4.4	-5.1	-10.2	-11.3	-3.2	-6.4	-4.9	+1.0	-10.0	-7.5	-5.8	-7.3	-4.9	-3.7	-12.4	-2.7	+1.1	-11.5
GROUP III																			
338 cities, 50,000 to 99,999; population 22,975,000:																			
1994	8,273	1,204	18,240	4,487	6,010	22,874	21,605	18,034	34,176	27,440	174,196	66,584	22,120	120,491	20,639	7,869	4,260	2,197	2,379
1995	7,941	971	17,851	4,338	4,462	23,393	19,060	18,086	34,023	28,061	160,824	66,303	20,978	115,350	19,812	7,471	4,374	2,112	2,213
Percent change	-4.0	-19.4	-2.1	-3.3	-25.8	+2.3	-11.8	+.3	-.4	+2.3	-7.7	-.4	-5.2	-4.3	-4.0	-5.1	+2.7	-3.9	-7.0

See footnotes at end of table.

Table 15.—Crime Trends, Offenses Known Breakdown, Population Group, 1994-1995 — Continued

Population group	Forcible rape		Robbery				Aggravated assault				Burglary			Motor vehicle theft			Arson[1]		
	Rape by force	Assault to rape—attempts	Firearm	Knife or cutting instrument	Other weapon	Strong-armed	Firearm	Knife or cutting instrument	Other weapon	Hands, fists, feet, etc.	Forcible entry	Unlawful entry	Attempted forcible entry	Autos	Trucks and buses	Other vehicles	Structure	Mobile	Other
GROUP IV																			
607 cities, 25,000 to 49,999; population 20,911,000:																			
1994	6,073	786	10,060	2,656	3,373	13,753	12,174	11,720	21,199	24,365	126,036	54,641	17,193	72,288	13,357	7,162	3,388	1,307	2,098
1995	5,905	786	9,369	2,569	2,849	14,239	11,036	11,544	20,816	24,825	120,951	55,222	16,173	69,483	12,360	6,265	3,314	1,279	2,190
Percent change	-2.8	—	-6.9	-3.3	-15.5	+3.5	-9.3	-1.5	-1.8	+1.9	-4.0	+1.1	-5.9	-3.9	-7.5	-12.5	-2.2	-2.1	+4.4
GROUP V																			
1,443 cities, 10,000 to 24,999; population 22,684,000:																			
1994	5,904	838	6,924	1,896	2,664	9,455	10,836	11,414	18,399	24,137	114,154	50,902	16,363	55,029	9,801	5,728	2,934	1,006	1,692
1995	5,379	754	6,490	1,783	2,211	9,537	9,775	11,241	18,779	23,437	109,446	51,393	15,777	54,561	9,439	5,926	2,911	974	1,653
Percent change	-8.9	-10.0	-6.3	-6.0	-17.0	+.9	-9.8	-1.5	+2.1	-2.9	-4.1	+1.0	-3.6	-.9	-3.7	+3.5	-.8	-3.2	-2.3
GROUP VI																			
5,383 cities under 10,000; population 18,951,000:																			
1994	3,988	684	3,554	930	1,023	5,268	6,765	8,138	12,282	26,341	85,212	46,163	12,594	32,024	6,725	4,536	2,712	663	1,524
1995	3,698	639	3,479	921	1,003	5,302	6,489	8,123	12,184	26,258	82,394	46,256	11,877	33,658	6,929	4,496	2,686	677	1,678
Percent change	-7.3	-6.6	-2.1	-1.0	-2.0	+.6	-4.1	-.2	-.8	-.3	-3.3	+.2	-5.7	+5.1	+3.0	-.9	-1.0	+2.1	+10.1
SUBURBAN COUNTIES																			
1,224 agencies; population 49,591,000:																			
1994	14,643	1,803	22,293	3,594	6,575	18,720	32,956	22,923	53,676	43,584	291,558	114,236	28,625	141,830	38,808	17,458	6,692	3,796	3,814
1995	13,613	1,659	22,227	3,822	4,746	18,682	31,524	22,800	54,390	43,154	273,703	112,443	26,788	139,843	38,177	16,418	6,489	3,717	3,836
Percent change	-7.0	-8.0	-.3	+6.3	-27.8	-.2	-4.3	-.5	+1.3	-1.0	-6.1	-1.6	-6.4	-1.4	-1.6	-6.0	-3.0	-2.1	+.6
RURAL COUNTIES																			
2,336 agencies; population 24,167,000:																			
1994	6,062	619	1,723	407	502	1,685	8,756	6,179	11,017	17,402	109,698	40,563	8,974	17,628	6,104	6,516	2,462	867	638
1995	5,688	552	1,720	413	525	1,714	8,824	6,484	11,453	19,461	110,869	42,483	8,722	19,463	6,410	6,814	2,654	895	718
Percent change	-6.2	-10.8	-.2	+1.5	+4.6	+1.7	+.8	+4.9	+4.0	+11.8	+1.1	+4.7	-2.8	+10.4	+5.0	+4.6	+7.8	+3.2	+12.5
SUBURBAN AREA[2]																			
5,680 agencies; population 91,840,000:																			
1994	23,673	3,085	36,534	6,952	11,569	36,926	48,835	39,189	84,370	88,988	485,448	209,841	57,340	262,299	59,790	28,804	12,231	5,760	7,516
1995	21,966	2,831	35,434	7,052	8,623	37,636	45,996	38,681	84,170	86,352	457,887	207,149	54,105	256,220	57,962	27,153	11,838	5,587	7,597
Percent change	-7.2	-8.2	-3.0	+1.4	-25.5	+1.9	-5.8	-1.3	-.2	-3.0	-5.7	-1.3	-5.6	-2.3	-3.1	-5.7	-3.2	-3.0	+1.1

[1] The number of agency reports used in arson trends is less than used in compiling trends for other Crime Index offenses.

[2] Includes suburban city and county law enforcement agencies within metropolitan areas. Excludes central cities. Suburban cities and counties are also included in other groups.

Forcible rape figures furnished by the state-level Uniform Crime Reporting (UCR) Program administered by the Illinois State Police were not in accordance with national UCR guidelines and were excluded from the forcible rape categories.

Aggravated assault figures for 1994 furnished by the state level Uniform Crime Reporting (UCR) Program administered by the Kentucky State Police were not in accordance with national UCR guidelines and were excluded for both years from the aggravated assault, violent crime, Crime Index total, and Modified Crime Index total categories.

Complete data for 1995 were not available for the states of Delaware, Illinois, Kansas, and Montana. See "Offense Estimation," pages 367–368 for details.

Table 16.—Crime Rates, Offenses Known to the Police, Population Group, 1995

[1995 estimated population. Rate: Number of crimes per 100,000 inhabitants]

Population group	Crime Index total	Modified Crime Index total[1]	Violent crime[2]	Property crime[3]	Murder and non-negligent man-slaughter	Forcible rape	Robbery	Aggravated assault	Burglary	Larceny-theft	Motor vehicle theft	Arson[1]
TOTAL ALL AGENCIES: 10,481 agencies; population 215,854,000:												
Number of offenses known	**12,140,423**		**1,611,442**	**10,528,981**	**19,450**	**84,040**	**540,015**	**967,937**	**2,269,007**	**6,921,896**	**1,338,078**	
Rate	**5,624.4**		**746.5**	**4,877.8**	**9.0**	**38.9**	**250.2**	**448.4**	**1,051.2**	**3,206.7**	**619.9**	
TOTAL CITIES: 7,196 cities; population 145,830,000:												
Number of offenses known	**9,789,480**		**1,341,526**	**8,447,954**	**15,681**	**63,162**	**487,864**	**774,819**	**1,716,756**	**5,612,094**	**1,119,104**	
Rate	**6,712.9**		**919.9**	**5,793.0**	**10.8**	**43.3**	**334.5**	**531.3**	**1,177.2**	**3,848.4**	**767.4**	
GROUP I												
63 cities, 250,000 and over; population 45,801,000:												
Number of offenses known . .	3,921,993		716,444	3,205,549	9,532	26,931	306,713	373,268	668,113	1,937,277	600,159	
Rate	8,563.1		1,564.3	6,998.9	20.8	58.8	669.7	815.0	1,458.7	4,229.8	1,310.4	
8 cities, 1,000,000 and over; population 20,085,000:												
Number of offenses known . .	1,500,962		339,751	1,161,211	4,181	8,278	154,170	173,122	244,417	662,976	253,818	
Rate	7,472.9		1,691.5	5,781.4	20.8	41.2	767.6	861.9	1,216.9	3,300.8	1,263.7	
19 cities, 500,000 to 999,999; population 12,830,000:												
Number of offenses known . .	1,158,303		175,813	982,490	2,572	8,994	74,336	89,911	199,373	616,704	166,413	
Rate	9,027.8		1,370.3	7,657.5	20.0	70.1	579.4	700.8	1,553.9	4,806.6	1,297.0	
36 cities, 250,000 to 499,999; population 12,885,000:												
Number of offenses known . .	1,262,728		200,880	1,061,848	2,779	9,659	78,207	110,235	224,323	657,597	179,928	
Rate	9,799.7		1,559.0	8,240.7	21.6	75.0	606.9	855.5	1,740.9	5,103.4	1,396.4	
GROUP II												
144 cities, 100,000 to 249,999; population 21,127,000:												
Number of offenses known . .	1,607,045		205,461	1,401,584	2,473	10,562	72,988	119,438	301,738	918,519	181,327	
Rate	7,606.8		972.5	6,634.2	11.7	50.0	345.5	565.3	1,428.2	4,347.7	858.3	
GROUP III												
322 cities, 50,000 to 99,999; population 21,978,000:												
Number of offenses known . .	1,351,988		157,727	1,194,261	1,459	8,728	49,292	98,248	244,694	809,682	139,885	
Rate	6,151.7		717.7	5,434.0	6.6	39.7	224.3	447.0	1,113.4	3,684.1	636.5	
GROUP IV												
577 cities, 25,000 to 49,999; population 19,988,000:												
Number of offenses known . .	1,072,649		104,720	967,929	852	6,691	28,604	68,573	193,168	687,448	87,313	
Rate	5,366.5		523.9	4,842.6	4.3	33.5	143.1	343.1	966.4	3,439.4	436.8	

See footnotes at end of table.

Table 16.—Crime Rates, Offenses Known to the Police, Population Group, 1995 — Continued

[1995 estimated population. Rate: Number of crimes per 100,000 inhabitants]

Population group	Crime Index total	Modified Crime Index total[1]	Violent crime[2]	Property crime[3]	Murder and non-negligent man-slaughter	Forcible rape	Robbery	Aggravated assault	Burglary	Larceny-theft	Motor vehicle theft	Arson[1]
GROUP V												
1,298 cities, 10,000 to 24,999; population 20,470,000:												
Number of offenses known ..	1,000,791		89,991	910,800	785	6,002	19,794	63,410	172,013	671,375	67,412	
Rate	4,889.1		439.6	4,449.5	3.8	29.3	96.7	309.8	840.3	3,279.8	329.3	
GROUP VI												
4,792 cities under 10,000; population 16,467,000:												
Number of offenses known ..	835,014		67,183	767,831	580	4,248	10,473	51,882	137,030	587,793	43,008	
Rate	5,070.7		408.0	4,662.7	3.5	25.8	63.6	315.1	832.1	3,569.4	261.2	
SUBURBAN COUNTIES												
1,106 agencies; population 47,299,000:												
Number of offenses known ..	1,836,240		212,415	1,623,825	2,575	14,931	47,928	146,981	396,035	1,040,129	187,661	
Rate	3,882.2		449.1	3,433.1	5.4	31.6	101.3	310.8	837.3	2,199.1	396.8	
RURAL COUNTIES[4]												
2,179 agencies; population 22,726,000:												
Number of offenses known ..	514,703		57,501	457,202	1,194	5,947	4,223	46,137	156,216	269,673	31,313	
Rate	2,264.9		253.0	2,011.8	5.3	26.2	18.6	203.0	687.4	1,186.6	137.8	
SUBURBAN AREA[5]												
4,926 agencies; population 84,667,000:												
Number of offenses known ..	3,594,222		362,552	3,231,670	3,707	24,267	86,491	248,087	694,528	2,207,462	329,680	
Rate	4,245.1		428.2	3,816.9	4.4	28.7	102.2	293.0	820.3	2,607.2	389.4	

[1] Arson rates are not presented in this table because fewer agencies furnished complete reports for arson than for the other seven Crime Index offenses. Independently tabulated arson rates appear on page 54 of this publication.

[2] Violent crimes are offenses of murder, forcible rape, robbery, and aggravated assault.

[3] Property crimes are offenses of burglary, larceny-theft, and motor vehicle theft. Data are not included for the property crime of arson.

[4] Includes state police agencies with no county breakdown.

[5] Includes suburban city and county law enforcement agencies within metropolitan areas. Excludes central cities. Suburban cities and counties are also included in other groups.

Population figures were rounded to the nearest thousand. All rates were calculated on the population before rounding.

Forcible rape figures furnished by the state-level Uniform Crime Reporting (UCR) Program administered by the Illinois State Police were not in accordance with national UCR guidelines. See Appendix I for details.

Complete data for 1995 were not available for the states of Delaware, Illinois, Kansas, Montana and Pennsylvania. See "Offense Estimation," pages 367–368 for details.

Table 17.—Crime Rates, Offenses Known to the Police, Suburban and Nonsuburban Cities,[1] Population Group, 1995

[1995 estimated population. Rate: Number of crimes per 100,000 inhabitants]

Population group	Crime Index total	Modified Crime Index total[2]	Violent crime[3]	Property crime[4]	Murder and non-negligent man-slaughter	Forcible rape	Robbery	Aggravated assault	Burglary	Larceny-theft	Motor vehicle theft	Arson[2]
Suburban Cities												
TOTAL SUBURBAN CITIES: 3,820 cities; population 37,369,000:												
Number of offenses known	1,757,982		150,137	1,607,845	1,132	9,336	38,563	101,106	298,493	1,167,333	142,019	
Rate	4,704.4		401.8	4,302.6	3.0	25.0	103.2	270.6	798.8	3,123.8	380.0	
GROUP IV												
405 cities, 25,000 to 49,999; population 13,865,000:												
Number of offenses known	644,714		61,226	583,488	458	3,650	18,433	38,685	115,049	404,907	63,532	
Rate	4,649.8		441.6	4,208.3	3.3	26.3	132.9	279.0	829.8	2,920.3	458.2	
GROUP V												
918 cities, 10,000 to 24,999; population 14,489,000:												
Number of offenses known	627,170		54,428	572,742	420	3,551	13,347	37,110	107,208	415,409	50,125	
Rate	4,328.6		375.7	3,953.0	2.9	24.5	92.1	256.1	739.9	2,867.1	346.0	
GROUP VI												
2,497 cities under 10,000; population 9,015,000:												
Number of offenses known	486,098		34,483	451,615	254	2,135	6,783	25,311	76,236	347,017	28,362	
Rate	5,392.3		382.5	5,009.8	2.8	23.7	75.2	280.8	845.7	3,849.5	314.6	
Nonsuburban Cities												
TOTAL NONSUBURBAN CITIES: 2,847 cities; population 19,556,000:												
Number of offenses known	1,150,472		111,757	1,038,715	1,085	7,605	20,308	82,759	203,718	779,283	55,714	
Rate	5,882.9		571.5	5,311.5	5.5	38.9	103.8	423.2	1,041.7	3,984.9	284.9	
GROUP IV												
172 cities, 25,000 to 49,999; population 6,122,000:												
Number of offenses known	427,935		43,494	384,441	394	3,041	10,171	29,888	78,119	282,541	23,781	
Rate	6,989.7		710.4	6,279.3	6.4	49.7	166.1	488.2	1,276.0	4,614.9	388.4	
GROUP V												
380 cities, 10,000 to 24,999; population 5,981,000:												
Number of offenses known	373,621		35,563	338,058	365	2,451	6,447	26,300	64,805	255,966	17,287	
Rate	6,246.9		594.6	5,652.3	6.1	41.0	107.8	439.7	1,083.5	4,279.7	289.0	
GROUP VI												
2,295 cities under 10,000; population 7,453,000:												
Number of offenses known	348,916		32,700	316,216	326	2,113	3,690	26,571	60,794	240,776	14,646	
Rate	4,681.7		438.8	4,242.9	4.4	28.4	49.5	356.5	815.7	3,230.7	196.5	

[1] Suburban places are within Metropolitan Statistical Areas (MSAs) and include suburban city and county law enforcement agencies within the metropolitan area. Central cities are excluded. Nonsuburban places are outside MSAs.

[2] Arson rates are not presented in this table because fewer agencies furnished complete reports for arson than for the seven Crime Index offenses. Independently tabulated arson rates appear on page 54 of this publication.

[3] Violent crimes are offenses of murder, forcible rape, robbery, and aggravated assault.

[4] Property crimes are offenses of burglary, larceny-theft, and motor vehicle theft. Data are not included for the property crime of arson.

Population figures were rounded to the nearest thousand. All rates were calculated on the population before rounding.

Forcible rape figures furnished by the state-level Uniform Crime Reporting (UCR) Program administered by the Illinois State Police were not in accordance with national UCR guidelines. See Appendix I for details.

Complete data for 1995 were not available for the states of Delaware, Illinois, Kansas, Montana, and Pennsylvania. See "Offense Estimation," pages 367–368 for details.

Table 18.—Crime Rates, Offenses Known to the Police, Suburban and Nonsuburban Counties, Population Group, 1995

[1995 estimated population. Rate: number of crimes per 100,000 inhabitants]

Population group	Crime Index total	Modified[1] Crime Index total	Violent crime[2]	Property crime[3]	Murder and non-negligent man-slaughter	Forcible rape	Robbery	Aggravated assault	Burglary	Larceny-theft	Motor vehicle theft	Arson[1]
Suburban Counties[4]												
100,000 and over												
115 counties;												
population 28,815,000:												
Number of offenses known . .	1,315,400		157,166	1,158,234	1,807	9,621	41,783	103,955	264,645	751,975	141,614	
Rate	4,565.0		545.4	4,019.5	6.3	33.4	145.0	360.8	918.4	2,609.7	491.5	
25,000 to 99,999												
310 counties;												
population 15,877,000:												
Number of offenses known . .	402,431		41,841	360,590	551	3,936	4,631	32,723	106,390	229,785	24,415	
Rate	2,534.7		263.5	2,271.1	3.5	24.8	29.2	206.1	670.1	1,447.3	153.8	
Under 25,000												
681 counties;												
population 2,606,000:												
Number of offenses known . .	118,409		13,408	105,001	217	1,374	1,514	10,303	25,000	58,369	21,632	
Rate	4,542.9		514.4	4,028.5	8.3	52.7	58.1	395.3	959.2	2,239.4	829.9	
Nonsuburban Counties[4]												
25,000 and over												
221 counties;												
population 8,742,000:												
Number of offenses known . .	203,562		21,844	181,718	386	1,895	2,077	17,486	60,722	109,944	11,052	
Rate	2,328.6		249.9	2,078.7	4.4	21.7	23.8	200.0	694.6	1,257.7	126.4	
10,000 to 24,999												
598 counties;												
population 9,557,000:												
Number of offenses known . .	177,869		20,807	157,062	407	1,764	1,304	17,332	56,562	90,367	10,133	
Rate	1,861.1		217.7	1,643.4	4.3	18.5	13.6	181.4	591.8	945.5	106.0	
Under 10,000												
1,251 counties;												
population 3,919,000:												
Number of offenses known . .	102,889		11,490	91,399	341	1,873	594	8,682	30,933	52,321	8,145	
Rate	2,625.2		293.2	2,332.0	8.7	47.8	15.2	221.5	789.3	1,335.0	207.8	

[1] Arson rates are not presented in this table because fewer agencies furnished complete reports for arson than for the other seven Crime Index offenses. Independently tabulated arson rates appear on page 54 of this publication.

[2] Violent crimes are offenses of murder, forcible rape, robbery, and aggravated assault.

[3] Property crimes are offenses of burglary, larceny-theft, and motor vehicle theft. Data are not included for the property crime of arson.

[4] Offenses include sheriffs' and county law enforcement agencies. State police offenses are not included.

Population figures were rounded to the nearest thousand. All rates were calculated on the population before rounding.

Forcible rape figures furnished by the state-level Uniform Crime Reporting (UCR) Program administered by the Illinois State Police were not in accordance with national UCR guidelines. See Appendix I for details.

Complete data for 1995 were not available for the states of Delaware, Illinois, Kansas, Montana, and Pennsylvania. See "Offense Estimation," pages 367–368 for details.

Table 19.—Crime Rates, Offenses Known Breakdown, Population Group, 1995

[1995 estimated population. Rate: number of crimes per 100,000 inhabitants]

Population group	Forcible rape: Rape by force	Forcible rape: Assault to rape–attempts	Robbery: Firearm	Robbery: Knife or cutting instrument	Robbery: Other weapon	Robbery: Strong-armed	Aggravated assault: Firearm	Aggravated assault: Knife or cutting instrument	Aggravated assault: Other weapon	Aggravated assault: Hands, fists, feet, etc.	Burglary: Forcible entry	Burglary: Unlawful entry	Burglary: Attempted forcible entry	Motor vehicle theft: Autos	Motor vehicle theft: Trucks and buses	Motor vehicle theft: Other vehicles	Arson[1]: Structure	Arson[1]: Mobile	Arson[1]: Other
TOTAL ALL AGENCIES: 10,397 agencies; population 214,693,000:																			
Number of offenses known	73,233	10,490	220,766	48,973	49,314	219,216	220,971	176,726	317,886	250,441	1,512,182	571,981	174,648	1,045,230	217,073	71,676			
Rate	34.1	4.9	102.8	22.8	23.0	102.1	102.9	82.3	148.1	116.7	704.3	266.4	81.3	486.8	101.1	33.4			
TOTAL CITIES: 7,126 cities; population 145,034,000:																			
Number of offenses known	54,546	8,324	197,572	44,888	44,171	199,520	181,482	148,325	254,315	188,986	1,143,067	424,963	139,916	891,386	174,273	49,670			
Rate	37.6	5.7	136.2	30.9	30.5	137.6	125.1	102.3	175.3	130.3	788.1	293.0	96.5	614.6	120.2	34.2			
GROUP I																			
63 cities, 250,000 and over; population 45,801,000:																			
Number of offenses known	23,067	3,864	131,555	28,613	27,194	119,351	103,358	77,677	126,285	65,948	474,266	140,691	53,156	482,975	98,552	18,632			
Rate	50.4	8.4	287.2	62.5	59.4	260.6	225.7	169.6	275.7	144.0	1,035.5	307.2	116.1	1,054.5	215.2	40.7			
8 cities, 1,000,000 and over; population 20,085,000:																			
Number of offenses known	6,980	1,298	64,821	16,424	14,209	58,716	44,842	38,655	56,077	33,548	160,053	60,467	23,897	209,530	38,392	5,896			
Rate	34.8	6.5	322.7	81.8	70.7	292.3	223.3	192.5	279.2	167.0	796.9	301.1	119.0	1,043.2	191.1	29.4			
19 cities, 500,000 to 999,999; population 12,830,000:																			
Number of offenses known	7,754	1,240	34,222	5,846	6,362	27,906	25,557	17,227	32,388	14,739	152,770	33,819	12,784	132,141	27,795	6,477			
Rate	60.4	9.7	266.7	45.6	49.6	217.5	199.2	134.3	252.4	114.9	1,190.7	263.6	99.6	1,029.9	216.6	50.5			
36 cities, 250,000 to 499,999; population 12,885,000:																			
Number of offenses known	8,333	1,326	32,512	6,343	6,623	32,729	32,959	21,795	37,820	17,661	161,443	46,405	16,475	141,304	32,365	6,259			
Rate	64.7	10.3	252.3	49.2	51.4	254.0	255.8	169.1	293.5	137.1	1,252.9	360.1	127.9	1,096.6	251.2	48.6			
GROUP II																			
143 cities, 100,000 to 249,999; population 20,920,000:																			
Number of offenses known	9,047	1,407	28,951	6,867	6,629	29,169	31,005	21,602	41,825	24,249	203,200	70,037	24,300	143,624	28,082	7,746			
Rate	43.2	6.7	138.4	32.8	31.7	139.4	148.2	103.3	199.9	115.9	971.3	334.8	116.2	686.5	134.2	37.0			
GROUP III																			
321 cities, 50,000 to 99,999; population 21,917,000:																			
Number of offenses known	7,759	954	17,734	4,224	4,409	22,892	18,991	17,839	33,795	27,424	159,248	64,544	20,422	113,041	19,466	7,303			
Rate	35.4	4.4	80.9	19.3	20.1	104.5	86.7	81.4	154.2	125.1	726.6	294.5	93.2	515.8	88.8	33.3			

See footnotes at end of table.

Table 19.—Crime Rates, Offenses Known Breakdown, Population Group, 1995 — Continued

Population group	Forcible rape		Robbery				Aggravated assault				Burglary			Motor vehicle theft			Arson[1]		
	Rape by force	Assault to rape–attempts	Firearm	Knife or cutting instrument	Other weapon	Strong-armed	Firearm	Knife or cutting instrument	Other weapon	Hands, fists, feet, etc.	Forcible entry	Unlawful entry	Attempted forcible entry	Autos	Trucks and buses	Other vehicles	Structure	Mobile	Other
GROUP IV																			
574 cities, 25,000 to 49,999; population 19,868,000:																			
Number of offenses known	5,863	763	9,263	2,549	2,838	13,746	11,249	11,718	20,924	24,471	119,857	55,363	16,182	67,764	12,459	6,234			
Rate	29.5	3.8	46.6	12.8	14.3	69.2	56.6	59.0	105.3	123.2	603.3	278.7	81.4	341.1	62.7	31.4			
GROUP V																			
1,286 cities, 10,000 to 24,999; population 20,300,000:																			
Number of offenses known	5,246	717	6,638	1,719	2,109	9,285	10,150	11,282	19,175	22,702	106,663	49,693	14,693	52,421	9,015	5,578			
Rate	25.8	3.5	32.7	8.5	10.4	45.7	50.0	55.6	94.5	111.8	525.4	244.8	72.4	258.2	44.4	27.5			
GROUP VI																			
4,739 cities, under 10,000; population 16,228,000:																			
Number of offenses known	3,564	619	3,431	916	992	5,077	6,729	8,207	12,311	24,192	79,833	44,635	11,163	31,561	6,699	4,177			
Rate	22.0	3.8	21.1	5.6	6.1	31.3	41.5	50.6	75.9	149.1	491.9	275.0	68.8	194.5	41.3	25.7			
SUBURBAN COUNTIES																			
1,101 agencies; population 47,091,000:																			
Number of offenses known	13,282	1,639	21,560	3,693	4,626	18,026	30,637	21,849	52,199	42,213	262,329	106,733	26,479	135,209	36,672	15,621			
Rate	28.2	3.5	45.8	7.8	9.8	38.3	65.1	46.4	110.8	89.6	557.1	226.7	56.2	287.1	77.9	33.2			
RURAL COUNTIES																			
2,170 agencies; population 22,568,000:																			
Number of offenses known	5,405	527	1,634	392	517	1,670	8,852	6,552	11,372	19,242	106,786	40,285	8,253	18,635	6,128	6,385			
Rate	24.0	2.3	7.2	1.7	2.3	7.4	39.2	29.0	50.4	85.3	473.2	178.5	36.6	82.6	27.2	28.3			
SUBURBAN AREA[2]																			
4,896 agencies; population 84,195,000:																			
Number of offenses known	21,427	2,747	34,739	6,829	8,372	36,269	45,290	37,654	81,901	82,789	441,260	198,773	51,989	246,438	55,922	25,815			
Rate	25.4	3.3	41.3	8.1	9.9	43.1	53.8	44.7	97.3	98.3	524.1	236.1	61.7	292.7	66.4	30.7			

[1] Arson rates are not presented in this table because fewer agencies furnished complete reports for arson than for the other seven Crime Index offenses. Independently tabulated arson rates appear on page 54 of this publication.

[2] Includes suburban city and county law enforcement agencies within metropolitan areas. Excludes central cities. Suburban cities and counties are also included in other groups.

Population figures were rounded to the nearest thousand. All rates were calculated on the population before rounding.

Forcible rape figures furnished by the state-level Uniform Crime Reporting (UCR) Program administered by the Illinois State Police were not in accordance with national UCR guidelines. See Appendix I for details.

Complete data for 1995 were not available for the states of Delaware, Illinois, Kansas, Montana, and Pennsylvania. See "Offense Estimation," pages 367–368 for details.

Table 20.—Murder, State, Types of Weapons, 1995

State	Total murders[1]	Total firearms	Handguns	Rifles	Shotguns	Firearms (type unknown)	Knives or cutting instruments	Other weapons	Hands, fists, feet, etc.
Alabama	459	346	309	10	27	—	46	38	29
Alaska	48	24	17	6	1	—	9	10	5
Arizona	429	325	249	18	21	37	35	39	30
Arkansas	258	190	130	10	27	23	22	32	14
California	3,531	2,593	2,288	140	125	40	405	369	164
Colorado	199	117	95	8	8	6	38	25	19
Connecticut	150	102	96	2	—	4	19	17	12
Delaware[2]	9	4	1	—	2	1	4	1	—
District of Columbia[3]	332	269					35	28	—
Florida	1,037	615	415	26	28	146	115	262	45
Georgia	649	454	389	21	32	12	88	70	37
Hawaii	56	25	19	6	—	—	9	8	14
Idaho	48	28	13	3	5	7	8	8	4
Illinois[2]	810	601	517	14	16	54	86	62	61
Indiana	350	248	190	11	18	29	42	37	23
Iowa	44	17	11	—	3	3	8	10	9
Kansas[2]									
Kentucky	258	163	114	17	19	13	27	48	20
Louisiana	715	568	480	19	32	37	65	54	28
Maine	18	10	5	4	—	1	3	4	1
Maryland	599	433	397	14	15	7	85	53	28
Massachusetts	208	109	53	2	1	53	59	35	5
Michigan	791	559	284	38	61	176	85	115	32
Minnesota	181	115	98	5	9	3	34	21	11
Mississippi	194	142	122	6	13	1	22	19	11
Missouri	433	314	242	21	21	30	50	50	19
Montana[2]									
Nebraska	21	13	8	2	3	—	3	3	2
Nevada	159	104	94	3	6	1	16	31	8
New Hampshire	18	8	7	—	1	—	5	1	4
New Jersey	409	239	231	3	3	2	61	63	46
New Mexico	109	71	63	1	1	6	20	11	7
New York	1,522	1,012	916	22	47	27	241	156	113
North Carolina	671	448	349	36	59	4	87	106	30
North Dakota	6	3	1	—	2	—	1	2	—
Ohio	525	335	297	7	23	8	65	86	39
Oklahoma	386	138	105	15	17	1	33	197	18
Oregon	124	72	59	7	6	—	19	27	6
Pennsylvania[2]	677	476	424	16	33	3	78	73	50
Rhode Island	32	23	16	—	1	6	5	2	2
South Carolina	292	175	135	8	21	11	56	37	24
South Dakota	9	1	1	—	—	—	5	2	1
Tennessee	451	307	253	9	37	8	63	54	27
Texas	1,652	1,143	838	62	119	124	228	188	93
Utah	73	50	36	5	3	6	7	12	4
Vermont	12	8	1	6	—	1	—	4	—
Virginia	500	351	306	11	20	14	67	48	34
Washington	259	149	111	17	11	10	41	53	16
West Virginia	89	65	48	4	11	2	6	14	4
Wisconsin	218	107	92	2	9	4	29	57	25
Wyoming	10	4	4	—	—	—	2	—	4

[1] Total number of murders for which supplemental homicide data were received.
[2] Complete data for 1995 were not available for the states of Delaware, Illinois, Kansas, Montana, and Pennsylvania. See "Offense Estimation," pages 367–368 for details.
[3] Firearm breakdowns were not provided by the District of Columbia.

Table 21.—Robbery, State, Types of Weapons, 1995

State	Total robberies[1]	Firearms	Knives or cutting instruments	Other weapons	Strong-armed	Agency count	Population
Alabama	6,251	2,396	1,008	1,039	1,808	277	3,881,000
Alaska	902	324	97	89	392	24	530,000
Arizona	7,101	2,974	700	656	2,771	81	3,869,000
Arkansas	3,115	1,561	199	252	1,103	186	2,474,000
California	100,558	40,248	10,653	8,250	41,407	714	31,168,000
Colorado	3,444	1,126	367	569	1,382	145	3,283,000
Connecticut	5,325	1,921	512	462	2,430	99	2,773,000
Delaware[2]	92	43	6	4	39	1	29,000
District of Columbia	6,864	2,820	630	327	3,087	2	554,000
Florida	39,488	15,358	2,590	3,051	18,489	378	12,681,000
Georgia	14,031	6,790	913	1,766	4,562	358	6,257,000
Hawaii	1,553	145	97	37	1,274	5	1,187,000
Idaho	263	72	24	38	129	107	1,145,000
Illinois[2]	31,632	15,894	1,944	1,571	12,223	4	3,114,000
Indiana	3,159	1,455	256	257	1,191	208	3,168,000
Iowa	1,184	296	110	176	602	178	2,277,000
Kansas[2]	1,399	573	135	170	521	2	433,000
Kentucky	3,478	1,337	382	288	1,471	457	3,376,000
Louisiana	11,035	6,731	865	676	2,763	153	3,743,000
Maine	306	59	34	32	181	124	975,000
Maryland	21,326	11,159	1,416	1,395	7,356	146	5,041,000
Massachusetts	8,499	2,000	1,562	1,061	3,876	251	5,158,000
Michigan	17,258	7,989	1,020	3,025	5,224	455	8,239,000
Minnesota	5,677	1,625	417	352	3,283	290	4,498,000
Mississippi	2,504	1,476	121	229	678	56	948,000
Missouri	10,512	4,622	672	863	4,355	190	4,054,000
Montana[2]	31	6	5	4	16	4	129,000
Nebraska	1,053	405	78	62	508	239	1,553,000
Nevada	4,946	2,220	445	387	1,894	29	1,495,000
New Hampshire	250	62	24	11	153	70	816,000
New Jersey	22,395	7,163	2,082	1,626	11,524	513	7,880,000
New Mexico	2,063	1,006	256	135	666	45	989,000
New York	71,203	22,709	9,405	9,000	30,089	666	16,187,000
North Carolina	12,765	5,813	932	1,164	4,856	474	7,070,000
North Dakota	63	15	7	24	17	68	549,000
Ohio	17,394	6,997	1,040	1,629	7,728	253	6,964,000
Oklahoma	3,786	1,379	284	262	1,861	285	3,275,000
Oregon	4,217	1,285	448	374	2,110	185	2,874,000
Pennsylvania[2]	16,444	7,664	947	713	7,120	4	2,099,000
Rhode Island	912	213	98	67	534	44	990,000
South Carolina	6,420	2,396	682	755	2,587	192	3,602,000
South Dakota	171	62	23	6	80	44	455,000
Tennessee	10,910	6,044	788	1,048	3,030	133	3,396,000
Texas	33,611	14,865	2,919	3,469	12,358	903	18,545,000
Utah	1,182	372	89	165	556	102	1,731,000
Vermont	19	2	6	7	4	17	278,000
Virginia	8,450	3,876	558	837	3,179	343	6,492,000
Washington	6,785	2,040	703	540	3,502	206	5,144,000
West Virginia	780	270	62	49	399	297	1,826,000
Wisconsin	5,381	2,883	347	340	1,811	326	5,035,000
Wyoming	82	25	15	5	37	64	467,000

[1] The number of robberies for which breakdowns were received for 12 months of 1995.
[2] Complete data for 1995 were not available for the states of Delaware, Illinois, Kansas, Montana, and Pennsylvania. See "Offense Estimation," pages 367–368 for details.

Table 22.—Aggravated Assault, State, Types of Weapons, 1995

State	Total aggravated assaults[1]	Firearms	Knives or cutting instruments	Other weapons	Personal weapons	Agency count	Population
Alabama	15,454	4,290	3,060	4,102	4,002	277	3,881,000
Alaska	2,933	719	649	658	907	24	530,000
Arizona	19,760	7,029	3,256	5,323	4,152	81	3,869,000
Arkansas	9,405	2,798	1,525	2,002	3,080	186	2,474,000
California	181,965	36,180	23,624	52,710	69,451	714	31,168,000
Colorado	10,158	2,855	2,066	3,080	2,157	145	3,283,000
Connecticut	7,022	841	1,133	2,413	2,635	99	2,773,000
Delaware[2]	134	33	39	35	27	1	29,000
District of Columbia	7,228	1,540	1,756	2,932	1,000	2	554,000
Florida	91,996	20,110	17,829	40,262	13,795	378	12,681,000
Georgia	26,230	6,936	5,739	8,604	4,951	358	6,257,000
Hawaii	1,564	256	149	299	860	5	1,187,000
Idaho	3,046	911	683	1,063	389	107	1,145,000
Illinois[2]	41,767	12,323	9,467	15,396	4,581	4	3,114,000
Indiana	8,807	886	655	1,751	5,515	208	3,168,000
Iowa	5,947	752	930	1,642	2,623	178	2,277,000
Kansas[2]	1,951	568	364	761	258	2	433,000
Kentucky	5,970	1,148	977	2,251	1,594	457	3,376,000
Louisiana	25,835	9,179	4,554	7,189	4,913	153	3,743,000
Maine	901	57	132	308	404	124	975,000
Maryland	25,694	5,430	4,831	10,602	4,831	146	5,041,000
Massachusetts	27,015	2,067	4,080	10,785	10,083	251	5,158,000
Michigan	38,313	10,338	6,932	16,892	4,151	455	8,239,000
Minnesota	7,839	1,969	2,263	1,884	1,723	290	4,498,000
Mississippi	3,529	1,276	617	605	1,031	56	948,000
Missouri	20,073	6,447	3,342	6,567	3,717	190	4,054,000
Montana[2]	173	57	44	34	38	4	129,000
Nebraska	4,741	932	715	1,624	1,470	239	1,553,000
Nevada	8,300	1,626	1,030	2,487	3,157	29	1,495,000
New Hampshire	416	54	87	97	178	70	816,000
New Jersey	22,801	3,773	4,727	6,860	7,441	513	7,880,000
New Mexico	6,071	1,827	1,157	1,692	1,395	45	989,000
New York	71,866	10,422	17,445	26,334	17,665	666	16,187,000
North Carolina	30,189	8,871	5,780	8,559	6,979	474	7,070,000
North Dakota	319	21	50	94	154	68	549,000
Ohio	22,178	5,132	3,995	6,462	6,589	253	6,964,000
Oklahoma	16,102	3,439	2,217	4,696	5,750	285	3,275,000
Oregon	10,227	2,287	1,715	3,444	2,781	185	2,874,000
Pennsylvania[2]	8,827	2,770	1,766	2,056	2,235	4	2,099,000
Rhode Island	2,432	248	403	972	809	44	990,000
South Carolina	27,168	6,510	6,407	9,902	4,349	192	3,602,000
South Dakota	802	149	185	160	308	44	455,000
Tennessee	20,446	6,143	3,575	6,219	4,509	133	3,396,000
Texas	80,082	21,685	16,918	24,271	17,208	903	18,545,000
Utah	3,753	724	728	1,434	867	102	1,731,000
Vermont	199	67	25	77	30	17	278,000
Virginia	12,565	2,042	2,547	3,405	4,571	343	6,492,000
Washington	14,747	3,569	2,729	4,449	4,000	206	5,144,000
West Virginia	2,581	319	439	494	1,329	297	1,826,000
Wisconsin	7,573	1,234	1,231	1,710	3,398	326	5,035,000
Wyoming	918	132	159	238	389	64	467,000

[1] The number of aggravated assaults for which breakdowns were received for 12 months of 1995.

[2] Complete data for 1995 were not available for the states of Delaware, Illinois, Kansas, Montana, and Pennsylvania. See "Offense Estimation," pages 367–368 for details.

Table 23.—Offense Analysis, 1995, and Percent Change from 1994

[12,105 agencies; 1995 estimated population 221,392,290]

Classification	Number of offenses 1995	Percent change over 1994	Percent distribution[1]	Average value
MURDER	17,549	−6.9	—	$77
FORCIBLE RAPE	78,692	−5.7	—	38
ROBBERY:				
Total	**462,310**	**−6.5**	**100.0**	**873**
Street/highway	251,173	−6.6	54.3	645
Commercial house	56,908	−8.8	12.3	1,351
Gas or service station	10,693	−4.3	2.3	959
Convenience store	23,908	−9.9	5.2	400
Residence	50,147	−4.8	10.8	1,082
Bank	7,306	−4.7	1.6	4,015
Miscellaneous	62,175	−4.3	13.4	987
BURGLARY:				
Total	**2,136,379**	**−4.6**	**100.0**	**1,259**
Residence (dwelling):	1,429,094	−4.3	66.9	1,211
Night	436,632	−5.3	20.4	1,008
Day	628,957	−4.4	29.4	1,314
Unknown	363,505	−2.8	17.0	1,275
Nonresidence (store, office, etc.):	707,285	−5.2	33.1	1,257
Night	308,317	−7.6	14.4	1,132
Day	194,081	−2.4	9.1	1,515
Unknown	204,887	−4.0	9.6	1,546
LARCENY-THEFT (EXCEPT MOTOR VEHICLE THEFT):				
Total	**6,574,478**	**+1.6**	**100.0**	**535**
By type:				
Pocket-picking	41,992	−6.7	.6	350
Purse-snatching	42,033	−10.0	.6	279
Shoplifting	989,872	+1.2	15.1	108
From motor vehicles (except accessories)	1,594,499	+5.0	24.3	531
Motor vehicle accessories	792,484	−6.8	12.1	329
Bicycles	411,398	−1.2	6.3	286
From buildings	825,061	+.6	12.5	891
From coin-operated machines	40,833	−6.5	.6	283
All others	1,836,306	+4.7	27.9	770
By value:				
Over $200	2,515,923	+3.2	38.3	1,307
$50 to $200	1,531,925	+.4	23.3	117
Under $50	2,526,630	+.7	38.4	20
MOTOR VEHICLE THEFT	1,279,135	−4.8	—	5,129

[1] Because of rounding, percentages may not add to totals.
Complete data for 1995 were not available for states of Delaware, Illinois, Kansas, and Montana. See "Offense Estimation," pages 367–368 for details.

Table 24.—Type and Value of Property Stolen and Recovered, 1995

[12,105 agencies; 1995 estimated population 221,392,290]

Type of property	Value of property		Percent recovered
	Stolen	Recovered	
Total1	**$13,188,633,000**	**$4,642,911,000**	**35.2**
Currency, notes, etc.	809,445,000	54,279,000	6.7
Jewelry and precious metals	1,066,978,000	101,981,000	9.6
Clothing and furs	268,058,000	37,285,000	13.9
Locally stolen motor vehicles	6,605,292,000	4,093,281,000	62.0
Office equipment	460,213,000	38,037,000	8.3
Televisions, radios, stereos, etc.	947,248,000	46,167,000	4.9
Firearms	111,567,000	11,812,000	10.6
Household goods	225,034,000	17,212,000	7.6
Consumable goods	78,775,000	15,372,000	19.5
Livestock	18,806,000	2,268,000	12.1
Miscellaneous	2,597,216,000	225,217,000	8.7

[1] All totals and percentages calculated before rounding.
Complete data for 1995 were not available for the states of Delaware, Illinois, Kansas, and Montana. See "Offense Estimation," pages 367–368 for details.

SECTION III
Crime Index Offenses Cleared

For UCR purposes, law enforcement agencies clear or solve an offense when at least one person is arrested, charged with the commission of the offense, and turned over to the court for prosecution. Clearances recorded in 1995 may be for offenses which occurred in prior years. Several crimes may be cleared by the arrest of one person, while the arrest of many persons may clear only one offense. Law enforcement agencies may clear a crime by exceptional means when some element beyond law enforcement control precludes the placing of formal charges against the offender. Examples of circumstances allowing such clearances are the death of the offender (suicide, justifiably killed by police or private citizen, etc.); the victim's refusal to cooperate with prosecution after the offender has been identified; or the denial of extradition because the offender committed another crime and is being prosecuted in a different jurisdiction. In all exceptional clearance cases, law enforcement must have identified the offender, have enough evidence to support arrest, and know the offender's location.

Law enforcement agencies nationwide recorded a 21-percent Crime Index clearance rate for 1995. Collectively, 45 percent of violent crimes were cleared. Among the violent offenses, the rates were 65 percent for murder, 51 percent for forcible rape, 25 percent for robbery, and 56 percent for aggravated assault. Clearances for crimes against persons (murder, forcible rape, and aggravated assault) are generally higher as these offenses are often given more intensive investigative efforts and the victims and/or witnesses can frequently identify the perpetrators.

The overall property crime clearance rate was 18 percent. Thirteen percent of the burglaries, 20 percent of the larceny-thefts, 14 percent of motor vehicle thefts, and 16 percent of arsons were cleared during the year.

When considering the Modified Crime Index total which includes arson, the overall clearance rate remained the same, 21 percent.

Geographically, the highest total Crime Index clearance rate was registered in the Southern States, with 22 percent. The Midwestern and Western States each recorded 21-percent clearance rates, and the Northeastern States registered a 20-percent clearance rate. For violent crime, the highest clearance rate, 48 percent, was also recorded in the South. In the West,

the rate was 47 percent; in the Midwest, 44 percent; and in the Northeast, 38 percent. Property crime clearance rates were 18 percent in the South and Midwest and 17 percent in the Northeast and West.

By community type, city law enforcement agencies and those in suburban counties showed clearances for 21 percent of the Crime Index offenses brought to their attention. Rural county agencies cleared 23 percent. Among the city population groups, those with 10,000 to 24,999 inhabitants registered the highest total Crime Index and property crime clearance rates, 26 percent and 23 percent, respectively. The highest violent crime clearance rate—61 percent—was recorded in cities with populations under 10,000 and in the rural counties. (See Table 25.)

Clearances Involving Only Persons under 18 Years of Age

Involvement of juveniles in crime can be measured by the number of crimes in which they have been identified as the offenders. Even though no physical arrest may have been made, a clearance by arrest is recorded when an offender under 18 years of age is cited to appear in juvenile court or before other juvenile authorities. Since the juvenile clearance percentages shown in this publication indicate only those offenses where no adults were involved, they should be considered a slight underestimation of juvenile involvement in crime. Juveniles (persons under 18 years of age) account for 26 percent of the United States population, according to 1995 Bureau of the Census estimates.

Twenty-two percent of the Crime Index offenses cleared by law enforcement during 1995 involved only young people under age 18. Persons in this age group accounted for 14 percent of the violent crime clearances and 25 percent of those for property crimes. Murder showed the lowest percentage of juvenile involvement (9 percent), while the highest percentage was shown for arson (47 percent).

Geographically, the Midwestern States recorded the largest percentage of Crime Index offense involvement by the under 18 age group—26 percent. Juveniles alone were the offenders in 22 percent of the clearances in the Western States, 21 percent of those in the Southern States, and 20 percent of those in the Northeastern States.

CHART 3.1

CRIMES CLEARED
by ARREST
1995

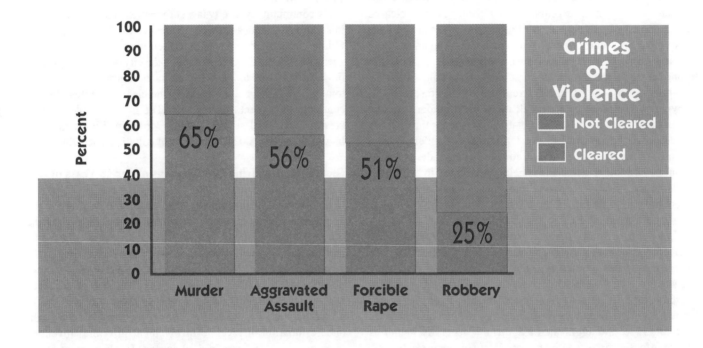

Crimes
of
Violence

Not Cleared

Cleared

Murder 65%
Aggravated Assault 56%
Forcible Rape 51%
Robbery 25%

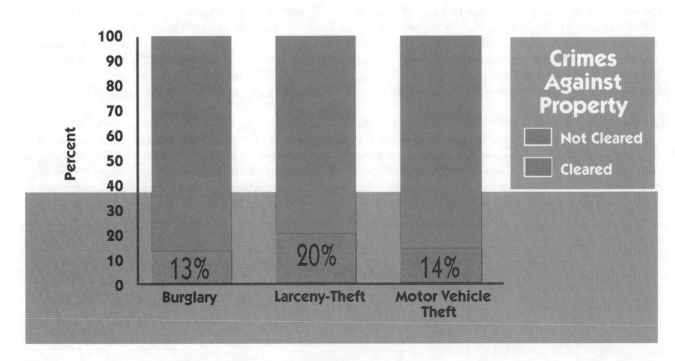

Crimes
Against
Property

Not Cleared

Cleared

Burglary 13%
Larceny-Theft 20%
Motor Vehicle Theft 14%

Table 25.—Offenses Known and Percent Cleared by Arrest,[1] Population Group, 1995

[1995 estimated population]

Population group	Crime Index total	Modified Crime Index total[2]	Violent crime[3]	Property crime[4]	Murder and non-negligent man-slaughter	Forcible rape	Robbery	Aggravated assault	Burglary	Larceny-theft	Motor vehicle theft	Arson[2]
TOTAL ALL AGENCIES: 11,884 agencies; population 220,918,000:												
Offenses known	11,859,129	11,948,988	1,531,703	10,327,426	18,324	82,538	502,352	928,489	2,216,954	6,808,490	1,301,982	89,859
Percent cleared by arrest . .	21.2	21.2	45.4	17.6	64.8	51.1	24.7	55.7	13.4	19.6	14.1	16.2
TOTAL CITIES: 8,278 cities; population 148,295,000:												
Offenses known	9,435,902	9,506,396	1,253,227	8,182,675	14,498	61,115	448,659	728,955	1,646,730	5,459,274	1,076,671	70,494
Percent cleared by arrest . .	21.1	21.1	43.5	17.7	63.2	50.8	24.2	54.4	12.8	20.1	13.2	15.5
GROUP I												
59 cities, 250,000 and over; population 41,961,000:												
Offenses known	3,541,050	3,571,971	630,943	2,910,107	8,486	24,842	270,774	326,841	607,076	1,748,249	554,782	30,921
Percent cleared by arrest . . .	17.8	17.8	37.2	13.6	57.3	51.3	21.1	49.0	10.7	15.7	10.1	11.8
7 cities, 1,000,000 and over; population 17,336,000:												
Offenses known	1,231,791	1,243,247	268,503	963,288	3,357	7,145	124,084	133,917	204,178	541,489	217,621	11,456
Percent cleared by arrest . . .	17.0	16.9	34.4	12.1	53.0	44.4	19.9	46.8	9.5	15.0	7.6	9.8
18 cities, 500,000 to 999,999; population 12,307,000:												
Offenses known	1,115,717	1,124,457	171,763	943,954	2,526	8,686	73,000	87,551	191,852	589,270	162,832	8,740
Percent cleared by arrest . . .	16.4	16.4	36.9	12.7	53.8	56.6	19.9	48.6	10.6	13.8	11.3	10.5
34 cities, 250,000 to 499,999; population 12,319,000:												
Offenses known	1,193,542	1,204,267	190,677	1,002,865	2,603	9,011	73,690	105,373	211,046	617,490	174,329	10,725
Percent cleared by arrest . . .	20.0	19.9	41.4	15.9	66.3	51.6	24.2	52.0	11.9	18.3	12.2	14.9
GROUP II												
136 cities, 100,000 to 249,999; population 19,931,000:												
Offenses known	1,497,023	1,508,925	192,800	1,304,223	2,287	9,960	67,714	112,839	274,369	857,159	172,695	11,902
Percent cleared by arrest . . .	21.3	21.3	46.9	17.6	66.8	52.4	27.5	57.6	12.8	19.8	14.0	15.4
GROUP III												
336 cities, 50,000 to 99,999; population 22,828,000:												
Offenses known	1,367,229	1,376,058	158,398	1,208,831	1,404	8,831	49,375	98,788	245,642	822,317	140,872	8,829
Percent cleared by arrest . . .	21.9	21.9	46.0	18.8	71.2	47.5	26.7	55.2	12.9	21.5	12.8	16.2
GROUP IV												
612 cities, 25,000 to 49,999; population 21,067,000:												
Offenses known	1,093,308	1,100,521	105,547	987,761	889	6,768	29,392	68,498	195,610	701,485	90,666	7,213
Percent cleared by arrest . . .	23.2	23.2	50.3	20.3	69.3	49.5	30.4	58.6	13.6	22.7	16.4	16.6

See footnotes at end of table.

Table 25.—Offenses Known and Percent Cleared by Arrest,[1] Population Group, 1995 — Continued

Population group	Crime Index total	Modified Crime Index total[2]	Violent crime[3]	Property crime[4]	Murder and non-negligent man-slaughter	Forcible rape	Robbery	Aggravated assault	Burglary	Larceny-theft	Motor vehicle theft	Arson[2]
GROUP V												
1,458 cities, 10,000 to 24,999; population 22,919,000:												
Offenses known	1,049,942	1,055,936	93,449	956,493	824	6,204	20,423	65,998	179,137	706,045	71,311	5,994
Percent cleared by arrest . . .	25.9	25.9	53.9	23.1	80.8	49.8	33.0	60.4	15.6	25.2	22.1	23.2
GROUP VI												
5,677 cities under 10,000; population 19,589,000:												
Offenses known	887,350	892,985	72,090	815,260	608	4,510	10,981	55,991	144,896	624,019	46,345	5,635
Percent cleared by arrest . . .	24.5	24.6	60.6	21.4	81.3	54.0	36.6	65.6	16.6	21.9	28.9	25.4
SUBURBAN COUNTIES												
1,234 agencies; population 48,543,000:												
Offenses known	1,887,805	1,902,218	220,290	1,667,515	2,603	15,121	49,329	153,237	407,687	1,067,275	192,553	14,413
Percent cleared by arrest . . .	21.0	21.0	52.1	16.9	66.2	52.2	27.9	59.7	15.0	17.8	16.1	17.9
RURAL COUNTIES												
2,372 agencies; population 24,080,000:												
Offenses known	535,422	540,374	58,186	477,236	1,223	6,302	4,364	46,297	162,537	281,941	32,758	4,952
Percent cleared by arrest . . .	23.2	23.2	60.9	18.6	80.1	51.6	40.3	63.6	16.4	18.3	32.0	21.7
SUBURBAN AREA[5]												
5,838 agencies; population 91,405,000:												
Offenses known	3,747,702	3,773,978	378,862	3,368,840	3,801	24,857	89,500	260,704	720,331	2,304,949	343,560	26,276
Percent cleared by arrest . . .	22.1	22.1	52.7	18.6	67.9	51.3	29.2	60.6	14.8	20.1	16.8	18.7

[1] Includes offenses cleared by exceptional means.

[2] The number of agency reports used in arson clearance rates is less than used in compiling clearance rates for other Crime Index offenses. It is not necessary to report clearances by detailed property classification to be included in this table. The Modified Crime Index total is the sum of the Crime Index offenses, including arson.

[3] Violent crimes are offenses of murder, forcible rape, robbery, and aggravated assault.

[4] Property crimes are offenses of burglary, larceny-theft, and motor vehicle theft. Data are not included for the property crime of arson.

[5] Includes suburban city and county law enforcement agencies within metropolitan areas. Excludes central cities. Suburban cities and counties are also included in other groups.

Forcible rape figures furnished by the state-level Uniform Crime Reporting (UCR) Program administered by the Illinois State Police were not in accordance with national UCR guidelines and were excluded from the forcible rape, violent crime, Crime Index total, and Modified Crime Index total categories.

Complete data for 1995 were not available for the states of Delaware, Illinois, Kansas, and Montana. See "Offense Estimation," pages 367–368 for details.

Table 26.—Offenses Known and Percent Cleared by Arrest,[1] Geographic Region and Division, 1995

[1995 estimated population]

Geographic region/division	Crime Index total	Modified Crime Index total[2]	Violent crime[3]	Property crime[4]	Murder and non-negligent man-slaughter	Forcible rape	Robbery	Aggravated assault	Burglary	Larceny-theft	Motor vehicle theft	Arson[2]
TOTAL **11,884 agencies;** **population 220,918,000:** Offenses known . . . . Percent cleared by arrest	11,859,129 21.2	11,948,988 21.2	1,531,703 45.4	10,327,426 17.6	18,324 64.8	82,538 51.1	502,352 24.7	928,489 55.7	2,216,954 13.4	6,808,490 19.6	1,301,982 14.1	89,859 16.2
NEW ENGLAND 671 agencies; population 11,490,000: Offenses known . . . . Percent cleared by arrest . .	491,187 21.4	497,883 21.2	57,433 52.5	433,754 17.3	435 67.8	3,163 50.6	15,363 28.0	38,472 62.3	96,278 13.9	278,801 19.4	58,675 12.9	6,696 6.2
MIDDLE ATLANTIC 2,154 agencies; population 35,466,000: Offenses known . . . . Percent cleared by arrest . .	1,467,017 19.8	1,479,008 19.7	240,135 34.3	1,226,882 16.9	2,598 57.0	8,574 49.2	114,120 20.1	114,843 46.7	261,710 13.3	774,964 20.1	190,208 8.8	11,991 13.9
Northeast **2,825 agencies;** **population 46,957,000:** Offenses known . . . . Percent cleared by arrest	1,958,204 20.2	1,976,891 20.1	297,568 37.8	1,660,636 17.0	3,033 58.6	11,737 49.6	129,483 21.1	153,315 50.6	357,988 13.5	1,053,765 19.9	248,883 9.8	18,687 11.1
EAST NORTH CENTRAL 1,410 agencies; population 24,367,000: Offenses known . . . . Percent cleared by arrest . .	1,184,864 19.7	1,195,259 19.7	135,897 40.5	1,048,967 17.0	1,686 64.2	11,720 45.5	44,284 23.3	78,207 48.9	210,617 12.0	708,087 18.8	130,263 15.4	10,395 15.8
WEST NORTH CENTRAL 1,090 agencies; population 13,631,000: Offenses known . . . . Percent cleared by arrest . .	615,688 23.4	620,292 23.4	58,193 53.1	557,495 20.3	631 84.2	4,665 56.0	15,276 29.3	37,621 61.9	104,602 13.7	405,352 21.8	47,541 22.5	4,604 16.0
Midwest **2,500 agencies;** **population 37,998,000:** Offenses known . . . . Percent cleared by arrest	1,800,552 21.0	1,815,551 20.9	194,090 44.3	1,606,462 18.2	2,317 69.6	16,385 48.5	59,560 24.9	115,828 53.1	315,219 12.5	1,113,439 19.9	177,804 17.3	14,999 15.9
SOUTH ATLANTIC 2,480 agencies; population 45,671,000: Offenses known . . . . Percent cleared by arrest . .	2,789,679 21.4	2,804,260 21.4	367,723 46.9	2,421,956 17.5	4,172 67.3	17,794 55.1	112,497 25.3	233,260 56.3	540,115 15.1	1,625,405 18.4	256,436 16.5	14,581 20.0
EAST SOUTH CENTRAL 673 agencies; population 8,056,000: Offenses known . . . . Percent cleared by arrest . .	410,164 23.4	413,236 23.3	53,567 52.6	356,597 19.0	899 64.3	3,759 58.4	17,271 30.5	31,638 63.6	87,296 14.5	223,396 21.1	45,905 17.4	3,072 20.1
WEST SOUTH CENTRAL 1,552 agencies; population 27,774,000: Offenses known . . . . Percent cleared by arrest . .	1,587,907 23.1	1,600,001 23.1	195,123 50.2	1,392,784 19.3	2,994 74.3	12,317 56.1	50,479 29.2	129,333 57.3	310,210 14.4	932,170 21.2	150,404 17.6	12,094 20.6

See footnotes at end of table.

Table 26.—Offenses Known and Percent Cleared by Arrest,[1] Geographic Region and Division, 1995 — Continued

[1995 estimated population]

Geographic region/division	Crime Index total	Modified Crime Index total[2]	Violent crime[3]	Property crime[4]	Murder and non-negligent man-slaughter	Forcible rape	Robbery	Aggravated assault	Burglary	Larceny-theft	Motor vehicle theft	Arson[2]
South												
4,705 agencies; population 81,501,000:												
Offenses known	4,787,750	4,817,497	616,413	4,171,337	8,065	33,870	180,247	394,231	937,621	2,780,971	452,745	29,747
Percent cleared by arrest	22.1	22.1	48.4	18.2	69.6	55.8	26.9	57.2	14.8	19.6	16.9	20.3
MOUNTAIN												
666 agencies; population 13,949,000:												
Offenses known	900,963	906,138	79,987	820,976	1,044	5,648	19,349	53,946	156,303	573,197	91,476	5,175
Percent cleared by arrest . .	20.1	20.1	41.7	18.0	62.8	36.8	23.5	48.4	10.6	20.6	14.7	19.4
PACIFIC												
1,188 agencies; population 40,514,000:												
Offenses known	2,411,660	2,432,911	343,645	2,068,015	3,865	14,898	113,713	211,169	449,823	1,287,118	331,074	21,251
Percent cleared by arrest . .	20.8	20.8	48.1	16.3	57.3	49.7	25.5	59.9	12.2	18.9	11.7	14.5
West												
1,854 agencies; population 54,463,000:												
Offenses known	3,312,623	3,339,049	423,632	2,888,991	4,909	20,546	133,062	265,115	606,126	1,860,315	422,550	26,426
Percent cleared by arrest	20.6	20.6	46.9	16.8	58.5	46.1	25.2	57.6	11.8	19.4	12.3	15.5

[1] Includes offenses cleared by exceptional means.

[2] The number of agency reports used in arson clearance rates is less than used in compiling clearance rates for other Crime Index offenses. It is not necessary to report clearances by detailed property classification to be included in this table. The Modified Crime Index total is the sum of the Crime Index offenses, including arson.

[3] Violent crimes are offenses of murder, forcible rape, robbery, and aggravated assault.

[4] Property crimes are offenses of burglary, larceny-theft, and motor vehicle theft. Data are not included for the property crime of arson.

Forcible rape figures furnished by the state-level Uniform Crime Reporting (UCR) Program administered by the Illinois State Police were not in accordance with national UCR guidelines and were excluded from the forcible rape, violent crime, Crime Index total, and Modified Crime Index total categories.

Complete data for 1995 were not available for the states of Delaware, Illinois, Kansas, and Montana. See "Offense Estimation," pages 367–368 for details.

Table 27.—Offenses Known Breakdown and Percent Cleared by Arrest,[1] Population Group, 1995

[1995 estimated population]

Population group	Forcible rape — Rape by force	Forcible rape — Assault to rape—attempts	Robbery — Firearm	Robbery — Knife or cutting instrument	Robbery — Other weapon	Robbery — Strong-armed	Aggravated assault — Firearm	Aggravated assault — Knife or cutting instrument	Aggravated assault — Other weapon	Aggravated assault — Hands, fists, feet, etc.	Burglary — Forcible entry	Burglary — Unlawful entry	Burglary — Attempted forcible entry	Motor vehicle theft — Autos	Motor vehicle theft — Trucks and buses	Motor vehicle theft — Other vehicles	Arson[2] — Structure	Arson[2] — Mobile	Arson[2] — Other
TOTAL ALL AGENCIES: 11,880 agencies; population 220,869,000:																			
Offenses known	72,412	10,100	203,181	46,219	46,970	205,876	205,933	166,400	304,853	251,066	1,480,939	565,868	169,213	1,017,879	212,851	70,657	45,549	21,900	20,594
Percent cleared by arrest	51.5	48.2	20.5	25.7	26.0	28.3	43.6	61.2	53.4	64.8	13.3	14.7	10.7	14.1	13.2	17.1	20.7	7.5	16.5
TOTAL CITIES: 8,275 cities; population 148,251,000:																			
Offenses known	53,188	7,903	179,343	41,988	41,692	185,531	165,365	137,012	238,662	187,679	1,100,009	412,570	133,364	860,177	168,345	47,600	35,931	17,108	15,888
Percent cleared by arrest	51.1	48.6	20.2	25.1	25.5	27.6	41.6	59.8	52.2	64.4	12.5	14.2	10.3	13.2	12.2	17.5	20.1	6.8	15.5
GROUP I																			
59 cities, 250,000 and over; population 41,961,000:																			
Offenses known	21,406	3,436	115,000	25,975	24,873	104,926	89,711	66,615	110,551	59,964	434,260	126,232	46,584	445,653	92,609	16,520	15,776	9,001	5,016
Percent cleared by arrest	51.6	49.2	17.7	21.6	21.6	24.5	36.9	55.5	47.4	62.8	10.6	11.6	9.0	10.1	9.8	11.8	16.6	4.6	12.1
7 cities, 1,000,000 and over; population 17,336,000:																			
Offenses known	6,025	1,120	49,556	14,638	12,788	47,102	33,193	29,643	41,560	29,521	131,524	51,869	20,785	178,002	34,273	5,346	5,857	3,671	1,928
Percent cleared by arrest	44.4	44.0	16.4	19.7	19.3	23.8	29.9	47.4	41.3	73.2	9.8	9.5	7.6	7.5	8.0	8.0	13.9	3.5	9.2
18 cities, 500,000 to 999,999; population 12,307,000:																			
Offenses known	7,512	1,174	33,829	5,688	6,085	27,398	24,724	16,501	31,764	14,562	148,165	31,766	11,921	129,326	27,095	6,411	4,217	2,676	965
Percent cleared by arrest	56.7	56.0	17.5	22.3	23.8	21.6	41.5	59.4	48.2	49.5	10.2	12.6	10.0	11.4	11.3	8.4	16.5	4.0	12.5
34 cities, 250,000 to 499,999; population 12,319,000:																			
Offenses known	7,869	1,142	31,615	5,649	6,000	30,426	31,794	20,471	37,227	15,881	154,571	42,597	13,878	138,325	31,241	4,763	5,702	2,654	2,123
Percent cleared by arrest	52.2	47.3	20.1	25.8	24.5	28.1	40.6	64.1	53.5	55.5	11.6	13.6	10.1	12.2	10.6	20.7	19.5	6.6	14.6
GROUP II																			
136 cities, 100,000 to 249,999; population 19,931,000:																			
Offenses known	8,678	1,282	27,363	6,358	6,133	27,860	29,377	20,416	40,107	22,939	188,662	64,609	21,098	139,360	26,595	6,740	6,392	2,895	2,528
Percent cleared by arrest	52.7	50.1	24.5	28.5	30.4	29.6	43.9	65.1	58.1	67.3	12.2	14.8	12.5	13.6	11.2	32.0	20.2	6.8	13.5
GROUP III																			
336 cities, 50,000 to 99,999; population 22,828,000:																			
Offenses known	7,869	962	17,365	4,291	4,464	23,253	18,704	18,070	34,062	27,952	158,903	65,781	20,936	113,774	19,697	7,397	4,323	2,092	2,287
Percent cleared by arrest	47.6	46.8	22.3	29.7	27.2	29.3	43.3	61.7	52.7	61.9	12.7	14.6	9.1	13.0	12.4	11.9	20.3	6.5	17.1
GROUP IV																			
612 cities, 25,000 to 49,999; population 21,067,000:																			
Offenses known	5,960	789	9,343	2,631	2,971	14,386	10,727	11,804	21,529	24,438	122,091	56,361	16,829	71,224	12,734	6,353	3,447	1,335	2,360
Percent cleared by arrest	50.4	43.2	25.6	31.8	32.6	32.9	49.5	62.3	55.1	64.0	13.6	14.6	10.7	16.8	15.5	14.5	19.7	9.7	16.3

See footnotes at end of table.

Table 27.—Offenses Known Breakdown and Percent Cleared by Arrest,[1] Population Group, 1995 — Continued

Population group	Forcible rape — Rape by force	Forcible rape — Assault to rape—attempts	Robbery — Firearm	Robbery — Knife or cutting instrument	Robbery — Other weapon	Robbery — Strong-armed	Aggravated assault — Firearm	Aggravated assault — Knife or cutting instrument	Aggravated assault — Other weapon	Aggravated assault — Hands, fists, feet, etc.	Burglary — Forcible entry	Burglary — Unlawful entry	Burglary — Attempted forcible entry	Motor vehicle theft — Autos	Motor vehicle theft — Trucks and buses	Motor vehicle theft — Other vehicles	Arson[2] — Structure	Arson[2] — Mobile	Arson[2] — Other
GROUP V																			
1,456 cities, 10,000 to 24,999; population 22,881,000:																			
Offenses known	5,435	766	6,689	1,793	2,218	9,699	9,997	11,565	19,569	24,639	111,170	51,877	15,727	55,645	9,584	5,958	3,081	1,031	1,813
Percent cleared by arrest	50.3	46.1	26.1	35.0	35.6	36.8	52.4	64.2	57.2	64.8	15.6	16.7	11.5	22.2	21.7	21.7	28.0	14.5	20.3
GROUP VI																			
5,676 cities under 10,000; population 19,582,000:																			
Offenses known	3,840	668	3,583	940	1,033	5,407	6,849	8,542	12,844	27,747	84,923	47,710	12,190	34,521	7,126	4,632	2,912	754	1,884
Percent cleared by arrest	53.8	54.8	29.8	39.5	37.6	40.4	59.5	67.8	61.6	68.4	17.2	16.9	11.3	29.8	27.1	24.2	30.9	19.2	19.8
SUBURBAN COUNTIES																			
1,234 agencies; population 48,543,000:																			
Offenses known	13,483	1,638	22,146	3,819	4,746	18,617	31,642	22,857	54,460	44,278	269,759	110,686	27,211	138,138	38,102	16,308	6,610	3,776	3,853
Percent cleared by arrest	53.0	44.9	22.1	30.5	29.9	33.8	49.1	67.2	57.5	66.1	14.9	16.0	11.8	16.7	14.9	14.5	23.4	8.7	17.9
RURAL COUNTIES																			
2,371 agencies; population 24,075,000:																			
Offenses known	5,741	559	1,692	412	532	1,728	8,926	6,531	11,731	19,109	111,171	42,612	8,638	19,564	6,404	6,749	3,008	1,016	853
Percent cleared by arrest	51.6	52.1	39.4	44.7	37.2	41.2	62.1	67.5	58.9	65.9	16.7	16.3	13.3	36.3	30.5	21.0	21.8	15.3	29.1
SUBURBAN AREA[3]																			
5,835 agencies; population 91,361,000:																			
Offenses known	22,001	2,832	35,647	7,118	8,743	37,890	46,137	39,404	85,611	89,315	457,256	207,284	55,051	257,347	58,428	27,251	12,256	5,762	7,976
Percent cleared by arrest	52.0	46.0	22.9	31.8	30.8	34.4	49.7	66.7	57.5	66.6	14.7	15.8	11.3	17.2	15.5	15.6	24.0	9.8	17.1

[1] Includes offenses cleared by exceptional means.

[2] The number of agency reports used in arson clearance rates is less than used in compiling clearance rates for other Crime Index offenses.

[3] Includes suburban city and county law enforcement agencies within metropolitan areas. Excludes central cities. Suburban cities and counties are also included in other groups.

Forcible rape figures furnished by the state-level Uniform Crime Reporting (UCR) Program administered by the Illinois State Police were not in accordance with national UCR guidelines and were excluded from the forcible rape, violent crime, Crime Index total, and Modified Crime Index total categories.

Complete data for 1995 were not available for the states of Delaware, Illinois, Kansas, and Montana. See "Offense Estimation," pages 367–368 for details.

Table 28.—Offenses Cleared by Arrest[1] of Persons Under 18 Years of Age, 1995

[1995 estimated population]

Population group	Crime Index total	Modified Crime Index total[2]	Violent crime[3]	Property crime[4]	Murder and non-negligent man-slaughter	Forcible rape	Robbery	Aggravated assault	Burglary	Larceny-theft	Motor vehicle theft	Arson[2]
TOTAL ALL AGENCIES: 11,715 agencies; population 210,149,000:												
Total clearances	2,434,005	2,448,417	661,255	1,772,750	11,181	40,884	113,770	495,420	288,726	1,306,318	177,706	14,412
Percent under 18	22.1	22.2	14.1	25.0	8.8	15.1	20.2	12.8	21.5	26.0	23.6	47.1
TOTAL CITIES: 8,245 cities; population 139,329,000:												
Total clearances	1,923,510	1,934,359	513,384	1,410,126	8,535	29,996	98,508	376,345	203,152	1,069,442	137,532	10,849
Percent under 18	22.2	22.3	14.1	25.1	9.0	13.3	20.2	12.7	20.7	26.1	24.1	49.5
GROUP I												
56 cities, 250,000 and over; population 33,831,000:												
Total clearances	578,746	582,386	206,805	371,941	4,292	11,951	47,875	142,687	59,773	259,388	52,780	3,640
Percent under 18	18.4	18.6	12.7	21.6	9.2	12.2	18.3	11.0	16.6	21.8	26.6	45.5
6 cities, 1,000,000 and over; population 10,016,000:												
Total clearances	166,865	167,988	68,322	98,543	1,349	2,489	16,281	48,203	15,300	69,155	14,088	1,123
Percent under 18	16.3	16.5	10.7	20.2	10.2	8.9	18.0	8.3	15.1	20.3	25.6	37.3
17 cities, 500,000 to 999,999; population 11,753,000:												
Total clearances	176,038	176,960	59,666	116,372	1,222	4,850	13,863	39,731	19,573	79,089	17,710	922
Percent under 18	17.3	17.5	13.2	19.4	5.9	14.6	17.4	11.8	14.2	19.4	25.4	45.7
33 cities, 250,000 to 499,999; population 12,062,000:												
Total clearances	235,843	237,438	78,817	157,026	1,721	4,612	17,731	54,753	24,900	111,144	20,982	1,595
Percent under 18	20.8	21.0	14.1	24.2	10.8	11.4	19.3	12.7	19.5	24.4	28.3	51.3
GROUP II												
134 cities, 100,000 to 249,999; population 19,573,000:												
Total clearances	310,918	312,688	87,988	222,930	1,483	5,033	17,949	63,523	34,055	165,344	23,531	1,770
Percent under 18	20.0	20.2	13.5	22.6	8.3	12.2	19.9	12.0	18.0	23.7	21.8	47.6
GROUP III												
335 cities, 50,000 to 99,999; population 22,745,000:												
Total clearances	298,083	299,511	72,352	225,731	995	4,182	13,121	54,054	31,521	176,190	18,020	1,428
Percent under 18	24.7	24.9	15.3	27.7	10.7	13.5	23.4	13.6	21.4	29.2	24.3	51.9

See footnotes at end of table.

205

Table 28.—Offenses Cleared by Arrest[1] of Persons Under 18 Years of Age, 1995 — Continued

Population group	Crime Index total	Modified Crime Index total[2]	Violent crime[3]	Property crime[4]	Murder and non-negligent man-slaughter	Forcible rape	Robbery	Aggravated assault	Burglary	Larceny-theft	Motor vehicle theft	Arson[2]
GROUP IV												
608 cities, 25,000 to 49,999; population 20,924,000:												
Total clearances	251,836	253,029	52,880	198,956	613	3,333	8,899	40,035	26,432	157,814	14,710	1,193
Percent under 18	24.8	24.9	15.7	27.2	7.3	14.9	23.4	14.2	23.8	28.3	21.6	54.9
GROUP V												
1,445 cities, 10,000 to 24,999; population 22,712,000:												
Total clearances	266,668	268,056	49,785	216,883	658	3,067	6,648	39,412	27,411	174,344	15,128	1,388
Percent under 18	25.1	25.2	16.1	27.2	9.6	16.1	23.0	15.0	24.2	28.1	21.3	52.4
GROUP VI												
5,667 cities under 10,000; population 19,544,000:												
Total clearances	217,259	218,689	43,574	173,685	494	2,430	4,016	36,634	23,960	136,362	13,363	1,430
Percent under 18	25.0	25.2	15.3	27.4	7.3	14.9	20.9	14.9	26.1	28.0	24.1	52.4
SUBURBAN COUNTIES												
1,182 agencies; population 47,278,000:												
Total clearances	388,934	391,444	113,280	275,654	1,689	7,696	13,533	90,362	59,446	186,321	29,887	2,510
Percent under 18	22.7	22.8	15.5	25.6	8.8	21.7	21.7	14.2	24.2	26.6	22.2	44.4
RURAL COUNTIES												
2,288 agencies; population 23,542,000:												
Total clearances	121,561	122,614	34,591	86,970	957	3,192	1,729	28,713	26,128	50,555	10,287	1,053
Percent under 18	18.4	18.5	10.6	21.5	7.3	16.0	13.9	9.9	21.8	21.4	21.5	28.1
SUBURBAN AREA[5]												
5,773 agencies; population 89,922,000:												
Total clearances	816,111	820,944	197,461	618,650	2,544	12,532	25,862	156,523	104,465	458,072	56,113	4,833
Percent under 18	23.5	23.6	16.1	25.8	9.0	19.4	23.1	14.7	24.3	26.7	21.8	49.2

[1] Includes offenses cleared by exceptional means.

[2] The number of agency reports used in arson clearance rates is less than those used in compiling clearance rates for other Crime Index offenses. It is not necessary to report clearances by detailed property classification to be included in this table. The Modified Crime Index total is the sum of the Crime Index offenses, including arson.

[3] Violent crimes are offenses of murder, forcible rape, robbery, and aggravated assault.

[4] Property crimes are offenses of burglary, larceny-theft, and motor vehicle theft. Data are not included for the property crime of arson.

[5] Includes suburban city and county law enforcement agencies within metropolitan areas. Excludes central cities. Suburban cities and counties are also included in other groups.

Forcible rape figures furnished by the state-level Uniform Crime Reporting (UCR) Program administered by the Illinois State Police were not in accordance with national UCR guidelines and were excluded from the forcible rape, violent crime, Crime Index total, and Modified Crime Index total categories.

Complete data for 1995 were not available for the states of Delaware, Illinois, Kansas, and Montana. See "Offense Estimation," pages 367–368 for details.

SECTION IV
Persons Arrested

Primarily a gauge of law enforcement's response to crime, arrest counts also provide definitive data concerning the age, sex, and race of perpetrators. Arrest practices, policies, and enforcement emphases vary from place to place and even within a community from time to time as, for example, during a local police campaign against residential burglary. While the practices for certain unlawful conduct such as drunkenness, disorderly conduct, vagrancy, and related violations may differ among agencies, those for robbery, burglary, and other serious crime arrests are more likely to be uniform and consistent throughout all jurisdictions. The Program's procedures require that an arrest be counted on each separate occasion a person is taken into custody, notified, or cited. Annual arrest figures do not measure the number of individuals arrested since one person may be arrested several times during the year for the same or different offenses.

Nationwide, law enforcement agencies made an estimated 15.1 million arrests in 1995 for all criminal infractions except traffic violations. The highest arrest counts among the specific crime categories were for larceny-theft and drug abuse violations, 1.5 million each. Driving under the influence accounted for 1.4 million arrests, and simple assault arrests numbered 1.3 million. (See Table 29.)

When the overall arrest volume was related to the total U.S. population, the rate was 5,807 arrests per 100,000 inhabitants. Among the city population groupings, those with more than 250,000 inhabitants recorded the highest rate, 7,783, while those with populations from 25,000 to 49,999 recorded the lowest rate, 5,355. (See Table 31.) For suburban county agencies overall, the arrest rate was 4,255, and for rural county law enforcement, it was 4,357 per 100,000 inhabitants. Regionally, the arrest rates per 100,000 population ranged from 5,626 in the West to 5,918 in the South. (See Tables 30 and 31.)

Because of reporting problems at the state levels, only limited arrest statistics were provided from Delaware and Pennsylvania, and no arrest data were available for New Hampshire. Due to NIBRS conversion efforts, arrest data were not received from contributing law enforcement agencies in Illinois, Kansas, and Montana. Therefore, tables showing the age, sex, or race of persons arrested contain limited or no data for these states. Arrest totals were estimated, however, for inclusion in Table 29, "Total Estimated Arrests, United States, 1995."

Arrest Trends

The number of arrests for all offenses excluding traffic violations increased 1 percent in 1995 as compared to the 1994 volume. Virtually no change was reported for violent crime arrests, while arrests for Crime Index offenses and those for property crimes decreased 1 percent.

During the same time period, juvenile and adult arrests for all offenses increased 1 percent. Violent crime arrests increased 1 percent for adults and decreased 3 percent for juveniles. For the 2-year period, property crime arrests declined 1 percent for adults and 2 percent for juveniles. (See Table 36.)

Two-year arrest trends showed a 1-percent increase in overall arrests for cities and 3-percent increases in arrests for suburban and rural counties. (See Tables 44, 50, and 56.)

The comparison of 1991 and 1995 data shows total arrests were up 5 percent. Juvenile arrests increased 20 percent, and adult arrests rose 2 percent for the same timeframe. (See Table 34.) Total Crime Index arrests declined 5 percent, and property crime arrests dropped 8 percent. Violent crime arrests increased 2 percent during the period.

For the decade 1986-1995, increases were recorded for total arrests, 17 percent; Crime Index offenses, 10 percent; violent crimes, 37 percent; and property crimes, 2 percent.

The 1995 drug abuse violation arrest total was 7 percent above the 1994 level, 41 percent higher than in 1991, and 65 percent higher than in 1986. The following table shows the types of drugs involved in violations resulting in arrests during 1995 by geographic region.

Table 4.1—Arrests for Drug Abuse Violations, 1995
[Percent distribution]

	United States total	North- eastern States	Mid- western States	Southern States	Western States
Total[1]	100.0	100.0	100.0	100.0	100.0
Sale/manufacture:	24.9	32.9	26.8	22.9	20.0
Heroin or cocaine and their derivatives	14.7	26.0	7.6	14.6	9.0
Marijuana	5.8	5.6	7.8	5.6	5.3
Synthetic or manufactured drugs	.7	.5	.4	1.2	.4
Other dangerous nonnarcotic drugs	3.7	.9	11.0	1.6	5.4
Possession:	75.1	67.1	73.2	77.1	80.0
Heroin or cocaine and their derivatives	27.8	33.6	15.1	26.8	29.3
Marijuana	34.1	30.7	44.2	43.3	22.4
Synthetic or manufactured drugs	1.5	.7	1.4	2.0	1.6
Other dangerous nonnarcotic drugs	11.8	2.1	12.5	5.0	26.6

[1]Because of rounding, percentages may not add to totals.

Age

Six percent of all persons arrested nationally in 1995 were under the age of 15; 18 percent were under 18; 31 percent were under 21; and 44 percent were under 25. Persons in the under-25 age group accounted for 46 percent of arrests in the cities, 41 percent in the suburban counties, and 39 percent in the rural counties.

Age distribution figures for persons arrested for Crime Index offenses showed 30 percent were under the age of 18; 44 percent, under 21; and 55 percent, under 25. The under-25 age group was also responsible for 46 percent of the violent crime arrests and 58 percent of property crime arrests in 1995.

Larceny-theft was the offense resulting in the most arrests of persons under age 18, while adults were most often arrested for driving under the influence. (See Table 38.)

Sex

Eighty percent of the persons arrested in the Nation during 1995 were males. (See Table 42.) They accounted for 76 percent of Index crime arrests, 85 percent of those for violent crimes, and 73 percent of the property crime arrests. Men were most often arrested for drug abuse violations and driving under the influence, which jointly accounted for 20 percent of all male arrests.

As in past years, larceny-theft was the crime for which females were most often arrested. This single offense accounted for 73 percent of arrests of women for Index crimes and 17 percent of all female arrests. Fifty-five percent of all female larceny-theft arrestees were under 25 years of age.

Two-year trends showed a 1-percent increase in the number of male arrests from 1994 to 1995, and a 4-percent rise in female arrests for the same period. (See Table 37.) Arrests of males rose 3 percent, and those of females were up 14 percent for the 5-year period from 1991 to 1995.

Race

Race distribution figures for the total number of arrests in the United States during 1995 showed 67 percent of the arrestees were white, 31 percent were black, and the remainder were of other races. (See Table 43.) Whites accounted for 62 percent of the Index crime arrests, 54 percent of the arrests for violent crimes, and 65 percent of those for property crimes.

Table 29.—Total Estimated Arrests,[1] United States, 1995

Total[2]	**15,119,800**	Embezzlement	15,200
		Stolen property; buying, receiving, possessing	166,500
Murder and nonnegligent manslaughter	21,230	Vandalism	311,100
Forcible rape	34,650	Weapons; carrying, possessing, etc.	243,900
Robbery	171,870	Prostitution and commercialized vice	97,700
Aggravated assault	568,480	Sex offenses (except forcible rape and prostitution)	94,500
Burglary	386,500	Drug abuse violations	1,476,100
Larceny–theft	1,530,200	Gambling	19,500
Motor vehicle theft	191,900	Offenses against family and children	142,900
Arson	20,000	Driving under the influence	1,436,000
		Liquor laws	594,900
Violent crime[3]	796,250	Drunkenness	708,100
Property crime[4]	2,128,600	Disorderly conduct	748,600
		Vagrancy	25,900
Crime Index total[5]	2,924,800	All other offenses	3,865,400
		Suspicion (not included in totals)	12,100
Other assaults	1,290,400	Curfew and loitering law violations	149,800
Forgery and counterfeiting	122,300	Runaways	249,500
Fraud	436,400		

[1]Arrest totals are based on all reporting agencies and estimates for unreported areas.
[2]Because of rounding, figures may not add to totals.
[3]Violent crimes are offenses of murder, forcible rape, robbery, and aggravated assault.
[4]Property crimes are offenses of burglary, larceny–theft, motor vehicle theft, and arson.
[5]Includes arson.

Table 30.—Arrests, Number and Rate, Regions, 1995

[Rate: Number of arrests per 100,000 inhabitants]

Offense charged	United States Total (9,498 agencies; population 196,440,000)	Northeast (1,510 agencies; population 34,627,000)	Midwest (2,033 agencies; population 34,012,000)	South (4,363 agencies; population 77,507,000)	West (1,592 agencies; population 50,293,000)
TOTAL	**11,407,288**	**1,984,783**	**2,006,017**	**4,586,785**	**2,829,703**
Rate	**5,807.0**	**5,731.9**	**5,897.9**	**5,917.9**	**5,626.4**
Murder and nonnegligent manslaughter	16,701	2,373	3,201	7,269	3,858
Rate	8.5	6.9	9.4	9.4	7.7
Forcible rape	26,561	4,513	5,345	11,314	5,389
Rate	13.5	13.0	15.7	14.6	10.7
Robbery	137,811	43,824	15,322	44,641	34,024
Rate	70.2	126.6	45.0	57.6	67.7
Aggravated assault.................	438,157	73,663	51,392	168,163	144,939
Rate	223.0	212.7	151.1	217.0	288.2
Burglary	292,315	43,461	36,893	121,056	90,905
Rate	148.8	125.5	108.5	156.2	180.7
Larceny–theft.....................	1,164,371	176,495	199,334	472,880	315,662
Rate	592.7	509.7	586.1	610.1	627.6
Motor vehicle theft	149,053	20,241	22,866	52,662	53,284
Rate	75.9	58.5	67.2	67.9	105.9
Arson	14,965	2,304	3,153	4,932	4,576
Rate	7.6	6.7	9.3	6.4	9.1
Violent crime[1]	619,230	124,373	75,260	231,387	188,210
Rate	315.2	359.2	221.3	298.5	374.2
Property crime[2]	1,620,704	242,501	262,246	651,530	464,427
Rate	825.0	700.3	771.0	840.6	923.4
Crime Index total[3]	2,239,934	366,874	337,506	882,917	652,637
Rate	1,140.3	1,059.5	992.3	1,139.1	1,297.7
Other assaults.....................	975,418	151,670	177,631	430,204	215,913
Rate	496.5	438.0	522.3	555.1	429.3
Forgery and counterfeiting	91,991	11,897	12,073	43,479	24,542
Rate	46.8	34.4	35.5	56.1	48.8
Fraud	320,046	64,760	45,319	186,542	23,425
Rate	162.9	187.0	133.2	240.7	46.6
Embezzlement	11,605	690	1,861	6,466	2,588
Rate	5.9	2.0	5.5	8.3	5.1
Stolen property; buying, receiving, possessing	127,844	27,175	23,117	35,952	41,600
Rate	65.1	78.5	68.0	46.4	82.7
Vandalism.........................	232,702	49,299	49,805	66,512	67,086
Rate	118.5	142.4	146.4	85.8	133.4
Weapons; carrying, possessing, etc.	187,237	26,325	31,106	74,132	55,674
Rate	95.3	76.0	91.5	95.6	110.7
Prostitution and commercialized vice	81,064	16,596	13,962	26,116	24,390
Rate	41.3	47.9	41.1	33.7	48.5
Sex offenses (except forcible rape and prostitution)	72,272	11,361	12,676	24,820	23,415
Rate	36.8	32.8	37.3	32.0	46.6
Drug abuse violations	1,144,228	265,538	140,473	388,632	349,585
Rate	582.5	766.9	413.0	501.4	695.1
Gambling	15,676	7,880	1,495	4,498	1,803
Rate	8.0	22.8	4.4	5.8	3.6
Offenses against family and children	104,952	27,848	34,027	32,965	10,112
Rate	53.4	80.4	100.0	42.5	20.1
Driving under the influence	1,033,280	105,209	200,332	416,208	311,531
Rate	526.0	303.8	589.0	537.0	619.4
Liquor laws	435,311	82,774	129,632	118,115	104,790
Rate	221.6	239.0	381.1	152.4	208.4
Drunkenness.......................	527,200	9,431	39,870	354,061	123,838
Rate	268.4	27.2	117.2	456.8	246.2
Disorderly conduct	561,642	149,471	153,999	185,589	72,583
Rate	285.9	431.7	452.8	239.4	144.3
Vagrancy.........................	20,521	6,526	1,917	3,915	8,163
Rate	10.4	18.8	5.6	5.1	16.2
All other offenses (except traffic)	2,919,723	577,917	529,198	1,174,258	638,350
Rate	1,486.3	1,669.0	1,555.9	1,515.0	1,269.3
Suspicion (not included in totals)	9,058	1,362	2,319	4,912	465
Rate	4.6	3.9	6.8	6.3	.9
Curfew and loitering law violations	114,946	10,777	33,633	28,333	42,203
Rate	58.5	31.1	98.9	36.6	83.9
Runaways.........................	189,696	14,765	36,385	103,071	35,475
Rate	96.6	42.6	107.0	133.0	70.5

[1]Violent crimes are offenses of murder, forcible rape, robbery, and aggravated assault.
[2]Property crimes are offenses of burglary, larceny–theft, motor vehicle theft, and arson.
[3]Includes arson.
Population figures were rounded to the nearest thousand. All rates were calculated before rounding.

Table 31.—Arrests, Number and Rate, Population Group, 1995

[Rate: Number of arrests per 100,000 inhabitants]

Offense charged	Total (9,498 agencies; population 196,440,000)	Cities — Total cities (6,541 agencies; population 132,932,000)	Cities — Group I (53 cities, 250,000 and over; population 38,820,000)	Cities — Group II (135 cities, 100,000 to 249,999; population 19,956,000)	Cities — Group III (310 cities, 50,000 to 99,999; population 21,040,000)	Cities — Group IV (543 cities, 25,000 to 49,999; population 18,755,000)	Cities — Group V (1,222 cities, 10,000 to 24,999; population 19,338,000)	Cities — Group VI (4,278 cities, under 10,000; population 15,023,000)	Counties — Suburban counties[1] (1,039 agencies; population 43,729,000)	Counties — Rural counties (1,918 agencies; population 19,780,000)	Suburban area[2] (4,680 agencies; population 82,984,000)
TOTAL	11,407,288	8,684,923	3,021,325	1,304,108	1,202,003	1,004,303	1,097,386	1,055,798	1,860,489	861,876	3,935,916
Rate	5,807.0	6,533.4	7,782.8	6,535.1	5,713.0	5,354.9	5,674.8	7,028.0	4,254.6	4,357.4	4,743.0
Murder and nonnegligent manslaughter	16,701	12,872	7,356	2,215	1,308	712	739	542	2,518	1,311	3,781
Rate	8.5	9.7	18.9	11.1	6.2	3.8	3.8	3.6	5.8	6.6	4.6
Forcible rape	26,561	19,698	8,531	3,159	2,527	1,858	2,053	1,570	4,613	2,250	8,285
Rate	13.5	14.8	22.0	15.8	12.0	9.9	10.6	10.5	10.5	11.4	10.0
Robbery	137,811	120,599	67,302	18,538	14,349	9,149	7,024	4,237	14,578	2,634	30,144
Rate	70.2	90.7	173.4	92.9	68.2	48.8	36.3	28.2	33.3	13.3	36.3
Aggravated assault	438,157	332,320	133,878	56,101	50,371	34,497	30,741	26,732	77,774	28,063	142,471
Rate	223.0	250.0	344.9	281.1	239.4	183.9	159.0	177.9	177.9	141.9	171.7
Burglary	292,315	212,154	66,478	37,929	34,731	25,528	25,038	22,450	53,594	26,567	102,950
Rate	148.8	159.6	171.2	190.1	165.1	136.1	129.5	149.4	122.6	134.3	124.1
Larceny—theft	1,164,371	967,859	265,692	156,637	164,254	136,401	139,641	105,234	153,169	43,343	405,123
Rate	592.7	728.1	684.4	784.9	780.7	727.3	722.1	700.5	350.3	219.1	488.2
Motor vehicle theft	149,053	116,806	54,637	18,184	15,448	9,838	9,517	9,182	24,661	7,586	44,390
Rate	75.9	87.9	140.7	91.1	73.4	52.5	49.2	61.1	56.4	38.4	53.5
Arson	14,965	11,286	3,395	1,702	1,635	1,492	1,602	1,460	2,414	1,265	5,476
Rate	7.6	8.5	8.7	8.5	7.8	8.0	8.3	9.7	5.5	6.4	6.6
Violent crime[3]	619,230	485,489	217,067	80,013	68,555	46,216	40,557	33,081	99,483	34,258	184,681
Rate	315.2	365.2	559.2	401.0	325.8	246.4	209.7	220.2	227.5	173.2	222.6
Property crime[4]	1,620,704	1,308,105	390,202	214,452	216,068	173,259	175,798	138,326	233,838	78,761	557,939
Rate	825.0	984.0	1,005.1	1,074.6	1,027.0	923.8	909.1	920.8	534.7	398.2	672.3
Crime Index total[5]	2,239,934	1,793,594	607,269	294,465	284,623	219,475	216,355	171,407	333,321	113,019	742,620
Rate	1,140.3	1,349.3	1,564.3	1,475.6	1,352.8	1,170.2	1,118.8	1,141.0	762.2	571.4	894.9
Other assaults	975,418	747,638	247,903	130,240	96,186	84,789	98,817	89,703	155,716	72,064	331,944
Rate	496.5	562.4	638.6	652.7	457.2	452.1	511.0	597.1	356.1	364.3	400.0
Forgery and counterfeiting	91,991	70,204	19,965	12,163	10,997	8,803	9,617	8,659	14,311	7,476	31,261
Rate	46.8	52.8	51.4	61.0	52.3	46.9	49.7	57.6	32.7	37.8	37.7
Fraud	320,046	194,825	60,189	26,747	24,447	26,038	30,032	27,372	75,775	49,446	125,134
Rate	162.9	146.6	155.0	134.0	116.2	138.8	155.3	182.2	173.3	250.0	150.8
Embezzlement	11,605	8,885	1,924	2,337	1,596	1,148	1,008	872	1,926	794	3,838
Rate	5.9	6.7	5.0	11.7	7.6	6.1	5.2	5.8	4.4	4.0	4.6
Stolen property; buying, receiving, possessing	127,844	101,561	32,643	18,447	16,290	13,732	11,548	8,901	19,289	6,994	44,988
Rate	65.1	76.4	84.1	92.4	77.4	73.2	59.7	59.2	44.1	35.4	54.2

See footnotes at end of table.

Table 31.—Arrests, Number and Rate, Population Group, 1995 — Continued

| Offense charged | Total (9,498 agencies; population 196,440,000) | Total cities (6,541 cities; population 132,932,000) | Cities | | | | | | Counties | | Suburban area[2] (4,680 agencies; population 82,984,000) |
			Group I (53 cities, 250,000 and over; population 38,820,000)	Group II (135 cities, 100,000 to 249,999; population 19,956,000)	Group III (310 cities, 50,000 to 99,999; population 21,040,000)	Group IV (543 cities, 25,000 to 49,999; population 18,755,000)	Group V (1,222 cities, 10,000 to 24,999; population 19,338,000)	Group VI (4,278 cities, under 10,000; population 15,023,000)	Suburban counties[1] (1,039 agencies; population 43,729,000)	Rural counties (1,918 agencies; population 19,780,000)	
Vandalism	232,702	185,661	55,640	26,511	26,532	23,983	27,166	25,829	30,807	16,234	81,481
Rate	118.5	139.7	143.3	132.9	126.1	127.9	140.5	171.9	70.5	82.1	98.2
Weapons; carrying, possessing, etc.	187,237	149,188	59,252	24,955	20,236	14,991	14,967	14,787	26,746	11,303	58,110
Rate	95.3	112.2	152.6	125.1	96.2	79.9	77.4	98.4	61.2	57.1	70.0
Prostitution and commercialized vice	81,064	75,209	53,199	11,955	6,009	2,848	958	240	5,611	244	9,349
Rate	41.3	56.6	137.0	59.9	28.6	15.2	5.0	1.6	12.8	1.2	11.3
Sex offenses (except forcible rape and prostitution)	72,272	53,166	22,499	8,162	7,423	5,492	5,088	4,502	13,052	6,054	23,480
Rate	36.8	40.0	58.0	40.9	35.3	29.3	26.3	30.0	29.8	30.6	28.3
Drug abuse violations	1,144,228	898,031	397,877	151,243	116,297	88,493	75,812	68,309	178,319	67,878	351,280
Rate	582.5	675.6	1,024.9	757.9	552.7	471.8	392.0	454.7	407.8	343.2	423.3
Gambling	15,676	13,913	10,559	1,029	975	462	429	459	1,293	470	2,131
Rate	8.0	10.5	27.2	5.2	4.6	2.5	2.2	3.1	3.0	2.4	2.6
Offenses against family and children	104,952	58,543	11,398	7,217	8,903	11,072	12,036	7,917	34,968	11,441	55,090
Rate	53.4	44.0	29.4	36.2	42.3	59.0	62.2	52.7	80.0	57.8	66.4
Driving under the influence	1,033,280	618,759	127,511	78,379	84,266	89,201	114,372	125,030	251,519	163,002	472,159
Rate	526.0	465.5	328.5	392.8	400.5	475.6	591.4	832.3	575.2	824.1	569.0
Liquor laws	435,311	356,691	113,238	35,417	43,250	37,222	58,993	68,571	42,747	35,873	131,780
Rate	221.6	268.3	291.7	177.5	205.6	198.5	305.1	456.4	97.8	181.4	158.8
Drunkenness	527,200	439,595	106,029	68,635	71,847	59,161	64,452	69,471	53,975	33,630	167,741
Rate	268.4	330.7	273.1	343.9	341.5	315.4	333.3	462.4	123.4	170.0	202.1
Disorderly conduct	561,642	493,141	159,705	61,522	71,222	55,605	72,791	72,296	42,415	26,086	168,605
Rate	285.9	371.0	411.4	308.3	338.5	296.5	376.4	481.2	97.0	131.9	203.2
Vagrancy	20,521	19,318	11,298	2,127	1,846	1,646	1,117	1,284	825	378	3,931
Rate	10.4	14.5	29.1	10.7	8.8	8.8	5.8	8.5	1.9	1.9	4.7
All other offenses (except traffic)	2,919,723	2,163,352	844,457	306,024	270,371	229,103	248,842	264,555	528,734	227,637	1,022,912
Rate	1,486.3	1,627.4	2,175.3	1,533.5	1,285.0	1,221.6	1,286.8	1,761.0	1,209.1	1,150.9	1,232.7
Suspicion (not included in totals)	9,058	6,965	3,337	223	543	909	793	1,160	1,648	445	3,279
Rate	4.6	5.2	8.6	1.1	2.6	4.8	4.1	7.7	3.8	2.2	4.0
Curfew and loitering law violations	114,946	108,897	44,695	12,118	13,074	12,420	14,282	12,308	4,482	1,567	29,992
Rate	58.5	81.9	115.1	60.7	62.1	66.2	73.9	81.9	10.2	7.9	36.1
Runaways	189,696	134,752	34,075	24,415	25,613	18,619	18,704	13,326	44,658	10,286	78,090
Rate	96.6	101.4	87.8	122.3	121.7	99.3	96.7	88.7	102.1	52.0	94.1

[1] Includes only suburban county law enforcement agencies.
[2] Includes suburban city and county law enforcement agencies within metropolitan areas. Excludes central cities. Suburban cities and counties are also included in other groups.
[3] Violent crimes are offenses or murder, forcible rape, robbery, and aggravated assault.
[4] Property crimes are offenses of burglary, larceny—theft, motor vehicle theft, and arson.
[5] Includes arson.
Population figures were rounded to the nearest thousand. All rates were calculated before rounding.

Table 32.—Total Arrest Trends, 1986–1995

[7,587 agencies; 1995 estimated population 176,320,000; 1986 estimated population 161,254,000]

Offense charged	Number of persons arrested								
	Total all ages			Under 18 years of age			18 years of age and over		
	1986	1995	Percent change	1986	1995	Percent change	1986	1995	Percent change
TOTAL	8,870,709	10,362,736	+16.8	1,446,133	1,881,586	+30.1	7,424,576	8,481,150	+14.2
Murder and nonnegligent manslaughter	14,297	15,384	+7.6	1,255	2,383	+89.9	13,042	13,001	−.3
Forcible rape	26,284	24,106	−8.3	3,994	3,853	−3.5	22,290	20,253	−9.1
Robbery	113,671	128,809	+13.3	25,607	41,841	+63.4	88,064	86,968	−1.2
Aggravated assault......................	260,451	399,414	+53.4	32,598	58,113	+78.3	227,853	341,301	+49.8
Burglary	324,002	266,363	−17.8	113,921	93,484	−17.9	210,081	172,879	−17.7
Larceny–theft..........................	988,925	1,056,145	+6.8	309,746	353,667	+14.2	679,179	702,478	+3.4
Motor vehicle theft	115,898	137,233	+18.4	44,675	57,209	+28.1	71,223	80,024	+12.4
Arson	12,698	13,569	+6.9	5,095	7,137	+40.1	7,603	6,432	−15.4
Violent crime[1]	414,703	567,713	+36.9	63,454	106,190	+67.3	351,249	461,523	+31.4
Property crime[2]	1,441,523	1,473,310	+2.2	473,437	511,497	+8.0	968,086	961,813	−.6
Crime Index total[3]	1,856,226	2,041,023	+10.0	536,891	617,687	+15.0	1,319,335	1,423,336	+7.9
Other assaults.........................	488,005	883,870	+81.1	69,554	146,543	+110.7	418,451	737,327	+76.2
Forgery and counterfeiting	64,005	84,068	+31.3	5,968	6,103	+2.3	58,037	77,965	+34.3
Fraud	245,779	295,584	+20.3	17,010	17,918	+5.3	228,769	277,666	+21.4
Embezzlement	8,857	10,832	+22.3	608	896	+47.4	8,249	9,936	+20.5
Stolen property; buying, receiving, possessing	97,711	114,982	+17.7	24,372	29,358	+20.5	73,339	85,624	+16.8
Vandalism.............................	175,589	208,705	+18.9	75,252	94,213	+25.2	100,337	114,492	+14.1
Weapons; carrying, possessing, etc.	142,488	170,335	+19.5	22,437	39,309	+75.2	120,051	131,026	+9.1
Prostitution and commercialized vice	91,764	74,644	−18.7	1,945	976	−49.8	89,819	73,668	−18.0
Sex offenses (except forcible rape and prostitution)	72,517	66,018	−9.0	11,616	11,180	−3.8	60,901	54,838	−10.0
Drug abuse violations	636,821	1,048,319	+64.6	61,960	133,323	+115.2	574,861	914,996	+59.2
Gambling	24,321	14,653	−39.8	552	1,093	+98.0	23,769	13,560	−43.0
Offenses against family and children	39,055	84,637	+116.7	2,287	4,077	+78.3	36,768	80,560	+119.1
Driving under the influence	1,215,983	917,167	−24.6	18,695	9,565	−48.8	1,197,288	907,602	−24.2
Liquor laws	372,532	394,621	+5.9	94,791	77,969	−17.7	277,741	316,652	+14.0
Drunkenness...........................	661,943	489,385	−26.1	23,474	14,252	−39.3	638,469	475,133	−25.6
Disorderly conduct	470,361	487,073	+3.6	65,517	109,305	+66.8	404,844	377,768	−6.7
Vagrancy..............................	31,264	19,582	−37.4	2,266	2,612	+15.3	28,998	16,970	−41.5
All other offenses (except traffic)	2,001,618	2,677,432	+33.8	237,068	285,401	+20.4	1,764,550	2,392,031	+35.6
Suspicion (not included in totals)	10,596	7,901	−25.4	1,866	1,383	−25.9	8,730	6,518	−25.3
Curfew and loitering law violations	58,930	103,436	+75.5	58,930	103,436	+75.5	—	—	—
Runaways..............................	114,940	176,370	+53.4	114,940	176,370	+53.4	—	—	—

[1]Violent crimes are offenses of murder, forcible rape, robbery, and aggravated assault.
[2]Property crimes are offenses of burglary, larceny–theft, motor vehicle theft, and arson.
[3]Includes arson.

Table 33.—Total Arrest Trends, Sex, 1986–1995

[7,587 agencies; 1995 estimated population 176,320,000; 1986 estimated population 161,254,000]

Offense charged	Males						Females					
	Total			Under 18			Total			Under 18		
	1986	1995	Percent change	1986	1995	Percent change	1986	1995	Percent change	1986	1995	Percent change
TOTAL	7,334,777	8,245,284	+12.4	1,124,942	1,399,547	+24.4	1,535,932	2,117,452	+37.9	321,191	482,039	+50.1
Murder and nonnegligent manslaughter	12,572	13,927	+10.8	1,170	2,245	+91.9	1,725	1,457	−15.5	85	138	+62.4
Forcible rape	26,016	23,809	−8.5	3,928	3,769	−4.0	268	297	+10.8	66	84	+27.3
Robbery	104,871	116,741	+11.3	23,848	37,978	+59.3	8,800	12,068	+37.1	1,759	3,863	+119.6
Aggravated assault....................	225,720	328,476	+45.5	27,593	46,695	+69.2	34,731	70,938	+104.2	5,005	11,418	+128.1
Burglary	297,599	236,495	−20.5	105,102	84,229	−19.9	26,403	29,868	+13.1	8,819	9,255	+4.9
Larceny–theft........................	687,289	704,565	+2.5	227,072	238,889	+5.2	301,636	351,580	+16.6	82,674	114,778	+38.8
Motor vehicle theft	104,886	119,175	+13.6	39,806	48,719	+22.4	11,012	18,058	+64.0	4,869	8,490	+74.4
Arson	10,918	11,413	+4.5	4,570	6,263	+37.0	1,780	2,156	+21.1	525	874	+66.5
Violent crime[1]	369,179	482,953	+30.8	56,539	90,687	+60.4	45,524	84,760	+86.2	6,915	15,503	+124.2
Property crime[2]	1,100,692	1,071,648	−2.6	376,550	378,100	+.4	340,831	401,662	+17.8	96,887	133,397	+37.7
Crime Index total[3]	1,469,871	1,554,601	+5.8	433,089	468,787	+8.2	386,355	486,422	+25.9	103,802	148,900	+43.4
Other assaults........................	413,578	710,249	+71.7	53,606	106,028	+97.8	74,427	173,621	+133.3	15,948	40,515	+154.0
Forgery and counterfeiting	42,281	53,878	+27.4	3,983	3,928	−1.4	21,724	30,190	+39.0	1,985	2,175	+9.6
Fraud	139,934	175,491	+25.4	12,871	13,242	+2.9	105,845	120,093	+13.5	4,139	4,676	+13.0
Embezzlement	5,498	6,105	+11.0	357	520	+45.7	3,359	4,727	+40.7	251	376	+49.8
Stolen property; buying, receiving, possessing	86,569	98,682	+14.0	22,112	25,799	+16.7	11,142	16,300	+46.3	2,260	3,559	+57.5
Vandalism...........................	157,051	180,511	+14.9	68,375	84,206	+23.2	18,538	28,194	+52.1	6,877	10,007	+45.5
Weapons; carrying, possessing, etc.	131,980	157,036	+19.0	21,006	36,161	+72.1	10,508	13,299	+26.6	1,431	3,148	+120.0
Prostitution and commercialized vice	31,959	29,576	−7.5	714	510	−28.6	59,805	45,068	−24.6	1,231	466	−62.1
Sex offenses (except forcible rape and prostitution)	66,795	60,672	−9.2	10,811	10,380	−4.0	5,722	5,346	−6.6	805	800	−.6
Drug abuse violations	545,008	872,834	+60.2	53,224	116,627	+119.1	91,813	175,485	+91.1	8,736	16,696	+91.1
Gambling	20,125	12,357	−38.6	514	1,038	+101.9	4,196	2,296	−45.3	38	55	+44.7
Offenses against family and children	33,064	66,351	+100.7	1,428	2,585	+81.0	5,991	18,286	+205.2	859	1,492	+73.7
Driving under the influence	1,076,712	784,253	−27.2	16,182	8,074	−50.1	139,271	132,914	−4.6	2,513	1,491	−40.7
Liquor laws	310,759	321,160	+3.3	70,123	55,548	−20.8	61,773	73,461	+18.9	24,668	22,421	−9.1
Drunkenness........................	603,473	431,851	−28.4	19,913	12,009	−39.7	58,470	57,534	−1.6	3,561	2,243	−37.0
Disorderly conduct	382,094	381,093	−.3	53,329	82,793	+55.2	88,267	105,980	+20.1	12,188	26,512	+117.5
Vagrancy	27,556	15,760	−42.8	1,855	2,329	+25.6	3,708	3,822	+3.1	411	283	−31.1
All other offenses (except traffic)	1,697,711	2,185,462	+28.7	188,691	221,621	+17.5	303,907	491,970	+61.9	48,377	63,780	+31.8
Suspicion (not included in totals)	9,075	6,699	−26.2	1,496	1,092	−27.0	1,521	1,202	−21.0	370	291	−21.4
Curfew and loitering law violations	44,288	72,649	+64.0	44,288	72,649	+64.0	14,642	30,787	+110.3	14,642	30,787	+110.3
Runaways...........................	48,471	74,713	+54.1	48,471	74,713	+54.1	66,469	101,657	+52.9	66,469	101,657	+52.9

[1]Violent crimes are offenses of murder, forcible rape, robbery, and aggravated assault.
[2]Property crimes are offenses of burglary, larceny–theft, motor vehicle theft, and arson.
[3]Includes arson.

Table 34.—Total Arrest Trends, 1991–1995

[7,051 agencies; 1995 estimated population 159,279,000; 1991 estimated population 153,397,000]

| Offense charged | Number of persons arrested | | | | | | | | |
| | Total all ages | | | Under 18 years of age | | | 18 years of age and over | | |
	1991	1995	Percent change	1991	1995	Percent change	1991	1995	Percent change
TOTAL	8,992,241	9,410,726	+4.7	1,435,389	1,723,311	+20.1	7,556,852	7,687,415	+1.7
Murder and nonnegligent manslaughter	16,712	14,166	–15.2	2,401	2,193	–8.7	14,311	11,973	–16.3
Forcible rape	25,184	21,322	–15.3	3,849	3,403	–11.6	21,335	17,919	–16.0
Robbery	126,882	118,501	–6.6	32,789	38,623	+17.8	94,093	79,878	–15.1
Aggravated assault......................	321,184	348,127	+8.4	45,401	50,359	+10.9	275,783	297,768	+8.0
Burglary	281,557	236,916	–15.9	92,363	81,873	–11.4	189,194	155,043	–18.1
Larceny–theft..........................	1,001,251	949,581	–5.2	298,521	316,554	+6.0	702,730	633,027	–9.9
Motor vehicle theft	145,265	126,265	–13.1	62,902	52,462	–16.6	82,363	73,803	–10.4
Arson	12,052	12,759	+5.9	5,598	6,732	+20.3	6,454	6,027	–6.6
Violent crime[1]	489,962	502,116	+2.5	84,440	94,578	+12.0	405,522	407,538	+.5
Property crime[2]	1,440,125	1,325,521	–8.0	459,384	457,621	–.4	980,741	867,900	–11.5
Crime Index total[3]	1,930,087	1,827,637	–5.3	543,824	552,199	+1.5	1,386,263	1,275,438	–8.0
Other assaults.........................	631,699	789,670	+25.0	99,093	134,726	+36.0	532,606	654,944	+23.0
Forgery and counterfeiting	62,288	74,705	+19.9	5,122	5,619	+9.7	57,166	69,086	+20.9
Fraud	247,195	251,951	+1.9	10,029	16,923	+68.7	237,166	235,028	–.9
Embezzlement	9,393	10,119	+7.7	727	790	+8.7	8,666	9,329	+7.7
Stolen property; buying, receiving, possessing	112,746	110,445	–2.0	30,213	28,411	–6.0	82,533	82,034	–.6
Vandalism............................	199,737	200,837	+.6	85,898	90,061	+4.8	113,839	110,776	–2.7
Weapons; carrying, possessing, etc.	156,291	160,983	+3.0	32,983	37,260	+13.0	123,308	123,723	+.3
Prostitution and commercialized vice	74,390	68,142	–8.4	920	867	–5.8	73,470	67,275	–8.4
Sex offenses (except forcible rape and prostitution)	69,521	62,311	–10.4	12,153	10,627	–12.6	57,368	51,684	–9.9
Drug abuse violations	685,157	963,871	+40.7	52,406	124,467	+137.5	632,751	839,404	+32.7
Gambling	11,364	13,730	+20.8	696	1,044	+50.0	10,668	12,686	+18.9
Offenses against family and children	61,388	85,657	+39.5	2,520	4,077	+61.8	58,868	81,580	+38.6
Driving under the influence	1,054,378	826,426	–21.6	10,460	8,665	–17.2	1,043,918	817,761	–21.7
Liquor laws	337,649	355,225	+5.2	75,396	74,848	–.7	262,253	280,377	+6.9
Drunkenness..........................	555,446	469,001	–15.6	14,051	13,862	–1.3	541,395	455,139	–15.9
Disorderly conduct	453,251	464,036	+2.4	77,246	111,811	+44.7	376,005	352,225	–6.3
Vagrancy.............................	29,594	18,325	–38.1	2,018	2,598	+28.7	27,576	15,727	–43.0
All other offenses (except traffic)	2,138,639	2,418,900	+13.1	207,606	265,701	+28.0	1,931,033	2,153,199	+11.5
Suspicion (not included in totals)	13,718	6,744	–50.8	2,600	1,121	–56.9	11,118	5,623	–49.4
Curfew and loitering law violations	56,817	104,532	+84.0	56,817	104,532	+84.0	—	—	—
Runaways.............................	115,211	134,223	+16.5	115,211	134,223	+16.5	—	—	—

[1]Violent crimes are offenses of murder, forcible rape, robbery, and aggravated assault.
[2]Property crimes are offenses of burglary, larceny–theft, motor vehicle theft, and arson.
[3]Includes arson.

214

Table 35.—Total Arrest Trends, Sex, 1991–1995

[7,051 agencies; 1995 estimated population 159,279,000; 1991 estimated population 153,397,000]

Offense charged	Males						Females					
	Total			Under 18			Total			Under 18		
	1991	1995	Percent change	1991	1995	Percent change	1991	1995	Percent change	1991	1995	Percent change
TOTAL	7,315,866	7,507,814	+2.6	1,110,455	1,292,152	+16.4	1,676,375	1,902,912	+13.5	324,934	431,159	+32.7
Murder and nonnegligent manslaughter	15,023	12,836	−14.6	2,291	2,063	−10.0	1,689	1,330	−21.3	110	130	+18.2
Forcible rape	24,879	21,068	−15.3	3,782	3,334	−11.8	305	254	−16.7	67	69	+3.0
Robbery	115,991	107,324	−7.5	29,889	35,025	+17.2	10,891	11,177	+2.6	2,900	3,598	+24.1
Aggravated assault	277,247	287,958	+3.9	38,513	40,771	+5.9	43,937	60,169	+36.9	6,888	9,588	+39.2
Burglary	255,506	209,428	−18.0	84,250	73,552	−12.7	26,051	27,488	+5.5	8,113	8,321	+2.6
Larceny–theft	682,006	632,602	−7.2	212,741	214,157	+.7	319,245	316,979	−.7	85,780	102,397	+19.4
Motor vehicle theft	130,762	109,722	−16.1	55,792	44,771	−19.8	14,503	16,543	+14.1	7,110	7,691	+8.2
Arson	10,459	10,733	+2.6	5,102	5,887	+15.4	1,593	2,026	+27.2	496	845	+70.4
Violent crime[1]	433,140	429,186	−.9	74,475	81,193	+9.0	56,822	72,930	+28.3	9,965	13,385	+34.3
Property crime[2]	1,078,733	962,485	−10.8	357,885	338,367	−5.5	361,392	363,036	+.5	101,499	119,254	+17.5
Crime Index total[3]	1,511,873	1,391,671	−8.0	432,360	419,560	−3.0	418,214	435,966	+4.2	111,464	132,639	+19.0
Other assaults	526,826	635,235	+20.6	75,499	97,875	+29.6	104,873	154,435	+47.3	23,594	36,851	+56.2
Forgery and counterfeiting	40,797	47,662	+16.8	3,428	3,631	+5.9	21,491	27,043	+25.8	1,694	1,988	+17.4
Fraud	142,453	151,268	+6.2	7,325	12,607	+72.1	104,742	100,683	−3.9	2,704	4,316	+59.6
Embezzlement	5,657	5,682	+.4	471	461	−2.1	3,736	4,437	+18.8	256	329	+28.5
Stolen property; buying, receiving, possessing	99,311	94,769	−4.6	27,114	24,971	−7.9	13,435	15,676	+16.7	3,099	3,440	+11.0
Vandalism	177,903	173,983	−2.2	78,757	80,556	+2.3	21,834	26,854	+23.0	7,141	9,505	+33.1
Weapons; carrying, possessing, etc.	145,176	148,449	+2.3	30,930	34,353	+11.1	11,115	12,534	+12.8	2,053	2,907	+41.6
Prostitution and commercialized vice	25,243	25,694	+1.8	449	433	−3.6	49,147	42,448	−13.6	471	434	−7.9
Sex offenses (except forcible rape and prostitution)	64,438	57,224	−11.2	11,291	9,858	−12.7	5,083	5,087	+.1	862	769	−10.8
Drug abuse violations	571,412	801,086	+40.2	46,663	108,620	+132.8	113,745	162,785	+43.1	5,743	15,847	+175.9
Gambling	9,911	11,556	+16.6	681	996	+46.3	1,453	2,174	+49.6	15	48	+220.0
Offenses against family and children	50,417	67,938	+34.8	1,653	2,543	+53.8	10,971	17,719	+61.5	867	1,534	+76.9
Driving under the influence	916,246	707,562	−22.8	9,028	7,306	−19.1	138,132	118,864	−13.9	1,432	1,359	−5.1
Liquor laws	273,100	288,733	+5.7	54,401	53,141	−2.3	64,549	66,492	+3.0	20,995	21,707	+3.4
Drunkenness	498,704	413,962	−17.0	11,880	11,710	−1.4	56,742	55,039	−3.0	2,171	2,152	−.9
Disorderly conduct	360,864	361,555	+.2	61,271	84,151	+37.3	92,387	102,481	+10.9	15,975	27,660	+73.1
Vagrancy	26,439	14,892	−43.7	1,765	2,311	+30.9	3,155	3,433	+8.8	253	287	+13.4
All other offenses (except traffic)	1,777,421	1,977,818	+11.3	163,814	205,994	+25.7	361,218	441,082	+22.1	43,792	59,707	+36.3
Suspicion (not included in totals)	11,457	5,722	−50.1	2,040	894	−56.2	2,261	1,022	−54.8	560	227	−59.5
Curfew and loitering law violations	41,777	73,540	+76.0	41,777	73,540	+76.0	15,040	30,992	+106.1	15,040	30,992	+106.1
Runaways	49,898	57,535	+15.3	49,898	57,535	+15.3	65,313	76,688	+17.4	65,313	76,688	+17.4

[1]Violent crimes are offenses of murder, forcible rape, robbery, and aggravated assault.
[2]Property crimes are offenses of burglary, larceny–theft, motor vehicle theft, and arson.
[3]Includes arson.

215

Table 36.—Total Arrest Trends, 1994–1995

[8,587 agencies; 1995 estimated population 184,792,000; 1994 estimated population 183,306,000]

Offense charged	Number of persons arrested											
	Total all ages			Under 15 years of age			Under 18 years of age			18 years of age and over		
	1994	1995	Percent change	1994	1995	Percent change	1994	1995	Percent change	1994	1995	Percent change
TOTAL	**10,793,150**	**10,925,520**	**+1.2**	**700,681**	**684,365**	**−2.3**	**1,987,209**	**2,003,657**	**+.8**	**8,805,941**	**8,921,863**	**+1.3**
Murder and nonnegligent manslaughter	17,270	16,214	−6.1	346	342	−1.2	2,917	2,498	−14.4	14,353	13,716	−4.4
Forcible rape	26,782	25,309	−5.5	1,594	1,489	−6.6	4,204	4,038	−3.9	22,578	21,271	−5.8
Robbery	137,422	134,767	−1.9	12,608	12,315	−2.3	44,075	43,655	−1.0	93,347	91,112	−2.4
Aggravated assault	415,112	420,270	+1.2	21,133	19,902	−5.8	64,016	62,031	−3.1	351,096	358,239	+2.0
Burglary	292,728	280,470	−4.2	42,630	38,667	−9.3	104,460	98,574	−5.6	188,268	181,896	−3.4
Larceny–theft	1,111,590	1,116,492	+.4	166,389	164,126	−1.4	369,155	372,570	+.9	742,435	743,922	+.2
Motor vehicle theft	153,319	144,311	−5.9	20,032	17,183	−14.2	67,116	60,787	−9.4	86,203	83,524	−3.1
Arson	14,670	14,224	−3.0	5,584	5,023	−10.0	8,102	7,461	−7.9	6,568	6,763	+3.0
Violent crime[1]	596,586	596,560	4	35,681	34,048	−4.6	115,212	112,222	−2.6	481,374	484,338	+.6
Property crime[2]	1,572,307	1,555,497	−1.1	234,635	224,999	−4.1	548,833	539,392	−1.7	1,023,474	1,016,105	−.7
Crime Index total[3]	2,168,893	2,152,057	−.8	270,316	259,047	−4.2	664,045	651,614	−1.9	1,504,848	1,500,443	−.3
Other assaults	876,508	936,694	+6.9	64,282	65,026	+1.2	151,890	157,002	+3.4	724,618	779,692	+7.6
Forgery and counterfeiting	82,906	86,560	+4.4	836	802	−4.1	6,225	6,253	+.4	76,681	80,307	+4.7
Fraud	301,654	302,944	+.4	4,267	4,702	+10.2	17,831	18,033	+1.1	283,823	284,911	+.4
Embezzlement	10,771	10,917	+1.4	84	88	+4.8	753	929	+23.4	10,018	9,988	−.3
Stolen property; buying, receiving, possessing	121,487	122,542	+.9	9,583	8,632	−9.9	32,207	31,436	−2.4	89,280	91,106	+2.0
Vandalism	227,922	222,376	−2.4	53,186	47,137	−11.4	107,593	99,672	−7.4	120,329	122,704	+2.0
Weapons; carrying, possessing, etc.	198,565	180,080	−9.3	15,079	12,741	−15.5	47,722	41,875	−12.3	150,843	138,205	−8.4
Prostitution and commercialized vice	81,420	80,137	−1.6	103	179	+73.8	932	1,033	+10.8	80,488	79,104	−1.7
Sex offenses (except forcible rape and prostitution)	73,768	69,362	−6.0	6,635	6,029	−9.1	12,831	11,767	−8.3	60,937	57,595	−5.5
Drug abuse violations	1,035,224	1,106,261	+6.9	20,028	24,094	+20.3	120,912	142,475	+17.8	914,312	963,786	+5.4
Gambling	15,022	15,463	+2.9	222	208	−6.3	1,365	1,253	−8.2	13,657	14,210	+4.0
Offenses against family and children	82,516	95,924	+16.2	1,289	1,338	+3.8	3,756	4,387	+16.8	78,760	91,537	+16.2
Driving under the influence	1,019,553	973,842	−4.5	290	308	+6.2	10,044	10,069	+.2	1,009,509	963,773	−4.5
Liquor laws	377,215	417,587	+10.7	8,626	8,704	+.9	81,014	83,434	+3.0	296,201	334,153	+12.8
Drunkenness	499,158	498,985	4	1,776	2,207	+24.3	13,022	14,606	+12.2	486,136	484,379	−.4
Disorderly conduct	520,794	534,048	+2.5	43,151	44,738	+3.7	119,736	126,002	+5.2	401,058	408,046	+1.7
Vagrancy	19,411	19,949	+2.8	694	556	−19.9	2,818	2,703	−4.1	16,593	17,246	+3.9
All other offenses (except traffic)	2,796,806	2,806,515	+.3	87,196	86,241	−1.1	308,956	305,837	−1.0	2,487,850	2,500,678	+.5
Suspicion (not included in totals)	10,464	8,657	−17.3	433	374	−13.6	1,492	1,409	−5.6	8,972	7,248	−19.2
Curfew and loitering law violations	97,911	111,715	+14.1	29,239	32,026	+9.5	97,911	111,715	+14.1	—	—	—
Runaways	185,646	181,562	−2.2	83,799	79,562	−5.1	185,646	181,562	−2.2	—	—	—

[1]Violent crimes are offenses of murder, forcible rape, robbery, and aggravated assault.
[2]Property crimes are offenses of burglary, larceny–theft, motor vehicle theft, and arson.
[3]Includes arson.
[4]Less than one-tenth of 1 percent.

216

Table 37.—Total Arrest Trends, Sex, 1994–1995

[8,587 agencies; 1995 estimated population 184,792,000; 1994 estimated population 183,306,000]

Offense charged	Males						Females					
	Total			Under 18			Total			Under 18		
	1994	1995	Percent change	1994	1995	Percent change	1994	1995	Percent change	1994	1995	Percent change
TOTAL	8,646,297	8,693,921	+.6	1,492,967	1,492,388	1	2,146,853	2,231,599	+3.9	494,242	511,269	+3.4
Murder and nonnegligent manslaughter	15,566	14,699	−5.6	2,744	2,345	−14.5	1,704	1,515	−11.1	173	153	−11.6
Forcible rape	26,504	25,019	−5.6	4,125	3,956	−4.1	278	290	+4.3	79	82	+3.8
Robbery	124,744	122,134	−2.1	40,044	39,626	−1.0	12,678	12,633	−.4	4,031	4,029	1
Aggravated assault	346,140	345,748	−.1	52,209	49,871	−4.5	68,972	74,522	+8.0	11,807	12,160	+3.0
Burglary	261,636	249,139	−4.8	94,397	88,870	−5.9	31,092	31,331	+.8	10,063	9,704	−3.6
Larceny–theft	742,767	744,793	+.3	251,237	251,659	+.2	368,823	371,699	+.8	117,918	120,911	+2.5
Motor vehicle theft	134,429	125,362	−6.7	57,778	51,896	−10.2	18,890	18,949	+.3	9,338	8,891	−4.8
Arson	12,523	11,962	−4.5	7,109	6,551	−7.8	2,147	2,262	+5.4	993	910	−8.4
Violent crime[2]	512,954	507,600	−1.0	99,122	95,798	−3.4	83,632	88,960	+6.4	16,090	16,424	+2.1
Property crime[3]	1,151,355	1,131,256	−1.7	410,521	398,976	−2.8	420,952	424,241	+.8	138,312	140,416	+1.5
Crime Index total[4]	1,664,309	1,638,856	−1.5	509,643	494,774	−2.9	504,584	513,201	+1.7	154,402	156,840	+1.6
Other assaults	712,679	752,937	+5.6	111,690	113,696	+1.8	163,829	183,757	+12.2	40,200	43,306	+7.7
Forgery and counterfeiting	53,625	55,613	+3.7	3,974	4,020	+1.2	29,281	30,947	+5.7	2,251	2,233	−.8
Fraud	184,309	179,184	−2.8	13,226	13,293	+.5	117,345	123,760	+5.5	4,605	4,740	+2.9
Embezzlement	6,296	6,107	−3.0	486	535	+10.1	4,475	4,810	+7.5	267	394	+47.6
Stolen property; buying, receiving, possessing	105,233	105,164	−.1	28,550	27,628	−3.2	16,254	17,378	+6.9	3,657	3,808	+4.1
Vandalism	198,542	192,270	−3.2	96,552	88,989	−7.8	29,380	30,106	+2.5	11,041	10,683	−3.2
Weapons; carrying, possessing, etc.	182,630	165,780	−9.2	43,914	38,461	−12.4	15,935	14,300	−10.3	3,808	3,414	−10.3
Prostitution and commercialized vice	31,343	31,241	−.3	487	532	+9.2	50,077	48,896	−2.4	445	501	+12.6
Sex offenses (except forcible rape and prostitution)	67,466	63,729	−5.5	11,857	10,910	−8.0	6,302	5,633	−10.6	974	857	−12.0
Drug abuse violations	864,637	921,262	+6.5	106,742	124,540	+16.7	170,587	184,999	+8.4	14,170	17,935	+26.6
Gambling	12,788	13,102	+2.5	1,301	1,193	−8.3	2,234	2,361	+5.7	64	60	−6.3
Offenses against family and children	65,261	76,319	+16.9	2,414	2,779	+15.1	17,255	19,605	+13.6	1,342	1,608	+19.8
Driving under the influence	875,350	832,193	−4.9	8,606	8,504	−1.2	144,203	141,649	−1.8	1,438	1,565	+8.8
Liquor laws	303,279	338,939	+11.8	57,590	59,267	+2.9	73,936	78,648	+6.4	23,424	24,167	+3.2
Drunkenness	442,267	439,991	−.5	10,999	12,285	+11.7	56,891	58,994	+3.7	2,023	2,321	+14.7
Disorderly conduct	411,341	417,933	+1.6	91,398	95,045	+4.0	109,453	116,115	+6.1	28,338	30,957	+9.2
Vagrancy	15,451	16,079	+4.1	2,371	2,403	+1.3	3,960	3,870	−2.3	447	300	−32.9
All other offenses (except traffic)	2,299,883	2,291,082	−.4	241,559	237,394	−1.7	496,923	515,433	+3.7	67,397	68,443	+1.6
Suspicion (not included in totals)	8,839	7,353	−16.8	1,200	1,120	−6.7	1,625	1,304	−19.8	292	289	−1.0
Curfew and loitering law violations	69,705	78,676	+12.9	69,705	78,676	+12.9	28,206	33,039	+17.1	28,206	33,039	+17.1
Runaways	79,903	77,464	−3.1	79,903	77,464	−3.1	105,743	104,098	−1.6	105,743	104,098	−1.6

[1] Less than one-tenth of 1 percent.
[2] Violent crimes are offenses of murder, forcible rape, robbery, and aggravated assault.
[3] Property crimes are offenses of burglary, larceny–theft, motor vehicle theft, and arson.
[4] Includes arson.

Table 38.—Total Arrests, Distribution by Age, 1995

[9,498 agencies; 1995 estimated population 196,440,000]

Offense charged	Total all ages	Ages under 15	Ages under 18	Ages 18 and over	Under 10	10–12	13–14	15	16	17	18	19	20	21
TOTAL	11,416,346	711,348	2,084,428	9,331,918	34,704	159,707	516,937	416,617	468,431	488,032	513,215	477,964	440,740	402,812
Percent distribution1 ..	100.0	6.2	18.3	81.7	.3	1.4	4.5	3.6	4.1	4.3	4.5	4.2	3.9	3.5
Murder and nonnegligent manslaughter	16,701	346	2,560	14,141	55	27	264	445	763	1,006	1,340	1,205	1,107	924
Forcible rape	26,561	1,542	4,190	22,371	72	372	1,098	752	887	1,009	1,180	1,095	1,012	946
Robbery	137,811	12,501	44,508	93,303	324	2,219	9,958	9,416	11,003	11,588	10,709	8,204	6,560	5,289
Aggravated assault.........	438,157	20,558	64,334	373,823	960	4,897	14,701	12,316	15,082	16,378	17,259	15,845	15,393	15,392
Burglary	292,315	40,150	102,722	189,593	2,530	10,013	27,607	20,362	21,456	20,754	19,524	14,458	10,935	9,032
Larceny–theft	1,164,371	170,945	388,533	775,838	8,719	48,080	114,146	72,784	74,699	70,105	62,439	47,477	37,374	31,291
Motor vehicle theft	149,053	17,717	62,545	86,508	203	2,083	15,431	15,791	15,637	13,400	10,702	7,822	5,986	4,945
Arson	14,965	5,268	7,834	7,131	952	1,764	2,552	1,082	812	672	543	441	339	283
Violent crime[2]	619,230	34,947	115,592	503,638	1,411	7,515	26,021	22,929	27,735	29,981	30,488	26,349	24,072	22,551
Percent distribution[1]	100.0	5.6	18.7	81.3	.2	1.2	4.2	3.7	4.5	4.8	4.9	4.3	3.9	3.6
Property crime[3]	1,620,704	234,080	561,634	1,059,070	12,404	61,940	159,736	110,019	112,604	104,931	93,208	70,198	54,634	45,551
Percent distribution[1]	100.0	14.4	34.7	65.3	.8	3.8	9.9	6.8	6.9	6.5	5.8	4.3	3.4	2.8
Crime Index total[4]	2,239,934	269,027	677,226	1,562,708	13,815	69,455	185,757	132,948	140,339	134,912	123,696	96,547	78,706	68,102
Percent distribution[1]	100.0	12.0	30.2	69.8	.6	3.1	8.3	5.9	6.3	6.0	5.5	4.3	3.5	3.0
Other assaults.............	975,418	67,446	163,068	812,350	3,863	17,809	45,774	31,064	32,379	32,179	31,317	30,395	30,377	31,902
Forgery and counterfeiting ...	91,991	844	6,640	85,351	58	140	646	938	1,878	2,980	4,382	4,600	4,389	3,965
Fraud	320,046	4,758	18,420	301,626	87	708	3,963	4,580	3,721	5,361	8,972	11,472	12,550	12,789
Embezzlement	11,605	93	955	10,650	8	17	68	50	278	534	624	659	584	589
Stolen property; buying, receiving, possessing......	127,844	9,046	32,851	94,993	327	1,612	7,107	6,660	8,230	8,915	9,441	7,610	6,079	5,185
Vandalism................	232,702	49,308	104,425	128,277	4,786	14,649	29,873	18,582	19,302	17,233	13,048	9,529	7,462	6,930
Weapons; carrying, possessing, etc.	187,237	13,135	43,211	144,026	585	2,857	9,693	8,384	10,017	11,675	12,610	10,617	9,278	8,518
Prostitution and commercialized vice	81,064	181	1,044	80,020	31	25	125	152	247	464	1,369	1,848	2,015	2,308
Sex offenses (except forcible rape and prostitution)	72,272	6,322	12,307	59,965	484	1,768	4,070	2,191	1,887	1,907	2,089	1,976	1,943	1,853
Drug abuse violations	1,144,228	24,847	147,107	997,121	545	2,614	21,688	27,553	41,291	53,416	66,258	60,030	53,355	47,263
Gambling	15,676	217	1,298	14,378	21	23	173	212	364	505	598	586	604	472
Offenses against family and children	104,952	1,536	5,040	99,912	116	289	1,131	1,121	1,186	1,197	2,513	2,343	2,676	3,027
Driving under the influence ..	1,033,280	324	10,749	1,022,531	150	20	154	490	2,794	7,141	16,566	21,779	26,344	35,299
Liquor laws	435,311	9,166	87,843	347,468	147	729	8,290	13,531	25,600	39,546	58,099	55,170	45,987	14,661
Drunkenness	527,200	2,268	15,337	511,863	143	213	1,912	2,485	3,481	7,103	12,821	13,382	13,820	17,185
Disorderly conduct	561,642	46,221	130,467	431,175	1,668	10,308	34,245	26,477	28,605	29,164	27,970	24,243	22,101	23,134
Vagrancy	20,521	573	2,776	17,745	14	99	460	496	790	917	1,209	972	805	681
All other offenses (except traffic)	2,919,723	89,574	317,495	2,602,228	5,280	17,345	66,949	60,953	74,251	92,717	119,281	123,896	121,365	118,670
Suspicion	9,058	412	1,527	7,531	26	65	321	309	376	430	352	310	300	279
Curfew and loitering law violations	114,946	33,052	114,946	—	553	4,915	27,584	27,107	31,523	23,264	—	—	—	—
Runaways.................	189,696	82,998	189,696	—	1,997	14,047	66,954	50,334	39,892	16,472	—	—	—	—

See footnotes at end of table.

218

Table 38.—Total Arrests, Distribution by Age, 1995 — Continued

Offense charged	Age											
	22	23	24	25–29	30–34	35–39	40–44	45–49	50–54	55–59	60–64	65 and over
TOTAL	383,620	375,051	384,642	1,657,000	1,632,047	1,308,829	815,217	451,759	226,410	119,031	68,039	75,542
Percent distribution[1]	3.4	3.3	3.4	14.5	14.3	11.5	7.1	4.0	2.0	1.0	.6	.7
Murder and nonnegligent manslaughter	860	711	722	2,380	1,643	1,209	828	479	273	207	104	149
Forcible rape	886	892	840	4,084	4,021	3,183	1,837	1,059	578	321	202	235
Robbery	4,685	4,284	4,200	17,631	14,723	9,488	4,542	1,790	670	255	124	149
Aggravated assault	15,064	15,064	15,555	69,048	69,089	54,271	33,117	18,245	9,289	4,852	2,830	3,510
Burglary	7,887	7,495	7,742	34,044	33,265	24,001	12,484	5,211	2,015	720	349	431
Larceny–theft	28,159	27,658	28,217	128,444	131,177	106,898	68,051	35,945	17,555	9,478	5,953	9,722
Motor vehicle theft	4,243	3,958	3,895	15,877	13,051	8,401	4,317	1,959	708	337	164	143
Arson	286	263	225	1,056	1,117	960	682	453	209	115	75	84
Violent crime[2]	21,495	20,951	21,317	93,143	89,476	68,151	40,324	21,573	10,810	5,635	3,260	4,043
Percent distribution[1]	3.5	3.4	3.4	15.0	14.4	11.0	6.5	3.5	1.7	.9	.5	.7
Property crime[3]	40,575	39,374	40,079	179,421	178,610	140,260	85,534	43,568	20,487	10,650	6,541	10,380
Percent distribution[1]	2.5	2.4	2.5	11.1	11.0	8.7	5.3	2.7	1.3	.7	.4	.6
Crime Index total[4]	62,070	60,325	61,396	272,564	268,086	208,411	125,858	65,141	31,297	16,285	9,801	14,423
Percent distribution[1]	2.8	2.7	2.7	12.2	12.0	9.3	5.6	2.9	1.4	.7	.4	.6
Other assaults	32,303	33,180	35,252	156,348	158,300	122,988	72,231	38,293	18,550	9,366	5,341	6,207
Forgery and counterfeiting	3,925	3,732	4,054	17,099	15,976	11,652	6,348	2,945	1,255	559	233	237
Fraud	13,179	13,144	13,818	60,526	55,117	43,000	27,561	14,980	7,267	3,410	1,752	2,089
Embezzlement	544	549	496	1,970	1,705	1,242	766	449	288	103	43	39
Stolen property; buying, receiving, possessing	4,633	4,227	4,273	17,097	14,808	10,596	5,974	2,742	1,201	597	278	252
Vandalism	6,113	5,634	5,783	23,083	20,462	14,536	7,905	3,919	1,823	878	502	670
Weapons; carrying, possessing, etc.	7,650	7,158	6,534	24,239	19,954	15,014	9,560	5,693	3,130	1,776	1,095	1,200
Prostitution and commercialized vice	2,553	2,820	3,209	17,818	19,113	13,816	6,827	3,207	1,414	751	418	534
Sex offenses (except forcible rape and prostitution)	1,832	1,790	1,886	9,344	10,658	9,133	6,355	4,150	2,568	1,655	1,120	1,613
Drug abuse violations	44,340	41,960	42,627	183,191	178,673	139,456	79,297	36,876	13,953	5,558	2,435	1,849
Gambling	482	454	425	1,869	1,896	1,858	1,433	1,293	787	697	444	480
Offenses against family and children	3,211	3,446	4,087	18,963	21,231	18,043	10,497	5,204	2,431	1,071	588	581
Driving under the influence	36,957	38,372	41,297	181,215	188,496	159,994	111,489	72,046	40,941	23,558	13,958	14,220
Liquor laws	11,225	9,602	8,837	33,609	31,741	28,159	20,612	13,297	7,540	4,372	2,405	2,152
Drunkenness	16,704	16,501	16,980	77,283	89,898	85,704	62,448	39,189	22,496	12,631	7,668	7,153
Disorderly conduct	20,949	19,384	19,310	74,509	70,471	56,163	33,544	18,831	9,545	4,965	2,897	3,159
Vagrancy	534	571	547	2,742	2,977	2,758	1,833	961	616	213	170	156
All other offenses (except traffic)	114,135	111,905	113,509	482,244	461,033	365,062	223,934	122,168	59,161	30,511	16,855	18,499
Suspicion	281	297	322	1,287	1,452	1,244	745	375	147	75	36	29
Curfew and loitering law violations	—	—	—	—	—	—	—	—	—	—	—	—
Runaways	—	—	—	—	—	—	—	—	—	—	—	—

[1]Because of rounding, the percentages may not add to total.
[2]Violent crimes are offenses of murder, forcible rape, robbery, and aggravated assault.
[3]Property crimes are offenses of burglary, larceny–theft, motor vehicle theft, and arson.
[4]Includes arson.

219

Table 39.—Male Arrests, Distribution by Age, 1995

[9,498 agencies; 1995 estimated population 196,440,000]

Offense charged	Total all ages	Ages under 15	Ages under 18	Ages 18 and over	Age									
					Under 10	10–12	13–14	15	16	17	18	19	20	21
TOTAL	9,084,133	502,047	1,551,874	7,532,259	28,745	119,444	353,858	299,118	356,833	393,876	426,505	396,205	364,605	333,821
Percent distribution1 . .	100.0	5.5	17.1	82.9	.3	1.3	3.9	3.3	3.9	4.3	4.7	4.4	4.0	3.7
Murder and nonnegligent manslaughter	15,120	308	2,402	12,718	52	22	234	420	710	964	1,272	1,137	1,032	865
Forcible rape	26,249	1,497	4,104	22,145	70	360	1,067	736	874	997	1,176	1,086	1,007	938
Robbery	124,942	11,011	40,430	84,512	307	1,965	8,739	8,444	10,134	10,841	10,056	7,699	6,102	4,914
Aggravated assault	360,522	15,989	51,743	308,779	847	3,993	11,149	9,609	12,298	13,847	14,738	13,333	12,928	12,947
Burglary	259,882	35,519	92,630	167,252	2,223	8,827	24,469	18,447	19,667	18,997	18,001	13,276	9,886	8,148
Larceny–theft	776,902	115,643	262,662	514,240	6,830	33,881	74,932	48,616	50,426	47,977	43,447	32,295	24,650	20,378
Motor vehicle theft	129,455	14,156	53,330	76,125	185	1,680	12,291	13,387	13,680	12,107	9,857	7,200	5,434	4,461
Arson	12,609	4,642	6,886	5,723	885	1,584	2,173	952	705	587	483	390	277	238
Violent crime[2]	526,833	28,805	98,679	428,154	1,276	6,340	21,189	19,209	24,016	26,649	27,242	23,255	21,069	19,664
Percent distribution[1]	100.0	5.5	18.7	81.3	.2	1.2	4.0	3.6	4.6	5.1	5.2	4.4	4.0	3.7
Property crime[3]	1,178,848	169,960	415,508	763,340	10,123	45,972	113,865	81,402	84,478	79,668	71,788	53,161	40,247	33,225
Percent distribution[1]	100.0	14.4	35.2	64.8	.9	3.9	9.7	6.9	7.2	6.8	6.1	4.5	3.4	2.8
Crime Index total[4]	1,705,681	198,765	514,187	1,191,494	11,399	52,312	135,054	100,611	108,494	106,317	99,030	76,416	61,316	52,889
Percent distribution[1]	100.0	11.7	30.1	69.9	.7	3.1	7.9	5.9	6.4	6.2	5.8	4.5	3.6	3.1
Other assaults	784,016	47,711	118,100	665,916	3,242	13,429	31,040	21,801	23,740	24,848	24,722	24,200	24,501	25,683
Forgery and counterfeiting . . .	58,990	495	4,292	54,698	33	95	367	588	1,206	2,003	2,836	2,965	2,959	2,712
Fraud	188,842	3,430	13,552	175,290	57	519	2,854	3,516	2,786	3,820	5,751	6,870	7,436	7,269
Embezzlement	6,545	68	553	5,992	4	16	48	34	151	300	337	374	313	297
Stolen property; buying, receiving, possessing	109,680	7,730	28,837	80,843	293	1,387	6,050	5,767	7,307	8,033	8,480	6,784	5,381	4,554
Vandalism	201,113	43,687	93,220	107,893	4,393	13,129	26,165	16,602	17,385	15,546	11,731	8,491	6,474	6,007
Weapons; carrying, possessing, etc.	172,358	11,669	39,704	132,654	553	2,530	8,586	7,635	9,361	11,039	12,007	10,136	8,808	8,056
Prostitution and commercialized vice	31,573	103	540	31,033	15	19	69	78	133	226	459	589	764	874
Sex offenses (except forcible rape and prostitution)	66,508	5,796	11,413	55,095	422	1,617	3,757	2,036	1,780	1,801	1,904	1,793	1,758	1,655
Drug abuse violations	953,499	20,089	128,493	825,006	484	2,014	17,591	23,723	36,699	47,982	59,453	53,681	47,559	41,816
Gambling	13,287	200	1,237	12,050	14	22	164	204	345	488	565	552	542	435
Offenses against family and children	83,735	870	3,172	80,563	69	184	617	686	777	839	1,962	1,880	2,079	2,387
Driving under the influence . .	882,735	260	9,080	873,655	132	15	113	388	2,355	6,077	14,430	19,069	23,239	30,727
Liquor laws	352,973	5,074	62,395	290,578	99	403	4,572	8,594	18,431	30,296	45,472	43,945	37,441	12,662
Drunkenness	464,742	1,647	12,907	451,835	117	154	1,376	1,968	2,915	6,377	11,623	12,151	12,634	15,730
Disorderly conduct	439,606	33,073	98,412	341,194	1,346	7,704	24,023	19,467	22,161	23,711	23,204	20,045	18,034	19,091
Vagrancy	16,532	490	2,463	14,069	12	90	388	428	706	839	1,077	832	696	584
All other offenses (except traffic)	2,382,236	65,187	246,311	2,135,925	4,208	13,347	47,632	45,350	58,655	77,119	101,151	105,154	102,399	100,149
Suspicion	7,681	309	1,205	6,476	22	52	235	237	297	362	311	278	272	244
Curfew and loitering law violations	80,935	21,633	80,935	—	429	3,316	17,888	18,859	22,940	17,503	—	—	—	—
Runaways	80,866	33,761	80,866	—	1,402	7,090	25,269	20,546	18,209	8,350	—	—	—	—

See footnotes at end of table.

Table 39.—Male Arrests, Distribution by Age, 1995 — Continued

Offense charged	Age											
	22	23	24	25–29	30–34	35–39	40–44	45–49	50–54	55–59	60–64	65 and over
TOTAL	315,815	305,532	310,426	1,315,352	1,274,905	1,035,285	661,476	376,040	191,994	102,562	58,843	62,893
Percent distribution[1]	3.5	3.4	3.4	14.5	14.0	11.4	7.3	4.1	2.1	1.1	.6	.7
Murder and nonnegligent manslaughter	811	660	666	2,127	1,393	1,023	689	399	239	181	94	130
Forcible rape	878	877	832	4,044	3,972	3,146	1,811	1,050	575	318	202	233
Robbery	4,340	3,901	3,804	15,719	12,929	8,294	4,036	1,614	621	239	116	128
Aggravated assault	12,592	12,453	12,885	56,365	55,605	44,046	27,506	15,492	8,015	4,224	2,533	3,117
Burglary	7,019	6,610	6,775	29,558	28,821	20,805	10,849	4,510	1,722	617	292	363
Larceny–theft	18,080	17,647	18,109	82,856	86,216	72,284	47,087	24,545	11,320	6,075	3,591	5,660
Motor vehicle theft	3,781	3,494	3,381	13,619	11,015	7,161	3,760	1,730	649	306	154	123
Arson	228	215	177	849	857	719	542	353	172	96	59	68
Violent crime[2]	18,621	17,891	18,187	78,255	73,899	56,509	34,042	18,555	9,450	4,962	2,945	3,608
Percent distribution[1]	3.5	3.4	3.5	14.9	14.0	10.7	6.5	3.5	1.8	.9	.6	.7
Property crime[3]	29,108	27,966	28,442	126,882	126,909	100,969	62,238	31,138	13,863	7,094	4,096	6,214
Percent distribution[1]	2.5	2.4	2.4	10.8	10.8	8.6	5.3	2.6	1.2	.6	.3	.5
Crime Index total[4]	47,729	45,857	46,629	205,137	200,808	157,478	96,280	49,693	23,313	12,056	7,041	9,822
Percent distribution[1]	2.8	2.7	2.7	12.0	11.8	9.2	5.6	2.9	1.4	.7	.4	.6
Other assaults	26,148	27,149	28,897	127,774	128,693	101,435	60,433	32,372	15,876	8,108	4,619	5,306
Forgery and counterfeiting	2,599	2,413	2,563	10,794	9,800	7,302	4,120	2,006	875	400	173	181
Fraud	7,583	7,414	7,641	33,944	31,348	24,954	16,678	9,156	4,534	2,248	1,161	1,303
Embezzlement	277	261	280	1,134	1,009	742	441	267	135	70	27	28
Stolen property; buying, receiving, possessing.	4,008	3,575	3,611	14,203	12,030	8,744	5,065	2,356	1,055	537	242	218
Vandalism	5,228	4,746	4,783	18,943	16,676	11,763	6,560	3,194	1,558	740	447	552
Weapons; carrying, possessing, etc.	7,203	6,655	6,034	22,132	17,795	13,343	8,591	5,235	2,867	1,661	1,019	1,112
Prostitution and commercialized vice	979	1,056	1,252	6,216	6,092	4,941	3,082	2,020	1,131	671	391	516
Sex offenses (except forcible rape and prostitution)	1,635	1,594	1,668	8,309	9,597	8,423	5,953	3,968	2,505	1,627	1,112	1,594
Drug abuse violations	38,716	36,000	35,910	148,745	138,687	108,905	63,870	30,885	12,083	4,894	2,182	1,620
Gambling	435	388	373	1,535	1,493	1,465	1,141	1,047	655	583	401	440
Offenses against family and children	2,574	2,749	3,300	15,189	16,867	14,434	8,721	4,452	2,108	909	476	476
Driving under the influence	32,249	33,417	35,644	155,664	156,904	133,216	94,056	62,190	36,101	21,169	12,695	12,885
Liquor laws	9,876	8,351	7,703	29,089	27,083	24,145	17,954	11,899	6,844	3,989	2,180	1,945
Drunkenness	15,213	14,876	15,168	67,708	76,495	73,501	54,905	35,309	20,716	11,803	7,272	6,731
Disorderly conduct	17,128	15,609	15,241	57,251	52,931	43,095	26,651	15,504	8,013	4,239	2,489	2,669
Vagrancy	426	455	404	1,837	2,174	2,144	1,517	860	571	194	159	139
All other offenses (except traffic)	95,565	92,708	93,045	388,683	367,197	294,196	184,815	103,293	50,922	26,595	14,725	15,328
Suspicion	244	259	280	1,065	1,226	1,059	643	334	132	69	32	28
Curfew and loitering law violations	—	—	—	—	—	—	—	—	—	—	—	—
Runaways	—	—	—	—	—	—	—	—	—	—	—	—

[1]Because of rounding, the percentages may not add to total.
[2]Violent crimes are offenses of murder, forcible rape, robbery, and aggravated assault.
[3]Property crimes are offenses of burglary, larceny–theft, motor vehicle theft, and arson.
[4]Includes arson.

Table 40.—Female Arrests, Distribution by Age, 1995

[9,498 agencies; 1995 estimated population 196,440,000]

Offense charged	Total all ages	Ages under 15	Ages under 18	Ages 18 and over	Age									
					Under 10	10–12	13–14	15	16	17	18	19	20	21
TOTAL	2,332,213	209,301	532,554	1,799,659	5,959	40,263	163,079	117,499	111,598	94,156	86,710	81,759	76,135	68,991
Percent distribution1 ..	100.0	9.0	22.8	77.2	.3	1.7	7.0	5.0	4.8	4.0	3.7	3.5	3.3	3.0
Murder and nonnegligent manslaughter	1,581	38	158	1,423	3	5	30	25	53	42	68	68	75	59
Forcible rape	312	45	86	226	2	12	31	16	13	12	4	9	5	8
Robbery	12,869	1,490	4,078	8,791	17	254	1,219	972	869	747	653	505	458	375
Aggravated assault.........	77,635	4,569	12,591	65,044	113	904	3,552	2,707	2,784	2,531	2,521	2,512	2,465	2,445
Burglary	32,433	4,631	10,092	22,341	307	1,186	3,138	1,915	1,789	1,757	1,523	1,182	1,049	884
Larceny–theft	387,469	55,302	125,871	261,598	1,889	14,199	39,214	24,168	24,273	22,128	18,992	15,182	12,724	10,913
Motor vehicle theft	19,598	3,561	9,215	10,383	18	403	3,140	2,404	1,957	1,293	845	622	552	484
Arson	2,356	626	948	1,408	67	180	379	130	107	85	60	51	62	45
Violent crime2	92,397	6,142	16,913	75,484	135	1,175	4,832	3,720	3,719	3,332	3,246	3,094	3,003	2,887
Percent distribution1	100.0	6.6	18.3	81.7	.1	1.3	5.2	4.0	4.0	3.6	3.5	3.3	3.3	3.1
Property crime3	441,856	64,120	146,126	295,730	2,281	15,968	45,871	28,617	28,126	25,263	21,420	17,037	14,387	12,326
Percent distribution1	100.0	14.5	33.1	66.9	.5	3.6	10.4	6.5	6.4	5.7	4.8	3.9	3.3	2.8
Crime Index total4	534,253	70,262	163,039	371,214	2,416	17,143	50,703	32,337	31,845	28,595	24,666	20,131	17,390	15,213
Percent distribution1	100.0	13.2	30.5	69.5	.5	3.2	9.5	6.1	6.0	5.4	4.6	3.8	3.3	2.8
Other assaults..............	191,402	19,735	44,968	146,434	621	4,380	14,734	9,263	8,639	7,331	6,595	6,195	5,876	6,219
Forgery and counterfeiting ...	33,001	349	2,348	30,653	25	45	279	350	672	977	1,546	1,635	1,430	1,253
Fraud	131,204	1,328	4,868	126,336	30	189	1,109	1,064	935	1,541	3,221	4,602	5,114	5,520
Embezzlement	5,060	25	402	4,658	4	1	20	16	127	234	287	285	271	292
Stolen property; buying, receiving, possessing.....	18,164	1,316	4,014	14,150	34	225	1,057	893	923	882	961	826	698	631
Vandalism.................	31,589	5,621	11,205	20,384	393	1,520	3,708	1,980	1,917	1,687	1,317	1,038	988	923
Weapons; carrying, possessing, etc.	14,879	1,466	3,507	11,372	32	327	1,107	749	656	636	603	481	470	462
Prostitution and commercialized vice	49,491	78	504	48,987	16	6	56	74	114	238	910	1,259	1,251	1,434
Sex offenses (except forcible rape and prostitution)	5,764	526	894	4,870	62	151	313	155	107	106	185	183	185	198
Drug abuse violations	190,729	4,758	18,614	172,115	61	600	4,097	3,830	4,592	5,434	6,805	6,349	5,796	5,447
Gambling	2,389	17	61	2,328	7	1	9	8	19	17	33	34	62	37
Offenses against family and children	21,217	666	1,868	19,349	47	105	514	435	409	358	551	463	597	640
Driving under the influence ..	150,545	64	1,669	148,876	18	5	41	102	439	1,064	2,136	2,710	3,105	4,572
Liquor laws	82,338	4,092	25,448	56,890	48	326	3,718	4,937	7,169	9,250	12,627	11,225	8,546	1,999
Drunkenness	62,458	621	2,430	60,028	26	59	536	517	566	726	1,198	1,231	1,186	1,455
Disorderly conduct	122,036	13,148	32,055	89,981	322	2,604	10,222	7,010	6,444	5,453	4,766	4,198	4,067	4,043
Vagrancy	3,989	83	313	3,676	2	9	72	68	84	78	132	140	109	97
All other offenses (except traffic)	537,487	24,387	71,184	466,303	1,072	3,998	19,317	15,603	15,596	15,598	18,130	18,742	18,966	18,521
Suspicion	1,377	103	322	1,055	4	13	86	72	79	68	41	32	28	35
Curfew and loitering law violations	34,011	11,419	34,011	—	124	1,599	9,696	8,248	8,583	5,761	—	—	—	—
Runaways	108,830	49,237	108,830	—	595	6,957	41,685	29,788	21,683	8,122	—	—	—	—

See footnotes at end of table.

Table 40.—Female Arrests, Distribution by Age, 1995 — Continued

Offense charged	Age											
	22	23	24	25–29	30–34	35–39	40–44	45–49	50–54	55–59	60–64	65 and over
TOTAL	**67,805**	**69,519**	**74,216**	**341,648**	**357,142**	**273,544**	**153,741**	**75,719**	**34,416**	**16,469**	**9,196**	**12,649**
Percent distribution[1]	2.9	3.0	3.2	14.6	15.3	11.7	6.6	3.2	1.5	.7	.4	.5
Murder and nonnegligent manslaughter	49	51	56	253	250	186	139	80	34	26	10	19
Forcible rape	8	15	8	40	49	37	26	9	3	3	—	2
Robbery	345	383	396	1,912	1,794	1,194	506	176	49	16	8	21
Aggravated assault	2,472	2,611	2,670	12,683	13,484	10,225	5,611	2,753	1,274	628	297	393
Burglary	868	885	967	4,486	4,444	3,196	1,635	701	293	103	57	68
Larceny–theft	10,079	10,011	10,108	45,588	44,961	34,614	20,964	11,400	6,235	3,403	2,362	4,062
Motor vehicle theft	462	464	514	2,258	2,036	1,240	557	229	59	31	10	20
Arson	58	48	48	207	260	241	140	100	37	19	16	16
Violent crime[2]	2,874	3,060	3,130	14,888	15,577	11,642	6,282	3,018	1,360	673	315	435
Percent distribution[1]	3.1	3.3	3.4	16.1	16.9	12.6	6.8	3.3	1.5	.7	.3	.5
Property crime[3]	11,467	11,408	11,637	52,539	51,701	39,291	23,296	12,430	6,624	3,556	2,445	4,166
Percent distribution[1]	2.6	2.6	2.6	11.9	11.7	8.9	5.3	2.8	1.5	.8	.6	.9
Crime Index total[4]	14,341	14,468	14,767	67,427	67,278	50,933	29,578	15,448	7,984	4,229	2,760	4,601
Percent distribution[1]	2.7	2.7	2.8	12.6	12.6	9.5	5.5	2.9	1.5	.8	.5	.9
Other assaults	6,155	6,031	6,355	28,574	29,607	21,553	11,798	5,921	2,674	1,258	722	901
Forgery and counterfeiting	1,326	1,319	1,491	6,305	6,176	4,350	2,228	939	380	159	60	56
Fraud	5,596	5,730	6,177	26,582	23,769	18,046	10,883	5,824	2,733	1,162	591	786
Embezzlement	267	288	216	836	696	500	325	182	153	33	16	11
Stolen property; buying, receiving, possessing	625	652	662	2,894	2,778	1,852	909	386	146	60	36	34
Vandalism	885	888	1,000	4,140	3,786	2,773	1,345	725	265	138	55	118
Weapons; carrying, possessing, etc.	447	503	500	2,107	2,159	1,671	969	458	263	115	76	88
Prostitution and commercialized vice	1,574	1,764	1,957	11,602	13,021	8,875	3,745	1,187	283	80	27	18
Sex offenses (except forcible rape and prostitution)	197	196	218	1,035	1,061	710	402	182	63	28	8	19
Drug abuse violations	5,624	5,960	6,717	34,446	39,986	30,551	15,427	5,991	1,870	664	253	229
Gambling	47	66	52	334	403	393	292	246	132	114	43	40
Offenses against family and children	637	697	787	3,774	4,364	3,609	1,776	752	323	162	112	105
Driving under the influence	4,708	4,955	5,653	25,551	31,592	26,778	17,433	9,856	4,840	2,389	1,263	1,335
Liquor laws	1,349	1,251	1,134	4,520	4,658	4,014	2,658	1,398	696	383	225	207
Drunkenness	1,491	1,625	1,812	9,575	13,403	12,203	7,543	3,880	1,780	828	396	422
Disorderly conduct	3,821	3,775	4,069	17,258	17,540	13,068	6,893	3,327	1,532	726	408	490
Vagrancy	108	116	143	905	803	614	316	101	45	19	11	17
All other offenses (except traffic)	18,570	19,197	20,464	93,561	93,836	70,866	39,119	18,875	8,239	3,916	2,130	3,171
Suspicion	37	38	42	222	226	185	102	41	15	6	4	1
Curfew and loitering law violations	—	—	—	—	—	—	—	—	—	—	—	—
Runaways	—	—	—	—	—	—	—	—	—	—	—	—

[1]Because of rounding, the percentages may not add to total.
[2]Violent crimes are offenses of murder, forcible rape, robbery, and aggravated assault.
[3]Property crimes are offenses of burglary, larceny–theft, motor vehicle theft, and arson.
[4]Includes arson.

Table 41.—Total Arrests of Persons under 15, 18, 21, and 25 Years of Age, 1995

[9,498 agencies; 1995 estimated population 196,440,000]

Offense charged	Total all ages	Number of persons arrested				Percent of total all ages			
		Under 15	Under 18	Under 21	Under 25	Under 15	Under 18	Under 21	Under 25
TOTAL	11,416,346	711,348	2,084,428	3,516,347	5,062,472	6.2	18.3	30.8	44.3
Murder and nonnegligent manslaughter	16,701	346	2,560	6,212	9,429	2.1	15.3	37.2	56.5
Forcible rape	26,561	1,542	4,190	7,477	11,041	5.8	15.8	28.2	41.6
Robbery	137,811	12,501	44,508	69,981	88,439	9.1	32.3	50.8	64.2
Aggravated assault............................	438,157	20,558	64,334	112,831	173,906	4.7	14.7	25.8	39.7
Burglary	292,315	40,150	102,722	147,639	179,795	13.7	35.1	50.5	61.5
Larceny–theft................................	1,164,371	170,945	388,533	535,823	651,148	14.7	33.4	46.0	55.9
Motor vehicle theft	149,053	17,717	62,545	87,055	104,096	11.9	42.0	58.4	69.8
Arson	14,965	5,268	7,834	9,157	10,214	35.2	52.3	61.2	68.3
Violent crime[1]	619,230	34,947	115,592	196,501	282,815	5.6	18.7	31.7	45.7
Property crime[2]	1,620,704	234,080	561,634	779,674	945,253	14.4	34.7	48.1	58.3
Crime Index total[3]	2,239,934	269,027	677,226	976,175	1,228,068	12.0	30.2	43.6	54.8
Other assaults................................	975,418	67,446	163,068	255,157	387,794	6.9	16.7	26.2	39.8
Forgery and counterfeiting	91,991	844	6,640	20,011	35,687	.9	7.2	21.8	38.8
Fraud	320,046	4,758	18,420	51,414	104,344	1.5	5.8	16.1	32.6
Embezzlement	11,605	93	955	2,822	5,000	.8	8.2	24.3	43.1
Stolen property; buying, receiving, possessing	127,844	9,046	32,851	55,981	74,299	7.1	25.7	43.8	58.1
Vandalism....................................	232,702	49,308	104,425	134,464	158,924	21.2	44.9	57.8	68.3
Weapons; carrying, possessing, etc.	187,237	13,135	43,211	75,716	105,576	7.0	23.1	40.4	56.4
Prostitution and commercialized vice	81,064	181	1,044	6,276	17,166	.2	1.3	7.7	21.2
Sex offenses (except forcible rape and prostitution)	72,272	6,322	12,307	18,315	25,676	8.7	17.0	25.3	35.5
Drug abuse violations	1,144,228	24,847	147,107	326,750	502,940	2.2	12.9	28.6	44.0
Gambling	15,676	217	1,298	3,086	4,919	1.4	8.3	19.7	31.4
Offenses against family and children	104,952	1,536	5,040	12,572	26,343	1.5	4.8	12.0	25.1
Driving under the influence	1,033,280	324	10,749	75,438	227,363	[4]	1.0	7.3	22.0
Liquor laws	435,311	9,166	87,843	247,099	291,424	2.1	20.2	56.8	66.9
Drunkenness..................................	527,200	2,268	15,337	55,360	122,730	.4	2.9	10.5	23.3
Disorderly conduct	561,642	46,221	130,467	204,781	287,558	8.2	23.2	36.5	51.2
Vagrancy....................................	20,521	573	2,776	5,762	8,095	2.8	13.5	28.1	39.4
All other offenses (except traffic)	2,919,723	89,574	317,495	682,037	1,140,256	3.1	10.9	23.4	39.1
Suspicion	9,058	412	1,527	2,489	3,668	4.5	16.9	27.5	40.5
Curfew and loitering law violations	114,946	33,052	114,946	114,946	114,946	28.8	100.0	100.0	100.0
Runaways....................................	189,696	82,998	189,696	189,696	189,696	43.8	100.0	100.0	100.0

[1]Violent crimes are offenses of murder, forcible rape, robbery, and aggravated assault.
[2]Property crimes are offenses of burglary, larceny–theft, motor vehicle theft, and arson.
[3]Includes arson.
[4]Less than one-tenth of 1 percent.

224

Table 42.—Total Arrests, Distribution by Sex, 1995

[9,498 agencies; 1995 estimated population 196,440,000]

Offense charged	Number of persons arrested			Percent male	Percent female	Percent distribution[1]		
	Total	Male	Female			Total	Male	Female
TOTAL	11,416,346	9,084,133	2,332,213	79.6	20.4	100.0	100.0	100.0
Murder and nonnegligent manslaughter	16,701	15,120	1,581	90.5	9.5	.1	.2	.1
Forcible rape	26,561	26,249	312	98.8	1.2	.2	.3	[2]
Robbery	137,811	124,942	12,869	90.7	9.3	1.2	1.4	.6
Aggravated assault	438,157	360,522	77,635	82.3	17.7	3.8	4.0	3.3
Burglary	292,315	259,882	32,433	88.9	11.1	2.6	2.9	1.4
Larceny–theft	1,164,371	776,902	387,469	66.7	33.3	10.2	8.6	16.6
Motor vehicle theft	149,053	129,455	19,598	86.9	13.1	1.3	1.4	.8
Arson	14,965	12,609	2,356	84.3	15.7	.1	.1	.1
Violent crime[3]	619,230	526,833	92,397	85.1	14.9	5.4	5.8	4.0
Property crime[4]	1,620,704	1,178,848	441,856	72.7	27.3	14.2	13.0	18.9
Crime Index total[5]	2,239,934	1,705,681	534,253	76.1	23.9	19.6	18.8	22.9
Other assaults.............................	975,418	784,016	191,402	80.4	19.6	8.5	8.6	8.2
Forgery and counterfeiting	91,991	58,990	33,001	64.1	35.9	.8	.6	1.4
Fraud	320,046	188,842	131,204	59.0	41.0	2.8	2.1	5.6
Embezzlement	11,605	6,545	5,060	56.4	43.6	.1	.1	.2
Stolen property; buying, receiving, possessing	127,844	109,680	18,164	85.8	14.2	1.1	1.2	.8
Vandalism................................	232,702	201,113	31,589	86.4	13.6	2.0	2.2	1.4
Weapons; carrying, possessing, etc.	187,237	172,358	14,879	92.1	7.9	1.6	1.9	.6
Prostitution and commercialized vice	81,064	31,573	49,491	38.9	61.1	.7	.3	2.1
Sex offenses (except forcible rape and prostitution)	72,272	66,508	5,764	92.0	8.0	.6	.7	.2
Drug abuse violations	1,144,228	953,499	190,729	83.3	16.7	10.0	10.5	8.2
Gambling	15,676	13,287	2,389	84.8	15.2	.1	.1	.1
Offenses against family and children	104,952	83,735	21,217	79.8	20.2	.9	.9	.9
Driving under the influence	1,033,280	882,735	150,545	85.4	14.6	9.1	9.7	6.5
Liquor laws	435,311	352,973	82,338	81.1	18.9	3.8	3.9	3.5
Drunkenness...............................	527,200	464,742	62,458	88.2	11.8	4.6	5.1	2.7
Disorderly conduct	561,642	439,606	122,036	78.3	21.7	4.9	4.8	5.2
Vagrancy.................................	20,521	16,532	3,989	80.6	19.4	.2	.2	.2
All other offenses (except traffic)	2,919,723	2,382,236	537,487	81.6	18.4	25.6	26.2	23.0
Suspicion	9,058	7,681	1,377	84.8	15.2	.1	.1	.1
Curfew and loitering law violations	114,946	80,935	34,011	70.4	29.6	1.0	.9	1.5
Runaways.................................	189,696	80,866	108,830	42.6	57.4	1.7	.9	4.7

[1]Because of rounding, the percentages may not add to total.
[2]Less than one-tenth of 1 percent.
[3]Violent crimes are offenses of murder, forcible rape, robbery, and aggravated assault.
[4]Property crimes are offenses of burglary, larceny–theft, motor vehicle theft, and arson.
[5]Includes arson.

Table 43.—Total Arrests, Distribution by Race, 1995

[9,495 agencies; 1995 estimated population 196,403,000]

Offense charged	Total arrests					Percent distribution[1]				
	Total	White	Black	American Indian or Alaskan Native	Asian or Pacific Islander	Total	White	Black	American Indian or Alaskan Native	Asian or Pacific Islander
TOTAL	11,386,627	7,607,522	3,523,409	129,843	125,853	100.0	66.8	30.9	1.1	1.1
Murder and nonnegligent manslaughter	16,691	7,245	9,074	134	238	100.0	43.4	54.4	.8	1.4
Forcible rape	26,519	14,739	11,234	260	286	100.0	55.6	42.4	1.0	1.1
Robbery	137,761	53,370	81,957	692	1,742	100.0	38.7	59.5	.5	1.3
Aggravated assault.........................	437,686	260,778	167,857	4,152	4,899	100.0	59.6	38.4	.9	1.1
Burglary	291,901	195,486	90,421	2,765	3,229	100.0	67.0	31.0	.9	1.1
Larceny–theft	1,162,674	753,868	377,143	12,811	18,852	100.0	64.8	32.4	1.1	1.6
Motor vehicle theft	148,899	87,159	57,060	1,743	2,937	100.0	58.5	38.3	1.2	2.0
Arson	14,931	11,083	3,543	150	155	100.0	74.2	23.7	1.0	1.0
Violent crime[2]	618,657	336,132	270,122	5,238	7,165	100.0	54.3	43.7	.8	1.2
Property crime[3]	1,618,405	1,047,596	528,167	17,469	25,173	100.0	64.7	32.6	1.1	1.6
Crime Index total[4]	2,237,062	1,383,728	798,289	22,707	32,338	100.0	61.9	35.7	1.0	1.4
Other assaults............................	973,672	613,098	338,038	11,983	10,553	100.0	63.0	34.7	1.2	1.1
Forgery and counterfeiting	91,782	59,630	30,336	509	1,307	100.0	65.0	33.1	.6	1.4
Fraud	319,404	204,473	110,920	1,559	2,452	100.0	64.0	34.7	.5	.8
Embezzlement	11,599	7,529	3,840	71	159	100.0	64.9	33.1	.6	1.4
Stolen property; buying, receiving, possessing	127,624	74,837	50,285	933	1,569	100.0	58.6	39.4	.7	1.2
Vandalism...............................	232,387	170,647	55,611	3,139	2,990	100.0	73.4	23.9	1.4	1.3
Weapons; carrying, possessing, etc.	187,046	111,123	72,494	1,235	2,194	100.0	59.4	38.8	.7	1.2
Prostitution and commercialized vice	81,050	49,334	29,866	439	1,411	100.0	60.9	36.8	.5	1.7
Sex offenses (except forcible rape and prostitution)	72,171	54,141	16,342	783	905	100.0	75.0	22.6	1.1	1.3
Drug abuse violations	1,143,148	709,704	421,346	5,286	6,812	100.0	62.1	36.9	.5	.6
Gambling	15,673	8,360	6,468	72	773	100.0	53.3	41.3	.5	4.9
Offenses against family and children	104,122	67,857	33,506	1,010	1,749	100.0	65.2	32.2	1.0	1.7
Driving under the influence	1,019,260	880,635	110,839	15,626	12,160	100.0	86.4	10.9	1.5	1.2
Liquor laws	433,585	345,127	75,137	10,212	3,109	100.0	79.6	17.3	2.4	.7
Drunkenness.............................	526,742	425,514	86,608	12,749	1,871	100.0	80.8	16.4	2.4	.4
Disorderly conduct	560,809	352,965	196,919	7,539	3,386	100.0	62.9	35.1	1.3	.6
Vagrancy................................	20,517	10,749	9,225	463	80	100.0	52.4	45.0	2.3	.4
All other offenses (except traffic)	2,915,568	1,840,568	1,012,616	30,274	32,110	100.0	63.1	34.7	1.0	1.1
Suspicion	9,055	4,697	4,302	35	21	100.0	51.9	47.5	.4	.2
Curfew and loitering law violations	114,702	86,902	24,445	1,519	1,836	100.0	75.8	21.3	1.3	1.6
Runaways................................	189, 649	145,904	35,977	1,700	6,068	100.0	76.9	19.0	.9	3.2

See footnotes at the end of table.

Table 43.—Total Arrests, Distribution by Race, 1995 — Continued

Offense charged	Arrests under 18					Percent distribution[1]				
	Total	White	Black	American Indian or Alaskan Native	Asian or Pacific Islander	Total	White	Black	American Indian or Alaskan Native	Asian or Pacific Islander
TOTAL	2,081,391	1,439,825	579,875	24,739	36,952	100.0	69.2	27.9	1.2	1.8
Murder and nonnegligent manslaughter	2,558	1,009	1,477	24	48	100.0	39.4	57.7	.9	1.9
Forcible rape	4,184	2,250	1,868	28	38	100.0	53.8	44.6	.7	.9
Robbery	44,498	16,725	26,799	239	735	100.0	37.6	60.2	.5	1.7
Aggravated assault...........................	64,255	35,981	26,765	652	857	100.0	56.0	41.7	1.0	1.3
Burglary	102,558	74,694	25,068	1,272	1,524	100.0	72.8	24.4	1.2	1.5
Larceny–theft................................	387,928	271,234	102,854	5,099	8,741	100.0	69.9	26.5	1.3	2.3
Motor vehicle theft	62,471	36,238	23,864	999	1,370	100.0	58.0	38.2	1.6	2.2
Arson	7,823	6,216	1,429	87	91	100.0	79.5	18.3	1.1	1.2
Violent crime[2]	115,495	55,965	56,909	943	1,678	100.0	48.5	49.3	.8	1.5
Property crime[3]	560,780	388,382	153,215	7,457	11,726	100.0	69.3	27.3	1.3	2.1
Crime Index total[4]	676,275	444,347	210,124	8,400	13,404	100.0	65.7	31.1	1.2	2.0
Other assaults...............................	162,773	100,988	57,389	1,882	2,514	100.0	62.0	35.3	1.2	1.5
Forgery and counterfeiting	6,630	5,208	1,252	66	104	100.0	78.6	18.9	1.0	1.6
Fraud	18,407	10,159	7,647	107	494	100.0	55.2	41.5	.6	2.7
Embezzlement	955	616	310	10	19	100.0	64.5	32.5	1.0	2.0
Stolen property; buying, receiving, possessing	32,794	19,669	12,184	320	621	100.0	60.0	37.2	1.0	1.9
Vandalism...................................	104,255	83,238	18,011	1,328	1,678	100.0	79.8	17.3	1.3	1.6
Weapons; carrying, possessing, etc.	43,164	27,364	14,730	382	688	100.0	63.4	34.1	.9	1.6
Prostitution and commercialized vice	1,043	664	349	10	20	100.0	63.7	33.5	1.0	1.9
Sex offenses (except forcible rape and prostitution)	12,277	8,584	3,439	103	151	100.0	69.9	28.0	.8	1.2
Drug abuse violations	146,938	93,721	50,952	947	1,318	100.0	63.8	34.7	.6	.9
Gambling	1,298	274	1,001	2	21	100.0	21.1	77.1	.2	1.6
Offenses against family and children	5,001	3,539	1,297	41	124	100.0	70.8	25.9	.8	2.5
Driving under the influence	10,651	9,677	660	214	100	100.0	90.9	6.2	2.0	.9
Liquor laws	87,581	79,339	4,807	2,687	748	100.0	90.6	5.5	3.1	.9
Drunkenness.................................	15,328	13,382	1,543	315	88	100.0	87.3	10.1	2.1	.6
Disorderly conduct	130,347	82,962	45,093	1,308	984	100.0	63.6	34.6	1.0	.8
Vagrancy...................................	2,775	1,784	958	15	18	100.0	64.3	34.5	.5	.6
All other offenses (except traffic)	317,021	220,286	87,411	3,377	5,947	100.0	69.5	27.6	1.1	1.9
Suspicion	1,527	1,218	296	6	7	100.0	79.8	19.4	.4	.5
Curfew and loitering law violations	114,702	86,902	24,445	1,519	1,836	100.0	75.8	21.3	1.3	1.6
Runaways...................................	189,649	145,904	35,977	1,700	6,068	100.0	76.9	19.0	.9	3.2

See footnotes at the end of table.

Table 43.—Total Arrests, Distribution by Race, 1995 — Continued

Offense charged	Arrests 18 and over					Percent distribution[1]				
	Total	White	Black	American Indian or Alaskan Native	Asian or Pacific Islander	Total	White	Black	American Indian or Alaskan Native	Asian or Pacific Islander
TOTAL	9,305.236	6,167,697	2,943,534	105,104	88,901	100.0	66.3	31.6	1.1	1.0
Murder and nonnegligent manslaughter	14,133	6,236	7,597	110	190	100.0	44.1	53.8	.8	1.3
Forcible rape	22,335	12,489	9,366	232	248	100.0	55.9	41.9	1.0	1.1
Robbery	93,263	36,645	55,158	453	1,007	100.0	39.3	59.1	.5	1.1
Aggravated assault	373,431	224,797	141,092	3,500	4,042	100.0	60.2	37.8	.9	1.1
Burglary	189,343	120,792	65,353	1,493	1,705	100.0	63.8	34.5	.8	.9
Larceny–theft	774,746	482,634	274,289	7,712	10,111	100.0	62.3	35.4	1.0	1.3
Motor vehicle theft	86,428	50,921	33,196	744	1,567	100.0	58.9	38.4	.9	1.8
Arson	7,108	4,867	2,114	63	64	100.0	68.5	29.7	.9	.9
Violent crime[2]	503,162	280,167	213,213	4,295	5,487	100.0	55.7	42.4	.9	1.1
Property crime[3]	1,057,625	659,214	374,952	10,012	13,447	100.0	62.3	35.5	.9	1.3
Crime Index total[4]	1,560,787	939,381	588,165	14,307	18,934	100.0	60.2	37.7	.9	1.2
Other assaults.............................	810,899	512,110	280,649	10,101	8,039	100.0	63.2	34.6	1.2	1.0
Forgery and counterfeiting	85,152	54,422	29,084	443	1,203	100.0	63.9	34.2	.5	1.4
Fraud	300,997	194,314	103,273	1,452	1,958	100.0	64.6	34.3	.5	.7
Embezzlement	10,644	6,913	3,530	61	140	100.0	64.9	33.2	.6	1.3
Stolen property; buying, receiving, possessing	94,830	55,168	38,101	613	948	100.0	58.2	40.2	.6	1.0
Vandalism	128,132	87,409	37,600	1,811	1,312	100.0	68.2	29.3	1.4	1.0
Weapons; carrying, possessing, etc.	143,882	83,759	57,764	853	1,506	100.0	58.2	40.1	.6	1.0
Prostitution and commercialized vice	80,007	48,670	29,517	429	1,391	100.0	60.8	36.9	.5	1.7
Sex offenses (except forcible rape and prostitution)	59,894	45,557	12,903	680	754	100.0	76.1	21.5	1.1	1.3
Drug abuse violations	996,210	615,983	370,394	4,339	5,494	100.0	61.8	37.2	.4	.6
Gambling	14,375	8,086	5,467	70	752	100.0	56.3	38.0	.5	5.2
Offenses against family and children	99,121	64,318	32,209	969	1,625	100.0	64.9	32.5	1.0	1.6
Driving under the influence	1,008,609	870,958	110,179	15,412	12,060	100.0	86.4	10.9	1.5	1.2
Liquor laws	346,004	265,788	70,330	7,525	2,361	100.0	76.8	20.3	2.2	.7
Drunkenness..............................	511,414	412,132	85,065	12,434	1,783	100.0	80.6	16.6	2.4	.3
Disorderly conduct	430,462	270,003	151,826	6,231	2,402	100.0	62.7	35.3	1.4	.6
Vagrancy.................................	17,742	8,965	8,267	448	62	100.0	50.5	46.6	2.5	.3
All other offenses (except traffic)	2,598,547	1,620,282	925,205	26,897	26,163	100.0	62.4	35.6	1.0	1.0
Suspicion	7,528	3,479	4,006	29	14	100.0	46.2	53.2	.4	.2
Curfew and loitering law violations	—	—	—	—	—	—	—	—	—	—
Runaways................................	—	—	—	—	—	—	—	—	—	—

[1]Because of rounding, the percentages may not add to totals.
[2]Violent crimes are offenses of murder, forcible rape, robbery, and aggravated assault.
[3]Property crimes are offenses of burglary, larceny–theft, motor vehicle theft, and arson.
[4]Includes arson.

Table 44.—City Arrest Trends, 1994–1995

[5,885 agencies; 1995 estimated population 127,451,000; 1994 estimated population 126,426,000]

Offense charged	Number of persons arrested								
	Total all ages			Under 18 years of age			18 years of age and over		
	1994	1995	Percent change	1994	1995	Percent change	1994	1995	Percent change
TOTAL	8,330,784	8,393,767	+.8	1,639,088	1,648,313	+.6	6,691,696	6,745,454	+.8
Murder and nonnegligent manslaughter	13,591	12,682	−6.7	2,464	2,045	−17.0	11,127	10,637	−4.4
Forcible rape	19,977	19,104	−4.4	3,162	3,124	−1.2	16,815	15,980	−5.0
Robbery	121,823	118,758	−2.5	39,903	39,317	−1.5	81,920	79,441	−3.0
Aggravated assault	320,147	321,766	+.5	51,225	49,563	−3.2	268,922	272,203	+1.2
Burglary	216,509	206,101	−4.8	75,435	70,913	−6.0	141,074	135,188	−4.2
Larceny–theft	933,805	934,696	+.1	315,391	318,557	+1.0	618,414	616,139	−.4
Motor vehicle theft	122,108	114,353	−6.4	54,559	49,017	−10.2	67,549	65,336	−3.3
Arson	11,103	10,836	−2.4	6,480	5,976	−7.8	4,623	4,860	+5.1
Violent crime[1]	475,538	472,310	−.7	96,754	94,049	−2.8	378,784	378,261	−.1
Property crime[2]	1,283,525	1,265,986	−1.4	451,865	444,463	−1.6	831,660	821,523	−1.2
Crime Index total[3]	1,759,063	1,738,296	−1.2	548,619	538,512	−1.8	1,210,444	1,199,784	−.9
Other assaults	684,011	723,637	+5.8	124,994	126,858	+1.5	559,017	596,779	+6.8
Forgery and counterfeiting	64,275	67,275	+4.7	5,033	5,079	+.9	59,242	62,196	+5.0
Fraud	189,701	185,751	−2.1	16,135	16,128	[4]	173,566	169,623	−2.3
Embezzlement	7,879	8,360	+6.1	607	803	+32.3	7,272	7,557	+3.9
Stolen property; buying, receiving, possessing	97,758	98,533	+.8	27,240	26,599	−2.4	70,518	71,934	+2.0
Vandalism	182,796	178,417	−2.4	87,009	80,535	−7.4	95,787	97,882	+2.2
Weapons; carrying, possessing, etc.	160,757	145,290	−9.6	40,534	35,349	−12.8	120,223	109,941	−8.6
Prostitution and commercialized vice	76,818	74,616	−2.9	864	957	+10.8	75,954	73,659	−3.0
Sex offenses (except forcible rape and prostitution)	54,472	51,623	−5.2	9,477	8,663	−8.6	44,995	42,960	−4.5
Drug abuse violations	817,631	878,301	+7.4	100,924	118,222	+17.1	716,707	760,079	+6.1
Gambling	13,546	13,755	+1.5	1,294	1,171	−9.5	12,252	12,584	+2.7
Offenses against family and children	47,262	53,363	+12.9	3,135	3,555	+13.4	44,127	49,808	+12.9
Driving under the influence	618,095	587,318	−5.0	6,426	6,529	+1.6	611,669	580,789	−5.0
Liquor laws	301,462	344,024	+14.1	61,177	63,847	+4.4	240,285	280,177	+16.6
Drunkenness	422,980	422,140	−.2	11,261	12,726	+13.0	411,719	409,414	−.6
Disorderly conduct	459,650	471,381	+2.6	107,996	113,215	+4.8	351,654	358,166	+1.9
Vagrancy	18,222	18,845	+3.4	2,516	2,501	−.6	15,706	16,344	+4.1
All other offenses (except traffic)	2,128,140	2,095,766	−1.5	257,581	249,988	−2.9	1,870,559	1,845,778	−1.3
Suspicion (not included in totals)	7,986	6,703	−16.1	1,259	1,210	−3.9	6,727	5,493	−18.3
Curfew and loitering law violations	92,122	105,978	+15.0	92,122	105,978	+15.0	—	—	—
Runaways	134,144	131,098	−2.3	134,144	131,098	−2.3	—	—	—

[1]Violent crimes are offenses of murder, forcible rape, robbery, and aggravated assault.
[2]Property crimes are offenses of burglary, larceny–theft, motor vehicle theft, and arson.
[3]Includes arson.
[4]Less than one-tenth of 1 percent.

Table 45.—City Arrest Trends, Sex, 1994–1995

[5,885 agencies; 1995 estimated population 127,451,000; 1994 estimated population 126,426,000]

Offense charged	Males						Females					
	Total			Under 18			Total			Under 18		
	1994	1995	Percent change	1994	1995	Percent change	1994	1995	Percent change	1994	1995	Percent change
TOTAL	6,656,342	6,665,589	+.1	1,232,450	1,228,479	–.3	1,674,442	1,728,178	+3.2	406,638	419,834	+3.2
Murder and nonnegligent manslaughter	12,292	11,565	–5.9	2,323	1,945	–16.3	1,299	1,117	–14.0	141	100	–29.1
Forcible rape	19,763	18,901	–4.4	3,101	3,060	–1.3	214	203	–5.1	61	64	+4.9
Robbery	110,409	107,505	–2.6	36,193	35,655	–1.5	11,414	11,253	–1.4	3,710	3,662	–1.3
Aggravated assault....................	265,357	263,003	–.9	41,592	39,674	–4.6	54,790	58,763	+7.3	9,633	9,889	+2.7
Burglary	192,377	182,153	–5.3	67,862	63,665	–6.2	24,132	23,948	–.8	7,573	7,248	–4.3
Larceny–theft......................	618,190	617,603	–.1	212,461	212,702	+.1	315,615	317,093	+.5	102,930	105,855	+2.8
Motor vehicle theft	107,198	99,564	–7.1	47,162	42,043	–10.9	14,910	14,789	–.8	7,397	6,974	–5.7
Arson	9,452	9,075	–4.0	5,680	5,259	–7.4	1,651	1,761	+6.7	800	717	–10.4
Violent crime[1]	407,821	400,974	–1.7	83,209	80,334	–3.5	67,717	71,336	+5.3	13,545	13,715	+1.3
Property crime[2]	927,217	908,395	–2.0	333,165	323,669	–2.9	356,308	357,591	+.4	118,700	120,794	+1.8
Crime Index total[3]	1,335,038	1,309,369	–1.9	416,374	404,003	–3.0	424,025	428,927	+1.2	132,245	134,509	+1.7
Other assaults......................	555,992	581,654	+4.6	91,588	91,524	–.1	128,019	141,983	+10.9	33,406	35,334	+5.8
Forgery and counterfeiting	41,460	43,196	+4.2	3,155	3,214	+1.9	22,815	24,079	+5.5	1,878	1,865	–.7
Fraud	124,618	116,846	–6.2	12,176	12,144	–.3	65,083	68,905	+5.9	3,959	3,984	+.6
Embezzlement	4,488	4,570	+1.8	381	458	+20.2	3,391	3,790	+11.8	226	345	+52.7
Stolen property; buying, receiving, possessing	84,592	84,511	–.1	24,203	23,395	–3.3	13,166	14,022	+6.5	3,037	3,204	+5.5
Vandalism..........................	158,900	154,077	–3.0	77,888	71,739	–7.9	23,896	24,340	+1.9	9,121	8,796	–3.6
Weapons; carrying, possessing, etc.	147,967	133,664	–9.7	37,285	32,469	–12.9	12,790	11,626	–9.1	3,249	2,880	–11.4
Prostitution and commercialized vice	29,000	27,707	–4.5	451	480	+6.4	47,818	46,909	–1.9	413	477	+15.5
Sex offenses (except forcible rape and prostitution)	49,290	46,955	–4.7	8,712	8,011	–8.0	5,182	4,668	–9.9	765	652	–14.8
Drug abuse violations	683,889	732,059	+7.0	89,467	103,874	+16.1	133,742	146,242	+9.3	11,457	14,348	+25.2
Gambling	11,525	11,632	+.9	1,232	1,115	–9.5	2,021	2,123	+5.0	62	56	–9.7
Offenses against family and children	33,724	38,691	+14.7	1,982	2,215	+11.8	13,538	14,672	+8.4	1,153	1,340	+16.2
Driving under the influence	527,073	498,734	–5.4	5,479	5,494	+.3	91,022	88,584	–2.7	947	1,035	+9.3
Liquor laws	243,623	281,973	+15.7	43,756	45,843	+4.8	57,839	62,051	+7.3	17,421	18,004	+3.3
Drunkenness.......................	375,031	372,479	–.7	9,549	10,714	+12.2	47,949	49,661	+3.6	1,712	2,012	+17.5
Disorderly conduct	362,326	368,353	+1.7	82,481	85,413	+3.6	97,324	103,028	+5.9	25,515	27,802	+9.0
Vagrancy	14,432	15,142	+4.9	2,128	2,229	+4.7	3,790	3,703	–2.3	388	272	–29.9
All other offenses (except traffic)	1,750,410	1,713,686	–2.1	201,199	193,854	–3.7	377,730	382,080	+1.2	56,382	56,134	–.4
Suspicion (not included in totals)	6,671	5,677	–14.9	1,003	965	–3.8	1,315	1,026	–22.0	256	245	–4.3
Curfew and loitering law violations	65,741	74,704	+13.6	65,741	74,704	+13.6	26,381	31,274	+18.5	26,381	31,274	+18.5
Runaways..........................	57,223	55,587	–2.9	57,223	55,587	–2.9	76,921	75,511	–1.8	76,921	75,511	–1.8

[1]Violent crimes are offenses of murder, forcible rape, robbery, and aggravated assault.
[2]Property crimes are offenses of burglary, larceny–theft, motor vehicle theft, and arson.
[3]Includes arson.

Table 46.—City Arrests, Distribution by Age, 1995

[6,541 agencies; 1995 estimated population 132,932,000]

Offense charged	Total all ages	Ages under 15	Ages under 18	Ages 18 and over	Under 10	10–12	13–14	15	16	17	18	19	20	21
TOTAL	8,691,888	591,879	1,705,675	6,986,213	29,362	133,960	428,557	341,753	379,895	392,148	398,595	367,610	336,241	305,424
Percent distribution[1]	100.0	6.8	19.6	80.4	.3	1.5	4.9	3.9	4.4	4.5	4.6	4.2	3.9	3.5
Murder and nonnegligent manslaughter	12,872	276	2,078	10,794	55	20	201	360	610	832	1,088	1,006	891	748
Forcible rape	19,698	1,209	3,217	16,481	63	302	844	565	679	764	819	783	737	679
Robbery	120,599	11,458	39,876	80,723	303	2,033	9,122	8,492	9,784	10,142	9,172	7,020	5,613	4,465
Aggravated assault	332,320	16,385	51,121	281,199	745	3,918	11,722	9,805	12,032	12,899	13,256	12,288	11,885	11,909
Burglary	212,154	29,696	73,284	138,870	1,895	7,541	20,260	14,622	15,057	13,909	12,535	9,361	7,269	6,104
Larceny–theft	967,859	148,886	331,116	636,743	7,771	42,385	98,730	61,952	62,528	57,750	50,491	38,146	29,984	25,128
Motor vehicle theft	116,806	14,438	50,105	66,701	174	1,760	12,504	12,582	12,481	10,604	8,462	6,114	4,576	3,801
Arson	11,286	4,279	6,246	5,040	815	1,415	2,049	838	619	510	358	294	229	197
Violent crime[2]	485,489	29,328	96,292	389,197	1,166	6,273	21,889	19,222	23,105	24,637	24,335	21,097	19,126	17,801
Percent distribution[1]	100.0	6.0	19.8	80.2	.2	1.3	4.5	4.0	4.8	5.1	5.0	4.3	3.9	3.7
Property crime[3]	1,308,105	197,299	460,751	847,354	10,655	53,101	133,543	89,994	90,685	82,773	71,846	53,915	42,058	35,230
Percent distribution[1]	100.0	15.1	35.2	64.8	.8	4.1	10.2	6.9	6.9	6.3	5.5	4.1	3.2	2.7
Crime Index total[4]	1,793,594	226,627	557,043	1,236,551	11,821	59,374	155,432	109,216	113,790	107,410	96,181	75,012	61,184	53,031
Percent distribution[1]	100.0	12.6	31.1	68.9	.7	3.3	8.7	6.1	6.3	6.0	5.4	4.2	3.4	3.0
Other assaults	747,638	55,317	131,153	616,485	3,163	14,653	37,501	24,980	25,462	25,394	24,283	23,670	23,790	25,196
Forgery and counterfeiting	70,204	704	5,360	64,844	56	120	528	770	1,538	2,348	3,347	3,543	3,320	2,990
Fraud	194,825	4,445	16,408	178,417	74	659	3,712	4,337	3,226	4,400	6,450	7,778	7,948	7,677
Embezzlement	8,885	78	827	8,058	6	16	56	44	241	464	522	534	469	501
Stolen property; buying, receiving, possessing	101,561	7,882	27,587	73,974	311	1,432	6,139	5,601	6,835	7,269	7,458	5,913	4,734	4,017
Vandalism	185,661	40,494	83,861	101,800	3,878	12,049	24,567	15,027	15,066	13,274	10,154	7,366	5,879	5,482
Weapons; carrying, possessing, etc.	149,188	10,969	36,305	112,883	505	2,359	8,105	7,091	8,481	9,764	10,331	8,656	7,512	6,942
Prostitution and commercialized vice	75,209	168	965	74,244	27	20	121	147	224	426	1,265	1,756	1,889	2,185
Sex offenses (except forcible rape and prostitution)	53,166	4,740	8,983	44,183	367	1,325	3,048	1,593	1,332	1,318	1,368	1,361	1,368	1,347
Drug abuse violations	898,031	20,711	121,471	776,560	507	2,135	18,069	23,123	34,288	43,349	51,780	46,595	41,108	36,316
Gambling	13,913	206	1,205	12,708	21	23	162	195	342	462	556	522	551	435
Offenses against family and children	58,543	1,287	4,096	54,447	105	242	940	916	953	940	1,756	1,546	1,709	1,830
Driving under the influence	618,759	259	6,974	611,785	134	14	111	318	1,820	4,577	10,254	13,399	16,016	21,680
Liquor laws	356,691	7,409	67,114	289,577	112	614	6,683	10,580	19,419	29,706	45,342	43,676	37,012	12,347
Drunkenness	439,595	2,014	13,245	426,350	133	183	1,698	2,188	2,996	6,047	10,217	10,830	11,259	14,166
Disorderly conduct	493,141	41,789	117,056	376,085	1,519	9,281	30,989	23,806	25,507	25,954	24,810	21,604	19,756	20,755
Vagrancy	19,318	520	2,562	16,756	12	88	420	454	738	850	1,145	920	756	633
All other offenses (except traffic)	2,163,352	74,299	258,530	1,904,822	4,584	14,264	55,451	49,976	59,675	74,580	91,102	92,685	89,742	87,674
Suspicion	6,965	358	1,281	5,684	21	54	283	273	327	323	274	244	239	220
Curfew and loitering law violations	108,897	31,324	108,897	—	538	4,663	26,123	25,701	29,847	22,025	—	—	—	—
Runaways	134,752	60,279	134,752	—	1,468	10,392	48,419	35,417	27,788	11,268	—	—	—	—

See footnotes at end of table.

Table 46.—City Arrests, Distribution by Age, 1995 — Continued

Offense charged	Age											
	22	23	24	25–29	30–34	35–39	40–44	45–49	50–54	55–59	60–64	65 and over
TOTAL	**287,936**	**280,227**	**285,571**	**1,237,170**	**1,211,654**	**975,260**	**606,778**	**334,769**	**166,243**	**87,103**	**49,787**	**55,845**
Percent distribution1	**3.3**	**3.2**	**3.3**	**14.2**	**13.9**	**11.2**	**7.0**	**3.9**	**1.9**	**1.0**	**.6**	**.6**
Murder and nonnegligent manslaughter	685	587	540	1,829	1,208	873	543	332	177	129	70	88
Forcible rape	643	640	631	3,136	3,031	2,433	1,324	742	390	209	128	156
Robbery	4,002	3,701	3,628	15,382	12,882	8,283	3,956	1,590	582	215	102	130
Aggravated assault	11,693	11,581	11,969	52,538	51,740	40,016	24,403	13,264	6,662	3,533	1,993	2,469
Burglary	5,539	5,320	5,528	25,690	25,909	18,918	9,924	4,114	1,538	540	272	309
Larceny–theft	22,530	22,301	22,645	105,286	108,633	89,175	56,963	29,770	14,509	7,819	5,000	8,363
Motor vehicle theft	3,274	2,973	2,928	12,201	10,090	6,484	3,309	1,478	547	251	115	98
Arson	204	186	145	762	811	705	500	324	142	80	50	53
Violent crime[2]	17,023	16,509	16,768	72,885	68,861	51,605	30,226	15,928	7,811	4,086	2,293	2,843
Percent distribution[1]	3.5	3.4	3.5	15.0	14.2	10.6	6.2	3.3	1.6	.8	.5	.6
Property crime[3]	31,547	30,780	31,246	143,939	145,443	115,282	70,696	35,686	16,736	8,690	5,437	8,823
Percent distribution[1]	2.4	2.4	2.4	11.0	11.1	8.8	5.4	2.7	1.3	.7	.4	.7
Crime Index total[4]	48,570	47,289	48,014	216,824	214,304	166,887	100,922	51,614	24,547	12,776	7,730	11,666
Percent distribution[1]	2.7	2.6	2.7	12.1	11.9	9.3	5.6	2.9	1.4	.7	.4	.7
Other assaults	25,154	25,889	27,225	120,729	119,586	91,678	53,301	27,943	13,330	6,594	3,733	4,384
Forgery and counterfeiting	2,912	2,807	3,033	13,124	12,098	8,910	4,857	2,210	936	428	153	176
Fraud	7,808	7,778	8,079	35,090	32,207	25,280	15,890	8,436	4,045	1,784	922	1,245
Embezzlement	432	419	383	1,479	1,255	865	556	309	218	64	25	27
Stolen property; buying, receiving, possessing	3,534	3,287	3,247	13,308	11,596	8,234	4,723	2,182	892	451	205	193
Vandalism	4,880	4,563	4,635	18,550	16,380	11,594	6,294	3,082	1,393	680	371	497
Weapons; carrying, possessing, etc.	6,189	5,732	5,174	19,102	15,366	11,300	7,149	4,218	2,268	1,293	769	882
Prostitution and commercialized vice	2,405	2,643	2,993	16,744	17,823	12,783	6,246	2,864	1,236	642	344	426
Sex offenses (except forcible rape and prostitution)	1,331	1,358	1,446	7,183	7,982	6,788	4,736	3,065	1,833	1,159	785	1,073
Drug abuse violations	34,088	32,167	32,751	142,652	139,309	109,475	62,553	29,136	11,035	4,351	1,848	1,396
Gambling	435	400	378	1,681	1,741	1,642	1,246	1,118	652	582	378	391
Offenses against family and children	1,885	1,989	2,309	10,249	11,165	9,535	5,375	2,583	1,231	538	338	409
Driving under the influence	22,533	23,151	25,171	109,231	112,213	95,106	65,843	42,616	23,958	13,907	8,261	8,446
Liquor laws	9,479	8,204	7,575	28,965	27,561	24,771	18,340	11,859	6,693	3,830	2,107	1,816
Drunkenness	13,824	13,560	13,950	63,960	74,739	71,787	52,539	33,094	19,123	10,752	6,520	6,030
Disorderly conduct	18,631	17,149	16,956	65,147	60,861	48,314	28,753	16,004	8,085	4,166	2,436	2,658
Vagrancy	500	529	519	2,560	2,801	2,629	1,734	915	594	202	168	151
All other offenses (except traffic)	83,121	81,093	81,477	349,585	331,608	266,717	165,176	91,264	44,079	22,861	12,671	13,967
Suspicion	225	220	256	1,007	1,059	965	545	257	95	43	23	12
Curfew and loitering law violations	—	—	—	—	—	—	—	—	—	—	—	—
Runaways	—	—	—	—	—	—	—	—	—	—	—	—

[1]Because of rounding, the percentages may not add to total.
[2]Violent crimes are offenses of murder, forcible rape, robbery, and aggravated assault.
[3]Property crimes are offenses of burglary, larceny–theft, motor vehicle theft, and arson.
[4]Includes arson.

Table 47.—City Arrests of Persons under 15, 18, 21, and 25 Years of Age, 1995

[6,541 agencies; 1995 estimated population 132,932,000]

Offense charged	Total all ages	Number of persons arrested				Percent of total all ages			
		Under 15	Under 18	Under 21	Under 25	Under 15	Under 18	Under 21	Under 25
TOTAL	8,691,888	591,879	1,705,675	2,808,121	3,967,279	6.8	19.6	32.3	45.6
Murder and nonnegligent manslaughter	12,872	276	2,078	5,063	7,623	2.1	16.1	39.3	59.2
Forcible rape	19,698	1,209	3,217	5,556	8,149	6.1	16.3	28.2	41.4
Robbery	120,599	11,458	39,876	61,681	77,477	9.5	33.1	51.1	64.2
Aggravated assault...................................	332,320	16,385	51,121	88,550	135,702	4.9	15.4	26.6	40.8
Burglary	212,154	29,696	73,284	102,449	124,940	14.0	34.5	48.3	58.9
Larceny–theft	967,859	148,886	331,116	449,737	542,341	15.4	34.2	46.5	56.0
Motor vehicle theft	116,806	14,438	50,105	69,257	82,233	12.4	42.9	59.3	70.4
Arson	11,286	4,279	6,246	7,127	7,859	37.9	55.3	63.1	69.6
Violent crime[1]	485,489	29,328	96,292	160,850	228,951	6.0	19.8	33.1	47.2
Property crime[2]	1,308,105	197,299	460,751	628,570	757,373	15.1	35.2	48.1	57.9
Crime Index total[3]	1,793,594	226,627	557,043	789,420	986,324	12.6	31.1	44.0	55.0
Other assaults.......................................	747,638	55,317	131,153	202,896	306,360	7.4	17.5	27.1	41.0
Forgery and counterfeiting	70,204	704	5,360	15,570	27,312	1.0	7.6	22.2	38.9
Fraud	194,825	4,445	16,408	38,584	69,926	2.3	8.4	19.8	35.9
Embezzlement	8,885	78	827	2,352	4,087	.9	9.3	26.5	46.0
Stolen property; buying, receiving, possessing	101,561	7,882	27,587	45,692	59,777	7.8	27.2	45.0	58.9
Vandalism...	185,661	40,494	83,861	107,260	126,820	21.8	45.2	57.8	68.3
Weapons; carrying, possessing, etc.	149,188	10,969	36,305	62,804	86,841	7.4	24.3	42.1	58.2
Prostitution and commercialized vice	75,209	168	965	5,875	16,101	.2	1.3	7.8	21.4
Sex offenses (except forcible rape and prostitution)	53,166	4,740	8,983	13,080	18,562	8.9	16.9	24.6	34.9
Drug abuse violations	898,031	20,711	121,471	260,954	396,276	2.3	13.5	29.1	44.1
Gambling	13,913	206	1,205	2,834	4,482	1.5	8.7	20.4	32.2
Offenses against family and children	58,543	1,287	4,096	9,107	17,120	2.2	7.0	15.6	29.2
Driving under the influence	618,759	259	6,974	46,643	139,178	[4]	1.1	7.5	22.5
Liquor laws	356,691	7,409	67,114	193,144	230,749	2.1	18.8	54.1	64.7
Drunkenness	439,595	2,014	13,245	45,551	101,051	.5	3.0	10.4	23.0
Disorderly conduct	493,141	41,789	117,056	183,226	256,717	8.5	23.7	37.2	52.1
Vagrancy..	19,318	520	2,562	5,383	7,564	2.7	13.3	27.9	39.2
All other offenses (except traffic)	2,163,352	74,299	258,530	532,059	865,424	3.4	12.0	24.6	40.0
Suspicion	6,965	358	1,281	2,038	2,959	5.1	18.4	29.3	42.5
Curfew and loitering law violations	108,897	31,324	108,897	108,897	108,897	28.8	100.0	100.0	100.0
Runaways..	134,752	60,279	134,752	134,752	134,752	44.7	100.0	100.0	100.0

[1]Violent crimes are offenses of murder, forcible rape, robbery, and aggravated assault.
[2]Property crimes are offenses of burglary, larceny–theft, motor vehicle theft, and arson.
[3]Includes arson.
[4]Less than one-tenth of 1 percent.

Table 48.—City Arrests, Distribution by Sex, 1995

[6,541 agencies; 1995 estimated population 132,932,000]

Offense charged	Number of persons arrested			Percent male	Percent female	Percent distribution[1]		
	Total	Male	Female			Total	Male	Female
TOTAL	**8,691,888**	**6,899,179**	**1,792,709**	**79.4**	**20.6**	**100.0**	**100.0**	**100.0**
Murder and nonnegligent manslaughter	12,872	11,729	1,143	91.1	8.9	.1	.2	.1
Forcible rape	19,698	19,486	212	98.9	1.1	.2	.3	[2]
Robbery	120,599	109,188	11,411	90.5	9.5	1.4	1.6	.6
Aggravated assault	332,320	271,700	60,620	81.8	18.2	3.8	3.9	3.4
Burglary	212,154	187,642	24,512	88.4	11.6	2.4	2.7	1.4
Larceny–theft	967,859	639,367	328,492	66.1	33.9	11.1	9.3	18.3
Motor vehicle theft	116,806	101,616	15,190	87.0	13.0	1.3	1.5	.8
Arson	11,286	9,464	1,822	83.9	16.1	.1	.1	.1
Violent crime[3]	485,489	412,103	73,386	84.9	15.1	5.6	6.0	4.1
Property crime[4]	1,308,105	938,089	370,016	71.7	28.3	15.0	13.6	20.6
Crime Index total[5]	1,793,594	1,350,192	443,402	75.3	24.7	20.6	19.6	24.7
Other assaults	747,638	600,606	147,032	80.3	19.7	8.6	8.7	8.2
Forgery and counterfeiting	70,204	45,001	25,203	64.1	35.9	.8	.7	1.4
Fraud	194,825	122,063	72,762	62.7	37.3	2.2	1.8	4.1
Embezzlement	8,885	4,892	3,993	55.1	44.9	.1	.1	.2
Stolen property; buying, receiving, possessing	101,561	87,034	14,527	85.7	14.3	1.2	1.3	.8
Vandalism	185,661	160,269	25,392	86.3	13.7	2.1	2.3	1.4
Weapons; carrying, possessing, etc.	149,188	137,263	11,925	92.0	8.0	1.7	2.0	.7
Prostitution and commercialized vice	75,209	27,912	47,297	37.1	62.9	.9	.4	2.6
Sex offenses (except forcible rape and prostitution)	53,166	48,409	4,757	91.1	8.9	.6	.7	.3
Drug abuse violations	898,031	748,791	149,240	83.4	16.6	10.3	10.9	8.3
Gambling	13,913	11,773	2,140	84.6	15.4	.2	.2	.1
Offenses against family and children	58,543	42,789	15,754	73.1	26.9	.7	.6	.9
Driving under the influence	618,759	525,022	93,737	84.9	15.1	7.1	7.6	5.2
Liquor laws	356,691	292,009	64,682	81.9	18.1	4.1	4.2	3.6
Drunkenness.............................	439,595	387,741	51,854	88.2	11.8	5.1	5.6	2.9
Disorderly conduct	493,141	385,280	107,861	78.1	21.9	5.7	5.6	6.0
Vagrancy	19,318	15,501	3,817	80.2	19.8	.2	.2	.2
All other offenses (except traffic)	2,163,352	1,766,891	396,461	81.7	18.3	24.9	25.6	22.1
Suspicion	6,965	5,890	1,075	84.6	15.4	.1	.1	.1
Curfew and loitering law violations	108,897	76,728	32,169	70.5	29.5	1.3	1.1	1.8
Runaways................................	134,752	57,123	77,629	42.4	57.6	1.6	.8	4.3

[1]Because of rounding, the percentages may not add to totals.
[2]Less than one-tenth of 1 percent.
[3]Violent crimes are offenses of murder, forcible rape, robbery, and aggravated assault.
[4]Property crimes are offenses of burglary, larceny–theft, motor vehicle theft, and arson.
[5]Includes arson.

Table 49.—City Arrests, Distribution by Race, 1995

[6,539 agencies; 1995 estimated population 132,911,000]

Offense charged	Total arrests					Percent distribution[1]				
	Total	White	Black	American Indian or Alaskan Native	Asian or Pacific Islander	Total	White	Black	American Indian or Alaskan Native	Asian or Pacific Islander
TOTAL	8,681,112	5,564,403	2,917,401	96,761	102,547	100.0	64.1	33.6	1.1	1.2
Murder and nonnegligent manslaughter	12,864	4,787	7,783	76	218	100.0	37.2	60.5	.6	1.7
Forcible rape	19,687	9,835	9,458	170	224	100.0	50.0	48.0	.9	1.1
Robbery	120,556	45,199	73,200	580	1,577	100.0	37.5	60.7	.5	1.3
Aggravated assault...........................	332,087	185,410	139,615	2,735	4,327	100.0	55.8	42.0	.8	1.3
Burglary	211,996	133,275	74,556	1,586	2,579	100.0	62.9	35.2	.7	1.2
Larceny–theft................................	966,681	616,295	322,524	11,389	16,473	100.0	63.8	33.4	1.2	1.7
Motor vehicle theft	116,716	63,987	48,877	1,308	2,544	100.0	54.8	41.9	1.1	2.2
Arson	11,265	7,963	3,056	114	132	100.0	70.7	27.1	1.0	1.2
Violent crime[2]	485,194	245,231	230,056	3,561	6,346	100.0	50.5	47.4	.7	1.3
Property crime[3]	1,306,658	821,520	449,013	14,397	21,728	100.0	62.9	34.4	1.1	1.7
Crime Index total[4]	1,791,852	1,066,751	679,069	17,958	28,074	100.0	59.5	37.9	1.0	1.6
Other assaults...............................	747,106	444,862	284,386	9,242	8,616	100.0	59.5	38.1	1.2	1.2
Forgery and counterfeiting	70,057	43,888	24,605	376	1,188	100.0	62.6	35.1	.5	1.7
Fraud	194,562	116,028	75,504	864	2,166	100.0	59.6	38.8	.4	1.1
Embezzlement	8,880	5,562	3,142	55	121	100.0	62.6	35.4	.6	1.4
Stolen property; buying, receiving, possessing	101,424	55,748	43,620	676	1,380	100.0	55.0	43.0	.7	1.4
Vandalism...................................	185,450	131,715	48,682	2,451	2,602	100.0	71.0	26.3	1.3	1.4
Weapons; carrying, possessing, etc.	149,078	83,766	62,640	846	1,826	100.0	56.2	42.0	.6	1.2
Prostitution and commercialized vice	75,198	45,064	28,367	421	1,346	100.0	59.9	37.7	.6	1.8
Sex offenses (except forcible rape and prostitution)	53,128	38,015	13,803	545	765	100.0	71.6	26.0	1.0	1.4
Drug abuse violations	897,415	527,214	361,256	3,523	5,422	100.0	58.7	40.3	.4	.6
Gambling	13,912	7,285	5,936	65	626	100.0	52.4	42.7	.5	4.5
Offenses against family and children	58,325	38,779	17,369	620	1,557	100.0	66.5	29.8	1.1	2.7
Driving under the influence	617,479	532,102	69,824	9,590	5,963	100.0	86.2	11.3	1.6	1.0
Liquor laws	355,155	274,707	69,609	8,304	2,535	100.0	77.3	19.6	2.3	.7
Drunkenness.................................	439,163	348,775	77,871	10,983	1,534	100.0	79.4	17.7	2.5	.3
Disorderly conduct	492,468	301,297	181,932	6,253	2,986	100.0	61.2	36.9	1.3	.6
Vagrancy....................................	19,314	9,831	8,958	451	74	100.0	50.9	46.4	2.3	.4
All other offenses (except traffic)	2,160,759	1,308,049	804,750	20,869	27,091	100.0	60.5	37.2	1.0	1.3
Suspicion	6,965	2,851	4,087	8	19	100.0	40.9	58.7	.1	.3
Curfew and loitering law violations	108,659	82,090	23,762	1,406	1,401	100.0	75.5	21.9	1.3	1.3
Runaways....................................	134,763	100,024	28,229	1,255	5,255	100.0	74.2	20.9	.9	3.9

See footnotes at the end of table.

Table 49.—City Arrests, Distribution by Race, 1995 — Continued

Offense charged	Arrests under 18					Percent distribution[1]				
	Total	White	Black	American Indian or Alaskan Native	Asian or Pacific Islander	Total	White	Black	American Indian or Alaskan Native	Asian or Pacific Islander
TOTAL	1,703,506	1,149,001	503,601	19,329	31,575	100.0	67.4	29.6	1.1	1.9
Murder and nonnegligent manslaughter	2,077	745	1,271	17	44	100.0	35.9	61.2	.8	2.1
Forcible rape	3,216	1,565	1,602	20	29	100.0	48.7	49.8	.6	.9
Robbery	39,868	14,677	24,324	206	661	100.0	36.8	61.0	.5	1.7
Aggravated assault......................	51,076	27,432	22,418	464	762	100.0	53.7	43.9	.9	1.5
Burglary	73,208	51,129	20,200	704	1,175	100.0	69.8	27.6	1.0	1.6
Larceny–theft	330,612	229,243	89,173	4,579	7,617	100.0	69.3	27.0	1.4	2.3
Motor vehicle theft	50,059	27,347	20,769	805	1,138	100.0	54.6	41.5	1.6	2.3
Arson	6,238	4,841	1,255	65	77	100.0	77.6	20.1	1.0	1.2
Violent crime[2]	96,237	44,419	49,615	707	1,496	100.0	46.2	51.6	.7	1.6
Property crime[3]	460,117	312,560	131,397	6,153	10,007	100.0	67.9	28.6	1.3	2.2
Crime Index total[4]	556,354	356,979	181,012	6,860	11,503	100.0	64.2	32.5	1.2	2.1
Other assaults............................	130,998	79,211	48,301	1,390	2,096	100.0	60.5	36.9	1.1	1.6
Forgery and counterfeiting	5,352	4,116	1,086	54	96	100.0	76.9	20.3	1.0	1.8
Fraud	16,400	8,544	7,292	86	478	100.0	52.1	44.5	.5	2.9
Embezzlement	827	517	284	9	17	100.0	62.5	34.3	1.1	2.1
Stolen property; buying, receiving, possessing	27,540	15,751	10,968	269	552	100.0	57.2	39.8	1.0	2.0
Vandalism............................	83,733	65,481	15,741	1,044	1,467	100.0	78.2	18.8	1.2	1.8
Weapons; carrying, possessing, etc.	36,275	22,463	12,939	282	591	100.0	61.9	35.7	.8	1.6
Prostitution and commercialized vice	965	612	324	10	19	100.0	63.4	33.6	1.0	2.0
Sex offenses (except forcible rape and prostitution)	8,975	5,934	2,855	57	129	100.0	66.1	31.8	.6	1.4
Drug abuse violations	121,359	74,455	45,254	662	988	100.0	61.4	37.3	.5	.8
Gambling	1,205	245	938	2	20	100.0	20.3	77.8	.2	1.7
Offenses against family and children	4,070	2,774	1,153	29	114	100.0	68.2	28.3	.7	2.8
Driving under the influence	6,951	6,289	474	144	44	100.0	90.5	6.8	2.1	.6
Liquor laws	66,892	59,959	4,285	2,063	585	100.0	89.6	6.4	3.1	.9
Drunkenness............................	13,236	11,481	1,415	262	78	100.0	86.7	10.7	2.0	.6
Disorderly conduct	116,947	73,623	41,348	1,072	904	100.0	63.0	35.4	.9	.8
Vagrancy............................	2,561	1,590	941	12	18	100.0	62.1	36.7	.5	.7
All other offenses (except traffic)	258,163	175,867	74,726	2,357	5,213	100.0	68.1	28.9	.9	2.0
Suspicion	1,281	996	274	4	7	100.0	77.8	21.4	.3	.5
Curfew and loitering law violations	108,659	82,090	23,762	1,406	1,401	100.0	75.5	21.9	1.3	1.3
Runaways	134,763	100,024	28,229	1,255	5,255	100.0	74.2	20.9	.9	3.9

See footnotes at the end of table.

Table 49.—City Arrests, Distribution by Race, 1995 — Continued

Offense charged	Arrests 18 and over					Percent distribution[1]				
	Total	White	Black	American Indian or Alaskan Native	Asian or Pacific Islander	Total	White	Black	American Indian or Alaskan Native	Asian or Pacific Islander
TOTAL	6,977,606	4,415,402	2,413,800	77,432	70,972	100.0	63.3	34.6	1.1	1.0
Murder and nonnegligent manslaughter	10,787	4,042	6,512	59	174	100.0	37.5	60.4	.5	1.6
Forcible rape	16,471	8,270	7,856	150	195	100.0	50.2	47.7	.9	1.2
Robbery	80,688	30,522	48,876	374	916	100.0	37.8	60.6	.5	1.1
Aggravated assault.......................	281,011	157,978	117,197	2,271	3,565	100.0	56.2	41.7	.8	1.3
Burglary	138,788	82,146	54,356	882	1,404	100.0	59.2	39.2	.6	1.0
Larceny–theft	636,069	387,052	233,351	6,810	8,856	100.0	60.9	36.7	1.1	1.4
Motor vehicle theft	66,657	36,640	28,108	503	1,406	100.0	55.0	42.2	.8	2.1
Arson	5,027	3,122	1,801	49	55	100.0	62.1	35.8	1.0	1.1
Violent crime[2]	388,957	200,812	180,441	2,854	4,850	100.0	51.6	46.4	.7	1.2
Property crime[3]	846,541	508,960	317,616	8,244	11,721	100.0	60.1	37.5	1.0	1.4
Crime Index total[4]	1,235,498	709,772	498,057	11,098	16,571	100.0	57.4	40.3	.9	1.3
Other assaults...........................	616,108	365,651	236,085	7,852	6,520	100.0	59.3	38.3	1.3	1.1
Forgery and counterfeiting	64,705	39,772	23,519	322	1,092	100.0	61.5	36.3	.5	1.7
Fraud	178,162	107,484	68,212	778	1,688	100.0	60.3	38.3	.4	.9
Embezzlement	8,053	5,045	2,858	46	104	100.0	62.6	35.5	.6	1.3
Stolen property; buying, receiving, possessing	73,884	39,997	32,652	407	828	100.0	54.1	44.2	.6	1.1
Vandalism..............................	101,717	66,234	32,941	1,407	1,135	100.0	65.1	32.4	1.4	1.1
Weapons; carrying, possessing, etc.	112,803	61,303	49,701	564	1,235	100.0	54.3	44.1	.5	1.1
Prostitution and commercialized vice	74,233	44,452	28,043	411	1,327	100.0	59.9	37.8	.6	1.8
Sex offenses (except forcible rape and prostitution)	44,153	32,081	10,948	488	636	100.0	72.7	24.8	1.1	1.4
Drug abuse violations	776,056	452,759	316,002	2,861	4,434	100.0	58.3	40.7	.4	.6
Gambling	12,707	7,040	4,998	63	606	100.0	55.4	39.3	.5	4.8
Offenses against family and children	54,255	36,005	16,216	591	1,443	100.0	66.4	29.9	1.1	2.7
Driving under the influence	610,528	525,813	69,350	9,446	5,919	100.0	86.1	11.4	1.5	1.0
Liquor laws	288,263	214,748	65,324	6,241	1,950	100.0	74.5	22.7	2.2	.7
Drunkenness............................	425,927	337,294	76,456	10,721	1,456	100.0	79.2	18.0	2.5	.3
Disorderly conduct	375,521	227,674	140,584	5,181	2,082	100.0	60.6	37.4	1.4	.6
Vagrancy..............................	16,753	8,241	8,017	439	56	100.0	49.2	47.9	2.6	.3
All other offenses (except traffic)	1,902,596	1,132,182	730,024	18,512	21,878	100.0	59.5	38.4	1.0	1.1
Suspicion	5,684	1,855	3,813	4	12	100.0	32.6	67.1	.1	.2
Curfew and loitering law violations										
Runaways..............................										

[1]Because of rounding, the percentages may not add to totals.
[2]Violent crimes are offenses of murder, forcible rape, robbery, and aggravated assault.
[3]Property crimes are offenses of burglary, larceny–theft, motor vehicle theft, and arson.
[4]Includes arson.

Table 50.—Suburban County Arrest Trends, 1994–1995

[961 agencies; 1995 estimated population 39,254,000; 1994 estimated population 38,792,000]

Offense charged	Number of persons arrested								
	Total all ages			Under 18 years of age			18 years of age and over		
	1994	1995	Percent change	1994	1995	Percent change	1994	1995	Percent change
TOTAL	1,698,638	1,743,002	+2.6	257,527	261,745	+1.6	1,441,111	1,481,257	+2.8
Murder and nonnegligent manslaughter	2,513	2,357	−6.2	311	331	+6.4	2,202	2,026	−8.0
Forcible rape	4,406	4,149	−5.8	717	624	-13.0	3,689	3,525	−4.4
Robbery	13,412	13,588	+1.3	3,750	3,804	+1.4	9,662	9,784	+1.3
Aggravated assault	69,534	72,862	+4.8	10,053	9,688	−3.6	59,481	63,174	+6.2
Burglary	51,092	49,960	−2.2	19,928	18,856	−5.4	31,164	31,104	−.2
Larceny–theft	138,493	142,198	+2.7	42,665	43,105	+1.0	95,828	99,093	+3.4
Motor vehicle theft	24,733	23,020	−6.9	9,838	8,935	−9.2	14,895	14,085	−5.4
Arson	2,439	2,255	−7.5	1,233	1,103	−10.5	1,206	1,152	−4.5
Violent crime[1]	89,865	92,956	+3.4	14,831	14,447	−2.6	75,034	78,509	+4.6
Property crime[2]	216,757	217,433	+.3	73,664	71,999	−2.3	143,093	145,434	+1.6
Crime Index total[3]	306,622	310,389	+1.2	88,495	86,446	−2.3	218,127	223,943	+2.7
Other assaults	132,204	145,419	+10.0	20,565	22,896	+11.3	111,639	122,523	+9.7
Forgery and counterfeiting	12,521	12,900	+3.0	743	798	+7.4	11,778	12,102	+2.8
Fraud	69,127	70,669	+2.2	1,037	1,049	+1.2	68,090	69,620	+2.2
Embezzlement	2,091	1,840	−12.0	83	89	+7.2	2,008	1,751	−12.8
Stolen property; buying, receiving, possessing	17,576	17,706	+.7	3,769	3,679	−2.4	13,807	14,027	+1.6
Vandalism	29,839	28,586	−4.2	14,428	13,134	−9.0	15,411	15,452	+.3
Weapons; carrying, possessing, etc.	26,996	24,369	−9.7	5,687	5,057	−11.1	21,309	19,312	−9.4
Prostitution and commercialized vice	4,417	5,285	+19.7	64	60	−6.3	4,353	5,225	+20.0
Sex offenses (except forcible rape and prostitution)	13,340	12,166	−8.8	2,286	2,059	−9.9	11,054	10,107	−8.6
Drug abuse violations	162,647	167,759	+3.1	15,568	18,575	+19.3	147,079	149,184	+1.4
Gambling	1,164	1,254	+7.7	62	62	—	1,102	1,192	+8.2
Offenses against family and children	26,304	32,785	+24.6	330	535	+62.1	25,974	32,250	+24.2
Driving under the influence	241,959	235,925	−2.5	1,837	1,820	−.9	240,122	234,105	−2.5
Liquor laws	41,413	40,447	−2.3	10,698	10,422	−2.6	30,715	30,025	−2.2
Drunkenness	46,844	48,227	+3.0	1,101	1,245	+13.1	45,743	46,982	+2.7
Disorderly conduct	38,268	39,104	+2.2	8,267	8,841	+6.9	30,001	30,263	+.9
Vagrancy	907	757	−16.5	238	143	−39.9	669	614	−8.2
All other offenses (except traffic)	478,877	502,354	+4.9	36,747	39,774	+8.2	442,130	462,580	+4.6
Suspicion (not included in totals)	1,767	1,627	−7.9	92	116	+26.1	1,675	1,511	−9.8
Curfew and loitering law violations	3,884	4,268	+9.9	3,884	4,268	+9.9	—	—	—
Runaways	41,638	40,793	−2.0	41,638	40,793	−2.0	—	—	—

[1]Violent crimes are offenses of murder, forcible rape, robbery, and aggravated assault.
[2]Property crimes are offenses of burglary, larceny–theft, motor vehicle theft, and arson.
[3]Includes arson.

238

Table 51.—Suburban County Arrest Trends, Sex, 1994–1995

[961 agencies; 1995 estimated population 39,254,000; 1994 estimated population 38,792,000]

Offense charged	Males						Females					
	Total			Under 18			Total			Under 18		
	1994	1995	Percent change	1994	1995	Percent change	1994	1995	Percent change	1994	1995	Percent change
TOTAL	1,367,033	1,391,300	+1.8	191,403	192,666	+.7	331,605	351,702	+6.1	66,124	69,079	+4.5
Murder and nonnegligent manslaughter	2,262	2,116	−6.5	296	296	—	251	241	−4.0	15	35	+133.3
Forcible rape	4,372	4,100	−6.2	708	615	−13.1	34	49	+44.1	9	9	—
Robbery	12,347	12,410	+.5	3,444	3,483	+1.1	1,065	1,178	+10.6	306	321	+4.9
Aggravated assault....................	58,939	60,977	+3.5	8,363	7,930	−5.2	10,595	11,885	+12.2	1,690	1,758	+4.0
Burglary	46,300	44,859	−3.1	18,181	17,155	−5.6	4,792	5,101	+6.4	1,747	1,701	−2.6
Larceny–theft........................	94,507	96,969	+2.6	29,997	30,213	+.7	43,986	45,229	+2.8	12,668	12,892	+1.8
Motor vehicle theft	21,725	19,959	−8.1	8,451	7,565	−10.5	3,008	3,061	+1.8	1,387	1,370	−1.2
Arson	2,084	1,905	−8.6	1,076	952	−11.5	355	350	−1.4	157	151	−3.8
Violent crime[1]	77,920	79,603	+2.2	12,811	12,324	−3.8	11,945	13,353	+11.8	2,020	2,123	+5.1
Property crime[2]	164,616	163,692	−.6	57,705	55,885	−3.2	52,141	53,741	+3.1	15,959	16,114	+1.0
Crime Index total[3]	242,536	243,295	+.3	70,516	68,209	−3.3	64,086	67,094	+4.7	17,979	18,237	+1.4
Other assaults......................	107,116	116,326	+8.6	15,329	16,815	+9.7	25,088	29,093	+16.0	5,236	6,081	+16.1
Forgery and counterfeiting	8,213	8,382	+2.1	535	554	+3.6	4,308	4,518	+4.9	208	244	+17.3
Fraud	37,179	38,259	+2.9	651	697	+7.1	31,948	32,410	+1.4	386	352	−8.8
Embezzlement	1,302	1,132	−13.1	57	54	−5.3	789	708	−10.3	26	35	+34.6
Stolen property; buying, receiving, possessing	15,269	15,270	[4]	3,314	3,234	−2.4	2,307	2,436	+5.6	455	445	−2.2
Vandalism.........................	26,342	24,960	−5.2	13,115	11,882	−9.4	3,497	3,626	+3.7	1,313	1,252	−4.6
Weapons; carrying, possessing, etc.	24,590	22,414	−8.8	5,237	4,622	−11.7	2,406	1,955	−18.7	450	435	−3.3
Prostitution and commercialized vice	2,247	3,389	+50.8	34	44	+29.4	2,170	1,896	−12.6	30	16	−46.7
Sex offenses (except forcible rape and prostitution)	12,507	11,462	−8.4	2,161	1,932	−10.6	833	704	−15.5	125	127	+1.6
Drug abuse violations	134,423	138,650	+3.1	13,488	15,858	+17.6	28,224	29,109	+3.1	2,080	2,717	+30.6
Gambling	988	1,096	+10.9	60	61	+1.7	176	158	−10.2	2	1	−50.0
Offenses against family and children	23,792	29,409	+23.6	217	344	+58.5	2,512	3,376	+34.4	113	191	+69.0
Driving under the influence	209,764	203,160	−3.1	1,589	1,536	−3.3	32,195	32,765	+1.8	248	284	+14.5
Liquor laws	32,651	31,154	−4.6	7,632	7,205	−5.6	8,762	9,293	+6.1	3,066	3,217	+4.9
Drunkenness........................	41,340	42,346	+2.4	907	1,027	+13.2	5,504	5,881	+6.8	194	218	+12.4
Disorderly conduct	30,665	30,887	+.7	6,303	6,666	+5.8	7,603	8,217	+8.1	1,964	2,175	+10.7
Vagrancy	786	646	−17.8	198	128	−35.4	121	111	−8.3	40	15	−62.5
All other offenses (except traffic)	394,289	408,432	+3.6	29,026	31,167	+7.4	84,588	93,922	+11.0	7,721	8,607	+11.5
Suspicion (not included in totals)	1,548	1,417	−8.5	80	97	+21.3	219	210	−4.1	12	19	+58.3
Curfew and loitering law violations	2,733	3,001	+9.8	2,733	3,001	+9.8	1,151	1,267	+10.1	1,151	1,267	+10.1
Runaways..........................	18,301	17,630	−3.7	18,301	17,630	−3.7	23,337	23,163	−.7	23,337	23,163	−.7

[1]Violent crimes are offenses of murder, forcible rape, robbery, and aggravated assault.
[2]Property crimes are offenses of burglary, larceny–theft, motor vehicle theft, and arson.
[3]Includes arson.
[4]Less than one-tenth of one percent.

Table 52.—Suburban County Arrests, Distribution by Age, 1995

[1,039 agencies; 1995 estimated population 43,729,000]

Offense charged	Total all ages	Ages under 15	Ages under 18	Ages 18 and over	Age									
					Under 10	10–12	13–14	15	16	17	18	19	20	21
TOTAL	**1,862,137**	**91,247**	**278,988**	**1,583,149**	**3,839**	**19,597**	**67,811**	**56,915**	**63,938**	**66,888**	**75,880**	**72,837**	**68,726**	**65,311**
Percent distribution1 ..	**100.0**	**4.9**	**15.0**	**85.0**	**.2**	**1.1**	**3.6**	**3.1**	**3.4**	**3.6**	**4.1**	**3.9**	**3.7**	**3.5**
Murder and nonnegligent manslaughter	2,518	48	353	2,165	—	6	42	61	117	127	198	139	157	117
Forcible rape	4,613	233	666	3,947	5	51	177	136	149	148	247	205	194	184
Robbery	14,578	930	4,068	10,510	17	173	740	827	1,076	1,235	1,285	989	791	669
Aggravated assault.........	77,774	3,345	10,250	67,524	187	803	2,355	1,954	2,325	2,626	2,893	2,601	2,510	2,505
Burglary	53,594	7,322	20,081	33,513	409	1,736	5,177	4,056	4,247	4,456	4,427	3,119	2,332	1,862
Larceny–theft	153,169	17,890	45,959	107,210	723	4,534	12,633	8,822	9,638	9,609	9,001	6,997	5,424	4,705
Motor vehicle theft	24,661	2,476	9,412	15,249	22	245	2,209	2,457	2,368	2,111	1,729	1,285	1,055	889
Arson	2,414	749	1,172	1,242	107	263	379	193	130	100	110	76	63	50
Violent crime[2]	99,483	4,556	15,337	84,146	209	1,033	3,314	2,978	3,667	4,136	4,623	3,934	3,652	3,475
Percent distribution[1]	100.0	4.6	15.4	84.6	.2	1.0	3.3	3.0	3.7	4.2	4.6	4.0	3.7	3.5
Property crime[3]	233,838	28,437	76,624	157,214	1,261	6,778	20,398	15,528	16,383	16,276	15,267	11,477	8,874	7,506
Percent distribution[1]	100.0	12.2	32.8	67.2	.5	2.9	8.7	6.6	7.0	7.0	6.5	4.9	3.8	3.2
Crime Index total[4]	333,321	32,993	91,961	241,360	1,470	7,811	23,712	18,506	20,050	20,412	19,890	15,411	12,526	10,981
Percent distribution[1]	100.0	9.9	27.6	72.4	.4	2.3	7.1	5.6	6.0	6.1	6.0	4.6	3.8	3.3
Other assaults..............	155,716	9,493	24,280	131,436	555	2,518	6,420	4,816	5,148	4,823	4,542	4,413	4,270	4,299
Forgery and counterfeiting ...	14,311	80	856	13,455	—	11	69	110	229	437	639	679	686	636
Fraud	75,775	153	1,121	74,654	6	17	130	124	249	595	1,394	2,158	2,706	2,986
Embezzlement	1,926	7	89	1,837	1	—	6	4	26	52	75	85	85	66
Stolen property; buying, receiving, possessing	19,289	897	4,001	15,288	12	141	744	826	1,060	1,218	1,457	1,245	949	825
Vandalism................	30,807	6,213	14,221	16,586	588	1,826	3,799	2,519	2,830	2,659	1,779	1,307	979	860
Weapons; carrying, possessing, etc.	26,746	1,688	5,358	21,388	57	383	1,248	1,009	1,184	1,477	1,769	1,459	1,289	1,144
Prostitution and commercialized vice	5,611	6	62	5,549	—	2	4	4	19	33	98	89	120	116
Sex offenses (except forcible rape and prostitution)	13,052	1,061	2,218	10,834	59	304	698	403	379	375	443	382	365	342
Drug abuse violations	178,319	3,177	19,519	158,800	23	351	2,803	3,443	5,304	7,595	10,469	9,609	8,549	7,771
Gambling	1,293	8	72	1,221	—	—	8	11	18	35	25	31	30	30
Offenses against family and children	34,968	175	602	34,366	3	35	137	138	144	145	523	538	692	867
Driving under the influence ..	251,519	43	1,957	249,562	6	5	32	93	480	1,341	3,528	4,815	5,950	8,280
Liquor laws	42,747	917	10,959	31,788	16	64	837	1,507	3,235	5,300	6,865	6,157	4,838	1,197
Drunkenness	53,975	170	1,364	52,611	4	22	144	201	350	643	1,588	1,521	1,497	1,813
Disorderly conduct	42,415	3,216	9,237	33,178	107	755	2,354	1,896	2,045	2,080	1,993	1,636	1,476	1,424
Vagrancy	825	35	153	672	—	5	30	28	36	54	43	37	32	31
All other offenses (except traffic)	528,734	10,858	41,687	487,047	464	2,129	8,265	8,059	10,258	12,512	18,700	21,222	21,640	21,599
Suspicion	1,648	34	131	1,517	3	3	28	14	19	64	60	43	47	44
Curfew and loitering law violations	4,482	1,224	4,482	—	9	154	1,061	1,058	1,279	921	—	—	—	—
Runaways................	44,658	18,799	44,658	—	456	3,061	15,282	12,146	9,596	4,117	—	—	—	—

See footnotes at end of table.

Table 52.—Suburban County Arrests, Distribution by Age, 1995 — Continued

Offense charged	Age											
	22	23	24	25–29	30–34	35–39	40–44	45–49	50–54	55–59	60–64	65 and over
TOTAL	**64,616**	**64,212**	**67,421**	**289,097**	**288,776**	**227,509**	**140,029**	**77,121**	**38,690**	**19,968**	**11,190**	**11,766**
Percent distribution[1]	**3.5**	**3.4**	**3.6**	**15.5**	**15.5**	**12.2**	**7.5**	**4.1**	**2.1**	**1.1**	**.6**	**.6**
Murder and nonnegligent manslaughter	128	95	115	350	274	205	155	83	52	41	23	33
Forcible rape	167	175	134	623	697	500	331	193	119	78	47	53
Robbery	554	480	480	1,893	1,534	1,025	514	157	73	32	17	17
Aggravated assault	2,435	2,459	2,609	12,270	12,877	10,507	6,306	3,544	1,851	895	564	698
Burglary	1,563	1,439	1,458	5,543	5,105	3,567	1,771	757	309	121	53	87
Larceny–theft	4,119	3,975	4,236	17,869	17,783	14,005	8,833	4,901	2,352	1,271	730	1,009
Motor vehicle theft	748	772	738	2,875	2,339	1,465	749	353	109	63	46	34
Arson	49	49	49	176	185	150	112	77	46	17	13	20
Violent crime[2]	3,284	3,209	3,338	15,136	15,382	12,237	7,306	3,977	2,095	1,046	651	801
Percent distribution[1]	3.3	3.2	3.4	15.2	15.5	12.3	7.3	4.0	2.1	1.1	.7	.8
Property crime[3]	6,479	6,235	6,481	26,463	25,412	19,187	11,465	6,088	2,816	1,472	842	1,150
Percent distribution[1]	2.8	2.7	2.8	11.3	10.9	8.2	4.9	2.6	1.2	.6	.4	.5
Crime Index total[4]	9,763	9,444	9,819	41,599	40,794	31,424	18,771	10,065	4,911	2,518	1,493	1,951
Percent distribution[1]	2.9	2.8	2.9	12.5	12.2	9.4	5.6	3.0	1.5	.8	.4	.6
Other assaults	4,694	4,825	5,393	24,163	26,510	21,465	12,747	6,902	3,344	1,686	1,041	1,142
Forgery and counterfeiting	626	615	667	2,645	2,563	1,835	977	494	216	79	60	38
Fraud	3,294	3,232	3,472	15,532	14,122	10,980	7,169	3,882	1,845	983	459	440
Embezzlement	82	98	91	350	317	273	134	97	42	24	10	8
Stolen property; buying, receiving, possessing	789	688	735	2,770	2,385	1,709	914	401	230	97	50	44
Vandalism	741	647	709	2,882	2,676	1,923	1,017	506	254	118	86	102
Weapons; carrying, possessing, etc.	1,067	1,027	987	3,518	3,082	2,420	1,500	924	507	294	221	180
Prostitution and commercialized vice	141	172	210	1,038	1,252	990	554	330	165	104	70	100
Sex offenses (except forcible rape and prostitution)	325	292	294	1,532	1,879	1,641	1,152	739	516	343	233	356
Drug abuse violations	7,229	6,968	6,924	29,538	28,623	21,644	12,062	5,599	2,146	901	427	341
Gambling	40	51	41	141	100	167	145	130	101	75	44	70
Offenses against family and children	954	1,061	1,362	6,682	7,726	6,556	3,855	1,998	895	391	164	102
Driving under the influence	9,169	9,646	10,291	46,007	46,627	38,883	27,031	17,417	10,175	5,528	3,117	3,098
Liquor laws	907	770	680	2,690	2,400	1,970	1,336	817	495	320	162	184
Drunkenness	1,702	1,814	1,847	8,358	9,475	8,673	6,208	3,765	1,995	1,108	624	623
Disorderly conduct	1,389	1,315	1,409	5,621	5,804	4,695	2,901	1,657	868	440	273	277
Vagrancy	25	33	14	113	131	82	72	37	11	6	2	3
All other offenses (except traffic)	21,629	21,462	22,426	93,683	91,985	69,937	41,316	21,261	9,928	4,925	2,643	2,691
Suspicion	50	52	50	235	325	242	168	100	46	28	11	16
Curfew and loitering law violations	—	—	—	—	—	—	—	—	—	—	—	—
Runaways	—	—	—	—	—	—	—	—	—	—	—	—

[1]Because of rounding, the percentages may not add to totals.
[2]Violent crimes are offenses of murder, forcible rape, robbery, and aggravated assault.
[3]Property crimes are offenses of burglary, larceny–theft, motor vehicle theft, and arson.
[4]Includes arson.

Table 53.—Suburban County Arrests of Persons under 15, 18, 21, and 25 Years of Age, 1995

[1,039 agencies; 1995 estimated population 43,729,000]

Offense charged	Total all ages	Number of persons arrested				Percent of total all ages			
		Under 15	Under 18	Under 21	Under 25	Under 15	Under 18	Under 21	Under 25
TOTAL	1,862,137	91,247	278,988	496,431	757,991	4.9	15.0	26.7	40.7
Murder and nonnegligent manslaughter	2,518	48	353	847	1,302	1.9	14.0	33.6	51.7
Forcible rape	4,613	233	666	1,312	1,972	5.1	14.4	28.4	42.7
Robbery	14,578	930	4,068	7,133	9,316	6.4	27.9	48.9	63.9
Aggravated assault............................	77,774	3,345	10,250	18,254	28,262	4.3	13.2	23.5	36.3
Burglary	53,594	7,322	20,081	29,959	36,281	13.7	37.5	55.9	67.7
Larceny–theft.............................	153,169	17,890	45,959	67,381	84,416	11.7	30.0	44.0	55.1
Motor vehicle theft	24,661	2,476	9,412	13,481	16,628	10.0	38.2	54.7	67.4
Arson	2,414	749	1,172	1,421	1,618	31.0	48.6	58.9	67.0
Violent crime[1]	99,483	4,556	15,337	27,546	40,852	4.6	15.4	27.7	41.1
Property crime[2]	233,838	28,437	76,624	112,242	138,943	12.2	32.8	48.0	59.4
Crime Index total[3]	333,321	32,993	91,961	139,788	179,795	9.9	27.6	41.9	53.9
Other assaults.....................................	155,716	9,493	24,280	37,505	56,716	6.1	15.6	24.1	36.4
Forgery and counterfeiting	14,311	80	856	2,860	5,404	.6	6.0	20.0	37.8
Fraud	75,775	153	1,121	7,379	20,363	.2	1.5	9.7	26.9
Embezzlement	1,926	7	89	334	671	.4	4.6	17.3	34.8
Stolen property; buying, receiving, possessing	19,289	897	4,001	7,652	10,689	4.7	20.7	39.7	55.4
Vandalism..	30,807	6,213	14,221	18,286	21,243	20.2	46.2	59.4	69.0
Weapons; carrying, possessing, etc.	26,746	1,688	5,358	9,875	14,100	6.3	20.0	36.9	52.7
Prostitution and commercialized vice	5,611	6	62	369	1,008	.1	1.1	6.6	18.0
Sex offenses (except forcible rape and prostitution)	13,052	1,061	2,218	3,408	4,661	8.1	17.0	26.1	35.7
Drug abuse violations	178,319	3,177	19,519	48,146	77,038	1.8	10.9	27.0	43.2
Gambling	1,293	8	72	158	320	.6	5.6	12.2	24.7
Offenses against family and children	34,968	175	602	2,355	6,599	.5	1.7	6.7	18.9
Driving under the influence	251,519	43	1,957	16,250	53,636	[4]	.8	6.5	21.3
Liquor laws	42,747	917	10,959	28,819	32,373	2.1	25.6	67.4	75.7
Drunkenness.....................................	53,975	170	1,364	5,970	13,146	.3	2.5	11.1	24.4
Disorderly conduct	42,415	3,216	9,237	14,342	19,879	7.6	21.8	33.8	46.9
Vagrancy..	825	35	153	265	368	4.2	18.5	32.1	44.6
All other offenses (except traffic)	528,734	10,858	41,687	103,249	190,365	2.1	7.9	19.5	36.0
Suspicion	1,648	34	131	281	477	2.1	7.9	17.1	28.9
Curfew and loitering law violations	4,482	1,224	4,482	4,482	4,482	27.3	100.0	100.0	100.0
Runaways.......................................	44,658	18,799	44,658	44,658	44,658	42.1	100.0	100.0	100.0

[1]Violent crimes are offenses of murder, forcible rape, robbery, and aggravated assault.
[2]Property crimes are offenses of burglary, larceny–theft, motor vehicle theft, and arson.
[3]Includes arson.
[4]Less than one-tenth of 1 percent.

Table 54.—Suburban County Arrests, Distribution by Sex, 1995

[1,039 agencies; 1995 estimated population 43,729,000]

Offense charged	Number of persons arrested			Percent male	Percent female	Percent distribution[1]		
	Total	Male	Female			Total	Male	Female
TOTAL	**1,862,137**	**1,487,237**	**374,900**	**79.9**	**20.1**	**100.0**	**100.0**	**100.0**
Murder and nonnegligent manslaughter	2,518	2,259	259	89.7	10.3	.1	.2	.1
Forcible rape	4,613	4,556	57	98.8	1.2	.2	.3	[2]
Robbery	14,578	13,339	1,239	91.5	8.5	.8	.9	.3
Aggravated assault.................................	77,774	64,966	12,808	83.5	16.5	4.2	4.4	3.4
Burglary	53,594	48,171	5,423	89.9	10.1	2.9	3.2	1.4
Larceny–theft	153,169	104,486	48,683	68.2	31.8	8.2	7.0	13.0
Motor vehicle theft	24,661	21,434	3,227	86.9	13.1	1.3	1.4	.9
Arson	2,414	2,050	364	84.9	15.1	.1	.1	.1
Violent crime[3]	99,483	85,120	14,363	85.6	14.4	5.3	5.7	3.8
Property crime[4]	233,838	176,141	57,697	75.3	24.7	12.6	11.8	15.4
Crime Index total[5]	333,321	261,261	72,060	78.4	21.6	17.9	17.6	19.2
Other assaults....................................	155,716	124,742	30,974	80.1	19.9	8.4	8.4	8.3
Forgery and counterfeiting	14,311	9,314	4,997	65.1	34.9	.8	.6	1.3
Fraud	75,775	41,051	34,724	54.2	45.8	4.1	2.8	9.3
Embezzlement	1,926	1,186	740	61.6	38.4	.1	.1	.2
Stolen property; buying, receiving, possessing	19,289	16,656	2,633	86.3	13.7	1.0	1.1	.7
Vandalism..	30,807	26,902	3,905	87.3	12.7	1.7	1.8	1.0
Weapons; carrying, possessing, etc.	26,746	24,569	2,177	91.9	8.1	1.4	1.7	.6
Prostitution and commercialized vice	5,611	3,513	2,098	62.6	37.4	.3	.2	.6
Sex offenses (except forcible rape and prostitution)	13,052	12,328	724	94.5	5.5	.7	.8	.2
Drug abuse violations	178,319	147,700	30,619	82.8	17.2	9.6	9.9	8.2
Gambling	1,293	1,129	164	87.3	12.7	.1	.1	[2]
Offenses against family and children	34,968	31,309	3,659	89.5	10.5	1.9	2.1	1.0
Driving under the influence	251,519	216,589	34,930	86.1	13.9	13.5	14.6	9.3
Liquor laws	42,747	32,933	9,814	77.0	23.0	2.3	2.2	2.6
Drunkenness......................................	53,975	47,396	6,579	87.8	12.2	2.9	3.2	1.8
Disorderly conduct	42,415	33,587	8,828	79.2	20.8	2.3	2.3	2.4
Vagrancy...	825	710	115	86.1	13.9	[2]	[2]	[2]
All other offenses (except traffic)	528,734	430,545	98,189	81.4	18.6	28.4	28.9	26.2
Suspicion	1,648	1,436	212	87.1	12.9	.1	.1	.1
Curfew and loitering law violations	4,482	3,167	1,315	70.7	29.3	.2	.2	.4
Runaways...	44,658	19,214	25,444	43.0	57.0	2.4	1.3	6.8

[1]Because of rounding, the percentages may not add to totals.
[2]Less than one-tenth of 1 percent.
[3]Violent crimes are offenses of murder, forcible rape, robbery, and aggravated assault.
[4]Property crimes are offenses of burglary, larceny–theft, motor vehicle theft, and arson.
[5]Includes arson.

Table 55.—Suburban County Arrests, Distribution by Race, 1995

[1,039 agencies; 1995 estimated population 43,729,000]

Offense charged	Total arrests					Percent distribution[1]				
	Total	White	Black	American Indian or Alaskan Native	Asian or Pacific Islander	Total	White	Black	American Indian or Alaskan Native	Asian or Pacific Islander
TOTAL	**1,849,812**	**1,371,282**	**460,092**	**8,456**	**9,982**	**100.0**	**74.1**	**24.9**	**.5**	**.5**
Murder and nonnegligent manslaughter	2,516	1,659	834	12	11	100.0	65.9	33.1	.5	.4
Forcible rape	4,588	3,225	1,309	20	34	100.0	70.3	28.5	.4	.7
Robbery	14,571	6,963	7,461	51	96	100.0	47.8	51.2	.4	.7
Aggravated assault.........................	77,599	55,345	21,400	410	444	100.0	71.3	27.6	.5	.6
Burglary	53,406	41,054	11,772	249	331	100.0	76.9	22.0	.5	.6
Larceny–theft	152,750	104,006	46,712	598	1,434	100.0	68.1	30.6	.4	.9
Motor vehicle theft	24,615	17,107	7,178	109	221	100.0	69.5	29.2	.4	.9
Arson	2,404	2,042	343	10	9	100.0	84.9	14.3	.4	.4
Violent crime[2]	99,274	67,192	31,004	493	585	100.0	67.7	31.2	.5	.6
Property crime[3]	233,175	164,209	66,005	966	1,995	100.0	70.4	28.3	.4	.9
Crime Index total[4]	332,449	231,401	97,009	1,459	2,580	100.0	69.6	29.2	.4	.8
Other assaults.............................	154,755	114,503	38,726	731	795	100.0	74.0	25.0	.5	.5
Forgery and counterfeiting	14,268	10,053	4,098	35	82	100.0	70.5	28.7	.2	.6
Fraud	75,438	52,045	22,977	246	170	100.0	69.0	30.5	.3	.2
Embezzlement	1,925	1,301	599	5	20	100.0	67.6	31.1	.3	1.0
Stolen property; buying, receiving, possessing	19,228	13,591	5,376	87	174	100.0	70.7	28.0	.5	.9
Vandalism................................	30,730	25,527	4,824	196	183	100.0	83.1	15.7	.6	.6
Weapons; carrying, possessing, etc.	26,684	18,724	7,664	92	204	100.0	70.2	28.7	.3	.8
Prostitution and commercialized vice	5,608	4,071	1,465	13	59	100.0	72.6	26.1	.2	1.1
Sex offenses (except forcible rape and prostitution)	13,000	10,908	1,943	62	87	100.0	83.9	14.9	.5	.7
Drug abuse violations	178,069	128,731	48,161	532	645	100.0	72.3	27.0	.3	.4
Gambling	1,291	796	464	5	26	100.0	61.7	35.9	.4	2.0
Offenses against family and children	34,378	20,486	13,765	59	68	100.0	59.6	40.0	.2	.2
Driving under the influence	243,706	219,170	21,573	978	1,985	100.0	89.9	8.9	.4	.8
Liquor laws	42,642	37,987	3,985	404	266	100.0	89.1	9.3	.9	.6
Drunkenness..............................	53,972	47,387	5,813	494	278	100.0	87.8	10.8	.9	.5
Disorderly conduct	42,299	31,075	10,681	325	218	100.0	73.5	25.3	.8	.5
Vagrancy................................	825	649	166	4	6	100.0	78.7	20.1	.5	.7
All other offenses (except traffic)	527,780	360,354	163,043	2,473	1,910	100.0	68.3	30.9	.5	.4
Suspicion	1,646	1,493	127	25	1	100.0	90.7	7.7	1.5	.1
Curfew and loitering law violations	4,477	3,823	597	17	40	100.0	85.4	13.3	.4	.9
Runaways................................	44,642	37,207	7,036	214	185	100.0	83.3	15.8	.5	.4

See footnotes at end of table.

Table 55.—Suburban County Arrests, Distribution by Race, 1995 — Continued

Offense charged	Arrests under 18					Percent distribution[1]				
	Total	White	Black	American Indian or Alaskan Native	Asian or Pacific Islander	Total	White	Black	American Indian or Alaskan Native	Asian or Pacific Islander
TOTAL	278,469	210,233	64,495	1,465	2,276	100.0	75.5	23.2	.5	.8
Murder and nonnegligent manslaughter	352	190	158	1	3	100.0	54.0	44.9	.3	.9
Forcible rape	662	449	206	1	6	100.0	67.8	31.1	.2	.9
Robbery	4,066	1,797	2,208	14	47	100.0	44.2	54.3	.3	1.2
Aggravated assault..........................	10,224	6,517	3,573	54	80	100.0	63.7	34.9	.5	.8
Burglary	20,022	15,845	3,875	117	185	100.0	79.1	19.4	.6	.9
Larceny–theft..............................	45,886	32,700	12,374	215	597	100.0	71.3	27.0	.5	1.3
Motor vehicle theft	9,389	6,396	2,793	50	150	100.0	68.1	29.7	.5	1.6
Arson	1,170	1,015	144	6	5	100.0	86.8	12.3	.5	.4
Violent crime[2]	15,304	8,953	6,145	70	136	100.0	58.5	40.2	.5	.9
Property crime[3]	76,467	55,956	19,186	388	937	100.0	73.2	25.1	.5	1.2
Crime Index total[4]	91,771	64,909	25,331	458	1,073	100.0	70.7	27.6	.5	1.2
Other assaults..............................	24,204	16,483	7,401	164	156	100.0	68.1	30.6	.7	.6
Forgery and counterfeiting	856	717	129	3	7	100.0	83.8	15.1	.4	.8
Fraud	1,116	852	249	4	11	100.0	76.3	22.3	.4	1.0
Embezzlement	89	64	23	—	2	100.0	71.9	25.8	—	2.2
Stolen property; buying, receiving, possessing	3,993	2,853	1,061	12	67	100.0	71.5	26.6	.3	1.7
Vandalism.................................	14,190	12,197	1,810	81	102	100.0	86.0	12.8	.6	.7
Weapons; carrying, possessing, etc.	5,346	3,742	1,504	29	71	100.0	70.0	28.1	.5	1.3
Prostitution and commercialized vice	61	37	23	—	1	100.0	60.7	37.7	—	1.6
Sex offenses (except forcible rape and prostitution)	2,197	1,705	476	6	10	100.0	77.6	21.7	.3	.5
Drug abuse violations	19,478	14,493	4,794	85	106	100.0	74.4	24.6	.4	.5
Gambling	72	15	56	—	1	100.0	20.8	77.8	—	1.4
Offenses against family and children	589	477	107	2	3	100.0	81.0	18.2	.3	.5
Driving under the influence	1,924	1,802	105	11	6	100.0	93.7	5.5	.6	.3
Liquor laws	10,940	10,386	405	95	54	100.0	94.9	3.7	.9	.5
Drunkenness................................	1,364	1,253	89	12	10	100.0	91.9	6.5	.9	.7
Disorderly conduct	9,234	6,169	2,939	72	54	100.0	66.8	31.8	.8	.6
Vagrancy..................................	153	142	10	1	—	100.0	92.8	6.5	.7	—
All other offenses (except traffic)	41,642	30,790	10,338	197	317	100.0	73.9	24.8	.5	.8
Suspicion	131	117	12	2	—	100.0	89.3	9.2	1.5	—
Curfew and loitering law violations	4,477	3,823	597	17	40	100.0	85.4	13.3	.4	.9
Runaways..................................	44,642	37,207	7,036	214	185	100.0	83.3	15.8	.5	.4

See footnotes at end of table.

Table 55.—Suburban County Arrests, Distribution by Race, 1995 — Continued

Offense charged	Arrests 18 and over					Percent distribution[1]				
	Total	White	Black	American Indian or Alaskan Native	Asian or Pacific Islander	Total	White	Black	American Indian or Alaskan Native	Asian or Pacific Islander
TOTAL	1,571,343	1,161,049	395,597	6,991	7,706	100.0	73.9	25.2	.4	.5
Murder and nonnegligent manslaughter	2,164	1,469	676	11	8	100.0	67.9	31.2	.5	.4
Forcible rape	3,926	2,776	1,103	19	28	100.0	70.7	28.1	.5	.7
Robbery	10,505	5,166	5,253	37	49	100.0	49.2	50.0	.4	.5
Aggravated assault..........................	67,375	48,828	17,827	356	364	100.0	72.5	26.5	.5	.5
Burglary	33,384	25,209	7,897	132	146	100.0	75.5	23.7	.4	.4
Larceny–theft	106,864	71,306	34,338	383	837	100.0	66.7	32.1	.4	.8
Motor vehicle theft	15,226	10,711	4,385	59	71	100.0	70.3	28.8	.4	.5
Arson	1,234	1,027	199	4	4	100.0	83.2	16.1	.3	.3
Violent crime[2]	83,970	58,239	24,859	423	449	100.0	69.4	29.6	.5	.5
Property crime[3]	156,708	108,253	46,819	578	1,058	100.0	69.1	29.9	.4	.7
Crime Index total[4]	240,678	166,492	71,678	1,001	1,507	100.0	69.2	29.8	.4	.6
Other assaults.............................	130,551	98,020	31,325	567	639	100.0	75.1	24.0	.4	.5
Forgery and counterfeiting	13,412	9,336	3,969	32	75	100.0	69.6	29.6	.2	.6
Fraud	74,322	51,193	22,728	242	159	100.0	68.9	30.6	.3	.2
Embezzlement	1,836	1,237	576	5	18	100.0	67.4	31.4	.3	1.0
Stolen property; buying, receiving, possessing	15,235	10,738	4,315	75	107	100.0	70.5	28.3	.5	.7
Vandalism................................	16,540	13,330	3,014	115	81	100.0	80.6	18.2	.7	.5
Weapons; carrying, possessing, etc.	21,338	14,982	6,160	63	133	100.0	70.2	28.9	.3	.6
Prostitution and commercialized vice	5,547	4,034	1,442	13	58	100.0	72.7	26.0	.2	1.0
Sex offenses (except forcible rape and prostitution)	10,803	9,203	1,467	56	77	100.0	85.2	13.6	.5	.7
Drug abuse violations	158,591	114,238	43,367	447	539	100.0	72.0	27.3	.3	.3
Gambling	1,219	781	408	5	25	100.0	64.1	33.5	.4	2.1
Offenses against family and children	33,789	20,009	13,658	57	65	100.0	59.2	40.4	.2	.2
Driving under the influence	241,782	217,368	21,468	967	1,979	100.0	89.9	8.9	.4	.8
Liquor laws	31,702	27,601	3,580	309	212	100.0	87.1	11.3	1.0	.7
Drunkenness..............................	52,608	46,134	5,724	482	268	100.0	87.7	10.9	.9	.5
Disorderly conduct	33,065	24,906	7,742	253	164	100.0	75.3	23.4	.8	.5
Vagrancy.................................	672	507	156	3	6	100.0	75.4	23.2	.4	.9
All other offenses (except traffic)	486,138	329,564	152,705	2,276	1,593	100.0	67.8	31.4	.5	.3
Suspicion	1,515	1,376	115	23	1	100.0	90.8	7.6	1.5	.1
Curfew and loitering law violations	—	—	—	—	—	—	—	—	—	—
Runaways................................	—	—	—	—	—	—	—	—	—	—

[1]Because of rounding, the percentages may not add to totals.
[2]Violent crimes are offenses of murder, forcible rape, robbery, and aggravated assault.
[3]Property crimes are offenses of burglary, larceny–theft, motor vehicle theft, and arson.
[4]Includes arson.

Table 56.—Rural County Arrest Trends, 1994–1995

[1,741 agencies; 1995 estimated population 18,087,000; 1994 estimated population 18,088,000]

Offense charged	Number of persons arrested								
	Total all ages			Under 18 years of age			18 years of age and over		
	1994	1995	Percent change	1994	1995	Percent change	1994	1995	Percent change
TOTAL	**763,728**	**788,751**	**+3.3**	**90,594**	**93,599**	**+3.3**	**673,134**	**695,152**	**+3.3**
Murder and nonnegligent manslaughter	1,166	1,175	+.8	142	122	−14.1	1,024	1,053	+2.8
Forcible rape	2,399	2,056	−14.3	325	290	−10.8	2,074	1,766	−14.9
Robbery	2,187	2,421	+10.7	422	534	+26.5	1,765	1,887	+6.9
Aggravated assault.......................	25,431	25,642	+.8	2,738	2,780	+1.5	22,693	22,862	+.7
Burglary	25,127	24,409	−2.9	9,097	8,805	−3.2	16,030	15,604	−2.7
Larceny–theft..........................	39,292	39,598	+.8	11,099	10,908	−1.7	28,193	28,690	+1.8
Motor vehicle theft	6,478	6,938	+7.1	2,719	2,835	+4.3	3,759	4,103	+9.2
Arson	1,128	1,133	+.4	389	382	−1.8	739	751	+1.6
Violent crime[1]	31,183	31,294	+.4	3,627	3,726	+2.7	27,556	27,568	[3]
Property crime[2]	72,025	72,078	+.1	23,304	22,930	−1.6	48,721	49,148	+.9
Crime Index total[4]	103,208	103,372	+.2	26,931	26,656	−1.0	76,277	76,716	+.6
Other assaults..........................	60,293	67,638	+12.2	6,331	7,248	+14.5	53,962	60,390	+11.9
Forgery and counterfeiting	6,110	6,385	+4.5	449	376	−16.3	5,661	6,009	+6.1
Fraud	42,826	46,524	+8.6	659	856	+29.9	42,167	45,668	+8.3
Embezzlement	801	717	−10.5	63	37	−41.3	738	680	−7.9
Stolen property; buying, receiving, possessing	6,153	6,303	+2.4	1,198	1,158	−3.3	4,955	5,145	+3.8
Vandalism............................	15,287	15,373	+.6	6,156	6,003	−2.5	9,131	9,370	+2.6
Weapons; carrying, possessing, etc.	10,812	10,421	−3.6	1,501	1,469	−2.1	9,311	8,952	−3.9
Prostitution and commercialized vice	185	236	+27.6	4	16	+300.0	181	220	+21.5
Sex offenses (except forcible rape and prostitution)	5,956	5,573	−6.4	1,068	1,045	−2.2	4,888	4,528	−7.4
Drug abuse violations	54,946	60,201	+9.6	4,420	5,678	+28.5	50,526	54,523	+7.9
Gambling	312	454	+45.5	9	20	+122.2	303	434	+43.2
Offenses against family and children	8,950	9,776	+9.2	291	297	+2.1	8,659	9,479	+9.5
Driving under the influence	159,499	150,599	−5.6	1,781	1,720	−3.4	157,718	148,879	−5.6
Liquor laws	34,340	33,116	−3.6	9,139	9,165	+.3	25,201	23,951	−5.0
Drunkenness...........................	29,334	28,618	−2.4	660	635	−3.8	28,674	27,983	−2.4
Disorderly conduct	22,876	23,563	+3.0	3,473	3,946	+13.6	19,403	19,617	+1.1
Vagrancy.............................	282	347	+23.0	64	59	−7.8	218	288	+32.1
All other offenses (except traffic)	189,789	208,395	+9.8	14,628	16,075	+9.9	175,161	192,320	+9.8
Suspicion (not included in totals)	711	327	−54.0	141	83	−41.1	570	244	−57.2
Curfew and loitering law violations	1,905	1,469	−22.9	1,905	1,469	−22.9	—	—	—
Runaways.............................	9,864	9,671	−2.0	9,864	9,671	−2.0	—	—	—

[1]Violent crimes are offenses of murder, forcible rape, robbery, and aggravated assault.
[2]Property crimes are offenses of burglary, larceny–theft, motor vehicle theft, and arson.
[3]Less than one-tenth of 1 percent.
[4]Includes arson.

Table 57.—Rural County Arrest Trends, Sex, 1994–1995

[1,741 agencies; 1995 estimated population 18,087,000; 1994 estimated population 18,088,000]

Offense charged	Males						Females					
	Total			Under 18			Total			Under 18		
	1994	1995	Percent change	1994	1995	Percent change	1994	1995	Percent change	1994	1995	Percent change
TOTAL	622,922	637,032	+2.3	69,114	71,243	+3.1	140,806	151,719	+7.8	21,480	22,356	+4.1
Murder and nonnegligent manslaughter	1,012	1,018	+.6	125	104	−16.8	154	157	+1.9	17	18	+5.9
Forcible rape	2,369	2,018	−14.8	316	281	−11.1	30	38	+26.7	9	9	—
Robbery	1,988	2,219	+11.6	407	488	+19.9	199	202	+1.5	15	46	+206.7
Aggravated assault....................	21,844	21,768	−.3	2,254	2,267	+.6	3,587	3,874	+8.0	484	513	+6.0
Burglary	22,959	22,127	−3.6	8,354	8,050	−3.6	2,168	2,282	+5.3	743	755	+1.6
Larceny–theft	30,070	30,221	+.5	8,779	8,744	−.4	9,222	9,377	+1.7	2,320	2,164	−6.7
Motor vehicle theft	5,506	5,839	+6.0	2,165	2,288	+5.7	972	1,099	+13.1	554	547	−1.3
Arson	987	982	−.5	353	340	−3.7	141	151	+7.1	36	42	+16.7
Violent crime[1]	27,213	27,023	−.7	3,102	3,140	+1.2	3,970	4,271	+7.6	525	586	+11.6
Property crime[2]	59,522	59,169	−.6	19,651	19,422	−1.2	12,503	12,909	+3.2	3,653	3,508	−4.0
Crime Index total[3]	86,735	86,192	−.6	22,753	22,562	−.8	16,473	17,180	+4.3	4,178	4,094	−2.0
Other assaults......................	49,571	54,957	+10.9	4,773	5,357	+12.2	10,722	12,681	+18.3	1,558	1,891	+21.4
Forgery and counterfeiting	3,952	4,035	+2.1	284	252	−11.3	2,158	2,350	+8.9	165	124	−24.8
Fraud	22,512	24,079	+7.0	399	452	+13.3	20,314	22,445	+10.5	260	404	+55.4
Embezzlement	506	405	−20.0	48	23	−52.1	295	312	+5.8	15	14	−6.7
Stolen property; buying, receiving, possessing	5,372	5,383	+.2	1,033	999	−3.3	781	920	+17.8	165	159	−3.6
Vandalism..........................	13,300	13,233	−.5	5,549	5,368	−3.3	1,987	2,140	+7.7	607	635	+4.6
Weapons; carrying, possessing, etc.	10,073	9,702	−3.7	1,392	1,370	−1.6	739	719	−2.7	109	99	−9.2
Prostitution and commercialized vice	96	145	+51.0	2	8	+300.0	89	91	+2.2	2	8	+300.0
Sex offenses (except forcible rape and prostitution)	5,669	5,312	−6.3	984	967	−1.7	287	261	−9.1	84	78	−7.1
Drug abuse violations	46,325	50,553	+9.1	3,787	4,808	+27.0	8,621	9,648	+11.9	633	870	+37.4
Gambling	275	374	+36.0	9	17	+88.9	37	80	+116.2	—	3	—
Offenses against family and children	7,745	8,219	+6.1	215	220	+2.3	1,205	1,557	+29.2	76	77	+1.3
Driving under the influence	138,513	130,299	−5.9	1,538	1,474	−4.2	20,986	20,300	−3.3	243	246	+1.2
Liquor laws	27,005	25,812	−4.4	6,202	6,219	+.3	7,335	7,304	−.4	2,937	2,946	+.3
Drunkenness........................	25,896	25,166	−2.8	543	544	+.2	3,438	3,452	+.4	117	91	−22.2
Disorderly conduct	18,350	18,693	+1.9	2,614	2,966	+13.5	4,526	4,870	+7.6	859	980	+14.1
Vagrancy	233	291	+24.9	45	46	+2.2	49	56	+14.3	19	13	−31.6
All other offenses (except traffic)	155,184	168,964	+8.9	11,334	12,373	+9.2	34,605	39,431	+13.9	3,294	3,702	+12.4
Suspicion (not included in totals)	620	259	−58.2	117	58	−50.4	91	68	−25.3	24	25	+4.2
Curfew and loitering law violations	1,231	971	−21.1	1,231	971	−21.1	674	498	−26.1	674	498	−26.1
Runaways..........................	4,379	4,247	−3.0	4,379	4,247	−3.0	5,485	5,424	−1.1	5,485	5,424	−1.1

[1]Violent crimes are offenses of murder, forcible rape, robbery, and aggravated assault.
[2]Property crimes are offenses of burglary, larceny–theft, motor vehicle theft, and arson.
[3]Includes arson.

Table 58.—Rural County Arrests, Distribution by Age, 1995

[1,918 agencies; 1995 estimated population 19,780,000]

Offense charged	Total all ages	Ages under 15	Ages under 18	Ages 18 and over	Age									
					Under 10	10–12	13–14	15	16	17	18	19	20	21
TOTAL	862,321	28,222	99,765	762,556	1,503	6,150	20,569	17,949	24,598	28,996	38,740	37,517	35,773	32,077
Percent distribution[1] ..	100.0	3.3	11.6	88.4	.2	.7	2.4	2.1	2.9	3.4	4.5	4.4	4.1	3.7
Murder and nonnegligent manslaughter	1,311	22	129	1,182	—	1	21	24	36	47	54	60	59	59
Forcible rape	2,250	100	307	1,943	4	19	77	51	59	97	114	107	81	83
Robbery	2,634	113	564	2,070	4	13	96	97	143	211	252	195	156	155
Aggravated assault	28,063	828	2,963	25,100	28	176	624	557	725	853	1,110	956	998	978
Burglary	26,567	3,132	9,357	17,210	226	736	2,170	1,684	2,152	2,389	2,562	1,978	1,334	1,066
Larceny–theft	43,343	4,169	11,458	31,885	225	1,161	2,783	2,010	2,533	2,746	2,947	2,334	1,966	1,458
Motor vehicle theft	7,586	803	3,028	4,558	7	78	718	752	788	685	511	423	355	255
Arson	1,265	240	416	849	30	86	124	51	63	62	75	71	47	36
Violent crime[2]	34,258	1,063	3,963	30,295	36	209	818	729	963	1,208	1,530	1,318	1,294	1,275
Percent distribution[1]	100.0	3.1	11.6	88.4	.1	.6	2.4	2.1	2.8	3.5	4.5	3.8	3.8	3.7
Property crime[3]	78,761	8,344	24,259	54,502	488	2,061	5,795	4,497	5,536	5,882	6,095	4,806	3,702	2,815
Percent distribution[1]	100.0	10.6	30.8	69.2	.6	2.6	7.4	5.7	7.0	7.5	7.7	6.1	4.7	3.6
Crime Index total[4]	113,019	9,407	28,222	84,797	524	2,270	6,613	5,226	6,499	7,090	7,625	6,124	4,996	4,090
Percent distribution[1]	100.0	8.3	25.0	75.0	.5	2.0	5.9	4.6	5.8	6.3	6.7	5.4	4.4	3.6
Other assaults	72,064	2,636	7,635	64,429	145	638	1,853	1,268	1,769	1,962	2,492	2,312	2,317	2,407
Forgery and counterfeiting ...	7,476	60	424	7,052	2	9	49	58	111	195	396	378	383	339
Fraud	49,446	160	891	48,555	7	32	121	119	246	366	1,128	1,536	1,896	2,126
Embezzlement	794	8	39	755	1	1	6	2	11	18	27	40	30	22
Stolen property; buying, receiving, possessing	6,994	267	1,263	5,731	4	39	224	233	335	428	526	452	396	343
Vandalism................	16,234	2,601	6,343	9,891	320	774	1,507	1,036	1,406	1,300	1,115	856	604	588
Weapons; carrying, possessing, etc.	11,303	478	1,548	9,755	23	115	340	284	352	434	510	502	477	432
Prostitution and commercialized vice	244	7	17	227	4	3	—	1	4	5	6	3	6	7
Sex offenses (except forcible rape and prostitution)	6,054	521	1,106	4,948	58	139	324	195	176	214	278	233	210	164
Drug abuse violations	67,878	959	6,117	61,761	15	128	816	987	1,699	2,472	4,009	3,826	3,698	3,176
Gambling	470	3	21	449	—	—	3	6	4	8	17	33	23	7
Offenses against family and children	11,441	74	342	11,099	8	12	54	67	89	112	234	259	275	330
Driving under the influence ..	163,002	22	1,818	161,184	10	1	11	79	494	1,223	2,784	3,565	4,378	5,339
Liquor laws	35,873	840	9,770	26,103	19	51	770	1,444	2,946	4,540	5,892	5,337	4,137	1,117
Drunkenness	33,630	84	728	32,902	6	8	70	96	135	413	1,016	1,031	1,064	1,206
Disorderly conduct	26,086	1,216	4,174	21,912	42	272	902	775	1,053	1,130	1,167	1,003	869	955
Vagrancy	378	18	61	317	2	6	10	14	16	13	21	15	17	17
All other offenses (except traffic)	227,637	4,417	17,278	210,359	232	952	3,233	2,918	4,318	5,625	9,479	9,989	9,983	9,397
Suspicion	445	20	115	330	2	8	10	22	30	43	18	23	14	15
Curfew and loitering law violations	1,567	504	1,567	—	6	98	400	348	397	318	—	—	—	—
Runaways	10,286	3,920	10,286	—	73	594	3,253	2,771	2,508	1,087	—	—	—	—

See footnotes at end of table.

Table 58.—Rural County Arrests, Distribution by Age, 1995 — Continued

Offense charged	Age											
	22	23	24	25–29	30–34	35–39	40–44	45–49	50–54	55–59	60–64	65 and over
TOTAL	**31,068**	**30,612**	**31,650**	**130,733**	**131,617**	**106,060**	**68,410**	**39,869**	**21,477**	**11,960**	**7,062**	**7,931**
Percent distribution[1]	**3.6**	**3.5**	**3.7**	**15.2**	**15.3**	**12.3**	**7.9**	**4.6**	**2.5**	**1.4**	**.8**	**.9**
Murder and nonnegligent manslaughter	47	29	67	201	161	131	130	64	44	37	11	28
Forcible rape	76	77	75	325	293	250	182	124	69	34	27	26
Robbery	129	103	92	356	307	180	72	43	15	8	5	2
Aggravated assault	936	1,024	977	4,240	4,472	3,748	2,408	1,437	776	424	273	343
Burglary	785	736	756	2,811	2,251	1,516	789	340	168	59	24	35
Larceny–theft	1,510	1,382	1,336	5,289	4,761	3,718	2,255	1,274	694	388	223	350
Motor vehicle theft	221	213	229	801	622	452	259	128	52	23	3	11
Arson	33	28	31	118	121	105	70	52	21	18	12	11
Violent crime[2]	1,188	1,233	1,211	5,122	5,233	4,309	2,792	1,668	904	503	316	399
Percent distribution[1]	3.5	3.6	3.5	15.0	15.3	12.6	8.1	4.9	2.6	1.5	.9	1.2
Property crime[3]	2,549	2,359	2,352	9,019	7,755	5,791	3,373	1,794	935	488	262	407
Percent distribution[1]	3.2	3.0	3.0	11.5	9.8	7.4	4.3	2.3	1.2	.6	.3	.5
Crime Index total[4]	3,737	3,592	3,563	14,141	12,988	10,100	6,165	3,462	1,839	991	578	806
Percent distribution[1]	3.3	3.2	3.2	12.5	11.5	8.9	5.5	3.1	1.6	.9	.5	.7
Other assaults	2,455	2,466	2,634	11,456	12,204	9,845	6,183	3,448	1,876	1,086	567	681
Forgery and counterfeiting	387	310	354	1,330	1,315	907	514	241	103	52	20	23
Fraud	2,077	2,134	2,267	9,904	8,788	6,740	4,502	2,662	1,377	643	371	404
Embezzlement	30	32	22	141	133	104	76	43	28	15	8	4
Stolen property; buying, receiving, possessing	310	252	291	1,019	827	653	337	159	79	49	23	15
Vandalism	492	424	439	1,651	1,406	1,019	594	331	176	80	45	71
Weapons; carrying, possessing, etc.	394	399	373	1,619	1,506	1,294	911	551	355	189	105	138
Prostitution and commercialized vice	7	5	6	36	38	43	27	13	13	5	4	8
Sex offenses (except forcible rape and prostitution)	176	140	146	629	797	704	467	346	219	153	102	184
Drug abuse violations	3,023	2,825	2,952	11,001	10,741	8,337	4,682	2,141	772	306	160	112
Gambling	7	3	6	47	55	49	42	45	34	40	22	19
Offenses against family and children	372	396	416	2,032	2,340	1,952	1,267	623	305	142	86	70
Driving under the influence	5,255	5,575	5,835	25,977	29,656	26,005	18,615	12,013	6,808	4,123	2,580	2,676
Liquor laws	839	628	582	1,954	1,780	1,418	936	621	352	222	136	152
Drunkenness	1,178	1,127	1,183	4,965	5,684	5,244	3,701	2,330	1,378	771	524	500
Disorderly conduct	929	920	945	3,741	3,806	3,154	1,890	1,170	592	359	188	224
Vagrancy	9	9	14	69	45	47	27	9	11	5	—	2
All other offenses (except traffic)	9,385	9,350	9,606	38,976	37,440	28,408	17,442	9,643	5,154	2,725	1,541	1,841
Suspicion	6	25	16	45	68	37	32	18	6	4	2	1
Curfew and loitering law violations	—	—	—	—	—	—	—	—	—	—	—	—
Runaways	—	—	—	—	—	—	—	—	—	—	—	—

[1]Because of rounding, the percentages may not add to totals.
[2]Violent crimes are offenses of murder, forcible rape, robbery, and aggravated assault.
[3]Property crimes are offenses of burglary, larceny–theft, motor vehicle theft, and arson.
[4]Includes arson.

Table 59.—Rural County Arrests of Persons under 15, 18, 21, and 25 Years of Age, 1995

[1,918 agencies; 1995 estimated population 19,780,000]

Offense charged	Total all ages	Number of persons arrested				Percent of total all ages			
		Under 15	Under 18	Under 21	Under 25	Under 15	Under 18	Under 21	Under 25
TOTAL	862,321	28,222	99,765	211,795	337,202	3.3	11.6	24.6	39.1
Murder and nonnegligent manslaughter	1,311	22	129	302	504	1.7	9.8	23.0	38.4
Forcible rape	2,250	100	307	609	920	4.4	13.6	27.1	40.9
Robbery	2,634	113	564	1,167	1,646	4.3	21.4	44.3	62.5
Aggravated assault..............................	28,063	828	2,963	6,027	9,942	3.0	10.6	21.5	35.4
Burglary	26,567	3,132	9,357	15,231	18,574	11.8	35.2	57.3	69.9
Larceny–theft..................................	43,343	4,169	11,458	18,705	24,391	9.6	26.4	43.2	56.3
Motor vehicle theft	7,586	803	3,028	4,317	5,235	10.6	39.9	56.9	69.0
Arson	1,265	240	416	609	737	19.0	32.9	48.1	58.3
Violent crime[1]	34,258	1,063	3,963	8,105	13,012	3.1	11.6	23.7	38.0
Property crime[2]	78,761	8,344	24,259	38,862	48,937	10.6	30.8	49.3	62.1
Crime Index total[3]	113,019	9,407	28,222	46,967	61,949	8.3	25.0	41.6	54.8
Other assaults...................................	72,064	2,636	7,635	14,756	24,718	3.7	10.6	20.5	34.3
Forgery and counterfeiting	7,476	60	424	1,581	2,971	.8	5.7	21.1	39.7
Fraud	49,446	160	891	5,451	14,055	.3	1.8	11.0	28.4
Embezzlement	794	8	39	136	242	1.0	4.9	17.1	30.5
Stolen property; buying, receiving, possessing	6,994	267	1,263	2,637	3,833	3.8	18.1	37.7	54.8
Vandalism.....................................	16,234	2,601	6,343	8,918	10,861	16.0	39.1	54.9	66.9
Weapons; carrying, possessing, etc.	11,303	478	1,548	3,037	4,635	4.2	13.7	26.9	41.0
Prostitution and commercialized vice	244	7	17	32	57	2.9	7.0	13.1	23.4
Sex offenses (except forcible rape and prostitution)	6,054	521	1,106	1,827	2,453	8.6	18.3	30.2	40.5
Drug abuse violations	67,878	959	6,117	17,650	29,626	1.4	9.0	26.0	43.6
Gambling	470	3	21	94	117	.6	4.5	20.0	24.9
Offenses against family and children	11,441	74	342	1,110	2,624	.6	3.0	9.7	22.9
Driving under the influence	163,002	22	1,818	12,545	34,549	[4]	1.1	7.7	21.2
Liquor laws	35,873	840	9,770	25,136	28,302	2.3	27.2	70.1	78.9
Drunkenness...................................	33,630	84	728	3,839	8,533	.2	2.2	11.4	25.4
Disorderly conduct	26,086	1,216	4,174	7,213	10,962	4.7	16.0	27.7	42.0
Vagrancy......................................	378	18	61	114	163	4.8	16.1	30.2	43.1
All other offenses (except traffic)	227,637	4,417	17,278	46,729	84,467	1.9	7.6	20.5	37.1
Suspicion	445	20	115	170	232	4.5	25.8	38.2	52.1
Curfew and loitering law violations	1,567	504	1,567	1,567	1,567	32.2	100.0	100.0	100.0
Runaways......................................	10,286	3,920	10,286	10,286	10,286	38.1	100.0	100.0	100.0

[1]Violent crimes are offenses of murder, forcible rape, robbery, and aggravated assault.
[2]Property crimes are offenses of burglary, larceny–theft, motor vehicle theft, and arson.
[3]Includes arson.
[4]Less than one-tenth of 1 percent.

Table 60.—Rural County Arrests, Distribution by Sex, 1995

[1,918 agencies; 1995 estimated population 19,780,000]

Offense charged	Number of persons arrested			Percent male	Percent female	Percent distribution[1]		
	Total	Male	Female			Total	Male	Female
TOTAL	**862,321**	**697,717**	**164,604**	**80.9**	**19.1**	**100.0**	**100.0**	**100.0**
Murder and nonnegligent manslaughter	1,311	1,132	179	86.3	13.7	.2	.2	.1
Forcible rape	2,250	2,207	43	98.1	1.9	.3	.3	[2]
Robbery	2,634	2,415	219	91.7	8.3	.3	.3	.1
Aggravated assault.................................	28,063	23,856	4,207	85.0	15.0	3.3	3.4	2.6
Burglary	26,567	24,069	2,498	90.6	9.4	3.1	3.4	1.5
Larceny–theft	43,343	33,049	10,294	76.2	23.8	5.0	4.7	6.3
Motor vehicle theft	7,586	6,405	1,181	84.4	15.6	.9	.9	.7
Arson	1,265	1,095	170	86.6	13.4	.1	.2	.1
Violent crime[3]	34,258	29,610	4,648	86.4	13.6	4.0	4.2	2.8
Property crime[4]	78,761	64,618	14,143	82.0	18.0	9.1	9.3	8.6
Crime Index total[5]	113,019	94,228	18,791	83.4	16.6	13.1	13.5	11.4
Other assaults....................................	72,064	58,668	13,396	81.4	18.6	8.4	8.4	8.1
Forgery and counterfeiting	7,476	4,675	2,801	62.5	37.5	.9	.7	1.7
Fraud	49,446	25,728	23,718	52.0	48.0	5.7	3.7	14.4
Embezzlement	794	467	327	58.8	41.2	.1	.1	.2
Stolen property; buying, receiving, possessing	6,994	5,990	1,004	85.6	14.4	.8	.9	.6
Vandalism...	16,234	13,942	2,292	85.9	14.1	1.9	2.0	1.4
Weapons; carrying, possessing, etc.	11,303	10,526	777	93.1	6.9	1.3	1.5	.5
Prostitution and commercialized vice	244	148	96	60.7	39.3	[2]	[2]	.1
Sex offenses (except forcible rape and prostitution) ...	6,054	5,771	283	95.3	4.7	.7	.8	.2
Drug abuse violations	67,878	57,008	10,870	84.0	16.0	7.9	8.2	6.6
Gambling	470	385	85	81.9	18.1	.1	.1	.1
Offenses against family and children	11,441	9,637	1,804	84.2	15.8	1.3	1.4	1.1
Driving under the influence	163,002	141,124	21,878	86.6	13.4	18.9	20.2	13.3
Liquor laws	35,873	28,031	7,842	78.1	21.9	4.2	4.0	4.8
Drunkenness.......................................	33,630	29,605	4,025	88.0	12.0	3.9	4.2	2.4
Disorderly conduct	26,086	20,739	5,347	79.5	20.5	3.0	3.0	3.2
Vagrancy..	378	321	57	84.9	15.1	[2]	[2]	[2]
All other offenses (except traffic)	227,637	184,800	42,837	81.2	18.8	26.4	26.5	26.0
Suspicion	445	355	90	79.8	20.2	.1	.1	.1
Curfew and loitering law violations	1,567	1,040	527	66.4	33.6	.2	.1	.3
Runaways	10,286	4,529	5,757	44.0	56.0	1.2	.6	3.5

[1]Because of rounding, the percentages may not add to totals.
[2]Less than one-tenth of 1 percent.
[3]Violent crimes are offenses of murder, forcible rape, robbery, and aggravated assault.
[4]Property crimes are offenses of burglary, larceny–theft, motor vehicle theft, and arson.
[5]Includes arson.

Table 61.—Rural County Arrests, Distribution by Race, 1995

[1,917 agencies; 1995 estimated population 19,762,000]

Offense charged	Total arrests					Percent distribution[1]				
	Total	White	Black	American Indian or Alaskan Native	Asian or Pacific Islander	Total	White	Black	American Indian or Alaskan Native	Asian or Pacific Islander
TOTAL	**855,703**	**671,837**	**145,916**	**24,626**	**13,324**	**100.0**	**78.5**	**17.1**	**2.9**	**1.6**
Murder and nonnegligent manslaughter	1,311	799	457	46	9	100.0	60.9	34.9	3.5	.7
Forcible rape	2,244	1,679	467	70	28	100.0	74.8	20.8	3.1	1.2
Robbery	2,634	1,208	1,296	61	69	100.0	45.9	49.2	2.3	2.6
Aggravated assault.............................	28,000	20,023	6,842	1,007	128	100.0	71.5	24.4	3.6	.5
Burglary	26,499	21,157	4,093	930	319	100.0	79.8	15.4	3.5	1.2
Larceny–theft	43,243	33,567	7,907	824	945	100.0	77.6	18.3	1.9	2.2
Motor vehicle theft	7,568	6,065	1,005	326	172	100.0	80.1	13.3	4.3	2.3
Arson	1,262	1,078	144	26	14	100.0	85.4	11.4	2.1	1.1
Violent crime[2]	34,189	23,709	9,062	1,184	234	100.0	69.3	26.5	3.5	.7
Property crime[3]	78,572	61,867	13,149	2,106	1,450	100.0	78.7	16.7	2.7	1.8
Crime Index total[4]	112,761	85,576	22,211	3,290	1,684	100.0	75.9	19.7	2.9	1.5
Other assaults...............................	71,811	53,733	14,926	2,010	1,142	100.0	74.8	20.8	2.8	1.6
Forgery and counterfeiting	7,457	5,689	1,633	98	37	100.0	76.3	21.9	1.3	.5
Fraud	49,404	36,400	12,439	449	116	100.0	73.7	25.2	.9	.2
Embezzlement	794	666	99	11	18	100.0	83.9	12.5	1.4	2.3
Stolen property; buying, receiving, possessing	6,972	5,498	1,289	170	15	100.0	78.9	18.5	2.4	.2
Vandalism	16,207	13,405	2,105	492	205	100.0	82.7	13.0	3.0	1.3
Weapons; carrying, possessing, etc.	11,284	8,633	2,190	297	164	100.0	76.5	19.4	2.6	1.5
Prostitution and commercialized vice	244	199	34	5	6	100.0	81.6	13.9	2.0	2.5
Sex offenses (except forcible rape and prostitution)	6,043	5,218	596	176	53	100.0	86.3	9.9	2.9	.9
Drug abuse violations	67,664	53,759	11,929	1,231	745	100.0	79.4	17.6	1.8	1.1
Gambling	470	279	68	2	121	100.0	59.4	14.5	.4	25.7
Offenses against family and children	11,419	8,592	2,372	331	124	100.0	75.2	20.8	2.9	1.1
Driving under the influence	158,075	129,363	19,442	5,058	4,212	100.0	81.8	12.3	3.2	2.7
Liquor laws	35,788	32,433	1,543	1,504	308	100.0	90.6	4.3	4.2	.9
Drunkenness	33,607	29,352	2,924	1,272	59	100.0	87.3	8.7	3.8	.2
Disorderly conduct	26,042	20,593	4,306	961	182	100.0	79.1	16.5	3.7	.7
Vagrancy.....................................	378	269	101	8	—	100.0	71.2	26.7	2.1	—
All other offenses (except traffic)	227,029	172,165	44,823	6,932	3,109	100.0	75.8	19.7	3.1	1.4
Suspicion	444	353	88	2	1	100.0	79.5	19.8	.5	.2
Curfew and loitering law violations	1,566	989	86	96	395	100.0	63.2	5.5	6.1	25.2
Runaways.....................................	10,244	3,673	712	231	628	100.0	84.7	7.0	2.3	6.1

See footnotes at the end of table.

253

Table 61.—Rural County Arrests, Distribution by Race, 1995 — Continued

Offense charged	Arrests under 18					Percent distribution[1]				
	Total	White	Black	American Indian or Alaskan Native	Asian or Pacific Islander	Total	White	Black	American Indian or Alaskan Native	Asian or Pacific Islander
TOTAL	99,416	80,591	11,779	3,945	3,101	100.0	81.1	11.8	4.0	3.1
Murder and nonnegligent manslaughter	129	74	48	6	1	100.0	57.4	37.2	4.7	.8
Forcible rape	306	236	60	7	3	100.0	77.1	19.6	2.3	1.0
Robbery	564	251	267	19	27	100.0	44.5	47.3	3.4	4.8
Aggravated assault........................	2,955	2,032	774	134	15	100.0	68.8	26.2	4.5	.5
Burglary	9,328	7,720	993	451	164	100.0	82.8	10.6	4.8	1.8
Larceny–theft	11,430	9,291	1,307	305	527	100.0	81.3	11.4	2.7	4.6
Motor vehicle theft	3,023	2,495	302	144	82	100.0	82.5	10.0	4.8	2.7
Arson	415	360	30	16	9	100.0	86.7	7.2	3.9	2.2
Violent crime[2]	3,954	2,593	1,149	166	46	100.0	65.6	29.1	4.2	1.2
Property crime[3]	24,196	19,866	2,632	916	782	100.0	82.1	10.9	3.8	3.2
Crime Index total[4]	28,150	22,459	3,781	1,082	828	100.0	79.8	13.4	3.8	2.9
Other assaults...........................	7,571	5,294	1,687	328	262	100.0	69.9	22.3	4.3	3.5
Forgery and counterfeiting	422	375	37	9	1	100.0	88.9	8.8	2.1	.2
Fraud	891	763	106	17	5	100.0	85.6	11.9	1.9	.6
Embezzlement	39	35	3	1	—	100.0	89.7	7.7	2.6	—
Stolen property; buying, receiving, possessing	1,261	1,065	155	39	2	100.0	84.5	12.3	3.1	.2
Vandalism................................	6,332	5,560	460	203	109	100.0	87.8	7.3	3.2	1.7
Weapons; carrying, possessing, etc.	1,543	1,159	287	71	26	100.0	75.1	18.6	4.6	1.7
Prostitution and commercialized vice	17	15	2	—	—	100.0	88.2	11.8	—	—
Sex offenses (except forcible rape and prostitution)	1,105	945	108	40	12	100.0	85.5	9.8	3.6	1.1
Drug abuse violations	6,101	4,773	904	200	224	100.0	78.2	14.8	3.3	3.7
Gambling	21	14	7	—	—	100.0	66.7	33.3	—	—
Offenses against family and children	342	288	37	10	7	100.0	84.2	10.8	2.9	2.0
Driving under the influence	1,776	1,586	81	59	50	100.0	89.3	4.6	3.3	2.8
Liquor laws	9,749	8,994	117	529	109	100.0	92.3	1.2	5.4	1.1
Drunkenness.............................	728	648	39	41	—	100.0	89.0	5.4	5.6	—
Disorderly conduct	4,166	3,170	806	164	26	100.0	76.1	19.3	3.9	.6
Vagrancy................................	61	52	7	2	—	100.0	85.2	11.5	3.3	—
All other offenses (except traffic)	17,216	13,629	2,347	823	417	100.0	79.2	13.6	4.8	2.4
Suspicion	115	105	10	—	—	100.0	91.3	8.7	—	—
Curfew and loitering law violations	1,566	989	86	96	395	100.0	63.2	5.5	6.1	25.2
Runaways...............................	10,244	8,673	712	231	628	100.0	84.7	7.0	2.3	6.1

See footnotes at the end of table.

Table 61.—Rural County Arrests, Distribution by Race, 1995 — Continued

Offense charged	Arrests 18 and over					Percent distribution[1]				
	Total	White	Black	American Indian or Alaskan Native	Asian or Pacific Islander	Total	White	Black	American Indian or Alaskan Native	Asian or Pacific Islander
TOTAL	756,287	591,246	134,137	20,681	10,223	100.0	78.2	17.7	2.7	1.4
Murder and nonnegligent manslaughter	1,182	725	409	40	8	100.0	61.3	34.6	3.4	.7
Forcible rape	1,938	1,443	407	63	25	100.0	74.5	21.0	3.3	1.3
Robbery	2,070	957	1,029	42	42	100.0	46.2	49.7	2.0	2.0
Aggravated assault............................	25,045	17,991	6,068	873	113	100.0	71.8	24.2	3.5	.5
Burglary	17,171	13,437	3,100	479	155	100.0	78.3	18.1	2.8	.9
Larceny–theft................................	31,813	24,276	6,600	519	418	100.0	76.3	20.7	1.6	1.3
Motor vehicle theft	4,545	3,570	703	182	90	100.0	78.5	15.5	4.0	2.0
Arson	847	718	114	10	5	100.0	84.8	13.5	1.2	.6
Violent crime[2]	30,235	21,116	7,913	1,018	188	100.0	69.8	26.2	3.4	.6
Property crime[3]	54,376	42,001	10,517	1,190	668	100.0	77.2	19.3	2.2	1.2
Crime Index total[4]	84,611	63,117	18,430	2,208	856	100.0	74.6	21.8	2.6	1.0
Other assaults................................	64,240	48,439	13,239	1,682	880	100.0	75.4	20.6	2.6	1.4
Forgery and counterfeiting	7,035	5,314	1,596	89	36	100.0	75.5	22.7	1.3	.5
Fraud	48,513	35,637	12,333	432	111	100.0	73.5	25.4	.9	.2
Embezzlement	755	631	96	10	18	100.0	83.6	12.7	1.3	2.4
Stolen property; buying, receiving, possessing	5,711	4,433	1,134	131	13	100.0	77.6	19.9	2.3	.2
Vandalism...................................	9,875	7,845	1,645	289	96	100.0	79.4	16.7	2.9	1.0
Weapons; carrying, possessing, etc.	9,741	7,474	1,903	226	138	100.0	76.7	19.5	2.3	1.4
Prostitution and commercialized vice	227	184	32	5	6	100.0	81.1	14.1	2.2	2.6
Sex offenses (except forcible rape and prostitution)	4,938	4,273	488	136	41	100.0	86.5	9.9	2.8	.8
Drug abuse violations	61,563	48,986	11,025	1,031	521	100.0	79.6	17.9	1.7	.8
Gambling....................................	449	265	61	2	121	100.0	59.0	13.6	.4	26.9
Offenses against family and children	11,077	8,304	2,335	321	117	100.0	75.0	21.1	2.9	1.1
Driving under the influence	156,299	127,777	19,361	4,999	4,162	100.0	81.8	12.4	3.2	2.7
Liquor laws	26,039	23,439	1,426	975	199	100.0	90.0	5.5	3.7	.8
Drunkenness.................................	32,879	28,704	2,885	1,231	59	100.0	87.3	8.8	3.7	.2
Disorderly conduct	21,876	17,423	3,500	797	156	100.0	79.6	16.0	3.6	.7
Vagrancy....................................	317	217	94	6	—	100.0	68.5	29.7	1.9	—
All other offenses (except traffic)	209,813	158,536	42,476	6,109	2,692	100.0	75.6	20.2	2.9	1.3
Suspicion	329	248	78	2	1	100.0	75.4	23.7	.6	.3
Curfew and loitering law violations	—	—	—	—	—	—	—	—	—	—
Runaways...................................	—	—	—	—	—	—	—	—	—	—

[1]Because of rounding, the percentages may not add to totals.
[2]Violent crimes are offenses of murder, forcible rape, robbery, and aggravated assault.
[3]Property crimes are offenses of burglary, larceny–theft, motor vehicle theft, and arson.
[4]Includes arson.

Table 62.—Suburban Area[1] Arrest Trends, 1994–1995

[4,157 agencies; 1995 estimated population 72,475,000; 1994 estimated population 71,314,000]

Offense charged	Number of persons arrested								
	Total all ages			Under 18 years of age			18 years of age and over		
	1994	1995	Percent change	1994	1995	Percent change	1994	1995	Percent change
TOTAL	3,347,038	3,422,962	+2.3	634,597	647,793	+2.1	2,712,441	2,775,169	+2.3
Murder and nonnegligent manslaughter	3,550	3,326	−6.3	517	498	−3.7	3,033	2,828	−6.8
Forcible rape	7,536	7,008	−7.0	1,310	1,154	−11.9	6,226	5,854	−6.0
Robbery	26,141	26,176	+.1	8,289	8,309	+.2	17,852	17,867	+.1
Aggravated assault	122,552	124,521	+1.6	19,960	18,919	−5.2	102,592	105,602	+2.9
Burglary	94,208	90,649	−3.8	38,230	35,914	−6.1	55,978	54,735	−2.2
Larceny–theft	346,650	350,638	+1.2	118,371	120,292	+1.6	228,279	230,346	+.9
Motor vehicle theft	42,382	39,567	−6.6	18,364	16,496	−10.2	24,018	23,071	−3.9
Arson	5,154	4,762	−7.6	3,113	2,839	−8.8	2,041	1,923	−5.8
Violent crime[2]	159,779	161,031	+.8	30,076	28,880	−4.0	129,703	132,151	+1.9
Property crime[3]	488,394	485,616	−.6	178,078	175,541	−1.4	310,316	310,075	−.1
Crime Index total[4]	648,173	646,647	−.2	208,154	204,421	−1.8	440,019	442,226	+.5
Other assaults	265,949	286,341	+7.7	50,472	53,294	+5.6	215,477	233,047	+8.2
Forgery and counterfeiting	25,499	26,880	+5.4	1,945	2,071	+6.5	23,554	24,809	+5.3
Fraud	106,068	108,613	+2.4	2,405	2,352	−2.2	103,663	106,261	+2.5
Embezzlement	3,562	3,434	−3.6	225	266	+18.2	3,337	3,168	−5.1
Stolen property; buying, receiving, possessing	38,954	39,583	+1.6	10,666	10,526	−1.3	28,288	29,057	+2.7
Vandalism	73,234	70,491	−3.7	39,166	36,555	−6.7	34,068	33,936	−.4
Weapons; carrying, possessing, etc.	55,844	49,976	−10.5	14,557	12,527	−13.9	41,287	37,449	−9.3
Prostitution and commercialized vice	7,038	7,709	+9.5	136	104	−23.5	6,902	7,605	+10.2
Sex offenses (except forcible rape and prostitution)	22,797	20,747	−9.0	4,432	3,957	−10.7	18,365	16,790	−8.6
Drug abuse violations	291,890	309,242	+5.9	36,234	44,124	+21.8	255,656	265,118	+3.7
Gambling	1,789	1,928	+7.8	178	183	+2.8	1,611	1,745	+8.3
Offenses against family and children	38,456	47,930	+24.6	1,243	1,693	+36.2	37,213	46,237	+24.2
Driving under the influence	432,510	421,198	−2.6	4,076	3,912	−4.0	428,434	417,286	−2.6
Liquor laws	115,960	113,837	−1.8	30,982	31,534	+1.8	84,978	82,303	−3.1
Drunkenness	130,915	131,617	+.5	4,000	4,578	+14.5	126,915	127,039	+.1
Disorderly conduct	137,585	139,636	+1.5	37,300	39,152	+5.0	100,285	100,484	+.2
Vagrancy	3,915	3,309	−15.5	1,035	654	−36.8	2,880	2,655	−7.8
All other offenses (except traffic)	854,282	899,649	+5.3	94,773	101,695	+7.3	759,509	797,954	+5.1
Suspicion (not included in totals)	3,231	3,010	−6.8	595	524	−11.9	2,636	2,486	−5.7
Curfew and loitering law violations	22,111	25,381	+14.8	22,111	25,381	+14.8	—	—	—
Runaways	70,507	68,814	−2.4	70,507	68,814	−2.4	—	—	—

[1]Includes suburban city and county law enforcement agencies within metropolitan areas. Excludes central cities. Suburban cities and counties are also included in other groups.
[2]Violent crimes are offenses of murder, forcible rape, robbery, and aggravated assault.
[3]Property crimes are offenses of burglary, larceny–theft, motor vehicle theft, and arson.
[4]Includes arson.

Table 63.—Suburban Area[1] Arrest Trends, Sex, 1994–1995

[4,157 agencies; 1995 estimated population 72,475,000; 1994 estimated population 71,314,000]

Offense charged	Males						Females					
	Total			Under 18			Total			Under 18		
	1994	1995	Percent change	1994	1995	Percent change	1994	1995	Percent change	1994	1995	Percent change
TOTAL	2,679,003	2,717,283	+1.4	478,481	483,122	+1.0	668,035	705,679	+5.6	156,116	164,671	+5.5
Murder and nonnegligent manslaughter	3,182	2,978	−6.4	484	453	−6.4	368	348	−5.4	33	45	+36.4
Forcible rape	7,469	6,930	−7.2	1,287	1,133	−12.0	67	78	+16.4	23	21	−8.7
Robbery	23,879	23,838	−.2	7,592	7,657	+.9	2,262	2,338	+3.4	697	652	−6.5
Aggravated assault....................	103,815	104,140	+.3	16,584	15,531	−6.3	18,737	20,381	+8.8	3,376	3,388	+.4
Burglary	85,097	81,105	−4.7	34,819	32,554	−6.5	9,111	9,544	+4.8	3,411	3,360	−1.5
Larceny–theft.......................	232,776	235,113	+1.0	83,518	83,957	+.5	113,874	115,525	+1.4	34,853	36,335	+4.3
Motor vehicle theft	36,956	34,039	−7.9	15,596	13,784	−11.6	5,426	5,528	+1.9	2,768	2,712	−2.0
Arson	4,448	4,080	−8.3	2,719	2,487	−8.5	706	682	−3.4	394	352	−10.7
Violent crime[2]	138,345	137,886	−.3	25,947	24,774	−4.5	21,434	23,145	+8.0	4,129	4,106	−.6
Property crime[3]	359,277	354,337	−1.4	136,652	132,782	−2.8	129,117	131,279	+1.7	41,426	42,759	+3.2
Crime Index total[4]	497,622	492,223	−1.1	162,599	157,556	−3.1	150,551	154,424	+2.6	45,555	46,865	+2.9
Other assaults........................	214,399	227,449	+6.1	37,779	39,071	+3.4	51,550	58,892	+14.2	12,693	14,223	+12.1
Forgery and counterfeiting	16,402	17,066	+4.0	1,306	1,376	+5.4	9,097	9,814	+7.9	639	695	+8.8
Fraud	57,842	59,426	+2.7	1,583	1,557	−1.6	48,226	49,187	+2.0	822	795	−3.3
Embezzlement	2,134	1,988	−6.8	161	166	+3.1	1,428	1,446	+1.3	64	100	+56.3
Stolen property; buying, receiving, possessing	33,465	33,705	+.7	9,430	9,258	−1.8	5,489	5,878	+7.1	1,236	1,268	+2.6
Vandalism..........................	64,748	61,753	−4.6	35,427	32,870	−7.2	8,486	8,738	+3.0	3,739	3,685	−1.4
Weapons; carrying, possessing, etc.	51,011	46,066	−9.7	13,457	11,580	−13.9	4,833	3,910	−19.1	1,100	947	−13.9
Prostitution and commercialized vice	3,677	4,634	+26.0	80	72	−10.0	3,361	3,075	−8.5	56	32	−42.9
Sex offenses (except forcible rape and prostitution)	21,474	19,636	−8.6	4,155	3,698	−11.0	1,323	1,111	−16.0	277	259	−6.5
Drug abuse violations	242,986	256,736	+5.7	31,246	37,623	+20.4	48,904	52,506	+7.4	4,988	6,501	+30.3
Gambling	1,548	1,685	+8.9	171	172	+.6	241	243	+.8	7	11	+57.1
Offenses against family and children	33,424	41,232	+23.4	824	1,075	+30.5	5,032	6,698	+33.1	419	618	+47.5
Driving under the influence	370,219	358,099	−3.3	3,476	3,288	−5.4	62,291	63,099	+1.3	600	624	+4.0
Liquor laws	91,812	88,902	−3.2	22,182	22,161	−.1	24,148	24,935	+3.3	8,800	9,373	+6.5
Drunkenness........................	115,488	115,705	+.2	3,380	3,827	+13.2	15,427	15,912	+3.1	620	751	+21.1
Disorderly conduct	110,075	110,909	+.8	28,869	30,190	+4.6	27,510	28,727	+4.4	8,431	8,962	+6.3
Vagrancy	3,284	2,837	−13.6	836	579	−30.7	631	472	−25.2	199	75	−62.3
All other offenses (except traffic)	700,469	729,293	+4.1	74,596	79,064	+6.0	153,813	170,356	+10.8	20,177	22,631	+12.2
Suspicion (not included in totals)	2,784	2,605	−6.4	501	445	−11.2	447	405	−9.4	94	79	−16.0
Curfew and loitering law violations	16,080	18,104	+12.6	16,080	18,104	+12.6	6,031	7,277	+20.7	6,031	7,277	+20.7
Runaways..........................	30,844	29,835	−3.3	30,844	29,835	−3.3	39,663	38,979	−1.7	39,663	38,979	−1.7

[1]Includes suburban city and county law enforcement agencies within metropolitan areas. Excludes central cities. Suburban cities and counties are also included in other groups.
[2]Violent crimes are offenses of murder, forcible rape, robbery, and aggravated assault.
[3]Property crimes are offenses of burglary, larceny–theft, motor vehicle theft, and arson.
[4]Includes arson.

Table 64.—Suburban Area[1] Arrests, Distribution by Age, 1995

[4,680 agencies; 1995 estimated population 82,984,000]

Offense charged	Total all ages	Ages under 15	Ages under 18	Ages 18 and over	Under 10	10–12	13–14	15	16	17	18	19	20	21
TOTAL	3,939,195	252,270	742,187	3,197,008	11,595	56,419	184,256	149,978	167,995	171,944	184,320	167,622	152,095	138,602
Percent distribution2 ..	100.0	6.4	18.8	81.2	.3	1.4	4.7	3.8	4.3	4.4	4.7	4.3	3.9	3.5
Murder and nonnegligent manslaughter	3,781	70	560	3,221	1	9	60	104	185	201	296	228	237	172
Forcible rape	8,285	476	1,347	6,938	14	112	350	250	294	327	458	369	342	319
Robbery	30,144	2,456	9,526	20,618	45	433	1,978	2,005	2,466	2,599	2,633	1,868	1,512	1,260
Aggravated assault	142,471	6,983	21,678	120,793	362	1,681	4,940	4,164	5,007	5,524	5,709	5,042	4,778	4,807
Burglary	102,950	15,384	40,514	62,436	842	3,701	10,841	8,175	8,502	8,453	8,040	5,525	4,119	3,357
Larceny–theft	405,123	58,677	139,446	265,677	2,655	15,876	40,146	26,283	27,780	26,706	23,807	17,679	13,542	11,339
Motor vehicle theft	44,390	5,088	18,471	25,919	44	512	4,532	4,892	4,604	3,887	3,156	2,235	1,762	1,434
Arson	5,476	2,174	3,265	2,211	337	775	1,062	475	333	283	208	154	117	94
Violent crime[3]	184,681	9,985	33,111	151,570	422	2,235	7,328	6,523	7,952	8,651	9,096	7,507	6,869	6,558
Percent distribution[2]	100.0	5.4	17.9	82.1	.2	1.2	4.0	3.5	4.3	4.7	4.9	4.1	3.7	3.6
Property crime[4]	557,939	81,323	201,696	356,243	3,878	20,864	56,581	39,825	41,219	39,329	35,211	25,593	19,540	16,224
Percent distribution[2]	100.0	14.6	36.2	63.8	.7	3.7	10.1	7.1	7.4	7.0	6.3	4.6	3.5	2.9
Crime Index total[5]	742,620	91,308	234,807	507,813	4,300	23,099	63,909	46,348	49,171	47,980	44,307	33,100	26,409	22,782
Percent distribution[2]	100.0	12.3	31.6	68.4	.6	3.1	8.6	6.2	6.6	6.5	6.0	4.5	3.6	3.1
Other assaults	331,944	24,714	60,755	271,189	1,374	6,521	16,819	11,893	12,354	11,794	10,829	10,054	9,516	9,864
Forgery and counterfeiting ...	31,261	283	2,386	28,875	5	42	236	337	680	1,086	1,635	1,679	1,601	1,371
Fraud	125,134	386	2,701	122,433	23	48	315	374	659	1,282	2,967	4,220	4,902	5,201
Embezzlement	3,838	36	288	3,550	3	7	26	15	86	151	226	210	191	172
Stolen property; buying, receiving, possessing	44,988	3,279	12,070	32,918	77	616	2,586	2,518	3,057	3,216	3,535	2,783	2,143	1,804
Vandalism.................	81,481	19,343	41,651	39,830	1,933	5,807	11,603	7,445	7,709	7,154	4,914	3,309	2,444	2,184
Weapons; carrying, possessing, etc.	58,110	4,776	14,450	43,660	176	1,061	3,539	2,816	3,215	3,643	4,029	3,144	2,793	2,411
Prostitution and commercialized vice	9,349	21	138	9,211	—	2	19	14	43	60	161	172	212	223
Sex offenses (except forcible rape and prostitution)	23,480	2,173	4,494	18,986	134	612	1,427	851	714	756	782	704	651	632
Drug abuse violations	351,280	8,541	49,943	301,337	100	889	7,552	9,192	13,913	18,297	23,573	20,580	17,439	15,308
Gambling	2,131	47	229	1,902	—	5	42	43	59	80	72	77	70	60
Offenses against family and children	55,090	549	2,075	53,015	27	103	419	495	531	500	1,110	1,075	1,239	1,467
Driving under the influence ..	472,159	140	4,468	467,691	52	11	77	186	1,081	3,061	7,429	9,811	11,789	15,996
Liquor laws	131,780	3,501	35,626	96,154	56	273	3,172	5,431	10,241	16,453	22,747	20,119	15,623	4,059
Drunkenness	167,741	859	5,734	162,007	37	87	735	943	1,489	2,443	4,731	4,820	4,786	5,834
Disorderly conduct	168,605	16,218	44,979	123,626	622	3,677	11,919	9,255	9,943	9,563	8,624	7,023	6,277	6,478
Vagrancy	3,931	213	761	3,170	6	48	159	146	179	223	250	193	162	137
All other offenses (except traffic)	1,022,912	33,877	115,927	906,985	1,714	6,867	25,296	23,286	27,571	31,193	42,227	44,438	43,734	42,514
Suspicion	3,279	162	623	2,656	16	25	121	114	153	194	172	111	114	105
Curfew and loitering law violations	29,992	8,849	29,992	—	110	1,262	7,477	7,149	8,361	5,633	—	—	—	—
Runaways.................	78,090	32,995	78,090	—	830	5,357	26,808	21,127	16,786	7,182	—	—	—	—

See footnotes at end of table.

Table 64.—Suburban Area[1] Arrests, Distribution by Age, 1995 — Continued

Offense charged	Age											
	22	23	24	25–29	30–34	35–39	40–44	45–49	50–54	55–59	60–64	65 and over
TOTAL	132,277	129,860	135,729	571,057	560,696	439,902	271,123	149,323	76,240	39,628	22,682	25,852
Percent distribution2	3.4	3.3	3.4	14.5	14.2	11.2	6.9	3.8	1.9	1.0	.6	.7
Murder and nonnegligent manslaughter	184	140	168	506	424	311	220	112	86	57	30	50
Forcible rape	288	294	259	1,191	1,198	911	547	314	181	108	68	91
Robbery	1,029	933	947	3,722	3,094	2,037	984	339	143	59	22	36
Aggravated assault......................	4,643	4,653	4,799	22,192	22,712	18,018	10,766	5,935	3,092	1,563	940	1,144
Burglary	2,843	2,611	2,655	10,724	9,970	6,734	3,423	1,420	544	220	100	151
Larceny–theft	9,865	9,598	10,053	43,244	43,511	34,431	21,909	11,799	5,974	3,300	2,135	3,491
Motor vehicle theft	1,264	1,267	1,207	4,868	3,926	2,488	1,284	582	209	112	67	58
Arson	92	73	81	308	331	276	200	125	70	28	26	28
Violent crime[3]	6,144	6,020	6,173	27,611	27,428	21,277	12,517	6,700	3,502	1,787	1,060	1,321
Percent distribution[2]	3.3	3.3	3.3	15.0	14.9	11.5	6.8	3.6	1.9	1.0	.6	.7
Property crime[4]	14,064	13,549	13,996	59,144	57,738	43,929	26,816	13,926	6,797	3,660	2,328	3,728
Percent distribution[2]	2.5	2.4	2.5	10.6	10.3	7.9	4.8	2.5	1.2	.7	.4	.7
Crime Index total[5]	20,208	19,569	20,169	86,755	85,166	65,206	39,333	20,626	10,299	5,447	3,388	5,049
Percent distribution[2]	2.7	2.6	2.7	11.7	11.5	8.8	5.3	2.8	1.4	.7	.5	.7
Other assaults........................	10,096	10,360	11,535	50,827	53,612	42,245	24,805	13,362	6,547	3,286	1,978	2,273
Forgery and counterfeiting	1,293	1,294	1,348	5,583	5,364	3,842	2,076	1,002	420	188	102	77
Fraud	5,616	5,557	5,920	25,320	22,596	17,158	11,036	6,002	2,934	1,452	703	849
Embezzlement	179	199	184	664	537	463	230	153	74	38	17	13
Stolen property; buying, receiving, possessing	1,601	1,466	1,585	5,831	5,090	3,517	1,949	844	399	193	96	82
Vandalism...........................	1,848	1,667	1,742	6,890	6,004	4,287	2,238	1,117	508	260	170	248
Weapons; carrying, possessing, etc.	2,157	2,032	1,958	7,182	6,135	4,755	2,917	1,792	1,013	585	371	386
Prostitution and commercialized vice	260	290	359	1,816	2,068	1,622	878	503	258	154	98	137
Sex offenses (except forcible rape and prostitution)	597	542	562	2,835	3,268	2,782	1,974	1,313	808	557	389	590
Drug abuse violations	13,946	13,343	13,229	55,159	52,645	39,056	21,465	9,454	3,520	1,390	679	551
Gambling	80	74	59	208	164	244	198	187	141	110	60	98
Offenses against family and children	1,577	1,694	2,120	10,225	11,555	9,777	5,764	2,951	1,370	580	272	239
Driving under the influence	16,995	17,808	19,338	84,219	86,681	73,251	50,567	32,530	18,767	10,464	6,015	6,031
Liquor laws	2,846	2,268	1,976	7,286	6,217	5,065	3,306	2,016	1,167	671	377	411
Drunkenness	5,552	5,550	5,557	25,208	28,586	26,132	18,983	11,665	6,697	3,638	2,199	2,069
Disorderly conduct	5,849	5,475	5,575	20,935	20,217	15,919	9,560	5,472	2,863	1,430	870	1,059
Vagrancy	114	148	130	513	533	417	283	156	65	38	16	15
All other offenses (except traffic)	41,354	40,423	42,273	173,185	163,755	123,761	73,326	38,041	18,319	9,111	4,866	5,658
Suspicion	109	101	110	416	503	403	235	137	71	36	16	17
Curfew and loitering law violations	—	—	—	—	—	—	—	—	—	—	—	—
Runaways...........................	—	—	—	—	—	—	—	—	—	—	—	—

[1]Includes suburban city and county law enforcement agencies within metropolitan areas. Excludes central cities. Suburban cities and counties are also included in other groups.
[2]Because of rounding, the percentages may not add to totals.
[3]Violent crimes are offenses of murder, forcible rape, robbery, and aggravated assault.
[4]Property crimes are offenses of burglary, larceny–theft, motor vehicle theft, and arson.
[5]Includes arson.

Table 65.—Suburban Area[1] Arrests of Persons under 15, 18, 21, and 25 Years of Age, 1995

[4,680 agencies; 1995 estimated population 82,984,000]

Offense charged	Total all ages	Number of persons arrested				Percent of total all ages			
		Under 15	Under 18	Under 21	Under 25	Under 15	Under 18	Under 21	Under 25
TOTAL	3,939,135	252,270	742,187	1,246,224	1,782,692	6.4	18.8	31.6	45.3
Murder and nonnegligent manslaughter	3,781	70	560	1,321	1,985	1.9	14.8	34.9	52.5
Forcible rape	8,285	476	1,347	2,516	3,676	5.7	16.3	30.4	44.4
Robbery	30,144	2,456	9,526	15,539	19,708	8.1	31.6	51.5	65.4
Aggravated assault............................	142,471	6,983	21,678	37,207	56,109	4.9	15.2	26.1	39.4
Burglary	102,950	15,384	40,514	58,198	69,664	14.9	39.4	56.5	67.7
Larceny–theft............................	405,123	58,677	139,446	194,474	235,329	14.5	34.4	48.0	58.1
Motor vehicle theft	44,390	5,088	18,471	25,624	30,796	11.5	41.6	57.7	69.4
Arson	5,476	2,174	3,265	3,744	4,084	39.7	59.6	68.4	74.6
Violent crime[2]	184,681	9,985	33,111	56,583	81,478	5.4	17.9	30.6	44.1
Property crime[3]	557,939	81,323	201,696	282,040	339,873	14.6	36.2	50.6	60.9
Crime Index total[4]	742,620	91,308	234,807	338,623	421,351	12.3	31.6	45.6	56.7
Other assaults....................	331,944	24,714	60,755	91,154	133,009	7.4	18.3	27.5	40.1
Forgery and counterfeiting	31,261	283	2,386	7,301	12,607	.9	7.6	23.4	40.3
Fraud	125,134	386	2,701	14,790	37,084	.3	2.2	11.8	29.6
Embezzlement	3,838	36	288	915	1,649	.9	7.5	23.8	43.0
Stolen property; buying, receiving, possessing	44,988	3,279	12,070	20,531	26,987	7.3	26.8	45.6	60.0
Vandalism....................	81,481	19,343	41,651	52,318	59,759	23.7	51.1	64.2	73.3
Weapons; carrying, possessing, etc.	58,110	4,776	14,450	24,416	32,974	8.2	24.9	42.0	56.7
Prostitution and commercialized vice	9,349	21	138	683	1,815	.2	1.5	7.3	19.4
Sex offenses (except forcible rape and prostitution)	23,480	2,173	4,494	6,631	8,964	9.3	19.1	28.2	38.2
Drug abuse violations	351,280	8,541	49,943	111,535	167,361	2.4	14.2	31.8	47.6
Gambling	2,131	47	229	448	721	2.2	10.7	21.0	33.8
Offenses against family and children	55,090	549	2,075	5,499	12,357	1.0	3.8	10.0	22.4
Driving under the influence	472,159	140	4,468	33,497	103,634	[5]	.9	7.1	21.9
Liquor laws	131,780	3,501	35,626	94,115	105,264	2.7	27.0	71.4	79.9
Drunkenness.....................	167,741	859	5,734	20,071	42,564	.5	3.4	12.0	25.4
Disorderly conduct	168,605	16,218	44,979	66,903	90,280	9.6	26.7	39.7	53.5
Vagrancy....................	3,931	213	761	1,366	1,895	5.4	19.4	34.7	48.2
All other offenses (except traffic)	1,022,912	33,877	115,927	246,326	412,890	3.3	11.3	24.1	40.4
Suspicion	3,279	162	623	1,020	1,445	4.9	19.0	31.1	44.1
Curfew and loitering law violations	29,992	8,849	29,992	29,992	29,992	29.5	100.0	100.0	100.0
Runaways....................	78,090	32,995	78,090	78,090	78,090	42.3	100.0	100.0	100.0

[1]Includes suburban city and county law enforcement agencies within metropolitan areas. Excludes central cities. Suburban cities and counties are also included in other groups.
[2]Violent crimes are offenses of murder, forcible rape, robbery, and aggravated assault.
[3]Property crimes are offenses of burglary, larceny–theft, motor vehicle theft, and arson.
[4]Includes arson.
[5]Less than one-tenth of 1 percent.

Table 66.—Suburban Area[1] Arrests, Distribution by Sex, 1995

[4,680 agencies; 1995 estimated population 82,984,000]

Offense charged	Number of persons arrested			Percent male	Percent female	Percent distribution[2]		
	Total	Male	Female			Total	Male	Female
TOTAL	**3,939,195**	**3,123,810**	**815,385**	**79.3**	**20.7**	**100.0**	**100.0**	**100.0**
Murder and nonnegligent manslaughter	3,781	3,378	403	89.3	10.7	.1	.1	[3]
Forcible rape	8,285	8,191	94	98.9	1.1	.2	.3	[3]
Robbery	30,144	27,468	2,676	91.1	8.9	.8	.9	.3
Aggravated assault	142,471	118,760	23,711	83.4	16.6	3.6	3.8	2.9
Burglary	102,950	92,229	10,721	89.6	10.4	2.6	3.0	1.3
Larceny–theft....................................	405,123	271,114	134,009	66.9	33.1	10.3	8.7	16.4
Motor vehicle theft	44,390	38,159	6,231	86.0	14.0	1.1	1.2	.8
Arson	5,476	4,700	776	85.8	14.2	.1	.2	.1
Violent crime[4]	184,681	157,797	26,884	85.4	14.6	4.7	5.1	3.3
Property crime[5]	557,939	406,202	151,737	72.8	27.2	14.2	13.0	18.6
Crime Index total[6]	742,620	563,999	178,621	75.9	24.1	18.9	18.1	21.9
Other assaults...................................	331,944	263,764	68,180	79.5	20.5	8.4	8.4	8.4
Forgery and counterfeiting	31,261	19,806	11,455	63.4	36.6	.8	.6	1.4
Fraud	125,134	68,367	56,767	54.6	45.4	3.2	2.2	7.0
Embezzlement	3,838	2,196	1,642	57.2	42.8	.1	.1	.2
Stolen property; buying, receiving, possessing	44,988	38,324	6,664	85.2	14.8	1.1	1.2	.8
Vandalism	81,481	71,146	10,335	87.3	12.7	2.1	2.3	1.3
Weapons; carrying, possessing, etc.	58,110	53,516	4,594	92.1	7.9	1.5	1.7	.6
Prostitution and commercialized vice	9,349	5,270	4,079	56.4	43.6	.2	.2	.5
Sex offenses (except forcible rape and prostitution)	23,480	22,228	1,252	94.7	5.3	.6	.7	.2
Drug abuse violations	351,280	292,031	59,249	83.1	16.9	8.9	9.3	7.3
Gambling	2,131	1,872	259	87.8	12.2	.1	.1	[3]
Offenses against family and children	55,090	47,165	7,925	85.6	14.4	1.4	1.5	1.0
Driving under the influence	472,159	401,103	71,056	85.0	15.0	12.0	12.8	8.7
Liquor laws	131,780	103,087	28,693	78.2	21.8	3.3	3.3	3.5
Drunkenness.....................................	167,741	147,473	20,268	87.9	12.1	4.3	4.7	2.5
Disorderly conduct	168,605	133,428	35,177	79.1	20.9	4.3	4.3	4.3
Vagrancy.......................................	3,931	3,374	557	85.8	14.2	.1	.1	.1
All other offenses (except traffic)	1,022,912	827,689	195,223	80.9	19.1	26.0	26.5	23.9
Suspicion	3,279	2,823	456	86.1	13.9	.1	.1	.1
Curfew and loitering law violations	29,992	21,386	8,606	71.3	28.7	.8	.7	1.1
Runaways.......................................	78,090	33,763	44,327	43.2	56.8	2.0	1.1	5.4

[1]Includes suburban city and county law enforcement agencies within metropolitan areas. Excludes central cities. Suburban cities and counties are also included in other groups.
[2]Because of rounding, the percentages may not add to totals.
[3]Less than one-tenth of 1 percent.
[4]Violent crimes are offenses of murder, forcible rape, robbery, and aggravated assault.
[5]Property crimes are offenses of burglary, larceny–theft, motor vehicle theft, and arson.
[6]Includes arson.

Table 67.—Suburban Area[1] Arrests, Distribution by Race, 1995

[4,678 agencies; 1995 estimated population 82,984,000]

Offense charged	Total arrests					Percent distribution[2]				
	Total	White	Black	American Indian or Alaskan Native	Asian or Pacific Islander	Total	White	Black	American Indian or Alaskan Native	Asian or Pacific Islander
TOTAL	**3,921,773**	**2,974,856**	**901,650**	**20,303**	**24,964**	**100.0**	**75.9**	**23.0**	**.5**	**.6**
Murder and nonnegligent manslaughter	3,778	2,396	1,335	22	25	100.0	63.4	35.3	.6	.7
Forcible rape	8,254	5,714	2,432	42	66	100.0	69.2	29.5	.5	.8
Robbery	30,111	14,663	15,126	120	202	100.0	48.7	50.2	.4	.7
Aggravated assault	142,160	101,062	39,300	769	1,029	100.0	71.1	27.6	.5	.7
Burglary	102,707	78,352	23,135	468	752	100.0	76.3	22.5	.5	.7
Larceny–theft	404,343	281,254	116,595	1,976	4,518	100.0	69.6	28.8	.5	1.1
Motor vehicle theft	44,302	31,477	12,132	243	450	100.0	71.1	27.4	.5	1.0
Arson	5,461	4,662	732	26	41	100.0	85.4	13.4	.5	.8
Violent crime[3]	184,303	123,835	58,193	953	1,322	100.0	67.2	31.6	.5	.7
Property crime[4]	556,813	395,745	152,594	2,713	5,761	100.0	71.1	27.4	.5	1.0
Crime Index total[5]	741,116	519,580	210,787	3,666	7,083	100.0	70.1	28.4	.5	1.0
Other assaults...........................	330,840	243,794	83,077	1,891	2,078	100.0	73.7	25.1	.6	.6
Forgery and counterfeiting	31,099	21,987	8,754	105	253	100.0	70.7	28.1	.3	.8
Fraud	124,724	88,376	35,394	357	597	100.0	70.9	28.4	.3	.5
Embezzlement	3,836	2,588	1,189	11	48	100.0	67.5	31.0	.3	1.3
Stolen property; buying, receiving, possessing	44,868	30,598	13,599	191	480	100.0	68.2	30.3	.4	1.1
Vandalism..............................	81,271	67,462	12,770	457	582	100.0	83.0	15.7	.6	.7
Weapons; carrying, possessing, etc.	57,993	41,653	15,652	192	496	100.0	71.8	27.0	.3	.9
Prostitution and commercialized vice	9,336	6,888	2,320	26	102	100.0	73.8	24.9	.3	1.1
Sex offenses (except forcible rape and prostitution)	23,412	19,525	3,591	117	179	100.0	83.4	15.3	.5	.8
Drug abuse violations	350,649	261,719	86,380	1,109	1,441	100.0	74.6	24.6	.3	.4
Gambling	2,128	1,159	889	8	72	100.0	54.5	41.8	.4	3.4
Offenses against family and children	54,452	36,347	17,768	159	178	100.0	66.8	32.6	.3	.3
Driving under the influence	463,646	419,102	38,703	2,379	3,462	100.0	90.4	8.3	.5	.7
Liquor laws	130,836	117,683	11,004	1,238	911	100.0	89.9	8.4	.9	.7
Drunkenness.............................	167,451	147,852	17,074	1,880	645	100.0	88.3	10.2	1.1	.4
Disorderly conduct	168,158	125,406	40,785	1,033	934	100.0	74.6	24.3	.6	.6
Vagrancy...............................	3,928	2,764	1,111	26	27	100.0	70.4	28.3	.7	.7
All other offenses (except traffic)	1,020,789	726,507	284,723	4,889	4,670	100.0	71.2	27.9	.5	.5
Suspicion	3,277	2,711	535	28	3	100.0	82.7	16.3	.9	.1
Curfew and loitering law violations	29,932	25,779	3,685	197	271	100.0	86.1	12.3	.7	.9
Runaways...............................	78,032	65,376	11,860	344	452	100.0	83.8	15.2	.4	.6

See footnotes at the end of table.

Table 67.—Suburban Area[1] Arrests, Distribution by Race, 1995 — Continued

Offense charged	Arrests under 18					Percent distribution[2]				
	Total	White	Black	American Indian or Alaskan Native	Asian or Pacific Islander	Total	White	Black	American Indian or Alaskan Native	Asian or Pacific Islander
TOTAL	**740,966**	**578,360**	**151,775**	**3,895**	**6,936**	**100.0**	**78.1**	**20.5**	**.5**	**.9**
Murder and nonnegligent manslaughter	559	315	236	4	4	100.0	56.4	42.2	.7	.7
Forcible rape	1,343	905	424	6	8	100.0	67.4	31.6	.4	.6
Robbery	9,519	4,468	4,914	42	95	100.0	46.9	51.6	.4	1.0
Aggravated assault.........................	21,633	14,389	6,937	123	184	100.0	66.5	32.1	.6	.9
Burglary	40,432	32,044	7,778	199	411	100.0	79.3	19.2	.5	1.0
Larceny–theft..............................	139,247	103,495	32,926	764	2,062	100.0	74.3	23.6	.5	1.5
Motor vehicle theft	18,425	13,027	4,979	115	304	100.0	70.7	27.0	.6	1.6
Arson	3,260	2,857	364	14	25	100.0	87.6	11.2	.4	.8
Violent crime[3]	33,054	20,077	12,511	175	291	100.0	60.7	37.9	.5	.9
Property crime[4]	201,364	151,423	46,047	1,092	2,802	100.0	75.2	22.9	.5	1.4
Crime Index total[5]	234,418	171,500	58,558	1,267	3,093	100.0	73.2	25.0	.5	1.3
Other assaults...............................	60,628	43,166	16,663	373	426	100.0	71.2	27.5	.6	.7
Forgery and counterfeiting	2,380	1,984	361	8	27	100.0	83.4	15.2	.3	1.1
Fraud	2,692	2,090	555	11	36	100.0	77.6	20.6	.4	1.3
Embezzlement	288	192	91	—	5	100.0	66.7	31.6	—	1.7
Stolen property; buying, receiving, possessing	12,041	8,411	3,352	55	223	100.0	69.9	27.8	.5	1.9
Vandalism..................................	41,543	35,921	5,047	218	357	100.0	86.5	12.1	.5	.9
Weapons; carrying, possessing, etc.	14,427	10,813	3,368	69	177	100.0	74.9	23.3	.5	1.2
Prostitution and commercialized vice	137	91	43	1	2	100.0	66.4	31.4	.7	1.5
Sex offenses (except forcible rape and prostitution)	4,472	3,497	923	16	36	100.0	78.2	20.6	.4	.8
Drug abuse violations	49,871	39,259	10,084	202	326	100.0	78.7	20.2	.4	.7
Gambling	229	72	155	—	2	100.0	31.4	67.7	—	.9
Offenses against family and children	2,057	1,699	338	8	12	100.0	82.6	16.4	.4	.6
Driving under the influence	4,429	4,140	247	26	16	100.0	93.5	5.6	.6	.4
Liquor laws	35,556	33,594	1,382	328	252	100.0	94.5	3.9	.9	.7
Drunkenness................................	5,729	5,337	309	52	31	100.0	93.2	5.4	.9	.5
Disorderly conduct	44,938	33,448	11,011	179	300	100.0	74.4	24.5	.4	.7
Vagrancy...................................	761	651	98	7	5	100.0	85.5	12.9	.9	.7
All other offenses (except traffic)	115,783	90,849	23,517	530	887	100.0	78.5	20.3	.5	.8
Suspicion	623	491	128	4	—	100.0	78.8	20.5	.6	—
Curfew and loitering law violations	29,932	25,779	3,685	197	271	100.0	86.1	12.3	.7	.9
Runaways...................................	78,032	65,376	11,860	344	452	100.0	83.8	15.2	.4	.6

See footnotes at the end of table.

Table 67.—Suburban Area[1] Arrests, Distribution by Race, 1995 — Continued

Offense charged	Arrests 18 and over					Percent distribution[2]				
	Total	White	Black	American Indian or Alaskan Native	Asian or Pacific Islander	Total	White	Black	American Indian or Alaskan Native	Asian or Pacific Islander
TOTAL	**3,180,807**	**2,396,496**	**749,875**	**16,408**	**18,028**	**100.0**	**75.3**	**23.6**	**.5**	**.6**
Murder and nonnegligent manslaughter	3,219	2,081	1,099	18	21	100.0	64.6	34.1	.6	.7
Forcible rape	6,911	4,809	2,008	36	58	100.0	69.6	29.1	.5	.8
Robbery	20,592	10,195	10,212	78	107	100.0	49.5	49.6	.4	.5
Aggravated assault............................	120,527	86,673	32,363	646	845	100.0	71.9	26.9	.5	.7
Burglary	62,275	46,308	15,357	269	341	100.0	74.4	24.7	.4	.5
Larceny–theft.................................	265,096	177,759	83,669	1,212	2,456	100.0	67.1	31.6	.5	.9
Motor vehicle theft	25,877	18,450	7,153	128	146	100.0	71.3	27.6	.5	.6
Arson	2,201	1,805	368	12	16	100.0	82.0	16.7	.5	.7
Violent crime[3]	151,249	103,758	45,682	778	1,031	100.0	68.6	30.2	.5	.7
Property crime[4]	355,449	244,322	106,547	1,621	2,959	100.0	68.7	30.0	.5	.8
Crime Index total[5]	506,698	348,080	152,229	2,399	3,990	100.0	68.7	30.0	.5	.8
Other assaults................................	270,212	200,628	66,414	1,518	1,652	100.0	74.2	24.6	.6	.6
Forgery and counterfeiting	28,719	20,003	8,393	97	226	100.0	69.7	29.2	.3	.8
Fraud	122,032	86,286	34,839	346	561	100.0	70.7	28.5	.3	.5
Embezzlement	3,548	2,396	1,098	11	43	100.0	67.5	30.9	.3	1.2
Stolen property; buying, receiving, possessing	32,827	22,187	10,247	136	257	100.0	67.6	31.2	.4	.8
Vandalism....................................	39,728	31,541	7,723	239	225	100.0	79.4	19.4	.6	.6
Weapons; carrying, possessing, etc.	43,566	30,840	12,284	123	319	100.0	70.8	28.2	.3	.7
Prostitution and commercialized vice	9,199	6,797	2,277	25	100	100.0	73.9	24.8	.3	1.1
Sex offenses (except forcible rape and prostitution)	18,940	16,028	2,668	101	143	100.0	84.6	14.1	.5	.8
Drug abuse violations	300,778	222,460	76,296	907	1,115	100.0	74.0	25.4	.3	.4
Gambling	1,899	1,087	734	8	70	100.0	57.2	38.7	.4	3.7
Offenses against family and children	52,395	34,648	17,430	151	166	100.0	66.1	33.3	.3	.3
Driving under the influence	459,217	414,962	38,456	2,353	3,446	100.0	90.4	8.4	.5	.8
Liquor laws	95,280	84,089	9,622	910	659	100.0	88.3	10.1	1.0	.7
Drunkenness.................................	161,722	142,515	16,765	1,828	614	100.0	88.1	10.4	1.1	.4
Disorderly conduct	123,220	91,958	29,774	854	634	100.0	74.6	24.2	.7	.5
Vagrancy....................................	3,167	2,113	1,013	19	22	100.0	66.7	32.0	.6	.7
All other offenses (except traffic)	905,006	635,658	261,206	4,359	3,783	100.0	70.2	28.9	.5	.4
Suspicion	2,654	2,220	407	24	3	100.0	83.6	15.3	.9	.1
Curfew and loitering law violations	—	—	—	—	—	—	—	—	—	—
Runaways....................................	—	—	—	—	—	—	—	—	—	—

[1]Includes suburban city and county law enforcement agencies within metropolitan areas. Excludes central cities. Suburban cities and counties are also included in other groups.
[2]Because of rounding, the percentages may not add to totals.
[3]Violent crimes are offenses of murder, forcible rape, robbery, and aggravated assault.
[4]Property crimes are offenses of burglary, larceny–theft, motor vehicle theft, and arson.
[5]Includes arson.

Table 68.—Police Disposition of Juvenile Offenders Taken into Custody, 1995

[1995 estimated population]

Population group	Total[1]	Handled within department and released	Referred to juvenile court jurisdiction	Referred to welfare agency	Referred to other police agency	Referred to criminal or adult court
TOTAL ALL AGENCIES: 8,112 agencies; population 176,175,000						
Number	1,365,108	388,062	896,576	22,937	12,582	44,951
Percent2	100.0	28.4	65.7	1.7	.9	3.3
TOTAL CITIES: 5,684 cities; population 121,279,000						
Number	1,106,195	303,500	738,769	18,660	8,707	36,559
Percent2	100.0	27.4	66.8	1.7	.8	3.3
GROUP I						
48 cities, 250,000 and over; population 37,170,000						
Number	278,512	71,919	192,384	5,261	2,199	6,749
Percent[2]	100.0	25.8	69.1	1.9	.8	2.4
GROUP II						
123 cities, 100,000 to 249,999; population 18,218,000						
Number	162,439	44,135	105,894	4,151	1,232	7,027
Percent[2]	100.0	27.2	65.2	2.6	.8	4.3
GROUP III						
281 cities, 50,000 to 99,999; population 19,124,000						
Number	182,642	54,311	120,452	3,494	816	3,569
Percent[2]	100.0	29.7	65.9	1.9	.4	2.0
GROUP IV						
492 cities, 25,000 to 49,999; population 17,001,000						
Number	157,632	45,092	103,126	1,876	1,914	5,624
Percent[2]	100.0	28.6	65.4	1.2	1.2	3.6
GROUP V						
1,070 cities, 10,000 to 24,999; population 17,001,000						
Number	170,387	46,116	114,336	2,025	1,464	6,446
Percent[2]	100.0	27.1	67.1	1.2	.9	3.8
GROUP VI						
3,670 cities under 10,000; population 12,765,000						
Number	154,583	41,927	102,577	1,853	1,082	7,144
Percent[2]	100.0	27.1	66.4	1.2	.7	4.6
SUBURBAN COUNTIES						
1,530 agencies; population 15,583,000						
Number	56,249	12,091	39,629	1,608	646	2,275
Percent[2]	100.0	21.5	70.5	2.9	1.1	4.0
RURAL COUNTIES						
898 agencies; population 39,313,000						
Number	202,664	72,471	118,178	2,669	3,229	6,117
Percent[2]	100.0	35.8	58.3	1.3	1.6	3.0
SUBURBAN AREA[3]						
4,214 agencies; population 82,945,000						
Number	583,932	192,712	358,368	6,865	6,557	19,430
Percent[2]	100.0	33.0	61.4	1.2	1.1	3.3

[1]Includes all offenses except traffic and neglect cases.
[2]Because of rounding, the percentages may not add to totals.
[3]Includes suburban city and county law enforcement agencies within metropolitan areas. Excludes central cities. Suburban cities and counties are also included in other groups.

Table 69.—Arrests by State, 1995

[1995 estimated population] Dashes indicate zero data.

State	Total[1] all classes	Crime[2] Index total	Violent[3] crime	Property[4] crime	Murder and non-negligent man-slaughter	Forcible rape	Robbery	Aggra-vated assault	Burglary	Larceny–theft	Motor vehicle theft	Arson	Other assaults	Forgery and counter-feiting	Fraud
ALABAMA: 284 agencies; population 4,130,000															
Under 18	16,051	6,725	1,200	5,525	33	40	519	608	869	4,285	344	27	1,218	48	98
Total all ages	202,946	34,903	11,152	23,751	426	466	2,405	7,855	3,662	18,390	1,577	122	26,165	1,964	12,685
ALASKA: 23 agencies; population 495,000															
Under 18	5,647	2,532	258	2,274	2	16	68	172	489	1,549	219	17	460	15	11
Total all ages	33,220	6,796	1,399	5,397	26	102	190	1,081	783	4,050	538	26	3,854	83	196
ARIZONA: 81 agencies; population 3,869,000															
Under 18	66,578	18,621	2,260	16,361	43	40	550	1,627	2,459	11,866	1,715	321	4,853	140	133
Total all ages	292,752	60,197	9,524	50,673	297	258	1,648	7,321	5,968	40,575	3,678	452	29,641	2,232	1,906
ARKANSAS: 188 agencies; population 2,477,000															
Under 18	19,829	6,513	875	5,638	34	57	262	522	1,106	4,237	269	26	918	112	114
Total all ages	195,353	24,924	5,431	19,493	255	415	1,003	3,758	3,430	15,294	646	123	8,633	2,337	17,926
CALIFORNIA: 685 agencies; population 30,950,000															
Under 18	254,143	99,448	21,266	78,182	520	404	8,877	11,465	20,832	42,598	13,462	1,290	20,877	842	811
Total all ages	1,578,277	392,717	150,152	242,565	2,796	3,068	26,603	117,685	63,630	139,906	36,609	2,420	77,504	14,600	11,202
COLORADO: 127 agencies; population 2,944,000															
Under 18	41,053	13,693	981	12,712	13	62	191	715	1,333	10,474	737	168	3,157	149	228
Total all ages	167,842	36,993	5,611	31,382	148	399	704	4,360	2,893	26,509	1,734	246	20,354	1,165	2,800
CONNECTICUT: 98 agencies; population 2,750,000															
Under 18	33,259	10,404	1,582	8,822	15	64	534	969	1,583	5,889	1,182	168	3,212	49	89
Total all ages	186,902	39,582	8,477	31,105	170	416	2,121	5,770	5,284	23,239	2,303	279	19,186	1,184	3,190
DELAWARE:6 1 agency; population 29,000															
Under 18	510	248	26	222	1	2	8	15	12	194	13	3	76	—	4
Total all ages	2,730	865	118	747	1	11	32	74	77	642	22	6	336	51	175
DISTRICT OF COLUMBIA: 1 agency; population 554,000															
Under 18	3,916	1,557	639	918	13	7	299	320	73	76	769	—	260	8	1
Total all ages	43,239	9,831	4,300	5,531	200	88	1,095	2,917	985	2,587	1,944	15	4,306	260	117
FLORIDA: 622 agencies; population 14,142,000															
Under 18	147,531	58,333	10,968	47,365	181	374	3,324	7,089	10,863	31,336	4,871	295	8,655	284	610
Total all ages	766,240	189,981	58,408	131,573	1,114	2,289	10,214	44,791	26,523	93,034	11,409	607	63,588	5,489	9,068
GEORGIA: 308 agencies; population 4,522,000															
Under 18	34,418	12,881	2,078	10,803	54	89	612	1,323	1,752	7,851	1,106	94	3,298	163	211
Total all ages	281,428	59,187	16,391	42,796	433	630	3,203	12,125	6,933	32,181	3,379	303	24,388	4,088	9,107
HAWAII: 5 agencies; population 1,187,000															
Under 18	18,662	4,066	368	3,698	18	13	219	118	445	2,746	487	20	1,388	21	42
Total all ages	69,959	12,720	1,493	11,227	76	105	607	705	1,305	7,935	1,934	53	5,335	389	574
IDAHO: 106 agencies; population 1,141,000															
Under 18	23,716	7,169	460	6,709	7	14	62	377	770	5,365	455	119	1,352	111	59
Total all ages	77,839	13,202	1,605	11,597	35	78	147	1,345	1,397	9,256	800	144	6,696	499	860
ILLINOIS:6															
INDIANA: 102 agencies; population 3,235,000															
Under 18	38,434	11,363	1,936	9,427	39	20	244	1,633	934	7,349	1,047	97	1,997	80	56
Total all ages	159,954	31,733	8,108	23,625	191	149	943	6,825	2,550	18,557	2,305	213	10,809	823	1,965

See footnotes at end of table.

Table 69.—Arrests by State, 1995 — Continued

Embezzlement	Stolen property; buying, receiving, possessing	Vandalism	Weapons; carrying, possessing, etc.	Prostitution and commercialized vice	Sex offenses (except forcible rape and prostitution)	Drug abuse violations	Gambling	Offenses against family and children	Driving under the influence	Liquor laws	Drunkenness[5]	Disorderly conduct	Vagrancy	All other offenses (except traffic)	Suspicion	Curfew and loitering law violations	Runaways
2	420	350	585	—	31	1,167	3	19	115	866	131	1,057	39	1,746	—	297	1,134
45	2,277	3,094	2,605	140	429	13,201	149	1,166	18,639	9,101	13,529	5,439	414	55,569	1	297	1,134
—	23	406	113	4	62	333	—	—	34	643	—	62	—	937	—	12	—
2	60	922	562	190	265	1,503	6	117	4,047	1,906	7	672	—	12,020	—	12	—
33	958	3,854	949	23	326	4,736	7	113	266	4,590	—	4,218	72	5,970	—	8,632	8,084
220	3,949	10,434	4,861	1,835	2,135	24,046	37	1,824	27,708	21,894	—	22,923	705	59,489	—	8,632	8,084
1	435	487	376	3	60	1,072	13	12	278	619	444	1,162	45	3,685	81	1,944	1,455
17	2,350	1,338	3,079	344	468	11,206	186	1,005	19,742	3,408	20,451	8,144	1,022	64,826	548	1,944	1,455
81	6,853	15,102	9,389	197	1,944	23,668	93	15	1,657	4,973	4,515	6,567	869	30,879	—	16,512	8,851
1,257	27,867	28,556	36,271	15,824	14,264	257,605	1,189	643	198,619	23,773	114,600	13,984	4,558	317,881	—	16,512	8,851
21	172	3,303	821	7	284	2,535	—	17	243	2,089	19	2,446	10	5,477	10	4,807	1,565
220	579	7,236	3,224	1,131	1,280	12,722	27	870	13,425	10,182	453	13,336	1,591	33,871	11	4,807	1,565
12	110	2,355	687	8	195	3,471	13	112	79	466	32	4,422	27	6,482	20	216	798
106	444	5,525	2,500	1,020	862	21,342	107	1,984	9,308	1,597	40	26,272	163	51,435	41	216	798
—	14	21	9	—	4	25	—	1	—	5	—	37	2	62	—	2	—
—	24	72	39	12	24	194	—	11	—	13	21	113	12	766	—	2	—
—	38	50	252	4	17	650	10	—	1	2	—	89	—	844	—	—	133
4	443	676	1,541	793	103	6,123	251	20	2,717	53	—	6,982	—	5,599	3,287	—	133
82	823	2,479	1,802	103	509	8,601	90	19	271	1,670	—	3,334	—	18,798	—	—	41,068
542	4,831	4,910	7,883	6,903	4,141	78,882	748	1,699	51,718	22,695	—	21,237	—	250,857	—	—	41,068
7	703	1,049	850	19	265	2,748	63	63	334	902	107	2,653	32	5,266	34	771	1,999
461	4,696	3,753	5,061	2,100	2,672	27,721	433	3,251	32,345	7,546	7,866	25,282	95	58,352	254	771	1,999
4	34	744	99	6	88	804	9	139	58	386	—	110	—	4,218	—	906	5,540
63	351	1,373	546	509	398	3,570	380	1,965	4,115	1,597	—	1,053	—	28,575	—	906	5,540
12	213	1,096	316	—	80	829	—	7	231	1,492	6	526	—	4,733	—	1,962	3,522
94	555	1,728	1,049	9	284	4,578	2	441	10,797	4,293	118	2,010	5	25,135	—	1,962	3,522
9	439	1,410	340	6	154	1,464	21	111	101	1,935	290	1,729	10	6,883	56	3,311	6,669
22	1,059	2,304	1,757	1,267	1,092	9,622	150	1,082	17,071	7,229	16,151	5,040	27	40,625	146	3,311	6,669

Table 69.—Arrests by State, 1995 — Continued

State	Total[1] all classes	Crime[2] Index total	Violent[3] crime	Property[4] crime	Murder and non-negligent man-slaughter	Forcible rape	Robbery	Aggra-vated assault	Burglary	Larceny-theft	Motor vehicle theft	Arson	Other assaults	Forgery and counter-feiting	Fraud
IOWA: 187 agencies; population 2,494,000															
Under 18	18,275	6,195	805	5,390	2	23	110	670	783	4,099	436	72	1,527	115	64
Total all ages	95,070	17,098	3,844	13,254	36	107	339	3,362	1,893	10,409	830	122	8,392	799	2,200
KANSAS:6															
KENTUCKY: 36 agencies; population 1,288,000															
Under 18	13,585	6,017	1,089	4,928	25	37	325	702	817	3,448	596	67	535	124	106
Total all ages	99,981	22,520	7,849	14,671	129	238	1,238	6,244	2,729	10,387	1,430	125	5,669	2,795	9,149
LOUISIANA: 144 agencies; population 2,933,000:															
Under 18	37,788	12,890	2,055	10,835	120	79	405	1,451	1,996	8,129	590	120	3,799	103	47
Total all ages	194,629	45,441	11,482	33,959	501	463	1,501	9,017	6,009	26,095	1,578	277	21,039	1,882	2,015
MAINE: 119 agencies; population 805,000															
Under 18	7,477	3,118	132	2,986	—	13	33	86	574	2,131	212	69	736	18	17
Total all ages	33,356	6,492	603	5,889	13	71	93	426	1,118	4,320	363	88	4,011	140	836
MARYLAND: 146 agencies; population 4,994,000															
Under 18	49,183	18,420	3,565	14,855	127	136	1,341	1,961	2,837	8,377	3,369	272	6,876	74	106
Total all ages	281,807	63,698	13,974	49,724	691	836	4,839	7,608	10,014	32,542	6,704	464	35,769	1,073	3,532
MASSACHUSETTS: 243 agencies; population 4,854,000															
Under 18	22,973	7,877	2,820	5,057	15	72	621	2,112	1,494	2,980	500	83	1,356	27	24
Total all ages	158,142	36,617	15,872	20,745	128	598	2,185	12,961	5,133	13,988	1,458	166	13,658	656	427
MICHIGAN: 421 agencies; population 8,038,000															
Under 18	55,758	20,422	3,712	16,710	161	296	1,047	2,208	3,057	11,779	1,598	276	3,843	79	781
Total all ages	384,263	67,064	22,379	44,685	1,410	1,685	4,063	15,221	8,870	31,887	3,200	728	37,160	1,165	6,897
MINNESOTA: 284 agencies; population 4,439,000															
Under 18	67,413	20,153	2,106	18,047	49	212	652	1,193	2,090	13,662	2,051	244	5,382	437	424
Total all ages	228,556	41,449	7,044	34,405	219	1,033	1,502	4,290	4,226	26,160	3,669	350	23,033	2,589	11,126
MISSISSIPPI: 41 agencies; population 666,000															
Under 18	7,518	2,658	202	2,456	16	12	88	86	502	1,629	303	22	641	21	22
Total all ages	53,172	10,407	1,576	8,831	114	141	411	910	1,614	6,254	890	73	5,779	511	1,266
MISSOURI: 155 agencies; population 3,141,000															
Under 18	36,309	11,552	1,864	9,688	90	97	640	1,037	1,320	7,088	1,108	172	4,123	143	101
Total all ages	263,054	46,942	11,285	35,657	500	580	2,443	7,762	5,072	26,968	3,226	391	31,709	1,728	2,710
MONTANA:6															
NEBRASKA: 237 agencies; population 1,470,000															
Under 18	17,202	5,943	325	5,618	10	28	131	156	449	4,776	278	115	1,668	96	86
Total all ages	81,118	12,690	1,548	11,142	55	166	294	1,033	1,001	9,455	527	159	8,098	667	2,550
NEVADA: 22 agencies; population 1,406,000															
Under 18	18,660	5,254	614	4,640	17	33	319	245	924	3,195	479	42	1,827	12	63
Total all ages	117,434	19,610	3,350	16,260	161	270	1,312	1,607	3,438	11,575	1,170	77	13,757	604	1,734
NEW HAMPSHIRE:6															

See footnotes at end of table.

Table 69.—Arrests by State, 1995 — Continued

Embezzle-ment	Stolen property; buying, receiving, possessing	Vandalism	Weapons; carrying, possessing, etc.	Prostitution and commercialized vice	Sex offenses (except forcible rape and prostitution)	Drug abuse violations	Gambling	Offenses against family and children	Driving under the influence	Liquor laws	Drunken-ness[5]	Disorderly conduct	Vagrancy	All other offenses (except traffic)	Suspicion	Curfew and loitering law violations	Runaways
11	50	1,264	147	2	64	618	2	—	294	2,425	309	1,406	—	2,348	—	774	660
102	115	2,491	850	253	259	6,278	17	237	12,824	10,969	7,554	4,917	83	18,198	—	774	660
1	737	419	219	8	81	1,088	26	21	66	433	296	753	—	1,855	—	60	740
340	2,061	1,673	1,646	751	701	10,634	77	1,777	8,134	1,447	12,145	4,964	—	12,698	—	60	740
—	894	1,484	610	26	179	2,214	53	151	216	493	149	3,093	60	7,463	36	1,626	2,202
14	3,021	4,224	2,573	421	1,143	15,446	160	1,369	14,043	1,892	6,348	14,043	514	54,992	221	1,626	2,202
1	89	719	46	—	50	417	—	5	83	452	8	132	—	1,197	—	53	336
11	240	1,373	191	2	223	2,198	—	166	5,267	1,857	26	977	—	8,957	—	53	336
27	97	2,360	1,239	10	404	7,579	59	17	201	1,283	—	1,374	10	7,279	145	326	1,297
439	474	4,443	4,829	2,077	1,675	43,707	210	1,649	22,526	5,009	—	6,070	275	82,325	404	326	1,297
—	903	971	341	20	69	2,907	8	208	132	1,262	444	1,903	38	3,118	58	113	1,194
12	3,416	2,760	1,495	2,835	877	23,229	44	3,542	15,130	4,191	8,484	11,452	416	27,121	473	113	1,194
144	1,972	2,816	1,446	64	392	4,028	29	1	691	2,076	26	2,651	48	7,587	—	2,554	4,108
1,334	9,009	6,923	7,509	4,889	2,241	33,045	236	4,026	46,711	15,375	372	23,089	384	110,172	—	2,554	4,108
—	1,204	4,725	1,296	32	254	3,443	18	30	373	8,044	—	6,792	18	5,543	—	6,047	3,198
4	2,908	8,257	3,089	945	872	14,844	107	795	32,979	21,495	—	16,752	119	37,948	—	6,047	3,198
6	52	197	171	4	13	606	23	47	53	241	78	678	1	1,364	18	373	251
301	373	653	724	73	122	5,439	267	692	5,162	2,338	4,407	4,641	12	9,341	40	373	251
22	346	1,933	785	18	269	2,446	15	78	152	1,068	48	1,371	58	6,106	149	2,249	3,277
116	1,615	7,353	5,255	2,007	1,934	19,899	89	3,388	15,219	5,546	1,339	10,726	540	97,595	1,818	2,249	3,277
11	532	1,208	269	5	71	749	5	45	261	2,104	—	674	—	2,353	—	516	606
88	1,335	2,574	1,375	396	601	6,367	81	1,499	11,903	7,937	—	4,279	3	17,553	—	516	606
27	518	730	509	13	106	1,021	23	33	55	912	32	458	66	2,972	—	3,012	1,017
396	2,462	1,634	2,303	2,965	991	9,325	138	822	6,102	4,393	424	3,045	1,208	41,480	12	3,012	1,017

Table 69.—Arrests by State, 1995 — Continued

State	Total[1] all classes	Crime[2] Index total	Violent[3] crime	Property[4] crime	Murder and non-negligent man-slaughter	Forcible rape	Robbery	Aggravated assault	Burglary	Larceny-theft	Motor vehicle theft	Arson	Other assaults	Forgery and counterfeiting	Fraud
NEW JERSEY: 536 agencies; population 7,587,000															
Under 18	88,724	23,718	5,535	18,183	60	184	2,247	3,044	3,179	13,269	1,412	323	8,657	73	201
Total all ages	400,392	75,157	20,886	54,271	380	972	6,075	13,459	9,315	41,867	2,517	572	39,522	1,357	5,584
NEW MEXICO: 42 agencies; population 460,000															
Under 18	9,262	2,288	305	1,983	6	3	27	269	523	1,337	105	18	811	28	16
Total all ages	44,049	5,554	1,327	4,227	42	62	103	1,120	895	3,026	274	32	3,629	152	274
NEW YORK: 451 agencies; population 15,810,000															
Under 18	150,774	43,824	16,415	27,409	172	245	10,719	5,279	5,134	19,495	2,380	400	11,062	433	10,605
Total all ages	1,091,274	174,218	66,793	107,425	1,345	1,962	28,629	34,857	19,000	78,012	9,577	836	65,464	8,061	52,921
NORTH CAROLINA: 462 agencies; population 6,957,000															
Under 18	53,240	17,714	3,187	14,527	86	77	893	2,131	3,953	9,611	813	150	6,551	165	894
Total all ages	482,641	83,467	25,905	57,562	733	727	4,012	20,433	15,889	38,867	2,381	425	52,601	4,193	52,131
NORTH DAKOTA: 44 agencies; population 481,000															
Under 18	7,836	2,193	94	2,099	9	10	12	63	163	1,725	195	16	360	61	12
Total all ages	23,841	3,843	214	3,629	9	36	27	142	268	3,067	272	22	1,144	217	2,936
OHIO: 231 agencies; population 5,204,000															
Under 18	63,407	15,110	2,401	12,709	61	166	1,073	1,101	2,391	8,281	1,742	295	5,417	122	56
Total all ages	307,506	43,926	10,654	33,272	350	868	3,359	6,077	6,131	23,244	3,326	571	29,290	1,640	3,785
OKLAHOMA: 283 agencies; population 3,250,000															
Under 18	29,535	12,731	1,502	11,229	30	68	415	989	1,820	7,825	1,340	244	1,105	125	124
Total all ages	153,252	29,951	7,161	22,790	236	430	1,094	5,401	4,146	15,787	2,462	395	7,067	1,428	2,088
OREGON: 177 agencies; population 2,144,000															
Under 18	34,532	11,571	858	10,713	7	41	284	526	1,464	8,049	925	275	2,374	151	119
Total all ages	117,987	30,820	3,454	27,366	67	224	996	2,167	3,389	20,629	2,872	476	12,986	1,670	1,314
PENNSYLVANIA:6 1 agency population 1,530,000															
Under 18	19,464	5,955	2,287	3,668	38	70	1,351	828	328	2,026	1,270	44	736	19	9
Total all ages	70,336	26,036	9,191	16,845	312	373	4,497	4,009	2,413	10,621	3,602	209	4,036	382	245
RHODE ISLAND: 44 agencies; population 990,000															
Under 18	9,745	3,082	498	2,584	1	13	89	395	440	1,869	172	103	1,011	4	27
Total all ages	41,753	8,118	2,428	5,690	23	88	224	2,093	1,035	4,122	402	131	5,301	96	1,438
SOUTH CAROLINA: 226 agencies; population 3,513,000															
Under 18	26,174	9,553	1,605	7,948	39	94	393	1,079	1,929	5,464	483	72	3,186	83	284
Total all ages	202,475	34,849	10,270	24,579	324	598	1,583	7,765	5,339	18,026	1,004	210	21,990	2,284	31,946
SOUTH DAKOTA: 45 agencies; population 462,000															
Under 18	10,013	2,728	179	2,549	—	20	23	136	354	2,008	143	44	489	32	45
Total all ages	33,285	5,429	704	4,725	7	77	75	545	649	3,809	214	53	2,722	179	844
TENNESSEE: 93 agencies; population 1,701,000															
Under 18	19,500	5,969	777	5,192	33	24	199	521	668	3,726	747	51	1,342	42	51
Total all ages	122,929	25,639	6,528	19,111	216	293	1,049	4,970	2,674	14,497	1,808	132	10,671	1,416	1,440
TEXAS: 890 agencies; population 17,993,000															
Under 18	220,652	62,565	8,523	54,042	243	490	2,861	4,929	10,654	37,618	5,240	530	16,739	701	657
Total all ages	1,071,300	179,148	37,780	141,368	1,413	2,766	7,996	25,605	22,779	106,165	11,392	1,032	89,276	7,588	14,562
UTAH: 95 agencies; population 1,688,000															
Under 18	36,754	13,091	847	12,244	5	31	193	618	987	10,065	986	206	2,529	200	94
Total all ages	110,736	24,682	2,240	22,442	37	120	394	1,689	1,762	18,928	1,486	266	9,491	1,103	784

See footnotes at end of table.

Table 69.—Arrests by State, 1995 — Continued

Embezzlement	Stolen property; buying, receiving, possessing	Vandalism	Weapons; carrying, possessing, etc.	Prostitution and commercialized vice	Sex offenses (except forcible rape and prostitution)	Drug abuse violations	Gambling	Offenses against family and children	Driving under the influence	Liquor laws	Drunkenness[5]	Disorderly conduct	Vagrancy	All other offenses (except traffic)	Suspicion	Curfew and loitering law violations	Runaways
7	3,068	6,749	2,087	25	409	10,214	41	17	219	2,906	9	9,946	364	10,876	—	3,204	5,934
70	9,494	11,567	6,203	2,254	2,020	53,600	464	18,311	24,581	9,910	24	36,564	2,847	91,725	—	3,204	5,934
11	114	312	165	—	16	658	—	116	134	1,224	13	258	6	1,616	196	679	601
114	444	432	404	4	96	2,713	—	1,216	7,709	2,856	303	1,289	13	15,260	307	679	601
17	2,535	8,811	2,729	73	1,345	15,273	257	358	304	3,260	—	11,749	754	31,788	—	—	5,597
346	12,627	24,815	13,533	8,925	6,747	150,319	7,108	3,071	44,731	63,111	—	62,079	3,012	384,589	—	—	5,597
182	1,380	2,589	1,592	6	304	3,861	16	108	885	1,396	—	3,143	26	10,309	—	94	2,025
2,004	6,594	10,310	8,576	847	2,650	32,248	358	6,913	68,246	8,393	—	15,113	163	125,715	—	94	2,025
—	74	491	55	—	28	99	—	112	47	1,245	2	493	—	1,155	—	341	1,068
3	130	673	116	3	72	502	—	308	2,829	3,629	365	1,350	20	4,292	—	341	1,068
—	1,650	2,385	872	27	277	4,136	114	1,937	276	2,554	336	3,459	26	14,354	54	6,173	4,072
10	4,946	4,866	4,144	2,234	1,790	28,359	565	18,633	21,616	15,508	13,542	17,947	526	83,790	144	6,173	4,072
67	807	809	510	17	100	1,416	1	72	276	899	720	557	—	3,743	—	2,421	3,035
603	2,575	1,458	2,923	314	888	13,971	51	945	21,319	5,083	28,695	2,816	—	25,621	—	2,421	3,035
3	147	2,120	423	1	254	1,639	—	11	170	3,523	—	1,015	—	4,841	—	3,110	3,060
121	556	4,174	2,133	120	1,075	10,183	9	525	13,837	9,415	—	4,570	—	18,309	—	3,110	3,060
—	27	686	620	12	70	1,553	9	3	15	358	9	1,439	2	831	—	7,111	—
2	221	1,380	1,939	1,257	301	10,341	115	26	2,780	775	808	9,061	22	3,498	—	7,111	—
6	182	882	149	6	56	663	4	66	20	211	9	557	25	1,336	463	80	906
131	684	1,793	462	303	316	4,233	42	608	1,929	1,123	49	2,867	66	10,360	848	80	906
2	598	1,404	680	7	159	2,546	16	69	140	1,127	175	2,338	1	2,393	1	83	1,329
46	2,250	4,061	3,044	928	736	19,222	392	1,437	15,635	12,667	11,195	14,927	281	23,168	5	83	1,329
17	59	493	90	2	41	344	—	81	41	1,416	33	405	—	1,890	—	568	1,239
36	146	801	196	8	181	1,662	1	284	4,126	5,920	341	1,672	4	6,925	1	568	1,239
—	96	662	410	12	80	1,129	55	29	101	473	214	1,389	17	3,369	3	2,345	1,712
89	294	1,853	2,654	1,394	414	9,710	387	584	12,102	2,212	13,639	5,198	41	29,025	110	2,345	1,712
42	403	9,242	3,836	98	887	13,348	127	239	630	5,032	5,771	17,008	93	31,788	21	14,161	37,264
295	1,256	15,990	17,966	7,490	5,742	82,856	689	7,140	84,806	22,122	182,354	40,081	1,047	259,425	42	14,161	37,264
1	308	2,859	656	30	318	1,935	—	19	165	2,907	164	1,559	3	7,066	10	1,952	888
14	695	4,006	1,351	875	874	8,521	6	714	6,721	10,988	6,281	4,122	21	26,604	43	1,952	888

Table 69.—Arrests by State, 1995 — Continued

State	Total[1] all classes	Crime[2] Index total	Violent[3] crime	Property[4] crime	Murder and non-negligent man-slaughter	Forcible rape	Robbery	Aggra-vated assault	Burglary	Larceny–theft	Motor vehicle theft	Arson	Other assaults	Forgery and counter-feiting	Fraud
VERMONT: 18 agencies; population 301,000															
Under 18	402	142	10	132	—	3	—	7	43	84	4	1	53	3	—
Total all ages	3,990	654	123	531	2	33	—	88	163	326	19	23	492	21	119
VIRGINIA: 341 agencies; population 6,533,000															
Under 18	54,462	16,001	1,885	14,116	47	123	773	942	2,085	10,205	1,592	234	4,898	295	312
Total all ages	385,760	58,893	11,628	47,265	396	798	2,686	7,748	6,776	36,457	3,529	503	44,526	5,553	15,133
WASHINGTON: 177 agencies; population 3,573,000															
Under 18	42,233	18,523	1,713	16,810	31	141	472	1,069	2,406	13,023	1,157	224	5,225	191	73
Total all ages	189,965	45,454	7,562	37,892	159	667	1,283	5,453	5,145	30,379	2,027	341	30,581	1,901	1,564
WEST VIRGINIA: 297 agencies; population 1,826,000															
Under 18	7,653	2,577	183	2,394	17	13	52	101	471	1,684	203	36	689	58	89
Total all ages	64,744	9,213	1,434	7,779	87	125	280	942	1,477	5,675	507	120	8,401	567	4,202
WISCONSIN: 327 agencies; population 5,048,000															
Under 18	138,396	32,112	2,539	29,573	68	131	938	1,402	3,253	22,616	3,363	341	5,478	568	433
Total all ages	431,689	67,332	9,480	57,852	424	644	2,277	6,135	6,233	45,778	5,297	544	25,274	2,266	10,306
WYOMING: 52 agencies; population 434,000															
Under 18	6,919	1,727	63	1,664	2	3	13	45	114	1,445	77	28	322	15	11
Total all ages	30,108	3,892	493	3,399	14	36	37	406	300	2,894	162	43	2,085	144	217

[1]Does not include traffic arrests.
[2]Includes arson.
[3]Violent crime includes offenses of murder, forcible rape, robbery, and aggravated assault.
[4]Property crime includes offenses of burglary, larceny–theft, motor vehicle theft, and arson.
[5]Drunkenness is not considered a crime in some states; therefore, the figures vary widely from state to state.
[6]Complete data for 1995 were not available for the states of Delaware, Illinois, Kansas, Montana, New Hampshire, and Pennsylvania. See page 207 for details.
NOTE: Direct comparisons of arrest totals listed in this table should not be made with prior years' issues. Some Part II offenses are not considered crimes in some states; therefore, figures may vary widely.

Table 69.—Arrests by State, 1995 — Continued

Embezzlement	Stolen property; buying, receiving, possessing	Vandalism	Weapons; carrying, possessing, etc.	Prostitution and commercialized vice	Sex offenses (except forcible rape and prostitution)	Drug abuse violations	Gambling	Offenses against family and children	Driving under the influence	Liquor laws	Drunkenness[5]	Disorderly conduct	Vagrancy	All other offenses (except traffic)	Suspicion	Curfew and loitering law violations	Runaways
—	6	26	1	—	2	32	—	1	16	76	—	21	—	23	—	—	—
12	49	86	2	—	15	276	—	140	1,483	210	—	199	—	232	—	—	—
62	392	2,552	1,179	94	413	3,229	10	82	349	2,057	605	1,701	—	10,132	—	3,396	6,703
1,167	1,871	6,715	7,716	1,373	2,615	27,315	160	2,528	30,175	12,175	44,183	8,665	14	104,884	—	3,396	6,703
5	1,295	2,625	816	20	266	1,935	—	36	195	3,076	20	608	16	5,026	6	266	2,010
80	4,009	6,178	2,736	926	1,641	13,428	9	806	14,089	9,488	252	3,864	52	50,575	56	266	2,010
1	76	352	161	1	33	376	4	8	68	373	196	223	2	1,208	—	434	724
99	562	1,289	1,273	156	297	3,537	129	779	8,899	1,961	9,228	1,874	25	11,095	—	434	724
18	988	6,656	2,400	31	1,268	4,366	64	399	402	11,075	80	22,412	35	26,889	134	11,100	11,488
146	1,854	13,563	6,815	1,960	3,634	19,895	249	3,775	35,054	36,024	206	68,227	211	112,100	210	11,100	11,488
—	17	188	114	—	10	270	—	13	51	1,224	47	490	1	1,697	32	353	337
7	73	413	234	2	112	1,391	—	169	4,362	4,005	1,400	1,715	10	9,151	36	353	337

Section V
Weapons Used in Violent Crime

The surge in the level of violent crime in the Nation over the past decade corresponded with a significant rise in firearm usage by the criminal population. The main focus of this study is to examine this dynamic nationally and regionally and to discuss trends for other types of weapons used in violent crimes. The data in this report are based on Uniform Crime Reporting (UCR) weapon information collected for the offenses of murder, robbery, and aggravated assault. These crimes constitute 95 percent of all violent crimes. Weapon data are not collected for forcible rape. The weapon categories are (1) firearms, (2) knives or cutting instruments, (3) other dangerous weapons, and (4) personal weapons (hands, fists, feet, etc.)

National Experience

During 1994, based on crimes reported to law enforcement agencies, there were 544,880 offenses in the United States in which victims were murdered, robbed, or assaulted with firearms. In other words, nearly 1 out of 3 (31%) murder, robbery, and aggravated assault offenses collectively involved firearms as the weapons used. Further, Table 5.1 shows that from 1985 to 1994 violent crimes committed with firearms increased by a much wider margin than those committed with other weapons. During this 10-year time period, firearm-related offenses were chiefly responsible for the overall 42-percent increase in murders, robberies, and aggravated assaults. When addressing the trends for the remaining weapon types, the increases did not exceed those for the firearm category. In contrast to crimes of violence nationwide, property crime (which is not weapon-oriented) increased only 9 percent during the period 1985 to 1994.

Weapon statistics have been collected since the mid-1970s by the UCR Program for each violent crime offense with the exception of forcible rape. Chart 5.1 shows that considering weapon types, the 1990s have become the decade most prone to firearm use in history for the violent crimes studied. The trends for firearm use in murders, robberies, and aggravated assaults were remarkably similar in pattern. After remaining stable or declining during the period 1980–1985, firearm-related violent crimes followed a distinctive upward trend with the number of firearm-related aggravated assaults showing the greatest increase—76 percent—in 1994 as compared to the 1985 level. (Table 5.1.)

Recently, the Bureau of Justice Statistics, Department of Justice, released a study concluding that of the victims of nonfatal violent crimes who faced an assailant armed with a firearm, 17 percent were injured in some manner (pistol-whipped, shot, etc.). Three percent of those confronted with a firearm suffered gunshot wounds. When applying this statistic to the 1994 UCR figure of 528,575 firearm-related robbery and

Table 5.1

Percent Changes in the Numbers of Murders, Robberies, and Aggravated Assaults, by Weapon Types, United States, 1994 over 1985

Offense	Total	Firearms	Knives or cutting instruments	Other dangerous weapons	Personal weapons
Murder	22.8%	46.3%	–25.6%	9.4%	–4.9%
Robbery	24.3%	46.3%	–10.5%	27.8%	15.9%
Aggravated assault . . .	54.8%	75.6%	21.5%	58.2%	63.2%
Total	42.1%	59.5%	11.7%	52.6%	37.5%

Table 5.2

Number of Firearm-Related Violent Crimes and Shooting Victims, United States, 1994

Offense	Firearms used to commit crime	Victims Shot
Murder	16,305	16,305
Robbery and Aggravated Assault ..	528,575	15,857*
Total	544,880	32,162

*According to the Bureau of Justice Statistics, Department of Justice, victims of nonfatal violent crimes are shot and wounded 3 percent of the time when the offender is armed with a firearm.

aggravated assault offenses, an estimated 15,857 offenses involved victims who suffered gunshot wounds. Moreover, when including firearm-related murders during 1994, there were an estimated 32,162 offenses where victims were shot (see Table 5.2). It should be noted that the aforementioned figures do not include criminals who have been shot during the commission of a crime.

Firearm-related violent crimes that result in injury or death are having a substantial impact on the Nation's public health system. A recent study by the Centers for Disease Control and Prevention, United States Department of Health and Human Services, indicated that 92 percent of patients who required hospitalization due to firearm-related injuries survived. Since firearm-related violent crime is the fastest increasing category, the number of hospital admissions due to these crimes may adversely affect the cost of health care since most of these victims are taken to trauma centers. The American Hospital Association reported in 1994 that approximately 23 percent of the Nation's 6,650 hospitals have trauma centers, up from 11 percent in 1991.

The advent of trauma centers in nearly all major urban areas may have influenced the recent decline in the Nation's

CHART 5.1

Number of Murders by Firearm, United States, 1975-1994

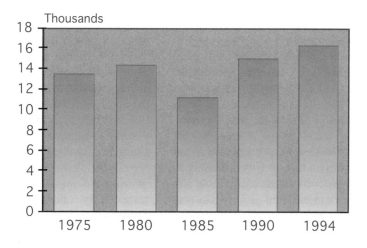

Number of Robberies by Firearm, United States, 1975-1994

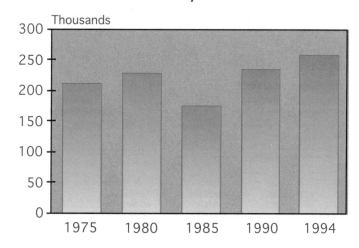

Number of Aggravated Assaults by Firearm, United States, 1975-1994

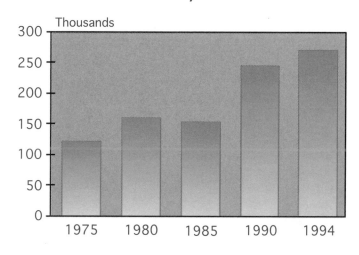

homicide rate. The Centers for Disease Control and Prevention reported that of people hospitalized with gunshot wounds, 9 out of 10 survived, as earlier mentioned. This may, in part, account for the recent significant decline in the number of homicides nationwide. Ostensibly, this is an area of criminal justice research that needs further examination.

Accompanying the unprecedented level of firearm usage in the violent crimes studied is the dramatic increase in the number of juveniles arrested for weapon violations. Specifically, estimates for the years 1985 and 1994 show juvenile arrests for this crime increased 113 percent nationwide. As shown in Table 5.3, substantial increases in arrests for weapon violations were experienced by all racial groups over the 10-year timespan. The overall increase for total weapon violation arrests was 43 percent, with adult arrests for this category increasing 30 percent for the 10-year period under consideration. It should also be noted that total juvenile violent crime arrests in 1994 rose considerably—80 percent—as compared to the 1985 total.

Regional Experience

An escalation in the violent crime volume was experienced by every region in the Nation over the past decade, 1985 to 1994. As with the national experience, the upward trend in violent crime for each region was fueled by significant increases in firearm-related murders, robberies, and aggravated assaults, as shown in Table 5.4. The Midwestern and Western Regions experienced exceedingly large increases for murders and aggravated assaults committed with firearms. When considering the trends for weapon types other than firearms (e.g., knives, clubs, hands, fists, etc.), there were no across-the-board increases as was experienced in the firearm category.

The South, the most populous region in the Nation, had a disproportionally high percentage of firearm-related murders and aggravated assaults during 1994. More specifically, while the South constituted 35 percent of the United States population in 1994, it accounted for 43 percent of murders and 44 percent of aggravated assaults that were firearm-related (see Chart 5.2). In contrast to the Southern Region, the Northeast recorded a disproportionally low number of firearm-related murders and aggravated assaults, 15 percent and 10 percent, respectively. This region accounted for 20 percent of the Nation's population in 1994. The regional percent distribution for firearm-related robberies mirrored the Nation's population distribution percentages.

The Western and Midwestern Regions experienced the most consistency in their proportions of firearm-related murders, robberies, and aggravated assaults in 1994, as delineated in Chart 5.2. The percentage of the total was roughly the same for each crime category.

Table 5.3

Percent Changes in the Number of Juvenile Arrests for Weapon Violations, by Race, United States, 1994 over 1985

Race	Number of Arrests for Weapon Violations		Percent Change 1994 over 1985
	1985	1994	
White	20,594	39,197	90.3
Black	8,787	22,820	159.7
Other.................	436	1,488	241.3
Total	29,817	63,505	113.0

Table 5.4

Percent Increases in the Number of Firearm-Related Murders, Robberies, and Aggravated Assaults, by Region, United States, 1994 over 1985

Region	Murder	Robbery	Aggravated assault
Northeast	49.6%	28.3%	52.0%
Midwest	45.9%	49.7%	79.9%
South	34.8%	57.4%	69.4%
West	71.6%	45.2%	97.0%

CHART 5.2

Distribution of Firearm
Murders by Region, United States, 1994

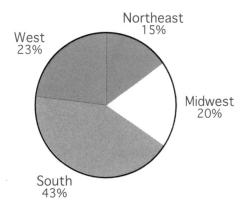

Distribution of Firearm
Robberies by Region, United States, 1994

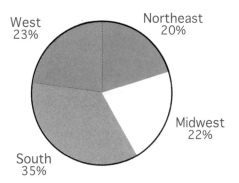

Distribution of Firearm
Aggravated Assaults by Region, United States, 1994

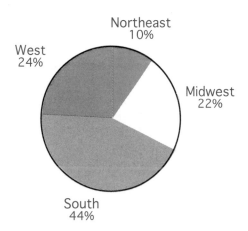

SECTION VI

Law Enforcement Personnel

The Nation's law enforcement community employed an average of 2.4 full-time officers for every 1,000 inhabitants as of October 31, 1995. Including full-time civilians, the overall law enforcement employee rate was 3.3 per 1,000 inhabitants according to 13,052 city, county, and state police agencies reporting in 1995. These agencies collectively employed 586,756 officers and 226,780 civilians, giving law enforcement service to over 245 million U.S. inhabitants. A listing of reported full-time law enforcement officers and civilian employees by state is shown in Table 77.

Varying demographic and other characteristics greatly affect the requirements for law enforcement service from one locale to another. The needs of a community having a highly mobile or seasonal population, for example, may be very different from those of a city whose population is relatively stable. Similarly, a small community situated between two large cities may require a greater number of law enforcement personnel than a community of the same size which has no urban centers nearby.

The functions of law enforcement are also significantly diverse throughout the Nation. In certain areas, sheriffs' responsibilities are limited almost exclusively to civil functions and/or the administration of the county jail facilities. Likewise, the responsibilities of state police and highway patrol agencies vary from one jurisdiction to another.

In view of these differing responsibilities and service requirements, care should be used when attempting any comparison of law enforcement employee rates. The rates presented in the following tables represent national averages; they should be viewed as guides or indicators, not as recommended or desirable police strengths. Adequate personnel for a specific locale can be determined only after careful study and analysis of the various conditions affecting service requirements in that jurisdiction.

Nationwide, cities collectively reported an average of 3.0 law enforcement employees per 1,000 inhabitants in 1995. The highest average among the city population groupings, 3.9 employees per 1,000 population, was recorded in cities with over 250,000 inhabitants. Rural and suburban county law enforcement agencies averaged full-time law enforcement employee rates of 4.4 and 3.8 per 1,000 population, respectively. (See Table 74.)

Regionally, the law enforcement employee rate was 3.3 in the Northeast and in the South, 2.7 in the Midwest, and 2.5 in the West. (See Table 70.)

Sworn Personnel

Rates based solely on sworn law enforcement personnel (excluding civilians) showed the national average for all cities was 2.3 officers per 1,000 inhabitants. By city population grouping, the rates ranged from 1.8 for cities with populations of 25,000 to 99,999 to 3.1 in cities with 250,000 or more inhabitants. Suburban county law enforcement agencies averaged 2.4 officers per 1,000 population, while agencies in rural counties averaged 2.8. (See Table 71.)

Geographically, the highest rate of officers to population was recorded in the Northeastern States where there were 2.7 officers per 1,000 inhabitants. Following were the Southern States with 2.6, the Midwestern States with 2.2, and the Western States with 1.8.

Males comprised 90 percent of all sworn employees both nationally and in cities. Ninety-three percent of those in rural counties and 88 percent in suburban counties were males.

Civilian Employees

Civilians made up 28 percent of the total United States law enforcement employee force in 1995. They represented 22 percent of the police employees in cities, 36 percent in rural counties, and 38 percent of the suburban county law enforcement strength. Sixty-two percent of all civilian employees were females.

Law Enforcement Officers Killed and Assaulted

Seventy-four law enforcement officers were feloniously slain in the line of duty during 1995, 3 fewer than in 1994. Accidents occurring while performing official duties claimed the lives of an additional 53 officers in 1995. The 1995 total for officers accidentally killed was 9 lower than the 1994 total of 62.

Extensive data on line-of-duty deaths and assaults on city, county, state, and federal officers can be found in the Uniform Crime Reporting publication, *Law Enforcement Officers Killed and Assaulted.*

Table 70.—Full-time Law Enforcement Employees,[1] Number and Rate per 1,000 Inhabitants, Geographic Region and Division by Population Group, October 31, 1995

[1995 estimated population]

Geographic region/division	Total (9,970 cities; population 165,542,000)	Group I (64 cities, 250,000 and over; population 46,205,000)	Group II (142 cities, 100,000 to 249,999; population 20,866,000)	Group III (360 cities, 50,000 to 99,999; population 24,505,000)	Group IV (684 cities, 25,000 to 49,999; population 23,564,000)	Group V (1,699 cities, 10,000 to 24,999; population 26,730,000)	Group VI (7,021 cities, under 10,000; population 23,672,000)
TOTAL: 9,970 cities; population 165,542,000:							
Number of employees	492,201	181,995	53,113	55,504	53,532	62,930	85,127
Average number of employees per 1,000 inhabitants	3.0	3.9	2.5	2.3	2.3	2.4	3.6
New England: 703 cities; population 11,761,000:							
Number of employees	30,600	2,854	4,142	6,023	6,029	6,605	4,947
Average number of employees per 1,000 inhabitants	2.6	5.2	3.6	2.4	2.2	2.2	2.8
Middle Atlantic: 1,600 cities; population 28,874,000:							
Number of employees	103,601	57,887	5,441	7,813	10,020	11,769	10,671
Average number of employees per 1,000 inhabitants	3.6	5.9	3.3	2.4	2.5	2.1	2.3
NORTHEAST: 2,303 cities; population 40,635,000:							
Number of employees	134,201	60,741	9,583	13,836	16,049	18,374	15,618
Average number of employees per 1,000 inhabitants	3.3	5.9	3.4	2.4	2.4	2.1	2.5
East North Central: 1,905 cities; population 28,295,000:							
Number of employees	79,139	27,315	5,619	9,485	10,239	13,160	13,321
Average number of employees per 1,000 inhabitants	2.8	4.9	2.3	2.1	2.0	2.1	2.9
West North Central: 859 cities; population 11,276,000:							
Number of employees	27,025	7,317	2,858	2,835	3,304	4,560	6,151
Average number of employees per 1,000 inhabitants	2.4	3.5	2.2	1.7	1.8	2.1	2.8
MIDWEST: 2,764 cities; population 39,571,000:							
Number of employees	106,164	34,632	8,477	12,320	13,543	17,720	19,472
Average number of employees per 1,000 inhabitants	2.7	4.5	2.3	2.0	2.0	2.1	2.8
South Atlantic: 1,636 cities; population 19,080,000:							
Number of employees	74,809	17,181	11,419	10,100	6,970	9,955	19,184
Average number of employees per 1,000 inhabitants	3.9	4.3	3.2	3.2	3.1	3.5	5.9
East South Central: 821 cities; population 8,831,000:							
Number of employees	27,567	7,121	3,585	1,390	3,130	4,639	7,702
Average number of employees per 1,000 inhabitants	3.1	3.1	2.8	2.7	2.8	2.8	4.0
West South Central: 1,125 cities; population 19,423,000:							
Number of employees	56,128	22,243	6,153	5,665	4,535	6,219	11,313
Average number of employees per 1,000 inhabitants	2.9	3.1	2.4	2.3	2.3	2.4	4.3
SOUTH: 3,582 cities; population 47,334,000:							
Number of employees	158,504	46,545	21,157	17,155	14,635	20,813	38,199
Average number of employees per 1,000 inhabitants	3.3	3.4	2.8	2.8	2.7	2.9	4.9
Mountain: 573 cities; population 10,793,000:							
Number of employees	28,161	11,326	3,489	3,361	2,387	2,298	5,300
Average number of employees per 1,000 inhabitants	2.6	2.7	2.3	1.9	2.3	2.4	4.2
Pacific: 748 cities; population 27,209,000:							
Number of employees	65,171	28,751	10,407	8,832	6,918	3,725	6,538
Average number of employees per 1,000 inhabitants	2.4	2.8	1.9	1.9	2.0	2.2	4.5
WEST: 1,321 cities; population 38,002,000:							
Number of employees	93,332	40,077	13,896	12,193	9,305	6,023	11,838
Average number of employees per 1,000 inhabitants	2.5	2.7	2.0	1.9	2.0	2.2	4.3

Suburban and County

Suburban:[2] 6,143 agencies; population 100,836,000:		County: 3,082 agencies; population 80,304,000:	
Number of employees	327,493	Number of employees	321,335
Average number of employees per 1,000 inhabitants	3.2	Average number of employees per 1,000 inhabitants	4.0

[1]Includes civilians.

[2]Includes suburban city and county law enforcement agencies within metropolitan areas. Excludes central cities. Suburban cities and counties are also included in other groups. Population figures were rounded to the nearest thousand. All rates were calculated before rounding.

Table 71.—Full-time Law Enforcement Officers, Number and Rate per 1,000 Inhabitants, Geographic Region and Division by Population Group, October 31, 1995

[1995 estimated population]

Geographic region/division	Total (9,970 cities; population 165,542,000)	Population group					
		Group I (64 cities, 250,000 and over; population 46,205,000)	Group II (142 cities, 100,000 to 249,999; population 20,866,000)	Group III (360 cities, 50,000 to 99,999; population 24,505,000)	Group IV (684 cities, 25,000 to 49,999; population 23,564,000)	Group V (1,699 cities, 10,000 to 24,999; population 26,730,000)	Group VI (7,021 cities, under 10,000; population 23,672,000)
TOTAL: 9,970 cities; population 165,542,000:							
Number of officers	**385,348**	**142,678**	**40,780**	**43,295**	**42,115**	**50,055**	**66,425**
Average number of officers per 1,000 inhabitants	**2.3**	**3.1**	**2.0**	**1.8**	**1.8**	**1.9**	**2.8**
New England: 703 cities; population 11,761,000:							
Number of officers	25,283	2,093	3,466	5,236	5,167	5,509	3,812
Average number of officers per 1,000 inhabitants	2.1	3.8	3.0	2.1	1.9	1.8	2.2
Middle Atlantic: 1,600 cities; population 28,874,000:							
Number of officers	85,727	47,080	4,593	6,541	8,402	10,004	9,107
Average number of officers per 1,000 inhabitants	3.0	4.8	2.8	2.0	2.1	1.8	2.0
NORTHEAST: 2,303 cities; population 40,635,000:							
Number of officers	**111,010**	**49,173**	**8,059**	**11,777**	**13,569**	**15,513**	**12,919**
Average number of officers per 1,000 inhabitants	**2.7**	**4.8**	**2.9**	**2.1**	**2.0**	**1.8**	**2.0**
East North Central: 1,905 cities; population 28,295,000:							
Number of officers	64,382	22,903	4,620	7,551	8,063	10,515	10,730
Average number of officers per 1,000 inhabitants	2.3	4.1	1.9	1.7	1.6	1.7	2.3
West North Central: 859 cities; population 11,276,000:							
Number of officers	20,965	5,305	2,164	2,286	2,588	3,603	5,019
Average number of officers per 1,000 inhabitants	1.9	2.5	1.7	1.3	1.4	1.7	2.3
MIDWEST: 2,764 cities; population 39,571,000:							
Number of officers	**85,347**	**28,208**	**6,784**	**9,837**	**10,651**	**14,118**	**15,749**
Average number of officers per 1,000 inhabitants	**2.2**	**3.7**	**1.8**	**1.6**	**1.6**	**1.7**	**2.3**
South Atlantic: 1,636 cities; population 19,080,000:							
Number of officers	57,485	13,345	8,745	7,582	5,379	7,594	14,840
Average number of officers per 1,000 inhabitants	3.0	3.3	2.4	2.4	2.4	2.7	4.6
East South Central: 821 cities; population 8,831,000:							
Number of officers	21,431	5,332	2,803	1,083	2,458	3,617	6,138
Average number of officers per 1,000 inhabitants	2.4	2.3	2.1	2.1	2.2	2.2	3.2
West South Central: 1,125 cities; population 19,423,000:							
Number of officers	42,579	17,022	4,802	4,361	3,396	4,789	8,209
Average number of officers per 1,000 inhabitants	2.2	2.3	1.9	1.8	1.7	1.9	3.1
SOUTH: 3,582 cities; population 47,334,000:							
Number of officers	**121,495**	**35,699**	**16,350**	**13,026**	**11,233**	**16,000**	**29,187**
Average number of officers per 1,000 inhabitants	**2.6**	**2.6**	**2.2**	**2.1**	**2.1**	**2.3**	**3.8**
Mountain: 573 cities; population 10,793,000:							
Number of officers	20,566	8,302	2,461	2,458	1,738	1,681	3,926
Average number of officers per 1,000 inhabitants	1.9	2.0	1.6	1.4	1.6	1.7	3.1
Pacific: 748 cities; population 27,209,000:							
Number of officers	46,930	21,296	7,126	6,197	4,924	2,743	4,644
Average number of officers per 1,000 inhabitants	1.8	2.0	1.3	1.3	1.4	1.6	3.2
WEST: 1,321 cities; population 38,002,000:							
Number of officers	**67,496**	**29,598**	**9,587**	**8,655**	**6,662**	**4,424**	**8,570**
Average number of officers per 1,000 inhabitants	**1.8**	**2.0**	**1.4**	**1.3**	**1.5**	**1.6**	**3.1**

Suburban and County

Suburban:1 6,143 agencies; population 100,836,000:		County: 3,082 agencies; population 80,304,000:	
Number of officers	225,217	Number of officers	201,408
Average number of officers per 1,000 inhabitants	2.2	Average number of officers per 1,000 inhabitants	2.5

[1]Includes suburban city and county law enforcement agencies within metropolitan areas. Excludes central cities. Suburban cities and counties are also included in other groups. Population figures were rounded to the nearest thousand. All rates were calculated before rounding.

Table 72.—Full-time Law Enforcement Employees, October 31, 1995

[Range in rate per 1,000 inhabitants]

Rate range		Total[1] (9,275 cities, population 165,542,000)	Group I (64 cities, 250,000 and over; population 46,205,000)	Group II (142 cities, 100,000 to 249,999; population 20,866,000)	Group III (360 cities, 50,000 to 99,999; population 24,505,000)	Group IV (684 cities, 25,000 to 49,999; population 23,564,000)	Group V (1,699 cities, 10,000 to 24,999; population 26,730,000)	Group VI (6,326 cities under 10,000; population 23,672,000)
.1–.5	Number	127	—	—	2	2	13	110
	Percent	1.4	—	—	.6	.3	.8	1.7
.6–1.0	Number	480	—	—	3	15	56	406
	Percent	5.2	—	—	.8	2.2	3.3	6.4
1.1–1.5	Number	1,085	—	7	39	84	170	785
	Percent	11.7	—	4.9	10.8	12.3	10.0	12.4
1.6–2.0	Number	1,849	9	41	124	206	424	1,045
	Percent	19.9	14.1	28.9	34.4	30.1	25.0	16.5
2.1–2.5	Number	1,837	9	35	96	193	475	1,029
	Percent	19.8	14.1	24.6	26.7	28.2	28.0	16.3
2.6–3.0	Number	1,264	15	25	49	93	266	816
	Percent	13.6	23.4	17.6	13.6	13.6	15.7	12.9
3.1–3.5	Number	843	12	17	25	53	140	596
	Percent	9.1	18.8	12.0	6.9	7.7	8.2	9.4
3.6–4.0	Number	539	5	11	9	21	90	403
	Percent	5.8	7.8	7.7	2.5	3.1	5.3	6.4
4.1–4.5	Number	352	5	5	7	9	37	289
	Percent	3.8	7.8	3.5	1.9	1.3	2.2	4.6
4.6–5.0	Number	227	2	1	3	3	16	202
	Percent	2.4	3.1	.7	.8	.4	.9	3.2
5.1 and over	Number	672	7	—	3	5	12	645
	Percent	7.2	10.9	—	.8	.7	.7	10.2
Total		9,275	64	142	360	684	1,699	6,326
Percent[2]		100.0	100.0	100.0	100.0	100.0	100.0	100.0

[1]The number of agencies used to compile these figures differs from the other Law Enforcement Employee tables because small agencies with no resident population are excluded from this table.

[2]Because of rounding, percentages may not add to totals.

Table 73.—Full-time Law Enforcement Officers, October 31, 1995

[Range in rate per 1,000 inhabitants]

Rate range		Total[1] (9,275 cities, population 165,542,000)	Group I (64 cities, 250,000 and over; population 46,205,000)	Group II (142 cities, 100,000 to 249,000; population 20,866,000)	Group III (360 cities, 50,000 to 99,999; population 24,505,000)	Group IV (684 cities, 25,000 to 49,999; population 23,564,000)	Group V (1,699 cities, 10,000 to 24,999; population 26,730,000)	Group VI (6,326 cities under 10,000; population 23,672,000)
.1–.5	Number	148	—	—	2	4	18	124
	Percent	1.6	—	—	.6	.6	1.1	2.0
.6–1.0	Number	653	—	3	23	49	94	484
	Percent	7.0	—	2.1	6.4	7.2	5.5	7.7
1.1–1.5	Number	1,965	9	45	127	210	429	1,145
	Percent	21.2	14.1	31.7	35.3	30.7	25.3	18.1
1.6–2.0	Number	2,449	19	40	116	240	615	1,419
	Percent	26.4	29.7	28.2	32.2	35.1	36.2	22.4
2.1–2.5	Number	1,602	11	26	52	118	315	1,080
	Percent	17.3	17.2	18.3	14.4	17.3	18.5	17.1
2.6–3.0	Number	958	12	20	27	40	133	726
	Percent	10.3	18.8	14.1	7.5	5.8	7.8	11.5
3.1–3.5	Number	518	3	6	7	16	64	422
	Percent	5.6	4.7	4.2	1.9	2.3	3.8	6.7
3.6–4.0	Number	284	3	2	3	4	20	252
	Percent	3.1	4.7	1.4	.8	.6	1.2	4.0
4.1–4.5	Number	191	4	—	3	—	8	176
	Percent	2.1	6.2	—	.8	—	.5	2.8
4.6–5.0	Number	119	1	—	—	1	1	116
	Percent	1.3	1.6	—	—	.1	.1	1.8
5.1 and over	Number	388	2	—	—	2	2	382
	Percent	4.2	3.1	—	—	.3	.1	6.0
Total		9,275	64	142	360	684	1,699	6,326
Percent[2]		100.0	100.0	100.0	100.0	100.0	100.0	100.0

[1]The number of agencies used to compile these figures differs from the other Law Enforcement Officer tables because small agencies with no resident population are excluded from this table.

[2]Because of rounding, percentages may not add to totals.

Table 74.—Law Enforcement Employees, Percent Male and Female, October 31, 1995

[1995 estimated population]

Population group	Total police employees			Police officers (sworn)			Civilian employees		
	Total	Percent male	Percent female	Total	Percent male	Percent female	Total	Percent male	Percent female
TOTAL AGENCIES: 13,052 agencies; **population 245,846,000:**	**813,536**	**75.7**	**24.3**	**586,756**	**90.2**	**9.8**	**226,780**	**38.0**	**62.0**
TOTAL CITIES: 9,970 cities; **population 165,542,000:**	**492,201**	**77.3**	**22.7**	**385,348**	**90.3**	**9.7**	**106,853**	**30.7**	**69.3**
GROUP I 64 cities, 250,000 and over; population 46,205,000:	181,995	73.9	26.1	142,678	85.3	14.7	39,317	32.6	67.4
8 cities, 1,000,000 and over; population 20,085,000:	97,454	73.3	26.7	77,717	84.4	15.6	19,737	29.8	70.2
19 cities, 500,000 to 999,999; population 12,816,000:	43,346	76.2	23.8	34,218	86.1	13.9	9,128	39.1	60.9
37 cities, 250,000 to 499,999; population 13,304,000:	41,195	73.0	27.0	30,743	86.9	13.1	10,452	32.2	67.8
GROUP II 142 cities, 100,000 to 249,999; population 20,866,000:	53,113	75.7	24.3	40,780	90.5	9.5	12,333	26.9	73.1
GROUP III 360 cities, 50,000 to 99,999; population 24,505,000:	55,504	78.1	21.9	43,295	92.8	7.2	12,209	25.9	74.1
GROUP IV 684 cities, 25,000 to 49,999; population 23,564,000:	53,532	79.7	20.3	42,115	93.8	6.2	11,417	27.5	72.5
GROUP V 1,699 cities, 10,000 to 24,999; population 26,730,000:	62,930	80.8	19.2	50,055	94.6	5.4	12,875	27.3	72.7
GROUP VI 7,021 cities, under 10,000; population 23,672,000:	85,127	81.0	19.0	66,425	93.5	6.5	18,702	36.7	63.3
SUBURBAN COUNTIES 844 agencies; population 52,497,000:	200,047	72.2	27.8	123,696	88.4	11.6	76,351	46.0	54.0
RURAL COUNTIES 2,238 agencies; population 27,807,000:	121,288	74.5	25.5	77,712	92.9	7.1	43,576	41.7	58.3
SUBURBAN AREA[1] 6,143 agencies; population 100,836,000:	327,493	75.7	24.3	225,217	90.8	9.2	102,276	42.3	57.7

[1]Includes suburban city and county law enforcement agencies within metropolitan areas. Excludes central cities. Suburban cities and counties are also included in other groups.

Table 75.—Civilian Law Enforcement Employees, Percent of Total, Population Group, October 31, 1995

[1995 estimated population]

Population group	Percent civilian employees	Population group	Percent civilian employees
TOTAL AGENCIES: 13,052 agencies; **population 245,846,000:**	**27.9**	GROUP IV 684 cities, 25,000 to 49,999; population 23,564,000:	21.3
TOTAL CITIES: 9,970 cities; **population 165,542,000:**	**21.7**	GROUP V 1,699 cities, 10,000 to 24,999; population 26,730,000:	20.5
GROUP I 64 cities, 250,000 and over; population 46,205,000:	21.6	GROUP VI 7,021 cities, under 10,000; population 23,672,000:	22.0
8 cities, 1,000,000 and over; population 20,085,000:	20.3		
19 cities, 500,000 to 999,999; population 12,816,000:	21.1	SUBURBAN COUNTIES 844 agencies; population 52,497,000	38.2
37 cities, 250,000 to 499,999; population 13,304,000:	25.4		
GROUP II 142 cities, 100,000 to 249,999; population 20,866,000:	23.2	RURAL COUNTIES 2,238 agencies; population 27,807,000:	35.9
GROUP III 360 cities, 50,000 to 99,999; population 24,505,000:	22.0	SUBURBAN AREA[1] 6,143 agencies; population 100,836,000:	31.2

[1]Includes suburban city and county law enforcement agencies within metropolitan areas. Excludes central cities. Suburban cities and counties are also included in other groups.

Table 76.—Full-time State Law Enforcement Employees, October 31, 1995

State	TOTAL	Officers Male	Officers Female	Civilians Male	Civilians Female	State	TOTAL	Officers Male	Officers Female	Civilians Male	Civilians Female
ALABAMA:						**MONTANA:**					
Department of Public Safety	1,197	598	12	191	396	Highway Patrol	279	196	16	19	48
Other state agencies	245	196	5	32	12	**NEBRASKA:**					
ALASKA:						State Patrol	637	429	20	95	93
State Police	528	302	19	71	136	**NEVADA:**					
ARIZONA:						Highway Patrol	540	340	26	66	108
Department of Public Safety	1,686	904	66	327	389	**NEW HAMPSHIRE:**					
Other state agencies	58	25	1	26	6	State Police	337	221	23	33	60
ARKANSAS:						**NEW JERSEY:**					
State Police	702	478	22	66	136	State Police	3,636	2,594	72	420	550
CALIFORNIA:						**NEW MEXICO:**					
Highway Patrol	9,162	5,640	533	1,262	1,727	State Police	558	423	12	29	94
Other state agencies	965	707	168	18	72	**NEW YORK:**					
COLORADO:						State Police	4,626	3,622	303	249	452
State Patrol	825	574	27	67	157	Other state agencies	199	126	8	54	11
Other state agencies	817	255	19	375	168	**NORTH CAROLINA:**					
CONNECTICUT:						Highway Patrol	1,673	1,294	11	211	157
State Police	1,523	946	70	240	267	Other state agencies	1,026	606	72	121	227
DELAWARE:						**NORTH DAKOTA:**					
State Police:	696	471	36	77	112	Highway Patrol	197	116	1	53	27
Other state agencies	205	148	13	16	28	**OHIO:**					
FLORIDA:						State Highway Patrol	2,457	1,277	95	547	538
Highway Patrol	2,085	1,463	173	145	304	**OKLAHOMA:**					
GEORGIA:						Department of Public Safety ...	1,318	759	9	258	292
Department of Public Safety	2,055	840	39	437	739	Other state agencies	66	63	2	—	1
Other state agencies	425	326	23	29	47	**OREGON:**					
IDAHO:						State Police	1,044	731	50	84	179
State police	244	176	7	19	42	**PENNSYLVANIA:**					
Other state agencies	77	59	4	2	12	State Police	5,351	4,027	153	542	629
ILLINOIS:						**RHODE ISLAND:**					
State Police	3,553	1,834	163	597	959	State Police	244	188	13	31	12
Other state agencies	597	479	37	37	44	Other state agencies	61	42	6	5	8
INDIANA:						**SOUTH CAROLINA:**					
State Police	1,779	1,075	60	270	374	Highway Patrol	1,775	1,094	47	176	458
IOWA:						Other state agencies	998	700	89	35	174
Department of Public Safety	869	588	35	104	142	**SOUTH DAKOTA:**					
KANSAS:						Highway Patrol	233	153	2	59	19
Highway Patrol	712	510	33	79	90	**TENNESSEE:**					
Other state agencies	339	219	2	35	83	Department of Public Safety ...	1,570	742	42	123	663
KENTUCKY:						**TEXAS:**					
State Police	1,651	923	23	392	313	Department of Public Safety ...	6,338	2,596	120	1,146	2,476
Other state agencies	837	658	35	37	107	**UTAH:**					
LOUISIANA:						Highway Patrol	410	361	18	9	22
State Police	1,351	815	16	179	341	Other state agencies	24	20	3	—	1
MAINE:						**VERMONT:**					
State Police	452	312	15	70	55	State Police	429	267	15	60	87
Other state agencies	121	35	2	44	40	**VIRGINIA:**					
MARYLAND:						State Police	2,243	1,614	52	194	383
State Police	2,262	1,413	131	344	374	Other state agencies	604	449	41	39	75
Other state agencies	1,667	976	172	281	238	**WASHINGTON:**					
MASSACHUSETTS:						State Patrol	1,882	907	44	488	443
State Police	2,532	2,049	215	130	138	**WEST VIRGINIA:**					
MICHIGAN:						State Police	921	592	16	89	224
State Police	3,156	1,916	248	477	515	Other state agencies	93	87	1	—	5
MINNESOTA:						**WISCONSIN:**					
Highway Patrol	699	465	37	121	76	State Patrol	676	439	70	77	90
MISSISSIPPI:						Other state agencies	271	212	19	19	21
Highway Safety Patrol	782	516	8	65	193	**WYOMING:**					
MISSOURI:						Highway Patrol	213	154	2	14	43
State Highway Patrol	1,988	1,067	48	414	459						

NOTE: The responsibilities of the various state police, highway patrol, and departments of public safety agencies range from full law enforcement duties to traffic patrol only. Any comparison of these data from state to state must take these factors and those on page iv into consideration.

Table 77.—Full-time Law Enforcement Employees, State, 1995

[1995 estimated population]

State	Total employees	Officers Male	Officers Female	Civilians Male	Civilians Female	State	Total employees	Officers Male	Officers Female	Civilians Male	Civilians Female
ALABAMA: 366 agencies; Population 4,292,000:	13,418	8,453	699	1,693	2,573	**MONTANA:** 98 agencies; Population 850,000:	2,206	1,358	70	302	476
ALASKA: 39 agencies; Population 604,000:	1,727	1,015	80	180	452	**NEBRASKA:** 163 agencies; Population 1,634,000:	4,212	2,732	260	357	863
ARIZONA: 98 agencies; Population 4,163,000:	14,488	7,790	823	2,642	3,233	**NEVADA:** 35 agencies; Population 1,529,000:	5,396	3,345	402	363	1,286
ARKANSAS: 191 agencies; Population 2,479,000:	6,824	4,306	354	852	1,312	**NEW HAMPSHIRE:** 100 agencies; Population 886,000:	2,488	1,793	102	173	420
CALIFORNIA: 454 agencies; Population 28,185,000:	90,281	54,857	6,711	9,667	19,046	**NEW JERSEY:** 529 agencies; Population 7,620,000:	34,973	26,239	1,458	2,446	4,830
COLORADO: 229 agencies; Population 3,353,000:	12,361	7,579	925	1,425	2,432	**NEW MEXICO:** 94 agencies; Population 1,661,000:	5,214	3,374	256	469	1,115
CONNECTICUT: 99 agencies; Population 2,773,000:	9,114	6,869	532	577	1,136	**NEW YORK:** 461 agencies; Population 17,033,000:	78,309	55,730	7,511	4,346	10,722
DELAWARE: 43 agencies; Population 544,000:	2,021	1,468	141	144	268	**NORTH CAROLINA:** 472 agencies; Population 6,967,000:	21,809	14,407	1,637	2,438	3,327
DISTRICT OF COLUMBIA: 2 agencies; Population 554,000:	4,349	2,826	865	210	448	**NORTH DAKOTA:** 100 agencies; Population 639,000:	1,411	958	63	139	251
FLORIDA: 335 agencies; Population 12,268,000:	50,822	26,671	3,500	8,497	12,154	**OHIO:** 459 agencies; Population 8,884,000:	24,365	15,112	1,436	3,658	4,159
GEORGIA: 552 agencies; Population 6,326,000:	26,411	16,226	2,187	3,143	4,855	**OKLAHOMA:** 286 agencies; Population 3,275,000:	9,865	6,140	442	1,613	1,670
HAWAII: 5 agencies; Population 1,187,000:	3,221	2,331	186	226	478	**OREGON:** 166 agencies; Population 2,567,000:	6,732	4,586	418	359	1,369
IDAHO: 109 agencies; Population 1,161,000:	2,869	1,938	120	149	662	**PENNSYLVANIA:** 746 agencies; Population 8,383,000:	24,883	19,235	2,004	1,360	2,284
ILLINOIS: 745 agencies; Population 11,796,000:	41,877	28,855	3,601	3,277	6,144	**RHODE ISLAND:** 43 agencies; Population 979,000:	2,894	2,217	125	260	292
INDIANA: 235 agencies; Population 5,386,000:	13,577	8,359	639	2,067	2,512	**SOUTH CAROLINA:** 241 agencies; Population 3,671,000:	10,830	7,516	686	778	1,850
IOWA: 231 agencies; Population 2,837,000:	6,487	4,415	266	601	1,205	**SOUTH DAKOTA:** 107 agencies; Population 728,000:	1,641	1,041	46	269	285
KANSAS: 323 agencies; Population 2,484,000:	8,479	5,625	429	884	1,541	**TENNESSEE:** 254 agencies; Population 4,731,000:	14,955	8,819	810	2,344	2,982
KENTUCKY: 392 agencies; Population 3,801,000:	9,209	6,452	625	869	1,263	**TEXAS:** 914 agencies; Population 18,719,000:	66,768	38,285	4,078	10,406	13,999
LOUISIANA: 205 agencies; Population 4,245,000:	17,213	11,617	1,989	1,327	2,280	**UTAH:** 124 agencies; Population 1,937,000:	4,869	3,565	314	251	739
MAINE: 133 agencies; Population 1,231,000:	2,658	1,921	90	318	329	**VERMONT:** 60 agencies; Population 348,000:	1,243	844	62	114	223
MARYLAND: 125 agencies; Population 4,917,000:	17,294	11,777	1,609	1,544	2,364	**VIRGINIA:** 269 agencies; Population 6,605,000:	18,139	12,888	1,356	1,049	2,846
MASSACHUSETTS: 314 agencies; Population 6,012,000:	18,351	14,481	1,021	1,180	1,669	**WASHINGTON:** 229 agencies; Population 5,276,000:	12,152	7,953	714	1,191	2,294
MICHIGAN: 563 agencies; Population 9,492,000:	25,759	17,250	2,128	2,682	3,699	**WEST VIRGINIA:** 238 agencies; Population 1,518,000:	3,881	2,764	106	477	534
MINNESOTA: 261 agencies; Population 4,314,000:	9,731	6,279	499	1,157	1,796	**WISCONSIN:** 320 agencies; Population 5,038,000:	15,226	10,371	1,280	1,161	2,414
MISSISSIPPI: 142 agencies; Population 1,754,000:	5,220	3,390	232	634	964	**WYOMING:** 68 agencies; Population 479,000:	1,642	1,084	59	118	381
MISSOURI: 279 agencies; Population 5,142,000:	15,149	9,883	937	1,782	2,547						

Table 78.—Number of Full-time Law Enforcement Employees, Cities, October 31, 1995

City	Total police employees	Total officers	Total civilians	City	Total police employees	Total officers	Total civilians
ALABAMA				**ALABAMA — Continued**			
Abbeville	15	11	4	Gadsden	140	114	26
Adamsville	16	11	5	Gardendale	26	20	6
Alabaster	34	27	7	Geneva	16	12	4
Albertville	41	32	9	Glencoe	5	5	—
Alexander City	62	44	18	Goodwater	9	5	4
Aliceville	9	5	4	Gordo	4	4	—
Andalusia	38	29	9	Graysville	10	6	4
Anniston	128	99	29	Greenville	34	28	6
Arab	23	18	5	Gulf Shores	31	23	8
Ardmore	8	5	3	Guntersville	35	29	6
Argo	1	1	—	Gurley	4	4	—
Ariton	4	1	3	Haleyville	18	13	5
Ashford	11	6	5	Hamilton	14	13	1
Ashland	12	9	3	Hanceville	11	8	3
Athens	44	34	10	Hartford	13	9	4
Atmore	26	23	3	Hartselle	27	22	5
Attalla	26	20	6	Hayneville	6	6	—
Auburn	78	65	13	Headland	15	10	5
Bay Minette	23	18	5	Heflin	8	8	—
Bayou La Batre	17	12	5	Helena	12	8	4
Bear Creek	3	3	—	Hokes Bluff	6	6	—
Bessemer	103	85	18	Hollywood	5	2	3
Birmingham	1,077	816	261	Homewood	90	65	25
Blountsville	7	7	—	Hoover	132	105	27
Boaz	29	24	5	Hueytown	33	26	7
Brantley	5	5	—	Huntsville	473	344	129
Brewton	24	19	5	Hurtsboro	3	3	—
Bridgeport	8	4	4	Irondale	34	27	7
Brighten	12	5	7	Jackson	21	16	5
Brilliant	2	2	—	Jacksonville	25	19	6
Brundidge	11	7	4	Jasper	61	41	20
Butler	9	5	4	Jemison	4	4	—
Calera	14	10	4	Killen	5	4	1
Camden	11	7	4	Kimberly	3	3	—
Camp Hill	5	5	—	Kingston	2	2	—
Cedar Bluff	4	4	—	Lafayette	18	14	4
Centre	12	8	4	Lanett	29	24	5
Centreville	5	5	—	Leeds	28	22	6
Cherokee	3	3	—	Level Plains	4	4	—
Chickasaw	20	20	—	Lexington	3	2	1
Childersburg	17	13	4	Lincoln	13	8	5
Citronelle	11	7	4	Linden	6	6	—
Clanton	24	23	1	Lineville	11	7	4
Clayton	3	3	—	Lipscomb	11	5	6
Clio	6	3	3	Livingston	15	10	5
Collinsville	7	4	3	Louisville	3	3	—
Columbiana	12	8	4	Loxley	6	6	—
Coosada	2	2	—	Luverne	15	11	4
Cordova	6	4	2	Madison	46	35	11
Courtland	6	5	1	Marion	12	8	4
Creola	9	7	2	Midfield	16	12	4
Cullman	47	38	9	Midland City	10	6	4
Dadeville	10	10	—	Millbrook	19	14	5
Daleville	20	15	5	Mobile	515	431	84
Daphne	46	29	17	Monroeville	28	23	5
Decatur	140	112	28	Montevallo	14	10	4
Demopolis	27	19	8	Montgomery	611	458	153
Dothan	175	113	62	Moody	13	12	1
East Brewton	7	5	2	Morris	3	3	—
Elba	20	16	4	Moulton	9	9	—
Enterprise	58	44	14	Moundville	7	4	3
Eufaula	49	38	11	Mountain Brook	60	46	14
Eutaw	12	8	4	Mount Vernon	7	6	1
Evergreen	21	15	6	Muscle Shoals	35	35	—
Fairfield	64	49	15	Napier Field	2	2	—
Fairhope	22	17	5	New Brockton	4	4	—
Falkville	4	4	—	New Hope	6	6	—
Fayette	11	11	—	Northport	56	46	10
Flomaton	12	8	4	Notasulga	9	5	4
Florala	8	5	3	Oneonta	14	13	1
Florence	112	86	26	Opelika	96	70	26
Foley	31	23	8	Opp	25	20	5
Fort Payne	43	32	11	Orange Beach	25	19	6
Fultondale	19	15	4	Oxford	38	30	8

Table 78.—Number of Full-time Law Enforcement Employees, Cities, October 31, 1995 — Continued

City	Total police employees	Total officers	Total civilians	City	Total police employees	Total officers	Total civilians
ALABAMA — Continued				**ALASKA — Continued**			
Ozark	45	36	9	Petersburg	12	8	4
Pelham	46	36	10	Seward	22	9	13
Pell City	25	23	2	Skagway	4	4	—
Pennington	2	2	—	Soldotna	12	10	2
Phenix City	77	61	16	Togiak	3	3	—
Phil Campbell	7	7	—	Wasilla	14	12	2
Pickensville	3	2	1	Wrangell	11	6	5
Piedmont	18	14	4				
Pleasant Grove	17	13	4	**ARIZONA**			
Prattville	58	52	6				
Priceville	4	4	—	Apache Junction	62	45	17
Prichard	81	59	22	Avondale	52	40	12
Rainbow City	25	18	7	Benson	19	12	7
Rainsville	15	11	4	Bisbee	20	14	6
Ranburne	3	2	1	Buckeye	24	17	7
Reform	4	4	—	Bullhead City	92	56	36
Roanoke	25	20	5	Camp Verde	22	14	8
Robertsdale	12	8	4	Casa Grande	72	49	23
Russellville	23	19	4	Chandler	244	180	64
Samson	11	7	4	Chino Valley	18	12	6
Saraland	33	28	5	Cottonwood	34	21	13
Satsuma	14	10	4	Douglas	45	33	12
Scottsboro	56	36	20	Eagar	9	7	2
Selma	98	60	38	El Mirage	16	12	4
Sheffield	34	29	5	Flagstaff	117	81	36
Slocomb	6	4	2	Florence	18	12	6
Somerville	4	2	2	Gilbert	94	67	27
Southside	12	7	5	Glendale	325	230	95
Springville	4	4	—	Globe	31	23	8
Stevenson	10	6	4	Goodyear	31	22	9
Sumiton	11	5	6	Hayden	6	5	1
Summerdale	4	4	—	Holbrook	22	17	5
Sylacauga	44	39	5	Huachuca City	12	6	6
Talladega	55	44	11	Jerome	3	3	—
Tallassee	17	13	4	Kearny	12	8	4
Tarrant City	23	18	5	Kingman	57	39	18
Thomasville	16	12	4	Lake Havasu City	78	58	20
Thorsby	3	3	—	Mammoth	10	4	6
Trinity	3	3	—	Marana	41	33	8
Troy	60	47	13	Mesa	829	550	279
Trussville	26	21	5	Miami	9	6	3
Tuscaloosa	251	194	57	Nogales	69	52	17
Tuscumbia	23	23	—	Paradise Valley	38	29	9
Tuskegee	50	38	12	Payson	33	24	9
Union Springs	15	11	4	Peoria	101	71	30
Valley	28	21	7	Phoenix	2,988	2,183	805
Vance	1	1	—	Pima	2	2	—
Vestavia Hills	43	41	2	Pinetop-Lakeside	21	15	6
Wadley	8	4	4	Prescott	80	53	27
Warrior	10	7	3	Prescott Valley	30	22	8
Weaver	7	6	1	Quartzsite	7	6	1
Wetumpka	22	17	5	Safford	19	17	2
Winfield	11	10	1	St. Johns	6	5	1
York	13	7	6	San Luis	23	18	5
				Scottsdale	393	249	144
ALASKA				Sedona	27	19	8
				Show Low	30	19	11
Anchorage	440	302	138	Sierra Vista	54	36	18
Bethel	22	12	10	Snowflake-Taylor	12	11	1
Bristol Bay Borough	11	4	7	Somerton	17	12	5
Cordova	10	5	5	South Tucson	31	23	8
Craig	9	4	5	Springerville	7	6	1
Dillingham	16	5	11	Superior	11	7	4
Fairbanks	48	32	16	Surprise	27	25	2
Haines	9	5	4	Tempe	377	262	115
Homer	22	11	11	Thatcher	10	9	1
Juneau	69	44	25	Tolleson	18	12	6
Kenai	24	16	8	Tombstone	7	6	1
Ketchikan	32	23	9	Tucson	1,086	834	252
Klawock	9	4	5	Wellton	4	4	—
Kodiak	31	15	16	Wickenburg	14	9	5
North Pole	11	7	4	Willcox	15	10	5
North Slope Borough	88	48	40	Winslow	29	20	9
Palmer	22	9	13	Youngtown	14	9	5

City	Total police employees	Total officers	Total civilians	City	Total police employees	Total officers	Total civilians
ARKANSAS				**ARKANSAS — Continued**			
Alma	7	5	2	Nashville	10	9	1
Arkadelphia	22	18	4	Newport	23	16	7
Ashdown	11	10	1	North Little Rock	210	180	30
Bald Knob	7	3	4	Osceola	37	25	12
Barling	8	7	1	Ozark	10	7	3
Beebe	10	5	5	Paragould	35	30	5
Benton	44	33	11	Paris	14	8	6
Bentonville	35	26	9	Piggott	8	7	1
Berryville	9	8	1	Pine Bluff	150	131	19
Blytheville	62	44	18	Pocahontas	17	12	5
Booneville	11	7	4	Prairie Grove	7	6	1
Brinkley	16	12	4	Prescott	6	6	—
Bryant	14	12	2	Rogers	79	56	23
Bull Shoals	3	3	—	Russellville	46	39	7
Cabot	20	15	5	Searcy	51	40	11
Camden	35	23	12	Sheridan	8	7	1
Carlisle	9	5	4	Sherwood	65	56	9
Clarksville	18	12	6	Siloam Springs	43	27	16
Conway	81	65	16	Smackover	5	4	1
Corning	13	9	4	Springdale	89	68	21
Crossett	19	13	6	Star City	4	4	—
Danville	6	5	1	Stuttgart	29	20	9
Dardanelle	11	8	3	Texarkana	110	72	38
De Queen	12	10	2	Trumann	19	14	5
Dermott	11	7	4	Van Buren	32	25	7
Des Arc	4	4	—	Waldron	6	6	—
De Witt	15	10	5	Walnut Ridge	13	9	4
Dumas	19	12	7	Warren	18	12	6
Earle	9	7	2	West Fork	3	3	—
Elaine	1	1	—	West Helena	28	21	7
El Dorado	65	52	13	West Memphis	78	59	19
England	8	5	3	Wynne	19	18	1
Eudora	11	7	4				
Eureka Springs	14	9	5	**CALIFORNIA**			
Farmington	5	4	1				
Fayetteville	111	74	37	Adelanto	33	23	10
Fordyce	14	9	5	Alameda	141	99	42
Forrest City	39	29	10	Albany	32	28	4
Fort Smith	175	137	38	Alhambra	147	100	47
Greenbrier	2	2	—	Alturas	9	8	1
Green Forest	6	4	2	Anaheim	549	382	167
Greenwood	8	8	—	Anderson	20	14	6
Gurdon	5	4	1	Angels Camp	6	5	1
Hamburg	7	6	1	Antioch	131	93	38
Hampton	4	4	—	Arcadia	102	78	24
Harrison	35	24	11	Arcata	30	22	8
Hazen	9	5	4	Arroyo Grande	32	23	9
Heber Springs	18	11	7	Arvin	17	11	6
Helena	24	18	6	Atascadero	37	28	9
Hope	30	23	7	Atherton	24	19	5
Horseshoe Bend	10	8	2	Atwater	32	24	8
Hot Springs	105	84	21	Auburn	23	17	6
Hoxie	7	5	2	Azusa	82	56	26
Jacksonville	76	59	17	Bakersfield	351	264	87
Jonesboro	84	74	10	Baldwin Park	96	73	23
Judsonia	4	3	1	Banning	47	31	16
Kensett	3	3	—	Barstow	59	44	15
Lake Village	13	9	4	Bear Valley Springs	10	6	4
Lincoln	5	4	1	Beaumont	23	17	6
Little Rock	572	494	78	Bell	51	37	14
Lonoke	13	8	5	Bell Gardens	70	54	16
Lowell	6	5	1	Belmont	43	30	13
Magnolia	23	18	5	Belvedere	7	6	1
Malvern	27	20	7	Benicia	50	34	16
Marianna	15	11	4	Berkeley	290	191	99
Marion	14	13	1	Beverly Hills	187	127	60
Marked Tree	13	9	4	Bishop	21	14	7
Maumelle	40	21	19	Blue Lake	4	4	—
McGehee	14	9	5	Blythe	32	19	13
Mena	11	11	—	Brawley	38	28	10
Monticello	21	16	5	Brea	124	100	24
Morrilton	20	14	6	Brentwood	23	18	5
Mountain Home	24	17	7	Brisbane	17	14	3
Mountain View	6	5	1	Broadmoor	9	8	1

Table 78.—Number of Full-time Law Enforcement Employees, Cities, October 31, 1995 — Continued

City	Total police employees	Total officers	Total civilians	City	Total police employees	Total officers	Total civilians
CALIFORNIA — Continued				**CALIFORNIA — Continued**			
Buena Park	138	89	49	Fresno	747	493	254
Burbank	247	158	89	Fullerton	215	147	68
Burlingame	63	44	19	Galt	27	17	10
Calexico	46	30	16	Gardena	111	89	22
California City	17	12	5	Garden Grove	230	165	65
Calipatria	6	5	1	Gilroy	89	53	36
Calistoga	13	10	3	Glendale	325	220	105
Campbell	59	43	16	Glendora	76	52	24
Capitola	32	23	9	Gonzales	11	10	1
Carlsbad	111	81	30	Grass Valley	27	19	8
Carmel	24	15	9	Greenfield	12	11	1
Cathedral City	67	43	24	Gridley	18	12	6
Ceres	51	35	16	Grover City	26	19	7
Chico	113	70	43	Guadalupe	9	8	1
Chino	115	79	36	Gustine	9	8	1
Chowchilla	19	13	6	Half Moon Bay	15	13	2
Chula Vista	263	174	89	Hanford	57	41	16
Claremont	53	36	17	Hawthorne	125	90	35
Clayton	13	10	3	Hayward	259	162	97
Clearlake	25	17	8	Healdsburg	24	15	9
Cloverdale	15	11	4	Hemet	73	56	17
Clovis	106	76	30	Hercules	23	20	3
Coachella	33	24	9	Hermosa Beach	50	35	15
Coalinga	24	16	8	Hillsborough	31	24	7
Colfax	5	5	—	Hollister	30	25	5
Colma	19	15	4	Holtville	10	8	2
Colton	76	61	15	Hughson	7	6	1
Colusa	8	7	1	Huntington Beach	355	223	132
Compton	182	130	52	Huntington Park	106	72	34
Concord	210	155	55	Huron	15	11	4
Corcoran	22	17	5	Imperial	18	15	3
Corning	16	12	4	Indio	64	45	19
Corona	173	121	52	Ingelwood	288	200	88
Coronado	54	39	15	Ione	4	4	—
Costa Mesa	202	137	65	Irvine	184	134	50
Cotati	17	12	5	Irwindale	27	21	6
Covina	77	52	25	Isleton	4	4	—
Crescent City	13	12	1	Jackson	11	9	2
Culver City	154	118	36	Kensington	10	10	—
Cypress	81	55	26	Kerman	14	14	—
Daly City	140	109	31	King City	18	16	2
Davis	72	51	21	Kingsburg	18	13	5
Delano	42	36	6	Laguna Beach	80	47	33
Del Ray Oaks	4	4	—	La Habra	77	72	5
Dinuba	26	20	6	Lakeport	14	12	2
Dixon	22	18	4	Lake Shastina	4	4	—
Dorris	4	3	1	La Mesa	85	63	22
Dos Palos	7	7	—	La Palma	29	23	6
Downey	158	115	43	La Verne	56	42	14
East Palo Alto	58	46	12	Lemoore	27	21	6
El Cajon	195	130	65	Lincoln	14	9	5
El Centro	80	50	30	Lindsay	20	14	6
El Cerrito	37	32	5	Livermore	112	65	47
El Monte	160	129	31	Livingston	25	19	6
El Segundo	84	63	21	Lodi	101	70	31
Emeryville	49	33	16	Lompoc	55	41	14
Escalon	10	8	2	Long Beach	1,258	822	436
Escondido	214	146	68	Los Alamitos	29	23	6
Etna	1	1	—	Los Altos	45	30	15
Eureka	81	51	30	Los Angeles	11,231	8,363	2,868
Exeter	14	13	1	Los Banos	38	26	12
Fairfax	15	11	4	Los Gatos	61	41	20
Fairfield	148	99	49	Madera	67	50	17
Farmersville	11	10	1	Mammoth Lakes	18	15	3
Ferndale	3	3	—	Manhattan Beach	68	63	5
Firebaugh	13	9	4	Manteca	65	44	21
Folsom	47	37	10	Marina	31	25	6
Fontana	165	112	53	Martinez	52	41	11
Fort Bragg	24	17	7	Marysville	40	26	14
Fortuna	20	15	5	Maywood	38	27	11
Foster City	54	40	14	Menlo Park	66	46	20
Fountain Valley	88	64	24	Merced	111	80	31
Fowler	8	7	1	Millbrae	31	25	6
Fremont	281	183	98	Mill Valley	33	22	11

Table 78.—Number of Full-time Law Enforcement Employees, Cities, October 31, 1995 — Continued

City	Total police employees	Total officers	Total civilians	City	Total police employees	Total officers	Total civilians
CALIFORNIA — Continued				**CALIFORNIA — Continued**			
Milpitas	108	79	29	San Carlos	48	35	13
Modesto	329	237	92	Sand City	6	6	—
Monrovia	82	58	24	San Diego	2,626	1,998	628
Montclair	75	53	22	San Fernando	48	35	13
Montebello	133	94	39	San Francisco	2,447	2,055	392
Monterey	74	58	16	San Gabriel	64	50	14
Monterey Park	119	78	41	Sanger	29	21	8
Moraga	13	12	1	San Jacinto	35	25	10
Morgan Hill	39	26	13	San Jose	1,664	1,241	423
Morro Bay	25	19	6	San Leandro	133	93	40
Mountain View	116	85	31	San Luis Obispo	80	55	25
Mount Shasta	14	9	5	San Marino	29	23	6
Murrieta	34	26	8	San Mateo	131	99	32
Napa	108	66	42	San Pablo	46	38	8
National City	94	68	26	San Rafael	100	67	33
Nevada City	10	9	1	Santa Ana	591	375	216
Newark	72	52	20	Santa Barbara	225	141	84
Newman	11	10	1	Santa Clara	171	140	31
Newport Beach	200	132	68	Santa Cruz	115	78	37
Novato	76	55	21	Santa Maria	115	81	34
Oakdale	30	22	8	Santa Monica	2	1	1
Oakland	1,009	661	348	Santa Paula	38	30	8
Oceanside	235	164	71	Santa Rosa	221	145	76
Ontario	310	193	117	Sausalito	21	21	—
Orange	212	146	66	Scotts Valley	29	21	8
Orland	9	8	1	Seal Beach	49	33	16
Oroville	33	23	10	Seaside	53	40	13
Oxnard	240	160	80	Sebastopol	18	14	4
Pacifica	53	41	12	Selma	36	24	12
Pacific Grove	37	28	9	Shafter	19	13	6
Palm Springs	123	80	43	Sierra Madre	24	15	9
Palo Alto	164	95	69	Signal Hill	44	30	14
Palos Verdes Estates	35	23	12	Simi Valley	161	106	55
Paradise	37	24	13	Soledad	15	12	3
Parlier	12	11	1	Sonoma	17	14	3
Pasadena	332	224	108	Sonora	17	13	4
Paso Robles	36	30	6	South Gate	127	93	34
Patterson	17	15	2	South Lake Tahoe	71	52	19
Perris	73	51	22	South Pasadena	51	36	15
Petaluma	88	62	26	South San Francisco	104	76	28
Piedmont	27	20	7	Stallion Springs	3	3	—
Pinole	45	24	21	Stockton	526	367	159
Pismo Beach	28	20	8	Suisun City	32	23	9
Pittsburg	87	71	16	Sunnyvale	171	122	49
Placentia	64	49	15	Susanville	18	16	2
Placerville	22	17	5	Sutter Creek	6	5	1
Pleasant Hill	61	42	19	Taft	16	11	5
Pleasanton	100	70	30	Tiburon	17	14	3
Pomona	280	167	113	Torrance	335	250	85
Porterville	64	43	21	Tracy	67	45	22
Port Hueneme	28	21	7	Trinidad	4	4	—
Red Bluff	36	22	14	Tulare	64	44	20
Redding	149	98	51	Tulelake	4	4	—
Redlands	109	75	34	Turlock	82	55	27
Redondo Beach	156	104	52	Tustin	119	83	36
Redwood City	117	83	34	Twin Cities	42	31	11
Reedley	29	21	8	Ukiah	35	25	10
Rialto	154	104	50	Union City	88	62	26
Richmond	264	182	82	Upland	121	87	34
Ridgecrest	40	28	12	Vacaville	133	80	53
Rio Dell	6	6	—	Vallejo	200	133	67
Rio Vista	9	8	1	Ventura	186	119	67
Ripon	20	13	7	Vernon	75	56	19
Riverside	508	331	177	Visalia	127	87	40
Rocklin	44	30	14	Walnut Creek	101	74	27
Rohnert Park	79	52	27	Waterford	13	12	1
Roseville	116	67	49	Watsonville	66	58	8
Ross	10	9	1	Weed	13	9	4
Sacramento	982	614	368	West Covina	152	110	42
St. Helena	17	12	5	Westminster	140	97	43
Salinas	212	151	61	West Sacramento	72	50	22
San Anselmo	23	17	6	Wheatland	4	4	—
San Bernardino	410	263	147	Whittier	176	128	48
San Bruno	59	48	11	Williams	8	7	1

Table 78.—Number of Full-time Law Enforcement Employees, Cities, October 31, 1995 — Continued

City	Total police employees	Total officers	Total civilians	City	Total police employees	Total officers	Total civilians
CALIFORNIA — Continued				**COLORADO — Continued**			
Willits	19	12	7	Greeley	151	89	62
Willows	10	9	1	Green Mountain Falls	2	2	—
Winters	11	10	1	Greenwood Village	66	49	17
Woodlake	11	10	1	Gunnison	23	14	9
Woodland	70	52	18	Haxtun	3	3	—
Yreka	19	12	7	Hayden	4	4	—
Yuba City	64	40	24	Holly	4	3	1
				Holyoke	4	4	—
COLORADO				Hotchkiss	2	2	—
				Idaho Springs	9	7	2
Alamosa	23	20	3	Ignacio	5	5	—
Alma	2	2	—	Johnstown	5	5	—
Arvada	184	124	60	Kersey	1	1	—
Aspen	35	26	9	Kremmling	5	5	—
Ault	4	4	—	Lafayette	32	26	6
Aurora	658	473	185	La Junta	19	16	3
Avon	9	8	1	Lakewood	320	211	109
Basalt	8	7	1	Lamar	26	21	5
Bayfield	3	3	—	La Salle	5	5	—
Berthoud	4	3	1	Las Animas	5	5	—
Black Hawk	29	19	10	Le Veta	2	2	—
Boulder	194	128	66	Leadville	10	8	2
Bow Mar	2	2	—	Limon	6	5	1
Breckenridge	24	17	7	Littleton	71	55	16
Brighton	40	29	11	Longmont	114	85	29
Broomfield	66	49	17	Louisville	29	23	6
Brush	14	11	3	Manitou Springs	19	14	5
Buena Vista	8	7	1	Manzanola	1	1	—
Burlington	7	7	—	Meeker	4	4	—
Canon City	37	28	9	Milliken	4	4	—
Carbondale	13	11	2	Minturn	5	4	1
Castle Rock	26	21	5	Monte Vista	20	14	6
Cedaredge	4	4	—	Montrose	32	27	5
Center	7	7	—	Monument	6	6	—
Central City	16	14	2	Morrison	1	1	—
Cherry Hills Village	24	22	2	Mountain View	2	2	—
Colorado Springs	688	485	203	Mount Crested Butte	7	6	1
Columbine Valley	3	3	—	Northglenn	63	49	14
Commerce City	69	47	22	Olathe	5	4	1
Cortez	34	22	12	Pagosa Springs	5	5	—
Craig	26	18	8	Palisade	7	6	1
Crested Butte	7	6	1	Palmer Lake	4	4	—
Cripple Creek	26	15	11	Paonia	4	3	1
Dacono	7	6	1	Parachute	9	4	5
De Beque	1	1	—	Parker	26	20	6
Del Norte	5	4	1	Platteville	4	4	—
Delta	14	12	2	Pueblo	227	176	51
Denver	1,546	1,347	199	Rangely	9	5	4
Dillon	6	5	1	Ridgway	3	3	—
Durango	56	33	23	Rocky Ford	9	8	1
Eaton	5	4	1	Salida	19	16	3
Elizabeth	4	4	—	Sheridan	25	16	9
Empire	1	1	—	Silverthorne	17	15	2
Englewood	93	63	30	Snowmass Village	12	9	3
Erie	7	6	1	Springfield	4	4	—
Estes Park	24	15	9	Steamboat Springs	27	19	8
Fairplay	2	2	—	Sterling	35	22	13
Federal Heights	29	20	9	Stratton	1	1	—
Firestone	3	3	—	Telluride	13	10	3
Florence	12	7	5	Thornton	127	96	31
Fort Collins	190	124	66	Trinidad	24	18	6
Fort Lupton	18	13	5	Vail	54	33	21
Fort Morgan	32	24	8	Victor	3	3	—
Fountain	25	16	9	Walsenburg	17	12	5
Fowler	6	6	—	Westminster	178	125	53
Frederick	4	4	—	Wheat Ridge	87	62	25
Frisco	10	9	1	Wiggins	1	1	—
Fruita	10	9	1	Windsor	10	9	1
Georgetown	4	4	—	Woodland Park	24	17	7
Glendale	39	29	10	Wray	11	7	4
Glenwood Springs	27	22	5	Yuma	8	7	1
Golden	40	29	11				
Granada	1	1	—				
Grand Junction	118	70	48				

Table 78.—Number of Full-time Law Enforcement Employees, Cities, October 31, 1995 — Continued

City	Total police employees	Total officers	Total civilians	City	Total police employees	Total officers	Total civilians
CONNECTICUT				**CONNECTICUT — Continued**			
Ansonia	40	34	6	Wallingford	91	72	19
Avon	37	30	7	Waterbury	365	313	52
Berlin	47	38	9	Waterford	54	47	7
Bethel	35	29	6	Watertown	40	33	7
Bloomfield	52	42	10	West Hartford	147	127	20
Branford	47	45	2	West Haven	126	110	16
Bridgeport	467	388	79	Weston	15	14	1
Bristol	122	113	9	Westport	72	64	8
Brookfield	35	29	6	Wethersfield	55	44	11
Canton	19	14	5	Willimantic	37	34	3
Cheshire	53	44	9	Wilton	42	40	2
Clinton	27	24	3	Windsor	60	52	8
Coventry	14	10	4	Windsor Locks	26	19	7
Cromwell	27	21	6	Winchester	26	21	5
Danbury	141	136	5	Wolcott	33	22	11
Darien	58	51	7	Woodbridge	32	24	8
Derby	25	24	1				
East Hampton	15	13	2	**DELAWARE**			
East Hartford	160	127	33				
East Haven Town	50	46	4	Bethany Beach	9	8	1
Easton	19	14	5	Blades	1	1	—
East Windsor	24	18	6	Bridgeville	5	4	1
Enfield	103	84	19	Camden-Wyoming	6	5	1
Fairfield	112	106	6	Clayton	2	2	—
Farmington	55	42	13	Dagsboro	1	1	—
Glastonbury	68	51	17	Delmar	12	11	1
Granby	17	12	5	Dewey Beach	9	6	3
Greenwich	175	158	17	Dover	99	80	19
Groton	38	32	6	Ellendale	2	2	—
Groton Long Point	5	5	—	Elsmere	13	12	1
Groton Town	69	63	6	Felton	1	1	—
Guilford	40	35	5	Fenwick Island	8	7	1
Hamden	122	100	22	Frankford	1	1	—
Hartford	554	443	111	Frederica	2	2	—
Madison Town	41	33	8	Georgetown	11	11	—
Manchester	137	107	30	Greenwood	6	5	1
Meriden	122	112	10	Harrington	13	10	3
Middlebury	12	10	2	Laurel	9	8	1
Middletown	113	94	19	Lewes	9	9	—
Milford	118	104	14	Milford	33	25	8
Monroe	42	35	7	Millsboro	8	7	1
Naugatuck	57	49	8	Milton	4	4	—
New Britain	179	156	23	Newark	66	51	15
New Canaan	46	42	4	New Castle	14	13	1
New Haven	523	419	104	Newport	7	7	—
Newington	54	42	12	Ocean View	3	3	—
New London	98	83	15	Rehoboth Beach	23	17	6
New Milford	54	41	13	Seaford	27	21	6
Newtown	45	36	9	Selbyville	5	5	—
North Branford	25	20	5	Smyrna	18	13	5
North Haven	56	47	9	South Bethany	6	6	—
Norwalk	196	171	25	Wilmington	298	244	54
Norwich	102	86	16				
Old Saybrook	27	25	2	**DISTRICT OF COLUMBIA**			
Orange	47	37	10				
Plainfield	17	16	1	Washington	4,328	3,671	657
Plainville	38	31	7				
Plymouth	22	18	4	**FLORIDA**			
Putnam	19	15	4				
Ridgefield Town	41	36	5	Alachua	23	17	6
Rocky Hill	38	30	8	Altamonte Springs	129	90	39
Seymour	30	28	2	Apalachicola	8	7	1
Shelton	51	47	4	Apopka	56	49	7
Simsbury	39	33	6	Arcadia	29	21	8
Southington	64	57	7	Atlantic Beach	31	23	8
South Windsor	40	31	9	Atlantis	17	11	6
Stamford	352	291	61	Auburndale	37	27	10
Stonington	43	34	9	Avon Park	29	20	9
Stratford	113	99	14	Bal Harbour	27	21	6
Suffield	19	14	5	Bartow	68	49	19
Thomaston	15	12	3	Bay Harbor Islands	28	23	5
Torrington	71	65	6	Belleair	15	10	5
Trumbull	75	65	10	Belleair Beach	8	7	1
Vernon	64	49	15	Belle Glade	62	48	14

Table 78.—Number of Full-time Law Enforcement Employees, Cities, October 31, 1995 — Continued

City	Total police employees	Total officers	Total civilians	City	Total police employees	Total officers	Total civilians
FLORIDA — Continued				**FLORIDA — Continued**			
Belleview	19	16	3	Indialantic	17	12	5
Biscayne Park	7	7	—	Indian Harbour Beach	23	16	7
Blountstown	12	7	5	Indian River Shores	20	19	1
Boca Raton	221	137	84	Indian Shores	13	12	1
Bowling Green	5	4	1	Inverness	18	16	2
Boynton Beach	156	121	35	Jacksonville	2,272	1,347	925
Bradenton	109	89	20	Jacksonville Beach	74	53	21
Bradenton Beach	9	8	1	Juno Beach	16	13	3
Bunnell	10	9	1	Jupiter	94	74	20
Bushnell	7	6	1	Jupiter Inlet Colony	6	5	1
Cape Coral	176	125	51	Jupiter Island	18	14	4
Casselberry	72	50	22	Kenneth City	17	15	2
Cedar Grove	5	5	—	Key Biscayne	34	24	10
Chattahoochee	11	10	1	Key West	101	74	27
Chiefland	12	9	3	Kissimmee	137	91	46
Chipley	9	8	1	Lady Lake	27	21	6
Clearwater	363	245	118	Lake Alfred	14	10	4
Clermont	26	18	8	Lake City	43	31	12
Clewiston	21	13	8	Lake Clarke Shores	10	10	—
Cocoa	80	60	20	Lake Hamilton	9	6	3
Cocoa Beach	46	34	12	Lake Helen	6	5	1
Coconut Creek	87	62	25	Lakeland	301	209	92
Coral Gables	199	140	59	Lake Mary	34	22	12
Coral Springs	236	151	85	Lake Park	34	26	8
Crescent City	8	7	1	Lake Wales	46	35	11
Crestview	30	23	7	Lake Worth	137	95	42
Cross City	5	5	—	Lantana	42	28	14
Crystal River	25	22	3	Largo	169	122	47
Davenport	8	7	1	Lauderdale-by-the-Sea	17	15	2
Davie	132	105	27	Leesburg	67	52	15
Daytona Beach	321	234	87	Lighthouse Point	40	31	9
De Funiak Springs	14	13	1	Longboat Key	26	20	6
De Land	77	56	21	Longwood	39	35	4
Delray Beach	209	141	68	Lynn Haven	33	26	7
Dundee	12	8	4	Madison	13	12	1
Dunnellon	11	9	2	Maitland	47	33	14
Eagle Lake	5	5	—	Manalapan	13	9	4
Eatonville	11	10	1	Mangonia Park	16	15	1
Edgewater	43	32	11	Margate	150	99	51
Edgewood	10	9	1	Marianna	24	17	7
El Portal	7	7	—	Mascotte	8	7	1
Eustis	48	36	12	Medley	37	31	6
Fellesmere	8	7	1	Melbourne	186	140	46
Fernandina Beach	36	29	7	Melbourne Beach	10	9	1
Flagler Beach	10	10	—	Melbourne Village	3	3	—
Florida City	35	25	10	Mexico Beach	4	4	—
Fort Lauderdale	745	474	271	Miami	1,438	998	440
Fort Meade	22	16	6	Miami Beach	474	335	139
Fort Myers	214	150	64	Miami Shores	42	34	8
Fort Walton Beach	66	53	13	Miami Springs	51	42	9
Frostproof	13	8	5	Miccosukee	24	16	8
Fruitland Park	9	8	1	Milton	19	14	5
Gainesville	379	249	130	Miramar	124	103	21
Golden Beach	15	14	1	Monticello	13	9	4
Graceville	10	6	4	Mount Dora	33	24	9
Greenacres City	76	38	38	Mulberry	14	10	4
Green Cove Springs	20	15	5	Naples	119	74	45
Groveland	12	8	4	Neptune Beach	23	17	6
Gulf Breeze	18	16	2	New Port Richey	40	32	8
Gulfport	38	29	9	New Smyrna Beach	61	45	16
Gulf Stream	9	9	—	Niceville	23	18	5
Haines City	52	40	12	North Bay Village	30	24	6
Hallandale	119	82	37	North Lauderdale	63	51	12
Havana	11	8	3	North Miami	150	112	38
Hialeah	417	306	111	North Miami Beach	154	90	64
Hialeah Gardens	37	28	9	North Palm Beach	42	33	9
Highland Beach	11	11	—	North Port	45	27	18
High Springs	11	7	4	Oak Hill	5	5	—
Hillsboro Beach	16	12	4	Oakland Park	107	76	31
Holly Hill	30	22	8	Ocala	190	131	59
Hollywood	562	315	247	Ocean Ridge	17	12	5
Holmes Beach	19	11	8	Ocoee	50	37	13
Homestead	118	93	25	Okeechobee	24	18	6
Howey-in-the-Hills	4	4	—	Opa Locka	51	43	8

Table 78.—Number of Full-time Law Enforcement Employees, Cities, October 31, 1995 — Continued

City	Total police employees	Total officers	Total civilians	City	Total police employees	Total officers	Total civilians
FLORIDA — Continued				**FLORIDA — Continued**			
Orange City	26	18	8	West Melbourne	23	20	3
Orange Park	27	21	6	West Miami	18	13	5
Orlando	872	619	253	West Palm Beach	347	234	113
Ormond Beach	75	54	21	White Springs	4	2	2
Oviedo	50	35	15	Wildwood	16	11	5
Pahokee	20	15	5	Williston	15	10	5
Palatka	41	34	7	Wilton Manors	42	31	11
Palm Bay	173	112	61	Windermere	8	8	—
Palm Beach	110	68	42	Winter Garden	44	34	10
Palm Beach Gardens	109	85	24	Winter Haven	113	79	34
Palm Beach Shores	8	7	1	Winter Park	97	75	22
Palmetto	37	28	9	Winter Springs	58	38	20
Palm Springs	31	24	7	Zephyrhills	34	25	9
Panama City	113	77	36	Zolfo Springs	1	1	—
Panama City Beach	42	33	9				
Parker	8	7	1	**GEORGIA**			
Parkland	25	23	2				
Pembroke Pines	207	163	44	Abbeville	4	4	—
Pensacola	200	145	55	Acworth	32	23	9
Perry	22	20	2	Adairsville	12	10	2
Pinellas Park	112	80	32	Adel	21	18	3
Plantation	238	154	84	Alamo	2	2	—
Plant City	79	60	19	Albany	239	212	27
Pompano Beach	288	233	55	Alma	22	16	6
Ponce Inlet	13	8	5	Alpharetta	63	43	20
Port Orange	78	60	18	Americus	52	41	11
Port Richey	14	9	5	Aragon	4	4	—
Port St. Joe	17	12	5	Arcade	4	3	1
Port St. Lucie	154	107	47	Arlington	3	3	—
Punta Gorda	36	24	12	Athens–Clarke County	242	194	48
Quincy	42	30	12	Atlanta	1,943	1,491	452
Redington Beach	10	9	1	Attapulgus	2	1	1
Rockledge	48	37	11	Auburn	10	9	1
Royal Palm Beach	51	36	15	Austell	16	12	4
St. Augustine	53	43	10	Avondale Estates	11	10	1
St. Augustine Beach	11	10	1	Bainbridge	47	35	12
St. Cloud	49	35	14	Baldwin	5	5	—
St. Petersburg	719	511	208	Ball Ground	2	2	—
St. Petersburg Beach	47	30	17	Barnesville	14	12	2
Sanford	112	90	22	Barwick	2	2	—
Sanibel	33	22	11	Baxley	20	15	5
Sarasota	274	182	92	Berlin	1	1	—
Satellite Beach	26	19	7	Blackshear	10	9	1
Sea Ranch Lakes	11	8	3	Blakely	22	17	5
Sebastian	37	26	11	Bloomingdale	10	9	1
Sebring	31	24	7	Blue Ridge	5	5	—
Sewall's Point	8	8	—	Blythe	1	1	—
Sneads	7	6	1	Boston	4	4	—
South Bay	16	11	5	Bowdon	11	7	4
South Daytona	32	23	9	Braselton	1	1	—
South Miami	54	45	9	Bremen	16	14	2
South Palm Beach	10	10	—	Brooklet	2	2	—
Springfield	21	16	5	Brunswick	18	15	3
Starke	23	17	6	Buchanan	5	5	—
Stuart	56	42	14	Buena Vista	6	6	—
Sunrise	190	139	51	Butler	5	5	—
Surfside	27	23	4	Byron	14	7	7
Sweetwater	26	21	5	Cairo	24	21	3
Tallahassee	462	319	143	Calhoun	36	34	2
Tampa	1,125	849	276	Camilla	21	17	4
Tarpon Springs	56	42	14	Canton	24	21	3
Tavares	27	20	7	Carrollton	63	53	10
Temple Terrace	65	44	21	Cartersville	49	40	9
Tequesta	22	17	5	Cave Spring	4	4	—
Titusville	106	73	33	Cedartown	22	20	2
Treasure Island	24	20	4	Chamblee	39	32	7
Umatilla	8	7	1	Chatsworth	18	13	5
Valparaiso	13	9	4	Chauncey	1	1	—
Venice	66	46	20	Chickamauga	6	5	1
Vero Beach	89	61	28	Clarkesville	5	5	—
Virginia Gardens	9	7	2	Clarkston	13	12	1
Waldo	9	8	1	Claxton	8	8	—
Wauchula	10	10	—	Clayton	10	9	1
Webster	3	3	—	Cleveland	8	8	—

Table 78.—Number of Full-time Law Enforcement Employees, Cities, October 31, 1995 — Continued

City	Total police employees	Total officers	Total civilians	City	Total police employees	Total officers	Total civilians
GEORGIA — Continued				**GEORGIA — Continued**			
Cochran	15	14	1	Hephzibah	3	3	—
Cohutta	1	1	—	Hiawassee	4	3	1
College Park	96	79	17	Hilltonia	1	1	—
Columbus	487	383	104	Hinesville	62	55	7
Comer	3	3	—	Hiram	5	5	—
Commerce	16	11	5	Hoboken	2	1	1
Conyers	51	37	14	Hogansville	13	9	4
Cordele	34	28	6	Holly Springs	6	6	—
Cornelia	17	16	1	Homerville	9	5	4
Covington	56	50	6	Homeland	2	2	—
Crawfordville	1	1	—	Hoschton	2	2	—
Cumming	8	8	—	Ideal	2	2	—
Cusseta	6	2	4	Ivey	3	3	—
Cuthbert	18	8	10	Jackson	20	13	7
Dallas	16	12	4	Jasper	10	10	—
Dalton	75	61	14	Jefferson	12	11	1
Damascus	1	1	—	Jeffersonville	6	5	1
Danielsville	1	1	—	Jesup	38	27	11
Danville	2	1	1	Jonesboro	13	13	—
Davisboro	2	2	—	Kennesaw	47	27	20
Dawson	22	17	5	Kingsland	25	23	2
Decatur	59	45	14	Lafayette	21	17	4
Demorest	3	3	—	La Grange	89	80	9
Dillard	2	2	—	Lake City	22	20	2
Doerun	5	4	1	Lakeland	9	8	1
Donalsonville	17	9	8	Lake Lanier Islands	8	8	—
Doraville	50	32	18	Lake Park	2	2	—
Douglas	47	39	8	Lavonia	12	9	3
Douglasville	59	46	13	Lawrenceville	59	44	15
Dublin	56	46	10	Leary	1	1	—
Duluth	39	27	12	Leesburg	5	5	—
East Dublin	9	8	1	Leslie	4	4	—
East Ellijay	7	5	2	Lilburn	29	21	8
Eastman	17	14	3	Lincolnton	5	4	1
East Point	140	107	33	Lithonia	12	8	4
Eatonton	11	10	1	Loganville	14	10	4
Edison	4	4	—	Lookout Mountain	8	7	1
Elberton	26	21	5	Louisville	9	9	—
Ellaville	4	4	—	Ludowici	8	5	3
Emerson	2	2	—	Lumber City	7	6	1
Enigma	2	1	1	Lumpkin	8	7	1
Eton	2	2	—	Macon	329	299	30
Fairburn	23	17	6	Madison	15	14	1
Fairmount	4	3	1	Manchester	19	14	5
Fayetteville	38	29	9	Marshallville	3	3	—
Fitzgerald	32	27	5	Marietta	138	114	24
Folkston	6	6	—	Matsville	1	1	—
Forest Park	100	52	48	McCaysville	4	4	—
Forsyth	23	18	5	McDonough	17	16	1
Fort Gaines	6	4	2	McIntyre	3	3	—
Fort Oglethorpe	21	15	6	McRae	10	7	3
Fort Valley	32	27	5	Meigs	5	5	—
Franklin Springs	2	1	1	Milan	3	3	—
Gainesville	99	78	21	Milledgeville	61	35	26
Garden City	24	22	2	Millen	11	11	—
Georgetown	3	2	1	Molena	1	1	—
Glenville	12	7	5	Monroe	33	29	4
Glenwood	3	2	1	Montezuma	15	12	3
Gordon	9	6	3	Monticello	16	11	5
Gray	6	5	1	Morrow	39	28	11
Greenville	8	7	1	Morven	3	3	—
Griffin	94	78	16	Moultrie	56	46	10
Grovetown	17	11	6	Mountain City	1	1	—
Hahira	8	5	3	Muscogee	15	14	1
Hamilton	1	1	—	Nahunta	3	3	—
Hampton	9	8	1	Nashville	14	11	3
Hapeville	39	34	5	Nelson	1	1	—
Harlem	11	8	3	Newnan	44	42	2
Harrison	1	1	—	Nicholls	3	2	1
Hartwell	21	17	4	Norcross	31	24	7
Hawkinsville	12	11	1	Oakwood	8	7	1
Hazlehurst	16	11	5	Ocilla	17	12	5
Helen	11	7	4	Oglethorpe	6	4	2
Helena	3	3	—	Omega	2	2	—

Table 78.—Number of Full-time Law Enforcement Employees, Cities, October 31, 1995 — Continued

City	Total police employees	Total officers	Total civilians	City	Total police employees	Total officers	Total civilians
GEORGIA — Continued				**GEORGIA — Continued**			
Oxford	2	2	—	Union Point	11	8	3
Palmetto	11	10	1	Uvalda	1	1	—
Patterson	1	1	—	Valdosta	91	80	11
Peachtree City	46	36	10	Vidalia	36	29	7
Pearson	4	4	—	Vienna	6	6	—
Pelham	16	12	4	Villa Rica	20	15	5
Pembroke	7	6	1	Wadley	9	6	3
Perry	33	26	7	Warner Robins	101	83	18
Pine Lake	2	2	—	Washington	16	15	1
Pinehurst	3	1	2	Watkinsville	5	5	—
Pine Mountain	6	6	—	Waverly Hall	2	2	—
Pineview	3	1	2	West Point	19	14	5
Plains	3	3	—	Whigham	3	3	—
Pooler	17	15	2	White	1	1	—
Portal	3	2	1	Willacoochee	4	4	—
Porterdale	12	10	2	Winder	37	31	6
Port Wentworth	16	14	2	Woodbury	8	6	2
Poulan	1	1	—	Woodstock	26	22	4
Powder Springs	24	18	6	Wrens	16	15	1
Preston	1	1	—	Zebulon	6	6	—
Quitman	20	15	5				
Ray City	1	1	—	**HAWAII**			
Reidsville	11	5	6				
Remerton	3	3	—	Hilo	236	126	110
Reynolds	3	3	—	Honolulu	2,188	1,742	446
Richland	5	5	—				
Richmond Hill	21	14	7	**IDAHO**			
Rincon	8	7	1				
Ringgold	5	5	—	Aberdeen	8	5	3
Riverdale	42	31	11	American Falls	10	8	2
Roberta	3	3	—	Bellevue	3	3	—
Rockmart	17	15	2	Blackfoot	23	20	3
Rome	97	86	11	Boise	247	207	40
Rossville	13	9	4	Bonners Ferry	8	7	1
Roswell	142	88	54	Buhl	9	8	1
Royston	13	10	3	Caldwell	44	33	11
St. Marys	31	29	2	Cascade	5	4	1
Sandersville	29	18	11	Chubbuck	24	16	8
Sardis	4	4	—	Coeur d'Alene	61	51	10
Savannah	512	421	91	Emmett	11	10	1
Screven	1	1	—	Filer	4	4	—
Senoia	9	8	1	Firth	3	2	1
Shellman	3	3	—	Fruitland	7	6	1
Shiloh	1	1	—	Garden City	31	24	7
Smyrna	120	88	32	Glens Ferry	6	4	2
Snellville	34	27	7	Gooding	6	6	—
Soperton	10	6	4	Grangeville	5	5	—
Sparks	1	1	—	Hailey	11	9	2
Springfield	7	6	1	Heyburn	6	5	1
Statesboro	682	333	349	Homedale	6	6	—
Statham	3	3	—	Idaho Falls	114	82	32
Stone Mountain	21	16	5	Jerome	16	15	1
Stone Mountain Park	24	19	5	Kamiah	3	3	—
Summerville	22	19	3	Kellogg	7	6	1
Suwanee	15	11	4	Ketchum	15	11	4
Swainsboro	24	16	8	Kimberly	6	6	—
Sycamore	1	1	—	Lewiston	63	45	18
Sylvania	18	10	8	McCall	12	10	2
Sylvester	19	15	4	Meridian	25	21	4
Talbottom	4	4	—	Montpelier	6	6	—
Tallapoosa	14	12	2	Moscow	38	28	10
Tallulah Falls	1	1	—	Mountain Home	26	19	7
Thomaston	46	39	7	Nampa	69	49	20
Thomasville	49	44	5	New Plymouth	4	4	—
Thomson	18	16	2	Orofino	8	7	1
Thunderbolt	12	8	4	Osburn	3	3	—
Tifton	55	45	10	Parma	4	4	—
Toccoa	33	27	6	Payette	12	11	1
Trenton	7	7	—	Pinehurst	2	2	—
Trion	7	7	—	Pocatello	105	82	23
Tunnel Hill	4	4	—	Ponderay	3	3	—
Tybee Island	23	17	6	Post Falls	37	23	14
Tyrone	11	9	2	Preston	4	4	—
Union City	34	25	9	Priest River	5	4	1

Table 78.—Number of Full-time Law Enforcement Employees, Cities, October 31, 1995 — Continued

City	Total police employees	Total officers	Total civilians	City	Total police employees	Total officers	Total civilians
IDAHO — Continued				**ILLINOIS — Continued**			
Rexburg	30	26	4	Broadview	41	35	6
Rigby	7	7	—	Brookfield	34	27	7
Rupert	14	13	1	Brooklyn	6	5	1
St. Anthony	8	8	—	Buda	1	1	—
St. Maries	4	4	—	Buffalo Grove	82	69	13
Salmon	7	6	1	Bull Valley	2	2	—
Sandpoint	23	15	8	Bunker Hill	4	3	1
Shelley	6	6	—	Burbank	55	46	9
Soda Springs	8	7	1	Burnham	14	10	4
Spirit Lake	4	3	1	Burr Ridge	25	22	3
Sun Valley	8	8	—	Byron	5	4	1
Twin Falls	61	47	14	Cahokia	42	31	11
Wallace	3	3	—	Cairo	22	17	5
Weiser	10	9	1	Calumet City	110	78	32
Wendell	5	5	—	Calumet Park	25	18	7
Wilder	3	3	—	Camp Point	1	1	—
				Canton	29	21	8
ILLINOIS				Carbon Cliff	3	3	—
				Carbondale	76	60	16
Abingdon	8	4	4	Carlinville	16	10	6
Addison	81	61	20	Carlyle	7	6	1
Albany	1	1	—	Carmi	9	8	1
Albion	3	3	—	Carol Stream	75	52	23
Aledo	9	8	1	Carpentersville	51	46	5
Alexis	1	1	—	Carrier Mills	2	2	—
Algonquin	32	25	7	Carrollton	6	6	—
Alsip	52	41	11	Carterville	4	4	—
Altamont	5	5	—	Carthage	3	3	—
Alton	79	67	12	Cary	30	22	8
Amboy	3	2	1	Casey	8	7	1
Andalusia	2	2	—	Caseyville	11	7	4
Anna	7	7	—	Central City	3	3	—
Annawan	1	1	—	Centralia	36	28	8
Antioch	26	18	8	Centreville	17	14	3
Arcola	4	4	—	Champaign	143	116	27
Arlington Heights	134	101	33	Channahon	13	11	2
Arthur	5	5	—	Charleston	36	28	8
Ashland	1	1	—	Chatham	10	8	2
Astoria	1	1	—	Chenoa	3	3	—
Atkinson	2	2	—	Cherry Valley	12	12	—
Atlanta	2	2	—	Chester	11	8	3
Auburn	8	4	4	Chicago	15,681	13,344	2,337
Aurora	303	239	64	Chicago Heights	108	78	30
Avon	1	1	—	Chicago Ridge	32	28	4
Bannockburn	7	7	—	Chillicothe	13	9	4
Barrington	43	30	13	Christopher	4	4	—
Barrington Hills	24	16	8	Cicero	145	103	42
Bartlett	52	39	13	Clarendon Hills	13	13	—
Bartonville	11	7	4	Clinton	16	12	4
Batavia	43	37	6	Coal City	10	6	4
Beardstown	12	8	4	Coal Valley	7	6	1
Bedford Park	33	27	6	Cobden	2	2	—
Beecher	6	6	—	Collinsville	45	35	10
Belleville	93	78	15	Colona	5	5	—
Bellwood	55	47	8	Columbia	16	11	5
Belvidere	29	28	1	Cordova	2	2	—
Benld	3	1	2	Coulterville	2	2	—
Bensenville	50	40	10	Country Club Hills	34	26	8
Benton	10	5	5	Countryside	28	22	6
Berkeley	18	14	4	Crest Hill	27	20	7
Berwyn	103	79	24	Crestwood	4	3	1
Bethalto	20	14	6	Crete	17	12	5
Bloomingdale	63	45	18	Creve Coeur	9	8	1
Bloomington	106	91	15	Crystal Lake	66	50	16
Blue Island	51	33	18	Cuba	1	1	—
Blue Mound	1	1	—	Dallas City	2	2	—
Bolingbrook	105	74	31	Danvers	1	1	—
Bourbonnais	23	17	6	Danville	84	68	16
Bradley	28	18	10	Darien	45	30	15
Braidwood	14	10	4	Decatur	154	149	5
Breese	8	5	3	Deerfield	51	38	13
Bridgeport	3	3	—	De Kalb	63	52	11
Bridgeview	53	43	10	Depue	1	1	—
Brighton	4	3	1	De Soto	3	3	—

Table 78.—Number of Full-time Law Enforcement Employees, Cities, October 31, 1995 — Continued

City	Total police employees	Total officers	Total civilians	City	Total police employees	Total officers	Total civilians
ILLINOIS — Continued				**ILLINOIS — Continued**			
Des Plaines	114	93	21	Glencoe	43	34	9
Divernon	3	3	—	Glendale Heights	73	51	22
Dixmoor	8	6	2	Glen Ellyn	42	34	8
Dixon	27	24	3	Glenview	90	66	24
Dolton	50	44	6	Glenwood	23	17	6
Downers Grove	94	70	24	Golf	1	1	—
Dupo	6	6	—	Grafton	2	2	—
Du Quoin	12	9	3	Granite City	62	53	9
Durand	1	1	—	Grant Park	4	4	—
Dwight	11	7	4	Grayslake	28	19	9
Earlville	3	3	—	Grayville	7	3	4
East Alton	18	12	6	Greenfield	3	3	—
East Carondelet	1	1	—	Green Rock	4	4	—
East Dubuque	8	7	1	Greenup	4	4	—
East Dundee	14	13	1	Greenville	14	10	4
East Galesburg	1	1	—	Gridley	1	1	—
East Hazel Crest	10	9	1	Gurnee	62	43	19
East Moline	47	36	11	Hamilton	3	3	—
East Peoria	44	33	11	Hampton	3	3	—
East St. Louis	119	85	34	Hampshire	6	6	—
Edwardsville	33	24	9	Hanover	1	1	—
Effingham	37	25	12	Hanover Park	63	45	18
Elburn	7	6	1	Harrisburg	17	14	3
Eldorado	10	7	3	Hartford	6	5	1
Elgin	183	140	43	Harvard	22	17	5
Elizabeth	2	2	—	Harvey	90	62	28
Elk Grove Village	111	97	14	Harwood Heights	26	19	7
Elmhurst	89	67	22	Havana	9	9	—
Elmwood Park	46	36	10	Hawthorn Woods	7	6	1
El Paso	4	4	—	Hazel Crest	32	24	8
Energy	3	3	—	Hebron	2	2	—
Enfield	1	1	—	Henry	3	3	—
Equality	1	1	—	Herrin	18	14	4
Erie	2	2	—	Herscher	2	2	—
Essex	2	2	—	Hickory Hills	33	27	6
Eureka	4	4	—	Highland	23	17	6
Evanston	202	150	52	Highland Park	75	58	17
Evergreen Park	65	55	10	Highwood	13	9	4
Fairbury	6	6	—	Hillsboro	6	6	—
Fairfield	14	10	4	Hillside	39	31	8
Fairmont City	12	8	4	Hinckley	2	2	—
Fairview	1	1	—	Hinsdale	37	27	10
Fairview Heights	48	37	11	Hodgkins	17	16	1
Farmer City	7	4	3	Hoffman Estates	115	91	24
Farmington	7	4	3	Holiday Hills	2	2	—
Fisher	2	2	—	Homer	1	1	—
Flora	15	10	5	Hometown	5	1	4
Flossmoor	23	17	6	Homewood	47	36	11
Ford Heights	12	5	7	Hoopeston	14	9	5
Forest Park	51	36	15	Huntley	10	9	1
Forest View	11	8	3	Indian Head Park	13	9	4
Fox Lake	24	18	6	Island Lake	16	11	5
Fox River Grove	9	9	—	Itasca	37	27	10
Fox River Valley Gardens	16	11	5	Jacksonville	43	36	7
Frankfort	21	18	3	Jerome	4	4	—
Franklin Park	72	52	20	Jerseyville	18	12	6
Freeburg	6	5	1	Johnsburg	9	8	1
Freeport	69	53	16	Johnston City	5	5	—
Fulton	6	6	—	Joliet	272	221	51
Galena	11	9	2	Jonesboro	2	2	—
Galesburg	75	52	23	Justice	38	30	8
Galva	4	4	—	Kankakee	92	68	24
Gardner	1	1	—	Kenilworth	14	11	3
Geneseo	16	10	6	Kewanee	24	19	5
Geneva	36	26	10	Kildeer	7	7	—
Genoa	8	7	1	Kincaid	1	1	—
Germantown	1	1	—	Kirkland	3	3	—
Gibson City	11	7	4	Knoxville	4	4	—
Gifford	1	1	—	Lacon	1	1	—
Gilberts	1	1	—	La Grange	37	27	10
Gillespie	9	6	3	La Grange Park	29	24	5
Gilman	2	2	—	Lake Bluff	15	13	2
Girard	4	4	—	Lake Forest	59	43	16
Glen Carbon	17	12	5	Lake-in-the-Hills	28	21	7

Table 78.—Number of Full-time Law Enforcement Employees, Cities, October 31, 1995 — Continued

City	Total police employees	Total officers	Total civilians	City	Total police employees	Total officers	Total civilians
ILLINOIS — Continued				**ILLINOIS — Continued**			
Lakemoor	6	6	—	Morton	23	18	5
Lake Villa	10	9	1	Morton Grove	66	46	20
Lakewood	4	4	—	Mount Carmel	18	13	5
Lake Zurich	50	34	16	Mount Carroll	2	2	—
Lanark	2	2	—	Mount Morris	8	5	3
Lansing	71	56	15	Mount Olive	4	3	1
La Salle	21	17	4	Mount Prospect	95	76	19
Lebanon	10	7	3	Mount Pulaski	2	2	—
Leland Grove	5	5	—	Mount Sterling	9	5	4
Lemont	23	21	2	Mount Vernon	41	39	2
Lenzburg	1	1	—	Mount Zion	10	9	1
Leroy	4	4	—	Moweaqua	5	2	3
Lewistown	3	3	—	Mundelein	45	35	10
Libertyville	50	38	12	Murphysboro	20	14	6
Lincoln	27	26	1	Naperville	227	141	86
Lincolnshire	28	18	10	Nashville	7	6	1
Lincolnwood	46	34	12	National City	1	1	—
Lindenhurst	14	12	2	Nauvoo	1	1	—
Lisle	48	35	13	Neoga	2	2	—
Litchfield	17	13	4	New Athens	4	4	—
Lockport	27	20	7	New Baden	4	4	—
Lombard	81	65	16	New Lenox	20	19	1
London Mills	1	1	—	Newman	1	1	—
Loves Park	33	25	8	Newton	7	6	1
Lynwood	17	13	4	Niles	67	52	15
Lyons	29	24	5	Nokomis	7	4	3
Mackinaw	1	1	—	Normal	70	56	14
Macomb	25	24	1	Norridge	50	37	13
Madison	14	11	3	North Aurora	15	14	1
Mahomet	4	4	—	Northbrook	82	59	23
Manhattan	6	6	—	North Chicago	69	49	20
Manito	3	3	—	Northfield	28	21	7
Manteno	9	9	—	Northlake	26	23	3
Marengo	17	13	4	North Pekin	1	1	—
Marion	25	18	7	North Riverside	36	27	9
Marissa	5	5	—	Oak Brook	52	38	14
Markham	41	34	7	Oakbrook Terrace	24	18	6
Maroa	3	3	—	Oak Forest	50	37	13
Marquette Heights	3	3	—	Oak Lawn	125	103	22
Marseilles	8	8	—	Oak Park	147	115	32
Marshall	9	9	—	Oakwood Hills	2	2	—
Martinsville	2	2	—	Oblong	1	1	—
Maryville	10	7	3	O'Fallon	40	29	11
Mascoutah	12	11	1	Ogden	1	1	—
Mason City	4	4	—	Oglesby	11	8	3
Matteson	47	36	11	Okawville	3	3	—
Mattoon	46	40	6	Old Shawneetown	1	1	—
Maywood	66	54	12	Olney	17	12	5
McCook	20	15	5	Olympia Fields	19	17	2
McCullom Lake	1	1	—	Oregon	6	6	—
McHenry	44	31	13	Orland Hills	11	10	1
McLean	1	1	—	Orland Park	106	83	23
McLeansboro	5	5	—	Oswego	20	17	3
Melrose Park	84	61	23	Ottawa	34	28	6
Mendota	15	13	2	Palatine	107	82	25
Meredosia	2	2	—	Palestine	3	3	—
Metamora	4	4	—	Palmyra	2	2	—
Metropolis	20	16	4	Palos Heights	26	24	2
Midlothian	28	22	6	Palos Hills	32	29	3
Milan	16	12	4	Palos Park	13	12	1
Milledgeville	2	2	—	Pana	14	10	4
Millstadt	5	5	—	Paris	19	15	4
Minier	1	1	—	Park City	13	8	5
Minonk	2	2	—	Park Forest	50	40	10
Minooka	9	8	1	Park Ridge	66	53	13
Mokena	19	18	1	Pawnee	5	5	—
Moline	103	76	27	Paxton	6	6	—
Momence	7	7	—	Pecatonica	2	2	—
Monee	5	5	—	Pekin	55	48	7
Monmouth	25	17	8	Peoria	273	224	49
Montgomery	17	11	6	Peoria Heights	14	11	3
Monticello	8	7	1	Peotone	13	7	6
Morris	25	19	6	Peru	21	18	3
Morrison	7	7	—	Petersburg	5	5	—

City	Total police employees	Total officers	Total civilians	City	Total police employees	Total officers	Total civilians
ILLINOIS — Continued				**ILLINOIS — Continued**			
Phoenix	5	2	3	Smithton	5	4	1
Pinckneyville	6	5	1	Somonauk	3	3	—
Pittsfield	6	6	—	South Barrington	12	11	1
Plainfield	18	16	2	South Beloit	11	8	3
Plano	15	13	2	South Chicago Heights	14	9	5
Plymouth	1	1	—	South Elgin	26	19	7
Polo	4	3	1	Southern View	3	3	—
Pontiac	26	20	6	South Holland	48	37	11
Pontoon Beach	16	11	5	South Jacksonville	7	6	1
Port Byron	2	2	—	South Pekin	2	2	—
Posen	12	10	2	South Roxana	6	5	1
Princeton	11	11	—	Sparta	14	10	4
Prophetstown	4	3	1	Springfield	292	239	53
Prospect Heights	25	22	3	Spring Grove	7	7	—
Quincy	86	71	15	Spring Valley	12	8	4
Rankin	1	1	—	Staunton	10	7	3
Rantoul	34	28	6	Steger	15	11	4
Raymond	1	1	—	Sterling	39	28	11
Red Bud	3	3	—	Stickney	20	15	5
Richmond	9	9	—	Stockton	3	3	—
Richton Park	26	21	5	Stone Park	28	17	11
Ridge Farm	2	2	—	Stonington	1	1	—
Ridgway	3	3	—	Streamwood	68	50	18
Riverdale	45	35	10	Streator	26	21	5
River Forest	41	31	10	Sugar Grove	6	5	1
River Grove	25	19	6	Sullivan	9	7	2
Riverside	21	17	4	Summit	33	26	7
Robbins	11	5	6	Sumner	2	2	—
Robinson	14	12	2	Swansea	19	15	4
Rochelle	25	19	6	Sycamore	27	21	6
Rochester	7	7	—	Tampico	1	1	—
Rockdale	5	5	—	Taylorville	24	18	6
Rock Falls	26	18	8	Thomasboro	1	1	—
Rockford	309	276	33	Thornton	11	10	1
Rock Island	112	84	28	Tilden	1	1	—
Rockton	9	8	1	Tilton	3	3	—
Rolling Meadows	71	51	20	Tinley Park	75	58	17
Romeoville	40	30	10	Tolono	3	3	—
Roodhouse	4	4	—	Tonica	2	2	—
Roscoe	10	9	1	Tower Lakes	2	2	—
Roselle	48	34	14	Tremont	4	3	1
Rosemont	79	66	13	Trenton	3	3	—
Rosiclare	1	1	—	Troy	18	13	5
Rossville	2	2	—	Tuscola	8	7	1
Round Lake	10	9	1	University Park	24	17	7
Round Lake Beach	37	31	6	Urbana	59	47	12
Round Lake Heights	3	3	—	Valier	1	1	—
Round Lake Park	8	7	1	Valmeyer	1	1	—
Roxana	6	5	1	Vandalia	15	11	4
Royalton	3	3	—	Venice	9	7	2
Ruma	1	1	—	Vernon Hills	54	36	18
Rushville	5	5	—	Vienna	2	2	—
St. Anne	4	4	—	Villa Grove	4	4	—
St. Charles	61	49	12	Villa Park	54	39	15
St. Francisville	1	1	—	Virden	9	5	4
Salem	19	14	5	Virginia	1	1	—
Sandwich	17	11	6	Wamac	2	2	—
Sauget	9	9	—	Warren	4	4	—
Sauk Village	23	17	6	Warrensburg	1	1	—
Savanna	7	7	—	Warrenville	23	18	5
Saybrook	1	1	—	Washington	18	13	5
Schaumburg	200	140	60	Washington Park	12	8	4
Schiller Park	38	30	8	Waterloo	10	9	1
Seneca	7	4	3	Watseka	17	12	5
Sesser	6	5	1	Wauconda	27	16	11
Shannon	2	2	—	Waukegan	191	139	52
Shawneetown	4	4	—	Wayne	4	4	—
Shelbyville	8	7	1	Westchester	48	35	13
Sherman	5	5	—	West Chicago	45	37	8
Shiloh	6	6	—	West City	8	4	4
Shorewood	18	16	2	West Dundee	18	16	2
Silvis	19	12	7	Western Springs	25	19	6
Skokie	138	105	33	West Frankfort	18	14	4
Sleepy Hollow	6	5	1	Westmont	48	33	15

Table 78.—Number of Full-time Law Enforcement Employees, Cities, October 31, 1995 — Continued

City	Total police employees	Total officers	Total civilians	City	Total police employees	Total officers	Total civilians
ILLINOIS — Continued				**INDIANA — Continued**			
West Salem	3	3	—	Hartford City	18	12	6
Westville	3	3	—	Highland	47	40	7
Wheaton	87	63	24	Hobart	61	48	13
Wheeling	75	56	19	Huntingburg	9	8	1
White Hall	5	5	—	Huntington	36	32	4
Williamsville	2	2	—	Indianapolis	1,343	975	368
Willowbrook	29	25	4	Jasonville	4	4	—
Willow Springs	15	11	4	Jasper	24	17	7
Wilmette	60	43	17	Kendallville	19	15	4
Wilmington	20	12	8	Kokomo	138	103	35
Winchester	4	2	2	Lafayette	110	81	29
Winfield	17	15	2	Lake Station	23	19	4
Winnebago	2	2	—	La Porte	47	41	6
Winnetka	38	27	11	Lawrence	56	40	16
Winthrop Harbor	14	9	5	Linton	13	9	4
Witt	1	1	—	Logansport	47	37	10
Wood Dale	48	34	14	Long Beach	5	5	—
Woodhull	1	1	—	Loogootee	4	4	—
Woodridge	65	45	20	Lowell	17	12	5
Wood River	26	19	7	Madison	31	24	7
Woodstock	39	28	11	Marion	77	67	10
Worth	27	25	2	Martinsville	23	18	5
Yorkville	13	13	—	Merrillville	55	45	10
Zeigler	5	4	1	Michigan City	105	87	18
Zion	57	41	16	Mooresville	20	15	5
				Mount Vernon	17	13	4
INDIANA				Muncie	127	117	10
				Munster	43	34	9
Alexandria	14	10	4	Nappanee	13	9	4
Angola	17	13	4	New Albany	74	58	16
Austin	4	4	—	New Castle	38	35	3
Batesville	12	8	4	New Chicago	5	2	3
Bedford	37	31	6	New Haven	21	16	5
Beech Grove	34	25	9	Noblesville	41	33	8
Berne	6	5	1	North Manchester	15	11	4
Bloomington	87	64	23	North Vernon	15	14	1
Bluffton	23	17	6	Plainfield	28	26	2
Boonville	12	11	1	Portage	52	39	13
Brazil	14	10	4	Portland	18	14	4
Bremen	15	10	5	Princes Lakes	3	3	—
Burns Harbor	9	5	4	Rensselaer	12	8	4
Carmel	72	59	13	Richmond	99	76	23
Cedar Lake	18	13	5	Schererville	44	35	9
Charlestown	13	9	4	Sellersburg	17	11	6
Chesterfield	7	6	1	Seymour	40	28	12
Chesterton	21	15	6	South Bend	311	244	67
Clarksville	41	33	8	Speedway	38	29	9
Clinton	15	10	5	Tell City	16	11	5
Connersville	34	33	1	Terre Haute	130	110	20
Corydon	7	7	—	Trail Creek	4	4	—
Crawfordsville	40	28	12	Union City	7	7	—
Crown Point	36	29	7	Valparaiso	55	40	15
Culver	6	4	2	Vincennes	37	31	6
Decatur	19	16	3	Wabash	31	25	6
Delphi	11	7	4	Warsaw	41	34	7
Dunkirk	8	4	4	West Lafayette	45	36	9
Dyer	25	19	6	West Terre Haute	5	5	—
East Chicago	141	113	28	Winchester	16	12	4
Elkhart	132	104	28				
Elwood	20	16	4	**IOWA**			
Evansville	293	266	27				
Fairmount	9	5	4	Adel	5	5	—
Fort Wayne	462	381	81	Albia	7	7	—
Fowler	3	3	—	Algona	13	9	4
Garrett	15	10	5	Altoona	16	15	1
Gas City	15	11	4	Ames	69	50	19
Georgetown	2	2	—	Anamosa	6	5	1
Goshen	46	41	5	Ankeny	32	26	6
Greendale	13	9	4	Atlantic	14	12	2
Greenfield	31	24	7	Audubon	3	3	—
Greenwood	62	46	16	Bedford	2	2	—
Griffith	36	28	8	Belle Plaine	3	3	—
Hagerstown	9	5	4	Belmond	4	4	—
Hammond	251	202	49	Bettendorf	50	39	11

Table 78.—Number of Full-time Law Enforcement Employees, Cities, October 31, 1995 — Continued

City	Total police employees	Total officers	Total civilians	City	Total police employees	Total officers	Total civilians
IOWA — Continued				**IOWA — Continued**			
Bloomfield	7	7	—	Newton	32	27	5
Boone	16	15	1	Norwalk	10	8	2
Burlington	60	42	18	Oelwein	14	10	4
Camanche	7	7	—	Onawa	5	5	—
Carlisle	5	5	—	Orange City	5	5	—
Carroll	20	13	7	Osage	6	6	—
Carter Lake	6	5	1	Osceola	9	8	1
Cedar Falls	47	44	3	Oskaloosa	20	18	2
Cedar Rapids	233	187	46	Ottumwa	39	34	5
Centerville	17	12	5	Palo	1	1	—
Chariton	8	7	1	Pella	14	12	2
Charles City	18	13	5	Perry	16	12	4
Cherokee	11	10	1	Pleasant Hill	9	9	—
Clarinda	15	10	5	Red Oak	14	10	4
Clarion	6	6	—	Rock Rapids	3	3	—
Clear Lake	18	13	5	Rock Valley	3	3	—
Clinton	53	44	9	Sac City	5	5	—
Clive	19	15	4	Sergeant Bluff	4	4	—
Coralville	26	24	2	Sheldon	10	6	4
Council Bluffs	104	92	12	Shenandoah	13	10	3
Cresco	7	7	—	Sioux Center	6	6	—
Creston	14	10	4	Sioux City	149	124	25
Davenport	192	153	39	Spencer	27	19	8
Decorah	17	12	5	Spirit Lake	7	6	1
Denison	16	12	4	Storm Lake	21	17	4
Des Moines	481	354	127	Story City	5	5	—
De Witt	6	6	—	Tama	5	5	—
Dubuque	87	81	6	Tipton	5	5	—
Dyersville	9	5	4	Urbandale	43	36	7
Eagle Grove	7	7	—	Vinton	7	7	—
Eldridge	6	6	—	Washington	10	10	—
Emmetsburg	6	5	1	Waterloo	140	123	17
Estherville	11	11	—	Waukee	7	6	1
Evansdale	8	7	1	Waukon	6	6	—
Fairfield	19	14	5	Waverly	14	13	1
Forest City	8	8	—	Webster City	21	15	6
Fort Dodge	44	40	4	West Burlington	9	8	1
Fort Madison	27	22	5	West Des Moines	61	48	13
Garner	5	5	—	West Union	5	5	—
Glenwood	13	11	2	Windsor Heights	12	11	1
Grinnell	15	14	1	Winterset	7	7	—
Grundy Center	4	4	—				
Guttenberg	6	4	2	**KANSAS**			
Hampton	12	7	5				
Harlan	9	8	1	Abilene	23	13	10
Hawarden	4	4	—	Andale	1	1	—
Hiawatha	7	7	—	Andover	14	9	5
Humboldt	7	7	—	Anthony	5	5	—
Independence	17	13	4	Argonia	1	1	—
Indianola	16	14	2	Arkansas City	31	24	7
Iowa City	74	65	9	Arma	4	4	—
Iowa Falls	15	11	4	Atchison	24	23	1
Jefferson	8	8	—	Attica	1	1	—
Johnston	10	9	1	Augusta	27	20	7
Keokuk	38	28	10	Baldwin City	7	6	1
Knoxville	15	11	4	Basehor	3	3	—
Lamoni	3	3	—	Baxter Springs	10	9	1
Le Claire	5	5	—	Belle Plaine	5	4	1
Le Mars	14	13	1	Belleville	5	5	—
Lenox	3	3	—	Beloit	12	9	3
Leon	4	4	—	Blue Rapids	1	1	—
Lisbon	1	1	—	Bonner Springs	22	18	4
Manchester	13	9	4	Buhler	3	3	—
Maquoketa	15	10	5	Burden	1	1	—
Marion	41	33	8	Burlingame	3	3	—
Marshalltown	46	40	6	Burlington	8	6	2
Mason City	56	40	16	Burrton	1	1	—
Missouri Valley	5	5	—	Bushton	1	1	—
Monticello	7	4	3	Caldwell	4	4	—
Mount Pleasant	15	13	2	Caney	9	5	4
Mount Vernon	5	5	—	Carbondale	2	2	—
Muscatine	42	34	8	Cawker City	1	1	—
Nevada	10	9	1	Cedar Vale	2	2	—
New Hampton	6	6	—	Chanute	22	19	3

Table 78.—Number of Full-time Law Enforcement Employees, Cities, October 31, 1995 — Continued

City	Total police employees	Total officers	Total civilians	City	Total police employees	Total officers	Total civilians
KANSAS — Continued				**KANSAS — Continued**			
Chapman	2	2	—	La Cygne	2	2	—
Chase	1	1	—	Lake Quivira	2	2	—
Cherokee	2	2	—	Lansing	11	10	1
Cherryvale	6	6	—	Larned	14	9	5
Chetopa	5	5	—	Lawrence	114	93	21
Cimarron	2	2	—	Leavenworth	73	56	17
Clay Center	6	5	1	Leawood	59	41	18
Clearwater	6	6	—	Lebo	2	2	—
Coffeyville	33	25	8	Lenexa	103	63	40
Colby	16	11	5	Le Roy	1	1	—
Columbus	8	7	1	Liberal	31	26	5
Colwich	2	2	—	Lindsborg	6	5	1
Concordia	16	10	6	Louisburg	6	6	—
Conway Springs	4	3	1	Lyndon	3	3	—
Council Grove	7	6	1	Lyons	7	6	1
Derby	36	27	9	Maize	5	4	1
Dodge City	50	37	13	Marion	3	3	—
Eastborough	7	7	—	Marquette	1	1	—
Edgerton	3	3	—	Marysville	7	6	1
Edwardsville	12	11	1	McLouth	1	1	—
El Dorado	29	24	5	McPherson	26	22	4
Elkhart	3	3	—	Meade	3	3	—
Ellinwood	5	5	—	Medicine Lodge	4	4	—
Ellis	4	4	—	Melvern	1	1	—
Ellsworth	6	6	—	Merriam	26	24	2
Elwood	2	2	—	Minneapolis	5	5	—
Emporia	53	44	9	Mission	23	21	2
Enterprise	1	1	—	Moundridge	3	3	—
Erie	3	3	—	Mound Valley	2	2	—
Eudora	4	4	—	Mount Hope	2	2	—
Fairway	7	6	1	Mulvane	16	11	5
Florence	2	2	—	Neodesha	8	7	1
Fort Scott	23	17	6	Newton	27	24	3
Fredonia	8	7	1	North Newton	1	1	—
Frontenac	10	6	4	Norton	6	5	1
Galena	12	8	4	Oakley	11	6	5
Garden City	83	56	27	Oberlin	4	4	—
Garden Plain	1	1	—	Olathe	128	98	30
Gardner	15	13	2	Osage City	6	6	—
Garnett	12	8	4	Osawatomie	13	8	5
Girard	4	4	—	Osborne	3	3	—
Goddard	3	3	—	Oswego	5	5	—
Goodland	14	8	6	Ottawa	27	21	6
Grandview Plaza	3	3	—	Overbrook	2	2	—
Great Bend	43	32	11	Overland Park	209	161	48
Halstead	5	5	—	Oxford	3	2	1
Harper	3	3	—	Paola	17	11	6
Hays	37	29	8	Park City	13	12	1
Haysville	27	17	10	Parsons	32	23	9
Herington	10	6	4	Pawnee Rock	1	1	—
Hiawatha	7	6	1	Peabody	2	2	—
Highland	4	4	—	Pittsburg	50	35	15
Hill City	4	4	—	Plainville	4	4	—
Hillsboro	4	4	—	Pleasanton	2	2	—
Hoisington	10	7	3	Prairie Village	49	40	9
Holcomb	5	4	1	Pratt	20	14	6
Holton	6	6	—	Quinter	1	1	—
Holyrood	1	1	—	Roeland Park	15	14	1
Hope	1	1	—	Rose Hill	5	5	—
Horton	9	5	4	Rossville	1	1	—
Hoxie	2	2	—	Russell	13	8	5
Hugoton	7	6	1	Sabetha	5	5	—
Humboldt	5	5	—	St. Francis	2	2	—
Hutchinson	97	67	30	St. George	1	1	—
Independence	28	20	8	St. John	3	3	—
Inman	2	2	—	St. Marys	4	4	—
Iola	25	18	7	Salina	94	72	22
Junction City	70	51	19	Scott City	12	7	5
Kanopolis	1	1	—	Scranton	3	2	1
Kansas City	468	356	112	Sedan	3	3	—
Kingman	10	6	4	Sedgwick	3	3	—
Kinsley	4	4	—	Seneca	5	5	—
Kiowa	2	2	—	Shawnee	82	66	16
La Crosse	3	3	—	Silver Lake	2	2	—

Table 78.—Number of Full-time Law Enforcement Employees, Cities, October 31, 1995 — Continued

City	Total police employees	Total officers	Total civilians		City	Total police employees	Total officers	Total civilians
KANSAS — Continued					**KENTUCKY— Continued**			
Smith Center	2	2	—		Devondale	3	3	—
South Hutchinson	7	6	1		Dixie Police Authority	11	9	2
Spearville	1	1	—		Dry Ridge	4	4	—
Spring Hill	5	5	—		Edgewood	10	10	—
Stafford	4	4	—		Edmonton	7	7	—
Sterling	5	5	—		Elizabethtown	44	33	11
Stockton	4	4	—		Elkton	6	6	—
Tonganoxie	5	5	—		Elsmere	10	9	1
Topeka	362	272	90		Eminence	6	6	—
Towanda	1	1	—		Erlanger	38	28	10
Udall	2	2	—		Evarts	2	2	—
Ulysses	9	9	—		Falmouth	16	10	6
Valley Center	7	6	1		Flatwoods	11	7	4
Valley Falls	2	2	—		Fleming-Neon	2	2	—
Wa Keeney	5	5	—		Flemingsburg	7	7	—
Wakefield	1	1	—		Florence	50	47	3
Wamego	11	6	5		Fort Mitchell	12	12	—
Waterville	1	1	—		Fort Thomas	22	21	1
Waverly	1	1	—		Fort Wright	9	9	—
Weir	2	2	—		Frankfort	57	51	6
Wellington	17	13	4		Franklin	26	19	7
Wellsville	4	4	—		Fulton	15	11	4
Westwood	8	7	1		Georgetown	48	36	12
Wichita	728	544	184		Glasgow	32	25	7
Wilson	1	1	—		Grayson	10	9	1
Winfield	26	21	5		Greensburg	9	5	4
Yates Center	4	3	1		Greenup	2	2	—
					Greenville	10	10	—
KENTUCKY					Guthrie	5	5	—
					Hardinsburg	3	3	—
Adairville	1	1	—		Harlan	15	11	4
Albany	8	5	3		Harrodsburg	26	17	9
Alexandria	8	8	—		Hartford	4	4	—
Anchorage	14	10	4		Hazard	29	23	6
Ashland	54	45	9		Henderson	61	54	7
Auburn	2	2	—		Hickman	12	8	4
Augusta	2	2	—		Highland Heights	8	8	—
Barbourville	15	12	3		Hillview	14	14	—
Bardstown	22	18	4		Hodgenville	11	8	3
Bardwell	2	2	—		Hopkinsville	57	50	7
Beattyville	5	5	—		Horse Cave	5	5	—
Beaver Dam	4	4	—		Independence	14	13	1
Bellevue	11	10	1		Indian Hills	5	5	—
Benham	1	1	—		Irvine	7	7	—
Benton	7	6	1		Irvington	3	3	—
Berea	25	19	6		Jackson	11	9	2
Bloomfield	3	2	1		Jamestown	5	5	—
Bowling Green	111	86	25		Jeffersontown	51	45	6
Brandenburg	4	4	—		Jenkins	4	4	—
Brooksville	2	2	—		Junction City	4	4	—
Brownsville	1	1	—		La Grange	9	8	1
Burkesville	7	4	3		Lakeside Park	7	6	1
Burnside	3	3	—		Lancaster	8	8	—
Butler	1	1	—		Land-between-the-Lakes	33	27	6
Cadiz	7	7	—		Lawrenceburg	19	15	4
Calvert City	5	4	1		Lebanon	20	13	7
Campbellsville	15	14	1		Lebanon Junction	4	4	—
Carlisle	8	5	3		Leitchfield	12	12	—
Carrollton	9	9	—		Lewisport	1	1	—
Catlettsburg	7	7	—		Lexington	541	407	134
Cave City	6	6	—		Liberty	5	5	—
Central City	8	8	—		Livermore	1	1	—
Clay City	3	3	—		London	20	19	1
Cloverport	3	3	—		Louisa	10	6	4
Cold Springs	6	6	—		Louisville	901	654	247
Columbia	8	8	—		Ludlow	8	8	—
Corbin	20	16	4		Lynch	3	2	1
Covington	127	106	21		Madisonville	58	47	11
Crittenden	1	1	—		Manchester	13	9	4
Cumberland	11	8	3		Marion	7	7	—
Cynthiana	19	15	4		Mayfield	36	29	7
Danville	31	26	5		Maysville	26	22	4
Dawson Springs	9	5	4		Middlesboro	25	21	4
Dayton	7	7	—		Millersburg	1	1	—

Table 78.—Number of Full-time Law Enforcement Employees, Cities, October 31, 1995 — Continued

City	Total police employees	Total officers	Total civilians	City	Total police employees	Total officers	Total civilians
KENTUCKY — Continued				KENTUCKY — Continued			
Monticello	12	8	4	Worthington	3	3	—
Morehead	24	17	7	Wurtland	1	1	—
Morganfield	15	9	6				
Morgantown	6	6	—	LOUISIANA			
Mount Sterling	20	15	5				
Mount Vernon	6	6	—	Abbeville	32	32	—
Mount Washington	8	8	—	Abita Springs	5	5	—
Muldraugh	2	2	—	Addis	4	4	—
Munfordville	2	2	—	Alexandria	170	139	31
Murray	33	27	6	Amite	19	19	—
New Castle	1	1	—	Arnaudville	5	5	—
Newport	51	43	8	Baker	32	31	1
Nicholasville	40	33	7	Baldwin	8	6	2
North Middletown	1	1	—	Bastrop	51	41	10
Oak Grove	10	7	3	Baton Rouge	788	672	116
Olive Hill	7	6	1	Bernice	5	5	—
Owensboro	113	97	16	Berwick	10	10	—
Owenton	3	3	—	Blanchard	3	3	—
Owingsville	6	4	2	Bogalusa	50	40	10
Paducah	82	76	6	Bossier City	176	127	49
Paintsville	17	11	6	Breaux Bridge	21	21	—
Paris	22	17	5	Brusly	5	5	—
Park Hills	4	4	—	Cheneyville	5	5	—
Perryville	1	1	—	Church Point	15	15	—
Pewee Valley	3	3	—	Clinton	4	4	—
Pikeville	21	16	5	Covington	35	28	7
Pineville	9	9	—	Crowley	32	30	2
Pioneer Village	3	3	—	Cullen	4	4	—
Prestonsburg	9	9	—	Delcambre	9	6	3
Princeton	14	13	1	Delhi	6	6	—
Prospect	7	7	—	Denham Springs	34	20	14
Raceland	5	5	—	De Ridder	25	24	1
Radcliff	44	30	14	Erath	10	10	—
Ravenna	2	2	—	Eunice	35	28	7
Richmond	52	42	10	Farmerville	12	12	—
Russell	13	13	—	Ferriday	19	18	1
Russell Springs	5	5	—	Franklin	24	22	2
Russellville	32	23	9	Franklinton	10	10	—
St. Matthews	33	27	6	Gibsland	2	1	1
Salyersville	5	4	1	Golden Meadow	6	5	1
Scottsville	15	11	4	Gonzales	29	29	—
Sebree	1	1	—	Gramercy	3	3	—
Shelbyville	19	18	1	Gretna	79	69	10
Shepherdsville	12	9	3	Gueydan	5	5	—
Shively	25	20	5	Hammond	78	78	—
Somerset	30	28	2	Harahan	24	24	—
Southgate	5	5	—	Harrisonburg	1	1	—
Springfield	7	7	—	Haynesville	6	6	—
Stamping Ground	2	2	—	Houma	73	59	14
Stanford	7	7	—	Iota	4	4	—
Stanton	6	6	—	Iowa	8	7	1
Sturgis	5	5	—	Jackson	3	3	—
Taylor Mill	8	7	1	Jeanerette	19	19	—
Taylorsville	3	3	—	Jena	5	5	—
Tompkinsville	7	7	—	Jennings	37	24	13
Uniontown	2	2	—	Jonesboro	15	14	1
Vanceburg	3	3	—	Kenner	173	132	41
Versailles	24	17	7	Kentwood	10	9	1
Villa Hills	9	8	1	Kinder	7	7	—
Vine Grove	6	5	1	Krotz Springs	7	4	3
Walton	4	4	—	Lafayette	270	208	62
Warsaw	4	4	—	Lake Charles	156	154	2
Wayland	1	1	—	Lake Providence	15	13	2
West Buechel	8	8	—	Lecompte	5	5	—
West Liberty	8	4	4	Leesville	28	28	—
West Point	5	3	2	Lockport	4	4	—
Wheelwright	1	1	—	Lutcher	3	3	—
Whitesburg	5	5	—	Mamou	17	17	—
Wilder	6	6	—	Mandeville	35	31	4
Williamsburg	8	7	1	Mansfield	17	17	—
Williamstown	10	4	6	Many	11	11	—
Wilmore	8	6	2	Marksville	11	11	—
Winchester	38	27	11	Minden	30	29	1
Wingo	2	1	1	Monroe	234	175	59

Table 78.—Number of Full-time Law Enforcement Employees, Cities, October 31, 1995 — Continued

City	Total police employees	Total officers	Total civilians	City	Total police employees	Total officers	Total civilians
LOUISIANA — Continued				**MAINE — Continued**			
Morgan City	51	41	10	Eastport	3	3	—
Natchitoches	53	39	14	Eliot	7	7	—
Newellton	2	2	—	Ellsworth	14	10	4
New Iberia	77	58	19	Fairfield	11	10	1
Newllano	8	8	—	Falmouth	18	13	5
New Orleans	1,656	1,372	284	Farmington	11	10	1
New Roads	22	17	5	Fort Fairfield	6	5	1
Oakdale	22	21	1	Fort Kent	8	4	4
Olla	4	4	—	Freeport	17	12	5
Opelousas	54	45	9	Fryeburg	4	4	—
Patterson	17	17	—	Gardiner	15	10	5
Pineville	42	35	7	Gorham	22	16	6
Plaquemine	32	29	3	Gouldsboro-Winter Harbor	1	1	—
Ponchatoula	16	15	1	Greenville	2	2	—
Port Allen	22	22	—	Hallowell	5	5	—
Rayne	23	19	4	Hampden	14	9	5
Rayville	9	9	—	Houlton	18	13	5
Richwood	5	4	1	Jay	11	7	4
Ruston	49	41	8	Kennebunk	21	16	5
St. Francisville	6	5	1	Kennebunkport	16	11	5
St. Joseph	3	3	—	Kittery	23	17	6
St. Martinville	20	14	6	Lewiston	96	79	17
Scott	13	12	1	Limestone	2	2	—
Shreveport	626	472	154	Lincoln	6	5	1
Simmesport	5	4	1	Lisbon	18	13	5
Slidell	94	63	31	Livermore Falls	11	6	5
Sorrento	2	2	—	Machias	3	3	—
Springhill	12	12	—	Madawaska	8	7	1
Sunset	12	12	—	Madison	7	6	1
Tallulah	18	18	—	Mechanic Falls	4	4	—
Thibodaux	52	43	9	Medway	2	2	—
Vidalia	20	19	1	Mexico	4	4	—
Ville Platte	29	29	—	Millinocket	16	12	4
Vinton	13	13	—	Milo	3	3	—
Vivian	16	16	—	Monmouth	2	2	—
Washington	5	5	—	Mount Desert	8	4	4
Welsh	10	10	—	Newport	4	4	—
Westlake	18	14	4	North Berwick	8	7	1
West Monroe	65	62	3	Norway	8	7	1
Westwego	20	19	1	Oakland	8	7	1
Winnfield	21	17	4	Ogunquit	12	7	5
Zachary	26	24	2	Old Orchard Beach	21	16	5
				Old Town	17	13	4
MAINE				Orono	18	13	5
				Oxford	5	4	1
Ashland	3	3	—	Paris	8	7	1
Auburn	53	45	8	Phippsburg	1	1	—
Augusta	52	39	13	Pittsfield	5	5	—
Baileyville	5	5	—	Portland	195	150	45
Bangor	77	63	14	Presque Isle	23	18	5
Bar Harbor	13	9	4	Richmond	4	4	—
Bath	23	16	7	Rockland	24	17	7
Belfast	15	11	4	Rockport	4	4	—
Berwick	11	10	1	Rumford	16	15	1
Bethel	3	3	—	Sabattus	7	6	1
Biddeford	53	41	12	Saco	32	26	6
Boothbay Harbor	7	6	1	Sanford	49	33	16
Brewer	20	15	5	Scarborough	39	26	13
Bridgton	12	8	4	Searsport	3	3	—
Brownville	2	2	—	Skowhegan	17	12	5
Brunswick	39	30	9	South Berwick	10	6	4
Bucksport	9	7	2	South Portland	57	52	5
Buxton	10	6	4	Southwest Harbor	9	5	4
Calais	12	8	4	Thomaston	8	5	3
Camden	14	9	5	Topsham	15	11	4
Cape Elizabeth	17	12	5	Van Buren	7	4	3
Caribou	15	14	1	Veazie	2	2	—
Carrabassett Valley	2	1	1	Waldoboro	5	4	1
Cumberland	15	10	5	Washburn	1	1	—
Damariscotta	2	2	—	Waterville	38	30	8
Dexter	6	5	1	Wells	22	21	1
Dixfield	4	4	—	Westbrook	36	30	6
Dover-Foxcroft	5	5	—	Wilton	5	5	—
East Millinocket	4	4	—	Windham	24	20	4

Table 78.—Number of Full-time Law Enforcement Employees, Cities, October 31, 1995 — Continued

City	Total police employees	Total officers	Total civilians	City	Total police employees	Total officers	Total civilians
MAINE — Continued				**MARYLAND — Continued**			
Winslow	7	6	1	University Park	8	8	—
Winthrop	13	9	4	Westernport	3	3	—
Wiscasset	8	7	1	Westminster	43	35	8
Yarmouth	15	10	5				
York	25	18	7	**MASSACHUSETTS**			
				Abington	26	25	1
MARYLAND				Acton	34	29	5
				Acushnet	15	13	2
Aberdeen	43	34	9	Adams	23	18	5
Annapolis	144	116	28	Agawam	53	47	6
Baltimore	3,662	3,110	552	Amesbury	38	30	8
Baltimore City Sheriff	116	111	5	Amherst	51	41	10
Bel Air	40	29	11	Andover	61	46	15
Berlin	18	13	5	Arlington	70	63	7
Berwyn Heights	5	5	—	Ashburnham	6	6	—
Bladensburg	23	15	8	Ashby	4	3	1
Brunswick	10	8	2	Ashfield	2	2	—
Cambridge	54	40	14	Ashland	20	19	1
Capitol Heights	8	7	1	Athol	23	19	4
Centreville	7	7	—	Attleboro	73	65	8
Cheasapeake City	1	1	—	Auburn	31	25	6
Chestertown	11	10	1	Avon	14	11	3
Cheverly	13	11	2	Ayer	21	16	5
Cottage City	4	4	—	Barnstable	100	91	9
Crisfield	10	7	3	Barre	8	5	3
Cumberland	67	60	7	Bedford	26	25	1
Delmar	12	11	1	Belchertown	20	15	5
Denton	12	11	1	Bellingham	29	24	5
District Heights	8	8	—	Belmont	50	47	3
Easton	52	40	12	Berkley	2	2	—
Edmonston	6	6	—	Berlin	7	4	3
Elkton	33	26	7	Bernardston	3	2	1
Federalsburg	10	9	1	Beverly	70	67	3
Forest Heights	5	5	—	Billerica	69	64	5
Frederick	103	81	22	Blackstone	16	13	3
Frostburg	18	14	4	Bolton	11	7	4
Fruitland	11	10	1	Boston	2,854	2,093	761
Glenarden	10	9	1	Bourne	37	30	7
Greenbelt	63	47	16	Boxboro	6	6	—
Greensboro	3	3	—	Boxford	12	12	—
Hagerstown	116	88	28	Boylston	9	8	1
Hampstead	3	3	—	Braintree	88	79	9
Hancock	4	3	1	Brewster	21	16	5
Havre de Grace	35	26	9	Bridgewater	33	31	2
Hurlock	7	7	—	Brockton	192	167	25
Hyattsville	35	25	10	Brookfield	1	1	—
Landover Hills	4	4	—	Brookline	149	136	13
La Plata	9	9	—	Buckland	2	2	—
Laurel	64	47	17	Burlington	59	56	3
Luke	2	2	—	Cambridge	318	266	52
Manchester	3	3	—	Canton	41	39	2
Morningside	4	3	1	Carlisle	9	9	—
Mount Rainier	21	14	7	Carver	18	13	5
North East	7	6	1	Charlton	16	12	4
Oakland	6	5	1	Chatham	22	21	1
Ocean City	108	91	17	Chelmsford	67	53	14
Ocean Pines	16	11	5	Chelsea	96	82	14
Oxford	3	3	—	Chicopee	114	111	3
Pocomoke City	17	13	4	Clinton	27	26	1
Preston	3	3	—	Cohasset	22	19	3
Princess Anne	7	7	—	Concord	39	33	6
Ridgely	4	4	—	Dalton	9	8	1
Rising Sun	5	4	1	Danvers	58	44	14
Riverdale	18	13	5	Dartmouth	71	60	11
Rock Hall	4	4	—	Dedham	63	59	4
St. Michaels	7	7	—	Deerfield	7	6	1
Salisbury	107	83	24	Dennis	43	34	9
Seat Pleasant	8	7	1	Dighton	13	10	3
Smithsburg	2	2	—	Douglas	11	8	3
Snow Hill	8	8	—	Dover	17	16	1
Sykesville	7	6	1	Dracut	39	35	4
Takoma Park	51	41	10	Dudley	17	13	4
Taneytown	8	8	—	Dunstable	3	3	—
Thurmont	7	7	—				

Table 78.—Number of Full-time Law Enforcement Employees, Cities, October 31, 1995 — Continued

City	Total police employees	Total officers	Total civilians	City	Total police employees	Total officers	Total civilians
MASSACHUSETTS — Continued				**MASSACHUSETTS — Continued**			
Duxbury	33	31	2	Marion	12	10	2
East Bridgewater	22	21	1	Marlborough	67	59	8
East Brookfield	3	3	—	Marshfield	43	40	3
Eastham	22	16	6	Mashpee	31	25	6
Easthampton	27	26	1	Mattapoisett	17	17	—
East Longmeadow	24	22	2	Maynard	24	22	2
Easton	34	31	3	Medfield	25	20	5
Edgartown	11	10	1	Medford	116	111	5
Essex	8	7	1	Medway	17	16	1
Everett	99	88	11	Melrose	50	47	3
Fairhaven	31	27	4	Mendon	5	4	1
Fall River	292	248	44	Merrimac	9	5	4
Falmouth	69	61	8	Methuen	85	72	13
Fitchburg	102	86	16	Middleboro	36	31	5
Foxboro	28	27	1	Middleton	12	11	1
Framingham	117	106	11	Milford	48	47	1
Franklin	43	36	7	Millbury	20	15	5
Freetown	18	14	4	Millis	17	13	4
Gardner	37	33	4	Millville	3	3	—
Gay Head	4	4	—	Milton	69	57	12
Georgetown	13	10	3	Monson	15	11	4
Gill	1	1	—	Montague	17	16	1
Gloucester	67	60	7	Nahant	14	12	2
Grafton	22	17	5	Nantucket	30	25	5
Granby	11	9	2	Natick	65	52	13
Great Barrington	15	15	—	Needham	53	47	6
Greenfield	41	36	5	New Bedford	305	275	30
Groton	20	13	7	Newbury	11	9	2
Groveland	13	8	5	Newburyport	37	35	2
Hadley	9	7	2	Newton	190	170	20
Halifax	13	9	4	Norfolk	18	17	1
Hamilton	18	14	4	North Adams	35	30	5
Hampden	12	9	3	Northampton	67	60	7
Hanover	29	27	2	North Andover	44	32	12
Hanson	21	17	4	North Attleboro	48	38	10
Hardwick	2	2	—	Northborough	24	18	6
Harvard	11	7	4	Northbridge	23	16	7
Harwich	34	28	6	North Brookfield	6	6	—
Hatfield	2	2	—	Northfield	4	3	1
Haverhill	93	86	7	North Reading	26	25	1
Hingham	54	44	10	Norton	22	20	2
Holbrook	19	18	1	Norwell	22	21	1
Holden	22	17	5	Norwood	70	61	9
Holliston	20	20	—	Oak Bluffs	12	11	1
Holyoke	133	119	14	Oakham	1	1	—
Hopedale	10	9	1	Orange	11	11	—
Hopkinton	20	15	5	Orleans	27	21	6
Hubbardston	6	3	3	Oxford	21	16	5
Hudson	34	28	6	Palmer	21	16	5
Hull	30	25	5	Paxton	8	7	1
Huntington	1	1	—	Peabody	95	88	7
Ipswich	24	23	1	Pelham	1	1	—
Kingston	30	20	10	Pembroke	27	25	2
Lakeville	18	14	4	Pepperell	16	15	1
Lancaster	6	6	—	Petersham	3	2	1
Lanesboro	4	4	—	Phillipston	1	1	—
Lawrence	135	128	7	Pittsfield	99	84	15
Lee	11	11	—	Plainville	17	13	4
Leicester	17	14	3	Plymouth	100	87	13
Lenox	10	10	—	Plympton	7	5	2
Leominster	77	73	4	Princeton	7	4	3
Lexington	61	49	12	Provincetown	23	18	5
Lincoln	17	12	5	Quincy	226	195	31
Littleton	19	13	6	Randolph	54	52	2
Longmeadow	32	31	1	Raynham	26	21	5
Lowell	267	219	48	Reading	46	38	8
Ludlow	31	30	1	Rehoboth	24	19	5
Lunenburg	11	11	—	Revere	126	103	23
Lynn	200	179	21	Rochester	8	8	—
Lynnfield	25	19	6	Rockland	32	30	2
Malden	105	99	6	Rockport	16	15	1
Manchester	16	13	3	Rowley	10	9	1
Mansfield	35	30	5	Rutland	2	2	—
Marblehead	39	35	4	Salem	97	88	9

Table 78.—Number of Full-time Law Enforcement Employees, Cities, October 31, 1995 — Continued

City	Total police employees	Total officers	Total civilians	City	Total police employees	Total officers	Total civilians
MASSACHUSETTS — Continued				**MASSACHUSETTS — Continued**			
Salisbury	23	17	6	Woburn	81	74	7
Sandwich	33	32	1	Worcester	479	425	54
Saugus	58	56	2	Wrentham	15	14	1
Scituate	36	29	7	Yarmouth	54	45	9
Seekonk	36	31	5				
Sharon	29	25	4	**MICHIGAN**			
Shelburne	2	2	—				
Sherborn	15	15	—	Adrian	37	30	7
Shirley	14	9	5	Albion	35	28	7
Shrewsbury	40	32	8	Algonac	6	5	1
Somerset	38	30	8	Allegan	12	10	2
Somerville	135	127	8	Allen Park	58	52	6
Southampton	13	7	6	Alma	14	13	1
Southborough	17	13	4	Almont	5	5	—
Southbridge	32	31	1	Alpena	18	17	1
South Hadley	30	25	5	Ann Arbor	221	171	50
Southwick	19	14	5	Argentine Township	5	5	—
Spencer	8	5	3	Armada	3	3	—
Springfield	592	499	93	Atlas Township	2	2	—
Sterling	15	10	5	Auburn	3	2	1
Stockbridge	6	6	—	Auburn Hills	47	37	10
Stoneham	45	35	10	Bad Axe	7	7	—
Stoughton	57	54	3	Bancroft	1	1	—
Stow	16	12	4	Bangor	4	4	—
Sturbridge	18	13	5	Baraga	4	4	—
Sudbury	31	25	6	Barry Township	2	2	—
Sunderland	2	1	1	Bath Township	7	6	1
Sutton	10	10	—	Battle Creek	164	120	44
Swampscott	37	35	2	Bay City	82	76	6
Swansea	36	27	9	Belding	10	9	1
Taunton	103	98	5	Bellaire	2	2	—
Templeton	7	7	—	Belleville	10	8	2
Tewksbury	58	51	7	Bellevue	3	3	—
Tisbury	15	12	3	Benton Harbor	34	26	8
Topsfield	11	7	4	Benton Township	32	24	8
Townsend	15	14	1	Berkley	34	30	4
Truro	16	11	5	Berrien Springs-Oronoko Township	7	6	1
Tyngsboro	22	18	4	Beverly Hills	28	24	4
Upton	12	9	3	Big Rapids	18	17	1
Uxbridge	19	15	4	Birch Run	5	4	1
Wakefield	48	46	2	Birmingham	54	35	19
Walpole	40	36	4	Blackman Township	26	25	1
Waltham	145	129	16	Blissfield	5	4	1
Ware	15	15	—	Bloomfield Hills	27	23	4
Wareham	48	42	6	Bloomfield Township	87	68	19
Warren	9	6	3	Bloomingdale	1	1	—
Watertown	74	63	11	Boyne City	11	8	3
Wayland	32	23	9	Breckenridge	3	3	—
Webster	27	22	5	Bridgeport Township	7	6	1
Wellesley	58	45	13	Bridgman	4	4	—
Wellfleet	15	10	5	Brighton	14	13	1
Wenham	11	10	1	Bronson	5	5	—
Westborough	31	26	5	Brown City	1	1	—
West Boylston	13	12	1	Brownstown Township	43	35	8
West Bridgewater	21	20	1	Buchanan	11	10	1
West Brookfield	6	6	—	Buena Vista Township	19	17	2
Westfield	73	68	5	Burr Oak	1	1	—
Westford	35	28	7	Burton	40	36	4
Westhampton	1	1	—	Cadillac	20	18	2
Westminster	13	9	4	Calumet	2	2	—
West Newbury	17	8	9	Cambridge Township	2	2	—
Weston	29	25	4	Camp Grayling	1	1	—
Westport	29	24	5	Canton Township	83	63	20
West Springfield	78	68	10	Capac	6	4	2
West Tisbury	6	6	—	Carleton	4	3	1
Westwood	32	27	5	Caro	9	8	1
Weymouth	105	93	12	Carrollton Township	7	6	1
Whitman	23	22	1	Carson City	2	2	—
Wilbraham	27	26	1	Carsonville	1	1	—
Williamstown	11	8	3	Caseville	2	2	—
Wilmington	43	41	2	Cass City	3	3	—
Winchendon	11	10	1	Cassopolis	6	5	1
Winchester	44	37	7	Cedar Springs	7	7	—
Winthrop	35	34	1	Center Line	31	25	6

Table 78.—Number of Full-time Law Enforcement Employees, Cities, October 31, 1995 — Continued

City	Total police employees	Total officers	Total civilians	City	Total police employees	Total officers	Total civilians
MICHIGAN — Continued				**MICHIGAN — Continued**			
Centreville	1	1	—	Fowlerville	6	6	—
Charleston Township	1	1	—	Frankenmuth	6	6	—
Charlevoix	7	7	—	Frankfort	5	5	—
Charlotte	18	17	1	Franklin	11	10	1
Cheboygan	9	9	—	Fraser	54	44	10
Chelsea	10	7	3	Fremont	8	7	1
Chesterfield Township	26	21	5	Frost Township	2	1	1
Chikaming Township	3	3	—	Gaines	1	1	—
Chocolay Township	4	3	1	Galesburg	2	2	—
Clare	7	6	1	Garden City	50	39	11
Clarkston	1	1	—	Gaylord	10	8	2
Clawson	26	23	3	Genesee Township	17	15	2
Clay-Algonac	16	12	4	Gerrish Township	4	4	—
Clinton	3	3	—	Gibraltar	15	14	1
Clinton Township	117	87	30	Gladstone	13	12	1
Clio	1	—	1	Gladwin	3	3	—
Coldwater	17	15	2	Gobles	1	1	—
Coleman	2	2	—	Grand Beach	2	2	—
Coloma	5	4	1	Grand Blanc	20	16	4
Coloma Township	5	5	—	Grand Blanc Township	30	26	4
Colon	3	3	—	Grand Haven	37	33	4
Columbia Township	4	3	1	Grand Ledge	16	15	1
Concord Township	3	3	—	Grand Rapids	377	303	74
Constantine	5	5	—	Grandville	22	19	3
Coopersville	7	6	1	Grayling	7	6	1
Corunna	5	5	—	Green Oak Township	13	11	2
Covert Township	7	7	—	Greenville	27	18	9
Croswell	6	6	—	Grosse Ile Township	21	16	5
Crystal Falls	5	5	—	Grosse Pointe	29	25	4
Crystal Township	1	1	—	Grosse Pointe Farms	40	32	8
Davison	10	8	2	Grosse Pointe Park	46	43	3
Davison Township	12	10	2	Grosse Pointe Shores	19	17	2
Dearborn	223	200	23	Grosse Pointe Woods	44	42	2
Dearborn Heights	107	90	17	Hamburg Township	11	10	1
Decatur	4	4	—	Hampton Township	12	11	1
Deckerville	1	1	—	Hamtramck	53	53	—
Denmark Township	1	1	—	Hancock	7	6	1
Denton Township	3	3	—	Harbor Beach	4	4	—
Detour Village	1	1	—	Harbor Springs	6	5	1
Detroit	4,337	3,819	518	Harper Woods	41	36	5
De Witt	8	7	1	Hart	4	4	—
De Witt Township	13	12	1	Hartford	5	5	—
Douglas	4	4	—	Hastings	18	16	2
Dowagiac	15	14	1	Hazel Park	44	37	7
Dryden Township	2	2	—	Hesperia	5	4	1
Durand	5	5	—	Highland Park	85	70	15
East Grand Rapids	33	30	3	Hillsdale	20	15	5
East Jordan	5	5	—	Holland	72	61	11
East Lansing	87	59	28	Holly	15	9	6
East Pointe	59	53	6	Homer	3	3	—
East Tawas	4	4	—	Houghton	9	9	—
Eaton Rapids	9	8	1	Howard City	1	1	—
Eau Claire	1	1	—	Howard Township	3	3	—
Ecorse	38	32	6	Howell	18	16	2
Edmore-Home	3	3	—	Hudson	4	3	1
Elk Rapids	3	3	—	Hudsonville	8	7	1
Elkton	2	2	—	Huntington Woods	16	15	1
Elsie	1	1	—	Huron Township	15	12	3
Emmett Township	8	7	1	Imlay City	8	7	1
Erie Township	2	2	—	Inkster	71	52	19
Escanaba	43	35	8	Ionia	17	16	1
Essexville	8	8	—	Iron Mountain	12	12	—
Evart	3	3	—	Iron River	5	5	—
Fairhaven Township	1	1	—	Ironwood	20	16	4
Farmington	28	22	6	Ishpeming	13	12	1
Farmington Hills	146	102	44	Ishpeming Township	1	1	—
Fenton	18	13	5	Ithaca	4	4	—
Ferndale	62	52	10	Jackson	85	65	20
Flat Rock	24	22	2	Jonesville	4	4	—
Flint	361	307	54	Kalamazoo	330	250	80
Flint Township	38	35	3	Kalamazoo Township	35	28	7
Flushing	12	11	1	Kalkaska	6	5	1
Flushing Township	7	6	1	Keego Harbor	6	5	1
Forsyth Township	6	6	—	Kentwood	56	50	6

Table 78.—Number of Full-time Law Enforcement Employees, Cities, October 31, 1995 — Continued

City	Total police employees	Total officers	Total civilians	City	Total police employees	Total officers	Total civilians
MICHIGAN — Continued				**MICHIGAN — Continued**			
Kingsford	18	18	—	Muskegon Township	12	11	1
Kinross Township	2	2	—	Napolean Township	3	3	—
Laingsburg	2	2	—	Nashville	1	1	—
Lake Angelus	2	2	—	Negaunee	14	13	1
Lake Linden	2	2	—	Newaygo	2	2	—
Lake Odessa	3	3	—	New Baltimore	12	11	1
Lake Orion	7	4	3	Newberry	4	4	—
Lakeview	2	2	—	New Buffalo	6	6	—
L'Anse	5	5	—	New Haven	4	4	—
Lansing	339	250	89	New Lothrup	1	1	—
Lansing Township	16	15	1	Niles	28	22	6
Lapeer	20	17	3	Niles Township	7	7	—
Lathrup Village	11	8	3	North Branch	1	1	—
Laurium	4	4	—	Northfield Township	8	7	1
Lawrence	2	2	—	North Muskegon	7	6	1
Lawton	5	5	—	Northville	17	15	2
Lennon	1	1	—	Northville Township	25	20	5
Leoni Township	5	4	1	Norton Shores	27	25	2
Leslie	4	4	—	Norvell Township	2	2	—
Lexington	3	3	—	Norway	6	6	—
Lincoln Township	13	11	2	Novi	77	52	25
Lincoln Park	60	60	—	Oak Park	75	69	6
Linden	4	4	—	Olivet	2	2	—
Litchfield	5	5	—	Onaway	2	2	—
Livonia	190	161	29	Ontonagon	1	1	—
Lowell	7	6	1	Ontwa Township-Edwardsburg	8	7	1
Ludington	15	14	1	Orchard Lake	9	8	1
Luna Pier	4	4	—	Oscoda Township	10	10	—
Mackinac Island	6	5	1	Otisville	1	1	—
Mackinac City	5	5	—	Otsego	8	7	1
Madison Heights	77	60	17	Ovid	3	3	—
Madison Township	1	1	—	Owosso	22	20	2
Mancelona	4	4	—	Oxford	18	13	5
Manchester Township	1	1	—	Parchment	5	4	1
Manistee	16	15	1	Parma	2	2	—
Manistique	10	9	1	Paw Paw	10	8	2
Manton	2	2	—	Peck	1	1	—
Maple Rapids	1	1	—	Pennfield Township	7	6	1
Marcellus	4	4	—	Pentwater	2	2	—
Marenisco Township	1	1	—	Perry	5	5	—
Marine City	9	8	1	Petoskey	17	13	4
Marion	1	1	—	Pierson Township	2	1	1
Marlette	3	3	—	Pigeon	1	1	—
Marquette	42	35	7	Pinckney	5	4	1
Marshall	19	14	5	Pinconning	2	2	—
Marysville	15	13	2	Pittsfield Township	32	24	8
Mason	10	9	1	Plainwell	7	6	1
Mattawan	4	4	—	Pleasant Ridge	8	7	1
Mayville	1	1	—	Plymouth	19	15	4
Melvindale	27	25	2	Plymouth Township	30	22	8
Memphis	2	2	—	Pontiac	184	145	39
Menominee	22	17	5	Portage	64	51	13
Meridian Township	43	38	5	Port Austin	1	1	—
Metamora Township	2	2	—	Port Huron	74	53	21
Michiana	2	2	—	Portland	6	6	—
Middleville	3	3	—	Port Sanilac	2	2	—
Midland	52	48	4	Potterville	3	3	—
Midland Township	2	2	—	Prairieville Township	1	1	—
Milan	13	9	4	Quincy	3	3	—
Milford	18	12	6	Redford Township	86	71	15
Millington	3	3	—	Reed City	5	5	—
Monroe	50	44	6	Reese	2	2	—
Montague	5	5	—	Republic Township	1	1	—
Montrose Township	10	8	2	Richfield Township (Roscommon County)	3	3	—
Morenci	3	3	—	Richfield Township (Genesee County)	8	7	1
Morrice	2	2	—	Richland	1	1	—
Mount Clemens	36	29	7	Richland Township	4	4	—
Mount Morris	7	6	1	Richmond	9	6	3
Mount Morris Township	36	33	3	Richmond Township	4	1	3
Mount Pleasant	28	24	4	River Rouge	41	37	4
Mundy Township	14	12	2	Riverview	31	27	4
Munising	5	5	—	Rochester	21	15	6
Muskegon	94	84	10	Rockford	12	9	3
Muskegon Heights	31	28	3	Rockwood	9	9	—

Table 78.—Number of Full-time Law Enforcement Employees, Cities, October 31, 1995 — Continued

City	Total police employees	Total officers	Total civilians	City	Total police employees	Total officers	Total civilians
MICHIGAN — Continued				**MICHIGAN — Continued**			
Rogers City	7	7	—	Watervliet	5	5	—
Romeo	9	6	3	Wayland	4	3	1
Romulus	66	56	10	Wayne	51	36	15
Roosevelt Park	7	6	1	Webberville	3	2	1
Roscommon Township	1	1	—	West Bloomfield Township	84	62	22
Rose City	1	1	—	West Branch	5	4	1
Roseville	97	84	13	Westland	122	101	21
Ross Township	2	2	—	Whitehall	6	6	—
Royal Oak	113	95	18	White Lake Township	29	21	8
Royal Oak Township	11	7	4	White Pigeon	4	4	—
Saginaw	163	147	16	Williamston	5	5	—
Saginaw Township	47	44	3	Wixom	19	16	3
St. Charles	4	4	—	Wolverine Lake	8	7	1
St. Clair	11	10	1	Woodhaven	31	28	3
St. Clair Shores	101	83	18	Woodstock Township	1	1	—
St. Ignace	6	6	—	Wyandotte	60	47	13
St. Johns	14	12	2	Wyoming	111	83	28
St. Joseph	25	20	5	Yale	3	3	—
St. Joseph Township	10	9	1	Ypsilanti	50	42	8
St. Louis	6	5	1	Zeeland	10	9	1
Saline	18	13	5	Zilwaukee	3	3	—
Sand Lake	2	1	1				
Sandusky	6	6	—	**MINNESOTA**			
Saugatuck	4	3	1				
Sault Ste. Marie	32	24	8	Albert Lea	37	28	9
Schoolcraft	4	3	1	Alexandria	18	15	3
Scottville	2	2	—	Anoka	36	28	8
Sebewaing	4	4	—	Apple Valley	54	37	17
Shelby	3	3	—	Austin	30	27	3
Shelby Township	63	49	14	Babbitt	4	4	—
Shepherd	2	2	—	Baxter	7	6	1
Somerset Township	1	1	—	Bayport	5	5	—
Southfield	205	159	46	Belle Plaine	6	5	1
Southgate	48	42	6	Bemidji	26	20	6
South Haven	25	19	6	Benson	6	5	1
South Lyon	13	11	2	Big Lake	5	4	1
South Rockwood	2	2	—	Blaine	47	39	8
Sparta	9	8	1	Blooming Prairie	3	3	—
Spaulding Township	1	1	—	Bloomington	131	102	29
Spring Arbor Township	2	2	—	Blue Earth	6	6	—
Springfield	14	13	1	Brainerd	24	20	4
Spring Lake-Ferrysburg	11	11	—	Breckenridge	11	7	4
Stanton	1	1	—	Brooklyn Center	59	44	15
Sterling Heights	208	151	57	Brooklyn Park	81	66	15
Sturgis	19	17	2	Buffalo	10	9	1
Summit Township	4	4	—	Burnsville	75	60	15
Sumpter Township	11	10	1	Caledonia	5	4	1
Sunfield	1	1	—	Cambridge	10	9	1
Swartz Creek	8	7	1	Canby	2	2	—
Sylvan Lake	5	5	—	Cannon Falls	5	4	1
Taylor	121	101	20	Champlin	20	19	1
Tecumseh	16	15	1	Chanhassen	4	2	2
Thomas Township	3	3	—	Chaska	18	15	3
Three Oaks	4	4	—	Chisholm	11	10	1
Three Rivers	18	15	3	Circle Pines–Lexington	15	12	3
Tittabawassee Township	3	3	—	Colquet	17	16	1
Traverse City	33	32	1	Cold Spring	4	4	—
Trenton	50	47	3	Columbia Heights	33	26	7
Troy	179	130	49	Coon Rapids	64	55	9
Tuscarora Township	5	5	—	Corcoran	3	3	—
Twin City	3	3	—	Cottage Grove	43	33	10
Ubly	2	2	—	Crookston	17	15	2
Unadilla Township	1	1	—	Crosby	10	6	4
Union City	4	3	1	Crystal	39	26	13
Unionville	2	2	—	Dawson	3	3	—
Utica	17	13	4	Dayton	3	3	—
Van Buren Township	24	18	6	Deephaven	8	7	1
Vassar	4	4	—	Detroit Lakes	14	12	2
Vicksburg	5	4	1	Dilworth	5	5	—
Walker	38	31	7	Duluth	157	132	25
Walled Lake	18	13	5	Eagan	79	55	24
Warren	280	237	43	East Grand Forks	22	21	1
Waterford Township	99	80	19	Eden Prairie	68	47	21
Watertown Township	1	1	—	Edina	62	49	13

Table 78.—Number of Full-time Law Enforcement Employees, Cities, October 31, 1995 — Continued

City	Total police employees	Total officers	Total civilians	City	Total police employees	Total officers	Total civilians
MINNESOTA — Continued				**MINNESOTA — Continued**			
Elk River	25	19	6	Proctor	6	5	1
Ely	8	7	1	Ramsey	15	13	2
Eveleth	10	9	1	Red Wing	28	25	3
Fairmont	19	16	3	Redwood Falls	9	8	1
Faribault	37	26	11	Richfield	54	43	11
Farmington	9	8	1	Robbinsdale	24	19	5
Fergus Falls	23	19	4	Rochester	136	102	34
Forest Lake	12	11	1	Roseau	4	4	—
Fridley	47	35	12	Rosemount	16	14	2
Gilbert	6	6	—	Roseville	47	41	6
Glencoe	9	8	1	St. Anthony	20	18	2
Glenwood	3	3	—	St. Bonifacius-Minnetrista	11	9	2
Golden Valley	40	30	10	St. Cloud	81	66	15
Goodview	4	4	—	St. James	7	6	1
Grand Rapids	16	11	5	St. Joseph	6	6	—
Granite Falls	5	5	—	St. Louis Park	68	50	18
Hastings	24	21	3	St. Paul	648	515	133
Hermantown	10	9	1	St. Paul Park	7	7	—
Hibbing	31	28	3	St. Peter	18	12	6
Hoyt Lakes	5	5	—	Sartell	9	8	1
Hutchinson	25	19	6	Sauk Centre	9	6	3
International Falls	13	13	—	Sauk Rapids	11	10	1
Inver Grove Heights	31	25	6	Savage	21	18	3
Jackson	6	6	—	Shakopee	24	21	3
Jordan	4	4	—	Silver Bay	4	4	—
Kasson	6	6	—	Slayton	3	3	—
Kenyon	3	3	—	Sleepy Eye	5	5	—
La Crescent	6	5	1	South Lake Minnetonka	15	14	1
Lake City	8	7	1	South St. Paul	26	25	1
Lakefield	3	3	—	Springfield	3	3	—
Lakeville	46	34	12	Spring Lake Park	12	10	2
Le Sueur	10	6	4	Staples	6	6	—
Lino Lakes	17	14	3	Stillwater	21	17	4
Litchfield	10	9	1	Thief River Falls	17	16	1
Little Falls	12	10	2	Tracy	4	4	—
Long Prairie	5	5	—	Two Harbors	7	6	1
Luverne	6	6	—	Virginia	24	23	1
Madison	4	4	—	Wadena	9	8	1
Mankato	47	40	7	Waite Park	9	8	1
Maple Grove	50	41	9	Warroad	5	4	1
Maplewood	55	42	13	Waseca	12	10	2
Marshall	22	18	4	Wayzata	10	8	2
Medina	7	6	1	Wells	4	4	—
Melrose	4	4	—	West Hennepin	10	8	2
Mendota Heights	18	16	2	West St. Paul	37	25	12
Minneapolis	1,045	860	185	White Bear Lake	36	29	7
Minnetonka	61	48	13	Willmar	34	29	5
Montevideo	9	8	1	Windom	8	7	1
Moorhead	63	48	15	Winona	40	37	3
Mora	7	6	1	Woodbury	34	31	3
Morris	8	7	1	Worthington	24	17	7
Mound	13	12	1				
Mounds View	16	15	1	**MISSISSIPPI**			
Mountain Iron	6	6	—				
New Brighton	24	22	2	Aberdeen	21	16	5
New Hope	36	27	9	Ackerman	5	5	—
Newport	8	8	—	Amory	22	17	5
New Prague	9	7	2	Baldwyn	13	9	4
New Ulm	20	18	2	Batesville	33	23	10
Northfield	21	16	5	Bay St. Louis	30	25	5
North Mankato	10	9	1	Belzoni	12	7	5
Oakdale	29	24	5	Booneville	26	21	5
Oak Park Heights	9	8	1	Brandon	26	18	8
Olivia	4	4	—	Calhoun City	6	6	—
Orono	17	15	2	Clarksdale	53	40	13
Ortonville	5	4	1	Cleveland	40	34	6
Osseo	4	4	—	Collins	13	9	4
Owatonna	28	26	2	Columbus	73	63	10
Park Rapids	6	6	—	Corinth	40	31	9
Pipestone	6	6	—	Edwards	4	4	—
Plainview	4	4	—	Flowood	24	18	6
Plymouth	71	55	16	Fulton	9	9	—
Princeton	8	7	1	Goodman	2	2	—
Prior Lake	20	18	2	Greenville	143	99	44

City	Total police employees	Total officers	Total civilians	City	Total police employees	Total officers	Total civilians
MISSISSIPPI — Continued				**MISSOURI — Continued**			
Greenwood	68	49	19	Charlack	11	10	1
Grenada	48	36	12	Charleston	22	20	2
Gulfport	205	149	56	Chesterfield	71	67	4
Hattiesburg	161	106	55	Chillicothe	19	14	5
Heidelberg	5	5	—	Claycomo	9	8	1
Hernando	12	12	—	Clayton	62	49	13
Indianola	34	26	8	Clinton	18	17	1
Inverness	4	4	—	Columbia	141	111	30
Kosciusko	28	21	7	Cool Valley	14	7	7
Laurel	69	49	20	Crestwood	37	30	7
Leakesville	3	3	—	Creve Coeur	56	45	11
Long Beach	35	23	12	Crystal City	17	13	4
Louisville	22	16	6	Des Peres	39	33	6
Lucedale	14	9	5	Edmundson	7	7	—
Macon	6	6	—	Ellisville	23	21	2
Madison	35	25	10	Eureka	20	17	3
Magee	16	16	—	Excelsior Springs	35	25	10
McComb	50	31	19	Farmington	30	21	9
Mendenhall	12	8	4	Fayette	7	7	—
Meridian	139	107	32	Ferguson	59	52	7
Moss Point	41	36	5	Festus	31	23	8
Natchez	83	59	24	Florissant	90	76	14
Newton	14	9	5	Frontenac	23	18	5
Ocean Springs	40	31	9	Fulton	28	21	7
Pascagoula	82	55	27	Gladstone	68	56	12
Pass Christian	23	18	5	Glendale	14	11	3
Petal	17	13	4	Grandview	59	48	11
Picayune	36	22	14	Hannibal	54	34	20
Purvis	10	7	3	Harrisonville	23	16	7
Ridgeland	51	33	18	Hazelwood	65	52	13
Rolling Fork	5	5	—	Hermann	7	6	1
Shaw	5	5	—	Hillsdale	14	13	1
Southaven	59	47	12	Independence	242	165	77
Starkville	49	37	12	Ironton	5	5	—
Tupelo	119	94	25	Jackson	21	16	5
Utica	8	8	—	Jefferson City	95	72	23
Vaiden	3	3	—	Jennings	64	39	25
Verona	11	7	4	Joplin	70	63	7
Vicksburg	112	92	20	Kansas City	1,811	1,175	636
Waveland	24	18	6	Kearney	8	8	—
Waynesboro	20	15	5	Kennett	27	20	7
Wiggins	13	9	4	Kirksville	29	22	7
Winona	16	11	5	Kirkwood	69	55	14
				Ladue	34	29	5
MISSOURI				Lake St. Louis	23	16	7
				Lamar	9	8	1
Arnold	52	41	11	Lebanon	24	18	6
Aurora	19	13	6	Lees Summit	99	70	29
Ballwin	59	47	12	Lexington	10	9	1
Bellefontaine Neighbors	24	24	—	Liberty	42	31	11
Bel-Nor	9	9	—	Louisiana	12	8	4
Bel-Ridge	21	14	7	Macon	11	10	1
Belton	38	27	11	Manchester	22	20	2
Berkeley	55	44	11	Maplewood	31	26	5
Blue Springs	82	59	23	Marceline	7	6	1
Bolivar	19	13	6	Marshall	32	23	9
Bonne Terre	8	8	—	Maryland Heights	72	58	14
Boonville	26	15	11	Maryville	21	14	7
Branson	49	34	15	Mexico	34	29	5
Breckenridge Hills	13	12	1	Moberly	41	35	6
Brentwood	28	22	6	Moline Acres	8	8	—
Bridgeton	67	56	11	Monett	24	15	9
Brookfield	17	10	7	Montgomery City	6	6	—
Buckner	6	5	1	Neosho	22	20	2
Butler	10	6	4	Nevada	28	18	10
California	5	5	—	Newburg	2	2	—
Calverton Park	6	6	—	Normandy	19	18	1
Cameron	14	10	4	North Kansas City	46	36	10
Canton	8	4	4	Northwoods	21	18	3
Cape Girardeau	88	67	21	Oakview	5	5	—
Carrollton	7	7	—	Odessa	8	8	—
Carthage	32	25	7	O'Fallon	55	41	14
Centralia	10	5	5	Olivette	27	22	5
Chaffee	10	6	4	Osage Beach	33	23	10

City	Total police employees	Total officers	Total civilians	City	Total police employees	Total officers	Total civilians
MISSOURI — Continued				**MONTANA — Continued**			
Overland	56	42	14	Fort Benton	3	3	—
Pacific	19	13	6	Glasgow	7	6	1
Pagedale	18	17	1	Glendive	14	10	4
Park Hills	14	13	1	Great Falls	102	69	33
Parkville	9	8	1	Hamilton	14	12	2
Pevely	17	12	5	Havre	22	19	3
Pine Lawn	19	17	2	Helena	58	42	16
Pleasant Hill	12	8	4	Kalispell	34	26	8
Poplar Bluff	53	43	10	Laurel	14	9	5
Potosi	14	13	1	Lewistown	18	12	6
Raytown	78	60	18	Livingston	19	12	7
Republic	18	14	4	Manhattan	2	2	—
Rich Hill	4	4	—	Miles City-Custer County	18	14	4
Richland	8	5	3	Missoula	86	70	16
Richmond	15	10	5	Plentywood	4	3	1
Richmond Heights	39	33	6	Polson	8	8	—
Riverside	18	13	5	Red Lodge	5	5	—
Riverview	9	9	—	Ronan	4	4	—
Rock Hill	16	12	4	Saint Ignatius	1	1	—
Rolla	43	25	18	Sidney	11	10	1
St. Ann	49	41	8	Thompson Falls	2	2	—
St. Charles	126	97	29	Three Forks	2	2	—
Ste. Genevieve	10	9	1	Troy	3	3	—
St. George	5	5	—	West Yellowstone	10	5	5
St. John	21	19	2	Whitefish	16	11	5
St. Joseph	145	108	37	Whitehall	3	2	1
St. Louis	2,254	1,538	716				
St. Peters	75	60	15	**NEBRASKA**			
St. Robert	13	9	4				
Salem	16	12	4	Albion	3	3	—
Savannah	4	4	—	Alliance	30	21	9
Sedalia	48	42	6	Ashland	4	4	—
Shrewsbury	20	17	3	Auburn	6	6	—
Sikeston	63	54	9	Aurora	8	7	1
Slater	9	6	3	Beatrice	29	20	9
Smithville	10	9	1	Bellevue	56	52	4
Springfield	306	240	66	Blair	13	12	1
Sugar Creek	17	15	2	Broken Bow	8	7	1
Sullivan	20	12	8	Central City	6	5	1
Sunset Hills	24	18	6	Chadron	19	12	7
Town and Country	34	31	3	Columbus	33	26	7
Trenton	16	11	5	Cozad	11	7	4
Union	13	11	2	Crete	13	9	4
University City	93	74	19	David City	6	5	1
Valley Park	11	10	1	Elkhorn	5	5	—
Vandalia	10	6	4	Fairbury	7	6	1
Warrensburg	35	31	4	Falls City	13	9	4
Warrenton	18	13	5	Fremont	40	33	7
Warson Woods	7	6	1	Geneva	4	4	—
Washington	27	23	4	Gering	18	15	3
Webb City	18	18	—	Gordon	8	6	2
Webster Groves	53	43	10	Gothenburg	10	6	4
Wentzville	28	21	7	Grand Island	67	60	7
Weston	3	3	—	Hastings	54	37	17
West Plains	20	18	2	Holdrege	11	7	4
Winchester	2	1	1	Imperial	4	4	—
Windsor	6	6	—	Kearney	44	36	8
Woodson Terrace	16	14	2	Kimball	6	6	—
Wright City	5	4	1	La Vista	22	19	3
				Lexington	16	14	2
MONTANA				Lincoln	374	276	98
				Madison	4	4	—
Baker	3	3	—	McCook	18	14	4
Belgrade	9	7	2	Milford	4	4	—
Billings	132	111	21	Minden	5	4	1
Boulder	2	2	—	Mitchell	5	5	—
Bozeman	44	33	11	Nebraska City	13	12	1
Bridger	2	2	—	Neligh	3	3	—
Columbia Falls	13	7	6	Norfolk	53	37	16
Conrad	5	5	—	North Platte	55	35	20
Cut Bank	6	5	1	Ogallala	10	8	2
Dillon	8	7	1	Omaha	831	673	158
East Helena	4	4	—	O'Neill	12	7	5
Eureka	3	2	1	Ord	8	4	4

City	Total police employees	Total officers	Total civilians	City	Total police employees	Total officers	Total civilians
NEBRASKA— Continued				**NEW HAMPSHIRE — Continued**			
Papillion	22	20	2	Hudson	43	32	11
Pierce	3	3	—	Jaffrey	12	11	1
Plainview	2	2	—	Keene	56	44	12
Plattsmouth	10	9	1	Lancaster	6	6	—
Ralston	11	10	1	Lebanon	42	30	12
Schuyler	9	7	2	Litchfield	9	8	1
Scottsbluff	34	30	4	Londonderry	45	32	13
Seward	13	9	4	Manchester	230	187	43
Sidney	16	12	4	Merrimack	44	32	12
South Sioux City	20	19	1	Milford	26	22	4
Superior	8	6	2	Milton	6	5	1
Syracuse	3	3	—	Moultonborough	7	5	2
Tecumseh	4	3	1	Nashua	193	142	51
Tekamah	4	4	—	New Castle	2	2	—
Valentine	5	5	—	New Hampton	4	4	—
Valley	4	4	—	Newington	10	9	1
Wahoo	6	6	—	Newport	16	12	4
Wayne	12	8	4	Northfield	8	7	1
West Point	6	6	—	Orford	1	1	—
Wilber	4	4	—	Pembroke	11	10	1
Wymore	3	3	—	Peterborough	13	11	2
York	19	14	5	Plaistow	18	12	6
				Plymouth	17	10	7
NEVADA				Rindge	8	7	1
				Rochester	48	38	10
Boulder City	33	27	6	Rollinsford	4	4	—
Carlin	6	5	1	Seabrook	30	23	7
Fallon	27	19	8	Somersworth	26	19	7
Henderson	211	158	53	Swanzey	7	6	1
Las Vegas Metropolitan Police Department				Tilton	10	9	1
Jurisdiction	2,355	1,585	770	Wakefield	9	8	1
Lovelock	6	5	1	Wilton	6	5	1
Mesquite	21	14	7	Winchester	6	5	1
North Las Vegas	181	125	56	Windham	20	15	5
Reno	437	300	137	Wolfeboro	14	10	4
Sparks	117	79	38				
Wells	5	5	—	**NEW JERSEY**			
West Wendover	13	10	3				
Winnemucca	17	14	3	Aberdeen Township	39	32	7
Yerington	10	9	1	Absecon	29	27	2
				Allendale	17	13	4
NEW HAMPSHIRE				Allenhurst	12	8	4
				Allentown	9	6	3
Amherst	15	14	1	Alpha	5	5	—
Auburn	7	5	2	Alpine	12	12	—
Barrington	8	7	1	Andover Township	11	7	4
Bedford	30	21	9	Asbury Park	73	63	10
Berlin	22	19	3	Atlantic City	535	404	131
Boscawen	5	4	1	Atlantic Highlands	19	14	5
Bow	11	7	4	Audubon	19	17	2
Bristol	7	6	1	Audubon Park	4	4	—
Candia	6	5	1	Avalon	29	20	9
Charlestown	9	5	4	Avon-by-the-Sea	10	10	—
Claremont	30	25	5	Barnegat Township	26	21	5
Concord	83	65	18	Barrington	16	15	1
Derry	59	48	11	Bay Head	9	8	1
Dover	60	42	18	Bayonne	215	180	35
Durham	16	14	2	Beach Haven	16	12	4
Enfield	6	5	1	Beachwood	17	15	2
Epping	7	6	1	Bedminster Township	16	15	1
Exeter	30	23	7	Belleville	99	95	4
Farmington	12	11	1	Bellmawr	26	20	6
Fitzwilliam	4	3	1	Belmar	27	21	6
Franklin	25	18	7	Belvidere	6	6	—
Gilford	19	13	6	Bergenfield	54	49	5
Goffstown	33	22	11	Berkeley Heights	30	25	5
Gorham	8	8	—	Berkeley Township	75	57	18
Hampstead	3	3	—	Berlin	16	15	1
Hanover	30	19	11	Berlin Township	18	16	2
Henniker	7	6	1	Bernards Township	36	27	9
Hinsdale	7	5	2	Bernardsville	21	16	5
Holderness	5	5	—	Beverly	9	8	1
Hollis	9	8	1	Blairstown Township	9	8	1
Hooksett	34	20	14	Bloomfield	142	122	20

Table 78.—Number of Full-time Law Enforcement Employees, Cities, October 31, 1995 — Continued

City	Total police employees	Total officers	Total civilians	City	Total police employees	Total officers	Total civilians
NEW JERSEY — Continued				**NEW JERSEY — Continued**			
Bloomingdale	15	14	1	Elizabeth	423	347	76
Bogota	20	20	—	Elk Township	7	6	1
Boonton	23	18	5	Elmer	4	4	—
Boonton Township	10	10	—	Elmwood Park	34	32	2
Bordentown	11	10	1	Emerson	19	19	—
Bordentown Township	25	19	6	Englewood	86	71	15
Bound Brook	23	18	5	Englewood Cliffs	27	26	1
Bradley Beach	22	18	4	Englishtown	3	3	—
Branchburg Township	21	20	1	Essex Fells	14	11	3
Brick Township	142	98	44	Evesham Township	54	48	6
Bridgeton	72	63	9	Ewing Township	92	77	15
Bridgewater Township	77	64	13	Fairfield	39	35	4
Brielle	15	13	2	Fair Haven	14	13	1
Brigantine	46	38	8	Fair Lawn	64	56	8
Brooklawn	5	5	—	Fairview	33	33	—
Buena	14	9	5	Fanwood	22	21	1
Burlington	35	31	4	Far Hills	4	4	—
Burlington Township	43	35	8	Flemington	13	11	2
Butler	15	15	—	Florence Township	25	20	5
Byram Township	14	12	2	Florham Park	31	30	1
Caldwell	23	22	1	Fort Lee	112	91	21
Califon	2	2	—	Franklin	13	12	1
Camden	416	341	75	Franklin Lakes	26	21	5
Cape May	24	18	6	Franklin Township (Gloucester County)	29	22	7
Carlstadt	30	26	4	Franklin Township (Hunterdon County)	4	4	—
Carney's Point Township	23	18	5	Franklin Township (Somerset County)	103	80	23
Carteret	63	51	12	Freehold	34	27	7
Cedar Grove Township	33	30	3	Freehold Township	59	48	11
Chatham	26	19	7	Frenchtown	4	4	—
Chatham Township	29	23	6	Galloway Township	48	44	4
Cherry Hill Township	156	126	30	Garfield	59	52	7
Chesilhurst	9	8	1	Garwood	18	16	2
Chester	9	8	1	Gibbsboro	2	2	—
Chesterfield Township	3	3	—	Glassboro	51	41	10
Chester Township	16	15	1	Glen Ridge	35	28	7
Cinnaminson Township	34	29	5	Glen Rock	22	19	3
Clark Township	54	45	9	Gloucester City	27	25	2
Clayton	23	15	8	Gloucester Township	90	72	18
Clementon	13	12	1	Green Brook	22	17	5
Cliffside Park	42	39	3	Greenwich Township (Gloucester County)	20	15	5
Clifton	168	141	27	Greenwich Township (Warren County)	6	5	1
Clinton	7	7	—	Guttenberg	26	23	3
Clinton Township	22	20	2	Hackensack	127	107	20
Closter	21	19	2	Hackettstown	22	18	4
Collingswood	29	26	3	Haddonfield	26	21	5
Colts Neck Township	17	16	1	Haddon Heights	21	16	5
Cranbury Township	12	11	1	Haddon Township	25	22	3
Cranford Township	66	50	16	Haledon	22	17	5
Cresskill	23	20	3	Hamburg	6	6	—
Deal	16	11	5	Hamilton Township (Atlantic County)	54	41	13
Delanco Township	8	7	1	Hamilton Township (Mercer County)	206	169	37
Delaware Township	7	7	—	Hammonton	35	28	7
Delran Township	30	26	4	Hanover Township	34	27	7
Demarest	12	12	—	Harding Township	15	14	1
Denville Township	34	26	8	Hardyston Township	20	14	6
Deptford Township	61	51	10	Harrington Park	11	11	—
Dover	38	35	3	Harrison	56	55	1
Dover Township	158	128	30	Harrison Township	10	9	1
Dumont	31	27	4	Harvey Cedars	8	7	1
Dunellen	18	14	4	Hasbrouck Heights	32	29	3
Eastampton Township	16	15	1	Haworth	13	11	2
East Brunswick Township	120	86	34	Hawthorne	31	30	1
East Greenwich Township	16	14	2	Hazlet Township	51	43	8
East Hanover Township	34	29	5	Helmetta	4	4	—
East Newark	9	9	—	High Bridge	6	6	—
East Orange	302	276	26	Highland Park	37	29	8
East Rutherford	24	23	1	Highlands	18	13	5
East Windsor Township	61	48	13	Hightstown	19	14	5
Eatontown	43	33	10	Hillsborough Township	51	42	9
Edgewater	23	22	1	Hillsdale	21	19	2
Edgewater Park Township	14	13	1	Hillside Township	84	73	11
Edison Township	223	180	43	Hi Nella	6	4	2
Egg Harbor City	21	13	8	Hoboken	144	133	11
Egg Harbor Township	88	68	20	Ho-Ho-Kus	14	14	—

Table 78.—Number of Full-time Law Enforcement Employees, Cities, October 31, 1995 — Continued

City	Total police employees	Total officers	Total civilians	City	Total police employees	Total officers	Total civilians
NEW JERSEY — Continued				**NEW JERSEY — Continued**			
Holland Township	7	6	1	Midland Park	13	12	1
Holmdel Township	37	29	8	Millburn Township	59	52	7
Hopatcong	31	24	7	Milltown	16	13	3
Hopewell Township	35	28	7	Millville	79	68	11
Howell Township	79	63	16	Mine Hill Township	10	9	1
Independence Township	6	5	1	Monmouth Beach	11	10	1
Interlaken	5	5	—	Monroe Township (Gloucester County)	61	50	11
Irvington	232	196	36	Monroe Township (Middlesex County)	46	33	13
Island Heights	5	5	—	Montclair	121	105	16
Jackson Township	88	62	26	Montgomery Township	30	21	9
Jamesburg	11	10	1	Montvale	23	21	2
Jefferson Township	39	33	6	Montville Township	41	36	5
Jersey City	955	851	104	Moonachie	21	18	3
Keansburg	40	30	10	Moorestown Township	42	32	10
Kearny	117	109	8	Morris Plains	22	16	6
Kenilworth	25	24	1	Morristown	64	57	7
Keyport	24	18	6	Morris Township	53	43	10
Kinnelon	16	15	1	Mountain Lakes	17	12	5
Lacey Township	44	35	9	Mountainside	27	22	5
Lakehurst	10	9	1	Mount Arlington	9	8	1
Lakewood	124	100	24	Mount Ephraim	13	12	1
Lambertville	12	10	2	Mount Holly	27	24	3
Laurel Springs	9	8	1	Mount Laurel Township	64	53	11
Lavallette	16	11	5	Mount Olive Township	48	40	8
Lawnside	11	9	2	Mullica Township	15	14	1
Lawrence Township	73	61	12	National Park	6	6	—
Lebanon Township	8	8	—	Neptune	22	18	4
Leonia	27	20	7	Neptune Township	81	65	16
Lincoln Park	26	24	2	Netcong	12	7	5
Linden	135	126	9	Newark	1,422	1,160	262
Lindenwold	40	37	3	New Brunswick	169	133	36
Linwood	22	18	4	Newfield	5	5	—
Little Egg Harbor Township	41	30	11	New Hanover Township	3	3	—
Little Falls Township	29	24	5	New Milford	37	34	3
Little Ferry	32	26	6	New Providence	27	22	5
Little Silver	18	15	3	Newton	27	19	8
Livingston Township	69	61	8	North Arlington	44	35	9
Lodi	45	34	11	North Bergen Township	141	118	23
Logan Township	14	13	1	North Brunswick Township	97	82	15
Long Beach Township	41	34	7	North Caldwell	19	19	—
Long Branch	105	87	18	Northfield	27	20	7
Long Hill Township	29	22	7	North Haledon	20	16	4
Longport	15	12	3	North Hanover Township	7	6	1
Lopatcong Township	11	10	1	North Plainfield	49	44	5
Lower Alloways Creek Township	17	12	5	Northvale	13	12	1
Lower Township	71	54	17	North Wildwood	34	26	8
Lumberton Township	21	19	2	Norwood	12	12	—
Lyndhurst Township	49	44	5	Nutley	72	64	8
Madison	40	36	4	Oakland	33	29	4
Magnolia	9	9	—	Oaklyn	10	9	1
Mahwah Township	56	50	6	Ocean City	76	60	16
Manalapan Township	59	46	13	Ocean Gate	6	6	—
Manasquan	24	18	6	Oceanport	20	14	6
Manchester Township	65	54	11	Ocean Township (Monmouth County)	68	56	12
Mansfield Township (Burlington County)	5	4	1	Ocean Township (Ocean County)	17	12	5
Mansfield Township (Warren County)	11	11	—	Ogdensburg	6	6	—
Mantoloking	8	7	1	Old Bridge	124	87	37
Mantua Township	30	20	10	Old Tappan	14	13	1
Manville	25	23	2	Oradell	22	21	1
Maple Shade Township	39	31	8	Orange	113	102	11
Maplewood Township	71	58	13	Oxford Township	4	4	—
Margate City	40	30	10	Palisades Park	35	32	3
Marlboro Township	80	61	19	Palmyra	18	16	2
Matawan	28	21	7	Paramus	113	86	27
Maywood	28	23	5	Park Ridge	23	20	3
Medford Lakes	9	8	1	Parsippany-Troy Hills Township	128	107	21
Medford Township	40	31	9	Passaic	161	146	15
Mendham	11	10	1	Paterson	431	356	75
Mendham Township	14	12	2	Paulsboro	20	14	6
Merchantville	14	13	1	Peapack and Gladstone	9	8	1
Metuchen	35	29	6	Pemberton	4	4	—
Middlesex	34	32	2	Pemberton Township	67	57	10
Middle Township	58	41	17	Pennsauken	119	92	27
Middletown Township	120	95	25	Penns Grove	21	16	5

Table 78.—Number of Full-time Law Enforcement Employees, Cities, October 31, 1995 — Continued

City	Total police employees	Total officers	Total civilians	City	Total police employees	Total officers	Total civilians
NEW JERSEY — Continued				**NEW JERSEY — Continued**			
Pennsville Township	34	27	7	Springfield	47	43	4
Pequannock Township	30	25	5	Springfield Township	5	5	—
Perth Amboy	129	117	12	Spring Lake	17	13	4
Phillipsburg	37	29	8	Spring Lake Heights	22	13	9
Pine Beach	7	6	1	Stafford Township	53	40	13
Pine Hill	19	17	2	Stanhope	8	7	1
Pine Valley	7	6	1	Stillwater Township	4	4	—
Piscataway Township	98	81	17	Stone Harbor	23	18	5
Pitman	19	14	5	Stratford	14	13	1
Plainfield	174	138	36	Summit	59	46	13
Plainsboro Township	38	29	9	Surf City	21	12	9
Pleasantville	54	46	8	Swedesboro	6	6	—
Plumsted Township	7	6	1	Teaneck Township	112	97	15
Pohatcong Township	8	7	1	Tenafly	32	26	6
Point Pleasant	35	27	8	Tewksbury Township	10	9	1
Point Pleasant Beach	29	21	8	Tinton Falls	38	30	8
Pompton Lakes	23	18	5	Totowa	27	25	2
Princeton	40	32	8	Trenton	434	383	51
Princeton Township	39	31	8	Tuckerton	7	7	—
Prospect Park	13	11	2	Union Beach	21	13	8
Rahway	89	77	12	Union City	189	171	18
Ramsey	36	31	5	Union Township	167	120	47
Randolph Township	45	38	7	Upper Saddle River	23	19	4
Raritan	15	15	—	Ventnor City	48	38	10
Raritan Township	34	28	6	Vernon Township	41	32	9
Readington Township	20	18	2	Verona	33	30	3
Red Bank	49	39	10	Vineland	140	122	18
Ridgefield	37	28	9	Voorhees Township	60	45	15
Ridgefield Park	31	28	3	Waldwick	19	16	3
Ridgewood	46	41	5	Wallington	21	21	—
Ringwood	26	20	6	Wall Township	63	51	12
Riverdale	15	12	3	Wanaque	22	18	4
River Edge	26	23	3	Warren Township	29	22	7
Riverside	14	13	1	Washington	13	12	1
Riverton	6	6	—	Washington Township (Bergen County)	22	22	—
River Vale	20	20	—	Washington Township (Gloucester County)	78	65	13
Rochelle Park Township	20	18	2	Washington Township (Mercer County)	23	17	6
Rockaway	15	14	1	Washington Township (Morris County)	37	29	8
Rockaway Township	58	48	10	Washington Township (Warren County)	11	10	1
Roseland	27	26	1	Watchung	33	26	7
Roselle	69	56	13	Waterford Township	23	21	2
Roselle Park	39	33	6	Wayne Township	138	110	28
Roxbury Township	44	39	5	Weehawken Township	49	45	4
Rumson	17	17	—	Wenonah	6	6	—
Runnemede	19	17	2	Westampton Township	21	18	3
Rutherford	47	41	6	West Amwell Township	5	4	1
Saddle Brook Township	35	33	2	West Caldwell	32	30	2
Saddle River	15	13	2	West Cape May	7	7	—
Salem	28	22	6	West Deptford Township	39	32	7
Sayreville	103	86	17	Westfield	68	59	9
Scotch Plains Township	51	45	6	West Long Branch	22	18	4
Sea Bright	13	10	3	West Milford Township	49	42	7
Sea Girt	14	11	3	West New York	119	110	9
Sea Isle City	28	21	7	West Orange	110	98	12
Seaside Heights	26	20	6	West Paterson	24	23	1
Seaside Park	17	13	4	Westville	14	10	4
Secaucus	58	51	7	West Wildwood	4	4	—
Ship Bottom	11	11	—	West Windsor Township	48	38	10
Shrewsbury	19	15	4	Westwood	30	27	3
Somerdale	12	11	1	Wharton	13	12	1
Somers Point	30	24	6	Wildwood	51	42	9
Somerville	40	34	6	Wildwood Crest	27	21	6
South Amboy	30	28	2	Willingboro Township	84	70	14
South Belmar	9	9	—	Winfield Township	9	9	—
South Bound Brook	13	13	—	Winslow Township	83	70	13
South Brunswick Township	93	64	29	Woodbridge Township	242	198	44
South Hackensack	21	18	3	Woodbury	34	27	7
South Harrison Township	5	4	1	Woodbury Heights	8	7	1
South Orange	65	56	9	Woodcliff Lake	17	16	1
South Plainfield	66	54	12	Woodlynne	8	7	1
South River	33	27	6	Wood Ridge	22	19	3
South Toms River	10	9	1	Woodstown	8	7	1
Sparta Township	37	29	8	Woolwich Township	5	4	1
Spotswood	23	19	4	Wyckoff	29	24	5

Table 78.—Number of Full-time Law Enforcement Employees, Cities, October 31, 1995 — Continued

City	Total police employees	Total officers	Total civilians	City	Total police employees	Total officers	Total civilians
NEW MEXICO				**NEW YORK— Continued**			
Acoma	10	5	5	Bath Village	16	12	4
Alamogordo	90	66	24	Beacon	39	37	2
Albuquerque	1,176	845	331	Bedford Town	44	38	6
Artesia	37	23	14	Binghamton	151	142	9
Aztec	21	14	7	Blooming Grove Town	13	12	1
Belen	26	18	8	Bolivar Village	1	1	—
Bernalillo	18	12	6	Bolton Town	1	1	—
Bloomfield	19	17	2	Boonville Village	3	3	—
Central	3	3	—	Brant Town	1	1	—
Chama	3	2	1	Briarcliff Manor Village	18	18	—
Clayton	15	5	10	Brighton Town	49	40	9
Cloudcroft	3	3	—	Brockport Village	10	10	—
Clovis	77	59	18	Bronxville Village	26	23	3
Corrales	20	13	7	Buchanan Village	7	7	—
Cuba	7	2	5	Buffalo	1,092	914	178
Deming	35	28	7	Caledonia Village	2	2	—
Eunice	10	6	4	Cambridge Village	2	2	—
Farmington	136	86	50	Camden Village	4	3	1
Gallup	115	60	55	Camillus Town and Village	20	18	2
Grants	31	23	8	Canajoharie Village	3	3	—
Hobbs	119	78	41	Canastota Village	4	4	—
Hurley	5	4	1	Canisteo Village	2	2	—
Jal	8	4	4	Canton Village	11	9	2
Las Cruces	169	132	37	Carmel Town	36	33	3
Los Lunas	32	24	8	Carroll Town	1	1	—
Las Vegas	61	40	21	Carthage Village	7	7	—
Lovington	26	20	6	Catskill Village	13	13	—
Mesilla	8	8	—	Cattaraugus Village	1	1	—
Milan	13	8	5	Cayuga Heights Village	7	6	1
Mountainair	3	2	1	Cazenovia Village	5	5	—
Portales	31	21	10	Centre Island Village	5	5	—
Questa	4	3	1	Chester Town	6	5	1
Raton	22	14	8	Cheektowaga Town	166	128	38
Red River	8	4	4	Chester Village	8	8	—
Rio Rancho	131	96	35	Chittenango Village	7	7	—
Roswell	106	85	21	Clayton Village	3	3	—
Ruidoso	36	23	13	Clay Town	23	19	4
Ruidoso Downs	11	7	4	Clifton Springs Village	2	2	—
Santa Rosa	11	7	4	Clyde Town	2	2	—
Silver City	38	29	9	Cobleskill Village	10	10	—
Socorro	26	15	11	Coeymans Town	6	3	3
Taos	34	19	15	Cohocton Town	1	1	—
Taos Pueblo Tribal	11	7	4	Cohoes	39	35	4
Tatum	6	2	4	Colchester Town	1	1	—
Texico	3	3	—	Cold Spring Village	2	2	—
Tucumcari	32	24	8	Colonie Town	150	109	41
Tularosa	13	8	5	Cooperstown Village	6	6	—
Village of Wagon Mound	2	2	—	Corning	28	24	4
				Cornwall-on-Hudson Village	4	4	—
NEW YORK				Cornwall Town	14	10	4
				Cortland	43	40	3
Addison Town and Village	21	20	1	Coxsackie Village	1	1	—
Albany	402	327	75	Crawford Town	11	9	2
Albion Village	13	12	1	Croton-on-Hudson Village	18	18	—
Alexandria Bay Village	2	2	—	Cuba Town	3	3	—
Alfred Village	6	6	—	Dansville Village	11	8	3
Allegany Village	3	3	—	Delhi Village	4	4	—
Altamont Village	2	2	—	Depew Village	39	31	8
Amherst Town	177	150	27	Deposit Village	3	3	—
Amity Town and Belmont Village	1	1	—	Dewitt Town	38	35	3
Amityville Village	29	26	3	Dobbs Ferry Village	26	25	1
Amsterdam	35	33	2	Dryden Village	4	3	1
Andover Village	1	1	—	Dunkirk	34	34	—
Angola Village	4	3	1	East Aurora – Aurora Town	20	16	4
Arcade Village	6	6	—	Eastchester Town	62	52	10
Ardsley	17	17	—	East Fishkill Town	28	20	8
Asharoken Village	3	3	—	East Greenbush Town	25	19	6
Athens Village	1	1	—	East Hampton Town	57	46	11
Auburn	71	63	8	East Hampton Village	24	22	2
Avon Village	4	4	—	East Rochester Village	8	7	1
Bainbridge Village	1	1	—	East Syracuse Village	11	8	3
Baldwinsville Village	15	12	3	Eden Town	5	4	1
Ballston Spa Village	12	7	5	Ellenville Village	15	13	2
Batavia	37	31	6	Ellicott Town	12	11	1

Table 78.—Number of Full-time Law Enforcement Employees, Cities, October 31, 1995 — Continued

City	Total police employees	Total officers	Total civilians	City	Total police employees	Total officers	Total civilians
NEW YORK — Continued				**NEW YORK — Continued**			
Ellicottville	3	3	—	Lake Placid Village	17	14	3
Elmira	82	77	5	Lake Success Village	24	21	3
Elmira Heights Village	10	10	—	Lakewood-Busti	11	10	1
Elmira Town	4	4	—	Lancaster Town	37	31	6
Elmsford Village	17	17	—	Lancaster Village	22	16	6
Endicott Village	46	36	10	Larchmont Village	31	28	3
Evans Town	25	20	5	Laurel Hollow Village	8	8	—
Fairport Village	11	10	1	Le Roy Village	11	8	3
Fallsburg Town	20	16	4	Liberty Village	19	16	3
Floral Park Village	45	35	10	Little Falls	14	13	1
Florida Village	1	1	—	Liverpool Village	12	11	1
Fort Edward Village	5	5	—	Lloyd Harbor Village	13	12	1
Fort Plain Village	3	3	—	Lloyd Town	6	6	—
Frankfort Village	4	4	—	Lockport	55	52	3
Franklinville Village	1	1	—	Long Beach	94	77	17
Fredonia Village	17	15	2	Lowville Village	6	6	—
Freeport Village	105	93	12	Lynbrook Village	52	45	7
Fulton	37	34	3	Lyons Village	12	10	2
Garden City Village	61	48	13	Macedon Town and Village	3	3	—
Gates Town	35	29	6	Malone Village	18	18	—
Geddes Town	17	15	2	Malverne Village	19	19	—
Geneseo Village	8	8	—	Mamaroneck Town	40	39	1
Geneva	38	34	4	Mamaroneck Village	52	46	6
Glen Cove	56	52	4	Manlius Town	45	40	5
Glens Falls	42	34	8	Marcellus Village	2	2	—
Glenville Town	31	19	12	Marlborough Town	8	5	3
Gloversville	35	33	2	Massena Village	24	22	2
Goshen	3	3	—	Mechanicville	12	12	—
Goshen Village	13	12	1	Medina Village	16	13	3
Gouverneur Village	12	8	4	Menands Village	13	10	3
Granville Village	6	6	—	Middleport Village	2	2	—
Great Neck Estates Village	15	12	3	Middletown	65	57	8
Greece Town	97	89	8	Mohawk Village	3	3	—
Greenburgh Town	125	102	23	Monroe Village	17	14	3
Greene Village	2	2	—	Montgomery Town	3	2	1
Green Island Village	4	4	—	Monticello Village	28	24	4
Greenport Town	1	1	—	Moravia Village	1	1	—
Greenwood Lake Village	14	11	3	Moriah Town	1	1	—
Guilderland Town	41	28	13	Mount Kisco Village	33	32	1
Hamburg Town	81	66	15	Mount Morris Village	5	5	—
Hamburg Village	17	15	2	Mount Pleasant Town	50	45	5
Hamilton Village	6	5	1	Mount Vernon	224	179	45
Hammondsport Village	2	2	—	Nassau Village	1	1	—
Harriman Village	6	6	—	Newark Village	20	19	1
Harrison Town	66	57	9	Newburgh	94	78	16
Hastings-on-Hudson	21	21	—	Newburgh Town	57	43	14
Haverstraw Town	30	29	1	New Castle Town	37	35	2
Haverstraw Village	22	22	—	New Hartford Town and Village	17	15	2
Hempstead Village	122	95	27	New Paltz Town and Village	24	19	5
Herkimer Village	24	23	1	New Rochelle	228	179	49
Highland Falls Village	12	8	4	New Windsor Town	44	31	13
Homer Village	5	4	1	New York	46,802	37,450	9,352
Hoosick Falls Village	2	2	—	New York Mills Village	2	2	—
Hornell	21	20	1	Niagara Falls	181	160	21
Horseheads Village	14	12	2	Niagara Town	4	4	—
Hudson	26	22	4	Niskayuna Town	39	29	10
Hudson Falls Village	16	12	4	North Castle Town	35	31	4
Hunter Village	1	1	—	North Greenbush Town	12	11	1
Huntington Bay Village	6	6	—	Northport Village	20	16	4
Hyde Park Town	13	11	2	North Syracuse Village	15	12	3
Ilion Village	18	16	2	North Tarrytown Village	23	23	—
Inlet Town	6	3	3	North Tonawanda	60	56	4
Irondequoit Town	64	53	11	Norwich	20	19	1
Irvington Village	21	21	—	Norwood Village	2	2	—
Ithaca	88	72	16	Ogdensburg	29	24	5
Jamestown	80	66	14	Ogden Town	15	12	3
Johnson City Village	46	39	7	Old Brookville Village	48	38	10
Kenmore Village	26	25	1	Old Westbury Village	28	23	5
Kensington Village	6	6	—	Olean	40	38	2
Kent Town	22	17	5	Oneida	23	20	3
Kings Point Village	22	22	—	Oneonta	28	25	3
Kingston	81	76	5	Orangetown Town	108	98	10
Kirkland Town	5	5	—	Orchard Park Town	32	30	2
Lackawanna	67	49	18	Ossining Town	13	13	—

Table 78.—Number of Full-time Law Enforcement Employees, Cities, October 31, 1995 — Continued

City	Total police employees	Total officers	Total civilians	City	Total police employees	Total officers	Total civilians
NEW YORK — Continued				**NEW YORK— Continued**			
Ossining Village	59	51	8	Trumansburg Village	1	1	—
Oswego	50	44	6	Tuckahoe Village	29	26	3
Owego Village	12	8	4	Tupper Lake Village	12	11	1
Oxford Village	2	2	—	Tuxedo Town	13	10	3
Oyster Bay Cove Village	11	11	—	Ulster Town	24	20	4
Painted Post Village	4	4	—	Vestal Town	41	33	8
Palmyra Village	7	6	1	Walden Village	13	9	4
Pawling Village	4	4	—	Wallkill Town	23	19	4
Peekskill	65	52	13	Walton Village	6	5	1
Pelham Manor Village	28	28	—	Wappingers Falls Village	7	5	2
Pelham Village	26	23	3	Warsaw Village	6	6	—
Penn Yann Village	11	10	1	Warwick Town	31	26	5
Perry Village	5	5	—	Washingtonville Village	10	9	1
Phoenix Village	2	2	—	Waterford Town and Village	13	10	3
Plattsburgh	50	44	6	Waterloo Village	9	8	1
Pleasantville Village	24	23	1	Watertown	66	62	4
Port Chester Village	63	59	4	Watervliet	25	25	—
Port Dickinson Village	3	3	—	Watkins Glen Village	4	4	—
Port Jervis	26	26	—	Waverly Village	15	10	5
Port Washington Village	65	56	9	Wayland Village	1	1	—
Potsdam Village	20	16	4	Webb Town	4	4	—
Poughkeepsie	103	88	15	Webster Town and Village	37	30	7
Poughkeepsie Town	86	77	9	Wellsville Village	16	12	4
Pound Ridge Town	1	1	—	Westfield Village	5	5	—
Pulaski Village	2	2	—	Westhampton Beach Village	20	16	4
Putnam Valley Town	16	11	5	West Seneca Town	76	66	10
Quogue Village	12	12	—	Whitehall Village	5	5	—
Ramapo Town	124	108	16	White Plains	240	200	40
Red Hook Village	3	3	—	Whitesboro Village	7	7	—
Rensselaer	35	28	7	Whitestown Town	5	5	—
Riverhead Town	85	70	15	Windham Town	2	2	—
Rochester	822	678	144	Wolcott Village	1	1	—
Rockville Centre Village	59	46	13	Woodbury Town	18	14	4
Rome	84	76	8	Woodridge Village	1	1	—
Rosendale Town	4	3	1	Woodstock Town	10	10	—
Rotterdam Town	55	42	13	Yonkers	631	544	87
Rouses Point Village	3	3	—	Yorktown Town	56	49	7
Rye Brook Village	22	22	—	Yorkville Village	3	3	—
Sag Harbor Village	13	12	1				
St. Johnsville Village	3	3	—	**NORTH CAROLINA**			
Salamanca	13	13	—				
Sands Point Village	20	20	—	Aberdeen	19	17	2
Saranac Lake Village	13	13	—	Ahoskie	21	17	4
Saratoga Springs	70	63	7	Albemarle	55	49	6
Saugerties Town	18	14	4	Andrews	7	7	—
Saugerties Village	12	10	2	Angier	9	9	—
Scarsdale Village	43	39	4	Apex	27	22	5
Schenectady	171	152	19	Archdale	22	17	5
Schodack Town	9	8	1	Asheboro	51	47	4
Schoharie Village	1	1	—	Asheville	209	164	45
Scotia Village	16	15	1	Atlantic Beach	25	20	5
Seneca Falls Village	16	12	4	Aulander	2	2	—
Shandaken Town	2	2	—	Aurora	1	1	—
Shawangunk Town	3	3	—	Ayden	21	16	5
Shelter Island Town	9	7	2	Banner Elk	6	6	—
Sherburne Village	1	1	—	Battleboro	3	3	—
Sherrill	4	4	—	Beaufort	15	15	—
Sidney Village	9	9	—	Beech Mountain	13	9	4
Silver Creek Village	6	5	1	Belhaven	12	9	3
Skaneateles Village	5	5	—	Belmont	27	24	3
Solvay Village	12	12	—	Benson	17	14	3
Southampton Town	107	87	20	Bessemer City	13	9	4
Southampton Village	35	25	10	Bethel	11	7	4
South Glens Falls Village	6	6	—	Beulaville	3	3	—
South Nyack-Grandview	6	6	—	Biltmore Forest	10	10	—
Southold Town	51	37	14	Biscoe	6	6	—
Southport Village	2	1	1	Black Creek	2	2	—
Stony Point Town	28	27	1	Black Mountain	18	14	4
Suffern Village	31	26	5	Bladenboro	5	5	—
Syracuse	572	474	98	Blowing Rock	13	9	4
Tarrytown Village	39	32	7	Boiling Springs	5	5	—
Tonawanda	34	31	3	Boiling Spring Lake	5	5	—
Tonawanda Town	152	106	46	Boone	34	34	—
Troy	123	114	9	Brevard	20	18	2

Table 78.—Number of Full-time Law Enforcement Employees, Cities, October 31, 1995 — Continued

City	Total police employees	Total officers	Total civilians	City	Total police employees	Total officers	Total civilians
NORTH CAROLINA — Continued				**NORTH CAROLINA — Continued**			
Broadway	3	3	—	Hendersonville	45	33	12
Brookford	1	1	—	Hertford	11	10	1
Bryson City	5	5	—	Hickory	112	87	25
Bunn	3	3	—	Highlands	9	9	—
Burgaw	7	7	—	High Point	210	180	30
Burlington	125	95	30	Hillsborough	19	19	—
Butner	42	37	5	Holden Beach	6	6	—
Candor	5	5	—	Holly Ridge	4	4	—
Canton	17	14	3	Holly Springs	11	7	4
Cape Carteret	5	5	—	Hope Mills	25	18	7
Carolina Beach	25	19	6	Hudson	11	10	1
Carrboro	33	30	3	Huntersville	23	21	2
Carthage	6	6	—	Indian Beach	4	4	—
Cary	93	73	20	Jacksonville	116	94	22
Caswell Beach	3	3	—	Jefferson	3	3	—
Catawba	1	1	—	Jonesville	7	7	—
Chadbourn	8	7	1	Kannapolis	84	71	13
Chapel Hill	114	95	19	Kenansville	3	3	—
Charlotte-Mecklenburg	1,534	1,208	326	Kenly	8	8	—
Cherryville	19	15	4	Kernersville	47	36	11
China Grove	8	8	—	Kill Devil Hills	25	22	3
Claremont	6	6	—	King	13	12	1
Clayton	25	20	5	Kings Mountain	30	24	6
Cleveland	3	3	—	Kinston	87	75	12
Clinton	34	28	6	Kitty Hawk	16	14	2
Clyde	4	4	—	Knightdale	10	9	1
Coats	5	5	—	La Grange	7	7	—
Concord	107	85	22	Lake Lure	9	9	—
Conover	20	19	1	Lake Waccamaw	2	2	—
Conway	1	1	—	Landis	4	4	—
Cooleemee	2	2	—	Laurel Park	5	5	—
Cornelius	28	19	9	Laurinburg	38	32	6
Cramerton	7	7	—	Leland	6	6	—
Creedmoor	11	8	3	Lenoir	60	50	10
Dallas	15	11	4	Lewiston	1	1	—
Davidson	11	11	—	Lexington	74	61	13
Denton	7	7	—	Liberty	9	9	—
Dobson	3	3	—	Lillington	8	8	—
Drexel	6	6	—	Lincolnton	33	28	5
Dunn	43	33	10	Locust	5	5	—
Durham	401	353	48	Long Beach	18	14	4
East Spencer	4	4	—	Longview	14	14	—
Eden	57	48	9	Louisburg	12	11	1
Edenton	18	16	2	Lowell	7	7	—
Elizabeth City	48	40	8	Lucama	2	2	—
Elizabethtown	17	16	1	Lumberton	81	71	10
Elkin	21	18	3	Madison	16	15	1
Ellerbe	2	2	—	Maggie Valley	3	3	—
Elm City	4	4	—	Maiden	14	13	1
Elon College	10	9	1	Manteo	7	6	1
Emerald Isle	20	16	4	Marion	21	16	5
Enfield	13	9	4	Mars Hill	5	5	—
Erwin	14	10	4	Marshville	6	6	—
Eureka	1	1	—	Matthews	44	34	10
Fair Bluff	5	5	—	Maxton	11	9	2
Fairmont	16	12	4	Mayodan	14	12	2
Farmville	20	16	4	Maysville	1	1	—
Fayetteville	346	264	82	McAdenville	4	4	—
Forest City	30	25	5	Mebane	16	13	3
Four Oaks	4	4	—	Middlesex	3	3	—
Foxfire Village	2	2	—	Mocksville	14	13	1
Franklin	15	14	1	Monroe	92	81	11
Franklinton	8	7	1	Montreat	5	5	—
Fremont	4	4	—	Mooresville	34	28	6
Fuquay–Varina	20	15	5	Morehead City	33	27	6
Garner	44	40	4	Morganton	95	78	17
Garysburg	3	3	—	Morrisville	13	11	2
Granite Quarry	2	2	—	Morven	1	1	—
Greensboro	568	446	122	Mount Airy	45	34	11
Greenville	159	126	33	Mount Gilead	6	6	—
Grifton	6	6	—	Mount Holly	26	21	5
Hamlet	23	18	5	Mount Olive	20	15	5
Havelock	27	22	5	Murfreesboro	13	9	4
Henderson	62	54	8	Murphy	12	8	4

City	Total police employees	Total officers	Total civilians	City	Total police employees	Total officers	Total civilians
NORTH CAROLINA — Continued				**NORTH CAROLINA — Continued**			
Nags Head	19	16	3	Star	4	4	—
Nashville	10	9	1	Stoneville	3	3	—
New Bern	96	73	23	Sugar Mountain	6	6	—
Newland	3	3	—	Sunset Beach	6	6	—
Newport	4	4	—	Surf City	8	8	—
Newton	42	33	9	Swansboro	4	4	—
Newton Grove	3	3	—	Sylva	9	9	—
Norlina	4	3	1	Tabor City	8	7	1
North Topsail Beach	9	8	1	Tarboro	33	23	10
North Wilkesboro	22	19	3	Taylortown	1	1	—
Norwood	6	6	—	Taylorsville	9	9	—
Oakboro	3	3	—	Thomasville	66	55	11
Ocean Isle Beach	7	7	—	Topsail Beach	5	5	—
Old Fort	5	5	—	Trent Woods	4	4	—
Oxford	34	28	6	Troutman	6	6	—
Parkton	2	2	—	Troy	10	10	—
Pembroke	14	10	4	Tryon	14	9	5
Pilot Mountain	9	8	1	Valdese	13	12	1
Pinebluff	3	3	—	Vanceboro	2	2	—
Pinehurst	27	22	5	Vass	4	4	—
Pine Knoll Shores	8	8	—	Wadesboro	25	20	5
Pinetops	9	6	3	Wagram	3	3	—
Pineville	34	24	10	Wake Forest	25	21	4
Pink Hill	1	1	—	Wallace	14	11	3
Pittsboro	7	7	—	Walnut Cove	5	5	—
Plymouth	11	10	1	Warsaw	14	11	3
Polkville	1	1	—	Washington	37	30	7
Princeton	3	3	—	Waxhaw	4	4	—
Raeford	16	15	1	Waynesville	34	29	5
Raleigh	622	554	68	Weldon	13	9	4
Ramseur	7	7	—	Wendell	14	10	4
Randleman	9	9	—	West Jefferson	5	5	—
Ranlo	6	6	—	Whispering Pines	7	7	—
Red Springs	19	15	4	Whitakers	3	2	1
Reidsville	48	41	7	White Lake	4	4	—
Rhodhiss	1	1	—	Whiteville	32	26	6
Richlands	5	5	—	Wilkesboro	17	16	1
River Bend	3	3	—	Williamston	19	18	1
Roanoke Rapids	43	34	9	Wilmington	180	159	21
Robbins	8	7	1	Wilson	100	87	13
Robersonville	8	8	—	Windsor	7	7	—
Rockingham	32	27	5	Winfall	1	1	—
Rocky Mount	179	145	34	Wingate	4	4	—
Rolesville	4	4	—	Winston-Salem	582	448	134
Roseboro	5	5	—	Winterville	11	10	1
Rose Hill	4	4	—	Winton	2	2	—
Rowland	8	5	3	Woodfin	8	8	—
Roxboro	31	28	3	Woodland	1	1	—
Rutherfordton	13	12	1	Wrightsville Beach	25	19	6
St. Pauls	14	10	4	Yadkinville	8	8	—
Salisbury	110	92	18	Yaupon Beach	4	4	—
Saluda	3	3	—	Youngsville	5	5	—
Sanford	86	71	15	Zebulon	20	19	1
Scotland Neck	14	8	6				
Seaboard	2	2	—	**NORTH DAKOTA**			
Selma	27	22	5				
Seven Devils	6	6	—	Beulah	7	6	1
Shallotte	9	8	1	Bismarck	96	74	22
Sharpsburg	5	5	—	Bowman	3	3	—
Shelby	74	62	12	Cando	3	3	—
Siler City	21	19	2	Carrington	4	4	—
Smithfield	36	30	6	Casselton	2	2	—
Southern Pines	32	26	6	Cavalier	3	3	—
Southern Shores	9	8	1	Cooperstown	1	1	—
Southport	14	9	5	Crosby	3	3	—
Sparta	5	5	—	Devils Lake	16	14	2
Spencer	8	8	—	Dickinson	35	24	11
Spindale	13	13	—	Elgin	1	1	—
Spring Hope	6	6	—	Emerado	1	1	—
Spring Lake	27	20	7	Fargo	118	91	27
Spruce Pine	9	9	—	Fessenden	1	1	—
Stanfield	2	2	—	Grafton	12	10	2
Stanley	12	9	3	Grand Forks	77	65	12
Stantonsburg	3	3	—	Gwinner	1	1	—

Table 78.—Number of Full-time Law Enforcement Employees, Cities, October 31, 1995 — Continued

City	Total police employees	Total officers	Total civilians	City	Total police employees	Total officers	Total civilians
NORTH DAKOTA — Continued				**OHIO — Continued**			
Harvey	3	3	—	Chillicothe	57	50	7
Hatton	1	1	—	Cincinnati	1,194	952	242
Hazen	4	4	—	Clear Creek Township	10	9	1
Hillsboro	2	2	—	Cleveland	2,180	1,727	453
Jamestown	32	28	4	Cleves	2	2	—
Larimore	2	2	—	Clinton Township	8	8	—
Lehr	1	1	—	Coitsville Township	3	3	—
Linton	2	2	—	Conneaut	26	21	5
Lisbon	2	2	—	Cortland	9	9	—
Mandan	32	27	5	Covington	6	5	1
Mayville	3	3	—	Crestline	14	10	4
Minot	73	54	19	Cuyahoga Falls	94	79	15
Napoleon	1	1	—	Deer Park	10	9	1
Northwood	2	2	—	Delaware	46	34	12
Oakes	2	2	—	Delta	6	6	—
Parshall	2	2	—	Dennison	4	4	—
Rugby	4	4	—	Deshler	2	2	—
South Heart	1	1	—	Dover	21	19	2
Stanton	1	1	—	Doylestown	4	3	1
Steele	1	1	—	Dublin	65	47	18
Thompson	1	1	—	East Canton	2	2	—
Valley City	13	11	2	East Cleveland	60	46	14
Wahpeton	20	13	7	Eastlake	42	32	10
Watford City	3	3	—	East Liverpool	28	22	6
West Fargo	24	17	7	East Palestine	10	6	4
Williston	28	20	8	Eaton	18	12	6
Wishek	2	2	—	Elmwood Place	8	5	3
				Elyria	116	98	18
OHIO				Englewood	23	17	6
				Euclid	167	100	67
Akron	558	514	44	Fairborn	54	42	12
Amberley	17	15	2	Fairfax	9	9	—
Amherst	22	17	5	Fairfield	66	50	16
Archbold	8	8	—	Fairfield Township	7	7	—
Ashland	42	30	12	Fairlawn	28	20	8
Ashtabula	44	37	7	Fairport Harbor	7	6	1
Athens	34	23	11	Fairview Park	29	28	1
Aurora	22	18	4	Fayette	3	3	—
Bainbridge Township	24	17	7	Forest	2	2	—
Barberton	50	41	9	Forest Park	39	32	7
Bazetta Township	9	8	1	Franklin	24	19	5
Beavercreek	51	40	11	Fremont	37	32	5
Beaver Township	13	9	4	Gahanna	48	42	6
Bedford	36	29	7	Gallipolis	19	15	4
Bedford Heights	46	33	13	Garfield Heights	70	57	13
Bellaire	13	13	—	Gates Mills	16	12	4
Bellbrook	11	7	4	Germantown	13	8	5
Bellefontaine	30	22	8	German Township	6	6	—
Bellevue	15	11	4	Gibsonburg	4	4	—
Belpre	16	11	5	Girard	25	21	4
Berea	39	30	9	Glendale	8	7	1
Bexley	35	27	8	Golf Manor	9	5	4
Blanchester	5	5	—	Goshen Township	7	6	1
Blue Ash	45	36	9	Granville	14	10	4
Bowling Green	42	31	11	Greenfield	12	10	2
Bradford	4	4	—	Grove City	51	37	14
Brecksville	30	26	4	Hamilton	134	114	20
Brewster	4	4	—	Harrison	20	17	3
Bridgeport	9	6	3	Hartville	5	5	—
Broadview Heights	31	24	7	Heath	24	19	5
Brooklyn	37	30	7	Hicksville	7	6	1
Brooklyn Heights	13	13	—	Hilliard	50	37	13
Brook Park	51	41	10	Hinckley Township	11	10	1
Bryan	24	19	5	Holgate	1	1	—
Buckeye Lake	5	5	—	Holland	5	5	—
Bucyrus	25	19	6	Hubbard	16	12	4
Burton	3	3	—	Huber Heights	49	45	4
Cadiz	4	4	—	Hudson	28	23	5
Cambridge	30	24	6	Hunting Valley	13	11	2
Canal Fulton	9	8	1	Huron	15	11	4
Carlisle	9	9	—	Indian Hill	24	19	5
Centerville	40	32	8	Jackson Township	36	31	5
Chagrin Falls	15	8	7	Johnstown	8	4	4
Chardon	13	8	5	Kent	59	40	19

Table 78.—Number of Full-time Law Enforcement Employees, Cities, October 31, 1995 — Continued

City	Total police employees	Total officers	Total civilians	City	Total police employees	Total officers	Total civilians
OHIO — Continued				**OHIO — Continued**			
Kettering	104	80	24	Ontario	20	16	4
Kirtland Hills	7	6	1	Oregon	53	43	10
Lakemore	6	5	1	Orrville	17	12	5
Lakewood	106	86	20	Ottawa Hills	15	11	4
Lancaster	91	67	24	Oxford	29	23	6
Lawrence Township	5	5	—	Parma	116	94	22
Lebanon	30	23	7	Pepper Pike	20	14	6
Lexington	11	7	4	Perkins Township	17	13	4
Liberty Township	26	24	2	Perrysburg	29	22	7
Lima	118	96	22	Perry Township (Stark County)	21	16	5
Lockland	10	10	—	Pierce Township	12	11	1
Logan	18	13	5	Piqua	34	30	4
Lorain	138	104	34	Plain City	3	3	—
Lordstown	12	8	4	Poland Township	8	8	—
Louisville	15	12	3	Poland Village	5	5	—
Loveland	16	15	1	Port Clinton	16	12	4
Lyndhurst	35	28	7	Portsmouth	48	44	4
Madeira	13	12	1	Randolph Township	13	12	1
Madison Township (Lake County)	18	16	2	Ravenna	28	21	7
Madison Township (Montgomery County)	24	19	5	Reading	22	19	3
Mansfield	135	94	41	Reynoldsburg	56	43	13
Maple Heights	64	47	17	Richmond Heights	25	20	5
Mariemont	10	9	1	Rittman	12	9	3
Marietta	36	29	7	Roseville	3	3	—
Marion	74	53	21	Rossford	19	18	1
Marlboro Township	2	2	—	St. Marys	18	14	4
Marysville	19	15	4	Salem	21	19	2
Mason	20	19	1	Salineville	4	4	—
Massillon	53	50	3	Sandusky	60	53	7
Maumee	51	41	10	Sebring	9	6	3
Mayfield Heights	44	33	11	Seven Hills	16	15	1
Mayfield Village	21	15	6	Shadyside	9	6	3
McConnelsville	7	5	2	Shaker Heights	101	70	31
Medina Township	17	15	2	Sharonville	41	31	10
Mentor	91	63	28	Sheffield Lake	10	7	3
Mentor-on-the-Lake	14	10	4	Shelby	18	14	4
Miamisburg	46	37	9	Silverton	13	10	3
Miami Township	31	28	3	Solon	48	38	10
Middleburg Heights	35	29	6	South Euclid	43	36	7
Middlefield	7	6	1	South Russell	8	8	—
Middletown	124	82	42	South Solon	3	3	—
Milford	16	13	3	Spencerville	4	4	—
Minerva	7	7	—	Springboro	20	14	6
Mingo Junction	15	13	2	Springdale	39	31	8
Mogadore	8	8	—	Springfield	154	115	39
Monroe	5	1	4	Springfield Township (Hamilton County)	39	34	5
Montgomery	19	18	1	Springfield Township (Mahoning County)	6	5	1
Montpelier	8	8	—	Stow	46	29	17
Moraine	38	31	7	Streetsboro	28	21	7
Mount Sterling	8	5	3	Strongsville	70	59	11
Munroe Falls	8	7	1	Sunbury	8	8	—
Napolean	19	14	5	Swanton	6	6	—
Navarre	4	4	—	Sylvania	36	30	6
Newark	72	62	10	Sylvania Township	36	27	9
Newcomerstown	11	6	5	Tallmadge	35	24	11
New Lebanon	8	7	1	Tiffin	43	30	13
New Lexington	10	6	4	Tipp City	15	14	1
New Paris	1	1	—	Toledo	779	701	78
New Philadelphia	24	20	4	Toronto	10	10	—
Newtown	5	5	—	Trenton	11	7	4
Niles	42	32	10	Trotwood	26	22	4
North Baltimore	5	5	—	Troy	40	37	3
North Canton	28	22	6	Twinsburg	32	24	8
North Olmsted	72	56	16	Uniontown	6	5	1
North Kingsville	4	4	—	Union Township (Butler County)	59	46	13
North Ridgeville	38	29	9	Union Township (Clermont County)	45	33	12
North Royalton	46	31	15	University Heights	39	31	8
Northwood	20	15	5	Upper Arlington	58	49	9
Norton	22	16	6	Upper Sandusky	11	9	2
Norwalk	26	22	4	Urbana	24	21	3
Norwood	44	44	—	Valley View	16	14	2
Oak Harbor	6	4	2	Vandalia	38	30	8
Oberlin	17	13	4	Vam Wert	28	22	6
Olmsted Township	16	12	4	Vermilion	23	18	5

Table 78.—Number of Full-time Law Enforcement Employees, Cities, October 31, 1995 — Continued

City	Total police employees	Total officers	Total civilians	City	Total police employees	Total officers	Total civilians
OHIO — Continued				**OKLAHOMA — Continued**			
Village of Highland Hills	6	6	—	Cordell	6	6	—
Wadsworth	29	24	5	Coweta	19	14	5
Waite Hill	5	5	—	Crescent	5	4	1
Walbridge	9	5	4	Cushing	25	18	7
Walton Hills	15	12	3	Davis	14	11	3
Warren Township	8	8	—	Del City	46	34	12
Washington Court House	24	17	7	Dewey	9	8	1
Waterville	13	12	1	Drumright	5	5	—
Waterville Township	2	2	—	Duncan	50	40	10
Wauseon	12	10	2	Durant	33	26	7
Waverly	17	12	5	Edmond	93	83	10
Wellington	7	6	1	Elk City	27	17	10
Wellsville	6	6	—	Elmore City	3	2	1
West Carrollton	32	25	7	El Reno	32	26	6
Westerville	62	54	8	Enid	112	86	26
West Jefferson	11	8	3	Erick	2	2	—
Westlake	53	40	13	Eufaula	12	9	3
Whitehall	52	42	10	Fairfax	7	4	3
Wickliffe	37	29	8	Fairview	10	6	4
Willard	20	15	5	Forest Park	3	2	1
Willoughby	5	5	—	Fort Gibson	9	6	3
Willoughby Hills	22	16	6	Frederick	16	10	6
Willowick	28	23	5	Geary	7	3	4
Wilmington	20	18	2	Glenpool	15	11	4
Windham	7	5	2	Goodwell	2	2	—
Woodsfield	6	6	—	Gore	3	3	—
Woodville	3	2	1	Granite	3	3	—
Wooster	36	34	2	Grove	20	13	7
Worthington	45	33	12	Guthrie	33	25	8
Wyoming	21	17	4	Guymon	20	14	6
Xenia	71	47	24	Harrah	8	8	—
Yellow Springs	12	9	3	Hartshorne	5	5	—
Youngstown	229	204	25	Haskell	6	6	—
Zanesville	96	58	38	Healdton	7	4	3
				Heavener	10	6	4
OKLAHOMA				Hennessey	9	4	5
				Henryetta	14	10	4
Ada	45	32	13	Hobart	17	11	6
Altus	51	43	8	Holdenville	12	8	4
Alva	13	8	5	Hollis	10	6	4
Anadarko	22	16	6	Hominy	6	3	3
Antlers	8	4	4	Hooker	5	3	2
Apache	4	4	—	Hugo	17	12	5
Ardmore	62	49	13	Hulbert	5	4	1
Arkoma	7	3	4	Idabel	25	19	6
Atoka	14	13	1	Inola	7	2	5
Barnsdall	6	4	2	Jay	10	7	3
Bartlesville	77	51	26	Jenks	17	12	5
Beggs	6	3	3	Jones	4	4	—
Bethany	34	24	10	Keyes	1	1	—
Bixby	16	12	4	Kingfisher	8	7	1
Blackwell	18	13	5	Kingston	4	4	—
Blanchard	7	4	3	Konawa	8	4	4
Boise City	3	3	—	Krebs	4	4	—
Bristow	15	13	2	Laverne	5	2	3
Broken Arrow	107	79	28	Lawton	171	149	22
Broken Bow	15	10	5	Lexington	10	6	4
Carnegie	8	4	4	Lindsay	12	8	4
Catoosa	11	11	—	Locust Grove	7	3	4
Chandler	13	9	4	Lone Grove	8	4	4
Checotah	12	8	4	Luther	3	3	—
Chelsea	5	5	—	Madill	9	9	—
Cherokee	6	3	3	Mangum	11	7	4
Chickasha	42	33	9	Mannford	12	7	5
Choctaw	18	17	1	Marietta	6	6	—
Chouteau	5	4	1	Marlow	10	9	1
Claremore	49	32	17	Maud	3	3	—
Clayton	8	4	4	Maysville	3	2	1
Cleveland	8	8	—	McAlester	51	39	12
Clinton	28	20	8	McLoud	9	5	4
Coalgate	5	5	—	Meeker	5	5	—
Collinsville	10	6	4	Miami	39	29	10
Comanche	4	4	—	Midwest City	121	98	23
Commerce	2	2	—	Minco	4	4	—

Table 78.—Number of Full-time Law Enforcement Employees, Cities, October 31, 1995 — Continued

City	Total police employees	Total officers	Total civilians	City	Total police employees	Total officers	Total civilians
OKLAHOMA — Continued				**OKLAHOMA — Continued**			
Moore	49	44	5	Westville	9	4	5
Mooreland	3	3	—	Wetumka	7	6	1
Morris	3	3	—	Wewoka	13	9	4
Muldrow	14	8	6	Wilburton	9	6	3
Muskogee	109	83	26	Woodward	30	20	10
Mustang	21	16	5	Wright City	5	3	2
Newcastle	17	9	8	Wynnewood	9	5	4
Newkirk	6	5	1	Yale	7	3	4
Nichols Hills	20	15	5	Yukon	39	29	10
Nicoma Park	5	5	—				
Noble	15	10	5	**OREGON**			
Norman	152	121	31	Albany	67	49	18
Nowata	8	6	2	Amity	2	2	—
Oilton	3	3	—	Ashland	36	25	11
Okeene	7	3	4	Astoria	22	15	7
Okemah	13	6	7	Athena	1	1	—
Oklahoma City	1,664	1,142	522	Aumsville	3	2	1
Okmulgee	31	24	7	Aurora	2	1	1
Oologah	3	3	—	Baker	16	12	4
Owasso	31	23	8	Bandon	7	6	1
Pauls Valley	20	14	6	Beaverton	111	91	20
Pawhuska	14	7	7	Bend	62	47	15
Pawnee	6	6	—	Boardman	4	4	—
Perkins	4	4	—	Brookings	19	13	6
Perry	17	13	4	Burns	10	5	5
Piedmont	6	5	1	Butte Falls	1	1	—
Pocola	10	7	3	Canby	22	16	6
Ponca City	87	56	31	Cannon Beach	9	8	1
Porum	4	4	—	Carlton	2	2	—
Poteau	22	16	6	Central Point	22	16	6
Prague	12	7	5	Clatskanie	7	6	1
Pryor	24	20	4	Coburg	2	2	—
Purcell	23	16	7	Columbia City	1	1	—
Ringling	3	3	—	Coos Bay	43	30	13
Roland	9	6	3	Coquille	10	8	2
Rush Springs	4	4	—	Cornelius	16	14	2
Salina	4	4	—	Corvallis	83	52	31
Sallisaw	24	17	7	Cottage Grove	23	15	8
Sand Springs	41	31	10	Creswell	2	2	—
Sapulpa	46	35	11	Culver	1	1	—
Sayre	8	5	3	Dallas	18	17	1
Seiling	2	2	—	Dundee	6	6	—
Seminole	17	14	3	Eagle Point	6	5	1
Shawnee	72	53	19	Elgin	3	3	—
Skiatook	15	11	4	Enterprise	4	4	—
Snyder	4	4	—	Eugene	323	164	159
Spencer	11	10	1	Florence	21	13	8
Spiro	5	5	—	Forest Grove	28	22	6
Stigler	13	9	4	Garibaldi	3	3	—
Stillwater	84	62	22	Gaston	1	1	—
Stilwell	19	13	6	Gearhart	2	2	—
Stratford	3	3	—	Gervais	1	1	—
Stroud	15	11	4	Gladstone	17	12	5
Sulphur	14	9	5	Gold Beach	7	6	1
Tahlequah	33	24	9	Grants Pass	38	26	12
Talihina	7	4	3	Gresham	128	90	38
Tecumseh	14	10	4	Heppner	3	3	—
The Village	30	24	6	Hermiston	26	19	7
Tishomingo	8	7	1	Hines	2	2	—
Tonkawa	12	7	5	Hood River	14	11	3
Tulsa	890	762	128	Hubbard	6	5	1
Tuttle	10	6	4	Independence	11	10	1
Valliant	7	4	3	Jacksonville	4	4	—
Vian	4	4	—	John Day	9	4	5
Vinita	20	14	6	Junction Ciy	13	9	4
Wagoner	11	11	—	Keizer	35	29	6
Walters	4	4	—	King City	3	3	—
Warner	4	4	—	Klamath Falls	34	32	2
Warr Acres	32	23	9	La Grande	32	17	15
Watonga	11	7	4	Lake Oswego	65	42	23
Waukomis	2	2	—	Lakeview	5	5	—
Waynoka	3	3	—	Lebanon	30	22	8
Weatherford	29	19	10	Lincoln City	28	20	8
Weleetka	8	4	4				

City	Total police employees	Total officers	Total civilians	City	Total police employees	Total officers	Total civilians
OREGON — Continued				**PENNSYLVANIA — Continued**			
Madras	10	9	1	Aldan	5	4	1
McMinnville	34	27	7	Aleppo Township	8	5	3
Medford	117	83	34	Aliquippa	18	17	1
Milton-Freewater	12	8	4	Allegheny Township (Blair County)	6	6	—
Milwaukie	42	30	12	Allegheny Township (Westmoreland County)	8	7	1
Molalla	11	9	2	Allentown	224	200	24
Monmouth	12	10	2	Altoona	90	73	17
Mount Angel	7	6	1	Ambler	13	12	1
Myrtle Creek	13	8	5	Ambridge	11	11	—
Myrtle Point	8	7	1	Amity Township	6	6	—
Newberg	30	22	8	Annville Township	5	5	—
Newport	27	23	4	Arnold	11	10	1
North Bend	24	17	7	Ashland	5	5	—
North Plains	4	3	1	Ashley	3	3	—
Nyssa	9	8	1	Aspinwall	7	6	1
Oakland	2	2	—	Aston Township	20	18	2
Oakridge	12	7	5	Athens	5	5	—
Ontario	29	20	9	Athens Township	6	6	—
Oregon City	32	28	4	Baldwin Borough	29	23	6
Pendleton	29	21	8	Baldwin Township	5	5	—
Philomath	9	8	1	Bally	1	1	—
Phoenix	8	7	1	Bangor	6	5	1
Pilot Rock	5	4	1	Barrett Township	5	5	—
Portland	1,260	996	264	Beaver	11	7	4
Powers	2	2	—	Bedford	6	5	1
Prairie City	2	2	—	Belle Acres	1	1	—
Prineville	17	10	7	Bellefonte	10	9	1
Rainier	7	6	1	Bellwood	2	2	—
Redmond	26	21	5	Bensalem Township	96	80	16
Reedsport	17	12	5	Berlin	1	1	—
Rockaway	3	3	—	Bern Township	7	7	—
Rogue River	4	4	—	Berwick	13	12	1
Roseburg	40	36	4	Bethel Park	46	38	8
St. Helens	21	18	3	Bethel Township (Lebanon County)	2	2	—
Salem	254	161	93	Bethlehem	159	136	23
Sandy	10	9	1	Bethlehem Township	21	20	1
Scappoose	11	9	2	Big Beaver	3	3	—
Seaside	25	18	7	Birdsboro	6	6	—
Shady Cove	5	4	1	Birmingham Township	2	2	—
Sherwood	10	8	2	Blair Township	3	3	—
Silverton	13	11	2	Blairsville	3	3	—
Sisters	7	6	1	Blakely	7	7	—
Springfield	87	61	26	Blawnox	4	4	—
Stanfield	3	3	—	Bloomsburg Town	15	12	3
Stayton	13	11	2	Blossburg	2	2	—
Sutherlin	14	12	2	Boyertown	7	7	—
Sweet Home	19	14	5	Brackenridge	5	5	—
Talent	9	8	1	Bradford	21	20	1
The Dalles	21	19	2	Bradford Township	6	5	1
Tigard	58	47	11	Briar Creek Township	2	2	—
Tillamook	10	9	1	Bridgeport	10	9	1
Toledo	13	8	5	Bridgeville	9	8	1
Troutdale	16	13	3	Bridgewater	2	2	—
Tualatin	30	27	3	Brighton Township	4	4	—
Turner	1	1	—	Bristol Township	74	65	9
Umatilla	8	7	1	Brockway	1	1	—
Umatilla Tribal	15	10	5	Brookhaven	8	7	1
Vale	4	4	—	Brookville	7	6	1
Veneta	6	6	—	Bryn Athyn	5	5	—
Vernonia	6	5	1	Buckingham Township	20	18	2
Waldport	4	3	1	Bushkill Township	5	5	—
Warrenton	8	7	1	Butler	21	21	—
West Linn	27	22	5	Butler Township (Butler County)	21	19	2
Winston	11	7	4	Butler Township (Luzerne County)	5	4	1
Woodburn	29	25	4	Butler Township (Schuylkill County)	2	2	—
Yamhill	2	2	—	California	7	6	1
				Caln Township	15	13	2
PENNSYLVANIA				Cambria Township	4	4	—
				Camp Hill	9	9	—
Abington Township	111	91	20	Canonsburg	17	15	2
Adams Township (Butler County)	1	1	—	Carlisle	37	30	7
Adams Township (Cambria County)	4	4	—	Carnegie	19	13	6
Akron	4	4	—	Carroll Township (Washington County)	4	4	—
Albion	1	1	—	Carroll Township (York County)	4	4	—

Table 78.—Number of Full-time Law Enforcement Employees, Cities, October 31, 1995 — Continued

City	Total police employees	Total officers	Total civilians	City	Total police employees	Total officers	Total civilians
PENNSYLVANIA— Continued				**PENNSYLVANIA— Continued**			
Castle Shannon	10	9	1	East Cocalico Township	20	18	2
Catawissa	1	1	—	East Conemaugh	2	2	—
Cecil Township	11	11	—	East Coventry Township	3	3	—
Center Township	9	9	—	East Donegal Township	4	4	—
Central Berks Regional	13	12	1	East Fallowfield Township	2	2	—
Chalfont	5	5	—	East Hempfield Township	27	23	4
Chambersburg	33	30	3	East Lampeter Township	27	24	3
Charleroi	10	9	1	East Lansdowne	3	3	—
Chartiers Township	9	9	—	East McKeesport	3	3	—
Cheltenham Township	90	80	10	East NorritonTownship	26	23	3
Chester	107	99	8	East Pennsboro Township	16	15	1
Chester Township	8	8	—	East Pikeland Township	5	5	—
Cheswick	3	3	—	East Stroudsburg	15	13	2
Chippewa Township	8	7	1	Easttown Township	14	13	1
Christiana	1	1	—	East Vincent Township	5	5	—
Churchill	10	10	—	East Whiteland Township	14	12	2
Clarion	9	8	1	Ebensburg	5	5	—
Clarks Summit	7	6	1	Economy	11	10	1
Clearfield	8	8	—	Edgewood	7	7	—
Cleona	2	2	—	Edgeworth	5	5	—
Coal Township	12	12	—	Edinboro	8	7	1
Coatesville	26	23	3	Edwardsville	5	5	—
Cochranton	2	2	—	Elizabeth	1	1	—
Colebrookdale Township	9	9	—	Elizabethtown	15	13	2
Collegeville	6	6	—	Elizabeth Township	16	15	1
Collier Township	10	10	—	Elizabethville	1	1	—
Collingdale	9	8	1	Elkland	3	3	—
Columbia	16	13	3	Ellwood City	19	15	4
Conemaugh Township (Somerset County)	4	4	—	Emmaus	16	14	2
Conestoga Township	3	3	—	Ephrata	23	20	3
Conewago Township	5	5	—	Ephrata Township	11	10	1
Conewango Township	4	4	—	Erie	232	192	40
Connellsville	17	15	2	Etna	5	4	1
Conoy Township	4	3	1	Everett	2	2	—
Conshohocken	13	12	1	Exeter Township (Berks County)	24	23	1
Conway	2	2	—	Fairview	1	1	—
Conyngham	3	3	—	Fairview Township (York County)	14	13	1
Coolbaugh Township	10	9	1	Falls Township	47	41	6
Coopersburg	5	5	—	Fawn Township	2	2	—
Coplay	4	4	—	Ferguson Township	15	13	2
Coraopolis	14	10	4	Ferndale	2	2	—
Cornwall	4	3	1	Findlay Township	19	13	6
Corry	16	12	4	Fleetwood	5	5	—
Covington Township	1	1	—	Folcroft	7	7	—
Crafton	13	9	4	Ford City	4	4	—
Cranberry Township	17	15	2	Forest City	2	2	—
Crescent Township	1	1	—	Forest Hills	19	10	9
Cresson	2	2	—	Forks Township	13	11	2
Cressona	2	2	—	Forty Fort	5	5	—
Cresson Township	1	1	—	Foster Township	5	5	—
Cumberland Township (Adams County)	6	6	—	Fountain Hill	5	5	—
Cumru Township	22	21	1	Fox Chapel	11	11	—
Curwensville	2	2	—	Frackville	6	6	—
Dale	1	1	—	Franklin (Cambria County)	2	2	—
Dallas	5	5	—	Franklin (Venango County)	22	16	6
Dallas Township	8	8	—	Franklin Park	8	7	1
Danville	9	8	1	Franklin Township (Beaver County)	1	1	—
Darby	13	11	2	Franklin Township (Carbon County)	4	4	—
Darby Township	15	14	1	Freedom-Greenfield Township	2	2	—
Derry Township (Dauphin County)	38	31	7	Freeland	5	5	—
Donora	5	5	—	Gallitzin	1	1	—
Dormont	14	13	1	Gettysburg	14	12	2
Douglass Township (Montgomery County)	10	9	1	Girard	5	4	1
Downington	11	9	2	Glenolden	9	8	1
Doylestown	17	15	2	Granville Township	5	5	—
Doylestown Township	22	19	3	Greencastle	5	5	—
Du Bois	14	10	4	Greensburg	33	27	6
Duboistown	1	1	—	Green Tree	12	11	1
Duncansville	1	1	—	Greenville	13	12	1
Dunmore	14	12	2	Grove City	7	7	—
Dupont	1	1	—	Halstead	2	2	—
Duquesne	13	13	—	Hamburg	7	7	—
East Bethlehem Township	1	1	—	Hampden Township	21	20	1
East Brandywine Township	8	7	1	Hanover Township (Luzerne County)	20	15	5

Table 78.—Number of Full-time Law Enforcement Employees, Cities, October 31, 1995 — Continued

City	Total police employees	Total officers	Total civilians	City	Total police employees	Total officers	Total civilians
PENNSYLVANIA — Continued				**PENNSYLVANIA— Continued**			
Hanover Township (Washington County)	7	7	—	Locust Township	2	2	—
Harmar Township	4	4	—	Logan Township	19	14	5
Harmony Township	3	3	—	Lower Allen Township	21	18	3
Hatboro	19	14	5	Lower Burrell	14	14	—
Hatfield Township	27	22	5	Lower Gwynedd Township	21	17	4
Haverford Township	79	65	14	Lower Heidelberg Township	5	5	—
Hazleton	31	25	6	Lower Merion Township	159	134	25
Heidelberg	2	2	—	Lower Moreland Township	26	19	7
Heidelberg Township (Lebanon County)	2	2	—	Lower Paxton Township	48	43	5
Hellam Township	7	7	—	Lower Pottsgrove Township	12	11	1
Hellertown	9	8	1	Lower Providence Township	32	25	7
Hempfield Township	7	6	1	Lower Saucon Township	15	10	5
Hermitage	28	25	3	Lower Southampton Township	29	26	3
Highspire	6	6	—	Lower Swatara Township	12	11	1
Hilltown Township	15	13	2	Lower Yoder Township	3	3	—
Hollidaysburg	12	7	5	Luzerne	3	3	—
Homer City	1	1	—	Luzerne Township	1	1	—
Honey Brook Township	2	2	—	Lykens	1	1	—
Hooversville	1	1	—	Macungie	4	4	—
Hopewell Township	14	14	—	Mahoning Township (Carbon County)	4	4	—
Horsham Township	45	37	8	Mahoning Township (Montour County)	7	6	1
Houtzdale	1	1	—	Malvern	6	5	1
Hughesville	3	3	—	Manheim	7	6	1
Hummelstown	6	6	—	Manheim Township	59	45	14
Huntingdon	14	11	3	Manor	2	2	—
Independence Township	2	2	—	Manor Township	18	16	2
Indiana	24	19	5	Mansfield	5	5	—
Indiana Township	8	8	—	Marietta	4	3	1
Ingram	6	6	—	Marlborough Township	3	3	—
Irwin	2	2	—	Marple Township	40	33	7
Jackson Township (Butler County)	3	3	—	Martinsburg	2	2	—
Jackson Township (Cambria County)	1	1	—	Marysville	2	2	—
Jackson Township (York County)	8	7	1	Masontown	5	5	—
Jeannette	19	16	3	Matamoras	2	2	—
Jefferson	15	14	1	Mayfield	1	1	—
Jefferson Township	3	3	—	McAdoo	2	2	—
Jenkintown	10	10	—	McConnellsburg	2	2	—
Jermyn	1	1	—	McDonald	2	2	—
Jersey Shore	7	6	1	McKeesport	32	30	2
Johnsonburg	6	5	1	McKees Rocks	12	8	4
Johnstown	54	45	9	McSherrystown	4	4	—
Jones Township	1	1	—	Meadville	29	22	7
Kane	6	6	—	Mechanicsburg	15	14	1
Kennedy Township	10	9	1	Media	20	14	6
Kennett Square	9	7	2	Mercer	4	4	—
Kidder Township	6	6	—	Mercersburg	2	2	—
Kilbuck Township	2	2	—	Meyersdale	4	4	—
Kingston	22	18	4	Mid-Cumberland Valley Regional	12	11	1
Kingston Township	10	10	—	Middlesex Township (Butler County)	6	6	—
Kittanning	9	8	1	Middlesex Township (Cumberland County)	7	7	—
Kutztown	10	9	1	Middletown	15	14	1
Lake City	3	3	—	Midland	6	5	1
Lancaster	148	137	11	Mifflin County Regional	20	19	1
Lansdale	29	22	7	Mifflin Town	1	1	—
Lansdowne	18	15	3	Milford	2	2	—
Lansford	5	4	1	Millbourne	3	3	—
Latrobe	13	12	1	Millcreek Township	65	53	12
Laureldale	4	4	—	Millersburg	3	3	—
Lawrence Park Township	7	6	1	Millersville	12	10	2
Lawrence Township	7	7	—	Milton	11	10	1
Lebanon	44	37	7	Minersville	7	6	1
Leetsdale	2	2	—	Mohnton	3	3	—
Leet Township	5	5	—	Monongahela	11	7	4
Lehighton	9	8	1	Monroeville	70	56	14
Lehigh Township (Northampton County)	9	8	1	Montgomery Township	40	31	9
Lehman Township	2	2	—	Montoursville	5	5	—
Lewisburg	7	7	—	Moon Township	31	26	5
Ligonier Township	2	2	—	Moore Township	5	5	—
Limerick Township	12	10	2	Moosic	2	2	—
Lincoln	1	1	—	Morrisville	13	11	2
Linesville	1	1	—	Morton	4	4	—
Lititz	13	11	2	Mount Holly Springs	3	3	—
Littlestown	7	7	—	Mount Jewett	1	1	—
Lock Haven	14	12	2	Mount Joy	11	9	2

Table 78.—Number of Full-time Law Enforcement Employees, Cities, October 31, 1995 — Continued

City	Total police employees	Total officers	Total civilians	City	Total police employees	Total officers	Total civilians
PENNSYLVANIA— Continued				**PENNSYLVANIA— Continued**			
Mount Joy Township	7	6	1	Patton Township	13	12	1
Mount Lebanon	55	41	14	Paxtang	3	3	—
Mount Pleasant	4	4	—	Pen Argyl	3	3	—
Mount Union	5	5	—	Penbrook	6	6	—
Muhlenberg Township	24	23	1	Penn Hills	62	53	9
Munhall	21	17	4	Pennridge Regional	16	14	2
Murrysville	22	18	4	Penn Township (Butler County)	5	4	1
Myerstown	4	4	—	Penn Township (Lancaster County)	6	6	—
Nanticoke	16	13	3	Penn Township (Westmoreland County)	21	19	2
Nanty Glo	2	2	—	Penn Township (York County)	18	17	1
Narberth	6	6	—	Pequea Township	3	3	—
Nazareth Area	12	10	2	Perkasie	12	11	1
Nesquehoning	3	3	—	Perryopolis	2	2	—
Nether Providence Township	13	13	—	Peters Township	21	19	2
Newberry Township	12	11	1	Philadelphia	7,319	6,376	943
New Britain	2	2	—	Philipsburg	2	2	—
New Britain Township	13	12	1	Phoenixville	23	21	2
New Castle	36	36	—	Pine Grove	3	3	—
New Cumberland	8	8	—	Pine Township	13	12	1
New Hanover Township	4	4	—	Pitcairn	4	4	—
New Holland	9	8	1	Pittsburgh	1,252	1,180	72
New Hope	8	7	1	Pittston	9	7	2
New Oxford	2	2	—	Plainfield Township	6	6	—
New Sewickley Township	6	5	1	Plains Township	7	7	—
Newtown	3	3	—	Pleasant Hills	19	15	4
Newtown Township (Bucks County)	20	18	2	Plum	25	21	4
Newtown Township (Delaware County)	14	13	1	Plumstead Township	10	8	2
Newville	2	2	—	Plymouth	2	2	—
New Wilmington	4	4	—	Plymouth Township	41	34	7
Norristown	77	65	12	Pocono Mountain Regional	19	17	2
Northampton	11	11	—	Pocono Township	10	10	—
Northampton Township	41	36	5	Point Township	5	5	—
North Belle Vernon	2	2	—	Portage	2	2	—
North Bethlehem Township	1	1	—	Port Allegany	3	3	—
North Charleroi	2	2	—	Port Carbon	3	3	—
North Cornwall Township	9	8	1	Pottstown	50	41	9
North Coventry Township	10	9	1	Pottsville	29	28	1
North East	7	6	1	Prospect Park	8	8	—
Northeastern Berks Regional	7	7	—	Pymatuning Township	4	4	—
Northeastern Regional	7	6	1	Radnor Township	55	45	10
Northern Cambria Regional	3	3	—	Rankin	1	1	—
Northern York Regional	42	38	4	Reading	234	204	30
North Fayette Township	19	13	6	Red Lion	9	8	1
North Franklin Township	7	7	—	Redstone Township	2	2	—
North Huntingdon Township	29	23	6	Reserve Township	3	3	—
North Lebanon Township	8	7	1	Reynoldsville	2	2	—
North Londonderry Township	6	6	—	Richland	1	1	—
North Middleton Township	7	7	—	Richland Township (Cambria County)	21	19	2
North Sewickley Township	2	2	—	Ridgway	6	6	—
North Strabane Township	12	11	1	Ridley Township	39	34	5
Northumberland	5	5	—	Riverside	3	3	—
North Versailles Township	11	11	—	Roaring Spring	1	1	—
North Wales	3	3	—	Robesonia Boro	2	2	—
Norwegian Township	1	1	—	Robeson Township	4	4	—
Norwood	6	5	1	Rochester	10	8	2
Oakdale	1	1	—	Rochester Township	2	1	1
Oakmont	8	7	1	Rockledge	3	3	—
O'Hara Township	12	12	—	Ross Township	50	40	10
Ohio Township	3	3	—	Rostraver Township	10	9	1
Ohioville	2	2	—	Royersford	7	6	1
Oil City	18	17	1	Rye Township	1	1	—
Old Forge	7	6	1	St. Clair	6	6	—
Old Lycoming Township	8	7	1	St. Marys	15	13	2
Oley Township	1	1	—	Salisbury Township	10	9	1
Olyphant	5	5	—	Sandy Lake	1	1	—
Orangeville	1	1	—	Sandy Township	6	6	—
Orwigsburg	4	4	—	Saxton	1	1	—
Oxford	9	9	—	Sayre	10	8	2
Paint Township	2	2	—	Schuylkill Haven	12	8	4
Palmerton	9	8	1	Schuylkill Township	8	7	1
Palmer Township	25	21	4	Scottsdale	7	7	—
Palmyra	7	7	—	Selinsgrove	4	3	1
Parkside	2	2	—	Seven Springs	7	5	2
Patterson Township	4	4	—	Sewickley	12	10	2

Table 78.—Number of Full-time Law Enforcement Employees, Cities, October 31, 1995 — Continued

City	Total police employees	Total officers	Total civilians	City	Total police employees	Total officers	Total civilians
PENNSYLVANIA — Continued				**PENNSYLVANIA— Continued**			
Sewickley Heights	7	7	—	Upland	2	2	—
Shaler Township	38	28	10	Upper Allen Township	14	13	1
Shamokin	11	11	—	Upper Chichester Township	21	19	2
Shamokin Dam	3	3	—	Upper Darby Township	112	97	15
Sharon	34	30	4	Upper Dublin Township	41	36	5
Sharon Hill	8	7	1	Upper Gwynedd Township	15	14	1
Sharpsville	6	5	1	Upper Makefield Township	7	7	—
Shenandoah	8	7	1	Upper Merion Township	72	54	18
Shenango Township (Lawrence County)	4	4	—	Upper Mount Bethel Township	4	4	—
Shenango Township (Mercer County)	4	3	1	Upper Nazareth Township	2	2	—
Shillington	8	7	1	Upper Perkiomen	6	5	1
Shippingport	2	2	—	Upper Pottsgrove Township	9	4	5
Shiremanstown	2	2	—	Upper Providence Township (Delaware County)	12	11	1
Sinking Spring	4	4	—	Upper Providence Township (Montgomery County)	12	11	1
Slatington	6	6	—	Upper St. Clair Township	36	29	7
Slippery Rock	5	5	—	Upper Saucon Township	14	13	1
Solebury Township	9	8	1	Upper Southampton Township	24	21	3
Souderton	7	6	1	Upper Uwchlan Township	7	6	1
South Abington Township	10	9	1	Upper Yoder Township	5	5	—
South Beaver Township	3	3	—	Uwchlan Township	22	20	2
South Coatesville	3	3	—	Vandergrift	9	9	—
Southern	7	6	1	Vanport Township	3	3	—
South Fayette Township	17	16	1	Vernon Township	4	4	—
South Greensburg	2	2	—	Verona	2	1	1
South Lebanon Township	7	6	1	Versailles	2	2	—
South Londonderry Township	4	4	—	Walnutport	3	3	—
South Park Township	16	15	1	Warminster Township	50	44	6
South Strabane Township	10	9	1	Warren	20	16	4
South Waverly	2	2	—	Warwick Township (Lancaster County)	14	13	1
Southwest Greensburg	2	2	—	Washington	31	30	1
S.W. Mercer County Regional	15	13	2	Washington Township (Westmoreland County)	3	3	—
South Whitehall Township	35	32	3	Wayneshoro	16	15	1
South Williamsport	6	6	—	Waynesburg	7	7	—
Springettbury Township	29	26	3	Wellsboro	6	6	—
Springfield Township (Bucks County)	4	4	—	Wernersville	2	2	—
Springfield Township (Delaware County)	40	33	7	West Brandywine Township	6	6	—
Springfield Township (Montgomery County)	31	30	1	West Chester	47	39	8
Spring Garden Township	18	17	1	West Conshohocken	8	7	1
Spring Township (Berks County)	21	20	1	West Deer Township	10	9	1
Spring Township (Centre County)	4	4	—	West Donegal Township	6	6	—
State College	63	54	9	West Earl Township	4	4	—
Steelton	10	9	1	Westfall Township	5	5	—
Stoneycreek Township	3	3	—	West Goshen Township	25	22	3
Stowe Township	7	6	1	West Grove	3	3	—
Strasburg	4	4	—	West Hempfield Township	16	14	2
Stroud Township	16	14	2	West Lampeter Township	12	11	1
Sugarcreek	5	5	—	West Manchester Township	24	22	2
Sugarloaf Township	2	2	—	West Manheim Township	6	6	—
Summerhill Township	1	1	—	West Mifflin	35	30	5
Sunbury	15	13	2	West Norriton Township	30	25	5
Susquehanna Township (Dauphin County)	33	30	3	West Pittston	7	4	3
Swarthmore	9	9	—	West Pottsgrove Township	8	7	1
Swissvale	12	9	3	West Reading	9	8	1
Swoyersville	4	4	—	West Shore Regional	12	10	2
Sykesville	1	1	—	Westtown Township	17	15	2
Tamaqua	10	9	1	West View	12	9	3
Teleford	7	6	1	West Whiteland Township	22	20	2
Temple	2	2	—	West Wyoming	2	2	—
Tinicum Township (Bucks County)	4	4	—	West York	6	6	—
Tinicum Township (Delaware County)	11	10	1	Whitehall	23	18	5
Titusville	14	13	1	Whitehall Township	53	44	9
Towamencin Township	20	18	2	White Haven	1	1	—
Towanda	4	4	—	Whitemarsh Township	30	27	3
Trafford	2	2	—	White Oak	11	11	—
Trainer	5	4	1	Whitpain Township	30	24	6
Tredyffrin Township	59	51	8	Wilkes-Barre Township	16	12	4
Troy	2	2	—	Wilkinsburg	37	30	7
Tunkhannock	4	4	—	Wilkins Township	11	11	—
Turtle Creek	9	6	3	Willistown	16	15	1
Tyrone	6	5	1	Wilmerding	1	1	—
Union City	5	4	1	Wilson	6	6	—
Uniontown	22	17	5	Windber	3	2	1
Union Township (Washington County)	6	6	—	Wind Gap	3	3	—
Union Township (Mifflin County)	2	2	—	Windsor Township	9	8	1

Table 78.—Number of Full-time Law Enforcement Employees, Cities, October 31, 1995 — Continued

City	Total police employees	Total officers	Total civilians	City	Total police employees	Total officers	Total civilians
PENNSYLVANIA — Continued				**SOUTH CAROLINA — Continued**			
Wrightsville	2	2	—	Calhoun Falls	8	7	1
Wyomissing	23	19	4	Camden	30	24	6
Wyomissing Hills	4	4	—	Campobello	1	1	—
Yardley	3	3	—	Cayce	47	35	12
Yeadon	17	15	2	Central	5	5	—
York	108	98	10	Chapin	2	2	—
York Springs – Latimore Township	3	3	—	Charleston	417	314	103
York Township	24	21	3	Cheraw	30	24	6
Youngsville	2	2	—	Chesnee	7	4	3
Zelienople	8	7	1	Chester	26	22	4
				Chesterfield	5	4	1
RHODE ISLAND				Clemson	29	24	5
				Clinton	30	25	5
Barrington	31	24	7	Clio	3	3	—
Bristol	46	36	10	Clover	15	12	3
Burrillville	26	20	6	Columbia	320	284	36
Central Falls	41	40	1	Conway	40	32	8
Charlestown	22	17	5	Cowpens	5	4	1
Coventry	63	50	13	Darlington	26	22	4
Cranston	174	145	29	Denmark	8	8	—
Cumberland	50	43	7	Dillon	16	15	1
East Greenwich	36	32	4	Due West	4	4	—
East Providence	106	88	18	Duncan	8	6	2
Foster	10	6	4	Easley	36	27	9
Glocester	14	10	4	Edgefield	8	8	—
Hopkinton	15	10	5	Edisto Beach	7	6	1
Jamestown	18	14	4	Ehrhardt	1	1	—
Johnston	84	67	17	Elgin	3	2	1
Lincoln	40	33	7	Elloree	4	4	—
Little Compton	12	8	4	Estill	7	6	1
Middletown	41	38	3	Eutawville	4	3	1
Narragansett	43	34	9	Fairfax	6	6	—
Newport	113	90	23	Florence	100	91	9
New Shoreham	5	3	2	Folly Beach	13	8	5
North Kingstown	60	49	11	Forest Acres	30	24	6
North Providence	91	68	23	Fort Lawn	2	2	—
North Smithfield	24	19	5	Fort Mill	20	15	5
Pawtucket	173	148	25	Fountain Inn	22	16	6
Portsmouth	29	27	2	Gaffney	33	27	6
Providence	492	422	70	Gaston	1	1	—
Richmond	8	6	2	Georgetown	43	33	10
Scituate	21	15	6	Goose Creek	41	32	9
Smithfield	45	36	9	Great Falls	8	6	2
South Kingstown	58	44	14	Greenville	212	174	38
Tiverton	32	23	9	Greenwood	64	56	8
Warren	27	21	6	Greer	46	35	11
Warwick	217	165	52	Hampton	9	8	1
Westerly	47	38	9	Hanahan	24	17	7
West Greenwich	12	7	5	Hardeeville	13	9	4
West Warwick	67	61	6	Harleyville	3	3	—
Woonsocket	106	99	7	Hartsville	40	36	4
				Hemingway	8	5	3
SOUTH CAROLINA				Holly Hill	6	6	—
				Honea Path	15	11	4
Abbeville	21	16	5	Inman	5	5	—
Aiken	106	88	18	Irmo	16	14	2
Allendale	12	7	5	Isle of Palms	24	17	7
Anderson	87	64	23	Iva	5	4	1
Andrews	17	13	4	Jackson	4	4	—
Aynor	9	4	5	Jamestown	1	1	—
Bamberg	10	9	1	Jefferson	5	5	—
Barnwell	11	10	1	Johnsonville	8	5	3
Batesburg-Leesville	24	19	5	Johnston	9	7	2
Beaufort	43	40	3	Jonesville	4	4	—
Belton	20	15	5	Kershaw	11	6	5
Bennettsville	31	28	3	Kingstree	21	17	4
Bishopville	19	14	5	Lake City	29	23	6
Blacksburg	8	7	1	Lake View	4	4	—
Blackville	8	7	1	Lamar	3	3	—
Bluffton	4	4	—	Lancaster	43	38	5
Bonneau	2	2	—	Landrum	7	7	—
Bowman	3	3	—	Latta	9	7	2
Branchville	1	1	—	Laurens	30	25	5
Briarcliffe Acres	1	1	—	Lexington	21	19	2

Table 78.—Number of Full-time Law Enforcement Employees, Cities, October 31, 1995 — Continued

City	Total police employees	Total officers	Total civilians	City	Total police employees	Total officers	Total civilians
SOUTH CAROLINA — Continued				**SOUTH CAROLINA — Continued**			
Liberty	12	8	4	Winnsboro	24	17	7
Loris	10	6	4	Woodruff	16	11	5
Lyman	6	5	1	Yemassee	4	4	—
Manning	19	17	2	York	25	20	5
Marion	29	22	7				
Mauldin	35	28	7	**SOUTH DAKOTA**			
Mayesville	2	2	—				
McBee	4	2	2	Aberdeen	47	39	8
McColl	8	3	5	Belle Fourche	8	7	1
McCormick	7	7	—	Brookings	31	26	5
Moncks Corner	20	18	2	Burke	1	1	—
Mount Pleasant	93	68	25	Canton	5	5	—
Mullins	21	21	—	Deadwood	11	10	1
Myrtle Beach	164	132	32	Eagle Butte	3	3	—
Newberry	27	24	3	Fort Pierre	3	3	—
New Ellenton	6	6	—	Harrisburg	1	1	—
Ninety Six	7	6	1	Hot Springs	8	7	1
North	2	2	—	Lead	7	6	1
North Augusta	59	47	12	Madison	11	10	1
North Charleston	253	192	61	McLaughlin	3	2	1
North Myrtle Beach	66	50	16	Miller	5	5	—
Norway	3	2	1	Mitchell	30	22	8
Orangeburg	85	73	12	Mobridge	11	7	4
Pacolet	5	4	1	Parkston	2	2	—
Pageland	15	11	4	Pierre	30	21	9
Pamplico	6	5	1	Rapid City	118	94	24
Pendleton	8	7	1	Salem	2	2	—
Pickens	12	10	2	Sioux Falls	183	153	30
Pine Ridge	2	1	1	Spearfish	18	12	6
Pinewood	3	3	—	Sturgis	14	13	1
Port Royal	12	11	1	Vermillion	17	16	1
Prosperity	3	3	—	Winner	12	8	4
Ridgeland	9	8	1	Yankton	44	22	22
Ridge Spring	4	4	—				
Ridgeville	5	3	2	**TENNESSEE**			
Ridgeway	3	3	—				
Rock Hill	123	100	23	Adamsville	10	7	3
St. George	10	9	1	Alcoa	28	24	4
St. Matthews	10	7	3	Algood	5	5	—
St. Stephens	6	6	—	Ardmore	14	5	9
Salley	1	1	—	Ashland City	9	8	1
Saluda	9	9	—	Athens	28	27	1
Santee	11	7	4	Baileyton	2	2	—
Sellers	1	1	—	Bartlett	69	49	20
Seneca	33	27	6	Benton	7	5	2
Simpsonville	36	28	8	Bolivar	27	21	6
Society Hill	6	5	1	Bradford	2	2	—
South Congaree	3	3	—	Brentwood	47	37	10
Spartanburg	187	146	41	Bristol	70	59	11
Springdale	8	7	1	Bruceton	5	5	—
Sullivans Island	8	7	1	Carthage	11	7	4
Summerton	6	4	2	Centerville	15	10	5
Summerville	48	46	2	Chattanooga	553	431	122
Sumter	121	89	32	Church Hill	8	8	—
Surfside Beach	16	11	5	Clarksville	165	148	17
Tega Cay	12	8	4	Cleveland	88	72	16
Timmonsville	9	7	2	Collegedale	10	9	1
Travelers Rest	17	11	6	Collierville	55	40	15
Turbeville	2	1	1	Collinwood	3	3	—
Union	41	35	6	Columbia	84	76	8
Vance	2	1	1	Cornersville	2	2	—
Varnville	6	3	3	Cowan	4	4	—
Wagener	4	4	—	Crossville	23	20	3
Walhalla	14	12	2	Cumberland Gap	2	2	—
Walterboro	32	24	8	Dandridge	5	5	—
Ware Shoals	8	7	1	Dayton	14	12	2
Wellford	5	5	—	Dyer	6	6	—
West Columbia	44	35	9	Dyersburg	65	53	12
Westminster	10	10	—	Elkton	1	1	—
West Pelzer	4	4	—	Erwin	10	10	—
West Union	2	1	1	Etowah	15	9	6
Whitmire	10	4	6	Fairview	12	11	1
Williamston	18	16	2	Fayetteville	27	21	6
Williston	8	7	1	Franklin	80	61	19

Table 78.—Number of Full-time Law Enforcement Employees, Cities, October 31, 1995 — Continued

City	Total police employees	Total officers	Total civilians	City	Total police employees	Total officers	Total civilians
TENNESSEE — Continued				**TENNESSEE — Continued**			
Gallatin	51	42	9	Sparta	16	15	1
Gallaway	2	2	—	Spring City	10	6	4
Gates	1	1	—	Springfield	40	29	11
Gatlinburg	46	38	8	Spring Hill	11	11	—
Gleason	4	4	—	Trenton	21	13	8
Goodlettsville	46	31	15	Trimble	3	3	—
Grand Junction	3	3	—	Tullahoma	36	29	7
Greeneville	44	42	2	Union City	37	29	8
Halls	6	6	—	Waverly	14	9	5
Hartsville	10	9	1	White House	17	10	7
Henderson	12	12	—	Winchester	23	18	5
Hendersonville	67	50	17	Woodbury	9	8	1
Hohenwald	10	10	—				
Hollow Rock	3	3	—	**TEXAS**			
Humboldt	30	24	6				
Huntingdon	15	11	4	Abernathy	3	3	—
Jacksboro	2	2	—	Abilene	231	172	59
Jackson	208	164	44	Addison	64	48	16
Jefferson City	17	16	1	Alamo	22	16	6
Jonesborough	16	12	4	Alamo Heights	27	19	8
Kenton	4	4	—	Alice	49	34	15
Kingsport	135	96	39	Allen	46	31	15
Knoxville	446	366	80	Alpine	15	9	6
Lafayette	15	12	3	Alto	4	3	1
Lake City	10	7	3	Alvarado	12	6	6
La Vergne	33	26	7	Alvin	51	34	17
Lawrenceburg	45	33	12	Amarillo	351	271	80
Lexington	27	23	4	Andrews	16	14	2
Livingston	19	14	5	Angleton	42	31	11
Loretto	4	4	—	Anson	5	4	1
Manchester	25	24	1	Anthony	9	9	—
Martin	29	23	6	Aransas Pass	21	16	5
Maryville	41	37	4	Argyle	5	5	—
Mason	3	3	—	Arlington	562	435	127
McEwen	3	3	—	Arp	3	2	1
McKenzie	16	12	4	Athens	30	23	7
McMinnville	37	32	5	Atlanta	18	13	5
Memphis	1,811	1,376	435	Austin	1,420	983	437
Milan	21	16	5	Azle	29	21	8
Millersville	8	5	3	Baird	2	2	—
Millington	34	27	7	Balch Springs	41	28	13
Minor Hill	5	2	3	Balcones Heights	25	19	6
Monterey	6	6	—	Ballinger	9	5	4
Morristown	65	61	4	Bangs	2	2	—
Mount Carmel	6	6	—	Bastrop	14	12	2
Mount Juliet	19	14	5	Bay City	47	37	10
Mount Pleasant	12	11	1	Bayou Vista	5	5	—
Murfreesboro	133	106	27	Baytown	141	114	27
Nashville	1,521	1,110	411	Beaumont	324	257	67
Newbern	16	10	6	Bedford	94	66	28
New Johnsonville	5	5	—	Beeville	26	20	6
New Tazewell	6	6	—	Bellaire	54	40	14
Oak Ridge	57	48	9	Bellmead	19	14	5
Obion	3	3	—	Bellville	11	9	2
Oliver Springs	13	8	5	Belton	31	21	10
Pigeon Forge	45	36	9	Benbrook	40	32	8
Portland	20	15	5	Bertram	2	2	—
Pulaski	25	23	2	Beverly Hills	7	6	1
Red Bank	26	20	6	Big Sandy	3	3	—
Ripley	25	22	3	Big Spring	64	45	19
Rockwood	13	12	1	Bishop	11	6	5
Rutherford	4	4	—	Blanco	4	4	—
Savanannh	14	14	—	Blue Mound	8	6	2
Sevierville	45	35	10	Boerne	16	14	2
Sewanee	12	8	4	Bonham	22	16	6
Sharon	4	4	—	Borger	28	20	8
Shelbyville	39	33	6	Bovina	2	2	—
Signal Mountain	16	14	2	Bowie	15	10	5
Smyrna	49	34	15	Brady	14	8	6
Soddy-Daisy	21	18	3	Brazoria	13	8	5
Somerville	12	10	2	Breckenridge	15	10	5
South Carthage	4	4	—	Brenham	42	28	14
South Fulton	9	7	2	Bridge City	18	13	5
South Pittsburg	9	9	—	Bridgeport	12	7	5

Table 78.—Number of Full-time Law Enforcement Employees, Cities, October 31, 1995 — Continued

City	Total police employees	Total officers	Total civilians	City	Total police employees	Total officers	Total civilians
TEXAS — Continued				**TEXAS — Continued**			
Brookshire	12	10	2	Dublin	7	6	1
Brownfield	24	18	6	Dumas	37	29	8
Brownsville	254	188	66	Duncanville	77	54	23
Brownwood	42	29	13	Eagle Lake	6	5	1
Bruceville-Eddy	5	4	1	Eagle Pass	69	54	15
Bryan	116	97	19	Early	6	5	1
Bullard	1	1	—	Earth	3	2	1
Burkburnett	18	14	4	Eastland	10	8	2
Burleson	47	35	12	Edcouch	7	6	1
Burnet	11	10	1	Eden	2	2	—
Caddo Mills	2	1	1	Edgewood	6	6	—
Caldwell	11	10	1	Edinburg	83	60	23
Cameron	13	9	4	Edna	9	8	1
Caney City	2	2	—	El Campo	30	23	7
Canton	14	9	5	Electra	11	7	4
Canyon	18	16	2	Elgin	16	10	6
Carrollton	197	134	63	El Paso	1,242	1,008	234
Carthage	20	13	7	Elsa	16	11	5
Castle Hills	23	18	5	Ennis	35	28	7
Cedar Hill	47	36	11	Euless	97	67	30
Cedar Park	28	20	8	Everman	17	12	5
Celina	4	4	—	Fairfield	7	7	—
Center	18	12	6	Fair Oaks Ranch	7	7	—
Childress	12	6	6	Falfurrias	8	8	—
Cisco	8	7	1	Farmers Branch	79	65	14
Clarksville	8	8	—	Farmersville	5	5	—
Cleburne	56	42	14	Farwell	1	1	—
Cleveland	26	17	9	Ferris	14	12	2
Clifton	6	5	1	Flatonia	3	3	—
Clute	26	19	7	Florence	1	1	—
Cockrell Hill	16	12	4	Floresville	10	9	1
Coffee City	1	1	—	Flower Mound	56	42	14
Coleman	14	9	5	Floydada	5	5	—
College Station	117	82	35	Forest Hill	28	22	6
Colleyville	31	24	7	Forney	14	10	4
Colorado City	14	8	6	Fort Stockton	26	17	9
Columbus	8	7	1	Fort Worth	1,429	1,112	317
Comanche	6	6	—	Frankston	8	4	4
Combes	4	4	—	Fredericksburg	19	16	3
Commerce	19	14	5	Freeport	32	25	7
Conroe	78	61	17	Freer	7	3	4
Converse	19	18	1	Friendswood	45	33	12
Coppell	43	32	11	Friona	10	6	4
Copperas Cove	59	45	14	Frisco	25	18	7
Corinth	11	10	1	Gainesville	42	32	10
Corpus Christi	558	396	162	Galena Park	21	16	5
Corrigan	10	6	4	Galveston	197	167	30
Corsicana	53	42	11	Garland	370	262	108
Crane	10	5	5	Gatesville	17	11	6
Crockett	16	14	2	Georgetown	47	31	16
Crowley	21	16	5	Giddings	14	9	5
Crystal City	12	8	4	Gilmer	13	11	2
Cuero	13	12	1	Gladewater	20	14	6
Cuney	1	1	—	Glenn Heights	11	7	4
Daingerfield	6	5	1	Gonzales	15	9	6
Dalhart	18	11	7	Graham	16	14	2
Dallas	3,539	2,833	706	Granbury	21	18	3
Dalworthington Gardens	11	8	3	Grand Prairie	254	169	85
Dayton	17	12	5	Grand Saline	5	5	—
Decatur	15	10	5	Granite Shoals	4	4	—
Deer Park	60	46	14	Grapevine	91	62	29
De Kalb	7	6	1	Greenville	64	44	20
De Leon	2	2	—	Groesbeck	7	6	1
Del Rio	74	57	17	Groves	17	16	1
Denison	50	41	9	Gruver	2	2	—
Denton	134	104	30	Gun Barrel City	15	12	3
Denver City	12	7	5	Hale Center	3	3	—
DeSoto	70	54	16	Hallettsville	5	4	1
Devine	12	8	4	Haltom City	70	53	17
Diboll	14	11	3	Hamlin	8	4	4
Dickinson	24	19	5	Harker Heights	38	28	10
Dilley	6	5	1	Harlingen	128	102	26
Dimmitt	8	7	1	Hart	1	1	—
Donna	26	19	7	Haskell	4	4	—

City	Total police employees	Total officers	Total civilians	City	Total police employees	Total officers	Total civilians
TEXAS — Continued				**TEXAS — Continued**			
Hawkins	3	3	—	La Grange	6	5	1
Hawley	1	1	—	La Joya	12	9	3
Hearne	21	14	7	Lake Dallas	14	8	6
Heath	6	6	—	Lake Jackson	50	34	16
Hedwig Village	22	16	6	Lakeside	2	2	—
Helotes	6	6	—	Lakeview	15	11	4
Hemphill	4	4	—	Lakeway Village	23	18	5
Hempstead	10	9	1	Lake Worth	25	19	6
Henderson	32	27	5	La Marque	31	24	7
Hereford	33	26	7	Lamesa	23	17	6
Hewitt	23	16	7	Lampasas	17	12	5
Hico	3	3	—	Lancaster	49	38	11
Hidalgo	27	20	7	La Porte	74	53	21
Highland Park	64	50	14	Laredo	297	244	53
Highland Village	20	14	6	La Vernia	3	3	—
Hill Country Village	16	16	—	La Villa	5	5	—
Hillsboro	26	20	6	Lavon	2	2	—
Hitchcock	19	14	5	League City	70	51	19
Holland	1	1	—	Leander	13	7	6
Holliday	1	1	—	Leon Valley	33	25	8
Hollywood Park	7	7	—	Levelland	26	19	7
Hondo	15	13	2	Lewisville	125	82	43
Hooks	4	4	—	Lexington	2	2	—
Horizon City	6	6	—	Liberty	21	14	7
Horseshoe Bay	7	6	1	Lindale	12	7	5
Houston	7,268	5,170	2,098	Littlefield	17	11	6
Hubbard	3	3	—	Live Oak	27	20	7
Humble	60	49	11	Livingston	19	11	8
Huntington	3	3	—	Llano	7	6	1
Huntsville	50	37	13	Lockhart	15	15	—
Hurst	90	59	31	Lockney	3	3	—
Hutchins	15	11	4	Lone Star	3	3	—
Hutto	1	1	—	Longview	196	144	52
Idalou	4	3	1	Lorena	3	3	—
Ingleside	18	13	5	Los Fresnos	17	12	5
Ingram	6	5	1	Lubbock	348	306	42
Iowa Colony	8	5	3	Lufkin	88	68	20
Iowa Park	16	10	6	Luling	14	8	6
Irving	387	273	114	Lumberton	13	11	2
Itasca	3	3	—	Lytle	5	5	—
Jacinto City	21	15	6	Madisonville	7	6	1
Jacksboro	8	7	1	Malakoff	5	5	—
Jacksonville	32	23	9	Manor	6	5	1
Jamaica Beach	5	5	—	Mansfield	36	23	13
Jasper	24	17	7	Manvel	6	6	—
Jefferson	6	5	1	Marble Falls	21	13	8
Jersey Village	20	13	7	Marfa	5	3	2
Johnson City	3	3	—	Marlin	14	10	4
Joshua	8	8	—	Marshall	59	45	14
Jourdanton	6	6	—	Marshall Creek	1	1	—
Junction	4	4	—	Mart	3	3	—
Karnes City	6	5	1	Martindale	4	4	—
Katy	25	18	7	Mathis	10	5	5
Kaufman	20	13	7	McAllen	281	184	97
Keene	15	8	7	McGregor	11	7	4
Keller	34	23	11	McKinney	51	37	14
Kemah	11	7	4	Meadows	13	13	—
Kemp	4	4	—	Memphis	4	3	1
Kendleton	3	2	1	Mercedes	33	23	10
Kennedale	18	13	5	Meridian	2	2	—
Kermit	14	9	5	Merkel	4	4	—
Kerrville	56	42	14	Mesquite	246	185	61
Kilgore	36	29	7	Mexia	23	17	6
Killeen	171	134	37	Midland	200	152	48
Kingsville	59	42	17	Midlothian	20	15	5
Kirby	16	12	4	Mineola	16	10	6
Kirbyville	3	3	—	Mineral Wells	31	25	6
Knox City	2	2	—	Mission	84	66	18
Kountze	6	5	1	Missouri City	52	40	12
Kress	1	1	—	Monahans	19	12	7
Kyle	5	4	1	Mont Belvieu	8	7	1
Lacy-Lakeview	15	10	5	Morgans Point Resort	5	5	—
La Feria	12	8	4	Mount Pleasant	31	23	8
Lago Vista	15	9	6	Muleshoe	12	6	6

Table 78.—Number of Full-time Law Enforcement Employees, Cities, October 31, 1995 — Continued

City	Total police employees	Total officers	Total civilians	City	Total police employees	Total officers	Total civilians
TEXAS — Continued				**TEXAS — Continued**			
Munday	2	2	—	Robinson	17	12	5
Mustang Ridge	1	1	—	Robstown	29	21	8
Nacogdoches	65	51	14	Rockdale	14	9	5
Naples	2	2	—	Rockport	23	17	6
Nassau Bay	16	11	5	Rockwall	41	28	13
Navasota	24	14	10	Rollingwood	5	5	—
Nederland	28	20	8	Roma	24	16	8
Needville	6	5	1	Roman Forest	1	1	—
New Boston	11	7	4	Ropesville	1	1	—
New Braunfels	71	54	17	Roscoe	1	1	—
New Deal	1	1	—	Rosebud	4	4	—
Nocona	10	6	4	Rose City	2	1	1
Nolanville	3	3	—	Rosenberg	60	44	16
Northcrest	4	3	1	Round Rock	86	66	20
North Richland Hills	109	76	33	Rowlett	63	46	17
Oak Ridge North	9	9	—	Royse City	6	6	—
Odessa	244	178	66	Rule	1	1	—
Olmos Park	11	11	—	Rusk	8	8	—
Olney	9	5	4	Sabinal	4	3	1
Olton	3	3	—	Sachse	18	13	5
Onalaska	4	4	—	Saginaw	25	19	6
Orange	55	42	13	St. Jo	1	1	—
Orange Grove	3	3	—	San Angelo	189	163	26
Ore City	3	3	—	San Antonio	2,015	1,809	206
Overton	9	6	3	San Augustine	5	5	—
Oyster Creek	9	5	4	San Benito	49	42	7
Palacios	7	4	3	San Diego	4	4	—
Palestine	47	36	11	Sanger	7	7	—
Palmer	3	3	—	San Juan	29	23	6
Pampa	34	29	5	San Marcos	82	65	17
Panhandle	5	4	1	Sansom Park Village	12	8	4
Pantego	15	10	5	Santa Anna	1	1	—
Paris	75	53	22	Sante Fe	22	15	7
Parker	1	1	—	Santa Rosa	5	4	1
Pasadena	261	206	55	Schertz	27	20	7
Pearland	67	44	23	Seabrook	25	22	3
Pearsall	10	9	1	Seadrift	1	1	—
Pecos	24	18	6	Seagoville	17	13	4
Pelican Bay	3	2	1	Seagraves	3	3	—
Perrytown	15	9	6	Sealy	13	12	1
Pflugerville	25	19	6	Seguin	57	40	17
Pharr	86	64	22	Selma	9	8	1
Pilot Point	5	5	—	Seminole	12	10	2
Pinehurst	8	5	3	Seven Points	10	6	4
Pittsburg	11	9	2	Seymour	7	6	1
Plainview	41	35	6	Shallowater	4	4	—
Plano	291	210	81	Shamrock	4	2	2
Pleasanton	20	13	7	Shavano Park	9	9	—
Port Aransas	17	11	6	Shenandoah	7	7	—
Port Arthur	143	111	32	Sherman	75	56	19
Port Isabel	26	19	7	Silsbee	20	15	5
Portland	32	21	11	Sinton	10	9	1
Port Lavaca	26	20	6	Slaton	15	8	7
Port Neches	18	16	2	Smithville	14	8	6
Poteet	5	5	—	Snyder	21	18	3
Pottsboro	4	4	—	Socorro	12	11	1
Premont	4	4	—	Somerset	3	3	—
Primera	3	3	—	Somerville	4	4	—
Princeton	5	5	—	Sonora	7	5	2
Quanah	5	4	1	Sour Lake	4	4	—
Quinlan	7	6	1	South Houston	41	32	9
Quitman	5	5	—	Southlake	34	27	7
Ranger	6	4	2	South Padre Island	29	21	8
Ransom Canyon	2	2	—	Southside Place	9	7	2
Raymondville	21	14	7	Spearman	8	4	4
Red Oak	13	8	5	Springtown	9	5	4
Refugio	5	4	1	Spring Valley	20	15	5
Richardson	236	152	84	Spur	1	1	—
Richland Hills	24	17	7	Stafford	40	29	11
Richmond	28	20	8	Stamford	12	7	5
Richwood	6	5	1	Stanton	5	5	—
Riesel	1	1	—	Stephenville	36	29	7
River Oaks	22	16	6	Stratford	3	3	—
Roanoke	21	11	10	Sugar Land	95	67	28

Table 78.—Number of Full-time Law Enforcement Employees, Cities, October 31, 1995 — Continued

City	Total police employees	Total officers	Total civilians	City	Total police employees	Total officers	Total civilians
TEXAS — Continued				**UTAH**			
Sulphur Springs	38	30	8	Alpine	9	9	—
Sunset Valley	5	5	—	Alta	8	4	4
Surfside Beach	5	4	1	American Fork	25	22	3
Sweeny	6	5	1	Blanding	6	5	1
Sweetwater	27	22	5	Bountiful	38	29	9
Taft	5	5	—	Brian Head	4	4	—
Tahoka	4	4	—	Brigham City	28	22	6
Tatum	6	1	5	Cedar City	25	21	4
Taylor	25	17	8	Centerville	16	13	3
Teague	7	6	1	Clearfield	29	25	4
Temple	129	106	23	Clinton	8	8	—
Terrell	44	32	12	East Carbon	4	4	—
Terrell Hills	16	16	—	Ephraim	5	5	—
Texarkana	90	81	9	Fairview	1	1	—
Texas City	92	76	16	Farmington	10	9	1
The Colony	32	23	9	Garland	3	3	—
Thrall	2	1	1	Genola	1	1	—
Three Rivers	5	4	1	Grantsville	7	7	—
Tomball	32	25	7	Gunnison	3	3	—
Tool	6	6	—	Harrisville	5	4	1
Trinity	13	5	8	Heber City	10	8	2
Trophy Club	8	7	1	Helper	5	5	—
Troup	5	5	—	Hildale	5	4	1
Tulia	10	7	3	Hurricane	10	8	2
Tye	2	2	—	Kamas	2	2	—
Tyler	223	164	59	Kanab	7	5	2
Universal City	33	25	8	Kaysville	15	13	2
University Park	41	34	7	Layton	65	52	13
Uvalde	26	19	7	Lehi	14	13	1
Van	4	4	—	Logan	62	51	11
Vernon	29	22	7	Mantua	1	1	—
Victoria	136	99	37	Mapleton	4	4	—
Vidor	27	20	7	Midvale	27	25	2
Village	36	30	6	Minersville	1	1	—
Village of Jones Creek	5	4	1	Moab	13	11	2
Waco	283	213	70	Monticello	4	4	—
Wake Village	5	5	—	Moroni	1	1	—
Waller	7	6	1	Mount Pleasant	6	5	1
Wallis	3	3	—	Murray	69	58	11
Watauga	40	31	9	Naples	8	5	3
Waxahachie	49	40	9	Nephi	8	6	2
Weatherford	53	35	18	North Park	5	5	—
Webster	45	32	13	North Ogden	14	12	2
Weimar	6	6	—	North Salt Lake	10	9	1
Wells	1	1	—	Ogden	128	106	22
Weslaco	58	47	11	Orem	90	68	22
West	4	4	—	Panguitch	2	2	—
West Columbia	13	8	5	Park City	26	20	6
West Lake Hills	17	12	5	Parowan	2	2	—
West Orange	8	7	1	Payson	15	14	1
Westover Hills	14	13	1	Perry	2	2	—
West Tawakoni	5	4	1	Pleasant Grove	18	17	1
West University Place	28	21	7	Pleasant View	5	4	1
Westworth	9	5	4	Price	17	16	1
Wharton	31	21	10	Provo	126	84	42
Whitehouse	11	9	2	Richfield	12	9	3
White Oak	15	11	4	Riverdale	18	16	2
Whitesboro	11	7	4	Roosevelt	11	10	1
White Settlement	40	31	9	Roy	39	25	14
Whitney	6	5	1	St. George	68	52	16
Wichita Falls	251	176	75	Salem	5	5	—
Willow Park	4	4	—	Salina	3	3	—
Wills Point	8	7	1	Salt Lake City	518	364	154
Wilmer	17	12	5	Sandy	110	91	19
Windcrest	24	18	6	Santaquin	4	4	—
Winnsboro	13	11	2	South Jordan	18	16	2
Winters	5	5	—	South Ogden	23	18	5
Wolfforth	4	4	—	South Salt Lake	51	41	10
Woodville	7	6	1	Spanish Fork	18	16	2
Woodway	27	18	9	Springville	24	18	6
Wylie	17	12	5	Sunset	9	8	1
Yoakum	15	10	5	Syracuse	6	5	1
Yorktown	3	3	—	Tooele	23	20	3
				Tremonton	9	7	2

City	Total police employees	Total officers	Total civilians	City	Total police employees	Total officers	Total civilians
UTAH — Continued				**VIRGINIA — Continued**			
Unitah	5	5	—	Cape Charles	2	2	—
Vernal	18	15	3	Cedar Bluff	2	2	—
Washington Terrace	12	10	2	Charlottesville	129	102	27
Wellington	4	4	—	Chase City	11	7	4
Wendover	6	5	1	Chatham	4	4	—
West Bountiful	5	5	—	Chesapeake	367	295	72
West Jordan	72	62	10	Chilhowie	6	6	—
West Valley	163	138	25	Chincoteague	12	9	3
Willard	2	2	—	Christiansburg	40	32	8
Woods Cross	9	8	1	Clarksville	7	6	1
				Clifton Forge	14	11	3
VERMONT				Clintwood	4	4	—
				Coeburn	8	7	1
Barre	22	17	5	Colonial Beach	12	8	4
Barre Town	8	7	1	Colonial Heights	57	43	14
Bellows Falls	12	8	4	Courtland	2	1	1
Bennington	28	24	4	Covington	19	14	5
Brandon	7	7	—	Crewe	5	5	—
Brattleboro	40	29	11	Culpeper	38	29	9
Bristol	3	3	—	Damascus	2	2	—
Burlington	122	91	31	Danville	136	119	17
Castleton	3	3	—	Dayton	4	4	—
Chester	5	4	1	Dublin	8	7	1
Colchester	27	23	4	Dumfries	12	11	1
Dover	6	5	1	Edinburg	2	2	—
Essex	31	25	6	Elkton	10	6	4
Fair Haven	3	3	—	Emporia	27	20	7
Hartford	27	21	6	Exmore	2	2	—
Manchester	13	8	5	Fairfax City	74	59	15
Middlebury	13	11	2	Falls Church	36	25	11
Milton	13	11	2	Farmville	28	19	9
Montpelier	20	15	5	Franklin	34	25	9
Morristown	7	6	1	Fredericksburg	79	59	20
Newport	13	11	2	Fries	1	1	—
Northfield	3	3	—	Front Royal	38	29	9
Norwich	5	4	1	Galax	27	21	6
Randolph	5	5	—	Gate City	3	3	—
Richmond	1	1	—	Glade Springs	4	4	—
Rutland	46	37	9	Glen Lyn	2	2	—
St. Johnsbury	16	11	5	Gordonsville	6	6	—
South Burlington	33	28	5	Gretna	3	3	—
Springfield	19	14	5	Grottoes	3	3	—
Stowe	13	11	2	Grundy	6	6	—
Swanton	4	3	1	Halifax	4	4	—
Vergennes	3	3	—	Hampton	321	245	76
Vernon	4	4	—	Harrisonburg	63	49	14
Waterbury	3	3	—	Haysi	1	1	—
Williston	5	4	1	Herndon	46	36	10
Windsor	9	6	3	Hillsville	6	6	—
Winhall	5	5	—	Honaker	3	3	—
Winooski	15	11	4	Hopewell	58	44	14
Woodstock	6	5	1	Hurt	3	3	—
				Independence	3	3	—
VIRGINIA				Iron Gate	1	1	—
				Jonesville	3	3	—
Abingdon	18	16	2	Kenbridge	5	5	—
Alexandria	385	264	121	Kilmarnock	4	4	—
Altavista	15	11	4	La Crosse	1	1	—
Amherst	4	4	—	Lawrenceville	5	5	—
Appalachia	8	7	1	Lebanon	10	9	1
Ashland	23	20	3	Leesburg	37	34	3
Bedford	27	21	6	Lexington	22	16	6
Berryville	8	7	1	Louisa	3	3	—
Big Stone Gap	15	13	2	Luray	15	14	1
Blacksburg	66	52	14	Lynchburg	191	147	44
Blackstone	15	10	5	Manassas	88	70	18
Bluefield	17	12	5	Manassas Park	21	13	8
Bowling Green	1	1	—	Marion	20	18	2
Boykins	1	1	—	Martinsville	59	53	6
Bridgewater	6	6	—	McKenney	1	1	—
Bristol	68	48	20	Middleburg	4	3	1
Brookneal	4	4	—	Middletown	2	2	—
Buena Vista	16	12	4	Mount Jackson	3	3	—
Burkeville	3	3	—	Narrows	6	6	—

City	Total police employees	Total officers	Total civilians	City	Total police employees	Total officers	Total civilians
VIRGINIA — Continued				**WASHINGTON — Continued**			
New Market	4	4	—	Brier	7	6	1
Newport News	480	345	135	Buckley	15	8	7
Norfolk	789	692	97	Burlington	23	16	7
Norton	22	16	6	Camas	19	15	4
Onancock	5	5	—	Carnation	3	3	—
Onley	2	2	—	Castle Rock	6	5	1
Orange	12	11	1	Centralia	34	29	5
Parksley	3	3	—	Chehalis	23	19	4
Pearisburg	6	6	—	Chelan	16	10	6
Pembroke	2	2	—	Cheney	14	12	2
Pennington Gap	9	5	4	Chewelah	6	5	1
Petersburg	142	104	38	Clarkston	17	14	3
Pocahontas	3	3	—	Cle Elum	6	5	1
Poquoson	22	17	5	Clyde Hill	8	7	1
Portsmouth	341	243	98	Colfax	5	5	—
Pound	4	4	—	College Place	12	8	4
Pulaski	41	29	12	Colville	12	11	1
Purcellville	7	7	—	Connell	6	6	—
Quantico	3	3	—	Cosmopolis	7	6	1
Radford	34	25	9	Coulee Dam	4	4	—
Rich Creek	1	1	—	Darrington	3	2	1
Richlands	21	16	5	Davenport	4	4	—
Richmond	775	684	91	Des Moines	41	31	10
Roanoke	294	254	40	Duvall	6	5	1
Rocky Mount	14	13	1	East Wenatchee	14	12	2
Rural Retreat	1	1	—	Eatonville	5	5	—
St. Paul	4	4	—	Edmonds	57	40	17
Salem	79	59	20	Ellensburg	25	19	6
Saltville	4	4	—	Elma	6	5	1
Shenandoah	3	3	—	Enumclaw	28	17	11
Smithfield	18	12	6	Ephrata	18	11	7
South Boston	20	17	3	Everett	190	154	36
South Hill	21	17	4	Ferndale	13	11	2
Stanley	2	2	—	Fife	24	15	9
Staunton	61	44	17	Fircrest	10	8	2
Stephens City	1	1	—	Forks	13	7	6
Strasburg	11	10	1	Gig Harbor	11	9	2
Suffolk	146	113	33	Goldendale	8	6	2
Tappahannock	8	8	—	Grand Coulee	3	3	—
Tazewell	11	10	1	Grandview	20	15	5
Victoria	4	4	—	Granger	4	4	—
Vienna	50	39	11	Granite Falls	6	6	—
Vinton	24	17	7	Hoquiam	25	20	5
Virginia Beach	879	671	208	Issaquah	30	20	10
Warrenton	22	20	2	Kalama	5	5	—
Warsaw	2	2	—	Kelso	31	27	4
Waverly	4	4	—	Kennewick	85	68	17
Waynesboro	48	44	4	Kent	142	93	49
Weber City	3	3	—	Kettle Falls	5	5	—
Williamsburg	41	29	12	Kirkland	80	56	24
Winchester	71	52	19	La Center	5	5	—
Wise	12	11	1	Lacey	45	38	7
Woodstock	13	12	1	La Conner	5	5	—
Wytheville	35	24	11	Lake Stevens	7	7	—
				Long Beach	8	7	1
WASHINGTON				Longview	57	51	6
				Lummi Tribal	15	14	1
Aberdeen	51	37	14	Lynden	13	10	3
Airway Heights	8	7	1	Lynnwood	72	62	10
Algona	8	6	2	McCleary	3	3	—
Anacortes	33	19	14	Medina	8	7	1
Arlington	12	10	2	Mercer Island	41	31	10
Auburn	97	73	24	Milton	11	10	1
Bainbridge Island	22	18	4	Monroe	22	17	5
Battle Ground	14	12	2	Montesano	9	7	2
Bellevue	246	160	86	Morton	5	4	1
Bellingham	151	97	54	Moses Lake	35	25	10
Bingen	2	2	—	Mossyrock	2	2	—
Black Diamond	8	7	1	Mountlake Terrace	35	30	5
Blaine	15	13	2	Mount Vernon	45	35	10
Bonney Lake	21	14	7	Mukilteo	23	20	3
Bothell	51	35	16	Napavine	4	3	1
Bremerton	78	62	16	Newport	4	4	—
Brewster	9	8	1	Nisqually Tribal	8	8	—

Table 78.—Number of Full-time Law Enforcement Employees, Cities, October 31, 1995 — Continued

City	Total police employees	Total officers	Total civilians	City	Total police employees	Total officers	Total civilians
WASHINGTON — Continued				**WASHINGTON — Continued**			
Normandy Park	18	12	6	Yelm	12	9	3
Oak Harbor	40	25	15	Zillah	8	6	2
Oakville	2	2	—				
Ocean Shores	11	8	3	**WEST VIRGINIA**			
Odessa	3	3	—				
Olympia	91	67	24	Alderson	2	2	—
Omak	14	12	2	Anmoore	2	2	—
Oroville	10	6	4	Ansted	3	3	—
Othello	17	11	6	Barboursville	15	14	1
Pacific	10	8	2	Beckley	60	45	15
Pasco	53	44	9	Belington	3	3	—
Pe Ell	2	2	—	Belle	5	5	—
Pomeroy	3	3	—	Benwood	8	4	4
Port Angeles	52	29	23	Bethlehem	3	3	—
Port Orchard	14	13	1	Bluefield	32	29	3
Port Townsend	14	12	2	Bridgeport	21	19	2
Poulsbo	18	15	3	Buckhannon	8	7	1
Prosser	15	10	5	Cameron	4	4	—
Pullman	35	25	10	Cedar Grove	3	3	—
Puyallup	64	46	18	Ceredo	8	5	3
Quincy	10	7	3	Chapmanville	4	4	—
Rainier	4	4	—	Charleston	201	177	24
Raymond	8	7	1	Charles Town	14	12	2
Reardan	1	1	—	Chesapeake	4	4	—
Redmond	82	57	25	Chester	5	5	—
Renton	116	86	30	Clarksburg	48	44	4
Republic	2	2	—	Clendenin :	3	3	—
Richland	51	45	6	Danville	3	3	—
Ridgefield	4	4	—	Delbarton	2	2	—
Ritzville	3	3	—	Dunbar	20	15	5
Royal City	3	3	—	Elkins	15	9	6
Ruston	2	2	—	Fairmont	44	34	10
Seattle	1,759	1,252	507	Fayetteville	5	4	1
Sedro Woolley	18	11	7	Follansbee	10	10	—
Selah	13	11	2	Fort Gay	2	2	—
Sequim	14	11	3	Gauley Bridge	1	1	—
Shelton	34	20	14	Glen Dale	6	5	1
Snohomish	20	17	3	Glenville	5	5	—
Snoqualmie	8	7	1	Grafton	12	7	5
Soap Lake	4	4	—	Grantsville	1	1	—
South Bend	5	4	1	Granville	3	2	1
Spokane	380	284	96	Harpers Ferry/Bolivar	3	3	—
Stanwood	10	8	2	Harrisville	2	2	—
Steilacoom	13	11	2	Hinton	6	6	—
Sultan	6	5	1	Huntington	114	104	10
Sumner	23	16	7	Hurricane	14	10	4
Sunnyside	31	22	9	Kenova	10	8	2
Swinomish Tribal	10	9	1	Kermit	3	3	—
Tacoma	427	376	51	Keyser	13	8	5
Tekoa	2	2	—	Kimball	3	3	—
Tenino	5	5	—	Kingwood	5	5	—
Tieton	2	2	—	Lewisburg	12	10	2
Toledo	2	2	—	Logan	12	9	3
Tonasket	5	4	1	Lumberport	2	2	—
Toppenish	24	17	7	Mabscott	3	3	—
Tukwila	77	64	13	Madison	6	6	—
Tumwater	26	22	4	Man	3	3	—
Twisp	3	3	—	Mannington	5	5	—
Union Gap	20	15	5	Marlinton	2	2	—
Vader	1	1	—	Marmet	4	4	—
Vancouver	129	109	20	Martinsburg	47	41	6
Waitsburg	2	2	—	Mason	3	3	—
Walla Walla	60	39	21	Matewan	3	3	—
Wapato	17	13	4	McMechen	4	4	—
Washougal	11	9	2	Milton	5	5	—
Wenatchee	55	39	16	Mitchell Heights	1	1	—
Westport	9	7	2	Monongah	3	2	1
West Richland	13	11	2	Montgomery	8	7	1
White Salmon	4	4	—	Moorefield	6	6	—
Wilbur	2	2	—	Morgantown	61	52	9
Winlock	5	3	2	Moundsville	20	14	6
Winthrop	3	3	—	Mount Hope	4	4	—
Woodland	7	6	1	Mullens	5	5	—
Yakima	148	110	38	New Cumberland	5	5	—

Table 78.—Number of Full-time Law Enforcement Employees, Cities, October 31, 1995 — Continued

City	Total police employees	Total officers	Total civilians	City	Total police employees	Total officers	Total civilians
WEST VIRGINIA — Continued				**WISCONSIN — Continued**			
New Haven	2	2	—	Black Earth	2	2	—
New Martinsville	14	10	4	Black River Falls	9	8	1
Nitro	15	11	4	Bloomfield	8	6	2
North Fork	3	3	—	Brillion	5	5	—
Nutter Fort	5	5	—	Brodhead	11	7	4
Oak Hill	14	11	3	Brookfield	83	62	21
Oceana	5	5	—	Brookfield Township	10	9	1
Paden City	7	4	3	Brown Deer	38	29	9
Parkersburg	77	61	16	Burlington	27	21	6
Parsons	2	2	—	Burlington Town	7	7	—
Pennsboro	1	1	—	Butler	10	8	2
Petersburg	4	4	—	Caledonia	32	26	6
Philippi	6	6	—	Campbell Township	5	5	—
Piedmont	2	2	—	Cedarburg	27	19	8
Pineville	4	4	—	Chenequa	8	8	—
Point Pleasant	8	7	1	Chetek	4	4	—
Princeton	24	22	2	Chilton	6	6	—
Rainelle	4	4	—	Chippewa Falls	33	25	8
Ranson	10	9	1	Clear Lake	1	1	—
Ravenswood	12	8	4	Clinton	5	5	—
Reedsville	1	1	—	Clintonville	16	12	4
Richwood	9	4	5	Columbus	13	9	4
Ripley	9	8	1	Combined Locks	4	4	—
Romney	4	3	1	Cornell	8	4	4
Ronceverte	4	4	—	Crandon	3	3	—
St. Albans	25	19	6	Cuba City	5	4	1
St. Marys	8	4	4	Cudahy	42	32	10
Salem	3	3	—	Darien	5	5	—
Shepherdstown	5	4	1	Darlington	5	4	1
Shinnston	5	5	—	De Forest	11	10	1
Sistersville	3	3	—	Delafield	11	10	1
Smithers	4	4	—	Delavan	19	15	4
Sophia	5	5	—	Delavan Town	8	8	—
South Charleston	36	30	6	De Pere	31	26	5
Spencer	9	7	2	Dodgeville	10	9	1
Star City	6	6	—	Durand	4	4	—
Stonewood	3	3	—	Eagle River	7	7	—
Summerville	13	13	—	East Troy	8	7	1
Sutton	3	3	—	Eau Claire	110	85	25
Vienna	22	14	8	Eleva	1	1	—
War	4	4	—	Elkhorn	16	14	2
Wayne	2	1	1	Elm Grove	23	17	6
Weirton	47	39	8	Elroy	3	3	—
Welch	14	11	3	Everest	21	19	2
Wellsburg	5	5	—	Fennimore	5	5	—
Weston	8	6	2	Fitchburg	30	23	7
Westover	10	8	2	Fond Du Lac	76	65	11
Wheeling	84	82	2	Fort Atkinson	23	18	5
White Sulphur Springs	7	7	—	Fox Lake	1	1	—
Whitesville	2	2	—	Fox Point	19	14	5
Williamson	9	8	1	Fox Valley	28	25	3
Williamstown	5	4	1	Franklin	50	39	11
				Germantown	36	26	10
WISCONSIN				Glendale	48	47	1
				Grafton	25	19	6
Adams	3	3	—	Grand Chute	21	18	3
Algoma	6	6	—	Green Bay	218	180	38
Altoona	9	8	1	Greendale	36	28	8
Amery	7	6	1	Greenfield	79	56	23
Antigo	18	17	1	Green Lake	3	3	—
Appleton	122	98	24	Hales Corners	21	17	4
Arcadia	4	4	—	Hartford	25	20	5
Ashland	24	18	6	Hartland	16	14	2
Ashwaubenon	39	35	4	Hayward	7	6	1
Bangor	3	3	—	Hillsboro	2	2	—
Baraboo	27	23	4	Holmen	7	6	1
Barron	5	5	—	Horicon	11	9	2
Bayfield	3	3	—	Hudson	20	17	3
Bayside	21	15	6	Hurley	7	6	1
Beaver Dam	37	28	9	Independence	2	2	—
Belleville	3	3	—	Jackson	4	3	1
Beloit	99	84	15	Janesville	104	91	13
Beloit Town	10	9	1	Jefferson	15	13	2
Berlin	16	12	4	Juneau	4	4	—

Table 78.—Number of Full-time Law Enforcement Employees, Cities, October 31, 1995 — Continued

City	Total police employees	Total officers	Total civilians	City	Total police employees	Total officers	Total civilians
WISCONSIN— Continued				**WISCONSIN — Continued**			
Kaukauna	22	21	1	Princeton	4	4	—
Kenosha	183	172	11	Pulaski	7	7	—
Kewaskum	5	5	—	Racine	243	209	34
Kewaunee	6	6	—	Reedsburg	17	12	5
Kiel	11	6	5	Rhinelander	29	19	10
Kohler	6	5	1	Rice Lake	23	16	7
La Crosse	112	90	22	Richland Center	12	10	2
Ladysmith	7	6	1	Ripon	18	13	5
Lake Delton	11	10	1	River Falls	22	19	3
Lake Geneva	24	17	7	River Hills	15	15	—
Lake Mills	10	9	1	Rome Town	4	4	—
Lancaster	8	7	1	Rothschild	9	8	1
Lodi	5	4	1	St. Croix Falls	3	3	—
Madison	397	336	61	St. Francis	20	19	1
Manitowoc	73	62	11	Sauk Prairie	11	10	1
Marinette	30	24	6	Saukville	8	7	1
Markesan	4	4	—	Shawano	25	18	7
Marshfield	52	38	14	Sheboygan	118	88	30
Mauston	7	6	1	Sheboygan Falls	10	10	—
Mayville	11	9	2	Shorewood	33	27	6
Mazomanie	3	3	—	Shorewood Hills	5	5	—
McFarland	11	9	2	Silver Lake	4	3	1
Medford	10	9	1	Slinger	6	5	1
Menasha	33	28	5	Somerset	5	4	1
Menasha Town	24	20	4	South Milwaukee	35	33	2
Menomonee Falls	72	55	17	Sparta	23	17	6
Menomonie	35	27	8	Spooner	7	6	1
Mequon	44	36	8	Stanley	4	4	—
Merrill	26	22	4	Stevens Point	51	42	9
Middleton	32	26	6	Stoughton	22	17	5
Milton	7	7	—	Strum	2	2	—
Milwaukee	2,580	2,086	494	Sturgeon Bay	19	18	1
Minocqua	17	11	6	Sturtevant	11	9	2
Mondovi	4	4	—	Summit	8	8	—
Monona	21	18	3	Sun Prairie	45	32	13
Monroe	32	24	8	Superior	63	60	3
Mosinee	7	6	1	Thiensville	8	7	1
Mount Horeb	8	7	1	Tomahawk	5	5	—
Mount Pleasant	30	22	8	Town of East Troy	7	6	1
Mukwonago	16	11	5	Town of Madison	20	18	2
Muskego	37	30	7	Twin Lakes	11	7	4
Neenah	49	41	8	Two Rivers	29	25	4
Neillsville	7	6	1	Verona	12	11	1
New Berlin	77	60	17	Viroqua	12	9	3
New Glarus	5	5	—	Walworth	5	5	—
New Holstein	10	6	4	Washburn	5	5	—
New London	17	17	—	Washington Island	1	1	—
New Richmond	11	10	1	Waterloo	7	6	1
North Fond du Lac	10	8	2	Watertown	50	36	14
Oak Creek	54	44	10	Waukesha	134	100	34
Oconomowoc	29	22	7	Waunakee	11	10	1
Oconomowoc Town	10	9	1	Waupaca	17	13	4
Oconto	7	7	—	Waupun	22	15	7
Oconto Falls	6	6	—	Wausau	72	59	13
Omro	6	5	1	Wauwatosa	116	85	31
Onalaska	27	25	2	West Allis	156	132	24
Oregon	11	10	1	West Bend	65	51	14
Osceola	4	4	—	Westby	3	3	—
Oshkosh	104	89	15	West Milwaukee	23	19	4
Palmyra	5	4	1	West Salem	4	4	—
Pardeeville	4	3	1	Whitefish Bay	28	24	4
Park Falls	8	7	1	Whitehall	3	3	—
Peshtigo	6	6	—	Whitewater	33	23	10
Pewaukee	16	14	2	Williams Bay	6	5	1
Pewaukee Township	11	10	1	Winneconne	5	4	1
Phillips	5	5	—	Wisconsin Dells	15	15	—
Platteville	24	19	5	Wisconsin Rapids	49	38	11
Pleasant Prairie	20	19	1				
Plover	13	12	1	**WYOMING**			
Plymouth	15	14	1				
Portage	28	21	7	Afton	4	4	—
Port Washington	25	20	5	Baggs	1	1	—
Prairie du Chien	17	12	5	Basin	4	4	—
Prescott	7	6	1	Buffalo	13	8	5

345

Table 78.—Number of Full-time Law Enforcement Employees, Cities, October 31, 1995 — Continued

City	Total police employees	Total officers	Total civilians	City	Total police employees	Total officers	Total civilians
WYOMING — Continued				**WYOMING — Continued**			
Casper	89	74	15	Lovell	8	4	4
Cheyenne	103	81	22	Lusk	5	5	—
Cody	17	15	2	Lyman	10	6	4
Diamondville	4	3	1	Mills	8	7	1
Douglas	20	13	7	Moorcroft	5	4	1
Encampment	2	2	—	Newcastle	9	5	4
Evanston	28	24	4	Pine Bluffs	5	2	3
Evansville	11	7	4	Powell	19	12	7
Gillette	54	38	16	Rawlins	32	20	12
Glenrock	10	6	4	Riverton	33	22	11
Green River	29	25	4	Rock Springs	55	31	24
Greybull	4	4	—	Saratoga	7	4	3
Guernsey	5	5	—	Sheridan	40	26	14
Hanna	4	2	2	Sundance	3	3	—
Hulett	2	2	—	Thermopolis	14	8	6
Jackson	25	19	6	Torrington	19	14	5
Kemmerer	12	9	3	Upton	3	3	—
Lander	18	17	1	Wheatland	11	10	1
Laramie	48	38	10	Worland	11	11	—

Table 79.—Number of Full-time Law Enforcement Employees, Universities and Colleges, October 31, 1995

University/College	Total police employees	Total officers	Total civilians	University/College	Total police employees	Total officers	Total civilians
ALABAMA				**CALIFORNIA — Continued**			
Alabama State University	28	26	2	Pasadena Community College	17	9	8
Auburn University:				San Diego State University	36	22	14
Main Campus	45	19	26	San Francisco State University	25	20	5
Montgomery	21	13	8	San Jose State University	44	23	21
Enterprise State Junior College	2	2	—	San Jose/Evergreen Community College	10	4	6
Jacksonville State University	19	15	4	Santa Rosa Junior College	15	10	5
Troy State University	10	9	1	Sonoma State University	17	8	9
University of Alabama:				State Center Community College	13	11	2
Birmingham	89	53	36	University of California:			
Huntsville	12	9	3	Berkeley	118	72	46
Tuscaloosa	42	36	6	Davis	74	44	30
University of Montevallo	15	9	6	Hastings College of Law	13	6	7
University of North Alabama	12	11	1	Irvine	33	26	7
University of South Alabama	31	23	8	Lawrence Livermore Laboratory	191	2	189
University of West Alabama	7	5	2	Los Angeles	81	54	27
				Riverside	26	19	7
ALASKA				San Diego	50	27	23
				San Francisco	51	25	26
University of Alaska:				Santa Barbara	36	26	10
Anchorage	17	11	6	Santa Cruz	29	17	12
Fairbanks	13	10	3	West Valley College	11	9	2
ARIZONA				**COLORADO**			
Arizona State University:				Adams State College	3	3	—
Tempe	61	42	19	Arapahoe Community College	6	5	1
West	16	8	8	Auraria Higher Education Center	33	17	16
Arizona Western College	9	8	1	Colorado School of Mines	7	6	1
Central Arizona College	6	6	—	Colorado State University	28	19	9
Northern Arizona University	31	19	12	Fort Lewis College	6	2	4
Pima Community College	35	25	10	Pike's Peak Community College	6	5	1
University of Arizona	72	43	29	Red Rocks Community College	3	2	1
Yavapai College	4	4	—	University of Colorado			
				Boulder	73	31	42
ARKANSAS				Colorado Springs	7	5	2
				Health Sciences	50	23	27
Arkansas State University	23	18	5	University of Denver	30	23	7
Henderson State University	9	8	1	University of Northern Colorado	18	11	7
Southern Arkansas University	5	5	—	Unviersity of Southern Colorado	10	3	7
University of Arkansas:							
Fayetteville	31	24	7	**CONNECTICUT**			
Little Rock	30	23	7				
Medical Science	47	36	11	Central Connecticut State University	27	23	4
Monticello	6	5	1	Eastern Connecticut State University	17	13	4
Pine Bluff	18	13	5	Southern Connecticut State University	27	21	6
University of Central Arkansas	22	19	3	University of Connecticut:			
				Avery Point	5	5	—
CALIFORNIA				Health Center	21	16	5
				Storrs	47	41	6
Allan Hancock College	3	2	1	Western Connecticut State University	20	17	3
Cabrillo Community College	6	4	2	Yale University	89	72	17
California State Polytechnic University:							
Pomona	29	12	17	**DELAWARE**			
San Luis Obispo	16	12	4				
California State University:				University of Delaware	72	45	27
Bakersfield	12	8	4				
Chico	15	10	5	**FLORIDA**			
Dominguez Hills	24	13	11				
Fresno	26	13	13	Florida A&M University	31	21	10
Fullerton	30	13	17	Florida Atlantic University	31	25	6
Hayward	19	10	9	Florida International Univeristy	47	35	12
Long Beach	26	21	5	Florida State University:			
Los Angeles	20	16	4	Panama City	3	2	1
Northridge	21	16	5	Tallahassee	69	49	20
Sacramento	20	14	6	Santa Fe Community College	14	12	2
San Bernardino	12	12	—	University of Central Florida	51	34	17
Stanislaus	14	9	5	University of Florida	129	80	49
College of the Sequoias	4	2	2	Univeristy of North Florida	29	20	9
Contra Costa Community College	24	19	5	University of South Florida:			
El Camino College	21	16	5	St. Petersburg	16	12	4
Foothill-De Anza College	7	6	1	Sarasota	17	13	4
Humboldt State University	15	10	5	Tampa	64	44	20
Long Beach Community College	13	12	1	University of West Florida	30	22	8
Marin Community College	9	9	—				

Table 79.—Number of Full-time Law Enforcement Employees, Universities and Colleges, October 31, 1995 — Continued

University/College	Total police employees	Total officers	Total civilians	University/College	Total police employees	Total officers	Total civilians
GEORGIA				**INDIANA — Continued**			
Abraham Baldwin College	11	10	1	Gary	14	10	4
Agnes Scott College	22	11	11	Indianapolis	55	34	21
Albany State College	23	13	10	New Albany	9	7	2
Armstrong State College	12	9	3	Purdue University	44	38	6
Augusta College	15	14	1				
Berry College	15	11	4	**IOWA**			
Brunswick College	5	5	—	Iowa State University	30	25	5
Clark Atlanta University	53	21	32	University of Iowa	47	26	21
Clayton State College	14	12	2	University of Northern Iowa	28	19	9
Columbus College	13	11	2				
Dalton College	7	7	—	**KANSAS**			
Emory University	46	30	16				
Fort Valley State College	20	18	2	Emporia State University	9	9	—
Georgia College	17	12	5	Fort Hays State University	11	10	1
Georgia Institute of Technology	52	38	14	Kansas State University, Manhattan	31	20	11
Georgia Southern University	37	29	8	Pittsburg State University	14	12	2
Georgia Southwestern College	11	10	1	University of Kansas:			
Georgia State University	75	66	9	Lawrence	54	31	23
Gordon College	4	2	2	Medical Center	41	30	11
Kennesaw College	28	19	9	Wichita State University	28	21	7
Medical College of Georgia	54	38	16				
Mercer University	33	25	8	**KENTUCKY**			
Middle Georgia College	10	7	3				
North Georgia College	9	5	4	Eastern Kentucky University	29	18	11
Reinhardt College	4	3	1	Jefferson Community College	6	6	—
Savannah State College	32	13	19	Kentucky State University	17	13	4
South Georgia College	7	7	—	Morehead State University	26	12	14
Southern College of Technology	15	11	4	Murray State University	20	12	8
University of Georgia	71	62	9	Northern Kentucky University	28	18	10
Valdosta State University	31	21	10	University of Kentucky	44	32	12
Wesleyan College	5	5	—	University of Louisville	49	25	24
West Georgia College	26	17	9	Western Kentucky University	27	20	7
ILLINOIS				**LOUISIANA**			
Black Hawk College	5	4	1	Grambling State University	23	22	1
Chicago State University	31	23	8	Louisiana State University:			
College of DuPage	17	12	5	Baton Rouge	60	58	2
College of Lake County	13	7	6	Medical Center	62	60	2
Eastern Illinois University	30	21	9	Shreveport	7	7	—
Governors State University	13	9	4	Louisiana Tech. University	19	17	2
Illinois State University	29	24	5	McNeese State University	13	11	2
John A. Logan College	3	2	1	Nichols State University	14	12	2
Joliet Junior College	8	6	2	Northeast Louisiana University	25	21	4
Loyola University of Chicago	48	21	27	Northwestern State University	15	14	1
Morton College	10	7	3	Southeastern Louisiana University	28	21	7
Northeastern Illinois University	25	18	7	Southern University and A&M College,			
Northern Illinois University	41	29	12	Baton Rouge	43	26	17
Northwestern University	17	13	4	University of Southwestern Louisiana	17	16	1
Oakton Community College	8	7	1				
Parkland College	16	8	8	**MAINE**			
Rock Valley College	7	6	1				
Sangamon State University	14	8	6	University of Maine:			
Southern Illinois University:				Farmington	4	4	—
Carbondale	55	42	13	Orono	35	23	12
Edwardsville	27	19	8	University of Southern Maine	24	18	6
School of Medicine	12	2	10				
South Suburban College	17	14	3	**MARYLAND**			
State Community College	1	1	—				
Triton College	15	10	5	Bowie State University	22	15	7
University of Illinois:				Coppin State University	15	13	2
Chicago	81	56	25	Frostburg State University	20	15	5
Urbana	51	38	13	Morgan State University	44	31	13
Waubonsee College	2	2	—	St. Mary's College	10	4	6
Western Illinois University	36	22	14	Salisbury State University	19	17	2
William Rainey Harper College	14	7	7	Towson State University	49	33	16
Wright College	2	1	1	University of Baltimore	45	13	32
				University of Maryland:			
INDIANA				Baltimore City	111	57	54
				Baltimore County	28	20	8
Ball State University	35	28	7	College Park	79	68	11
Indiana State University	28	23	5	Eastern Shore	19	11	8
Indiana University:							
Bloomington	51	42	9				

Table 79.—Number of Full-time Law Enforcement Employees, Universities and Colleges, October 31, 1995 — Continued

University/College	Total police employees	Total officers	Total civilians	University/College	Total police employees	Total officers	Total civilians
MASSACHUSETTS				**NEVADA**			
Bentley College	26	16	10	University of Nevada:			
Boston College	57	44	13	Las Vegas	33	22	11
Boston University	52	44	8	Reno	18	15	3
Brandeis University	24	21	3				
Clark University	11	11	—	**NEW HAMPSHIRE**			
Emerson College	14	12	2				
Fitchburg State College	15	13	2	University of New Hampshire	33	17	16
Framingham State College	14	8	6				
Massachusetts Institute of Technology	65	55	10	**NEW JERSEY**			
North Adams State College	13	9	4				
Northeastern University	69	44	25	Brookdale Community College	17	12	5
Salem State College	21	19	2	Essex County College	52	18	34
Tufts University	53	39	14	Kean College	36	21	15
University of Massachusetts:				Middlesex County College	17	12	5
Amherst	94	54	40	Monmouth College	19	15	4
Harbor Campus, Boston	40	28	12	Montclair State College	31	14	17
Worcester	20	16	4	New Jersey Institute of Technology	53	22	31
Wentworth Institute of Technology	25	10	15	Rowan College	34	2	32
Westfield State College	42	12	30	Rutgers University:			
				Camden	39	16	23
MICHIGAN				Newark	60	29	31
				New Brunswick	145	67	78
Central Michigan University	25	15	10	Stockton State College	21	17	4
Delta College	11	8	3	Trenton State College	24	18	6
Eastern Michigan University	29	24	5	University of Medicine and Dentistry:			
Ferris State University	19	14	5	Camden	19	18	1
Grand Valley State University	9	8	1	Newark	125	48	77
Hope College	10	6	4	Piscataway	37	28	9
Lansing Community College	10	8	2	William Paterson College	32	25	7
Macomb Community College	33	22	11				
Michigan State University	55	49	6	**NEW MEXICO**			
Michigan Technological University	13	9	4				
Northern Michigan University	17	14	3	Eastern New Mexico University	8	7	1
Oakland Community College	18	16	2	New Mexico Highlands University	14	7	7
Oakland University	19	15	4	New Mexico State University	26	19	7
Saginaw Valley State University	8	6	2	University of New Mexico	44	39	5
University of Michigan:							
Ann Arbor	73	37	36	**NEW YORK**			
Flint	16	5	11				
Western Michigan University	35	26	9	Cornell University	59	45	14
				Ithaca College	32	16	16
MINNESOTA				Rensselaer Polytechnic Institute	23	21	2
				State University of New York:			
University of Minnesota:				Albany	43	34	9
Duluth	9	8	1	Binghamton	40	25	15
Twin Cities	47	39	8	Buffalo	62	55	7
				Downstate Medical Center	106	25	81
MISSISSIPPI				Maritime College	9	7	2
				Oswego	27	21	6
Itawamba Community College	3	3	—	Stony Brook	81	48	33
Jackson State University	39	35	4	Upstate Medical Center	56	2	54
Mississippi State University	37	28	9	State University of New York Agricultural and Technical College:			
University of Mississippi:				Alfred	17	12	5
Medical Center	75	68	7	Cobleskill	11	10	1
Oxford	46	25	21	Farmingdale	17	16	1
				Morrisville	11	10	1
MISSOURI				State University of New York College:			
				Brockport	20	18	2
Lincoln University	10	7	3	Buffalo	32	27	5
University of Missouri:				Canton	10	9	1
Columbia	47	33	14	Cortland	18	16	2
St. Louis	27	18	9	Environmental Science and Forestry	14	10	4
Washington University	26	18	8	Fredonia	16	15	1
				Geneseo	18	16	2
MONTANA				New Paltz	22	20	2
				Old Westbury	22	21	1
Montana State University	14	10	4	Oneonta	18	17	1
University of Montana	15	11	4	Optometry	3	1	2
				Plattsburgh	18	13	5
NEBRASKA				Potsdam	12	11	1
				Purchase	19	16	3
University of Nebraska				Technology	13	11	2
Kearney	7	6	1	Utica-Rome	14	12	2
Lincoln	41	23	18				

Table 79.—Number of Full-time Law Enforcement Employees, Universities and Colleges, October 31, 1995 — Continued

University/College	Total police employees	Total officers	Total civilians	University/College	Total police employees	Total officers	Total civilians
NEW YORK — Continued				**PENNSYLVANIA — Continued**			
Syracuse University	43	39	4	Clarion University	17	11	6
				East Stroudsburg University	15	14	1
NORTH CAROLINA				Edinboro University	15	14	1
				Elizabethtown College	12	7	5
Appalachian State University	23	18	5	Indiana University	24	19	5
Beaufort County Community College	1	1	—	Kutztown University	18	11	7
Davidson College..........................	10	9	1	Lehigh University	25	14	11
Duke University...........................	132	63	69	Lock Haven University	11	9	2
East Carolina University	44	27	17	Mansfield University	12	12	—
Elizabeth City State University	12	11	1	Millersville University	20	15	5
Fayetteville State University	24	16	8	Moravian College	9	7	2
Mars Hill College	6	4	2	Pennsylvania State University:			
Methodist College	24	6	18	Altoona..............................	6	5	1
North Carolina A&T State University,				Behrend College	7	5	2
Greensboro.........................	51	25	26	Capital Campus	6	5	1
North Carolina Central University, Durham	36	19	17	Mount Alto	2	2	—
North Carolina School of the Arts	9	8	1	University Park	62	48	14
North Carolina State University, Raleigh	48	31	17	Shippensburg University	16	14	2
Pembroke State University	13	10	3	Slippery Rock University	16	15	1
Pfeiffer College	2	2	—	University of Pittsburgh, Bradford	5	5	—
Queens College	8	7	1				
University of North Carolina:				**RHODE ISLAND**			
Asheville	10	7	3				
Chapel Hill	58	29	29	Brown University.........................	63	21	42
Charlotte............................	28	25	3	University of Rhode Island	27	16	11
Greensboro..........................	37	25	12				
Wilmington	23	17	6	**SOUTH CAROLINA**			
Wake Forest University	24	13	11				
Western Carolina University	16	13	3	Clemson University	33	30	3
Winston-Salem State University	13	11	2	Denmark Technical College	3	3	—
				Francis Marion University	11	11	—
NORTH DAKOTA				Lander University	12	11	1
				Medical University of South Carolina	113	68	45
University of North Dakota.................	17	11	6	South Carolina State University	33	22	11
				The Citadel.............................	16	13	3
OHIO				Trident Technical College	20	18	2
				University of South Carolina:			
Bowling Green State University	26	17	9	Aiken	2	2	—
Cleveland State University	37	30	7	Coastal Carolina	14	9	5
Cuyahoga Community College	34	28	6	Columbia	65	55	10
Kent State University	38	28	10	Spartanburg	9	9	—
Lakeland Community College	11	7	4	Winthrop University	21	14	7
Marietta College	4	4	—				
Miami University.........................	36	28	8	**SOUTH DAKOTA**			
Ohio State University	58	47	11				
Ohio University	32	22	10	South Dakota State University	12	7	5
University of Akron	35	29	6				
University of Cincinnati	97	47	50	**TENNESSEE**			
University of Toledo	33	28	5				
Wright State University	26	18	8	East Tennessee State University	24	18	6
Youngstown State University	22	19	3	Middle Tennessee State University	22	17	5
				Tennessee Technological University...........	15	13	2
OKLAHOMA				University of Tennessee:			
				Knoxville	57	49	8
Cameron University.......................	7	6	1	Martin...............................	16	12	4
Central State University	19	13	6	Memphis	36	23	13
East Central University	4	4	—				
Murray State College	3	3	—	**TEXAS**			
Northeastern Oklahoma State University	12	10	2				
Oklahoma State University:				Alamo Community College	58	29	29
Main Campus.........................	35	25	10	Alvin Community College	12	10	2
Okmulgee............................	8	8	—	Amarillo College	7	5	2
Southeastern Oklahoma State University	7	7	—	Amarillo Technical Center	6	6	—
Tulsa Junior College	16	8	8	Angelo State University	11	9	2
University of Oklahoma:				Austin College	8	7	1
Health Science Center	22	18	4	Baylor University	26	17	9
Norman	34	23	11	Baylor University Medical Center	81	49	32
				Central Texas College	9	8	1
PENNSYLVANIA				College of the Mainland	6	5	1
				Eastfield College	8	8	—
Beaver County Community College	1	1	—	East Texas State University, Commerce	24	14	10
Bloomsburg University	18	17	1	Grayson County Junior College	4	4	—
California University	15	11	4	Hardin-Simmons University	7	5	2
Cheyney University	15	14	1	Houston Baptist University	8	8	—

Table 79.—Number of Full-time Law Enforcement Employees, Universities and Colleges, October 31, 1995 — Continued

University/College	Total police employees	Total officers	Total civilians	University/College	Total police employees	Total officers	Total civilians
TEXAS — Continued				**VERMONT**			
Houston Community College	23	22	1	University of Vermont	26	17	9
Lamar University, Beaumont	22	10	12				
Laredo Community College	11	10	1	**VIRGINIA**			
McLennan Community College	4	3	1				
Midwestern State University	8	7	1	Christopher Newport College	13	13	—
North Lake College	9	8	1	Clinch Valley College	5	5	—
Paris Junior College.	3	1	2	College of William and Mary	21	16	5
Prairie View A&M University	26	17	9	George Mason University	39	32	7
Rice University	38	25	13	Hampton University	27	19	8
Richland College	9	8	1	James Madison University	27	17	10
Southern Methodist University	33	22	11	Longwood College	12	11	1
South Plains College	4	4	—	Mary Washington College	18	13	5
Southwestern University	6	6	—	Norfolk State University	47	22	25
Southwest Texas State University	40	22	18	Northern Virginia Community College	26	26	—
Stephen F. Austin State University	34	17	17	Old Dominion University	27	24	3
Sul Ross State University	8	6	2	Radford University	23	16	7
Tarleton State University	12	11	1	Thomas Nelson Community College	9	8	1
Texas A&M University:				University of Richmond	28	15	13
College Station	111	40	71	University of Virginia	107	57	50
Corpus Christi	18	10	8	Virginia Commonwealth University	71	54	17
Galveston	7	7	—	Virginia Military Institute	5	5	—
Kingsville	21	15	6	Virginia Polytechnic Institute and			
Texas Christian Univeristy	28	16	12	State University	45	33	12
Texas College Osteo. Med.	21	12	9	Virginia State University	32	12	20
Texas Southern University	31	19	12	Virginia Western Community College	5	5	—
Texas State Technical College:							
Harlingen	9	6	3	**WASHINGTON**			
Waco.	15	12	3				
Texas Tech. University:				Central Washington University	11	10	1
Health Science Center	42	19	23	Eastern Washington University	7	6	1
Lubbock	48	30	18	University of Washington	70	50	20
Texas Woman's University	34	16	18	Washington State University	24	17	7
Trinity University	25	10	15	Western Washington University	15	11	4
Tyler Junior College	4	3	1				
University of Houston:				**WEST VIRGINIA**			
Central Campus	44	32	12				
Clearlake	17	10	7	Bluefield College	4	2	2
Downtown Campus	26	16	10	Concord College	4	4	—
University of North Texas	50	24	26	Glenville State College	3	3	—
University of Texas:				Marshall University	26	20	6
Arlington	62	29	33	Potomac College	6	6	—
Austin	166	67	99	West Liberty State College	6	6	—
Brownsville and Texas Southmost College . . .	13	6	7	West Virginia State College	12	10	2
Dallas.	32	12	20	West Virginia Tech.	8	8	—
El Paso	47	17	30	West Virginia University	63	42	21
Health Science Center, San Antonio	57	17	40				
Health Science Center, Tyler	15	5	10	**WISCONSIN**			
Houston	162	51	111				
Medical Branch	92	35	57	University of Wisconsin:			
Pan American	20	11	9	Eau Claire	12	10	2
Permian Basin	11	5	6	Green Bay	10	5	5
San Antonio	35	26	9	La Crosse	9	8	1
Southwest Medical School	60	20	40	Madison	92	41	51
Tyler	8	5	3	Milwaukee	34	30	4
West Texas A&M University	13	9	4	Oshkosh	11	10	1
				Parkside	10	7	3
UTAH				Platteville	7	7	—
				Stout	8	7	1
Brigham Young University	34	24	10	Superior	5	4	1
College of Eastern Utah	1	1	—	Whitewater.	14	10	4
Salt Lake Community College	17	12	5				
Southern Utah University	5	4	1	**WYOMING**			
University of Utah	45	36	9				
Utah State University	18	12	6	Sheridan College	2	2	—
Utah Valley State College	7	5	2	University of Wyoming	23	13	10
Weber State University	16	11	5				

Table 80.—Number of Full-time Law Enforcement Employees, Suburban Counties, October 31, 1995

County by State	Total police employees	Total officers	Total civilians	County by State	Total police employees	Total officers	Total civilians	County by State	Total police employees	Total officers	Total civilians
ALABAMA				**CALIFORNIA —** **Continued**				**GEORGIA —** **Continued**			
Autauga	29	17	12	Sutter	73	53	20	Columbia	154	127	27
Baldwin	114	54	60	Tulare	268	209	59	Coweta	120	57	63
Blount	44	21	23	Ventura	1,103	676	427	Dade	36	17	19
Calhoun	64	28	36	Yolo	195	77	118	Dekalb	555	146	409
Colbert	32	20	12	Yuba	68	44	24	Dougherty Police			
Dale	18	12	6					Department	50	50	—
Elmore	52	21	31	**COLORADO**				Douglas	203	138	65
Etowah	91	40	51					Effingham	70	35	35
Houston	111	38	73	Adams	352	226	126	Fayette	108	81	27
Jefferson	594	469	125	Arapahoe	459	314	145	Forsyth	93	68	25
Lauderdale	59	24	35	Douglas	139	103	36	Fulton	829	732	97
Lawrence	27	19	8	El Paso	473	358	115	Fulton Police			
Limestone	46	25	21	Jefferson	515	357	158	Department	324	222	102
Madison	167	88	79	Larimer	230	80	150	Gwinnett	294	228	66
Mobile	459	146	313	Pueblo	223	109	114	Gwinnett Police			
Montgomery	203	101	102	Weld	162	132	30	Department	499	346	153
Morgan	69	40	29					Harris	55	31	24
Russell	65	22	43	**DELAWARE**				Henry	88	46	42
Shelby	87	68	19					Henry Police			
St. Clair	38	21	17	New Castle Police				Department	147	131	16
Tuscaloosa	112	67	45	Department	317	294	23	Houston	117	75	42
								Jones	43	40	3
ARIZONA				**FLORIDA**				Lee	30	21	9
								McDuffie	23	12	11
Maricopa	1,696	445	1,251	Alachua	323	208	115	Newton	70	44	26
Mohave	214	87	127	Bay	217	149	68	Oconee	39	25	14
Pima	1,033	385	648	Brevard	657	290	367	Paulding	113	65	48
Pinal	258	134	124	Broward	2,869	890	1,979	Peach	49	24	25
Yuma	196	53	143	Charlotte	368	219	149	Pickens	27	17	10
				Collier	735	379	356	Pickens Police			
ARKANSAS				Dade	4,082	2,846	1,236	Department	10	10	—
				Escambia	849	350	499	Richmond	606	482	124
Benton	89	40	49	Flagler	101	52	49	Rockdale	120	108	12
Crawford	39	17	22	Gadsden	56	28	28	Spalding	110	76	34
Crittenden	62	27	35	Hernando	247	161	86	Twiggs	13	9	4
Faulkner	52	17	35	Hillsborough	2,473	925	1,548	Walker	96	66	30
Jefferson	50	44	6	Lee	771	369	402	Walton	98	49	49
Lonoke	22	12	10	Manatee	728	295	433				
Miller	42	20	22	Marion	637	202	435	**IDAHO**			
Pulaski	463	365	98	Martin	300	202	98				
Saline	41	27	14	Nassau	114	58	56	Ada	187	84	103
Sebastian	110	27	83	Okaloosa	185	144	41	Canyon	79	44	35
Washington	84	41	43	Orange	1,457	976	481				
				Osceola	477	259	218	**ILLINOIS**			
CALIFORNIA				Pasco	752	324	428				
				Pinellas	2,022	784	1,238	Boone	43	24	19
Alameda	1,240	747	493	Polk	1,122	415	707	Champaign	56	50	6
Butte	185	134	51	St. Johns	324	141	183	Clinton	21	17	4
Contra Costa	882	620	262	St. Lucie	463	208	255	Cook	657	533	124
El Dorado	289	143	146	Santa Rosa	224	112	112	De Kalb	65	51	14
Fresno	492	337	155	Sarasota	735	336	399	Du Page	195	141	54
Kern	481	295	186	Seminole	591	255	336	Grundy	40	28	12
Los Angeles	6,704	4,454	2,250	Volusia	530	352	178	Henry	46	46	—
Madera	82	62	20					Jersey	10	10	—
Marin	265	184	81	**GEORGIA**				Kane	143	88	55
Merced	91	69	22					Kankakee	109	61	48
Monterey	373	285	88	Barrow	69	31	38	Kendall	61	54	7
Napa	82	64	18	Bibb	242	214	28	Lake	377	174	203
Orange	2,285	1,226	1,059	Bryan	33	19	14	Macon	139	44	95
Placer	332	216	116	Carroll	93	55	38	Madison	94	74	20
Riverside	1,993	1,081	912	Catoosa	83	53	30	McHenry	233	194	39
Sacramento	1,621	1,159	462	Chatham	378	319	59	McLean	69	49	20
San Bernardino	1,920	1,128	792	Chatham Police				Menard	12	7	5
San Diego	2,731	1,664	1,067	Department	190	147	43	Monroe	22	11	11
San Joaquin	307	152	155	Chattahoochee	3	2	1	Ogle	59	43	16
San Luis Obispo	307	227	80	Cherokee	211	164	47	Peoria	114	62	52
San Mateo	528	312	216	Cherokee Police				Rock Island	83	53	30
Santa Barbara	323	229	94	Department	2	2	—	St. Clair	163	150	13
Santa Clara	525	415	110	Clayton Police				Sangamon	216	72	144
Santa Cruz	288	220	68	Department	246	218	28	Tazewell	61	37	24
Shasta	130	88	42	Cobb	384	282	102	Will	411	322	89
Solano	385	87	298	Cobb Police				Winnebago	145	124	21
Sonoma	557	198	359	Department	440	381	59	Woodford	27	18	9
Stanislaus	471	182	289								

Table 80.—Number of Full-time Law Enforcement Employees, Suburban Counties, October 31, 1995 — Continued

County by State	Total police employees	Total officers	Total civilians	County by State	Total police employees	Total officers	Total civilians	County by State	Total police employees	Total officers	Total civilians
INDIANA				**KENTUCKY — Continued**				**MICHIGAN — Continued**			
Allen...............	250	120	130	Pendleton	3	2	1	Jackson.............	99	50	49
Clark...............	75	31	44	Scott	19	19	—	Kalamazoo	159	129	30
Dearborn	53	17	36	Woodford	5	5	—	Kent	157	135	22
Elkhart	154	64	90	Woodford Police				Lapeer.............	62	48	14
Harrison	31	11	20	Department........	20	19	1	Lenawee	65	45	20
Howard............	95	34	61					Livingston	85	53	32
Huntington	31	11	20	**LOUISIANA**				Macomb	372	174	198
Lake	226	162	64					Midland	57	34	23
Marion	814	409	405	Acadia	96	63	33	Monroe	156	85	71
Porter	118	47	71	Ascension	159	158	1	Muskegon	92	36	56
St. Joseph	191	133	58	Bossier	142	113	29	Oakland	712	579	133
Tippecanoe	113	41	72	Caddo	595	414	181	Ottawa	86	75	11
Tipton	12	7	5	Calcasieu	487	486	1	Saginaw	128	87	41
Vanderburgh	157	100	57	East Baton Rouge	662	662	—	St. Clair	110	65	45
Vigo	68	36	32	Jefferson	1,315	875	440	Van Buren..........	60	34	26
Warrick	59	28	31	Lafayette	444	444	—	Washtenaw	230	131	99
Wells..............	30	10	20	Lafourche	195	121	74	Wayne.............	1,447	736	711
				Livingston	158	116	42				
IOWA				Ouachita	241	240	1	**MINNESOTA**			
				Rapides............	274	197	77				
Black Hawk	150	105	45	St. Charles	232	144	88	Anoka	165	79	86
Dallas	34	12	22	St. James	93	71	22	Benton	26	15	11
Dubuque	48	40	8	St. John the Baptist	140	138	2	Carver.............	106	46	60
Johnson	71	47	24	St. Landry..........	121	114	7	Chisago	51	25	26
Linn	127	90	37	St. Martin	147	120	27	Dakota	142	69	73
Polk	213	170	43	St. Tammany	339	159	180	Hennepin	602	290	312
Pottawattamie........	60	32	28	Terrebonne	255	255	—	Houston	19	11	8
Scott	128	40	88	Webster............	77	56	21	Isanti..............	36	17	19
Warren	27	19	8	West Baton Rouge	77	53	24	Olmsted	51	50	1
Woodbury	87	31	56					Polk	26	16	10
				MAINE				St. Louis	177	98	79
KANSAS								Scott	87	30	57
				Androscoggin	16	11	5	Sherburne	68	29	39
Butler	50	36	14	Cumberland	60	43	17	Stearns	105	41	64
Douglas	67	35	32					Washington	182	70	112
Harvey	21	13	8	**MARYLAND**				Wright	126	71	55
Johnson	366	294	72								
Leavenworth	50	36	14	Allegany	28	20	8	**MISSISSIPPI**			
Miami	26	14	12	Anne Arundel........	42	37	5				
Sedgwick	316	159	157	Anne Arundel Police				Harrison	252	252	—
Shawnee	123	104	19	Department........	772	587	185	Madison	61	30	31
Wyandotte	156	52	104	Baltimore County				Rankin	80	28	52
				Sheriff...........	73	53	20				
KENTUCKY				Baltimore County				**MISSOURI**			
				Police Department ...	1,730	1,477	253				
Bell...............	9	5	4	Calvert	69	62	7	Andrew	11	9	2
Boone	22	19	3	Carroll	37	31	6	Boone	91	45	46
Boone Police				Cecil	54	43	11	Buchanan	71	63	8
Department........	54	50	4	Charles	207	144	63	Cass	48	20	28
Bourbon	6	6	—	Frederick	107	80	27	Christian	34	34	—
Boyd	21	21	—	Harford	287	167	120	Clay	126	96	30
Boyd Police Department ..	13	13	—	Howard	45	28	17	Franklin	91	80	11
Bullitt	15	12	3	Howard Police				Greene	134	115	19
Campbell	11	11	—	Department........	383	314	69	Jackson	111	84	27
Campbell Police				Montgomery	1,224	962	262	Jasper	91	78	13
Department........	34	24	10	Montgomery Police				Jefferson	207	161	46
Christian	14	14	—	Department........	111	98	13	Platte..............	62	48	14
Christian Police				Prince George's	272	205	67	St. Charles	148	105	43
Department........	4	4	—	Prince George's				St. Louis County			
Clark	9	9	—	Police Department ...	1,525	1,225	300	Police Department ...	804	595	209
Daviess	38	37	1	Queen Anne's.........	31	29	2	Warren	28	22	6
Gallatin	3	3	—	Washington	149	60	89	Webster............	14	14	—
Grant..............	6	4	2								
Greenup	9	9	—	**MICHIGAN**				**MONTANA**			
Henderson	15	15	—								
Jefferson Police				Allegan	89	52	37	Cascade	53	30	23
Department........	563	421	142	Bay	36	30	6	Yellowstone	108	47	61
Jessamine	11	11	—	Berrien	170	59	111				
Kenton Police				Calhoun	87	50	37	**NEBRASKA**			
Department........	48	33	15	Clinton	55	21	34				
Madison	14	10	4	Eaton	133	73	60	Cass	30	16	14
Oldham	12	12	—	Genesee	240	130	110	Dakota	24	10	14
Oldham Police				Ingham	208	113	95	Douglas	165	112	53
Department........	17	16	1								

Table 80.—Number of Full-time Law Enforcement Employees, Suburban Counties, October 31, 1995 — Continued

County by State	Total police employees	Total officers	Total civilians	County by State	Total police employees	Total officers	Total civilians	County by State	Total police employees	Total officers	Total civilians
NEBRASKA — Continued				**NEW YORK —** Continued				**OHIO —** Continued			
Lancaster	79	61	18	Erie	641	538	103	Auglaize	33	18	15
Sarpy	120	100	20	Genesee	56	40	16	Belmont	39	19	20
Washington	25	11	14	Herkimer	55	46	9	Champaign	36	28	8
				Livingston	78	66	12	Clark	122	100	22
NEVADA				Madison	24	19	5	Clermont	163	69	94
				Monroe	272	228	44	Columbiana	82	33	49
Nye	105	73	32	Nassau	4,193	3,051	1,142	Crawford	33	17	16
Washoe	515	339	176	Niagara	158	139	19	Cuyahoga	1,060	159	901
				Oneida	154	110	44	Delaware	86	44	42
NEW JERSEY				Onondaga	235	204	31	Franklin	680	551	129
				Ontario	90	57	33	Fulton	29	19	10
Atlantic	111	85	26	Orange	97	88	9	Geauga	66	34	32
Atlantic Prosecutor	149	65	84	Orleans	38	25	13	Greene	93	83	10
Bergen	452	364	88	Oswego	73	62	11	Hamilton	949	237	712
Bergen Police Department	106	81	25	Putnam	89	64	25	Lake	151	40	111
Bergen Prosecutor	259	115	144	Rensselaer	38	33	5	Lawrence	34	27	7
Burlington	67	54	13	Saratoga	112	85	27	Licking	130	98	32
Burlington Prosecutor	120	42	78	Schoharie	52	42	10	Lorain	141	46	95
Camden	208	183	27	Suffolk	154	114	40	Lucas	432	260	172
Camden Prosecutor	213	99	114	Suffolk Police Department	3,310	2,710	600	Mahoning	214	151	63
Cape May	127	111	16	Tioga	48	32	16	Medina	99	87	12
Cape May Prosecutor	45	18	27	Warren	82	63	19	Miami	69	39	30
Cumberland	61	54	7	Wayne	76	49	27	Pickaway	74	40	34
Cumberland Prosecutor	52	17	35	Westchester	282	232	50	Portage	118	39	79
Essex	462	416	46					Richland	100	48	52
Essex Police Department	49	44	5	**NORTH CAROLINA**				Stark	182	105	77
Essex Prosecutor	426	296	130	Alamance	106	65	41	Trumbull	78	40	38
Gloucester	184	154	30	Alexander	26	17	9	Wood	93	89	4
Gloucester Prosecutor	74	29	45	Brunswick	80	72	8				
Hudson	178	142	36	Buncombe	288	177	111	**OKLAHOMA**			
Hudson Police Department	124	83	41	Burke	79	59	20	Canadian	32	17	15
Hudson Prosecutor	272	102	170	Cabarrus	128	122	6	Cleveland	90	37	53
Hunterdon	30	22	8	Caldwell	77	47	30	Comanche	45	26	19
Hunterdon Prosecutor	42	17	25	Catawba	105	99	6	Creek	25	15	10
Mercer	119	91	28	Chatham	65	41	24	Garfield	21	11	10
Mercer Prosecutor	124	79	45	Cumberland	424	267	157	Logan	14	8	6
Middlesex	197	163	34	Currituck	32	25	7	McClain	16	7	9
Middlesex Prosecutor	223	137	86	Davidson	144	84	60	Oklahoma	444	102	342
Monmouth	359	301	58	Davie	38	27	11	Osage	28	20	8
Monmouth Prosecutor	244	107	137	Durham	334	98	236	Pottawatomie	25	12	13
Morris	270	190	80	Edgecombe	65	39	26	Rogers	26	12	14
Morris Prosecutor	139	90	49	Forsyth	440	233	207	Sequoyah	15	6	9
Ocean	186	76	110	Franklin	64	32	32	Tulsa	382	189	193
Ocean Prosecutor	125	56	69	Gaston Rural Police	164	112	52	Wagoner	12	7	5
Passaic	675	499	176	Guilford	376	206	170				
Passaic Prosecutor	184	70	114	Johnston	96	47	49	**OREGON**			
Salem	150	131	19	Lincoln	73	54	19	Clackamas	219	184	35
Salem Prosecutor	32	10	22	Nash	79	45	34	Columbia	15	13	2
Somerset	170	132	38	New Hanover	239	177	62	Jackson	67	47	20
Somerset Prosecutor	94	61	33	Onslow	124	74	50	Lane	108	65	43
Sussex	114	100	14	Orange	97	81	16	Marion	95	70	25
Sussex Prosecutor	50	32	18	Pitt	90	76	14	Multnomah	164	115	49
Union	170	150	20	Randolph	106	79	27	Polk	28	22	6
Union Prosecutor	221	126	95	Rowan	122	104	18	Washington	210	152	58
Warren	22	18	4	Stokes	49	30	19	Yamhill	47	42	5
Warren Prosecutor	53	33	20	Union	121	92	29				
				Wake	421	192	229	**PENNSYLVANIA**			
NEW MEXICO				Wayne	96	44	52	Allegheny Police Department	285	243	42
Dona Ana	96	80	16	Yadkin	44	24	20	Beaver	29	24	5
Sandoval	35	30	5					Cambria	20	15	5
				NORTH DAKOTA				Centre	9	9	—
NEW YORK				Burleigh	53	39	14	Chester Detective	19	16	3
				Cass	67	44	23	Cumberland	23	21	2
Albany	143	93	50	Grand Forks	27	21	6	Lebanon Detective	6	5	1
Broome	215	200	15	Morton	31	17	14	Washington	28	24	4
Cayuga	40	26	14					Westmoreland Detective	51	12	39
Chautauqua	97	73	24	**OHIO**							
Chemung	48	34	14	Allen	137	58	79				
Dutchess	125	108	17	Ashtabula	75	40	35				

County by State	Total police employees	Total officers	Total civilians	County by State	Total police employees	Total officers	Total civilians	County by State	Total police employees	Total officers	Total civilians
SOUTH CAROLINA				**TEXAS —** Continued				**VIRGINIA —** Continued			
Aiken	107	82	25					Mathews	15	9	6
Anderson	136	112	24	Hunt	53	22	31	New Kent	20	13	7
Berkeley	106	65	41	Jefferson	405	86	319	Pittsylvania	82	41	41
Charleston	317	232	85	Johnson	116	47	69	Powhatan	18	15	3
Cherokee	50	37	13	Kaufman	65	28	37	Prince George	41	32	9
Dorchester	104	57	47	Liberty	94	36	58	Prince William Police			
Edgefield	28	16	12	Lubbock	242	151	91	Department	436	316	120
Florence	188	78	110	McLennan	234	56	178	Roanoke Police			
Greenville	346	285	61	Midland	156	88	68	Department	128	97	31
Horry	25	13	12	Montgomery	378	271	107	Scott	40	31	9
Horry Police				Nueces	376	327	49	Spotsylvania	78	54	24
Department	146	134	12	Orange	128	62	66	Stafford	118	81	37
Lexington	266	164	102	Parker	68	29	39	Washington	58	45	13
Pickens	89	63	26	Potter	168	157	11	York	79	71	8
Richland	331	292	39	Randall	72	59	13				
Spartanburg	229	211	18	Rockwall	42	15	27	**WASHINGTON**			
Sumter	98	91	7	San Patricio	68	31	37				
York	180	86	94	Smith	228	62	166	Benton	59	47	12
				Tarrant	1,162	758	404	Clark	194	141	53
SOUTH DAKOTA				Taylor	125	69	56	Franklin	24	21	3
				Tom Green	104	54	50	Island	42	34	8
Pennington	111	43	68	Travis	1,105	416	689	King	848	610	238
				Upshur	36	19	17	Kitsap	115	93	22
TENNESSEE				Victoria	123	81	42	Pierce	331	284	47
				Waller	42	18	24	Snohomish	244	174	70
Carter	46	28	18	Webb	208	154	54	Spokane	264	180	84
Hawkins	48	38	10	Wichita	131	36	95	Thurston	112	79	33
Knox	739	283	456	Williamson	207	123	84	Whatcom	69	58	11
Madison	61	61	—	Wilson	21	17	4	Yakima	97	67	30
Marion	26	16	10								
Montgomery	124	116	8	**UTAH**				**WEST VIRGINIA**			
Robertson	74	29	45								
Rutherford	147	86	61	Davis	177	131	46	Brooke	21	14	7
Shelby	1,366	483	883	Salt Lake	819	644	175	Cabell	84	31	53
Sullivan	186	85	101	Utah	156	111	45	Hancock	34	22	12
Sumner	120	54	66					Kanawha	85	68	17
Union	17	11	6	**VERMONT**				Marshall	21	19	2
Washington	126	52	74					Mineral	11	5	6
Williamson	121	60	61	Chittenden	10	8	2	Ohio	26	19	7
				Grand Isle	2	1	1	Putnam	26	22	4
TEXAS								Wayne	29	12	17
				VIRGINIA				Wood	39	29	10
Archer	11	7	4								
Bastrop	95	30	65	Albemarle Police				**WISCONSIN**			
Bell	213	71	142	Department	101	83	18				
Bexar	1,502	374	1,128	Amherst	47	39	8	Brown	197	130	67
Bowie	159	49	110	Arlington Police				Calumet	32	24	8
Brazoria	270	100	170	Department	413	334	79	Chippewa	52	52	—
Brazos	125	56	69	Bedford	84	84	—	Dane	416	337	79
Caldwell	48	11	37	Botetourt	51	40	11	Douglas	40	23	17
Cameron	227	59	168	Campbell	61	52	9	Eau Claire	77	49	28
Chambers	58	20	38	Charles City	14	8	6	Kenosha	167	103	64
Collin	317	108	209	Chesterfield Police				La Crosse	74	33	41
Comal	108	47	61	Department	411	356	55	Marathon	126	61	65
Coryell	39	17	22	Clarke	18	11	7	Milwaukee	774	573	201
Dallas	1,562	429	1,133	Culpeper	71	53	18	Outagamie	185	71	114
Denton	431	126	305	Dinwiddie	35	26	9	Ozaukee	87	66	21
Ector	146	56	90	Fairfax Police				Pierce	40	39	1
El Paso	666	197	469	Department	1,301	1,024	277	Racine	248	179	69
Ellis	116	39	77	Fauquier	108	81	27	Rock	165	94	71
Fort Bend	294	194	100	Fluvanna	15	11	4	Sheboygan	128	73	55
Galveston	324	277	47	Gloucester	66	56	10	St. Croix	54	49	5
Grayson	68	49	19	Goochland	17	13	4	Washington	106	55	51
Gregg	131	71	60	Greene	16	10	6	Waukesha	305	147	158
Guadalupe	86	29	57	Hanover	144	131	13	Winnebago	156	89	67
Hardin	45	27	18	Henrico Police							
Harris	3,271	2,511	760	Department	621	445	176	**WYOMING**			
Harrison	85	30	55	Isle of Wight	27	21	6				
Hays	168	57	111	James City Police				Laramie	57	37	20
Henderson	75	28	47	Department	56	53	3	Natrona	49	39	10
Hidalgo	314	125	189	King George	28	27	1				
Hood	50	34	16	Loudoun	207	167	40				

Table 81.—Number of Full-time Law Enforcement Employees, Rural Counties, October 31, 1995

County by State	Total police employees	Total officers	Total civilians
ALABAMA			
Barbour	23	12	11
Bibb	20	8	12
Butler	12	6	6
Chambers	50	16	34
Cherokee	22	13	9
Chilton	27	15	12
Choctaw	16	5	11
Clay	9	3	6
Cleburne	6	5	1
Coffee	30	10	20
Conecuh	19	7	12
Coosa	11	6	5
Covington	28	15	13
Crenshaw	15	7	8
Cullman	70	53	17
Dallas	45	41	4
De Kalb	37	21	16
Escambia	41	15	26
Fayette	12	12	—
Franklin	32	16	16
Geneva	16	8	8
Greene	14	6	8
Hale	12	5	7
Henry	19	10	9
Jackson	45	27	18
Lee	80	37	43
Lowndes	21	7	14
Macon	23	14	9
Marengo	19	9	10
Marion	19	9	10
Marshall	36	20	16
Monroe	32	16	16
Perry	15	7	8
Pickens	12	6	6
Pike	18	10	8
Randolph	12	12	—
Sumter	4	3	1
Talladega	56	20	36
Tallapoosa	48	17	31
Walker	38	32	6
Wilcox	18	8	10
Winston	18	11	7
ARIZONA			
Apache	55	28	27
Cochise	161	64	97
Coconino	123	58	65
Gila	108	50	58
Graham	30	15	15
Greenlee	25	15	10
Lapaz	75	32	43
Navajo	87	47	40
Santa Cruz	64	38	26
Yavapai	182	89	93
ARKANSAS			
Arkansas	8	8	—
Ashley	25	11	14
Baxter	31	19	12
Boone	24	13	11
Bradley	5	4	1
Calhoun	7	4	3
Carroll	26	13	13
Chicot	8	6	2
Clark	23	11	12
Clay	14	7	7
Cleburne	20	12	8
Cleveland	9	5	4
Columbia	22	10	12
Conway	15	8	7
Craighead	49	17	32
Cross	32	10	22
ARKANSAS — Continued			
Dallas	6	5	1
Desha	15	7	8
Drew	14	8	6
Franklin	14	7	7
Fulton	8	4	4
Garland	79	32	47
Grant	11	6	5
Greene	37	10	27
Hempstead	34	11	23
Hot Spring	24	11	13
Howard	18	7	11
Independence	60	37	23
Izard	13	8	5
Jackson	17	10	7
Johnson	15	10	5
Lafayette	13	5	8
Lawrence	18	8	10
Lee	6	5	1
Lincoln	14	4	10
Little River	15	7	8
Logan	18	8	10
Madison	16	9	7
Marion	15	6	9
Mississippi	46	19	27
Monroe	13	6	7
Montgomery	10	5	5
Nevada	17	7	10
Newton	9	4	5
Ouachita	27	13	14
Perry	10	6	4
Phillips	30	8	22
Pike	10	6	4
Poinsett	54	11	43
Polk	19	9	10
Pope	43	21	22
Prairie	12	6	6
Randolph	8	7	1
St. Francis	32	14	18
Scott	12	5	7
Searcy	12	4	8
Sevier	17	9	8
Sharp	17	8	9
Stone	18	6	12
Union	45	20	25
Van Buren	14	9	5
White	45	22	23
Woodruff	10	6	4
Yell	19	7	12
CALIFORNIA			
Alpine	12	9	3
Amador	46	34	12
Calaveras	73	42	31
Colusa	40	27	13
Del Norte	44	40	4
Glenn	50	19	31
Humboldt	193	162	31
Imperial	109	73	36
Inyo	34	25	9
Kings	167	73	94
Lake	140	57	83
Lassen	88	28	60
Mariposa	56	47	9
Mendocino	132	109	23
Modoc	11	11	—
Mono	43	25	18
Nevada	110	72	38
Plumas	64	35	29
San Benito	39	22	17
Sierra	15	10	5
Siskiyou	62	47	15
Tehama	52	32	20
CALIFORNIA — Continued			
Trinity	24	19	5
Tuolumne	72	50	22
COLORADO			
Alamosa	30	26	4
Archuleta	27	7	20
Baca	9	5	4
Bent	9	5	4
Chaffee	24	15	9
Cheyenne	8	5	3
Clear Creek	31	18	13
Conejos	12	6	6
Custer	12	7	5
Delta	36	14	22
Dolores	7	4	3
Fremont	54	35	19
Garfield	48	15	33
Gilpin	32	18	14
Grand	40	26	14
Gunnison	21	20	1
Hinsdale	4	3	1
Kiowa	4	3	1
Kit Carson	12	6	6
Lake	16	9	7
La Plata	74	61	13
Las Animas	19	11	8
Lincoln	17	6	11
Logan	23	10	13
Mineral	5	3	2
Moffat	32	16	16
Montezuma	35	19	16
Morgan	41	24	17
Otero	17	17	—
Ouray	7	6	1
Park	27	17	10
Phillips	3	3	—
Pitkin	39	21	18
Prowers	26	7	19
Rio Blanco	17	10	7
Rio Grande	18	8	10
Routt	35	22	13
Saguache	10	5	5
San Juan	5	4	1
Sedgwick	9	5	4
Summit	41	33	8
Teller	36	27	9
Washington	12	8	4
Yuma	10	6	4
FLORIDA			
Baker	55	27	28
Bradford	28	18	10
Citrus	225	137	88
Columbia	147	111	36
De Soto	73	31	42
Dixie	46	21	25
Gilchrist	30	16	14
Glades	47	24	23
Gulf	40	23	17
Hardee	74	30	44
Hendry	104	50	54
Highlands	206	94	112
Holmes	26	10	16
Indian River	363	159	204
Jackson	51	34	17
Jefferson	40	15	25
Levy	116	61	55
Liberty	16	10	6
Madison	53	19	34
Monroe	546	198	348
Okeechobee	125	48	77

Table 81.—Number of Full-time Law Enforcement Employees, Rural Counties, October 31, 1995 — Continued

County by State	Total police employees	Total officers	Total civilians	County by State	Total police employees	Total officers	Total civilians	County by State	Total police employees	Total officers	Total civilians
FLORIDA— Continued				**GEORGIA— Continued**				**IDAHO— Continued**			
Putnam	189	90	99	Mitchell	22	12	10	Elmore	16	12	4
Sumter	96	45	51	Monroe	58	46	12	Franklin	15	6	9
Suwannee	87	46	41	Morgan	30	22	8	Fremont	15	15	—
Taylor	74	60	14	Murray	41	19	22	Gem	18	9	9
Union	15	7	8	Pierce	15	8	7	Gooding	15	7	8
Wakulla	68	27	41	Pike	18	10	8	Idaho	29	18	11
Walton	85	48	37	Polk	44	42	2	Jefferson	21	14	7
Washington	44	27	17	Polk Police Department	18	16	2	Jerome	19	11	8
				Pulaski	15	8	7	Kootenai	86	62	24
GEORGIA				Putnam	72	18	54	Latah	35	24	11
Atkinson	10	5	5	Quitman	3	2	1	Lemhi	12	6	6
Bacon	13	6	7	Rabun	20	16	4	Lewis	11	6	5
Baker	8	3	5	Randolph	13	11	2	Lincoln	4	3	1
Baldwin	72	40	32	Schley	7	3	4	Madison	19	13	6
Banks	23	15	8	Screven	18	9	9	Minidoka	18	10	8
Ben Hill	22	12	10	Seminole	12	8	4	Nez Perce	31	18	13
Berrien	17	11	6	Stephens	30	20	10	Oneida	11	6	5
Bleckley	17	8	9	Stewart	8	4	4	Owyhee	17	9	8
Brantley	15	9	6	Sumter	45	24	21	Payette	20	11	9
Brooks	20	12	8	Talbot	12	6	6	Power	15	9	6
Bulloch	50	22	28	Telfair	12	7	5	Shoshone	16	13	3
Butts	37	20	17	Terrell	20	12	8	Teton	12	6	6
Calhoun	12	5	7	Thomas	54	27	27	Twin Falls	55	40	15
Camden	72	62	10	Tift	62	38	24	Valley	22	13	9
Charlton	19	9	10	Toombs	28	12	16	Washington	14	7	7
Chattooga	42	23	19	Towns	13	9	4				
Clay	7	4	3	Treutlen	12	8	4	**ILLINOIS**			
Clinch	12	9	3	Troup	86	48	38	Adams	55	40	15
Coffee	49	31	18	Union	19	14	5	Alexander	13	12	1
Colquitt	64	30	34	Upson	38	26	12	Bond	17	8	9
Crawford	21	10	11	Ware	54	26	28	Brown	5	4	1
Crisp	57	38	19	Ware Police Department	14	2	12	Bureau	27	26	1
Dawson	25	18	7	Warren	2	2	—	Calhoun	3	3	—
Decatur	57	20	37	Washington	33	18	15	Carroll	22	14	8
Dodge	18	10	8	Wayne	30	28	2	Cass	7	6	1
Dooley	21	12	9	Webster	3	2	1	Christian	29	15	14
Early	21	15	6	Wheeler	3	1	2	Clark	8	8	—
Echols	4	4	—	White	33	15	18	Clay	12	7	5
Elbert	39	24	15	Wilcox	9	4	5	Coles	41	37	4
Emanuel	18	13	5	Wilkes	18	10	8	Crawford	16	9	7
Fannin	17	13	4	Wilkinson	16	8	8	Cumberland	12	7	5
Floyd	80	54	26	Worth	27	15	12	De Witt	26	16	10
Floyd Police Department	62	57	5					Douglas	21	9	12
Franklin	39	18	21	**HAWAII**				Edgar	20	18	2
Glynn	95	30	65	Hawaii Police Department	232	210	22	Edwards	9	3	6
Glynn Police Department	126	99	27	Kauai Police Department	164	132	32	Effingham	35	14	21
Gordon	65	35	30	Maui Police Department	401	307	94	Fayette	22	10	12
Grady	24	11	13					Ford	5	4	1
Greene	23	11	12	**IDAHO**				Franklin	43	18	25
Habersham	33	20	13	Adams	11	6	5	Fulton	24	20	4
Hall	259	210	49	Bannock	56	35	21	Gallatin	3	2	1
Hancock	31	10	21	Bear Lake	11	5	6	Greene	11	5	6
Hancock Police Department	1	1	—	Benewah	14	14	—	Hamilton	8	8	—
Irwin	11	6	5	Bingham	42	22	20	Hancock	17	8	9
Jackson	55	34	21	Blaine	30	20	10	Hardin	10	3	7
Jasper	20	9	11	Boise	14	9	5	Henderson	12	8	4
Jeff Davis	16	9	7	Bonner	47	38	9	Iroquois	26	17	9
Jenkins	8	4	4	Bonneville	62	44	18	Jackson	63	19	44
Lamar	38	11	27	Boundary	16	8	8	Jasper	20	9	11
Lanier	9	5	4	Butte	4	4	—	Jefferson	32	18	14
Laurens	70	38	32	Camas	5	5	—	Jo Daviess	30	27	3
Liberty	70	40	30	Caribou	13	7	6	Johnson	11	6	5
Long	9	8	1	Cassia	45	33	12	Knox	44	41	3
Lowndes	164	77	87	Clark	5	2	3	La Salle	61	48	13
Lumpkin	31	23	8	Clearwater	24	16	8	Lawrence	8	5	3
Marion	12	4	8	Custer	11	7	4	Lee	26	25	1
McIntosh	28	20	8					Livingston	29	26	3
Meriwether	26	15	11					Logan	29	20	9
Miller	16	7	9					Macoupin	32	20	12
								Marion	26	22	14
								Marshall	18	8	10
								Mason	10	9	1

Table 81.—Number of Full-time Law Enforcement Employees, Rural Counties, October 31, 1995 — Continued

County by State	Total police employees	Total officers	Total civilians	County by State	Total police employees	Total officers	Total civilians	County by State	Total police employees	Total officers	Total civilians
ILLINOIS — Continued				**IOWA — Continued**				**IOWA — Continued**			
Massac	23	9	14	Buena Vista	14	9	5	Washington	28	14	14
McDonough	19	13	6	Butler	14	9	5	Wayne	8	4	4
Mercer	17	11	6	Calhoun	11	6	5	Webster	28	15	13
Montgomery	13	13	—	Carroll	9	9	—	Winnebago	7	5	2
Morgan	40	17	23	Cass	9	7	2	Winneshiek	16	10	6
Moultrie	14	10	4	Cedar	18	6	12	Worth	12	5	7
Perry	21	13	8	Cerro Gordo	27	13	14	Wright	7	6	1
Piatt	18	9	9	Cherokee	14	4	10				
Pike	19	9	10	Chickasaw	13	8	5	**KANSAS**			
Pope	6	5	1	Clarke	8	4	4				
Pulaski	8	4	4	Clay	12	7	5	Allen	12	7	5
Putnam	11	6	5	Clayton	14	10	4	Anderson	14	13	1
Randolph	19	11	8	Clinton	38	26	12	Atchison	13	8	5
Richland	19	13	6	Crawford	11	9	2	Barber	10	5	5
Saline	45	32	13	Davis	4	3	1	Barton	36	18	18
Schuyler	4	4	—	Decatur	6	3	3	Bourbon	6	6	—
Scott	8	4	4	Delaware	11	9	2	Brown	19	19	—
Shelby	24	12	12	Des Moines	21	17	4	Chase	10	4	6
Stark	9	4	5	Dickinson	17	8	9	Chautauqua	7	3	4
Stephenson	33	31	2	Emmet	15	8	7	Cherokee	22	13	9
Union	14	13	1	Fayette	18	8	10	Cheyenne	4	4	—
Vermilion	75	32	43	Floyd	14	8	6	Clark	7	3	4
Wabash	10	5	5	Franklin	9	7	2	Clay	13	6	7
Warren	11	11	—	Fremont	15	6	9	Cloud	15	10	5
Washington	11	6	5	Greene	11	6	5	Coffey	21	9	12
Wayne	13	7	6	Grundy	12	8	4	Comanche	8	5	3
White	7	7	—	Guthrie	10	5	5	Cowley	30	30	—
Whiteside	30	20	10	Hamilton	11	9	2	Crawford	52	24	28
Williamson	55	23	32	Hancock	8	7	1	Decatur	7	3	4
				Hardin	15	8	7	Dickinson	21	14	7
INDIANA				Harrison	15	6	9	Doniphan	8	4	4
				Henry	19	10	9	Edwards	9	5	4
Bartholomew	68	37	31	Howard	8	7	1	Elk	7	3	4
Benton	12	4	8	Humboldt	9	9	—	Ellis	16	10	6
Blackford	11	7	4	Ida	14	9	5	Ellsworth	12	7	5
Carroll	17	7	10	Iowa	13	9	4	Finney	56	53	3
Daviess	22	9	13	Jackson	14	8	6	Ford	32	15	17
Decatur	23	8	15	Jasper	29	9	20	Franklin	42	15	27
Gibson	28	11	17	Jefferson	12	6	6	Geary	47	16	31
Grant	82	37	45	Jones	17	9	8	Gove	4	3	1
Henry	33	18	15	Keokuk	6	4	2	Graham	7	3	4
Jackson	27	11	16	Kossuth	11	9	2	Grant	22	14	8
Jefferson	23	12	11	Lee	30	15	15	Gray	4	4	—
Jennings	17	10	7	Louisa	18	10	8	Greeley	7	3	4
Kosciusko	48	27	21	Lucas	11	5	6	Greenwood	24	10	14
La Grange	25	13	12	Lyon	14	8	6	Hamilton	7	4	3
La Porte	103	50	53	Madison	11	5	6	Harper	11	6	5
Lawrence	44	17	27	Mahaska	18	9	9	Haskell	15	10	5
Martin	16	5	11	Marion	20	11	9	Hodgeman	9	4	5
Montgomery	25	13	12	Marshall	29	15	14	Jackson	13	13	—
Newton	23	10	13	Mills	11	9	2	Jefferson	36	18	18
Pulaski	20	8	12	Mitchell	7	6	1	Jewell	7	3	4
Putnam	20	10	10	Monona	14	7	7	Kearny	17	12	5
Ripley	15	9	6	Monroe	10	5	5	Kingman	7	6	1
Rush	22	10	12	Montgomery	18	8	10	Kiowa	11	11	—
Starke	20	11	9	Muscatine	43	18	25	Labette	27	14	13
Steuben	50	19	31	O'Brien	18	10	8	Lane	9	5	4
Switzerland	9	4	5	Osceola	14	10	4	Lincoln	8	7	1
Wabash	28	13	15	Page	10	5	5	Linn	13	8	5
Wayne	72	28	44	Palo Alto	11	7	4	Logan	3	2	1
White	25	11	14	Plymouth	17	8	9	Lyon	56	10	46
				Pocahontas	10	5	5	Marion	12	5	7
IOWA				Poweshiek	12	7	5	Marshall	18	6	12
				Ringgold	7	3	4	McPherson	31	13	18
Adair	6	5	1	Sac	9	6	3	Meade	11	4	7
Adams	7	3	4	Shelby	10	6	4	Mitchell	5	5	—
Allamakee	12	7	5	Sioux	21	11	10	Montgomery	25	18	7
Appanoose	13	8	5	Story	51	36	15	Morris	7	7	—
Audubon	8	5	3	Tama	23	12	11	Morton	8	4	4
Benton	19	7	12	Taylor	8	4	4	Nemaha	10	5	5
Boone	13	8	5	Union	11	5	6	Neosho	19	9	10
Bremer	15	10	5	Van Buren	10	5	5	Ness	11	6	5
Buchanan	21	13	8	Wapello	26	8	18	Norton	9	4	5

County by State	Total police employees	Total officers	Total civilians	County by State	Total police employees	Total officers	Total civilians	County by State	Total police employees	Total officers	Total civilians
KANSAS — Continued				**KENTUCKY —** Continued				**LOUISIANA —** Continued			
Osage	29	27	2	Hickman	3	3	—	Bienville	39	33	6
Osborne	12	7	5	Hopkins	16	13	3	Caldwell	15	15	—
Ottawa	9	5	4	Jackson	4	4	—	Cameron	73	53	20
Pawnee	12	6	6	Johnson	8	8	—	Catahoula	29	29	—
Phillips	15	10	5	Knott	8	6	2	Claiborne	27	18	9
Pottawatomie	30	19	11	Knox	8	5	3	Concordia	42	20	22
Pratt	14	8	6	Larue	6	6	—	De Soto	60	60	—
Rawlins	8	3	5	Laurel	15	15	—	East Carroll	23	23	—
Reno	64	54	10	Lawrence	6	4	2	East Feliciana	41	31	10
Republic	12	5	7	Lee	2	2	—	Evangeline	48	48	—
Rice	5	5	—	Leslie	5	5	—	Franklin	76	29	47
Riley Police Department	125	86	39	Letcher	10	10	—	Grant	41	41	—
Rooks	10	7	3	Lewis	5	5	—	Iberia	118	118	—
Rush	10	4	6	Lincoln	4	4	—	Iberville	129	57	72
Russell	12	6	6	Livingston	5	5	—	Jackson	32	28	4
Saline	76	71	5	Logan	12	11	1	Jefferson Davis	58	23	35
Scott	5	4	1	Lyon	3	3	—	La Salle	36	19	17
Seward	16	9	7	Lyon Police Department	4	4	—	Madison	20	8	12
Sheridan	4	3	1	Magoffin	4	4	—	Morehouse	135	31	104
Sherman	11	5	6	Marion	3	2	1	Natchitoches	62	60	2
Smith	7	3	4	Marshall	14	11	3	Pointe Coupee	80	67	13
Stafford	8	4	4	Martin	5	5	—	Red River	41	38	3
Stanton	11	6	5	Mason	8	8	—	Richland	38	38	—
Stevens	6	6	—	McCracken	38	38	—	Sabine	61	61	—
Sumner	25	12	13	McCreary	3	3	—	St. Helena	23	12	11
Thomas	11	8	3	McCreary Police Department	1	1	—	St. Mary	123	123	—
Trego	7	3	4	McLean	4	4	—	Tangipahoa	204	199	5
Wabaunsee	9	5	4	Meade	7	7	—	Tensas	47	8	39
Wallace	2	1	1	Menifee	3	3	—	Tensas Basin Levee	3	2	1
Washington	12	8	4	Mercer	6	6	—	Union	32	20	12
Wichita	8	4	4	Metcalfe	2	2	—	Vermilion	99	98	1
Wilson	16	6	10	Monroe	3	3	—	Vernon	113	113	—
Woodson	8	4	4	Montgomery	10	10	—	Washington	90	57	33
				Morgan	4	3	1	West Feliciana	26	25	1
KENTUCKY				Muhlenberg	10	10	—	West Carroll	20	20	—
				Nelson	9	6	3	Winn	31	31	—
Anderson Police Department	2	2	—	Nelson Police Department	6	6	—				
Ballard	5	5	—	Nicholas	3	3	—	**MAINE**			
Barren	10	8	2	Ohio	10	10	—				
Bath	4	3	1	Owen	4	4	—	Aroostook	15	10	5
Boyle	7	7	—	Owsley	4	4	—	Franklin	21	14	7
Bracken	2	2	—	Perry	11	11	—	Hancock	13	12	1
Breathitt	6	6	—	Pike	28	12	16	Kennebec	26	19	7
Breckinridge	6	6	—	Powell	6	6	—	Knox	19	14	5
Butler	4	4	—	Pulaski	21	14	7	Lincoln	18	15	3
Caldwell	3	3	—	Robertson	1	1	—	Oxford	19	12	7
Calloway	7	5	2	Rockcastle	3	3	—	Penobscot	27	17	10
Carlisle	3	3	—	Rowan	7	7	—	Piscataquis	11	7	4
Carroll	4	4	—	Russell	7	6	1	Sagadahoc	19	16	3
Casey	5	5	—	Shelby	10	10	—	Somerset	17	11	6
Clay	6	6	—	Simpson	7	6	1	Waldo	15	10	5
Clinton	3	3	—	Spencer	3	3	—	Washington	16	10	6
Crittenden	3	3	—	Taylor	6	6	—	York	28	19	9
Cumberland	2	2	—	Todd	12	12	—				
Edmonson	5	5	—	Trigg	5	5	—	**MARYLAND**			
Elliott	1	1	—	Trimble	3	3	—				
Estill	4	3	1	Union	9	5	4	Caroline	20	19	1
Fleming	5	5	—	Warren	22	21	1	Dorchester	32	23	9
Floyd	14	10	4	Washington	4	4	—	Garrett	31	17	14
Franklin	10	10	—	Wayne	9	7	2	Kent	20	19	1
Fulton	3	3	—	Webster	6	6	—	St. Mary's	151	76	75
Garrard	4	4	—	Whitley	7	7	—	Somerset	12	11	1
Graves	11	8	3	Wolfe	3	2	1	Talbot	16	14	2
Grayson	9	9	—					Wicomico	68	54	14
Green	4	4	—	**LOUISIANA**				Worcester	29	24	5
Hancock	6	6	—								
Hardin	17	17	—	Allen	37	28	9	**MICHIGAN**			
Harlan	10	7	3	Assumption	45	24	21				
Harrison	6	6	—	Avoyelles	228	228	—	Alcona	18	13	5
Hart	4	4	—	Beauregard	60	49	11	Alger	14	9	5
Henry	5	5	—					Alpena	24	14	10
								Antrim	35	16	19
								Arenac	22	14	8

County by State	Total police employees	Total officers	Total civilians	County by State	Total police employees	Total officers	Total civilians	County by State	Total police employees	Total officers	Total civilians
MICHIGAN — **Continued**				**MINNESOTA —** **Continued**				**MISSOURI**			
								Atchison	8	4	4
Baraga	5	5	—	Hubbard	21	10	11	Audrain	20	20	—
Barry	40	23	17	Itasca	45	41	4	Barry	19	11	8
Benzie	41	15	26	Jackson	14	7	7	Barton	12	11	1
Branch	39	18	21	Kanabec	18	7	11	Benton	16	15	1
Cass	61	32	29	Kandiyohi	53	28	25	Bollinger	10	6	4
Charlevoix	23	15	8	Kittson	11	5	6	Caldwell	9	4	5
Cheboygan	26	14	12	Koochiching	16	10	6	Camden	34	28	6
Chippewa	28	16	12	Lac Qui Parle	10	6	4	Cape Girardeau	41	29	12
Clare	32	23	9	Lake	17	11	6	Carroll	17	7	10
Crawford	24	14	10	Lake-of-the-Woods	8	4	4	Chariton	9	9	—
Delta	27	13	14	Lincoln	7	3	4	Clark	6	4	2
Dickinson	23	12	11	Lyon	20	9	11	Cole	46	37	9
Emmet	28	16	12	Mahnomen	10	5	5	Cooper	6	6	—
Gladwin	35	19	16	Marshall	14	9	5	Crawford	17	16	1
Gogebic	20	15	5	Martin	22	8	14	Dallas	11	11	—
Grand Traverse	85	51	34	McLeod	32	17	15	Daviess	5	4	1
Gratiot	36	22	14	Meeker	20	9	11	Dent	12	9	3
Hillsdale	35	23	12	Mille Lacs	31	15	16	Douglas	8	4	4
Houghton	27	19	8	Morrison	36	13	23	Dunklin	16	11	5
Huron	47	24	23	Mower	39	18	21	Grundy	10	5	5
Ionia	46	18	28	Murray	9	5	4	Holt	10	5	5
Iosco	24	5	19	Nicollet	20	8	12	Howell	20	18	2
Iron	9	8	1	Nobles	15	7	8	Lawrence	22	21	1
Isabella	42	22	20	Norman	8	5	3	Linn	6	5	1
Kalkaska	37	18	19	Otter Tail	58	25	33	Livingston	11	11	—
Keweenaw	4	4	—	Pennington	11	6	5	McDonald	15	14	1
Lake	39	12	27	Pine	31	19	12	Mercer	7	3	4
Leelanau	36	15	21	Pipestone	16	6	10	Moniteau	10	5	5
Luce	3	2	1	Pope	10	4	6	Monroe	12	7	5
Mackinac	14	8	6	Renville	15	8	7	Montgomery	12	10	2
Manistee	27	14	13	Rice	37	34	3	Morgan	12	11	1
Marquette	44	30	14	Rock	10	5	5	Nodaway	15	8	7
Mason	30	19	11	Roseau	15	9	6	Oregon	8	4	4
Mecosta	39	25	14	Sibley	17	8	9	Osage	9	4	5
Menominee	30	14	16	Steele	30	16	14	Ozark	9	6	3
Missaukee	23	12	11	Stevens	10	5	5	Perry	20	13	7
Montcalm	53	25	28	Swift	12	6	6	Pike	30	8	22
Montmorency	24	12	12	Todd	22	13	9	Polk	26	20	6
Newaygo	24	21	3	Traverse	6	3	3	Pulaski	17	17	—
Oceana	33	19	14	Wabasha	21	11	10	Reynolds	9	5	4
Ogemaw	30	18	12	Wadena	14	5	9	Ripley	8	8	—
Ontonagon	13	9	4	Waseca	22	10	12	St. Clair	35	16	19
Osceola	30	16	14	Watonwan	13	7	6	St. Francois	44	42	2
Oscoda	15	10	5	Wilkin	7	6	1	Ste. Genevieve	47	36	11
Otsego	22	11	11	Winona	46	18	28	Saline	12	11	1
Presque Isle	20	13	7	Yellow Medicine	12	6	6	Scotland	8	8	—
Roscommon	23	18	5					Scott	25	19	6
St. Joseph	46	26	20	**MISSISSIPPI**				Shelby	8	3	5
Sanilac	50	25	25					Stone	26	20	6
Schoolcraft	5	5	—	Adams	43	26	17	Sullivan	7	5	2
Shiawassee	56	33	23	Attala	11	6	5	Taney	43	33	10
Tuscola	49	29	20	Chickasaw	10	10	—	Vernon	15	10	5
Wexford	49	19	30	Claiborne	19	8	11	Washington	25	14	11
				Clarke	12	7	5	Worth	4	3	1
MINNESOTA				Covington	12	6	6				
				Franklin	8	4	4	**MONTANA**			
Aitkin	27	13	14	Holmes	17	8	9				
Beltrami	58	19	39	Humphreys	10	7	3	Beaverhead	13	7	6
Big Stone	7	4	3	Issaquena	6	4	2	Big Horn	28	13	15
Blue Earth	37	18	19	Jones	44	15	29	Blaine	13	5	8
Brown	31	8	23	Lowndes	54	31	23	Broadwater	6	6	—
Carlton	34	17	17	Montgomery	7	3	4	Carbon	11	7	4
Cass	45	28	17	Oktibbeha	32	14	18	Carter	2	2	—
Chippewa	16	7	9	Simpson	29	9	20	Chouteau	13	7	6
Cook	13	8	5	Tishomingo	14	8	6	Custer	11	5	6
Cottonwood	11	6	5	Walthall	8	4	4	Daniels	7	3	4
Dodge	26	18	8	Warren	55	25	30	Dawson	11	6	5
Douglas	46	16	30	Wayne	10	6	4	Deer Lodge	37	24	13
Faribault	18	8	10	Winston	10	5	5	Fallon	3	2	1
Fillmore	26	13	13	Yalobusha	10	5	5	Fergus	19	7	12
Freeborn	33	17	16					Flathead	82	41	41
Goodhue	56	33	23					Gallatin	57	30	27
Grant	9	4	5					Garfield	4	2	2

County by State	Total police employees	Total officers	Total civilians	County by State	Total police employees	Total officers	Total civilians	County by State	Total police employees	Total officers	Total civilians
MONTANA — **Continued**				**NEBRASKA —** **Continued**				**NEW HAMPSHIRE**			
								Belknap	18	8	10
Glacier	14	8	6	Garfield	2	2	—				
Golden Valley	2	2	—	Gosper	5	4	1	**NEW MEXICO**			
Granite	7	3	4	Grant	1	1	—				
Hill	18	9	9	Greeley	2	1	1	Catron	10	5	5
Jefferson	19	10	9	Hall	29	23	6	Curry	18	14	4
Judith Basin	4	3	1	Hamilton	13	7	6	Eddy	66	32	34
Lake	28	14	14	Harlan	8	4	4	Guadalupe	8	3	5
Lewis and Clark	54	31	23	Hayes	2	2	—	Hidalgo	20	11	9
Liberty	9	4	5	Hitchcock	10	4	6	Lincoln	23	16	7
Lincoln	35	22	13	Holt	10	4	6	Luna	46	23	23
Madison	14	9	5	Hooker	2	2	—	McKinley	54	36	18
McCone	3	3	—	Howard	3	2	1	Quay	8	6	2
Meagher	7	4	3	Jefferson	10	5	5	Roosevelt	23	9	14
Mineral	18	8	10	Johnson	7	2	5	San Juan	69	55	14
Missoula	84	48	36	Kearney	12	6	6	San Miguel	15	10	5
Musselshell	11	7	4	Keith	15	8	7	Sierra	27	11	16
Park	17	10	7	Keya Paha	1	1	—	Socorro	13	10	3
Petroleum	1	1	—	Kimball	7	3	4	Taos	20	17	3
Phillips	14	9	5	Knox	15	7	8	Torrance	16	14	2
Pondera	11	8	3	Lincoln	40	21	19				
Powder River	7	3	4	Logan	3	2	1	**NEW YORK**			
Powell	14	10	4	Loup	1	1	—				
Prairie	9	3	6	Madison	27	18	9	Allegany	35	30	5
Ravalli	42	20	22	McPherson	1	1	—	Cattaraugus	58	39	19
Richland	15	6	9	Merrick	8	4	4	Chenango	33	20	13
Roosevelt	21	10	11	Morrill	9	3	6	Clinton	38	33	5
Rosebud	33	17	16	Nance	8	4	4	Columbia	43	35	8
Sanders	14	8	6	Nemaha	8	3	5	Cortland	47	31	16
Sheridan	13	5	8	Nuckolls	6	4	2	Delaware	18	11	7
Silver Bow	71	43	28	Otoe	17	8	9	Essex	26	26	—
Stillwater	14	7	7	Pawnee	4	3	1	Fulton	48	33	15
Sweet Grass	10	4	6	Perkins	8	4	4	Greene	21	19	2
Teton	10	6	4	Phelps	11	4	7	Jefferson	56	32	24
Toole	17	12	5	Pierce	9	4	5	Lewis	25	19	6
Treasure	2	2	—	Platte	21	12	9	Otsego	17	14	3
Valley	16	7	9	Polk	11	6	5	St. Lawrence	36	33	3
Wheatland	6	4	2	Red Willow	7	5	2	Seneca	33	23	10
Wibaux	3	3	—	Richardson	7	3	4	Steuben	40	23	17
				Rock	8	3	5	Sullivan	45	33	12
NEBRASKA				Saline	14	10	4	Tompkins	35	25	10
				Saunders	26	11	15	Ulster	57	46	11
Adams	26	18	8	Scotts Bluff	19	14	5	Wyoming	41	30	11
Antelope	11	6	5	Seward	20	9	11	Yates	34	20	14
Arthur	1	1	—	Sheridan	4	3	1				
Banner	1	1	—	Sherman	3	2	1	**NORTH CAROLINA**			
Blaine	1	1	—	Sioux	1	1	—				
Boone	12	4	8	Stanton	7	6	1	Alleghany	25	10	15
Box Butte	14	4	10	Thayer	9	5	4	Anson	36	21	15
Boyd	2	2	—	Thomas	3	1	2	Ashe	29	16	13
Brown	7	3	4	Thurston	8	3	5	Avery	24	19	5
Buffalo	50	19	31	Valley	6	2	4	Beaufort	64	37	27
Burt	8	5	3	Wayne	5	4	1	Bertie	23	16	7
Butler	8	4	4	Webster	9	6	3	Bladen	54	35	19
Cedar	9	5	4	Wheeler	2	1	1	Camden	7	7	—
Chase	8	2	6	York	17	8	9	Carteret	36	32	4
Cherry	10	4	6					Caswell	45	28	17
Cheyenne	12	5	7	**NEVADA**				Cherokee	20	11	9
Clay	9	4	5					Chowan	12	12	—
Colfax	13	4	9	Carson City	106	76	30	Clay	18	9	9
Cuming	8	4	4	Churchill	41	34	7	Cleveland	96	59	37
Custer	7	6	1	Douglas	103	90	13	Columbus	68	44	24
Dawes	8	3	5	Elko	56	45	11	Craven	94	51	43
Dawson	50	16	34	Esmeralda	15	11	4	Dare	107	48	59
Deuel	6	3	3	Humboldt	42	20	22	Duplin	58	35	23
Dixon	9	5	4	Lander	36	33	3	Gates	4	4	—
Dodge	19	16	3	Lincoln	19	17	2	Granville	48	30	18
Dundy	7	4	3	Lyon	68	47	21	Greene	30	20	10
Fillmore	8	4	4	Mineral	30	24	6	Halifax	74	44	30
Franklin	7	3	4	Pershing	16	11	5	Harnett	98	60	38
Frontier	9	5	4	Storey	22	21	1	Haywood	35	31	4
Furnas	12	7	5	White Pine	28	21	7	Henderson	106	78	28
Gage	15	9	6					Hertford	40	12	28
Garden	9	4	5					Hoke	57	46	11

County by State	Total police employees	Total officers	Total civilians	County by State	Total police employees	Total officers	Total civilians	County by State	Total police employees	Total officers	Total civilians
NORTH CAROLINA — Continued				**NORTH DAKOTA — Continued**				**OKLAHOMA — Continued**			
Hyde	12	8	4	Rolette	12	9	3	Jackson	13	7	6
Iredell	97	85	12	Sargent	4	3	1	Jefferson	7	4	3
Jackson	31	26	5	Sheridan	2	2	—	Johnston	10	10	—
Jones	14	8	6	Sioux	1	1	—	Kay	28	12	16
Lee	58	27	31	Slope	1	1	—	Kingfisher	10	7	3
Lenoir	65	44	21	Stark	12	9	3	Kiowa	12	11	1
Macon	26	25	1	Steele	3	3	—	Latimer	11	8	3
Martin	20	18	2	Stutsman	11	9	2	Le Flore	23	12	11
McDowell	45	32	13	Towner	2	1	1	Lincoln	15	7	8
Montgomery	39	25	14	Traill	8	4	4	Love	15	6	9
Moore	83	50	33	Walsh	13	7	6	Major	7	3	4
Northampton	23	16	7	Ward	39	17	22	Marshall	17	6	11
Pamlico	22	12	10	Wells	3	3	—	Mayes	21	12	9
Pasquotank	24	21	3	Williams	26	21	5	McCurtain	24	14	10
Pender	52	29	23					McIntosh	12	7	5
Perquimans	8	8	—	**OHIO**				Murray	9	4	5
Person	61	33	28					Muskogee	51	12	39
Polk	29	17	12	Ashland	47	39	8	Noble	10	5	5
Richmond	52	35	17	Athens	37	17	20	Nowata	12	8	4
Robeson	166	72	94	Clinton	34	30	4	Okfuskee	11	6	5
Rockingham	94	74	20	Coshocton	54	42	12	Okmulgee	18	12	6
Rutherford	71	42	29	Darke	59	27	32	Ottawa	19	16	3
Sampson	61	43	18	Defiance	24	19	5	Pawnee	17	9	8
Scotland	52	32	20	Erie	66	30	36	Payne	24	22	2
Stanly	46	33	13	Hardin	19	15	4	Pittsburg	27	21	6
Surry	64	50	14	Harrison	10	9	1	Pontotoc	14	8	6
Swain	23	10	13	Henry	20	17	3	Pushmataha	13	6	7
Transylvania	46	32	14	Hocking	22	15	7	Roger Mills	13	8	5
Tyrrell	14	8	6	Huron	31	20	11	Seminole	13	13	—
Vance	28	28	—	Logan	55	26	29	Stephens	19	11	8
Warren	35	14	21	Muskingum	94	55	39	Texas	15	7	8
Washington	25	13	12	Noble	13	7	6	Tillman	11	6	5
Watauga	37	25	12	Ottawa	46	39	7	Washington	25	14	11
Wilkes	77	53	24	Paulding	20	9	11	Washita	9	8	1
Wilson	113	55	58	Preble	59	33	26	Woods	8	4	4
				Ross	84	57	27	Woodward	14	8	6
NORTH DAKOTA				Seneca	58	16	42				
				Shelby	56	29	27	**OREGON**			
Adams	4	3	1	Tuscarawas	71	26	45				
Barnes	14	8	6	Union	35	24	11	Baker	8	7	1
Benson	3	3	—	Van Wert	23	17	6	Benton	36	29	7
Billings	4	3	1	Williams	22	20	2	Clatsop	17	13	4
Bottineau	12	8	4	Wyandot	18	10	8	Coos	39	32	7
Bowman	2	1	1					Crook	13	10	3
Burke	4	3	1	**OKLAHOMA**				Curry	23	15	8
Cavalier	9	5	4					Deschutes	67	55	12
Dickey	5	4	1	Adair	11	7	4	Gilliam	4	3	1
Divide	4	4	—	Alfalfa	9	5	4	Grant	5	4	1
Dunn	4	3	1	Atoka	10	5	5	Harney	5	4	1
Eddy	5	5	—	Beaver	9	5	4	Hood River	16	14	2
Emmons	3	3	—	Beckham	12	10	2	Jefferson	17	10	7
Foster	3	2	1	Blaine	8	7	1	Josephine	41	27	14
Golden Valley	9	3	6	Bryan	22	10	12	Klamath	31	24	7
Grant	2	2	—	Caddo	19	8	11	Lake	5	5	—
Griggs	2	2	—	Carter	35	10	25	Lincoln	30	24	6
Hettinger	3	3	—	Cherokee	24	17	7	Linn	76	54	22
Kidder	3	2	1	Choctaw	10	4	6	Malheur	17	11	6
Lamoure	4	3	1	Cimarron	9	4	5	Morrow	19	11	8
Logan	2	2	—	Coal	8	4	4	Multnomah	164	115	49
McHenry	6	5	1	Cotton	9	4	5	Sherman	5	4	1
McIntosh	3	3	—	Craig	13	7	6	Tillamook	22	20	2
McKenzie	8	5	3	Custer	18	8	10	Umatilla	30	15	15
McLean	24	20	4	Delaware	14	8	6	Umatilla Tribal	15	10	5
Mercer	18	7	11	Dewey	8	4	4	Union	8	7	1
Mountrail	8	4	4	Ellis	8	4	4	Wallowa	10	5	5
Nelson	5	4	1	Garvin	15	8	7	Wasco	27	19	8
Oliver	4	3	1	Grady	23	12	11	Wheeler	2	2	—
Pembina	20	14	6	Grant	8	4	4				
Pierce	7	3	4	Greer	5	4	1	**PENNSYLVANIA**			
Ramsey	6	5	1	Harmon	3	3	—				
Ransom	5	5	—	Harper	6	3	3	Elk	3	2	1
Renville	5	5	—	Haskell	12	8	4	Jefferson	5	5	—
Richland	16	10	6	Hughes	8	3	5	Warren	46	22	24

Table 81.—Number of Full-time Law Enforcement Employees, Rural Counties, October 31, 1995 — Continued

County by State	Total police employees	Total officers	Total civilians
SOUTH CAROLINA			
Abbeville	32	24	8
Allendale	8	7	1
Bamberg	12	11	1
Barnwell	21	13	8
Beaufort	138	126	12
Calhoun	12	11	1
Chester	36	32	4
Chesterfield	33	30	3
Clarendon	45	29	16
Colleton	47	40	7
Darlington	43	39	4
Dillon	30	19	11
Fairfield	55	39	16
Georgetown	55	47	8
Greenwood	79	50	29
Hampton	24	11	13
Jasper	44	22	22
Kershaw	39	36	3
Lancaster	61	47	14
Laurens	58	51	7
Lee	24	22	2
Marion	28	23	5
Marlboro	22	17	5
McCormick	19	8	11
Newberry	26	24	2
Oconee	55	41	14
Orangeburg	74	58	16
Saluda	24	11	13
Union	30	26	4
Williamsburg	40	20	20
SOUTH DAKOTA			
Aurora	4	3	1
Beadle	16	5	11
Bon Homme	5	2	3
Brookings	15	7	8
Brown	37	12	25
Charles Mix	10	4	6
Clay	6	5	1
Corson	3	2	1
Day	6	3	3
Deuel	7	4	3
Douglas	2	2	—
Edmunds	6	4	2
Fall River	11	4	7
Faulk	5	3	2
Harding	2	1	1
Hughes	22	7	15
Hyde	1	1	—
Jerauld	1	1	—
Kingsbury	3	2	1
Lake	9	4	5
Lawrence	33	11	22
Lyman	4	3	1
Marshall	9	5	4
McCook	3	2	1
Meade	40	14	26
Miner	4	3	1
Moody	9	6	3
Perkins	2	2	—
Potter	8	3	5
Sanborn	3	2	1
Spink	14	9	5
Sully	2	2	—
Todd	2	1	1
Yankton	7	6	1
TENNESSEE			
Bradley	95	83	12
Cannon	22	10	12
Chester	18	7	11
Coffee	45	44	1

County by State	Total police employees	Total officers	Total civilians
TENNESSEE— Continued			
Crockett	21	10	11
Gibson	51	25	26
Giles	26	16	10
Greene	94	34	60
Hamblen	45	41	4
Hardeman	36	17	19
Henderson	28	16	12
Henry	46	43	3
Houston	17	8	9
Humphreys	15	7	8
Lawrence	38	25	13
Lincoln	44	14	30
Macon	25	12	13
Marshall	33	14	19
Maury	48	26	22
McMinn	46	24	22
Meigs	16	8	8
Monroe	31	31	—
Obion	27	18	9
Perry	16	11	5
Putnam	78	31	47
Stewart	14	9	5
Trousdale	15	6	9
Van Buren	10	10	—
Warren	56	32	24
Wayne	13	9	4
Weakley	28	16	12
White	29	17	12
TEXAS			
Anderson	53	24	29
Andrews	24	12	12
Angelina	66	26	40
Aransas	36	17	19
Armstrong	7	3	4
Atascosa	60	20	40
Austin	36	19	17
Bailey	9	4	5
Bandera	27	14	13
Baylor	13	3	10
Bee	34	16	18
Blanco	12	6	6
Borden	4	3	1
Bosque	21	15	6
Brewster	12	8	4
Briscoe	3	2	1
Brooks	30	15	15
Brown	35	18	17
Burleson	21	10	11
Burnet	48	25	23
Calhoun	39	22	17
Callahan	11	5	6
Camp	14	5	9
Carson	10	7	3
Cass	33	11	22
Castro	16	8	8
Cherokee	49	23	26
Childress	12	5	7
Clay	15	9	6
Cochran	14	8	6
Coke	5	4	1
Coleman	5	5	—
Collingsworth	11	7	4
Colorado	32	16	16
Comanche	24	8	16
Concho	7	3	4
Cooke	31	16	15
Cottle	3	1	2
Crane	11	7	4
Crockett	12	8	4
Crosby	16	7	9
Culberson	12	6	6

County by State	Total police employees	Total officers	Total civilians
TEXAS — Continued			
Dallam	10	4	6
Dawson	11	6	5
Deaf Smith	35	18	17
Delta	12	7	5
Dewitt	21	8	13
Dickens	6	2	4
Dimmit	17	10	7
Donley	4	4	—
Duval	29	20	9
Eastland	14	7	7
Edwards	11	5	6
Erath	38	12	26
Falls	8	4	4
Fannin	19	14	5
Fayette	33	16	17
Fisher	10	6	4
Floyd	10	6	4
Foard	5	3	2
Franklin	21	7	14
Freestone	21	9	12
Frio	17	9	8
Gaines	17	8	9
Garza	14	10	4
Gillespie	24	12	12
Glasscock	2	2	—
Goliad	18	7	11
Gonzales	28	15	13
Gray	30	14	16
Grimes	10	9	1
Hale	47	47	—
Hall	12	3	9
Hamilton	20	8	12
Hansford	7	3	4
Hardeman	8	4	4
Hartley	6	3	3
Haskell	6	3	3
Hemphill	14	9	5
Hill	32	13	19
Hockley	19	9	10
Hopkins	42	22	20
Houston	19	8	11
Howard	15	12	3
Hudspeth	28	8	20
Hutchinson	30	12	18
Irion	8	4	4
Jack	14	9	5
Jackson	22	12	10
Jasper	29	15	14
Jeff Davis	4	3	1
Jim Hogg	32	16	16
Jim Wells	27	13	14
Jones	19	9	10
Karnes	15	7	8
Kendall	38	16	22
Kenedy	8	8	—
Kent	4	2	2
Kerr	51	24	27
Kimble	9	5	4
King	2	2	—
Kinney	9	3	6
Kleberg	41	39	2
Knox	6	5	1
La Salle	8	8	—
Lamar	57	18	39
Lamb	14	8	6
Lampasas	21	12	9
Lavaca	20	9	11
Lee	15	10	5
Leon	17	9	8
Limestone	37	14	23
Lipscomb	9	5	4
Live Oak	24	14	10
Llano	25	13	12

County by State	Total police employees	Total officers	Total civilians	County by State	Total police employees	Total officers	Total civilians	County by State	Total police employees	Total officers	Total civilians
TEXAS — Continued				**TEXAS — Continued**				**VIRGINIA — Continued**			
Loving	3	2	1	Willacy	31	14	17	Giles	32	26	6
Lynn	13	6	7	Winkler	24	9	15	Grayson	27	21	6
Madison	21	7	14	Wise	60	27	33	Greensville	31	29	2
Marion	10	9	1	Wood	46	21	25	Halifax	49	39	10
Martin	7	3	4	Yoakum	19	12	7	Henry	93	84	9
Mason	6	4	2	Young	24	16	8	Highland	16	11	5
Matagorda	68	49	19	Zapata	43	21	22	King and Queen	11	6	5
Maverick	34	13	21	Zavala	5	5	—	King William	21	15	6
McCulloch	11	7	4					Lancaster	27	23	4
McMullen	3	3	—	**UTAH**				Lee	44	42	2
Medina	27	15	12					Louisa	27	21	6
Menard	6	2	4	Beaver	16	14	2	Lunenburg	13	7	6
Milam	22	8	14	Box Elder	44	35	9	Madison	15	10	5
Mills	9	5	4	Cache	60	55	5	Mecklenburg	64	24	40
Mitchell	9	4	5	Carbon	27	24	3	Middlesex	17	11	6
Montague	19	8	11	Daggett	5	4	1	Montgomery	56	44	12
Moore	26	11	15	Duchesne	21	18	3	Nelson	22	22	—
Morris	20	7	13	Emery	33	28	5	Northampton	34	30	4
Motley	2	2	—	Garfield	10	10	—	Northumberland	25	25	—
Nacogdoches	65	17	48	Grand	24	16	8	Nottoway	18	13	5
Navarro	70	29	41	Iron	55	49	6	Orange	32	22	10
Newton	12	12	—	Juab	18	18	—	Page	19	19	—
Nolan	18	9	9	Kane	16	10	6	Patrick	26	20	6
Ochiltree	17	7	10	Millard	33	25	8	Prince Edward	17	15	2
Oldham	10	5	5	Morgan	9	8	1	Pulaski	66	54	12
Palo Pinto	44	24	20	Piute	4	3	1	Rappahannock	7	7	—
Panola	31	7	24	Rich	8	3	5	Richmond	14	8	6
Parmer	12	5	7	San Juan	29	24	5	Rockbridge	24	16	8
Pecos	19	12	7	Sanpete	20	15	5	Rockingham	125	108	17
Polk	55	27	28	Sevier	43	38	5	Russell	41	39	2
Presidio	19	5	14	Summit	36	20	16	Shenandoah	50	50	—
Rains	16	7	9	Tooele	52	38	14	Smyth	40	38	2
Reagan	10	6	4	Uintah	40	16	24	Southampton	66	58	8
Real	8	2	6	Wasatch	15	14	1	Surry	13	8	5
Red River	18	8	10	Washington	47	42	5	Sussex	34	32	2
Reeves	28	14	14	Wayne	5	4	1	Tazewell	52	43	9
Refugio	32	15	17					Warren	50	49	1
Roberts	5	4	1	**VERMONT**				Westmoreland	24	17	7
Robertson	19	7	12					Wise	59	44	15
Runnels	14	7	7	Addison	11	5	6	Wythe	41	32	9
Rusk	47	26	21	Bennington	9	5	4				
Sabine	16	7	9	Caledonia	4	3	1	**WASHINGTON**			
San Augustine	10	4	6	Essex	1	1	—				
San Jacinto	22	12	10	Franklin	19	13	6	Adams	19	17	2
San Saba	11	4	7	Lamoille	11	5	6	Asotin	14	12	2
Schleicher	9	4	5	Orange	4	3	1	Chelan	59	46	13
Scurry	17	7	10	Orleans	5	5	—	Clallam	44	36	8
Shackelford	13	4	9	Rutland	9	7	2	Columbia	14	9	5
Shelby	28	10	18	Washington	9	6	3	Cowlitz	53	47	6
Sherman	9	5	4	Windham	18	12	6	Douglas	37	25	12
Somervell	29	15	14	Windsor	10	8	2	Ferry	16	10	6
Starr	91	31	60					Garfield	11	4	7
Stephens	10	6	4	**VIRGINIA**				Grant	54	37	17
Sterling	4	3	1					Grays Harbor	49	40	9
Stonewall	6	2	4	Accomack	47	44	3	Jefferson	23	19	4
Sutton	15	5	10	Alleghany	34	32	2	Kittitas	43	23	20
Swisher	9	7	2	Amelia	13	8	5	Klickitat	23	17	6
Terrell	5	3	2	Augusta	85	73	12	Lewis	59	46	13
Terry	16	7	9	Bath	17	17	—	Lincoln	15	13	2
Throckmorton	7	2	5	Bland	20	13	7	Mason	43	36	7
Titus	37	16	21	Brunswick	31	23	8	Okanogan	33	29	4
Trinity	12	7	5	Buchanan	44	34	10	Pacific	31	15	16
Tyler	26	13	13	Buckingham	12	9	3	Pend Oreille	21	15	6
Upton	14	9	5	Caroline	41	33	8	San Juan	24	17	7
Uvalde	15	13	2	Carroll	38	30	8	Skagit	59	44	15
Val Verde	76	21	55	Charlotte	22	20	2	Skamania	22	19	3
Van Zandt	42	22	20	Craig	11	6	5	Stevens	28	26	2
Walker	69	28	41	Cumberland	13	8	5	Wahkiakum	8	7	1
Ward	28	15	13	Dickenson	35	34	1	Walla Walla	22	19	3
Washington	37	16	21	Essex	14	14	—	Whitman	16	14	2
Wharton	49	30	19	Floyd	21	14	7				
Wheeler	10	6	4	Franklin	67	55	12				
Wilbarger	17	6	11	Frederick	70	59	11				

County by State	Total police employees	Total officers	Total civilians	County by State	Total police employees	Total officers	Total civilians	County by State	Total police employees	Total officers	Total civilians
WEST VIRGINIA				**WEST VIRGINIA— Continued**				**WISCONSIN— Continued**			
Barbour	10	5	5					Price	23	18	5
Berkeley	35	27	8	Wirt	5	2	3	Richland	26	26	—
Boone	19	18	1	Wyoming	18	18	—	Rusk	24	24	—
Braxton	5	4	1					Sawyer	28	24	4
Calhoun	2	2	—	**WISCONSIN**				Shawano	81	34	47
Clay	4	4	—	Adams	44	43	1	Taylor	23	17	6
Doddridge	2	2	—	Ashland	20	20	—	Vernon	23	23	—
Fayette	32	30	2	Barron	35	34	1	Vilas	44	29	15
Gilmer	4	4	—	Bayfield	27	26	1	Washburn	21	10	11
Grant	7	6	1	Buffalo	18	9	9	Waupaca	39	39	—
Greenbrier	27	18	9	Burnett	25	14	11	Waushara	28	27	1
Hampshire	9	4	5	Clark	38	35	3	Wood	70	42	28
Hardy	6	5	1	Columbia	69	33	36				
Harrison	62	27	35	Crawford	20	19	1	**WYOMING**			
Jackson	20	11	9	Dodge	74	41	33				
Jefferson	14	11	3	Door	44	37	7	Albany	19	17	2
Lewis	9	8	1	Dunn	33	20	13	Big Horn	14	6	8
Lincoln	6	5	1	Florence	12	12	—	Campbell	46	29	17
Logan	39	19	20	Fond du Lac	99	90	9	Carbon	21	14	7
Marion	48	25	23	Forest	18	17	1	Converse	16	9	7
Mason	27	12	15	Grant	40	24	16	Crook	11	6	5
McDowell	14	13	1	Green	41	33	8	Fremont	46	26	20
Mercer	27	21	6	Green Lake	29	15	14	Goshen	9	7	2
Mingo	37	11	26	Iowa	22	22	—	Hot Springs	11	6	5
Monongalia	50	21	29	Iron	12	12	—	Johnson	12	8	4
Monroe	5	5	—	Jackson	33	19	14	Lincoln	34	16	18
Morgan	4	4	—	Jefferson	110	86	24	Niobrara	16	4	12
Nicholas	19	15	4	Juneau	30	23	7	Park	35	26	9
Pendleton	4	2	2	Kewaunee	28	25	3	Platte	7	6	1
Pleasants	10	6	4	Lafayette	18	12	6	Sheridan	26	13	13
Pocahontas	13	5	8	Langlade	24	20	4	Sublette	22	15	7
Preston	24	13	11	Lincoln	41	26	15	Sweetwater	57	37	20
Raleigh	49	40	9	Manitowoc	110	54	56	Teton	34	16	18
Randolph	15	6	9	Marinette	50	26	24	Uinta	38	24	14
Ritchie	9	4	5	Marquette	26	25	1	Washakie	14	7	7
Roane	6	5	1	Menominee	10	9	1	Weston	6	6	—
Summers	4	3	1	Monroe	40	38	2				
Taylor	19	5	14	Oconto	42	20	22	**OTHER AREAS**			
Tucker	8	4	4	Oneida	45	25	20				
Tyler	9	4	5	Pepin	10	10	—	American Samoa	221	145	76
Upshur	16	7	9	Polk	35	32	3	Guam	557	428	129
Webster	4	4	—	Portage	87	41	46	Virgin Islands	637	493	144
Wetzel	11	7	4								

SECTION VII
APPENDIX I
Methodology

The information compiled by UCR contributors is forwarded to the FBI either directly from local law enforcement agencies or through state-level UCR Programs in 44 states and the District of Columbia. Agencies submitting directly to the FBI are provided continuing guidance and support on an individual basis.

State-level UCR Programs are very effective intermediaries between local contributors and the FBI. Many of the Programs have mandatory reporting requirements and collect data beyond the national UCR scope to address crime problems germane to their particular locales. In most cases, these agencies are also able to provide more direct and frequent service to participating law enforcement agencies, to make information more readily available for use at the state level, and to contribute to more streamlined operations at the national level.

With the development of a state UCR Program, the FBI ceases direct collection of data from individual law enforcement agencies within the state. Instead, information from local agencies is forwarded to the national Program through the state data collection agency.

The conditions under which these systems are developed ensure consistency and comparability in the data submitted to the national Program, as well as provide for regular and timely reporting of national crime data. These conditions are: (1) The state Program must conform to national Uniform Crime Reports' standards, definitions, and information requirements. The states are not, of course, prohibited from collecting other statistical data beyond the national requirements. (2) The state criminal justice agency must have a proven, effective, statewide Program and have instituted acceptable quality control procedures. (3) Coverage within the state by a state agency must be, at least, equal to that attained by the national Uniform Crime Reports. (4) The state agency must have adequate field staff assigned to conduct audits and to assist contributing agencies in record practices and crime reporting procedures. (5) The state agency must furnish to the FBI all of the detailed data regularly collected by the FBI in the form of duplicate returns, computer printouts, and/or magnetic tapes. (6) The state agency must have the proven capability (tested over a period of time) to supply all the statistical data required in time to meet national Uniform Crime Reports' publication deadlines.

To fulfill its responsibilities in connection with the UCR Program, the FBI continues to edit and review individual agency reports for both completeness and quality; has direct contact with individual contributors within the state when necessary in connection with crime reporting matters, coordinating such contact with the state agency; and upon request, conducts training programs within the state on law enforcement records and crime reporting procedures. Should circumstances develop whereby the state agency does not comply with the aforementioned requirements, the national Program may reinstitute a direct collection of Uniform Crime Reports from law enforcement agencies within the state.

Reporting Procedures

Based on records of all reports of crime received from victims, officers who discover infractions, or other sources, law enforcement agencies across the country tabulate the number of Crime Index or Part I offenses brought to their attention each month. Specifically, the crimes reported to the FBI are murder and nonnegligent manslaughter, forcible rape, robbery, aggravated assault, burglary, larceny-theft, motor vehicle theft, and arson.

Whenever complaints of crime are determined through investigation to be unfounded or false, they are eliminated from an agency's count. The number of "actual offenses known" is reported to the FBI regardless of whether anyone is arrested for the crime, stolen property is recovered, or prosecution is undertaken.

Another integral part of the monthly submission is the total number of actual Crime Index offenses cleared. Crimes are "cleared" in one of two ways: (1) at least one person is arrested, charged, and turned over to the court for prosecution; or (2) by exceptional means when some element beyond law enforcement control precludes the arrest of an offender. Law enforcement agencies also report the number of Index crime clearances which involve only offenders under the age of 18; the value of property stolen and recovered in connection with the offenses; and detailed information pertaining to criminal homicide and arson.

In addition to its primary collection of Crime Index (Part I) offenses, the UCR Program solicits monthly data on persons arrested for all crimes except traffic violations. The age, sex, and race of arrestees are reported by crime category, both Part

I and Part II. Part II offenses include all crimes not classified as Part I.

Various data on law enforcement officers killed or assaulted are collected on a monthly basis. The number of full-time sworn and civilian personnel are reported as of October 31 each year.

Editing Procedures

Each report submitted to the UCR Program is thoroughly examined for arithmetical accuracy and for deviations which may indicate errors. To identify any unusual fluctuations in an agency's crime count, monthly reports are compared with previous submissions of the agency and with those for similar agencies. Large variations in crime levels may indicate modified records procedures, incomplete reporting, or changes in the jurisdiction's geopolitical structure.

Data reliability is a high priority of the Program and noted deviations or arithmetical adjustments are brought to the attention of the state UCR Program or the submitting agency through correspondence. A standard procedure of the FBI is to study the monthly reports and to evaluate periodic trends prepared for individual reporting units. Any significant increase or decrease is made the subject of a special inquiry. When it is found that changes in crime reporting procedures or annexations are influencing the level of crime, the figures for specific crime categories, or if necessary, totals are excluded from trend tabulations.

To assist contributors in complying with UCR standards, the national Program provides training seminars and instructional materials in crime reporting procedures. Throughout the country, liaison with state Programs and law enforcement personnel is maintained, and training sessions are held to explain the purpose of the Program, the rules of uniform classification and scoring, and the methods of assembling the information for reporting. When an individual agency has specific problems in compiling its crime statistics and remedial efforts are unsuccessful, FBI Headquarters' personnel may visit the contributor to aid in resolving the difficulties.

The *Uniform Crime Reporting Handbook,* which details procedures for classifying and scoring offenses, is supplied to all contributors as the basic resource document for preparing reports. Since a good records system is essential for accurate crime reporting, the FBI also furnishes the *Manual of Law Enforcement Records.*

To enhance communication among Program participants, letters to UCR contributors and State UCR Program "Bulletins" are utilized. They address Program policy, as well as present information and instructional material, and are produced as needed.

The final responsibility for data submissions rests with the individual contributing law enforcement agency. Although the Program makes every effort through its editing procedures, training practices, and correspondence to assure the validity of the data it receives, the statistics' accuracy depends primarily on the adherence of each contributor to the established standards of reporting. Deviations from these established standards which cannot be resolved by the national UCR Program may be brought to the attention of the Criminal Justice Information Systems Committees of the International Association of Chiefs of Police and the National Sheriffs' Association.

NIBRS Conversion

Several states provided their UCR data in the expanded NIBRS format. For presentation in this book, NIBRS data were converted to the historical summary UCR formats. The NIBRS data base was constructed to allow for such conversion so that UCR's long-running time series could continue.

Offense Estimation

Tables 1 through 5 and 7 of this publication contain statistics for the entire United States. Because not all law enforcement agencies provide data for complete reporting periods, estimated crime counts are included in these presentations. Offense estimation occurs within each of three areas: Metropolitan Statistical Areas (MSAs), cities outside MSAs, and rural counties. Using the known crime experiences of similar areas within a state, the estimates are computed by assigning the same proportional crime volumes to nonreporting agencies. The size of agency; type of jurisdiction, e.g., police department versus sheriff's office; and geographic location are considered in the estimation process.

Because of efforts to convert to the National Incident-Based Reporting System (NIBRS), in recent years, it has become necessary to estimate totals for some states. Also, the inability of some state UCR Programs to provide forcible rape figures in accordance with UCR guidelines and other problems at the state-levels have required unique estimation procedures. A summary of state- and offense-specific estimation procedures are outlined below:

1985 through 1995—The Illinois (1985–1995), Michigan, and Minnesota (1993 only) state UCR Programs were unable to provide forcible rape figures in accordance with UCR guidelines. The rape totals were estimated using national rates per 100,000 inhabitants within the eight population groups and assigning the forcible rape volumes proportionally to each state.

1988 and 1991—Reporting problems at the state levels resulted in no usable data for Florida and Kentucky for 1988. In 1991, Iowa NIBRS conversion required estimation during the transition. State totals were estimated during these years by updating previous valid annual totals for individual jurisdictions, subdivided by population group. Percent changes for each offense within each population group of the geographic divisions in which the states reside were applied to the previous valid annual totals. The state totals were compiled from the sums of the population group estimates.

1993—NIBRS conversion efforts resulted in estimation for Kansas and Illinois. Kansas totals were estimated by updating previous valid annual totals for individual jurisdictions, subdivided by population group. Percent changes for each offense within each population group of the West North Central Division were applied to the previous valid annual totals. The state totals were compiled from the sums of the population group estimates.

Since valid annual totals were available for approximately 60 Illinois agencies, those counts were maintained. The counts for the remaining jurisdictions were replaced with the most recent valid annual totals or were generated using standard estimation procedures. The results of all sources were then combined to arrive at the 1993 state total for Illinois.

1994—State totals for Kansas and Illinois, both undergoing NIBRS conversion, were generated using only the valid crime rates for the geographic division in which the state resides. Within each population group, each state's offense totals were estimated based on the rate per 100,000 inhabitants within the remainder of the division. Montana state totals were estimated by the same method as were Kansas state totals in 1993.

1995—The Kansas state-level UCR Program was able to provide valid 1994 state totals which were then updated using 1995 crime trends for the West North Central Division. Concerning Illinois, valid Crime Index counts were available for most of the largest cities. For other agencies, the only available counts were generated without application of the UCR Hierarchy Rule. (The Hierarchy Rule requires that only the most serious offense in a multiple-offense criminal incident is counted.) To arrive at a state estimate comparable to the rest of the Nation, the total supplied by the Illinois State Program (which was inflated because of the nonapplication of the Hierarchy Rule) was reduced by the proportion of multiple offenses reported within single incidents in the available NIBRS data. Valid totals for the large cities were excluded from the reduction process. Montana state estimates were computed by updating the previous valid annual totals using the 1994 versus 1995 percent changes for the Mountain States.

Crime Trends

Showing fluctuations from year to year, trend statistics offer the data user an added perspective from which to study crime. Percent change tabulations in this publication are computed only for reporting units which have provided comparable data for the periods under consideration. Exclusions from trend computations are made when figures from a reporting agency are not received for comparable timeframes or when it is ascertained that unusual fluctuations are due to such variables as improved records procedures, annexations, etc.

Care should be exercised in any direct comparison between data in this publication and those in prior issues of *Crime in the United States*. For example, upon receiving 1995 aggravated assault figures for the state of Kentucky, it was determined the 1994 aggravated assault figures previously submitted were not valid; therefore, the Kentucky aggravated assault figures are not included in Tables 12 through 15 of this edition. Also, 1994 estimates for Delaware, Kansas, and Kentucky were updated in certain offense categories. These updates are in the national trends.

Table Methodology

Although most law enforcement agencies submit crime reports to the UCR Program, data are sometimes not received for complete annual periods. To be included in this publication's Tables 8 through 11, showing specific jurisdictional statistics, figures for all 12 months of the current year must have been received at the FBI prior to established publication deadlines. Other tabular presentations are aggregated on varied levels of submission. Unless consisting of estimates for the total population of the United States, each table in this publication shows the number of agencies reporting and the extent of population coverage.

Designed to assist the reader, this appendix explains the construction of many of this book's tabular presentations. The following key refers to the columnar headings used throughout the appendix.

Key: A) Column 1 shows the table numbers. Included are Tables 1 through 69, *Crime in the United States—1995*.
B) Column 2 indicates the level of submission necessary for an agency's statistics to be included in a table.
C) Column 3 explains how each table was constructed. Data adjustments, if any, are discussed along with various definitions of data aggregation.
D) Column 4 contains general comments regarding the potential use and misuse of the statistics presented.

(1) Table	(2) Data Base	(3) Table Construction	(4) General Comments
1	All law enforcement agencies in the UCR Program (including those submitting less than 12 months).	The 1995 statistics are consistent with Table 2. Pre-1995 crime statistics may have been updated, and hence, may not be consistent with prior publications. Crime statistics include estimated offense totals for agencies submitting less than 12 months of offense reports for each year. Population statistics represent July 1 provisional estimations for each year except 1980 and 1990, which are Bureau of the Census decennial census data (see App. III). Crime volume statistics are rounded to the nearest 10 for violent crime and the nearest 100 for property crime. Percent changes and rates are computed prior to rounding.	Represents an estimation of national reported crime activity from 1976 to 1995.
2	All law enforcement agencies in the UCR Program (including those submitting less than 12 months in 1995).	Statistics are aggregated from individual state statistics as shown in Table 5. Crime statistics include estimated offense totals for agencies submitting less than 12 months of offense reports. Population statistics represent July 1, 1995, Bureau of the Census provisional estimates. See Appendix III for UCR population breakdowns.	Represents an estimation of national reported crime activity in 1995.
3	All law enforcement agencies in the UCR Program (including those submitting less than 12 months in 1995).	Regional offense distributions are computed from volume figures as shown in Table 4. Population distributions are based on July 1, 1995, Bureau of the Census provisional estimates (see App. III).	Represents the 1995 geographical distribution of estimated Crime Index offenses and population.
4	All law enforcement agencies in the UCR Program (including those submitting less than 12 months).	The 1995 statistics are aggregated from individual state statistics as shown in Table 5. Crime statistics include estimated offense totals for agencies submitting less than 12 months of offense reports for 1994 and 1995. Population statistics represent July 1 provisional estimates for both years (see App. III).	Represents an estimation of reported crime activity for Index offenses at the: 1. national level 2. regional level 3. division level 4. state level Any comparison of UCR statistics should take into consideration demographic factors.
5	All law enforcement agencies in the UCR Program (including those submitting less than 12 months in 1995).	Crime statistics include estimated offense totals for agencies submitting less than 12 months of offense reports. Population statistics represent 1995 estimates (see App. III). Statistics under the heading "Area Actually Reporting" represent reported offense totals for agencies submitting 12 months of offense reports and estimated totals for agencies submitting less than 12 but more than 2 months of offense reports. The statistics under the heading "Estimated Totals" represent the above plus estimated offense totals for agencies having less than 3 months of offense reports.	Represents an estimation of reported crime activity for Index offenses at the state level. Any comparison of UCR statistics should take into consideration demographic factors.
6	All law enforcement agencies in the UCR Program (including those submitting less than 12 months in 1995).	Statistics are published for all Metropolitan Statistical Areas (MSAs) having at least 75% reporting and for which the central city/cities submitted 12 months of data in 1995. Crime statistics include estimated offense totals for agencies submitting less than 12 months of offense statistics for 1995. Population statistics represent July 1, 1995, Bureau of the Census provisional estimates. The statistics under the heading "Area Actually Reporting" represent reported offense totals for agencies submitting all 12 months of offense reports plus estimated offense totals for agencies submitting less than 12 but more than 2 months of offense reports. The statistics under the heading "Estimated Total" represent the above plus the estimated offense totals for agencies submitting less than 3 months of offense reports. The tabular breakdowns are according to UCR definitions (see App. II).	Represents an estimation of reported crime activity for Index offenses at individual MSA level. Any comparison of UCR statistics should take into consideration demographic factors.
7	All law enforcement agencies in the UCR Program (including those submitting less than 12 months in 1995).	Offense totals are for all Index offense categories other than aggravated assault. Crime statistics include estimated offense totals for agencies submitting less than 12 months of offense reports for each year.	Represents an estimation of national reported crime activity from 1991 to 1995. Aggravated assault is excluded from Table 7, because if money or property is taken in connection with an assault, the offense is robbery.

(1) Table	(2) Data Base	(3) Table Construction	(4) General Comments
8	All law enforcement agencies submitting complete reports for 12 months in 1995.	"Cities and Towns" are defined to be agencies in Population Groups I through V (App. III). The agency populations are 1995 estimates for each agency (see App. III).	Represents reported crime activity of individual agencies in cities and towns 10,000 and over in population. Any comparison of UCR statistics should take into consideration demographic factors.
9	All university/college law enforcement agencies submitting complete reports for 12 months in 1995.	The 1994 student enrollment figures, which are provided by the U.S. Department of Education, are the most recent available. They include full- and part-time students. No adjustments to equate part-time enrollments into full-time equivalents have been made.	Represents reported crime from those individual university/college law enforcement agencies contributing to the UCR Program. These agencies are listed alphabetically by state. Any comparison of these UCR statistics should take into consideration size of enrollment, number of on-campus residents, and other demographic factors.
10	All law enforcement agencies submitting complete reports for 12 months in 1995.	"Suburban Counties" are defined as the areas covered by noncity agencies within an MSA (App. III). Population estimates of suburban counties are as of July 1, 1995, (see App. III).	Represents crime reported to individual law enforcement agencies in suburban counties, i.e., the individual sheriff's office, county police department, highway patrol, and/or state police. These figures do not represent the county totals since they exclude city crime counts. Any comparison of UCR statistics should take into consideration demographic factors.
11	All law enforcement agencies submitting complete reports for 12 months in 1995.	"Rural Counties" are those outside MSAs and whose jurisdictions are not covered by city police agencies (App. III). Population classifications of rural counties are based on 1995 estimates for individual agencies (see App. III).	Represents crime reported to individual rural county law enforcement agencies covering populations 25,000 and over, i.e., the individual sheriff's office, county police department, highway patrol, and/or state police. These figures do not represent the county totals since they exclude city crime counts. Any comparison of UCR statistics should take into consideration demographic factors.
12–15	All law enforcement agencies submitting complete reports for at least 6 common months in 1994 and 1995.	The 1995 crime trend statistics are 2-year comparisons based on 1995 reported crime activity. Only common reported months for individual agencies are included in 1995 trend calculations. Populations represent July 1, 1995, estimates for individual agencies. See Appendix III for UCR population breakdowns. Note that "Suburban and Nonsuburban Cities" are all municipal agencies other than central cities in MSAs.	Slight decrease in national coverage for Table 15 due to editing procedure and lower submission rate.
16–19	All law enforcement agencies submitting complete reports for 12 months in 1995.	The 1995 crime rates are the ratios of the aggregated 1995 crime volumes and the aggregated 1995 populations of the contributing agencies. Population statistics represent 1995 estimates for individual agencies. See Appendix III for UCR population breakdowns. Note that "Suburban and Nonsuburban Cities" are all municipal agencies other than central cities in MSAs.	The forcible rape figures furnished by the Illinois state-level UCR Program were not in accordance with national guidelines. For inclusion in these tables, the Illinois forcible rape figures were estimated by using the national rates for each population group applied to the population by group for Illinois agencies supplying all 12 months of data. Slight decrease in national coverage for Table 19 due to editing procedure and lower submission rate.
20	All law enforcement agencies submitting Supplementary Homicide Report (SHR) data in 1995.	The weapon totals are the aggregate for each murder victim recorded on the SHRs for calendar year 1995.	The SHR is the monthly report form concerning homicides. It details victim and offender characteristics, circumstances, weapons used, etc.
21, 22	All law enforcement agencies submitting complete reports for 12 months in 1995.	The weapon totals are aggregated 1995 totals. Population statistics represent 1995 estimates.	
23, 24	All law enforcement agencies submitting complete reports for at least 6 months in 1995.	Offense total and value lost total are computed for all Index offense categories other than aggravated assault. Percent distribution is derived based on offense total of each Index offense. Trend statistics are derived based on agencies with at least 6 common months complete for 1994 and 1995.	Aggravated assault is excluded from Table 23. For UCR Program purposes, the taking of money or property in connection with an assault is reported as robbery.
25–28	All law enforcement agencies submitting complete reports for at least 6 months in 1995.	The 1995 clearance rates are based on offense and clearance volume totals of the contributing agencies for 1995. Population statistics represent 1995 estimates. See Appendix III for UCR population breakdowns.	

(1) Table	(2) Data Base	(3) Table Construction	(4) General Comments
29	All law enforcement agencies in the UCR Program (including those submitting less than 12 months in 1995).	The arrest totals presented are national estimates based on the arrest statistics of all law enforcement agencies in the UCR Program (including those submitting less than 12 months). The "Total Estimated Arrests" statistic is the sum of estimated arrest volumes for each of the 29 offenses. Each individual arrest total is the sum of the estimated volumes within each of the eight population groups (App. III). Each group's estimate is the reported volume (as shown in Table 31) divided by the percent of total group population reporting (according to 1995 Bureau of the Census provisional estimates; see App. III).	
30, 31	All law enforcement agencies submitting complete reports for 12 months in 1995.	The 1995 arrest rates are the ratios, per 100,000 inhabitants, of the aggregated 1995 reported arrest statistics and population. The population statistics represent July 1, 1995, estimates. See Appendix III for UCR population classifications/geographical configuration.	
32, 33	All law enforcement agencies submitting complete reports for 12 months in 1986 and 1995.	The arrest trends are the percentage differences between 1986 and 1995 arrest volumes aggregated from common agencies. Population statistics represent July 1, 1995, estimates (see App. III).	
34, 35	All law enforcement agencies submitting complete reports for 12 months in 1991 and 1995.	The arrest trends are the percentage differences between 1991 and 1995 arrest volumes aggregated from common agencies. Population statistics represent 1995 estimates (see App. III).	
36, 37	All law enforcement agencies submitting complete reports for 12 months in 1994 and 1995.	The arrest trends are 2-year comparisons between 1994 and 1995 arrest volumes aggregated from common agencies. Population statistics represent 1995 estimates (see App. III).	
38–43	All law enforcement agencies submitting complete reports for 12 months in 1995.		Slight decrease in coverage for Table 43 due to editing procedure and lower submission of race data.
44, 45	All city law enforcement agencies submitting complete reports for 12 months in 1994 and 1995.	The 1995 city arrest trends represent the percentage differences between 1994 and 1995 arrest volumes aggregated from common city agencies. "City Agencies" are defined to be all agencies within Population Groups I-VI (App. III).	
46–49	All city law enforcement agencies submitting complete reports for 12 months in 1994 and 1995.	"City Agencies" are defined as agencies within Population Groups I-VI (App. III).	Slight decrease in coverage for Table 49 due to editing procedure and lower submission of race data.
50, 51	All suburban county law enforcement agencies submitting complete reports for 12 months in 1994 and 1995.	The 1995 suburban county arrest trends represent percentage differences between 1994 and 1995 volumes aggregated from contributing agencies. "Suburban Counties" are defined as the areas covered by noncity agencies within an MSA (App. III).	
52–55	All suburban county law enforcement agencies submitting complete reports for 12 months in 1995.	"Suburban Counties" are defined as the areas covered by noncity agencies within an MSA (App. III).	Slight decrease in coverage for Table 55 due to editing procedure and lower submission of race data.
56, 57	All rural county law enforcement agencies submitting complete reports for 12 months in 1994 and 1995.	The 1995 rural county arrest trends represent percentage differences between 1994 and 1995 volumes aggregated from contributing agencies. "Rural Counties" are defined as noncity agencies outside MSAs (App. III).	
58–61	All rural county law enforcement agencies submitting complete reports for 12 months in 1995.	"Rural Counties" are defined as noncity agencies outside MSAs (App. III).	Slight decrease in coverage for Table 61 due to editing procedure and lower submission of race data.
62, 63	All suburban area law enforcement agencies submitting complete reports for 12 months in 1994 and 1995.	The 1995 suburban area arrest trends represent percentage differences between 1994 and 1995 arrest volumes aggregated from contributing agencies. "Suburban Area" is defined as cities with fewer than 50,000 inhabitants and all counties within MSAs (App. III).	

(1) Table	(2) Data Base	(3) Table Construction	(4) General Comments
64–67	All suburban area law enforcement agencies submitting complete reports for 12 months in 1995.	"Suburban Area" is defined as cities with fewer than 50,000 inhabitants and all counties within MSAs (App. III).	Slight decrease in coverage for Table 67 due to editing procedure and lower submission of race data.
68	All law enforcement agencies submitting complete reports for 12 months in 1995.	Arrest totals are aggregated for individual agencies within each state. Population figures represent July 1, 1995, estimates (see App. III).	Any comparison of statistics should take into consideration variances in arrest practices, particularly for Part II crimes.
69	All law enforcement agencies submitting complete reports for 12 months in 1995.	Population statistics represent July 1, 1995, estimates for individual agencies. See Appendix III for definitions of the population classifications presented.	Data furnished are based upon individual state age definitions for juveniles.

APPENDIX II
Offenses in Uniform Crime Reporting

Offenses in Uniform Crime Reporting are divided into two groupings, Part I and Part II. Information on the volume of Part I offenses known to law enforcement, those cleared by arrest or exceptional means, and the number of persons arrested is reported monthly. Only arrest data are reported for Part II offenses.

The Part I offenses are:

Criminal homicide.—a. Murder and nonnegligent manslaughter: the willful (nonnegligent) killing of one human being by another. Deaths caused by negligence, attempts to kill, assaults to kill, suicides, accidental deaths, and justifiable homicides are excluded. Justifiable homicides are limited to: (1) the killing of a felon by a law enforcement officer in the line of duty; and (2) the killing of a felon, during the commission of a felony, by a private citizen. b. Manslaughter by negligence: the killing of another person through gross negligence. Traffic fatalities are excluded. While manslaughter by negligence is a Part I crime, it is not included in the Crime Index.

Forcible rape.—The carnal knowledge of a female forcibly and against her will. Included are rapes by force and attempts or assaults to rape. Statutory offenses (no force used–victim under age of consent) are excluded.

Robbery.—The taking or attempting to take anything of value from the care, custody, or control of a person or persons by force or threat of force or violence and/or by putting the victim in fear.

Aggravated assault.— An unlawful attack by one person upon another for the purpose of inflicting severe or aggravated bodily injury. This type of assault usually is accompanied by the use of a weapon or by means likely to produce death or great bodily harm. Simple assaults are excluded.

Burglary-breaking or entering.—The unlawful entry of a structure to commit a felony or a theft. Attempted forcible entry is included.

Larceny-theft (except motor vehicle theft).—The unlawful taking, carrying, leading, or riding away of property from the possession or constructive possession of another. Examples are thefts of bicycles or automobile accessories, shoplifting, pocket-picking, or the stealing of any property or article which is not taken by force and violence or by fraud. Attempted larcenies are included. Embezzlement, "con" games, forgery, worthless checks, etc., are excluded.

Motor vehicle theft.—The theft or attempted theft of a motor vehicle. A motor vehicle is self-propelled and runs on the surface and not on rails. Specifically excluded from this category are motorboats, construction equipment, airplanes, and farming equipment.

Arson.—Any willful or malicious burning or attempt to burn, with or without intent to defraud, a dwelling house, public building, motor vehicle or aircraft, personal property of another, etc.

The Part II offenses are:

Other assaults (simple).—Assaults and attempted assaults where no weapon is used and which do not result in serious or aggravated injury to the victim.

Forgery and counterfeiting.— Making, altering, uttering, or possessing, with intent to defraud, anything false in the semblance of that which is true. Attempts are included.

Fraud.—Fraudulent conversion and obtaining money or property by false pretenses. Included are confidence games and bad checks, except forgeries and counterfeiting.

Embezzlement.—Misappropriation or misapplication of money or property entrusted to one's care, custody, or control.

Stolen property; buying, receiving, possessing.— Buying, receiving, and possessing stolen property, including attempts.

Vandalism.—Willful or malicious destruction, injury, disfigurement, or defacement of any public or private property, real or personal, without consent of the owner or persons having custody or control.

Weapons; carrying, possessing, etc.—All violations of regulations or statutes controlling the carrying, using, possessing, furnishing, and manufacturing of deadly weapons or silencers. Included are attempts.

Prostitution and commercialized vice.—Sex offenses of a commercialized nature, such as prostitution, keeping a bawdy house, procuring, or transporting women for immoral purposes. Attempts are included.

Sex offenses (except forcible rape, prostitution, and commercialized vice).—Statutory rape and offenses against chastity, common decency, morals, and the like. Attempts are included.

Drug abuse violations.—State and/or local offenses relating to the unlawful possession, sale, use, growing, and manufacturing of narcotic drugs. The following drug categories are specified: opium or cocaine and their derivatives (morphine, heroin, codeine); marijuana; synthetic narcotics—manufactured narcotics that can cause true addiction (demerol, methadone); and dangerous nonnarcotic drugs (barbiturates, benzedrine).

Gambling.—Promoting, permitting, or engaging in illegal gambling.

Offenses against the family and children.—Nonsupport, neglect, desertion, or abuse of family and children.

Driving under the influence.— Driving or operating any vehicle or common carrier while drunk or under the influence of liquor or narcotics.

Liquor laws.—State and/or local liquor law violations, except "drunkenness" and "driving under the influence." Federal violations are excluded.

Drunkenness.—Offenses relating to drunkenness or intoxication. Excluded is "driving under the influence."

Disorderly conduct.—Breach of the peace.

Vagrancy.—Vagabondage, begging, loitering, etc.

All other offenses.—All violations of state and/or local laws, except those listed above and traffic offenses.

Suspicion.—No specific offense; suspect released without formal charges being placed.

Curfew and loitering laws (persons under age 18).—Offenses relating to violations of local curfew or loitering ordinances where such laws exist.

Runaways (persons under age 18).—Limited to juveniles taken into protective custody under provisions of local statutes.

APPENDIX III
Uniform Crime Reporting Area Definitions

The presentation of statistics by reporting area facilitates analyzing local crime counts in conjunction with those for areas of similar geographical location or population size. Geographically, the United States is divisible by regions, divisions, and states. Further breakdowns rely on population figures and proximity to metropolitan areas. As a general rule, sheriffs, county police, and state police report crimes committed within the limits of counties but outside cities, while local police report crimes committed within the city limits.

Community Types

UCR data are often presented in aggregations representing three types of communities:

1. Metropolitan Statistical Areas (MSAs)—Each MSA includes a central city of at least 50,000 people or an urbanized area of at least 50,000. The county containing the central city and other contiguous counties having strong economic and social ties to the central city and county are also included. Counties in an MSA are designated "suburban" for UCR purposes. An MSA may cross state lines. The MSA concept facilitates the analysis and presentation of uniform statistical data on metropolitan areas by establishing reporting units which represent major population centers. Due to changes in the geographic composition of MSAs, no year-to-year comparisons of data for those areas should be attempted.

New England MSAs are comprised of cities and towns instead of counties. In this publication's tabular presentations, New England cities and towns are assigned to the proper MSAs. Some counties, however, have both suburban and rural portions. Data for state police and sheriffs in those jurisdictions are included in statistics for the rural areas.

MSAs made up approximately 81 percent of the total U.S. population in 1995. Some presentations in this book refer to "suburban area." A suburban area includes cities with less than 50,000 inhabitants in addition to counties (unincorporated areas) within the MSA. The central cities are, of course, excluded. The concept of suburban area is especially important because of the particular crime conditions which exist in the communities surrounding the Nation's largest cities.

2. Cities Outside MSAs—Cities outside MSAs are mostly incorporated. They comprised 8 percent of the 1995 population of the United States.

3. Rural Counties Outside MSAs—Rural counties are comprised of mostly unincorporated areas. Law enforcement agencies in rural counties cover areas that are not under the jurisdiction of city police departments. Rural county law enforcement agencies served 11 percent of the national population in 1995.

The following is an illustration of the community types:

	MSA	NON-MSA
CITIES	CENTRAL CITIES 50,000 AND OVER	CITIES OUTSIDE METROPOLITAN AREAS
	SUBURBAN CITIES	
COUNTIES (including unincorporated areas)	SUBURBAN COUNTIES	RURAL COUNTIES

Population Groups

The population group classifications used by the UCR Program are:

Population Group	Political Label	Population Range
I	City	250,000 and over
II	City	100,000 to 249,999
III	City	50,000 to 99,999
IV	City	25,000 to 49,999
V	City	10,000 to 24,999
VI	City[1]	Less than 10,000
VIII (Rural County)	County[2]	N/A
IX (Suburban County)	County[2]	N/A

[1]Includes universities and colleges to which no population is attributed.
[2]Includes state police to which no population is attributed.

The major source of UCR data is the individual law enforcement agency. The number of agencies which are included in each population group will vary slightly from year to year due to population growth, geopolitical consolidation, municipal incorporation, etc. Population figures for individual jurisdictions are estimated by the UCR Program in noncensus years. In this year's publication, the state and national populations used are 1995 Bureau of the Census provisional estimates. Population figures for individual jurisdictions were updated by applying 1995 state growth rates to 1994 city and county estimates. The estimate of United States population showed a 1-percent increase from 1994 to 1995.

The following table shows the number of UCR contributing agencies within each population group for 1995.

Population Group	Number of Agencies	Population Covered
I	65	46,543,793
II	150	21,840,202
III	385	26,081,446
IV	732	25,253,076
V	1,775	27,916,143
VI[1]	8,000	25,703,290
VIII (Rural County)[2]	3,628	31,964,511
IX (Suburban County)[2]	2,030	57,451,539
Total[3]	16,765	262,755,000

[1]Includes universities and colleges to which no population is attributed.
[2]Includes state police to which no population is attributed.
[3]Because of Bureau of the Census rounding, the population covered does not add to total.

Regions and Divisions

As shown in the accompanying map, the U.S. is comprised of four regions: the Northeastern States, the Midwestern States, the Southern States, and the Western States. These regions are further divided into nine divisions. The following table delineates the regional, divisional, and state configuration of the country.

NORTHEASTERN STATES

New England	Middle Atlantic
Connecticut	New Jersey
Maine	New York
Massachusetts	Pennsylvania
New Hampshire	
Rhode Island	
Vermont	

MIDWESTERN STATES

East North Central	West North Central
Illinois	Iowa
Indiana	Kansas
Michigan	Minnesota
Ohio	Missouri
Wisconsin	Nebraska
	North Dakota
	South Dakota

SOUTHERN STATES

South Atlantic	East South Central
Delaware	Alabama
District of Columbia	Kentucky
Florida	Mississippi
Georgia	Tennessee
Maryland	West South Central
North Carolina	Arkansas
South Carolina	Louisiana
Virginia	Oklahoma
West Virginia	Texas

WESTERN STATES

Mountain	Pacific
Arizona	Alaska
Colorado	California
Idaho	Hawaii
Montana	Oregon
Nevada	Washington
New Mexico	
Utah	
Wyoming	

REGIONS
AND DIVISIONS
OF THE UNITED STATES

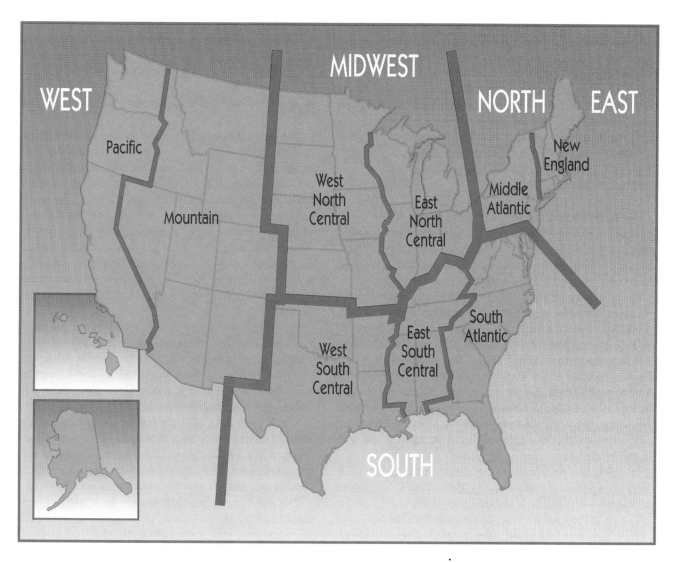

WEST

MIDWEST

NORTH   EAST

Pacific

New England

Mountain

West North Central

East North Central

Middle Atlantic

West South Central

East South Central

South Atlantic

SOUTH

APPENDIX IV
The Nation's Two Crime Measures

The U.S. Department of Justice administers two statistical programs to measure the magnitude, nature, and impact of crime in the Nation: the Uniform Crime Reporting (UCR) Program and the National Crime Victimization Survey (NCVS). Each of these programs produces valuable information about aspects of the Nation's crime problem. Because the UCR and NCVS programs are conducted for different purposes, use different methods, and focus on somewhat different aspects of crime, the information they produce together provides a more comprehensive panorama of the Nation's crime problem than either could produce alone.

Uniform Crime Reports

The FBI's UCR Program, which began in 1929, collects information on the following crimes reported to law enforcement authorities: homicide, forcible rape, robbery, aggravated assault, burglary, larceny-theft, motor vehicle theft, and arson. Arrests are reported for 21 additional crime categories.

The UCR data are compiled from monthly law enforcement reports or individual crime incident records transmitted directly to the FBI or to centralized state agencies that then report to the FBI. Each report submitted to the UCR Program is examined thoroughly for reasonableness, accuracy, and deviations that may indicate errors. Large variations in crime levels may indicate modified records procedures, incomplete reporting, or changes in a jurisdiction's boundaries. To identify any unusual fluctuations in an agency's crime counts, monthly reports are compared with previous submissions of the agency and with those for similar agencies.

In 1995, law enforcement agencies active in the UCR Program represented approximately 251 million United States inhabitants—95 percent of the U.S. population.

The UCR Program provides crime counts for the Nation as a whole, as well as for regions, states, counties, cities, and towns. This permits studies among neighboring jurisdictions and among those with similar populations and other common characteristics.

UCR findings for each calendar year are published in a preliminary release in the spring, followed by a detailed annual report, *Crime in the United States,* issued in the following calendar year. In addition to crime counts and trends, this report includes data on crimes cleared, persons arrested (age, sex, and race), law enforcement personnel (including the number of sworn officers killed or assaulted), and the characteristics of homicides (including age, sex, and race of victims and offenders, victim-offender relationships, weapons used, and circumstances surrounding the homicides). Other special reports are also available from the UCR Program.

Following a 5-year redesign effort, the UCR Program is currently being converted to the more comprehensive and detailed National Incident-Based Reporting System (NIBRS). NIBRS will provide detailed information about each criminal incident in 22 broad categories of offenses.

National Crime Victimization Survey

The Bureau of Justice Statistics' NCVS, which began in 1973, provides a detailed picture of crime incidents, victims, and trends. After a substantial period of research, in 1993 the survey completed an intensive methodological redesign. The redesign was undertaken to improve the questions used to uncover crime, update the survey methods, and broaden the scope of crimes measured. The redesigned survey collects detailed information on the frequency and nature of the crimes of rape, sexual assault, personal robbery, aggravated and simple assault, household burglary, theft, and motor vehicle theft. It does not measure homicide or commercial crimes (such as burglaries of stores).

U.S. Census Bureau personnel interview all household members at least 12 years old in a nationally representative sample of approximately 49,000 households (about 101,000 persons). Households stay in the sample for 3 years and are interviewed at 6-month intervals. New households rotate into the sample on an ongoing basis.

The NCVS collects information on crimes suffered by individuals and households, whether or not those crimes were reported to law enforcement. It estimates the proportion of each crime type reported to law enforcement, and it summarizes the reasons that victims give for reporting or not reporting.

The survey provides information about victims (age, sex, race, ethnicity, marital status, income, and educational level), offenders (sex, race, approximate age, and victim-offender relationship), and the crimes (time and place of occurrence, use of weapons, nature of injury, and economic consequences). Questions also cover the experiences of victims with the criminal justice system, self-protective measures used by victims, and possible substance abuse by offenders. Supplements are added periodically to the survey to obtain detailed information on topics like school crime.

The first data from the redesigned NCVS were published in a BJS bulletin in June 1995. BJS publication of NCVS data includes *Criminal Victimization in the United States,* an annual report that covers the broad range of detailed information collected by the NCVS. BJS publishes detailed reports on topics such as crime against women, urban crime, and gun use in crime. The NCVS data files are archived at the National Archive of Criminal Justice Data at the University of Michigan to enable researchers to perform independent analysis.

Comparing UCR and NCVS

Because the NCVS was designed to complement the UCR Program, the two programs share many similarities. As much as their different collection methods permit, the two measure the same subset of serious crimes, defined alike. Both programs cover rape, robbery, aggravated assault, burglary, theft, and motor vehicle theft. Rape, robbery, theft, and motor vehicle theft are defined virtually identically by both the UCR and NCVS. (While rape is defined analogously, the UCR Crime Index measures the crime against women only, and the NCVS measures it against both sexes.)

There are also significant differences between the two programs. First, the two programs were created to serve different purposes. The UCR Program's primary objective is to provide a reliable set of criminal justice statistics for law enforcement administration, operation, and management. The NCVS was established to provide previously unavailable information about crime (including crime not reported to police), victims, and offenders.

Second, the two programs measure an overlapping but nonidentical set of crimes. The NCVS includes crimes both reported and not reported to law enforcement. The NCVS excludes, but the UCR includes, homicide, arson, commercial crimes, and crimes against children under age 12. The UCR captures crimes reported to law enforcement, but it excludes sexual assaults and simple assaults from the Crime Index.

Third, because of methodology, the NCVS and UCR definitions of some crimes differ. For example, the UCR defines burglary as the unlawful entry or attempted entry of a structure to commit a felony or theft. The NCVS, not wanting to ask victims to ascertain offender motives, defines burglary as the entry or attempted entry of a residence by a person who had no right to be there.

Fourth, for property crimes (burglary, theft, and motor vehicle theft), the two programs calculate crime rates using different bases. The UCR rates for these crimes are per-capita (number of crimes per 100,000 persons), whereas the NCVS rates for these crimes are per-household (number of crimes per 1,000 households). Because the number of households may not grow at the same rate each year as the total population, trend data for rates of property crimes measured by the two programs may not be comparable.

In addition, some differences in the data from the two programs may result from sampling variation in the NCVS and

from estimating for nonresponse in the UCR. The NCVS estimates are derived from interviewing a sample and are therefore subject to a margin of error. Rigorous statistical methods are used to calculate confidence intervals around all survey estimates. Trend data in NCVS reports are described as genuine only if there is at least a 90 percent certainty that the measured changes are not the result of sampling variation. The UCR data are based on the actual counts of offenses reported by law enforcement jurisdictions. In some circumstances, UCR data are estimated for nonparticipating jurisdictions or those reporting partial data.

Each program has unique strengths. The UCR provides a measure of the number of crimes reported to law enforcement agencies throughout the country. The UCR's Supplementary Homicide Reports provide the most reliable, timely data on the extent and nature of homicides in the Nation. The NCVS is the primary source of information on the characteristics of criminal victimization and on the number and types of crimes not reported to law enforcement authorities.

By understanding the strengths and limitations of each program, it is possible to use the UCR and NCVS to achieve a greater understanding of crime trends and the nature of crime in the United States. For example, changes in police procedures, shifting attitudes towards crime and police, and other societal changes can affect the extent to which people report and law enforcement agencies record crime. NCVS and UCR data can be used in concert to explore why trends in reported and police-recorded crime may differ.

Apparent discrepancies between statistics from the two programs can usually be accounted for by their definitional and procedural differences or resolved by comparing NCVS sampling variations (confidence intervals) of those crimes said to have been reported to police with UCR statistics.

For most types of crimes measured by both the UCR and NCVS, analysts familiar with the programs can exclude from analysis those aspects of crime not common to both. Resulting long-term trend lines can be brought into close concordance. The impact of such adjustments is most striking for robbery, burglary, and motor vehicle theft, whose definitions most closely coincide.

With robbery, annual victimization rates based only on NCVS robberies reported to the police are possible. It is also possible to remove from analysis UCR robberies of commercial establishments such as gas stations, convenience stores, and banks. When the resulting NCVS police reported robbery rates are compared to UCR non-commercial robbery rates, the results reveal closely corresponding long-term trends.

APPENDIX V

Directory of State Uniform Crime Reporting Programs

Alabama

Alabama Criminal Justice
   Information Center
Suite 350
770 Washington Avenue
Montgomery, Alabama 36130
(334) 242-4900

Alaska

Uniform Crime Reporting Section
Department of Public Safety
   Information System
5700 East Tudor Road
Anchorage, Alaska 99507
(907) 269-5708

American Samoa

Department of Public Safety
Post Office Box 1086
Pago Pago
American Samoa 96799
(684) 633-1111

Arizona

Uniform Crime Reporting
Arizona Department of Public Safety
Post Office Box 6638
Phoenix, Arizona 85005
(602) 223-6638

Arkansas

Arkansas Crime Information Center
One Capitol Mall, 4D-200
Little Rock, Arkansas 72201
(501) 682-2222

California

Law Enforcement Information Center
Department of Justice
Post Office Box 903427
Sacramento, California 94203-4270
(916) 227-3473

Colorado

Uniform Crime Reporting
Colorado Bureau of Investigation
Suite 3000
690 Kipling Street
Denver, Colorado 80215
(303) 239-4300

Connecticut

Uniform Crime Reporting Program
Post Office Box 2794
Middletown, Connecticut 06457-9294
(860) 685-8030

Delaware	State Bureau of Identification Post Office Box 430 Dover, Delaware 19903 (302) 739-5875
District of Columbia	Information Services Division Metropolitan Police Department Room 5054 300 Indiana Avenue, Northwest Washington, D.C. 20001 (202) 727-4301
Florida	Uniform Crime Reports Section Florida Crime Information Center Bureau Post Office Box 1489 Tallahassee, Florida 32302-1489 (904) 487-1179
Georgia	Georgia Crime Information Center Georgia Bureau of Investigation Post Office Box 370748 Decatur, Georgia 30037 (404) 244-2840
Guam	Guam Police Department Planning, Research and Development Pedro's Plaza 287 West O'Brien Drive Agana, Guam 96910 (671) 472-8911
Hawaii	Crime Prevention and Justice Assistance Division Department of the Attorney General 1st Floor 425 Queen Street Honolulu, Hawaii 96813 (808) 586-1416
Idaho	Criminal Identification Bureau Department of Law Enforcement Post Office Box 700 Meridian, Idaho 83680 (208) 884-7156
Illinois	Uniform Crime Reporting Program Division of Administration, Crime Studies Illinois State Police Post Office Box 3677 Springfield, Illinois 62708-3677 (217) 782-5791

Iowa	Iowa Department of Public Safety Wallace State Office Building East Ninth and Grand Des Moines, Iowa 50319 (515) 281-8494
Kansas	Kansas Bureau of Investigation 1620 Southwest Tyler Street Topeka, Kansas 66612 (913) 296-8200
Kentucky	Information Services Branch Kentucky State Police 1250 Louisville Road Frankfort, Kentucky 40601 (502) 227-8783
Louisiana	Louisiana Commission on Law Enforcement Room 708 1885 Wooddale Boulevard Baton Rouge, Louisiana 70806 (504) 925-4847
Maine	Uniform Crime Reporting Division Maine State Police Station #42 36 Hospital Street Augusta, Maine 04333 (207) 624-7004
Maryland	Central Records Division Maryland State Police Department 1711 Belmont Avenue Baltimore, Maryland 21244 (410) 298-3883
Massachusetts	Crime Reporting Unit Massachusetts State Police 470 Worcester Road Framingham, Massachusetts 01701 (508) 820-2110
Michigan	Uniform Crime Reporting Section Michigan State Police 7150 Harris Drive Lansing, Michigan 48913 (517) 322-1150
Minnesota	Bureau of Criminal Apprehension Minnesota Department of Public Safety Criminal Justice Information Systems 1246 University Avenue St. Paul, Minnesota 55104 (612) 642-0610

Montana	Montana Board of Crime Control 303 North Roberts Helena, Montana 59620-1408 (406) 444-2077
Nebraska	Uniform Crime Reporting Section The Nebraska Commission on Law Enforcement and Criminal Justice Post Office Box 94946 Lincoln, Nebraska 68509 (402) 471-3982
Nevada	Criminal Information Services Nevada Highway Patrol 555 Wright Way Carson City, Nevada 89711 (702) 687-5713
New Hampshire	Uniform Crime Reporting Unit New Hampshire Department of Public Safety Division of State Police 10 Hazen Drive Concord, New Hampshire 03305 (603) 271-2509
New Jersey	Uniform Crime Reporting Division of State Police Post Office Box 7068 West Trenton, New Jersey 08628-0068 (609) 882-2000 x 2392
New York	Statistical Services New York State Division of Criminal Justice Services 8th Floor, Mail Room Executive Park Tower Building Stuyvesant Plaza Albany, New York 12203 (518) 457-8381
North Carolina	Crime Reporting and Field Services Division of Criminal Information State Bureau of Investigation 407 North Blount Street Raleigh, North Carolina 27601 (919) 733-3171
North Dakota	Information Services Section Bureau of Criminal Investigation Attorney General's Office Post Office Box 1054 Bismarck, North Dakota 58502 (701) 328-5500

Oklahoma

Uniform Crime Reporting Section
Oklahoma State Bureau of Investigation
Suite 300
6600 North Harvey
Oklahoma City, Oklahoma 73116
(405) 848-6724

Oregon

Law Enforcement Data Systems Division
Oregon Department of State Police
400 Public Service Building
Salem, Oregon 97310
(503) 378-3057

Pennsylvania

Bureau of Research and Development
Pennsylvania State Police
1800 Elmerton Avenue
Harrisburg, Pennsylvania 17110
(717) 783-5536

Puerto Rico

Puerto Rico Police
Post Office Box 70166
San Juan, Puerto Rico 00936-8166
(787) 793-1234

Rhode Island

Rhode Island State Police
Post Office Box 185
North Scituate, Rhode Island 02857
(401) 444-1121

South Carolina

South Carolina Law Enforcement Division
Post Office Box 21398
Columbia, South Carolina 29221-1398
(803) 896-7162

South Dakota

South Dakota Statistical Analysis Center
500 East Capitol Avenue
Pierre, South Dakota 57501-5070
(605) 773-6310

Texas

Uniform Crime Reporting
Crime Information Bureau
Texas Department of Public Safety
Post Office Box 4143
Austin, Texas 78765-9968
(512) 424-2091

Utah

Data Collection and Analysis
Bureau of Criminal Identification
Utah Department of Public Safety
4501 South 2700 West
Salt Lake City, Utah 84119
(801) 965-4445

Vermont	Vermont Crime Information Center 103 South Main Street Waterbury, Vermont 05671-2101 (802) 244-8786
Virginia	Records Management Division Department of State Police Post Office Box 27472 Richmond, Virginia 23261-7472 (804) 674- 2023
Virgin Islands	Records Bureau Virgin Islands Police Department 2nd Floor Nisky Center Saint Thomas, Virgin Islands 00802 (809) 774-6400
Washington	Uniform Crime Reporting Program Washington Association of Sheriffs and Police Chiefs Post Office Box 826 Olympia, Washington 98507 (360) 586-3221
West Virginia	Uniform Crime Reporting Program West Virginia State Police 725 Jefferson Road South Charleston, West Virginia 25309 (304) 746-2159
Wisconsin	Office of Justice Assistance 2nd Floor 222 State Street Madison, Wisconsin 53702-0001 (608) 266-3323
Wyoming	Uniform Crime Reporting Criminal Records Section Division of Criminal Investigation 316 West 22nd Street Cheyenne, Wyoming 82002 (307) 777-7625

APPENDIX VI

National Uniform Crime Reporting Program Directory

Administration . . . . (304) 625-3690
    Program administration; management; policy

Information Dissemination . . . . (304) 625-2823
    Requests for published and unpublished data; printouts, magnetic tapes, books   (202) 324-5015

    Send correspondence to: Federal Bureau of Investigation
                            Criminal Justice Information
                                Services Division
                            Attention: Uniform Crime Reports
                            1000 Custer Hollow Road
                            Clarksburg, West Virginia 26306

Training/Education . . . . (304) 625-4831
    Requests for training of law enforcement; information on police reporting systems; technical assistance

Statistical Analysis/Processing . . . . (304) 625-3601
    Statistical models; special studies and analyses; crime forecasting; processing of summary and   (202) 324-3821
    incident-based reports from data contributors; reporting problems; requests for reporting forms;
    data processing; data quality

APPENDIX VII
Uniform Crime Reporting Publications List

Crime in the United States (annual)

Law Enforcement Officers Killed and Assaulted (annual)

Hate Crime Statistics (annual)

Killed in the Line of Duty: A Study of Selected Felonious Killings of Law Enforcement Officers (special report)

UCR Preliminary Release, January–June (semiannual)

UCR Preliminary Annual Report (semiannual)

Uniform Crime Reporting Handbook:
Summary System
National Incident-Based Reporting System (NIBRS)

NIBRS:
Volume 1—*Data Collection Guidelines*
Volume 2—*Data Submission Specifications*
Volume 3—*Approaches to Implementing an Incident-Based Reporting (IBR) System*
Volume 4—*Error Message Manual*
Supplemental Guidelines for Federal Participation

Manual of Law Enforcement Records

Hate Crime:
Hate Crime Data Collection Guidelines
Training Guide for Hate Crime Data Collection
Hate Crime Statistics, 1990: A Resource Book

Age-Specific Arrest Rates and Race-Specific Arrest Rates for Selected Offenses

Population-at-Risk Rates and Selected Crime Indicators

Periodic Press Releases:
Crime Trends (semiannual)
Law Enforcement Officers Killed (semiannual)
Hate Crime (annual)

Evaluation Form For
Crime in the United States - 1995

1. For what purpose did you use this issue of *Crime in the United States?*

2. Was the publication adequate for that purpose?

    ____ Quite adequate   ____ Somewhat adequate   ____ Quite inadequate
    ____ Adequate   ____ Not Adequate

3. Are there presentations not included that you would find particularly useful?

4. What changes, if any, would you recommend for subsequent issues?

5. Can you point out specific table notes or presentations which are not clear or additional terms which need to be defined?

6. In what capacity did you use *Crime in the United States?*

    ____ Criminal justice/law enforcement   ____ Researcher
         agency employee *(specify functional area)*   ____ Student
                                                   ____ Legislator
    ____ Other government employee   ____ Media
    ____ Private citizen   ____ Other *(specify)*
    ____ Educator

7. Add any additional comments you care to make.

OPTIONAL

— — — —(Fold here)— — — —

U.S. Department of Justice
Federal Bureau of Investigation
Washington, D.C. 20535

PLACE
STAMP
HERE

Uniform Crime Reports
Federal Bureau of Investigation
1000 Custer Hollow Road
Clarksburg, West Virginia 26306

— — — —(Fold here)— — — —